THE REGULARS

AN ACCOUNT OF THE MILITARY CAREER OF COLONEL DONALD A. SEIBERT, USA RET.

DONALD A. SEIBERT

Order this book online at www.trafford.com
or email orders@trafford.com

Most Trafford titles are also available at major online book retailers.

Printed in Victoria, BC, Canada.

ISBN: 978-1-4269-2886-4 (sc)

*Our mission is to efficiently provide the world's finest, most comprehensive book publishing
service, enabling every author to experience success. To find out how to publish your book, your
way, and have it available worldwide, visit us online at www.trafford.com*

Trafford rev. 4/9/2010

 www.trafford.com

North America & international
toll-free: 1 888 232 4444 (USA & Canada)
phone: 250 383 6864 ♦ fax: 812 355 4082

ABOUT THE AUTHOR

COLONEL DON SEIBERT passed away peacefully on January 15, 2010 at age 89.

Like his life, he was fully aware of his serious condition and did not want to be a burden to his family and friends, and so, deciding it was time, his life support was removed at his insistence, and he passed on, with family at his side.

To his family and friends, of which there are legions of, he was, a true American hero, spending his entire life in the service of his country and serving it proudly and gallantly. Years earlier, in 1980, he wrote these memoirs, entitled "The Regulars", and kept it in a bound manuscript, giving a few copies to friends and family. He stated:

""....it is a small part of the story of the Regular Army as one insider knew it. The author was no great captain making monumental decisions, no hero whose deeds should be recorded, no malcontent with a cause to plead. It is the record of an average soldier in ability and performance. To this account I bring an abiding love for America and a great admiration for the Regulars who serve her."

As a final tribute to him, we wanted to finally publish this book and memorialize this man's incredible career. He was certainly our hero.

The Family of Don Seibert
April 2010

DEDICATED

TO THE REGULARS

AND ALL THOSE WHO HAVE SERVED

CONTENTS

FOREWORD

THE REGULARS is not really my story, and does not pretend to speak of grand strategy or great leadership. Rather, it is a small part of the story of the Regular Army as one insider knew it. The author was no great captain making monumental decisions, no hero whose deeds should be recorded, no malcontent with a cause to plead. It is the record of an average soldier in ability and performance. To this account I bring an abiding love for America and a great admiration for the Regulars who serve her. Many of the officers and soldiers I knew and served with were not Regulars. This in no way detracts from their service, their dedication, their loyalty, or the warm friendship and high esteem in which I hold them. But it is the Regulars who provide the continuity, the expertise, the framework on which America must build in times when larger military forces are needed. It is the Regulars who respond first in any crisis. And it is to the credit of the Regulars that the Armed Forces of the United States have never posed a threat of a coup d'etat or interference in the orderly administration or civil affairs of the Government.

THE REGULARS records a career that is in no way unique. All of my contemporaries could tell of similar activities if they wished, and most could recount adventures far more entertaining, gripping and significant than those set down here. Yet THE REGULARS reflects a typical career, the usual way of life in the United States Army. If there is a central theme, a motivating force, or a principal idea in this account, it is the friendships made and cherished, the reappearance of old friends in unexpected places, the recurring assignments with people with whom I had previously served.

To the best of my recollection, the incidents and events recorded here are true. Many of them can be documented; others have been verified by those who served with me at specific times; several are related solely from my own imperfect memory. Though I kept no diary or journal, I am certain that they are factual. Obviously, conversations have been reconstructed based on my own recollections. No doubt, many incidents and impressions have been colored by later experiences, prejudices and desires. Hindsight may mellow an event, but it does not alter it. If there has been a revision of the facts, it has been done unconsciously. It is my regret that it has not been possible to include the names of all those with whom I have served and recall with pleasure. Those names mentioned have been carefully checked and are, in fact, those with whom I served. It is not my intention to embarrass or ridicule anyone, but rather to tell the story as I recall it. In a few instances the names of individuals have been deliberately omitted to spare them or their survivors pain or embarrassment. To my shame and regret, I have not been able to recall the names of some fine soldiers with whom I served.

A number of people have helped me put this narrative together; to them I am deeply indebted. Howard Wickert suggested I set down such an account, encouraged me to complete it and read the first draft His criticisms and guidance set the style and format. Jeanette Rosenberg read critically the second draft and her advice is in large measure responsible for the readability of the chronicle. General William B. Rosson read and carefully edited the final draft. COLs Herbert V. Mansfield and William P. DeBrocke proofed the current manuscript.

Many friends read those parts of the initial draft which deal with periods during which they served with me. Among them are: Alvin Cedarbaum, Frederick Rothert, William Long, William Homen, Leslie Clarke, Henry Balough, Nicholas Ditrano, Harry Natelson, Colin Bury, Fitzgerald Cookson, Arnold Dempewolf, Eli Vukovich, Carl Johnson, Richard Thorn, Howard Leifheit, Olin Baggett, Thomas Tackaberry, Henry Alsup, Franklin Mashburn, John Kiser, Edward Morris, Aldo

Bettelli, Henry Hand, George McLendon, Herbert Mansfield, James Elsbecker, Joseph McAteer, William Lindahl, Richard Norcross, Raymond McClean, Hershell Murray, Charles Jackson, Harrison Merritt, Irving Carpenter, Levin Broughton, Richard Hooker, John Hermann, Samuel Barth, John Mess, William Rosson, Kyle Gruene, Emil Schaerer, Richard Wise, Chris Melonson, Fr. Leonard Stegman, Sidney Hack, Douglas Morgan, Ralph Zimmer, Jack Frankeberger, Jaan Kurgvel, Sidney Steele, Hans Hoffman, Kenneth Renaud, George Skinner, C. Edward Miller, Peter Kelley, Joe Foster, Lewington Ponder, Alec Kovalevsky, William DeBrocke, Ron Aman, Robert Reid, and Robert Apt. These friends confirmed many of the incidents recorded, corrected errors of omission and commission, recalled additional facts, and augmented the text or related incidents which they experienced. A few of the latter are included verbatim with appropriate attributions. Other comments were incorporated into the text with minor changes and without crediting authorship. To all these friends I owe much for the interest, color and verity they have given this record. Finally, I would like to acknowledge my debt to the four ladies who typed the manuscript: Judith Wilson, who started the transcription from the initial tapes and developed the procedures which made that transcription more manageable, Katherine Rockford who transcribed most of the maundering tapes and produced the first usable draft from my hieroglyphics, and Carla and Gladys Stanley who completed the final draft.

Whatever merit is in this account belongs to those mentioned above. The errors and blame are mine alone.

Fayetteville, NC
Fairfax County, VA
1981 -1995
Donald A. Seibert
Colonel USA RET

Colonel Donald A. Seibert, U.S. Army May 1974

CHAPTER 1

RECRUIT

December 7, 1941 was a typical winter day in New York, except that I had a physics test the next day and my brother Bill was out on the North Atlantic on convoy duty with the Navy. It was a bright, sunny, bitter-cold Sunday afternoon. The house was redolent with the aromas of the customary Sunday dinner we had just finished. Mother and Dad were busy in the back of the house with minor chores after the noon meal. I was in the living room studying physics. The radio was tuned to WQXR, the good music station of the New York Times, to block out the distracting sounds in the house. The exam on Monday was to cover electrochemical effects and I was not in my element in physics. About 2:15 or 2:30, Chadwick's "Jubilee Overture" was suddenly interrupted and the announcer's voice penetrated my concentration as he said shakenly, "We interrupt this program for a special bulletin. The White House has announced that Japan has attacked Pearl Harbor. Stand by for additional details."

I couldn't believe my ears. It had to be another Orson Welles hoax. I listened carefully as the announcement was repeated, then rushed to tell Mother and Dad, who dropped everything to listen to the news releases that followed. The physics exam was forgotten, my books and notes put aside, as we sat glued to the radio the rest of the day. The news was sketchy and confusing, the details sparse, but as nearly as we could make out, a great deal of damage had been done to our fleet in Pearl Harbor, to the Army at Schofield Barracks, and to the Air Corps at Hickam Field, all of which were close to Honolulu. It was estimated that many people had been killed or wounded. The newscasters kept raising the possibility of an attack on the West Coast. President Roosevelt announced that he would address a Joint Session of Congress on Monday.

The next morning I went to work at the Valspar Corporation as usual (I was carrying a full semester at Washington Square College at night and working as a credit clerk during the day), but went about my duties with a distracted air. Office conversation was concerned exclusively with the attack the day before. I had called my best friend, George Gabelia, and discussed the matter the previous night, he had promised to call me as soon as there were any new developments.

Taking an early lunch, I was back in the office by 11:45. George called just as I returned and said that the President was ready to address the Emergency Joint Session of Congress and that everyone was speculating that he would ask for a declaration of war. "As a matter of fact," he added, "the President is entering the House now. Why don't I put the phone next to the radio so you can hear him?" My desk was close to the switchboard, and I asked the operator if it was okay to tie up the phone for a while. She saw no problem, indeed, she wanted to listen herself, and so plugged into my line. By the time the President started to speak there were some 10 or 15 people plugged into the switch board to hear him. We all sat in silence as President Roosevelt described December 7 as a "day that would live in infamy" and requested a declaration of war against Japan.

Certain that the declaration would be passed by Congress I could not stay in the office when such important events were going on. While talking with George we had agreed to meet later at Queens College which both our girls were attending. About 1:00 o'clock I left the office and took the subway to Jamaica. George picked me up and then we met his girl, Shirley Martin (my girl, Winnie Buckley, had no classes that day) and discussed what we should do. Because I was taking a pre-medical course, I had a deferment from the draft. George was vulnerable, he had been classified 1-A when he dropped out of the University of Georgia several months before. We decided that we would rather select our way of serving, since war was inevitable, and elected to enlist in the Marines. We thought that this was the first service that would get into action against the Japanese in the Pacific.

When we got to the Marine Recruiting Station in Jamaica, there was already a considerable line in front of it, we joined the end of it. Shirley walked along with us until we actually went in to talk to the Marine Recruiter. The first thing he asked was if we had any physical disabilities. We told him we had none. Then he gave us a quick eye examination, neither of us could pass the eye test. We did not have 20-20 vision, though our eyes were correctable. This immediately eliminated us since the declaration of war had happened too suddenly to permit any of the services to alter their physical requirements. The Marines were not yet waiving even minor eye deficiencies.

We were stunned! We talked about what other service we might join. We both agreed we had to get involved right away. Because of my pre-med studies, I decided to go to the Federal Building in Manhattan the next morning and volunteer for the Navy Pharmacy Corps. Having completed all the biology and chemistry courses needed for medical school, I was sure the Navy would take me immediately as a medical corpsman. George and I parted, determined to get into service as soon as possible.

When I arrived at 90 Church Street at 7:30 on 9 December, there was already a line winding halfway around the block. Once again I took my place at the end of the slowly moving queue. At 9:30 I was talking with a Navy Recruiter. He was eager to enlist me in the Pharmacy Corps, but he also took a quick check of my vision and immediately eliminated me. The Navy had not revised its standards either, though all the services would soon do so because of the war.

After this second rejection, I talked with my Uncle Ed, who worked close by and had been in the Navy in WWI. He had many Navy friends, both officers and Chief Petty Officers, and I thought he might know somebody who could help me get in. He immediately called Chief Pharmacist's Mate James Durkin and sent me back with a note to him. When I finally got to see Durkin, I found that he was in charge of giving physical examinations to recruits. He checked my eyes and we talked at great length, but he could find no way that my deficient eyesight could be waived at that time.

Disappointed, I went back to the Valspar Corporation, Needless to say, I had little enthusiasm for my duties, but continued to attend to my work as best I could. Determined to get in the war one way or another, I decided to drop out of college, I wasn't going to sit around and wait. That evening I went to Washington Square College and talked to Dr Girard, Director of the Evening Division of the College, a part of NYU. He advised me to continue my schooling since I would graduate in June, strongly urging me to get my degree and then get into service. He was sure the degree would lead to a better job, might even lead to a commission. But I was impatient to get into action and told Girard I would think about it, but I knew then that I would never attend another class at NYU until the war was over.

My good friend in the University, Jack Ormsby, suggested we enlist in the Coast Guard as Bosun's Mates. He had heard that anyone who had any sailing experience could get a rating. My experience was limited to some sailing in a Comet and Jack had about the same qualifications. The first question the recruiter asked us was the difference between a halyard and a lanyard! We didn't know, so he said they were not interested in us.

Again George Gabelia, whom I had known since we were both in the third grade, and I consulted. His father suggested that we see a friend of his, a Russian emigre who was an eye specialist. We went to his office and he examined us carefully, writing prescriptions for reading glasses. He also suggested some eye exercises which he thought might strengthen our eyes, and a diet which included a lot of raw carrots. He advised that before we took any eye exams, we rest our eyes, in a dark room if possible. He wouldn't take any money for the examination and said he hoped we'd have the opportunity to get into uniform and serve our country.

The Marines didn't want me, the Navy didn't want me, the Coast Guard didn't want me, so my only recourse was the Army. The Army had a fine Medical Corps and could undoubtedly use people with my background. The following week the 15th or 16th of December, I took the day off again and went to the Whitehall Building, where the Army Recruiting Center was located. By this time I was even more determined to get into service, on 11 December Germany and Italy had declared war against the US and Congress had adopted a resolution recognizing a state of war between the US and those countries. Again I had to wait in a long line. The recruiters were extremely fast in their processing so it wasn't more than an hour before I was talking to someone. After quickly filling out the papers, I was up against my old nemesis, a physical, which included an eye test. As luck would have it, we waited outside the cubicle in which the eye exam was being given so I heard over and over, the recruits as they read the eye chart. It was a simple matter to memorize the chart, since the examiner never varied the procedure. He instructed each man to start at one line and read until he told him to stop. When my turn came, I was able to call the chart from memory. I was accepted in the Army!

Although accepted, with all of the necessary papers completed and signed, I was not sworn in. The Army could not absorb the tremendous number of people who had surged to enlist, so my swearing in was deferred until the 27th of January, 1942. That 1941 Christmas would be spent at home after all. Although impatient to get to get into service, I could live with this relatively short delay, at least I had been accepted. I did not attend any more classes at Washington Square College, but I did go to talk with Dr Girard again. He was disappointed that I had decided that I was not going to continue and get my degree, but sympathized with me and said that he would do everything possible to help me. However, I did continue to work at the Valspar Corporation.

George received his draft notice just before Christmas and reported to Camp Upton on Long Island immediately after. His mother gave each of us a small icon which had been blessed in the Russian Orthodox Cathedral in Manhattan. She told us it would keep us safe during the war. I put it in my shaving kit and forgot about it.

The time passed quickly. It was a wonderful Christmas despite the fact that Bill was still on convoy duty in the North Atlantic and my sister Margaret's husband had been recalled into the Army immediately after Pearl Harbor. He had been drafted, had finished his year of training and been released in November. My other sister, Arlene's husband was subject to call at any moment.

The 27th of January came at last. Reporting to 30 Whitehall Street together with several hundred other men, I raised my right hand and undertook "to defend the Constitution of the United States and to obey the orders of the officers appointed over me." I was a member of the Army of the United States!

We were ordered to report to Penn Station at eight o'clock the next morning where we would entrain for Fort (FT) Dix. They told us to bring only our toilet articles and something in which to send our civilian clothes home.

The entire household was stirring the next morning. Mother was preparing the sort of breakfast usually reserved for Sunday mornings, and the aroma of coffee and frying bacon filled the house. My ablutions were conducted with the studied care preceding special dates. As we ate breakfast, conversation was spotty. Dad was proud, delighted with my decision to enlist, and concerned, but trying to appear unmindful that something special was occurring that morning. Mother fought a trembling lip. Finally Dad had to leave. We shook hands. "Good Luck, Don. I hope you get in the Medical Corps. Let's hear from you.

"Good bye, Dad. Take care."

Dad disappeared precipitously. I finished breakfast and got my small suitcase containing only a change of underwear and my toilet articles, my civilian clothes would be sent home in it. Mother busied herself aimlessly until it was time for me to go.

She kissed me. "Take care, Don. Write to us. And don't take any chances." Before she broke down, I turned quickly and left the house.

When I arrived at Penn Station, it was crowded. There seemed to be thousands of young men like myself milling around. Nobody knew where to go or what to do. Finally three harassed sergeants (SGTs) appeared and called for all inductees. We bunched around them while they issued each of us one of the many thousands of sack lunches I would consume before I left the Army again. We were herded down the steps and onto tired, grimy, decrepit coaches that had been resurrected from some storage yard. The seats were upholstered in soot-impregnated green mohair. We clambered on board, found seats, and looked at one another silently. The usual traveling time to FT Dix is only about an hour, but we didn't have a very high priority because we started, stopped, were side-tracked and all but ran backwards, finally arriving at FT Dix in the early afternoon. Having eaten our sack lunches on the train, we were not going to get any other lunch.

We scrambled off the train and were shepherded to a tent city consisting mostly of pyramidal tents, where we were assigned six to a tent. One double-decked bunk was on each side of the tent with the exception of the side with the entrance. A coal stove, identified by someone as a "Sibley Stove", occupied the center. The company street was mud. In the center of the company was a latrine, which fortunately had duck boards in front of it so some of the mud could be scrapped from our shoes before entering. This was a tar-paper covered building with a cement floor that smelled of sweat, soap and urine. The air was always steaming from the showers. That week at FT Dix, people seemed to be taking showers all the time.

We were assigned to a Reception Company (Co) and the processing began. After bedding was issued we were ordered to make up our beds, an easy task for any one who had been to Scout camp, but difficult for some of my tent-mates who had never made their own beds before. We were then moved in bunches to a test center to take a battery of tests. The cadre called them the Army Qualification Test and told us that they were supposed to measure not only our intelligence, ability in reading, math and logic, but also our ability to fit into the many different military jobs. We were hungry, tired, cold and confused. It was late on a bitter winter day, some snow was left on the ground and there was ice where water had spilled in the Co street. With considerable misgivings we entered the baralike building, sat on student chairs and were "oriented" on the test for an interminable amount of time. Over the years I learned that the Army addressed the slowest learner in a group. Finally we began the endless series of tests. We did not complete them until about 11 o'clock at night. At last, bored guides led us to the mess hall.

The next day at 5:30 we awoke to a whistle and a loud call to "FALL OUT". It was bitter cold in that tent! None of us knew how to tend the Sibley Stove, so it had gone out during the night. Getting to the latrine early, I was able to get washed and shaved before the mob descended. That was a trick learned at Scout camp, beat the crowd to the latrine.

We were herded, I won't say marched yet, to the mess hall where we had a good, but heavy breakfast. Lots of eggs, bacon, bread, all served family style so we could eat as much as we liked. After breakfast a corporal (CPL), who couldn't have been in the Army much more few weeks himself, finally got us to the clothing issue point in anything but a military formation, to continue our processing. Here we stripped down to our skivies and put our civilian clothes into a "barracks bag". We then walked through an assembly line and were handed clothing, our Government Issue (GI). Since I was of medium height (5'1O") and slender, I was easy to fit and got a uniform that hung on me fairly well. Others were not so fortunate and were dispensed clothing far too large. We were issued an Olive Drab uniform consisting of trousers, shirt, blouse, overcoat, gloves, flannel underwear, shorts, T-shirts, handkerchiefs, towels, belt, cap, a couple of sets of what the CPL called "fatigue clothes", and a duffle bag. The duffle bag was for transporting our clothing and other items when traveling.

Finally we were fitted carefully with ankle high shoes, standard issue for the field. On top of those shoes we soon learned to put canvas leggings , combat boots had not yet been designed.

We then settled down to wait for the personnel clerks to analyze our test scores and civilian backgrounds and match them to military requirements. The next two or three days were crowded and unvaried. At reveille formation, the cadre checked to see that we were all there and then turned us loose for morning ablutions and chow. After breakfast, which now became almost a tactical feeding with clean garbage cans filled with hot soapy water in which to wash messkits, there was another formation. We "policed" the area, picking up papers and cigarette butts, and then were told off into various details: latrine, fire, supply, or coal. We pulled many details, in the post supply warehouses, loading beds and mattresses and other supplies onto trucks and delivering them to newly activated reception areas around the post, in barracks, tents, offices, recreation halls, test rooms and Post Exchanges (PXs) which we swept and mopped. The coal detail was the worst, loading trucks with soft coal and delivering it to various areas. We loathed Kitchen Police (KP) because we had to be on the job by 4:00 in the morning and rarely got off until 10:30 at night. Guard was merely a fire watch to see that none of the tents or buildings burned. Latrine "orderlies" scrubbed toilets, sinks, mirrors, shelves, duckboards and floors, only to re-do them after another surge passed. If we weren't on a detail we huddled around the Sibley stove in our pyramidal tent and speculated about the war, our shipment, our assignment, and our future. We traded experiences and told tales. We wrote letters with nothing of note in them, we read, and learned to cope with the Sibley stove.

I met many people, on details, in the mess hall, and in my tent. Most of them I never saw again. A few I liked, men with similar backgrounds, part of a college education, and I started to hang around with them. Al Cooperman was a heavy set Jewish lad from Brooklyn. He too had taken a pre-med course. We had the same aspirations, to the Medical Department in the Army and to medical school when the war was over. Bob Kempner, an overweight and apparently wealthy young man from Manhattan, was big and uncoordinated, and was almost always on the coal detail. He would go to the PX barber shop when dismissed from the detail and get hot towels and mud packs to get the coal dust out of his pores. Both of them were later assigned to the same basic training unit that I was. The other men are a blur, they passed through my life but left no impression.

There was not much to do at FT Dix. New men would come and old men would ship out. Names would appear on a roster on the bulletin board for shipment or for KP or for fire guard. We were warned to read the bulletin board at least twice a day, and most of us read it every hour.

The PX provided the nightly diversion. After evening chow, or after we got off details, which was frequently close to 10:00 p.m., we would walk over to the huge, barnlike structure. On entering, the barber shop was in a separate room on the right, the latrines and office on the left, and a broad hallway led into the large common room. There were tables and chairs in the open middle floor where people sat drinking beer or eating ice cream, sandwiches and goodies. The floors were always wet and muddy from shoes which were rarely scraped as the recruits entered the building. Counters on three sides displayed the basics, toilet articles, stationery, cleaning materials, cigarettes, and food. These wares were dispensed by young girls from nearby communities.

That first Sunday, Mother and Dad took bus, subway, and train from College Point to visit me. I was sitting on my bunk when the runner from company headquarters thrust his head in the tent and yelled, "Seibert"

"Right here."

"You got visitors at the service club." The head disappeared.

Grabbing my jacket and shrugging into it, I was out the tent opening putting on my overcoat before the runner cleared the company street, jamming my cap on my head and buttoning the coat as I ran to the service club. There was bedlam in the club. Built for a group of 500, there must have been three times that many people in it. The air was thick with smoke, the juke box was blaring out

Harry James' "Two O'clock Jump", people were talking and the noise was deafening. Looking about uncertainly I finally spotted Mother and Dad off in a corner. They saw me at the same time and we quickly met and embraced.

"Let's get out of here and take a walk," I suggested. "We can't hear ourselves over all of these people." Without waiting for their concurrence, I led the way outside, chattering about my experiences during the first week. We took a walk around my company area and I pointed out my tent. The Co area was off limits to civilians, so I could not take them into it.

Mother and Dad told me the news of the family, a letter from Bill almost a month old indicated that he was in Iceland. George, Margaret's husband, had been assigned to the 2nd Armored Division and was already out on maneuvers. Many friends had been drafted during the week. On top of this they had a lot of questions. Of course they wanted a good look at me in uniform, and seemed satisfied with what they saw. They took a picture of me.

We made our way through the slush and mud and I told them about my tent mates. They were surprised that I had not been shipped out or received orders. There was little to do, and no place to take them to eat. The snack bar in the service club was too crowded to get even a cup of coffee. Finally Dad looked at his watch and then a timetable. "Mother, let's catch the early train back. We can get a bus in ten minutes."

"Let's do. I am getting a little tired."

We talked quietly as we walked to the bus station. This time, Mother was more composed when I kissed her goodbye. She seemed to accept the fact that everything was going well and that I was satisfied with my lot. Though delighted to see them when they arrived, I was glad to see them leave. It was just too much to try to entertain visitors in a reception center.

One of the few things I remember vividly from FT Dix was a lecture given us by the captain (CPT) who was the Commanding Officer (CO) of the Reception Co. He insisted that we should never turn up the collar of our overcoats, because that merely funneled cold air down inside the overcoat and made you colder. He told us we should leave the collar of the overcoat flat, fasten the top button and seal ourselves inside the coat. It is strange, the trivial things that made a lasting impression on me at that time.

After a week at Dix I was assigned to the Medical Department. The Air Corps had top priority on personnel who scored high on the Army Qualification Test. My scores were in the upper quarter so there had been some debate among the assignment people as to whether I would go to the Air Corps or to the Medics. Because of my pre-med training and my expressed interest, they finally assigned me to the Medical Department.

My name, along with Al Cooperman's and Bob Kempner's appeared on a shipping roster on the bulletin board. We were informed to be ready for shipment the following morning.

We fell out after breakfast the next day with stuffed duffel bags, were loaded onto a train; a SGT told us that we were going to the Medical Training Center at Camp Lee, VA. It was a long trip once again because the troop train had low priority. Getting through the Washington yards was a real problem, it took us several hours to do just that. We finally got to Camp Lee at 9 o'clock at night. We had been issued another sack lunch for the noon meal, but we hadn't anything else to eat. The mess halls were closed when we arrived but someone managed to get some dehydrated soup heated, and made available coffee, bread and jam, and that had to suffice for the evening meal. We were issued bedding about midnight, and tumbled onto cots too tired to know what it was all about, or to care much.

We had hardly gotten to sleep when the lights were turned on in the barracks, whistles blew and loud voices insisted that we "FALL OUT in overcoats and shoes immediately." We stumbled outside and were introduced to the infamous "short arm" inspection.

"Okay, line up behind Corporal Best. When you reach the doctor, unbutton your coat, take out your penis and milk it. Now MOVE!"

With no conscious effort, I found myself in a line which inched forward slowly. Suddenly I was in front of an officer seated in a chair under the fire light on the building. I froze. A non-commissioned officer (NCO) standing next to the doctor snapped, "Take it out and milk it." Somehow I managed to comply, and as I moved on another NCO said not unkindly, "Move back into the barracks and get ready for reveille."

We were told later that this technique was used to identify soldiers infected with gonorrhea. It was usually done at reveille, though I have seen such inspections held at almost any time. If a discharge was noted, that soldier was marked for further examination. It was one of the most degrading experiences I had in the Army, though I understand it was of great assistance in controlling this venereal disease. The Army had a massive VD program which included monthly lectures and graphic movies, frequent testing using Wassermans, Kahns and the "short arm", and the free provision of prophylaxis.

After reveille and a welcome breakfast, I was assigned to the 3rd Platoon of Company C, 4th Medical Training Battalion. Where it was located on Camp Lee is now a mystery although at the time I thought I'd never forget the area. Most of the people in Co C who had been to college were assigned to the 3rd Platoon (Plt). We became the butt of Co C, every mistake or goof the platoon made gave rise to sarcastic comments about the "smart-ass college boys" who couldn't do as well in training as the rest of the company. In the end we did come out on top in everything, but that was much later. Co C was commanded by CPT James L. Prejean, a doctor, who had a neat moustache, wore riding britches and boots and fit the image most of us had of the "Old Army" officer (OFF). The First Sergeant (1SG) was a tough career soldier named Paul Reichert. He was the one, rather than the Co CO, with whom we had to deal. The 3rd Plt Leader (Ldr) was a dentist, First Lieutenant (1LT) Robert F. Hand. Lieutenants (LTs) Hand and Lee, a veterinarian who commanded the 4th Plt, were the two officers whom we liked and got to know best. We were fortunate in having one of the senior NCOs in C Co as our Platoon Sergeant (PSG), Staff Sergeant (SSG) James. His assistants, CPLs Best and Robbins, were eager NCOs who were both humane and dedicated.

One of the men in the platoon, Al Cedarbaum, became a life long friend. Al was a sturdy individual about my height with sandy hair, a round face and a smile which displayed dazzling white teeth. This was in character, since Al was a licensed dentist from New York who had volunteered to enlist in order to get into the Army early, rather than wait for the routine and extended processing necessary to be called to active duty as an officer. By the end of our training cycle, however, the paperwork was completed and he was commissioned a First Lieutenant in the Dental Corps. Al and I were assigned to the same squad and shared the same interests, likes and dislikes. We agreed almost completely on our evaluations of our fellow trainees.

The military service is a powerful catalyst in the formation of close friendships. The time spent together is apparently not important, but the circumstances, the experiences shared, the conditions under which you meet a person exert influences which quickly cement warm relationships. This was to be one of the greatest rewards of my military career -the formation of close and lasting friendships.

As is the case in every unit, there was a character; Bob Kempner, who I had met at FT Dix, kept us howling with his stories and with his griping. He was a nonconformist but a good guy, who would do anything to help a friend. There were forty men in the 3rd Plt and 200 in C Co, but I can recall only those two, plus Claude Lipe, Al Coooperman, John Thompson and Fred Buch. At the time I was sure that I would never forget any of them, now most are names without faces and only Al Cedarbaum is real.

The day after we arrived at Camp Lee we received our first shots, typhoid and tetanus. It was interesting to watch the reaction to the needle of various individuals. As we stood in line awaiting our turn to be inoculated, even some of the most apparently virile had qualms. Some men passed out, not from reaction to the serum but from dread of the needle.

We soon got into the swing of the routine, up at 5:00 with the blast of the whistle and the lights turned on in the squad bays. Radios, plugged into outlets controlled by the light switches, began to play when the lights went on. All we heard at that time was what we called "hill-billy music". The radio stations in the area carried nothing but what is now termed "country and western music", which drove wild those of us from New York. We longed for music by the great name bands, such as Glen Miller, Artie Shaw and Harry James. Reveille, barracks cleaning, breakfast and the first training formation followed each other inexorably day after day.

Our training (tng) began immediately, as the cadre attempted to turn us into effective soldiers in a few short weeks. Probably the most important training we received was the result of community living rather than any particular lecture or instruction. On the drill field, in the barracks, in the mess hall, on details, in practical work, we soon learned the need for teamwork, for cooperation and coordination of the entire group's effort.

The first Saturday inspection brought it home to us in a graphic way. As latrine orderly, I had finally gotten the place scrubbed and gleaming. Suddenly, one of the men on the mop detail burst into the latrine, carrying a mop dripping duty water over the floor. He rushed to the sink, squeezed his mop and made a mess of the sink. Just as he was leaving, the outside man dashed in to wash his hands. In no time the latrine was a shambles. There were shouts from the barracks as similar incidents disrupted other areas.

The latrine was not fully restored to order when the door burst open and a loud "TEN HUT" announced the arrival of the Commander and inspecting officer. The latrine received eight "gigs" and the rest of the barracks many more. The 3rd Plt was restricted to the company area for the weekend!

Thus we became aware of how one individual's lack of consideration made more work or greater difficulty for all, how quickly and easily any job was accomplished if everyone concerned did his full share, how one person could disrupt a formation or task. Involuntarily we put pressure on one another to insure group participation and team work. It was an unconscious process, but one which was all the more effective.

Our training, once begun, continued at a fast pace. We absorbed military lore even as we slept! We learned to salute, to say "Sir", to take off our hats indoors, to move off with the left foot, to police the area without being told, to refrain from littering {"What you don't drop you don't have to pick up."), to sound off when our name was called, to repeat our serial number on command (can I ever forget 12056708?), to move on the double when an NCO spoke, to use the twenty-four hour clock (5:00 P.M. became 1700 in a short time), and to do all these things without thinking about them.

Our professional training was also conducted at breakneck speed; the cadre shook their heads as they groaned "Nine weeks to make soldiers out of you recruits!" An endless succession of lectures, problems and practical work in military courtesy and customs of the service, military law, first aid, litter drill, defense against chemical attack, military medicine, Articles of War, field sanitation, camouflage, cover and concealment, field fortifications, ever-longer hikes with ever increasing equipment on our backs. We learned the art of packing knapsacks in the dark and putting on leggings with the hooks on the outer side of the leg; when put on incorrectly the hooks were on the inner side and caught and tripped the unwary. Then more first aid, camping and bivouacs, there seemed no end to the training and little reason for much of it. Yet it all seemed to coalesce into a single theme, the Medical Department Soldier prepared for combat.

In addition to our training there were details. A barracks orderly was left behind each day, as a guard and to restore the squad bays to inspection condition after we departed for training. A Co Runner was held back as was a supply room helper. And periodically a small group reported to

Battalion Headquarters (HQ) to clean it up; some of the details, including fire watch, were after training hours.

KP was the most frequent and disliked detail that we pulled in Basic Training. We ate family style at picnic type tables in the mess hall. Food was placed on each table in large platters and bowls, though bread, butter and jam were always on the tables when we filed in. We stood at attention at the table until everyone was in place and were then given permission to sit down; food was passed from soldier to soldier. Anything left could be eaten by the first person who asked for it. It was a grave sin to "short stop" a dish that had been asked for. Frequently there were "seconds" to be obtained by holding up an empty dish for the Dining Room Orderly (DRO). Coffee was in large aluminum pitchers, as was fruit juice in the morning, and iced tea or Kool-aid when on the menu. Milk was usually served in individual cartons.

When assigned to KP on the duty roster, you never knew what job you would be given. The Mess Sergeant was all powerful in this area, and rewarded some with light tasks such as DRO, and punished others with the outside detail. The later was despised not only because it entailed washing out the garbage cans, but also because the outside man had to clean the grease trap. This was a large cast iron box with a baffle to trap the grease. Cleaning it was a messy and smelly job, thoroughly disliked by everyone. The one reward of KP was getting extra food, especially milk.

The DRO had to set the tables and clean the dining room. Every item on the table had to be meticulously aligned, plates, cups, silverware, salt and pepper shakers, sugar bowls, jam jars and catsup bottles were zeroed in across as well as lengthwise. Each item not specifically washed every meal, such as salt shakers or catsup bottles, had to be wiped clean of dirty finger marks. The center board of the table had to be turned, and all crumbs removed. And of course the floor had to be mopped after each meal. Still it was an easier job than being in the kitchen. Others had to wash dishes or pots and pans, assist the cooks by peeling potatoes and other vegetables, or do other chores as directed by the Mess Sergeant.

KP involved a longer day than usual. At 0400 the Charge-of-Quarters (CQ) would awaken the KPs who had tied towels to the end of their bunks. And it was rare when a KP got away from the mess hall before 2100, even though the evening meal was served immediately after retreat, about 1715.

The mess hall was the scene of my first real trouble in the Army. One morning, following my normal routine, I had gotten to the latrine early, made my ablutions before it became mobbed, quickly made up my bunk and straightened up my area, and then arrived at the door of the mess hall to be one of the first in. Just before the Mess Sergeant admitted us Marlarski, a big Polish kid in my platoon, pushed in line ahead of me muttering, "I've got to eat in a hurry to take care of something." I became incensed. He was always one of the last people in formation, and had held up the platoon on more than one occasion. He wouldn't make any effort to get up early so that he could take care of his chores. My temper flared, and I pushed him out of line. "Get to the end of the line where you belong."

"Don't push me. I got to get out fast." With that he pushed back in line ahead of me.

Although he was large and muscular, and outweighed me by almost 30 pounds, I punched him. Immediately there was a battle going during which I got in some pretty fair licks before the cadremen separated us. Had the fight continued, eventually he would have beat me up badly, I'm afraid. Finally we were pulled apart. SSG James told us both to report to him after chow. When we went to his cadre-room in the barracks later, he chewed us out and gave each of us a couple of days extra KP. Marlarski had been surprised at my response, and gave me grudging respect for standing up to him. Certainly I earned the respect of the other men in the company for asserting my rights.

For the first three weeks we were at Camp Lee, we were restricted to the post. This was considered the normal incubation period for most diseases which we might have contracted before we came into the Army. After that we were permitted to go into Petersburg. The town was so overwhelmed with troops from Camp Lee, that there wasn't much to do but go to the USO club. There was an Episcopal Church which I attended whenever I could get into town on Sunday But there were few things that could be bought downtown that were not available in the PX. The principal one was the garrison belt cherished both as an ornament and a weapon. Basically there was everything needed on post: entertainment, movies, PX, beer garden, chapel, and there was no real point in going into town except for the chance to get away from the barracks, the routine and the supervision of the noncoms.

The day that we were turned loose on Petersburg, February 28th, was my first official payday in the Army. After inspection, which was held in Class A uniforms, the whistle blew and the now familiar "OUTSIDE" resounded through the barracks. We rushed into formation under the watchful eyes of the cadre. SSG James took the report from the squad leaders (SLs), and turned the Plt over to 1LT Hand, as 1SG Reichert ordered "POST", turned, and saluted CPT Prejean.

"At ease, men." CPT Prejean then gave us our first "payday lecture." He talked briefly about our training, venereal disease, military courtesy, soldier's savings and safety. Then he called, "First Sergeant." As the 1SG strode out to salute him, 1LT Hand moved to the rear of the Plt and SSG James took his place.

"PARADE REST. Now when your name is called, line up at the Orderly Room door. When the man ahead of you comes out, walk in, remove your hat with your left hand, stop two paces in front of the Captain's desk and salute him. He will not return your salute. I repeat, he will not return your salute. Report as follows, 'PVT Jones reports for pay, sir.' Step forward, sign your payroll signature on the payroll. That is your first name, middle initial and last name just as it appears on your records. The Captain will count out your pay. Scoop it up into your hat with your right hand, do a left face without saluting and move out of the way. Any questions?"

No one dared ask any questions, even if a legitimate one had occurred to any of us. 1SG Reichert was not one you questioned. He told you and that was it. After the briefest pause he said, "Platoon Sergeants take charge", and moved smartly to the Orderly Room. He stepped inside and returned outside almost immediately. He opened the payroll he now held in his hand.

"James!"

"Stephen C." SSG James trotted to the Orderly Room door. And so it went as the 1SG called the company alphabetically according to rank. Responses varied from the professional one SSG James had given to "Yo", "Present", and the "Here, SGT," that we recruits gave. The line stretched long, S is far down the alphabet and there was no one more junior in the company.

Finally I stood at the Orderly Room door. A soldier came out and I stepped in, took off my hat with my left hand and walked forward looking for the CPT's desk. It was immediately apparent, and I stopped two paces before it, rendered my best salute and hesitated before returning my hand to my side when the CPT failed to return it. "Private Seibert reports for pay, Sir." The Captain motioned to the payroll lying open on the desk. Even as I bent to sign it, he was counting out the eighteen dollars due me. Privates were then paid twenty-one dollars a month. Three dollars were deducted for laundry service. Scooping the money into my cap, I turned to the left. Already the next man was crowding into the Orderly Room behind me.

On turning, I encountered several NCOs sitting at a folding field table. One was selling a book of movie tickets for two dollars, I bought one, the next was selling PX coupons, redeemable for merchandise in the PX, I asked for a five dollar book, the third "urged" me to contribute a dollar to the mess fund to buy additional condiments, I contributed. When finally clear of the Orderly Room, I had ten dollars to show for my first month in the Army. Despite our impoverished pay, card and dice games flourished in the barracks. Gambling a dollar, I made two, and quit. That was not my forte, I knew that I would lose all of my money if I did not quit then. Others had lost their month's pay by the time Al Cedarbaum and I got back from our short-lived trip to Petersburg.

By the fourth week we were getting on well, doing litter drill, carrying patients, learning advanced first aid, and learning how to live in the communal atmosphere of the barracks. It was at this time that we received our yellow fever shot. We lined up after chow on a Monday night and got the usual assembly line treatment. We were told that there was a possibility of a reaction four to five days later. That same week one of the men in our company came down with spinal meningitis, was rushed off to the hospital and subsequently died. A second man was diagnosed as having the disease on Friday morning. That evening retreat was a battalion (Bn) formation.

The Adjutant (Adj) took his position.

"REPORT."

Each Co CO in turn rendered his report. CPT Prejean saluted as he intoned "C Company all present or accounted for, Sir." The Adj did an about face and saluted the Bn Commander standing behind him. "All present or accounted for, Sir."

"Take your post. AT EASE. Men, Company C has been placed off limits to all men not assigned to it. All men of Company C are restricted to their company area except when on required training. This is a precautionary measure only, to prevent a possible epidemic."

Everyone in the Battalion knew that one man in C Co had died of spinal meningitis and that a second man had been hospitalized for it. A stir rippled through the formation at the Commander's announcement of the quarantine of C Company.

"Battalion, ATTENTION. Parade, REST."

As I assumed a rigid parade rest position I felt myself getting dizzy and swayed a bit. I had never felt that way before, and the thought raced through my mind that perhaps I was coming down with spinal meningitis! Gulping some air, I managed to calm myself as the last notes of Retreat sounded.

"ATTENTION."

We popped to. As the bugle sounded "To the Colors" I became light headed, grabbed the arm of the man next to me and momentarily recovered. Then I blacked out. When I came to, I was in my bunk with five or six doctors hovering over me. A thermometer was thrust under my tongue. When it was removed a doctor examined it and announced, "Normal."

"Is your neck stiff?" "No, sir." A grunt greeted this response.

"Bend your head forward." A pair of hands felt the back of my neck, as I bent my head forward with no discomfort or effort. "The neck is not rigid," reported the doctor whose hands held my neck. This was greeted with a sigh of relief. Some one looked into my eyes. "Some Jaundice," he said.

"When did you get your yellow fever shot, Private?"

"Monday, sir."

There was a whispered consultation between the doctors. One then came to me and said,

"It appears that you have had a reaction to the yellow fever serum. We have had several cases like this so far, and your symptoms seem to fit the pattern. There is nothing to worry about and you will be back to normal in a day or so. We will put you on light duty tomorrow, and then you can go back to normal training. If you have any further discomfit, go on sick call immediately. Understand?"

"Yes, Sir."

The doctors cleared out and my platoon crowded around my bed. There were many questions. Someone brought a tray over from the mess hall, but I did not feel like eating.

Later, Al Cedarbaum told me that when I passed out there was a strong reaction through the Bn. Everyone was sure that another case of spinal meningitis had surfaced and that C Co was completely infected with it. The platoon was happy with the doctors' diagnosis and started to kid me about passing out in ranks. The only good thing that came out of it was that I got out of inspection the next morning.

Monday, I was in formation as usual and training continued.

The next Friday, Al and I went up to Richmond in an Army truck to hear Ezio Pinza sing in the Mosque. It was good to hear something other than "hill-billy" music and doubly so to hear a concert by such a famed artist. It was also good to see the Mosque again. The last time had been in 1928 when the family moved from Richmond to New York.

In the sixth week of training I caught a cold. It did not respond to my studied neglect, and overcoming my reluctance, I went on sick call. A bored aid man took my temperature and asked a few questions. When he discovered that I had a fever of 103, he sent me in to see the doctor, who sent me to the hospital with a "Strep Throat." The station hospital was a series of one story buildings connected with covered or inclosed walkways. There were about fifteen beds on each side of the ward. Most patients in the ward were there for like ailments.

Treatment was symptomatic and effective, one of the new wonder drugs, sulfanilimide, aspirin, lots of fluids and bed rest. In two days I was eager to get out. As soon as my temperature was normal, I took my turn in cleaning the ward and serving the sicker patients. This was routine in military hospitals, those able to do so assisted the ward man in his duties. Finally I was released back to duty.

The week before the end of our training, men in the company began to get assignments. Two of the men who had volunteered to become paratroopers received orders to FT Benning. Up to that time I hadn't heard about the Airborne (ABN) and asked them to tell me about it. It sounded good, but it was too late for me to put in for jump school at that point. Many of our company were assigned to the 1st Infantry Division which was getting ready to move overseas. About 20 of us were selected for advanced training at Walter Reed Hospital. We were to be trained as Senior Surgical Technicians to assist in operations, serve on surgical wards or in Bn Aid Stations.

Trucks took us the 150 miles to Walter Reed which we reached late in the afternoon. We were assigned to new brick barracks and were impressed with the treatment we received. Al Cooperman, John Thompson, and Fred Buch from my Plt were in the same barracks as myself. I struck up a conversation with Ted Rothert, a slim, dark haired soldier who appeared a bit older than the rest of us, wore glasses and sported a neatly trimmed moustache. He was interested in singing, enjoyed eating and liked to talk about Purdue, his Alma Mater. He and I enjoyed the same interests and became life long friends. Vic Maslon, a short energetic individual who had gone to NYU uptown, formed the other member of a close triumvirate which lasted all through the course. Vic and I corresponded for many years.

The three of us were more or less inseparable. In fact, Ted, Vic, and I took the train to New York one Saturday afternoon after training for a quick weekend. Vic's father was in the city so Vic did not come home with me. Ted did. As luck would have it, my brother Bill was home. We went out on the town. I think we hit every bar on 8th Avenue that night and got gloriously drunk. In those days a soldier in uniform was the pride of the country, and it was rare indeed to pay for a drink. We got home about three in the morning. Sometime during the night Bill got up to go to the bathroom. On his way back to bed, he became confused and first tried to crawl into bed with Ted. When Ted pushed him out, he wandered into the dining room and crawled on the dining room table between the cloth and the mat and there the family found him in the morning. It was quite a weekend!

The course at Walter Reed was from 1 April to 23 May. Under the direction of CPT Cross, an articulate group of doctors gave us truly professional training. Primarily, we were trained to help out at aid stations in the forward areas where emergency surgery was required.

As part of our training, we were assigned to various wards on which we worked under experienced ward masters. Classes were interspersed with ward duties. My first duty was on a medical ward. The principal chores were cleaning rooms and halls and giving medication, fluids and chow. It was not very challenging or interesting, but served to familiarize me with paper work, forms, reports and ward procedures. Next I drew an assignment to the Neuropsychiatric (NP) Ward. This was more interesting because of the patients. It was a locked ward. Each of us carried a key, not only to the main door, but also to each of the rooms. Here too, I learned several techniques, the use of hydrotherapy to calm violent patients, the importance of eternal vigilance, the need that people have for their fellow humans. Several patients were truly pathetic. There was an elderly Infantry Colonel (COL) who developed a trembling in his hand and was put into this ward pending diagnosis. He was horrified, as was his wife, when she visited him. I finally let them into a locked dining room for privacy. There was a West Point Cadet who declaimed and orated and insisted he had to study for a "writ". There was a SGT who tried to grab the nurse or any other female who came within his sight.

My final duty was on an orthopedic ward. Here I learned the bed care of patients, bathing them, taking care of urinals and bed pans, giving back rubs, making beds with patients in them, turning long term patients, changing dressings, assisting in putting on, changing and removing casts, making rounds with the doctors and Grand Rounds with the Chief of Service, giving shots for pain, and feeding patients in traction. Each of the ward tours lasted only a week, but the ward masters worked us while they had us.

We did not get into the operating room (OR) except to assist in scrubbing it. There was a mock-up of an OR in the school where we practiced many techniques, adjusting the operating table for various operations, draping patients, preparing or "prepping" patients for an operation to include shaving the area of the incision, setting up instrument (Mayo) stands, identifying and passing instruments, and counting sponges..

Finally the two month course came to an end, and we eagerly awaited our orders. Ted Rothert received his first. He and several other members of the class were selected to take an additional month of training in the OR in preparation for assignment as instructors either at Walter Reed or at a new medical training center being opened in Atlanta. The rest of us hoped that we would join battalion medical teams or division clearing companies. None of us did. My assignment was to the Station Hospital at Indiantown Gap Military Reservation (IGMR) northeast of Harrisburg, PA.

During the process of clearing the Student Co at Walter Reed, I was given a Travel Request (TR) which could be exchanged for a bus ticket. The trip to Indiantown Gap involved several changes, but finally my duffel bag and I arrived at the small post nestled in the mountains. After signing in, the CQ escorted me to a barracks and told me where to get bedding and white uniforms. And that was all. For three days I was used by the CQ for details, cleaning the dayroom and Orderly Room and policing up around the Detachment (Det) Headquarters (HQ). This irked me because I had an exalted opinion of my training at Walter Reed. On the fourth day I marched into the First Sergeant's office and demanded a job, pointing out that I was a trained Senior Surgical Technician and wanted to get to work. 1SG Flynn, an old Regular Army NCO, looked at me as if I was insane. He told me, in barracks room terms no soldier could fail to grasp, to get the hell out of his Orderly Room. He further indicated that I would be assigned when and where he decided. My confrontation had some effect on him, however, because the next day, Sunday, I was told to report to the "locked ward", a psychiatric ward.

Despite the fact that I would be deprived of a day off, I eagerly donned starched white trousers and jacket and made my way to Ward 24. This was at the far end of the hospital. The ward was enclosed by a chain link fence and the windows were barred. Opening the wooden doors from the corridor I was faced with a heavy metal grill door. There was a door bell, which I pushed.

The door was unlocked by an attractive dark-haired nurse. She was a second lieutenant, and came up to my shoulder. "What can I do for you, soldier?"

"I am Private Seibert, Ma'am, reporting for duty on this ward."

"Come in, we can use you." She led the way into the nurses' office. "Have you had any experience with neuropsychiatric patients?"

Standing awkwardly, not sure if I was supposed to be at attention while talking to a nurse, I responded, "I spent a week in the NP Ward at Walter Reed during my Surgical Technicians Course, Lieutenant."

"So, you are a surgical technician and they send you here! Typical. Well, sit down a minute and let me tell you about your duties. I'm Second Lieutenant Federonko, and I am here on this ward temporarily, myself."

With that she proceeded to tell me about the ward. It was a combination prison and neuropsychiatric ward. There were several patients who periodically became violent. She warned me to stay alert, not to let the patients irritate me, to handle them with care and cautioned me against beating them or mistreating them. While we were talking a tall, muscular SGT came into the office and the second lieutenant (2LT) introduced me to the Ward Master. He took me in hand and gave me further, specific, terse instructions.

After working on Ward 24 for four days, I got to know 2LT Dana Federonko well, we became as good friends as the difference in our rank and position permitted. She and other nurses dated enlisted men (Federonko was dating the SGT in Ward 24), finding some of them more compatible than many of the medical officers, most of whom were married. But all were spoken for, so I never got to take any of them out.

Finally I was assigned to permanent duty on Medical Ward 45. Indiantown Gap was a staging center for units being shipped overseas. Just before my arrival the 28th Division (Div), Pennsylvania National Guard, had left and most of the patients in the hospital were soldiers it had left behind. The ward had 10 or 12 men on it recovering from flu, colds or other respiratory ailments. There was little medical care for them, most of my duties were cleaning and supply details. My life in the hospital became boring.

Once a week all enlisted men had military training under the supervision of the Detachment Commander (Det CO) or 1SG. Drill, required subjects, reading of the Articles of War every six months, VD lectures, and medical classes were the norm. At one session 1SG Flynn announced that we would fire on the range in two months. The next six training periods were devoted to the US Rifle, Caliber 30, Springfield '03. There had been no rifle training in basic, so this was new and interesting. We learned to field strip and clean the rifle and then had preliminary marksmanship training, sighting, aiming, windage adjustment, dry firing and trigger squeeze.

The day for our familiarization firing came. It was a bright sunny day and I SG Flynn fell the Det in to march to the range. When he gave "RIGHT SHOULDER ARMS", several of the wardmen were almost decapitated. He had not taught us the Manual of Arms so few of us knew how to get the rifle to our shoulders and weapons swung wildly as we lifted them into place. A disgusted First Sergeant took us over back roads so we would not be seen. Firing was almost as much of a disaster. There had not been enough or proper training. Most of us hit somewhere on the target, but that was about all. Ten rounds to zero, 10 rounds at slow fire and five rounds rapid fire was all that was allotted. This was familiarization in name only.

Though unhappy at not being in the Operating Room or on a surgical ward, I settled into the ward routine. The NCO-in-charge (NCOIC) of the OR told me that there were too many technicians for the work load. The surgical wards were likewise fully staffed. So I made the best of it, trying to learn as much as possible and asking everyone who would listen to me to get me transferred to a ward or section where I could learn more. The hospital was not busy as there were no troops on the post and it was handling the remnants of the 28th Div and cadre personnel. Then word came that the 1st Infantry (IN) Div was enroute.

The 1st IN Div arrived at Indiantown Gap directly from maneuvers, hence the men were dirty, their personal equipment was dirty and it appeared that they had been unable to shower for a week or more. The first outbreak of diarrhea occurred immediately after the 1st Div arrived. It soon became epidemic as several hundred men were hospitalized with a virulent form of shigella dysentery. Ward 45 was turned into a dysentery ward. It was impossible to count the bed pans I handled in the next few weeks! Wardmen were kept busy taking samples of feces to the lab for culture to determine whether or not the patients still had the organism causing the dysentery. The doctors were trying a new sulpha drug to control the disease.

At the height of the epidemic I was shifted to night duty and had time to study a little. After my 2100 check of the ward one evening I turned out the lights, settled at the desk in the ward office and took out paper, pencil and the book on the chemistry of the sulpha drugs that the ward doctor had lent me. Intent on constructing the spatial formula for sulphaguanadine, the medication being used to treat the dysentery, I became completely absorbed. The drug had several benzine radicals and the linkages were giving me trouble. Just as I tore up the fifth attempt to derive the formula, there was a slight sound and I turned to find the stocky SSG in charge of the Lab watching me. "Say, whatcha doing there, young fella?"

"Trying to figure out the spatial formula for sulphaguanadine. I can't balance these damn bonds and linkages, though."

"You had Organic?

"Yeah, I have a minor in chemistry."

"Where did you go?"

"I took a pre-med course at NYU, Washington Square College."

"What are you doing on a medical ward?"

"The damn Top won't put me where I belong. I graduated from Walter Reed as a Senior Surgical Technician, but I can't get near the OR or a surgical ward."

"Think you might be interested in working in the Lab? We're short a couple of people and with your chemistry you would be a natural."

"Sure, I'd like to get away from pushing bed pans in this dysentery ward. It sounds good. Lab work would help me in Med School. But how do I get 1SG Flynn to transfer me?"

"I'll take care of that. Come down to the Lab tomorrow about three. I want you to talk to CPT Irey, the Officer-in-Charge. Can you make it?"

"Sure. I'll be there."

"Okay. My name is Long. What's yours?"

"Seibert. Don Seibert."

"Okay Seibert. I'll see you tomorrow at three. So long."

"So long, SGT Long. Thanks."

The chubby SSG disappeared into the corridor. I mulled over what had taken place. Certainly lab work would be more interesting than work on the medical ward. But would I be giving up all chance of getting into the OR? Well, I would wait and see what developed.

The next day I went to the Lab at 1500 as agreed. SSG Long met me and took me into the Laboratory office. CPT Irey, the Officer-In-Charge (OIC) of the Lab, was about my height and build, but about 30 years old. He was very business-like, asked me about my college education and seemed impressed with the amount of biology and chemistry lab courses I had taken. He told me before I left that he was going to have me transferred to the Lab as soon as possible, but that it might take a day or so. Satisfied that I had done the right thing, I left, certain that I would enjoy working for CPT Irey and SSG Long. Work in the dysentery ward became intolerable and I was impatient to get started in the Lab.

In those last few days on Ward 45, for the first and only time in my Army career, I got drunk on duty. Miss McKeehan, who supervised three or four medical wards, including 45, at night, brought back from Harrisburg a pint of rum, which she presented to me because she said I was doing a good job on the ward. Due to frustration over the pending transfer I proceeded to drink the whole pint.

That was just too much alcohol for me and about 0400 I called Miss McKeehan and told her I was in no condition to work. She came to the ward, took over my duties, let me go to bed and woke me up just before the day shift took over. It was a lesson to me and I felt miserable, physically as well as mentally in that I had let her down, let the Army down and let myself down. I swore that never again would I be under the influence of alcohol while I was on duty. To this day I drink, and will always drink, but memory of that lesson remained and never again was I under the influence of alcohol on duty.

Finally, I was transferred to the Lab and began doing much of the routine work. Under the watchful eye of SSG Long and other military and civilian technicians I soon learned many procedures, taking blood samples and making white and red cell counts, typing blood, doing urine analyses, and running Wassermans and Kahns, the two standard tests for syphilis. In pipetting urine one day, I inadvertently got some in my mouth and can attest that diabetic urine is sweet! When SSG Long showed me how to use the dark field microscope and I saw for the first time the beautiful but deadly *Treponema Pallidum,* the organism that causes syphilis, it opened up a new world. Lab work was more interesting than ward work, at least on the dysentery ward, so I was pleased. It was an opportunity to learn lab procedures, some biochemistry and blood work.

SSG Long, the rotund NCO who had gotten me assigned to the Lab, was now my boss. He had attended Gettysburg College where he had studied chemistry with a view toward going on to medical school. He was an interesting extrovert, who loved to argue, and had the intelligence and general knowledge to push his points logically and forcefully. He had a keen sense of humor and his throaty chuckle befitted his moon-faced appearance. He smoked a pipe, usually one with a curved stem, which imparted an academic look to him. As he taught me my duties, I got to know and appreciate Bill and we became life long friends. We had similar interests and ideas, we both hoped to go to medical school and we began to do things together. We took long walks about the Reservation, swam in the reservoir, snacked in the Lab in the evenings, and talked on and on. Frequently we went into Harrisburg when off duty. One of our favorite places to eat was a small hotel which served excellent onion soup, cheap. We could rarely afford to eat in the more expensive Perm-Harris or Harrisburger Hotels, though when we went into the bars in those hotels we were frequently treated to drinks paid for by some WWI veteran or deferred individual. Men in uniform were still held in high esteem. One week I went home with Bill to visit his parents in Williamsport.

It was a good trip.

Bill was not only a good friend, he was also an excellent NCO. He ran an efficient laboratory, knew his business, kept the fine line between friendship and authority, and handled both the civilian and military personnel in the Lab fairly and effectively.

Some time in the summer of 1942 we were told that Congress had raised our pay, privates henceforth were to get $50.00 per month. That more than doubled my pay! There had not been much trouble with money. Civilians were eager to buy soldiers a drink in a bar. There always seemed to be enough to buy toilet articles, see an occasional movie and eat in Harrisburg once in a while. Most soldiers seemed to get along on $21.00. Now we were to get twice that much! But we were "urged" to take out an allotment for a War Bond. For $ 18.75 per month we could get a $25.00 Bond. AND THE PRESSURE WAS APPLIED. It seemed like a good idea, so I signed up to have $18.75 deducted from my pay each month. Even after that deduction, I still had more money than in the past.

Just before our pay raise went into effect, I went into Harrisburg one Saturday. The bus stop was at the railroad station, which I entered on a whim, just as the public address system crackled and a voice announced, "Train for Paoli, Philadelphia, Trenton and New York. Track Three. All aboard."

Without thinking I rushed to the ticket window. The agent looked at me and asked, "Where to,son?"

"Round trip to New York."

"Here you are. That will be three fifty."

I reached into my wallet and pulled out three dollars. I felt in my pocket and it was empty!

"Gosh, I've only got three dollars. Guess I can't go."

"Well soldier, we won't keep you in camp for fifty cents." He smiled at me and handed me the ticket.

"Gee, thanks. I sure appreciate it." But I was already racing for the train which had just rumbled into the station. I had no weekend pass, just my Class A pass, no toilet articles, and not a cent to my name. Well, I could borrow some money when I got home.

The trip to New York took about three hours, before long the train was easing into Pennsylvania Station. From track 12 I walked thoughtfully toward the IRT Subway. When I got there I squared my shoulders and went up to the change booth.

"I'm on a pass for the weekend and I'm broke. I need to get to Flushing to see my family. Can I duck under the turnstile?"

The man looked at me keenly for a minute, then smiled and waved me over to the turnstile.

"Thanks." I ducked under while several people stared, then walked to the uptown platform.

The 45 minute ride to Flushing seemed interminable. Finally the train reached the end of the line. I walked to the College Point Causeway and started to thumb each car that passed. The third car slowed and stopped. I ran up to it.

"Going to the Point?"

"Sure, hop in."

It turned out the driver knew my brother, and we talked about mutual friends in College Point. Though now classified 4F because of an injury, he had played on the College Point Football Team, and knew many people I did. He told me where they all were. He dropped me off at my front door. The family was surprised and delighted to see me. I called my girl friend, Winnie, and went over to her house. Mother and Dad gave me a few dollars {they would not lend it to me) to tide me over until pay day. The return trip was uneventful.

Periodically, each soldier assigned to the Lab pulled night duty. When Bill was convinced that I could handle most of the routine procedures he put me on the roster. The "on duty" Lab man did any emergency procedures required, if they were too much for him, he called SSG Long. Most of the requests were for blood counts in suspected appendicitis cases, though occasionally other tests were required. The night man also delivered the slips showing the results of the lab work. This meant an hour's trek throughout the rambling cantonment type hospital. It was a chance to talk to some of the ward men and nurses and to see what was going on in the hospital.

Lab work became routine. Assigned to Hematology, I drew blood for white and red counts, made smears for differential counts and drew gallons of blood for the Kahn's, which I ran. Fate seemed to punish me for defecting from the dysentery ward when I was called upon to take rectal smears from half of the 1st Div to see how many men still harbored any *Shigella Paradysenteriae,* the organism that caused the dysentery. That was not a pleasant job!

CPT Irey was the hospital pathologist as well as the Lab Officer. He came in early one morning and told me to follow him. We went over to the morgue , a separate building near the boiler room. As we went he told me that a body had been brought in the evening before and he would have to perform an autopsy. I was to assist him! This would surely give me some experience I could use later!

Dr Irey instructed me to get the body out of the refrigerator which had four long drawers each of which could hold one body. Together we lifted the metal tray and slid the body onto the stone table in the center of the mortuary. The odor was terrible despite the refrigeration! It got worse as we proceeded. Handing Irey instruments as required, I retracted, pulled, snipped and tagged specimens, under his directions. It turned out that the individual had died as a result of drowning, his lungs were full of water and quite decomposed, which accounted for the odor. When finished, CPT Irey showed me how to sew up the body taking care to keep the blood vessels tied so it could be embalmed. We did several other autopsies while I was at IGMR which stood me in great stead later.

The months passed. It didn't look as though I was going overseas. Just before the 1st Div left Indiantown Gap, I had gone with Saul Miller, a buddy from NYU, into Lebanon where we had a couple of drinks, dinner and a great deal of talk. Saul was also a medic, but with an IN Bn. Now he was overseas and I was still in the hospital at Indiantown Gap with no indication that I was ever going to leave the place. Impatience overwhelmed me. Though learning a great deal, I was not satisfied, and went to see 1SG Flynn again about the possibility of being assigned to the operating room. He still remembered my initial outburst to him and was unforgiving. He told me that I was lucky to be where I was! When asked about my chances for an assignment overseas, he laughed unpleasantly and ordered me out of his office. About this time the Army mounted a major campaign to urge qualified soldiers to apply for Officer Candidate School (OCS). Bill and I came back from a walk the evening the notice appeared on the bulletin board. It was too early to go to bed, so we stopped off at the Lab, and got cokes and a package of cheese which Bill had stashed in the refrigerator among the reagents that required refrigeration.

"Bill, have you seen that poop on OCS? What do you think of the idea?"

"Waal, I don't know about it. I don't want to be a Medical Administrative Corps (MAC) officer, and I am not sure I would like to be in the Infantry. So I am not going to jump on the bandwagon. What about you?"

"I don't know. It sure looks like I am not going to get any place here as long as Flynn is the first soldier. I won't get promoted, and I won't get in the OR. I like it here in the lab, but I want to do something else. I want to get overseas for one thing, and maybe this is the way to do it."

"What branch are you thinking of putting in for?"

"I don't know. And I hate to think of leaving the friends I have made. If I became an officer, I wouldn't be able to pal around with you and the other men I know well. I think that officers are basically snobs. Look at some of those we see on the Officers Ward. They are pretty hard to get along with."

"Yeah, but then there are some good eggs like Irey. He is a pretty good Joe. Look at all the fun we had with him on the picnic last week. You will make other friends. And the damn war is not going to last forever. When you get out of the Army, you can associate with anybody you please. Why don't you talk to Irey about it. He's got a good head and will steer you straight."

"Good idea. Well I think I'll hit the sack. Coming?"

In the next few days, I had a chance to sit down and talk with CPT Irey. He told me, "You'll make new friends and once the war is over the old friends you made while you were an enlisted man couldn't care less what your rank was, so by all means go to OCS. It will give you a great opportunity for service, and use your college education to a greater degree."

He persuaded me to apply and I did, though determined not to apply for the Medical Administrative Corps and shuffle papers. If I couldn't get into the operating room or do work that would help me in medical school, then I would try to get into one of the combat arms. Mother and Dad were concerned when I wrote them about my plans. They tried to persuade me to continue in the Medical Department so that when I got out and went to medical school I would have practical knowledge and experience. To satisfy them, one of the choices I put down was the Chemical Warfare Service (CWS) in which I would be able to use my chemistry. Infantry and Anti-aircraft Artillery (AA) were my First and second choices. The OCS Screening Board was very tolerant and selected me. The list of recommended enlisted men (EM) then went to II Corps Command, where the personnel people assigned me to attend the CWS OCS at Edgewood Arsenal, MD. Army policy dictated that a soldier be a noncommissioned officer when entering OCS. But I had never been promoted to Private First Class (PFC). 1SG Flynn nursed his grudge with Spartan tenacity, and somehow kept me from getting promoted. Although Bill Long had recommended me, indorsed by CPT Irey, Flynn managed to block my promotion each time. Instead of a CPL, I became a Technician Fifth Class, a specialist instead of an NCO. It didn't matter, because stripes were not worn at OCS.

That fateful 3rd of October I reported for duty at the OCS at Edgewood Arsenal and was assigned to the 4th Platoon, Company C, 15th Officer Candidate Class. We were billeted in WWI barracks with kitchen and mess hall attached. Latrines were in the buildings, though we had to go out on the porch to get to them. Second Lieutenant (2LT) Electus B. Ward was the Tactical Officer of the 4th Plt. A tall, thin, ascetic looking IN OFF, he was largely responsible for my graduation and commissioning. First Lieutenant (1LT) Linville A. Baker, the Co CO, was a prissy little guy with no discernible leadership ability. Fortunately 2LT Ward was able to make up for the Co CO's lack of ability and we were able to graduate.

There was no change in status that I could see. After signing in and surrendering my records for the inevitable processing, a cadreman pointed to the supply room and I drew my bedding. As one of the last Candidates to report in, I had to be satisfied with an upper bunk. While making my bed, I surreptitiously sized up the men already there. The patches indicated that many had come from tactical units, and stripes ranged from PFC to 1SG; the 1SG was a National Guard (NG) NCO.

A trim, dark haired, swarthy TSG walked over to me holding out his hand. As we shook hands I looked him over. His uniform was tailored to his frame, and his manner indicated a self assurance, almost a cockiness, which characterized so many competent Regular Army (RA) EM. He spoke quickly and always seemed to have an appropriate response to any sally. As he gave me a firm hand clasp he said, "Hi, I'm Bill Homen. I'm from California, where are you from?"

"I'm Don Seibert from New York."

"Not the City?"

"Sure, well from Queens, which is part of the City. Have they put out any instructions yet?"

"Only that we have to have our stripes off before the first formation tomorrow and have the OCS tab sewn on by inspection next Saturday. I sure as hell hate to take off these stripes. They were mighty hard to come by."

Several others joined us and a general bull session ensued. I met George Reid from Ocala, FL who immediately got into an argument with Homen over the relative virtues of California versus Florida. It was still going on when we went to chow.

Upon our return to the barracks, we sat on our bunks and talked. The NCOs among us reluctantly finished removing the stripes from their shirts and coats. They meticulously cut the stitches, leaving only the needle holes to attest to their former lofty status. The mood of the entire group was somber, tinged with uncertainty, even fear. Though having no stripes to remove, I soon became infected with the depression that gripped the entire platoon.

We had been issued a large number of field manuals and instruction sheets. Among them was the Program of Instruction (POI) for the entire 13 weeks, which I studied before going to sleep. The CWS OCS was designed to qualify graduates as platoon commanders in Chemical Mortar Battalions and other CWS units. Hence the emphasis was on general military subjects rather than special chemical training. Most of the instruction was in the field, with the remainder divided between lectures, conferences, class room exercises and training films. The latter was a sure cure for insomnia, whenever anybody had difficulty falling asleep at night, a rarity with our crowded and strenuous schedule, the Candidate would call out, "Show us a training film so I can go to sleep."

Many subjects were covered, the largest single block of instruction being devoted to Chemical Mortar techniques. The 4.2 inch mortar was the pride of the CWS, a highly versatile and accurate weapon Another large block of time was devoted to defense against chemicals. Tactics, both Chemical and Infantry, the school of the soldier, map reading, meteorology, and company administration were also featured subjects. The remainder of the time was allocated to a myriad of subjects from camouflage to training management. There was a course in public speaking, which I thought was a good idea, but it was far too short. We even had a course in table manners!

COL Milton T. Hankins, the Assistant (Asst) Commandant (CMDT) of the CWS School, was a portly, dynamic individual who left no doubt as to his rank and authority. He completely overshadowed and overwhelmed Lieutenant Colonel (LTC) Richard S. Danek, the Director of the OCS. So it was a very special occasion when the entire Regiment (Regt) of Cadets marched into the Riding Hall and found COL Hankins on the stage behind a table set for a formal dinner.

When the Regt had been reported to him and taken its seats, he informed us that he was going to discuss etiquette with us, and more particularly, good table manners He pointed out that as officers and gentlemen we would be expected to conduct ourselves in the best traditions of polite society. Despite the dead silence which indicated our indignation at being subjected to such treatment, he proceeded to go through the motions of eating dinner, while he lectured on table manners and gentlemanly conduct.

He carefully placed his napkin on his lap, broke his bread before buttering it, dabbed his lips with his napkin before sipping from the various glasses before him, cut his meat into bite sized pieces, and fully covered the essentials of good table manners. As the class progressed there was a stir as some ridiculed the instruction and others became more incensed at the thought that the school believed that we needed instruction in good manners. Finally COL Hankins ate his pie after selecting the correct fork. At this point the instruction took a turn. COL Hankins grabbed a piece of bread and started to smear excessive butter on it with exaggerated motions all the while talking about those who resembled plasterers at work. The class dissolved in laughter as he proceeded to show us how not to eat in polite company. He soon had the entire Regt of Cadets weak with laughter as he emphasized one rule after another in the "how not to" demonstration.

As we fell in outside the Riding Hall after the class, most of us burst into laughter as we thought of COL Hankins' antics. Bill Homen was having difficulty controlling himself and all during the march back to the barracks would suddenly give vent to a burst of laughter. It was certainly a highlight of the instruction at Edgewood and one that brought home the teaching points in a never-to-be-forgotten fashion. In was also one of the funniest one-man shows ever.

Not all of the instructors were that effective, in fact it appeared to me they were generally poor. Most had recently graduated from OCS, not only Edgewood but many of the combat arms schools also, and then been immediately assigned to the Chemical Warfare (CW) School. Obviously Edgewood did not have a high priority for outstanding graduates. While most of the instructors were technically qualified, they lacked experience in military training and leadership. Hence, we suffered.

Much of our tactical instruction and all Infantry training was given or supervised by 1LT Marshall S. Marshall, who stood out because he was an Infantry OFF and a 1LT. The bulk of our instructions were 2LTs of the CWS. Marshall soon communicated to all of us that he considered himself a fine tactician, and strode arrogantly about the field supervising our practical exercises. We took this as a mark of superiority until Homen and several others came upon him on a hill top directing an Infantry charge up the slope with his right hand slipped into his shirt front. He was immediately dubbed Napoleon and became a joke to the entire class, which lost respect for him. The experienced "old soldiers" like Bill Homen, Bernie Ryle and even Bill Binkowski baited him into expounding on grand strategy and intricate tactical maneuvers. He was so conceited that he failed to recognize that he was being ridiculed. It was sad that we only had a few officers such as 2LT Ward we could respect.

As part of our weapons training, we received instruction and preliminary marksmanship training with the rifle. One of those we handled was the British Enfield. When we did sighting and aiming exercises I was not happy with the sight, remembering the definitive one on the Springfield I had fired at Indiantown Gap. We were trucked to Aberdeen Proving Ground (APG) just a few miles from Edgewood, for range firing. It was difficult to get a proper sight picture with the Enfield sight because it seemed to take in too much of the landscape, but I managed to qualify as a marksman.

We also fired the Browning Automatic Rifle, BAR, for familiarization. While on the range, one of the Candidates had a BAR on which the sear broke and it began to fire full automatic. The Candidate panicked and dropped the weapon, which continued to spew rounds over the range as it slowly revolved. A cadreman jumped on it and held it down range until the magazine was empty. The Cadet was severely reprimanded for lack of confidence and failure to take proper action.

The course was set up in blocks of instruction. At the conclusion of each block, an evaluation was made of every student. Those who were academically deficient or weak in leadership were counseled by one of the staff or faculty, and some placed on probation. HQ of the CWS OCS was in Building 416, all counseling took place there. We commiserated with our classmates who were "416ed". If they did not improve sufficiently during the next block of instruction, these Candidates were placed before a Board of Officers who considered their cases and recommended elimination, turn back one or more classes, or continuation on probation. The threat of "416" hung over all of us during the course.

The attrition was high. Much of it resulted from lack of motivation on the part of Candidates. Many had been selected from other arms and services and were oriented toward those branches. Particularly the men from the combat arms tended to look down on CW and hence did not exert themselves fully. Some said they had applied for OCS in their original branch and had not been selected, so they took Chemical Warfare which was considered a breeze. They found out differently. Later we learned that our class, the 15th, set a record with a 33.4% attrition rate, the highest of any CWS OCS class in WWII.

Despite the failures attributed to leadership, lack of force, aggressiveness or military bearing, we all thought that several weak individuals got through because of their high academic scores. We were not impressed with them.

The senior National Guard NCO in the class, 1SG Kerr, was caught cheating. Despite his almost tearful denials, he was forced to resign. This resulted from the rather unevenly administered honor system at the school. Very few were eliminated because of honor violations.

Returning from class at the noon break one day, I noted that I had three demerits on the "gig list" for "unsatisfactory area". There was also a note for me to report to 2LT Ward, the Tactical Officer, as soon as possible. Alarmed, I mentally checked my grades and peer ratings. Three times during the course the class listed every Candidate according to his leadership potential, I had ranked in the upper quarter on the last one. Vainly trying to recall how many demerits I had amassed I took heart from the fact that this was not a summons to 416, perhaps 2LT Ward wanted to see me concerning the year book of which I was the C Co representative. After the last class that afternoon I approached 2LT Ward's office with considerable doubt in my mind, and knocked. "Come in."

"Sir, Candidate Seibert reports as ordered," rendering my sharpest salute. LT Ward returned my salute. "Sit down Seibert." He ruffled some papers on his desk and then looked me in the eye.

"Seibert, I have been worried about you. You have the potential of becoming a good officer. You seem to like the military, have adapted well, and get along with the men in your unit. But your area is one of the most untidy ones of all the Candidates in C Co. You just seem indifferent to spit and polish. I have given you many demerits in the past, but have seen no improvement. You are not sloppy, but your area shows less effort and concern than those of the rest of the men in the Company. What's the problem?"

"There's no problem, sir. I hadn't realized that my area was so bad. I try to keep things neat, but somehow, I just can't get the shine or the arrangement that some of the other men seem to. I'll do better, you can depend on it, sir."

"Well, I would hate to see you wash out because of demerits. You had better make a major effort to improve your area. Now, I am not going to let you get in any deeper. I am going to stop giving you demerits on your area. But I want some real improvement."

"Yes, sir. You'll see it, sir. Thank you, sir."

"All right, keep this to yourself, and let me see some improvement. That will be all."

"Thank you, sir". I saluted and left the office as fast as I could. My heart was pounding. Washed out because of lack of spit and polish! That would really be something. I made a resolution to spend more time on my shoes, bed, clothing display and footlocker. And I tried sincerely to improve. But even to my biased eye, there appeared to be little improvement. But 2LT Ward, true to his commitment, never again "gigged" me for area.

Again a "Strep Throat" hospitalized me. This time, I fought it vigorously, concerned that I might be dropped back a class. But I was ordered on sick call and ordered to the hospital. It was another small cantonment-type hospital with individual buildings joined by an enclosed walkway. It was smaller than the one at Indiantown Gap. My stay was only four days and I never did have to help with the ward work. Once my temperature was down, I was released. Homen, Reid and several others came over for a few minutes each night and gave me help with the assignments and notes from the classes I missed. Fortunately, "416" decided to let me continue in Class 15.

Shortly after discharge from the hospital, I reported on sick call again. A bored medic looked at me with an expression that clearly denoted that he thought I was a "goldbrick".

"What's your problem, Candidate?"

"I need a Wasserman or a Kahn."

The medic jerked upright and stared at me. "Do you have VD?" he asked incredulously.

"No, but I worked in a hospital lab before I came here. I handled the VD tests and the doctor in charge of the lab thought it would be a good idea if I had a periodic check up for the next six months. I am sure I don't have it, but I don't want to take any chances."

"Who you tryin' to kid, soldier? Nobody, least of all an Officer Candidate comes in here for a VD check unless he thinks he has it. You know this could get you thrown out of OCS?"

"Sure. But this is a legitimate request. Check my records. You'll see that I came here from the Station Hospital at Indiantown Gap. Where do I go to have my blood taken?"

"Well, it's your ass, but I wouldn't do it if I was you. I'll take the blood, but the report will have to go to your Orderly Room, and if it is positive, you've had it."

"Okay, okay. Just take the blood and let me get to class."

He got a syringe and needle and took the 10cc's of blood required for a Kahn. As I left for class he was still shaking his head over my stupidity. When the slip was sent to the Orderly Room it caused as stir among the people there and I was looked at suspiciously and watched a bit more closely from then on.

While there was competition among all of us for cadet rank and class standing, it was mostly in the spirit of good sportsmanship. Our classmates rarely resorted to cut-throat competition, and only reported a fellow Cadet if there was an honor violation involved or if it had to be done to avoid being skinned yourself. There was a real spirit of cooperation, sometimes too much of it. I was "Section Marcher" (the individual who marched the group from one class to another) one day. This was intended to give training in voice and command, and to provide a basis for evaluation and comparison of Cadet performance. Just before we left the barracks area, I was handed a slip of paper which indicated that our second period class room had been changed. I did not have a chance to say anything to the group about it.

After the first period, I assembled the group and marched them to the next class. All went well, until I gave the command "Column Left, MARCH." Normally we went to the right for the second period class. The Platoon Guide, and I suppose the entire group, thinking I had made a mistake and not wanting to see me "gigged", executed a smart column right and marched off. I had to run to catch them, finally halting them. Because a Tactical Officer was present I had to do something. After a short speech in which I told the Platoon to be more alert to orders, I gave the Guide ten push-ups for not paying attention. Finally, I told them that the next class area had been changed and proceeded to march them to the correct class room. That evening in study hall, I apologized to the class for chewing them out, told them I appreciated what they had tried to do, and had only reprimanded them because a Tac OFF was present. Everyone understood and no one took the incident seriously. This was the sort of cooperation that was given to all of the Cadets who worked together with the group.

During the course, the Candidates maintained a practice interior guard. The Cadet cadre established a duty roster and posted a guard detail each day. It included a Cadet Officer of the Day (OD), Officer of the Guard (OG), Sergeant, Corporals and Privates of the Guard. Informal guard mount was conducted and the guard posted each evening. The guard was relieved at 2200 hours so that everyone could get some sleep and not miss any instruction. As Cadet OD one night, I completed my check of the guard, made my reports and got into bed about 2215. Just as I dozed off I heard a plaintive but loud voice calling, "Corporal of the Guard, Post Number Six." It was obvious that the OG or SGT of the Guard had forgotten to relieve one of the sentinels. Jumping out of bed, I dressed and rushed to Post Number Six, the OD brassard still on my field jacket. The sentinel challenged me correctly and I relieved him on the spot. He was a friend, as were the OG and SGT. By mutual consent no report was made of the incident.

But it impressed me and I was conscious of this matter when I was OG or OD after receiving my commission.

My poor opinion of 1LT Baker, CO of Co C, Regt of Cadets, OCS CWS, Edgewood Arsenal, MD was shared by most of the Candidates. It seemed that those who looked up to him had the lowest peer ratings in the Company.

At one point during the course, it was customary for each class or company to contribute entertainment to a general gathering of the Candidates. C Co was warned of the requirement and told to come up with some skit or other form of entertainment. We were so immersed in the course, trying to keep our heads above water, that the deadline passed. Baker had a meeting of the Company one evening. He asked what we had come up with. There was a silence. Finally one hand went up. Cadet O'Dowd, a tall thin, ungainly individual with a large adams apple was recognized by our erstwhile leader.

"Sir, I can sing Irish songs, if that would be appropriate."

Lieutenant Baker beamed.

"Step right up, Mr O'Dowd. Show the Company what you can do."

O'Dowd sang one of the familiar Irish ballads in a deep resonant voice, which we all reluctantly admitted was very well done. O'Dowd was not one of our favorites. Upon completion of the number, 1LT Baker jumped excitedly to his feet and shrilled in his almost feminine falsetto, "That's LEADERSHIP, men."

The situation was ludicrous! The Commander with little leadership ability complimenting the Cadet, who had less leadership potential, on his better-than-average singing and perhaps speaking voice! Everyone recoiled in embarrassment and disgust. What influence Baker had up to that point was immediately lost.

One day in December the schedule called for OD uniforms. We were to provide an honor cordon for President Roosevelt, who was to present an "E" Pennant to the Arsenal for efficient production. It was a cold, sleeting day. The entire Regt was in files closely spaced on each side of the road from the OCS area to the Riding Hall We had been instructed that we would be given the command "ATTENTION!" as the Presidential limousine approached and would render eyes right and a hand salute as he passed, following the President with our eyes until our heads came to the front at which time we would drop our salute. The Regt stood in the cold and wet for over an hour. By the time the command "ATTENTION!" was given we were stiff. We could barely make a snappy salute we were so frozen. We remained until after the ceremony and then repeated the performance as the President left.

You serve with many fine people in the US Army. Their consideration, loyalty and generosity are legend. That is one of the most attractive features of military service. Edgewood OCS was no exception. Christmas passes were to be issued on the results of a lottery. Fourteen men in my platoon who lived too far away to get home and back in three days put my name in the hat instead of their own. My name was drawn consecutively four times (!) so I was able to go home for Christmas of 1942. We had only three days and I made the most of them. Christmas seemed very special that year, and the war was far away. Mother and Dad had a large tree as usual, the heirloom stand which revolved the tree and played German Christmas carols did not seem too objectionable even though we were at war with Germany. Despite rationing, Mother had the traditional turkey feast with all the trimmings I liked so much. Dad uncorked some wine with which we toasted those missing, Bill, George and Bob. It was wonderful to be with the family again that year.

On returning to Edgewood, Homen told me that LLT Baker had ordered an inspection of the barracks Christmas morning on the basis that OCS billets should be ready for inspection at all times. The gig list was horrendous. Fortunately 2LT Ward was able to reduce the demerits when he returned from his own leave.

As C Company's representative on the Yearbook committee, my duties consisted of insuring that the Company picture was turned in to the editors, that the Co history was written, and that orders were taken for the book and the money collected. During one study period I wrote a short doggerel poem about our three months at Edgewood. Some thought it was funny, certainly different, and suggested that it be used for the Co history, my scribbling thus became history.

FIFTEENTH CLASS HISTORY

Company C

ODE IN RETROSPECT

1

'Twas a rainy day at Edgewood
When we headed there to school.
We all were mighty eager
To learn the Army's rule.

2

That night we cut off chevrons
'Midst a haze of doubt and dread.
We thought of graduation
And dreamed of bars in bed.

3

Lt. Ward addressed us,
Which made our woes seem light.
Thanks and appreciations
We owe him-'tis his right.

4

They warned us then of "C" Block
And things that still would come.
Then 416 began to work-
They thinned our ranks quite some.

5

Yes, they gassed us as we studied,
They gassed us as we walked.
CBS became our perfume.
We cried as much as talked

6

Jack Regon couldn't sleep one night,
He thought he had the cure;
"Just show us all a training film
To give us sleep so sure."

7

"Is California better,
Or does Florida have appeal (?)"
Was the question long debated
In the squad room and at meal.

8

Lieutenant Colonel "A"
Then made a graceful bow.
The dud we found in "49"
Sure caused an awful row.

9

"In trucks we place our ranges
If we want travel while
We are cooking all our goodies,
Understand me Mr. Ryle."

10

The winter came in earnest
And snow was on the ground,
Which made it hard to march on-
As Churchhill quickly found.

11

We finally go to "E" Block
With Tactics and its woes.
Al Pearson gave on order
To penetrate our foes.

12

At last came Merry Christmas
Some had their passes then;
While others stood inspections-
"Your squad room's dirty, Men!"

13

Binkowski learned to whistle,
Cliff Arch- he learned to shout.
Seibert counted riffles
While the others milled about.

14

We've come to graduation,
The bars we've earned are gold.
So I'll end this little ditty,
The tale I have is told.

At last the three month ordeal came to a close. We had all ordered uniforms, their arrival was the occasion for a great deal of trying on and strutting about. The cadre inspected us in our officers' uniforms without insignia, and there were compliments and criticisms. "Pinks and greens" were our favorite uniforms, some even bought Sam Brown belts, though they were being phased out. The evening before the graduation and commissioning exercises, the school authorities had arranged a "Graduation Ball". A group of young ladies from the surrounding area had been invited and transportation to and from the Riding Hall provided. The dance had not been well publicized so most of us decided not to go. Our experience with such affairs in the past presaged a line of "wall flowers" with an overabundance of chaperons. It did not sound attractive. A number of us went to bed about 2100 that evening. At 2115 the lights were suddenly put on and the order to "FALL OUT" was given. We assembled in the study hall and were addressed by an irate 1LT Baker, who told us we would dress and attend the dance. The discourtesy of leaving so many young ladies with no dancing partners was dinned in our ears.

Reluctantly we donned our tired O.D.s, in most cases retained only for the final parade on the next day. We trudged through the cold to the Riding Hall and danced our "duty dances" with the invited guests. LTC Danek, resplendent in blue mess jacket, was in evidence as chaperon and Commandant. He kept an eagle eye out for any untoward behavior on the part of these future officers and gentlemen. At midnight the ladies were shepherded home and we plodded back through the icy evening to the barracks and bed.

Mother and Dad had been invited for graduation exercises on Saturday, 23 January 1943. Dad had accepted and written that his train was due at Edgewood Station at 0900 hours. This would give him plenty of time to get to the service club, where I planned to meet him, by 1000 hours, parade time. By the time we had to fall in for the graduation parade, he had not arrived, I was disappointed and worried, hoping that nothing serious had delayed him.

It was a bitterly cold day. The wind was blowing off the Chesapeake Bay and readily penetrated our enlisted overcoats. The thought of that Replacement Co CO at FT Dix occurred to me as I buttoned the top button of the coat and flattened the collar. It was our last formation in enlisted uniforms.

Again I looked for Dad as we hurried to the barracks after the parade to change into our "pinks and greens" the standard semi-dress uniform. As we marched to the Riding Hall where the graduation was to be held, I was still on the look-out for him. There was no sign of him or any other parents who had been keenly anticipated by my classmates.

The commissioning ceremony was relatively short and simple. As we repeated the oath "...to support and defend the Constitution of the United States against all its enemies foreign and domestic, that I will bear true faith and allegiance to the same..., SO HELP ME GOD", a chill ran down my spine. I have been part of many other commissioning ceremonies and always got that same chill. It was over except for the final ritual, pinning on the second lieutenant's gold bars.

Just as I asked Bill Homen and George Reid, two of my closest friends in OCS, to pin on my bars, a group of angry people burst into the Riding Hall, Dad was among them. They were livid with anger. There had been some foul up at the Security Gate and they had been held there waiting for clearance to get onto the post since the tram had arrived at 0900 hours. Dad did get to pin my bars on me. He also had the opportunity to witness the receipt of my first salute as a commissioned officer from one of the NCOs on the post.

We were coming from the barracks, where we had gone to get my suitcase. The class had been given 10 days leave which I would spend in College Point. As I stepped onto the sidewalk a stentorian voice barked, "GOOD MORNING, LIEUTENANT." Starting slightly, I grinned sheepishly as I returned the Supply Sergeant's salute.

"Thank you, Sergeant." Quickly removing the dollar bill from my pocket where I had carefully placed it for just such a contingency, I gave it to the expectant NCO.

"Thank you, sir. Good luck." He walked swiftly away looking for other newly commissioned officers.

"Why did you give him that dollar, Don?" Dad asked.

"It is traditional to give a dollar to the first enlisted man who salutes you after you have been commissioned. They used to give silver dollars, but we couldn't get any here. Some of the cadre NCOs make quite a bundle whenever a class graduates. I'll bet the Supply Sergeant has been lying in wait for some of us since early this morning." Dad laughed.

It had been a long three months. We had learned a lot, but had much more to learn. We had been through a rigorous schedule, under stress, to insure that we could operate under pressure. Reconciling myself to the fact that I was not going to be a combat arms OFF, I did hope to be assigned to a Chemical Mortar Battalion (Bn) which would see combat in support of the Infantry. It seemed to me that we had received quality basic officer training, in spite of some short-comings in the in-structors, and that most of us would be able to handle ourselves in whatever assignments we would draw. Some weak ones had gotten through though. My request for a Chemical Mortar Bn was disapproved, I was ordered to report to the Officers' Replacement Pool at Edgewood Arsenal on the conclusion of my 10 day leave. Homen, Reid and several other friends received the same orders. With the assumption of a commission, I also acquired a new serial number. Once again, it was committed to memory so deeply that I can never forget it, 0-1038113. The 0 identified it as an officer's serial number.

CHAPTER 2

SHAVETAIL

It was great to be home, and I enjoyed the 10 days with the family. Bill was home on convalescent leave. He looked terrible but we had an opportunity to talk and be with each other for a few days before he had to rejoin his ship in the Pacific. The 10 days ended before the realization that OCS was over and I was now a second lieutenant finally struck me. Back at Edgewood, there were still no orders for us. We were put to work in various departments of Edgewood Arsenal: helping in the manufacture of gases, testing and checking chemical defense equipment, test-firing flame throwers, administrative details and other odd jobs. After a week of such make-work projects we were thoroughly disgusted with the Chemical Warfare Service. Finally, orders assigning us to the First Air Chemical Officers Course were published. Morale plummeted still further. We were going to school again for another month right there at Edgewood Arsenal!

We moved into the CW School Bachelor Officers Quarters (BOQ) near the main gate. After more processing, the student body was organized into a company and we attended our first class. During the orientation we were told that a need had been identified for Chemical Officers trained in the Army Air Corps applications of CW. We were to study both offensive and defensive aspects, the protection from chemical agents of airfields, aircraft and personnel, the decontamination of aircraft, personnel and airfields in the event they were attacked with chemicals, and the offensive dispersal of smoke, incendiaries and poison gases from aircraft. A pilot program had been developed for which we were the trial group. Upon completion of the course, we were to be assigned to Air Corps installations either overseas or in the Continental United States (CONUS). This was a far cry from a Chemical Mortar Battalion, but there appeared no way out. We reluctantly faced the month ahead.

The class began the First Air Chemical Officers Course with a bad attitude. The School authorities imposed restrictions on us which we thought unnecessary and inconsistent with our status as OFFs. Because a few OFFs had abused their new-found freedom in the past, we were given a set of rules which resembled OCS Barracks Regulations; lights out at 2200, no gambling in the BOQs, rooms ready for inspection when we left for class, were a few of the more onerous.

Since the School was quite far from the Main Officers Club, the theater and other entertainment, the gambling edict was particularly irksome and in fact was ignored. Almost every night the windows of one room or another were blanketed and a tense game dealt. Not a particularly astute poker player, I thought the stakes too high for an amateur, and contented myself with watching.

One evening the game was played in Bill Homen's room while I watched with bated breath as several large pots were contested. Bill Binkowski was the big winner that evening. Finally I turned in about 2300. Just as I got to sleep people began scurrying about and talking in hoarse whispers. Drowsily, I heard someone say that the OD had discovered the game and taken names. Bill Homen told me the story the next day.

"Sometime after midnight, in walks the OD. All I could think of was Reclassification Board here I come! The OD asked whose room it was, I told him mine. He asked who put the blankets on the windows, I admitted I had. He then listed the violations we were guilty of, lights on after 2200 and gambling. I protested, in the face of a lot of visible money on the table, that it was for small stakes and therefore the game itself was not a violation. He glanced at the pile of bills on the table and asked how I stood. Quick as a bunny I said, 'Well, sir, I've lost quite a bit, but I can afford it.'

"He asked, 'How much?'

"Oh, two or three dollars,' I said.

"Everybody caught on and as he went around the circle they each told him that they had won or lost from $1.50 to $3.00. Finally he got to Binkowski. What does he say? He shifted his unlit cigar to the other side of his face and says, I'm up three or four hundred!'

"Christ, I thought it was lights out for old Willy Homen. The OD looked at me with a look that said, 'I guess it's just not your day, Lieutenant!' He told us to break it up and get to bed."

We all sweated for Homen, Binkowski and the others. They were good friends and good guys and we did not want to see them get into trouble. Time passed, nothing happened. We finally concluded that the OD was a regular egg and had not reported the matter.

Much of the subject matter of the First Air Chemical Officers Course was a repetition of that we had just studied in OCS. There was additional emphasis on incendiaries, aerial chemical bombs, smoke or spray tanks, and other offensive uses of CW materials by the Army Air Corps. We received some instruction on the decontamination of aircraft which was new to us. But the course was designed for officers coming into the Army from civilian life, or those who had been out of school for some time. Essentially it was a bore to recent graduates of the CWS OCS, understandably, we were less than enthusiastic about our studies.

Bill Homen and I continued to pal around and took every opportunity to go into Baltimore to sample the night life, or just to have a meal in one of the many fine restaurants for which the city was famous. Bill's first son, Billy, had been born just before he reported to OCS and he had seen him only once, briefly. He was anxious to see both Lucy and Billy and to get settled into some kind of a job.

Finally, the course ended, Bill and I were both assigned to the Army Air Corps Flying Training Command (FTC) HQ, at Fort Worth, TX. We cleared post the afternoon of graduation, caught the first train into Baltimore and managed to find seats on the night train to St Louis. It was crowded and dirty, as all trains were during WWII. There were no Pullmans, no dining car, no club car, but when we arrived at St Louis the following day we were able to get berths on the next train to Fort Worth. We wanted to beat the crowd there, sign in early and hopefully select our job, preferably one overseas. However, that was not to be the case. We signed in, but the FTC had no orders for us as yet. The Air Chemical Officer concept was new, and the personnel and training people had not yet determined where we were going or what we were going to do.

Bill and I registered at the Blackstone, one of the better hotels in Fort Worth, and decided that we would enjoy ourselves until the Army found a use for us. We did! In fact, our boss, MAJ Jones, eventually called us in and told us to stop visiting with the secretaries because we were disturbing the functioning of the FTC HQ! During the day we wandered from office to office and if a girl seemed interesting or receptive, we sat down, chatted with her and tried to make a date for that evening. The girls in Fort Worth and Dallas were truly impressive, there appeared to be more beautiful and personable girls in those cities at that time than in any other cities I visited.

MAJ Jones dropped by our hotel room one evening to have a drink with us. Bill and I complained bitterly about the fact that we weren't doing anything or making any contribution. He tried to convince us that when our assignments came in we would have more work than we could handle. We remained skeptical.

During a pause in the conversation, I seized the chance to ask a question that had been bothering me since I had received my commission. "MAJ Jones, you are an Old Army OFF. Do you ever get used to having senior NCOs salute you?

"What do you mean, Seibert?"

"Well, today as I was leaving the Headquarters, a Master Sergeant with eight or ten hash marks saluted me. I returned the salute of course, but as I looked at those hash marks, it occurred to me that the sergeant knew more about the Army than I did, and maybe I ought to be showing him a bit of respect."

"Get that idea out of your head right away, Seibert. You don't owe any NCO that sort of respect. Every senior noncommissioned officer in the Army was offered the opportunity to apply for a commission or OCS. If they had any real ability they did. The ones you see are the ones who couldn't make it, or did not have the guts to accept the responsibilities of a commission. Perhaps he has more years in the Army man you have, and I certainly hope that he knows more about his particular job than you do about chemical warfare. But you don't owe him any respect, other than the loyalty and consideration you normally give to all subordinates. Stop feeling inferior to those old timers. Do I make myself clear?"

"Yes, sir. I never thought of it in that light."

"Well, you have asked for more responsibility and have completed a very demanding and discriminating course at Edgewood, which weeded out the weak people along the way. You can be proud of your achievement, and you will soon supervise or command such men as you are concerned about. You deserve the salute as an officer, and take it in that light. The salute is to the uniform and the grade as much as it is to the individual, so the old soldier has no reluctance to salute a shavetailDOU like you."

"That makes me feel better, sir. I don't want recognition I do not merit."

"As an officer you should demand the salute."

Perhaps as a result of this episode, though more likely to keep us away from the secretaries throughout the HQ, Bill and I were given the task of computing the FTC's yearly allocation of expendable Chemical Warfare material for training. When we multiplied the number of "Brushes, decontaminating, with handle, each" authorized per thousand personnel per year by the authorized strength of the command, we found that MAJ Jones could order 2 and 2/3 brushes per year. This seemed stupid, so we changed the figure to three. MAJ Jones gave us a heated and interminable lecture on being precise in our calculations and the statutory responsibility ofOFFs to order only what was expressly authorized.

The rest of our First Air Chemical Officers Course classmates drifted into the FTC HQ. At the end of the week we received orders. Bill and I, along with several other OCS and Air Chemical classmates were assigned to the Western Flying Training Command (WFTC) at Santa Ana Army Airbase (SAAB) just south of Los Angeles. We were issued transportation requests (TRs) which we took to the HQ's Transportation Office. A clerk gave us reservations on the Southern Pacific RR with Pullman accommodations. Just before checking out we asked the hotel clerk to make reservations for us at a similar class hotel in Los Angeles. Before we left he handed me a slip with the name of the hotel on it. It meant nothing to me as I put it into my pocket.

Bill and I departed from Fort Worth, again ahead of our less energetic classmates. The trip from Fort Worth to Los Angeles was a three day ordeal, a long, hard trip through uninteresting desert. The train was crowded with people standing in the aisles or sitting on suit cases. Among those in our car were several Navy wives enroute to join their husbands somewhere in Arizona. We had a good time with them, they were young, friendly and lonely. They also needed assistance. We played bridge and other games with them, swapped life stories and generally enjoyed their company. Because of the crowding and shortages the dining car fed military personnel first, civilians got what was left. Since it was mandatory to wear the uniform during wartime, we were in pinks and greens and were moved to the head of the line in the dining car. We took our new friends in as our dependents and they were able to eat with us. After they got off in Arizona the trip became boring. Arriving at Los Angeles late at night, we hailed a taxi and I fished from my pocket the paper handed to me by the hotel clerk in Fort Worth. "Baltimore Hotel, please." The driver turned and looked at us as if we were insane.

"That's a dump on skid row. Officers don't belong there."

"It can't be too bad. The best hotel in Fort Worth made the reservations. We'll take a look anyhow. It's too late to shop around."

The driver shrugged and drove off. As we proceeded, the area became dingier and dirtier. We saw drunks lying in the gutter. Finally the taxi stopped before a "flop house" in the middle of "skid row".

Apparently the hotel in Fort Worth had confused the Baltimore with the Biltmore. But by this time it was 2300 and Bill and I were tired. We needed a shower and a bed anchored to an unmoving floor, so we went in anyway. Walking through the lobby in our uniforms created a sensation. The room was worse than we thought possible, with no shower, only a tub. We gingerly hung up our clothes and fell into bed, careful to secure the door and our wallets. We got up at dawn and checked out as fast as we could.

An early train took us to Santa Ana where we found HQ, WFTC in an office building downtown. After signing in, we were directed to the Air Base. Santa Ana Army Air Base was a pre-flight training center where the young men entering any of the Air Corps flying programs were given basic ground instruction. Here they were processed, issued uniforms, and given mental and physical examinations. The fledgling pilots then began their pre-flight training. During this early training, which included a bit of administration, mathematics, weather and basic aero-dynamics, we were to give them CW training including the role of the Army Air Corps in the use of chemicals.

We were assigned to the Base Chemical Office, headed by 1LT Ludecke, a gangling, pompous character much impressed with his own importance and education. He was immediately nicknamed the "Street Car Conductor" because his garrison cap circa 1920, resembled the hats worn by those who collected fares on local trolleys. Ludecke was condescending to all 2LTs, and was aghast to find that most of us had not yet finished college. He was outraged that Bill Homen had not even finished high school.

We were all assigned classes in the pre-flight school, all of us, that is, except Bill Homen, who was assigned to the Base Gas Office which gave instruction to the EM on the base and handled routine, unimportant base gas defense plans. We had several weeks to prepare our instruction before our classes. Bill frequently came over to spend the day with us, to the discomfiture of the Street Car Conductor.

One day when we were discussing CW materiel, the Street Car Conductor interrupted us and began to pontificate about the agent under discussion. He put the spatial formula for diphenylamine chlorarsine - Adamsite - on the black board, but omitted the double bonds in the phenol ring and had one radical wrong. When he paused for breath, I walked to the blackboard and calmly corrected his formula. The group howled as Ludecke left in high dudgeon.

Once we started to teach, we found that the aviation cadets were not at all interested in Chemical Warfare, they wanted to fly, navigate or drop bombs, and they wanted to know what it was like to be an officer. Grudgingly, they gave us their attention, and I found my instruction slowly changing from emphasis on CW to an emphasis on leadership and administration. Though all of the required material was covered in a condensed program, I tried to answer the questions put to me by the cadets, to explain the responsibilities of a commissioned officer as I understood them, although I had less than three months of commissioned service. None of the CWS OFFs were convinced we were making a real contribution. Nonetheless we attempted to put together a decent program of instruction.

Those of us in the BOQ also set about enjoying ourselves. Bill had joined his wife, Lucy. They had found some sort of accommodations at Newport Beach about a half hour's drive from the Air Base. Bill was no longer around to enjoy off duty time with me, however, I met three Air Corps OFFs who shared similar interests and we started to pal around. It was hard to find dates in Santa Ana because of the large number of officers and aviation cadets stationed there. Recalling my days in the Medics and the ready availability of nurses, who were officers too, I mentioned to the other three that I was sure the hospital on Base had a periodic open house in the nurses quarters. It was an opportunity for them to meet other officers and aviation cadets and to have their boyfriends over to their area. This might be a way to meet some gals in this area.

They had never heard of such a thing, but I persisted, and suggested that we call the Chief Nurse. We flipped to see who would make the call, I lost. On the third try I got through to the Chief Nurse, a 1LT, and asked her if they planned to have an open house in the near future.

"No, we haven't had one since I arrived here. Why?"

"Well, that's too bad, because there are four fine young lieutenants here trying to meet some nice nurses."

She said almost with a laugh, "Perhaps I can arrange it for you. Call me back about 1300 tomorrow. I'll ask some of my 'girls' if they are interested." Promptly at 1300 hours the following day, I called back, the other three crowding around me.

"Nurses Quarters. Chief Nurse speaking."

"This is LT Seibert. I called yesterday about meeting some nurses."

"I remember. Four of my 'nicest girls' are interested. They are all off this evening. Why don't you meet me in the nurses' day room after retreat, make that 1800, and I'll introduce you. I'll be in my white uniform."

"Great, we'll see you about 1800." When I hung up we all whooped. But as we walked across the parade ground to the hospital that evening we became more and more certain that we had made a mistake. We envisioned some real "dogs" and our steps slowed as we neared the nurses' day room. As it turned out we were introduced to four of the nicest young ladies I ever met. One was beautiful, the other three pretty. They had outgoing personalities, were interested in dancing, and generally enjoying themselves. We paired off through some mysterious chemistry, I began dating Nellie Steele. The eight of us became inseparable. Any time all of us were free we were together. We went to all the dances and parties at the Officers' Club their duties permitted. We bowled, we walked, picnicked, danced, ate, went to the movies, did everything together.

One night coming home from bowling, the girls were late for duty and wanted to run. Away we went! It became a race of couples. One of the nurses, not Nellie, tripped, fell, cut her knee and twisted her ankle. We carried her to the Emergency Room in great embarrassment. She had to be hospitalized. The Chief Nurse was mildly unhappy with us because she was short of nurses. But we had long since learned how to get around her. We moved our operations to the hospital and brought the patient martinis every night. She was in a private room so we were able to visit her almost any time. Her fellow nurses looked the other way at what went on.

Shortly after I arrived at Santa Ana, I had a letter from my brother Bill. He told me that he coming to the west coast to join his ship, the destroyer *Murray,* and said he would stop by to see me as he passed through the area. Since he would be in uniform, I asked the Club Officer if it would be okay to have him for lunch at the Officers' Club. The answer was an emphatic NO so I planned to take him to the cafeteria in the service club. He arrived about 1000 one Saturday morning. I had no transportation and could not borrow any, so I met his bus at the depot on base. During the Battle of Savo Island in 1942 when the *Quincy* had been sunk, he had been blown free but had spent a number of hours in the water before being rescued. He still looked gaunt, not much improved from the condition I had seen him in during my leave after OCS. We walked around the Base for an hour or so, talked about the family and the war, and had lunch in the cafeteria He left in the afternoon for San Diego where he was to join the *Murray.*

Several CWS OFFs at Santa Ana made us cringe 2LT Perry was short (5ft 6in), dark, and slender and seemed to hold himself in a perpetual brace. He was much concerned about his appearance. When he was assigned to the Army Air Corps, he soaked his garrison cap in water, after removing the grommet, rolled it up and slept on it to produce a spectacular "50 mission crush". He took great delight in harassing the aviation cadets, often stopping a group marching to class and unmercifully chewing out the cadet-in-charge for any irregularities he noted in the formation or in the dress of the cadets. He spent his time wandering about Santa Ana Army Air Base collecting salutes. Any enlisted man or cadet who failed to salute 2LT Perry when he was within 300 yards of him, was sure to feel the ire of this little egoist.

Another OFF, who made it through Edgewood on his academic rating, but who lacked leadership and soldierly bearing, made us ashamed to be in the same branch of service as he was. He was not OFF material as we understood it; perhaps he could have made a contribution in research or production at Edgewood Arsenal, but he was not one to inspire troops. One day several of our classmates from OCS saw him in a restaurant in Santa Ana. He had just finished his meal and was walking out. He passed a table on which there were several coins, left as a tip by another customer. Without any hesitation or attempt to conceal his action, he reached out and took the coins. The waitress happened to be behind him and asked him to give her the money because it was her tip. He protested and only turned over the coins when she threatened to make a scene. He was in uniform, of course; our classmates left as inconspicuously as possible. We could not believe it when they related the incident.

Life settled into a routine at Santa Ana Army Air Base. That I was still out of combat concerned me. When one of my Air Corps buddies, Bill Braun, rejected for pilot training because of his eyes, decided to apply for navigation or bombardier training, I went with him. We were both eliminated as soon as they checked our vision. Although waivers could be obtained, neither of us qualified for them. Life was pleasant but relatively dull. Even our nurses did not compensate for what I perceived as rear echelon duty. Finally I went over Ludecke's head and asked CPT Janz, the WFTC Chemical Officer, to get me transferred overseas. He told me he could not get me released from the FTC which enjoyed a high priority on personnel, but he could assign me to a job that would give me more to do. As a result, I received orders assigning me as Base Chemical Officer at Roswell Army Air Field (RAAF), NM.

SAAB was cleared in record time, goodbyes were said to my nurse friends, my Air Corps buddies, Bill and Lucy Homen and other OCS classmates. The Santa Fe Railroad's crack *Superchief* took me to Roswell. Enroute, I had an interesting experience. As usual, I got up early to shave before a crowd gathered in the Pullman lavatory. When I finished, I wiped the sink clean and generally policed the area I had utilized. A gentleman, whom I found out later was CPT Henderson, and commanded one of the squadrons at RAAF (he was in a tee shirt), was waiting to freshen up.

"You must have been a soldier before you became an officer", he said.

"I was, sir, but what made you say that?"

"Only a soldier who is used to sharing facilities and who has to clean up any mess made takes the trouble to clean up for the next person."

This pleased me, even this early in my career being called a "soldier" seemed to me an accolade rather than a put down.

The *Superchief* arrived at Roswell early in the day. There was transportation at the station; recovering my footlocker, I made the half hour trip to the Air Base. After signing in, I went through the routine processing.

RAAF was a still-growing post, with much construction going on. It had been a glider training base, an advanced flying training base, and a bombardier training school. The advanced flying training and glider programs were ending and a B-17 transition program to familiarize air crews with that aircraft was being phased in. The bombardier training was to continue. It was a busy, active Army Air Corps training base.

Roswell was a small town which serviced the sheep and cattle ranches in the area. It was the county seat and an important rail shipment point. But its chief claim to fame was the presence of the

New Mexico Military Institute (NMMI) which had an outstanding polo team and was still dedicated to the horse cavalry.

The Blue Moon and the Yucca, on the outskirts of the town, featured juke box music and were the two most popular night clubs in the area. The Varsoviana, familiarly called "Put Your Little Foot", in which the gentleman danced beside his partner changing sides as he and his lady put their little feet forward, was popular in the Southwest and was a local favorite. Soon Roswellites from all over the country were swaying to the catchy tune.

One of the QM Officers, 2LT Sheehy, was acting Base Chemical Supply Officer when I arrived. He had completed a Unit Gas Officers' Course, but had been assigned the extra duty primarily to account for the property rather than to conduct chemical training. I took over from him as soon as we could jointly inventory the property and complete the paperwork to transfer accountability.

The Chemical Warfare office and warehouse were in a company supply building in the former glider training area. It was manned by two outstanding young CW EM, CPL Strohmetz and PVT Daniels. Both had majored in chemistry in college and were interested in getting back to school as soon as the war was over. They were delighted to welcome a CWS OFF. Despite specific directives from the various echelons of the Army Air Corps from its HQ in Washington, through the FTC at Fort Worth and the WFTC at Santa Ana, almost no CW training had been accomplished since the last Base Chemical Officer had departed six months earlier.

Determined to get the chemical training program under way immediately, I plunged into my duties. In a short time I was oriented on the base, had organized my section and began to badger the Base Operations Officer to give me time and people to accomplish the required training. He kept putting me off. He and his staff were most cooperative in permitting me to put out training directives to implement those of higher HQ, and all the buildings and equipment needed for the training program were made available. This resulted in a truly excellent CW establishment, but I couldn't use it for any training.

As the new Base Chemical Officer, I stood out, the only officer wearing CWS insignia on the base. Since most of officers ate lunch at the club, and a large percentage ate dinner there, I soon met many people Several became close friends: Clarence Kettler, a handsome, blond Ordnance OFF from Illinois, Larry Hartz, a wiry, bespectacled lawyer from Cleveland, who spoke in clipped, precise terms and loved tennis, Nick Ditrano, a stocky, easy-going Italian engineer from New York, Les Clarke, a tall, lanky Californian who had been with the State Board of Equalization (tax office),

Hank Balough, a bombardier instructor from Canton, OH, and Gene Boilletat, another bombardier instructor from New Jersey. The group of us were compatible, liked to dance and generally enjoy life, so we naturally started to do things together. Les Clarke lived in town, and though Mildred, his wife, frequently joined us, we did not see as much of him or her as we would have liked. The rest of us became inseparable and were in the middle of any activity going on.

In addition to Nick Ditrano, there were quite a few officers at Roswell from New York. Bob and Derry Wellman were from Flushing. They had been seniors in Flushing High when I was a sophomore. We became good friends and I enjoyed many a good meal at their house. Harry Natelson, from White Plains, was the Adj of the 42nd (Colored) Squadron. A ILT who was a little older than the rest of us, he lived in the BOQ with the more senior officers, so we saw less of him than we did of our age group. T J. Reilly had been with an insurance firm in New York before the war. He and I chaperoned a trip to Ruidoso, a nearby mountain resort, for the Special Service Office.

Though my efforts to conduct CW training produced few results, I got into other activities on the Base. There were opportunities to hop rides on cross country flights. Usually it was not possible to fly on routine training (tag) flights, but when pilots or navigators had to satisfy requirements for cross country flying, it was normal policy to take passengers. Thus I was able to get to Fort Sumner, an air base just north of Roswell, to Marfa Army Air Field to see Bill Binkowski and Nellie Steele, who had been transferred there shortly after Heft Santa Ana, and to other Army Air Bases where I had friends. The flights offered an opportunity to see more of the country, to get away from the boredom at Roswell, to talk over training problems with friends, and to look at their CW set-ups, or to meet Chemical Officers I had not served with before. The pilots frequently permitted me to fly the aircraft once we were airborne. My greatest thrill was to fly a B-17 for an hour. We ascended to 10,000 feet, just below the level at which oxygen was required. The complexity of the cockpit, the bombardier's plexiglass bubble in the nose, and the huge bomb bays all fascinated me.

Perhaps because of my outspoken statements that I had nothing to do, I was assigned as a defense counsel on one of the Special Courts-Martial. The first and second cases I defended resulted in acquitals. Immediately my reputation as a defense counsel was established! Every hood on the Base requested me to defend him. My first cases had been unusual in the sense that the evidence had not been clear cut; if the pre-trial investigations had been more complete, they probably would not have been brought to trial. The cases I got from then on were open and shut. The pre-trial investigations were thorough and in most instances I advised the defendants to plead guilty and throw themselves on the mercy of the court. Still I had more requests than I could handle.

Larry Harlz, one of my buddies, was the Assistant Staff Judge Advocate and hence the Trial Judge Advocate (TJA) or District Attorney in most of the cases I defended. We thus found ourselves on opposite sides. It was obvious that most of my clients were guilty, but I thought it my duty to insure that they received a fair trial, to be sure that all evidence for them was presented to the court, to argue that any reasonable doubt be resolved in their favor, and to explain to the court all mitigating and extenuating circumstances. But I became convinced that except in very unusual circumstances, the pre-trial investigations weeded out the innocent and those cases in which the evidence was marginal. It seemed to me an essentially fair system and justice was done more often than in civilian courts, where technicalities or emotion frequently overrode common sense. These legal duties continued as long as I was at RAAF. Initially I spent more time on them than I did on my chemical duties.

Once I had become an accepted member of the RAAF establishment and had my section functioning as I wanted it, I became impatient to get started on CW tng. Other officers were busy and active on the Base while I chaffed because I was not permitted to do the job I had been trained for and sent to Roswell to do. Even the Physical Training Director seemed more productive than I.

CPT Ken Loeffler, a college basketball coach, was the Director of Physical Training at RAAF. He faced much the same problems I did in getting his directed programs implemented. But he was aided by the enthusiasm, the natural interest in athletics and the need of the young men on the Base, especially pilots and other aircrewmen, to keep in top physical condition.

Loeffler, who coached LaSalle's 1952 national championship college basketball team after the war, was an achiever. With the aid of his assistants, 1LT Dave Bewick, a high school physical education teacher and coach from New Jersey, and 2LT Dave Goldenberg, a short, heavily muscled weight lifter, he built acceptable physical training and recreational facilities on the Base. "Scrounging", swapping, pleading and threatening, he got softball fields, tennis courts, volley-ball courts and other facilities completed. He convinced RAAF HQ to send letters requiring a reply by indorsement (RBI) to everyone who failed to turn out for their three hours of mandatory Physical Training (PT) each week.

After four or five months of inactivity I finally convinced the Base Command Section that the directives from higher HQ were too strong to ignore. When the Commander became aware that my reports were so unfavorable that RAAF was getting a reputation for noncompliance with orders, he directed a change in policy. He finally authorized a Base-wide gas mask drill or alert. I determined that this first alert would be special to get the interest and cooperation of everyone on Base. My two NCOs and I planned in great detail. The hospital commander and his staff became interested in the treatment of gas casualties, and agreed to set up a treatment station where simulated gas casualties, anyone caught during the alert without a mask properly worn, would be given a shower and other standard decontamination treatment. A carefully worded directive was issued.

Finally the day of the first gas alert arrived. On my instruction the engineer at the post laundry blew the steam whistle signaling the alert. Immediately chaos ensued. Every activity on the base ground to a halt. The landing and take off of aircraft, maintenance, classroom instruction, administration, all functions were interrupted. The order had gone out that everybody had to wear gasmasks regardless of where they were. Many OFFs tried to end the alert, but the man on the whistle had instructions to blow it and to end the alert only on my orders. Because I was all over the base checking on compliance, no one could locate me. Over 75 people, many of them OFFs, were tagged and ambulances hauled them to the hospital. Some refused to cooperate, but the doctors were caught up in the exercise and threatened to take air crew members off flight status if they did not follow the procedures. That ended the protests. The alert continued for 40 minutes. Finally I directed that the All Clear signal be sounded. At lunch and later at dinner, people stopped me to tell me how stupid they thought the drill and I were. But it showed clearly that training was needed, and just how disruptive a gas attack could be.

A complete report on the alert was made and sent to Base Headquarters. In it, the problems and accomplishments were reviewed and suggested changes to minimize interference with the flight line were made. The 42d Aviation Squadron and its CDR were complimented on their gas discipline and training. My report triggered a letter of commendation to CPT Monroe, the Squadron CDR. One of the staff officers in HQ commented that "Seibert never has anything good to say about anyone so far as gas training is concerned. If he says Willie Monroe's outfit is good, it must be good." This was a good lesson, one I remembered all of my Army career. Give commendation and appreciation where it is deserved, but do so sparingly. CPT Monroe thanked me for the recognition.

CPT, (later MAJ) William, "Willy", Monroe was a lean, tanned individual from New Orleans. When I first met him, I was sure he was from New York, probably Brooklyn. It was a long while before I was convinced that anyone who mispronounced the English language the way he did could hail from New Orleans rather than "Greenpernt" (Greenpoint), Brooklyn. Willie tried as hard as I did to get sent overseas, but he too was not successful.

CPT Monroe commanded the 42d Aviation Squadron, ably assisted by his Adjutant, 1LT Harry Natelson, whose authentic New York, Westchester, accent was far less abusive of the language than his commander's. Except for the officers, the 42d was composed of all colored troops, as Negroes or blacks were still called in those days. It provided the service personnel for the Base, drivers, warehousemen, duty soldiers of all types. Willy Monroe, a true Southerner, handled the squadron well, it was one of the most effective units on RAAF.

He succeeded in prying from the tight-fisted Quartermaster, MAJ Ratigan, instruments to outfit a full drum and bugle corps, an achievement which astounded everyone. Part of his success, the result of dogged persistence, was due to the support he received from the Base Commander, who remembered the authority for instruments in Army Regulations. The resulting drum and bugle corps provided the music for several parades.

Each evening there was an informal retreat ceremony and guard mount at the flag pole in front of Base Headquarters. Some of the older officers had difficulty doing a proper about face without swinging their arms wildly or almost losing their balance. We OCS graduates, smug in our own competence in drill, took delight in putting them to shame on this matter.

But it was during the few parades that the lack of practice in drill really became apparent. Lead by the enthusiastic, if unprofessional, 42d Aviation Squadron Drum and Bugle Corps, the Pass-in-Review was less than precise. The absence of good command voice and presence gave rise to confusion in orders and an uneven pace. This was exacerbated by the WAACs who were unable to maintain a 30 inch step and lagged far behind. Someone suggested that the formation be lead by the WAACs, which only resulted in the male units half stepping around the parade field. Finally, the press of training, the lack of opportunity to practice close order drill, and the poor showings led to longer and longer intervals between parades.

Shortly after the first gas alert, The Chemical Office put on an incendiary demonstration. Strohmetz and Daniels worked hard to set the demonstration up. Its purpose was to show the Base how effective incendiaries were and how vulnerable aircraft were to a fire bomb attack. Many aircraft parts contained an alloy of magnesium, which burns with an intense heat and is difficult to extinguish once ignited. In the salvage yard we located about 90 aircraft wheels which had a high magnesium content. As part of the demonstration, a large pile of wheels and chips (which Strohmetz and Daniels made with sledge hammers) would be ignited. The Base Fire Department was asked to attempt to extinguish the magnesium fire. The Fire Chief was delighted to work with me on this as it was training for his firemen.

The incendiary demonstration was held in the evening and many off-duty airmen came because they had nothing else to do. The display went according to plan The climax came when the pile of wheels was ignited and the Fire Department went to work. The more water they put on it, the brighter it burned. There was a spectacular flare up on several occasions. The troops cheered and were highly impressed with incendiaries.

With these opening events, I was able to implement in slow stages a full CW program. But the more I did the less the people in charge of training liked it. This was particularly true after the aviation training at Roswell had been reduced to B-17 transition flying and bombardier training. There were just too many priority subjects to cram into the training day, and aviation training rightly took precedence. Chemical Warfare training suffered as a result.

Though the training was slighted, the facilities provided for it were out-standing. My Chemical empire was located in the former Glider School area, where many empty buildings were assigned to me by the Base authorities. The engineers did a great deal of work for me. My office and warehouse were in one of the WWII orderly/supply room buildings. There was a fine class room building with a training aids room and latrine. We constructed a decontamination facility from one of the central latrines in the former tent city, with a regulation gas shelter entrance built onto it. The gas chamber was at the south end of the cantonment area, and space had been allocated in a bunker in the Ammunition Dump for detonators, incendiaries, and smoke grenades. It was a splendid establishment if only it could be used for training.

The only thing denied me was a Jeep. These were in short supply, highly sought after and my priority was low. A bicycle was issued in lieu of a jeep, which saved many steps. But relief came when the Chemical Office received an M3A1 Decontaminating Apparatus (Farquhar). This was a modified, skid mounted, commercial agricultural spray tank. HQ was persuaded to assign me a "deuce and a half1, a GMC 2 1/2 ton truck to carry it. By means of a crane the M3A1 Apparatus was mounted in the truck bed; the Decon Truck soon became a familiar sight on the Base. AH of my EM had licenses; I got one too, though OFFs did not normally drive trucks in those days. The truck was used for many things besides decontamination

The Operations (OPS) OFF let me use tear gas and smoke in the bivouac areas where pilots and maintenance personnel were learning to operate under primitive conditions. One day, just as Daniels released the grenades, the wind changed and blew the smoke and tear gas over the runway where the B-17s were making touch-and-go landings. The training had to be suspended for over an hour, irritating everyone. Then the wind veered again and blew the gas into the housing area and into the dependents quarters. Such incidents were used by the Base CDR as excuses to restrict the CW Tng Program more and more until there was not much left of it. Finally, little or no chemical training was conducted and I had difficulty finding enough to keep me busy.

During this period I attended the ground school phase of a B-17 Crew Chiefs Course and learned about how those aircraft were constructed and functioned. When my request for permission to attend the course reached the Base authorities, they were pleased at my interest in the Air Corps and delighted that I would not be insistent on conducting chemical training for the duration of the course. After the Crew Chiefs Course, I took a Weather Course, but still did not have enough to keep me busy. During these courses, I learned a great deal about the psychology of Air Corps personnel, met a lot of OFFs and EM and became well known around the Base. As I result I got more cooperation from the rank and file than I normally might have expected.

The Women's Army Auxiliary Corps (WAAC) barracks were directly across from the Officers' Club. The four OFFs assigned to the Det ate at the Club so I got to know them. The Det CDR ILT Rita O'Donnell, was very conscious of her rank and prerogatives, I did not particularly like her. Two of the others were quiet types who seemed to fit the stereotype of librarians more than of Army officers. The fourth, Bertha Schwartz, the XO of the Det, was an interesting person. Bertha was rather plain, but she had a good sense of humor, an outgoing personality, lots of energy and was interested in everything. She was a graduate chemist and had been a control chemist for Schenley's, one of the large liquor firms in New York. We soon found that we had many common interests, not the least of which was dancing. Bertha was a good dancer, but more important she could follow me easily; in addition, she was from New York. I began escorting her to the dances at the club. This led to other activities we shared; we found ourselves as chaperons on several Special Service trips. The fact that we had dated had not escaped the gossip-mongers in the WAAC Detachment, so we were in turn chaperoned by all the enlisted WAACs on the trip. We enjoyed a close friendship until she was transferred to one of the Air Corps wings in England.

On 2LT Schwartz's suggestion, I requested a WAAC be assigned to the Chemical Office as secretary or clerk. Many OFFs would not use women soldiers and there were more WAACs than jobs for them. Almost immediately I was notified that PVT Bertha Lambion would report to me for duty. My Chemical Empire continued to expand, but I still had little to do! PVT Lambion, a matronly forty year old, reported for duty. After she settled into her duties, I asked her how she happened to enlist in the Army. She told me that she had a sixteen year old son (her husband was dead) who kept fretting to enlist and get into the war. He told his mother that somebody in the family had to fight in the war. Lambion made an agreement with him that she would go into the Army if he would finish his high school education. If the war was still going on after he graduated, he could enlist. Each was fulfilling his and her part of the agreement.

PVT Lambion was a prize. Formerly the private secretary to the Regional Manager of the General Motors Corporation in Colorado, she was the type of secretary I could give a letter to and say, "Answer this, tell them no", she would then produce a much better letter than I could. She had mastered military correspondence before she reported to us. With minimum guidance, she took over the administration of the Chemical Office She rapidly put the files in order and kept me out of trouble administratively. Strohmetz and Daniels readily accepted her in our organization, and the three of them often spent off duty time together. Surprised that I managed to get such a paragon, I learned that the cute young WAACs were being assigned to the Air Corps Officers; because Lambion was older, she was exiled to the Chemical Section. My sincere and constant praise of Lambion eventually led to her transfer to Base HQ when I departed from RAAF.

In the summer of 1943, I was asked to go to Fort Sumner Army Air Base, about 75 miles north of Roswell, to assist with some Chemical Warfare training. At Fort Sumner I helped the two Chemical NCOs assigned put on a gas alert and other training. It was a welcome change from my inactivity at RAAF. Later in the summer Bill Homen was assigned as Chemical Officer at Fort Sumner. We began an active campaign of mutual assistance which included sharing equipment, ideas, munitions and training aids; it also involved several visits back and forth. I was able to spend Thanksgiving

(1943) with Bill, his wife Lucy, and their son, Billy. But these were occasional activities in a usually monotonous existence.

During one of my visits to Fort Sumner, Bill and I came up with the idea of having a Command-wide Chemical Officers meeting. It would give us an opportunity to see some of our OCS classmates, but also give us a chance to exchange ideas on how to cope with our problems, particularly the low priority given to CW training. We wrote a joint letter to CPT Janz, the West Coast Chemical OFF. He approved our recommendation; it was held at Roswell. Every one of the Chemical OFFs in the WFTC came. It was good to see Bill Binkowski and the others. But LTC Jones, the FTC Chemical OFF invited himself; he dominated the meeting precluding the open exchange of ideas Bill and I had hoped for.

Since there was nothing else to do, I began to apply for every school and assignment listed in Army Circulars. On a regular basis, I entreated my superiors at Fort Worth and Santa Ana to send me overseas, but was always turned down. In desperation, I wrote a letter to MG Porter, Chief of the Chemical Warfare Service, asking him to assign me to a Chemical Mortar Battalion. He had been the guest speaker at our OCS graduation and had told us that if we ever had a problem to remember that we had a friend in Washington. Back came a warm letter telling me that he (MG Porter) would be glad to grant my request and post me to a Chemical Mortar Bn, but that since I was assigned to the Army Air Corps, unless General (GEN) Arnold released me, he was powerless. If I could get released from the Air Corps, he would insure that I was ordered to a Chemical Mortar Bn. My immediate application through channels did not get off Base.

One Army Circular identified the need for Foreign Area Specialists to go to the Far East to work with the Air Corps units flying the hump, I applied and my application was returned. The Base Adj, MAJ Becker, for whom I had little use, would not forward any requests even with a "Recommend Disapproval" indorsement.

Between applications, a minimum of chemical training was accomplished, but CW continued to enjoy a very low priority in the training program at Roswell. I must have made a pest of myself trying to push my program, trying to do my job as I understood it from the directives.

Personnel matters in the CW Section were minimal; it took considerable effort to get Strohmetz promoted to SGT, Daniels to CPL, and Lambion to PFC. Almost as soon as he was promoted, Strohmetz was transferred over my protests and SSG Michael Duchane was assigned in his place. Duchane, an older, more experienced NCO, had less enthusiasm and imagination that Strohmetz. The section was augmented by PFC Waldo Junge. an inexperienced, but eager soldier.

Now there was a sizeable detachment and an excellent training facility, but no training was authorized. After a spell of inactivity, I wrote a letter requesting a transfer from RAAF, and asked for an appointment with the Base Commander, COL John Horton, to discuss it. In my letter I charged that CW tag was being neglected at RAAF, thus there was no need for a full time Chemical OFF. The letter contained my request to be assigned overseas. An appointment was granted me.

On the day of the appointment, the Colonel's secretary greeted me coolly and motioned me into the Commander's office. Knocking at the door, I entered at the words "Come In", marched across the office to the Colonel's desk, saluted and said, "LT Seibert has permission to speak tothe Base Commander Sir". COL Horton returned my salute, looked at me expectantly, but said nothing more. Since he had not put me At Ease, I remained at Attention. "Sir, I would like to ask you to approve my request for a transfer from Roswell. I prefer to go overseas, but I want to go anywhere my training will be utilized. I am doing nothing of importance here, certainly nothing in the Chemical Warfare area. With the amount of Chemical Warfare training being conducted at Roswell, there is no need for a full time Chemical Officer."

Box 395
Roswell Army Air Field
Roswell, N. M.

22 November 1943

Major General William N. Portar
Chief Chemical Warfare Service
Washington, 25, D.C.

Dear Sir,

Since my entrance into the Armed Forces I have tried to obtain service in one of the overseas theaters of operation. Second only to the above was my desire to serve with the Army Ground Forces.

After graduation from Officer Candidate School at Edgewood Arsenal, I attended the First Air Chemical Officer's Course and was assigned to duty with Headquarters, Army Air Forces Flying Training Command, Ft North, Texas, by paragraph 3, dated 2 March 1943, Office Chief Chemical Warfare Service. For the nine months I have been on duty with the Army Air Forces it has been my hope to once again be assigned to the Ground Forces. Attempts at reassignment through channels have met with failure due to extremely literal interpretations of Army Regulations.

The new Army Air Force organization which will force all Arms and Service Officers now on duty with the Army Air Force to wear Air Force insignia will settle forever any hope I have of duty with an Arm in which I feel that I could contribute more tha n I have here-to-fore in the Army Air Forces.

I would appreciate any information or aid you can give me in applying for reassignment to duty with some Army Service Force or Army Ground Force unit. I am especially desirous of overseas duty with a Chemical Weapons Company or some Infantry organization
Sincerely yours,

DONALD A. SEIBERT
2nd Lt., C. W. S.
0-1038113

HEADQUARTERS, ARMY SERVICE FORCES
OFFICE CHIEF OF CHEMICAL WARFARE SERVICE
WASHINGTON 25, D. C.

In reply refer to: 201 Seibert , Donald A. (2nd lt)
25 November 1943

Second Lt. Donald A Seibert, CWS
Box 395
Roswell Army Air Field
Roswell, New Mexico

Dear Seibert:

Thanks very much for your letter 22 November 1943, expressing your desire for overseas assignment or duty with the Army Ground Forces.

You probably realize that, in your present assignment as a chemical officer on duty with Army Air Forces, you are under the jurisdiction. You have the prerogative, of course, to write a request, through channels, for reassignment for duty with Chemical Warfare Service with the ultimate ail of going out with a chemical weapons battalion if you so desire. This, if approved all the way through, will allow you to be transferred for further training for a Ground Force Unit.

I am of the opinion, however, that if it is you desire for overseas duty that you probably have as good a chance, if not a better chance with the Army Air Forces than you do with one of the Ground Force units, in view of the fact that all of the presently activated unites under the Ground Forces are fully staffed and activations are temporarily postponed. However, if you are still desirous of this type of duty and your request is approved, I shall instruct my Personal Division to give you additional training as is necessary for assignment to a Ground Force unit and then to give you such an assignment as soon as available.

Very truly yours,
Willam N. Porter
Major Genral
Chief of the Chemical Warfare Service

PLEASE ADDRESS ALL COMMUNICATION TO "CHIEF OF THE CHEMICAL WARFARE SERVICE WAR DEPARTMENT, WASHINGTON 25, D. C.

"Lieutenant, I'll decide whether we need a Chemical Officer at Roswell Army Air Field. You are too junior to understand the problems I am faced with in conducting the flying training program here, in administering this Base and in complying with all of the directives of higher headquarters. Although you are one of my staff officers, you do not have the perspective to assist me in reconciling all of the many requirements placed upon me and the Base."

"Sir, I am aware of the excessive nature of the chemical training requirements. I believe that I have made constructive recommendations on complying with most of the directives while interfering with the primary mission of RAAF to the minimum. But even my short cut approach has been disapproved. You are not using me and I want to be reassigned."

COL Horton stared at me for a moment, obviously becoming incensed that I would dispute with him even as respectfully as I had.

"Don't all of the training bases in the Western Flying Training Command have Chemical Officers?"

"Yes, sir."

"Well how do you think it would look if Roswell Army Air Field, the largest and most important Base in the Command, did not have a Chemical Officer when all of the smaller fields did? We would be looked down on. No, as long as the Table of Organization authorizes a Chemical Officer, Roswell will have one."

It was my turn to stare at the Colonel. I could not believe the rationale he presented, and groped for words to tell him as politely as I could how asinine his logic was. I failed. We traded arguments for almost 45 minutes. This surprised me, because as Base Commander, COL Horton was a busy man, yet he was taking the time to debate with his most junior staff officer All this time I was at Attention. Though I never went so far as to take up an "At Ease" position, I relaxed the rigidity of my brace somewhat. Finally the Colonel said,

"Seibert, I am not going to forward your request for a transfer. That matter is closed And I cannot authorize a complete chemical training program on the Base. I will have MAJ O'Piel, the Operations Officer, see what can be done to fulfill the essential chemical training requirements. I will authorize a Chemical NCO Course and a Unit Gas Officers Course. And you can continue to have monthly alerts, subject to certain restrictions. We can't interfere with flight operations, so any installation on the flight line concerned with flying, will be declared a gas shelter. Now work out the program with MAJ O'Piel's people. That's all."

"Yes, sir. Thank you, sir." Saluting, I did an about face and walked out of the office. I was actually pleased. The COL had given me the guts of the chemical program I had been asking for.

We had parted on strained terms. He took the matter quite personally, because several times when I passed him and wished him a courteous "Good morning, Colonel" he completely ignored me.

Plans for the two courses he had authorized were immediately completed, but they could not be scheduled until after the Christmas holidays. During the Christmas period many people planned to go on leave and all of my training would be reduced to a minimum. My own request for leave over Christmas was disapproved because only 15% of the officers could be absent from the Base at anytime, and my request had been late. The flying training program continued at the same pace, but all other programs were cut back.

It appeared that this would be a good time to try a few experiments on my own. While talking with one of the medical officers in the hospital, I asked him if he had ever seen blisters raised by either Mustard or Lewisite, the two blister gases. He had not, nor had I, nor had he ever treated such a case. I said to him, "I'm going to burn myself on the arm. We can watch the development of the blisters and you can experiment on them."

The doctor was reluctant to get involved in this uncontrolled (and unauthorized) experiment, even though I assured him I would use only weak solutions and be very careful. Despite his reservations,

I went ahead with the project. Mustard and Lewisite were available for demonstration purposes. I put a drop of Mustard on my right forearm and one of Lewisite on my left. The Base Photographer agreed to take pictures every three hours for the first three days, then once a day after the blisters developed. It was an interesting study as some large blisters developed. Once the blisters appeared, the medics were fascinated, examining them frequently. They read all of the medical literature available; the hospital Commander organized a seminar on the subject. Together we wrote a detailed account of the development of the blisters caused by Mustard and Lewisite.

Just before the Christmas holidays, the Chemical Office conducted the annual post-wide gas chamber exercise. In this exercise one room was saturated with tear gas in which to check the mask and its fit, to make sure that everyone understood how to use the mask, and to develop confidence in it. The other chamber contained a heavy concentration of chlorine. The NCOs handled the tear gas side, while I handled the chlorine side. A group already masked entered the chlorine chamber, talking through my mask I explained that they were in a lethal concentration of gas and that their masks were protecting them from any dangerous effects. They were kept in the chlorine chamber for several minutes, during which I stressed that in that time they would have become gas casualties. They were then required to "Check for Gas" before they left the chamber to be sure they knew what chlorine smelled like and that they had in fact been exposed to a heavy concentration of it. The exercise was designed to and did instill confidence in the mask. All post personnel were scheduled by roster to go through the exercise. Wearing my uniform to convince everyone of my own status, I spent four days in the chlorine chamber. I reeked of chlorine and my brass turned green, but we finally got through it.

Suddenly the Christmas season was on us. Activities on Base lessened as people went on leave. Those remaining enjoyed a heavy social schedule. There had been a dance at the Officers' Club on Christmas Eve. LT Schwartz and I had attended and then she left on leave for New York. It had been a good dance after which we had gone into Roswell for breakfast about two in the morning. When we gathered at the Club on Christmas Day about 1000, we were not too spry. Someone suggested that we needed an eye opener to start the day. We collected some liquor, got the necessary makings from the kitchen and proceeded to mix egg nogs. A distinguished looking COL was sitting in the corner of the club, obviously alone. Filled with Christmas spirit, I said, "Hey, guys. There's a COL over there by himself. We can't let him spend Christmas alone. Let's invite him to join us."

"Sure, Don. You ask him. But no COL is going to have anything to do with a bunch of 2LTs like us."

Disregarding the doubters, I walked over to the COL. "Merry Christmas, Sir. I'm LT Seibert. Will you join us for some egg nog? No one should be alone on Christmas."

"Merry Christmas to you, LT. I am COL Smith, here with the IG Team. Thanks, egg nog sounds good."

We joined the group and I made the introductions. The COL was human! We were surprised that anyone with such an exalted rank could be interested in the routine things we were all concerned with. Everyone was having a good time; after we ran out of bourbon, the only liquor we could find was tequila. Tequila egg nog was different, but not too bad!

While we were enjoying the egg nog, the Base Commander, COL Horton, and his wife came in. COL Horton had been less than cordial with me since our recent confrontation. He noticed the COL with our group and he and his wife headed our way. Apparently he wanted to extend his courtesy to the COL, whom I gathered was senior to him in rank. We asked the Hortons to join us for a drink, and they did. The two COLs stepped aside to talk and Mrs Horton told us about her husband's promotion.

It appeared that Jack, as she called him, had been in the Army Air Corps for many years after he graduated from the Military Academy before he made captain. He married just as the war started, and was promoted with minimum time-in-grade to MAJ, LTC, and COL. Mrs Horton's grandmother, who didn't understand about the military and the war, said, "Isn't it wonderful what Virginia has done for Jack. She got him promoted to COL in three years."

Without giving it a second thought, I looked her in the eye and said, "That is a good idea, maybe I ought to get married."

At the time we were all sweating out our first lieutenancies . All of the officers laughed, but Mrs Horton didn't think it was funny. Shortly thereafter she and the COL departed coolly. But we enjoyed Christmas.

Aphrodite Kalabokus, one of the WAACs assigned to Les Clarke's personnel section, was quite a little sex-pot. Her major aim in life seemed to be to date an officer and possibly marry one. She was constantly making eyes at the OFFs going in and out of Les's office, and was the topic of conversation all over the base. She worked on the personnel files which were in tubs in a narrow hallway, if an officer had to pass by, she would bend over the tub and make sure she pressed up against him as he passed her. This had happened to me several times, so Aphrodite and I were well acquainted.

During Christmas week the Ordnance Detachment had a party for its personnel. WAACs were invited, as were the nurses who dated some of the Ordnance Officers. There was food and music for dancing. The Chemical Det had been invited to attend as we were considered allied to the Ordnance by virtue of the munitons we had and the proximity of Edgewood and Aberdeen Proving Ground. Kettler had asked me to go as his guest.

It was a good party. During the course of the evening, one of the NCOs came to me and said that Aphrodite was eager to dance with me. She had seen me dancing with several of the nurses and thought that I was a great dancer. The SGT said that he knew her reputation but she had asked him to approach me. Larry Hartz, who was also at the party, thought this was a huge joke and urged me to dance with her. They made an agreement, If I would ask her to dance, one of the other officers would cut in after a few steps and finally the sergeant would cut in and that would end it. Because of too much Christmas spirit(s), I forgot my natural caution, walked over to Aphrodite who was standing with some WAACs and enlisted men and asked her if I could have the pleasure of the next dance. She beamed at me, fluttered her long eye lashes, wiggled her little bottom and appeared to be in ecstasy. When the music started we whirled away. My pals let me dance the whole number! Obviously I had been set up. Aphrodite clung, clung, clung, she couldn't get close enough to me. Everybody at the party was watching us and laughing at my discomfiture. Despite my pleading looks no one cut in. It seemed hours before the number ended and I could disengage.

Such pranks were constantly being played on brother officers. In the BOQ these were sometimes carried to extremes. We all kept a bottle of our favorite liquor on a shelf in our rooms. Someone slipped into Larry's room and glued his bottle to the shelf. Larry found it hell to get the liquor out without breaking the bottle, sipping it through a straw was no fun. "Dagwood" Dorwart, an energetic but fiendish officer, lugged 20 or 30 huge tumbleweeds into the BOQ and crammed them into Nick Ditrano's room. His masterpiece, however, was filling a condom with five or si quarts of water, tying it and putting it on Nick's bed. Trying to remove it without getting his bed wet was a test of genius. Nick finally slipped newspapers under it and carried it out.

Another big dance was scheduled at the Officers' Club onNew Year's Eve. Bertha Schwartz was on leave and for one reason or another, the others did not have dates (there must have been 10 officers for every eligible girl in the area). Kettler, Hartz, Ditrano and I decided to go stag. By getting to the club early, we pre-empted a choice table and proceeded to have a good time. We table-hopped, danced almost every set and sang a great deal. By midnight we were in rare form.

The band began to play Auld Lang Syne as everyone kissed everyone else. The four of us kissed the ladies closest to us, heedless of husbands and escorts. On the way back to our table, we passed

COL and Mrs Horton, sitting in regal dignity. As we dropped into our seats, I glanced again at the Hortons and muttered.

"Why don't we all go over and kiss Virginia?"

"Naw, the COL'll get sore. We're too drunk. Besides, you wouldn't dare, Don. Not after the chewing the Old Man gave you."

"Who says I wouldn't dare? I'll bet you a drink that I'll go over and wish them both a Happy New Year and kiss Virginia. But you guys gotta do it after me. Okay?"

All three of them agreed. Lurching to my feet, I threaded my way to the Horton's table with the exaggerated care of one who has had too much to drink. Bowing formally to COL Horton, I extended my hand and said, "Sir, may I wish my Commanding Officer a very Happy New Year?"

COL Horton looked surprised for a moment, then took my hand and shook it cordially.

"Thank you, LT Seibert. The same to you."

"Thank you, sir. May I have your permission to kiss Mrs Horton and wish her a Happy New Year?"

With a quizzical look on his face he said, "Er, why of course, Seibert. Go ahead."

When I leaned over, maintaining my balance with difficulty, I heard a cheer from our table. As I pecked Mrs Horton on the cheek, I murmured, "A very Happy New Year to you Ma'am. I hope that 1944 will be a great year for you."

She flushed and responded, "Thank you, Lieutenant."

Bowing again to both of them, I managed to turn around and make my way back to our table. "Okay, you guys, it's your turn. Go ahead. And where's the drink you owe me?"

Nick Ditrano laughingly signaled the waitress and ordered a Scotch and water for me. Kettler groped his way over to the Hortons and repeated my performance.

We all cheered. Larry and Nick followed. Shortly afterwards, the Hortons left.

We had one more drink, by the time the band played Army Blue and the National Anthem, we could barely hold ourselves at Attention. It was a great party.

On January 2nd, word was put out that all OFFs would report to the theater for a special officers call. There was considerable speculation as we crowded into the theater. After we were all assembled, LTC Tubbs, the Executive Officer (XO) of the Base, mounted the stage and talked about military courtesy. He said that he was disappointed at the lack of military courtesy among the officers on the Base and the failure to observe old traditions. He cited as an example that only four officers on the entire Base had the courtesy to wish their Commanding Officer a Happy New Year! Needless to say, the four of us nearly choked trying to stifle our laughter. He went on to say that three of the four were not Army Air Corps Officers, but were of other branches of service. Finally he pointed out that this did not reflect favorably on the Air Corps; he then chewed out the entire group. Others who knew what had happened at the Club, found it all they could do to suppress their laughter until LTC Tubbs dismissed the group. That night at the Club we really took a razzing. It was an interesting insight into how you can hoodwink some senior officers. EM call that a "Snow Job". We had unintentionally done the proper thing, but had created an erroneous impression.

After the holidays we settled down to training. Though I had to modify the program of instruction (POI) prescribed by higher headquarters in order to minimize interference with the flying training mission we managed to complete a Gas Noncommissioned Officers Course and a Unit Gas Officers (UGO) Course. I was satisfied that the students got adequate training. During the course I got to know many of the officers and noncommissioned officers involved with the flying program and enlisted their aid in our gas alerts. Many were happy to cooperate. It made my job easier.

One evening, while the Gas NCO Course was in progress, a fire broke out in an engineer warehouse. Nick, who was the only Engineer Officer living on Base, was notified of the fire. He and I had just finished dinner and raced to the scene. The fire was in a small building used to store materials for the water purification plant. There were several cylinders of chlorine stored there. As we arrived breathless, several firemen staggered out of the building, shouting, "The chlorine cylinders have blown. The place is full of gas. Clear the area."

Everyone looked at me for advice. "Stand clear of the building until I get back." There was a jeep at hand and I leaped in it. "Take me to the Chemical Warehouse. Quick". The driver took me literally and we raced the short way to my section. Bursting into the class room where Daniels was teaching, assisted by Junge, I shouted,

"Put about 20 gas masks on the jeep outside right away. And find all the rags you can. Junge, get the decon apparatus down to the Engineer Warehouse as fast as you can."

The Students looked at me in stunned surprise. "There's a fire in the warehouse and the chlorine cylinders have blown. We have to move fast. GO!"

The entire class galvanized into action. Junge ran to start up the decon truck, while Daniels and his students seized handfuls of rags and gas masks and put them in the jeep Daniels leaped in with me as I shouted to the driver, "Back to the warehouse." The round trip had taken less then 10 minutes. When we got back to the burning building, the firemen were still playing water on it, but were following my instructions not to go inside. Several men were stretched out on the ground.

"Get those men to the hospital. Don't wait for an ambulance."

Immediately the crowd began to help the three stricken men into available transportation. Meanwhile, Junge arrived with the decon truck. Daniels and I donned masks. "Junge, issue those masks to the firemen and make sure they know how to adjust them." Daniels and I entered the burning building and groped our way to the chlorine cylinders which we could identity by the green gas erupting from one of them. The others seemed intact.

Getting the cylinder, we started rolling it to the door, as I tried to recall everything I had ever heard about chlorine and how to neutralize it. Suddenly I shouted through my mask at Daniels, "Run ahead and wet all the rags we brought down. We'll wrap the top of the cylinder in them. The water may absorb the chlorine and turn it into hydrochloric acid." Daniels nodded his understanding and ran out of the building. By the time I had rolled the cylinder to the doorway, he had a pile of wet rags waiting for me.

Motioning everyone except those in gas masks to back away from the area, I rolled the cylinder out the door. Five or six fireman had put on masks and were waiting to get a hose into the building. Daniels handed me one wet rag after another. These were wrapped over the cylinder head, where the safety plug had blown out due to the increased pressure occasioned by the heat. With the application of the second or third rag, the cloud of gas escaping from the cylinder was reduced appreciably. By the time seven or eight layers of rags had been applied, there was almost no seepage. My wild idea seemed to be working. "Get the other cylinders out of the building before they blow", I instructed the firemen. They quickly rolled them out. "We'll put them on the decon truck and take them out to the gas demonstration area until they are safe. You can go into the building now with masks on." Willing hands helped us hoist the three cylinders on the truck. Junge headed for the open area we used for our demonstrations. There were no buildings nearby; fortunately the wind was blowing off post into the desert. Daniels and I clutched the cylinders to prevent them from falling off. The other cylinders cooled and presented no problems. Apparently, we had put enough wet rags on the leaking cylinder to render it harmless.

The Chemical Office got a bit of publicity from the incident; we used it as an example of how CW training could assist in coping with unusual situations. It also generated a bit more tolerance for our training program at Base HQ.

Toward the end of January I was called by my friend 1LT Bill Stratford, the Postal Officer. He told me that my promotion to first lieutenant had come in. It had to go to Base HQ first, and he urged me to get over to the PX to buy cigars and bars because they were in short supply. Forewarned,

I sat and waited for the official call. When the office closed at 1700 there had been no call. At the club I had a drink with friends and waited, the box of cigars hidden. Finally about 1830 Nick, Larry and I went in to dinner. Just as we sat down, I was paged to answer the phone. It was MAJ Becker, who chewed me out for some trumped up reason (the usual "cute" way of notifying an officer of his promotion in those days) and then told me I had been promoted. It was official at last. Larry Hartz or Nick Ditrano pinned the silver bar on me as I passed out the cigars. Finally I was a 1LT after one year in grade almost to the day!

We all sweated out our promotions in those days. To be eligible, an officer had to be assigned to a unit for six months, there had to be a vacancy in the grade in which he was to be promoted, and he had to be recommended by his commanding officer. Those who stayed in one unit, especially a unit with many grade vacancies, made rapid promotions. Those who moved frequently, or who were in units in which there were few grade vacancies, marked time. At Roswell, it was more a matter of getting HQ to put in the recommendations, there were many vacancies and we had all been there longer than six months.

During slack periods in CW Tng, I often went to the small arms range run by CPT Chris Vrang, a geology professor from one of the western universities. In time I became a fairly good shot with the carbine. This experience stood me in good stead when I went out on periodic bomb range clean-ups with Kettler and his boss, the Base Ordnance Officer. The bomb target ranges were on land leased from various ranches within a 50 mile radius of the Base. There were many duds which posed threats to people, cattle or sheep on the ranges. Smoke canisters in the base of the bombs normally exploded on contact with the ground and released smoke marking the point of impact, this enabled the bombardier students and their instructors to evaluate their accuracy. We fired at the smoke canisters, igniting them and eliminating any danger. The practice bombs were then collected, those that could be used again were refused, those broken or smashed were sold as scrap metal.

In early spring of 1944, MAJ Chapman, CDR of the 95th Squadron to which I was assigned, approved a two week leave. It was good to see Mother and Dad again. Mother fed me as if I had not had a good meal since I left home. The local merchants cooperated. She got extra meat, sugar and other rationed items. The butcher, who knew the family sold her a huge roast beef and only took the routine number of ration stamps. Additional ration points were available for service men on leave, but merchants gave out items far in excess of those authorized when any of the local boys came home.

Since liquor was in short supply, I wanted to take some Scotch back with me. It was hard to buy Scotch in Roswell, liquor dealers there required customers to buy two bottles of cheap liquor (mostly tequila) to get one bottle of Scotch As there was only one bottle available in College Point, I called Uncle Ed, the family wheeler-dealer. We had lunch in downtown Manhattan, then he took me to a liquor store he dealt with. After a short conversation, the owner sold me five bottles of precious Scotch. I nursed my heavy suitcase gingerly back to RAAF.

Shortly after I returned from leave, we held another of our now routine monthly gas alerts. During this alert we wore the mask for two hours, our requirement was to develop the ability to wear the mask for four hours without major interference with routine tasks. Walking back to the BOQ, I hung the mask over my shoulder to let the perspiration dry (an accepted procedure) before restoring it to the carrier.

Just as I passed one of the BOQs, a major, one of the flying instructors, stepped out. He looked at me sharply as he returned my salute. "LT, that's no way to handle a gas mask. You will ruin it. Put it back in the case immediately. You ought to be setting a better example to the enlisted men around here. We have trouble enough trying to teach them any Chemical Warfare training."

It struck me he was serious, that he did not realize that I was the Base Chemical Officer! It was obvious that he could not see my Chemical Warfare Service insignia because the hose of the mask was covering it Delighted that he was taking an interest in C W tog, I was at a loss to know how to get out of the predicament without curtailing his enthusiasm. But I had to correct him.

"Major, this is an accepted procedure. I am drying my mask after having worn it for two hours. It should not be put away wet."

"Now don't argue with me, LT. You young officers are always trying to get away with something. You have got to realize that your example is followed by the enlisted men. Now get that mask off your shoulder and into the case."

Some movement must have uncovered my insignia, because he took a hard look at my collar and turned red. Before he could say anything, I intervened, "MAJ, I am delighted that you are taking training and discipline seriously. I know this looks strange, but it is really accepted procedure. Please continue to help me by correcting any errors you see. I appreciate it". I saluted and walked on. He returned my salute, still embarrassed. "Sorry, LT. Yeah, I'll continue to work on it." He spun around and walked off rapidly.

About 25 miles from RAAF was a prisoner of war camp. Most of the prisoners there were from the German Afrika Korps, and were extremely arrogant. There were some serious incidents in the camp, in fact it was widely rumored that a kangaroo court had executed (hanged) a prisoner because he had cooperated with the Americans.

One day in April 1944, as Officer of the Day, I received a call from the OD of the Roswell POW Camp. He wanted to know if we could fly one of their seriously ill patients to Oklahoma, where the hospital for the POWs was located. In order to arrange it, I asked him what the problem was. He told me the prisoner had a blockage in his intestinal tract. My Army medical training flashed a caution light, so I called the Medical OD at the Base Hospital, told him about the request, and asked him about the medical justification for the air evacuation.

When the MOD heard that there was a suspected stricture of the intestines, he directed me to stop working on air evacuation, explaining that flying at high altitudes in an unpressurized cabin would aggravate the condition. He told me to have the doctor at the POW camp contact him. As a result of that conversation, the POW was brought to the RAAF hospital where the necessary surgery could be performed.

Since he was a POW, he had to be under guard at all times. Due to these unusual circumstances the head of the hospital requested that I be present during the entire procedure. It was a fairly routine operation, and no difficulty was experienced. One of the doctors, a Jewish CPT from St Louis, who had a keen sense of humor, stopped the proceedings in the middle of the operation and said in an exaggerated Jewish accent, "If my orthodox grandmother could see what I am doing now". We all broke out into laughter.

The patient was sent to the recovery room under guard. In connection with the report I had to make I visited him. He had just finished reading *Life* Magazine, which showed activities going on in several US cities, New York among them. He threw the magazine at me and muttered half in English, half in German, "DAS BLAVE VOM HIMMEL HERUNTERLUGEN (lie in the throat). DIE LUFT WAFFENEUE YORK AUFREIBEIN (the German Air Force has destroyed New York)". He continued to mutter that most of our big cities had been bombed so there could not be such activities in them now. I told him that they were not lies, that no German bombers had ever crossed the ocean, but he refused to believe me. Apparently German propaganda was very effective, or the hard core Afrika Korps would not accept our evidence.

One of my friends from NYU, Betty Elbaum, wrote and asked me if I wanted a subscription to *IN FACT,* a liberal newsletter "for the millions who want a free press". Always interested in various points of view, I told her that I did. She took out a subscription in my name and shortly I began receiving *IN FACT at* RAAF. The day I received the third issue, Bill Stratford, my good friend the Postal Officer, called me into his office as I was picking up my mail.

"Say, Don, do you know that your mail is under surveillance?"

"What do you mean, Bill?"

"Well, I have orders to report to the Base Intelligence Officer (S-2) anyone who gets certain publications. *IN FACT* is one of them. I had to send your name to the S-2. Now MAJ Bailie wants to know who you receive letters from, and I have to send your mail to him before I put it out. I don't think he opens it, just looks at the return addresses. What do you want to do about it?"

"Thanks, Bill That's funny. My friends at NYU always thought I was ultraconservative, now I am suspected of being subversive. That's a real laugh. Wait till I tell my friends in the Young Communist League about this! Don't do anything. Let's see what happens."

But the specter would not go away. A few weeks later, I was setting up a demonstration and wanted to know how incendiary bombs worked. CPL Daniels and I made some jellied gasoline, the forerunner of NAPALM, which was a constituent of our incendiary bombs. Needing an igniting device I went to the library to look at a handbook for chemists containing the formulas for various combinations which would set off explosives. After checking the index, I turned to the pages I wanted , they were not there! Three or four pages were missing from the book. When I reported this to the Librarian, she looked at me oddly and said,

"Yes, I know. The S-2 directed me to cut them out. He has them in his office."

This seemed to be carrying security too far. The book was available in most book stores and at all libraries. Shaking my head, I proceeded to the S-2 office and asked for the pages. The clerk told me that I would have to talk with MAJ Bailie personally, and that he was not in. His secretary set up an appointment for me. The next day, when I went to see MAJ Bailie, he seemed quite agitated. He wanted to know how I knew the pages were missing and what I wanted them for. Patiently, I explained why I was interested in them and that I found the pages missing from the book in the library. Completing my explanation, I asked him why they had been removed from the book.

"Why to prevent sabotage, of course! We have been warned that saboteurs might try to damage some of the B-17s here on base. So I am taking no chances."

"But Major, that book is available in every library and in most book stores. Surely you don't believe that any one who wants to blow up the aircraft at Roswell will go to the Base Library to find out how to do it!"

"Well we can't take any chances. I will let you read them here, officially, but you cannot take the pages from this office. I keep them in my safe."

He went to the safe and got out an envelope, for which I had to sign a receipt. When finished with the pages, read at a table in his office, I turned them back. After he had verified that all the pages were indeed in the envelop, he lined through my signature and initialed it. It struck me that he might conclude from my receipt of *IN FACT* and my interest in explosive compounds that I was the long heralded saboteur!

A short time later I was called to MAJ Bailie's office. He took me into a room within a room, mysteriously swore me to secrecy, then told me that there had been a suspected case of sabotage against some of the aircraft on the flight line. An inspection of the parts that were giving trouble revealed powder in the casings. MAJ Bailie's people had collected a sample of the powder and he wanted to know if I could tell them what it was. I looked at it. It seemed to be filings or scrapings resulting from two metal parts rubbing together. Bailie dismissed this theory, he asked me to make a chemical analysis of the powder to see if it was an incendiary agent. There were no lab facilities on the Base so I suggested that one of the druggists might be able to analyze it for him. Again Bailie impatiently passed this off, it might violate security. A military person had to do it. Recalling that one of the professors of chemistry at NMMI had told me there was a fully equipped chemistry laboratory at the school, I told Bailie that perhaps CPL Daniels, who had majored in chemistry in college, could do it. I was tied up with a court-martial which could not be postponed. This pleased Bailie, who had me sign for an envelope of powder, asking me to expedite the matter, Daniels and I went to NMMI where the faculty was happy to let him use the facilities. Daniels was delighted with the chance to work with chemicals again. I glumly went about my duties on the military court. In two days Daniels had a complete analysis. The powder proved to be scrapings from the housing of the aircraft part. Bailie was disappointed.

Shortly after this Daniels was transferred and was replaced by SGT Young. A Mexican-American from Colorado, he was a loyal, resourceful and hardworking NCO, who loved to drive the decon truck. Young gave a Chemical Warfare Course in Spanish to other Hispanic airmen which proved both popular and useful.

Once again, Bill Homen and I plotted together. The first All-WFTC Chemical Officers conference had proved to be so valuable, despite LTC Jones' presence, that we recommended another one be held. The recommendation was approved. We were notified that LTC Fain, the new West Coast Chemical Officer, would chair the meeting at Roswell. It was our first meeting with LTC Fain; we were not impressed. He was intelligent, ambitious, and ruthless in pushing his own views. He could not understand our problems, which he dismissed as excuses to avoid compliance with the training directives. He told us that all training directed by higher HQ would be completed within the time limits imposed. Because LTC Fain refused to hear our views, the meeting was a disaster. My relations with West Coast Headquarters were cool from then on.

In early summer of 1944, COL Horton was reassigned and COL Orin Bushey succeeded him as Base Commander. We all sensed an immediate change in tempo and outlook. It struck me then, how powerful an impact a commander can have on a unit. I have never lost that belief.

My chemical training program began progressing slowly but steadily and we gradually accomplished all of the training required by higher HQ. We did not always complete the requirements by the date specified, but eventually it got done. In certain instances, I cut comers to accommodate other activities on the Base, we devised ingenious methods of working incendiary and decontamination training into the regular schedule.

In addition I was busy with legal work because Larry Hartz made sure that I remained on all the courts. As a result, I sat on several General Courts, was defense counsel on many Special Courts, and on several occasions served as Summary Court Officer to dispose of the personal effects of airmen or officers killed in flying or automobile accidents. I accompanied Larry to the State Prison in Las Vegas where he was to take a deposition from a prisoner who was a key witness against one of our EM accused of having homosexual relations with him and other people. My mission was to represent the accused and ask questions which might discredit the prisoner's testimony. It was a sticky case, but an interesting experience.

On one occasion I went to Albuquerque to obtain a statement from the family of a young girl who accused an RAAF airmen of assaulting her. PFC Lambion went with me to take the statement in shorthand, transcribe and type it there, so I could get it signed. A problem developed in fitting her with a parachute. The straps had to go between her legs, but she had no slacks. We finally decided that she could fly with the straps free until anything happened, nothing did. She was the envy of the WAAC Detachment, the first of the WAACs on Base to fly.

Summary Court duty was always sad. I had to collect the belongings of the deceased, turn in government property, pay his debts, settle his accounts, ship home his personal property and write a report to his family. In the effects of one deceased I found not only letters to the man's wife, but also to his girl friend. The girl friend's letters were destroyed. Pornographic pictures and literature I also destroyed without authority. Two B-25s from Marfa Army Air Base collided in mid-air and crashed close by. Ten men were killed. Sorting out the bodies and personal effects was a problem. Fortunately, Marfa sent up its own Summary Court Officer so I merely assisted him.

Despite the improvement in my Chemical Warfare duties, I was still anxious to get overseas, preferably with a Chemical Mortar Bn. When the landings on D-Day were announced, I was frantic. The possibility that I might spend the entire war in the United States was intolerable. I had to get out of Roswell! Just as I reached a point of desperation, War Department Circular 229 passed over my desk. The circular authorized any OFF, regardless of branch or assignment, to transfer to the Infantry (IN). Circular 229 made it clear that all applications for transfer to the IN would be approved. The transferees would be sent to FT Benning, GA to complete the Basic Infantry Officers Course and then be assigned either overseas or wherever the need was greatest. This appeared to be a sure way of getting overseas so I immediately submitted my application according to the instructions in the circular. A month passed with no response. The circular had led me to believe that orders would be forthcoming within a week or two at most. A second month passed and still no word.

On the 7th of September I found myself on duty as OD at HQ. During the early evening a LTC walked into the OD's office and began to talk with me. He was a member of an Inspector General (IG) Team from Washington doing a routine Annual General Inspection of RAAF.

"You don't have any problems, do you, Lieutenant?"

"No, sir. Everything is going fine."

"Good. We are setting up a special session for any one who wants to bring complaints to us. Do your think there will be many?"

"I don't know, sir. Everyone I have talked to on base seems to be satisfied."

"Well, I am mostly looking at administration. That is my specialty."

"Say, sir, how long does it usually take for a request to get from a base like Roswell to the War Department and orders to be cut?" He looked at me sharply, "What do you mean?"

"Well, how long would it be before orders are cut on an officer who applied for a transfer to the Infantry under Circular 229?"

"Funny you should ask that. That is a matter of special interest to all IGs this month. It should not be over two weeks at most."

"That's odd I submitted my request in June and have not heard a word."

"Someone is sitting on it someplace. You should have had orders in July. It is very rare for a request under that circular to be disapproved. You should follow up on it. Write a tracer letter under the provisions of Army Regulation 340-15. Include a copy of your original request. That has to be forwarded through all channels that your application must go through, and a report made on the action. But to expedite things, make an extra copy. Put on the bottom of the letter, cc, Information copy direct to the Adjutant General. The cc stands for carbon copy. If I were you, I would mail that copy to the Adjutant General (AG) before you put the original through channels. Just put it in an envelope addressed to the Adjutant General, War Department, Washington, D.C. While the original is going through channels the War Department will take action on your request. You should have orders in two weeks at most. But mail that carbon copy first, in case someone is holding up your request."

"Thanks a lot, sir. I'll get it out the first thing in the morning." The next morning, Lambion typed up the tracer in accordance with the IG's instructions. She made the extra copy which I took into Roswell before lunch and mailed in the Post Office. The original was hand carried to Base HQ that afternoon. Almost immediately, there was action. MAJ Becker, the Base Adj, called me to his office the next morning.

"What is this note on the bottom of your letter about a copy direct to the AG. Where is that copy?"

"Why I mailed it yesterday, MAJ Becker."

"Who authorized you to do that? All correspondence from this Base must come through this office."

"There is nothing in regulations that prohibits a copy of a letter from being mailed direct. I think the War Department may act on that carbon and I'll get my orders in a couple of days."

"Well, I don't like it. It sounds as if you don't trust the Commander. Going behind his back is serious business."

"I don't mean to indicate distrust of COL Bushey, but I want that transfer."

"We'll see about that. Don't start packing yet. That's all." I saluted and left.

Becker was very agitated. Apparently my letter had never cleared Base HQ, contrary to Army policy and certainly the provisions of that circular. Later, I was told that a letter came down through channels from Washington seeking information as to the disposition of the original request. Now I waited impatiently for action.

Several days after my talk with MAJ Becker I received a telephone call to report to LTC Andrews, now Base XO. The order sounded urgent, and was unusual as I rarely had dealings with LTC Andrews. The thought occurred to me that I might be in trouble about the carbon copy direct to the AG. When I reported to Andrews he was grim. He told me that COL Bushey, MAJ Bailie and SSG John Nemetz had been killed in an aircraft accident at Fort Worth. A plane was waiting to take me there to secure the personal effects of all three, I would be the Summary Court Officer for them. This duty would take priority over all others. After calling my office I was quickly airborne. When I returned, I had all the information available on the accident and the personal effects of the three men. Because of his grade and the complexity of the case, a legal officer replaced me as Summary Court for COL Bushey. But I completed the other two cases. This was my last official act at Roswell Army Air Field.

Eight days after mailing that carbon copy, I received orders transferring me to the Infantry (IN) and directing me to report to FT Benning to attend Infantry Officers Special Basic Course Number 43 (0SB43). With orders in hand, I walked into MAJ Becker's office, tore off the Army Air Corps patch I was wearing, threw it on his desk and said, "I'm going back to the Army."

"Well you needn't get hostile."

That night I exchanged my CW insignia for the crossed rifles of the IN. Fortunately the PX had a few sets of crossed rifles. There was quite a celebration at the club. Within days I cleared the post, turning the chemical property back to CPT Sheehy, the OFF I had taken it from a year and a half earlier; again he would be the Base Chemical Supply OFF until another CW officer was assigned.

Although I left behind many good friends, I was delighted to bid farewell to RAAF. Now I would surely get overseas immediately.

CHAPTER 3

DOUGH BOY

Upon arrival at FT Benning in October 19441 was assigned to the 5th Company, 1st Student Training Regiment, The Infantry School (TIS). We were billeted in temporary wooden enlisted barracks, in a section of the post set aside for student officers. We slept in squad bays, about 18 OFFs to each floor of the barracks. Most of the OFFs in the 5th Co had been transferred to the Infantry involuntarily from Antiaircraft Artillery (AA) or Tank Destroyer (TD) units and wanted no part of it. Only about 20 of us had volunteered for the Infantry under the provisions of Circular 229, among them Cal Bury, a former Army Air Corps OFF and Bill Geislinger. Cal was a husky, good looking 1LT from California who had studied mining engineering before the war. Bill was a slender, exuberant character from Paramus, NJ. Those of us who had volunteered for the IN were approaching the course with great enthusiasm. The reluctant doughboys who had not volunteered obviously did not want to go into combat.

An entire bus load of former AA LTs pulled up in front of the barracks followed by a "deuce and a half truck. The superior attitude of the "ack-ack" boys as they scrambled out, turned to astonishment, disbelief and horror as several enlisted men unloaded their footlockers and duffel bags, stacked them on the grass and drove off. What a come down! They made no attempt to conceal their contempt for the Infantry. Whenever a section of Quad 50's, Twin 40's, 90's, or other AA weapons went by, they would cheer heedless of the instruction going on. The OFFs transferred involuntarily were uncooperative, heckled the instructors and made it difficult for everyone concerned.

FT Benning was a model of military training procedures. The instructors knew their subjects, used training aids well to enhance their instruction, and presented their material in a clear and interesting manner. The Infantry School did an outstanding job of cramming a great deal of information into those of us who were willing to receive it. However, the bulk of the class refused to accept the instruction. Cal Bury, Bill Geislinger, the other volunteers and I tried to get as much as we could out of the class in spite of the distractions.

Frequently when an instructor had finished a particularly involved period of instruction, the "disenchanted retreads" would chant in unison.

"FORTY EIGHT!"

"FORTY NINE!"

"FIFTY!"

"SOME SHIT!"

The instructors, of course, reported the entire class for discourtesy. The 5th Company Commander's lectures on military courtesy and cooperation were of no avail, the majority of the class was completely turned off and would not cooperate. Finally COL Brown, Commander of the 1st Student Training Regiment, talked to the 5th Co and laid it out plainly. Whether we liked it or not, we were assigned to the Infantry, we were assigned to the course, we were going to complete the course. The COL said that he would take whatever steps were necessary to insure that no further disturbances took place in class. He told the class that if it thought that such juvenile conduct would get it out of the Infantry or to some state-side sinecure, they were mistaken. The purpose of the course was to prepare Infantry lieutenants for their combat role. All of us were destined for combat and we had better learn as much as we could to improve our chances of survival. COL Brown, an RA OFF (he wore riding boots and breeches when he addressed us), then informed us that he was going to inspect our Co the following Saturday.

The wiseheads in the Co decided that we had to pass that inspection or we'd be harassed by the cadre for the rest of the course. Everyone fell to, determined to pass. It was amazing how those men could cooperate and organize themselves if they saw the need. We organized teams, each team having a specific part of the barracks to clean or arrange. Some teams organized the books on the shelves so that every officer's set was exactly the same. Some aligned clothing so that every item hung exactly the same. Others made sure the beds were lined up, and were tightly made. Since we had to lay out our rifles, detailed stripped, a team made sure that the weapons were properly broken down and that all pieces were laid out exactly the same. It was a major effort in uniformity and spit and polish.

The essence of an inspection is organization. When every soldier has his equipment in exactly the same place as every other soldier, it is a simple matter to determine missing or damaged equipment. Thus the task of the inspector is expedited, hence he gains a more favorable impression of the unit. When COL Brown came through the barracks, he was amazed at the appearance of the 5th Co. He told us after the inspection that in all his Army career he had never seen a more professional looking organization. This is what this group was capable of; they simply would not put out routinely.

One of the major blocks of the Basic Course was rifle marksmanship. We were told that we had to qualify with the M-1 rifle. This should present no problem as far as I could see. The preliminary marksmanship training was complete, extensive and well done. We moved to the known distance (KD) range early one morning for zeroing, practice and record firing. The initial firing for zeroing the M-1 rifles was disastrous; despite careful sighting and trigger squeeze I couldn't seem to hit the target. Others had the same difficulty. Immediately the instructors started to berate us and emphasize that the ability to hit what we aimed at was necessary for our survival. They were convinced that we were trying to bolo (fail to qualify) as part of the protest against the unwilling retraining of most. That was not the case with me, nor with Bury or Geislinger. Even though we never got a satisfactory zero, we went through several orders of practice firing, and through record firing twice. More than a third of the class did not attain the minimum score, 140, to qualify. I finished with a miserable 117. Cal eked out a 110, while Bill Geislinger managed to qualify with 161. We were ordered to appear before an investigating board.

When called, I walked into the room in which three grim faced officers were seated behind a table, stopped three paces from them, saluted and reported. "LT Seibert reports to the Board of Officers as directed, Sir." The senior OFF, a MAJ, returned my salute. "Sit down LT Seibert. As you are aware, the Board is investigating the range firing of OSB 43, and the reason so many OFFs failed to qualify. Any statement you make to this Board is considered an official statement. You are aware of the penalty for uttering false official statements?"

"Yes, Sir."

"Very well, do you have any explanation for your failure to qualify?"

"No, sir, I do not. I took very careful sight pictures, followed the correct procedure and squeezed the trigger carefully. My coach said that I did not flinch. But I never got my rifle zeroed. I ran out of windage and elevation, and could not get the strike of the bullet into the bull's eye."

"Are you sure you did not jerk off your rounds?"

"Yes, sir. My coach can verify that."

"Who was your coach?"

"Lieutenant Bury, sir."

"Did you volunteer for transfer to the Infantry?"

"Yes, sir. Under Circular 229. LT Bury did also."

"Don't you want to complete this course successfully?"

"Yes, sir, I do. I am sure there is something wrong with the sight on my rifle. I had the armorer on the range check it, but he said it was okay. Somehow, I thought the bullet was tumbling when it was enroute to the target, but of course, I couldn't really see it."

"The bullet was tumbling? Can you get your rifle?"

"Yes, sir. It is outside with LT Bury. I'll get it immediately."

I stepped outside, grabbed my rifle, checking the serial number to make sure it was mine, returned to the Board Room and handed the President the M-1. He inspected the sight and then looked through the bore. Immediately he started laughing. Without a word he handed the rifle to the CPT on his right, who looked through the bore and laughed also. The M-1 was passed to the ILT who completed the Board who likewise broke out in laughter as he examined the rifle. "What have you cleaned this rifle with, Lieutenant?" asked the CPT.

"Why bore cleaner and oil. sir."

"There are almost no lands and grooves in this rifle, Lieutenant. They are completely worn.

Are you sure you didn't use steel wool on that bore?"

"No, sir."

"It looks like your Co was issued rifles used by one of the OCS classes. They often use steel wool on their bores to get out rust and pits. No wonder you thought the bullet was tumbling. I'll bet the strike on the target was a keyhole. This is basically a shot gun now. I can understand why you couldn't zero it. You are dismissed, LT." He laughed again as he handed me my rifle. Giving a rifle salute, I faced about and walked from the room, relieved.

There was not enough time to refire a third time due to the foil schedule, so many of us left FT Benning without qualifying with our basic arm.

Just after I arrived at Benning, my sister, Arlene, wrote and told me that her friend, Helen Baker, was also there. Arlene and Helen had worked together before the war, Helen had been to the house many times, so I knew her. She had enlisted in the WAACs and was stationed at TIS. Arlene suggested that I take her out to dinner. She wanted first hand information about Helen, particularly how she looked in uniform.

Since I had no idea of Helen's schedule, I called the WAAC Detachment (Det). After several busy signals, I finally got through to the Orderly Room. The CQ was quick to locate Technician Third Class Baker for me when I identified myself as LT Seibert. Helen and I exchanged pleasantries, then I asked her if she would like to have dinner with me the following Tuesday. She thought it would be fun as we had much to talk about.

On the night of our "date" I walked into the WAAC Det Orderly Room in pinks and greens. The CQ jumped to attention and squealed, "ATTENTION"!

"As you were, Corporal. I would like to see Technician Third Grade Helen Baker." Her eyes grew wide as she gasped, "Yes, sir. Just a minute, sir." and ran from the room. In a short time she returned with Helen, followed by a WAAC 1LT. Seizing Helen I gave her a brotherly kiss under the disapproving gaze of the Det CO and the CQ.

"Hi, Helen. How are you? How is your family?"

Helen glanced uneasily at her Commanding Officer and responded tightly, "Everyone is fine, Don. It's good to see you. How is Arlene?" Just then the Detachment Commander stepped forward.

"Lieutenant, you know it is against Army Regulations for officers to fraternize with enlisted women except under unusual circumstances, such as your prior friendship with Technician Baker. I have here an authorization for you and Baker to be together. This will avoid any incidents with the Military Police." With that she handed me a document which certified that Helen had official permission to be in my company on 24 October. I glanced at it and began laughing.

WAC DETACHMENT #2
THE INFANTRY SCHOOL
FORT BENNING GEORGIA

24 October 1944

C E R T I F I C A T E

This certifies that Dec 3 Helen Baker A 202952 of WAC Detachment #2 Academic Regiment The Infantry School Fort Benning Georgia has permission to be in the company of 1st Lt Donald A Seibert 0138113 Tuesday, 24 October 1924.

FRANCES E. VAN NICE
1st Lt. WAC
Commanding

"You've got to be kidding, Lieutenant. Helen and I are old friends and the Army is not going to tell me who I can be seen with."

"This is a serious problem here at FT Benning, LT Seibert. We have to protect our girls as well as maintain discipline. Baker must have a copy of this authorization with her all the time you are together, and this copy is for you. Please have her back to the barracks by taps."

I could only gape at her. Finally I managed to get out a strangled, "I understand, Lieutenant. I'll have her back on time. Come on Helen." before I was convulsed with laughter. Once outside Helen dissolved in laughter also.

"Did you see LT Van Nice's face when you started to laugh, Don?"

We talked about what we would do in view of Helen's curfew; taking a bus into Columbus would consume too much of our time together. It seemed a good idea to stay on Post. Remembering the experience when Bill had visited me at Santa Ana, we went to the PX cafeteria for dinner. There was an initial silence when the two of us walked into the cafeteria together. This occurred wherever we went. Finally we decided to go to a movie. At that time all Army theaters had a reserved section for officers. Dependents and EM where in other sections. As I surrendered the tickets, I requested seats in the Officers' Section. There was a short confrontation with the usher when he questioned whether Helen could sit with me. With a flourish, I produced my certificate, which overwhelmed the young PFC. Yielding to my authority as a 1LT he hurriedly seated us in the Officers' Section. It was both a frustrating evening as well as a hilarious one. I was glad to see Helen, but I told her that I would not go through that drill again as long as such rules and regulations remained in force for WAACs.

OSB 43 included several hours of instruction in hand-to-hand combat. Bill Geislinger and I were buddies in this training, as we were paired off by height. We tossed each other about with more enthusiasm than technique.

Several bivouacs were included in the POI, an attempt to teach us how to get along in the field with minimum comforts. Many of the AA OFFs boarded the vehicles taking us to the bivouac site with everything they owned, some even brought the mattresses from their bunks! We were still using 1917 type packs and they cunningly fastened the rolled mattress to the pack by means of the bedding flap. If it had not been serious it would have been comical.

Bayonet training was one of the most disliked blocks of training we had during the course. It was considered important, not only as a weapon of last resort in close-in fighting, but also because the training was supposed to instill in us "the Spirit of the Bayonet", a will to close with and destroy our enemy.

The Head of the Bayonet Committee, a thickset Major with a German accent named Bronckhorst was Prussian in the worst sense of the word - a true martinet. He would deliberately hold us in an awkward position until someone lost balance or lowered his rifle, then he would deride the culprit unmercifully. "Long thrust and HOLD", "Smash and HOLD", "Short thrust and HOLD" became all too common. We hated him; perhaps that was what he wanted, part of his technique.

One day OSB 43 and an OCS Class had bayonet training on opposite the sides of a large field. Bronckhorst strode between the two classes apparently in his element. At one point we noted some disturbance in the OCS Class while Bronckhorst was in that area. After the class I was talking with one of the Officer Candidates and asked him what the problem was.

"Bronckhorst" he said disgustedly. "He kept riding Jones for some reason. Most of it was unjustified. He pulled one that was real bad. Jones walked off the field and grabbed his shirt. Bronckhorst followed him, chewing him out and razzing him about not having any guts. Finally Jones had enough.

"Have you ever killed a man with a bayonet, MAJ Bronckhorst?"

"Well, no. But I could if I had to."

"Jones threw his khaki shirt around his shoulders, pointing to a deep blue ribbon with red and white borders (a Distinguished Service Cross or DSC) he said,' See this ribbon? I got that for killing a Jap with a bayonet on Guadalcanal. I think your bayonet training stinks.'

"He walked away. Bronckhorst was too surprised to say anything. I don't know what they will do to Jones."

The story was told throughout FT Benning, but never verified. It was rumored that Jones had appeared before a Board, which permitted him to complete OCS.

Finally the course came to a close, there was a simple graduation at which the Regt CO presented our diplomas. The retreads were not to be denied their last formation. As we fell in to march back to the barracks after graduation, some wag sounded off with an order.

"Prepare to ground diplomas, GROUND DIPLOMAS."

With the exception of a few of us, everybody put their diplomas on the ground as the Student Co CO marched us off. The diplomas were left on the ground to blow away; that they had to be picked up by some detail, did not bother these bull-headed retreads.

Cal Bury and I were assigned to the Infantry Replacement Training Center (IRTC) at Fort McClellan, AL. We were unhappy because we had transferred to the Infantry to get into combat, but were doomed to another Stateside assignment, training recruits. We spoke to the Personnel Officer about getting the orders changed. He told us that all current overseas quotas were full, that this was a priority assignment, a "good deal", an important mission. We were going to train combat replacements during which we would have an opportunity to review what we had learned in OSB 43, to become more experienced IN OFFs before we were reassigned to a combat unit overseas. He assured us that there was a continuing requirement for IN Plt Ldrs so that we need not worry about getting into combat. Again he reiterated that the orders could not be changed. We made up our minds to make the best of it.

Cal and I cleared the Post and caught the L&N Railroad to Anniston, AL, the closest town to FT McClellan. As we embarked on our new assignment we determined that we would get into combat before the war ended.

At the Anniston Station, a SGT escorted us to a bus which would take us to the Post, while a detail collected our footlockers and put them on a truck. The trip from the Anniston Railroad Station to the IRTC HQ was a short one. Along with a dozen other IN LTs we signed in; I was assigned to the 3rd Replacement Training Regt, Cal to another.

On reaching the HQ of the 3rd Regt, I entered first, more by happenstance than by seniority, although I was the only 1LT in the group. After glancing about, I spotted the Sergeant Major (SGM) sitting at a desk and writing. When I walked up to him he glanced up and then continued writing.

My temper, always on short lead, started to boil. Finally, as he and all of the personnel in the office continued to ignore the five lieutenants, I took matters in hand, and asked politely, "Pardon me SGT, where do we sign in?"

"Don't bother me now, can't you see I'm busy?" he said petulantly. In no mood to tolerate this treatment in front of other EM and civilian clerks, I barked an order.

"SGT, on your feet and stand at attention. Your conduct is disrespectful and insulting. I would expect more military courtesy in an Infantry Replacement Training Center. Now, I asked you a question. Where do we sign in?"

At this a CPT came over and asked, "What's the trouble, LT?"

"The trouble is, sir, you don't have NCOs who have any respect for commissioned officers. Your SGM, who should set an example for other enlisted men, is insolent and discourteous. He is too self important to answer a polite question."

"The SGM is busy on a project."

"That's no excuse for discourtesy to an officer."

The CPT gave me a look which said, "Keep quiet. I'll talk to you later." I shut up.

After signing in we talked with the Regt Adj (the CPT who had intervened in the altercation) who then took us in to see the Regt CO, LTC Chester Haisley. He interviewed us, asked about our backgrounds, then told us to report to the 26th Bn for duty. He informed us that the Bn was to start training Infantrymen in the use of the 4.2 inch mortar which had just been transferred from the CWS to the IN. This was welcome news and I mentioned my training in the 4.2 mortar. He officially welcomed us to the Regiment, then dismissed us. As we were leaving, he said,

"Just a minute LT Seibert, I'd like to talk to you."

After the others had gone he closed the door to his office and told me that no one disciplined his SGM or anyone else in his HQ except him. He took exception to my discussion with the SGM which he had heard through the open office door. When he paused, I apologized, but said that I thought it appropriate to make spot corrections whenever required. The SGM had been deliberately and publicly discourteous to a group of newly assigned officers, his military courtesy left much to be desired, and this could not be permitted to pass without action. In my view, it was particularly serious in an IRTC and in front of trainees who were present in the HQ. The COL ignored my comments and proceeded to inform me that his SGM had been with him for some 14 years and he worked for the Regt CDR and no one else. In those days a SGM was a title rather than a grade. Senior MSGs were given the title if they were in a headquarters.

Obviously I was off on the wrong foot with my new CO. The COL seemed eager to drop the matter after calling me to task for disciplining his SGM. The SGM was wrong and the COL was wrong in supporting him, but it was a case in which a deep sense of loyalty and camaraderie clouded the issue. Perhaps I should have been less obvious in my correction, but the discourtesy had been intentional and highly visible.

The 26th Bn was a short walk from Regt HQ. After signing in, the Adj, 1LT Goodwin, further assigned me to Co B. Goodwin was also Billeting Officer, he pointed to a tarpaper covered hut close to the HQ which I was to share with another officer.

The entire IRTC was in tarpaper covered shacks. Twelve to 16 recruits slept double-decked in shacks about four times the size of our BOQ huts. The latrines, also tarpaper covered, were separate, in the officers area we had to walk about 50 yards to the closest one. Some of the recruits had to walk as much as 250 yards to get to a latrine. Already it was beginning to get cold in Alabama. The shacks were heated by coal stoves, I greeted the Sibley stove in my hut like an old friend.

Later that day, we met the Bn CO, MAJ Anderson. He was a homesteader, he had reported to the IRTC two years before as a 2LT, had stayed and been promoted successively every six months. Now a MAJ commanding a Bn, he had just been recommended for promotion to LTC. Under similar circumstances I would have been a senior MAJ by this time. During WWII promotions were decentralized, local commanders recommended officers with six months in grade for promotion if there were vacancies. Those who had stable assignments in units which had vacancies in higher grades were promoted more rapidly than their often more-deserving contemporaries who moved frequently. MAJ Anderson was not an inspiring officer, rather he seemed a politician.

After getting my footlocker and other luggage stowed in my hut, I reported to Co B. CPT Lloyd C. Lineberger, the Co CO, had recently returned from combat in Italy. He was an outstanding officer, had sound judgement, knew his weapons and tactics, was firm but fair in handling his subordinates, had confidence in himself and was not afraid to stand up for his views. He taught me a great deal about leadership and discipline. The two most important things I learned from him were, to never back down when right, but make sure you were right, and that "no senior can say 'NO' loud enough to hurt you". These guided my actions my entire career.

CPT Lineberger assigned me as Plt Ldr of the 1st Plt and also as Chief of the Bn Heavy Machine Gun (HMG) Committee. Most training in the IRTC was conducted by committees which taught a subject to all companies in a battalion. When CPT Lineberger put me in charge of HMG training, I explained to him that while I had been exposed to the weapon both in OCS and at Benning, I was by no means proficient in it. I assured him I would learn the weapon thoroughly, but suggested that I was much more familiar with the 4.2 inch mortar and would like to teach it. The CPT dismissed my comments lightly. He told me that SGT Bean, the Committee NCO-in-Charge (NCOIC), was not only highly proficient with the weapon, but was also one of the best instructors he had ever served with, and urged me to rely on him. He explained that there were already two ex-CWS officers assigned to 4.2 instruction and there was no requirement for a third. He gave me the additional duty of Co Mess OFF.

The Co Clerk, CPL Alexander, an excellent administrator, kept us all out of trouble. He was over 6 1/2 feet tall (I wondered how he fit on a GI cot), was from Queens, and had gone to Jamaica High, an arch rival of my alma mater, Flushing.

The following day I was introduced to the IRTC Standing Operating Procedures (SOP). It was a volume of over a 1,000 pages, which encompassed everything concerned with the Basic Training of the recruits from how to carry the cadre stick to foot inspections. Almost every action or contingency had been anticipated and laid down in explicit detail in the SOP. It helped when you had time to consult it in connection with a specific problem. Certainly it standardized administration and procedures, even instruction. It was a curse to innovative and imaginative officers who handled unexpected problems in their own manner, only to find later that the solution in the SOP differed from theirs. It was not a guide, but standing orders. Even an SOP of this size could not cover every contingency; it was frustrating if followed too rigidly. Unfortunately, both LTC Haisiey and MAJ Anderson considered every word sacred and permitted no deviation from it. The SOP soon became a mill stone around my neck.

Almost before I got settled, I was placed in charge of some training not handled by a committee. My third day in Co B, the officer handling the problem on "Calibration of Night Noises" became ill and I was put in charge of that training. The NCOIC assured me that everything was ready for the night's class. There was just time to check the SOP and make a quick reconnaissance of the firing range. The training consisted of identifying noises in the dark, digging, rattling mess kits, truck movements, and firing of weapons. In the case of the latter, the recruits were to learn to distinguish the sounds of different weapons. There was much emphasis on night training in the IRTC at the time. Almost every night except Saturday and Sunday, there was some night exercise. Night operations have traditionally been a weakness of American combat forces.

On the way back from my reconnaissance late in the afternoon, I reported to the Range Control Office, received my instructions, got the red range flag, and was convinced that I had complied with the necessary procedures giving me range clearance. That evening the Company marched out to the range; at the appointed time the instruction began with noises such as digging and rattling mess kits. Meanwhile, I called Range Control to inform them that we would commence firing in 10 minutes. When Range Control told me that I did not have clearance to fire, I was astounded. "Why not?" I asked. The NCO on duty explained that I had failed to report in one hour before I was to fire. "But I was there this afternoon and understood that I had range clearance," I declared. The conversation became heated. Finally I asked to speak to the Duty Officer in Range Control. After receiving the same negative answer from him, I told him that I would be right in to get the range clearance.

"You can't do it. It is too late now. You are over the deadline."

"How can I possibly get range clearance so that we will not waste the recruits training time?"

"The only person who can give you that is the CG, or the DO acting for him."

When I asked for the DO he switched me to the IRTC HQ. I explained what had happened, pointing out that in order to continue the training it was necessary to have range clearance, if unable to fire, the training would have to be rescheduled, a difficult matter in the already crowded training cycle. The DO was sympathetic and cooperative; he said that he would get the clearance and call back. Within 15 minutes he called with the clearance. The training continued and from then on went well, due primarily to the efforts of the NCOIC.

About a half hour after firing started, the Bn CO drove up in a jeep and asked for me. In accordance with the stylized report required by the SOP, I said, "Sir, I am LT Seibert, Plt Ldr, 1st Plt, Co B, 26th Bn, 3d IRTC Regt, FT McClellan, AL. The Co is in the third week of its cycle. We are conducting the Calibration of Night Noises and are now firing the M1919A6 LMG. If you wish to observe the training, please follow me, sir." MAJ Anderson said that he had not come out to observe the training but to talk about something more serious. He had been called by the Regt CO, who had been called by the CG about my failure to get range clearance. He was astounded that I had failed to follow the SOP in securing range clearance. But even worse was bypassing channels and going directly to IRTC HQ.

I apologized and told him that in my eagerness to give the trainees the scheduled training I had followed the Range Control Officer's lead without thinking. I assured him that I did not normally go out of channels. He didn't say much more, but told me to see him in his office the following day.

After he left, the training continued, the recruits seemed to get a great deal out of it. The NCOs had the practical work well in hand and all I had to do was exercise a minimal amount of supervision. We got the Company back to the barracks without any losses and put the troops to bed. It was well after midnight before I finally turned in.

Four thirty arrived only minutes after I crawled into bed. As usual, I awoke before the alarm went off, reached over and pushed the button so it would not ring. The Sibley had gone out during the night; it was cold in the hut. The latrine was also cold, but in a few minutes it was steaming as I completed my ablutions. After dressing, I walked the few hundred yards to the Co. The moon was bright, hanging just above the horizon, the stars brighter and more plentiful than I ever recalled seeing them. The air was brittle and dry. There was almost no activity in the Battalion area.

When I inspected the mess hall, the cooks were busy, the KPs had all reported on time, and breakfast was almost ready. This prereveille mess inspection was adopted when I was appointed Mess Officer to insure the cooks had things in hand, the mess hall was warm, and that everything was done to start the day with a good meal. It remained a habit for my entire military career. Finding all in order at the mess, I proceeded to the Orderly Room just as the 1SG blew his whistle for reveille. As Co DO, I received the "All Present or Accounted For, Sir" report and turned the Co back to the 1SG, For breakfast there was creamed beef on toast, dubbed Shit-on-a-Shingle, or SOS, by the troops. It was a favorite of mine so the day was off to a good start.

After breakfast, I explained to CPT Lineberger the difficulty I had encountered with range clearance the evening before. He was not concerned, though he indicated that I could expect a real "ass-chewing" from MAJ Anderson. Walking to Bn HQ, I meditated on the problem. 1LT Goodwin was at his desk and I said to him, "MAJ Anderson told me to report to him right after breakfast, Jim."

"Yeah, he mentioned it to me. Have a seat, Don. I'll get you in as soon as I can." Goodwin gave me a resigned look.

In about five minutes, the Adjutant went into MAJ Anderson's office. He returned almost immediately. "You can go in now, Don."

Walking to the open door, I knocked. Upon the invitation to "Come in", I marched in, stopped three paces from MAJ Anderson's desk, rendered my best salute and reported, "LT Seibert reports to the Bn CO as ordered, Sir."

MAJ Anderson returned my salute. "Close the door, Seibert." I stepped over, closed the door, then returned to my former position in front of the Major's desk resuming my position of attention.

"At ease, LT. You seem to have gotten off to a bad start in the 3d Regt. Are you trying to make trouble."

"No, sir. I am sorry if I have given a bad impression. I am trying to do my job as well as I can. I am new to the Infantry, but I think I will show you that I am a dedicated and effective officer, Major Anderson."

"Well, your actions so far would not lead me to believe that you are a good officer. You embarrassed the Regt SGM and incidentally the Regt CO when you reported in. Last night you failed to comply with the SOP and not only delayed training, but went out of channels to IRTC HQ. You really caused a flap. In my opinion you are a sub-standard officer. Have you read the SOP yet, LT?"

"Not completely, sir. I have been reading as much of it each day as I can, and do read each section which pertains to the training scheduled for the day. I will have it completed before the week is out."

"Well, you should have read it by this time. As I said, this indicates to me that you are a sub-standard officer."

"Sir, I do not think you should come to such a hasty and false conclusion. Certainly the two incidents you mentioned were unfortunate, but I took appropriate action in each case as I saw it. The SGM was publicly insolent and unmilitary; I thought it my duty to make a spot correction. I believe that it is the duty of every officer to make corrections when he sees a violation. To fail to do so condones the dereliction."

MAJ Anderson squirmed a bit in his chair. He was obviously not happy with me for speaking up and defending myself. Before he could speak, I continued. "Last night I was tempted to call off the problem when I found that we didn't have range clearance. I was certain that I had obtained it when I reported to Range Control yesterday afternoon. Since I had not obtained it, I was responsible for any lost training, and did not want those recruits going into combat half-trained because I goofed. They are going overseas with only a minimum of training as it is. I will not jeopardize their training, perhaps their chance for survival, to cover up for myself. When the Range Control Officer mentioned the Duty Officer, I acted on his lead and went to the IRTC DO. I was wrong not to contact the Bn DO first, and I assure you that I will not jump channels again. In time you will find me a dedicated and responsible officer."

"Well, the burden is on you to prove that to me. I will not have my officers going behind my back to higher headquarters. I expect you to be fully aware of the SOP for this IRTC and to follow it to the letter all times. Now, I don't want to hear of any more difficulties caused by you. Do you understand?"

"Yes, sir."

"That will be all. Dismissed." I popped to attention, saluted, made an about face and marched from the office. Goodwin winked at me as I passed him on the way out of the HQ. Obviously, IRTC, FT McClellan and I were at odds, I resolved to correct the situation.

During OSB 43 at Benning we had been "talked through" the obstacle course, but never ran it against time or on a routine basis. Shortly after my arrival at McClellan, I found myself OIC of Co B while it was negotiating the obstacle course. It was the last hour of the training day. The NCOs had the men go through the course several times, even though they were tired. Some men could not get over all of the obstacles. The SGTs demonstrated, talked, cajoled, threatened, but some men simply could not complete the course. As it was almost dark, I told the NCOs to double time the men back to the Co area.

Concerned by the recruits' difficulty in managing the obstacles, I decided to run the course once before I followed the Company. Everything went well until I reached the wall. This was a wooden palisade (about 8 feet) which had to be surmounted by leaping up, getting a firm grip on the top, pulling with the arms and pushing with the feet against the wall to get over the top, vaulting over, then dropping to the far side. I could not get over it! It took an hour and a half of trial and error until I was finally able to get over it with any degree of speed. When I dragged myself back to the Co area, I was more tired than the trainees. From then on, I made it a point to run the obstacle course several times a week.

The following week we were to begin training on the "Browning Machine Gun, Caliber 30, Ml 917A1 (water cooled)". My committee was to give this training to all four companies in the 26th BN. After Reading the Training Manual (TM) and checking the SOP, I talked to SGT Bean. He was a neat, wiry man, about my height, who spoke with confidence and respect. Confiding in him that although I had been exposed to the HMG at OCS and Benning, I was not expert in it and depended on him to teach me the weapon. We set up a training program; every night SGT Bean and I spent an hour going over some detail of the weapon. Both of us were busy with other duties, which created problems in scheduling the time; in addition I tried to avoid keeping him on Post too late as he lived with his family in town. We started with nomenclature, went on to functioning and then to gun drill. Gradually SGT Bean made a machine gunner out of me.

When the actual training started, I told SGT Bean to teach the first period as I was not yet sure of myself. I knew from firsthand experience that he was an outstanding instructor. The first hour went well due to SGT Bean's knack for instruction. The second hour, to be given the following day, was devoted to the functioning of the weapon. Although functioning was not difficult to comprehend, the instruction made it necessary to isolate each movement in sequence, to identify each part as it entered into movement, and to relate the movement of each part to every other part during the firing cycle. Rearward movement of the bolt, forward movement of the bolt, loading, locking, firing, recoil, ejection - each phase had to be isolated and explained. Though SGT Bean and I had gone over it many times, I still stumbled when I discussed it. Since the SGT was so much more knowledgeable at that time than I, he was told to teach that particular class. He pointed out the SOP required an officer teach all classes on the functioning of weapons.

"SGT Bean, I know what the SOP says. But it is more important that we teach the trainees the HMG. You'll teach this class."

"Yes, sir." He was delighted to do so, taking pride in his knowledge and ability. The following day the class got off to a good start. SGT Bean was doing a fine job with the training, making the functioning clear to all the recruits. Standing in the rear of the group, I was finally getting the sequence set in my mind, I was sure that I would be able to teach functioning the next time it was scheduled.

MAJ Anderson inopportunely drove up in his jeep to inspect training. When I reported to him in the prescribed SOP manner, his first question was, "Why isn't an officer teaching this class?"

Donald A. Seibert

"Sir, I am the officer-in-charge. I was not quite sure of the subject matter. SGT Bean is much more knowledgeable than I am in the functioning of the HMG. I believe that he can put the subject across at this time better than I can. I am learning from him and feel confident that when functioning is scheduled again, I will be able to take over the class."

"Aren't you ashamed to admit that a SGT knows more than you do about the machine gun?"

"No, sir. I am never ashamed to admit that I do not know something. If I don't know it, it is unfortunate, but the shame is in concealing ignorance. I intend to overcome this deficiency immediately."

MAJ Anderson once again instructed me in the virtues of the IRTC SOP and the dangers of not following it completely. Though aware of the importance of standardizing training, I thought quality of instruction was more important than the letter of the SOP. When he heard this he was incensed. I had failed to follow the SOP which he told me was wrong; another black mark went against my record. It seemed I could do nothing right; obviously I was not going to please MAJ Anderson. The Battle of the Bulge had started a few days before, perhaps this would be a good time to ask for a transfer. By going overseas, I would get out of the mess I had created at FT McClellan and satisfy my desire to get into combat. Rumor had it that there was a pressing requirement for Infantry LTs in Europe. Cal Bury, my buddy in OSB 43, already had orders. But when I spoke to LT Goodwin, though he told me to submit my request, he said that he was sure it would be disapproved at Bn, Regt and IRTC HQ. It was the policy to retain OFFs in the IRTCs to stabilize training. While recognizing the importance of training, I had transferred to the Infantry to get into combat. As predicted by the Adj, my request for transfer was disapproved.

The serious matter of training men for combat proceeded at a fast, intensive pace. All of the techniques required for survival on the battle field were crammed into that 17 week course. Perhaps no single subject was given more attention than rifle marksmanship. Only after weeks of intensive preliminary marksmanship instruction (PRI), did the recruits actually fire the M-1 rifle. That training included sighting and aiming, trigger squeeze and correct sight pictures. The men were assured that once the rifle was zeroed, the bullet would hit the target if the proper sight picture was obtained and the trigger squeezed, not jerked.

Finally B Co was ready to fire on the range. The first morning of actual fire was devoted to zeroing the rifles. CPT Lineberger was called back to the Co area for some administrative work, so I was left in charge of the range. All was going well, we had just completed zeroing as the IRTC Commanding General (CG,) arrived on the range. The officer in the Tower called for the first round of slow fire as I hurried over to report to the Major General (MG). He waved aside the formal report and asked what we were doing.

"Sir, we have just completed the zero of the M-1 rifles and are starting record fire. The men will be firing slow fire momentarily."

"Good, I want to see how they are doing. Let's walk along the firing line." By this time, individual shots were being fired and targets were being pulled and marked by the pit detail. When the target was run up after a soldier had fired a round, discs were hoisted to the point of impact so that scores could be recorded and the sight picture verified. A red flag was waved when there was a miss. There were several "Maggie's Drawers", as these red flags were called, waving along the 50 points on the range. The CG stopped behind one recruit just as his target was marked. The pit detail raised a white disc to the center of the target indicating that he had hit the bull's eye. "That's his 8th bull's eye, sir," his coach proudly reported. The MG leaned over, patted the man on the back and complimented him on his Firing.

"What's your sight-setting, son?" he asked.

"Two clicks left windage, three clicks elevation, sir," replied the soldier proudly.

"That's fine, keep up that kind of shooting and you'll be an expert."

"Yes, sir. Thank you, sir."

We moved on down the range and halted behind another recruit. This time the pit detail signaled a Maggie's Drawers. "That's his fourth miss, sir," the Range Safety NCO, standing observing the poor shooting, reported. The CG, appeared disturbed and asked, "What's your sight-setting, young man?"

"Four clicks right windage, four clicks elevation, sir," reported the unhappy soldier. The CG turned to me furiously. "I thought you told me that these rifles had all been zeroed, LT. This soldier does not have the proper zero on his rifle. What was it the other lad had? Two clicks left windage, three clicks elevation." As the Range NCO and I looked on incredulously, he leaned down to the prone firer, "Soldier, change your sighting to two clicks left windage and three clicks elevation. That will put you on target." With that the MG strode to the next firer as the SGT and I trailed along.

Once again he asked the recruit what his sight-setting was. With a sense of alarm, I listened as the soldier reported his zero to be one click right windage, two clicks elevation. Again the CG turned to me angrily. "LT, it is obvious that you have not checked all of these men to insure that they have the proper zero. Now cease firing and get all of these rifles set properly. Make sure every one puts on the proven zero, two clicks left windage, three clicks elevation. You wasted valuable training time by not having attended to that."

"But, sir, every rifle is made differently, therefore each requires a different zero. What is correct for one man, will not be correct for the others. We have spent three hours getting the rifles zeroed this morning." My amazement at his ignorance was tempered by my own unfamiliarity with the HMG. "Now, LT, I want no more argument. Announce the proper setting for the M-1, check to make sure that all the troops put it on their rifles, and get on with the firing."

"Sir, that will set us behind three hours. Those rifles are zeroed. What is correct on Point 26 is not correct for any other rifle on the range. The men have found their zeroes. Please let them continue firing with them."

"LT, I want no more argument. Get those zeroes corrected now." He turned on his heel and strode to the control tower as the SGT and I looked at each other in disbelief.

"LT!" The Control Officer looked over the railing and immediately came to attention and saluted. "Yes, sir."

"Cease Firing and get the proper sight-setting on all of these rifles. It is three clicks elevation and two clicks left windage. That man on Point 26 has the correct setting and is hitting the bull's eye every time. Now that is an order! I don't want any more time wasted on this range. Do you understand?"

"Er, yes, sir." The skeptical look on the LT's face belied his answer. He was not sure whether the CG was spoofing him or not. But one look at the MG's grim features and my unhappy countenance convinced him. In a daze he clicked on the microphone. "Cease firing. CEASE FIRING!"

The NCOs and I quickly checked the entire range to insure that all men had cleared and locked their pieces. "Listen carefully. Everyone is to place the following sight-setting on his rifle, three clicks elevation, two clicks left windage. I say again, everyone will place three clicks elevation and two clicks left windage on their sights. Coaches, check your pupils. NCOs check the settings." The NCOs looked at the officer in the tower in stunned surprise, then looked at me. I shrugged, nodding to the MG, who was walking to his jeep with the air of one who has done a good job of setting junior officers straight.

When he had left the range, I went to the tower and seized the microphone. "As you were on that last order. There has been a mistake. Return to your proper zeroes and continue your slow fire." When I explained the situation to the OFF in the tower, he was still too dazed to comprehend that the CG of the IRTC knew so little about rifle marksmanship. The recruits slumped over their firing points, not sure of what was going on. Quickly, I called the NCOs together to explain what had happened. They were exhorted to try to convince the trainees that we knew what we were doing. Raggedly, firing got underway again. Fortunately, CPT Lineberger arrived at the range shortly thereafter and assisted in getting things back to normal.

Training settled back to its old routine. The cadre attacked their duties with all the dedication and enthusiasm they could muster in the face of such serious shortcomings in leadership. Each day I picked up additional subjects, becoming more and more involved in the training.

Among the subjects I taught was Combat Drill, squad and platoon extended order drill in combat formations. Squad members were divided into "Able, Baker and Charlie" teams which constituted elements of various formations, Wedge, Inverted V, On Line, Column Echelon Right or Left, designed to suit the terrain or situation. The object was to get members of a squad responsive to both verbal and hand orders to shift formations rapidly in changing combat situations, so that a squad or platoon's maximum fire power could be brought to bear on an enemy. At that time the squad had 12 men with two BARs, the two BAR teams were designated Able and Baker, while the support/command team was Charlie. This was before the phonetic alphabet was standardized to enable our allies to understand us more easily. I was never convinced that Keebec (Quebec) was easier to understand than Queen or Delta than Dog. In a like fashion, squads replaced teams in Platoon Combat Drill, though the same formations were used.

GI's, including Basic Trainees, have an earthy sense of humor. This was brought home one Saturday. Going through the latrine to see if it had been prepared for the routine inspection, I noted that the toilet seats had been raised and propped up at exactly ninety degrees. All, that is, except the last one in line. That was the one set aside for those with VD or other contagious diseases. That seat was propped up at forty-five degrees with a note to the effect that it was ill!

That same afternoon, after the troops had been released for rest and relaxation, one of the trainees rushed into the Orderly Room and shouted that I was needed in Hut H right away. Dropping the paper work I was engaged with I followed him over to Hut H. As I entered, someone bellowed "ATTENTION" loud enough to be heard at Bn HQ. Everyone popped to a rigid attention -except one man. He had been lying on his bunk, apparently asleep. He leaped from his bed, hit the floor, let out a scream and doubled over. While he was sleeping, naked, his fellow trainees managed to get a string noose around his penis. The other end had been tied to the bed spring. When ATTENTION was called he almost castrated himself. I had given "As You Were" almost as soon as the command "ATTENTION" had sounded, so the delighted troops doubled up in laughter pointing to the embarrassed and agonized trainee trying to untie himself and get some clothes on. Giving the group a good-natured chewing for tormenting a fellow trainee and using me for their purposes, I beat a hasty retreat.

At one point during the cycle, the recruits did not fall out as quickly as the First Sergeant thought they should. The following Saturday afternoon, he gave them extra training. He fell out everyone in the Company Street, and announced that they would have additional drill to sharpen their responsiveness. When dismissed, they would return to the barracks, put on overcoats, leggings and gasmasks, and on the next whistle would fall out in that uniform with barracks bags in hand. He gave them a few minutes before blowing the whistle. The men fought each other getting out into formation. He repeated this exercise several times, changing the uniform and items carried each time. When he ordered the men to fall out with footlockers, they almost destroyed the huts, as well as injuring themselves trying to get out the doors. The men did learn to fall out promptly with the required uniform and equipment.

Several weeks before Christmas, I was notified to report to Bn HQ. Reviewing my performance to date to determine what portion of the SOP I had violated recently, I reported to the Bn CO. MAJ Anderson informed me that I had been selected to go to Edgewood Arsenal on the 5th of January to attend the UGO Course! At that I really exploded. I reminded MAJ Anderson that I was a graduate of the CWS OCS and the Air Chemical Officers Course, that for a year and a half I had taught

UGOs at RAAF, NM, that I had the necessary credentials to be a Regt Gas Officer (RGO) without further schooling, that it would be a waste of money and my time for me to go to Edgewood. At the end of my tirade the Bn CO informed me bluntly that the Regt CO had personally selected me and that he was the only one who could revoke the orders. Immediately, I requested permission to see the Regt CO. Permission was granted.

Seething with frustration, I trudged to Regt HQ, ignored the SGM who glared at me balefully, and went to the Regt Adj. "Sir, I have MAJ Anderson's permission of to speak with the Regimental Commander."

"Yes, LT Goodwin has already called me. You can go right in. COL Haisley is free." I knocked on the COL's door and entered at his peremptory "Come in."

"Sir, LT Seibert has permission to speak with the Regt CO". I saluted and dropped my hand as COL Haisley returned my salute. "At ease, LT Seibert. What did you want to see me about?"

"Sir, I would like to be taken off orders to attend the UGO Course at Edgewood Arsenal. I graduated from CWS OCS and attended the First Air Chemical Officers Course. For a year and a half after that I was the Base Chemical Officer at RAAF and taught both UGO Courses and NCO Courses. I am a qualified CWS OFF. It is a waste for me to go to the UGO Course at Edgewood. I need more Infantry training. It would be much better for me and the Army to stay here at FT McClellan. I don't need any more Chemical Warfare Training."

LTC Haisley interrupted my plea, saying, "Do you mean to say that you can't learn anything at Edgewood?"

"Of course I can learn a bit, sir, but the amount of new material I would learn would be minimal, only the most recent advances. That would not justify the time, effort and expense. I believe it is more important that I remain here to get as much Infantry training as I can before I get sent into combat."

"LT, I am more concerned with the reputation of this Regiment and IRTC than I am with your particular needs and desires. We have had strong criticism of the officers we have sent to Edgewood Arsenal in the past. They have not done well academically, apparently their motivation was poor. I personally selected you to insure that the next officer from the 3rd Regiment, IRTC, FT McClellan would be at the top of his class. Now, you are going to that course and I expect you to be at the head of your class. Do you understand?"

"Yes, sir. But I think it would be better for the Army and me to stay here and learn to be an Infantryman. It is a waste of money and manpower to send me to the UGO course. If you want to make me the RGO, I am more than qualified to assume those duties. You should fill the quota with some one who will get more out of the course than I will."

"LT, the matter is closed. You will attend the course. If you finish first in your class and get a superior rating on our next CWS Inspection, I will approve your request for transfer to a combat unit. Now, that is all." As I dejectedly left the Col's office, I reflected that it was no wonder that Haisley was still a LTC, an officer with limited vision, bad judgement and poor reasoning ability should never be promoted to higher rank!

And so I lost again. I was going to attend a course I had taught. Since the decision was made, I prepared to leave immediately after the first of the year. My only hope was to graduate first in my class and get a superior rating on the next Chemical Warfare Inspection.

The Post was preparing for the imminent Christmas holidays, as I got ready to go to Edgewood. At this time we were told that LTG Ben Lear, Commander (CDR) of the Replacement and School Command, would visit FT McClellan on 15 December. Immediately there was a flurry of orders and activity to prepare for the visit. Lear was considered a martinet. We heard how he got his name, "Yoohoo".

Donald A. Seibert

During the Tennessee Maneuvers in mid-1941, a convoy of 2 1/2 ton trucks loaded with men from tile 35th IN Div passed a golf course just outside Memphis. Several young ladies in shorts were playing golf. The soldiers whistled, shouted "Yoohoo", and waved at the girls. LTG Lear, who was also playing on the course, became incensed. He had the convoy stopped, dismounted the soldiers and lectured them. When he ascertained their unit, he ordered the entire Regt to march from Memphis to nearby Camp Roberts. This march was made on a hot day; many men dropped out of the formation due to dehydration or heat exhaustion. There was an investigation, but after Pearl Harbor the matter was dropped. As a result, the troops dubbed Lear "Yoohoo" and the name stuck.

On 15 December almost the entire cadre of the IRTC was assembled in the Field House to hear LTG Lear give his evaluation of the IRTC, and to receive his guidance, encouragement or condemnation. As we gathered, there was considerable coughing; the weather had been cold and damp and the trainees and cadre had been out in the wet much of the time. Finally, some one roared "ATTENTION!" and we all popped to. LTG Lear, followed by the two IRTC generals and a host of staff officers marched down the center aisle to the stage. Lear had on a short overcoat and scarf. Reaching the stage, he looked for a place to hang his coat, found none, turned and handed it to the MG commanding the IRTC. The MG, a bit nonplused, passed it to the BG - and so it went down the line. Finally a LTC was left holding the coat. After a brief introduction by the IRTC CG.LTG Lear got up to speak. His opening remarks went something like this.

"There is entirely too much coughing in this Field House. I have a great deal to say, but cannot compete with the coughing. I want it stopped. As members of the chain of command you should have enough self discipline to stop coughing. No officer or non-commissioned officer who lacks self control can command the confidence and respect of troops. Now stop that coughing." LTG Lear then launched into his remarks. For the first few minutes there was a noticeable lack of wheezing. But some people in my vicinity were turning purple with their efforts to suppress their coughs. Finally hacking broke out again, a little at first, then swelling to a roar. LTG Lear could stand it no longer. He slapped his hand on the podium and almost shouted, "Stop that coughing, God damn it. Where is your self control?"

Then he coughed loudly. The assembled group convulsed in laughter! Lear became so incensed that he stomped over to the LTC holding his coat, snatched it from him and stormed toward the Field House exit. Some one did have the presence of mind to call ATTENTION as he left. The coughing broke out again, more loudly than before. Just as he reached the nearest door he stopped, glared at the assembled group, then stormed out.

CPT Lineberger received orders at this time; he would go on leave then on to his next assignment without returning to McClellan. 1LT Jake Heyman was to take command of Co B after the first of the year, until then I would be acting Co CO.

On Christmas Eve a choir from a Baptist Church in Anniston was to sing Christmas carols for the troops in the Post Field House; orders were issued to pack the house, which could seat several thousand men. Each Co was given a quota of 50 men to be in formation in front of Regt HQ; transportation to the Field House had been provided for. The cadre got the formation together, there was a sizeable group from the 3rd Regt. As Acting CO, I accompanied the Co B troops to the Field House, which was filled. The troops seemed to enjoy the carols.

Later that evening I was told that a message had been received from Bn HQ that the next day, Christmas, another Anniston church choir was to be at the Main Post Chapel which the CG wanted filled. Therefore, each Co would provide 14 soldiers plus an officer to attend church. The 1SG asked me how I wanted to handle it. I said, "Tomorrow morning we'll just ask for volunteers."

He looked at me and said, "That won't work, sir."

"Well, that's the way we're going to handle it."

The next morning I checked the mess early as usual wearing pinks and greens. While the Co was eating breakfast one of the NCO's announced the Christmas Service and told the men to fall out in Class A uniforms if they wanted to attend. There was little response, so I sent a messenger through the recruit barracks calling for volunteers. Six men fell out. Since an officer was required, I marched the detail to Bn HQ where the troops would be entrucked for the Main Post Chapel. At Bn HQ MAJ Anderson was checking each detail as it arrived.

"Where are the 14 men from B Co, Seibert?"

"Here, sir." I pointed to my six men.

"Wasn't the requirement 14?"

"Yes, sir, but these are the only men who want to go to church."

"That is not the issue, you are required to provide 14 men."

"Sir, I cannot order a man to go to church."

"LT, you will have 14 men here in five minutes."

Returning to the Co, I ordered the 1SG to send the CQ through the huts again. Two more men fell out, I marched the detail back to Bn HQ, reported to MAJ Anderson and said, "These are all of the troops from B Co who wish to go to Christmas service."

"LT, I gave you an order and I expect it to be obeyed."

"Sir, that is an illegal order and I will not require any man to go to church against his will. We officers have neither the right authority or the fight to order a man to go to church."

"I don't care how you get the men; whether you order them out or not. I want 14 men."

"Sir, I am not going to harass the troops any further on Christmas."

MAJ Anderson turned purple with rage. The 1SG who had come up to Bn HQ with me had listened to this conversation. He slipped back to the Co, got six more men, unknown to me, marched them up and reported them to the Bn Adj. Our quota was satisfied. MAJ Anderson had been called to LTC Haisley's office so our conversation had been terminated without being settled. Throughout the service, I assumed that I had only the eight men I had marched up. It wasn't until I got back that I found out from CPL Alexander what the 1SG had done. He hadn't ordered any men to go to church, but had gone to several huts and told the men that the LT was in a bind. If they didn't want to see one of their officers get into trouble, they'd go to church for him. He got the six extra men. There was genuine satisfaction in knowing that the troops rallied behind me. But I never forgot the fear and moral bankruptcy of that Bn Co who was willing to strip every vestige of freedom and dignity from his troops to meet a quota.

On New Year's Eve I took a nurse from the hospital to the Main Post Officers' Club. Many of my friends were there and we welcomed 1945 royally. The next day, New Year's Day, I didn't feel very good, but fortunately there were no crises that day.

On 3 January I left Anniston by train. At Edgewood some of my old instructors and friends wanted to know what I was doing there. When I told them I was going to the UGO Course, they couldn't believe the stupidity of sending a graduate of the CWS OCS and First Air Chemical Officers Course to take a UGO Course. Obviously, the course was a sinecure for me; I didn't have to study, with free time, I coached several of the officers through it.

Almost all of the material covered in the UGO Course was repetitious for me. The faculty readily assented to my request to miss some of the instruction in order to attend classes on the 4.2 inch mortar. This enabled me to take back information on the latest mortar techniques to the officers teaching that weapon at FT McClellan. In spite of my protracted absence from the UGO Course, I graduated at the top of my class. This made LTC Haisley happy.

When I returned to FT McClellan B Co was in the Chocaloca Bivouac area, I was ordered not to join it. I was sorry to miss this training, probably the most interesting and meaningful training we gave the recruits. Not only did I want to see how the tactical field training was conducted at the IRTC, but I also believed that I could profit from it.

As I signed in at HQ, I was informed that I was now the RGO, with responsibility for all CW Training in the 3rd Regt. Each Bn in the 3rd Regt provided one NCO assigned as Asst Instructor. All of them proved to be outstanding. Two of the four were graduates of an NCO Gas Course and were proficient in CW Training. The other two were knowledgeable but a bit unsure of themselves. During the next few days I worked with all of them, wrote the POI, checked the SOP, assembled training aids, re-checked the SOP, and was all set when the first unit reported for CW Training.

The first classes went well, the NCOs were effective instructors, the recruits absorbed the training. During instruction on gas identification, LTC Haisley made a training inspection. Upon completion of the training day I was told to report to the Regt CO. Without preliminaries, LTC Haisley told me that my instruction was unsatisfactory, that I was teaching CW improperly! Instinctively, I went on the offensive, pointing out that I had just completed the UGO Course at Edgewood Arsenal as the top student in the class, that I had learned there the latest methods of instructing CW, and that those were the methods I was using. What was wrong with the training? He mentioned several procedures which had been used years before, but which had long since been discarded. I told him that those procedures were no longer approved doctrine. LTC Haisley told me not to argue with him, he wanted CW Training conducted in his Regt as he had just outlined.

"Sir, that is not approved CW doctrine and I cannot teach it. As RGO I must teach only approved doctrine. You made me the expert on CW by insisting I attend the UGO Course at Edgewood. In addition I have attended the CWS OCS and the First Air Chemical Officers Course. I assure you that your information is out of date and no longer approved. Please trust me to teach this subject properly."

"LT, I have just given you your instructions. I expect them to be carried out. That is all."

"Sir, I cannot do that. I refuse to teach unapproved doctrine. I request that this be referred to the IRTC Chemical Officer for decision."

Not sure that I was on firm ground according to military protocol, but certain of my CW doctrine, this appeared to be the only logical thing to do. My insistence gave him pause, then he said he would think about it. Not hearing further from Haisley, I continued to use the methods he had criticized.

The CW Training in the 3rd Regt proceeded smoothly for the next three weeks, all but one Co had completed it when word of a CW Training Inspection filtered down to us. A team was arriving from Washington to inspect C W Training at the IRTC. The War Department was concerned that as the war drew a close, the Germans might resort to desperate measures which could include CW.

LTC Haisley sent for me. He reiterated his concern about the way I was conducting the training and told me that I must get a superior on this inspection. I told him to rest assured, we would be rated superior on our training. The block of instruction the inspectors would evaluate was on the recognition of chemical agents and gas mask drill. LTC Haisley wanted to know how I was going to handle it. The recognition of agents would be introduced with a 15 minute lecture, I explained, then practical work would follow using a "county fair". The troops would move from station to station sniffing bottles of the more common gases such as Phosgene, Lewisite, and Mustard. The gas mask drill would be conducted with the troops in an extended Co mass formation with the instructor, myself, and a demonstrator on a PT platform in front of them. As we proceeded through gas mask drill by the numbers, my Asst Instructors together with the Co NCOs would circulate and make corrections. LTC Haisley, obviously nervous, was not satisfied with my plan of instruction, and made suggestion after suggestion, each of which I vetoed. Finally I said, "Sir, leave me alone, let me do it my way. I assure you, we will get a superior."

He wasn't sure. The following day he called me in once more. The inspectors had been to the 1st Regt and declared the training unsatisfactory. They had recommended that the OIC of the training be relieved. The CG had sent word to the other Regts to buck up their training. LTC Haisley was extremely concerned. Once again I reassured him that we would get a superior. Again, he insisted that I change my instruction; again, I argued against it, leaving without any positive decision because Haisley was torn between his own convictions and my very definite views.

The next day the 2nd Regt was inspected. Again, an unsatisfactory rating was given with the recommendation that the training officer be relieved. The CG was irate and LTC Haisley even more agitated. For the third time I made the trek to his office, only to go over the same arguments.

"Sir, I know what these people are looking for. Believe me, they'll get it." We parted with Haisley obviously nervous but undecided what to do about the training. The next day, the day of our inspection, was gray and overcast. Though I got to the training area early to be sure that all was ready, the NCOs had preceded me, everything was set up as planned. The Company arrived promptly and I started the instruction even though the inspectors had not appeared. One of my NCOs was to report to them in the SOP manner to explain what was going on. Toward the end of my 15 minute orientation on chemical agents the inspecting party arrived. When we broke up for practical work, I moved from group to group, answering questions, assisting the NCOs if they needed it and generally supervising. Despite LTC Haisley's frantic gestures to me to report to the visitors, I ignored the inspectors. They made the rounds, looked at everything, questioned the recruits and my Asst Instructors and missed nothing.

After the SOP 10 minute break, which I spent getting prepared for the next hour of instruction, the Company formed for gas mask drill.

The trainees had kept their gas masks with them all during the first hour and were now ready for gas mask drill. It was a good class, the troops knew they were on display and were at their best. At the conclusion of the period, I finally reported to the group of inspectors who had remained for the entire session. There were three CWS COLs in addition to LTC Haisley, MAJ Anderson and the IRTC Chemical Officer. The colonel in charge said, "LT, I want to tell you that this is the best CW instruction that I have ever seen. You know your job. These men are qualified as the result of this fine training." He turned to LTC Haisley, "This is superior training."

Not able to resist the opportunity I said, "COL, we have some problems with training. I wonder if you could straighten us out."

"Glad to, Lieutenant."

With an air of deep concentration, I enumerated the points of difference between LTC Haisley and me, and asked which was the accepted doctrine. On each point the inspector supported my position. LTC Haisley became annoyed and tried to end the discussion, but the inspectors were interested; I really did not care what Haisley thought. The worst he could do was make me available for a combat assignment, which was exactly what I wanted.

The 3rd Regt was officially rated superior on its CW Training; everybody in the chain of command was happy. The next day I requested permission to see LTC Haisley. I reminded him that he had promised to send me overseas if the Regt received a superior on the CW Training.

"No", he said, "Now that we've got a superior we want to keep it and we're going to keep you. In fact I've had to fight to keep you here in the 3rd Regt because they want to take you up to IRTC HQ."

With difficulty I suppressed my rage. There was nothing I could do. Haisley was the Commander. An obviously mediocre officer, he had now proven that he lacked integrity, repudiating an agreement he had made with a subordinate. With a smart salute, I did an about face and left the office without a word.

Despite my disappointment, training proceeded. With the CW instruction completed for this cycle, I became immersed in the IRTC routine once again. In addition to my duties as 1st Plt Ldr, RGO, and OIC of the HMG Committee, I was also the B Co Mess OFF. There was a good crew in the mess, much work had been done to make the mess hall an attractive place to eat. By dint of much hard work on the part of the 1SG, Mess SGT and cooks, the cadre and the trainees, we won first the Bn, then the Regt and finally the IRTC Best Mess Award. We were all pleased, but MAJ Anderson was proudest of all. He was almost civil to me for a time!

Shortly after the visit of the CW Inspectors, I was scheduled to take B Co through the gas chamber. That morning, I checked the mess as usual. The cooks had things well in hand, preparing to serve the typical GI breakfast, bacon, scrambled eggs, toast, milk, coffee, oranges. Since I had to get to the gas chamber early, the cooks served me breakfast before the Company ate. Departing for the chamber immediately, I had the tear gas and chlorine concentrations at the desired levels by the time the Company arrived.

All went well at first. Then a few men came out of the chamber vomiting and complaining of stomach cramps. Concerned that the concentrations were too strong, I checked them. Nothing seemed wrong in the gas chamber and there was nothing wrong with the gas masks, which I checked carefully. Several more men got sick. Reporting the matter to Bn HQ, I requested an ambulance, mentioning that it appeared the men might have a touch of food poisoning. Instead of an ambulance, I got MAJ Anderson!

Meanwhile, quite a few more men had gotten sick. In questioning the men, it finally came out that after the first 50 trainees had gone through the chow line, the cooks discovered some potatoes left over from the night before, hurriedly fried them, and set them on the serving line. Those who were sick had eaten the potatoes, those who were not sick had not. It was obvious what had happened.

After reporting to MAJ Anderson I explained this to him and asked when the ambulance was due to arrive. "We have not called an ambulance", he said. "I am not sure that this is food poisoning. B Co has a superior mess and I am not going to jeopardize that rating with the suspicion of food poisoning."

With ill suppressed fury I expostulated, arguing that the men came first. Only after several men who had not been through the gas chamber became ill did Anderson authorize medical assistance. A team from the hospital investigated, reporting that the potatoes, which had not been properly refrigerated, had caused food poisoning. MAJ Anderson held me responsible as Mess Officer!

HMG training continued. Towards the end of the training cycle it took on added impetus. Most of the instruction was practical and tactical work. Range firing would culminate the training. Late in February we were practicing Placing the Gun in Action (PGIA). This involved breaking the HMG down into its major components (gun, tripod, steam condensing device and ammo can) moving to a selected gun position, setting up the gun, engaging a target, then repeating the procedure. CPT Lineberger, who had commanded a Heavy Weapons Co in Italy, had given me some pointers on how to handle this phase of training. The Field Manual (FM) on the HMG was also clear on this matter and in consonance with CPT Lineberger's suggestions. My instruction was based on Lineberger's recommendations, the FM and SGT Bean's experience. MAJ Anderson visited the training area with an inspector from IRTC HQ. He questioned our procedures. I told him that they were not only prescribed in the FM, but were also being practiced in combat. He dismissed these authorities and referred to the SOP (apparently he had it memorized). Though I had read it before preparing this particular class, I was not sure of the SOP on this point.

"Sir, I can't vouch for the SOP, but I can assure you it's in the manual, I think the manual should be our bible."

MAJ Anderson did not know what the FM said, but was sure that what we were doing was not according to the SOP. There was no authority higher than the SOP in his opinion. He told me to modify the training.

"But, sir, it is in the FM," I said, taking a copy from my back pocket where I always kept it during training, and offering it to him. He became annoyed that I had referred him to the manual in front of an IRTC inspector, and became irate when the manual bore me out. Another black mark against Seibert. No matter, I knew I was going to get a low efficiency report from this assignment. Since I was not a career officer, it didn't make much difference to me. My conscience was clear, I was doing the best possible job I could to prepare the trainees for combat.

At the end of February, LT Heyman decided that we would have a "graduation party" for the trainees upon completion of their training cycle. Elaborate plans were made to hold it in a private club in Anniston. My mission was to find girls for the party. A girls college in Jackson, about 15 miles from Anniston, was agreeable to permitting some of their girls to attend the dance if no liquor was served, the school would provide the chaperons, if the Army would provide buses to and from the dance. The Post Transportation Office agreed to supply the buses, LT Heyman was more than willing to ban alcohol.

On the evening of the dance the troops were in neatly pressed Olive Drab (OD) uniforms, their faces scrubbed and shoes shined. They looked ready for inspection. All went well until some of the men started drinking in the latrine. B Co had been under such rigid discipline for so long that the men broke loose. Although there were only a few of them, it was necessary to get them out of the club and back to the Post. It marred what would have been otherwise a fine occasion. None of the girls was insulted or molested, but the chaperons insisted we take the girls home since alcohol had been in evidence. The dance broke up an hour or so before we had planned.

Late in the training cycle, I had the Co on the Infiltration Course. A few men, lacking confidence in themselves or the cadre, were afraid to crawl under the machine gun bullets or close to the demolitions. I had crawled through the course with one young trainee who was almost immobile with fear. He made it after much coaching, though I had to physically put his head down at one point to keep it out of the line of fire. Despite the fact that the machine guns were clamped in racks with the barrels fixed so that the fire was always at a specified height, some men could not be convinced that it was safe to crawl under our own fire.

Because I had crawled through the course with the frightened trainee, I was at the far end of the course when the next order started through. Just before the training had started that morning, an elderly gentlemen, clad in coveralls had come out to the range. Veterans from WWI sometimes came to watch the training, so I thought he was one of them. As I looked down the lanes, I saw with alarm that he was going through the course, obviously encouraging one of the less confident trainees. Incensed that the NCOIC had permitted a civilian to go through the course, I was waiting for the unauthorized crawler when the order reached the end of the course. As he got to his feet, I spoke to the gentleman about unapproved entry into a live firing area which might result in injury. He smiled and told me not to worry. It was only then that I noted his khaki shirt beneath his coveralls. On the collar were four stars! He introduced himself as General Joseph Stillwell, CG of Army Ground Forces and in charge of all Army training in the United States. He explained that he had come to FT McClellan on a surprise inspection and no one was given advance notice of his visit.

"I want to see how things go on routinely, not how they go when you are prepared for a senior officer. You are doing a fine job, LT. Keep it up."

Stammering an apology, I tried to report to him in the approved SOP manner but he waved me off. He wanted to talk to the men. I did manage to notify Bn of his presence in the area. By the time the cavalcade of senior officers arrived from Bn, Regt and IRTC, GEN Stilwell had left to visit some other training area. I never did find out if the cortege caught up with him. In my opinion, GEN Stillwell had the right idea on inspections.

Spring came early to Alabama that year, with it a spring party in the Regt Officers' Mess. The 3rd Tng Regt had one of the best Officers' Field Messes I have ever eaten in. It was operated by German POWs, some of whom were true chefs. The food was outstanding, the service impeccable. The mess was in a typical wooden GI mess hall building located in the center of the Regt area.

Each Bn in turn sponsored parties in the Mess. Most of us were unmarried, though a few officers, including the Regt and Bn COs, had their wives in the area. This spring it was the 26th Bn's turn to host the party, MAJ Anderson was determined to outdo all of the other Bns. He sent two cadre NCOs to buy special whiskey for the party, paid for by the 26th Bn officers. On the way back to FT McClellan, the SGTs were apprehended in a dry county. The car and whiskey were confiscated and the two NCOs jailed. The MAJ was responsible, he had ordered the whiskey, so he had to pay the fine to get them out of jail. He had to get the car released, he had to make sure the NCOs records were not blemished, and he had to get more whiskey. We all got a big chuckle out of this and thought he was getting just retribution, until we got the bill for the party. Each officer was prorated not only the cost of the party, but also of the fines and the confiscated whiskey. We protested, but the Regt CO ruled that those expenses were a legitimate part of the cost and should be shared by all officers. We probably could have gotten out of paying it by going to the Inspector General (IG), but officers did not do so in those days.

The party was a good one. The mess hall was decorated with sprays of peach and apple blossoms which had bloomed early in 1945. They looked romantic in the candlelight. The German POW cooks had prepared a superb meal and liquor flowed freely. Indeed, I was so carried away with the spirit of the evening that I asked both LTC Haisley's wife and MAJ Anderson's wife to dance!

Shortly after the party, my HMG Committee was giving preliminary marksmanship training prior to actual range firing. The trainees were doing manipulation exercises, covering targets that were wide, long or obliquely dispersed. To do this it was necessary to traverse and search, that is, to move the point of impact of the rounds. The key words were "pull up, push down, pull right, push left", referring to the manipulation of the elevating and traversing knobs on the tripod. By twisting or pulling the elevation knob, the barrel was elevated and the rounds would strike farther out, when the traversing knob was twisted or pulled right, the barrel swung to the right moving the strike of the rounds in that direction. The gunners had to track and trace the targets indicated by an Asst Instructor.

It was raining steadily, a wretched day. The SOP required that the steam condensing device (which resembled a one gallon water can) be filled with water and attached to the gun by means of a rubber hose, and the water jacket which cooled the gun barrel, be filled and the calking checked, this was to get the troops in the habit of taking care of those chores. The trainees were miserable, weren't paying attention and were getting nothing from the exercise. During a break I found out why. They were sitting behind the guns in mud puddles. After the break I ordered the guns placed on "high tripod". The tripods were adjustable so the gun could be emplaced to take advantage of the terrain and the gunner could either lie behind a gun on "low tripod" or sit behind one on "high tripod". After emphasizing that the steam condensing devices must always be in position to conserve water and prevent the steam from giving the gun position away, the men were told to sit on the steam condensing devices. This got them out of the mud puddles, instruction proceeded beyond all expectation. The men sensed that somebody was looking after them, they appreciated getting their butts off the wet ground, so they paid a great deal more attention to the training and began doing well on the manipulation exercises.

But things were going too good! MAJ Anderson made a routine training inspection and exploded when he saw the trainees sitting on the steam condensing devices instead of having them properly placed according to the SOP. He chewed me out, dismissing my rationale as "pampering the troops". He was right about the SOP, I was wrong. But he cut short his lengthy tirade and went off in his jeep.

In a short time, 1LT Goodwin, the 26th Bn Adj, appeared. He asked me if I preferred to go to the European or to the Pacific Theater if I had a choice. The Battle of the Bulge was over. All reports indicated that the war in Europe was grinding to a halt. The fighting in the Pacific was still heavy, in addition, my brother Bill was there. With only the shortest consideration, I opted for the Pacific.

"I am directed to tell you that you are to consider yourself on orders to the Pacific Theater of Operations. The 3rd Regt has a quota for one IN LT and MAJ Anderson thinks that you should fill it." Goodwin, a good egg, grinned and continued, "Well, you finally made it, Don. Best of luck."

In response to my question as to whether I was relieved of my training duties as of that time, Goodwin said, "Yes. You will have to clear Post immediately if you want to take pre-embarkation leave."

Smiling broadly, I saluted SGT Bean and turned the instruction over to him. Having been relieved of my duties I did not have to make the night training and indulged myself with a drink and a leisurely dinner at the club that evening. My friends in the 3rd Regt not involved in night training, joined me to celebrate my orders and pending combat assignment.

My thoughts turned to Cal Bury at this point. While I was at Edgewood, Cal left for Europe. Just before I received my orders, I had a letter from him from a hospital in England. He had left McClellan, had a short leave with his wife, then reported for transport to England. A fast, five day trip on the *Queen Mary,* a few days in Southampton and a trip across the Channel put him in a Replacement Depot in France. He was transported by the famed "forty and eight" box cars to Germany where he joined the 35th Division. Assigned as a Weapons Plt Ldr in a Rifle Co, he was leading a patrol after only a few days with his unit. He stepped on a "shoe mine", lost his foot, and was evacuated speedily to England. He wanted to get into combat as an Infantryman so much, but had less than a week of it. I wondered about my fate.

The next morning, 1LT Goodwin, who had helped me celebrate the night before, gave me copies of my orders. Clearing Post was soon accomplished, though I had to pay for a lensatic compass that had been lost by a trainee. As OIC I had signed for all equipment on the problem and so was responsible. Rather than taking the time and energy to locate the compass, I paid the $6.00, glad to get away. That afternoon I caught a train that would connect in Washington with a New York express. Ten days delay enroute and four days travel to FT Ord, CA had been authorized in my orders, which required me to report to Army Ground Forces Replacement Depot No 2 not later than 3 April 1945. The leave, a good one, passed quickly.

Before my departure from McClellan I was given a certificate of priority for air travel. Armed with this I decided to fly to San Francisco, thus giving me more time in New York. My departure from LaGuardia Airport on the 1st of April was an omen; it was the day US troops landed on Okinawa. But that coincidence did not strike me until later. The flight west was crowded, the weather was bad. To avoid being delayed by a snow storm at Denver, the pilot curtailed our stop-over there. Even so we took off as a heavy snow began to fall. Fortunately, aside from severe turbulence, the flight was uneventful and we landed in San Francisco just about on time.

As in most large cities, it was difficult to find a hotel room in San Francisco. Every available lodging was filled with military personnel or their dependents who were seeing them off to the Pacific. Finally the Sir Francis Drake Hotel agreed to put six of us in a single room. My room mates were a group of Naval officers enroute to join their ship at Pearl Harbor. We all had a rousing night on the town. The following day I was able to see the Messineos, friends of my parents, and have dinner with Les and Mil Clarke, friends from Roswell. Les had been transferred shortly after I was.

Arriving at FT Ord by train, I reported to the Replacement Depot. The post was a mad house, as it was a staging area not only for individual replacements, but also for units. Processing began immediately. This included issuance of all the field equipment needed in combat including carbines. We had a chance to zero our carbines, which I found to be an accurate weapon. There was also some last minute training, which Washington had decreed we should take. One of the items issued was the officers bedding roll. After carefully packing it with the regulation two shelter halves, tent pins, poles and ropes, blankets and sleeping bag, I stenciled it, turned it in to the Transportation Office and forgot it. It was the last I saw of it.

During the processing at Ord, I met several compatible LTs who were destined to go with me to my eventual unit. Ed Schmitt, Jim Waggoner, Isadore Ressler, Pugsley and a number of others. We had an opportunity to get into Carmel and Monterey, where we enjoyed some good meals and sampled the night life.

In a few days we were on orders to FT Lawton, WA, the Port of Embarkation (POE) for many troops going overseas. The few days we spent there enabled us to learn that there was much action in Seattle. You only had to walk down the streets in uniform to be propositioned. We had several interesting evenings before we shipped out.

Late one afternoon we boarded a transport, in single file, answering to a roster. Officers and a contingent of nurses and Red Cross girls loaded first. The loading took several hours. All of us had smuggled on board one or more bottles of whiskey, and that evening we had a final celebration with some of the nurses and Red Cross girls who were to make the trip with us. As a result, I slept too soundly that night.

When I awoke the next morning I found that somebody had taken my wallet from my fatigues left hanging on the end of my bunk. There were six of us in a tiny compartment (complete with wash basin), all were missing something. What concerned us most was the loss of identification, both our official ID cards as well as the regulation Geneva Convention POW card were in our wallets. Most of my money was in travelers checks, so I was not concerned about that. Surprisingly, a few days later, someone found my wallet in one of the companion ways with the travelers checks and my identification still in it. The few dollars I had in cash were gone.

The ship started down Puget Sound very early that morning. We were underway only a few hours, when we reversed course and went back to Seattle. It was announced over the public address system that there was trouble with the propeller shaft. We tied up at a different dock and remained there for three days while the ship was repaired. Since we had been processed and briefed, we were restricted to the ship, and barred from having any contact with civilians. It was grim to be in port three days watching the civilian workers come and go while we had to stay on the ship.

The time was spent in organizing the passengers for the trip. There was an Army Transportation Unit on the ship, a converted Danish luxury liner manned by civilian merchant seaman, as well as a small Navy Detachment to man the AA guns. All housekeeping chores (police, KP, entertainment and guard) were accomplished by the Army replacements. Every OFF was assigned a duly, I was an Asst Mess OFF in charge of one of the shifts in the EM mess. Though there were three shifts for each meal, most troops ate only twice a day. In the troop mess the men had to eat standing up.

The steward in charge of the EM mess I was assigned to supervise, was a young civilian merchant mariner. He kept protesting that he wanted to join the Army, but he knew he couldn't cut it in the Army; that he wasn't worth anything because he wasn't in the Army. That sort of talk always disgusted me; in his case it infuriated me because he was drawing three times the money I was with very little responsibility or training. He was simply a glorified mess SGT. There was no reason he could not join the Army.

Ressler, Schmitt, Waggoner, Pugsley, Mester and McGrath, the OFFs I had met at Ord, were all on board. All were IN OFFs who became close friends, learned to know each other well, and looked forward to serving with each other in combat.

Finally the transport was repaired and under way. This time there was no turning back. The ship ran blacked out; as we were not in a convoy, we headed directly for Hawaii at full speed. The time passed quickly; we awoke one morning to see a haze on the horizon which rapidly resolved itself into Diamond Head. We scurried about getting ready for debarkation, then hurried on deck.

The big troop ship was inched toward the Honolulu pier by a tooting, self-important tug. We crowded the rail looking down on the dock on which a military band was playing Aloha Oe. A group of Red Cross workers stood waiting with leis to give to the nurses and the Red Cross girls on board our ship. As the vessel touched the wharf, an announcement came over the public address system that all personnel report to quarters to secure baggage. My duties in the EM mess had long since been discharged, the cabins, mess halls and ward rooms cleaned, inspected and approved. Debarkation began almost immediately; the nurses and Red Cross girls first, the senior OFFs next, then the junior OFFs, finally the EM.

By the time we junior OFFs reached the pier the welcoming activities were over; we were herded to waiting 2 1/2 ton trucks which took us to the 13th Replacement Depot, about a two and a half hour ride from the pier. Occasionally, we were able to catch glimpses of Oahu out of the back of the truck, but the canvas sides had not been rolled up so there was not much sightseeing.

On arriving at the Replacement Depot, which, we were told, was somewhere in the vicinity of Schofield Barracks, we tumbled off the trucks and assembled into a ragged formation. The EM were marched off to another part of the camp. The OFFs were given a brief orientation and assigned beds in the familiar WWII temporary barracks. All IN OFFs were assigned to the same barracks. When we were settled we explored the area. On that first short walk I bumped into an old friend, Ray Carroll, from College Point.

The inevitable processing began the next morning with the surrender of our records, The personnel people at first assigned me as a member of the cadre of the Replacement Depot. When I protested vehemently, they changed my orders sending me to a Replacement Depot on Saipan. During the processing we were told that we had an important, mandatory briefing at 1630 that day.

Mail which had been accumulating for many weeks was distributed, I had almost 50 letters. The first one I opened was from Mother. She wrote that my brother Bill's ship, the *Murray,* had been dive-bombed by a Japanese Kamikaze and was at Pearl Harbor for repairs. She wanted me to try to see him if I got to the Hawaiian Islands.

Determined to see Bill, I looked for a telephone. The Red Cross at Pearl Harbor verified that the *Murray* was in port and that I could get on board. I told them that I would be down later that evening and asked them to stay open for me if possible.

At 1630 we attended the mandatory formation, a film on the rotation point system instituted to return men to the United States who had been overseas and in combat for prolonged periods of time. It was a waste of time for us, although we had amassed a large number of points by virtue of total service, we did not approach the number required for rotation, nor was that my objective at this time. The system was rightly weighted to give more points to those overseas, especially to those who had seen combat duty.

Immediately after the formation I went to see the Replacement Depot Co CO and asked for a pass. He told me that I was restricted to the Depot because our group was scheduled to leave on short notice. My explanation about my brother's bombed ship and his wounds fell on deaf ears. The CPT was adamant, I could not have a pass. I told him that if he didn't give me a pass, I would go to Pearl Harbor without one, so that he might as well make it legitimate rather than cause me to go AWOL. I was a strong-headed young LT at that time and nothing was going to stop me from seeing Bill. The

CPT not only refused to give me the pass, but warned me that disciplinary action would be taken against me in the event I broke the restriction. He let slip that our group was flying to Saipan in the morning. This made me even more determined.

Since I did not have a pass, I could not take the shuttle bus to Pearl Harbor. Getting out the gate was no problem for an OFF and I started to hitchhike to Honolulu. It was some time before I was picked up because gasoline was rationed and there were relatively few private cars on the road at that time. Finally a generous soul shared his car and dropped me off at Pearl Harbor about 2000. The Red Cross Office was ready to close, but the girl on duty hurriedly told me that the USS *Maury* was at Xray Anchorage and that I should take Liberty Boat 10. When I protested that Bill was on the *Murray* she assured me that it was just a question of pronunciation, Bill's ship was the *Maury,* it was at Xray Anchorage, I was to walk to the Liberty Pier take Boat Number 10, and ask the coxswain to let me off at the *Maury.* As I left the office someone informed me that this was the last Liberty Boat for the evening and that I had better take it or wait until morning.

It was only a short walk to the pier where I found Liberty Boat 10 already loaded with sailors. They looked at me askance. An Army 1LT boarding an seaman's Liberty Boat was apparently a serious breach of protocol in the Navy. There appeared to be a greater gulf between Naval officers and sailors than there was between Infantry officers and soldiers. Despite the obvious discomfiture of the sailors, I was determined to get to Bill's ship, so I jumped into Liberty Boat 10. Immediately, the space around me was evacuated. I sat next to the coxswain and asked him to let me off at Xray Anchorage. With an "Aye, Aye, sir", we were under way.

It took about 30 minutes to get to Xray Anchorage and locate the ship. There was a rope ladder over the side and the coxswain indicated that I should climb that to get aboard. Even as I climbed Liberty Boat 10 took off. I was stranded! Upon reaching the deck, I saw a Lieutenant Junior Grade (LTJG), equivalent to an Army 1LT, walked over to him, put out my hand and said,

"I'm Don Seibert. I'm looking for my brother, Bill."

He scowled at me and said, "Don't you Army people know anything about protocol? You're supposed to request permission to come aboard, then salute the ensign (the flag at the stern), then the Officer of the Deck (OD) and state your business."

Shrugging, I went back to the top of the ladder and said, "Request permission to come aboard, sir."

"Permission granted."

I saluted the ensign and the OD, and said, "I'm looking for Ship Fitter First Class William Seibert."

The OD became a bit more affable and replied , "We don't have a Seibert aboard."

"Sometimes its pronounced "Seabert", perhaps you know him as Bill Seabert, he's a Ship Fitter."

"No, I know most of the men on the destroyer but I don't recognize the name. However, I'll check the rolls just to make sure."

This he proceeded to do. There was no Seibert listed; this I verified by looking over his shoulder to make sure he didn't miss the name. When I mentioned the *Murray* he told me it was several miles away in the Harbor. During the conversation, the LTJG informed me that he was "Annapolis, '43". It was obvious that he was punctilious about matters nautical. He told me he could do nothing to get me to the *Murray,* indeed he could not get me to shore. The last liberty boat for the night had brought me to the *Maury,* and a 2200 curfew was in force at Pearl Harbor, in fact all over Hawaii, no further boats would be moving to the mainland.

"I've got to get back to the Replacement Depot by 0600. Isn't there any way I can get back to shore? Can't you put one of your little boats in the water and have someone take me in?"

"No, indeed, that's against standing orders."

"Well, can I talk to the Captain?"

"Oh, no, he's asleep and I can't disturb him unless it is an emergency."

We argued and both got hot under the collar. My cracks about the stuffiness of the Navy further aggravated him and he responded with cracks about ignorant Army officers. We reached an impasse. Just at that point I saw a small boat heading toward the shore, and rushed to the side shouting, "Ahoy! Hey, I need help."

The LTJG almost had apoplexy. He tried to grab me, to shut me up; he did everything possible to silence me short of throwing me over the side. But I would not be silenced. Even if couldn't get to see Bill I was determined to get back to the Replacement Depot in time to make the shipment. As the little boat veered toward the *Maury,* I didn't notice anything unique about it. Someone said, "Ahoy, the *Maury.* What's the problem?"

"I'm an Army officer stranded aboard this ship, I need to get back to shore as soon as possible."

A voice said, "Come aboard, we'll take you ashore."

It wasn't until I clambered down the rope ladder and jumped into the cockpit of the boat that I noticed the tasseled fringe around the roof of the barge and the blue flag in the stem with three stars on it! No wonder the LTJG was excited. The Admiral sitting there asked me what my problem was. Immediately assuming my best military manner, I introduced myself and explained my problem. "Well," he said, "We can't let you miss the opportunity to see your brother. We'll get you to the *Murray* at Zebra Anchorage and back to shore in time to make your shipment."

He directed the coxswain to take us to the "Quartermaster Shack" with all possible speed. The little boat, or Admiral's Barge, made good time, we reached the Quartermaster Shack about 2130. The Admiral gave instructions to "break out a communications launch" and take the LT to the *Murray* at Zebra Anchorage, even farther from the main pier than was the *Maury.* Thanking the Admiral, I threw him my smartest salute and boarded the other boat.

It was almost 2300 by the time we got to the *Murray.* Determined not to embarrass Bill, I caught the bottom of the ladder and shouted, "Request permission to come aboard, sir."

"Permission granted."

After struggling up the ladder, I started to salute the ensign, the OD and follow the protocol the LTJG on the *Maury* had instructed me in. The LTJG who was the OD of the *Murray* said, "Oh, stop it. We don't bother with that shit aboard this ship."

Apparently there is a big difference between ships and their commanders. Later, I learned the *Maury* was officered by "Regular Navy" and the *Murray* by "Reserve Navy". Things seemed to be more relaxed on the *Murray,* although it was equally clean and efficient.

When I told the OD that I had come to see my brother, Bill Seibert, he was immediately helpful. He knew Bill and sent someone to wake him up. Meanwhile, he offered me every courtesy.

Bill came on deck half asleep. He was astonished to see me and we shook hands warmly. He looked terrible, tired and drawn. But he was soon awake, and took me on a tour of the ship during which we talked about home. Having been home more recently than he, I was able to tell him how Mother and Dad were and give him the latest news about College Point.

The OD, over my protest, awakened the Captain (a Commander or LTC) of the *Murray.* He officially welcomed me aboard on behalf of the crew. It was a good feeling. It eased the bad taste I had gotten on the *Maury.* The Captain told me that the *Murray* was going out for a shakedown cruise the next morning and would be out about three days. He urged me to remain aboard and go with them. He offered me the freedom of the ship, I could spend time with Bill, I could see how the Navy operated. He was truly sincere in his offer. Regretfully, I pointed out that I was due to ship out in the morning and had to make that shipment; indeed, I had to get back to the Replacement Depot or face charges of desertion to avoid hazardous duty. He reluctantly agreed with me.

At 0200, the Captain ordered his gig into the water and had his coxswain take me to Pearl Harbor. Once ashore I was in violation of curfew regulations. Fortunately, no one challenged me, nobody stopped me. On reaching the main gate of Pearl Harbor Naval Base I started to walk toward Schofield Barracks without exact knowledge of its location or how long it would take me to walk there. I hoped that there would be some vehicles moving at that time of night (0330) to give me a ride. Only then did I begin to worry about my situation.

A civilianized Jeep driven by an elderly man finally came along. The driver stopped and offered me a lift, which I accepted gratefully. He was glad to have my company and asked if this was my first trip to the Islands. When I told him it was, he said, "Then I'll have to take you the long way and show you the pineapple plantations and what the Island really looks like,"

"I've got to get back in time to meet a formation at six o'clock, sir, and its almost four. I really ought to go directly, so let's take the short way."

But he would have no part of that. He was determined to show me the Island even though it was still dark and I could see only a few feet off the side of the road by the light of the headlights. He kept up a running commentary about the cultivation of pineapples, how they were picked and processed and the routine of the plantations.

We arrived at the main gate of the Replacement Depot at 0600. As I looked through the gate I saw a formation in my Co area with a convoy of trucks, motors running, behind it. Ed Schmitt spied me and called,

"Hey, Don, I've got your gear, just make it to the truck." He had also reported me **present" to the CPT, who appeared ready to apprehend me, but shrugged and let me go. I sprinted to the trucks from the main gate, managed to catch the tailgate of the last one, and was hauled aboard by my friends.

CHAPTER 4

DEADEYE

The convoy took us directly to Hickam Field. There we were briefed on flight procedures, issued "Mae Wests" and manifested. We checked our Mae Wests, including fitting them and inflating them by mouth. Finally everyone was satisfied that we were ready to go. As we were preparing to board the plane we were told to assemble back in the briefing room, where we were informed that the weather between Honolulu and Saipan was so dangerous that the flight had been delayed. We were assigned transient billets and put on-call for the next day.

Although eager to get to our final units, we were not too dejected. Surprisingly, with stem warnings about talking loosely, we were permitted to go into Honolulu. The now inseparable group (Seibert, Schmitt, Pugsley, Mester, McGrath, Waggoner) had dinner in one of the famous restaurants and saw a little of the City. We walked along Waikiki Beach, which appeared to me rather small and pebbly. Probably, this was due to the anti-invasion barriers (hedge-hogs and barbed wire) installed on it.

The next day we assembled again, only to be told that the weather was still too dangerous for flight. We spent the day wandering around Hickam Field; the damage inflicted by the Japanese on 7 December 1941 was still visible - gutted buildings, bullet marks and burn smudges. That night we had dinner at the Hickam Officers' Club. The following day our flight was again postponed. I reflected that I might have spent those three days on the *Murray*.

At 0500 on the fourth day we boarded the "gooney bird", (C-47), that was to take us to Saipan, with great anticipation. The plane was rigged for medical evacuation and manned by four flight nurses in addition to the Army Air Corps crew. When the nurses found out that most of us were IN LTs they predicted that they would be seeing us on their return trip in not more than two days. Of course this was very comforting. But we were gung-ho and exacted their assurances that they would give us special care. The C-47 also carried medical supplies, mostly whole blood, according to the labels on the O.D. boxes.

The flight was bumpy, but we made good time and about 1600 hours we landed at Saipan. Again, we followed the routine we had learned to expect. We were herded on trucks and taken to the 23rd Replacement Depot, high on the spine of the Island. Here we received the inevitable briefing and assignment to billets. The 23rd "Repple Dep", as it was called by the troops, was in squad tents and had few of the amenities enjoyed on Oahu. We slept on canvas cots, provided with a mattress cover in lieu of sheets and a mosquito bar on a wooden frame, and ate from mess kits, going through a GI chow line as all soldiers do in the field.

During the briefing we were told that we were all being assigned to Okinawa but that the Landing Ships Tank (LSTs) that were to take us there would not leave for two days. It struck me that the invasion had started the day I left College Point for FT Ord, I April. In the morning we marched to a temporary rifle range to test fire our carbines. Later we were issued an individual basic load of ammunition, and then moved out on the hill behind the Replacement Depot.

Here, the cadre informed us that many Jap soldiers had hidden in spider holes (a Japanese fox hole), caves and bunkers on this hill when the Americans had retaken Saipan. We had already noted the occasional rifle shot into the Depot, especially at chow time. We were to sweep the hill to try to flush out these stay-behind enemy soldiers. After the briefing we were organized into a parody of a skirmish line. It was a frightful formation! About 300 LTs, senior NCOs and inexperienced privates were on line, ordered to raise arms, touch the finger tips of the men on either side, and dress to the right and left. Then the half mile line of soldiers, maintaining a ragged dress, moved slowly forward looking for Japs. None of us spotted a thing; nothing moved as we swept forward. When we had progressed a mile or so down the slope, we were assembled and marched back to the Depot. We retained the live ammo.

Early the next morning 10 officers (five 1LTs, myself among them, and five 2LTs) boarded *LST 810*. All five 2LTs were Infantry Officers, Glen Herndon, Bill Hollinger, Jim Lamb III, Paul McGrath and Ed Mester. The other four 1LTs were doctors who generally kept to themselves. An exception was Bob Nims, a slender, blond-headed officer, who took pictures of everything. We shared many interests and became fast friends on the 10 day trip.

The skipper, LT R. Coburn, a pleasant, considerate, competent young officer, welcomed us aboard. After assigning us to cabins (which we shared, some with Navy officers), the Captain briefed us, informing us that the convoy would move out later that day, perhaps about 1700. "I might as well level with you. We will be at the tail end of the convoy because we are loaded with supersensitive artillery fuses. The other LSTs are carrying the artillery shells. If we have to go to General Quarters, we will break away from the convoy. We could detonate every ship in it if we blew." That was enough to add interest to an already provocative trip! We left Saipan, joining the right rear of a convoy of 20 ships, 15 LSTs, several destroyers and one cargo ship. The weather was clear and calm. We Army OFFs had the run of the ship, the crew of *LST 810* did everything possible to make us comfortable. We got to know most of them and to appreciate their professionalism. As the senior Army officer aboard, I had responsibility for the rest to include signing vouchers for food.

During the voyage our conversation inevitably turned to the combat situation we were going to face. I had some qualms about my own performance in combat. Perhaps everyone who faces battle has these same doubts. A major concern was how the troops would react to me when I finally joined my unit, a "stateside" LT with no combat experience joining a unit that had already been blooded. Would the men accept my leadership; would I have a problem getting to them? There were reservations about my preparation for duty as a leader in combat. Although I thought I knew my tactics, my weapons, my leadership, did I know enough? These thoughts I kept to myself but mulled over. There wasn't much that could be done about it now. Among the six IN OFFs there were a limited number of Field Manuals, I leafed through one or two but this was not like cramming for an exam in physics. Everyone has to rely on his judgement when he faces battle. Though apprehensive, I was still eager to fight.

General Quarters sounded only once during the trip; as briefed, we dropped to the rear and became an obvious target. The Destroyer Escort reported sonar contact with an enemy sub, but it fired no torpedoes. We rejoined the convoy and continued on our way. We did see several enemy aircraft but before we went to General Quarters they disappeared.

At dawn on the tenth day, the Skipper pointed to a smudge on the horizon he said was Okinawa. We arrived at Brown Beach, Okinawa, in mid-morning. It was interesting to see the LSTs beached. Their Captains lined up certain visual references on shore, then moved dead ahead until the keels grounded. The large clam shell doors in the bow had been opened, the ramp partially lowered and an anchor dropped while we were in deep water. The anchor would be used in withdrawing from the beach. When the LST beached the ramp was lowered, enabling us to walk ashore without getting our boots wet. We said goodbye to the crew of *LST 810* and moved up the beach to the Beachmaster's Control Shack. We were given instructions on where to report for transportation to yet another Repple Dep.

The 74th Replacement Bn, located on the beach, quickly processed us. Though the procedures were familiar they were accomplished with a more purposeful attitude. Everybody seemed to know what had to be done and did it with the least possible delay. It was hard to forget that troops were fighting just a few miles away. Facilities at the 74th were minimal; a number of squad tents, cots with mosquito bars, a latrine and a mess tent. The chow was better than I expected in a combat zone; although there were no fresh vegetables, there were cold drinks which I was surprised to get on Okinawa. We were briefed, our records collected and told that we would have orders later that evening.

Just about dark we were assembled, all IN LTs were assigned to the 96th IN Div, the "Deadeyes". The Div was on line outside Shuri Castle about a third of the way from the southern tip of the Island. Bob Nims was assigned to a separate Artillery (ARTY) Bn and the other Medical OFFs were assigned to units other than ours.

At dark, about 2130, we hit the sack; there was nothing else to do. As I lay on my bunk the pending introduction to combat tormented me; the same questions recurred; how would I be accepted by the troops I would command; how would they accept an officer who had never been under fire; how well did I know my Infantry tactics and weapons; how, above all, would I react under fire? This time I mentioned my thoughts to my friends, who admitted that they had much the same concerns. But we were young and optimistic, confident that we would rise to any situation; as my doubts disappeared, I fell asleep.

During that night on Brown Beach, we were entertained with a Jap air raid. When the siren sounded we awakened, leaped from our cots, some shredding their mosquito bars, rushed from the tents putting on helmets, and dropped into slit trenches close to the tents. We could see the antiaircraft tracers and the search lights trying to finger the aircraft. The rythmic booming of twin forties drowned out the sound of the enemy propellers. Although the search lights illuminated one aircraft, on which all of the fire was directed, it escaped. We heard later that the air raid had done no damage to friendly units.

Next morning we arose early in the gray, rainy dawn. After a breakfast of dehydrated eggs, we were loaded on trucks and driven to the 96th Replacement Co. Here we were again processed, surrendering orders, 201 files and qualification cards to the personnel clerks. We were informed almost immediately that six of us were going to the 382nd Infantry. Despite speedy processing, we spent the night at the 96th Replacement Co located in a Japanese commercial facility. There was a wooden floor to sleep on, a luxury, because it had been raining all day and it was muddy. Someone told us that the end of the rainy season was at hand, though we could expect quite a bit more rain.

The trip to the 382nd Infantry Regiment next morning was a slow truck ride through sticky mud. Our records had accompanied us from the Div Rear, so the Adj (S-1) and his Personnel OFF quickly made the final determination as to the units to which we would be assigned. Three were to go to the 2nd Bn, two to the 1st Bn, and I was to stay at Regt HQ as the Asst Regt Adj and the RGO. My previous CW training continued to plague me, I was to be denied the opportunity to serve in combat in a rifle Co. When I protested vehemently, the Personnel OFF told me that I would have to take my case to the Regt Adi, a MAJ. He pointed to an office. Losing no time, I knocked on the door jamb, walked in, saluted and intoned the formula "LT Seibert reports, sir."

The busy MAJ returned my salute and enquired, "What is it, LT?"

"Sir, I want to go to a rifle Co or at least to a Bn. I do not want to stay at Regt HQ in any capacity. I volunteered for the Infantry, and I want to fight with a rifle company."

"I understand your feelings, but we have to think of the best interests of the Regiment. You are a trained UGO and we need one. And I've got to have some help with this damn paperwork. You look like the logical prospect."

"Sir, I got out of the CWS because I wanted to be an Infantryman. I don't want to do CW work again. I could have stayed in CWS for that. I have fought every Personnel Officer I have encountered to get here. I won't be side-tracked now. I want to get to a rifle Co. I am not going to be satisfied until I do."

"Well, you'll have to be satisfied with whatever we give you, Seibert. Now, I can't take the time to review every OFF's assignment. That's why I have a Personnel Officer. If he thinks you should be assigned to Regt that's where you'll go."

"You don't need anyone with special qualifications, MAJ Any one can help you with your paper work. Give me a break. Send me down to the 2nd Bn with my buddies."

"Sony, I can't do that. You'll go where the Personnel Officer assigns you."

"Sir, I request permission to see the Regimental XO."

"What? What are you trying to pull?"

"I want to go to a rifle Bn, and I will go to the Regt CO if I have to."

"OK, if you feel that strongly about it tell LT Smith that I said you were to be assigned to the 2nd Bn. They need all the officers they can get. Now get out of my hair."

"Yes, sir. Thank you, sir." I saluted and left before he could change his mind, not at all concerned with who would take my place at Regt. I ran to the Personnel Office and informed the amazed 2LT of my change of orders. He grinned resignedly as he told the clerk to change the orders. Strand, McGrath, Mester and I were on the same order to the 2nd Battalion, 382nd infantry.

Late in the afternoon we were introduced to the Regimental CO, COL Macey Dill. We spent the night at Regt HHC, were able to speak to the COL and his staff, and were briefed on the situation. The Asst S-3 (Operations Officer) told us that the attack to the south had bogged down around Shuri Castle. The "Deadeyes" had not made much progress in the last few days, not only because of increasing Japanese resistance, but also because of the heavy rains which had made the countryside almost impassable. The S-4 (Supply Officer) mentioned that the only way of getting needed supplies to the troops was by means of tracked vehicles called "weasels". These were open, lightly armored, cargo vehicles, almost like bathtubs on tracks. They could negotiate through almost any mire on the Island. The S-3 informed us that the 2nd Bn was dug in at the foot of a ridge line dominated by two hills called Hector and Hen. The Bn had made three attacks on that ridge, but had been unable to take it; heavy losses had been incurred in those attacks.

The situation was not reassuring; once again doubts arose. I wondered if I had done the right thing in fighting to go to an IN Bn. But I was determined, having gotten this far, that I was not going to stop until I reached a rifle Co. It was raining when we bedded down, but once again we had wooden floors to sleep on. HHC was in a school building made of thin boards, with paper covered doors and windows. At least we had a roof over our heads and did not have to sleep in the muck and mire.

Early next morning we boarded a weasel and started out to the 2nd Bn. The trip was a revelation to us. We passed many vehicles stuck in the mud, ammunition and supplies waiting for weasel transport forward; body bags containing dead soldiers awaited return to the rear. Each weasel that went forward with supplies picked up dead on the way back. We wondered how long the bodies had been there; when we got to the 2nd Bn we were told that it was less than 24 hours. It was a beautiful and fertile island with tiny villages and individual farm houses scattered throughout terraced hills. Finally we reached the 2d Bn HQ where we were introduced to the Bn CO, LTC Cyril Dean Sterner. We heard a call over the radio asking for Dean; this shocked us until we found that it was SOP in the 382nd to call OFFs by a nickname rather than by grade or last name. LTC Sterner, a young, good looking, very erect OFF, with a high forehead, yellow hair and piercing blue eyes, welcomed us. He was the picture-book image of a soldier; reputedly, he was doing an outstanding job as Bn CO. He left shortly after we arrived, to return to his forward observation post (OP). The Adj, CPT Tracy, took us in tow, found us chow (it was long past noon) and took our records. He promised to give us our final assignments before the evening meal. Meanwhile we were turned over to an OFF in the S-3 section who briefed us on the 96th IN Div and the current situation.

From the briefings we had at Div, Regt and now Bn, a history of the 96th IN Div emerged. Activated in August 1942, at Camp Adair, OR, the Div was destined for amphibious operations in the Pacific. Training was conducted at various military installations on the West Coast, including FT Lewis and Yakima. Following amphibious training at Camp Callan and San Louis Obispo, CA, and an uncertain Odyssey across the Pacific Ocean, the "Deadeyes" participated in the amphibious assault on Leyte. From all accounts it acquitted itself well during that campaign, hence it was selected to make the assault landing on Okinawa. The initial days after the landing had been relatively easy for the 382nd IN Regt as it fought its way inland. On the third day, the 382nd relieved its sister Regt, the 381st, and had fought hard and steadily ever since. A short break to rest and assimilate replacements had done little to ease the fighting. Now the Div was held up by fanatic resistance and the mud and rains.

The name "Deadeyes" had resulted from the emphasis the Asst Div CDR, BG Claudius Easley, had placed on rifle marksmanship in the early training of the Div. This had produced an unusually high percentage of experts which was quickly capitalized upon by the troops who enthusiastically adopted the nickname "Deadeyes". Now I was a Deadeye.

The S-3 OFF went over the current situation with us in detail. For the first time we saw on a map the disposition of the 382nd IN including the Cos of the 2nd Bn. The low "foxhole" strength of the rifle Cos shocked us. The final summary of the fighting in the current area and the S-2's estimate of the Japanese forces facing the 382nd Infantry revealed a grim picture.

Following the briefing, the Adj, CPT Tracy, told us that we would be given our assignments as soon as he cleared them with the "Old Man" when he came back from the OP for chow. Just before the evening meal, about 1800, Tracy called us together "Okay, the COL has just approved your assignments. Seibert, you're assigned to Head and Read as Anti-tank Platoon Leader and UGO, Strand to E Co, McGrath to F and Mester to H. Any questions?"

"Hey, Captain, why can't I go to one of the rifle companies? That's where I want to go, and that's where I think I can do the best job. Don't let that CW stuff influence my assignment."

"Well, it was a toss up between Head and Head and Heavy Weapons Co. They need a HMG Plt Ldr in H Co and we thought of sending you there. You're sort of senior for a Rifle Plt; all of our Rifle Cos have XOs we don't want to change."

"I don't give a damn about being an XO. I want a rifle platoon. Send me to one of the rifle companies."

"Okay, okay. No problem. All of the line Cos need platoon leaders. I'm sure the Old Man will approve a switch to, let's see, I guess Fox needs officers more than any other Co. So we'll send you down to Fox. Bourdeau is Co CO and Ed Foley the XO."

"Fine, thanks a lot, Captain."

"We've got some other officers coming down from Regiment tomorrow and they can go to Head and Head and H."

The officers following were those I had met at Ord and who had come through the Replacement Depots with me. Ressler got the job I was slated for at Bn; Ed Schmitt came down to F Co. But that was later.

Finally, I was on my way to a rifle company, F Co. Once again that night I reviewed everything I knew about leadership and Infantry tactics; there was more soul-searching, but the decision was made, so I got a good night's sleep. At breakfast, LTC Sterner said he would take us to the OP to show us on the ground what was going on, then we could join our companies. We went on foot; Sterner set out at a rapid gait. I didn't know whether he was trying to test us or whether that was the way he normally walked (I learned later that he was renowned for his long stride and fast pace). The trip took longer than it should have because of the mud. We finally reached the OP, a sandbagged revetment behind which we could crouch to look across the valley The BN CO's BC scope (powerful binoculars on a tripod) was set up and brought the positions and terrain out plainly. A field table with a map on it, was next to the BC scope.

Sterner pointed out F Co almost directly ahead, across an open valley. A slope led to a ravine in which the Co HQ was located. The ground then rose, at first gently, then took an abrupt turn upward to Hector Hill. F Co platoons were dug in along the base of the hill. "Dean" pointed out Hen Hill, on the right of Hector and the ridge which extended right to the Marine sector. G Co was located at the base of the ridge. We were the right flank Bn of the right flank Regt of the 96th Div. The 77th Div was on our right flank, the 1st Bn of the 382nd was to our left.

After about a half hour of talk and advice, LTC Sterner said, "Are you set to go to your companies?"

"Yes, sir."

"Move out."

Thinking he meant to take off down the hill to the F Co CP which he had pointed out directly ahead of the OP, I jumped over the revetment and started to slog through the mud down the slope.

There were some shouts, but I did not relate them to my action. Without realizing it, I was completely exposed to Jap observation and fire. The Japanese, who were extremely accurate marksmen, had been sniping at the OP; in fact, they had wounded a man in the OP the day before. But luck was with me. If I was shot at, I was too green to know it. Rounds went off now and then, but it was desultory fire, which I didn't pay much attention to. Finally, I got to the F Co CP without incident.

The XO, 1LT Ed Foley, a wiry, talkative Irishman from Massachusetts, met me. He had been alerted to go to the OP by a covered route to pick up McGrath and me and lead us to the Co so that we would not be exposed to fire. When I jumped over the parapet before anyone could stop me, everyone held their breath until I reached cover. Ed gave me hell, directing that next time I wait for an escort.

He took me to the Co CO, CPT Cledith Bourdeau, a tall, husky, handsome, dark headed officer with a darling smile. Although he showed strain from lack of sleep, he looked like an Infantryman; I learned, firsthand, that he was a good soldier and an excellent CDR. Bourdeau, who hailed from California, talked to me about my background, experience and training. He told me bit more about the unit, what it had done on Leyte and what had gone on so far on Okinawa. But he was more interested in what F Co had done and what F Co was going to do. He had been with the Co only a short time, having recently replaced a casualty. Until taking over F Co he had been with the 1st Bn. While we were talking, Foley returned with McGrath. There was a brief exchange of gibes, as Paul told me of the reaction to my trek down the hill.

Then Bourdeau assigned us to Plts, me to the 2nd, McGrath to the 1st. Fred Steed had the 3rd Plt. Foley told me that the 2nd PSG, SSG Schroeder, had been with the unit all through Leyte, although he had been wounded. He was an experienced, steady NCO; Bourdeau was certain that he would break me in fast. Bourdeau gave McGrath and me a quick orientation on the tactics being used and how the enemy operated. When I asked about the strength of the 2nd Plt, Bourdeau said it numbered 20 men, including me; the authorized strength was 40 men. Despite that, the Plt was expected to operate on a normal front, about 100 yards.

As we were talking the field phone rang, Ed Foley answered it, then silently gave it to Bourdeau. "Yes, sir, I'll be right there," and Bourdeau hung up.

He turned to us saying that he had been called to the Bn OP to receive an order. As he left, Bourdeau told Foley to alert the Co. Ed called the Plts on the sound-powered telephone, directing the Plt Ldrs to report to the CP. Foley surmised that Bourdeau would get an attack order. 1LT Fred Steed, 3rd Plt Ldr, arrived first; as we shook hands I sized him up; he was a tall, muscular, blond officer from Seattle. We immediately liked each other. SSG Schroeder came up and Foley introduced us. Bourdeau returned at that time.

With few preliminaries, other than introducing McGrath and myself, the Co CO issued the attack order. The 2nd Bn was to assault the Hector-Hen Hill ridge and seize and hold it. This was the fourth attempt to take the hill mass, so we were to be supported by all the fire support available to the 382nd. An Artillery preparation would be Fired. F Co would attack in a column of Plts, 2nd Plt leading. We would take off from the line of departure (LD), our present location) at 1230. The Co Command Group (CMD GP) would follow 2nd Plt. He looked around,"Any questions?"

There were none from the other Plt Ldrs, and I was too dumb or green to think of any. I hadn't even met my Plt yet. SSG Schroeder said, "Let's go, sir."

He took off with me at his heels. As we proceeded to the 2nd Plt area, I formulated my plan for the attack. Looking up at Hector Hill, I reviewed the accounts Bourdeau had told me about the three previous attacks and how or why they had failed. It became clear to me how I was going to attack it. We quickly reached the Plt CP, a three-man fox hole. PFC Robert Laird, the Plt Runner, and the Medic were there. After introducing us Schroeder asked, "What's the first order of business, sir?"

There was less than an hour an a half before H hour. "The first order of business is to meet the Platoon," I said.

Since it was obviously impossible for the troops to come to the Plt CP, we proceeded to make the rounds of the squad positions. SSG Schroeder took me to each of the foxholes in turn (most were two-man holes), and introduced me to the 16 men in the Plt. They were strange faces, dirty, drawn, tired, yet the men appeared to have high morale and to be intelligent and professional soldiers, That is a strange sense you develop in the service. You can enter a unit area and know immediately what kind of outfit it is. A quick evaluation, based on appearance, condition or feel, but correct 90% of the time. This was the case, I knew it was a good outfit, though I could not have told you how I knew it. It was impossible to connect all of the names and faces of the men, but I did take particular note of the three squad leaders (SLs), Rylant, Waxman and Rose.

The three SLs returned with us to the Plt CP, which had a bit more cover than the rest of the Plt area. When everyone was under cover, I issued my order. The formation I had decided on was two BAR teams, a demolition man (a rifleman familiar with demolitions and armed with satchel charges) and the CMD GP, Plt Ldr, PSG, Plt Runner and Plt Medic, a total of 11 men. Everyone would carry as many satchel charges and hand grenades as possible. After reaching the Jap positions, we would blow them up with the satchel charges. Eleven of the 20 men in the Plt would make the attack, supported by the fire of the rest. SGT Rylant, the senior SL, would command the base of fire.

When I completed issuing my order, the NCOs looked at me strangely. They had made three determined attacks in force on this position without taking it, now a green 1LT new in combat, had decided that a very small force could take it. Noting their skepticism, I explained my plan. Hector was a narrow, conical hill. It appeared to me that more than two BAR teams, more than four or six men abreast, would be ineffective on it. The fire of any additional men would be masked; they would almost have to be in single file behind the leading BAR teams. Hence there appeared to be little need for additional men; they could do more good firing from their present positions. I was even more sure of my plan since we were to have a thorough preparation by fire.

My NCOs shrugged and moved out, unconvinced I am sure. Since the 2nd Plt was on the right flank of the Co, I wanted to establish liaison with G Co, on our right, and the Plt that was on my flank. There were 45 minutes until H-Hour, so I double-timed to the G Co CP which SSG Schroeder pointed out to me. The Co CO gave me his plan; he had to take Hen Hill, a little nipple next to Hector and part of the ridge to the right of it. His left flank Plt Ldr, who was going to be on my immediate flank, and I arranged signals and coordinated zones. He looked at me oddly when I told him my plan, but said nothing.

When I got back to the Plt CP just a few minutes before H-Hour, I did manage to recognize SSG Schroeder and PFC Laird, my runner. He was a wiry individual, who wore glasses. Despite the fact that he was a little older than most of us in the Plt, he had lots of energy. He would tag along behind me in case I had messages to send. He also carried the Signal Corps Radio (SCR) 536, the handietalkie radio which operated in the F Co net.

The Artillery preparation began; it was every bit as intense as had been promised. Promptly at 1230, H-Hour, we moved out. The two BAR teams went first, followed immediately by me, SSG Schroeder, the rifleman with the satchel charges, PFC Laird and the Medic. The preparatory fire lifted off the hill as we moved. The BAR men had been told to lay down a steady fire and move as fast as they could. They took me at my word and made those BARs sing. The riflemen were firing also as was the base of fire at the line of departure. We moved steadily without opposition until we were two-thirds of the way to the objective. Suddenly, the top of the hill erupted with rifle fire, grenades and knee mortar rounds. The knee mortar fired a smaller round than our 60mm mortar and the rounds detonated into fine shrapnel which sprayed a 15 yard area.

Our attack, which had been going so well, suddenly halted. We all hit the ground, seeking some fold or cover which would give us protection from the fire. Faintly I heard SGT Rylant below me, "Put all your fire on the top of the hill, and shoot like hell!"

The Japanese rifle bullets zipped over our heads doing little damage. Their grenades, lobbed over the entrenchments blindly, fell with no accuracy and so were ineffective. But several knee mortar rounds fell in the middle of our formation. Fortunately, the BAR teams were beyond the bursting radius of the rounds. Not so, SSG Schroeder and myself. I felt several pinpricks in the back as some of the tiny shrapnel, almost like bits of wire, cut through my fatigue jacket, but I was not hurt. The rounds impacted close to SSG Schroeder, who was riddled with bits of steel. He shouted, "I've been hit!" I glanced over at him; he was bleeding from several wounds, but did not appear to be in serious danger as he began to slide back down the hill. Even as I looked, the Medic reached him, I was sure he would be okay.

I turned my attention back to the fire-fight, shouting to the BAR men, "Fire automatic! The rest of you throw grenades." We were close enough to the top of the hill so that the natural ability of the American to throw a baseball or rock carried the grenades over the edge of the trenches at the top of it.

A few more mortar rounds came in but they landed down the hill, between the assault group and the base of fire. Apparently the Japs were searching the hill, trying to prevent our ascent. They were not putting observed fire on us. Scrambling forward, I urged the men up toward the top; hand grenade range became easier; we threw grenades as fast as we could. Laird went back for more and returned with another man lugging an entire case of them. As we neared the crest, I called forward the demolition man, SGT Pauley, who armed his satchel charges, then threw them into the trenches. When the charges went off we jumped up and ran to the top of the hill, firing at anything moving in the trenches or behind. Some Japs tried to escape to the rear, but we killed most of them. None volunteered to surrender.

Once to the top of the hill I glanced to my right at the G Co attack. A single soldier was standing astride the trenches on the ridge, firing into them. The thought crossed my mind that he was unusually courageous, braving enemy fire to do his job. Surely he deserved some sort of award, a Silver Star, at least. We were able to bring the fire of our BARs to the rear of the ridge and Hen Hill to cut down some of the Japs, thus preventing them from firing up at this soldier. But he apparently needed little help from us.

Now that we were in control of Hector Hill, I waived the rest of my Plt forward. They came up out of their holes on the double, scrambling to the top of the hill. We found the body of an American soldier, killed on the last attack. Bourdeau had mentioned that the Co had reluctantly had to leave him there when the Plt Ldr was badly shot up, and the Plt was forced off the hill. It was bloated by this time; all bodies lying unburied on Okinawa were immediately attacked by the climate and the flies to start the decaying process within hours. As I took his dog tags, I noticed that there were half a dozen bullet wounds in him; he must have been killed instantly during that attack. Laird called back to request that the Graves Registration people come forward to take care of him.

We set about clearing the area, examining the bunkers and trenches, making sure that all the Japs were dead. We searched the bodies for intelligence material. My men looked at the waists of the Japs, where most carried flags, which were highly prized souvenirs. Weapons and swords were also prized as souvenirs. SGT Rose finally amassed five swords which he carried with him, since we had no rear area to store them in; it was a chore for him.

After our position on Hector Hill was consolidated, Bourdeau ordered me to move forward, sweep the reverse slope of the hill, then take the high ground beyond it. Ahead and to the left of our position was Shuri Castle. Unfortunately, F Co never entered that area, so I did not get to see that famous land mark; it was badly damaged by artillery fire. To the right, down the valley, was a high steel tower, apparently a radio tower. There were orders to preserve it for use by our own communications personnel. But an artillery shell hit at its base and the tower toppled.

During the advance from Hector, we were engaged several times. At one point, a small group of Japs dashed at us with hand grenades and bayonets, firing as they came. One by one they were cut down. I fired at one, hitting him again and again, but he came on. Jap soldiers reportedly took drugs and refused to give up, but I could not understand why he was not stopped by my bullets. I was sure I was hitting him. Others were stopped by a single shot from an M-1. He finally dropped; when the action ended, I walked over to him to make sure that I had hit him. I had. Holes made by a carbine round in flesh are distinct from the gouging and tearing action of an M-1 bullet. There were at least three carbine hits in vital areas readily apparent, and other hits in less critical places. This convinced me that the carbine had little or no shock action; if I wanted to stop a man in his tracks, I had better get an M-1 rifle. When I mentioned this to Laird, he eagerly offered to exchange his M-1 for my carbine. The radio made it difficult to carry the M-1, which he rarely got to fire.

By the time we had cleared the reverse slope of Hector and taken the high ground beyond it, it was 1500. We stopped to dig in for the night. I assigned squad positions and the men began digging in. We were on a level plateau, which gave us good observation and fields of fire. Since SSG Schroeder had been evacuated because of his wounds, I made SGT Roy Rylant, the senior SL, the PSG. His Asst SL took over his squad. I also selected a location for the Plt CP; Laird and the Medic started to dig a four-man hole, assisted occasionally by Rylant and me. In the next two hours, I checked to satisfy myself that the SLs had picked good sites for their Squad holes, complimented the men on their performance, checked on supplies, particularly ammo and water, and started to get to know the men in the Plt, who were digging two-man holes.

When satisfied with the Plt, I helped with the digging. It was hard work (the ground was rocky) so it was unfair to let only two people do all the digging. On the other hand I had responsibilities as Plt Ldr which frequently required my absence from the Plt CP. This was an understood principle, one of the reasons a runner or messenger was provided for each Plt Ldr, to assist him in getting settled and organized; to help him in the exercise of his command.

By 1700 hours everybody was well dug in; the men needed no urging to dig adequate shelter as they had experienced both artillery and automatic weapons fire and knew the value of a good foxhole. One final check assured me that all the men had ammo, water and C Rations. One five gallon can of water per squad, with one extra for the Plt CP and other use, had been delivered by the Co Supply Personnel, along with extra grenades, satchel charges, bandoleers of rifle ammo and C Rations. Everyone seemed to be provided for.

It was standard procedure each evening to go into a defensive position before dark. As mentioned before, one of the weaknesses of the American Army in combat was night operations. We did little fighting at night, almost no movement. Although all service schools taught the principles of night fighting, and it was included in all training directives, we were never comfortable with it. On the other hand, the Japs used the darkness; they fought, moved, and resupplied in it. The current defensive perimeter, tied in with other Plts and Cos in the Bn was an outgrowth of our concern for the night. The Co Commo SGT (Communications NCO) laid wire to the Plt CP; I was informed over the sound-powered telephone that there would be harassing and interdiction (H&I) fires to discourage and disrupt any movement to our front. Despite this, the Japs took over the night and had almost complete freedom of movement.

It started to rain as I settled down for my cold C Ration meal. About dark it became a steady downpour. We covered ourselves with our ponchos as best we could, preparing for the evening vigil. The necessary reports were made to Bourdeau over the sound-powered telephone; he was complimentary about the action that afternoon. I was relieved that it had gone as well as it had. My first day with this unit, as well as my first fire fight had gone better than I dared hope for; it appeared that I had been fully accepted by the troops. In fact, I got the impression that the men were hungry for leadership, that they willingly gave their loyalty and confidence to each officer placed over them until such time as he might prove himself inept, or for some other reason unacceptable. As a result of this desire for leadership, for some one to make the decisions, these men had accepted me with far less reserve than I had anticipated.

As the night grew darker, a thunder storm struck. There was much loud rumbling and vivid lightning. It was my turn to be awake and on watch; I was half sitting, half crouched with the tip of my helmet and my eyes over the lip of the foxhole so that I could observe any movement. A bolt of lightning struck the ground about 50 or 75 yards from the foxhole; I watched the crackling arc travel along the sound-powered telephone line toward our hole. It seemed to move slowly, almost leisurely down the wire, but I know it was only micro seconds before the lightning hit me; in the interim I could do nothing. The sound-powered telephone was resting on my thigh on top of the poncho. The electricity reached the telephone and was transmitted to my leg. It seemed as if my knee had been hit with a sledge hammer. The telephone was knocked into the water in which we crouched and the electricity drained off through the water and grounded.

As the jolt transited my body all of my muscles contracted. I found myself standing rigidly at attention in the foxhole. I was so stunned, that I cannot remember how it affected the other people who shared the hole. Whether they were standing and exposed as I was, remains unclear. Though my muscles were spastic, my mind was alert; I heard voices over the sound-powered telephone, even through the water at the bottom of the fox hole. Foley and Bourdeau were calling; then there were conversations with the other Plts as Bourdeau checked each in turn. Co HQ seemed to think that a shell landing in our position had wiped out the Plt CP. I tried in vain to reach down to grab the phone to tell them we were all right. In fact I wasn't all right because I was exposed to Jap fire.

Fortunately the Japs did not fire so I managed to get through the incident without any injuries, not even a burn. As soon as I was able, I forced myself to crouch down. Once down, all of my muscles began to jump; my knee bounced up and down with a rhythm all its own. It was about a half hour before I could grab the telephone and report to the CP that we were all right.

The other men in the fox hole were in no better shape than I. They had been knocked out of a sound sleep; it took them some time to realize what had happened. Fortunately there were no after affects. No one was burned or otherwise hurt. After two or three hours the stimulation left my muscles enabling me to get a little sleep before daylight.

The next morning we pushed on, with little contact at first. We exchanged a few rounds with fleeting Japs but had no real fire fight until late in the afternoon. Just as we were looking for a night position, there was a flurry of shots to our front. I watched in horror as one of my soldiers fell to the ground, it was obvious from the way he fell that he was dead. Busy at the time directing the Plt fire fight, I couldn't get to him immediately, but was sure the Medic would take care of him. When I finally did get back to him after the skirmish was over and we had reverted to a normal formation, I found that he had been killed instantly.

It was a traumatic thing for me; he was the first of my men to be killed; it was the first time that I felt responsible for the death of someone. I didn't even know his name! Suddenly I was aware of a strange dichotomy in my thinking in combat (it remains to this day). Killing the enemy did not bother me, though I took no pleasure or pride in it; there was no sense of responsibility for the enemy's death; it was simply the job to be done. On the other hand, the death of one of my men, although I was not directly responsible for it, placed a heavy burden on me. I could never, and have never, gotten over that feeling. I actually cried a little when that first man was killed, but soon got myself in hand; nobody noticed it but me. it is a feeling I have never ceased to have in combat; where had I erred that this individual was killed? Was my plan or my leadership lacking? This is probably healthy if you do not let it overwhelm you. As a result you analyze plans, orders or leadership more carefully in order to make the best possible decision. Certainly I did not go into a great depression or permit it to disturb me to the point that I couldn't think of anything else, but it was a difficult thing to accept.

We halted for the night shortly afterwards; as the Plt was digging in Bourdeau called me to the Co CP, where I met the PSG of the 1st Plt, TSG Dempewolf. He told me that his new Plt Ldr had been hit in the fire fight a few minutes before. "McGrath went out front up on a big rock to observe. I yelled, 'Get your ass down', but it was too late, and he was hit in the throat" A few weeks later I received a letter from McGrath, written from the hospital. He said that all he could think of when he was hit was whether or not he would be able to play his trumpet or trombone (an accomplished musician, he played in a dance band). To his great relief the doctor in the Clearing Company assured him that the wound would not interfere with his playing. I never saw McGrath again.

Bourdeau told me that the 2nd Bn would be squeezed out of line the next morning to become the Regt reserve. This was good timing. The men were tired, it would give me a chance to get to know the Plt. The following morning F Co stayed in position as the rest of the Regt pushed on, then moved to a small valley which gave us good cover. Being in reserve merely meant being to the rear of the attacking elements. There were no facilities other than those we carried with us or made. We did get our packs and so had pup tents to cover our foxholes (the Supply SGT found me some field equipment since my officers bedding roll never did catch up with me). We still dug fox holes; the pup tents kept a little of the water off us and the foxholes from flooding. Though it continued to rain, the men told me there was a noticeable slacking off.

While we were in reserve I was able to get fully acquainted with the men in my Plt as well as some of the other men in F Co. I was struck immediately with the caliber of the people I was serving with. A good percentage of them had received some college education in the Army Specialized Training Program, ASTP.

Foreseeing a need for technically trained people, engineers, doctors, military government specialists, and linguists, not only during the war but in the occupation, the Army had established this specialized college program. The men selected for it were high caliber people. Some had been in college when drafted, others had been screened and found to have high potential as leaders and students, hence assigned to the ASTP. Late in 1944 an urgent requirement for Infantrymen developed. It was suddenly realized that the Army had creamed off most of its top flight personnel, sending them to the Air Corps or the ASTP. There was a shortage of potential small unit leaders, SLs, PSGs, and other junior Ldrs. Combat had taken its toll; the Army had run short of people, not only riflemen but potential leaders. The myth that it takes no brains, training or skill to be an Infantryman was exploded forever. At the same time the need for specialists was found to be greatly overestimated. Reversing previous priorities, many of the ASTP students were transferred to the IN. They made superb soldiers.

F Co was fortunate in having many ex-ASTP men. Perhaps a fourth of the Co had such training. There were a number of them in my Plt with whom I was delighted. This is not to say that the other men in the Plt were less effective. There were many fine soldiers who were not ASTP transferees, as I soon learned. Many of them became close friends; Bob Laird, Ivan Iverson, Bob Neuharth, Wayne Page, Lloyd Sanders were all excellent soldiers; none of them had been in the ASTP. To me the reserve period was truly important as I got to know my men and how they worked. In addition, I met men in other Plts and in the Co HQ: Fitz Cookson, Bill Preece, Arnold Dempewolf. At this time I received the nickname "Si" which everyone used instead of LT Seibert.

While in reserve it was necessary to do much patrolling. We were constantly out checking caves and buildings to make sure that no Japs had been bypassed or that none had infiltrated to our rear. On one patrol we checked out a small valley. Before I realized it we were in the middle of a mine field. Whether to go forward or back, how to handle the situation were the questions which confronted me. I decided to go forward, the forward edge appeared a bit closer than the rear. My men were told of our situation and to carefully close into a single file, stepping where the men ahead did. Gingerly, I picked my way through the mine field, the patrol in file behind me. Fortunately the rains had scoured the earth so that some of the mines were exposed giving me some idea of the pattern. It wasn't the best solution; we should have probed with our bayonets then defused the mines we found. But time was important. There was still some terrain to be checked before we returned in the afternoon. I did not want to abort the mission to clear the mine field. Fortunately, no mines were detonated. The coordinates of the mine field were carefully established and reported in the debriefing. Later an engineer unit cleared the field.

All troops like to test their leaders; mine were no different. While we were cleaning weapons one day, putting a heavy coat of oil on them to prevent rusting, SGT Rylant suddenly grabbed the operating rod of his M-1 rifle and said, "Si, my operating rod is bent, my weapon won't fire. I need a new operating rod. I can't reassemble my rifle with this one."

Knowing that the operating rod was made slightly bent in order to permit assembly of the weapon, it struck me immediately that Rylant was testing me; he was too experienced an Infantryman not to know about the configuration of the operating rod. He was obviously trying to see what I knew about the M-1 and whether I would fall for his gag. Several other men in the vicinity paused to see what my response would be. Feigning concern, I told him that if he did not know how to reassemble his rifle, I would do it for him or get the Armorer from Co HQ to do it. The other men who had listened to the conversation turned away grinning.

While the Bn was in reserve, the XO, MAJ Harbison, was reassigned. He was replaced by a quiet, wiry MAJ from Lead, SD. When he visited F Co, I talked with him about that part of the country; he waxed enthusiastic about the Black Hills. The fact that he worked for the famous Home Stake Gold Mine intrigued me. MAJ Harold V. Christianson visited us frequently; we became good friends.

During this period, the 2nd Bn received a large influx of officers and men returning from the hospital, as well as replacements. F Co was reorganized to assimilate these veterans, many of whom were senior NCOs. Where possible the veterans were returned to their former Plts and positions. As a result, many acting PSGs and SLs were ranked out of their jobs. Rylant was one. TSG Arnold A. Dempewold was transferred to the 2nd Plt. He was a farmer from Kansas with the walk of a plowman and a mid-western drawl. Dempewolf was an experienced and outstanding Infantryman and a natural leader, well known and well liked by the men. We made a good team, I was pleased to have him. Ed Schmitt joined F Co at this time, too.

The 2nd Bn did not remain in reserve long. Back on line we joined with other units in the push to the south. The US Divs were on line across the Island moving south and driving the Japanese into the sea. We were constantly on the alert for a Banzai attack, a suicidal attack to break through our lines to get to the north end of the Island, the most beautiful part of it. There ammo and supplies were stored. One US Army Div was heavily engaged in clearing Japanese guard and supply troops from that end of the Island.

The night we went back on line, for the first time since I had joined F Co, we came under heavy Arty fire. The Japs had a great deal of artillery on Okinawa; in fact, the Island had been an Artillery Training Center for the Japanese Army. But the Jap Arty had been used sparingly. Their Artillery pieces had been dug into the hills. They would be run out on railroad tracks, fired, and then quickly moved back under cover. The Japs knew that US counter-battery fire was devastatingly effective. That evening we came under a sustained barrage; my men said that it was the heaviest barrage they had experienced since they had landed on Okinawa. It is hard to sit in a hole, even though you know that you are relatively safe, and watch the artillery dancing around you. The concussions of the exploding rounds, the blast of heat, the whine of shrapnel, the bright flare of flame as the round explodes, can really get to you. As this was my first experience under enemy Arty, I gritted my teeth and prayed. After 15 or 20 minutes, during which none of the rounds hit any of my positions, the barrage was over and we reverted to our normal night posture.

The days passed rapidly with relatively light combat activity. We moved southward each day, searching area after area, engaging in an occasional fire fight. There were no major attacks, no massive resistance, just a steady grinding toward the southern end of the Island. Some evenings it was extremely difficult to dig in, especially when we stopped on volcanic rock. Other days we were in the middle of old rice paddies or fields of soft dirt where digging was easy. But always we kept moving south. There was no letup in the routine. We were tired all the time. The rain gave way to bright sunshine which baked us as we toiled across the terrain. The tension of combat was present always. This tension was often broken by some inane remark by an unintentional wit such as, "Wonder what's for chow tonight?" which would strike a note, relieving the strain as we laughed. These comedians are priceless as they cause the troops to forget for a second the stress, permit relaxation for a flash, thus yielding a new perspective.

We neared an escarpment made of the Yuza-Dake and Yaeju-Dake hill masses. This escarpment was the last major terrain feature on the Island The north side, which we approached, was steep, about 150 feet in height. The 383rd fought for most of the Yuza-Dake ridge, while the 381st tackled the Yaeju-Dake ridge. The 383rd was so badly mauled that the 382nd was ordered to relieve two of its Bns. The 2nd Bn relieved the 2/383 and the 3rd relieved the 1/383.

The 2/382, initially attached to the 383rd, was to attack in a narrow zone to gain a foot-hold on the escarpment. Leading the assault was F Co, with my Plt providing the point. We had been told during the attack order that we had reached the maximum range of our Artillery and mortars, which were displacing, thus we could expect minimum supporting fires. I was pleased with the role of point Plt. In the short time I had been in combat I had learned that it was better to lead an attack. It appeared to me that after getting beyond the enemy's prearranged defensive fires, the Plt was in comparative safety. This developed my firm belief that success lies forward. Reserves and following units seemed to get more artillery and mortar fire than the lead elements.

The attack went well, we got to the top of the escarpment with no great difficulty, then slipped to the west to permit the rest of the Co and Bn to come on line. We had gone about 50 or 100 yards when we came up against a small raised strip of rocks and dirt. As we started over it we came under intense small arms, sniper and machine gun fire. One of my men was killed instantly, another was wounded. We fell back behind the cover of the knob or ridge. Crawling forward I looked over the situation; there was a completely open field to our front, pock marked with positions, bunkers, foxholes and spider holes, so that the entire area was completely covered with Japanese fire. Immediately calling for Arty or mortar fire, I repositioned the Plt. Bourdeau informed me that no Arty was available at the time because one element was firing a mission and the other was displacing forward. The mortars were already out of range and were also displacing in echelon. There was no fire to support us! We did have the Co 60mm mortars, but they could not help much in this situation.

As the machine gun positions seemed poorly constructed, I called for grenades. There were only three, and only one grenade launcher. So few grenades had been used, that the PLT had gradually stopped carrying them; the launchers had been lost. I had failed to check on the matter since I had assumed command, now my neglect was to be costly. None of the men in the Plt had fired grenades, so I became the grenadier. Since there were no launcher sights, I had to use the field expedient of putting my foot in the sling and measuring the angle with my eye. Surprisingly, I did pretty well; the first round was short and did no damage, but the second and third destroyed two positions.

As I was sighting the second round, the Plt Medic came up behind me and looked over my helmet. There was an instant report from a sniper and the Medic fell. He had been shot squarely between the eyes with deadly accurate fire. He lived for a few minutes but died before he could be evacuated.

It was obvious what the Plt was up against. I called again for supporting fire, Bourdeau told me that none was available but that the 2nd Plt had to keep moving to permit the remainder of the Co and Bn to get into position. I told him it was suicide to take the Plt into that fire and asked if there were any tanks available. None were. Finally Bourdeau came up and looked over the situation As I pointed out the enemy positions which permitted the Japs to cover the area in a cross fire, his radio operator looked over his shoulder. There was a characteristic report and the man fell dead. A sniper round had struck him, too, squarely between the eyes. Bourdeau agreed that it was suicidal to continue; he went back to talk to LTC Sterner to see what could be done. He called shortly, ordering me to move on regardless of the odds. I argued, telling him that I would not feel right if I took my Plt into certain death. Finally he said grimly, "I am giving you a direct order, Si."

"I know you are, Cledith, but I can't obey it. We have to have some support." There was a silence on the radio.

Suddenly Bourdeau appeared, a grave look on his face. "Dammit, Si, move out! That's a direct order. You know what it means if you fail to follow orders in the face of enemy fire."

"1 know, but I'll be damned if I move the Plt into that area without some support."

LTC Sterner arrived just then. "What's the hold up, Cledith?"

"Si thinks we need some support before we move out.

"Look at those positions, Dean. They have us in a cross fire. We have already lost three men. It is suicide to move out there until we knock out some of those positions. We need Artillery or tanks." All the while I was cautiously showing him the many positions we could see from our location. An occasional round kept our heads low.

"I see what you mean, but we have to get this hill and move on. Move out!"

Torn with doubt, I called to the Plt, "Let's move out." I started forward, sensing that some of the men were with me. As we raised above the protection of the knob, a withering fire caused us to fall back behind the little ridge.

"I can't take this Plt out there. You have to get us some support."

Sterner stared at me grimly. "You have violated a lawful order in the face of the enemy. You will have to face the consequences after the campaign is over."

"I realize that. Am I relieved of my Plt?"

"No, you will continue to command. Now let's see what can be done."

While we were discussing ways of getting my Plt through that maze of enemy positions, a single tank suddenly appeared. Immediately Sterner and Bourdeau turned to me and told me that the tank was attached to my platoon.

Quickly, I oriented the tank CDR and told him what I wanted him to do. Fortunately, he could get around the southern end of the small ridge to fire on the enemy machine gun positions. We formed a Tank/Infantry team, my men on both sides of the tank as it moved forward, firing on the

Jap positions. After he had destroyed several of the bunkers he stopped. I got up on the tank deck to determine what was wrong, drawing quite a bit of small arms fire while there. He opened the pistol port to talk to me; the tank itself remained buttoned up. There were two more bunkers I wanted him to destroy; if they were neutralized, my Plt could take care of the foxholes and the rest of the resistance. As I was talking to the LT, the tank gunner spotted something and fired. My ear was about an inch from the barrel of the gun; the concussion knocked me off the tank deck and blasted my ears! It was five days before the ringing stopped and I could hear clearly again. As a result, I have a permanent loss of part of my hearing.

Other than the ringing in my ears I was not hurt. The tank knocked out the two bunkers that I had indicated. My Plt moved out, passed ahead of the tank, then swept over the area. A quick survey of the Jap defensive position revealed that it was a nest of tunnels and pillboxes, completely covered by machine gun fire from positions on the reverse slope of the small ridge behind which we had taken cover. Had we charged over that knob, we would have been taken in the back by those machine guns. I was glad that I had stood fast to protect my Plt; I was sure that it would have been wiped out if I had not refused to move out without support. But I knew the seriousness of having disobeyed an order in combat. For the next month I lived with the dread of what would happen to me when the campaign was over.

Once we had a firm hold on the escarpment we continued to move southward under constant but relatively light resistance. The enemy seemed to have no shortage of ammunition, though Artillery fire was sporadic. Certainly and machine gun fire did not let up and hand grenades were thrown continuously. The effectiveness of hand grenades was demonstrated as we moved down the escarpment. One detonated close to my point man; a piece of shrapnel nicked his neck, cutting either his jugular vein or carotid artery. It took me only seconds to reach him, hoping that I could help, but in that short time he bled to death. Once again I felt the great responsibility for the lives of those fine men I was leading in combat.

After we had progressed only a short distance, the hill mass fell off into a small valley to our right. We were receiving considerable fire from the area, so I requested permission from Bourdeau to clear it. It appeared to be sniper or fire, though there was a possibility that there was one machine gun there. The Regt was readjusting areas of responsibility; the 1/382 was to come up on our right flank to take care of that particular area, which would be in its sector. Bourdeau, therefore, refused permission to clear it. This was dangerous because it left enemy firing in our rear until the 1/382 got the area cleared out. Bourdeau told me that he had passed on the information about the position that we had bypassed.

The next morning the Asst Div CDR (ADC), BG Easley, came up to the position from which I had observed the enemy fire. As he was assessing the situation, he was killed instantly. In my opinion it was very accurate sniper fire, but it may have been machine gun fire, that killed him. Easley was an aggressive ADC, the type of individual who was always up with the troops. He had an obsession for marksmanship; his emphasis on well aimed shots had earned the Division its nickname the Deadeyes. The troops respected him, hence his death was a blow.

Col Macey Dill, The Regt CO, was also frequently up on the front lines with us. A short, wiry, dynamic officer, he urged us forward in a relatively high pitched voice. He, too, was greatly admired by the troops. It was rumored that he had turned down a promotion to BG (possibly after BG Easley's death) in order to fight with the Regt till the end of the campaign. He was the kind of soldier who preferred to fight with the troops on the ground, rather than direct from the rear. LTC Sterner was always up with us, so we had plenty of supervision.

We continued south steadily. One night we dug in at the edge of a large field. Immediately after dark I heard a rustling and movement to our front. Others heard it also. We were not sure if it was Jap soldiers trying to infiltrate, or refugees trying to get through our lines. We could take no chances.

Flares were requested, but revealed nothing. The movement continued when the flares burned out. I ordered my men to fire the next time they heard a noise. Shortly, we heard rustling. Several men fired; at least one round found a target. We heard a moan. Then a baby started to cry, its wails covered all other sounds. The possibility that it was a ruse to lure some of the Americans out of their holes occurred to me. But I was also concerned that under cover of the crying, we might be infiltrated by Japs. Much against my instincts, I ordered the Plt to open fire; we must have killed the youngster, because there were no more cries. Though depressed by the firing at a baby, I believed that it was necessary in order to protect the lives of my men. The next morning we could find nothing in front of the Plt position - no body, no baby, no civilian, no soldier, not even blood stains. Whoever had been there, had been removed before daylight.

We remained alert to the possibility of a final Banzai attack, but did not slow our move south. We reached an open area about 100 yards in depth which we had to cross to get to cover on the far side. Sporadic rifle fire came from the other side of the field. Normally, we moved by fire and movement, taking advantage of any cover that was available. But there was no cover in that field, so I decided to use marching fire. This was the first situation I had encountered in which I thought the use of "assault fire", much touted at FT Benning, was appropriate. I ordered the Plt on line and to move out with marching fire. The men were reluctant to move into the open that way, so I led the way. When they saw me walking forward firing my M-1, they quickly got on line with me, firing rapidly. We kept up a high volume of fire as we moved across the field. It was not uniform at all times; the men had never practiced or used such a technique since basic training; there were spurts and slackenings, but overall the fire was constant. The BARs provided most of the fire, the gunners slowly moving the strike of their bullets from right to left; the M-1 s instinctively increased their rate of fire when the BAR gunners changed magazines. It was the only time I employed marching fire in combat. It got us across the area without casualties, despite the small enemy force located on the far side. We overran their positions, took several prisoners and killed a number Japs.

Still we moved relentlessly south, herding the Japanese toward the sea; crowding them into less and less space; making them more and more desperate. One day we moved into a small rock-studded, tree grown valley. As we advanced, I had an uneasy feeling that something was wrong. I halted the Plt to take stock; the men went into alert positions in accordance with our standard procedure. We reconed the area visually, but saw nothing unusual. Still I had a premonition that something was not right. Sitting on a rock I took off my helmet as usual. (This was a classic joke in my Plt; every time we stopped I took off that damned helmet. Half the time I left it and Laird had to run back to get it for me.)

Fixing our position on the map, I reported our situation to Bourdeau, then ordered the Plt to move out. We moved cautiously because I still had that uneasy feeling. Suddenly, heavy small arms fire was directed on the Plt. Though there appeared to be no machine guns, I decided to pull the Plt back until we got a more accurate assessment of the situation. I ordered the men to fall back to some rocks and rubble. I was the last one to find cover from the enemy fire. Suddenly a bullet struck my cartridge belt in the back. In a one-in-a-million chance it struck the primers of several cartridges (perhaps it struck and fragmented the clip); one clip of cartridges fired, kicking up rocks and dust at my feet. I danced and ran like a rabbit. One of the rounds gouged the heel of my boot, but fortunately none hit me. My cartridge belt was shredded. Once the Plt knew I was not hurt, they howled at my expense.

When I had caught my breath, I took stock. As the firing continued, we were able to pinpoint where it was coming from. One squad was directed to circle the Jap position while the rest of the Plt laid down a base of fire. Soon the maneuvering squad was able to fire into the flanks of the enemy position ending the action. It was a small force; again, we killed several and took a few prisoners.

The Okinawan hillsides were honeycombed with natural caves and burial tombs. The latter were small caves dug in the hillside and faced with stone. Many had elaborate, stone arches and patios built around them. The Okinawans are ancestor worshipers who take great pains with the burial of their dead. The bodies are placed in the tombs until all of the flesh has disintegrated. Then the bones are placed in ceramic or porcelain urns, some very ornate and beautiful. Each tomb is a family shrine. Japanese soldiers used these caves and tombs for defensive positions. They were ideal for this purpose, despite the universal presence of flies, fleas and the often rotting bodies. As it was not uncommon for the Japs to hole up in the tombs, we rarely came upon one that was not searched and blown if time and demolitions were available.

On one occasion we came across a fairly large cave. In accordance with our standard procedure, one of the men threw a grenade into the cave, then went in to check it out. His squad stood ready outside. Suddenly he emerged with a whoop, throwing handsful of 1,000 yen notes in the air. The cave was the office of a Japanese paymaster! He and his clerks were in the cave, most of them wounded (one dead) from the grenade. There also were boxes of Japanese money. We reported our find to Bourdeau, who ordered us to leave things as they were for the intelligence people and continue our mission. We did move on, but not until each of us had seized a sheaf of 1,000 yen notes. We took them as souvenirs, not realizing they had any monetary value. I sent many home in letters to friends and relatives. Since I censored the Plt mail, I noted that many of the men did likewise.

Another time, we came to the crest of a hill which sloped gently southward. A number of tombs were dug in the slope, too many to stop to blow. I decided to move ahead. As we passed the line of tombs, we received fire from one large and ornate one. Fortunately, no one was wounded. Immediately deploying the Plt, I ordered one of the SLs, SGT Rose, to throw a satchel charge into the tomb.

Rose quickly ran in front of the tomb entrance, threw a satchel charge, and hit the ground. Instantly, the satchel charge was thrown out of the tomb, detonating harmlessly in the open. Rose armed another, ran across the top of the tomb and repeated the procedure; he threw it in, the Japs threw it out; this time the charge exploded in the air, again without doing any damage. A third time Rose ran across the tomb entrance throwing in a charge; again it was thrown out.

By this time I was concerned for Rose's safety since he had exposed himself so often and had set a pattern. There was a good possibility that someone inside the tomb would try to pick him off; on the previous attempts there had been scattered shots fired from the tomb at him, I called to him to throw a white phosphorous grenade in first, then throw in the satchel charge. Just as Rose began his fourth run across the entrance of the tomb, four sabers were thrown out. Rose had pulled the pin from the white phosphorous grenade and armed the satchel charge before he started his run. He tossed in the grenade, stooped down, grabbed the sabers, then threw the satchel charge. This time it detonated and destroyed the tomb and the Japs in it.

Rose clutched the four sabers as he returned to his squad. He gave two to the men who had assisted him, but kept the best two, one a fine samurai. Shortly after this action he was wounded for the fifth time. When he was evacuated he was separated from his souvenirs and personal belongings. I was not in his vicinity when he was evacuated, so was unable to take care of his personal effects. It was unfortunate because he deserved those souvenirs.

Censoring mail was one of the required duties no officer liked to perform. I was always uncomfortable reading the personal mail of my men. In F Co, each Plt Ldr censored the mail of the men in his Plt. It was amazing how or when the men found time to write, minutes taken in breaks, just at dawn before we moved out or just before darkness. Every day I was handed several letters to censor. I felt it incumbent upon me to do it as soon as possible, so that was usually my last task before dark. After I had made my final check of the Plt to insure that adequate holes had been dug, that everyone had received food, water and ammo, I would take out letters carried in a plastic bag in my pack.

Mail was censored to insure that no unauthorized information was sent to family and friends which might result in the compromise of operations or in identifying dead before the family had been officially notified. I could understand the need for it when troop movements were imminent, especially overseas movements. But the day-to-day operations we were conducting could not be compromised. Nonetheless, the requirement existed. Like most censors, I soon got to know my men well enough so that I was sure who would write about unauthorized matters and who would not. On the envelopes of the letters from the men who could be depended on not to reveal impermissible information, I noted, "Censored by Donald A. Seibert, 1st LT Inf" and sent them on without reading them. There were some men, however, who invariably talked about forbidden subjects. These men seemed to write the longest, and in many cases the most personal and embarrassing letters. As if realizing they were writing for an audience, they would reveal intimate details of their lives. One wrote 15 page letters telling his wife in the most graphic and explicit detail what he planned to do on his first night home. Interspersed with this personal pornography would be comments about operations, men killed and other proscribed matters. These had to be cut out with a razor blade. If any officers found enjoyment or satisfaction in reading the letters of their men, I never met them. It was a matter which was never discussed between us. The contents of our soldiers letters were held confidential. There was an occasional wag who would include a parenthetical note to the censor, but most of the mail was written without thought for him.

Souvenirs were eagerly sought after. As mentioned before, the most prized were sabers and flags (which Nipponese soldiers carried wrapped around their waists). Some of these flags were lovingly stitched by wives, mothers or sweethearts and contained the symbolic "thousand stitches". I was never lucky enough to get either souvenir. The men raced to search each dead soldier, becoming elated when an authorized and valued souvenir was obtained. I could never bring myself to race the men for a souvenir, nor would I ask for one. Even when some of the men tried to barter prized souvenirs for money or other things, I could not enter into it. On one occasion the 2nd Plt overran an enemy Arty OP. Much of the equipment was still in place. I picked up a Jap aiming circle, an exact copy of the one used in the US Army. I wrapped it in my jungle sweater, put it in my pack, and have it to this day. After another fire fight, I gingerly picked up an unexploded knee mortar round. Our Armorer was an expert at inactivating such rounds and made it a safe souvenir for me.

We continued south. Our advance took on the aspect of a mopping up operation rather than an assault. More and more prisoners were taken as many of the enemy began to realize the futility of their resistance. Many extracted from caves had old wounds. Our advance continued.

We finally reached the last of the high ground and could almost smell and see the sea and the southern tip of the Island. We were continually warned about the possibility of a Banzai attack, but none developed. About the 18th of June, we approached a small town, Aragachi. The Div fought for it for several days. Finally it fell under the assault of three battalions (one of them the 2/82) supported by heavy Artillery and Naval gun fire. In the afternoon we made a coordinated Tank/Infantry sweep through the town. The troops took up a modified marching fire formation supported by the tanks. One of my squads, under SGT Whitaker, had six of its eight men wounded in a skirmish with eight Japs trying to blow up one of the tanks. All of the Japs were killed in that action.

That night was one of the most frustrating and bloodcurdling ones that I spent in combat. We dug in on the outskirts of the town after turning in our prisoners and rendering reports. There was a good deal of enemy equipment in our area. One of my men, a farmer who was adept in making balky tractors run, managed to start a Nip truck. The men asked me if we could keep it to carry our packs, water and their souvenirs. I shrugged. I knew that we would eventually have to give it up, but we could enjoy the luxury of our personal transportation until it taken from us.

Our position for the night was located just forward of a water hole. After designating the squad positions, I walked to my right flank to tie in with the left flank Plt of the 3/382. After the Plt Ldr and I exchanged the usual information and banalities, I settled down for the night. It was nearing dark. As I looked at the slope opposite us, we were on one side of a wide, shallow valley, I saw moving figures. The men on the slope opposite us seemed to be forming a line, getting ready to come our way. It was hard to distinguish what was actually going on in the dusk. I looked again, then called the Arty FO who happened to be in my Plt area, pointed to the opposite slope and asked, "Is that the Banzai attack coming?"

He looked, becoming as excited as I was. "Sure looks like it to me."

I took one more look, then suggested, "Let's get some Artillery on it."

Meanwhile I called Bourdeau to report the sighting. The FO checked his map, then called for a Time on Target (TOT) concentration on the area. The Direct Support (DS) Artillery Bn had a concentration plotted on the area. When the FO described the target as a possible Banzai attack, it was given a Corps TOT concentration. Fortunately only one or two rounds were fired before somebody called CEASE FIRE. We almost put a Corps TOT on the 305th IN {attached to the 96th Div from the 77th Div), which was moving into position. Word had not been passed down about this disposition. Fortunately, no one was hurt. After sorting out the lines, we resumed our usual night posture.

During the night, Japs kept sneaking up to the hole for water. One man, under the supervision of TSG Dempewolf, killed five of them at the site. Some time later in the night or early morning Japs infiltrated our position. One jumped into a foxhole and began to fight, hand-to-hand, two Americans for it. One of the men, a small, dark-haired guy, grabbed his and swung with all his might. He hit the Jap on the head, breaking the stock and killing the Nip. The two men dumped the body outside the foxhole until morning.

Two days later, 22 June, 10th Army declared that organized resistance on Okinawa had ended. The 383rd still had several days of hard fighting in its area, but the 382nd IN Regt and the rest of the 96th IN Div began the final mopping up. We reversed direction and started back north. This time we were in a broader formation. We had a multiple mission, to locate, flush out, capture or kill any enemy bypassed during the fighting south, to seal all caves and tunnels, to recover all Japanese and usable US equipment, and to bury enemy dead. This last was done as a sanitary measure. So many Jap soldiers had been killed in the last ten days of the fighting that it had been impossible to remove the bodies for identification and burial. Now these bodies were blackened and bloated, swarming with flies. Maggots were eating the flesh away; every attempt to move a body resulted in the rupture of taut skin permitting the escape of foul smelling gas. It was impossible to recover, identify or give proper burial to all of the enemy dead, hence, it was difficult to estimate the number of unidentified bodies we placed in unmarked graves. Certainly we could not account for all the enemy missing and presumed dead in our area.

Distasteful as this burial task was, it had to be done. About ten days were spent in this final sweep to bury Japanese dead, flush out hidden enemy and recover equipment. There were occasional fire fights as fanatic Nipponese sought "honorable death" rather than surrender. Some bodies and equipment were booby trapped. These last days of combat on Okinawa took its toll of American soldiers; these casualties were all the more difficult to accept now that the Island was "secure".

The truck we had commandeered was very handy to carry supplies, tools and equipment, to haul prisoners to the POW collecting points and for other purposes. Finally we were ordered to turn it in. The men wanted to conceal it, to be recovered later, but the truck was turned in as ordered.

After the 382nd had policed its sector, it moved to a bivouac area to await further orders. The 96th Div, an amphibious Div, was alerted as one of the units selected for the initial assault landing in the invasion of Japan; plans were made to go to the Philippines to train and marshal for the invasion.

During this period in the rest area, the soldiers' infatuation with sports reasserted itself. Almost every free minute, the men were playing some game, softball, volleyball and touch football were the favorites. Every company had a recreation chest containing such items as softball bats, balls and gloves, volleyballs and nets, and footballs. If a game could not be organized, men tossed a football or threw softballs to each other. No matter how tired the troops were when free time occurred, there seemed to be unlimited energy for these sports. There was interest in other sports, horseshoes, basketball, baseball, but they did not hold the same attraction that softball, volleyball and touch football did. Throughout my military career the unceasing lure these three sports had for American soldiers continued to amaze me.

While we were in the rest area, orders were published awarding me the Combat Infantryman Badge (CIB). I was proud to have earned it. The Combat Infantryman Badge was awarded to troops in and forward of the Regimental area, after a minimum of 30 days in combat and under enemy fire. If an infantryman had been wounded, the 30 day requirement was waived. Though not given lightly, it was conferred on all Infantry troops who qualified for it. It seemed to me that Artillery FO Parties might be given the CIB. They shared the Infantryman's fortunes and were always with us in fire-fights, but the CIB was given only to Infantrymen until the war in Vietnam.

In the bivouac area a great deal of time was spent on the paperwork that had been neglected. Letters of condolence had to be written, a difficult task for any commander. Bourdeau asked me to draft many of the letters for his signature. One letter was particularly hard for both of us; it was in response to one received from the family of the soldier who had been left on Hector Hill. Apparently some thoughtless soldier who had been evacuated wrote to the family, telling them that their son had been wounded and abandoned - that he was alive when his Plt had withdrawn. The parents wrote an angry letter calling Bourdeau and the members of F Co murderers for abandoning a wounded comrade. It made Bourdeau and the men of the Co, particularly the individual's Plt Ldr who had been badly wounded, depressed, not only because great risks had been taken attempting to evacuate the body, but also because a soldier had heedlessly caused the family such anguish.

It was a difficult letter to write, but since I had recovered the body, I was in a position to tell the facts. These were fully explained; in addition, the family was given a brief account of the circumstances surrounding the attack, based on reports from the PSG and others in the Plt, as well as what I had seen when we recovered the body. I stressed that their son had not been abandoned while he was still living; that he was dead at the time of the withdrawal; that to send men back to recover a body in the face of the opposition confronting F Co at that time would have risked more lives, possibly resulting in more deaths. In fact, at one point during the campaign it was Division Policy that unless the body of a soldier could be recovered without risk to other soldiers, it would be left - bypassed until later on.

Another letter from the father of a soldier whose son had been wounded, excoriated the Army for putting his son into combat without proper training. He wrote that the type of basic training the men had gotten at Camp Roberts was inadequate. The only response to such a letter was to point out the thousands of other Infantrymen trained at that Camp who survived combat without being wounded.

All units used this period to write recommendations for awards. Bourdeau made me the Awards and Decorations Officer for F Co. Awards were submitted for gallantry in action, as well as for meritorious service. Proud of my Plt's performance in combat, I was pleased to have a hand in rewarding them for their courage and dedication. One of the first was a recommendation for the Silver Star for SGT Don Pauley for his action in blowing up the Japanese positions on Hector Hill. I was delighted when it was approved. Initially, awards for gallantry were given priority over those for meritorious service. Most of the awards were for Bronze Star with "V" device (the lowest award for valor), but a number were for Silver Stars. The Silver Star recommendation had to be accompanied by a statement from at least one eye witness. Other recommendations for Silver Stars I was happy to write were ones for SGT Rose for his tomb incident, for 1LT Bill Stocks for his action near Kochi (before I joined F Co) and for SGT Loren Heaton. All of my recommendations for the Silver Star were approved except the one for SGT Rose; he was awarded a Bronze Star with "V". TSG Dempewolf was awarded a Bronze Star with "V" for his action at the water hole outside Aragachi.

The matter of awards became quite an undertaking. COL Dill had been at Div HQ when several of the "rear echelon" troops, including the Div Information and Education (I&E) OFF, had been awarded the Bronze Star Medal for meritorious service. Upon his return from that ceremony he held an Officers' Call at which he told us that if Div HQ Troops earned Bronze Star Medals, then every man in his Regt deserved one. He directed a major effort to see that his men were recognized. We started cranking out recommendations for awards. There had to be a specific action or service to justify a recommendation, but many were "stretched" to meet the criteria for the Bronze Star Medal. For some reason which still escapes me, most of the recommendations I wrote were approved, hence I achieved quite a reputation.

At this time I first became aware that Clarence Craft, the individual who had been on the ridge line on Hen Hill firing down into the trenches, had been recommended for the Medal of Honor (MOH). It amazed me that no one had asked me for a statement because I was probably closer to him than most of the people in his own Co. It incensed me that he was being credited for many of the Japs the 2nd Plt had killed on the reverse slope of Hen hill firing to his rear to protect him. When I questioned the matter, I was told to stop my carping, the decision had been made to recommend Craft for the MOH, which was thought to be deserved. I did not want to take credit from Craft, but I wanted the men in my Plt to get the credit they deserved. During a particularly heated discussion on this matter, someone at Bn HQ told me that I had been recommended for the Silver Star for the action on Hector Hill. It immediately occurred to me that I was being recommended for the Silver Star to shut me up, thinking that I would not protest the award for Craft if it would jeopardize my award. At once, I told Bourdeau and the Bn Adj that I did not deserve the award; that there were men in my Plt who deserved one far more than I did; certainly I did not want an award under the circumstances.

Bourdeau told me he had recommended me for the Silver Star when Craft was being considered for the Distinguished Service Cross (DSC) before the decision had been made to recommend him for the MOH. He thought I had earned it. As the recommendation had to be considered by a Div Awards Board, I was sure it would be disapproved so I dropped the issue, having made my point. I did not want to do anything to influence any one else's award, particularly Craft's, whose action I thought deserved recognition; all I wanted was credit for the men in my Plt, which I thought equally deserved. Craft was awarded the Medal of Honor which he had certainly earned.

One day MAJ "Dog" Carter came over from the 1st Bn to ask me to write up a recommendation for a DSC for Bourdeau for an action on Leyte. He had heard about my reputation in getting awards approved, hence he had sought me out. He said that he would provide the two eye- witness accounts if I would write it up. I had the highest regard for Cledith Bourdeau as a man, as a soldier, and as a commander, so I was more than delighted to do so. In a short time we heard the Bourdeau's DSC had been approved.

When 1SG Hawkins left F Co, a young ASTP soldier, SGT Bill Preecs, who had understudied him, took over as 1SG. Preecs was energetic, enthusiastic and likeable, far better suited to handle the Co at this particular time. He learned quickly and did an outstanding job.

While we were busy with awards, Bob Nims, one of the doctors who had been with me on *LST 810* on the trip from Saipan, called. He was with an Arty Bn on the tip of the Island and asked me to visit his unit, spend the night, have a drink and share my experiences with him. Bourdeau had no objections; our jeep driver (there was only one jeep in an amphibious Co) took me to Bob's unit on the rocky shore. When Bob heard about our adventures on the Yuza Dake/Yaeju Dake, he suggested we go out to look at the area. An avid photographer, he offered to take pictures of it for me. He got a jeep and driver from his unit in which we retraced the line of F Co's attack. He took many good pictures, including one of the monument erected in memory of BG Easley on the site on which he had been killed. Before returning to his unit, Bob suggested we go to the base of the escarpment to find the site of my Plt's ascent. Bob directed the driver to the location using my map. Without difficulty we found the path to the top of the hill mass and stopped the jeep. Just as I jumped from the vehicle two Japs popped up and ran around a small knoll. Without a second thought I grabbed my rifle and went after them. Fortunately Bob Nims, although a Medic, was an expert man. He had been on the team in college and had a carbine with him, which he grabbed as he followed me, backing me up. The fugitives disappeared for a moment. As I jumped over a ditch to follow their trail, I looked down and saw them in it. Aware that I had spotted them, they immediately jumped up, cocking their arms to throw grenades. Both Bob and I fired, killing them before they could lob the grenades. The jeep driver was upset about the incident; as a Medic, he had not volunteered to get into this sort of combat. But Bob was elated that he had been in on the kill of two of the enemy.

On returning to the Arty Bn, Bob had quite a party, serving "GI Cocktails" (straight government issue (GI) alcohol with fruit juice) during which he related the story of our afternoon adventure several times. Bob Nims was a likeable person; the evening spent with him was enjoyable. His pictures turned out fine.

Back at F Co, I was told that I had been transferred to E Co. Several of the F Co OFFs who had been wounded returned from the hospital, making me surplus. I protested that if we were going to fight another campaign I wanted to do it with my 2nd Plt of F Co. I had gotten to know and depend on the men in my Platoon and had confidence in Bourdeau as a Co CO. Bourdeau wanted to keep me, but he could not deny the former OFFs their place in F Co. CPT Porter, CO of E Co, did not inspire the same esteem I had for Bourdeau; with great reluctance I moved to my new organization, determined to do my best for my new Company and Commander.

Following my transfer to E Co, Bourdeau came over to ask if I would write up an award for MAJ Carter as a favor for him. I told him I would be happy to do so. He outlined exactly the same incident that Carter had used to justify Bourdeau's DSC; he even had similar affidavits. When I pointed this out to Bourdeau, he explained that the two of them had been together during the action and that Carter had contributed to it as much as he had. The eye-witness statements he had only confirmed Bourdeau's heroism. The situation did not seem proper to me, so I refused to write up that particular award. There was no question that Bourdeau deserved his DSC, but I believed he was showing misguided loyalty in trying to get one for Carter. Someone else wrote up the citation resulting in the award of the DSC to Carter. It was explained to me that there were many cases of this sort in which two people involved in an incident received identical awards for it. It still smacked of collusion to me, so I was glad I had no part in it.

Early in July we received word that the Deadeyes were going to the Island of Mindoro in the Philippines. The beaches there were similar to those we were to face in Japan. On Mindoro we would practice beach landings and get organized and reconstituted for the assault on Japan. The move was to be by LST convoy. As Co E XO, I was appointed the Transport Quartermaster (TQM). Most officers in the Div had gone to TQM school at San Luis Obispo before leaving for the Pacific, hence it was a routine duty for them. Because I had not attended such a school, I had to learn the hard way.

The TQM's job was to prepare the loading plan so that troops and equipment were put on the LST in the proper order to be off-loaded as needed for combat on the beach. Since Mindoro was secure, it would be an administrative move; we would not be combat loaded, so the job was comparatively simple.

After consulting with the LST Captain and his officers I made the plan. All of E Co, most of F Co, and part of the Bn HQ were to be with us. MAJ C.C. Crall, who had replaced MAJ Christianson as the Bn XO, would be on our LST, LTC Sterner would be on the other LST assigned to the 2nd Bn. Sterner was not with us because the LST assigned to E Co was the Flotilla Command Ship with the Commander and his staff aboard. As a result, there were few officer billets available. In fact the Captain of the LST, a Navy LT, had yielded his Quarters to the Flotilla CDR and had to use another cabin. He managed to find a cabin for MAJ Crall, and most of the Army CPTs were in "Officers' Country", but all Army LTs were in petty officers quarters. Most of the men, except for the most senior NCOs, would bunk on the tank deck of the LST. The cargo would be stored forward near the landing ramp. This cargo was mostly C Rations, a few vehicles and Co supplies. The center of the hold, or tank deck, was to be the dormitory, with cots set up. The crew rigged tarps on the main deck to shield the troops from the sun; most of the men would sleep there unless there was bad weather.

Upon approval of my plan we began to organize for the move. Suddenly, orders were issued to load immediately for an early departure. A typhoon warning had been received and the Naval Command wanted to get the LSTs off the beach and out to sea before it struck. The loading was rushed with the result that we did not do as good a job as we should have. Nonetheless, all personnel and equipment were hastily loaded, so much so that the troops were still tying down the cargo as the LST began to move. In getting under way, powerful winches pulled against the anchor to assist in getting off the beach.

The typhoon struck soon after we put out to sea. Riding out that storm was a terrifying experience! There were high winds, torrential rains, and mountainous waves. Naturally, the men had to stay off the deck. Waves washed overboard everything not tied or bolted down. The men suffered below, not only from the motion of the ship, translated directly to their area, but also for lack of ventilation. The odors of gasoline, diesel fuel, stale bodies, mildewed canvas and other unpleasant aromas, combined with a lack of fresh air, did as much to make the men sick and nauseated as did the rough seas.

The LST climbed to the crest of a wave, hesitated, hanging over the top, shuddering, while the bow seemed to waggle, almost as if the ship would break in two at the middle. Then it would plunge with a sickening drop into the trough below. This was accompanied by loud buckling and cracking sounds which were magnified in the tank deck where the troops huddled. Some of the waves were as high as the top of the mast of the LST, at least 60 feet. It was a harrowing experience for land-lubbers who were convinced that the ship would break into several pieces any moment.

After three days of high winds there was a sudden calm, almost as frightening as the storm. The waves were still mountainous, but the wind stopped. The men could get on deck for a bit of fresh air as we passed through the eye of the typhoon. Then the storm struck anew with slashing rain and howling winds. The men were confined again to the fetid tank deck. I shared some of their discomfit as I periodically inspected the cargo to insure that none of it shifted during the gyrations of the ship, or talked with them to try to take their minds from their misery and fear.

Unpleasant as was our situation on board the LST, we were thankful for being at sea when we heard of the devastation the typhoon wreaked on Okinawa. Most of the shore installations were leveled. What tents and shacks had not been taken down were blown away. Many ships were hurled far up on the beach by the tidal waves; destruction and death were wide-spread.

After the typhoon experience we settled down to enjoy the trip as much as we could. The Army had the run of the ship, with only minimum duties. The GIs pulled KP for our own troops, although we OFFs ate in the ward room. We also provided cleaning and guard details. Army OFFs inspected the cargo, cabins and compartments used by our personnel. One of my duties was to inspect the cargo daily. During one inspection I found that some of the C Ration cases had been opened. Apparently the men were snacking on them, which amazed me because Navy chow, especially on this LST, was good.

The remainder of the trip was fairly comfortable. Except for the hostility between the Flotilla Commander and his staff and the Captain of the LST and the ship's complement, it would have been enjoyable. Unfortunately, as a result of that acrimony the Army OFFs were involved, courted by each faction to get at the other.

A few days after the ordeal of the typhoon had passed, we were suddenly awakened by the clanging of bells and hoot of sirens. "General Quarters!" Feet pounded on the metal decks, hatchways slammed closed and battened down. Army personnel had no function during "General Quarters", we were locked in compartments or the tank deck with no information about what was going on. When the LST secured from "General Quarters" we were told that the escort had contacted an enemy submarine which had launched at least one torpedo at the convoy. No ship was hit.

The daily news broadcasts became rampant with rumors of peace negotiations. One day it seemed the Japanese were on the verge of surrender, the next day it was all denied. Then on the 6th of August came the electrifying news that an "atomic bomb" had been dropped on Hiroshima. The troops, certain that the war was at an end, discussed nothing but the super bomb for the next few days. Three days later, excitement escalated with the news that another "atomic bomb" had been dropped on Nagasaki. A great cheer arose on 14 August when it was announced that the Japanese had surrendered unconditionally. The ship's whistle blew; some of the antiaircraft guns on the escorts were fired, the troops were ecstatic! This meant we would not have to make the amphibious assault on the coast of Japan; we now awaited our arrival at Mindoro with impatience.

During the voyage, I convinced MAJ Crall to transfer me back to F Co. Once ashore, I would revert to my familiar unit and comrades. I was indeed happy.

When the convoy reached Mindoro shortly after the middle of August, the calm seas, the lush green jungles, the clear blue skies, seemed a fantasy world after that voyage through the typhoon. Our assigned Regt area was in a flat meadow along a small river. Squad tents had been pitched by an advance party, arranged in Co groups. But there was much else to do. Many of the tents were rotten and leaked, but each man had a cot and mosquito bar. Ponchos were rigged to divert leaking water from the sleeping men. We quickly added "niceties", latrines were screened and roofed for protection against both the blazing sun and the predictable afternoon rain shower.

The ingenuity of the American soldier is boundless. I am always amazed at what he can do to make himself comfortable. Salvaged airplane wing tanks were converted into showers, wash stands were improvised from helmets. Fifty-five gallon drums were used for many things, burn-out latrines, clothes washing tubs, even bath tubs! Lumber was scrounged from sources which escaped me, soon there were tables, chairs, flooring and shelving in the tents. Within 10 days, given a little freedom of action and a minimum of equipment, the men had a complete and comfortable camp.

The awards writing culminated when we reached Mindoro. There was a flurry to get the last awards written and approved. The Bronze Star with "V" I had written up for Fred Steed was disapproved. When rewritten with more gore and adjectives, it was approved for a Silver Star. It was well deserved and should have been written that way in the beginning. While I was away from the Island, an awards ceremony was held on the air strip. There was some grumbling as almost every other man called out to receive an award was from F Co. When I returned someone chided me about having an in with the Awards Committee. "Wait until I get Ken Kone his CIB. Then you'll really appreciate my clout!" A muttered imprecation was the only response. Ken was a newly commissioned 2LT who had joined the Bn on Okinawa after the Island was declared secure.

We soon settled into a routine. We did minimal housekeeping, kept a guard on our area and did a bit of patrolling. Since the war was over, there was no need for a major military training program. One of the features of this era was the Information and Education (I&E) Program. There was a serious effort by the Army to bring the troops up to date on news and issues and to direct their thinking toward post-war problems. In addition to my other duties, I became the F Co I&E Officer The ASTP men contributed much to the debates. Some sessions covered controversial subjects such as post-war planning, individual aspirations and the atomic bomb. I learned more from the deliberations than the men did. My job was to introduce the subject, presenting some background material from pamphlets provided, then lead the discussion. I tried not to become too involved in the arguments, but encouraged everyone to air his views. I also tried to keep the discussions on track.

Other than those few duties and the I&E program, time was spent in recreation. A comprehensive sports program, built around softball, volleyball and touch football was first on the agenda. Softball and volleyball tournaments were the order of the day. The softball program probably appealed most to the EM. Each Co team competed in a Bn Championship playoff. The best teams from each Bn vied for Regt championships, these in turn played for the Deadeye Crown. The Div HQ field was lighted for night games. Uniforms were made from cut off fatigues, cut down combat boots and T-shirts with unit insignia stenciled on them. Great enthusiasm and support was generated throughout the Division.

In addition to the Deadeye League, there was wild interest in the 1945 World Series between the Chicago Cubs and the Detroit Tigers. Mindoro and the United States were on opposite sides of the International Date Line, therefore entire units would get up at 0300 to hear the game being played the night before. There were many large bets on the outcome of the games.

Swimming parties were organized and the men trucked to nearby beaches. Movies were shown every night, though we frequently saw the same film twice in a week. Several USO shows visited the Island. The Division Engineers built an amphitheater on a hillside that could seat a thousand troops. A visiting company put on *Oklahoma* there, a great show, well done, and especially welcome at the time.

The Red Cross established a recreation center called "Fatigue Junction" in a sugar mill in the village near our camp. The enlisted men used this whenever they could get away from their companies. Gambling, while officially condemned, was tacitly condoned.

Despite these activities, the troops were bored. They wanted to go home, all else was secondary now that the war was over. They looked for other diversions.

Across the river were the houses of a number of Filipinos. As might be expected, some of the women presented themselves for prostitution. I went over to see what was attracting the men. It was not pretty. One woman, about 30 years old and not particularly nice-looking, was lying on an air mattress she had apparently bought from one of the GIs. She had a towel over her middle which she would flip aside. A man would get on after paying her 10 or 20 pesos. She really kept up a fast pace, I am not sure how many she took on in an hour. The venereal disease rate soared. Our Bn Surgeon, CPT Fisher, wanted to inspect the prostitutes and mark the bellies of those who had a venereal disease with silver nitrate or some other permanent marking, but the Chaplains thought that improper. Fisher and his asst,lLT Goldman (MAC) were kept busy. COL Dill was determined to find another outlet for his men.

A week or so after our arrival on Mindoro, LTC Sterner sent for me. This was the long-dreaded summons to account for my actions on Yuza Dake. Dempewolf was with me when I received word that LTC Sterner wanted to see me.

"What's he want, Si?"

"I guess its about the time I wouldn't move the Plt without support on the last escarpment. There were spider holes and Jap positions all over the place. Bourdeau's radio operator and the Medic had been hit between the eyes by snipers. It was suicide to go out there. I wanted either Artillery or tank support. Sterner did not want to wait for either. He gave me a direct order to move the Plt and I refused. A tank came up a short time later and knocked out most of the positions and we moved on. Sterner told me when I refused to move that he would court-martial me."

"Hell, Si, he told me the same thing and never did it. He sent me and five others out on a patrol with one of those damn SCR 300s. A tank had gone out a short time before and been blown up by Jap Artillery. We were sent out to observe. There wasn't any cover. We went out a ways and all of us got that uneasy feeling. There was just no place to hide; not a damn bit of cover or concealment. So we asked to come in. Sterner said, 'No, stay out and observe.' I said, 'If you wanna see what's out here come see for yourself, and we'll come back in.' Sterner met us and said, 'I'll have you court-martialed'.

I reported the whole thing to Bourdeau, who says, 'You didn't!' 'I did.' Just then Bourdeau was called in to see Sterner. When he got back he called me in and says, 'Sterner is going to court-martial you when we get back to the rest area. And no Silver Star for you.' But nothin' ever come of it. Same with you, Si. He ain't gonna do nothin 'cept chew your ass."

Despite Dempewolfs encouragement, I reported to LTC Sterner at Bn HQ with foreboding. Sterner told me to sit down and began to talk about various things. Eventually he got around to the action on the Yuza-Dake Hill Mass. He reviewed it for both of us and told me that I was absolutely wrong. I admitted that I was. He said that he had considered what action to take against me. He felt that my refusal of an order in combat warranted some action, but after wrestling with his conscience and in view of my subsequent conduct and performance in combat, he concluded that this was an isolated case. In the heat of combat I had acted rashly and the circumstances were a bit cloudy. He admitted that I had probably saved a number of lives as a result of my stubbornness. On balance he had decided to take no action on the matter, which was now a closed issue. I heaved a sigh of relief, saluted and left.

Many local Filipinos came into our Co area during the day. The men hired them to do some of the unpleasant chores; burning out latrines, digging garbage pits, washing clothes. Almost every native who came into the area carried a small tin pail. After each meal they would line up and ask for left over food. Though our food became better as frozen vegetables and meat arrived, the men ate little. Because of the inactivity, the heat, the monotonous fare, the men did not need the heavy meals the Army provided. As a result there was a great deal of waste. These leftovers provided meals for many local families for several months until they could re-establish their lives.

All of F Co personnel chipped in and bought a cow. It was scrawny and bony, but we thought we would have a couple of good meals of fresh meat from it. The Medics were not happy, they had no idea whether or not the animal was diseased, but they did not stop us. Our cooks butchered the cow one afternoon; the men were looking forward to the first feast. That evening, several nurses came to the Officers' Club (a squad tent in the Regt HQ area) to visit. F Co officers seemed to attract them, because we eventually had five of them at our table. Bourdeau, who did not drink, suggested that we go to the mess hall for steaks. He invited the nurses; about ten or twelve people drifted down to the Co mess tent. The cooks soon had the ranges going, they cooked up some very tasty steak sandwiches on good GI bread. Later, Dempewolf told me that as a result of that midnight snack, there were not enough steaks for all the men who resented it very much. Bourdeau had been a good Commander in combat, but this did not set well with the troops.

G Co not to be outdone, decided that they would also get some fresh meat. They sent out a raiding party which stole a cow, they thought. It turned out to be a water buffalo whose meat was stringy and tough. Carabaos were valuable animals; a complaint was lodged against the Army for the loss of the buffalo. G Co had to pay for it.

Because of the help 1SG Preecs and his Co Clerk, CPL Clyde Phillips, gave to one family, they were invited to a barbecue. The invitation urgently requested that the Co OFFs attend also. It was to be a gala affair, a combination victory celebration, birthday party, and back to work ceremony. Bill Preecs urged Bourdeau and the rest of the officers to go. We decided we would. The affair was to be held at a house deep in the jungle; the way to it entailed wading at least one river and a trek through the jungle.

Setting out late in the afternoon, with a change of clothes and some candy and other food in waterproof bags, we arrived at the site of the festivities about 1700. We were astonished to find there three large spits over a huge bed of coals. On one was a pig, on another a lamb, and on the third, a calf. The aroma was mouth-watering. Donning our dry clothes, we greeted our host, offering our gifts. Our host was a chemist who had managed the sugar plant and distillery in San Jose, the principal village on the Island. He had made a batch of whisky (alcohol) which he offered to us. There were cokes, brought by Preecs and Phillips for the non-drinkers including Bourdeau, Foley, Steed and both Preecs and Phillips. The rest of us drank the hard liquor. A lime tree in the yard provided variety to the alcohol and water; we had only to reach out, pick one, squeeze it into the glass for a tasty drink. There was also coconut milk, too sweet with alcohol for me.

We ate inside. The houses were on stilts, as much to keep out animals as to keep them out of the floods during the monsoons. The bamboo slats with which the houses were floored were highly polished; the host apologetically asked us to remove our boots before climbing into his home. The food, served by the women, consisted of thick, luscious cuts of meat, light bread made of rice flour, cooked rice, and local vegetables including scallions and small hot red peppers. A most enjoyable feast, a welcome change from our own fare. How we made our way back in the dark, especially after drinking so much , remains unclear. But we returned without incident.

Shortly after the 96th Div reached Mindoro, each officer received a liquor ration, about six bottles of assorted whisky, for which we of course paid. Taking three of my bottles, I went to the tents in which my Plt slept and gave them to TSG Dempewolf. One bottle was opened; after I had a drink with my men, I left. They enjoyed the whisky so much, I sent down another bottle. Much as I liked to drink, I thought it should be shared with my men.

A few weeks after we had landed on Mindoro, high point men began to rotate back to the United States. Dempewolf was one of the first to go. I missed that salty farmer when he left. Many officers left also; when LTC Sterner rotated MAJ Crall assumed command of the 2/382. The remaining men became even more impatient to get home.

Just at this time, word came in from some Filipino that the wreckage of an aircraft which had crashed early in the war was in the hills northeast of our camp. The 382nd was ordered to recover the remains of the crew if possible. The 2nd Plt of F Co was selected for the mission.

Departing early in the morning with a Filipino guide and a very poor map of the area, we had only a general idea of the location of the wreckage. We carried body bags, water, rations, machetes and weapons, a fairly heavy load for that hot, humid climate. Cutting a trail through the jungle was slow, hot work, especially since I determined to make a fairly wide path in the event we had to carry back remains or personal effects.

About 1030 there was a great thumping and crashing behind us; we halted to determine what was going on. The F Co jeep appeared, maneuvering with great difficulty over the primitive trail we had cut. Another F Co Plt Ldr jumped out as the vehicle reached us. He announced that he was to relieve me on this mission, freeing me to report immediately to the Regt CDR. He had no other information about what was going on, only that it wasn't bad. He assumed charge of the patrol as I got into the jeep to return to base camp.

When I got back to F Co about 1130, tired, dirty and sweaty, Bourdeau would not let me take time to wash up. He said the Regt CO wanted to see me immediately. I reported to COL Dill in his tent; he asked me to sit down. "Would you like to go to Manila?" he asked without preamble.

Almost speechless at the request, I blurted out, "Yes, sir!

"There is a plane leaving at 1230. I want you on it. I'm sending you to Manila to buy whisky, playing cards and any games you can for the Regt. Not only for the OFFs, but mostly for the enlisted men. There isn't much for the troops to do, so I'm setting up EM clubs throughout the Regt. We're going to buy whisky, cards and other games not provided through the Red Cross or Special Services. I don't know how much money you will have to spend. Make the best deal for as much whisky as you can. A little later, after we've collected the money from the troops, I'll send an officer to Manila with it and with information on how you are going to get it back to Mindoro. Your mission is to find out what is available, get the best price possible, the best and most whisky for the price. See what cards and games you can buy or get from the Special Services or Red Cross. Then wait at the Manila Leave

Center until my representative comes to give you the information. Now here is a letter order which will authorize you to be in Manila. Any questions?"

"No, sir."

I saluted, did an about face and sprinted to the Co area. Taking a quick shower, I put on well creased khakis which had not been out of my duffle bag since I had packed them at FT Ord. The rest of my khakis, some underwear and my shaving gear were stuffed in my musette bag, I was ready to go! There was no chance to eat, Bourdeau had the jeep ready to take me to the airstrip. I had just been paid, the first pay since Hawaii, so I had about $400 in my wallet.

At the airstrip I discovered that the trip to Manila was to be made in a B-26, a night fighter aircraft, black, with two engines and a small bomb bay. There was not much room for passengers, but two other people crowded in the aircraft in addition to the pilot and crew chief. The trip, which lasted just under an hour, was routine.

The pilot asked me if I had a way to get into Manila. When I told him that I did not, he offered me a lift to the city. He parked the aircraft, filed the necessary forms, then led the way to a parking lot. Expecting a jeep, I was astonished when he got into a GI ambulance which he said he had appropriated from some unit. No one claimed it, so he and his crew chief used it whenever they got to Manila. If worse came to worse, they could sleep in it. It provided an ideal means of transportation; nobody challenged an ambulance driving about the city. During the short trip into Manila, I had a chance to see something of FT Stotsenberg, Clark Field and the Luzon countryside. Once in the City, I located the recently opened Manila Leave Center. A tent city near Rizal Stadium, the Leave Center had all the necessary facilities, latrines with hot showers (a treat), cots with mosquito bars and sheets (a real luxury), a good mess hall with free meals, a recreation pavilion with pool and other games, an outdoor theater, and a PX. When I signed in I was informed that I could stay there five days without charge; a cot was assigned me in the OFFs' section.

The pilot had suggested that I meet him for drinks and dinner that evening so he could show me some of the sights. I was more than willing to do that. As he drove around the city he pointed out many interesting landmarks. It was a devastated city. The City Hall appeared to be the only building intact, even it had been hit with bombs or artillery shells and was pock-marked with bullet scars.

About 1800 we went to the Hacienda, a recently opened club. For two pesos I was given an exclusive membership in the club good for an entire year! We had tasty but stringy steak, cooked rare as I like it with fresh vegetables. There was a small band, many Filipino women were dancing with Americans, mostly OFFs. Getting into the swing, we danced quite a bit. About 2300 the pilot dropped me off at the Leave Center, he wanted to turn in early because he had to fly back to Mindoro the next day.

After a leisurely breakfast the next morning, I set out on my mission to locate the distilleries in Manila. The manager of the club at the Leave Center gave me the names of five operating distilleries from which he was buying liquor. Armed with a map provided by the Red Cross, I set out for the first one on the list, reaching it about 1000. The negotiations were difficult because I had no idea how much whisky we would order. Finally, I estimated that we would buy about $10,000 worth. This impressed the manager; 20,000 pisos was a lot of money at that time. He took me to his office to sample his wares. The "bourbon", "Scotch", and "brandy" were basically all straight alcohol to which coloring and flavoring had been added to make each different type. Not accustomed to drinking in the morning (I have never gotten used to drinking before Retreat), I was slightly drunk by the time I had finished sampling, somehow I managed to get the information I needed.

Making my way back to the Leave Center, I had lunch and took a nap. About 1400 I set out for another distillery, this one run by Indians from Calcutta. They were high pressure salesmen who tried to get me to commit myself, but I would not buy from anyone until I had checked all of the distilleries. Their operation looked shoddy, I wasn't sure they could produce everything ordered. I eliminated that distillery from further consideration.

That night I went to the Cielita Lindo, another night club I had heard of. It was an enjoyable evening which included a few drinks, a good meal, some dancing, and the opportunity to meet some OFFs from other units and a few Filipino girls who were extraordinarily friendly.

The next day I again visited two distilleries, one in the morning, another in the afternoon. Each time I sampled too freely and paid the price. That evening I enjoyed Manila night life at Club Ciro. The number of night clubs and bars already open was surprising.

By noon of the third day I narrowed the choice to two distilleries. That afternoon, I visited them both, finally deciding to buy from the Tanduay Distillery, operated by Elizalde and Company, probably the largest holding company in the Philippines. It had interests on many islands, timber, sugar cane, refineries, the distillery, land and real estate. Mr Jesus Cabarus, the individual I dealt with, was an interesting gentlemen; we decided to meet the following day to try to reach some sort of agreement. Once again I went out on the town in the evening and had a grand time.

At 0900 on my fourth day in Manila, I went to see Mr Cabarus. He assured me that he could give me any amount of whisky in any configuration; Scotch, gin, bourbon, brandy, blackberry brandy, apricot brandy, name your poison, Tanduay could provide it. His only problem was a shortage of containers. He suggested that if we were going to buy a lot of whisky, I go to the PX to see if there were any empty Coca-Cola hogsheads for sale. The Manila Warehouse supplied the entire Southwestern Pacific area, hence they received many 55 gallon oak barrels in which the coke syrup was shipped. Mr Cabarus explained that his firm had a steam device which could get the coke out of the barrels which he said were ideal for storing whisky.

In response to my inquiry, the PX Manager told me there were 29 hogsheads available for sale. Taking no chances, I bought all 29 on the spot, putting a deposit on them from my fast dwindling bankroll. They were relatively cheap, $25 or $30 each and the PX was glad to get rid of them. That same afternoon, Mr Cabarus sent me back with a truck to pick them up. Tanduay paid for them in scrip, which Mr Cabarus gave to me to complete the transaction. Scrip was readily available to civilians in Manila. The barrels, when emptied of our whisky, were to be delivered to the Elizalde Sugar Refinery on Mindoro. While at the PX, I was assured that there were plenty of cards, checkers and other games that could be bought in any quantity. The Red Cross Center agreed to give me 200 packs of cards, poker chips and some games. My mission now appeared accomplished. The only thing remaining was the arrival of the messenger with the money and the exact order.

By this time I had been in Manila five days and my authorized stay at the Leave Center was up. The Manager, when he saw my orders and heard that I was waiting for information from Mindoro as to how I would get back, agreed to extend my stay another five days.

During that time I explored Manila and enjoyed its amenities. I roamed the city, exploring, gaping, awed. An enjoyable stroll was along Dewey Boulevard which skirts Manila Bay. It is the resort area of Manila. From it there was access to a broad beach; along it were many famous buildings, the Army Navy Club, now just a shell, the famous Manila Hotel, some of the embassies, and many beautiful homes, most occupied by high ranking officers, one by General MacArthur's wife. Dewey Boulevard was also popular with lovers at night.

It became more apparent during these ramblings that the city had been very badly damaged, mostly by artillery, much of it American, as our Army tried to recapture the city. The Cathedral had just one wall standing, the main portal; the Opera House had no roof, although it looked as if it could be easily repaired. The Legislative Building was a heap of rubble. The one solid building was City Hall which housed HQ, Armed Forces Western Pacific, AFWESTPAC, or AFWPC.

While in AFWESTPAC HQ, I chanced upon an interesting Special Order, which pertained to GEN MacArthur's enlisted aide, driver, or clerk. Under the authority exercised by MacArthur as

Supreme Commander in the area, the Special Order made the individual a WO1, then commissioned him a 2LT; in successive paragraphs he was promoted in turn to 1LT, CPT, MAJ, LTC, and COL. The entire order concerned only that one individual.

Since the population of Manila is predominantly Roman Catholic, it is a city of churches. The Church of the Black Nazerene contained a life sized crucifix depicting Christ as a black man, carved in ebony. This crucifix was apparently greatly venerated by the local population. Many worshipers traversed the long, granite, paved nave from the rear entrance to the altar on their knees. It was explained to me this ordeal was undertaken in expiation of sins or in thanksgiving for a special favor or deliverance.

Another church had a monastery or seminary attached to it. It was beautifully decorated with *trompe l'oeil* friezes on the ceiling which did, indeed, "fool the eye"; they looked as if they had been carved instead of painted. A primitive gasoline motor and air pump had replaced the hand-pumped bellows on the ancient organ. Another church had organ pipes made from bamboo. Most of the churches retained their beauty in spite of the destruction sustained.

During my travels I came in possession of a jeep. When I noted that it had not moved in three days, I remembered the ambulance commandeered by the pilot who had flown me to Manila. Since it was not secured, I appropriated it. With a vehicle I could go farther abroad to see more of the city and countryside. I boldly filled the tank at one of the military gas pumps!

That jeep covered much of Manila during the short time I was able to keep it. In it I went to many interesting places; Santa Tomas University, where the Japanese had imprisoned most of the American civilians, largely women and children, during the war; Rizal Stadium, taken over by Army Special Services for athletic events, very usable despite damage to several tiers of seats; the grounds of San Lazarus Hospital. Enclosed behind a brick wall, the buildings looked to be a hundred years old. Yet, it was the major hospital in Manila.

While in possession of the jeep, I met CPT Charles R. Thorn and Mr Bill Soeberg from the 381st IN. They were in Manila on a mission similar to mine, though they were buying whisky in limited quantity for the 381 st Officers' Club. Dick Thorn, a lawyer from Port Jefferson, Long Island, was a stocky, cigar smoking individual with a mop of curly black hair and a round face. He spoke with an odd combination of southern drawl and New York twang. Since we were both from Long Island we became fast friends. Bill Soeberg was the Red Cross representative to the 381st. I showed them much of Manila using the jeep. We also enjoyed the night life, which I was able to introduce them to. Dick received word that the cargo ship he was to take to Mindoro was leaving. It seemed strange that COL Dill had not made arrangements for me to go back on the same ship, but no messenger had arrived with money. Dick and Bill had several demijohns, five gallon cans and assorted bottles filled with whisky. I drove them to the pier. It was comical to watch them trying to climb the rope ladder from the bobbing small boat, which took them out to the ship anchored in the bay, balancing those whisky containers. Within the year, I visited Dick at Port Jefferson and met his delightful wife, Dorothy. We have enjoyed a close friendship ever since.

One of the night spots I liked best was the Stars and Bars Club. As the name implies this was a club for officers, run by civilians. Here companionship was offered, for a price. On entering the building, attention was drawn to a bench along one wall on which a group of young ladies was seated. They ranged from a statuesque White Russian to the most fragile oriental beauty. These young women were available for hire for the evening's entertainment. For five pisos ($2.50) the girl who appealed to you came to your table. She would dance with you, smile at you, talk with you (if she spoke English) and drink with you. She would not leave the club with you. In addition to the "rental fee" you paid for whatever drinks she had. Of course she tea, but you paid for the most expensive drink served. During my stay in Manila, I went to the Stars and Bars Club several times to enjoy dancing and talking to some of these girls.

One of the things that intrigued me about Manila was the operation of the local prostitution syndicate. Despite an edict banning it (issued by both MacArthur and the local military government officials) the racket flourished. It was supposedly run by "The Fat Man". In almost any bar or restaurant, an obvious pimp, would approach a likely prospect, point out a girl or woman, and ask if the soldier was interested. If so, he negotiated for her services. If a price was agreed upon, the man would be told where to go, for instance, Rizal Alley No 13 (the alley off Rizal Avenue at House No 13). On arrival the customer found a bare room with a bed, mosquito bar, fairly clean sheets, a bald electric light bulb, sometimes a small table or stand and a chair. The prostitute would be waiting for him. The minimum was 75 pisos (about $37.50) but ranged much higher. What the split was between "Fat Man", pimp and prostitute, I never could learn.

Toward the end of my second five day period at the Leave Center, things began to fall apart. MPs repossessed my jeep, with a stern warning about misappropriating government property, and there was no word from COL Dill. In an attempt to expedite matters, I sent a TWX from AFWESTPAC HQ to the 382nd IN requesting instructions. COL Dill's cryptic reply ordered me to await further orders. I was told that I could not stay any longer at the Leave Center. After an impassioned plea, the Officer-in-Charge extended my stay another five days. He did so reluctantly and advised me that it was absolutely the last extension I would get. Finally, my money began to run out, I had to eat all of my meals at the Leave Center, where the meals were free and excellent.

With no money, I had to find free diversions. I continued to explore the city during the day. Tours to Corregidor had been canceled for safety reasons - duds in the tunnels and structural weaknesses due to bombings - so I did not get to see that landmark. From the shore I could see FT Drum, a small concrete pill box which controlled the entrance to the harbor. In the distance was Bataan Peninsula, infamous as the scene of the "Death March".

At night I stayed at the Leave Center or attended Special Services activities. I did get to hear the Manila Symphony several times. It was an excellent orchestra, conducted twice by an Army Band Master (WO1) as guest conductor. GEN MacArthur's wife was in attendance both times.

On returning from a walk late one afternoon, I found CPT Porter, my old E Co CO sitting on the cot opposite mine. I was overjoyed to see someone from my outfit. He told me he had the money and that arrangements for getting the liquor to Mindoro had been made. He handed me a check for $35,000. I looked at it and gasped. Then he handed me a list of what was wanted. It included a great deal of bourbon and rye, a little Scotch, some gin and a small quantity of brandy of assorted kinds. He told me that in two days two PT boats would arrive in Manila from the PT base on Mindoro. The liquor would be split between them; he would go on one and I on the other, both of us armed. Although COL Dill had promised the crews of the two PT boats some of the whiskey for transporting it, he wanted to take no chances of losing any of it.

The following morning CPT Porter and I went to see Mr Cabarus. He said the distillery would have no problem filling the order. It would be loaded on a truck in his compound that evening. In the morning he would deliver it to the pier and have it loaded on the PT boats. He indicated that the bouncing of the boats across the waves would "age the whiskey" in the oak barrels. Our next stop was the Finance Office, where we cashed the Government check issued at Mindoro. We were able to get enough pisos to cover Mr Cabarus' bill. We took the rest in scrip which we used to buy cards and games at the PX. We left our purchases in the office of the Leave Center for safe keeping.

In the afternoon I was able to show Porter a bit of the city. That evening, he treated me to dinner. We went to the Shangri La, one of the liveliest night clubs, where we had a great time. Porter regretted that he did not have more time to spend in Manila.

HEADQUARTERS 3824 INFANTRY
APO 96

11 September 1945

TO WHOM IT MAY CONCERN:

CAPTAIN WILLIAM C PORTER, 0126887, and FIRST LIEUTENANT DONALD A SEIBERT, 01038113, members of the 382d Infantry, have the permission of the Headquarters to visit Manila on official business, for the purpose of purchasing beverages and playing cards for the 382d Infantry Officers' Club.

Macey L. Dill
Colonel Inf
Commanding

HEADQUARTERS COMPANY 2D 3N 382D INF
APO 96

30 OCT 45

(Company Order)
(Number 12)

2d Lt Kenneth M Kone 01330193, asgd additional duties:
Co Ex O (1542)
Bn MTO (00600)
Actg A & P Plat Ldr (4510-9)
Actg Anti-Tank Plat Ldr (1542)
EM & Off Mess (chge)
Bn Malaria Control Off
Bn Armament Off
Co I & E Off
Co Bond Sale Off
Co Insurance Off
Co Voting Off
Co Athletic Off
Co PX Off
Class "A" Finance Off
Co TQN Off
Custodian (EM Club)
Co Shipping Adm Off
Co Supply Off
Bn Gas Off
2d Kt Donald H McCullough 013310193:
Comm Off

By Order of Lt Seibert
1st Lt., Inf.,
Commanding.

DISTRIBUTION:
1 Copy-Lt Seibert
1 Copy Maj Crall
1 Copy 382d Pere Off
1 Copy Lt Kone
1 Copy Lt McCullough

The next morning when we arrived at the pier, both PT boats and the truck from the Tanduay Distillery were already there. The liquor, in 21 hogsheads, two small casks, a number of five gallon cans, and several demijohns was quickly loaded on the two PT boats. Two 382nd NCOs had come up with the PT boats; one OFF and one NCO went on each boat. The speedy PT boats made the trip to Mindoro in 5 or 6 hours. We ate one meal on board. It was an interesting experience, my only trip on a PT boat. They bounced across the waves, just skimming the surface of the water at about 30 knots. Fortunately the water was calm, so the trip was an enjoyable one.

When the PT boats arrived at their base on Mindoro in mid-afternoon, a detail unloaded the liquor which COL Dill put under guard until his Athletic and Recreation (A&R) OFF could distribute it. The A&R OFF also collected the cards and games I had obtained from the Red Cross and bought at the PX.

During my absence from the Island, an Awards Review had been held. My first evening back I received some kidding about my clout with the Awards Committee.

I learned on my return that my runner, Bob Laird, was in the 13th Station Hospital, which was on a hill overlooking San Jose, the largest "city" on Mindoro. The next morning I went to the Hospital, where I found Laird in bed in one of the huge ward tents. As I was telling him about my trip, I heard the voice of the ward nurse, who was talking with one of the wardmen. Though I couldn't see her, I recognized the voice. Laird did not know her name, but he said it sounded Russian or Polish. "It wouldn't be Federonko, would it?", I asked.

The man in the next bed spoke up, "Yes, sir, that's her name."

What a surprise to meet Daria Federonko, an old friend from Indiantown Gap days on Mindoro! With a wink at Laird, I walked up to the nurses station. When Daria was finished talking to the ward man, she looked up at me questioningly, half recognizing someone she knew.

"How are you Daria, do you remember me?", I said.

"You are either Bill Long or Don Seibert. I think Bill Long was short and stocky, so you must be Don Seibert."

We embraced and kissed to the amusement of the ward men and patients and made arrangements to get together for dinner in the Nurses' Dining Room very shortly. Bob Laird told me that Daria had quite a reputation among the patients, who called her "Ma Feddy", more in appreciation than in derision. She would call units that had patients on her ward, informing them that it was their turn to furnish sheet pies or cakes for the ward. She also managed to cajole ice cream from the Seabee Base, which had an ice cream maker. Her ward always had extras. Laird said that she was "stern but lovable" and that the men respected and liked her. They knew, for instance, that she bought baby powder at the PX for back rubs when there was no GI issue available.

The 382nd IN had permission to use a wooden school building with many louvered windows for an Officers' Club. Screens were installed and the building painted inside and out. By the time I returned from the whiskey run a bar had been set up; the grand opening awaited the arrival of the liquor.

The pending opening of the 382nd Officers' Club gave a certain urgency to seeing Daria again soon. On my next visit we had a great time talking, drinking and reminiscing. When asked if she would like to attend the opening of our Officers' Club, Daria was delighted. Not only would she come but she would persuade all of the off-duty nurses in her hospital and possibly in the other hospital on the Island to come. She did just that.

Except those nurses on duty, every American female on the Island, nurses and Red Cross workers, attended the opening of our club. It was quite an affair! The Div Band Combo played the hit tunes of the time. We danced, Daria is a superb dancer, talked, sang and ate. There was a buffet of sorts: cheese, cold cuts, pickles, crackers, deviled eggs, whatever could be found. The bar did a land office business in Manila Whiskey. It was quite a sight to see COL Dill dancing the polka! He loved the dance and had phenomenal stamina; he could dance two or three consecutive polkas without breathing too heavily. I also love to polka and Daria was an outstanding polka dancer. As there were several officers of Polish descent in the Regt, the polka was popular. Everyone enjoyed the party.

Daria and I saw quite a bit of each other after that. She followed a policy which I thought was wise, of dating only one officer from a Regt. I wasn't the only person she dated, but she did not date any one else in the 382nd, hence there was never any hard feelings. We had many good times; Fred Steed or some of the other officers would accompany me to the Nurses Club to play bridge, dance or just talk. After one such expedition, Fred and I went out to get the F Co jeep which we had driven to the hospital, only to find that someone had stolen the rotor. We tried to find another but were unsuccessful. The Hospital CO's jeep was parked next to ours; we "borrowed" his rotor!

A few weeks after that trip to Manila, MAJ Crall called me to his tent. He was redistributing officers to cover vacancies created by the rotation of high point officers to the United States. He told me that he was going to make me the Bn HQ Co (HHC) CO, a dual assignment since the HHC CO was also the Bn Adj. Delighted to get a Co command, I would have preferred a rifle Co, especially F Co. But the combined duties would make it an interesting assignment; though I hated to leave F Co, I could not protest too strenuously.

Bourdeau asked MAJ Crall to reconsider, but the need to fill vacancies was too great. My Plt invited me to go to San Jose with them before I left. They took me to an off limits restaurant where we had good hamburgers and other food we were not getting in the mess. An MP was all ready to prevent us from going in, but when he saw my silver bar he decided not to. It was a good party from which the men brought me back to camp slightly intoxicated.

The F Co OFFs had a party at the Officers' Club the night before I transferred. When we got back to the Co area after midnight, 2LT Bob Ely got out a bugle that SGT Preecs had captured and blew Reveille. The troops tumbled out. SGT Drozd, realizing what had happened, called out, "What's the uniform?" The men took the incident good naturedly, laughing at the antics of their OFFs. Bourdeau, Foley and Steed did not drink, but Stocks, Farnsworth, Ely and I made up for them. It was a tribute to all of us that the men took the occurrence in such good spirits - they found it a humorous change from the boring routine.

On assuming command of Bn HHC, I immediately set about learning the men and my new duties. This was temporarily suspended when I was again sent to Manila to buy more whiskey; this time I took a check for only $12,000 with me. Mr Cabarus, who had now become a friend as well as the 382nd agent, invited me to his home for drinks the night I spent in Manila. He introduced me to Planters Punch, which he called Haciendero Punch. Later I was asked to go to Manila a third time to buy more liquor, but by then I had become enmeshed in my duties as Co CO and Bn Adj and begged off. The officer who went took a letter of introduction from me to Mr Cabarus, who, as in the past, served us well.

When the Deadeyes arrived on Mindoro, there was a sizeable Naval contingent on the Island, a battalion of Seabees which had built the airfield and the naval installation, a PT Squadron, a US Navy Shore party, and a logistical element. When these Naval forces were abruptly ordered elsewhere, their installation was turned over to the 96th Div. It was in excellent shape, had good quarters for troops, fine facilities such as mess halls equipped with ice cream machines, ice makers, reefers (walk-in refrigerators), an electric generating plant which powered such appliances as electric stoves, and running water. There were both OFFs' and EM Clubs. The Div Engrs had built such a comfortable camp on the high ground above San Jose that the Div CG decided not to move his HQ to the beach area. The excellent Naval facility was turned over to the 382nd IN.

The Regt moved just after I was transferred to HHC. Everyone was delighted with our new area. The EM had screened Quonset huts with wooden floors, as well as latrines with running water, hot showers and other amenities. Most OFFs had individual huts (built up pyramidal tent frames, so well

113

screened that it was not necessary to use mosquito bars). Each hut was equipped with a cold water shower, all were located on the beach. We could run from our quarters for an early morning swim before breakfast.

This move was accomplished just before Thanksgiving. A special shipment of supplies was issued for the Thanksgiving dinner; frozen turkeys, canned fruits, vegetables, nuts, shrimp and cranberry sauce - everything to make that Thanksgiving a traditional and memorable one. As Bn Adj, I decided to invite all of the Bn OFFs to eat with the Bn CO in the Officers' Dining Room the Seabees had constructed onto the EM mess. My cooks outdid themselves. Some Red Cross girls manned the serving line, joking with the men as they came through. After observing the first half of the Co go through the chow line, I went back to the Officers' Dining room. It was a good meal and there seemed to be plenty of turkey for all. As we were finishing up, I went back into the EM's mess hall to make sure that everything was going well. I was stunned to find the cooks serving cold cuts to the last 10 or 15 men who came through the chow line. When I confronted the Mess SGT, he told me that I had fouled up by inviting all of the OFFs for dinner and not having rations switched from their Cos. The other Cos had excess rations while HHC was feeding 20 extra OFFs with rations allocated for our normal strength.

It was a bitter lesson for me. Because of my ignorance some of my men were deprived of a superb Thanksgiving meal. It was a lesson I never forgot. From that time on I insisted that all OFFs eat last to ensure that the EM received everything they were entitled to before the OFFs ate. This is standard procedure which all good commanders follow even now.

Just after Thanksgiving, a ship load of liquor arrived at Mindoro. Before the Div left California, OFFs were given an opportunity to buy shares in a liquor fund, specifying their preference. The liquor was ordered (where or how this was accomplished in those days of liquor shortages I never found out) to be delivered whenever transportation was available. The liquor had finally caught up with the Div, but many OFFs who had paid into the fund had been killed, wounded, evacuated or rotated back to the United States. Those of us who had joined the Div after its departure from the States were able to buy the shares of those OFFs no longer present for duty. We were charged the same price per share, the money to be refunded to those who had left. I bought two shares, which turned out to be two cases of Mount Vernon Rye! We had to take what was left after the original subscribers received their preference; apparently little Scotch had been ordered. Not a rye drinker before, I soon became one, I had a lot of it to drink!

There were two OFFs assigned to HHC, in addition to those assigned to the HQ itself: 2LT Kenneth M. Kone and 2LT Donald H. McCullough. Ken Kone was an outstanding young officer who had joined the 2/382 on Okinawa, just after the end of hostilities, directly from IN OCS at FT Benning. Ken, a trim, intelligent, good-looking officer with a mane of thick black hair, was a born leader, respected and liked by the men because he demonstrated a sincere interest in their welfare. He had boundless energy, was exceptionally well coordinated, and was a superb ball player. He also had an excellent tenor voice. Though he was into every activity in the unit, it was hard to keep Ken fully occupied. McCullough, though a good officer, was less eager, less personable.

Kone had so much energy that I published a Company Order assigning duties to the two officers. Ken was given 20 responsibilities, McCullough but one. Nothing daunted, 2LT Kone ably discharged all of his duties. During an inspection of his Ammunition and Pioneer (A&P) Platoon, Ken was showing off a bit, twirling the rifles as he brought them up to his eye to inspect the bores. His performance was impressive until one soldier failed to drop his hands as Ken reached for his rifle. As a result, the spin was faulty and the rifle smashed into Kone's head. He rocked a bit, tears came to his eyes and he bled from a gash, but he recovered, completing the inspection without pause. There was nothing but admiration in the eyes of his men as he dismissed them

In addition to Kone and McCullough, there were three NCOs who helped me in my duties as Adj and Co CO: TSG Walter Cohen, SSG Carl C. Johnson and SSG Mark B. Townsend. Walt Cohen, a wiry, energetic, articulate Texan, was the Bn SGM. He kept the duty rosters, allocated details to the Cos and took care of most of the paper work. Carl Johnson, a husky Scandinavian from Chicago, was the Commo PSG. He kept the Bn in touch with Regt and the Cos. He also helped with some of the disciplinaiy problems in HHC. Mark Townsend, from Springfield, IL, the 1SG, handled all Co admin. Between the three of them, they kept me out of trouble and the Co and Bn running smoothly. Over the years, I have maintained correspondence with them and hold them in high esteem.

Life settled into a monotonous pattern. The men were reduced to performing housekeeping chores and recreation: police of the area, details such as KP, guard or supply, mandatory training such as I&E, Articles of War, VD lectures and other repetitive subjects, reading, playing cards, and athletics, including swimming. My own routine was simple; I appeared at the Co after reveille (which 1SG Townsend took care of), signed the morning report, made necessary inspections, attended to the minimal training requirements, took care of any administration that needed my attention, ate lunch and departed. In the afternoon, the men played ball, swam or sun bathed, gambled and drank. The clubs COL Dill had organized opened immediately after lunch. For those who needed something earlier, "Raisin Jack", a primitive moonshine derived from fermented raisins and other fruits, made by the cooks, was usually available.

The Bn SGM and the 1SG handled routine Bn and Co matters. The PSGs, Carl Johnson of the Commo Plt and Jack Berger of the A&P Plt took care of routine Co chores. SGT Jack Berger was a tall, muscular, exceedingly handsome soldier who had been a bouncer at the Palladium in Los Angeles before the war. Berger, strong enough to handle most men easily, adopted a protective attitude toward his Plt Ldr, 2LT Kone, whom no one dared defy on any matter. Ken, Berger, and one of the younger soldiers in the A&P Plt, Eli Vukovich, were seen together frequently, as they shared common interests and played most sports well. After the war Berger had a career in movies and TV under the name Chris Alcaide, mostly Grade B westerns. Vukovich became a teacher and retired as Superintendent of one of the California County School Systems.

SSG Johnson, the Commo PSG, was technically well qualified, but did not take the enforced, "make work" duties of the post-war era too seriously. I had to intervene in his behalf when 2LT McCullough wanted to discipline him for not pushing the intensive training program McCullough developed for the Commo Plt. Johnson could see little need for training men who were only awaiting discharge. I agreed.

We officers enjoyed life! There was little for us to do other than sign our names periodically and exercise minimum supervision. We were immediately available if any matters arose that the NCOs could not handle (those were few); the Navy had left intact a comprehensive telephone system with phones in every OFF's hut. Like the enlisted men we enjoyed the beach, sports, reading, gambling, bull sessions and writing letters. That supply of Mount Vernon Rye shrank noticeably. Every evening we would go to the Officers' Club to drink, play cards or sing.

There was a close knit group in the Bn comprised of Schmitt, Ressler, Mester, Pugsley and I, who had traveled overseas together, and Deadeyes such as Steed, Stocks, Ely and Kone. Almost every night we would have a few drinks and sing Army songs, old ballads, and of course the current hits. Ken Kone had an exceptional voice; the rest of us left much to be desired in that area. We were the bane of the Officers' Club, used by all Regt OFFs. The 3rd Bn CO, LTC James (Jabo) Stell, who thought our singing terrible, vainly tried to shut us up. In fact, he gave me several direct orders not to sing or let other OFFs sing in the club at night. Apparently I was considered the leader of this sour note chorus. I told him bluntly that they were illegal orders which we would not obey. He could take it up with MAJ Crall or COL Dill, but the rules of the club gave us license.

It got to be a touchy situation. He tried to send his officers to the club early to get the tables filled up so there would be no place for us. The Club Officer, a good friend, heard of it, called me, so the plan was thwarted. The situation came to a head on New Year's Eve. The Div CG decided that there would be a Div OFFs' New Year's Parry at the 382nd Club. The Div Band was to play and all of the nurses and Red Cross girls on the Island had been invited. Unfortunately, Daria had rotated, so I had no date. Preparations were grand. Christmas Eve I went to Midnight Mass with some of the Catholic OFFs. They had organized a choir which not only sang the familiar Christmas Carols, but also participated in the Gregorian Chant used during the solemn High Mass. It was a meaningful occasion, that first Christmas after the end of the war.

Head and Head had a delicious Christmas dinner, in part because I did not repeat the blunder I had made Thanksgiving. We all approached 1946 with eagerness. The party at the Officers' Club was to be a gala affair. Tables were allocated to units so that all would be represented. LTC "Jabo" Stell, the 3/382 Commander told me that he did not want our singing to disrupt the party. I promised nothing, not knowing what might develop, but Jabo admonished me that he would take strong disciplinary action against me and the other OFFs if we interrupted the party to sing.

The festivities got underway early and it was a festive event. Just before midnight (our group had been drinking quite heavily), someone suggested that during the next orchestra break we take over the microphone and sing. Shortly later, the band took a breather. We all surged to the microphone and started a song. Stell leaped to his feet and advanced towards us threateningly. Before he reached us the Div CG, MG Bradley, joined our group. When we finished the number he complimented us. His words went over the public address system so everyone in the club including Jabo could hear. He went on, "I wonder if you can sing my favorite song, Old Black Joe?"

Of course we could sing his favorite song; we sang Old Black Joe with ribald solemnity, led and accompanied by the General. We sang several other songs he liked. By that time the band reassembled to welcome 1946 and we quit. We enjoyed the evening, in no small measure because of LTC Stell's discomfiture. After the first of the year, life settled back into its former monotony

Whenever two or more soldiers or officers were together, the conversation invariably turned to post-war plans. Many expected to finish college and go into the professions, some wanted to master a trade, but most wanted to return to their prewar jobs and resume their lives where they had dropped them to fight the war. The GI Bill figured in many plans, as it provided the means to complete college, the capital to start a business or farm, or the security for a mortgage on a home. Every facet of the problem was examined in detail. Speculation about these plans only lead to greater impatience to get back home. As the boring routine continued, the soldiers became more and more restive. Activists urged mass meetings to force the government to speed our return. Manila was the scene of soldier riots.

Shortly after the beginning of 1946, I was again reassigned, first as CO of Service Co, then given the additional duty as Regimental Supply OFF (S-4 or RSO). Both are normally time consuming duties, but the Div was slowly phasing down so one individual could handle the two jobs readily. Service Co was assigned all personnel who handled administration and supply functions for the Regt. There no longer was much supply activity, other than the issue of rations, some gasoline and replacement clothing and the turn in of equipment as it became obvious that it was no longer needed. My assignment was based on the fact that I was one of the senior 1LTs remaining in the Regt, not because I knew anything about supply.

We were informed about this time that the Deadeyes would be leaving Mindoro between the middle of January and the middle of February. The bulk of our remaining equipment was transferred to a rear detachment or given to Filipinos. Arrangements were made to turn the former Navy Base back to the Filipino who owned the land. We crated the colors and Regimental memorabilia so they would be immediately available on arrival in the States. The troops were prepared for embarkation.

A contest was held at this time to select "Miss 96th Infantry Division". One of the EM in the Div was married to a starlet in Hollywood. Her name, one of the first considered, had a great deal of support. Then some wag suggested that the Deadeyes was a rough, tough outfit which a pretty little starlet could not properly symbolize. As a joke, Marjorie Main was nominated. When the ballots were counted, Marjorie Main easily won the title "Miss 96th IN Div ".

The remnants of the Div embarked on the USS *General W.C. Langfitt* on the 17th of January, we watched Mindoro fade from view with delight. We were impatient when the troop ship stopped at Manila to let troops off and to take on additional men from other units. This was necessary because the Div had shrunk to such a size that it did not fill the ship.

The Commander of the USS *General W.C. Langfitt,* a Regular Navy Captain, observed to the letter the exaggerated protocol I so detested about the Navy. BG McCunniff was the ranking Army officer aboard, hence the Commander of Troops. The Navy Captain was most attentive to him. By chance, both BG McCunniff and the Captain were Episcopalians. An Army Chaplain (LTC) aboard, was an Episcopal priest who arranged to hold a Communion Service each Sunday in the Ward Room. As a life long Episcopalian and an acolyte for many years, I offered to assist during these services.

The first Sunday at sea the Episcopal Communion was scheduled for 0800. By 0730 I was in the wardroom to help in setting up the altar. There had been a party in the Ward Room the night before and sailors were just finishing cleaning it when I arrived. It took us some time to set up the altar and arrange the seats. Promptly at 0800 the Captain of the *Langfitt* marched in followed by his Marine orderly. BG McCunniff was already there, in less than five minutes arrangements for the service would have been completed. The ship's chaplain, a LTJG, was assisting us to set up. The Captain immediately went to him and addressed him in a loud tone, "I thought this service was to start at 0800."

The chaplain responded, "Yes, sir, it was. We are a little late in getting set up, but the service will start in one or two minutes."

The Army chaplain went over and explained that the Ward Room had not been ready, but the ship's Captain ignored him, as he chewed out the LTJG,

"When events are scheduled on this ship, they go as scheduled. Send my orderly to my quarters when you are ready for the service."

"Sir, we are ready to start any minute, you might as well stay. Please have a seat next to BG McCunniff."

But the Captain did an about face and marched off leaving his Marine orderly. The arrangements were quickly completed and the Marine was sent to notify the Captain, who arrived promptly dressed in a white uniform. The ship was rolling due to a heavy ground swell. During that part of the service when I had to pour the wine into the chalice, the ship gave a lurch, causing me to skid across the deck. I ended up in front of the Captain, spilling the red wine on his white uniform! I thought it was poetic justice. He ignored me and the wine, received Communion and stomped out.

Irritated by such antics, I decided that I would needle this pompous ass. The next time I saw him parading the deck, I confronted him,

"Captain, I notice that you play Church Call for every religious service conducted on the ship except the Episcopal Service. I think it should be blown for that service."

The Captain got red in the face, harrumped a few times, allowed that I was right and that he would rectify the matter, and quickly departed. Apparently it had been an oversight due to the fact that the Episcopal Service had been added to the ship's schedule at the last minute and was not a regular part of the routine. The next Sunday, the Service started at exactly 0800, but no bugle had called the faithful to worship. Just as the priest reached the most solemn part of the service, the bugle call started. Church Call is a beautiful but long call; it completely blanked out the consecration of the elements.

I glanced over at the Captain; red faced, he turned to say something to his Marine orderly, but decided that it would be disrespectful to do so. As soon as there was a break in the service, he sent the young Marine on an errand. I am sure someone caught hell. The third Sunday, everything went smoothly.

We finally pulled into San Pedro, the harbor for Los Angeles. The pilot boat which came to meet us had a huge sign *"Yonabaru Maru"*. Yonabaru was a city on Okinawa for which the Deadeyes had fought, Maru is the Japanese word for ship. Sitting on the rail on the top deck was Marjorie Main dressed in her western regalia. She was shooting off her pistols and shouting, "Welcome home, Deadeyes.

Somehow she was transferred to the *Langfitt,* a difficult task because of the ground swell. Finally she was literally handed from one vessel to the other. She kidded with the men, kissed them, gave them autographs and wished them well. There was a band on the pilot boat which played on and on as the *Yonabaru Maru* escorted us to the pier, whistles blowing. Fire boats squirted streams from every nozzle; all ships in the harbor blew their fog horns and whistles. We were home!

We debarked rapidly from the USS *General W.C. Langfitt* and were trucked to Camp Anza near Riverside. A sumptuous meal was served that first night back: huge steaks, fresh vegetables and salad, whole milk, French fries, pie-ala-mode. There were seconds and thirds if desired; the mess personnel could not have done better for a welcome home meal; the fresh milk and ice cream were particularly welcome, since only reconstituted milk was available overseas.

The morning after our arrival we turned in all of the Division equipment - colors, records and memorabilia. I bought my GI watch, which kept excellent time and had a receipt for that. I also had authorization to retain the aiming circle, several Japanese bayonets, the knee mortar round and a Japanese hand grenade. I kept some records not required to be turned in such as an after action report. Things were handled expeditiously so we finished up early in the day. Some of us went to the Mission Inn in Riverside for a fantastic dinner that evening. The next day orders were published transferring me to the Separation Center at FT Dix, NJ, I was manifested on an Army Air Corps plane for the flight to the east coast. I called home to tell the family that I was in the States. I would give them more information when I got to Dix.

CHAPTER 5

RESERVIST

The trip from Camp Anza to FT Dix for those who lived on the East Coast was made in an Army Air Corps C-47 airplane. It was a slow uncomfortable flight; 20 or 30 men occupied canvas "bucket seats" along each side of the aircraft. The plane developed engine trouble and landed at Tulsa, OK for repairs. We arrived mid-morning, with nothing to do until the plane was flyable. Tulsa was dry, and we were impatient to be on our way. The local citizens did their best to entertain us. A prominent family invited us to their lovely home where we were treated to tea, cakes, and coffee. Someone played the piano with rare skill, a delightful concert which I would have enjoyed under other circumstances. However, this was not the kind of entertainment for which we were in the mood. Most of the men could not conceal their boredom and irritation. Though the Welcoming Committee did its best, nothing could please this impatient group of returnees except a speedy flight home.

Finally we became airborne again about 1500 and landed at FT Dix (McGuire Air Field) late in the evening. We were told that processing would begin at 0800 in the morning. After a late meal in a poorly run consolidated mess, we fell on our bunks. The first step in our processing the next morning was the completion of a questionnaire which explored our interest in remaining on active duty, applying for Regular Army (RA), or immediate release from active duty (AD), in which case we were asked to state a preference for assignment to the National Guard (NG) or Reserves (RES). I elected to get out of the Army immediately and join the RES. The processing proceeded apace, during which I was given a terminal leave promotion to CPT. Terminal leave promotions, designed for those who had the misfortune to serve in units in which no vacancies occurred, were to compensate for inequities in the system which permitted advancement only to fill vacancies in a unit. In two days the processing, which included a final physical examination, was complete. Although I actually left FT Dix on 17 February 1946, my discharge was not effective until 26 April, due to accrued leave.

At 1400 on 17 February I called home to tell Mother and Dad that I would take the next train from Trenton. When I arrived home about 2200, the entire family, including George and Bob, my sisters' husbands, were waiting to welcome me; it was quite a celebration. We missed my brother Bill who was still in the Navy.

In two days my plans were complete; I would re-enroll immediately in the Evening Division of Washington Square College, NYU, to complete the requirements for my BA degree. Even though I would still draw active duty pay, I would work to pay my expenses in order to save the education benefits of the GI Bill for medical school. On applying for my old job at the Valspar Corp, my right to it guaranteed by law, I was immediately rehired. My old friends at Valspar greeted me with acclaim. Some one in the office had read in the *New York Times* of my award of the Silver Star. I was the hero of the Valspar Corp!

When I went to register at NYU, Doctor Girard and Professor Gordon welcomed me warmly. Both assisted me in planning my courses and in preparing applications for medical school. The spring term had started the week before, but I was admitted to Physics I, the one course I needed for medical school. At the end of the semester I found that the requirements for my BA, with the exception of Physics II, could be satisfied with the credits given me for OCS and other Army schools I had attended plus three additional courses. These could only be taken in the two-month summer session during the day. To attend these courses, Physics II, Histology, Histological Techniques, and Math Analysis

I quit my job and went to school full time. Surprisingly, my grades were much better than they had been before I served in the Army. In that intensive two month period I got a C (Physics II), a B and two A's. Evidently I had learned how to apply my mind.

Once settled in school and the job, I wrote to each member of my Plt, as well as to some of the men who had served with me in HHC, to thank them, particularly the Plt members, for the support they had given me and the fine job they had done. This initiated a correspondence which has lasted over the years. A few fall out of the net each year, but for the rest of my military career, I continued to hear from many of the men I had served with in combat in WWII; they gave a lot of encouragement to me in my years as a Regular Army Officer.

The first six months after my return to New York, I saw many old friends, not only those I had known before the war, but also a number I had made in the Army. Of course, I encountered people I had known at NYU. Among those was Howard Clark, who had taken several courses with me. He had been ordained an Episcopal priest. I visited his parish at Bellport, Long Island and met his lovely wife, June.

Kettler, my buddy from Roswell, and I met in Washington one weekend. Later I showed his fiance, Elizabeth, some of the sights of New York. Nick Ditrano lived in the Bronx, and Larry Hartz often visited his brother, Milan, a musician who played in many Broadway shows. There were others from Roswell in the area, so there were occasional RAAF reunions.

Harry Goldman, Irving Paley, and Joe Pasternak, all from the 382nd lived in New York. We got together to entertain Ed Foley and his wife when they came to see the sights. I had dinner with Chris Christianson, also from the 382nd, and his new bride on their honeymoon in New York.

Daria Federonka spent some time with her relatives in New York; we had several dates which included dancing at the Hotel Pennsylvania and the Rainbow Grill. It was a good feeling to have friends like these and to see them or correspond with them over the years.

Early in April I began completing applications for admission to medical school. Though submitted late, with the help of Professor Gordon and other friends, I was admitted to the Long Island College of Medicine (LICM) in Brooklyn in the fall of 1946.

In May 1946 the Army assigned me to the 305th IN, 77th IN Div (a Reserve Div based in New York City). It was not until September, however, that I attended my first meeting. With considerable surprise and delight I found that Dick Thom, who had been promoted to MAJ, was the S-3 of the Regt. I had last seen him juggling whiskey containers while climbing up the side of a ship in Manila Bay. There were many experienced officers in the unit. One who became a close friend, was Hanz Druener, a New York City Policeman, who had been with the 82nd Airborne Div during the war. He was a husky, square faced, Teuton who always seemed ready for inspection. He had a fine combat record and we shared an identification with the Army that made us close friends. His wife Jean, whom I immediately liked, was vivacious and friendly.

The 77th IN Div was a remarkable unit. Its CG was Julius Ochs Adler, the Managing Editor of the *New York Times*. The Asst Div CDR was President of the American Bar Association; the 305th Regt CO, COL Gardener, was a Vice President of the Anaconda Copper Corp. Almost every OFF and many of the EM assigned to the Division had some combat or meritorious service award from WWII.

With all that clout the Div got pretty much what it wanted in the way of training areas and exercises. The 305th Regt Advisor, MAJ Vincent Abrignani (who was to play a significant role in my future), and the other RA Advisors, were kept busy trying to comply with the demands of these highly qualified and well-connected leaders. We spent several weekends at FT Dix where excellent Command Post Exercises (CPXs) were conducted. On most of these I acted as Dick Thorn's assistant. My actual assignment was CO of HHC but there was no play for Co COS in CPXs. One weekend we went to the Military Academy at West Point, one of the few Reserve units to go there for training.

We stayed in the Cadet Barracks at Camp Popalopin, where the Cadets have their field training. On Saturday we witnessed a parade reviewed by MG Adler and dedicated to the 77th Div. The weekend included familiarization firing on the range conducted by the USMA cadre.

Early in September I reported to the Long Island College of Medicine. Because my undergraduate academic record was mediocre, and because I had no money, I was lucky to be able to go. Fortunately, I was entitled to four years of schooling under the GI Bill of Rights, which paid not only my tuition and expenses, including books, but also a monthly stipend on which I could live. During the week I stayed in a furnished room in Brooklyn Heights; most weekends I went home to College Point.

My first year in medical school passed swiftly with studies, Army Reserve meetings, and extra-curricular activities at school. There were several compatible people in the class who became close friends: Caroline Lydecker, Dee Starr, Tom Samartino (a registered nurse with a master's degree in biology) and Walt Stankewick. The five of us were together most of the time in school.

Frequently our group included a student from British Guiana, Mir Safda Ali Shaw. We played a lot of bridge and went to all the parties and dances. It was an enjoyable year in spite of the long hours we were in classes and the time spent on our books. I adopted a schedule which stood me in good stead; I would get up early, between 0300 and 0400 to do most of my studying. My mind was fresh and there were no distractions. I could accomplish twice as much in two or three hours as I could in the evenings. It also left the evenings free for other activities. My first year I squeezed through with a high C average, neither encountering great difficulty in any subject, nor setting any records.

The BI received in Biochemistry was more the result of baksheesh than knowledge. When taking an examination, I go through it thoroughly and rapidly, answering all the questions I can. When finished with it, I glance over it, then turn it in and leave. That first time through the test I put down everything I know; if the answer evades me there is no point in agonizing over it or waiting for the flash of inspiration or recall. It simply does not come. Though not a top student in the class, I was always the first to leave the Biochemistry exams (and most others). The Professor told me that my early departures were demoralizing to other students. Before the final exam he offered to give me a B without correcting my paper if I would sit through the entire exam. Since I was a borderline B student in Biochemistry, I was perfectly willing to gamble for the grade. It was a hard bargain! I finished in about half the time allotted, then sat and fidgeted, barely managing to control myself until the end of the exam. I always wondered if I would have made that B on the merits of my answers on the exam.

It was an interesting year; all our first year subjects were basic science courses. Anatomy was fascinating; Dee Starr, Walt Stankewick, Jules Schwimmer, Ali Shaw and I dissected one cadaver. Even Psychiatry proved provocative.

The summer of 1947 I badly needed a job to pay my expenses and to buy some instruments, but was unable to find one at first. Finally, Mr Gabelia, who was General Manager of the Lily Tulip Cup Plant in College Point, got me a job as a printers' devil in the press room. It was messy but it paid more than any similar level job in the plant. Working with my hands was a refreshing change of pace after the intensive first year of medical school, I also learned a lot about printing, unions, and work in factories.

After only a month at Lily Tulip, Howard Clark, my former NYU classmate and now an Episcopal priest, called and asked if I would accept the position of camp doctor at the Boy Scout Camp in Wading River near Port Jefferson, Long Island, where he was Camp Chaplain. It was a tempting offer. Mr Gabelia urged me to take the job as it would give me more experience in my chosen field, dismissing my concern about quitting so soon after he had found the job for me. It was an instructive summer, during which my military experience stood me in good stead. There was one serious incident when I missed a notation on a physical exam and permitted a boy with an allergy to receive a tetanus shot. He had a violent reaction, necessitating his confinement to the camp hospital for several days. Fortunately he recovered completely. It was a shock; I learned a fundamental lesson about checking paperwork fully.

The camp had a good medical facility. There was a room for me in the small hospital, with a ward containing two beds for boys who needed constant care. My duties were not too demanding, I got in lots of swimming, reading, and relaxation. There was only that one boy hospitalized with the reaction. At the end of the leisurely camp season, during which I learned much about myself and the medical profession, I spent a few days at Port Jefferson with Dick and Dorothy Thom. We did some sailing and planned the activities for the 305th IN for the year.

On returning to LICM in September of 1947, I was filled with some disturbing thoughts. There was no longer a burning interest in medicine, though I still wanted to become a doctor, certainly I would complete medical school. But the fascination had worn off, I missed the Army! The second year was crammed with engrossing courses: Physiology, Pharmacology, Parasitology, Pathology, Bacteriology, Applied Anatomy, Obstetrics, Hematology and Psychiatry. The Professor of Psychiatry, Dr Potter, was particularly impressive; a common-sense sort of doctor - the most normal psychiatrist I have ever known.

The same group gravitated together again: Caroline Lydecker, Dee Starr, Walt Stankewick, Tom Samartino and I. Unfortunately, Ali Shaw had flunked out but was trying to get into an English medical school. Tom, Walt and I pledged the Theta Kappa Psi Medical Fraternity. We were almost rejected because we laughed during the secret part of the initiation ritual; the secret ceremony, the trappings and symbols appeared hilarious if not immature. We had joined for fellowship and shared interests, not for prestige or snobbery. Our group was active in school affairs, appeared in several school plays, attended all social functions and worked on the school newspaper. My application to studies suffered - my grades were even more borderline that second year.

That year was also an active one in the Reserves; the 305th IN met twice a month on Wednesday from 1930to 2130. I attended all of the meetings. At those meetings I saw a great deal of Dick Thom and Hanz Druener. There was a constant turn over of personnel in the 305th but those two were stalwarts.

As the year wore on, I began to miss the Army more and more, frequently dwelling on the possibility of getting back into the service. At first I put these thoughts aside, but they persisted so I finally decided to investigate the possibilities of returning to active duty (AD). All friends I discussed the matter with, including those in the Army, were unanimous in discouraging such a course of action. They all thought that I would be foolish to give up medicine for the military. Most were sure the Army would stabilize and stultify, and that I would find myself bored, frustrated and repressed. Since I am an energetic individual interested in many different activities, my mentors thought I might be severely limited in the Army.

Yet there were many things that were attractive about the Army. One of them was my strong perception of the integrity and dedication of most of the officers I had met during WWII. Some OFFs were stupid, a small number were lazy, but few lacked integrity. The image I had long cherished of the Doctor, the bastion of truth, wisdom, dedication and compassion, had been altered by things I saw on the wards and in the clinics. Doctors were all too human; I began to feel less comfortable with them and their profession. The Army seemed more and more attractive as a career.

While I was mulling this matter, I received a call from Ken Kone who had been with me in the 2/382. We maintained an active correspondence. He had decided to return to AD and asked me to write a letter of recommendation for him. Ken, who had been of great assistance to me in HHC, was a personable, highly moral, competent OFF who would be an asset to the RA. My letter urged his recall in the strongest terms. Whether it helped is debatable, but Ken was ordered back to AD. We never served together again, unfortunately, but I did see him off and on, especially during my tours in the Pentagon. This incident bolstered my own inclination to get back in the Army.

As the school year went on I became more convinced that I had made a mistake in getting out of the Army. In fact it became such an obsession that I asked Dr Potter, the Professor of Psychiatry, for an interview. He listened to my concerns thoughtfully, giving them careful consideration. He first suggested that I complete medical school, then go into the Army Medical Corps. This had been an option I had considered, but to me the essence of the Army is the combat arms, particularly the IN. If I reentered the Army, it would be as an Infantryman. Dr Potter pointed out that some people are not cut out to be physicians and that I might be one of them. He suggested that possibly I had been carried away with the romance and mystique of the profession. Perhaps the Army was the place for me. He recommended that I go on AD during the summer between my sophomore and junior years, to see if the peacetime Army had the same appeal as the wartime Army, and to provide a comparison of the two fields. This seemed sound advice.

MAJ Abrignani told me that there was an opportunity for RES OFFs to be recalled to active duty for two weeks, a month, or even three months for summer training. He located a circular which outlined a need for RES OFFs to cadre for three months the summer camp for NG and RES units at Pine Camp, NY. They were looking especially for OFFs with operations experience (Asst S-3). We both thought that I qualified and he helped me complete an application. Toward the end of my second year in LICM orders were published recalling me to AD and assigning me to Pine Camp from mid-June to mid-September which fitted the LICM summer break exactly.

The end of that second year at medical school brought with it a blow to my ego. Not only did my grade point average fall to a C minus, but I flunked Obstetrics, my only failure in medical school. Strangely, that was the course I had most interest in. I wanted to be an Obstetrician! The idea of bringing new life into the world appealed to me. In spite of that interest, I failed the course. This failure could be made up by studying during the summer and passing a reexamination in the fall. This I determined to do. At the end of the school year, the entire class took Part I of the examination given by the National Board of Medical Examiners. My ego was restored a bit, late in the summer, when I learned that I had passed all of the tests in that section.

The school term finally ended. After a week at home with Mother and Dad, during which I got out my uniforms and made preparations for the summer, I took the train to Watertown and Pine Camp with great pleasure and anticipation.

An Army bus took all military personnel from the railroad station at Watertown to the Camp. At HQ I signed in, then went to see the Personnel Officer, who told me that there was a problem with my assignment. First Army had ordered to AD more CPT Asst S-3s than were needed. Apparently everyone who had applied had been accepted. I was the ninth OFF assigned as an Asst S-3, against a requirement for four or five. The Post CO, COL England, was going to decide which were to be Asst S-3s based on training and experience. The rest would be assigned to other duties. I was told to report back at 1000 the next day.

The Billeting Office assigned me a room in a wooden WWII BOQ. Even in that bare and temporary BOQ, I felt at home. My first night on post, I met many of the officers who were to cadre the summer camp. Some were on extended AD, some like myself were there for only three months. It was an interesting mixture of people as I have found every military organization to be.

Promptly at 1000 the next morning I presented myself at HQ, where I was ushered into the office of the XO. He informed me that after examining my records, COL England had decided that I could best serve the summer camp as the Post Chemical Officer! Leaping to my feet, I said, "You must be kidding, COL. I left the CWS in 1944 because I didn't like it. I went into the IN and am here to learn something that will enhance my RES Commission in the IN. I want no part of the CWS again."

He tried to calm me, saying, "Well, we all have to make a few sacrifices."

"I am not here to make sacrifices. I am here to learn, to gain experience which will make me a better officer so I can be of greater value to my unit and the Army. I also want to determine if I want to apply for extended AD. This job will not let me do any of those things."

"Well, if you feel that strongly about it I'll go back and talk to COL England. Come by this afternoon and we'll discuss your assignment."

At 1400 I reported to him. He looked at me quizzically. "Well, CPT, you're out of the frying pan and into the fire,"

"What do you mean?"

"COL England said that the only job he had that you could fit into was Club and Billeting Officer."

"I didn't come up here to be a housemaid. I came up here to learn something", I protested.

The XO was sympathetic, but carrying out his instructions. "Apparently that is the only job we have for a CPT with your background and qualifications. We don't need IN OFFs except in the S-3 shop, and we have more of those than we can use, most with more training and experience than you have. Don't underrate this job. You will meet every OFF on the post; you will also learn a lot of useful information and procedures. If you have any interest in the Army at all, it's a job that will stand you in good stead."

Unconvinced, I said, "I want my summer encampment orders rescinded."

"Don't make a decision now. Think about it. Sleep on it tonight. Come back and see me tomorrow morning at 0800."

There appeared to be no reason to rush matters, so I agreed to do so. That night I went to the club which I would run if I stayed, examining it with a critical eye. While there, I saw the 77th Div Advisor, a very senior RA COL. We had met several times at 77th Div functions. I went over to say hello. During our conversation I told him my dilemma, explaining that I had come to Pine Camp to decide whether or not to drop out of medical school and make the Army my career. So far my impressions were all negative, though I did not think this was representative of the Army. The COL listened thoughtfully.

"If I were you, I'd take the job. I think the XO is right. Hopefully you will never get such a job again. But it will give you good experience. You will appreciate what goes into the management of the club, the mess and the billets, and you'll get a feel for the Army that perhaps you wouldn't get in a job to your liking. Every job you get in the Army is not going to be one you prefer. You're going to get varied assignments some of which will be ideal, others you'll just have to tolerate. If you still like the Army after a job like this, then you know that it is for you. I recommend you take it."

That sounded like good advice, I thanked him and told him I would think about it. When I woke in the morning, I knew that I would take the Club and Billeting Officer assignment.

The XO, when told of my decision, was delighted. He took me to meet the Billeting OFF I would relieve. At the time, the club and mess were in one of the small bungalows found on all WWII posts, provided for Regt COs. Two bedrooms, a large living room, a dining room, kitchen, bath and orderly's room in the back. Within a day or so the club and mess were to move to a WWII type service club in order to handle the large number of OFFs expected during the summer. My responsibilities would include billeting and messing both cadre and visiting OFFs. RES and NG OFFs training with their units would be billeted by those units. EM billeting, mess and club would be handled by another OFF.

The cadre officers were housed in five standard WWII BOQs, no better, no worse than many I had been in. We would operate an Officers' Field Mess in the dining room attached to the Officers' Club.

An outstanding TSG, experienced in running clubs and messes, was assigned as my Asst. He held the Military Occupational Speciality (MOS) code of Mess SGT, but he was more than a Mess SGT.

He was a caterer and chef, fully capable of putting on delicious dinners and spectacular parties, of setting out a banquet, or good GI chow at a reasonable cost. With him as my principal NCO I felt more confident, I entered into the job if not enthusiastically, at least energetically.

COL England called me to his office to talk about the importance of the club, the mess and the billets to the morale of the OFFs, both those assigned as cadre and those here for the summer training. He closed by saying,

"By the way, I expect you to make enough money from the RES and NG OFFs here for the camp to take care of the cadre OFFs during the next winter."

I looked at him rather strangely. Surely he must know that I was one of those "RES OFFs" assigned for summer training. To ask me to take advantage of my fellow Reservists didn't seem very politic. I said nothing but made up my mind I would do the best I could for him, the Post and the officers I was to serve, though I would do so without taking advantage of anyone.

My NCO and I set up a social calendar. We contracted with several local dance bands in Black River and Watertown for one dance in each two week encampment. These were most successful and I was highly conspicuous at each of them. There were many excellent dancers among the cadre OFFs' wives, so I rarely missed a dance.

One of the first couples I met was Howard and Dorothy Leifheit. CPT Howard Leifheit was the Asst PM for the summer camp. We had many things in common: he, too, was a RES OFF on AD for the summer; had graduated from the CWS OCS at Edgewood in the class after mine; had transferred to the Military Police Corps during WWII; and he lived in Queens! Dorothy was a smart, articulate, attractive woman, and an excellent dancer. The three of us were drawn together and became life long friends. A special table was set up for the Club Officer and his guests at which the Leifheits joined me for all of the dances. Both Dorothy and I liked to polka; she did it well. The bands were instructed to play several polkas each night; as a result, I earned, through Dorothy's excellent dancing, a reputation as the "Polka King" of Pine Camp. The dances were well attended and greatly enjoyed.

COL England's wife, kept asking me when I was going to have Bingo. The OFFS (most of whom were without their wives) did not appear interested in that type of entertainment while they were at camp. This was explained to Mrs England several times but she insisted she wanted Bingo. She was finally told bluntly that during the summer the social functions were being tailored to the desires of the RES and NG OFFs training at Pine Camp, rather than those of the permanent party. In the winter the permanent party could have all the Bingo parties it wanted. She persisted, saying that I was very uncooperative not to do what the "Colonel's Lady" wanted. It was apparent what the OFFs wanted and it did not include Bingo. The officers' views prevailed; I was not impressed with the desires of "Colonels Ladies."

When I had been on the job for about three weeks, I contracted a lingering summer cold.

Usually I stayed at the Club until midnight, when it closed, to make the final checks for fire and security. One night I felt so miserable that I called my NCO, told him to close the Club that evening, went to the BOQ, took several aspirin and crawled into bed. Suddenly the phone in the hall rang. Normally someone in a nearby room would answer it immediately, then shout for the OFF receiving the call. That night it rang at least a dozen times before someone finally answered it. There was a knock on my door and a voice said,

"CPT Seibert, COL England would like to speak to you." COL England informed me that he had tried to reach me at the Club, but had finally tracked me down at the BOQ. His tone implied dereliction of duty, but I was too miserable to explain. He went on to tell me that LTG W.A. Burress, CG of 1st Army, was scheduled to arrive the next day to make his annual visit to Pine Camp, and wanted to be sure that the VIP cottage was in good shape. I assured him it was. He persisted,

"Are there any towels for the General?"

"Only GI issue, sir. If you recall, COL, at the last Board of Governors' meeting, we voted money to purchase towels and soap for the VIP quarters and some of the other visitors quarters. When it got to your office for approval, you redlined that item, so I was not able to buy any good towels."

"Well, for LTG Burress, in fact for any general officer, we should have special towels and soap. I think you should put them in."

"How am I going to get them, sir? You refused permission to buy them, I can't spend the Club's money without authorization."

"You'll find a way to get them, Captain."

"No, sir. I can't find a way to get them. Since you turned the request down, I don't see how we can get the money. We can't get the Board of Governors together before the General arrives tomorrow."

"You know we have to take care of these senior officers. They expect to be treated properly. You'll just have to find a way."

"COL, I didn't come to Pine Camp to take care of senior officers or to coddle them or act as nursemaid to them. I came on AD hoping to contribute something to the Army and to learn more about being an OFF. I just can't find a way of getting any towels for a General."

My German stubbornness combined with that miserable cold made me completely uncooperative. "Well," he said, "I'll bring some towels and soap from my quarters in the morning."

"That is a good idea, COL. Good night, sir." I hung up and went to bed.

When I checked the VIP quarters early next morning, I noted that the COL had put beautiful towels from his quarters there. LTG Burress arrived on time, everything went well, and the Colonel never mentioned the incident again.

I felt a little better and went to the Club as usual. About 1000 the Colonel's Lady arrived as was her custom. She checked to see what was on the menu for lunch, looked at the cleaning going on, then flounced into my office. As she sat down she said,

"You know, Colonel England was very unhappy with you last night."

"Oh?"

"Yes, you know you just can't ignore general officers. You've got to take care of them."

"Mrs England, I try to take care of all visiting officers but your husband will not let me. Therefore, I am not going to make a special effort for one general when he shows up."

"Well, you certainly made Colonel England unhappy. He does not have a high opinion of your performance of duty and I am sure it will reflect in your efficiency report."

I shrugged. "If that is the way the Colonel evaluates his officers, so be it. There is nothing I can do about it. Good day, Mrs England." She got up and left in a huff.

By the time I had been at Pine Camp about a month, I had settled into a routine. A great deal of time was spent with the Leifheits and other friends I made. Some officers, including the Leifheits, had found temporary housing in the resort areas in the vicinity. Several times I managed to get away from the club to have dinner with Dorothy and Howard. As I had no car there were few opportunities to see the area around Pine Camp, although I did get into Black River and Watertown on business occasionally. What little I saw whetted my appetite, I hoped to see more of it before I left. That hope was filled in an unusual way.

One day, the Post Maintenance Officer, a WO1 and the only Negro officer on the cadre, came to see me. (In 1948 the Army was still segregated and the term "black" had not acquired widespread usage. When a colored officer was sent on TDY he was usually accommodated with white officers.) He was obviously uneasy, but he finally got around to telling me that his wife was coming to visit him. He wanted to know if he could bring her to the Club and whether there was any possibility of finding her a place in the guest house.

"Of course," I said. "You're a member of the Army, a member of the staff here, and a member of the Club. Your wife is welcome, just like any other officers'. She has the freedom of the Club. I'll reserve a room in the guest house for her."

He was relieved and thanked me profusely. He told me that she was arriving the following Friday.

At about 1600 on Friday, Mr Sowder came into the Club to introduce me to his wife. She was a charming, vivacious, blonde, German girl; I surmised they had been married during the occupation. This was a shock because at that time there were few mixed marriages. Recovering my aplomb, I showed them to the quarters reserved for them in the guest house, meanwhile explaining that they were free to use all of the Club's facilities. That evening we had a drink together.

The next say Mr and Mrs Sowder came in early for lunch, selecting a table in a corner at the far end of the dining room. After they had been seated, Mrs England sailed in. She got halfway through the dining room, skidded to a halt, did an about face and marched up to the cashier's desk. It was my custom to supervise the dining room during meal hours, so I was standing at the entrance.

Looking me in the eye, Mrs England demanded, "What is the meaning of this?"

"What do you mean, Mrs England?"

"Why do you permit that colored officer to associate with that white girl over there?

"Why Mrs England, she is Mr Sowder's wife."

"Well, I have never seen anything like that. I will not eat in this dining room as long as those two are in here."

"I'm sorry, Mrs England, but the Sowders have no place to eat except in this dining room. It is their Club as much as it is yours. You have a home here on Post; if you don't want to associate with them or don't want to eat with them, I would suggest that you eat at home. They are going to eat here as long as Mrs Sowder is on Post.'

"Well, I will not." She strode out and did not eat at the Club again until Mrs Sowder left.

Co F of the 505th Airborne (ABN) IN Regt was on TDY from FT Bragg to support the summer training. The appearance, courtesy and performance of the paratroopers impressed me. I enjoyed watching the men on their run every morning. They were a coordinated unit which moved as one. The Co CO routed the run around the BOQs and the Club. To avoid the heat, they ran at 0600, sounding off with special volume as they counted cadence or chanted Airborne jingles while passing the BOQs to make sure that all the OFFs were awake. Always an early riser, this did not bother me, but some of the other officers became indignant.

CPT David Tracy, the F Co CO, recommended that one of his NCOs be reduced. The case came before the Pine Camp Reduction Board, of which I was a member. Although the SGT looked sharp, Tracy presented a long list of derelictions. The NCO did not measure up to his high standards, the Board approved his reduction. The spirit, morale and professionalism of Co F aroused my interest in the ABN.

There were many outstanding officers at Pine Camp that summer, including two that I would serve with later, LTC Albin E. Irzyk, an Armor (AR) Officer, assigned to the Weapons Department for the summer camp, was a professional with whom I served in the Pentagon. MAJ Ed Markey, an IN OFF and the Post S-4, was later in my class at the Command and General Staff College at FT Leavenworth.

Midway through my tour I received a phone call from the Post Adj, who told me that I had been selected for a special function. A prominent local summer resident of he area was giving a birthday party for his step-son. Among the guests invited were five unescorted ladies, COL England and Pine Camp had been requested to provide squires for these ladies. The host was a well known millionaire whom the COL was happy to oblige. By some cute personnel manipulation, HQ (COL England?) had come up with the names of five bachelors, COL Carl Metz, a Dentist, LTC Scofield, the Post XO,

MAJ George Moore the IG, CPT Seibert, and 1LT Larry Sharpe, the A&R Officer. We were given no choice; this was an assignment. With some reservations, I went as directed. We all wore tropical worsted shirts and trousers with no tie. The party was at Deerlick Farm in the Cape Vincent area on Lake Ontario where the St Lawrence River enters it. When we arrived, we found the party underway in "The Barn", a 200 year old structure that had been converted into a play house. The hay loft had been made over into a dance hall. The area formerly occupied by the cow stalls, which was field stone, was the playroom with pool and ping pong tables. On the wide ledge formed by the stone foundation were a dozen or so slot machines of all denominations. Next to each slot machine was a bowl of the coins to play it. Players used the host's coins, but any winnings were to be pocketed.

After cocktails, there was a beautifully served sit down dinner for several hundred people. The social elite of the area were there, an area in which many of the wealthy spent their summers. The ladies we were to escort were all married but their husbands were "in town taking care of business". The vivacious lady I paired off with, about my own age, came from the vicinity of Pittsburgh. Two dance bands played for our pleasure; one a regular dance band which played the hits of the day, the other a country-western combo for square dancing. My "date" danced well, we were compatible, thus had an enjoyable time. All five Pine Camp Squires, together with our "dates" sat at the same table. It was a hilarious group; indeed we thoroughly enjoyed the evening. We had several follow-up invitations for dinners and cocktail parties.

Several days after the party, COL England's secretary notified me that the owner of Deerlick Farm was so appreciative of our efforts on behalf of the "business widows" and what we had done for the party (apparently our group was the "life of the party") that he wanted to take us fishing. Though not an avid fisherman, I do enjoy it occasionally; the trip would be a break from the Club routine. I was more than agreeable. COL England had also been invited and he, together with the five of us, would drive to the lake in two sedans.

On Friday we left Pine Camp about 0530 for the short drive to Lake Ontario, where our host met us. With him was the lady I had "dated", apparently a particular favorite of the old gentleman. Two launches had been hired for the occasion; we boarded by rank, the host, the young lady and the two COLs in one boat, the rest of us in the other. Since we would be fishing in Canadian waters, we went first to the Canadian shore where our host bought each of us a Canadian fishing and hunting license good for one year.

The guides, one in each boat, were well paid and knew their business. They headed directly for a favorite fishing spot. Our guide slowed the boat and suggested that we start fishing.

"Where is the bait?" I asked.

"Oh sir, I'll bait your hook", replied the guide, whereupon he put bait on my hook. As soon as it struck the water, I had a bite. Reeling in a nice lake trout, I prepared to take the fish off the hook.

"Oh sir, I'll do that."

It got to be boring. Not accustomed to people waiting on me, half the fun in fishing was lost when someone else took care of my bait, tackle and catch. There was some compensation in the fact that the fish were actively biting. We continued to reel in bream, trout and sunfish; the guide continued to bait hooks, take the fish from them, rebait the hooks and take care of the catch. By 1030 we had a nice string. Obviously we were not going to take that many fish back to Pine Camp with us and there was a limit to the number we could eat for lunch. Having had nothing to drink since breakfast, I suddenly felt thirsty and asked the guide, "Is there anything to drink on board?"

"What would you like, sir? We have Scotch, bourbon, wine, beer and gin."

"Really, all I want is a drink of water, a coke or some fruit juice."

"I've got those, of course, but wouldn't you like a drink?"

Against my better judgement, I yielded, saying, "I could be persuaded to take a Scotch and water."

At that, all of the fishermen put down their poles and started to drink. Fortunately, I have never been able to drink in the middle of the day; I fall asleep when I do and so it was. By noon I was dozing, slightly inebriated but still in full control of my faculties. The others were in similar shape. We rendezvoused with the other boat at Wolf Island, where the two guides built a fire, cleaned the fish and began to fry them.

"Has anybody ever had Bees Knees?" our host asked.

All of us shook our heads, not knowing whether it was something to eat, or to drink. It turned out to be something to drink, one of his favorite concoctions. He took an agate coffee pot, emptied a can of Birdseye Lemon Juice into it, added three heaping tablespoons of honey and then filled it with gin. After stirring it, he handed each of us a large coffee mug, and proudly prepared to pour. The two COLs politely extended their cups but cut off the supply with only a bit in the bottom of their mugs. So it went, our host was obviously disappointed until he came to me. I said, "Fill her up, sir."

He beamed, complied gladly, then filled his own cup. A pleasant drink, it was very potent. He insisted that I have another cup, which made almost a pint that I drank. Luckily lunch was ready at that time. The fish was indescribable, crisp and tasty. There were many other delightful things to go with the fish; potato salad, cucumber and watercress sandwiches, all sorts of relishes, cold cuts, bread, coffee and dessert. We sat around the fire talking for almost an hour. This made me even more sleepy. As we had brought our bathing suits, I suggested we go swimming. Everyone was too comfortable, so I elected to go alone. There was some concern about my going swimming in view of what I had imbibed and that it was just an hour after lunch. Something had to be done to dispel my lethargy, and I did know my capacity and ability to swim. Despite the half-hearted protests, I stepped behind some bushes, quickly donned my swimming trunks and plunged into the lake. Swimming a mile out, I felt invigorated upon returning to the Island.

As soon as I dressed, we boarded the boats and fished a little more. Our luck deserted us, I caught only two more fish; mainly we talked and drank. The guides got us back to the dock about 1730. Our invitation included dinner at Deerlick Farm that evening. A magnificent dinner it was, served in the beautiful old farm house which had been restored and redecorated. Everything in the house - linens, silverware, china - bore the insignia of the estate - the words "Deerlick Farm" encircled by a horseshoe. The roast turkey with oyster dressing was simple but delicious. The vegetables had been picked that very afternoon. Dinner was served by several white gloved waiters under the careful supervision of the butler. Elegant hardly does justice to that repast. It was a delightful evening of talk; our return to Pine Camp about 2300 ended the fabulous fishing trip of 1948.

Back at Pine Camp, I returned to my routine. Colonel England decided to institute a liquor locker system in the Club. Liquor would no longer be sold across the bar, but everyone would provide his own bottle. To make the system convenient, COL England directed the Post Engineer to build lockers just large enough to hold four quart bottles. Officers could rent these lockers, thus eliminating the need for carrying liquor to and from the club every day. The bar tender would mix drinks using the customer's liquor. The Colonel was in consultation with me constantly about that project. Hence, I expected him in my office almost daily.

At this same time Mrs England gave me more and more trouble. She became quite obnoxious, criticizing, complaining, even correcting my EM. If she found something that displeased her when I was out of the office, she would find my SGT or one of the other EM and berate them unmercifully. The men rightly resented it and complained to me. Things came to a head one day late in July. My senior NCO reported that Mrs England had "made an inspection" of the bar, found some chewing gum stuck under the ledge, located him and began chewing him out. He had cut her tirade short, whereupon she informed him that she was going to speak to me about his conduct. I told him to forget the incident and go on with his duties.

In due time Mrs England came to my office, visibly angry. Without preamble she started to tongue-lash me about the Club, the cleanliness, general appearance, food, parties, the gamut. She continued her harangue for a minute or two before I stopped her,

"Mrs England, stop right there. I am perfectly satisfied with the way the Club looks and operates. If you have any complaints, take them to your husband so that he can bring them to me. I do not work for you, and I will not take any abuse from you or anyone else."

She started her diatribe again, again I cut her short.

"Apparently you didn't hear me, Mrs England. I am not going to listen to your tirades. Now get out of the Club. If you have any complaints, tell your husband; I will discuss them with him."

Again she tried to launch into a petulant criticism of the Club and its personnel. By now my patience was at an end. Interrupting her, I said, "I don't think you understand, Mrs England. You are not a member of this Club. You are an Associate Member by virtue of your husband's membership. Now, I am ordering you out of the Club. You will not set foot in this Club unless you are with your husband, your sponsor. Is that clear?"

She looked at me aghast; for a moment I thought she was going to faint or cry.

"Well, I'll tell John about this and he'll be right down and straighten things out. You can't talk to me that way."

"Mrs England, I tried to talk to you in a courteous manner but you are so overwrought that you would not listen. I had to take some means of getting through to you. I am deadly serious in what I have said. I do not want to see you in this Club except with COL England from now on. Is that clear?"

She heaved herself out. Within 15 minutes, COL England was in my office. He spent 45 minutes talking about the liquor lockers, the upcoming dance, the Officers' Field Mess, about everything but the fact that I had thrown Mrs England out of the Club. Since he did not bring up the subject, I did not. The Colonel never did mention the matter to me, nor did Mrs England come into the Club for the next few weeks unless she was with the COL.

Mrs England did not set foot in the cub unaccompanied until near the end of the season. One day my NCOIC reported that Mrs England, alone, had ordered a chocolate sundae at the ice cream bar. He asked if he should serve her. Believing she had learned her lesson, I told him to do so. She ate her sundae and left. Long afterwards I learned that Mrs England even at that time was suffering from a cancer from which she eventually died. It was an unfortunate situation, but I could not let her interfere with my people.

Toward the end of the summer, Howard Leifheit made his decision to return to the Army. He actually entered on extended AD in January 1949 and was later commissioned in the RA.

The summer finally came to an end. In transferring the Club accounts back to the Permanent Party, I gave them $10 more than had been turned over to me at the beginning of the season. I had made a profit but not the bonanza England expected. However, the Club had provided good food and entertainment to many officers on temporary duty. This was my mission and I believe that I accomplished it.

During the audit associated with the transfer, a discrepancy in the accounts was discovered. To minimize the handling of cash, chit books used in lieu of cash at the bar and for meals were sold in the Club Office. It was a procedure which had been recommended by the Post IG. During the inventory, I noticed that the books had not been sold in the proper sequence, hence all were not accounted for. The PM was notified and asked to investigate. COL England was also notified. The ensuing investigation revealed that a young CPL who worked in the Club office, had been selling books and not putting the money into the cash drawer. Charges were preferred against him and I was alerted to return to Pine Camp to testify against him during his General Court-martial.

Financially, the summer had been profitable for me. I had drawn captain's pay for a little more than three months; with limited expenses, I had accrued a nice cash reserve. While attending LICM under the GI Bill, my tuition, fees and books were paid for and about $75.00 per month was provided for living expenses. It was good to have a cash reserve to fall back on.

In late September I returned for my third year of medical school with little enthusiasm. Duty at Pine Camp had reawakened my interest in the military; I now found that I missed even the mundane duties I had performed during summer camp. Perhaps the camaraderie enjoyed in the military environment was the single most important factor which influenced me. Sharing the experiences, life and rewards of service, somehow strengthens friendships, indeed, develops them more rapidly and deeply than is possible in civilian life. It was hard to refocus my interest back on medicine. Despite my attitude, I retook the examination in Obstetrics, passed it, and accepted my D (the only grade given on re-examination).

Third year medical school brings the aspiring physician abruptly in contact with patients. The first quarter consisted of lectures in various specialities: Obstetrics, Gynecology, Pediatrics, Psychiatry, and General Medicine. We made rounds on the Wards of the Long Island College Hospital with attending physicians who used the patients as training aids to show us various symptoms and disease characteristics. We listened to the sounds made by the heart and lungs in certain disorders. All of this was done with the permission of the patients, many of whom were charity cases. It was always embarrassing to me when our group of 15 students trooped up to listen to a "crack pot resonance", a diastolic murmur, rales, or some other characteristic symptom. It must have been tiring, and difficult for the patients, even though they had given their consent. The doctors, however, seemed oblivious to the possible embarrassment the patients.

After the first quarter we were assigned to "junior clerkships", during which we worked on the wards of hospitals associated with LICM, supervised closely by interns, residents and attending physicians. My first clerkship was on the Obstetrics Ward of the Bedford-Stuyvesant Hospital. It was a city hospital in a run-down part of Brooklyn in which crime and poverty flourished; most of the patients were charity cases. For that reason it was a very busy hospital in which a junior clerk could expect to get a lot of hands on training. In fact, we got too much. There was no time to absorb the information and experience thrown at us, to review what we had learned or the mistakes we had made. Walt Stankewick and I were on the same clerkship.

Before reporting to Bedford-Stuyvesant, I went back to Pine Camp to testify at the court-martial. The CPL was found guilty and sentenced to two years in prison. During the three days there, I had another brief opportunity to look at Army life; at that time I finally made my decision to go back into military service. On my return to LICM I had another long talk with Dr Potter, since he had advised me to go on active duty during the summer before making my decision. Dr Potter applauded my decision, saying that he thought I was showing a great deal of courage and sense in making the decision now. "Once you are in the field and have your MD, it will be difficult not to practice, and the profession does not need an undedicated doctor." I certainly agreed with him.

MAJ Abrignani informed me that Department of the Army (DA) Circular 382 provided for recall to active duty officers who desired to apply for an RA commission. There were two ways to obtain such a commission under Circular 382: by direct appointment, or through "competitive tour". Individuals who had served as commissioned officers during WWII and who had college degrees were eligible for direct appointment as a 2LT, RA. The date of rank of such a commission would be,1 January 1948, for those on active duty; for those, like myself, who were in the RES, the date of rank would be adjusted for time not served on active duty. In other words, an OFF lost all rank prior to I Jan 1948. Most OFFs were integrated into the RA according to age or total length of service, but Circular 382 limited both the grade and date of rank. OFFs on "competitive tours" were required to serve in four duty assignments during a one year period. Based on the four efficiency reports, a Board would determine those to be commissioned as 2nd LTs, RA. Again, date of rank would be I January 1948 (adjusted for those not on extended active duty).

MAJ Abrignani suggested that I apply under both criteria, and helped me prepare the paperwork required. In due course, notification that I had been accepted for competitive tour was received. In my request, I had asked to serve my competitive tour with the 82nd Airborne Division at FT Bragg, NC, and attend The Parachute School at FT Benning, GA enroute. Both requests were approved; I was directed to report to the nearest military installation for a physical examination. Orders were to be issued directing me to report on Active Duty at Benning on 10 Jan 1949 to attend The Parachute School. This information was in a letter, but I had no orders. The Army also acknowledged receipt of my application for a direct commission.

There was an Army Dispensary and Examining Facility in the Federal Building at 90 Church Street in Manhattan to which I reported for my physical exam. The physical went well until the hearing test. The young medical technician conducting the examination shook his head as he told me that I had a loss of hearing in the conversational range frequencies which would disqualify me as an RA OFF. My morale plummeted. Was my military career to end even before it began? The technician noting my dejection, suggested that the hearing loss could be waived.

In making conversation, the NCO asked me what unit I had served with in WWII. When I told him the 96th Div, he became excited. He had served with the "Dead-eyes" also! I was the first person he had come across since the end of the war who had been in the 96th Div; no one he had encountered up to this point had even heard of it. He immediately became my friend and advocate.

"We can't let a hearing loss keep a Deadeye out of the Army. I think I can fix it." With that he made an adjustment on the record, and told me to proceed with the examination. So began a long and difficult cover up; I often felt guilty, since I was not completely honest with the Army about my physical profile. I compromised my integrity on this matter and would continue to hide my hearing loss throughout my career. It is the only time I knowingly and deliberately made or tacitly approved a false official statement. I have rationalized that it never affected my performance of duty, but the fact remains that I compromised my integrity.

Up to this time I had not told anyone of my decision to leave medical school for the Army except Dr Potter and MAJ Abrignani. When notification of acceptance arrived, I confided in Hanz Druener, who was highly sympathetic. He, too, was thinking of returning to AD as he was having second thoughts about a career as one of "New York's Finest" policemen. He asked me to write him as soon as I got settled to let him know how things were in the Army, he might follow me in.

Despite my intention to leave medical school I reported for the junior clerkship in Obstetrics at Bedford-Stuyvesant Hospital. It was a busy clerkship during which we observed, assisted and handled many deliveries. As we gained experience, we were permitted to handle routine deliveries under supervision. If any problem was anticipated, an intern or resident handled the case. In the ensuing two weeks, I delivered six babies, one of which was stillborn. The stillborn was traumatic, when I informed the mother that her baby was dead on birth, she became hysterical. It took the efforts of both the Ward Nurse and myself to quiet her.

At the beginning of the Christmas vacation, I still hadn't told my family or friends. The last school day in December 1948, I went to see Dean Clarke, informing him that I was leaving LICM at the Christmas break. He was shocked. A dedicated doctor, he could not understand why anyone would aspire to any other profession. In fact, he suggested that I talk with one of the Psychiatrists. I laughed as I told him that I had already talked with Dr Potter who concurred in my decision.

Walt Stankewick and I had rooms in the same boarding house; he was puzzled when I cleaned out all my belongings and terminated my lease. But I still did not tell him or any of my other classmates of my decision.

That Christmas seemed brighter, more joyous, than any I remembered. Even the stars shone brighter. During the early part of the leave, I measured a one mile stretch of road and began to run it every day.

Finally, after Christmas, I told Mother and Dad that I was leaving medical school. They were stunned. They did not say much and did not try to talk me into continuing on. It was my decision, which they accepted. But I knew they were hurt and disappointed, certainly they were not enthusiastic about my decision to go back into the Army. Over the years they reconciled themselves to my new profession, taking as much pride and delight in my Army career as I did.

On the 2nd of January I still had no orders. Though I had given my parents' home address for all my official correspondence with the Army, I checked back at the boarding house and LICM to see if any mail had come for me, it had not. In desperation, I called the Pentagon. I don't know to this day how I managed to get in touch with the right party, but finally I talked to an officer who knew my case. He told me that I should report to the Pentagon to get my orders, giving me his name and room number.

On 6 January I packed my uniforms, kissed Mother goodbye, shook hands with Dad, and left for Penn Station. They were still unaware that I was going to Jump School. On leaving, I promised to get home to see them as soon as possible. For the second time, I boarded a train at Penn Station to begin a career in the Army.

I stopped off in Baltimore to see Ted Rothert, my classmate at Walter Reed. I met his wife, Amy, a former Army nurse. Continuing my journey the next day, I finally got to the Pentagon, found my way through that confusing maze of rings, corridors, and bays to the room I had been told to report to. When I gave my name and serial number to the MAJ who handled recalls to AD, he looked startled. Rummaging through his desk, he pulled out a folder and said,

"Oh, didn't you get the word?"

"No, what do you mean?"

"Well, your application for active duty has been disapproved."

It seemed as if I had been struck in the stomach with a sledge hammer. "Damn! Have I thrown away medical school for nothing? I received word that everything had been approved."

As I leaped to my feet I looked at the file in his hand. It was marked Donald W. Seibert, AR. This immediately alerted me.

"Hell, that's not my file. I'm not AR, I'm IN." He checked the file, then asked for my serial number. "01038113", I rattled off.

"That's not the serial number on this file. Wait a minute." As I waited with renewed hope, he searched through the files on his desk. It seemed like hours before he pulled out another file. "This is your file, Donald A. Seibert, Inf, 01038113. And, yes, your application for AD has been approved. You are assigned to the 82nd Airborne Division with TDY enroute at the Airborne School at Fort Benning, reporting 10 January. Yep, it's all in order."

"Thank God. You sure gave me a jolt." My heart was still pounding.

"My secretary will type out a couple of copies of the order to get you to Benning. We'll mail the official orders to you. However, you can get these reproduced at The Infantry School (TIS)."

Heaving a great sigh, I took the orders, went to Union Station and caught the next train to Columbus, GA. I arrived there early on 9 January 1949.

CHAPTER 6

PARATROOPER

The train came to a halt at the Columbus Railroad Station, launching me on my Airborne career. Alighting from it, I noticed the large sign, which I had first seen in 1944, "Students for the Parachute School, report to the NCO at the Information Desk for transportation". A neat, courteous paratrooper popped to attention when I identified myself as an Airborne Student. He escorted me to a bus which took all those reporting to Jump School to the Post. The route looked familiar. I remembered Victory Boulevard and other sights along the way as we drove out to FT Benning. Very shortly the four 250-foot towers came into view, I looked at them with a different feeling this time.

The bus pulled into the Jump School area, on the hill above Lawson Air Field. After signing in at the Parachute School I had to go to the Post AG's Office to sign in on extended active duty. I was assigned to G Company, Airborne Training Battalion, Student Training Regiment, The Infantry School, and also to a room in the BOQ in the Biglerville area. This was the same area I had lived in when attending OSB 43, though this time we were in BOQS with individual rooms.

All the officers in my BOQ were Airborne Students in the same Co and the same class. We quickly sized each other up as we introduced ourselves. Most were younger than I; all were in top physical condition. Since I had done very little PT since 1946, I was in marginal condition, but determined to use the few days before classes began to get into better shape. A number of other officers wanted to improve their condition, so an impromptu PT class was organized which included a run twice a day, the "Army Dozen" (calisthenics), and whatever else we could think of. Those few days paid off; once we got into the course, I was able to keep up. During the next few days the inevitable processing took place, including another physical examination and hearing test. Since this was a spoken test rather than one using the audiometer, I managed to get by once again. There were many forms to fill out, papers to sign and circulars to read.

We reported to school on 17 January. The senior OFF in the class, LTC John R. Pugh, a United States Military Academy (USMA) graduate and former Cavalryman, was appointed Student Co CO. He organized the class as a "squadron". As his "Adjutant" as contrasted to 1SG, I did the detail work in getting the Co organized for classes, passed orders, got messages to people and handled other administrative and military chores. There were 19 OFFs in our class (2 LTCs, 5 CPTs, 8 1LT, 3 2LTs, and a CW2) and double that number of EM.

The first week of the four week course was devoted to PT and air transportability. The latter emphasized techniques in lashing vehicles and other equipment in C-46, C-47 and C-82 aircraft, and in gliders. We loaded jeeps and other equipment in mock-ups of gliders and aircraft, tied them in, then unloaded them. We went through hell in PT; the cadre poured it on, for good reasons. A Paratrooper must be in good shape to stand the strains put on his body during jumping. It was not that a great deal of strength is needed, but the body takes much punishment from the opening shock and landing. During the Orientation, we rode the "buddy seat" to the top of the 250-foot tower and made a controlled descent, much like the parachute ride at the New York World's Fair or at Coney Island.

Physical conditioning and responsiveness were stressed that first week. Each morning we were inspected; push-ups were meted out as punishment for any shortcoming in the shine of our boots or belt buckles, haircut or uniform. Even though we wore fatigues we were expected to look sharp. Sharp as used in the Airborne meant a soldier who was alert, professional, physically fit, and superlatively groomed - looking as if ready for inspection - everything that could be shined (brass, belt buckle, boots) gleaming, fatigues or khakis heavily starched with knife edge creases, hats blocked, trousers bloused, hair cut short (the "flat-top" was much admired, as were "white side-walls"), posture erect, attitude alert. OFFs received the same treatment as EM in the class. The only exception was that the two LTCs stood inspections separately from the Co. Whether or not they were ever gigged or required to do push-ups for imperfections was never revealed to the rest of the class. They also took PT separately, we would occasionally pass them on runs, being shepherded along by a self-conscious NCO. Co grade OFFs took PT with the EM; this gave us an added incentive not to fall out in front of the troops, and served to weld ABN OFFs and EM more closely together because both shared the same training. There were two periods of PT a day. In that first week, a few students (OFFs and EM), fell by the wayside; they either could not or would not accept the discipline and physical conditioning required. The highlight of this week was a glider ride which earned us our glider wings.

The second week we reported to the Ground Training Area to begin Parachute Training. We continued PT, especially the running. We learned and practiced exits from a "mock door" of an, parachute landing falls (PLFs) from a three foot platform, and how to recover when being dragged. This was accomplished by inflating a chute by means of a huge fan, the "wind machine" which created a rush of air powerful enough to blow the chute and drag the harnessed student across the ground. We learned to collapse the chute by hauling on the bottom risers to spill out the air, or getting to our feet and running around the parachute to collapse it. This second method could only be used in light winds.

The big challenge in the second week was the 34-foot tower. With much trepidation we put on the web harness with its four canvas "risers" ending in hooks; with increasing dread we doubled timed up the steps to the platform 34 feet above the ground. Here two burly NCOs hooked us onto a pulley which rolled along a sloping steel cable to a mound about 100 yards from the tower. After last minute instructions and checks an NCO shouted "Stand in the Door". We shuffled to the mock door in the approved manner holding our "static line" with the proper bight or loop, pivoted and stamped into the correct exit position (all of which we had practiced in our mock door exercises). Then came the real test! The cadreman ordered us to look down and then straight ahead. The NCO suddenly shouted "GO!", at the same time slapping us on the butt. It took much soul searching to spring into the air, trusting to that pulley and harness. As we leaped we had to assume a faultless body position (hands on the reserve, chin tucked into the chest, eyes on our feet, legs extended and joined) and count loudly "One thousand, two thousand, three thousand". Suddenly there was a jolt as the slack in the risers was expended and our weight was caught up by the harness, simulating the "opening shock". At this time we had to reach up, spread the risers apart, and look up to "check our canopy". Each movement was graded by the cadre. Meanwhile we were rolling toward the mound and had to take up a "prepare to land" attitude. Upon reaching the mound we were unhooked. We then double timed to the grading OFF or NCO seated in a student chair at the foot of the tower, and were critiqued. Before we were permitted to advance to the next stage of training it was necessary to make three satisfactory exits. A student detail ran the pulley or trolley back to the tower by means of a drag rope.

PLFs were practiced by jumping from platforms three or six feet high. We placed our toes at the edge of the platforms, facing the sawdust pit beneath it for a front fall, back to the sawdust pit for a rear fall, and right or left to the sawdust pit for a right or left fall. The instructor would call out the type PLF he wanted" "LEFT REAR PARACHUTE LANDING FALL!" We would assume the proper position, our toes at the edge of the platform, knees slightly bent, hands over head as if we held our risers in a "prepare to land position". "Ready, GO!" We leaped off to the side, back or front to make the appropriate PLF. In a correct PLF there were four points of contact: the balls of the feet, calf, thigh, and what was known as the "push-up muscle", or the latisimus dorsi and teres major as I knew from medical school. We were drilled in the "five points of performance" in the air, CHECK YOUR BODY POSITION AND COUNT; CHECK YOUR CANOPY; KEEP A SHARP LOOKOUT DURING DESCENT; PREPARE TO LAND; LAND.

It was during this week that the eliminations began in earnest. Several OFFs and EM voluntarily signed "quit slips" and withdrew from the course, especially on encountering the 34-foot tower. Others were flunked out because of excessive demerits, or because in the opinion of the cadre they lacked sufficient determination or coordination to complete the training.

At this time I had the bad luck to run afoul of the cadre. One morning, as we were getting ready to assemble preparatory to double timing to the Tower Area, a group of cadre NCOs was looking at us critically. A young private (PVT) ran to get into the formation. Just at that moment, a cadre 2LT stepped around the corner of the building. Obviously the PVT did not see him and failed to salute. The cadre NCOs immediately descended on him, took him out of the formation, dressed him down for lack of alertness and military courtesy, and made him do 50 push-ups. It appeared to me that this was excessive; I also thought the NCOs had been abusive in making their correction for improper military courtesy. That failure to salute was an innocent error.

Satisfied with their diligence, the cadremen reassembled to talk among themselves. At that moment LTC Pugh walked past them preparing to take charge of the Co. They looked at him but failed to salute. My blood boiled! I walked over, called the group to attention, and dressed them down in much the same manner they had dressed down the PVT, though with no verbal abuse. When asked why they had not saluted LTC Pugh, they replied that he was "just a student". I really boiled at that! In clipped tones I instructed them that regardless of his status as a student, LTC Pugh was still a lieutenant colonel in the United States Army, entitled to all the rights and privileges of his grade, including the respect of NCOs such as themselves. They were advised that in class formations, some saluting could be eliminated in the interests of time and efficiency, but in all other circumstances proper military courtesy was in order. After suggesting that they set an example in alertness and courtesy, I ordered them to do 50 push-ups, the same punishment they had exacted from the PVT. They were bitter about it and told me that I was out of line.

"I'm a lieutenant in the United States Army, I gave you NCOs a direct order to do 50 pushups. Now MOVE!"

The cadre NCOs reluctantly did the push-ups and moved out.

The formation got organized and we double timed over to the Tower Area. By the time we arrived there, word of my action had reached the cadre. From then on I could do nothing right. Every one of my PLFs was criticized; I had to do them over and over again. Everything I did was watched with a jaundiced eye; I was on parade from then on. The worst came when we were jumping from the 34-foot tower. I hated it! I hated to make exits out of it, not only because of a certain psychological reaction (fear?) to jumping from it as contrasted with actually jumping out of an aircraft, but also because of the bruising jolt received. There is a theory that the fear of height is a function of still being connected with the earth while looking down, as contrasted with being free of such fear while flying because of being completely divorced from the earth when looking down from an aircraft in flight. At any rate, I hated the 34-foot tower, but I had to make three satisfactory exits from it. Usually a student made a couple of practice jumps, then was rated satisfactory unless he was completely uncoordinated. Every exit I made was considered unsatisfactory: my hands were too close together on my reserve; my hands were too far apart on my reserve; my feet were not together; my feet were crossed; my body was arched; my body was straight; my exit was too vigorous; my exit was not vigorous enough. All my exits were unsatisfactory.

When the last day of training on the 34-foot tower arrived, I hadn't made a single satisfactory exit from it according to the cadre. That Friday, I climbed up the steps of that 34-foot platform 35 times! I jumped, recovered, ran from mound to tower, was criticized in a snide manner bordering on disrespect, harnessed up again, was re-inspected, double timed up the steps and made another unsatisfactory exit. I was so tired that I didn't know what I was doing and literally fell out of the tower the last few jumps. Finally three jumps were declared satisfactory. I am certain that of all the jumps I made from the tower during that week, these were the least satisfactory, but the cadre was obviously afraid to eliminate me from the course because they knew I was determined to qualify, they knew I would fight to stay in the course and call them to account for their harassment if necessary. My ordeal on the 34-foot tower seemed to satisfy them, although I still had to watch my step carefully. In the long run it probably redounded to my benefit because I got to practice every procedure over and over, and got more physical conditioning than anybody else!

The 34-foot tower training continued into the third week. Also in that third week, in addition to PT, mock door and PLF training, we worked in the "suspended harness" - agony training. We got into harnesses similar to those used in the 34-foot tower, were hooked up to a ring or wheel, which was then hoisted by ropes and pulleys until our feet were off the ground. Thus suspended, we learned to maneuver the parachute, slipping by pulling down on the risers. We also packed the five parachutes we would use for our qualifying jumps. We were taught to shake them out, untangle the suspension lines, smooth out the panels and fold them properly before stowing them and the suspension lines in the back packs. It was excellent training; not only did we get to understand the functioning of the parachute, but it was an impressive exercise in confidence. We learned to appreciate the job the riggers do. It is too bad that such training has been deleted in the interest of economy.

During the third week we dropped from the 250-foot towers. Each of the three towers used for uncontrolled descent had four arms at right angles to the others. From the arms cables were let down, to which large metal rings were attached. Special parachutes, with standard harnesses were used. The apex of the canopies had plugs which fit into sockets at the end of the cables, this was the means of releasing the parachutes on command. The skirts of the canopies were clipped to the metal rings, fully deploying them. The class was split, some doing suspended harness or other training, while about half worked on the 250-foot towers. That half was divided into three groups, one to an arm as only three arms were used on each tower. One student, the pole man, inserted the plug into the socket by means of a long pole. The remainder of the group snapped the canopy to the ring while the man in the harness stood in the center under the canopy. The student was then raised 250 feet, on command he was dropped. This gave practice in checking the canopy, slipping, preparing to land and making an actual parachute landing fall. It was good training and great fun. Occasionally we dropped from a "dirty arm". The arm pointing into the wind was not used because the jumper would be blown into the tower on release. Sometimes the wind would shift during the period and blow at an angle to the arm being used. The shift would not be enough to be considered dangerous, but might blow a jumper into the tower occasionally. This was the "dirty arm". Some students did get blown into the tower, especially if the wind was gusting or fishtailing. I was fortunate never to get the dirty arm or to be blown into the tower. In one or two cases, students blown into the tower became panic stricken and froze. One of the cadreman then had to climb out on the girders and talk the individuals down. Though the 250-foot tower was great run, we only made three or four jumps from it.

The other two events handled by the Tower Committee in the third week were a final run and a PT test. The final run was led by MAJ H. V. Mansfield, a stocky, enthusiastic, energetic OFF with beetling eyebrows, the OIC of the Tower Training Committee. We followed Mansfield from the Tower Area, down the hill to Lawson Air Field, around Lawson Field, along the Chattahootchee River, then up the steep hill to the Airborne Area. It was a long drag up that hill; the cadre harassed anyone who fell out on that run; several did.

The PT Test was the Standard Army PT Test, however, the Airborne Cadre demanded higher standards than the minimum usually considered satisfactory. We had to perform eight pull-ups, 25 push-ups, 75 sit-ups in two minutes, 100 squat jumps in three minutes and a 50 yard dash in

10 seconds. Only exercises done in exact form were counted. Having applied myself in PT (and benefitting no doubt, from the additional push-ups and other "training" the Tower Committee had given me) I made an acceptable score. During the exam, I questioned the rating of one EM and had to report to MAJ Mansfield. After chewing me out royally, he sent me back to the group considering myself fortunate that I did not have to work for him. He appeared to be hard headed and unreasonable!

The last week of the course was jump week, which we had trained for and looked forward to - both with great anticipation, as well as trepidation. Any one who said they were completely indifferent to those first jumps was either a damn fool or a liar. We were all much concerned and keyed up for the first jump.

The great day finally came. We reported to Lawson Field to what was called the "sweat shed", a wooden addition on the end of the hanger in which we had packed our parachutes. After we were manifested (assigned to a "stick" in random order) we secured one of the 'chutes we had packed and struggled into the harness. We took special care in adjusting it you may be sure, and were then checked by NCOs or riggers. The initial jump was to be an individual tap out; the second, a two man tap out; the rest stick jumps (all men following the first jumper without command). On the last jump we were to jump with weapons.

Once in the parachute harness we sat on benches, waiting. The reason it was called the sweat shed was because jumpers sat and waited and sweated. Jumpers sweat for many reasons: because it is hot; because they are confined in parachute harnesses which are adjusted snugly to minimize the opening shock; because of concern about the outcome of the jump. The risers deployed first from the T-7 parachute, which caused a terrific jolt or "opening shock" when the canopy was inflated; if the harness was not adjusted so that there was no slack in it, the opening shock was magnified and the quick release box often shifted and struck the careless in the chin. Tightening of the harness was sometimes carried to extremes, but however adjusted, it was always uncomfortable to be in one before the chute was deployed; a cause to sweat. Jumpers were always faced with the possibility of a malfunction of the chute, of problems in the air (oscillation due to wind or poor body position, of collisions or entanglements with inexperienced jumpers), of missing the Drop Zone (DZ) due to wind or faulty estimates by pilot or ground control personnel, of making a poor landing. All causes to sweat.

The individual tap out went well. The procedure was the same as that used in the 34-foot tower so this was an old routine for me! Each jumper shuffled up to and took position in the door. Jumpers were then tapped out three or four seconds apart. This was done to preclude the possibility of colliding in the air, to enable instructors on the ground to monitor our descent and make corrections in our performance, as well as to facilitate grading. The manifest or list of jumpers was available to the cadre on the ground. While in the air we were barraged with instructions; Number Two Jumper slip to your right; Number Six Jumper check your canopy; Number Ten Jumper get your legs together. We jumped from a C-82 aircraft onto Lee Field, which was so well plowed that it seemed impossible to get hurt, nobody was. The wind was ideal for that first jump; we recovered with relief and considerable confidence. After getting out of our chutes, we "rigger rolled" (a hasty twirling to get the skirt of the parachute tight, like preparing to store a collapsible umbrella) the parachute, put it in our kit bag, which we threw over our shoulders, double timed to the assembly point, reported in, turned in parachutes, then listened to a critique of our performance.

The next day the weather turned foul; we sat in the sweat shed about an hour and a half before the jump was canceled. On the third and fourth days the jumps also had to be canceled. Each day the adrenalin pumped as we sweated for an hour or two. The fifth day, which was to have been our graduation day, we made our second jump, the two man tap out. On Monday of the fifth week we were able to get in one jump early in the morning, then the weather closed in again. Tuesday there were no jumps but lots of sweating. On Wednesday we got in a jump at 0800. Without pause, we were trucked hastily back to Lawson Field, issued weapons and a Griswold Container (a padded carrier for the M-1 rifle with snaps so it could be fastened to the harness) and hurried into our parachutes. As soon as we received our rigger checks, we were loaded into waiting C-82s with engines running, which took off immediately. We made our fifth and qualifying jump without injuries or incidents.

The graduation ceremony was at 1400 in the ABN Co Area. We were proud and happy; happy to be away from the harassment of the cadre, proud of ourselves for having qualified as paratroopers.

One of the members of the class, Chief Warrant Officer, Second Grade (C W2) Charlesworth, Director of the 82nd ABN Div Band, who was driving to FT Bragg immediately after graduation, offered me a ride. We hurriedly cleared the Post, then departed without bothering to change into civilian clothes. After a 10 hour drive we reached FT Bragg about midnight Charlesworth drove to Div HQ where we signed in. The DO got me a temporary billet after instructing me to report to the G-l (personnel staff OFF) in the morning for my assignment within the Div.

The next morning I donned a starched khaki uniform with gleaming brass, and spit-shined jump boots before reporting to the G-1. After examining my appearance closely, he instructed me, "In this Division you wear your jump wings on top of all other decorations, including the CIB. You are a paratrooper and should be proud to show it."

I was proud of being a paratrooper, but I was also proud of my CIB. Though not convinced that jump wings outranked the CIB or that Army Regulations prescribed that order of rank, I did not question the matter. With a clipped, "Yes, sir", I shifted the jump wings. The G-l then told me that I was assigned to the 504th ABN IN Regt. Hanz Druener had fought with the 504, and the cadre at Jump School had mentioned it with approval, it had an illustrious record in WWII. As the 504th Regt HQ was just across the street from Div HQ, I walked quickly over, signed in, and reported to the Adj, who informed me that I was further assigned to HHC. Though I would have preferred an assignment to a rifle Co I did not protest. Since I was on a Competitive Tour for an RA commission, I would spend only three months in HHC before being reassigned.

The Adj pointed out the Head and Head Orderly Room across the parade field, where I reported to 1LT Charles Stevens, the Co CO. Stevens, a stocky, unimpressive officer, seemed prone to jump to questionable conclusions, he made me his XO. He introduced me to the two other HHC OFFs 1LT Ed Morris, the Commo Plt Ldr, and 1LT Charles Dubsky, the Intelligence and Reconnaissance (I&R) Platoon Leader. Morris was a fine looking soldier, well built, neat, dark headed, friendly, a true professional. He inspired confidence, I liked him immediately, we began a warm and close friendship which has continued throughout the years. Dubsky, a husky, tall, blond, almost arrogant, USMA graduate, lived in the same BOQ that I did. We formed a close association. Three of the Co NCOs I met that day made immediate, favorable and lasting impressions on me, SFC Carbajal (later MSG), of the Commo Plt, SFC (later MSG) James Tryon, PSG of the I&R Plt, and SGT Watts, a SL in the I&R Plt. None of them worked directly for me, but they drew attention wherever they were by their impressive appearance and performance. They were the kind of NCOs who came to mind when you thought of the ABN, proud, sharp, competent, the true elite.

Stevens gave me an additional duty, Motor Officer. The Regt Motor OFF, CPT Gray (assigned to Service Co), when he found that I had no Motor OFF experience, took me under his wing. He and the HHC Motor SGT, an experienced and competent NCO, taught me the rudiments of my duties and kept me out of trouble. The number of motor vehicles in HHC surprised me, I had the impression that ABN Divs, like Amphibious ones, had only a few critical vehicles. But after the war, vehicles had been added to meet specific needs, hence the large number I found in the 504.

The 504 BOQ, in which I was assigned a room, was a typical WWII wooden BOQ, with one big improvement, an additional latrine had been installed on the second floor to augment the original one on the ground floor, a convenience since I was on the second floor. The rooms were not finished, the studs were still exposed but the cats between them made good shelves for glasses and liquor bottles. Furniture was minimal: a metal GI cot, a dresser and a shelf with a clothing rack under it. Eventually a folding field table and chair were provided. It was convenient, next to the Officers' Field Mess and across the parade ground from the buildings housing the companies.

There was a wild crowd in that BOQ. The senior officer was MAJ (Wild Bill) Martin, CO of the 1st Bn. He had two rooms, one furnished with a comfortable leather living room set which I bought from him later. CPT Stieber lived on the second floor, down the hall from me. The rest of the OFFs were 1LTs and 2LTs, including Frank Mashburn, Bud Hillman, Jack Philips, Hal Langerman, Charlie Dubsky, Frank Westling, Sherwood Stutz and Frank Gilmore. There were three dogs: Stieber's beautiful but neurotic German Shepherd, Hillman's friendly but slobbering Boxer, and Langerman's Kerry Blue, Hood. It was a boisterous and active crew which got along well together. I liked most of them though but my special friends were Mashburn and Hillman.

A number of married officers in the 504 became good friends. At least once a week some couple invited me to their home for dinner and the evening. Those who became life long friends and whose careers touched mine again and again included Tom and Lilian Tackaberry, Peanut and Marjie Hinton, Bob and Betty Whitelaw, Bill and Betty Ankley, Ed and Betty Morris, Dave and Sara McNaught, John and Lorraine Kiser, Al and Hela Bettelli, and Ted and Kay Fuller.

A routine soon emerged; reveille at 0600, breakfast at the Regimental Officers Field Mess, then back to HHC by 0730 for duty. A check of the motor pool was usually my first business. The other officers went out on various training or administrative assignments.

Co PT was lead by each of the Co OFFs in turn. The first day I had that duty I learned a quick lesson. As was customary, after the "Army Dozen", calisthenics were concluded by doing 25 push-ups. After the 25th push-up that first morning, some wag in the back of the formation shouted, "More, more". Not sure whether the call was serious, or that the company usually did a second set of 25, and pleased that the men were so gung-ho, I naively gave a second set of 25 push-ups. Some of the men had difficulty with that set, but again came the call "More, more". Foolishly, I again capitulated, finding it difficult to finish that last set of push-ups myself. Three fourths of the Co failed to do so. Then it struck me that these characters were testing me, but I had been stupid enough to punish the entire Co because I was taken in by their feigned interest in PT. There were a few mutters of "Chicken", but I'd learned my lesson and never again listened to anonymous comments from the ranks. In all future PT sessions I posted an NCO at the rear of the Co to make sure there were no remarks in the ranks.

Shortly after joining Head and Head, I was at the motor pool when there was a commotion at the Regt Motor Office. CPT Gray came out of his office with a tall, thin officer, and headed directly toward the HHC area. When he got close, I noticed that the OFF was wearing one star. He was obviously BG Charles D.W. Canham, the Asst Div CDR. The troopers called Canham "The Skull" because his head and face were gaunt.

I reported to Canham, who informed me that he wanted to inspect HHC's vehicles. With an air of confidence I led him to the first in line. He inspected it thoroughly and professionally, obviously well versed in such matters; he pointed out that the grease fittings were not shining. They had not been cleaned after the grease gun had been disconnected from them. He then worked me over as he looked at the other vehicles. He asked me questions about such details as CVU joints, TOE IN and other matters I knew little about. He demonstrated to me that I had much to learn to do my job competently.

After BG Canham had gone CPT Gray consoled me, "Don't worry, the General always finds something wrong. He knows where to look and what to look for. Yours isn't the only company he has gigged today." But Canham had shown me how little I knew about motor vehicles. I determined to learn as much as I could as fast as I could. Even though the Table of Organization and Equipment

(TO&E) provided for a Motor OFF, HHC was so short of OFFs that those of us assigned to it had to assume additional duties I prayed for the early arrival of a Motor OFF!

The shortage of OFFs was not unique in Head and Head. Few of the line units had more that two or three OFFs when I first joined the Regt. When OFFs did begin to arrive, all-too-often they were placed on Special Duty (SD) as instructors in the Jumpmaster School, the NCO Academy, in the Basic Training Unit, or as coaches of the various Regt athletic teams. The shortages were partially filled as we neared the summer.

The NCOs, through default, really ran things. Most of them were combat veterans of high quality who impressed me with their knowledge of basic soldiering and field work; a few were worthless.

As I got to know the men in the Co, I was convinced that most were of high caliber. They could always put on a good show! They were impressive in parades and at civil functions; if their performance in the field was not always tactically sound, it was spirited. Wherever I looked in the Co, the Regt, the Div, I was struck with the esprit de corps of the ABN. There was a compulsion to outshine (literally) every other unit.

Just about the time that I had become comfortable with my Motor OFF duties, 1LT Stevens was superseded by CPT Paul T. Ingle, a short, stocky, nervous, likable officer who was also on Competitive Tour. He was a fuss-budget, who didn't trust his subordinates when he gave them a mission. 1LT Stevens became the XO (and, happily, the Motor OFF); I was assigned as the Antitank Plt Ldr. The Plt, very much under strength, was used more for detail and security missions than for antitank missions. TSG Brown, the PSG, was more than capable of handling all missions assigned.

Once again I settled into a new routine. A full day with the Co was followed by equally hard entertainment at night. The Regimental Officers' Club, just a few buildings from our BOQ, got much use from us. When money permitted, we often ate at the Main Officers' Club or in Fayetteville.

Late in March, LTC Edward Lahti, the Acting Commander of the 504, was replaced by COL Charles C.W. Allan, a tall, slender, USMA graduate with a deep feeling for the traditions and customs of the service. Shortly after he assumed command he re-instituted the custom of junior officers calling on their Commanding Officer. Every Thursday 25 officers were scheduled (by roster) to call on the CO and his wife at their quarters. We were briefed on the proper protocol; in groups of five, we were to call in semi-dress uniform (pinks and greens), accept the first drink, refuse the second, make polite conversation (you and your CDR were expected to get to know each other so he would henceforth be able to recognize you), and excuse yourself after 15 minutes. It seemed to me that these calls served a useful function because they put younger OFFs on a proper social footing with their CDR. Most OFFs objected; it was too much trouble to dress for a 15 minute visit. But many old customs were beneficial to morale and discipline of a unit.

A month after joining the 504 I still had not made my sixth jump and began to sweat it out. I wanted to get that jump with the Division as soon as possible, I especially wanted to get a jump with full equipment so that I would know what to expect in the future. When I mentioned the matter to CPT Ingle, he told me that HHC had jumps coming up. In a day or so a manifest appeared on the bulletin board with my name on it. The 504 had been designated to make a Regimental jump for President Truman. There would be a practice jump the day before to enable the Air Force (USAF) to check its formation and timing which would give many of us an opportunity to jump. The Regt XO, LTC John T. Berry, was to be the jumpmaster; I was third in the stick.

The day before the jump LTC Berry canceled because of some other commitment; a staff officer in Regt HQ, the next name on the manifest, was to be the jumpmaster. Since I was the senior officer after the jumpmaster, I was charged with getting the troopers from HHC, who were to jump in the lead ship, to the marshaling area. It was SOP to make several exits from the mock door and a few practice PLFs before each jump. NCOs in the Co actually handled this. We drew and put on our chutes, were checked by the riggers, then lined up in stick order. While I was supervising these activities, I received word that the jumpmaster had canceled out due to some unexpected business and that I was therefore the jumpmaster. This was challenging; to be jumpmaster on my sixth jump. I had never actually stood in the door except for that individual tap out at FT Benning, but was too keyed up at the time to really know what was going on. Now, faced with the responsibilities of the jumpmaster, I was not sure what I was supposed to do. About all I knew were the commands to get the troops to the door. I discussed this with TSG Tryon and TSG Brown, suggesting that one of them lead the stick. They assured me that there was nothing to do except jump on the green light. TSG Tryon pointed out that it would be good experience for me, though he suggested that he or TSG Brown get in the stick behind me to prompt me if needed. Reluctantly, I agreed to proceed with the mission as jumpmaster, secretly both apprehensive and exhilarated at the idea of leading the stick.

This jump was a Regt jump on Sicily South Drop Zone (DZ). At that time Sicily was actually two DZs, Sicily North and Sicily South, South being the larger of the two. The two have been combined into Sicily DZ since. Twenty-seven C-82 aircraft carrying over a thousand paratroopers would fly in a formation of "Vee of Vees in trail"; a Vee formed by the three leading aircraft, with similar Vees echeloned to the right and left of the leading Vee. This nine ship formation would be followed by two similar nine ship formations. Just before we loaded the aircraft the Marshalling Area Control Officer (MACO) reminded me that this was a "jump on silk". That meant that the jumpmasters of the following aircraft would execute the jump only when the plane they were in passed over parachutes ("silk") from my aircraft.

The MACO directed that the planes be loaded. As we fastened the seat belts across our laps, I looked at the men in the stick. The more experienced jumpers were bored or unconcerned. Of the novice jumpers like myself, a few displayed obvious bravado; one or two were patently terrified. There was little opportunity for me to become terrified! Things happened too rapidly. As I fastened my seat belt, the plane lumbered toward the runway, halted, then shuddered as the pilot went through his pre-flight procedures, revving the engines to maximum RPM. Then we were moving forward at increasing speed. Seated next to the open left jump door, I could see the runway passing beneath us. The nose tilted up and I watched with horror as the rear clam-shell doors seemed to scrape the concrete. The ship lifted hesitantly, laboring as if unsure that it had enough power to get the load airborne. Suddenly the plane eased its laboring, flying easily and lightly; we were airborne with wheels up! Almost before my stomach returned to its proper position, the red light came on. Training took control, I quickly stood up and hooked up, putting the safety wire through the holes in the static line snap fastener to lock it to the cable. Using hand signals, I also shouted to initiate the jump sequence, "GET READY, STAND UP, HOOKUP, CHECK YOUR EQUIPMENT, SOUND OFF FOR EQUIPMENT CHECK," pausing between each command to give time for compliance. Finally TSG Brown, behind me in the stick slapped my thigh and shouted in my ear "ALLOKAY". With a final glance along the line of poised jumpers, I shouted "STAND IN THE DOOR", pivoted on my right foot and stamped into the door. Instinctively I assumed the proper door position: left foot ahead of the right, body slightly crouched, hands with fingers extended and joined plastered on the outside of the door frame, fully prepared to spring out of the aircraft vigorously. Then I looked down!

Since this was the first time I had stood in the door, I became absorbed by the scene below me. The aircraft was just crossing Little River, one of the checkpoints. Manchester Road passed under my feet as the edge of the DZ appeared. There were jeeps, the ambulance, the Tee (a ground marker, two panels forming a Tee, designating the jump point) and people milling about; it was a fascinating sight. So fascinating that my eyes remained on the ground instead of on the jump light. Suddenly TSG Brown said in my ear,

"Sir, the green light is on."

The thought occurred to me that the troops believed that I had frozen in the door. Glancing down once again, I noted abstractedly that the Tee had passed under my boot. Looking up at the horizon,

I leaped out! The stick followed. It was a good jump. Nobody was hurt, nobody went into the trees, and I made one of my better PLFs (I never made really good PLFs in my entire career). That first experience at jumpmastering was a memorable occasion. On most of my jumps from then on, I was the jumpmaster; this had been a good indoctrination.

Only a small element of HHC made the jump for President Truman. The IN Bns were scheduled for that. A heavy drop which included Artillery followed the personnel jump. Just to make sure that everything went off as scheduled, a battery of Artillery was already set up in the woods over the brow of the hill in case of malfunctions. The Div *CG*, MG Clovis Byers, wanted to get the first round off fast. I'm not sure which Battery actually fired the first shot, the one just derigged or the one prepositioned. It was a good demonstration for the President. One of the WWII veteran jumpers, SSG Bennie Weeks, landed very close to the stands and presented the President with a copy of the Division History, *The Saga of the All American.*

A week or so after that first jump with the Div, I was informed by the Club Officer that there was to be a Prop Blast (the traditional initiation of a new jumper into the Airborne community) in three weeks and I was to be one of the blastees. No self respecting jumper considers himself a full fledged paratrooper until he has been prop blasted. This is a hazing formation during which experienced jumpers have fun at the novices' expense. It is a parody of jump school. A Board of Officers, usually the most experienced ABN OFFs in the unit, evaluates each blastee as he makes an exit from a mock door. The blastee reports to the Board after his exit and PLF or tumble. The Board critiques the exit and the PLF; if not considered satisfactory, the blastee is sent back after taking a drink from the "Prop Blast Mug". Blastees are pro-rated the cost of the affair. At that time, only blasted Troopers were permitted to witness the ceremony as spectators and harassers of the blastees. In later years some units permitted wives to attend in an attempt to reduce the amount of drinking. Originally it was a stag affair.

The "Blast Juice" was 75% champagne, 25% vodka, with lemon juice and sugar for flavoring. It was served very cold. Non-drinkers were not required to partake of the prop blast mixture, but they were given a foul tasting concoction instead, ketchup, hot sauce, Worcestershire Sauce, vinegar or some such combination. After a blastee makes a satisfactory exit and PLF, the President of the Board asks the group whether it wants him to take a long count or a short count. During the count the blastee drinks as everybody counts: "1,000,2,000,3,000". If it is a short count the group quickly shouts the numbers and the neophyte gets little to drink. If a long count, the numbers are counted slowly, on-n-n-e thou-s-s-s-and, tw-ooo thou-s-s-s-and, thr-eeee thou-sss, and during which the postulate has to chug-a-lug the contents of the blast mug. Usually these mugs are loving cups or cut down Artillery shells. Some of them hold a liter or so. I was fortunate to get a short count, but two or three of the blastees got drunk as a result of long counts. On conclusion of the count, the blastee signs the "Prop Blast Register"; he can then join the group to enjoy the fun. Some of the signatures in that Register are indecipherable! Unfortunately, Prop Blast ceremonies have been discontinued. At one such affair in April 1967 an individual died, supposedly as a result of drinking too much. It is the old story of the Army over re-acting, discontinuing something because of one unfortunate incident. It served a purpose by welding the ABN community closer together and adding to the esprit of units.

Following that sixth jump with HHC in the spring of 1949,I managed to jump on the average of once a month. Most of these jumps were tactical mass jumps, with full equipment and weapons, made in connection with some training exercise. A few were "Hollywood" or "Staff" jumps, with only a pistol belt for equipment. Hollywood jumps were frowned on by most CDRs and were resorted to only when aircraft were not available (due to lack of funds for fuel, or poor weather), and it was necessary to get the troops a "pay jump". Every trooper on jump status had to jump once each quarter to be eligible for his hazardous duty (jump) pay. By the time I transferred from the 504 I had over 30 jumps.

In May 1949 the 82nd participated in a maneuver called "Tarheel". To start the maneuver, the 504 moved by convoy to Camp Mackall, SC. The motor march went smoothly. "Tarheel" was to culminate in a jump on Sicily DZ on FT Bragg followed by another motor march back to the cantonment area. Unfortunately, as XO (Stevens had been transferred) I was not going to jump in the operation. My main job in the maneuver was to see that the EM of HHC were taken care of, and that work details set up the CP. CPT Ingle, the Co CO, was also the Headquarters Commandant (HQ CMDT). He took care of the Regt CO and his staff. Providing for the EM was a far more satisfying job, in fact a much easier job in most respects. Between us we split the chores of supervising the erection of latrines, mess tents, kitchen and supply tents.

Upon arrival at Camp Mackall, HHC personnel immediately set up the Tactical Operations Center (TOC), staff offices (tents), mess and billeting facilities, kitchen, sump and latrines. During the maneuver I saw little of either Morris or Dubsky because they were out on their individual missions. Ed Morris supervised the wire and radio, a full time job on any maneuver, while Charley Dubsky had the I&R Plt out screening the advance of the Regiment.

Midway through Tarheel, orders were published placing me on temporary duty (TOY) at FT McPherson in Atlanta for the purpose of appearing before an RA Screening Board. I was delighted. This meant that my application for a direct commission in the RA was going forward.

1LT Sanders, an AR OFF in the Div Recon Co, called me. He, too, was going before the RA Board, and offered to drive me to Atlanta. He was going by his home enroute, but would be delighted to have me accompany him. I was happy to accept. It wasn't until we got to Atlanta that I discovered that Joe Fix, Gordon Lippman and Tom Tackaberry, all friends in the 504, were also appearing before the same Board. Separate orders had been published covering those on Competitive Tour and those being considered for direct appointment.

Just before the big jump which ended the maneuver, I returned to the cantonment area at FT Bragg. The Division Area was desolate! The barracks were boarded up and the place deserted. This was the first time I had seen the area without the hustle and bustle of troop activity. Fortunately, I was able to get into the BOQ to get uniforms prepared.

Early on the morning of 7 May, LT Sanders picked me up at the BOQ. We drove first to Dillon, SC, where we had breakfast with Sanders' uncle, a tobacco farmer, then proceeded to Walterboro, where his family lived in a large antebellum plantation house. His parents made me welcome and we enjoyed a short respite. On 9 May we drove on to Atlanta, arriving at FT McPherson about 1600. After determining the location of the building to which we were to report in the morning, we got rooms in the Transient BOQ. In view of the gravity of the occasion the next day, we had an early dinner with only one or two drinks, then got a good night's sleep.

Promptly at 0750 we presented ourselves at Building 1088. Both of us were at our best. My boots gleamed with a spit-shine, my brass blinded the eye, my hair was in a short, flat crewcut. The tropical worsted shirt and trousers (summer uniform) I wore had been tailored to fit me. LT Sanders was similarly arrayed in Cavalry (CAV) splendor.

After a short wait, my name was called. I strode puposefully into the conference room, having knocked and been invited to enter. Walking to within three paces of the COL sitting in the middle of the long table, I halted and saluted, "LT Seibert reports to the Regular Army Screening Board as directed, sir." When my salute was returned, I dropped my hand smartly.

"Sit down, Lieutenant." As I complied I looked at the Board composed of two COLs, two LTCs and a MAJ; two of the OFFs were IN, one AR, one QM and one MC. They began firing questions at me.

"Why do you want to be a Regular Army Officer?" "I want to be a career officer, a Regular, sir."

"How did you get your original commission?" "OCS, Edgewood Arsenal, 1943, sir."

"Where did you serve in World War II?" "In the 96th Division in the Pacific, sir." "Why did you become a paratrooper?" "I wanted to join the best, sir."

The QM OFF asked, "What do you think of cutting down or tailoring the Ike Jacket?" This generated a discussion of the pros and cons of tailoring uniforms, the QM OFF saying it made reissue of such uniforms difficult. My response was to point to the morale value, especially in the Airborne units.

Many more questions were asked about current events, leadership, almost any topic to get me to talk, to see how I reacted to various questions. Finally the President said,

"Thank you, LT. That will be all. You will hear from DA in due course."

Instantly, I popped to attention, saluted, did a smart about face and marched from the room. Outside I collapsed in relief that it had gone so well. LT Sanders was next. We left immediately after he was finished and drove directly to FT Bragg. Since Tarheel would terminate shortly, I remained in the Div area.

After the maneuver, 1LT Boris Yankoff, a boxer born in Poland, was assigned to HHC to coach the Regimental Boxing Team. His assignment evoked recollections of the book *From Here to Eternity*. Yankoff was not much of an OFF; he was basically a "jock", more interested in athletics than in performing the routine duties expected of an OFF in a tactical unit. A likeable guy, he gave us many laughs. His favorite sally was, "What's the most important thing in a parachute jump?" The immediate response was, "Shiny boots."

He did organize and train a winning boxing team for the Regt, so I should not be too hard on Yankoff. At times it appeared that there was too much emphasis on competitive athletics in the Army. Every soldier should have the opportunity to play one sport, but he shouldn't be permitted to be a professional jock, doing nothing but competing in one sport after another for his entire enlistment. This is unfair to the individual as well as the unit. Somebody else has to do the details normally performed by the trooper who is on SD to an athletic team.

Yankoff's comment about shiny boots was not too far from the mark. Boots were the paratroopers most prized possession. Almost all troopers, including officers, spent an inordinate amount of time "spit-shining" their boots. Most bought Corcoran boots, because the hard toe took such a good shine, the ankles were reinforced, and the boots looked better than those issued. The preferred color was a deep cordovan; new boots were stained immediately. Kiwi Ox-blood Shoe Polish sold quickly in the PXs in Airborne unit areas. Though never able to achieve the ultimate in spit-shines, my boots always had a gleam on them. When I stood inspection or some other important formation, I usually paid some trooper whose boots I especially admired to give mine a good shine.

As expected, just after we got back from maneuvers, my three month stint in HHC was up and I was transferred to M Co, the Heavy Weapons Co of the 3rd Bn, commanded by CPT William Victor Stieber. The most memorable thing about CPT Stieber was his beautiful German Shepherd dog, unfortunately neurotic, which cringed whenever anyone reached out to pet it. CPT Stieber and his dog lived in the same BOQ I did; his pet was incessantly messing the hall floor, which made for bad footing when we came home from the Club late at night. Since no one else would clean up after the dog, Stieber, rightly, was forced to do so.

CPT Stieber was a handsome soldier, but his abilities did not seem to match his appearance. He ran a poor Co which was held together by the XO, Bucky Karnap and the 1SG, both outstanding soldiers. On reporting for duty, I was assigned as HMG Plt Ldr. My PSG, TSG Wooten, was a superb soldier. Frank Mashburn, a wiry, prematurely gray officer with a keen sense of humor, was the Recoilless Rifle Plt Ldr. Bud Hillman, a stocky, cocky, pipe-smoking individual, commanded the Mortar Plt. Both Frank and Bud lived in my BOQ, and we were close friends. Frank Mashburn and I continue to see each other and reminisce of our days in the 504. The Acting CO of the 3rd Bn, was

MAJ Nealson. In WWII, serving as a LT in the Philippines, he had been captured. In my opinion, he never developed beyond that grade. He was one of the poorest OFFs with whom I ever served.

True to my promise, I kept in contact with Hanz Druener during the first few months of my duty with the 82nd, my glowing report of how much I enjoyed the Army and particularly the 82nd precipitated his own application for recall on Competitive Tour. Since he had served with the 504 during WWII, he asked to be assigned to the 82nd; late in the summer he arrived. Unfortunately he was assigned to the 1st Bn, hence we did not see much of each other on duty, but he and Jean had me over for dinner occasionally, and of course I saw them at all the Regimental functions.

Just as I settled in to my duties with M Co, we were alerted that the Bn was going to Philadelphia for the American Legion Convention; we were to take part in the parade and act as an honor guard for President Truman who was to address the legionnaires. We practiced close order drill days on end before departure and held several inspections to make sure the troopers had their uniforms and accessories in top-notch condition. The Bn entrained at Fort Bragg and went directly to the Philadelphia Navy Yard, where it was billeted on a troop ship. Remembering my experience with the Navy in WWII, I reminded everybody about the proper protocol of saluting the Ensign and OD as they went aboard. The Navy did dispense with requesting permission to come aboard.

We had the opportunity to get into Philadelphia several times during the four days we were there. In company with Dave McNaught, Frank Mashburn, Bud Hillman and several others I enjoyed the hospitality of the legionnaires. We marched in the parade in a battalion mass formation. It was reported that we were the sharpest looking unit in the parade. The day President Truman arrived to address the Convention the Bn joined with other units to provide a cordon on either side of the street, from the railroad station to the convention hall. As the presidential limousine drove down the street, the EM presented arms with their M-1 rifles, while OFFs rendered the hand salute. It was quite a sight to see those rifles brought to Present Arms in an orderly ripple, hear the crisp cracks as the troopers slapped their rifle butts into position, and then returned to the Order and Parade Rest.

Just before we left FT Bragg, a LTC with close cropped, grizzled hair joined the 3/504, but stood aloof and watched everything that went on. We were told that LTC Wilbur Wilson was the new Bn CO. He had elected not to take over immediately since MAJ Nealson had planned the trip to Philadelphia. Rather, LTC Wilson was content to let him handle it. He came along, observed the performance of the OFFs, in particular, but also of the NCOs, and watched the conduct of the men. By the time he actually assumed command on our return to Bragg, he had a good insight into the operation of the Battalion.

LTC Wilson struck the 3rd Bn with hurricane force. He swept through buildings and barracks letting in fresh air and new ideas. He was a controversial officer, but I thought he was one of the finest officers I have been privileged to serve with. In fact, I learned more from him than from any other officer. We became good friends, despite the disparity in our age and grade, basically because we were in harmony in our thinking about the Army. The fact that we were both bachelors also entered into it. Of course, this friendship developed later on, not while I was serving directly under him.

The new Bn CO's primary concern was professionalism. He believed that the 82nd Airborne Division was the pride of the Army, it's most professional unit. He expected every OFF, NCO and soldier in it to act as a professional. When he got less proficient performance he was outraged; the culprit, EM, NCO or OFF , was told on the spot, regardless of who was present, in vivid terms, of his dereliction. Many people faulted Wilson for correcting OFFS and NCOs in front of their troops. I cannot defend him on this, but he was so wrapped up in the Army that he could not abide a shoddy performance of duty.

The welfare of the troopers was one of his primary concerns. This was manifested in many ways; a simple illustration will suffice. Whenever a convoy was being organized, it was the practice of the S-4 and Motor Officer to locate trucks in an area where they could be lined up in the order in which they were to move. In many cases this meant that the men had to carry heavy loads several hundred yards or more. LTC Wilson directed that the trucks be parked in the unit areas, as close to barracks, mess halls, supply rooms and storage facilities as possible to minimize the distance the troops had to carry equipment. We organized the convoys on the move!

He also contended that a professional unit should live in a professional manner. He insisted that we do as much as possible to make the WWII barracks in which our men were living as comfortable as circumstances permitted; mess halls, day rooms, orderly rooms and supply rooms were also to be improved. Every Co began paneling, laying linoleum, painting, even repairing the buildings we occupied. Much time, labor and expense were lavished on them, particularly the barracks. The men appreciated the fact that LTC Wilson was trying to improve their lot, though they grumbled about the extra work it made for them.

A great deal of time was spent scrounging lumber, then planing and finishing it. The Regt had a hobby shop well equipped with all manner of woodworking machines. With LTC Wilson's approval men were detailed to it for a week at a time to work on paneling for their units. If word reached the Bn that any post buildings were being torn down, a detail was rushed to it to try to get good looking wood for the many paneling jobs underway. The results were impressive. Every barracks was much more pleasant than it had been.

The 3rd Bn CO supervised everything carefully, if men were careless in lining up the nail holes in paneling a building, he corrected them and then reprimanded the OFF in charge. He maintained that anything the 82nd ABN Div did should be first class and professional. Of course he was right, but his exceedingly high standards made us all edgy.

Police received due emphasis. LTC Wilson stressed that if you didn't throw it down, you didn't have to pick it up. He was forever wandering through the Battalion area, calling attention to cigarette butts or other carelessly discarded trash. He refused to pick such items up, rather he called on an NCO or OFF to get someone to do it. In that way he taught us all to be alert to the appearance of the area.

Of particular concern were the large concrete coal bins outside each building The troopers stoked the boilers in the summer and the furnaces in the winter to maintain hot water and heat in the barracks. They were frequently careless about overloading the shovels and dribbled coal along the ground between the coal bins and the furnaces. Police of this coal was often perfunctory, as was tidying up the coal bins. LTC Wilson believed that the coal should be kept in a neat pile toward the back of the coal bin to facilitate handling and to avoid getting coal dust rather than lumps.

This insistence upon proper police of the coal bins got to the men. One day TSG Wooten, my HMG PSG, noticed that LTC Wilson was in the area and called out to warn everyone that "Coal Bin Willie" was near. The troops gleefully seized upon that name; from then on LTC Wilson was always referred to (affectionately by most, but in derision by some) as "Coal Bin Willie".

Training received the same supervision and emphasis on professionalism. Classes were inspected and critiqued. Except for authorized absences, troopers were expected to be at unit training sessions. The "Status Report" was checked regularly; woe to the 1SG who could not account for all of his men.

Not the least of the Bn CO's concerns were the messes, which he demanded serve the best possible food to the men. He inspected messes each morning, forcing Co COs and Mess OFFs to get there at 0530 to insure that all was ready when he appeared. Perhaps that was his purpose. He wanted the metal trays, then being used in the mess halls, heated on cold mornings so that the grease on eggs or bacon would not congeal when served. He instructed the Mess SGTs to heat them in the ovens or elsewhere; of course he checked this point. One morning my Mess SGT "Pappy" Howell, heated one tray to almost red heat. He carefully placed this tray on the top of the pile just before LTC Wilson made his anticipated morning check. Wilson grabbed the tray to see if it was warm, threw it down and roundly chewed out the mess personnel because the trays were too hot for the men to handle; there were some poorly suppressed grins among the KPs and troopers in the mess hall.

Each spring the 82nd conducted a Div Review. It was always a chore to prepare for them; intensive close order drill was on the training schedule for several weeks before the event, plus inspections of uniforms and equipment. We all complained, but once the more then 10,000 troops were massed on Pike Field with colors flying and the Band playing, we experienced a thrill which more than made up for the extra work. I am always stirred by a parade; when I am a part of it, that feeling is magnified. The Band invariably played the "All American Soldier" as we passed in review and every trooper stepped out a bit more proudly to the official 82nd Airborne Division March. So far as I know this is still true.

Toward the end of the summer, we heard that MG Byers was leaving. The new CG's name, Williston B. Palmer, was not familiar to us, but rumor had it that he was a BG, a former Artilleryman, currently in Jump School, who would be promoted to MG when he assumed command of the 82nd. Then word filtered down that BG Palmer had failed to qualify because of an old football injury which bothered his legs so that he could not make the PLFs. The CofS of the Army decided that he would command the Div despite the fact that he was not a qualified parachutist. Immediately the troopers dubbed him "Wingless Willy".

It was the 504's turn to provide the Aide for the CG. Five OFFs were selected by Regt, based on recommendations from the Bns and separate Cos, for consideration as the General's Aide. For some reason, I was one of them. One afternoon we reported to the CofS, LTC William C. Westmoreland, for interview. As a Plt Ldr, I had seen the CofS only once or twice. He was ramrod straight, with a jutting jaw, always in a freshly starched uniform. In his office at Div HQ he spent about a half hour outlining the duties of an aide and telling us how important such an assignment would be for our careers. Based on this approach, I assumed he was going to make up his mind from our records and appearance. Finally, he asked if we had any questions. I raised my hand, "Yes, sir. I have a question. Do we have any choice in the matter of this assignment?"

"What do you mean, Seibert?"

"Well, sir, if I had a choice, I would rather not be General Palmer's Aide. I have never been an Aide, and I don't like the idea of being a servant to a General. I have just come back on AD and prefer to stay with the Regt in order to get more experience in an ABN IN Co. There is much that I am rusty on."

LTC Westmoreland turned livid. I thought he was going to explode. When he finally calmed down he began to chew me out. He told me that I would not be a servant but an assistant; that I would meet people who would be able to help my career in the years ahead. Finally he dismissed all of us summarily; apparently he had become so incensed at my question that he decided that the 504 did not have suitable candidates for the position. In time he selected John R.D. Cleland, an officer from the 505.

By chance one Sunday afternoon late in the summer, Frank Mashburn, Bud Hillman and I were in the Regimental Officers' Field Mess. A shortage of funds toward the end of the month frequently necessitated this; though the 1630 supper hour was inconvenient, we could either charge the meal or pay the very reasonable fee. An elderly gentleman walked into the dining room and looked around. As we were the only officers there, he came over and asked if he could join us. We assumed that he was a retired officer, visiting the Post. He was gray headed, a bit disheveled as though he had been driving for a long time. He had on a sport shirt, rumpled trousers and wore glasses. We politely asked him to join us, affording him every courtesy routinely given to older gentlemen. He talked about the Army and asked us questions about the 82nd. As brash LTs we bragged about the Div and particularly the 504. We extolled the abilities, military courtesy and professionalism of the troopers, intimating that any one of them was better than five Marines. We got into several interesting arguments with the gentleman, who made his points forcefully; we were equally vigorous in defending our views. We weren't about to yield to anyone on the virtues of the Airborne. Finally we excused ourselves; he left the dining room with us.

The next morning Bud, Frank and I were in the Field Mess for breakfast as usual. Again there was a vacant seat at our table. The same gentleman walked in. He was in uniform wearing stars on his collar! He looked around the crowded dining room, spotted us in our corner, walked over and asked if he could join us. We popped to and said, "Yes, sir". He introduced himself, BG Williston B. Palmer, the new Div CG. As he was a bachelor, he continued to eat at the 504 mess until a General Officers' Mess had been set up at Div HQ. He knew us well and joined us on several occasions; we became known in the Regt as the "General's Boys". We were embarrassed about our arguments the evening before, though we had said nothing to apologize for. In due course BG Palmer was promoted to MG and installed as the Div CG.

One morning during this period, Frank Mashburn got up from the breakfast table to go to duty. His feet became entangled in his steel folding chair and he fell into the lap of the individual at the next table. As luck would have it, MG Palmer had just lifted his coffee cup to his lips when Frank landed on him. Frank and the coffee went flying. Mashburn, scarlet with embarrassment, stuttered an apology. He was sure his career was ended. However, MG Palmer took it with reasonable grace.

In the fall of 1949, during an official visit to Bragg of The Secretary of Defense, General George Catlett Marshall, a Corps Review was held in his honor. We practiced for weeks; the troops grumbled as usual. But there was great interest in seeing the legendary Marshall. It took at least an hour to mass the troops on Pike Field; in addition to the 82nd, V Corps Artillery and Corps Support Troops participated. Commands, given by a bugler standing next to the CDR of Troops, rippled down the line of units as they were repeated verbally by subordinate CDRs. General Marshall, in civilian clothes, declined the use of the specially appointed jeep, electing to troop the line on foot. It took almost an hour for him to inspect the units, despite the length of the inspection, the troopers were thrilled to get a look at the famous Five Star General, who stopped frequently to ask a soldier about a decoration or award. It was one of the most impressive reviews I have ever seen.

Late in October 1949, DA orders reached FT Bragg announcing that I had been integrated into the RA by direct commission under Circular 382, ranking as a 2LT from 16 October 1948. The fact that I had lost about eight and a half months of rank did not bother me except on the few occasions when I just missed the zone of consideration for promotion. Again I memorized a new serial number, 060224.

At this same time, another OFF in the 3/504, 1LT William C. Sibert, a USMA graduate, was getting ready for his wedding. He was constantly being congratulated on making RA, to his disgust, and I was congratulated on my forthcoming marriage to my amusement and that of my friends.

Tom Tackaberry and I reported to the hospital to take our RA physicals together. He passed with flying colors. Again, the audiometer caught me. On routine physicals it was customary to give a whispered hearing test; the doctor stood behind the patient and whispered numbers; the patient covered each ear in turn and repeated the numbers. It was easy to cheat; I had done so several times, but the audiometer was difficult to fool.

In the closing interview the certifying officer told me that everything was fine except my hearing, which disqualified me. He asked the purpose of the examination. When I told him it was for an appointment in the RA, he said, "You look like a fine officer to me. I don't think we should keep you out of the RA for a slight hearing loss. Has it given you any trouble in the field, understanding orders or radio transmissions?"

"No, sir. I have never noticed it."

"Well, we'll just adjust this a bit." With that he retraced the curve with his pen so it fell within the accepted level, then signed the certification. A short time later I took my oath and signed it; I was a Regular at last.

In late 1949 the 82nd Airborne Division began to implement President Truman's order to integrate all units of the Armed Forces. At Bragg, there were two all-Negro Bns of the 82nd located in the Spring Lake area of the Post: the 3rd Bn, 505 (formerly the 555th Parachute Infantry Battalion) and the 80th Antiaircraft Bn. There were also some Negro service units billeted there. When the order for integration was received there was some apprehension over the possibility of fights in the OFF and NCO Clubs and in the barracks. The night the order was effective, I was at the Officers' Club Annex, a huge barn-like building which was located behind the Main Club. We went there because the dress code was less rigid than in the Main Club. Two colored (the term "black" was not yet in vogue) couples came in, sat by themselves off to the side, danced, enjoyed themselves and left. They were left strictly alone. After that, it became normal to see colored officers and their wives or dates in the Club.

At first colored officers and soldiers were assigned to the formerly all-white units one or two at a time. For many years Puerto Rican and other Hispanic soldiers far outnumbered Negro soldiers in most units of the 82nd. Only one fight occurred outside the Officers' Club during the period, that I knew of, and the blame was placed on the white officer involved. There were occasional fights in the barracks, but they were more the result of disagreements between short tempered soldiers rather than between whites and Negroes. There did not appear to be any problems of true racial nature until the beginning of the sixties. At that time black soldiers (and white ones for that matter) began to be affected by the civil rights movement in the civilian world resulting in polarization. Until then relations between the races in the Army, as I remember them, were pleasant if not cordial.

Four of us (Hillman, Mashburn, Phillips and myself) decided to have a Christmas Party. Our printed invitations read, "Four of the '04 invite you to a Christmas Party". In addition to all our friends, we sent invitations to COL Allan, the Regt CO, LTC Wilson, our Bn CO, and our Co COs. When I suggested that we invite MG Palmer, everybody laughed, convinced that he would not come. However, all agreed that we should invite him. As expected, he did not attend, but regretted cordially, explaining he had an official function that evening.

We wanted to use the "Tucker Tumbler" for the eggnog. This was a large sterling silver loving cup, given to the 504 by the Tucker Family. A base of beautifully carved, or engraved, silver, with two stirring battle scenes and the insignia of all units with which the 504 had served in WWII had been crafted for it. The silver for the base came from the CIBs the troopers of the Regt donated for that purpose. It was indeed a magnificent piece of art. The entire assembly was kept in a locked trophy case at Regt HQ. The Regt Adj, designated as Custodian, safeguarded the key to the trophy room. The other three insisted that I ask for permission to use the Tumbler.

One afternoon, I reported to the Regt Adj, CPT Kennedy, and asked if we could use the Tucker Tumbler for our eggnog party. CPT Kennedy was shocked that we would even consider such a thing; any party given by LTs would probably become rowdy with the possibility of damage to the Tumbler. In my argument I suggested that COL Tucker had commissioned the Tumbler and its Base for use by the OFFs and EM of the 504, not as a museum piece. Upon joining the Regiment, each officer had paid to have his name engraved on a cup, therefore they should be ours to use. Even my suggestion that we use the Tumbler without the Base, failed to move CPT Kennedy. When it was obvious that he would not consider my request, I asked for permission to speak with the Regt XO. LTC Berry gave me much the same brush off. Determined to use the Tumbler, I asked for permission to talk to COL Allan the Regimental Commander. He listened attentively to my plea, which included the thought that COL Tucker had not meant the service to be a museum piece. When I ended my speech by assuring him that we would be very careful with it, he nodded and said, "Certainly. Tell CPT Kennedy I approve your request."

On the night of the party, the Duty Officer unlocked the trophy case, I signed for the Tumbler and cups. It was a great hit at the party; nobody had seen it used at an informal party, so they examined it carefully, and handled it equally carefully. There were other drinks of course, but we doled out the eggnog from the Tucker Tumbler with great pride. After the party, we carefully cleaned it and returned it to the DO, who put it in its special display case.

MG Palmer did not attend the party, but he did send the four of us invitations to his New Year's Reception. It was customary to invite commanders down to Co level; Lieutenants, except aides, the Pathfinder Platoon Leader, and other special personnel, were rarely invited. However, Mashburn, Hillman, Phillips and Seibert were there in pinks and greens. It proved to be a stuffy affair, as such receptions usually are: too many people, too little to drink, everyone very conscious of his conversation and behavior. But it was interesting because it was the first formal reception any of us had ever attended. MG Palmer greeted us cordially in the receiving line.

Late in December, I was transferred to I Company as a Rifle Platoon Leader. The Company Commander, 1LT Dave McNaught, an fine CO, a sound tactician and a good supervisor, ran a professional unit. Unfortunately, he was afflicted with some form of chronic ulcerative colitis, which resulted in constant diarrhea. He might be briefing the CG, he might be conducting a formal inspection, or he might be firing on the range, when he would be seized and have to run for the nearest latrine. It was a great burden; despite it, he did an outstanding job. We thought alike on many things; we argued incessantly about tactics and other matters, but I enjoyed serving with Dave. He and his wife Sara became close friends. First Sergeant Lattimore was a no-nonsense NCO, well versed in Co Administration.

My PSG, TSG Zoltan Kollat, was a weight lifter with a Herculean physique. The men respected his ability and leadership as much as they did his muscles. He was knowledgeable, forceful and effective; I was fortunate to have him and I learned a great deal from Kollat. There were also many eager junior NCOs in the Platoon.

One of the duties Dave assigned me was the annual inspection of the quarters of the EM assigned to the Co. An Army Regulation required that an OFF inspect the quarters of all men not living in the barracks to make sure that they had all of the necessities and were liveable. The inspection was not intended as a check on the housekeeping of the wives. Quarters both on and off Post were inspected, though I believe the original intent was to insure that off Post quarters met a minimum standard. It appeared to me an imposition to have an officer inspect your home; the regulation has since been rescinded.

The first quarters I inspected were those of my Platoon Sergeant. The Kollats lived in converted barracks on Smoke Bomb Hill. My mission was to make sure that our men and their families were well housed: Did the stove, furnace and toilet work? Were the quarters properly maintained by the Post Engineer or landlord? Were they free of vermin? Mrs Kollat's housekeeping was impeccable, the apartment was spotless. The inspection was as painless as they could make it, including an invitation to partake of coffee and cake. The quarters were adequate but small. WWII barracks had been converted to make four apartments in each building. The rent was reasonable (as substandard quarters, the occupants still drew quarters allowances, but paid a rental fee) and included utilities. However, heat and hot water were provided by coal-fired furnaces or water heaters; during the day or when their husbands were in the field, the wives had to do hard, dirty work to keep them stoked. I was relieved when all of my mens' quarters had been inspected, and that mission completed.

Because I had recently been transferred to I Co, I did not ask for leave for the holidays. It was an enjoyable Christmas on Post with dinner in the mess hall with the troops. LTC Wilson invited his Co COs and Staff to have dinner with him at the Main Officers' Club on New Year's Eve before the big bash at the Field House. I was invited to fill out the table. Later in the evening, the LTs from the 504 BOQ, all without dates, monopolized other OFFs' wives and dates. I don't remember sitting out a dance.

Though I enjoyed serving under Dave McNaught, I remained in I Co only a short time. Just after the first of the year, LTC Wilson told me I was to take Command of K Co. CPT Lindstrand, the present CO, was being reassigned as the BN S-3. Delighted to have the privilege of command, I wondered why LTC Wilson had selected me. He had observed me in my duties in the Bn, of course. Probably what impressed him most was that he could never predict what I was going to do or say next and had no hesitation in voicing my opinion.

As an example, during the newly initiated "Officers Call" program, I ran afoul of the Regt CO. Officers Calls provided opportunities to talk about the traditions of the service, leadership and other matters. LTC Wilson conducted the first "Officers Call" for the 504. The subject was "The Responsibilities of the Officer". After LTC Wilson's introductory remarks, he called on the two LTs Seibert/Sibert for comment. Bill Sibert, a Military Academy Graduate, spoke first. He gave a standard pitch, duty, honor country, the responsibility of an officer to his men and his mission, the traditional and very real role of the officer. LTC Wilson then turned to me. Standing up I said,

"When commanders learn to trust their subordinates, then I think the subordinates will measure up to their responsibilities. In this Regt, OFFs are not trusted. We are required constantly to sign certificates indicating compliance with routine orders. We certify that we have read the bulletin board, read certain publications, complied with certain regulations, obeyed certain orders. Such certification is not necessary. It is our responsibility to do those things. If we don't follow instructions or obey orders, then we should be disciplined or eliminated from the service. But to require us to sign a paper indicates a lack of confidence, a lack of trust, a lack of faith in us; as a result, many officers do nothing unless they are required to sign a certificate for it. I think it should be assumed that officers are trustworthy and can be depended upon to do their duty. Confidence and trust breed responsibility and loyalty."

There was silence when I finished. Everyone waited. The Regt CO, COL Allan, who had directed that we sign those certificates, was present. LTC Wilson broke the tension by asking for questions or comments. Shortly afterwards the officers were dismissed.

Later that morning I was directed to report to the Regimental Commander at 1400. He let me stand at attention after I had reported to him. He really chewed me out for criticizing his policy in public. I tried to explain that I hadn't meant to be critical of 504 policies. The example of the certificates popped into my head as a clear example of the mutual confidence and trust that must exist between subordinates and senior officer. Obviously I was wrong in publicly denouncing 504 procedures; had I thought before I spoke I would not have done so. COL Allan lectured me on loyalty and courtesy, but did not seem to be as irate as he sounded. He made it clear that further public criticism was not to be made.

CPT Lindstrand had been a strict, effective Co CO. K Co reflected his leadership. It was well-organized and well trained, I was happy to command it. A bit of confusion resulted from the fact that my XO was 1LT Bill Sibert. It was sometimes not clear which LT Seibert/Sibert was referred to. Bill did an excellent job for me. First Sergeant Jim Lowe was a knowledgeable and forceful NCO who kept the paper work moving. LTs George S Jones III, Tom Modisett and Bill (Peanut) Hinton were my Plt Ldrs. Peanut (as short as the name implies) had the tallest NCO in the Company, TSG Whelan. Later 1LT Jack O'Shaughnessy and 2LT Angel Torres were assigned. Immediately, I made a few changes to fit my own style of leadership. I have never believed that a new commander should make changes merely to impress his troops, nor did I accept the idea that he should hold off making changes simply because he is new. If something merits change, it should be changed.

K Co had many excellent NCOs in addition to 1SG Lowe; MSG Cooper, the 1st PSG (who had jumped with the 101st in WWII), TSG Whelan, the 2nd PSG, MSG Wyatt, the 3rd PSG, and MSG Prieto the Weapons PSG were competent, knowledgeable and effective. Mess SGT "Pappy" Howell and Supply SGT Johnson, were outstanding in their fields and needed little supervision. One of the CPLs, Arif Zaky, a well-trained machine gunner with a keen sense of humor, made an immediate impression on me. The troopers in K Co were some of the best soldiers in the Army , there were, unfortunately, a few duds.

1SG Jim Lowe, Infantry personified, was a sharp, articulate, aggressive, athletic and well trained NCO, who had one fault not too uncommon in the Army. He was a "pay day drinker". Almost without fail, the day after pay day, his wife Mary called or came to the Orderly Room to tell me that Jim was in no condition to come to work. He was put on pass, usually for two days, enough for his bout. The rest of the month he was an exemplary soldier. 1SG Lowe ran a good Orderly Room and kept me out of trouble. He was the star pitcher on the 504 Soft Ball Team, and rarely lost a game. Except for his monthly aberration, he was a model soldier.

LTC Wilson and 1SG Lowe had great respect for each other. Wilson found some trash under the 1st Pil barracks one day. He stomped into the Orderly Room to tell Lowe about it, who said, "Yes, sir, I'll check it out."

LTC Wilson snapped back, "Check it hell, I've done that, you get it out."

When Warrant Officer (WO) Olin L. Baggett reported in as Unit Administrator, ISG Lowe was not sure how to take him. The Unit Administrator concept was new. Highly qualified Administrative NCOs were appointed WOs and assigned to tactical companies to handle the administration. They operated somewhere between the 1SG and the Co XO. Baggett was a great asset; he knew both the Infantry and Army administration. When we finally worked out the proper procedures, he was of inestimable value to me, freeing not only the XO for some field duty, but also getting the First Sergeant out of the Orderly Room more often.

Administratively, K Co had no major problems. Probably we would have been hard-put in a no-notice IG Inspection or AGI, but the routine administration was well handled. One of the most aggravating things 1SG Lowe faced was use by doctors of green, red or any other color ink but blue or blue-black when signing the Sick Book If signed with these off-colors the *Co* had to accept the "gig" on an IG. Lowe in desperation, gave every trooper going on sick call a pen with blue-black ink and warned him that he would really need a Medic if the Sick Book was not signed with that pen! Mr Baggett finally solved the problem by talking with the Regimental Surgeon.

Problems in the Mess area were minor: cold trays and occasional failure to follow the Cooks' Work Sheet. Daily inspections solved these. There was always a shortage of condiments. Donations by the troopers was the answer. The shortage of silverware was taken care of by visiting the Pig Farm near Raeford, NC. The pig farmer had a contract with FT Bragg to pick up edible garbage at no expense to the Government. Troopers lost their silverware in the garbage while wiping out their trays. Some didn't have the fortitude to take it out and some were unaware that it had fallen into the garbage. Thus, the farmer accumulated silverware. He also accumulated more cans of issue (GI) coffee than the Ration Breakdown Point. Mess SGTs traded him coffee for silverware.

K Co had efficient, well supervised, dedicated cooks. It even had dedicated KPs. They were motivated by the fact that the last man reporting was assigned as Outside Man. Among other things his duties included cleaning the grease trap at the end of the day. SSG Howell's reasoning was: the last man to arrive should be the last to leave.

Supply was handled by SSG Johnson. Equipment was properly accounted for; I had no pecuniary worries and the troops were properly served. During the austerity of the day, expendables were a never-ending problem. At times the troopers had to buy their own toilet paper. But SSG Johnson was a poor record keeper. All the Property Records in the 82nd ABN Div dated from WWII, and had not been audited since. Accordingly, with Mr Baggett's help, Johnson set about preparing the K Co Property Records for a Final Audit. They spent long and tedious hours preparing them. Here SSG Johnson received his education in records keeping. Their efforts resulted in K Co's Property Records being the first in the entire Div to be audited by the IG. Johnson was justly proud of this feat.

Once I had settled into Command of K Company, I initiated a policy of designating a "Trooper of the Month"; based on the recommendations of the four Plt Ldrs, the final selection was made by a committee consisting of the 1SG, The XO and myself. The winner was presented with a small silver cup and a three day pass. For the first three or four months PFC Jerome Sullivan won hands down. He was a sharp looking and capable soldier. I tried to convince him to go to West Point or OCS, but he had no desire to do so.

It was my policy to give calisthenics each morning. Most Co COs rotated the PT chore among the Plt Ldrs to give them experience and exposure. Since I believed that physical conditioning was one of the most important items in our training, I wanted to highlight my interest by conducting it myself.

My priorities evolved over the next months. Discipline and physical fitness were on the top of the list. It was my belief that if Infantry troops had both, the technical training would come naturally. Technical or military skills were important, of course, but less so than the other two. With discipline came the ability to complete the task, with physical fitness the ability to stay when others fell along the way.

Payday was always hectic, not only because of the activities associated with that important event, but also because it posed some philosophical problems for me. Each payday the Troopers were confronted with a series of bowls or a number of OFFs or NCOs with their hands out for contributions. Much of it stemmed from pressure from Div or Regt to make a good statistical showing; to have 100% participation in Savings Bonds, in Soldiers Savings, in the Combined Federal Campaign, in the Heart Fund, in the Red Cross, or in AUSA membership. They were also asked for contributions to buy extra condiments and other items for the Mess Hall and to buy material to fix up the barracks. Our troops were constantly belabored for money. It is true that they received an additional $55.00 per month incentive or jump pay, hence the rationale that they could afford such contributions more than "leg" troops. After some thought, I decided that the two money matters I would emphasize were Soldiers' Savings and the Combined Federal Campaign. I had little guilt about pressuring the men to deposit money into their accounts each month, this was for their benefit. Once the money got into a Soldiers' Savings Account it was difficult to withdraw except in an emergency. Savings Bonds, on the other hand, could be cashed within 60 days. All of the causes the troopers were asked to contribute to were worthy ones, but they were not necessarily important to my soldiers. It was another of my contentions that if a soldier contributed once a year to the Combined Federal Campaign, he should not be asked to give to any other causes throughout the year. These became the two items I gave priority to. I would mention the others and suggest that contributions served good purposes, but only in the matters of Soldiers' Savings and the Combined Federal Campaign were they pressured.

Payday was a special day in the life of a soldier in those days. The first few paydays after I assumed Command I paid the troops myself. Then the duty was rotated among the other OFFs to give them the experience. It was a drill! Each pay officer, duly designated on orders, reported to the Finance Officer with an armed enlisted guard (he himself carried a loaded forty-five pistol). After his identity was properly established, he was given a paper sack of money (containing twenties, tens, fives and singles in amounts determined by a formula), copies of the unit payroll and a receipt. An ABN IN Co payroll at that time was about $25,000. Tables were available at which to sit and count the money. When satisfied that the amount stated on the receipt was in the sack, the receipt was signed and returned to the Finance Officer. The pay officer was responsible for the money from then on.

Many officers returned to their companies and counted out each man's pay which he then put in an envelope marked with his name. This insured that the pay, which they handed to the trooper in the envelope, was correct. I didn't like the procedure, preferring to count out the money to each man. This insured that the men got paid earlier in the day. Fortunately, I was never short.

Before paying their men, most Commanders held a Company formation. This was the one time that all of the men present for duty were assembled. Policies were published, orders issued, outstanding soldiers recognized, forms signed, announcements made, critiques given, future plans discussed, special checks made, precautions or admonitions given, and donations requested. As Co CO I also used the time to compliment the men on things they had done well. I pressed them to put part of their pay in Soldiers Savings and asked for whatever donations were needed or in vogue that month. Once the troops were paid, they were normally free to take care of personal business, hence the importance of paying as early as possible.

Each payday my thoughts flashed back to my first payday in the Army at FT Lee in 1942. The procedure had not changed much. Now as then, the 1SG called off the names in payroll order (alphabetically by rank). Each trooper reported to the pay table saluting smartly, "Sir, PFC Sullivan reports for pay." The salute was not returned because the pay officer was occupied with money. The man signed the payroll which listed all deductions (eventually individual pay slips were made available). The money was counted out, scooped up by the soldier, who turned away without saluting again. It was then that he was badgered to put money in Soldiers' Savings and to make contributions as he ran the gauntlet of soliciting OFFs and NCOs to the door.

It was the responsibility of the pay officer to track down and pay every man if possible. This often necessitated visits to the hospital or stockade. Returning the payroll was also a chore. All entries red lined (not paid because a soldier was not present on Post or refused his pay for some reason) had to be totaled and that amount of money refunded. Only then did the Finance Officer give the pay officer his receipt. Every payday some officer was short.

LTC Wilson directed that each Co in the 3/504 be best in one area such as supply, mess, or barracks. The Bn was thus able to sweep the 504 competitions. K Co was to have the Best Supply.

Our records were the best in the Regt because we had just gone through the IG audit and had new ones, therefore we concentrated on security and appearance. Mr Baggett and SSG Johnson did a fantastic job, stripping Camp Mackall of its usable lumber. When LTC Wilson inspected the K Co Supply, he was impressed with the office, warehouse and arms room. When he saw the baggage room (where suitcases and hand bags were stored for the troopers) he became irate. New shelving had been built and freshly painted IN Blue; baggage and other items were arranged neatly. But it was not paneled and varnished! LTC Wilson turned to Mr Baggett and asked why.

"Sir, we've run out of resources."

"Horse shit! Go buy lumber and varnish."

"We don't have that kind of money, sir."

"Hell, I didn't tell you to pay for it; charge it to the 504 Hobby Shop."

Baggett did as directed; K Co had the most beautiful knotty pine baggage room in the Div. Everyone was pleased except 1LT Cecil Kidd, the Regt Hobby Shop OIC. When Kidd tried to get Baggett to account for the huge charge, he referred him to LTC Wilson. Nothing further was heard about the matter. Funds for the hobby shop were generated by profits from the slot machines in the OFFs' and EM Clubs. K Co won the Best Supply Competition without difficulty.

In February, the annual training cycle began; it would culminate in the yearly maneuver in May. This included individual refresher training, squad, Plt, and Co problems, as well as Bn, Regt and combined exercises.

Range firing was scheduled in this training cycle. Preliminary marksmanship training was conducted in the close-in training areas around the Bn area. LTC Wilson directed each Co to bivouac on the range for actual firing to take advantage of the best light and to minimize movement. It was my first experience with RA range firing; camping on the site made for a more efficient range. K Co pitched tents in a small grove of trees just behind the 500 yard points. The mess was in the field with us, so the cooks were able to fire handily. During those three days on the range, every man in K Co fired, including myself. I was pleased to fire Sharpshooter, my best score yet. It was an honest scoring as I made sure that 1SG Lowe had not ordered someone to use an "M-l pencil" in rating me. We had to refire several troopers in order to get the entire Co qualified.

As part of this training, each Plt conducted an exercise in which it jumped into an area from which the Plt Ldr maneuvered his unit through a tactical problem. An umpire or observer went along to critique the Plt and its Ldr. I jumped with the 2nd Plt commanded by Peanut Hinton. We jumped with minimum equipment; a sudden cold snap the first night prevented many of us from sleeping. However the problem went well under Peanut's leadership.

One of the final exercises before the annual maneuver was a river crossing, actually conducted on Mott Lake. The lake was ideal for such training; there were good assembly areas for troops and river-crossing equipment, excellent launching sites, and a sandy beach on which to land on the far side. The mission of the 504 was to establish and secure a beachhead for the Div. K Co, leading, the assault, crossed without difficulty, then moved out rapidly to the 02 line, the second phase of consolidation of a beachhead. An inspection satisfied me that my men were digging tactically sound positions.

As I returned to the Co CP, there was a garbled report about some problem on the front line. Simultaneously a jeep came clattering through the Co area, finally stopping at the CP. A loud voice called for the Co CO - it was MG Palmer. I ran forward, reporting, "Sir, LT Seibert, K Co CO, reports to the CG. The Co is tactically deployed to defend the 02 line of the Regt beachhead."

"What kind of a Co do you run, LT?" he shouted at me.

"The best damn company in the 82nd Airborne Division, sir!"

"It is like hell! There is no discipline, no military courtesy in this Co." I was stunned. These were two things that I stressed, I thought K Co exemplified them.

"What is the matter, sir?"

"I approached from the enemy side to see how you were deployed. I got to the front line and stopped to talk to some of the troops. Not one of them got out of his fox hole, stood at attention or saluted."

"But, sir, those are their instructions. We are playing this tactically and obviously you don't stand at attention and salute an OFF on the front lines."

He continued his tirade about K Go's lack of discipline, chewing me out as he stated that troops always stand at attention and salute their Div CG. He ended saying, "I fought all through WWII and my troops always saluted me or any other officer."

By this time I was completely exasperated and responded, "Yes, sir! But you and the artillery were far behind the front lines."

At this he became enraged, jumped into his jeep and headed for the Bn CP. I am sure that the confrontation between BG Palmer and LTC Wilson was a warm one, though I heard no more about the incident. I remained convinced that my troopers lacked neither discipline nor military courtesy.

The 1950 maneuver, Operation Assembly, was held, as in 1949, on the Bragg/Mackall complex. Once again, I missed the mass tactical jump that ended the exercise. K Co was air landed in C-82s. Despite this, it was both interesting and satisfying training. During the air landing I sat in the cockpit, watching and listening to the Ground Control Approach (GCA) landing as the controllers talked the pilot to a landing on the Mackall Airfield.

The night of the landing was cold. Since K Co had gone in light, keeping warm was a problem until the land tail caught up with us at daylight with our warm clothing and bedrolls.

Early in 1950, two significant events occurred which affected me profoundly. The first was my decision to buy a car. An OFF in our BOQ had bought one in Monroe, a small town southwest of Ft Bragg, which did a large volume of business by minimizing the profit on each car. It sounded like a good place to get mine. One evening after chow, Frank Mashburn drove me to Monroe. The car that struck me immediately, was a fire engine red, convertible, Pontiac Star Chief. It was a beautiful car; without hesitation, I bought it. The Griffin Motor Company processed the paperwork for the GMAC loan on the spot. With great pride I drove it back to the Post. That convertible became well known on FT Bragg, everybody recognized me by it. I still meet sons and daughters of friends who recall riding in my red convertible as children.

The second was the reassignment of COL Allan who was replaced by COL Joseph P. Cleland. Prior to COL Cleland's assumption of command, there were a number of farewell functions for the Allans, culminating in a formal dance at the Main Post Officers' Club.

Periodically, the Regt held dances at the Club. Some were command performances such as this one for COL and Mrs Allan. Most bachelors protested the requirement to attend, but always enjoyed themselves once there. Dances were held in the Hodge Room of the Main Club, at that time the only formal ballroom on Post. I alternated between finding a date and going stag. During the formal for the Allans, to which I went stag, I found myself sitting on the floor eating barbecued chicken with Mrs Allan. I commented on the absurdity of the formal dress and the messy buffet only to learn that the Allans had specifically requested that menu!

COL Cleland had been a BG during WWII, but like many others, had been reduced in grade after the war. It was rumored that he would soon get his star again. He was an outstanding commander. I learned a great deal from him and enjoyed serving under him. He was a distinguished looking officer with a thick mane of silver hair and a neatly trimmed mustache. Overnight he became the "Great White Father", much admired by the troops.

Life returned to whatever passed for normal in the BOQ. Three dogs continued to reside there with us: Hillman's salivating Boxer, Stieber's beautiful but cringing German Shepherd, and Langerman's beloved Kerry Blue Terrier, Hood. Only Hood was a field dog, the other two were strictly garrison residents. Hood was always with Hal in the field and was a great favorite with the troops. Their admiration and love for Hood was cemented when he lifted his leg on the shiny boot of the 1st Bn CO, LTC Joe Ryneska, during a Bn formation, in full view of the incredulous but highly approving troops.

The OFFs in the BOQ were constantly looking for something to do at night. Fayetteville did not offer much entertainment and we got tired of drinking or playing the slot machines in the 504 Officers' Club. Frequently, when we heard of a night jump, we would go down to the Marshalling Area to see if we could get on the manifest. About half the times we were successful. Whenever the NCO Academy jumped, as part of their Jumpmaster Training, we could usually get to jump as a wind dummy.

One night three of us from the 504 BOQ were accepted as wind dummies for an NCO Academy jump. The fourth wind dummy, a LTC from the Div staff, was obviously nervous. He and I were manifested on the same flight. Once we were chuted up, he took me aside and asked, "Will you tap me out, LT? I might miss the green light."

"Sir, it doesn't make any difference. You go when you want to as a wind dummy. After the green light goes on, pick your time and exit. Remember though, that you don't slip unless you are going into the trees. Just drop naturally so the DZSO can plot the wind and adjust the Tee."

"But, LT, I might not see the green light and I don't want the NCOs to think that I hesitated in the door. Please tap me out."

At that time we were jumping an early model C-82 which did not have jump lights on the tail booms. They were located to the right of the door, so if the Jumpmaster was looking out checking the Tee, it is conceivable that he might miss the change from red to green. Remembering my own sixth jump, I agreed to tap him out.

We made a good approach to Sicily South. When the green light came on, I slapped the LTC's butt. He grabbed the sides of the door so tightly that his knuckles turned white. Through clenched teeth he shouted, "ONE THOUSAND, TWO THOUSAND, THREE THOUSAND" then leaped out into the night. I was shocked; the counting is done only after exiting the aircraft; if a jumper fails to get his opening shock by the end of the count, he pulls his reserve. The LTC, after counting in the aircraft, might have discovered a malfunction too late to pull his reserve, or not feeling an opening shock at the end of the count, he might have pulled his reserve in the aircraft. Fortunately he landed without any problem. As I jumped out on his tail I heard the laughter of the NCOs. I never saw that LTC again.

After Operation Assembly, convinced that K Co was functioning well, and anxious to showoff my new car, I decided to go on leave. In mid-June I drove to New York for an enjoyable but all too short period of relaxation. I saw several girl friends and some of my old friends, was able to get in some swimming, attended the wedding of George Gabelia's sister (the three hour rite in the Russian Orthodox Cathedral was something!), and spent some time with Mother and Dad. Finally, it was time to return to Bragg. I was just north of Baltimore when the radio program was interrupted by an announcement that the North Koreans had crossed the Demilitarized Zone and invaded South Korea. All military personnel were directed to report to their posts immediately because President Truman had indicated that he was going to intervene. Defying speed controls, I reached Fort Bragg in six hours.

In anticipation of the widely rumored deployment of the 504 to Korea, COL Cleland directed an intensive training program. Physical training and road marches were stressed. COL Cleland was in superb physical condition himself. He could do hand stands and run with the rest of us. Among other things he increased the length and number of road marches.

One day Cleland directed that every trooper scour out his helmet before leaving on a twenty five mile road march. Nobody understood the order, When we got back from the particularly demanding hike, the Div Band met us as we entered the cantonment area, and escorted us to the Regt Parade Field. In front of each mess hall were kegs of cold beer for the troops. Everyone got a helmet full of beer! There were soft drinks also,

All troopers did not drink beer, but none refused his ration. You can imagine where that ration went. Late into the night small clusters of troops could be seen on the parade field. While it was a morale factor for the troops it was a headache for the Regt OD, who had to clear the field by taps.

All of the 504 Co COs were certain that the Regt would be sent to Korea shortly, so extra steps were taken to insure that our men were ready. Each CO evaluated his Co for deficiencies and emphasized training to eliminate them. Concerned about the antitank defense of K Co, and with the skill of the 60mm Mortar Section, I had the 57m Recoiless Rifle and Mortar Squads out after chow in the evening for additional training. Before the first night session, I explained to them the areas in which I thought they were weak and stressed my desire that they go into combat as well trained as I could make them. The men appeared willing to participate, though K Co was alone in this intensive, off-duty training. After several weeks, I thought the Co ready for any mission, ready to go to Korea. However, it was not to be.

Word soon filtered through the Div that MG Palmer had made a strong plea to the CofS, GEN Collins, that the loss of the 504 would materially degrade his capability to reinforce Europe if required (the primary mission of the 82nd in 1950). Apparently the CofS and the JCS agreed; it was directed that the 187th AIR of the 11th Abn Div, at cadre strength, be reconstituted at Fort Campbell, KY and deployed to Korea. The logic for the decision still mystifies me; it seemed more sensible to send into combat a unit which had trained and operated together in the field, with procedures well developed, thus giving it the best possible chance to survive or accomplish the missions assigned to it. The 504 could be replaced in the 82nd by activation of another AIR (perhaps the 508 which had fought with the Div in WWII). It could be organized, equipped and trained, assisted by the remainder of the Div, in a minimum amount of time, which in 1950 did not seem significant. The US still had a monopoly on atomic weapons. Instead a newly reconstituted, less well-trained unit was ordered into combat in Korea.

In fact, the 82nd Abn Div was tasked to provide additional personnel to bring the 187 up to strength. Each unit was given a quota; K Co's was I MSG, E-7, and two TSGs, E-6. Almost all of my TSGs wanted to go. Dumas, Townsend, Whelan and others were eager to volunteer. However, the E-7 presented a real problem. There were four MSGs in K Co: 1SG Lowe, MSGs Cooper (1st Plt), Wyatt, (3rd Plt), and Prieto (4th or Weapons Plt). I called the four in and asked if any of them wanted to volunteer. None did, for good reasons which I respected. Since the quota had to be filled, I told them that I would put the four names in a hat, the NCO whose name was pulled would go.

I am a great believer in the fairness of a lottery for the draft, or for selecting an individual from a group of equally qualified people. The Co Clerk pulled Cooper's name from a helmet.

Immediately MSG Cooper made excuses and gave me reasons why he should not be sent. He was an old combat jumper; he had a bad back; he was not sure that he would be able to bear up under the rigors of combat in Korea. This incensed me because all of our troopers were supposed to be combat ready. It seemed to me an unprofessional attitude for an NCO in the 82nd. I ordered him to go to the hospital for a physical examination. If there was, in fact, a problem with his back which would preclude his being sent to combat, he would be removed from jump status. If there was no problem, he would go to the 187. Neither prospect pleased Cooper, but I made arrangements for the examination to determine his physical status.

Cooper went to the Bn XO, MAJ Nealson, who came to my office to dissuade me from my action. He became more and more angry when I refused to take Cooper off the levy. My question to him was, "Who do you want me to put on it? Why should I take J.B. off and put Wyatt, Prieto or Lowe on? They are all combat veterans, all equally fine NCOs, all have legitimate reasons for not volunteering. The lottery was the only fair way to make the decision."

MAJ Nealson had no answer for my arguments. He would not select one of the others, but kept insisting that Cooper should not go to Korea. One of them had to go, J.B. was going as far as I was concerned.

Finally, Nealson exploded, "Well, all I can say, Seibert, is that this reflects on your judgement as a commander and I'll make sure that it is made a matter of record."

Leaping to my feet, I said, "Sir, you and I had better go to see the BN Co." He was reluctant to go, LTC Wilson awed him. He tried to back off, but I insisted, practically dragging him to the BN HQ. Without ceremony we walked into LTC Wilson's office. Fortunately, he was in. I saluted, requesting permission to speak with the Bn CO. Permission was granted. I explained my dilemma in selecting an E-7 to fill the quota for the 187.

LTC Wilson heard me out, then said, "I do agree with MAJ Nealson that you showed poor judgement in this. You should not have included 1SG Lowe in the consideration. He is far too valuable to you and the Division to cadre out this way. Otherwise, I agree with you. As far as I am concerned Cooper is your cadre choice."

Cooper never did go to the 187. In some strange machination of the personnel system by the NCO Old Boy Net, a TSG in Div Artillery who had volunteered to go under a different MOS and in a lower grade filled that particular quota. K Co only provided two TSGs. The incident disturbed me. I lost respect for MSG Cooper; although he remained in the Company, he seemed less effective.

In those days a Company Commander was responsible for answering Congressional inquiries concerning men in his unit. When a member of Congress wrote to ask about a constituent, the letter was forwarded to the individual who could best answer it. This was a far cry from the current policy of designating a staff officer to answer all Congressional, requiring him to collect the information on which to base his reply, and then writing it without a full appreciation of the situation. It again demonstrates the lack of trust in junior officers. One day I received such a Congressional concerning a young PVT in K Co. The Senator wrote that it was his understanding that this man was undernourished and losing weight. He was alleged to be in such poor health that his mother was concerned about him. This made me laugh because the trooper in question was one of the huskiest and healthiest in K Co. He had come to us as a shy, raw recruit with a lot of puppy fat still on him. After a few months he had slimmed down into a well developed, physically fit, confident soldier.

When I talked to him about the letter, he told me that during his recent leave his mother had commented about the weight he had lost. He accompanied me to the hospital where I asked to have him checked to see if he was suffering from malnutrition. The doctor laughed when I explained about the Congressional inquiry. He found the trooper in excellent health. In my reply, I told the Senator that his constituent was a mature, healthy, vigorous paratrooper. In a short time I received a direct reply from the Senator, who explained that he was an old family friend. Since his father's death, his mother had been overly protective of her only son. He had advised the young man to go into the Army to grow up, but had not foreseen that he might volunteer for the Airborne. He was happy to hear that he had adjusted so well, thanked me for my effort, and said that he would take care of the mother.

Unfortunately, the Senator failed to follow through. A few week's later, the young trooper's mother appeared. 1SG Lowe showed her into my office. She was sniffing and complaining that her poor boy was losing weight and becoming a savage. The trooper, who had been summoned by Lowe, reported smartly. Extremely embarrassed, he tried to convince his mother to go home, telling her he felt fine and was happy in the Army. She wept over him. Finally, I dismissed him. Then I spoke to the mother in plain terms, pointing out what a sturdy young man he was, how mature he had become and how proud she should be of him. I urged her to let him live his life, to stop trying to live it for him. She did not like my candor and began to cry. This did not impress me, I repeated my advice that she let her son live his own life.

In a short time there was another Congressional from the Senator about my treatment of the mother. My reply reviewed the visit in detail. The Senator wrote another personal letter in which he thanked me for my candor, saying that he had given the lady much the same advice. He was sure that henceforth she would leave the young man alone. Apparently, she did.

TSG Townsend, a handsome, sharp, effective NCO came to see me about becoming an officer. He wanted to get a commission in any way, but he especially wanted to go to West Point. He had graduated from the 82nd NCO Academy with the highest grade given up to that time. He was not only a "spit and polish soldier", he was a good field soldier. He asked me if he would be barred from going to the USMA or VMI if he divorced his wife! Of course I discouraged that idea, explaining that a divorced individual could not go to West Point. I suggested that he go to one of the State Colleges where he could participate in the ROTC program. With his ability he would undoubtedly be designated a Distinguished Military Graduate and offered an RA Commission. Before he could take any action, he was transferred to Korea, where he earned a battlefield commission.

Periodically, battalions spent a week at the shore in the Fort Fisher area (near Wilmington). It was partly rest and recreation, partly water safety, partly compensatory time. Under LTC Wilson's supervision, the 3rd Bn left early one Monday morning in July and returned on Friday afternoon. The convoy took about three hours. On arrival at Fort Fisher, we found squad tents already erected. Each Co CO signed for tents, cots and mess tables. Our kitchen trucks and mess gear had accompanied us as well as a loaded supply truck which even had bed sheets. Despite the mosquitoes it was a comfortable camp.

We enjoyed a relaxed schedule, minimum training which included mandatory lectures on the Articles of War and I& E, much swimming, including instruction on water safety, and lots of sports. LTC Wilson was everywhere, yet he did not inhibit the troops. Only sloppy police brought forth an expected reaction. We returned to Bragg much refreshed.

During Officers' Call one Saturday morning, someone burst into the room and asked if any officers had A-Positive blood. A few of us raised our hands. We were told that a set of twins at Wrightsville Beach (about 100 miles southeast of the Post) needed blood. Of course we all volunteered. The Adj selected four of us and told us to take off immediately. Jack O'Shaughnessy, who knew the father of the twins, offered to drive us to Wrightsville Beach in his Packard sedan. He covered those miles in record time.

When we arrived at the hospital, the condition of the children was so critical that the doctors decided to do a direct transfusion, rare even in those days. On cross-matching us with the twins, my blood was compatible with one of the youngsters. We went immediately to an operating room where I laid on one table with a little girl on a table beside me. With needles, syringes and tubes, blood was drawn directly from me and transfused into the child. After the transfusions, the father of the twins, "Duke" Elvington, insisted on taking us to Faircloths, a well-known seafood restaurant. He recommended roast oysters, which I had never had. We all agreed to try them, whereupon Duke ordered a bushel! A young boy stood by the table and shucked them as fast as we could eat them. There were all sorts of condiments on the table to make any sauce we could devise. Later, Duke returned to AD with the 82nd, so we got to know the twins. Their parents said that the youngsters owed their lives to the troopers who had given them blood. Every trooper in the 82nd would have volunteered to give his blood to a young child under the circumstances. No paratrooper hesitated in such a situation!

The period immediately preceding the Korean War in 1950 was one of austerity for the Armed Forces. Most OFFs blamed Secretary of Defense Louis Johnson for the problems we faced, believing that he had accepted an inadequate budget without a fight. As a result of the shortage of funds, there was little gasoline allocated for administrative or training purposes. Many times the troops marched back from the DZs because the trucks were held in the motor pools to conserve fuel.

Wives of OFFs and NCOs frequently drove out to the DZ to pick up their husbands, and more and more civilian cars began to appear at the Marshalling Area. Although there were orders against using private transportation to and from the Marshalling Area and Drop Zone, they were violated with impunity.

The lack of gasoline was felt critically in Co administration. The two-wheeled carts assigned to each Co for minor pick-up and delivery chores, were inadequate for most tasks and of no use when issues were made outside the Regt area. As a result, everyone resorted to the use of personal transportation. The Supply and Mess Sergeants were especially hard hit, using their own cars routinely for Co business. My red convertible was pressed into service frequently; it was not unusual to see it with top down, loaded with laundry bundles, cartons of toilet paper, or waving mop heads. On several occasions permission was given to use the Co jeep or truck provided the gasoline expended was paid for. It was strange to see tactical vehicles lined up at the PX service station waiting to have the tanks topped off at Co COs' expense.

Among the measures COL Cleland initiated after the start of the Korean War was a periodic show-down inspection. Everyone in the 504 had alert gear including packs ready to go at all times. The packs contained minimum essentials needed to live in the field for a short time such as toilet articles, changes of socks and underwear and such comfort items as the trooper desired. At a July Muster, he directed the men of the 2nd Bn to lay out their alert gear. The results were embarrassing. There was everything but the required equipment in the packs: brassieres, ladies pants and hose, beer cans, cardboard and much more. But the most humiliating time was when he dismissed the EM and directed the OFFs to lay out their equipment. We were pretty straight in the 3rd Bn because LTC Wilson kept us on our toes. One of the other Bns opened their packs to reveal nothing but cardboard to make the packs look good. COL Cleland, incensed, ordered the Bn CO to double-time his OFFs to their area to make up proper packs. I have a feeling that many NCO packs were borrowed by OFFs to display. It was an object lesson to all of us. From then on nobody was caught short in the 504.

At this time the DA began to promote officers on an accelerated basis. When the first promotions were announced, all officers who had been integrated into the RA after WWII, including those of us commissioned under Circular 382, became enraged. The promotions, made in the Army of the United States, AUS, should have been based on temporary or AUS date of rank. Instead, they were made on permanent or RA date of rank. This meant that most of us were passed over by officers many years our junior in service and experience.

The day after the first promotions were made, Dave McNaught, John Kiser and I were discussing the matter. All of us had been overtaken by juniors and were irate. We decided to go to the Pentagon see to about it. Each of us obtained a three day pass; that evening after duty we drove to Washington in my convertible. Early the next morning, we were in the Infantry Branch office, when LTC Porteus arrived and asked our business. Interrupting each other, we poured out our concern about the obvious breach of faith inherent in the policy of basing temporary promotions on permanent date of rank. He heard us with increasing irritation.

During a pause in our tirade he pontificated, "You accepted your RA Commissions, didn't you? That means you accepted the system. You asked for it."

With this profundity, he turned to go to his desk. His remarks and attitude so angered me that I started to climb over the counter to punch him in the nose! Dave and John pulled me back, we left still seething.

On returning to Bragg, we learned that there were other personnel actions, even more odious, which the DA had imposed on us. Many of the OFFs who had been forced to leave the service the year before in a reduction in force (RIF) were being recalled to active duty. Most had accepted Reserve Commissions upon their release from AD, and some had re-enlisted as NCOs in order to complete the AD service requirements for retirement, in almost all cases, their rank in the RES was at least one grade higher than the one they held when released. Now they were recalled to AD in the higher grade; some came back to taunt us.

These personnel policies were clearly indefensible. They made us wonder about the advantages of our RA Commissions, called into question the integrity and leadership of senior officers, including the CofS, and raised doubts about the decision-making process in the Pentagon. Many never recovered their relative rank as a result of these incomprehensible decisions. Later we heard that Army Regulations barred an OFF from holding a grade higher than one above his Regular grade. Non-Regular OFFs on AD were under no comparable restrictions. If there was any logic behind these policies, DA failed to explain it. The Officers' Call program would have been an ideal forum for such an explanation. Certainly this failure to "keep the troops informed" caused unnecessary speculation and discontent.

The 504 was scheduled to have its Annual General Inspection (AGI) toward the end of the summer. Just as we received this word, I was notified that SSG Johnson was reassigned to Civilian Component Duty. On the recommendations of Mr Baggett and 1SG Lowe, SSG Harold Alsup was transferred from the Weapons Plt to the Supply Room. 1LT O'Shaughnessy, his Plt Ldr, and MSG Prieto vehemently protested; Alsup was one of the best weapons NCOs in the Regt. But supply was important to the Co and especially to me as Co CO, so Alsup went to the Supply Room to understudy Johnson for three weeks before his departure. Alsup was a trained supply man who owed no debts or favors to anyone in the supply field. A top-notch soldier, he became an outstanding Supply Sergeant.

There was never any suspicion that he was "wheeling or dealing' in government property. Later SSG Alsup was appointed a WO and retired as a W04.

In lieu of an inspection in ranks, the IG decreed that the men in all Cos pitch pup tents, lay out their full field equipment in front of them, and stand by their displays. There was also to be an inspection of the barracks, of all records, supplies, arms rooms, mess halls, dayrooms and motor pools. It was a good procedure in that it forced a check of every aspect of unit performance once a year.

We prepared for the AGI a month in advance, laying out equipment according to the SOP. The Plt Ldrs and Co COs inspected and re-inspected their units to make sure that all men had all of the clothing and field equipment authorized, required and issued. The supply records, mess records, Co Fund records, the entire administration of the Co, received careful scrutiny. The 1SG checked and retyped many morning report entries. The files were screened carefully and excess paper was retired. Everybody was busy. It was an ordeal.

Finally the day of the AGI arrived, the Div IG, his experts and clerks, descended on the 504 together with the Asst Div CDR, who made the actual inspection of the troops in formation beside their tents and full field equipment displays. Every piece of equipment was identical for every man; even toothbrushes, bars of soap, and razors were alike. Everyone had issue shorts and T-shirts. Uniformity was supreme. Each item was laid in the same place in each display, lined up by string so there would be no deviation. Again, the purpose was to permit the Inspecting Officer to tell at a glance whether there was anything missing, broken or otherwise out of the ordinary. Obviously, we went to extremes in the 82nd as attested by the starched GI shorts and T-shirts folded over cardboard.

K Co passed the AGI with flying colors. It was my final formation with the unit. I had received orders to attend the Infantry Officers' Advance Course at Fort Benning beginning the latter part of August, 1950. With the AGI completed, I turned over K Co to Bill Sibert.

CHAPTER 7

RED DEVIL

As MAJ Ted Fuller, the Adj of the 3/504, was slated to take the Associate Advance Course at the same time I was in the Regular Course, he and I drove to Fort Benning in my convertible. The trip took about ten hours in those days, easily accomplished in one day. Ted's course was only three months long, after which he returned to Fort Bragg to become the S-4 of the 504.

The Regular Advance Course was both an informative and pleasant experience. It was announced at the start that the course was being shortened; all of the essential material would be concentrated in the first three or four months It had not yet been decided how long the course would be, as the entire class was alerted for shipment to Korea on short notice. However, we were assured that we would have a minimum of three months in school, probably until Christmas. Thus, in the first three months we were kept busy with a concentrated immersion in Infantry tactics and leadership. After the Christmas holidays, the pace let up, and we spent more time on staff procedures, map exercises and "nice-to-have" courses. Finally it was announced that we would graduate in April.

The BOQ in which I was billeted was in the Biglerville area, now almost a second home. In that BOQ there were a number of compatible classmates: Frank Barnhart, Jim McAmis, Jim McRay, Tom Tarpley. Del Townsend, and Larkin Tully. In addition to those in the BOQ there were many married officers who became good friends: Al Burdette, Fred Davidson, Jim Dunn, Spike Harris, Bill Humphrey, Brick Krause, Jake Lance, Jim Russell, Bob Selton and Gene Walters. "Dog" Carter, who had been in the 96th Div was in the class also. Alec Kovalevsky, a friend of George Gabelia's, of whom I had seen a great deal before WWII, was on the faculty of The Infantry School (TIS). Over dinner with him and his wife, Frances, we recalled those pre-Army years. Many members of the class served with me in other units thereafter.

That crew in the BOQ was a wild one. We spent a great deal of our off-duty time in Phenix City where the favorite spot was Shad's Rose Room. Of course we went occasionally to Beachy Howard's, and to other night spots, but the Rose Room was preferred. Gambling, floor shows, dancing, liquor, and food were available in all of them; we always had a gala evening, though it was likely to be expensive. Since I had no steady date, I would go out with one group or another from the BOQ, rarely with the same girl twice.

LTC Wilson, assigned to the Ranger Department at TIS, arranged a night jump for me with the Rangers (TIS would not give me permission to miss class for a day jump). MAJ Jack Singlaub was the jumpmaster; the soft landing on Lee Field reminded me of Jump School. It was the only jump I made during the Course. Normally students were not permitted to jump to maintain their proficiency.

Frequently LTC Wilson and I had dinner together at the Club. A group of bachelors met for dinner most Sunday evenings, LTC Wilson asked me to join them occasionally. It was there I met COL Edwin C. Walker, LTC Bill Bond and MAJ Jack Singlaub. All were promoted within the year.

A two-week administrative leave was authorized at Christmas, which I spent with the family in New York. As expected, Mother and Dad followed traditions developed over the years in the family; the tree was spectacular in its revolving stand. With three grandchildren now a part of the family group, it was a spirited affair. An early return enabled me to attend the New Year's Eve Party at the

Main Club; following it I found myself in Phenix City, wandering in and out of the night clubs. It seemed that half our class was there.

As we entered Wharton Hall one morning for a leadership class, the instructor, a very tall major, was already positioned behind the podium. Normally, the instructors waited until the class assembled before mounting the dais. The Class Leader reported the class present and the lecture began. The instructor, MAJ William Fulton, announced that the topic was "Planning and Follow Through". He told us not to get so wrapped up in the details of a plan that we lost sight of the main elements of our program.

"For instance, although I was concerned about this class, I just relaxed and thought of my opening remarks. I knew the rest would come naturally."

With that, he stepped from behind the podium. He had on long Johns (winter underwear) with no trousers. The class howled as Bill, feigning great embarrassment, rushed behind the podium again. He made his point well.

In the curriculum were several hours on methods of conducting bayonet training. It amazed me to see MAJ (perhaps he was a LTC by then) Bronckhorst still in charge of that Instruction.

We learned a great deal in the Advance Class, I don't think we realized just how much we did learn. MAJ Donnelly Bolton taught us the reverse slope defense, a concept difficult to accept in spite of his excellent presentation. Other controversial tactics were covered equally well. The instructors were outstanding; the scheduling and facilities at Fort Benning faultless.

Toward the middle of March we received our orders. Though the Advance Class had prepared us for duty in Korea, few went directly into combat there. For some reason it had been decided not to send our class to Korea. On transfer to Benning I had asked for an assignment to the Ranger Department, more specifically, to one of the newly activated Ranger Companies being readied for Korea. Assigned to the Ranger Department, LTC Wilson indicated that I would be in a good position to transfer to one of the Ranger Cos if any of the OFFs fell out of the system.

At the graduation ceremony, the guest speaker announced the authorization of new accouterments: the IN Blue Shoulder Cord, and IN Blue Backgrounds for the insignia on EM's uniforms.

The Expert Infantryman Badge (EIB) was to be given added emphasis and status. These actions were taken to enhance the prestige of the Infantryman.

Immediately after graduation, my orders were changed; I was assigned to the508th Airborne Infantry Regimental Combat Team (dubbed the "Red Devils") at FT Bragg. When I protested the orders, the Personnel Officer at FT Benning told me that the 508th RCT, just being reactivated, had top priority on personnel. Therefore, he could do nothing for me.

Still determined to fight the change, I drove to Bragg, and was instructed to sign in at the 504 HQ. My disappointment in not getting the Ranger assignment was somewhat eased when I was told that COL Cleland was to command the 508. Though I had great respect for the "Great White Father", I made one last effort to be a Ranger. On reporting to COL Cleland I told him of my original assignment to the Ranger Department and of my desire to stay there. Cleland advised me to stick with the 508th, which had a high priority, a special mission and would be an outstanding unit.

That evening I had dinner with Ted and Kay Fuller. During our conversation I voiced my dissatisfaction with the 508 assignment. Ted suggested I call LTC Wilson at the Ranger Department. I did so. He advised me to stick with the 508, but said he would look into the matter for me. He could do nothing.

A number of OFFs and NCOs I knew, respected and liked were being assigned to the 508, Ted Fuller as the S-4, Ed Morris, as Commo OFF, as well as BUI Ankley, Al Bettelli, Hanz Druener, Hal Langerman (and Hood), Jack O'Shaughnessy and Ted Seely. Apparently COL Cleland had the pick of the OFFs and NCOs of the 82nd. The troops to be assigned to the 508 were currently undergoing basic training with the 82nd Airborne Division. They were probably the most gung-ho and best trained recruits the Army ever had. The Red Devils also got a number of OFFs from the Advance Class: Jack Wright to command a Bn, Spike Harris to be a Bn XO, Al Burdette, Arch Hamblen, Art Hyman, George McLendon, Larkin Tully, Horst Yost, and others. With those OFFs I knew it would be a fine outfit.

Duty with the 508 began to look as attractive as that with the Ranger Department. Still, the chance of getting into a Ranger Co and going into combat with it intrigued me. Finally, it became apparent that my protests were in vain; when COL Cleland gave me command of F Co, I settled down to enjoy the 508. In retrospect I am glad that I was assigned to the 508 Airborne Infantry Regimental Combat Team. Though it delayed my entry into combat for the second time, it was one of the highlights of my military career. The 508 RCT was one of the best units I served in from many facets: the caliber of people, OFF, NCO, and EM, the training, the support it received from DA.

COL Cleland continued to command the 504, even while supervising the organization and administration of the 508. Those of us assigned early formed the nucleus and did much of the initial administrative work.

In order to start drawing jump pay, I needed a jump, I had only jumped once in the past year and wanted to get into the swing of it again. COL Cleland arranged for me to jump at Camp Mackall with the 504 one morning. An Air Force (USAF) COL and I were picked up by a jeep at the 504 HQ at 0500. The driver got lost enroute, with the result that we arrived at the Marshalling Area just as the aircraft were being loaded. COL Cleland spotted us and called,

"Come on! We have chutes for both of you".

We jumped on the aircraft, helmets in hand. As soon as the plane was airborne we unhooked our seat belts to put on our chutes. This was the first time I had chuted up in flight. A qualified rigger in the stick gave us a quick check. Almost immediately the red light came on, triggering the jump sequence.

The AF COL commanded one of the wings which supported the 82nd and later the508; both units received exceptional cooperation from his unit.

As preparations fort he official activation continued, COL Cleland decided that the 508 cadre should take a Jumpmaster's Course. Art Hyman had been in the Pathfinder Group of the Airborne Department, which ran Jumpmaster Courses for TIS; he was directed to conduct the course. He organized a concentrated three day school which covered all of the essentials needed by Jumpmasters: how to inspect the aircraft, how to handle a marshalling area, how to organize a DZ (including the duties of both MACO and DZSO), how to inspect a trooper for proper parachute adjustment, how to inspect the stick in the aircraft, how to handle the assembly on the ground, how to compute drop time or point. Much of the subject matter concerned procedures many of us had been following as Co COs and Plt Ldrs but in which we had not had formal training. After our graduation jump we were awarded certificates of completion of the Jumpmaster's Course, which meant little; we had gained added confidence and fulfilled a requirement for qualification as a Master Jumper.

The 82nd Airborne Division, providing much of the cadre for the 508, was to hold a formal activation ceremony during which the colors of the RCT would be presented at a Division Review. COL Cleland had the words of the "All American Soldier" modified to fit the 508, and arranged to have the 508 Cadre sing it during the review. Fortunately I escaped that duty because I was designated as the Escort Officer for BG Roy C. Lindquist, the WWII Commander of the Red Devils. There were other WWII combat veterans of the 508 present for the function, among them Medal of Honor winner Leonard Funk.

The activation ceremony was impressive. The 508 cadre, seated in bleachers next to the Reviewing Stand, sang the modified version of "The All American Soldier", but the group was small, and there was no public address system so the words were unintelligible. A luncheon for the officers and civilian guests was held at the Club after the ceremony. It was my duty to see that BG Lindquist got to the appointed place at the proper time. This was no problem; I enjoyed escorting that exceptional OFF.

Thus, the 508 Airborne Infantry Regimental Combat Team was launched a second time. For a few weeks it operated under the 504, although several buildings were assigned for a HQ. Then the Red Devils were ordered to move to Fort Benning. An advance party, under the S-4, MAJ Ted Fuller, was ordered to proceed there immediately. I volunteered to be a part of it. CPT Jim Dunn (from the Advance Class and assigned as the Asst S-3) was also a member. We drove to Benning once again in my red convertible. The three of us spent many hours preparing for the arrival of the RCT.

The 508 was to occupy the Sand Hill area. Our first task was to sign for the buildings. In the process, I signed for those F Co was to occupy, getting an early start on organizing the area. Slowly the cadre drifted down. My 1SG, Henry Tucker, a tall, heavy- set individual arrived early. A likeable bachelor, he was intelligent, efficient, well-schooled in Army administration, and a doer. TSGs Kollat, Richter, Barnes and Chesney reported in as PSGs. MSG Cooper was a member of the cadre, but I made sure he was assigned to another Bn.

My XO, 1LT Bob Whitelaw, had been in the 504 with me and was an old friend. The Rifle Plt Ldrs, all newly commissioned, came from the Basic IN OFFs Course: 2LTs A.R. Stevens, Salvatore Fastuca, and Frank Costello. LT Jim Lattimore, who had been the I SG of I Co when I served under Dave McNaught, recently called to AD as an officer, was to be my Weapons Platoon Leader.

The filler personnel completed their basic training with the 82nd ABN Div. They had been exposed to the Airborne Spirit and were gung-ho. The men were assigned to their companies in the 508, then placed on TDY at Jump School. It was a stroke of luck, since we were able to talk with our men periodically, get to know them, fire them up and encourage them. When they made their jumps, the cadre of the 508 jumped with them. This was a boost to morale and did much to get the 508 off to a flying start. One of the OFFs I had words with while I was in Jump School, LTC Herbert V. Mansfield, now headed the Jump Committee; he was not overjoyed when we all trooped down to jump with our men. I avoided him.

Tom Mesereau, a Major, was assigned as CO of the 2nd Bn with Spike Harris as his XO. The staff consisted of three CPTs and a MAJ: George McLendon, S-1, Larkin Tully, S-2, MAJ Keith Honacker, S-3 and Mike Chester, S-4. The other Co COs were CPTs Warren Conlon, E Co, Doug Gilbert, G Co, Art Hyman, H Co, George Marr, HHC.

Before the fillers actually joined the Regt, we had a chance to send many of our NCOs to classes in TIS, as well as to conduct our own cadre training. Each Co set up a different tactical problem, through which all cadre personnel maneuvered.

Our filler personnel set a record while in Jump School; there were fewer wash-outs than in any previous class. As soon as they were settled in the barracks, their Advanced Individual Training, (AIT) began. They were a fine group to lead. With excellent NCOs and OFFs it was both enjoyable and rewarding to train that Co, to bring it along, to see it develop. The men learned fast, were eager in excellent physical condition and had discipline. With these attributes we could go full speed on technical military training. It was exhilarating to command a unit like that! My 1SG, Henry Tucker, and Bob Whitelaw, lifted much of the burden of administration from me. Bob was Supply OFF, Mess OFF, as well as XO.

The men were amused when they came over from the Airborne Area; for the first two days I stood in the mess line every meal and had each trooper tell me his name as he went into the mess hall. After six meals, I knew every man, every face, every name in F Co; when I spotted a man I could call him by name immediately. It proved helpful to me throughout my tenure as Co CO.

Almost before we were launched into our AIT program, F Co received a mission to put on a demonstration of physical training. TSG Kollat, the best physical specimen in the Co, was put in charge. Based on recommendations from LT Lattimore and TSG Kollat, I approved a two-part exhibition; twelve repetitions of the Army Dozen, the callisthenics routine, and a "Butts Manual" routine. A copy of an old ROTC manual which detailed the use of rifle drill for physical training was located. The demonstration platoon went through a silent "Butts Manual". It was an impressive show, but very strenuous physical exercise. TSG Kollat picked a group of sturdy young warriors, who put on a superb demonstration. They enjoyed the opportunity to display their physical prowess.

After we received our fillers, some of the splendid NCOs, who held RES commissions, began to be recalled to AD as commissioned officers. A month or so after the physical training exhibition, TSG Kollat was recalled as a 2LT. I never had the privilege of serving with him again, though I did bump into him once. Many other NCOs left the RCT at the time.

The Army was still looking for NCOs, particularly I SGs, who excelled in administration, to further the Unit Administrator Program. At my instigation, 1SG Tucker applied for his warrant and was immediately appointed a WO1. With unexpected good fortune he was assigned as the F Co Unit Administrator. For a short time he acted as both Administrator and First Sergeant.

Eventually 1SG Henry Hand was assigned to the Company. In another stroke of luck for F Co, it was decided that the NG Co of which he was 1SG, would not be deployed as a unit when it completed its Ranger training. Hand, who was looking for an Airborne billet, heard that F Co needed a 1SG and came to see me about the job. There was instant rapport between us resulting in 1SG Hand's immediate assignment.

Hand brought with him five or six young stalwarts who had completed the Ranger Course. Several were NCOs, the rest PVTs. One of them, Paul E. Bucey, I made my Co Runner or Messenger. Bucey, a first string football player from a Midwestern college, was not only a fine physical specimen, but also a quick and intelligent soldier who responded instantly to any orders or situation. He was tireless, which enhanced his value in a tactical situation. Another, SSG Haywood, became TSG Richter's second in Command, the 1st Plt Guide. The 1st Plt Ldr, 2LT Fastuca, a star football player for West Point, had been transferred there as an Asst Coach, leaving the 1st Plt under the Command of TSG Richter. Initially there was some animosity between them, but they fought it out behind the barracks one night and became a great team. Several of the Rangers were accepted for OCS shortly after joining F Company.

One of my first tasks was to provide a good mess for my troopers. One experienced cook, SGT Short, and one Cook's Helper, a semi-trained cook, had been assigned from the 82nd as part of the cadre. When the fillers arrived, volunteers were requested for mess hall duty; several excellent prospects came forward. SGT Short took those troopers in hand and taught them to cook; shortly we had a first class mess that gave the soldiers good chow.

One meal in particular F Co Troopers were not likely to forget. Tom Mesereau, the Bn CO, was married to Jean Leone, the daughter of the owner of the famous New York restaurant, Mama Leone's. Whether he had married into the family because he was a great chef himself was never revealed, but LTC (promoted since assuming Command of the 2nd Bn) Mesereau was indeed an outstanding chef. During an informal conversation, I mentioned to my Bn CO that we needed a good Italian meal in F Co. He responded,

"The next time you are scheduled to have spaghetti, let me know and I will come down and cook it for you."

A short time later, on learning that the menu three days hence called for spaghetti, I notified LTC Mesereau. He agreed to cook the meal, but asked me to get certain condiments and spices. With certain other extras, I expended over $50.00 to make that meal spectacular. On the day appointed, LTC Mesereau spent the morning cooking the sauce, simmering it slowly. That night the Co enjoyed a magnificent meal. With Tom's tacit approval, I had bought wine as well as some good Italian bread. The troopers had a gourmet treat.

Shortly after the spaghetti dinner, Bob Whitelaw was reassigned to take command of E Co. He lost and regained command several times, due to his rank. 1LT Phil Akins, a tall, quietly efficient OFF, who had been recalled to active duty for the Korean War, replaced him. He easily fit in, and did an outstanding job. He and his wife, Julie, became lifelong friends.

In every unit in the Army, rifles and other weapons are kept in the Arms Room, usually a part of the Supply Room. This, of course, was a security measure. Together with some of the other Co COs, I fought for permission to keep the rifles in the barracks so that the men would have access to them at any time. This was approved reluctantly, with the stipulation that the racks be secured to the buildings with chains. The rifles in their racks were moved to the barracks promptly. Each morning at Reveille the CQ opened the racks and just before Taps he counted the rifles and locked them. The men could clean their rifles, oil them, practice the manual of arms, field strip or otherwise familiarize themselves with their weapons at any time. It was a good system which enabled the men to know and respect their weapons. It is unfortunate that the theft of weapons has made extreme security measures necessary. Ready access to their rifles helped mold better soldiers.

Early in July I was promoted to Captain and threw a promotion party one Saturday afternoon in the Patton House. Every OFF in the RCT was invited for beer, dips and other "finger food". It was one of the cheapest promotion parties I have ever thrown, though it was a good one. I was delighted to be a CPT and wore my new bars proudly.

Just after I pinned on my Captain's bars, TSG Richter was promoted to MSG, the first of the NCOs I was able to get promoted. A talented PSG, he looked very young. Despite his baby-face, he was a demanding NCO who exercised good control over his men. After his promotion, many people who saw his MSG stripes on his sleeves, could not believe that he had earned them.

The training was in full swing by midsummer. Everything was going well. Then we heard that LTC Mesereau was leaving the Bn to become the Regt XO, replacing LTC Clyde Dillender who was to take Command of the 1st Bn. We wondered who was going to take Command of the 2/508. Finally word filtered down that LTC Herbert V. Mansfield from the Airborne Department was to be our new CO. My heart sank, he was the OFF I had a problem with when I was going through Jump School. My only hope was that he would not remember me.

LTC Mansfield bounced into the Battalion and immediately took charge. At the first Officers' Call he looked at me closely, finally recalling where he had known me. It did not influence our relationship. Like Wilbur Wilson, Herb Mansfield was a controversial character; a superb soldier, he was a firm but exemplary Commander. I suppose we were both mavericks, but we operated well together, developed a mutual respect for each other, and became friends, a friend I still cherish.

Herb was a dynamic individual, more aggressive in training than Tom Mesereau. Tom, a splendid officer and an effective Commander, lacked the enthusiasm and energy that Herb brought to training. He reconstituted the staff; Tully became the S-1, 1LT Phil Akins the S-2, McLendon the S-3 (an inspired choice), while Mike Chester remained the S-4. This staff performed well. Training now became more intensive. As a former member of the Airborne Department, Herb knew FT Benning and everyone on it; he knew how to get airplanes, parachutes and approval to jump on unprepared (we called them "unknown") DZ's; he instituted a policy of jumping frequently and on short notice. The 2nd Bn made Co and Plt jumps long before the rest of the RCT.

1LT Charles T. Reese, who had been in Ranger training with 1SG Hand, replaced Akins as XO. He was a fine one; but perhaps his greatest contribution was his assistance to the men in minor legal scrapes. A lawyer, he was especially helpful to the troopers picked up by the Columbus Police.

In mid-1951 the so-called "duck-tail" haircut was still very much in vogue in civilian life. Several of my young troopers let their hair grow and combed it back into a duck-tail. Spotting them immediately, I took action; at the next Reveille formation I removed my helmet liner, announcing, "This is the longest hair in Company F". At that time I had a very short crew cut. Those with the duck-tails groaned, but got the point. The haircut standard for F Co was then announced in an unmistakable fashion so everyone understood it. At the same time I laid down a policy that no one in the unit would have a moustache. In establishing both policies, I explained to the troops that long hair and moustaches required additional care and caused problems in the field; short hair and a clean shaven face were easy to maintain. Since we spent a great deal of time in the field this would reduce problems and permit the Co to move at a moment's notice.

One young trooper, whose Plt Ldr and PSG had ordered him to get his hair cut in accordance with Company policy, complained to the IG about it. The IG called me, informing me that in his opinion the young trooper had short enough hair, hence my order was illegal.

I asked the COL to quote me the Regulation that made me wrong. He hesitated then quoted, "Hair will be kept short and neatly cut at all times."

"Who determines whether hair is neat and short?"

"The Unit Commander."

"I am this man's Unit Commander, am I not?"

"Yes."

"I have already indicated to my soldier that his hair is too long, where am I wrong?"

Reluctantly the IG agreed that I was within my authority. This was before the Army joined the ranks of permissiveness. The trooper came back with his hair cut. I made sure his PSG did not lean on him for going to the IG. He was a good lad and gave no more trouble.

Toward the end of the summer The 508 scheduled a Prop Blast. COL Cleland, determined to make it a bit more tame, invited the wives to attend. This did indeed put a damper on the proceedings, to the extent that it was not the wild affair that we had attended in the 504. Most of the LTs in the RCT were Blasted, so it seemed to last forever. Despite the presence of the wives, it was an enjoyable occasion.

Just after the Prop Blast, football fever gripped the RCT. The 508 had a team which practiced daily under Tom Mesereau, who had been an outstanding player at West Point and was considered a fine service coach. One of the reasons he had been assigned as the RCT XO was to make him available to coach the football team. As the players were put on special duty (SD) with the team, I lost my runner, Bucey, and several other good troopers. These young men had played college football before they had been drafted, hence the 508 fielded an excellent team. The day of the first game, the entire RCT marched into and took over one side of Doughboy Stadium. The Red Devils easily defeated the FT Benning team. In fact, the 508 had an outstanding season. One of the virtues of ABN football is that the troopers are in superb physical condition and have the stamina and drive to win.

Early in the fall, LTC Mansfield scheduled a night jump on Lee Field to be followed by a 20 mile road march back to the 2/508 area. A minor tactical problem was involved for which F Co was designated to provide DZ security. My plan was to jump with a reinforced Plt to secure the DZ; the Co-minus would jump with the Bn mass. In the morning chutes were drawn, fitted and lined up in stick order in the Co street. The Plt Ldrs were briefed and in turn briefed their men. After lunch the Co was dismissed to relax until chow time. Following chow, the 3rd Platoon and I left the Co area at 1730. The rest of the Co was to marshall at 1800 for the night jump.

The 3rd Plt, reinforced, made an uneventful jump and assembled quickly and silently. The squads then dispersed rapidly to security positions while I established my CP in the F Co assembly area. At the appointed time, the aircraft came over Lee Field in a Vee of Vees. There were no serious injuries, though several jumpers drifted into the trees. Shortly after the jump, troopers began to arrive in the assembly area. It surprised me to see Mr Tucker come limping in with a twisted ankle, but not seriously hurt. He had not been scheduled to jump; as rear echelon commander he was to make sure that breakfast was ready when the Co arrived after the 20 mile hike. Tucker was out of sorts, not only because of his ankle, but for other reasons he explained to me.

The 1st Plt Ldr, a 1950 Military Academy graduate, had not shown up for the jump. He had received my briefing and had briefed his Plt (I heard part of his briefing as I wandered around the unit area). But he had failed to show up for chow or in time to load the trucks for Lawson Field. Tucker had called over to the BOQ but had not been able to locate him. He had heard some muttered comments from the 1st Plt about "chicken officers". Although MSG Richter was fully capable of handling the jump, Tucker had decided to lead the Plt in accordance with my policy that an officer lead each unit on such problems.

The officer in question had been in Easy Co but had received such a low efficiency report from CPT Warren Conlon, his Commander, that he had been transferred to Fox Co for "rehabil-itation". I was directed to take him in hand and make an officer of him. In spite of the fact that he did not impress me, I accepted him. Before sending him to the 1st Plt, I had a long talk with him concerning his duties and responsibilities. I also talked with MSG Richter, explaining to him that one of the duties of senior NCOs was the training of new officers. This LT was being turned over to him to make an officer out of him. While the OFF was nominally in Command of the Plt, MSG Richter was directed to take action to see that the Plt did not suffer as a result of his assignment. I instructed him to lead him by example, suggestion, or gentle nudging into proper leadership techniques. Richter was enthusiastic about this mission for several weeks. Later he came to me to report that the task was impossible. The LT did not learn; he would not take hints, suggestions, or recommendations; he curried favor with the troops and failed to provide positive leadership; the same problems CPT Conlon had identified.

Again, I counseled the officer carefully; pointing out his responsibilities to his troops, explaining the need for clear, sound orders and a requirement for unobtrusive supervision; emphasizing the necessity for consistency in his dealings with the men in his Plt, and reviewing other basic leadership techniques. He assured me that he understood and would do better. But there was little improvement. By the time of the jump he had been with F Co a little over a month and everyone was thoroughly disgusted with his performance. Now he had committed the ultimate Airborne sin - he had not jumped as scheduled.

It was traditional in the Airborne that when a name appeared on the manifest it was equivalent to a direct order to jump. Failure to jump without being excused by competent authority automatically resulted in a court-martial for failure to obey a lawful order. At least this was the case with EM. To my knowledge the situation had never occurred with an OFF. But now I was faced with the problem. Tucker was sent back to the Company area on one of the parachute trucks. MSG Richter would command the 1st Plt on the road march. Tucker was given instructions to tell the LT to wait for me in the Orderly Room; to be there when I arrived from the road march.

After a rapid assembly, the Bn moved out on the road march without delay. LTC Mansfield rotated the lead companies; by chance F Co was the last to lead. I set a good pace as we turned into the Sand Hill area about 0800. We arrived at the Company shortly after, the cooks had a good breakfast waiting for us. Together with the Plt Ldrs I inspected the feet of the troops, got the Co bedded down and was ready for a little sleep myself about 1100. But before I could leave the Company area there was one more chore to complete.

When I entered the Orderly Room, the errant LT was not there. The CQ told me that he had come in about 1930 last night quite upset, saying that he had overslept. The CQ gave him my message to be in the Orderly Room when I returned, but he told the CQ that he did not want anyone to think that he had missed the jump because of the road march! So he disobeyed my order and set out to follow our route, though we had started the march from Lee Field. Every Plt Ldr had a strip map of the route. The road march did not concern me, the missed jump, the violation of orders did. Needless to say, I was furious; now I had to wait for the lieutenant to return.

When he finally dragged himself into the Orderly Room about 1500, I was very tired, very frustrated and very angry. I really worked that LT over! While waiting, I had thought about the matter a great deal; probably I should not have made a decision while I was so angry; but it seemed to me that the only acceptable course of action was to court-martial the officer. He did not respond to suggestions, to counseling, to leadership, to guidance. He was apparently marching to a different drum beat than the rest of us, and he needed to be eliminated from the service.

He explained that he had overslept, that his alarm had not gone off and that the orderly in the BOQ had not awakened him as requested. We went over to the BOQ where we found his alarm set for Reveille, not chow time. The orderly swore that he had not requested him to awaken him; he showed me a list of the OFFs who had; all had made the jump. His blatant lying was the final straw.

After explaining that I was going to prefer charges against him and detailing the reasons why, I dismissed him.

Mr Tucker typed up the charge sheets so that the matter would not get all over the unit area. I took them to LTC Mansfield to explain my purpose in requesting a court-martial. Not only should the same criteria apply to OFFS as well as EM, but the individual should be eliminated from the service before he harmed men under him or himself. LTC Mansfield agreed and forwarded the charges to Regt. However, COL Cleland decided that the LT would not be court-martialed. Mansfield argued the point, but Cleland remained firm. When Mansfield told me of the decision, I requested to see COL Cleland. After reporting smartly, I gave my rationale on the need for a court-martial. COL Cleland said that he understood my point of view but that court-martialing a West Point officer during his initial tour of duty would ruin his career.

"Sir, that is exactly what we should do. He has had two chances now; two Commanders have judged him inept. He should be dismissed from the service."

"Don, I think we can salvage this young man. I want to give him another chance."

"Then please transfer him out of F Co immediately, sir. The men have lost respect for him and I cannot do anything further with him."

COL Cleland agreed to this. The LT was transferred to another unit and shortly thereafter he was on orders to Korea. Astounded, I protested to LTC Mansfield that we could not let that man go into combat as an officer, he would get good men killed. Though he agreed with me, LTC Mansfield could do nothing. The lieutenant went to Korea; on one of his first combat actions he took out a ten man patrol. Almost the entire patrol, including the lieutenant, was killed. When this report reached the 508,I wondered if COL Cleland had any second thoughts about contributing to the death of those men. I was badly shaken by the incident.

Early in October, LTC Mansfield called me to the Battalion CP to give me the mission of putting on a demonstration jump and assembly problem for a very select VIP. Herb did not know who the VIP was, but he was someone for whom the Pentagon had requested a demonstration of the US Airborne capability. F Co was to jump on an "unknown DZ"; I was to select the DZ and write up a simple assembly problem. It was a great experience to have the total package thrown at me this way. After careful reconnaissance, I selected a suitable DZ, decided where I wanted the bleachers for the VIPs, then wrote the assembly problem. LTC Mansfield approved the DZ and the scenario without change.

One of the pieces of guidance given me was that the heavy weapons were to drop as close to the bleachers as possible so the derigging could be observed. LT Lattimore the Weapons Platoon Leader, was assigned the mission of insuring that the 60m mortars and 57mm recoiless rifles landed directly in front of the bleachers after I had placed his Plt in an appropriate spot in the jump formation. My men were enthusiastic about the mission, despite the extra work it generated. This was the first time that any Co in the reactivated 508 had made a Co drop; the fact that it was a demonstration added to the excitement. We had not yet begun Company Tactical Training, but we leaped ahead to accomplish the necessary instruction to insure that this would be a good jump. The practice jump the day before was flawless; the heavy weapons bundles landed within 50 feet of the bleachers, while the Co landed squarely in the center of the DZ. The assembly took only a few minutes. The dry run was so perfect that I was concerned as I believe in the adage that a good dress rehearsal portends a poor performance. But I had faith in F Company.

The day of the demonstration was bright and clear with a slight breeze, a perfect day for a jump. Everything went according to plan; the marshalling was efficient, the aircraft took off on time, we exited over the DZ exactly on schedule. The recoilless rifle bundle skimmed the top of the bleachers so closely that everybody cringed and some even jumped out of the stands thinking they were going to be struck by it. However it landed ten feet directly in front of the stands. Two or three of the troopers (including LT Lattimore) who were to recover the bundle landed close by. It was a spectacular demonstration! I doubt if we could have repeated it. The remainder of F Co fared equally well; all troopers landed on the DZ, quickly got out of their chutes and assembled in the designated area. The chutes were left on the DZ as they would be in combat; after the VIPs left they were recovered. Nothing marred the assembly. It was a realistic demonstration of the rapidity with which we could organize a defensive position after a drop.

At the conclusion of the demonstration I reported to COL Cleland and the VIPs, and was introduced to the special guest, General Speidel of the German Army who had been the CofS to Field Marshall Rommel of Afrika Korps fame. At that time the US was authorizing, indeed, encouraging the Germans to reorganize their military forces as a part of NATO. This was General Speidel's initial briefing on the United States Army. He and the other spectators seemed impressed by our performance; certainly they were highly complimentary about our jump.

F Co had developed well and I was proud of it. With quite a bit of money in the Company Fund, I thought the troopers deserved a special party, instead of the usual beer bust. LT Reese was given the mission of organizing a dinner dance to be held in the Ralston Hotel in Columbus. The hotel was reluctant to book us, having reservations about paratroopers, but LT Reese persuaded them to do so. The married NCOs and OFFs would bring their wives, unmarried OFFs and troopers were permitted to bring dates. Only a few did. In Class A uniforms they were a sharp looking group of men. The festivities were everything I had wanted.

Just as the party was about to break up, MSG Richter went into the latrine. Several soldiers from a different unit refused to believe that the youthful looking Richter was a MSG. They tried to embarrass him in front of several Fox Company troopers. MSG Richter, whose penchant for fighting was well known in the Company, took care of the matter in his own way. Later, someone accidently knocked over a tray of glasses onto the parquet dance floor. The Ralston Hotel tried to hold us responsible for the scratched floor. LT Reese's legal expertise helped us out of that one. The troopers enjoyed the party, which enhanced the esprit de corps of Fox Company.

In the fall, Cleland was promoted to BG and reassigned as Asst Div CDR of the 82nd ABN Div. We were pleased that such an outstanding and charismatic leader had been promoted, but were sorry to see him leave the RCT. The day he left the Post the route from his quarters to the Main Gate of FT Benning was lined with 508 troopers. As he and his wife, Florence, passed in their car, we saluted him, a fitting gesture to a Fine Commander.

BG Cleland was replaced by COL Joe S. Lawrie, a short, stocky, dynamic individual who was determined to replace BG Cleland in our affections and esteem. He, too, was a good soldier, but he was not the charismatic leader Cleland was. Resolved to become involved in everything the 508 did, COL Lawrie decided to play on the Red Devil Football Team. LTC Mesereau, the coach, was hesitant to have his CDR on the team, but accepted the decision. Tom kept trying to get Lawrie out for practice, for PT, to learn the plays, to become part of the team. As commander of the RCT he obviously was too busy. Only rarely did he make practice.

One Saturday most of the RCT was in the stands when COL Lawrie trotted onto the field in uniform with the rest of the team. The troopers gave him a loud cheer. He did not start the game, but went in early in the first quarter. The ball was snapped; the play developed; one of the 508 players was down on the field. As the teams separated we saw that COL Lawrie was hurt. One play and our CO was a casualty. He was carried off the field with a broken foot. The troopers went wild; though respectful, they razzed their Commander, calling him "One Play Lawrie". The Colonel had his foot in a cast for several months.

Late in the fall of 1951 I had a confrontation with Art Hyman, the H Co CO. We were in the field frequently as we were now in Co and Bn training. The rifle Cos were supported by the Heavy Weapons Company in many exercises. Normally the HMGs were attached to the Co they supported, occasionally the recoiless rifles were. The mortars were never attached. Art came to me one day to tell me that his HMGs would no longer be attached to any Co regardless of the tactical situation. He claimed that rifle company commanders did not understand how to use the HMGs, did not take care of the gun crews, and often withdrew leaving them behind. He went on and on about how only the H Co CO could properly employ and support heavy weapons. He was going to talk to LTC Mansfield and urge that the guns never again be attached. As H Co CO, he would take care of them, he would decide where they would be emplaced and when they would be withdrawn.

After listening to this nonsense with growing irritation, I pointed out to Art that we had all received the same instruction in the Advance Course and were as competent in the employment of weapons as he was. In my Company area I was supreme; if his guns came into that area they would go where I wanted them to go and move when I wanted them to move. The only exception would be if the Bn Order placed them in direct support, then I would work with the Plt Ldr to employ them to best advantage. Finally the matter was resolved by LTC Mansfield, who agreed with me that the guns would be attached to the rifle Cos except under unusual circumstances; the rifle Co CO, in other words, would control the guns.

Neither the Machine Gun Plt Ldr nor the Plt had experienced difficulty in F Co. I believed that they had been used effectively and supported fully. They in turn, gave F Co good coverage. Art was always competing, always trying to get ahead of the other Co COs. Our relations were never cordial and we were frequently at odds on tactics and policy.

Immediately after the football season ended, the F Co troopers on TDY with the team returned to duty and were reintegrated into the Company. I had plans for most of those troopers; they were aggressive, disciplined and had great potential as NCOs, I wanted to train them and promote them as soon as possible. One man, Sarter, appeared to have unusual ability.

Early in December, several of the athletes, including Sarter, the spokesman, came to see me. The Regt was organizing a basketball team on which they wanted to play. Explaining that my policy was to permit each trooper to play one major sport a year, I told them they would not be able to play basketball. To permit a small group to continue to participate in athletics was unfair to the Company, the other troopers and the men themselves. While a soldier was on SD to a team, other men in the Company had to pull his share of the work; KP, guard duty, and other details came around a little faster because there were fewer men to pull the duties. I also pointed out that I had a high regard for their potential, especially Sarter's, but that I could not promote them unless they demonstrated their ability by training and pulling duty with the Company.

Sarter argued that the men had played college basketball and would be assets to the team. Though I acknowledged this, I stuck to my policy. They left unhappy. The Special Services Officer, the basketball coach, even LTC Mesereau called me to request that I make exceptions in the case of these men. Patiently, I explained my policy. I stood firm. Finally they went to LTC Mansfield, who called me to his office to find out what the problem was. I explained my position and the implications, using Sarter as an example; a natural, all-around athlete, he wanted to play baseball after the basketball season. Herb agreed with me; he tried to stem the tide, but had to yield to orders from RCT HQ. Sarter and one other man were to play basketball. When told of this decision, I requested that the men be transferred from F Co. Sarter and the other man did not want to leave their friends in F Co, but were equally adamant about playing basketball. They were transferred. My reputation for being hard-headed, uncooperative and putting F Co before the RCT was established. No one seemed to think of the other men in the Company, of the individuals themselves, or the real purpose of the Regt. There is little question that winning teams provide entertainment and enhance morale. But isn't it possible to build teams without developing "professional jocks"?

In the Sand Hill area in which the 508 was located was a large log cabin reputedly built by GEN George Patton when the 2nd Armored Div was temporarily stationed at FT Benning in WWII.

A spacious building with a large stone fireplace, it was now a branch Officers' Club. Patton House was where most of the 508 officers congregated on Saturday afternoons to drink, watch TV, brag about their troopers and units, and shoot the bull. The short order kitchen served an excellent steak, among other offerings, and many bachelors ate there if they did not eat in their unit messes. The Special Services Golf Course surrounded it, so when any of the 508 officers played a round they invariably dropped into the Patton House for a drink as they passed.

One warm, fall Saturday afternoon I was sitting at the bar talking with friends. A golfer came in the side entrance and sat at the end of the bar. My eyes casually wandered in that direction and suddenly locked on the golfer sitting at the end of the bar. I stared, dumbfounded. PVT Radatz of Fox Company was sitting at the bar of the Officers' Club!

He looked at me with a friendly smile on his face until he caught the look on mine. As I walked over to him he slowly slipped off the stool and stood uncertainly before me.

"Radatz, what are you doing in the Officers' Club?"

"I was playing golf, sir, and got hot and thirsty. I saw the players ahead of me stop in here and come out with a paper cup of cold beer and thought I would get one too."

"Don't you know this is an Officers' Club?"

"Yes, sir."

"Well, don't you know it is off limits to enlisted men?"

"I guess so, Captain, but everyone else seemed to be wandering in here, so I thought I would too. It's too far down to the Enlisted Club."

"Get your butt out of here, Radatz, and don't let me ever catch you in here again."

"Can I finish me beer, sir?" He had ordered a stein.

"Hell, no you can't finish your beer! Get out of here now!"

"But, sir...."

"Out! Now! Before I throw you out."

Muttering under his breath, Radatz moved quickly out of my vicinity and left the Club. When he was gone, everyone at the bar broke into laughter. My friends asked if I was going to send Radatz to OCS. At that I laughed too; Radatz was not one of my better soldiers. The matter required immediate attention, but I did not want to punish Radatz officially. The incident was too humorous, too trivial for that. The obvious solution was to let 1SG Hand take care of the matter.

Early Monday morning, just before Reveille, I told Hand about the incident. He chuckled, saying that is about what he would expect of a "hero" like Radatz. "Don't worry, CPT Seibert, that won't happen again."

After I turned the Company back to him at Reveille, he put the men at ease and ordered Radatz front and center. Retreating to the Orderly Room, I peeked out of the window to find out what would happen. Hand pointed to Radatz, as he said to the Company, "I want you to look at this man. He drinks beer with the Company Commander in the Officers' Club."

He proceeded to relate the incident in his inimitable fashion. The troops laughed. The 1SG then gave Radatz a little "extra training" to teach him proper military courtesy and discipline. He had him march through the Co area with a pack loaded with sand. Radatz got the message. As he walked through the area he was needled from time to time, "When are you going up to the Officers' Club for a drink?" or "CPT Seibert is up at Patton House having a drink. Why don't you go up and join him, Radatz?" There were no more incidents of this sort.

One of LTC Mansfield's major concerns was light equipment. He tried to reduce the load the Infantry soldier carried in combat. His solution was to use the existing web gear, the shoulder harness and cartridge belt with the shovel, canteen with cup and spoon in the carrier, and the first aid packet on it. A poncho was tied onto the rear. All other needed equipment would be brought up with the ammunition and chow. We jumped "clean". We didn't bother with mess gear, but ate with a spoon out of the canteen cup. When we had spaghetti, salad and ice cream, this became a little complex. The obvious solution was to eat each item separately; after one item was eaten, the troopers could go back for the second one. But most of the troopers went through the serving line and got all of the items on top of one another. Many thought this hilarious.

As a result of Mansfield's efforts, he did develop load bearing equipment that the Army adapted and adopted. It was the first change in the Army's load bearing equipment since 1917. To lighten the Infantryman's load was a worthy aim, but Herb's solution was more drastic than most were willing to accept.

Each pay day many of the unit commanders of the 508th set up "pay day patrols" in Phenix City. All of our troopers went to Phenix City occasionally, but they really let loose on pay day night and the first week end after it. Regardless of the day of the week on which the troopers were paid, from that night until after the first weekend after pay day Fox Co maintained a patrol. Usually WO1 Tucker and I went together; 1SG Hand and several NCOs picked by him went separately. The one truck available to F Co (the kitchen truck was modified and could not be used) was dispatched to Phenix City where it was parked strategically. If any of our troopers had too much to drink or we found them in trouble we ordered them (or took them) to the truck which transported them back to the unit area. We eliminated much trouble this way, sparing them fines they might have incurred if the police had picked them up.

In Phenix City most enlisted troopers frequented Beachy Howard's. All during WWII, it had been a traditional hangout for paratroopers, and so it was for the troopers of the 508, the Airborne Department, and the Rangers. Ma Beachy's was a pretty wild place. It had a large bar, gambling tables, food, dancing, and a floor show, mostly strip-tease dancers. The troopers let go when they went there. It was where Tucker and I would frequently park ourselves, because this was were most of the action was.

Ma Beachy was a great friend of the individual trooper. Many times I saw her go into the cash register and hand a jumper enough money to go home on leave. When asked about this she told me that only once in ten years has she ever lost any money. The troopers always returned and paid her back except for that one time. Apparently it was such a popular place that the troopers were afraid that if they didn't pay her back, they would never get in again. Eventually, when Phenix City was cleaned up, her place became a church.

Many amazing things went on at Beachy's. Perhaps one of the funniest occurred the night Mr Tucker, a tall, husky man, attempted to pick up a rather large girl, just the right height for him. When he made his pitch, "she" turned out to be a homosexual male in female dress. The Fox Company troopers there joined me in laughing at Tucker's discomfiture.

As Thanksgiving approached, SSG Short, 1SG Hand, Mr Tucker and I determined that our troops would enjoy a very special feast. Printed menus, paid for out of the Unit Fund, decorated with jump wings and the 508 insignia, were made up for every place. SSG Short recommended two sittings so that our married troopers, NCOs and OFFs could enjoy Thanksgiving dinner with their families in the mess. We couldn't seat that many people at one time. Special condiments and supplements were issued for that meal, in addition there were extras bought from a fund the OFFS and NCOS contributed to. The mess hall was decorated and sheets were used as tablecloths. The cooks outdid themselves to produce a truly memorable occasion.

Later in the year we heard that Gene Krupa and his band were going to be at Benning for an overnight stand. They would play in the Field Rouse for the EM and then at the Officers' Club for a dance. I suggested to the Special Services Officer that it would be a good idea to have Gene Krupa and his band eat chow in one of the mess halls. It would give the troopers a chance to meet him and be good publicity. He was taken with the idea; of course I volunteered to host the band in F Co. It was a great affair; we all had a chance to meet the celebrated drummer and the members of his band. Each musician sat at a different table so that more troopers had a chance to eat and to talk with them. The band could only remain for a short time, but appeared to enjoy the GI chow. As many of the men were fans of Krupa and his band, they enjoyed the occasion. Many of the troopers who normally did not eat the Saturday evening meal with the Co were there to meet the famous musician.

MAJ Robert Spillman (the troops called him "Rapid Robert") had been the S-3 of the 504 under COL Cleland and had been assigned to the 508 as one of the original cadre members. LTC Mansfield was not happy with him as the RCT S-3. He complained to COL Lawrie that Spillman's field training was insufficient and that operations were too important to trust to someone with so little troop experience. COL Lawrie agreed, but decreed that MAJ Spillman be assigned to the 2nd Bn for "additional training". I suppose he followed the reasoning which made those who complained of the mess, the Mess Officer. Upon Spike Harris' departure for Civilian Component Duty, Bob Spillman became the XO of the 2/508.

Following MAJ Spillman's arrival in the Bn, LTC Mansfield informed us at an Officers' Call that the RCT was going to FT Rucker, AL to act as aggressor against the 47th NG Div, federalized for the Korean War, which was scheduled to take its Div Annual Training Test. An Advance Party, including all Co COs, would go to Fort Rucker to make a reconnaissance and select defensive positions for the opening phase of the test.

A convoy, consisting of one jeep from each company left one cold December morning. Bucey and my driver were with me. The FT Rucker cadre opened BOQs and a field mess for us. There was time to drive over the entire area of operations as well as to make a detailed reconnaissance for the initial phase. Defensive positions were selected and routes to and from them scouted. By the time we returned to Benning, we were all familiar with the terrain we would operate over.

Shortly thereafter, the entire RCT moved by truck convoy from FT Benning to FT Rucker. It was an easy one day trip. The convoy arrived at Rucker without incident and the 508 bivouacked in the field. It was cold, but we were prepared for it. Defensive positions were readied first. The troopers put themselves to the task despite the fact that the RCT had not yet completed its Advanced Unit Training. The men dug first-rate positions, provided good overhead cover and camouflaged them well. I was proud of the professional job my men did.

All of the 508 CDRs attended the briefing for the 47th NG Div; we were not impressed with the OFFs or their EM. They did not inspire confidence in their professionalism, in fact, the exercise featured one fiasco after another.

During the briefing I had a long talk with LTC Harold Christianson who had been with the 382nd Infantry on Okinawa and Mindoro. He had been recalled to active duty and was at Fort Rucker for the Division Training Test.

An excited Plt Ldr reported that a wild boar had fallen into a fox hole in his area. He told me that since it had broken a leg, it was impossible to get the animal out of the fox hole and wanted permission to kill it. Knowing there were no wild boars in the area, I thought it was a farmer's pig.

But if the pig had fallen into a fox hole and broken its leg, it might be dangerous to try to get it out alive. Not wishing to expose any of my men to possible injury, I gave permission to kill it. I was never sure how they did it, though I suspect they clubbed it to death. Many of the men were farmers who would know a way. SSG Short and his cooks barbecued the pig, serving a delicious meal.

During the maneuver, MAJ Spillman lost his pistol. LTC Mansfield carried his pistol in his belt in the small of his back. Bob Spillman decided to do the same. One morning as we were preparing to move out of the assembly area, word came down to hold fast, a pistol was missing. All units were ordered to conduct a show-down inspection. It took an hour to find the weapon, a Fox Co trooper had it. Furious at my trooper for picking up a pistol without turning it in, I was equally irate that the pistol had been left on the ground by MAJ Spillman the night before. Apparently it had slipped from his belt (or he had removed it to be more comfortable) while watching the field movie. The loss of time did not endear him to the Battalion.

During the first phase of the test, the RCT was on the defensive. The 508 troopers threw themselves into the aggressor mission, acquitting themselves well. Disciplined, physically fit, they were already professional soldiers.

The final assault of our defensive position by the 47th Div was a shock. The Guardsmen stomped up to our positions as if they were robots. It was cold that morning, but they moved lethargically. They had no enthusiasm, no interest in the training, no aggressive spirit at all. They plodded along without regard for the tactical situation. Needless to say, we took many prisoners. TSG Vick and two F Co troopers captured the Asst Div CDR, who claimed that he was sick.

The aggressors had been briefed not to take a soldier's personal belongings, but they were to search for identification and intelligence information. We were amazed at the number of whiskey bottles found in the packs. I don't know how many, if any, of my men had liquor (I am sure that several of the NCOs did) but if they did, they kept it well concealed because I would not tolerate drinking in the field. There was considerable controversy over what to do with the whiskey we found in the packs. Finally orders came down to confiscate and destroy it. This did not endear us to the National Guard.

The day of the attack on our defensive positions there was a heavy frost on the ground. The 508 troopers held out until the last minute (the "enemy" was almost in our fox holes), then withdrew in good order to prearranged rallying points. We then moved on to the next phase of the operation.

The I&R Plt, under 1LT Hal Langerman (and Hood), was given the mission of raiding deep into the rear of the 47th Division Trains area and destroying its ammunition dump. The Plt, with Langerman and Hood in the lead jeep, captured the enemy ammo dump marked with a red flag. It was adjacent to the actual ammo storage area at FT Rucker. In order to inject a little realism into the exercise, Langerman and his PLT surrounded not only the area of the red flag but also the actual Post Ammunition Dump.

Rumors immediately flew through the maneuver area that the 508 had broken into the ammo dump, obtained live ammo, and were preparing to use against the NG troops. All action was halted immediately. COL Lawrie, without investigation, relieved 1LT Langerman of command of the I&R Plt in front of the highly approving CG of the 47th Division and his assembled staff.

Obviously, COL Lawrie took this action to calm any rumors and to make sure there was no misunderstanding. It was precipitate action on his part to relieve Langerman without ascertaining whether or not his men had in fact gotten into the Post Ammunition Dump or otherwise conducted themselves improperly. An inspection of the I&R Plt disclosed no live ammunition in possession of the ABN personnel. Certainly Langerman had not exercised good judgement in letting his enthusiasm override common sense, but this hardly seemed cause for relief. Hanz Druener was placed in Command of the I&R Platoon.

The troopers of the I&R Platoon wanted to retain Hood, even though Langerman had been relieved. They didn't mind losing Langerman, but they were very unhappy about having Hood leave the Platoon. But Hal refused to give up his dog, so the both of them went off in disgrace. Hal actually became a folk hero among the old Airborne types who claimed "that was the way troopers used to be, too bad we are now like the straight leg Army".

The maneuver began again as the 508 took the offensive after the National guard had been given a chance to dig in. On the last day, we assaulted the NG positions and swept right through them. There was no question about the trace of their line as their positions were readily discernible. They were poorly dug in, the fox holes were too shallow, and there was no overhead cover or camouflage. The 2/508 moved so fast that Herb Mansfield was suddenly in one of the Regt CPs and took the Commander and his staff prisoners. They protested that he couldn't do that, that he could not have gotten there tactically. Herb gleefully said, "Here I am and here are my troops all around you. Your Regt pulled back from their front line positions before the determined assault and fire power of the Double Blitz Bn." Several RA General Officer observers as well as the umpire were in the CP at the time. The umpire ruled, and the observers agreed, that the action had been tactically sound and the Regt overrun. The test ended at that point. The 47th Div was ordered to undergo retraining. They had failed to meet the minimum objectives of the Training Test, as a result they did not go to Korea.

The cocky Red Devils returned to Fort Benning just before Christmas. The operation had been a great shot in the arm for the 508, however it made it difficult for the RCT to settle back into its training routine. The exercise gave the troopers a greater regard for their own ability than was warranted at the time. Unit training still had to be completed, but it was hard to re-motivate the men to continue their training.

Preparations to make the dinner on Christmas even better than the one on Thanksgiving were immediately begun. The Army, as usual, issued many supplements to make it a special feast. My mess personnel told me that they could make a delicious eggnog if I would authorize the alcoholic contents. I not only agreed, but volunteered to provide the liquor, and wine for the meal as well. The cooks saved milk, cream, vanilla extract and other things to make the eggnog. They made one batch, with liquor, in a 15 gallon stock pot; a smaller portion of non-alcoholic eggnog was also made. Everyone who came to dinner had their choice.

The mess hall was decorated with a Christmas tree, sheets on the tables in lieu of tablecloths, and candles. We again had two servings. All OFFs were in pinks and greens and the men were in Class A uniforms. I ate with the single troopers at the first sitting, but stayed to greet the married men and their families as they arrived for the second sitting. It was a gala meal.

What went on in F Co was typical of what most Co COs in the RA were doing at that time. Out of his own pocket he was constantly supplementing or buying things for his unit, trying to raise the morale of his troops. No one in the military was making a great deal of money in those days, but what money an OFF could spare was ungrudgingly given to the unit. As a bachelor, I could afford to spend my money on the Company because I had no dependents to support, only myself and my car. The married officers, especially those with children, had more pressing expenses, but they too were constantly spending money on their units. All of this was to buy needed supplies that were not available or not issued, or to supplement what was issued to insure that the troops got the best possible support. It was characteristic of their dedication to their men and their position at that time.

There was a riotous New Year's Eve party at the Officers' Club that year. The 508 made early reservations for five or six tables. I attended with Ed and Betty Morris, Al and Hela Bettelli, and several other couples and did not miss a dance. Without a date, I did a lot of table-hopping. Just before midnight, I ordered two magnums of champagne and filled everyone's glass. When they were empty I ordered more, and then more. It was quite a party! There was a special feeling celebrating with such friends, a closeness unique to the military.

After the first of the year things settled down again as training was resumed. It was hard to get the Company back into routine training. Not only had the men done an excellent j ob on the jump for General Speidel, but they had also been far superior to the 47th Division in military tactics. While the troopers believed they were trained professional soldiers, they still had much to learn. Platoon and company training had to be completed before we undertook combined arms training and battalion exercises. All of this would culminate in late spring in the Battalion Army Training Test (ATT).

Physical training, including the daily dozen and then a run, was scheduled every morning. There was great spirit on those runs. When the weather permitted, we were in shorts, T-shirts and jump boots. To see an entire battalion, 700 or more soldiers, running in a column of companies with no stragglers, everyone in step, guidons waving, the troopers' heads high, all in excellent physical condition, was a thrilling sight and a symbol of esprit de corps. Of course we chanted or counted cadence as we ran. Normally Herb Mansfield led the Battalion; now and then each Company would run on its own, but most days we ran as a Battalion. I continued to follow my policy of giving PT to my troops before the runs, though the task was rotated among the Plt Ldrs at times to give them experience in handling it.

The start of unit training presented a great challenge to me to develop Co problems that would exercise the Platoon Leaders, the Squad Leaders and the troopers, while giving me an opportunity to perfect my Company procedures.

Eventually an F Co SOP (Standing Operating Procedures) was published. The page and a half document gave the Plt Ldrs some guidance on routine procedures. Its main purpose was to eliminate detailed orders. We got used to thinking that it was <u>SOP</u> to do certain things under certain circumstances, hence it clarified my thinking and made it easier for my Plt Ldrs and SLs. SOPs are helpful if their use is limited; all too often, they become too voluminous, too detailed and too stereotyped with the result that neither the CDR nor his subordinates uses any imagination or initiative. Certainly the FT McClellan SOP had that effect. But the brief F Co SOP served a good purpose, initially.

We spent four or five days every week in the field. Sometimes the Cos went out individually. More often the Bn went as a unit. On most of these field trips I tried to arrange for a free half day, or at least a couple of hours break in the training during which we had a "beer bust". The beer and soft drinks were purchased from the Unit Fund. This gave the men a change of pace and added to the morale of F Co. The men enjoyed these beer busts in the field as much or more than those in garrison. Not only did they provide a good opportunity for healthy young men to blow off steam, but there was always a lot of horseplay, Softball, touch football or volleyball to burn off their animal spirits. Again, F Company was not unique in this; most Co COs did everything possible to make their units cohesive ones.

Throughout the first year I had commanded F Co, there had been no major disciplinary problems. The few minor infractions were handled swiftly and easily through Company Punishment. In the second quarter of 1952, however, I had to court-martial two men. The first was for barracks thievery, a particularly despicable crime in the military, the second for AWOL. In both cases, the culprits had been roughed up prior to their official punishment. The men in his barracks had worked over the thief, while the AWOL's PSG or SL had "punished" him. This could not be countenanced. I lectured the Co about not taking matters into their own hands; obviously it was difficult to find the men who had worked over the barracks thief. The PSG of the AWOL left for Korea before I could make a thorough investigation. There were few other disciplinary problems for the rest of my tenure in F Company.

In the Spring of 1952 F Company conducted its annual range firing. After intensive preliminary marksmanship training, we moved to the range. Through Herb Mansfield's wide contacts on the Post, we received permission to fire on one of the excellent ranges used by TIS, perhaps the very one on which I had boloed in 1944. The Company hiked from the Sand Hill Area the afternoon before we were to begin firing. By the time we arrived at the range, about 1630, the mess truck, which had left immediately after lunch, had been on the scene for about three hours. The cooks had a good meal ready for the men. Before eating, we checked the range, drew and set up targets, and established our bivouac. Thus we were able to fire the first shot in the morning as soon we had good light. Some fired while others ate breakfast. The pit detail was rotated periodically so firing continued without pause. When the afternoon sun made it difficult to get good sight pictures, we ceased firing, cleaned rifles, relaxed, played softball, touch football or volleyball, and prepared for the next day's firing. As on the previous day, the first shot was fired as soon as it was light enough. All but a handful of the men qualified with the M-1; I managed to keep my sharpshooter rating. It was a good range.

Finally the 508 began battalion, regimental and combined arms training. On one Regt problem the 2nd Bn was on the outpost line of resistance (OPLR). Fox Company was in an exposed position overlooking Shell Creek. Hanz Druener and his I&R Plt, the aggressor force, attacked our position. LTC Mansfield was kept informed as the action proceeded. COL Lawrie was at my Company position during the attack and became excited. He kept telling me to withdraw. I refused,

"No, sir, I can't withdraw until my Battalion Commander tells me to."

"Well, I'm ordering you to. I am the Regimental Commander." So far as I knew, COL Lawrie was not in communication with his CP and had no current information about the tactical situation.

"Sir, I recognize that, but my Bn CO told me to hold at all costs until he ordered me to withdraw. If I withdraw now, I may expose the Bn and perhaps the entire Regt to a flank attack. Let me check with LTC Mansfield first."

"Well, I want you to withdraw." The problem apparently called for the 2nd Bn to withdraw at this point. When LTC Mansfield heard that I had been ordered to withdraw by higher authority, he shouted, "No, hold!"

COL Lawrie, when told that I had been ordered to hold, got on the field phone to the Bn CP, he and Herb argued it out. Finally COL Lawrie left. Later the 2nd Bn withdrew in an orderly fashion. It points up a principle which is all too often violated: Unity of Command. Senior commanders bypass one or more echelons of command to give orders to small units that conflict with those of the immediate commander on the ground. Frequently, as in this case, they are not fully informed of the situation, or see only one aspect of it. Instead of bettering the situation, they only confuse it more. The helicopter and excellent communications (plus an excessive command structure) contribute to this. As a result there has been an erosion of confidence in the chain of command, which needs to be reinforced as never before.

CPT Sam King replaced George Gilbert as the CO of G Co. Sam was a strong Commander which resulted in friendly but keen competition between our two Cos. We saw eye to eye on most policies and on tactics and consulted each other frequently. Quite often, Betty, Sam's wife, a gourmet cook, would have me over for dinner, during which Sam and I would argue tactics and leadership.

Betty planned a dinner party to which she invited a friend of hers to meet me. (Like all wives she was trying to get me married off.) The Bn was in the field all the week before the Friday night dinner party. F Co returned from the field later than anticipated. By the time the inspections were made, reports rendered and administrative matters discussed with Hand and Tucker, it was well into the evening. After a quick shower and change of clothes I arrived at the King's to find the party well underway. Sam handed me a double Old Fashioned, telling me I was two behind. While gulping down that first drink I met the young lady Betty had invited for me, a delightful person. After another double Old Fashioned, we went into dinner. There was wine with the delicious but all too filling meal, then drinks after dinner. The ladies went into the kitchen to help Betty clean up. The next I knew somebody was shaking me and saying, "Don't you think you ought to wake up and take Mary home?" I had only talked with her during the meal! I had fallen asleep! Mortified I mumbled an apology citing the week in the field, and drove her home. I did not see her again until four years later at a cocktail party in Washington, but by that time she was married to another officer. Betty and Sam kidded me, saying it was a hell of a way to get out of dating a girl.

In the midst of our intensive training, a newcomer joined Fox Company. Remembering the pleasure the troops had derived from Langerman's Hood, I thought we should have a mascot. One of the men had seen an ad in a magazine advertising foxes for sale. I hoped we would be able to train a fox as a pet. A tiny ball of fur arrived in a box, frightened, starving and very hostile. The Post Veterinarian examined it, gave it rabies shots, and prescribed a formula. The Co Clerk, Buz Marcinko, took on the task of feeding the little critter by eye dropper. A cage was built outside the Orderly Room. But we were never able to fully tame or train that little fox, which eventually had to be destroyed.

Training continued; the Cos, Bns, and the RCT were honed into professional and skilled fighting forces Finally, I was satisfied that Fox Co was ready for combat in Korea if that was to be our mission. The training program provided a means of validating that judgement. Late in the Spring, our training climaxed with a Battalion Army Training Test (ATT). This was an evaluated maneuver to determine if the 2nd Bn was ready for combat (Just as the 47th Div Test had proven that outfit unprepared, so every unit must undergo an annual ATT to prove itself). The ATT, an ABN Field Training Exercise (FTX), would include marshalling the 2/508 in a sealed area, a jump, reorganization and every element of combat: approach march, meeting engagement, defense, attack and withdrawal. Every facet of military preparedness would be rated: the collection of information and use of intelligence, planning, issuance of orders, security, military discipline, stamina, field sanitation, camouflage, field mess, antiaircraft and chemical discipline, and more. It would be a measure of what we were.

The test was conducted in late April. Just before we were sealed in the marshalling area in the Old Frying Pan Area our umpires joined us. The Chief Umpire, LTC Stovall, started out being critical. A team was assigned to each Company which lived with that Co throughout the Test, observing and evaluating everything it did. Detailed forms were provided on which they recorded their notes.

We jumped onto one of the unknown DZs LTC Mansfield was so expert in ferreting out. It was a good jump with few injuries, the Bn assembled rapidly. The umpires were astounded that we reorganized on the DZ so quickly and effectively. But training paid off; we had a lot of practice. Every jump the 2nd Bn made was a tactical jump after which we practiced assembly.

Things went smoothly; my umpire was impressed that F Co was trained so well; operated so smoothly with minimum orders or explanations. That simple SOP paid off! The biggest problem we encountered was that the umpires found it difficult to keep up with us in the field. When the route lead cross country those troopers of mine moved out with no lingering. The men really put out. Each phase seemed better than the one preceding it. The umpire and I had a few sticky moments, I reported information that he did not believe or positions he thought were wrong. But in all cases he found that we were right

The umpires had to live in the field just as we did. They did not like our light equipment, especially eating out of canteen cups. The night before the attack which would end the ATT, we had arranged for a hot meal to be served under tactical conditions in the assembly area. LTC Stovall decided to eat with F Co. The menu was spaghetti, salad and ice cream. The troops went through the mess line with their canteen cups and spoons, as if this was the normal way to eat in the field. Some of them had spaghetti in the bottom of their cup, salad on top of it and ice cream on top of that. Others came back for each course. Normally they finished up with coffee and there was plenty of bread and jam. When the troops had finished eating, I invited LTC Stovall to proceed through the line. He asked for mess trays. I told him we had none. He was annoyed. "How do you expect the umpires to eat?" he asked. "The same as the troops", I replied. "If you do not have a canteen cup, I can lend you one." My explanation about lightening the soldiers' load failed to impress Stovall who stomped off to find the Bn CP. He made an official protest to Mansfield who told him in no uncertain terms that this was the way the troops ate and he would eat the same way or go hungry.

The attack began at dawn, F Company crossed the line of departure on time and the Platoons moved forward rapidly. My Plt Ldrs kept me informed and I kept Bn informed. Bucey carried my SCR 300, his own equipment and M-1, and ran with the pack as if he had nothing on his back. The ATT ended when we had captured our main objective and consolidated on it.

There was an on the spot critique; a written report was rendered later. Stovall was grudgingly complimentary. The Battalion had done well so he could not downgrade its tactical performance. He did have some critical things to say about how we lived in the field. He did not really understand the light Infantry concept we were trying to utilize and the idea of eating out of canteen cups just blew his mind.

After the ATT, I submitted my request for transfer to an Infantry unit in Korea. Mansfield reluctantly approved it. There was no immediate response.

Following the ATT the 508th Airborne Infantry RCT had its picture taken on a Saturday morning after inspection. The men were in Class A uniforms. The entire RCT assembled on the parade field for a wide angle shot. It is one of my proudest possessions; that fine outfit, four thousand strong, in full array. It is probably the last picture of its kind taken in the Army; Regts are no more. Later we had Co pictures taken. Buz Marcinko held the fox in ours.

We now geared up for the big maneuver of the year, a joint Army/Air Force exercise called "Longhorn", which would be conducted in the vicinity of FT Hood, TX. It necessitated a cross country move by the RCT from FT Benning to San Angelo, TX where we were to marshall on a former Army Air Corps training field. Planning at every level was outstanding. Al Burdette, the RCT S-3 prepared a comprehensive plan, including march tables, which was implemented with little change. George McLendon prepared a detailed plan for the 2/508 which was complete in every detail. The Acting S-4, Evan Riley, made the Logistical Plan (Ted Fuller was attending the short course at FT Leavenworth). The plan required the RCT to travel 300 or 350 miles each day, bivouacking on a military installation if one was in the vicinity of our evening halt, or in parks or on farms. A hot meal was to be served each evening and a hot breakfast very early the next morning The "foraging party" or trains was to move out at 0300 each day. One mess truck per battalion would remain to serve breakfast, and then it too, moved out before cleaning all the utensils. When it caught up with the trains at the next bivouac area the gear would be cleaned and the evening meal cooked. The troopers would be provided sack lunches for the noon meal. It meant a real workout for the cooks, who would get little sleep. The plan was well conceived and Riley did a fine job in arranging for the delivery of rations and water.

Just before we left Benning, COL Lawrie had an RCT briefing in one of the theaters. Each Bn sat in a group as COL Lawrie and his staff briefed us. Then COL Lawrie said, "I want to talk to all of the drivers. Commanders dismiss your units, but have your drivers stay."

LTC Mansfield stood up and said, "2nd Battalion, Stand Fast.

All the other Commanders dismissed their troops except for the handful of drivers they had. COL Lawrie said to Mansfield, "You can dismiss your Bn, Herb. I only want to talk to the drivers."

Herb proudly pointed to the Bn and said, "These are my drivers. They are going to spell each other. Everybody in the Bn is going to take his turn driving." LTC Mansfield had established a policy that everyone in the 2nd Bn including officers, be qualified and hold valid drivers' licenses for every vehicle the 2/508 had. There were only three types of vehicles in the ABN IN Bn at that time, the 2 1/2 ton truck, the 3/4 ton truck, and the jeep. We had all practiced driving, been tested on, and held licenses to drive these vehicles.

Though amazed, COL Lawrie proceeded to exhort the drivers, including the entire 2nd Battalion, to exercise care and diligence. He emphasized defensive driving and safety. The drivers were then dismissed.

It was an interesting convoy. We started from FT Benning early in the morning, reaching the Mississippi before we halted for the night. The Advance Party had preceded us by five hours, so each Co mess truck was set up and ready to serve a hot meal. The Bn and Co bivouac areas had been staked out and all was in readiness for us when we arrived. After pitching our tents and getting set for the night, we ate. That first night there was a terrific storm. Tents were blown down and the bivouac turned into a quagmire. It took some time to get reorganized, but discipline and training paid off. According to plan one Co served breakfast while the rest of the mess trucks moved out to set up at the next bivouac. The sack lunches for the noon meal were too much, in view of the hot meal at night and the hot breakfast. Henry Tucker was in charge of my Advance Party, so I had nothing to worry about. He was of great assistance to the entire Bn, I am sure. Though the advance party, especially the cooks, got little sleep except in the moving trucks, they did an outstanding job.

LTC Mansfield's policy paid off. We rotated drivers at every rest break, hence our drivers never became sleepy. All of the troopers enjoyed driving the vehicles. A three tier duty schedule was followed, driving, watching, resting. The 2nd Bn made the trip from FT Benning to San Angelo without incident. In fact, it made it to San Angelo and back with only one minor accident involving slight damage to a 3/4 ton truck.

MSG Richter chewed tobacco in the field. Gradually, the entire 1st Plt picked up the habit. On the way to Texas, each spot on which the 1st Plt took a rest break was clearly marked before the Platoon pulled out. The men said that it was easier than trying to light a cigarette in the wind, and of course they could chew to their hearts' content in an aircraft. Although smoking was permitted once an aircraft became airborne, unless cigarettes, lighters or matches had been located for easy access, it was impossible to get at them when encumbered by parachute and web gear. To minimize clean-up, crew chiefs on all aircraft provided butt cans, hung along the bulkheads; chewers also used these. In this way the 1st Plt solved its craving for nicotine.

On arrival at San Angelo we went into an RCT Assembly Area on a WWII Army Air Corps training airfield which was in a standby status. Tents had been erected prior to our arrival; the original latrines with showers and toilets still functional provided the necessary facilities. The 508 remained in the San Angelo area for about three days, during which the troopers were permitted to go into town in fatigues because we had brought no Class A uniforms or civilian clothing. The men behaved themselves well, as they usually do when away from their home station. The Red Devils were made honorary citizens of the city.

All COs had an opportunity to reconnoiter the area in which the operation was going to take place. The 2nd Bn was to drop first and secure the LZ. Once the RCT had reorganized, it would break out of its perimeter to attack the 82nd. During the reconnaissance we were able to look at the DZ and the Reconnaissance and Security (R&S) Line that the 2/508 would occupy. Each Co CO was permitted to take his Plt Ldrs. I used PSGs as drivers, so the entire chain of command got to scout routes to the R&S Line. I designated on the ground, to each Plt Ldr, the segment of the perimeter his Platoon would secure. The maneuver was artificial from that tactical point of view (commanders would always like the opportunity to look over the ground, but it is impossible to do so when jumping behind enemy lines). The Maneuver Director authorized the reconnaissance to insure that there would be no problem in getting the RCT prepared for the final attack against the 82nd. In tracing the R&S Line, we passed many ranch houses. The people were most friendly, plying us with cold drinks, lemonade, iced tea, water and cookies. They showed great interest in the maneuver and wanted to question us about it. Many of the ranchers had leased their land to the Army for "Longhorn". Unfortunately, we were pressed for time and could not linger.

The day we were to make the jump was very windy. (In Texas there always seemed to be a wind, frequently sand storms.) Because we were to jump in midmorning, we held an early Reveille, had a good breakfast, then issued and fitted parachutes. Faces were streaked with camouflage grease to reduce highlights, all our troopers marked themselves with the "double blitz", two lightning flashes on each cheek, the sign of the 2/508. LTC Mansfield had directed this as an assembly aid and recognition signal. Herb had dubbed the 2nd Bn the "double blitz battalion", two streaks of lightning were used to mark anything associated with it: assembly areas, equipment, troopers.

The troopers were keyed up for the jump and the tactical maneuver. Though eager to go, some had misgivings about the wind. Walking from the Marshalling Area to the aircraft with parachutes adjusted and equipment hanging from our harnesses we had to lean into the wind, walking was difficult. Troopers with GP bags had to be assisted. The 508 was to jump from both C46s and C47s.

Finally everybody was loaded and the "gooney birds" became airborne. Almost half of the troopers became air sick due to the extreme turbulence. Fortunately I was standing at the door most of the time; adrenalin and the rush of air kept me from becoming nauseated. Though thoroughly familiar with the route of the flight, it was difficult to locate the check points because many were obscured by blowing sand. The wind followed us all the way to the Drop Zone.

"Longhorn" was the largest mass Airborne drop since WWII. Many VIPs, including the Army Chief of Staff had come to witness it. The morning of the jump, after the first wind readings had been taken on the DZ, the Protocol OFF told the spectators that there would be no drop, most returned to their billets and thus missed seeing us jump.

As we neared the DZ, it became questionable whether we would drop; the winds exceeded 15 knots, the safe limit for Airborne operations. Everyone hoped we would jump, however, as all dreaded the thought of returning with so many sick troops aboard.

Finally the red light came on; the troopers cheered as we went through the jump sequence. As I stood in the door there was dust on the DZ. When the green light flashed on, I heaved a sigh of relief as I leaped out of the door. The winds were gusting on the DZ; I was dragged about 100 feet before I could pull in my bottom risers to collapse the canopy. Fortunately we still had T-7 parachutes. If we had used T-10s, I'm sure we would have had more difficulty.

Of the 175 parachutists that jumped with F Co, about 120 of them were injured, ranging from light scratches through sprained ankles, twisted knees, to a broken leg (most serious). Most of the injured returned to the Co later in the day. Doctors at the Aid Station checked those with sprains, strains or bruises, returning most to duty. Many men, despite sprains or bruises, refused to go to the Aid Station but insisted on continuing with the Company. CPL Luby, a husky Texan, literally crawled to the Co Assembly Area. The final accounting revealed that F Co had six seriously injured, one with a broken leg. This was true of the entire 2nd Bn, but was insignificant compared to the rest of the RCT; due to our light loads and constant training in tactical jumps on unprepared DZs, the 2nd Bn minimized its losses.

As soon as I landed I located Bucey, my radio operator, who had jumped behind me and fortunately landed close to me with his GP bag. He got the radio out and made immediate contact with LTC Mansfield's radio operator. We left the chutes on the DZ to be recovered by a detail later. In a very short time F Co was partially assembled. When there was an acceptable force (I did not wait for the entire Co) I left Tucker on the DZ at the Assembly Area and moved my troopers out. The men literally loped off the DZ. In less than an hour we were in position on the R&S Line. When I reported to LTC Mansfield that F Co's sector of the R&S Line was secure, he expressed surprise. The other Cos in the Bn did equally well. I'm not sure which of us got to the line first, but it was a fast, well executed move. When Mansfield reported to his umpire and the RCT that the R&S Line was secure neither umpire nor staff would believe him. They found it difficult to accept that we had assembled, moved several miles, deployed and dug in that rapidly. But there were no false reports; those men were fired up; their excellent physical condition paid dividends. They could easily do anything reasonable asked of them. The problem stemmed from the fact that umpires did not jump with us, but joined us on the ground; they were late due to the uncertain jump and our fast movement; some even got lost! But F Co was in position and prepared to fight when I made the report; I am sure the other companies were too. The remainder of the Co straggled in all afternoon and even after dark.

The next morning the 82nd jumped in winds about like ours. There was little more to the maneuver after that; a day spent getting into position for future action. Immediately after "Longhorn" ended the 508 assembled in a staging area close to FT Hood without returning to San Angelo. The Rear Detachment joined us as we prepared to move back to Fort Benning.

COL Lawrie assembled the entire RCT on a hillside for a critique of the 508's conduct during "Longhorn". The troopers morale was high. They had done a good job in their view; certainly the jump had gone well despite the injuries sustained. Such injuries were expected with winds gusting on the DZ, but they were proud there had been so few. COL Lawrie had a superb opportunity to weld the 508 together even more closely, and to enhance his own image among the men, had he only said a few words about how well the troopers had done under adverse conditions. Instead he spent a half hour discoursing on the agony he and BG Murrow, the Air Force Commander, experienced, while flying over the DZ, getting constant readings on wind conditions from MAJ Arch Hamblen, the DZSO, as they debated scrubbing the jump. The troops listened with increasing disinterest, if not outright disbelief, as he told them that when finally the winds slackened, he and BG Murrow had quickly decided that it was safe for the RCT to jump. I am in no position to know what the winds were when we exited the aircraft; a reliable authority told me they gusted to 20 knots on the DZ. Nor is it germane to the principle. The troopers were convinced that the winds were marginal, if not beyond the safety limits, but the RCT had jumped successfully in spite of that. A short speech voicing his pride in his troopers, mentioning the gusting winds as obstacles they had surmounted, would have been appropriate. The lengthy defense of his decision was lost on the troopers; he never again regained the full respect of the 508 RCT. To them he was just another colonel commanding, not the leader COL /BG Cleland had been.

The trip back to Fort Benning was a repeat of the one out. The weather was good, the leap frogging procedure well practiced and the move went smoothly. As usual, there was a break every hour to let the men stretch, relieve themselves and change drivers. It was a good trip, a good jump and a good exercise. Though they found the 1100 mile convoy tiring, the men enjoyed "Longhorn".

Immediately after the 508 returned to Benning, it was announced that in order to make the Sand Hill Area available for NG, RES, or Recruit summer training, the 508 would move to the Harmony Church Area. This caused some unhappiness because the men had spent much effort fixing up their billets, day rooms and mess halls.

As we were preparing to move, orders arrived assigning me to Korea. My reporting date would allow time to make the move, get the Company settled into Harmony Church and take a short leave. I was proud of F Co and the troopers in it, and proud of the 508. It was unbelievable that no mission had been found for it in Korea or elsewhere. Certainly it would have acquitted itself well. That wealth of talent was not used for any purpose; the 508 was again deactivated without accomplishing a thing.

The move to the Harmony Church Area was made with few problems. After considerable labor, the buildings, newer and in better condition than those we had in Sand Hill, were ready for our troops. The 508 settled down in its new area.

LTC Mansfield decided that 1LT Lattimore, now the XO and Supply Officer of F Co would assume Command. In the short time before my departure there were a number of affairs in my honor, which helped make the parting less painful. The troopers were coerced by their NCOs, unknown to me, into contributing to a fund with which a map case and a Savings Bond were purchased as farewell gifts for me. This was illegal, but I accepted the gifts with pride.

When Lattimore and I inventoried the Company, the Supply Room was short many sleeping bags and field trousers as a result of the "Longhorn" Maneuver. This represented a considerable amount of money, so I tentatively decided to cancel my leave to try to make up the shortages. But Lattimore and SGT Fowler, the Supply Sergeant, insisted that they could make up the shortages and urged me to go ahead with my leave. Lattimore said that he would accept responsibility for the property if I would sign a blank Report of Survey form to cover any shortages they might not be able to make up. This was against every principle and instinct I had learned over the years; it was like signing a blank check; but the lure of a short leave in New York, plus my desire to get into the Korean War overcame my better judgement, I signed the blank forms and entrusted my property to Lattimore and Fowler.

After clearing F Co, I signed out. Just before I left, there was a Co formation at which the map case and Savings Bond were presented to me. This farewell moved me, indicating to me that the troopers had considerable respect and regard for me. Certainly, I had a great deal of both for all of the officers and men in F Company.

My trip home and my leave were enjoyable. I hated to sell that fire engine red convertible, but finally did so on the last day of my leave. Since I had not seen much of the Northwestern United States, I decided to take the Northern Pacific Railroad to FT Lawton, my port of embarkation. After signing in at Lawton, I was informed that the flight to Korea would not leave for several days. This provided an opportunity to see my Deadeye buddy, Fred Steed.

While at FT Lawton, I went to a bank in downtown Seattle. Rather apologetically, I asked the teller to cash an out-of-state check. In many places banks would not cash a check on an out-of-state bank, particularly for military personnel, without considerable hassle. But the teller said, "Why of course, Captain. We would be delighted to. Just show me your identification."

After seeing my ID card she asked, "How much do you want?" There was no question about okaying the check. It was the first time since I had returned to the Army that my check (and word) had been taken at face value. It was good to know that some people still trusted officers.

The group of Infantry lieutenants with whom I was to fly to Korea was taken by bus from FT Lawton to McChord AF Base, where we were first manifested, then herded onto a Northwest Orient Airlines DC-6 charter aircraft. Everything about the operation was third rate, the cleanliness of the plane, the appearance of the crew, the service of the stewardesses. The latter seemed more concerned with talking to some of the more attractive males on board than they were in taking care of their duties. We almost starved.

Almost as soon as we took off, the plane developed engine trouble. Though crippled, we made it to Elmendorf AF Base at Anchorage, AK. We were told that there would be a two or three hour delay while the engine was changed. After sitting in the lobby for almost four hours, during which the airlines provided breakfast in the terminal dining room, we reboarded the plane. As soon as we were airborne, the pilot announced that he was not satisfied with the repair job and was returning to Elmendorf. I was glad that he had such good sense.

We put down again at Elmendorf, where we were on a three hour alert, which prevented our leaving the terminal. Finally it became apparent that the aircraft would not be repaired for at least six or eight hours. Northwest Airlines arranged dinner for us and billets at the transient quarters on the Air Base. About 0300 we were called to board. We took off with considerable doubt that we would make it all the way. But our doubts were groundless.

The DC-6, a four engine propeller-driven plane, had to stop enroute for refueling at Shemya, one of the Aleutian Islands. Shemya, which is not very big, seemed to have room for little more than the Air Force Base. Facing constant winds that swept Shemya, the aircraft had to land by "crabbing" into the air current. When we deplaned I was reminded of San Angelo, TX - we had to lean into the wind to get to the dining hall for our meal, which we ate while the plane was refueled. When we took off our next stop was Tokyo.

CHAPTER 8

GUERRILLA

The charter flight landed at Tachikawa Air Base outside Tokyo, from which the entire packet of replacements was bussed to Camp Drake, an old Japanese Army camp taken over by the Americans at the beginning of the occupation. The comfortable, well run installation employed Japanese civilians to do the house keeping chores: KP, police and cleaning of the transient billets. Transients, officer or enlisted, had no duties.

The Officers' Club was particularly good. The meals were inexpensive and delicious, the drinks very cheap. There was excellent entertainment every night: singers, bands, shows, circuses. It was a pleasant place to spend time. OFFs going into combat fed the hundreds of slot machines, providing the funds for the entertainment and reasonable prices.

We all relaxed that first evening, had a good meal at the Club and enjoyed the entertainment. I had written to COL Wilson, who was then commanding the 9th Infantry Regiment of the 2nd Div, asking for a rifle company. In his reply, assuring me of command of a company, he told me to call him when I got to Tokyo. He had included instructions on how to put the call through. Shortly after dinner, I placed the call, finally reaching the 9th IN after going through four switchboards including Major Command, Corps, Division and finally Regiment. COL Wilson was not available, but I talked with John Kiser his S-1, who had been with me in the 504, was happy to hear from me, and assured me that I had been requested and would be assigned to the 9th Infantry.

The next morning orders were posted on the bulletin board. Several OFFs were assigned to the 2nd Div, but my name was not among them. When I asked the Personnel Officer why I was not on the list to the 2nd Div, he responded, "You are being screened for a particular job which I can't tell you about. You'll get details about it later on." He couldn't or wouldn't tell me more.

About 1000 the next morning a call came over the PA system for four OFFs, including me; the Personnel OFF directed us to report to the Mitsubishi Building in downtown Tokyo for inter-views. We were told nothing about the jobs for which we were to be interviewed. A sedan took us into Tokyo.

We reported to the suite in the Mitsubishi Building to which we had been directed, which was occupied by an element of the 8th Army Intelligence Office. The other three were interviewed first. Each of them came out and left without talking to me. Finally I went in, found a COL seated behind a desk and reported to him.

The COL began the interview by informing me that he could tell me nothing about the job I was being considered for because it was highly classified. Then he asked several questions. He wanted to know if I got along with people of other nationalities and races; my answer was affirmative; I had no trouble working with people of any type. He asked about my Infantry background, what training and assignments I had in that Branch. In the brief outline of my IN experience, I emphasized that I had commanded two rifle Cos and many Plts.

"Good, you're just the man we want. Are you interested in volunteering for this job?"

"Before I volunteer for the job, sir, I want to know what it is."

"I can't tell you that until you volunteer."

"I won't volunteer until I know what the job is."

We went around and around. I thought it a ridiculous approach to any assignment, finally telling him that I wanted to go to the 9th Infantry. The Colonel became exasperated, saying, "I need a definite yes or no answer. Now take a walk for an hour; when you come back I want to know whether you want to volunteer or not."

While walking about downtown Tokyo, I thought about the matter. It seemed to me that this was the most fantastic situation I had ever been faced with. I wanted to go to the 9th EN, and I would not volunteer for an unknown assignment under any circumstances. In an hour I returned to the COL's office and told him that I would not volunteer for the job.

"It doesn't make any difference. I've got clearance to assign you to the job anyway. You're exactly the type of officer we are looking for, so you are going to be assigned to CCRAK (Combined Command for Reconnaissance Activities in Korea), specifically, you are being assigned to the Far East Command Liaison Detachment (FEC/LD), an element of CCRAK. FEC/LD has the mission of raising and supporting guerrilla fighters behind the North Korean lines. There is a need for advisors and support personnel for this mission; you fit the need as an IN CDR with a good knowledge of small unit tactics and leadership. Your assignment will be as a guerrilla pack advisor. You will not discuss our talk or this assignment with anybody outside this organization. Clear?"

I objected, stating my desire to command a US Army rifle company in combat. My objections went unheeded; I was ordered to move from Camp Drake to a hotel in Tokyo pending shipment to Korea.

Reluctantly, I followed orders. I called the 9th Infantry again to tell John Kiser that I had been diverted to another assignment. Before leaving for Korea I had a chance to see a little of Tokyo and to call Mother and Dad to give them the APO address provided by the COL. Officially I was assigned to the 8240th Army Unit, a cover. The other three officers who had been interviewed before me were in the same hotel awaiting transportation to Korea. They were going to other elements of CCRAK, however.

Finally we were notified of the special flight that was to take us to Korea from Tachikawa When we got to Seoul, we were picked up by an American OFF with several jeeps driven by Koreans. He explained that many of the people working for CCRAK were Korean nationals; only the OFFs and a few EM in the HQ were US Army personnel. We were driven to CCRAK HQ located in a compound which had been a Presbyterian or Methodist seminary. The former chapel was now used as a recreation hall and theater for the CCRAK personnel.

My new boss, LTC Jay D. Vanderpool, an ARTY OFF, who greeted me warmly, was in charge of all guerrilla activities supported by the US Army. He was intrigued with the guerrilla concept and envisioned raising a corps of guerrillas that would tie down many Chinese Communist Forces (CCF) as well as elements of the North Korea Army (NKA) to relieve the pressure on the UN troops on the 38th Parallel Truce Line. He communicated some of his enthusiasm about his mission to me. In the following five days I attended a series of briefings and met many people; among them were ILT George Laland, who was eventually assigned to the same island I went to, CPT Al Roegge, an able and effective OFF who usually took care of me whenever I was in the HQ, and LTC Mac Austin, in the Intelligence Section, but with whom I worked frequently. Al and Mac became good friends.

After the briefings, LTC Vanderpool sent me to the nearest guerrilla base for some practical experience. One of the Korean drivers took me to Inchon, where an LCVP belonging to FEC/LD ferried me to the Island of Kanghwa Do. MAJ Richard M. Ripley was in charge of guerrilla operations there. During the next three days he explained how his organization functioned; the receipt of intelligence, the planning of raids, the recruiting, outfitting, training and support of guerrillas. He was an autonomous operator, with access to a large quantity of Won (Korean Currency); the funds were almost unlimited, as was his authority to use them. The American advisors lived in a compound guarded by Korean guerrillas. A large Korean labor pool, paid out of the Won fund, did all the work, so the American soldiers had no housekeeping chores to perform. Defenses were constructed, supplies handled, and transportation maintained and driven by Korean laborers, screened, hired and paid by the guerrilla advisors. Thus they could devote all of then-energies to the advisory effort. MAJ Ripley made it clear that neither he nor his advisors commanded the guerrilla forces. Their own leaders did that. But the allocation of resources gave the Americans such great leverage that control was effectively exercised by them. Only in matters of recruiting the guerrillas themselves and in conducting tactical operations were the guerrilla leaders independent. Communications between the HQ in Seoul and the American advisors were handled by US soldiers. A separate guerrilla radio network was manned by Korean personnel.

While on Kanghwa Do I was afforded no chance to go on any raids, but did sit in on several debriefings. Later Ripley was replaced by MAJ Harry H. Hiestand.

On my return to Seoul, LTC Vanderpool told me that I was going to Operation Leopard or Leopard Base, located on Paengnyong Do (Pangyang Do the Americans called it); Do in Korean means island). The day after returning from Kanghwa Do I left for Pang-Yang-Do.

The C-46 took 45 minutes to fly from Seoul to Paengnyong Do, an Island off the western tip of Korea, just south of the 38th Parallel. The only landing field on the Island was the beach, so flights were scheduled to take advantage of the low tide. The hard packed sand made a smooth runway. The beach was used as an emergency landing field by aircraft flying over North Korea; several, shot up by MIGs, landed while I was on the Island. Mail, supplies, and personnel arrived or went out on the daily plane, which provided diversion to the monotony of the island routine. Among those on the beach to meet my flight was MAJ Tom Dye, my new boss. He introduced himself as he drove me in his jeep to the Leopard Compound. Enroute he listed the military organizations on Paengnyong Do.

There were three American units on the Island: a USAF radar installation on the highest hill, which controlled most of the aircraft flying over North Korea; The Leopard Complex including the Advisors1 compound, guerrilla training area and a support area; and a USMC Advisory Det with the Republic of Korea (ROK) Marine Regt responsible for the security of Paengnyong Do. Each of the American commanders was independent. There were over 100 Americans on the Island. MAJ Dye explained that all of our supplies came either by ship or C-46.

The Leopard Compound consisted of several Quonset huts, a prefabricated mess hall and a commo bunker. The troops lived in a large Quonset, the OFFs in two half Quonsets, all of which had been sandbagged to a height well above the level of the cots inside. Initially I shared a hut with several 1LTs, Ben Malcolm and another OFF. There were four cots in our half Quonset, several field tables and folding chairs, and a diesel stove. A second full Quonset was being erected, under the direction of Ben Malcolm, the S-2 of Leopard, as a Tactical Operations Center (TOC).

The US Army complement of Leopard consisted of MAJ Dye, the Commander, a CPT, S-3, 1LT Malcolm, the S-2, a 1LT Guerrilla Training Officer, and one other 1LT who conducted special operations. In addition there were about 25 EM, Commo, mess, administrative, supply and operations personnel. This unit was dedicated to the support of 17 teams (packs) of partisans which operated from the 38th Parallel north to the Yalu River. Several of the guerrilla bands operated from islands, Cho Do and Sin Do north of the 38th Parallel, and Sunwi Do and other small Islands to the east of Paengnyong Do. Each pack was identified by a "Donkey Number" such as Donkey 13; that number also identified the leader.

Ben Malcolm was about my height, a well knit, handsome 1LT with boundless energy and enthusiasm. In addition to his very important duties as S-2, he was the Advisor to Donkey 4, a group based on the tip of the mainland just north of Paengnyong Do. This area was defended with extensive mine fields and excellent utilization of terrain.

After several days of briefings, MAJ Dye informed me that I was to be the Advisor to Donkey 13 and Donkey 3, both operating from Sunwi Do. The ANGRC 9 radio, an effective but complicated instrument, was to be my link with Leopard Base. The Commo NCO gave me intensive instruction in' how to "zero bead" the ANGRC 9 in order to get good reception. It had a hand-cranked generator, but could also be operated on batteries.

The trip to Sunwi Do was made in Donkey 13's motorized junk, purchased with Leopard funds. As mentioned before, the way in which the US Army controlled the guerrillas was by providing (or withholding) support: supplies, including rice, ammunition, weapons, clothing, communications equipment and medicines; fire support including naval gun tire as well as direct air support or bombing; medical support, including hospitalization of critically wounded in the US Army hospitals; and intelligence. Successful partisan teams were rewarded immediately and well. The ultimate prize was a motorized junk, which every Donkey leader wanted. They knew they could get them only after they had proven their ability in operations. Otherwise they were relegated to the use of sailboats and rowboats, we called them "wiggle boats", propelled with a stick or oar in the rear that was "wiggled" back and forth. Donkey 13 had obviously proven himself enough to merit a motorized junk.

On the junk with me were the ANGRC 9 radio with both generator and batteries, a good supply of C Rations and other food, several bottles of Scotch and enough toilet articles to last a month. An interpreter accompanied me. Both Donkey 13 and Donkey 3 were based on Sunwi Do; though I would advise them both, I would live with Donkey 13, adding to his prestige.

Donkey 13, who controlled the Island, assigned me two rooms in the schoolhouse. There was a Korean outhouse in the back which I shared with the children; to obtain privacy I was up and finished with my ablutions each morning before they arrived. The rest of the building was still used as a school. Disrupted by the war, it was now operating under the protection of Donkey 13.

My job was to support Donkey 13 and Donkey 3; to advise them on operations, to share intelligence with them, to receive reports, to verify results (if possible), to insure timely resupply, to coordinate fire support, and to obtain medical support. In no sense did I command the packs; my influence was exerted through the leaders by virtue of my control of assets. I could suggest operations, promising support, or I could discourage questionable operations by withholding support. But the leaders made the final decisions on all operations. One of the shortcomings of LTC Vanderpool's concept of guerrilla warfare was that operations would have become more and more paramilitary, resulting in actual light Infantry combat. As a result the cumbersome supply system and administrative procedures would have destroyed the advantages enjoyed in true guerrilla warfare.

It is disquieting to be the only American in an area, knowing that you have only limited influence over the local people. There was always the specter of infiltrators, agents, bandits or racists. Ben Malcolm assured me that the guerrilla units had no problem with infiltrators or double agents. Each guerrilla leader recruited his partisans from the same community or area of the mainland that he came from. Therefore, when a man was accepted into a partisan unit, his background was well known. Several enemy agents did try to pass themselves off as friends of the Donkeys, but none was ever successful. Of course, any adverse action against me would reflect upon Donkey 13, so I was well guarded.

Donkey 13 proudly introduced me to all of the civilian leaders on Sunwi Do. Since he had the military might, he completely controlled them. They invited me to several affairs; as the honored guest, I was served first and given the choicest parts. Fish was a staple at any dinner; the choicest part of the fish was considered the eye, which was always offered to me. It was like chewing rubber. I found the best way to eat one is to swallow it whole. Korean food is palatable if you like fish and highly spiced food.

Kimshi, marinated cabbage, is highly seasoned, consequently very hot; it gives all who eat it very bad breath. The "summer kimshi" was good, but "winter kimshi" was too hot for me. There was always rice, which I like, and stir fried vegetables. Some small minnows, crisply fried and salted, eaten with drinks (much as we eat salted peanuts) I enjoyed. About 80% of the Korean food I could eat with no problem, 10% of it I thoroughly enjoyed. Most meals I ate with my Donkey leaders. Occasionally I would share C Rations with them. They ate them to be polite, and as a matter of prestige, but preferred local fare. They did enjoy the canned fruit. We usually shared a drink before each evening meal.

At all affairs to which I was invited as the guest of honor, drinking was a ritual. Normally only males were present at such events. Using small porcelain cups which held about an ounce of local liquor, each one present, in order of precedence, would raise his cup in both hands, bow to me from the waist, still seated, and say "Kompai". The spelling and pronunciation varies from country to country, but the root word seems to be the same throughout the Orient. I would respond in like fashion, as we both tossed down the drink in one gulp. If there were 20 guests, then I "Kompai'd" 20 times. I soon learned to bring a can or other container into which I would inconspicuously pour the liquor, which was pretty bad. Perhaps one in 10 times I would actually drink; the other times I went through the motions.

My counterparts were usually receptive to suggestions. Donkey 13 was a college graduate, Donkey 3 a former political figure. Both recognized good military and political advice. The two guerrilla packs mounted raids onto the mainland with mixed results, returning with wildly exaggerated accounts of great damage to the enemy. When these reports were sifted and checked, the results were more prosaic. But the guerrillas did achieve one important objective; they diverted and pinned down significant enemy forces to provide security to military and political targets. That was perhaps their major contribution to the war effort, and a substantial one it was. The other results usually credited to the guerrillas appeared to be less conclusive. Just how effective they were in disrupting transportation or communications, destroying supplies, or eliminating important military and civilian leaders was never very clear. Perhaps I underestimated them. In any event, their reports were interesting and often quite lyrical.

To assess the results of the raids, verify the combat effectiveness of the partisans and gain a greater appreciation of just how the two guerrilla bands operated, I wanted to accompany them on occasional missions. Whenever a suitable operation was proposed, I would ask the leader to let me accompany his unit. There were always reasons which precluded my participation; the intelligence was tenuous, the forces too small, the inland approach too long, the timing not suitable, the area too difficult for me. It was never clear whether they were concerned about my safety or that I might witness something they wanted to conceal. I never did make a raid with those two units.

While I was on Sunwi Do, 1LT Malcolm accompanied Donkey 4 on a raid. The OPS plan and report inclosed are typical of those developed and rendered. Ben was awarded The Silver Star for his part in the operation. When I heard what Ben was able to contribute to the effort, my desire to participate with my Donkey units became almost unbearable. Ben Malcolm wrote a definitive account of this operation and of Operation Leopard after he retired from The Army called *"White Tigers, My Secret War in North Korea"*.

Some three weeks after my move To Sunwi Do, a radio message informed me that an NCO was coming to my location. MSG Roy Meeks arrived a few days later to work under my control. Airborne, sharp, good-looking, muscular, gung ho, he wanted to win the war all by himself. He confided to me that he had returned to Korea for a second tour to win The Medal of Honor. After briefing him on the situation and procedures, I sent him to Kirin Do to advise Donkey 1. He was to report through me. I made it clear to him that he was not to go on any raids without my express approval; however I am inclined to believe that he did not comply with those instructions.

OPERATIONS PLAN – LT. MALCOOOOM
ATTACK PLAN

1. DONKEY 4 UNIT WILL MOVE FROM WOLLAE-DO TO MAINLAND AND ENTER AT XC 624187 AT 0300 14 JULY. BY SAILING AND MOTOR LAUNCH – 120 men IN ATTACK.

2. THE UNIT WILL MOVE UNDER COVER OF DARKNESS INTO OSITIONS ALONG RIDGE LINES XC 6120 AND XC 617206, HILL 285, AND WILL REMAIN HERE DURING BOMBARDMENT.

3. BOMBARDMENT OF 628199, XC 638203, XC 631197, XC 638238 FROM 0430 UNTIL 0500 HRS.

4. AIRSTRIKE BEGINNING AT 0500 TO 0510 ON FOLLOWING TARGETS: PRIMARY TARGETS, XC 564227, 250 NKA, XC 638238, BN CP. SECONDARY TARGETS, XC 634205, M4G PLAT. XC 631197, AT GUN POSITIONS. AIRCAP WILL REMAIN IN AREA ON CALL FROM SHIP RADIO AND WILL HIT ANY TROOPS MOVING EAST OF XC 640 LINE OR NORTH OF XC 220.

5. D-4 UNIT WILL REMAIN IN POSITION DURING NAVAL AND AIR FIRE UNTIL 0530, THEN MOVE IN DIRECTION OF XC 628219, HILL 269, THEN TO XC 631197.

6. ANY ADDITIONAL BOMBARDMENT OR AIRSTRIKES NEEDED WILL BE CALLED IN BY LT. MALCOM TO SHIP BY RADIO (BRITISH) DOG CHANNEL, USING COORDIANTES FROM 1: 50,000 MAP.

7. D-4 UNIT WILL TAKE TIME TO PICK UP ANY SUPPLIES AND MATERIAL AT HAND AND WITHDRAW TO BOATS LOCATED AT XC 633191 AT APPROX 0730 HRS. D-4 WILL CONTACT HIS BOATS BY SCR 300 ON CHANNEL 32. EMERGENCY EXIT, CHANGSAN-GOT, XC 4521.

8. D-4 TROOPS WILL IDENTIFY THEMSELVES BY USING WHITE PANNELS.

TO: 8240
FW: LEOPARD
-H-
OFSUM #320

XC 625187, 13 JULY, 11:45 HRS LT. MALCOM, 120 D-4 MEN LANDED THIS LOCATION, MOVED INTO MOUNTAINS AT XC625202, XC 632212.

14 JULY 0430 NAVY BOMBARDED XC 631197, AT GUN, XC 63205 HMG PLATOON. FIRE LIFTED 0500 D-4 UNIT ATTACKED BOTH POSITIONS FROM REAR KILING 63 NKA WOUNDING 9 NKA. DESTROYED 76MM AT GUN, I MAXIM HMG, 19 CASES AMMO, 170 HANDGRENADES, 3 BARRACKS, I MESS HALL, 2 UNDERGROUND FORTIFICATIONS 4 ROOMS EACH, I RUSSION TYPE RADIO, 100 FT TELEPHONE LINE, BURNED 25 BAGS RICE. CAPTURED I PFSH 1952 MODEL, 65 HANDGRENADES, 43,---NK WON, 5 OXEN, MANY DOCUMENTS. FRIENDLY LOSSES 6 KIA, 7 WIA. AIRSTRIKES WERE CONTROLED FROM HILL XC 625202 ON NKA RE-ENFORCEMENTS MOVING UP VALLEY FROM XC 639238 WITH FOLLOWING RESULTS: 162 KIA, 18 WIA, DESTROYED ED BN CP, 2 MESS HALLS, 8 BARRACKS BUILT IN HILL, COMMO EQUIPMENT, 15 CASES AMMO.

Control of naval gunfire and air strikes was a major concern. This fire support was planned carefully, but with no Americans on the ground to adjust it, the fire power was often ineffective and some times disastrous to friendly forces. One solution was careful marking of targets. Early in August a well coordinated AF bomber raid was conducted on hydroelectric plants deep in North Korea. Just before the bomb run, guerrillas set off flares on all four sides of the plants, the bombers targeted their bombs on the center. The plants had been so well camouflaged that the Air Force could not find them in the daytime. This worked only on fixed targets, not against a fighting enemy.

After only a month on Sunwi Do, MAJ Dye directed me to return to Paengnyong Do to replace the S-3 who was rotating home. I did not want to leave Sunwi Do at this time because I had achieved good rapport with my counterparts. After much effort, I had persuaded both the Donkey Leaders and MAJ Dye that I could make a substantial contribution on several raids planned for the immediate future, if I accompanied the guerrillas on them. This was a sensitive issue, the partisans could fade into the countryside or hide in a village behind enemy lines, whereas I would be all too obvious. It was also possible that too much effort might be expended protecting me; my death would have resulted in great loss of face. Only under unusual circumstances was the American advisor an asset on a raid. At least two of the planned raids seemed to justify the risk, I would be able to adjust air strikes or control naval gunfire if necessary. It was a simple matter to coordinate air or naval fire on preplanned targets. The problem arose when fires had to be lifted or shifted; too few guerrillas understood the procedures or spoke English well enough to direct or call for air or naval support. There was also the matter of security; the enemy could compromise our plans and call in the fire on friendly elements. We normally preplanned fires to go on call; the guerrillas on the ground contacted the advisor at the base, who then relayed the request to the Navy or AF. But this took time and did not provide for proper adjustment. I wanted to go to handle support directly, but it was not to be. I collected my equipment and returned to Paengnyong Do.

The new job was interesting. As Leopard S-3, I helped coordinate 17 guerrilla packs, ranging in size from 75 to 400 partisans. Leopard was fielding and supporting in excess of 3,000 guerrillas. The US Army was spending a great deal of money, principally in the form of rice to sustain them.

Rice was shipped to Leopard Base on a small cargo vessel owned by FEC/LD but manned by Koreans. About once a month the ship loaded with rice, ammo, weapons and other supplies, arrived in the harbor, where it was unloaded. The rice was stored and later issued at a warehouse near the beach. Several NCOs handled this operation for Leopard. The warehouse was well guarded by partisans at all times; the Koreans were consummate thieves; indeed, they were called "slicky, slicky, boys" because of their ability to steal anything that was not well guarded. Leopard contracted with local Koreans on the island to unload the rice. The NCOs had to watch them closely because they would slit bags, fill the huge pockets in their flowing garments or handkerchiefs tied around their necks or heads, resulting in a surprising loss over the course of the unloading. The laborers were inspected each time they took a break to make sure they were not carrying off rice.

The planning and scope of the guerrilla operations was extensive. Ben Malcolm, The S-2, and I worked closely together on all projects. Raids had to be coordinated with the tides, so the small boats used to transport the partisans to the mainland could land on the incoming tide and leave on the outgoing tide. The boats otherwise would be marooned on the beach and the guerrillas trapped with their backs to the sea. Some raids involved a link-up with irregulars remaining on the mainland, always a difficult maneuver.

Naval gunfire from ships on station in the area was planned on likely targets, either in conjunction with a raid or as a separate bombardment. Land-based planes also hit prearranged targets, then stood by for targets of opportunity. But they could only stay in the area a short time. Carrier-based air craft had a longer time over the combat zone. The relay of target information was time consuming and usually not too effective.

Two ROK PT Boats which patrolled the islands, sometimes provided close-in support of operations. When available, or when they could be persuaded to work with the guerrillas, they were effective because communications between the two elements were good. The PT Boats mounted 16 five inch rockets on each side which were particularly effective against coastal defenses.

Naval gunfire support was provided in large part by the British: The Royal Navy, The Royal Canadian Navy, The Royal New Zealand Navy or The Royal Australian Navy. Several of the ships returned again and again so we got to know their Captains, OFFs and crews in arranging naval gunfire support for our guerrillas, or bombardment of targets the partisans identified. The *Ro-To-Iti,* a New Zealand frigate was in the area quite often. *Worthington,* a British cruiser, was occasionally on station. Once even The USS *Misssouri,* stood far offshore and bombarded targets for us.

Tactical air support was provided by the AF, the Navy and the Marines. We found The Marines gave us the best support of any of the services, followed by the Navy; support provided by the Air Force was the least effective. Perhaps the Marines, because their air wing is an integral part of the USMC Div, had worked out the procedures; we never seemed to be able to work them out with the Air Force. At times, Canadian or other British Air Forces supported us with preplanned air strikes; very few were on call and none were responsive to changes in plans or targets.

This was the support we were able to give the irregular forces, whose leaders especially liked the naval gunfire. On occasion, Donkey Leaders who were fluent in English would be given a radio with which they could commentate directly with a ship.

Partisan agents sent in daily reports of enemy locations; these reports were passed to 8th Army, the Navy and the Air Force for their use. One agent operated a tobacco shop beside a bridge over the Yalu River and reported the daily traffic by number and type.

Boats, carelessly called junks, were the key to success in our operations. Small boats made frequent trips to the mainland hauling rice, ammunition, and other supple and returned with captured material and cattle. The British Navy was constantly surprised to see a "junk" with a number of oxen tied to the sides heading across the straits from the mainland to the islands.

Raids into coves and inlets were usually successful, resulting in the sinking of many North Korean and Chinese boats. The partisan would leap from boat to boat dropping hand grenades into the open hatches, sinking as many as 10 or 12 fishing boats or supply vessels on each raid. North Korean gunboats would occasionally chase the guerrillas, but the 105mm Recoiless rifles mounted on the partisan motorized junks usually frightened them off.

Refugees often posed problems on raids to the mainland. As the guerrillas withdrew to the beach, refugees would flock to the shore begging to be evacuated. The irregulars took as many as possible, particularly the families and friends of members of the teams, but many had to be left, often beaten away from the small boats so they would not swamp them with overwhelming numbers.

Donkey 10 was captured when his motor junk broke down and he was forced to land on the mainland. He was executed and buried face down. Koreans believe that only those buried face up can get to heaven. The Donkey 10 Team lost almost half its men in attempts to retake the village and rebury their leader face up. Well-entrenched North Korean soldiers, anticipating just such an attempt, repulsed three attacks in as many weeks, killing over 50 partisans.

The raids and operations varied widely, and the type of administrative and logistical support provided the irregular effort was equally diverse. A monthly meeting was held at Leopard Base to which all Donkey Leaders came. They made their reports, discussed their plans and submitted their requests for supples. MAJ Dye would tell each leader how many partisans he would support; rice, weapons, ammunition and clothing were issued based on that figure. The Donkey Leaders continually tried to increase the size of their bands, but Dye would not approve additional support unless the results achieved justified a larger force.

The British Navy helped resupply our most northerly units. Supplies were loaded onto the frigate on station, which would take them and one of the Leopard advisers as far as the mouth of the Yalu, where they would rendezvous with 1LT Jim Mapp (whose code name was Himong), advisor to the units in that area.

Shortly after I became the S-3, 1LT Mapp, a tall, well built OFF reported in. He had been either in the hospital or on R&R when I arrived. MAJ Dye told me that Jim had just been awarded the Distinguished Service Cross (DSC) for action very close to the Chinese/Korean border near the Yalu River. The mission was the location and destruction of an enemy radar site. Jim and another American had been badly wounded and his guerrilla team decimated in that operation. Jim was going to organize another guerrilla unit for the north, but would spend a few weeks with us on the Island. I got to know him well, during some interesting discussions.

One evening, Jim, after drinking a bit too much, became extremely violent. Apparently he had a mental flashback and thought he was again on the Yalu River fighting for his life. In reality he was fighting us. We were the enemy overrunning his positions. It took four of us to get him under a cold shower, which calmed him down. Later Jim confided to me that the other American, who had also gotten a DSC, had "bugged out" leaving him and a few irregulars to fight their way back. It had been tough, hand-to-hand fighting, but Mapp was a husky football player from Georgia, who had the will to survive. Talking to me about the matter seemed to relieve a lot of pent-up tension. Jim never had problems of this type again.

One time I was chewed out royally because I broke security. In trying to get permission to run a sensitive operation, I used the "One Time Pad", a highly classified code. Three successive messages were sent via the "One Time Pad", none of which was answered. The deadline to launch the operation was only three hours away. In desperation I called on the radio telephone, referring to my three previous messages, and urgently requesting an answer. The security people thought I had compromised the "One Time Pad", eliciting the reprimand. In addition to the upbraiding, I also got permission to launch the operation.

In late fall of 1952 Ben Malcolm was replaced by Bill Watson also an IN 1LT. Bill learned quickly, becoming an effective S-2; Dye, Watson and I soon had a good operation going. I did not always agree with the way MAJ Dye handled the Donkey Leaders, but he was the boss. We had frequent discussions during which I would make my arguments, but once he had made a decision, I implemented it.

About this time 1LT George Laland arrived on Paengnyong Do to train an ABN Guerrilla Unit. Tom Dye took the opportunity to give our local guard force ABN Training. The guard detachment did not go on operations, got no loot or glory, hence had morale problems. By completing jump school they qualified for ABN pay, which improved their esprit.

All US advisors who were qualified parachutists were on jump status. Periodically, we were able to make arrangements to jump from the daily C-46 or C-47 or a wandering helicopter, using the beach or an open field as a DZ. We tried to avoid rice paddies, even after the harvest, because they were fertilized with human waste; landing in them was a smelly affair. We rarely jumped more than every other month because of the difficulty in arranging for aircraft, but we did manage to collect jump pay on a regular basis. I made four or five jumps while on Paengnyong Do.

In late October MSG Meeks came to the CP with a plan for a raid on the mainland, which he and Donkey I had developed. He wanted permission to accompany Donkey I on the raid. After only a cursory glance it was obvious that it had been written by Meeks. He accepted without hesitation, the few changes I suggested. Finally, I told him that I would approve the plan and his participation, subject to MAJ Dye's veto, only if I went along. I hastened to explain that I would be along solely as a Liaison Officer (LNO) to direct fire support provided by the Navy and Air Force based on the wishes of Donkey I (and Meeks), thus freeing him to work with Donkey I and to maintain communications.

The plan called for a two pronged approach, requiring firm and constant control of both elements. One American would accompany each of them. Meeks was not happy with this solution, but when he saw that his objection would lead only to disapproval of the plan, he reluctantly agreed. Dye approved the plan with the stipulation that I go along.

In coordinating with the captain of HMNZS *Ro-To-Iti,* he informed us that the British cruiser *Worthington* would be in the area on the day of the raid and would be available to support it. We gave it the call sign Abuse 2, *Ro-To-Iti* was Abuse 1, changed at the last minute to Jackstone. Air strikes and direct support from Navy Air were also coordinated. The aircraft's ability to loiter over the target area was limited, but that posed no problem since having them over our area would be a give away of our position and mission. When all of the details were buttoned down, Meeks and I went back To Donkey 1's HQ on Kirin Do to prepare for the operation.

The guerrilla moved out about 0200 in wiggle boats, sail boats, and motorized junks. AT 0300 all motors were stopped in order to make a silent move to shore. The initial elements lead by Donkey I and Meeks landed at 0400, I landed with the main force at 0500. My military interpreter, LT Pak, who became ill at the last minute, had been replaced by a young civilian who had volunteered to come with me as interpreter. He was a translator of documents, not trained for conversational work, so I initially opposed his coming. He pleaded to come; as there was no one else, he came along. He carried the radio which was our link with HMNZS *Ro-To-Iti.*

At dawn it became apparent that the operation, which was essentially a pincers movement with Meeks on one set of the jaws and me on the other, had been compromised. Both forces came under intense fire. The enemy knew exactly where we were and where we were going and had the routes covered with small arms and mortars. We sustained a few casualties in the initial I fire fight. When the enemy fire became really intense, Donkey I decided to pull back. Unfortunately, the withdrawal turned into a route as most of the partisans faded into the country side, leaving only a few of us, including my civilian interpreter, to fight our way back. I was not sure where Donkey I and Meeks were. We had established several rally points and the group I was with headed for the nearest one. In their haste, the irregulars headed for the beach hoping to find boats to get off the mainland. I tried desperately to convince them not to abandon the high ground, to stay as high on the hillside as possible. Once on the beach the enemy could fire down and pick us off at will. Just at that time, my interpreter was killed. I spoke no Korean and the Commander of my element spoke little or no English. The guerrillas flowed onward, sweeping me with them, unable to retrieve the radio. I had no communication with Meeks or *Ro-To-Iti,* and found it virtually impossible to make the element leader understand me. He became excited as the situation turned chaotic. Though concerned for me, he was more concerned for himself. Finally, he panicked and plunged down to the beach, drawing the rest of his troops with him. I had no alternative but to go with him or remain alone on the hill, which was suicide.

We got to the beach but found no boats. At this point the Element Commander tried to rally his men to make a stand, but the odds against us were overwhelming. It is not in the nature of guerrilla operations to stand and fight, they are not organized, armed or trained for it. As our boats were not scheduled to meet us until hours later, there was no alternative but to take to the water and swim. By good fortune, there was a log in the surf which I pushed ahead of me; it would keep me afloat until we were picked up.

Ultimate disaster was staved off when Meeks, who still had commo, called in the preplanned air strikes. Donkey I and MSG Meeks had been able to keep some control over their element. Donkey I also had commo with his boats, which he called in to pick us up. They were a welcome sight when they appeared.

HEADQUARTERS
OPERATION LEOPARD
APC 301

28 October 1952

OPERATIONAL ORDER # 6

1. a. 70 NKA, 2 LMG, IC 782008, in houses.

30 NKA, 2 LMG, XB 769996, in houses.

120 NKA, 4 LMG, I HMG, XB 789983, in trenches, Hill 125.

200 NKA, 2 LMG, 3 60mm mortar, I 80mm mortar, I ASMG, XC 815034, in trenches E hill 190, in pine grove extending 8 from Hill.

70 NKA, 3 LMG, XC 812091, in air raid shelters in gardens of houses.

100 NEA, 4 LMG, XB 795020, in houses. Civilians reported evacuated, only camp followers with Army.

b. Guerrilla Unit D-1 supported by HWBZA Rotoiti, and Worthington destroyer and by air craft of CTA 95.11.

2. 200 Partisans of guerrilla Unit D-1, led by Able Sugar 3, and King Able, lend at XB 738997 at 290200 I Oct. Attack 70 NKA XC 782008 at 290630 I Oct. Destroy enemy, S7 documents and prisoners and withdraw by 290930 I Oct. Bombline; WS XC 79 line to 0 EM XC AB.

3. a. 50 D-1 Partisans land from 2 sail junks XB 738997 at 290200 I Oct, move N and SZ high ground vicinity, XC 770028. Secure rear of main force, and cover withdrawal.

b. 150 D-1 Partisans land from 3 sail and I engine junks at XB 738997, at 290200 I Oct. Move N and E to objective, set up assault line along road, W and E of town. Attack 290630 I, Destroy enemy and installations, capture prisoners and documents. Withdraw by bounds on order.

c. HWN.S Rotoiti and Worthington destroyer supported by Naval gunfire from closest off shore positions. On station 290500 I Oct. Bombard enemy positions XC 811035 and XC 812019 at 290630 I or on call. Prepare to support with fire on call. Cover withdrawal of land forces.

d. Aircraft of CTA 95.11 strike enemy concentrations at XB 763996, XB 729983 and XB 713020 at 290635 I Oct. Provide TACAP until 290630 I Oct, to be extended if necessary. Strike targets of opportunity and on call from ground.

x. Land forces withdraw 5 by bounds on 0 to XB 745986. Leave mainland for Mahap-to by 290930 I Oct.

4. Casualties treated by D-1 aidman. Serious casualties evacuated to abuse 2 by engine boat from XC 783030.

5. a. CP XC 770028

Ship to shore communication;

SCR 300, channel 20, alt 25, alt 615, channel Baker alt Charlie. Call sign ship Abuse 2 shore Able Sugar 3, and King Able.

AM/CRC 9 on engine boat- 7305 XC. Call sign TOGNOGY ONE. HWMZS Rotoiti controls Worthington destroyer.

Air ground communications VHF channel white alt channel BLUE controlled by Able Sugar Three and King Able. Alt relay through Abuse 2. White panels, T shirts or handkerchiefs, air ground identification.

Radio and time check 2402013 I Oct.

6. Able Sugar Three at CP.

King Able at forward Bn Cp.

DYE

CMDG

DISTRIBUTION:
1 - 8240
1 - 95.12.2
1 - Tognogy
1 - AS-3
1 - KA
1 - File
OFFICIAL
SEIBERT S-3

TOR/010940 I NOV

TO: DONKEY

FM: D-1

#1. ON 29 I OCT THE FOLLOWING OPERATION TOOK PLACE AT XC 784009 (PULONG-MOL):

(1) LANDING AREA AND TIME

A. LANDED AT THE AREA OF XC 739997

B. LEADER ADVISOR (SGT MEEKS) LANDED ON 290350 I OCT.

C. LEADER WHO IS VICE COMMANDER (CAPT SEIBERT) LANDED ON 290500 I OCT

(2) COMBAT POSITION:

A. ON 290540 I OCT WE TRIED TO SEIZE BY AN ENVELOPING MOVEMENT FROM XC 785009 TO XC 784007 BUT WE WERE DISCOVERED BY THE ENEMY GUARD AT 290605 WHICH WAS TEN BEFORE THE PLANNED TIME OF ATTACK AND WE WERE FORCED TO FIGHT.

B. POSITION OF CP:

OUR FIRST CP WAS LOCATED AT XC 752014 (HILL SOUTH OF HONUN-RI)

THE SECOND CP POSITION WAS LOCATED AT XC 757019 (HONUN-NI HILL)

AFTER WE HAD FOUGHT FOR ABOUT 30 MINUTES AGAINST 170 ENEMIES, AT XC 785009, THERE ARRIVED 100 ENEMY REENFORCEMENTS FROM XC 795020, 70 MEN FROM XB 812019, 30 MEN FROM XB 775997, AND 150 MEN FROM XC 810036 (KAERONG MOUNTAIN). THESE MEN WERE COMPOSED OF BOTH NKA AND CCF, UNITED TO DRIVE OUR PARTISANS FROM THE AREA.

PART OF OUR PARTISANS RETREATED FROM THE AREA XC 774017 TO XC 770015, AND MADE A STRAIGHT DEFENSE LINE THERE. THE REST OF THE PARTISANS IN THE AREA XC 785009 RETREATED TO THE AREA XC 750015. OUR WOUNDED WERE EVACUATED TO XB 943982. A PART OF OUR AGENTS SUPPORTED THE COMBAT OF OUR PARTISANS, but THE PARTISANS HAD ALREADY RETREATED TO XC 758003. 90 NKA WERE ATTACKING OUR CP AND WE RETREATED TO XB 746017 TO XB 738992 AND CAME BACK TO OUR BASE MOSUM-DO.

We were pursued by fire from the shore, but happily *Ro-To-lti* monitored the radio transmissions to the Air Force. It shelled the beach, which ended any further enemy fire and enabled the junks to pick us up.

Ten guerrillas were dead in addition to my interpreter. Some of the dead were recovered, but most, including my interpreter, were left behind. In addition there were five seriously wounded and 12 slightly wounded partisans. Both Meeks and I escaped without a scratch.

We were on non-motorized boats with many casualties which I wanted to get to the guerrilla hospital on Paengnyong Do. Donkey I wanted to take his wounded and dead back to his Island HQ.

Before we could decide which course to follow, *Worthington* appeared and asked if there was anything it could do. I suggested that we put all of the wounded aboard so *Worthington's* medical personnel could treat them. Donkey I agreed to this. I went aboard with the wounded, MSG Meeks elected to accompany Donkey 1, the dead, and the remainder of the irregulars back to Kirin Do. The wounded received immediate and excellent medical care, which no doubt saved several lives.

It was well after dark when this was accomplished. When the wounded had been cared for, the captain of *Worthington* took me to the Ward Room. It was now about 2000 and I had not eaten for over 36 hours. The Captain ordered the bar opened and bought me a drink. After the Captain's initial gesture, almost every OFF aboard decided to follow suit. I finally had to beg off to avoid getting drunk. About midnight, after recounting the events of the day to various groups of interested and sympathetic Royal Naval Officers, a steward led me to a stateroom. Tired, completely drained physically and emotionally, I sank onto the bed without even taking a shower.

The next thing I was aware of was a rap on the door. A cockney voice said, "Sir, here's your tea."

A mess steward came in with a huge steaming mug of muddy looking liquid. It turned out to be very strong tea, liberally cut with evaporated milk, to which a huge amount of sugar had been added. It was horrible sweet and tasted terrible, but it revived me. As did the shower I took, though I had no clean clothes.

In the Ward Room I received a quick lesson in Royal Navy protocol. The steward told me to sit anyplace. Sitting between two officers I cheerfully said, "Good morning, gentlemen, how are you?" My efforts to start a conversation were met. with grunts and stares. It wasn't until later that I found out that it was the practice aboard ship that no one spoke until after breakfast. Despite my gaffe, the officers were most kind to me and the wounded guerrillas.

Worthington, through *Ro- To-Iti,* had contacted Leopard, whose motorize cargo junk, *The Ark,* was enroute to take the wounded and myself to Paengnyong Do. *Worthington* could not get close into shore because of her draft. Despite the hospitality aboard *Worthington,* I was delighted to see *The Ark* arrive and the wounded partisans transferred to it. CPL Brown was aboard *The Ark* as well as some of the medical personnel from our hospital.

Immediately after returning to Paengnyong Do I started to write my report, to rethink the entire sequence of the operation, what had gone wrong, lessons learned, how to insure that we would never again have such a disaster. Additional communications, a better interpreter, more detailed planning, all occurred to me. It seemed that there was a leak in the Leopard or Donkey organization; somebody had gotten information of the operation to the enemy. The order had been issued the afternoon before, so it was unlikely that a copy could have gotten into the hands of the north Koreans. Perhaps someone Donkey I had briefed, or discussed the raid with, had gotten word to the mainland (was LT Pak really sick?). In any event the enemy was waiting for us and had taken their toll.

It also appeared that we were using the guerrillas incorrectly; we were trying to fight conventional land warfare with troops whose training, temperament and desire was to hit and fade into the landscape. Was this the result of American pressure or the desire on the part of the advisors to participate in the raids? A more critical look at the plan showed that the tactics were more paramilitary than guerrilla. I was definitely at fault in not seeing that.

Our adversaries had consisted not only of NKA, but also Chinese Communist Forces (CCF). I had seen two different types of uniforms, one a CCF uniform. This was not only of considerable intelligence value, but was good news because it indicated that the irregular activities were causing the diversion of CCF to security missions. In that event our effort was successful.

The report (inclosed) from Donkey I was obviously inflated. How he arrived at the enemy casualty figures, I do not know. Even assuming naval gunfire and air strikes had hit lucrative targets, these casualty figures could not be justified.

Early in December, MAJ Dye, Bill Watson, Jim Mapp and I were playing cards in the officers Quonset hut. Suddenly there was a loud explosion, just outside our hut, followed by at least one more. Had a bomb struck the Island? We had expected that the enemy would someday determine that Paengnyong Do held both the HQ of the guerrilla activities and the AF radar station which controlled UN air strikes against North Korea and would try to knock out one or both. The explosions seem to come from the well area, which was in the center of our compound. Some stones or shrapnel had rattled on the roof of our hut, but there appeared to be no damage to it. The lights went out immediately, turned off by someone on duty in the commo shack (we were always blacked out at night). Or perhaps the generator had been knocked out. We were unable to get the commo shack on the telephone.

Someone had to make a check and notify our HQ in Seoul. As the S-3, that chore was clearly mine. I ducked out the door and headed for the Commo shack. The other three fanned out to various locations to get estimates of damage and to make certain that the compound defenses were fully manned. We were not sure if we would be bombed again or if there would be any follow-up on the ground by CCF or NKA forces.

Groping in the dark I managed to find my way to the radio bunker. The Commo SGT arrived at the same time. He quickly determined that the radio was intact, though some of our antennas had been blown down. A flash message notified FEC/LD that we had been bombed. The two of us then manned the switchboard which was flooded with reports. When we sorted them out, it appeared that the bomb (or bombs) had landed on the hillside just outside our perimeter doing little damage to Leopard Base.

The next day Paengnyong Do was inundated with AF personnel who made detailed studies of the bomb craters and collected the scrap for analysis. Later it was reported that "Bed Check Charlie" (a North Korean propeller-driven aircraft) had dropped the bombs. The raid coincided with the departure of President-elect Eisenhower from Seoul that evening. Eleven planes had participated in the raid, all of which had been shot down by antiaircraft fire or jet fighters.

A short time later, one of the guerrilla units reported that US or UN POWs were being held in the vicinity of Pyongyang, in North Korea. FEC/LD thought that it might be feasible to mount a partisan operation (OPN) to liberate them. As we began developing plans for the raid, it became obvious that more definite information was needed about the area before we could decide what forces to commit or the route by which we would extract the POWs to minimize danger to them. Leopard submitted a request for an aircraft in which 1LT Watson and I could make a recon of the reported POW location. At the same time, we could look at several other areas in which we were interested in conducting irregular operations. We were informed that the recon flight would be made on 8 Dec.

Bill Watson and I left Leopard Base on 7 December in order to be ready for the early morning take off on the 8th. On 8 Dec we arrived at K-16 at 0700; MAJ Freligh, the pilot, 1LT Hicks, the navigator and TSG Ledford, the flight engr met. us in the briefing room. We gathered around a map on which I pointed out the areas of interest to us, paying particular attention to the reported POW camp. The flight crew could not be told what was at those locations, because HQ had classified that information. The various recon zones would preclude pinpointing the POW camp as our primary area of interest; however, I emphasized that the Pyongyang location was our highest priority.

As I pointed out each location, MAJ Freligh groaned. He showed us an overlay on which was plotted the antiaircraft activity in the north. At each of the areas designated by us, heavy flak had been reported. MAJ Freligh wanted to modify the mission; I refused, telling him we had to look at those locations or abort the recon. He checked with his control and was told to attempt it.

The B26 Night Fighter/Bomber took off from K-16 about 1015. The aircraft has only one set of controls, the flight engr sits next to the pilot to monitor information recorded on the instruments and to make adjustments as needed, the navigator operates from the observation deck or "green house". Here he not only does his computations for navigation, but also for bombing runs. Our aircraft was not armed as its primary mission was reconnaissance. I was familiar with the B-26 as a result of my flight from Mindoro to Manila in 1945, and sat. in a jump seat between the pilot and the flight engr.

Between me and the pilot was a console of electronic gear including direction finding equipment, radios, radio compass, and the Identification, Friend or Foe (IFF). Bill Watson was in the "green house" with Hicks. We proceeded to all of the locations we were interested in, except the POW camp, which we were unable to get close to because of heavy antiaircraft activity.

As we reconned one site I noticed about 200 trucks of various types in a grove of trees. I pointed them out to Freligh and Hicks, suggesting that they request an air strike on the truck park. About 1145 our mission was complete except for the all-important POW camp. MAJ Freligh insisted that we could not get into that area. After checking with his controller, who concurred, we headed back for K-16. Aside from the fact that we had not been able to look at the area of primary interest, the mission had been uneventful and successful as far as the other reconnaissance targets were concerned.

We had been enroute to Seoul for 5 minutes when Freligh made an abrupt 180 degree turn heading the plane back north. When asked what was going on, the pilot explained that "Godfrey controller" had directed us to orbit over Cho Do and then lead in a flight of bombers on the truck concentration. We were to act as a spotting plane to pinpoint the target for the high performance jets.

Although interested in seeing those trucks knocked out, I protested, our mission might be put in jeopardy; it was important that we get back with the information gleaned from the recon, and that CCRAK be informed of our inability to determine anything further about the POW camp. However, Freligh said that he had to obey his controller. We orbited over Cho Do for about 45 minutes, which appeared to me an excessive amount of time to scramble a flight of bombers. Not being an expert on aerial tactics, however, I kept quiet. Eventually we received word that the bombers were approaching.

We led the way to the target area. Some of the trucks had disappeared but there was still significant numbers of them. As we swooped down directing the bombers to the target, I noticed that an antiaircraft gun had moved into the area. I was not familiar with NKA or CCF antiaircraft weapons, but I thought this might be a 37mm radar controlled gun, which had recently been reported in the theater. An intelligence bulletin had contained a picture which seemed to match this gun.

When we pulled out of our dive, the bombers dropped their ordnance, after which we went back for a bomb damage assessment. Even my inexperienced eyes could see that little damage had been done. The bombs dropped had been armed with delayed fuses, to judge by the craters; it seemed that by penetrating into the ground, the shrapnel effect had been lost. Only one or two trucks were burning and a like number were actually destroyed. Needless to say, the remaining trucks were moving out of the area.

Once again we headed back toward K-16 and once again we made a 180 degree turn. This time we headed back to the target area. MAJ Freligh explained that he had been ordered to orbit over the target; another flight of bombers armed with different ordnance had been scrambled and would be in the area soon. We were to keep an eye on the target to make sure all the trucks did not escape.

Protesting again, I became uneasy about our mission . We had been in that area for over an hour, and if there was in fact any antiaircraft capability there we were very vulnerable. Not only was the mission in jeopardy, but I was getting hungry! However, Freligh said that he had no choice; Godfrey controller directed him and his aircraft.

We orbited over the target area making wide circles; more of the trucks left, but there were still at least 50 remaining. As the bombers arrived and we started our dive toward the target, I saw the antiaircraft gun point toward us and fire. At least I saw smoke pour from the bore. Suddenly there was a sharp crack that sounded like a huge firecracker exploding. There was a hole in the side of the ship, just to the left of the pilot and the electronic console was a shambles. Apparently a round had detonated in it. That meant we were without electronics; we had no IFF, radio direction finder, or radio. But that was not the worst. The round had cut across the back of the pilot, perhaps damaging his spinal cord. He passed out and the plane immediately started to fall.

Instinct prompted me to grab the control and pull back on it so the plane headed up. Ledford, the flight engr, reached over and took action to put the plane back on an even keel. Making a hasty examination of the pilot, I could see there was some bleeding from his lower back, however, it was in a place difficult to get to. I got out the first aid kit, managed to stuff some sterile gauze and sulpha powder into the wound, and secured the dressing in place, hoping that I had at least stemmed the bleeding.

MAJ Freligh came to and said that he thought he could fly the aircraft if we set a direct course back. Now we were faced with the problem of entering friendly airspace, guarded by antiaircraft guns, without being able to identify ourselves. Of course the plane would be visually recognized, but when challenged we could not respond. But that was the least of our problems. When Freligh tried maneuver the aircraft, he discovered that he had no control over his legs. Apparently the wound had pinched some nerves or actually damaged the spinal cord, resulting in the paralysis of his lower limbs. In great pain, he kept blacking out. We attempted to get Freligh out of the pilot's seat to let either Ledford or Hicks fly the plane, but the cockpit was so cramped that we could not get enough leverage to lift him. Each time we tried, Freligh cried out in pain. Finally we gave up the attempt to move him. Freligh said he thought he could fly the aircraft without the use of the pedals if we would assist him. He could make wide, sweeping turns without the rudder. It would be difficult, but it seemed all we could do. My job was to keep the pilot conscious by lightly slapping his face and applying cold cloths to his forehead.

I suppose this is one of those times when we all prayed. With the pilot passing in and out of consciousness, the plane making frightening dives or rolls until I revived him or the engineer could get us back in a proper flying attitude, we faced death constantly. The plane entered friendly skies without incident, and MAJ Freligh headed directly for K-16. Several minutes out from the air field we watched as a fog rolled in completely obscuring the runway. A consultation between pilot, navigator and crew chief resulted in a decision to try for K-14 on the coast near Inchon. MAJ Freligh quickly headed for it, hoping that it might still be open.

A new worry, fuel, beset us. When departing from Seoul, we had anticipated a two hour flight; by this time we had been in the air for over four hours. We had little more leeway for additional changes of destination.

Shortly K-14 appeared and it was clear! Without attempting to get into the pattern or make a proper approach, the pilot lined up with the runway and began his descent. Just at that time a flight of jets took off. The fighters zoomed straight up at us, swerving just in time to avoid us. Their pilots must have cursed us; it was a touchy situation. MAJ Freligh did a fine job in landing the aircraft in his crippled condition. As soon as the wheels touched down, everyone took action! I turned off the ignition, the flight engr grabbed the brakes and the navigator readied a fire extinguisher. Immediately, there was a herd of vehicle around us, ambulances, fire trucks, MP jeeps.

When we attempted to slide open the canopy to get out of the cockpit, we found that it was stuck. The only way to leave the ship was to use the emergency exit, a trap door in the "green house". Watson, Hicks, Ledford and I crawled out of the navigator's compartment. People on the ground said they would take care of MAJ Freligh and the aircraft. It took them ten minutes to get the canopy off and to lift him out. We heard later that his paralysis was only temporary, he recovered fully.

We were whisked to the Air Field HQ where we were debriefed at length by the intelligence personnel. They were particularly interested in our description of the antiaircraft gun.

Ironically, the AF contemplated court-martialing MAJ Freligh for jeopardizing our reconnaissance mission. He had protested when Godfrey controller had ordered him back, and had shown true courage and professionalism in flying us back. I wrote a strong certificate outlining the events which had taken place and commending Freligh for saving the aircraft and the people on board. Following that experience, I gained new respect for AF pilots, their courage, skill and determination.

We finally got back to FEC/LD headquarters in Seoul late in the afternoon. Mac Austin carefully extracted every bit of intelligence from us. Later, a drink, a hot shower and a good dinner restored our spirits. Bill Watson and I flew back to Paengnyong Do the next morning. We still considered the raid on the POW camp, but intelligence began to flow back to us that the prisoners had been moved. Finally, after consultation with MAJ Dye, we recommended to HQ that we scrub efforts to locate or raid the POW camp.

By the time we recovered from the recon flight, preparations for Christmas were well under way. Christmas was a clear, cold day. All of the guerrilla leaders called on MAJ Dye and the Americans at Leopard Base, bringing presents and flowers. Local school children, dressed in colorful Korean clothes, visited the compound, sang carols, and presented OFFs and EM with bouquets, hand lettered and illustrated cards addressed to their "American Friends", and handkerchiefs and towel embroidered with Christmas decorations. Similar activities were conducted at the AF radar site and the USMC Advisory Team.

An Army Mess SGT, assisted by one US cook, supervised five Korean cooks, who produced good GI chow by carefully following instructions. When I visited the mess hall about 1000, I found it decorated colorfully in preparation for the traditional Christmas feast at 1300. Like all GI messes, ours had been issued extras to make the Christmas dinner very special. About 1230 someone noticed smoke coming from the mess hall. Within two minutes the whole structure erupted in flames and burned down completely. Fortunately, no one was injured or burned. What caused the fire we never determined. Though destruction of the building took only a few minutes, we could hear cans of juice and vegetables exploding as the heat intensified. Our mess personnel had worked hard to give us a special treat, but everything was now destroyed: the meal, the building, cooking equipment and food supplies. The Air Force and Marines rallied to our aid, first inviting us to share their Christmas dinners, then loaning us cooking gear until we could get more and rebuild our kitchen. This started immediately as we began erecting a prefabricated building already on the Island.

After the first of the year, I renewed my efforts to get transferred to the 2nd Div. Previous requests had been turned down. When I arrived in Korea, I had a job waiting ing for me in the 9th Infantry. Although COL Wilson had rotated back to the CONUS by this time, he had provided me with a letter of acceptance for transfer to the 2nd Div if I was released by FEC/LD. My third request, accompanied by a commitment for a one year extension to serve with the 2nd Div, was successful; both transfer and extension were approved. Orders assigning me to the 2nd Div arrived on the same day as orders placing me on TDY in Japan for five days of rest and recuperation (R&R). Although sorry to miss the chance to see Tokyo, I was happy with my transfer.

Leopard was informed by HQ in Seoul that a captain would arrive toward the end of January to replace me The day he was to arrive, I was at the beach to meet the aircraft as it landed on the hard packed sand. When it came to rest, out stepped an old buddy from the 504 and 508, Aldo Bettelli. We literally hugged each other. I was happy to see him, happier still that he was going to be my replacement. In the next few days, I briefed Al, recommended him highly to MAJ Dye and introduced him into the good graces of the Donkey Leaders.

The day before I left Paengnyong Do a ROK Army COL visited the Island. He pinned the Order of Wharang with Gold star on me and made other awards to Leopard personnel.

That night the Donkey Leaders had a party for me in the village. They presented me with a beautiful sterling silver saki pot. Local wisdom decreed that saki be heated only in sterling silver; wine heated in vessels of baser metals reacted with those metals to produce a toxic substance (most saki is heated in porcelain). Inscribed "To Captain Donald Seibert from all the Donkey Leaders", it is still a prized possession.

The next day I was at the beach early to meet the aircraft that would take me and my baggage to the beginning of a new assignment. As we took off for Seoul, I thought of the last landing we had attempted there - this landing at K16 was without incident. I spent the night at CCRAK HQ where I was first debriefed, then wined and dined by my friends Mac Austin and Al Roegge.

My orders directed me to report to the 100th Replacement Depot for movement to the 2nd Div. It proved to be a hectic, poorly supervised installation. Fortunately, I remained only overnight. The next morning, in company with many others, I mounted trucks for the short ride to the railroad station.

CHAPTER 9

MANCHU

The train station in Seoul was a barn-like building, through which a cold wind blew. Throngs of people were milling about as I arrived. At the Transportation Office I showed my orders to a bored NCO who informed me that the tram to Chorwon was on Track 3 and would leave in an hour and a half, 45 minutes late. I walked over and examined the train; an engine even then huffing steam, several box cars still being loaded, and five passenger cars. These last were primitive affairs, mostly wood, with cracked or broken windows and peeling paint. The seats were made of wood; some cars had small potbellied stoves which barely heated the corners in which they stood.

I wandered around the station, observing the mixed crowd: ROK soldiers and civilians; soldiers of the UN countries fighting in Korea: Belgian, British, Dutch, French and Turkish, as well as US soldiers. Several I took for Korean were in fact Thais. It was a fascinating scene.

The cold was intense; that winter of 1952 - 53 was an unusually cold one. The wind blowing across the Hahn River seemed to chill every bone in my body. Though well prepared for frigid temperatures, with longjohns, fatigues, field jacket and parka, the layers of clothing did little to keep the cold from penetrating to my skin. I was glad when the departure of the train was announced.

Shouldering my duffle bag and lifting my val-pak, I managed to find a seat in one of the wooden passenger coaches. With much jolting and rattling, with giant gasps of escaping steam from the engine, and with shrill whistle tooting, we began to move over the narrow gauge track out of Seoul north toward Chorwon. The engine chugged and strained for hours. It became colder and colder. Finally, we reached the end of the line. As I descended from the coach, I saw the twisted and mangled tracks on the road bed to the north.

A representative of the 2nd IN Div rounded up all of us destined for it; trucks took us to the Div Replacement Co. The OFFs were taken to Div HQ nearby where the G-L LTC Jim Bartholomees, greeted us. He took me to meet MG James C. Fry, the Div CG, who impressed me. During dinner at the Div HQ Mess, I was delighted to see Tom Tackaberry, Joe Lagatutta, Chester McCoid and other old friends, all on the Div Staff. The next morning John Kiser arrived and drove me to the 9th Infantry. John, now the Regt 8-2, was my sponsor. I was happy to see him, and later, Dave McNaught, the S-3, and other friends. When COL Wilson commanded the 9th Infantry, he had tried to get former 504 OFFs and NCOs assigned to it, so it was not surprising to find many of them there. John found me a place to sleep, then introduced me to the Regt Staff, who briefed me on the situation. Kiser told me that I would meet the Regt CO, COL Richard Steinbach, at the evening meal. The 9th was on line with three Bns committed and one in reserve (the Regt had a Thai Bn attached).

About 1700 John took me to the Regimental Officers' Mess Tent. The sight amazed me. There was a small bar in one end of the tent with a complete choice of drinks. Sipping Scotch and water I enjoyed a pleasant hour getting acquainted with the officers of the HQ. Just before dinner (1800) COL Steinbach came in. An imposing individual, most affable and friendly, he greeted me warmly, indicating that he would talk to me later about my assignment. He said that it was his policy to send all company-grade OFFs who joined the Regt to a rifle company initially to get them oriented on the terrain, situation, conditions, policies and fighting. Eventually he planned to bring me up to his Staff. Both COL Steinbach and his XO, LTC William Zimmerman, impressed me.

All the 9th IN HQ OFFs wore Infantry Blue scarves around their necks with a Regimental crest as a stickpin. John Kiser ceremoniously put me in uniform with the group just before we went to dinner. The other end of the mess tent contained a T-shaped table with sheets as table cloths. Candles in silver candelabra and china with the Regimental Crest and the Manchu Dragon adorned the dining table. When the 9th Infantry had been stationed in China during the Boxer Rebellion, it had adopted the five-toed dragon as its symbol, acquiring the name *Manchu*. The Regimental memorabilia was much in evidence. It was a pleasant meal. The food was outstanding considering that it was GI fare. I was told that one of the cooks had been a chef at the "21 Club" in New York City before he had been drafted. He could do wonders with government issue rations and made the best cream puffs (in combat!) I ever tasted.

Newly arrived officers were seated at the head of the table; being the senior one that evening, I sat between COL Steinbach and LTC Zimmerman. Steinbach told me he was assigning me to B Co, the worst unit in the 9th. Since I was an older, more experienced officer, he thought that I could bring it up to the standard he expected every Co in the Regt to meet. There is no better assignment in the Army than command of a rifle company, and no greater challenge or privilege than to work with the "worst company in the Regiment". I assured COL Steinbach that B Co would soon be the best one in the 9th Infantry, He went on to say that he planned to make me the S-3 when Dave McNaught left, but that I would spend a minimum of two months in B Co. If it was in shape by then, he would bring me up to understudy Dave until he left. All of this pleased me.

After dinner a projector was brought in and we watched a fairly current movie. The EM of HHC and the Reserve Bn also had movies every night. As I fell asleep in a tent with John Kiser and Dave McNaught, I felt at home. I was happy to be with them and with an American unit rather than with a guerrilla pack.

The next morning, John Kiser took me to the 1st Bn HQ where I reported to the Bn CO, Major John W. Carley, another friend from the 504. The XO, Bill Graves and the S-3, CPT George Jones, both of whom I knew, were Airborne and solid Infantrymen.

The 1/9 Staff briefed me. Later, John Carley talked with me about B Co, whose problems stemmed from a lack of leadership. Due to rotation and combat losses, an inexperienced and junior 1LT was commanding. While he was a good combat Plt Ldr, he was unable to get B Co to operate professionally. Carley told me that I would not assume command immediately. 1LT Anderson, the Co CO, was short several thousand dollars worth of equipment, mostly armored vests, and was to be given an opportunity to make up those shortages. Having left F Co under similar circumstances, I could sympathize with Anderson. John assured me that I would assume command the moment Anderson had his supplies under control. He told me to come back to the Bn CP for dinner that evening so that we could talk further and I could meet the other OFFs in HHC. He placed a jeep at my disposal so that I could go to B Co to meet the OFFs and key NCOs.

Immediately after lunch, I went to B Co. When I walked into the Orderly Tent, 1SG Cafora popped to and called Attention. He came forward, saluted and reported to me thinking that I was a staff officer from either Regt or Div. I introduced myself, shook hands with the First Sergeant, and told him that I was taking command of B Co shortly, whereupon he took me to 1LT Anderson's arctic tent (a small eight-sided tent used by officers in the field).

First Lieutenant Wayne E. Anderson was young, sharp, Airborne, too eager, too apologetic and too defensive. He had an excuse for everything before any question was raised. This is typical of many inexperienced officers, rather than being completely open with more senior officers, letting them see what is going on, permitting them to assess the situation, and waiting until asked about shortcomings or deficiencies, then explaining the reasons for them, they try to place blame elsewhere. The weak OFF gives excuses; the good OFF gives reasons.

There was an almost patronizing air about 1LT Anderson, as if he felt that I could not handle the job. He seemed to imply, "I am an experienced combat veteran who can clue you in before you take over so that you will not make any mistakes." After I had taken off my parka and he saw my CIB and jump wings, he became more tolerant. He briefed me on B Co, minimizing its capabilities, and gave me his assessment of the strengths and weaknesses of the OFFs and NCOs. He discussed the administration of the Co, as well as his combat experience with it, this last at great length. About 1500 1SG Cafora popped his head into the tent to remind the CO that there was a patrol briefing. Anderson asked if I wanted to hear the briefing. I did. He led the way. On the way I asked the First Sergeant to have my gear brought over from Bn, arrange a place for me to sleep (I had decided to stay with the Co), and dismiss the BN jeep. We arrived at the briefing tent, a squad tent with a make-shift sand table, where 1LT Anderson introduced me to 2LT Milton Benz and the patrol.

It was the policy in the 9th Infantry to use the Reserve Bn for most of the patrolling forward of the positions. By the time I joined the Regt, the lines had been stabilized and UN forces were in static defensive positions. Occasionally a unit would make a limited objective attack against the NKA or CCF to straighten the line, or conversely, the enemy did the same tiling, but basically there was little movement. The troops were in bunkers connected by trenches. The area between the UN/ROK/US lines and those of the NKA/CCF was a no man's land covered with plotted artillery and mortar concentrations and direct fire weapons. It was patrolled at night by both the enemy and our own troops.

The patrol before me would make a routine sweep of the Regt front. Benz was to lead the 10 or 12 men, essentially a squad. It surprised me that an OFF was going to lead the patrol instead of the SL or PSG, I had heard rumors of patrols going out only a few yards in front of their units and sitting down until it was time to return. Perhaps this was to prevent such action. During the briefing, Benz turned to Anderson and asked him what position he wanted to take in the patrol. Anderson opted to be the third man behind the point. It shocked me that the Co CO would accompany such a patrol. 1LT Anderson then turned to me and said,

"Captain, would you like to accompany the patrol?"

"No thank you. I see no need for me."

Anderson gave me an odd look before telling Benz to continue the briefing. Benz impressed me as a confident, stable young Plt Ldr; the men seemed to relate to him fully. He gave a good order, with everything in hand. At the conclusion of the briefing he asked me if I had any questions. My two queries concerned supporting fires and reserves. There was a back-up unit, a squad similar in size to that of the patrol, which was to stay behind the Main Line of Resistance (MLR) ready to reinforce or rescue the patrol if it got into trouble. Artillery and mortar concentrations were available on call On the spur of the moment I said that I would remain with the back-up squad at the MLR. It would give me an opportunity to see how the patrol went, to learn the procedures, and to get to know something of the terrain. This was more important than going back to Bn for dinner with John Carley.

As we were walking back to the Orderly Tent after the briefing, Anderson said, "You know, CPT, that was a bad mistake you made. You shouldn't have refused to go on the patrol."

Looking at him coldly, surprised at such a blunt statement, I asked, "What do you mean, LT?"

"Well, the troops like to know that you aren't afraid. I go on every patrol and I think they respect me for it."

Stopping short, I said, "LT, you and I need to talk. You're entirely wrong. You've a Co of 185 men to take care of. But you are putting yourself in the position of a Squad Leader or rifleman. You are going on patrol to convince yourself of your personal courage. You are not leading your Co. The 170 men staying behind need your guidance, need your leadership. The patrol needs your support if it gets into trouble. You can't give them any if you are pinned down with a 10 man patrol. You should be back on the MLR monitoring, ready to react. You're entirely wrong. The troops don't respect that kind of nonsense. They are not going to question your bravery if you don't go on every patrol. They want to know that someone is looking out for them."

Continuing in the same vein for another few minutes, I noted that my remarks did not sink in; Anderson still thought a Co CO should lead every combat action, regardless of size. I pointed out to him that if it was a Co operation, obviously he should lead it. If it was a reinforced Plt he might consider leading it, although he should have enough confidence in his Plt Ldrs to permit them to do their job. To go on every patrol was an admission that he distrusted his OFFs and NCOs. I talked at length because the lieutenant seemed to need guidance in leadership and command.

At the Orderly Tent, I called MAJ Carley to tell him that I would remain with B Co. The 1SG had another arctic tent pitched close to the Co CO's and the Orderly Tent. He had also had the Supply Sergeant assemble a set of organizational equipment, including a carbine. I asked that it be exchanged for an M-1 and a cartridge belt.

Chow was served at 1700 in the usual field mess line. A little disorganized, but adequate. While the men were going through the mess line I talked with the Mess Sergeant. He was an old pro; with proper guidance and supervision he would soon have an outstanding mess. But it was not yet my Co, so I gave no instructions or advice. All I did was look and think. I met the XO, 1LT Jim Johnson and the other two Rifle Plt Ldrs, 2LTs Ken Powers and Jim Black.

It had gotten dark about 1630, so the men ate in the dark. Then the patrol and back-up loaded onto trucks for the move to the MLR. I was completely disoriented on the move forward. Although I had a map and tried to follow the road, there was not much to see in the dark. The trucks stopped at the bottom of a hill; as we started to climb toward the bunkers on the reverse slope, there was the telltale "Plop" and "whoosh", which signaled a mortar attack, several rounds landed in the valley just below us. Our trucks had moved out the instant the last man dismounted, so were in no danger. We took cover in the mess bunker of the Co we were to patrol through. Mortar rounds peppered the reverse slope of the hill we were on, but no one was injured. It appeared to be Harassing and Interdiction (H&I) fire which ceased as suddenly as it started. It put us all on alert, a good thing in the case of the patrol.

Benz, Anderson and I went to the Co CP Bunker to coordinate the patrol's passage through the lines and back. The Co had been alerted by Regt and Bn but last-minute details had to be nailed down. While Benz was talking with the Arty FO, I talked with the Co CO (another Captain). During the half hour till H-Hour I talked with some of the men. At the appointed time, 2LT Benz called his group together and they silently filed into the dark. The SGT bringing up the rear of the patrol muttered as he passed me, "Sir, thank God we've finally got somebody to look out for us." Smiling in the dark I wondered if Anderson had heard the remark and if he had, whether he would now understand what I had tried to explain to him. These troops wanted to know, deserved to know, that somebody was indeed looking out for them.

The patrol completed its mission with no contact. The sweep took several hours, so it was midnight by the time we got back to the Co area. The cooks had hot coffee" waiting for the troops who shortly bedded down.

The First Sergeant told me that reveille was at 0600. Getting up a little after five, I wandered over to the kitchen. The Mess Sergeant was there working harder than his cooks or KPs. He gave me a hearty "good morning", offered me a cup of coffee and was amazed when I refused it. There was no can of hot water at the head of the mess line. I suggested to the Mess Sergeant that if he had an extra GI can, he might put it at the head of line filled with hot water so the men could rinse the metal trays to take the chill from them. If fried eggs are put on cold trays, the grease congeals and makes them unappetizing. He immediately went to do that. It is a routine procedure which apparently had not been emphasized before. No OFFs other than myself were in evidence as I wandered about the Co area.

At 0600 1SG Cafora blew his whistle. The men stumbled out of their tents and fell into ranks, reports were given. I stood behind the Co facing the 1SG, expecting the Co CO or DO to step forward. No OFF appeared. This was a combat situation; the Co was part of the Regt Reserve, ready for immediate commitment. Seeing me standing behind the formation the 1SG tried to report to me, but I waved refusal, telling him to carry on. He received the reports from the PSGs, made a few announcements, then dismissed the men.

Returning to the chow line, I replaced the KP serving the coffee, kidding with the men without holding up the line, asking them about themselves, associating names and faces, especially those of the NCOs. They looked like a good bunch. There was nothing wrong with the men in B Co. In fact, there was nothing wrong with B Company except the leadership at the top.

As the day passed I became more and more impatient to take command. In the afternoon I pushed Anderson, asking when he would be ready to turn over the Co. He gave me an evasive answer. He was short about 40 armored vests which represented quite a bit of money. I told him to concentrate on the property as I did not want a prolonged overlap. Not a great believer in long break-in periods, I particularly disliked overlaps in command. Obviously there are a few tilings a new commander has to be briefed on, but that can be done in a matter of hours, not days. Again that night Anderson went on patrol; again, I stayed with the back-up force. While waiting, the Co CO whose area we operated through gave me a good appreciation of the situation facing the 9th Infantry.

The next morning was a repeat of the one before, except that I avoided the reveille formation. While I was in the chow line serving coffee, there was a commotion in the line. Turning the coffee ladle over to one of the KPs, I went to the head of the line to find out what the trouble was.

"Get out of the line, gook."

"Me in hurry."

"I don't give a shit, take your turn."

"Officers in hurry."

Snatches of talk reached me. The men were complaining because some Korean "houseboys" for the Co OFFs, were trying to break into the chow line. When I asked what the problem was, the first Korean said, "Me LT Anderson's houseboy. Me get chow for LT Anderson. GI no let me in."

The next one was LT Johnson's houseboy, the third LT Benz's and so on. The men were visibly upset. It was a petty matter but one which reflected their dissatisfaction with the leadership of B Co. It was time to take Command.

"Okay, you houseboys get at the end of the line. When the troops are all finished, you can go through."

"Oh, this is terrible, this is terrible. Lieutenant won't like."

"I don't care whether the Lieutenant likes it or not. That is the way it is going to be. Move!"

The Koreans reluctantly went to the end of the line. Acting on my decision I went to the Orderly Tent, called MAJ Carley and told him I wanted to assume command right away. LT Anderson would be relieved of his duties as Co CO and could spend the next few days getting his property straightened out. I would sign for the property currently available but the final turn over in accountability would be delayed until he was ready to do so, provided he didn't string it out too long. MAJ Carley agreed.

"Okay, I'll be up there right after breakfast and we'll effect the change."

About 0800 MAJ Carley arrived, formerly relieved LT Anderson and installed me as Co CO. There was no ceremony, but Carley thought he should officially notify Anderson that he was no longer Commander.

Without preamble I took over. The first order of business was a meeting of the OFFs, during which they were instructed to be at reveille every morning prepared to be with their units throughout the day. In a few sentences I outlined my views on command and control, advised the officers that I expected them to command their platoons, and laid down my basic policies. I told the Plt Ldrs that

I would get into internal Plt affairs only after they had exhausted all their means and came to me for help. As stated before, I have never believed that a new commander should delay making changes if he sees something wrong. It is counter-productive to make changes simply to demonstrate that a new order has arrived, but every individual, every commander, has different priorities, different views, different ways of handling a situation. If he doesn't exercise his best judgement and leadership from the time he assumes command of a unit, then it will not be an effective one.

Next was a meeting with the NCOs, with their Plt Ldrs present. Again, my plans and policies were outlined. Without further explanation I announced that I would not accompany a patrol unless it was larger than a reinforced platoon, and even then it would depend on the situation. It was evident, though no one said so, that this was a relief. They understood and welcomed such a policy. When the meeting was opened for questions, one of the PSGs asked my policy on beer. When I looked puzzled, he explained that in reserve the men were authorized four cans of beer per night. They bought the beer in case lots, however. There was an administrative hassle in doling out the beer each evening. Would I permit them to keep the cases in their tents? "Certainly. But I expect you NCOs to see that the policy is enforced and that every man is in condition to move out at a moment's notice. Our men are not children. They can police themselves. But I don't want to hear about any beer being stolen or about any fights over it. You NCOs exert your leadership and watch the weak ones."

The next morning B Co fell out for reveille as usual with all Plt Ldrs present. After taking the report from the 1SG, I put the Co at ease, formally introduced myself as their new Commander, told them how proud I was to have such a position of trust, and promised them that with their support we would soon be the best Company in the 9th Infantry. When I turned the Co back to 1SG Cafora, he announced that training that day would be a conditioning march and terrain orientation. The uniform was light packs and weapons. The men then went to breakfast, the OFFs had been told that they would eat after the troops.

At 0800 Cafora fell the Company out again; the troops had their light combat packs and weapons as prescribed for the march. But none of the NCOs or Plt Ldrs had their packs. All they had were cartridge belts and a weapon. I called them together and gave them three minutes to get their equipment before the Company moved out. Both OFFs and NCOs were told that from then on they would carry the same equipment as the troops. This was not a training session at Fort Benning, but a rifle company in combat! I was incensed.

As we moved out I set a brisk but normal pace - about three miles per hour. We took the usual breaks every hour, during which the lead platoon was rotated to the rear, and I walked the length of the column inspecting the men and talking with them. I noticed that 2LT Benz, who had made a very favorable impression on me as a solid Infantry commander even that early, started to limp. It was only after we got back that I realized that he had on thermal boots (the troops called them Mickey Mouse boots). The arctic or thermal boot was made of rubber with air pockets for insulation. They did not "breathe" like leather boots and were not suited for road marches. The feet sweat and rub and become sore when the wearer does much walking or other exercise. They were really made for static situations. Apparently, Benz had fallen out with them and hadn't had time to change to his regular boots. He acquired many blisters. It was a lesson for him, but also another lesson for me; make sure that I inspected all the troops, including OFFs, thoroughly. Routinely I had done this before, but it never occurred to me to do the same for the Plt Ldrs. I had assumed that they could take care of themselves. It was a mistake Benz never repeated.

When we arrived back in the Co area about 1600, 1SG Cafora informed me that the Co had been alerted. At Bn HQ the S-2 briefed me that there was reliable intelligence that forward Manchu elements would be attacked that evening. Our alert was a routine precaution.

After chow, the Plt Ldrs were directed to inspect their units for readiness. Though the only beer was so-called military beer (3.2 percent alcohol), consumption was limited to two cans per man for this evening. The routine patrol returned about 2300, permitting me to crawl into my sleeping bag a bit early. I had just gotten to sleep, when Cafora shouted that I was wanted on the phone. The S-3 advised me that the Reserve had been ordered to a forward assembly area because the CCF had attacked the 2nd Bn. The 1SG had waited for my orders; as soon as I hung up I ordered him to fall out the Co on the double. Trucks were already moving into the Company area.

The troops responded well. Within 20 minutes we were on our way to the assembly area, where MAJ Carley briefed the Co COs on the situation. I also had an opportunity to talk briefly with Dave McNaught who was at the Regt FWD CP.

The 1/9 was prepared to either counterattack or relieve the 2/9. The situation was grim; the CCF had gotten into the trenches where hand-to-hand fighting was taking place. Though the 2nd Bn was holding its own, the Bn CO had called for Variable Time (VT) fire on his position. He ordered his men into the bunkers just before the VT concentration arrived on target; it caught the CCF in the open, killing many of them. By 0600 the situation had stabilized; the 2/9 had driven the enemy off, and the 1st Bn was released to return to its area.

A week after assuming Command I signed for the property from 1LT Anderson. Though given every opportunity to locate or account for the armored vests, he had not reduced the shortage very much. Apparently he had made no effort to control them. They were a hot item on the Black Market. Anderson could drop some of them on a Korean Certificate of Loss (KCL), an avenue open to accountable OFFs for losses suffered during combat, but in our stabilized situation, this would be scrutinized critically. One of the problems was that the vests were not taken from the wounded when they were evacuated. I told the XO and Supply Sergeant to give me their recommendations on procedures for control over the vests within a few days. The detailed accounting procedures, including having each man sign for his vest, were onerous, but necessary. This was a specific mission given to the XO, one I supervised closely.

By the time I signed for the property, things started to fall into a pattern that I liked. Company B settled into a routine, accepting my policies readily. In addition to the careful instructions I gave to the Supply Sergeant, I told the Mess Sergeant that I wanted the best mess in the 9th IN, not to win any contests but because the troops deserved it. LT Johnson, the XO, was made both Supply and Mess Officer.

Two weeks after I assumed command of B Co, I was called to the Bn CP for a meeting. During the meeting it was announced that Bill Graves, who was rotating to the CONUS, was being replaced by MAJ Leroy Stanley. Stanley had been in my Advance Class at Benning. While I was sorry to see Bill leave, I was pleased that he was going to be replaced by an old friend. But the main purpose of the meeting was to alert us that the 1st Bn was relieving the 3rd; B Co would take over I Co's position. Hill 159, the I Co position, was an exposed finger covering the "Bowling Alley" (a flat straight valley). One Plt was located at the very tip of the ridge looking into the valley. That position, we discovered, could be reached only by a series of trenches in a bad state of police and repair.

On my return to B Co I briefed my OFFS and the First sergeant. The relief was classified as "need to know", but the Plt Ldrs, XO and Cafora definitely needed to know. Regt had authorized a small recon party to establish liaison. The XO, Plt Ldrs and Commo SGT went forward with me. We used 3/9 vehicles to get to the I Co positions.

The condition of both I Co and its area was a shock. The troops were literally cowering in their bunkers, afraid to move around. The entire Co area, particularly the trenches, was in need of work. The trenches had crumbled in spots and were loaded with junk: commo wire, ammunition boxes, debris of all kinds. It was a messy position, but worse still was the morale of the men. Everyone kept telling me how exposed they were, that they were under constant fire, that B Co would have to be extremely careful during the relief because the position might be overrun.

When I talked to the Co CO, the reason for this situation became obvious. He was the one who was completely whipped. He was either worn out or he was a very weak OFF. He apparently exerted no positive leadership, was afraid and exuded fear. I Co took its cue from its CO; he admitted that he had ordered the tanks, recoilless weapons and mortars not to fire because the fire was returned by the enemy and that meant that someone might be killed! When the mortars registered a new concentration, for instance, the enemy immediately fired several mortar rounds also. Each time the attached tank platoon fired, there was instant retaliation.

Not only was the situation shocking, but it was hard to believe that it had existed for several weeks. The problem was that it was difficult to get to the I Co position. The rear dropped to a valley which led north and was under direct Chicom observation. Every time a vehicle entered the valley, it was subjected to artillery or recoilless weapons fire. Even foot movement would evoke fire. Hence, traffic was restricted to essential medical, supply and commo vehicles, and other traffic had been curtailed. The Bn and Regt CDRS must have visited I Co periodically, but for some reason no corrective action had been taken. It was a miserable situation over which my Plt Ldrs shook their heads as we compared notes after our recon.

While at I Co, I discussed with its CO the exchange of equipment to minimize the relief, some would be left on site for us, but my OFFS wanted their own weapons. The Commo NCO, SGT Oswald, was speechless over the amount of wire in the trenches.

CPT James Denby, the Arty FO, who was also a Battery Commander in the New Zealand (NZ) Arty Bn supporting the area, introduced himself. We discussed the custom of British Commonwealth Armies which dictated that the battery commander be the FO for his battery. It got good results! When the FO called, the battery responded. Of course he was not at his gun positions to run his battery, his XO (called No 1) did that for him. CPT Denby and his party were impressive contrasts to the I Co personnel.

All possible coordination was effected for the relief as this was the only opportunity we would have to effect liaison due to security and the problem of enemy observed fire. It was essential that the routine and traffic flow remain unchanged because any deviation would signal the relief. 2LT Powers remained on the position to maintain contact and learn everything he could about it and the situation.

On the night scheduled, the relief was effected without serious incident. But my convoy got lost. I was in the lead truck (we had decided not to take any jeeps), the driver of which had made many supply trips to I Co. He assured me that he knew the way. Our liaison trip had been made in the daytime, so I found it hard to follow our route on my map in the dark. At one fork the driver continued straight. I had the uneasy feeling that we should have turned right. Suddenly we were in the open. A quick reading of the terrain indicated that we had passed into the valley between the opposing forces! Without urging, the driver turned the vehicle (fortunately the terrain was flat and clear at that point) and the convoy moved out rapidly regardless of noise. We were highly exposed; if the enemy had fired at that time we would have sustained a great many casualties. Strangely, there was no fire though the CCF must have heard the sound of the truck engines, possibly even seen the black out lights. We found the fork, took the correct branch and soon reached the bottom of the hill behind I Co. Lessons relearned: post guides at all critical junctions; have a knowledgeable guide in the lead vehicle.

The relief itself went well. There was the normal confusion of people getting lost in the dark, misplaced packs or stumbling over unseen obstacles. But my Plt Ldrs had mapped their positions carefully, knew exactly where each squad was to go, and the I Co guides were unexpectedly effective, so things moved smoothly and rapidly.

The 1st Plt, under 2LT Benz, whom I considered the strongest Plt Ldr I had, was assigned the most exposed position. As the worst position, it would require strong leadership to get it up to the standard I expected. 2LT Powers' Plt had the second most critical position. By midnight I assumed control of the area and relieved the I Co CO of his responsibilities. It was with great relief that he left to go into the Reserve area. We received an H&I mortar round that night but no one was hurt. Nothing occurred to mar the relief.

As soon as it was daylight, my Plt Ldrs began calling the CP. There were signs forward of the bunkers reading, "Welcome Baker Company". Little "ditty bags" stuffed with peace propaganda were hung in the barbed wire in front of the positions. Chinese intelligence was good.

The Mess Sergeant had a good breakfast that first morning. CPT Denby's batman (orderly), Paddy, immediately made friends with him. Paddy loved GI pancakes. That was the menu that first morning; Paddy must have eaten a dozen. He once ate 57 at one sitting in a contest with one of my soldiers. Paddy took good care of CPT Denby. He was a natural comic who always said something funny at a critical time that broke the tension. Such people are invaluable in any tense combat situation.

There was a small combat command on Hill 159. In addition to B Co and the NZ FO party, there were attached tank and 75mm recoilless rifle Plts, a section of HMGs, an intelligence unit with radar and radios, a counter-mortar radar and other elements. Since the position thrust into the enemy area, there were a few more people than would normally be found in a rifle company area. That first morning I had a meeting with the attached unit CDRS and LNOs to introduce myself and establish my policies. During the meeting I asked the Tank Plt Ldr (a MSG) what his targets had been. With a sheepish look he admitted that he had not fired his tanks in two weeks!

"Why there are all sorts of targets available for tank gunnery. I can see a dozen exposed bunkers at a glance. Can't your tanks knock out bunkers? Don't you have enough ammunition? What's the problem?"

"Sir, we have lots of ammo; I've been scrounging it. And we can really do a job on bunkers. I have all kinds of targets spotted, but I was ordered not to fire." This last was said almost pleadingly.

"Well, after this meeting you and I will set priorities and you will start firing your tanks daily."

He beamed. He was so pleased he wanted to go right out and start firing. I had to restrain him. He had been a tank gunnery instructor at the Armor School at FT Knox before being assigned to Korea, knew tank gunnery well and how to get the most out of his tanks. He had been denied the opportunity to exercise his skill and was frustrated. After the meeting we discussed procedures. The tanks would fire daily on a random time schedule. He was to contact the Plt Ldrs to get their targets, as well as develop his own. Then he would set up his missions in accordance with the priorities I established. The Regt was under an available supply rate (ASR) which limited the number of rounds which could be fired each day, but since he had stockpiled ammo the ASR proved no handicap. He and his Platoon destroyed a large number of bunkers taking of several potential threats to the area.

The same was true of the attached 75mm recoilless rifle Plt. The recoilless rifles drew so much response whenever they were fired, that it became necessary to warn the troops when they were to shoot so they could get under cover to avoid the immediate counterfire that rained in on us.

I insisted that not only the tank guns and recoilless rifles be fired daily, but all weapons on the hill. The Plt Ldrs took some license with this directive. Each evening just before chow, there erupted a mini-mad-minute during which all small arms as well as crew served weapons were fired. The only exceptions I directed after the first startling outburst (the Plt Ldrs had gleefully coordinated with all elements on the hill and set a time for that initial demonstration without informing me) were the 75s and those weapons under an ASR. The tanks joined happily in the firing. I also insisted that crew served weapons, as well as the tanks, fire on identified targets. The firing lasted only a minute or two, insured that all weapons were firing, gave the men a charge of adrenalin and added to our readiness posture. The expenditure of ammunition was fully justified in my view.

It took only a day or two to shake down, but it took two or three weeks to get the area cleaned up and repaired. The basic position was well organized, but had deteriorated from lack of care. On each visit COL Steinbach would mention commo wire in the trenches (each time a round cut a wire I Co had laid another instead of tracing down the break and splicing it;, hence there was a jumble of wire which no one could sort out). I knew we had to do something about it, and eventually we just got rid of the tangle in the trenches; but it was a matter of priorities. We got it cleaned up in time.

A week after B Co went on line, we were alerted one day that an intelligence unit would arrive to coordinate an operation with us. That night 1LT Bud Hillman, a friend from the 504, arrived. He was assigned to CCRAK as a Technical Liaison Officer (TLO). His job was to put Korean intelligence teams through American lines to infiltrate enemy positions, gather information and bring it back. Bud brought his teams to a forward Co, put them through the lines, then came back to pick them up as they returned at a prearranged time. I was familiar with the TLO effort, knew what to expect and how to support it. Though not convinced that the teams were overly successful, nevertheless, it seemed it was worth the effort if one out of 15 returned with usable information. It was good to talk with Bud while he was on this mission.

B Co quickly settled into an orderly procedure. A master plan was developed to clean up and rebuild the position and ready it for combat. Within several weeks there was a noticeable difference. COL Steinbach visited our position frequently, MAJ Carley almost daily, and MAJ Stanley often, all had helpful "suggestions" on each trip!

When Stanley first arrived, he told the Co COs that he would take care of all supply problems (as Bn XO he supervised administration and logistics for the Bn Co). B Co had the usual minor supply problems. Restrictions on ammo (ASR), especially on 6Omm Mortar ammo, precluded firing in response to reports from listening posts during the night. The men liked the 6Omm mortar flares which could illuminate the area directly to their front. But we never had enough to satisfy them. Sandbags always seemed in short supply. They rotted in the rainy season and had to be replaced periodically. The delivery of supplies and rations posed the biggest problem, since the supply vehicles usually came under fire. This necessitated random scheduling of deliveries. A minor but annoying problem resulted from the length of time it took to get supply vehicles to B Co. Whenever there was ice cream on me menu (in combat!!), it arrived soft. Since Stanley had offered to take care of our supply problems, I mentioned it to him, half in jest. Leroy tried his best to find a solution, there was none. I continued to needle him, until it became a standing joke. Years later I would greet him with "My ice cream's melted", causing both of us to laugh,

B Co proved its mettle by adjusting quickly to the situation and the position. There was none of the low morale or abject fear apparent in the unit we had replaced. There were problems, of course, but none serious. We settled into a routine. Normally, I went to bed after the patrols were in, a little after midnight, and got up about 0400. Bn had ordered a pre-dawn stand-to or 100% alert. This is ordinarily the time of minimum alertness of American troops, because they are tired, cold, and miserable. The theory was that placing the unit on 100% alert just before dawn would frustrate any effort to take advantage of the fatigue and boredom of the men. The Co would "stand-to" a half hour before dawn and go back to its normal schedule after daylight, when breakfast would be served.

In the winter, the morning stand-tos were particularly unpleasant. The troops were routed from warm sleeping bags to don cold-soaked parkas and boots. The period just before dawn was the coldest part of the night. Still drugged with sleep, with little movement to increase circulation or generate warmth, the men shivered as they peered into the dark. Familiar bushes and rocks became enemy soldiers that seemed to move, convincing the half awake watchers that the NKA or CCF were about to infiltrate their position. As it became colder, the black gave way to gray; the sky slowly lightened, surroundings became more distinct and once more familiar. Many days it was overcast so there was no pink dawn or sudden appearance of the sun. Finally at daylight, the cramped, frigid soldiers were permitted to leave their positions to prepare for the day's activities. When the intense cold of winter gave way to chilly summer mornings, the "rosy-fingered dawn" more frequently cheered the bored, weary troops.

The normal schedule called for a third of the Company sleeping, a third on alert, and a third working. This was difficult to follow fully, and rather than insist on a rigid split, I left it to the Plt Ldrs to organize the work shifts as they saw fit. Some form of this three-way split schedule insured that the position was secure, the men rested and alert, and that work was accomplished to improve the defenses. For chow, one third of each Plt or unit rotated back to the mess bunker in turn.

Several bunkers had to be rebuilt. Rains had weakened the foundations under the heavy twelve foot long 12X12s. Replacing them, getting the timbers delivered to the bottom of the hill behind the Co, then manhandling them into position on the ridge, was hard work. But the men did a fine job for me; very soon I was proud of the position.

In the evenings while the patrols were out, CPT Denby and I talked at length. He was a school teacher in New Zealand, a member of the Territorial Forces, or Reserves, which had been called up for Korea. Jim was articulate, enthusiastic, interested in everything, an excellent Artilleryman; we became fast friends. He was an asset, because of him, we never wanted for fire.

Bn notified us late one afternoon that intelligence sources had determined that the NKA or CCF to our front planned to attack our position that evening. Such information was obtained by radio intercept of messages and analysis of radio traffic. It was predicted that the attack would come about 0200. Many NCOs and OFFS doubted the validity of the warning. With more confidence in that kind of intelligence and determined that we would be prepared for the attack, I gave orders that a minimum lookout be maintained prior to midnight, while the majority of the men turned in early to get as much rest as possible. A 100% alert would be called sometime after midnight; the exact time of the stand-to would be decided as additional information came in. The alert posture would be maintained as long as appropriate.

We had been subjected to intermittent H&I mortar fire every evening; rarely, there would be a prolonged mortar or artillery attack. During such attacks Oswald, the Commo SGT, was constantly out under fire, repairing breaks in the wires to maintain communications within the Co and to Bn.

One of the problems that most units in Korea faced after the lines had stabilized was a penchant on the part of senior commanders to play squad leader. As soon as a unit was under fire, some higher HQ (often back to Corps) tried to get into direct communications with the unit commander (in some cases the patrol leader!). They wanted continuing and immediate reports without giving the commander on the ground an opportunity to sort out the reliable from unreliable accounts or to evaluate the raw information. They flooded him with questions, advice, and orders; in general they distracted him from fighting his unit. This is perhaps inherent in static warfare, but I doubt if any Army was ever plagued before by the degree of high level command of such lowly forces as we experienced in Korea. Good communications made the problem worse. It is a lesson needing constant emphasis. Commanders must trust their subordinate unit leaders to fight their battles. If it becomes apparent that a subordinate cannot handle the job, then he must be replaced. Senior CDRs should have faith in the OFFs they accord the privilege of command.

SGT Oswald had a standing order to pull the wires from the switchboard as soon as we were under fire. This prevented harassment by Bn, Regt, Div and Corps. It was not overly forthright, but I believe that many junior commanders did the same thing. There was still communication by radio and the wires could be reattached whenever necessary. In addition, it was possible to communicate through the Artillery net in an emergency. It left me free to handle the reports from my subordinates, to evaluate what was going on, to get to the Platoons if necessary and to fight the battle. There was always a nagging concern that a Bn wire team would begin tracing the wire from their end looking for a break in it (fortunately, none ever did).

On this particular night Hill 159 was on full alert by 0049. The men were out of their sleeping bags, had on steel helmets and "flak jackets" (armored vests) and were manning their weapons. Patrols had been established between positions to insure that the trench system was not infiltrated. All of the FOs (artillery, tank, recoilless rifle and mortar) were vigilant and their crews ready. B Co, reinforced, was prepared to repel an attack.

About 0130 mortar rounds began to come in. As this occurred nightly, no great significance was attributed to it at first. It did happen to coincide with the time intelligence indicated that the attack was to come. The intensity of the mortar fire increased. At exactly 0200 the CCF did attack. The 1st Plt on the exposed end of Hill 159 took the brunt of the assault, although the entire ridge was hit. Very heavy mortar fire continued. I wanted to go to the 1st Plt, but the fighting was heavy throughout the entire Co position so I elected to stay at the CP with the communications rather than try to get to any one Plt. I did not want to be one of the senior OFFs usurping command.

Benz did a superb job and the 1st Plt fought well. The attack was repelled after some limited hand-to-hand fighting in the trenches. When the enemy was reported in the trenches, I had all of the Co HQ personnel alerted and gathered in the mess bunker to provide a reaction force if needed. The major attack had been stopped forward of the position with a mass of fire. Every weapon fired. Planned concentrations were fired by all indirect fire weapons from 60mm mortars to Corps Artillery. CPT Denby shifted fires as I followed the course of the battle, literally encircling the hill (Point 159 he called it) with a "ring of steel". It was a well-fought battle, though essentially an exchange of fire power.

As soon as it was apparent that the attack was checked, I went to the 1st Plt area, where I was given graphic accounts of the battle. Moving from bunker to bunker, I told all members of the Plt how well they had fought. I also talked with the wounded which we finally evacuated (my medical training came in handy as I was able to alert the Bn Aid Station as to the type of casualties to expect). The only man killed in the attack was my Commo NCO, SGT Oswald. When the line went out to the 1st Plt, he plunged out of the CP bunker to repair it and was killed by a mortar round. He was a great loss to me personally as well as to the Co. An excellent soldier, a fine man, he was determined to maintain communications even at the cost of his life.

Bn had been kept well informed by radio and through the ARTY net. When the fighting was over we reconnected our switchboard and gave a full report. At daylight, MAJ Carley came up to look at the area and discuss the situation with me. Each Plt Ldr gave him a report on the action in his sector. Though reluctant to disturb the 1st Plt with too many visitors, MAJ Carley did go to the position. He understood my concern about giving the men time to unwind, to get themselves and the position cleaned up. It was wrecked from the fire it had received. There was debris in the trenches and the men were tired and still taut. MAJ Carley understood this and made no comments other than to commend the men for a good fight.

Later that morning COL Steinbach visited Hill 159. He went out to talk with Benz and to assess the situation. He did not compliment the 1st Plt on their action. Perhaps he did not fully understand that it had taken the brunt of the attack, although I thought that I had made this clear in my report Instead he displayed considerable annoyance at the amount of debris in and around the position and wanted an immediate police. This is one of the few times I disagreed with him. I tried to point out to him that the men were tired and drained, that some were on alert, some sleeping and the few available for work couldn't do it all at once. Benz had a plan, using the three squad system, to get it all done in an orderly fashion and in a reasonable time. But Steinbach was insistent that the position be cleaned up immediately. Perhaps he did not want the men to relax their guard, or engage in either self-congratulation or self-pity. But it appeared to me that he did not appreciate time and manpower limitations. Overall he seemed satisfied with the way B Co, reinforced, had performed.

The immediate problem, in addition to a thorough police of the position, was to insure that our communications were in and functioning. SGT Oswald was sorely missed at this point. We had a back up; Oswald's asst took over effectively, but it was hard to replace the good Sergeant.

There, was also the letter of condolence to write to his father. As I mentioned before, one of the hardest tasks a commander has is to write letters of condolence to the families of the men. in his unit who were killed This was before the Army developed its sterile, unfeeling form letter which it now requires all commanders to use. With difficulty I .wrote the letter to SGT Oswald's father. He replied cordially, and for many years I continued to write to Mr Oswald to let him know that his son was remembered.

We quickly got the position back into fighting shape. When I told the 1st Plt that it was going to be rotated out of its exposed position, Benz asked me to leave it there. The men took pride in the fact that they were in the forefront; I left them there.

The UN forces, in static positions, were constantly trying to improve their defenses. For a year or more various units had planted mines in the barbed wire in front of the bunkers, but there was no complete plot of all the mines in the area. As a result, when SGT Garrighty went out to mend the wire after the attack, he detonated a mine and was killed. Another sad and needless loss. He was a sharp soldier and an excellent Squad Leader. The letter to his wife was also difficult to write, in view of the fact that he had not been killed directly by enemy action, but rather as a result of incomplete information on the location of friendly mines. It brought home pointedly the need to make and keep exact records of the locations of all mines laid down by friendly forces. The men in his Squad and Platoon took up a collection, to which most of the men in B Co contributed, to buy a Savings Bond for his son, recently born, whom he had never seen.

By March of 1953 the UN forces in Korea had been in defensive positions for over a year so that the lines were permanently set. Occasionally there would be a probe by either side to try to try to straighten the line, gain an advantage, reduce a salient or capture a key piece of terrain. But there was little maneuver or movement. The line was roughly on the original demilitarized zone (38th Parallel); President Truman had made further offensive action a political decision. As a result, the enemies traded shots or engaged in limited attacks while negotiations were going on. It was frustrating for a soldier, but as military force is an extension of national policy, it was our lot.

The UN Forces generally commanded the top of hills, but gave the floor of the valleys to the enemy, particularly at night when visibility was poor. Despite the periodic patrols UN Forces conducted on the valley floor, the enemy had almost complete freedom of movement because friendly positions were not, in all cases, on the military crest of the hills. MAJ Carley was well aware of this. He wanted to examine the possibility of moving some B Co bunkers forward to gain better observation and fields of fire which might give greater control of the "Bowling Alley", the major avenue of approach into the Regimental and Divisional sectors. He had talked to me bout this on several occasions, expressing a desire to get forward of the lines to take a look at the terrain. He was particularly interested in the area occupied by LT Powers' 2nd Plt. There were several bulges in the hill mass that restricted vision and aimed direct fire. Carley wanted to see if it was possible to adjust the line forward to remedy this. A daylight reconnaissance was out of the question. Whenever friendly troops appeared on the forward slope of the hill, the CCF or NKA immediately took them under fire. It was not worth risking the lives of any men to make this recon, MAJ Carley reasoned. However, he told me that if the area was ever blanketed in fog or otherwise obscured, he wanted to get out to take a look at the terrain.

One morning we had just such a situation. At daylight a thick fog rolled in. It appeared that it would stay for several hours. Daring our usual morning discussion of the situation on Hill 159, I mentioned the fog and the opportunity to effect the reconnaissance. MAJ Carley told me that he was leaving his CP immediately for B Co; he arrived within a half hour. Once he saw how thick the fog was he elected to go forward of the position. I wanted to accompany him but he insisted (I think rightly) that I remain back to command B Co, precluding any possibility of the two of us being pinned down or hit with the same fire. However, 2LT Powers and CPL Alioto, one of his SLs went with him. Of course, it was not possible to see to the floor of the valley, but they got to see the ground and to evaluate the feasibility of moving the bunkers forward.

While they were still forward of the lines, the fog lifted suddenly. Completely exposed, they were taken under fire immediately. The three of them took cover in some old trenches dug many years before. We suspected that these trenches had been mined or booby trapped at the time they had been abandoned but it was the only cover available. CPL Alioto was in the lead, 2LT Powers was immediately behind him and MAJ Carley brought up the rear. As they proceeded, Alioto's foot triggered a mine. It blew his foot off and killed Powers instantly. MAJ Carley, shielded by LT Powers' body, was not wounded.

The recon party was in radio contact with the CP and MAJ Carley immediately informed me of the situation (we could not see them due to the configuration of the terrain and the fact that they were in the trench). I ordered the front lines to open fire and requested CPT Denby to smoke the area. A relief team was quickly organized and extracted the three members of the recon party. Again my medical background enabled me inform the medics of Alioto's situation, so they were prepared to give him instant care. He was evacuated first to Japan, later to the CONUS. He lost his lower leg and had to be fitted with a prosthesis.

Major Carley was highly distraught. He blamed himself for LT Powers' death and for the loss of CPL Alioto's foot. I attempted to calm him, pointing out that this was a risk we all took in our profession. Almost any action a CDR orders in combat involves risk to his men. He was trying to make a sensible assessment of the need to reposition the bunkers. Ground recon was essential to do so. It was unfortunate that this sound action had resulted in the loss of a fine officer.

The letter to Ken's father was especially troubling to write. In a few weeks I received a friendly reply in which Mr Powers asked me to visit him when I returned to the United States. I also wrote to Mr and Mrs Alioto, and received a cordial reply. Both families mentioned that food and coffee pots (every bunker had one) were on the way and asked that I make sure that the members of the 2nd Plt received those items they had sent. Unfortunately, once a man is evacuated or killed his mail is no longer delivered to his unit, but is automatically stamped "Deceased, return to sender" or marked appropriately for wounded or rotated personnel. I was unable to follow their wishes. Another sad duty was to gather, inventory and forward Ken's belongings to his family. Alioto's possessions were likewise forwarded to his home.

CPL Alioto wrote to me while he was in the hospital. He was bitter about his disability, placed the blame squarely on MAJ Carley, and had unkind things to say about "higher brass" who unduly risked their subordinates. In my reply I tried to make him see the rationale for the recon mission. I continued to correspond with him to try to boost his morale. Certainly he was a fine soldier; I was fortunate to have people like him under my command.

Despite such untoward events and daily enemy mortar fire, B Co continued to improve its positions on Hill 159. I refused to permit the men to think that our position was overly dangerous. Though access to and from it was always hazardous, I occasionally tried to rotate as many of them as possible for a night off the hill, for a change of pace and location, to see a movie and to get showers and clean clothes. A shower point, maintained by a QM unit, was located in each Regt area. These QM Shower points were all set up alike; on entering the dressing tent on one end of the shower point, dirty domes were turned in. After showering in a connecting tent, along with 20 other men, clean clothes were issued in the third tent in line. On two occasions I got there myself, once when I went to attend a Commanders' meeting and once just to get cleaned up. But I didn't like to be away from the hill, particularly at night. This is the curse of most commanders. We believe that nobody can handle the situation as well as we can, so we never take a break or leave. It is a ridiculous attitude because if a commander is wounded or killed, there is always someone to take his place who does equally well. No one is indispensable, but we like to believe that the unit depends on us. Every worthwhile commander has a feeling of responsibility for and dedication to his men; he doesn't want to let them down; he doesn't want to be away during an attack because he knows them best and can fight them best. I spent little time off the hill.

When we had been in position a little over a month, during which we had traded fire frequently with the enemy, but had no other attacks, word was received that the 9th IN, indeed, the 2nd Div, was to be relieved by the British Commonwealth Division. One day a British MAJ (Co CO), his SGT MAJ, (equivalent to a WO1) and his Commo OFF arrived to coordinate the relief. They looked over the position carefully. First Sergeant Cafora explained to the SGM our billeting arrangements and the details of our operation. The British were shocked that my XO, 1SG, Commo SGT, Co Clerk and runner all slept in the same bunker with me (there were six bunks in it). They planned to put the Co CO alone in my bunker. The Co CP complex consisted of three connecting bunkers: the sleeping bunker just described; the main CP bunker, a combination TOC and Orderly Room in which all of the communications, including the switchboard, terminated; and a sleeping bunker for the New Zealand FO party. The SGM was going to fix up the ammunition bunker for himself.

All possible measures were taken to prevent the CCF from seeing the British recon parry. A relief is at best a tricky operation during which a unit is extremely vulnerable. Hence the effort to avoid giving any indication to the enemy that a new unit would take over.

On the night of the relief, the British arrived in trucks at the bottom of the hill, just as we had. There was a bit more noise and confusion than I wanted, but it seemed unavoidable. Since a British IN Co does not have the same organization or weapons as a US Rifle Co, the relief was more complicated than usual; there was no one-for-one exchange of weapons. In addition, the 9th In was withdrawing the tanks, recoilless rifles, HMGS and other elements.

The routine patrols included British as well as American personnel. B Co maintained normal communications throughout me relief. Despite the difference in grade between the British Co CO and myself, I remained in command of Hill 159 until about 0200; when three-quarters of the British Co was in position, the British MAJ assumed responsibility. I stayed until daylight to insure that all of my troops were out. LT Johnson, my XO, was already in the reserve area getting things organized as the troops came off the hill.

At daylight, we viewed a repeat of the scene which had greeted B Company's arrival on the hill; there were signs reading "Welcome Commonwealth Division" and ditty bags stuffed with peace propaganda hung on the barbed wire. Once again I was struck by the phenomenal intelligence of the enemy. No doubt information was leaked as a result of the intermixing of American and Korean personnel. There were no houseboys on the hill, but there were KATUSA (Korean Augmentation to the US Army), ROK soldiers assigned as members of squads to give them training and to provide American units with additional manpower. It is hard to believe that KATUSAs were relaying information to the enemy. However, in the rear areas, the houseboys and Korean Service Corps (KSC) personnel who handled supplies and baggage knew about the relief. Somehow word got to the NKA and CCF.

The 9th In went to Camp Casey at Tondu-Chon. Bns were set up in compact formations with each Co allotted sufficient squad tents for all its men, an Orderly Tent, Supply Tent and Mess Tent. The OFFs' arctic tents were in a Bn OFFs' Section. There were latrines, wash areas and a shower point.

Awaiting in the reserve area were orders conferring on me the Second Award of the Combat Infantryman Badge. Having fulfilled the requirements, 30 days in combat with a line unit and under enemy fire, I was now entitled to wear the Badge with one star on it. I was proud of the award, not for what I had done, but because it signified that I had again served. That is what the Regular Army existed for, that was why I was a Regular.

As was customary, a memorial service for those men in the Bn who had been killed while we were on line was ordered. To get to the area designated for the service, it was necessary to march between tent rows, which made for poor close order drill Detailed instructions had been issued specifying which row of tents each company was to march through. I missed the one B Co was to use and took the wrong one. The men were given Route Step to climb over the tent ropes. We arrived in the area behind another company. Because of lack of space, it was impossible to maneuver the formation with any standard close order drill. I could not flank or oblique, give columns right or left; there was no way I could get B Co into its proper position. Assessing my options, I dismissed the Company and ordered them to Fall In on me once I had positioned myself properly. This created some mirth, I was kidded for days afterwards. Several of my friends dropped by with copies of FM 22-5, "Drill". No one was more amused than I was.

Despite the poor beginning, the memorial service proceeded in solemn dignity. In such a ceremony there is nothing more moving than the sound of Taps. Tears well up in my eyes and I get a lump in my throat every time I hear Taps played specifically for the dead, it is something I cannot control. I am sure that all military personnel feel it. The mournful call is even more poignant when blown for a buddy or a soldier who died under your command.

The day after the memorial service orders were issued transferring me to HQ, 9th IN. In keeping with his policy, COL Steinbach had permitted me to command B Co for about 70 days. Though I wanted the experience as Regt S-3, I was reluctant to leave the men for whom I had formed a warm attachment. But orders had been given; it was time to take on a new challenge.

On reporting to the 9th IN HQ, I was again amazed at the elaborate facilities it enjoyed. One of the curses of the US Army is the penchant of OFFs and EM to be "pack rats". In their efforts to make themselves as comfortable as possible, a goal I fully support, much extraneous equipment not authorized by the Table of Organization and Equipment (TO&E) is acquired. From then on it must be carted from position to position or abandoned. For instance, the 9th IN had several Jamesway huts. These shelters, erected by covering collapsible frames with canvas, were designed as maintenance facilities. The Manchus used them for billets and -administrative offices.

There were many extra tents: an Officers' Mess Tent and one for the troops; in addition to the regular kitchen fly, another squad tent used for storage and cooking;, tents for each staff section as well as for the TOC; tents for troop billets, Supply, Orderly Room, Personnel Section, and other activities. Most of them had wooden floors to keep everyone out of the mud, an important consideration in a country which has a monsoon season. But this extra tentage and flooring required an inordinate amount of transportation when the Regt displaced its HQ. Again, the outstanding Regimental Officers' Mess impressed me.

My assignment was as one of two Asst Regt S-3s. The other was CPT Charley Zagata. who had been in the 2nd Bn of the 504 when I was in the 3rd. He had been a Commo OFF most of his career, and a good one. When he was displaced as the Regt Commo by the assignment of a Signal Corps Officer (a trial procedure), Dave McNaught had suggested that Charley get out of the communications field, in which he had no place to go as an Infantryman. Dave, who ranked Charley by several months, agreed to train him in the operations field, a transition not too difficult since the Commo worked closely with the S-3 in combat. Charley was a loyal and dedicated officer who would do anything for a friend. But he and Scagnelli had acquired reputations in the 504 of being trouble makers; an image he found hard to lose. It was always my impression that Charley was maneuvered into the fights and other questionable situations by Scagnelli, who played on Zagota's loyalty to a friend.

Charley's presence posed a problem. Until Dave left, I would be his understudy, at which time I would assume the duties of Regt S-3, and Charley would then be my asst. Zagata ranked me as a CPT by about six months. COL Steinbach made the decision anyhow; when I talked with Charley he was content to work under those conditions. Despite his concurrence it made things awkward.

The overlap with Dave was of uncertain length. I do not like overlaps, though they serve a purpose in some circumstances. In this case, it was not exactly an overlap, since I would be an Asst S-3. The temporary assignment would give me an opportunity to get to know everyone in the 9th IN as well as the OFFs I would work with at Div and in other Regts. It would also give me an opportunity to familiarize myself with Manchu procedures and operations. But after the first week, I became impatient to take over from Dave and began to look at everything he did with a super-critical eye. He was an excellent S-3 so there was little to criticize. Despite his continuing ailment (his ulcerative colitis and consequent diarrhea were unabated), Dave did more work than most. His condition must have sapped his energy, but it was difficult to tell it by the schedule he kept. The weather alone made his condition difficult and painful. But Dave forced himself to visit units daily, read and write endless documents and supervise the details of our operations. In spite of his excellence as an S-3 and his ailment, I began analyzing how I would have handled a situation, many times I would have done things differently.

Dave, aware of the situation, worked out a solution. He was transferred to the 1st Bn as Leroy Stanley's XO when John Carley left and Leroy took command of the Bn. Shortly after Dave reported to the 1st Bn a MAJ was assigned who displaced him as XO. Dave then became the Bn S-3, a strange regression in assignments. Relieved to see Dave go, I was elated to become the Regimental S-3.

LTC William Zimmerman, the Regimental XO, supervised and coordinated the staff and rated the principal staff officers. However, a special relationship exists between the Commander and his S-3. Figuratively, the S-3 is in the back pocket of his Commander with direct access to him on most matters. And so it was with COL Steinbach. He talked to me directly. He did not issue orders through LTC Zimmerman (it was my duty to keep the XO informed). I immediately liked COL Steinbach. Several incidents which had occurred while I commanded B Co had left a bad taste in my mouth, but now I began to understand the man, the pressures he was under and the way he operated. Every commander functions uniquely, gets results through different means. He may be criticized for the way he does things, but results count. COL Steinbach had his own methods; once I learned them, we quickly formed a warm relationship.

John Kiser, an old friend from the 504, was the S-2. The S-2 and the S-3 work closely together; having a friend in that spot made it easier for me to fit into my new job. He kept me straight! CPT Will (Rod) Rogers was the S-1 and MAJ Ralph "Rass" Rasmussen, the S-4. It was a good team which worked well together. In a short time I developed respect and admiration for all of them; I learned much from them and they supported me fully.

The Commo, LT Chester Phillips, was a SC OFF. The concept of using SC OFFs as Regt communications officers was under test. Each of the Combat Arms had its own Communications Course. The Army was trying to determine if the expertise of SC OFFs could be put to use in the regiment; if the communications in each of the Combat Arms could be standardized; if the duplicative schools could be eliminated. Both systems worked well, there were many excellent Infantry Communications Officers like Ed Morris or Charley Zagota, Phillips was also an excellent Regimental Commo. He became so impressed with the Infantry that he eventually transferred from the Signal Corps to the Infantry.

One of my first requirements as S-3 was to become familiar with the fourth Bn of the Regt. Each regiment in the 2nd Div, as in most US Divs in Korea, had a Bn from one of the UN members supporting South Korea. The 9th had the Royal Thai Bn, the 23rd a French Bn, and the 38th a Dutch

Bn. It was necessary to learn the organization, strengths and weaknesses of the Thais. They had fought valiantly at Pork Chop Hill in 1992.

On my first visit to the Thais I met MAJ Boon Rangaratna, the CDR, MAJ Chalard Hiransiri, his S-3, and CPT Bill Lindahl, the 9th IN's LNO to the Thais. All seemed solid professionals. The Thai Bn was larger than any American Bn because it was reinforced or augmented with supporting elements which made it independent. The Thais received special rations, supplemented from US supplies. Each Thai soldier received a bottle of Hot Sauce per week with his rations!

The American Liaison Team lived separately in arctic tents, with a mess of its own. An American cook was assigned to the Team and US Army rations were issued to them Thai food, highly spiced, was good once in a while, but Americans found it too much as a steady diet.

An important member of my S-3 Section was my driver, CPL Jim Elsbecker, an Iowa farmer, who had originally been assigned as an MP guarding POWs in Pusan. He hated guard duty and had volunteered for duty with an Infantry division. He wanted to get into a rifle company, but because of his civilian truck driving experience, he was made a truck driver. After six months of some very exciting driving, he switched jobs with a jeep driver who wanted to drive trucks. At that point he became my driver. He was a conscientious, highly proficient driver with a good sense of direction. I never had to tell him anything twice; once he had been to a place he never forgot it. This was important because it left me free to look at the terrain or think as we drove.

CPL Elsbecker and I shared some close calls together. We went to the front line units every day when the Regt was committed. On one occasion, we took a short cut from one position to another which led in front of one of our units. This was not particularly dangerous because the route was often used. However, on this occasion, the enemy began firing artillery at us; little black puffs began marching down the road toward us. Fortunately there was a bunker a shot distance off the road and we took shelter in it until the firing stopped. Then we beat it and never used that route again!

Jim told me some of his experiences as a truck driver. One day when he was driving his truck in convoy in January, it was snowing and ice formed on the roads. To get across the mountain the drivers had to keep the inside wheels in a shallow drainage ditch next to the hillside to keep from slipping off the road. Occasional tracers lighted the way for them.

About the same time that I was transferred to Regt, the Asst Div CDR, BG Lionel C. McGarr left to take charge of the POW camp at Koje Do and COL Louis W. Truman was assigned to replace him. Truman was on the promotion list but had not yet received his star. Enroute to the 2nd Div, he had undergone surgery to repair a hernia. When he arrived at the Div he was still recovering from that operation. This was unfortunate because Korea, particularly in our area, is hilly. There was no way to get to the Regt training areas or to most of the units without walking up a hill. This put a strain on COL Truman's incision.

Just after he arrived, one Bn of the 9th IN was to rehearse a counterattack plan. COL Truman decided that he wanted to see it. I was selected to meet him and escort him to the area in which the rehearsal was to be held. After reconnoitering the area I found that a jeep could get very close to the rehearsal area, but it would be necessary to walk about 50 yards up a small hill. A low spot or saddle would permit Truman to look down into the valley in which the rehearsal was to take place. There was no other vantage point. I met the Colonel and escorted him to the observation point, explaining that he would have a short walk. He said it would be no problem. But when he got out of the jeep and I pointed to the way he became irritated and said, "You know that I had this operation. I can't walk that far. Now take me to some place that I can watch it without getting out of the jeep."

COL Truman was told that this was the only vantage point that did not require a more vigorous climb. He finally managed to get up the easy slope without too much difficulty. But he was irritable throughout the evening, which made him critical of everything that was done. Later I learned that he had been in the class behind COL Steinbach at West Point and was inclined to throw his weight around because he had been promoted before Steinbach. In small ways this became evident to all of us in the 9th IN.

COL Truman, later BG Truman, became the bane of my existence. He did not seem to have a complete grasp of IN tactics. It may have been that he was rusty on some things but he operated on the principle that he was going to inspect one item each day. It became routine for the "word of the day" to be sent out. For instance, if he mentioned at breakfast "range cards", that would immediately alert the junior staff officers that "range cards" was the "word of the day". They would call all Divisional elements to put out the "word". We were fortunate that Jim Holt and Tom Tackaberry, both of whom had been in the 9th IN, were in the Div G-3 Section. They kept the regiments posted daily on what Truman was going to look for.

The more I saw of BG Truman the more convinced I became that he was not a nice guy. There are ways to reprimand, there are ways to make corrections, there are ways to handle situations without stripping an individual of his dignity. Truman, unfortunately, didn't realize that. I'm afraid that I might have a similar fault. I have frequently reprimanded an OFF in front of other OFFs and lost my temper in front of a group. But I don't think that I ever forgot myself to the extent that BG Truman did; I don't think I was ever as nasty or as personal, in reprimanding someone as he was. He made an individual feel small, insignificant, completely ineffective; people hated it when he visited their area. Rather than a positive influence, he had in fact, a very negative effect, not only on the morale but on the performance of the 2nd Div. This is something commanders must always consider; overdoing the negative aspect of inspections and supervision. There has to be a positive side. At any rate, BG Truman visited the 9th Infantry frequently.

It devolved on me more often than not to meet him, to report to him, and to explain what was going on. The Div was in reserve so every unit was rehabilitating equipment, conducting refresher training, preparing alternate positions, or writing and rehearsing counterattack plans. The reserve area made units readily accessible to visitors by helicopter or jeep The 9th IN got more than its share of supervision from BG Truman; I got to know him well because I met him more frequently than most. If COL Steinbach or LTC Zimmerman were out of the CP for any reason (they visited all the units daily) it devolved on me to meet the Asst Div CDR when he came in.

One day Tom Tackaberry notified us that the "word of the day" was "Fire Support Plan". We quickly prepared to demonstrate our mastery of this technique, something used routinely to coordinate all fire power elements available to a unit. The OPS SGT notified all fire support elements that they could expect Truman to ask questions about their fire support plans. Even in reserve we maintained a functioning TOC which included a Fire Support Coordination Center (FSCC). In the FSCC were, the LNOs from our Direct Support (DS) ARTY Bn and the AA ARTY, and NCOs from the 4.2-inch Mortar and Tank Cos (organic to the Regt). All had direct communications to their units.

The Regiment was preparing to rehearse one of its counterattack plans at the time "Fire Support Plan" was passed down as the "word of the day". BG Truman appeared late in the afternoon, announcing that he planned to observe the night counterattack rehearsal. True to form, he asked to visit the FSCC. By this time we were well prepared. The OPS SGT had labeled each field desk and phone so there would be no Question as to which LNO handled which weapon. Truman was obviously pleased at our highly functional set-up. He asked the ARTY LNO for his fire support plan. The captain rolled out his "measle chart" with its numerous concentrations plotted. He then questioned the AA LNO. The Quad 50s were used in a ground support role in Korea; the Chinese hated the weapon which they called "whispering death" because the bullets struck with only a faint swish to warn of their approach. Hence, concentrations were plotted similar to those for tube artillery. The AA LNO showed Truman his plan. He then accosted the 4.2-inch mortar NCO, who had an overlay with numbered "goose eggs" representing prepared concentrations (data for which had been calculated and was available at the gun positions). Finally Truman reached the SGT from the Tank

Co who didn't have a fire support plan. When Truman asked for it, I immediately answered for both COL Steinbach and the NCO,

"Sir, the Tank Co is in direct support of the 2nd Bn and fire plans are being worked out between the Bn CO and Co CO. Therefore, we do not have a fire support plan here."

"Just because the Tank Co is in direct support of the 2nd Bn is no reason not to have a fire support plan here," BG Truman snapped. "I want to see a fire support plan for every weapon and fire element that you have available to the Regiment."

"But, sir, we can't make a fire support plan for the Tank Co. The two CDRs are working out fires. The Bn CO has the option of adjusting the fire to his plan of maneuver. If we dictate the fire plan from here, we negate putting the Tank Co in direct support of the Battalion."

"CPT, don't argue with me. I want a fire support plan for the Tank Co."

"Sir. I think it needs further discussion."

COL Steinbach at this point gave me a nod to shut up. But I believed it essential to establish the principle of direct support between units. Truman, obviously annoyed, snapped at me,

"CPT, don't bother me with any of those text book definitions. I want a fire support plan for every weapon in this Regt. Now do you understand that?"

"Sir, I understand you want a fire support plan for every weapon in this Regiment."

"That is correct."

Turning to the OPS SGT, I said, "SGT, put out to all units that a fire support plan will be prepared for every weapon in the Regt, including M-1 rifles and 45 caliber pistols."

Truman looked at me as if he was going to brain me with his swagger stick.

COL Steinbach grabbed him by the arm, saying, "General, don't you want to watch the 2nd Bn cross the line of departure?"

He eased him out of the TOC. Perhaps he saved my life, at least he saved me from a tongue lashing by a very irate general officer. I should have shut up, but I thought that the principle should be established at the cost of tact.

At the end of June, John Kiser and Will Rogers rotated back to the CONUS. They were good friends and we made a good team so I was sorry to see them go. Bill Lindahl came from the Thai Bn to replace John as S-2 and Lou Williams became the S-1. Williams was a MAJ who had been in and out of command several limes. Every time he assumed command of a Bn someone senior to him would be assigned to the Regt bumping him from the position. These were top flight replacements which made the Regt Staff another cohesive and effective team.

While the Regiment was in reserve, I attempted to go on R&R. Each time I put in for it, some problem surfaced which caused COL Steinbach to ask me to stay. In one instance, my request was turned down because the 187th ABN RCT rotated from Japan to Korea for its annual combat OPN. The RCT was attached to the 2nd Div and the 9th IN was tasked to support it during refresher training. Specifically, we were to provide the Regt Tank Co for Tank/Infantry training. While coordinating with the S-3, MAJ Pete Kelley, I saw several people I knew; BG Westmoreland the CDR, COL "Bud" Russ his Deputy, Larry Mowery, and of course Pete, with whom I worked on other projects besides the Tank Co.

In desperation, I applied for the Air-Ground School in Japan, thinking that might provide a change of pace and an opportunity to see something of the country. However, the week I submitted my application, a new policy went into effect; only senior officers, Bn and Regt CDRS and higher level staff officers were eligible to go from then on. COL Steinbach was scheduled to go at the time I had requested. I never got to Japan.

While in reserve, all units worked on "switch positions". These were fall-back positions in the event the CCF or NKA once again tried to push across the 38th Parallel; reserve positions to which a unit could withdraw in the event it was overrun. The switch positions, situated at an angle to the

MLR, had been well plotted by Corps and the UN Command/8th Army. Regts had little leeway to change the general trace, fixed by limiting points. The actual trace could be modified to take advantage of the terrain, of course.

MAJ Don Bolton, who commanded the 2nd Bn, and I got into a heated discussion over this. We had first met at FT Benning where he taught the tactics of defense to our Advance Class. His particular speciality at TIS had been the Reverse Slope Defense. Consequently, he wanted to establish a reverse slope defensive position in the area that his Bn was preparing. He recommended it, urging that the terrain was ideal for such a defense. After a careful recon of his sector, with due consideration of his expertise, I disapproved his recommendation for the Regt CO. MAJ Bolton and I argued the matter on several occasions, neither of us budging in our positions. Finally Don told me that he was going to put in a reverse slope defense in spite of my objections. Whereupon, I insisted that we take the matter to COL Steinbach, who listened carefully to both views. He agreed with me that the terrain was not suitable for the reverse slope defense, and not appropriate for the switch position. Reluctantly, MAJ Bolton ordered his men to dig their positions on the forward slope.

Just before COL Steinbach left for Air-Ground School, LTC Zimmerman was replaced by LTC Donald K. Armstrong. The new XO was not an impressive officer; the more I worked with him, the less I thought of him. He was not without intelligence, but he was not well-versed in Infantry tactics; certainly he was no leader. We suspected that COL Steinbach had accepted his USMA classmate to get him promoted. With great trepidation I saw COL Steinbach leave for Japan, knowing that I would have trouble with LTC Armstrong, the Acting Commander.

The trouble began immediately. Two days after COL Steinbach's departure, the TOC was notified that the Regt CO was required at Div for a meeting. It was intimated that the purpose of the meeting was to issue a warning order. After informing Armstrong that he was to go to Division I asked him what time we would be leaving. He said, "What do you mean 'we'? I thought I was to go."

"Sir, I am sure that this meeting is for the purpose of issuing a warning order for our rotation back on line. You must take me with you. It is essential that I get the details while you are getting the big picture. I have to coordinate with the units on our flanks."

"Well, I am not sure that is true or that I should take you since Div did not specifically ask for you."

"Sir, the S-3 always goes with his CDR to receive an order, I insist that you take me with you."

Reluctantly he agreed to let me ride with him to Div. As expected, it was a warning order for our rotation back on line; the 9th IN would relieve the 7th. Attached to the 7th Infantry (the "Cotton Balers") was the Belgian Bn entrenched on a position called the "Boomerang" located just west of the Kumhwa valley. The warning order specified that the 187 RCT would relieve the unit on the right of the 7th IN, spanning the Kumhwa Valley and extending slightly to the east of it, two days before the 9th Infantry relieved the 7th.

Div emphasized the usual security and counter-intelligence measures, warning that recon was to be limited. Information concerning the relief was to be held on a need to know basis until the actual order was issued. I tried to discuss the matter with LTC Armstrong on the way back to the 9th IN CP, but because his driver was not cleared, he refused to let me talk about the matter. On our return to the Regt area I went to LTC Armstrong's hootch and asked him at what time he would like to issue his warning order.

"What do you mean?"

"We must inform the Bn COs and the Staff so that we can get our planning underway. We need to arrange to visit the "Cottonbalers" early so we don't telegraph our intention."

"This is on a need to know basis, so we can't tell anyone about it yet. We will have to wait until the order comes down."

"Sir, although the warning order is classified "need to know" there are people in the Regt who have to know; the Bn COs who in turn must have their staffs start making plans, the S-2 has to gather intelligence, the Commo has to get a communications plan worked out; the S-4 has to estimate his requirements for transportation to move troops, supplies and equipment, and the S-1 has to plan for replacements, medical coverage and other matters under his purview." Armstrong refused to hold a meeting to issue a warning order, but finally yielded, reluctantly and with much protest, to my request that I be permitted to tell the Bn COs and some of the Regimental Staff, but he would not authorize me to tell the S-1!

After leaving him, I called together, without his knowledge, the 1, 2, 4, the Commo and the HQ CMDT to inform them of the impending relief. They were warned that the subject was closely held, particularly in light of the way Armstrong was treating the matter. They looked at each other and nodded then- heads. Knowing the problem, they gave no unnecessary information to anyone. I felt guilty about going behind LTC Armstrong's back, since I owed my Commander, even the acting one, loyalty. Nonetheless, there were certain plans and actions that had to be initiated; I was sure that COL Steinbach would have approved.

Next I went to each of the Bn COs, told them of the impending relief, and warned them of LTC Armstrong's concern about need to know. I am sure they used their own judgement regarding the classification; they had much to do.

A reconnaissance plan was developed; the Commo and I went initially to talk with the 7th IN S-3 and his commo people. We made plans for other Manchu elements to come forward. They would check in at the Cottonbalers CP where they would be provided with 7th IN vehicles and field jackets with 3rd Div patches so they would not be conspicuous. The visits by the Manchus would be spaced so as to conform with the normal traffic pattern of the Cottonbalers. The S-3 showed me the Regt sector; I tentatively assigned the Bns that would go on line, subject to LTC Armstrong's or COL Steinbach's approval. LT Phillips completed arrangements for the communications takeover. Rasmussen, Williams, Lindahl, Phillips and I put together a workable plan. I was appalled at the number of trucks it took to move the Manchu CP; over 100 trucks were needed to move the tent floorings, Jamesways, generators and the rest of the equipment that had been collected to make us comfortable. The plan included a march table; Elsbecker and I drove the route. The rainy season was just beginning in early July; flash floods were common due to heavy downpours. During the route recon I identified several critical points and bridges which could be disrupted or destroyed by flash floods. On my return I insisted that several alternate routes be designated. The only available alternate routes were quite circuitous; because they would require a longer time to negotiate, it would throw off the timetable of the relief if they had to be used. But they were the only routes with no bridges exposed to flash floods; we had to have those contingencies available.

Fortunately COL Steinbach returned a few days before we were directed to implement the plan. When I explained exactly what I had done and why, he approved my actions and the plan. The next week promised to be hectic. The 187 was going on line on the 14th of July, the Manchus on the 16th. Immediately after the relief COL Julian J. Ewell would replace COL Steinbach, who would rotate.

The night of the relief there was a cloud burst. All of my worst fears were realized, flash floods washed out several bridges on our primary convoy route; use of the alternate routes played havoc with the timetable. Luckily, the 7th IN had enough leeway to accommodate our delayed schedule. I was like a caged lion, constantly harassing the Bns for reports, making a general pest of myself. I was apprehensive about this delicate operation.

Finally, COL Steinbach told me to get out of the CP. "You're making me nervous. Why don't you coordinate the status of our relief with the 187 on our flank?"

Jim Elsbecker was scheduled to rotate the next day, but had insisted upon driving me through the relief because he knew all the routes. I had protested that he should not be exposed on his last night, but he contended that in the dark and under the circumstances it would be easier for me if I had a driver who was familiar with the routes and positions. I appreciated this; he was of great help.

Elsbecker and I got in the jeep and headed toward the Kumhwa Valley, where the CP of the 187 was located. I warned him that he would see a professional outfit; airborne, gung-ho, aggressive, so that we should be prepared to stop suddenly as we would be challenged all the way to the CP. To my surprise and chagrin no one halted us. We drove into the CP and directly to the TOC bunker without being challenged. Certainly it was miserable night, rainy and windy, but that did not excuse the lack of security in that RCT CP. I walked into the TOC still unchallenged. Spotting Pete Kelley, I started to tell him our situation, but he cut me off. The 187th had a minor contact for which he was coordinating fire support. The S-2 was also too busy to speak with me. COL Russ, with great good sense, was asleep. There was no one to coordinate with in the confusion except BG Westmoreland, who was sitting at a field table in the corner of the bunker studying a contour map of the Kumhwa area. My helmet was off and my poncho concealed my name and insignia as I walked over to Westmoreland's table. He was dictating to an enlisted stenographer, making it a matter of record that he disagreed with the disposition of the 187th RCT. The 187 CDR was so intent that he did not notice me until I leaned over and inadvertently dripped on his map. He looked up, saying, "Messenger, wait over there". At my protest that I was not a messenger, Westmoreland recognized me and asked my business. I explained that COL Steinbach thought he should know about the situation on his flank. "Oh? What?" he said, as if he had not heard of our relief. Probably it had slipped his mind, but it was a critical time because his flank could be exposed. When he had been briefed on the delay due to the loss of the bridges, he thanked me for the information, assuring me that he would inform his S-2 and S-3 of the situation.

"Sir, as long as I am here, I'd like your permission to make coordination on the ground tomorrow morning between your left flank units and ours, at Bn, Co, and Plt. If you have no objection, I would like to do that directly rather than coming back through your CP." He gave me the necessary permission, after which Elsbecker and I returned to the Cottonbalers CP. By the time I reached it, the relief was well in progress with no further difficulties. About 0300I suggested to COL Steinbach that he assume responsibility for the position as most of our units were in place. He agreed, the 9th IN took control of the sector, and I became so busy that I could not harass anyone.

The next morning I collected the right flank Bn, Co and Plt CDRs who accompanied me to their counterparts in the 187. We were appalled at what we saw. The 187th RCT was anything but professional! Men were walking around the position in white T-shirts, drying their clothes on commo wire stretched around the area. Their position was dominated by the largest hill mass in the area called "Papasan", occupied by the CCF and NKA, who looked directly into the US position. They could see every move the Americans made; the trace of the trenches, the routes to latrines, mess halls, ammo bunkers and gun positions were indicated to the enemy by men in white T-shirts. The police of the area was atrocious. The papers, cigarette butts and minor trash did not bother me. These things accumulate in combat. But there were ammunition crates, C-ration cans and cartons, and a great deal of wire, including reels, in the trenches, making movement difficult. The general lack of professionalism embarrassed me because I had been touting the 187 as a top-notch unit.

Coordination between the 9th IN and 187th RCT CDRs was quickly effected. As the other Manchus returned to their units, I asked permission of the Bn Co to go to one of the 187 outposts, a platoon occupying two small knobs about 200 yards forward of the MLR. It seemed advisable to talk with the Plt Ldr because the break in the wire through which all of the 9th IN patrols in that sector would leave and return was directly in front of that outpost position. I wanted to make sure that no trigger-happy trooper fired on our patrols.

The Bn CO pointed the way. For some reason I had not worn my jump wings, though both the Bn and Co CDRs knew I was Airborne. On arrival at the outpost I was greeted disdainfully by the Plt Ldr. Obviously I was a "leg"; as a jumper he was going to give me short shrift. His insolence irritated me; I called the OFF to task, explaining the courtesy a 2LT owed a CPT, Airborne or not. In disabusing him of the notion that I was a "leg", I told him that his lack of respect was a reflection on the 187th RCT.

Once we had established the proper relationship between us, I told him about the patrols which would pass through the break in the wire in front of his position, assuring him that we would keep the 187 informed of their timing. He minimized my concern for our patrols. This also irked me because it is exactly the attitude that gets men killed,

Just as I was about to leave, mortar rounds landed in the position causing utter chaos. Collaring the LT, I shouted, "Lieutenant, those are friendly rounds. They are 81mm Mortar rounds! Get on the horn back to your unit and tell them to cease fire."

He looked at me and said, "Don't you think I know the difference between friendly and enemy rounds. Those are Chink."

"No, they're not. They are friendly rounds."

He refused to believe me. Grabbing the field phone and cranking frantically I told the operator to get to Bn immediately to have them cease firing all mortars because they were firing on their own position. Unfortunately one man was killed, another lost an arm and several others had lesser wounds. After doing what I could to help, once the situation seemed to be in hand, I left. Enroute I met the SGT FO who was on his way to the outpost to adjust the final protective fires of the Bn 81mm Mortars. Perhaps the Lieutenant was finally convinced that he had been fired on by his own mortars. It was inexcusable that an FO was not at the position when the rounds were fired.

With the relief completed, the Manchus settled down as COL Ewell assumed command. A tall, thin, bespectacled officer with a dry voice and a rather aloof air, he was an excellent commander with a firm grasp of Infantry tactics, who knew what was going on and what he wanted to do. In the following days, I saw a great deal of COL Ewell, but I never felt that I penetrated his reserve. Perhaps this is a good attitude for a commander; it lessens the impact emotion can have on decisions. Command is a lonely honor because only the commander makes decisions. No one can share the burden, the responsibility, the authority inherent in such a position.

COL Ewell, frustrated by our static situation, was constantly seeking ways of improving it and keeping the men on their toes. He asked me to draw up a plan for a tank shoot, indicating the area he thought it should be in. There were many excellent targets for direct fire weapons in the zone, but I pointed out to him the difficulties in getting the tanks in and out of that particular sector. It consisted largely of abandoned rice paddies, crisscrossed by dikes; in wet weather, the paddies became bogs. If the tanks got mired down, recovery crews would be exposed to enemy observation and fire. The dikes between paddies were too narrow to permit the tanks to traverse them. COL Ewell thought the results warranted the risks; me tank shoot was an excellent idea except for the problem of trafficability.

The Tank Co CO and I developed a plan which we submitted to COL Ewell together with our recommendation against implementing it. COL Ewell ordered the plan executed. The tanks moved out, fired their mission successfully, began to withdraw, and mired down. It took almost a day and half to retrieve them. Though the recovery team was fired on, no one was wounded. The tank shoot destroyed a number of enemy defenses forward of our position and threw the enemy off balance for a limited time.

Everyday I visited the forward units, either with COL Ewell, who also went forward daily, or alone. Frequently we would each take a different sector, look at different things, then compare notes. During one visit I concentrated on HMG positions. Units had been notified that I was going to inspect every front line HMG position. Since this would take considerable time, I requested that I be permitted to do this without having the Bn S-3s or Co COs accompany me. I did not want to tie them down for that long. I was interested in having the NCOs show me their positions, range cards, fields of fire, and final protective fires, especially the latter. It took a full day because I crawled into every gunners' position, sighted the gun with them, checked range cards and dead space, and had them show me the stake on which they would lay their guns if ordered to fire final protective fires. The positions and knowledge of the men ranged from outstanding (one ABN HMG PSG had the best positions and most knowledgeable gunners I encountered) to worthless. The men were surprised to see a Regt Staff OFF crawl into then- positions. But I gained first hand knowledge on the state of training of our gun crews and of the interlock between unit fires. Needless to say, any comments I had were made to the Bn S-3s.

MG General Fry, who commanded the 2nd Div when I first joined it, was an outstanding soldier and tactician, a soldier's soldier, a true Infantryman, a strong commander and a gentleman. When he rotated he was replaced by MG William L. Barriger, who did not impress me. He was more a staff OFF than a CDR. He was not inspiring when he talked with the men, nor did he have the presence that more charismatic leaders did. A rather heavy-set individual, the sobriquet "Willy Lump-lump" was applied to him. This immediately caught the fancy of the troops and the name spread throughout the Div. The troops never referred to him as MG Barriger, it was always "Willy Lump-lump". Eventually the Div Staff learned of the wide-spread use of the term and the G-2 was given the task of determining who had dubbed the Commanding General thus.

MAJ Chester McCoid, who had been in my Advance Class, was the 2nd Div G-2. A very serious-minded and conscientious officer, Chet could not see the humor in the situation. When he reached the 9th IN in his quest to find the bastard who had defamed the Div CDR, I pointed out to him that the more an issue was made of it, the more the troops would relish the name "Willy Lump-lump". It appeared to me that the best thing to do was to ignore it. Trying to pin blame or convince the troops not to use such a descriptive title only added more zest to it. But Chet was determined to find the culprit; he investigated and interrogated to no purpose. It was particularly amusing because Tom Tackaberry and Jim Holt, two CPTs on the Div Staff, had first coined the name. It stemmed from Div HQ; almost from his own office, yet the G-2 was looking to the units. He never did find out who had christened MG Barriger "Willy Lump-lump".

Since Eisenhower's visit to Korea in December 1952 when he pledged to end the war, peace negotiations had dragged on. Finally in July there appeared to be real progress. Just as the Manchus went back on line, the CCF and NKA launched a major drive to the right of our position. Apparently they wanted to insure that they held the key terrain when the truce became effective.

The attack was on a broad front and in great strength. The 187 came under heavy pressure and the Capitol ROK Division on their right was almost overrun. The 7th IN was moved behind the CAP ROK Division to bolster it. Since the CAP ROK was one of the best Korean Divisions, its difficulties indicated the force of the attack. We received little more than occasional shelling and probes. With great relief we learned on 26 July that the truce would be effective the next day.

The 27th of July dawned sunny and clear. After constant firing, the sudden stillness was almost frightening; there was no test firing of weapons, no H&I fires, no artillery attacks. The change that struck us most, however, was the number of people who suddenly arrived on the front lines. Many who had never been forward of the Regt rear areas found reasons to look at the front lines before we withdrew to the truce positions. One wag in the 9th IN CP put up a sign, "Guided Tour of the Front for Rear Echelon Personnel, Non-combat Personnel Report Here". Though a few people took umbrage, most thought it amusing.

The 9th IN moved to new positions as the Demilitarized Zone was marked out. This meant more digging. The plan had been developed over the weeks as the negotiations dragged on, but its implementation became a nightmare. Div required a daily report on the number of yards of dirt moved, how many feet of barbed wire had been emplaced, the number of bunkers started or finished, and many more details. Although the reports undoubtedly were used to indicate the progress achieved in building defensive positions on the south side of the Demilitarized Zone, it was not the kind of thing I took to readily.

After several days of reporting minutiae and filling out interminable forms, I asked COL Ewell if he had any objections to the curtailment of my tour. When I transferred from FEC/LDI extended for a full year. If completed, my tour in Korea would last another six months. At this time I had been in country about 13 months. COL Ewell interposed no objection. Lou Williams, the S-1, told me that since he truce, all extensions were subject to review. The necessary paperwork was submitted; in only a few days, I was notified that my tour had been curtailed; I was free to leave Korea immediately. Charlie Zagata would replace me as S-3.

Since Lou Williams was also rotating, he suggested that we drive to the Replacement Depot at Inchon in one of the Manchu jeeps rather than wait for the normal personnel processing. By getting ahead of the bulk of rotating personnel, we might be able to get on the next ship out. Accordingly, we left the 9th IN CP in a jeep with all of our gear in the trailer, stopped at the Div Replacement Co to clear, then headed for Inchon. On arrival at Inchon about 1600 we were told that a ship had left an hour or two before. Had we gotten there that morning, we would have sailed on it. The Depot Staff informed us that the next regular ship would not leave for several weeks. The next three ships leaving Inchon would carry only repatriated POWs and the people who were to process them during the voyage. An intensive rehabilitation program had been set up for the return trip: thorough physical examinations, psychiatric examinations, counseling and therapy if required, and an information and education program to bring the released POWs up-to-date on what was going on in the United States. The only OFFs on those ships were those concerned with the rehabilitation program or housekeeping and administration and the only other EM were those assigned to work details so the ex-POWs would not have to pull KP or other duty. The OFFs for those ships were at Inchon and had already been assigned their duties for the trips. There appeared no chance for an early return for Lou and me.

Three days after Lou and I had reported to Inchon, the 9th IN personnel who were also scheduled to rotate caught up with us. When they saw us in the OFFs' Club, several of them greeted me strangely, "Congratulations, Major Seibert."

"What do you mean?"

"Sir, you have been promoted to major."

"I don't believe it." They explained that shortly after Lou and I had left the 9th IN, orders promoting me "out of zone" to MAJ had been received. I still would not believe it, since nothing had been said at the Div Replacement Co when we cleared. When I checked with the Depot HQ they had no information about promotions, but suggested that I find out from the AG in Seoul. Since our group would not be leaving for some time, the CO offered me a pass to go there. With friends still present in FEC/LD, I requested three days to visit them as well as check on the matter of my alleged promotion.

Before I left, Lou Williams received word that in two days he was sailing as an I&E OFF on the next ship going out. He had to read up on current events so he could conduct briefings for the repatriated POWs. Only field grade OFFs (MAJ through COL) were assigned these duties. The Depot carried me as a CPT with a departure date at least two weeks in the future.

There was a steady flow of traffic between Inchon and Seoul, so I had no trouble getting a ride. At FEC/LD, Joe Lagatutta, an old buddy and another admirer of COL Wilson, slapped me on the back, pointed to his shiny new major's leaf and said, "Hey, Don, you're out of uniform. You were promoted on the 29th of July. Get with it fella."

"You're kidding me, Joe."

"No, I'm serious. We're on the same order. SO 147, 29 July."

"Do you have a copy of it?"

"Only an extract with my name on it. Come on you Doubting Thomas, I'll take you over to the AG Library and you can see for yourself."

At the AG Library, located in the huge HQ complex, an NCO quickly located a copy of SO 147. Paragraph 11 contained about 100 names of CPTs promoted to MAJ. My name was on that list! I was surprised and delighted as I had not expected to be promoted for some years.

Several months before, each Div was authorized to nominate a number of CPTs for out of zone (early) promotion. COL Steinbach had nominated me; somehow his recommendation made it through the screening process. MG Fry had written a strong indorsement for each officer on the 2nd Div list. COL Steinbach had told me about it at the time, but events had pushed the matter out of my mind. Now the recommendation had been approved, I was a new major!

Joe drove me to the PX where I bought several sets of leaves. Since I wanted my records to reflect my new status, I immediately returned to Inchon. If being a MAJ would enhance my chance to get home early, I wanted to take advantage of it. The Pers OFF at the Repl Dep took down the information, called Seoul to verify the promotion, and transferred my name to the field grade officers list. But he quickly dashed any hopes for an early sailing, since all jobs on the three POW ships had been filled.

That night I gave a promotion party in the Inchon Officers' Club. All of the Manchu Officers in the Depot helped "wet down" the new leaves. It was a simple, inexpensive affair.

With no prospect for immediate shipment, the CO of the Replacement Depot gave me another three day pass. Once again I said goodbye to Lou Williams who was leaving the next day. Joe Lagatutta had invited me to stay with him in Seoul. That evening we had a good session celebrating our promotions, recalling old friends and drinking too much. During the night a "slicky-boy" came into my room and rifled my wallet. A measure of how soundly I slept as a result of that drinking spree, the thief casually located my wallet, took all the cash from it, about $50.00, then threw the wallet on the floor. At least I still had my ID and other important documents.

An insistent ringing of the field telephone on the desk next to my cot awakened me. Groping my way to the phone I said from habit, "Captain Seibert."

"Hey Don, this is Lou Williams. Get your ass back down here right away. I'm on my way to a briefing for you. You must be here by noon."

"Why? What's going on?"

"I can't talk now. I'm already late. But you get here as soon as you can. Goodbye."

I looked at the phone, thought a minute then began moving. After a quick shave and shower I was ready to go. Joe got a jeep to take me to Inchon. Throwing my musette bag into the vehicle, I told the Korean driver to get me to Inchon as fast as he could. We arrived at Inchon just before noon, where Lou was impatiently waiting for me.

He handed me a pad with some notes on it, saying, "Hurry up. The troop ship is leaving in two hours and you have to get on board. They forgot to appoint a Commander of Troops and as you are the only field grade OFF left in the Depot, you have been appointed CDR of Troops. I've taken notes, but you still have to report in to get additional information including the manifest."

I was astounded. Normally the Commander of Troops is the senior officer on board. Because of the repatriation mission, officers had been selected for various jobs based on their specialities or training. Why a more senior OFF wasn't taken off his assignment and made CDR of Troops is a mystery. Perhaps their jobs with the POWs were considered more important than CDR of Troops, who is little more than a HQ CMDT or a channel to transmit orders to passengers.

At HQ I was given a thick sheaf of paper containing a list of the passengers. The POWs were listed separately from the processing OFFs and detail EM. After a final briefing, we were trucked to the pier, together with our baggage.

Boarding a ship at Inchon Harbor was tricky because of the tides. There is such a difference between water levels in the harbor at high and low tides, that ships have difficulty getting in and out. They come in on one high tide, are unloaded and loaded, then leave on the next high tide. We were hurried along as the ship had to sail before the tide dropped too much. As the CDR of Troops, I was the first person aboard. Someone showed me to a large cabin with a private bathroom. This was luxurious compared with what I had experienced on other troop ships. As I found out later, I was the only passenger on board with a private cabin; even the senior medical OFFs (COLs and LTCs) shared staterooms.

Hurriedly dropping my duffle bag and suitcase in the cabin, I returned to the deck to attend to my duties as CDR of Troops. It was my responsibility to certify that all of the POWs boarded the ship. They trooped aboard last, each sounding off with his last name, first name and middle initial as I checked off his name on my roster. The boarding went smoothly; shortly after 1600 the troop ship headed out to sea.

Life on board ship quickly settled into a routine. A number of CPTs, LTs and senior NCOs supervised the housekeeping functions. I checked on them periodically, found them conscientious and competent, so left them alone.

In my stateroom there was a table and four chairs. A continuing bridge game was quickly organized. On board from the 9th IN were Lou Williams and 1LT Joe D. McAteer. As the Counterfire Plt Ldr when I was the S-3, I had become acquainted with Joe.. While he and Lou had specific duties, they were not demanding; everyone had lots of free time. The three of us formed the nucleus of the bridge game; a fourth was always available. There was some cutthroat play in that cabin!

As is normal with soldiers, we frequently talked about our experiences. Joe McAteer related the story of his arrival in Korea. It impressed me because it seemed typical of what went on. As Joe told it,

"When I arrived in Seoul, all I had was a set of orders. I called HQ of the 9th and asked what to do and where to report. All I got was to report to Regt HQ. Fortunately, a WO found me a place to stay overnight. The next day I hitch-hiked to Regimental Headquarters.

"I was assigned to a platoon position on either Erie or Arsenal, behind the T-Bone. As a dumb second lieutenant I reported to CPT Roberts, the Co CO. He and a LT Phillips were the most frightened people I have ever seen. They failed to inform me that there was no ammo available. The whole position was a mess. Bunkers were dug with pilings sitting around waiting for someone to put lids on.

"Roberts and Phillips never left the HQ Bunker. When I reported on my daily visit that there was no ammunition, they did not say a word and did nothing. I had the men in my Platoon pick up unused rounds in the trenches, clean them and clip them so we had something to fire."

Everyone had similar stories, but there were more which reflected the dedication, professionalism and courage of the troops and officers than those like McAteer's, which revealed ineptness and terror.

The voyage was relatively uneventful. Several nights I was awakened to receive messages. They were usually intelligence reports (based on debriefings of other POWs) that one of our ex-POWs was threatened by his fellow prisoners because he had reported them for some infraction or had cooperated with their captors. Each time I posted a guard on the soldier named to insure that he was not molested. Toward the end of the trip there were frequent messages concerning arrival times and debarking instructions. Other than such minor interruptions there was little to do. There were no major crises and none of the POWs was killed or molested. I usually ate in the Ward Room with Lou Williams and Joe McAteer, but occasionally I would be invited to eat at the Captain's table. It was a slow, boring trip. Even the sea remained calm.

As the ship pulled into San Francisco Harbor, there was a warm welcome home as we passed under the Golden Gate Bridge. For once I was able to enjoy the festivities on deck; as a minor VIP I had the run of the ship.

The Personnel Center at Camp Mason took charge of us when we debarked. As soon as I had completed the paperwork incident to my duties as CDR of Troops, I enquired about leave and my next assignment. Due to the curtailment of my extension, I had no orders. The Pers OFF at Camp Mason had received no assignment instructions concerning me. He queried DA but told me it would be several days before a reply could be expected. Meanwhile I would have to wait at the Personnel Center there at Mason.

That first night in San Francisco, I called Les Clarke, my buddy from RAAF, who picked Lou and me up. He and his wife Mildred took us out to a fine restaurant for dinner. Les was progressing rapidly in the State Board of Equalization (tax department) of California. It was good to see old friends like Mil and Les. Lou Williams caught a plane for home later that evening.

The next day I badgered the Pers OFF until he suggested that I go on leave while awaiting orders. When my assignment had been determined, the orders could be sent to my parents' home in College Point. That was fine with me; I managed to catch a direct flight to La Guardia Field within the next few hours. The family met me on arrival. I enjoyed being with them again, and spending time with old friends.

In about four days, an envelope arrived from DA containing orders assigning me as "Professor of Military Science and Tactics, PMS&T, Kentucky Military Institute (KMI), Lyndon KY". I had no idea where Lyndon was, had never heard of KMI, and was not at all interested in ROTC duty. At the library, I learned from a book listing educational institutions, that KMI was a small private military school, which offered the 7th through 12th grades, located in the suburbs of Louisville. This was not my type of assignment so I decided to spend part of my leave visiting the Pentagon to see if I could get the orders changed.

The day after I arrived in College Point I bought a car, another Pontiac convertible. After an enjoyable week with the family, I drove to Washington. MAJ Josephs, the OFF handling majors' assignments in Infantry Branch, listened to my request, then said, "I don't see any problem in changing these orders. Where do you want to go?"

"I'd like to go back to the 82nd. How about FT Bragg?"

"The 82nd is over in Infantry majors, but I think I can handle it."

He got my file out. "Wait a minute. There's a flag on your file. No one can change your orders without the approval of the Chief of Infantry, MG Fry."

This was the same MG James C. Fry, who as Commander of the 2nd IN Div, had recommended me for an out of zone promotion.

"I know General Fry, I'm sure he will change my orders."

Fry was out when I went to his office, but I waited. It was almost an hour before he returned. Several years later, when I was assigned to the Pentagon, I talked with the secretary, who still worked for the Chief of Infantry, then BG Reuben Tucker. She remembered me well, "You're the major who wore out my carpet, pacing back and forth waiting for General Fry."

Once he had settled in his office, the secretary announced me. I walked in, saluted, and gave him a hearty hello. He was very cordial. After the amenities were over I explained my purpose in visiting him, "Sir, there is a problem with my orders For some strange reason somebody has assigned me as PMS&T at the Kentucky Military Institute. I'm certainly not the man for that job. I don't have enough diplomacy. I think you need someone with a little more tact, perhaps a married officer who has children of his own."

General Fry looked at me strangely and said,

"Seibert, I am the one who selected you for that job. I did it with a purpose in mind. The school asked for a bachelor and you obviously fulfill that requirement. The Army is having problems with KMI; we're not satisfied with the way the ROTC program is running there. I want you to go there and straighten it out. I remember you well from Korea and you're a hard head. Once you set your sights on something, there is no stopping you. So I want you to do exactly that; straighten out that ROTC program at Kentucky Military Institute. Now let's have no more talk of your assignment. Let's talk about our mutual friends from Korea. Colonel Wilbur Wilson, for instance."

After a brief but friendly conversation, I excused myself. Well, the boss had given me an order. I heard it, I understood it, but I still would not accept it. Since I had another week of leave, I left Washington and drove to FT Bragg to spend a few days with COL Wilson and other friends there. COL Wilson commanded the 325 AIR and lived in one of the WWII Regt CDRs shacks. Located in the Old Division Area, it was a two bedroom cottage with kitchen, bath, dining room, living room and a room and bath in the back for an orderly. His driver slept there and took care of him and the place. I'm sure he was paid a nice supplement to his RA pay for that extra duty,

It was good to see COL Wilson, who insisted that I inspect the mess halls with him in the morning! He was still checking them between 0530 and 0600. During the short visit with him I got to see more of his leadership techniques.

The night before my departure he hosted a cocktail parry for m, one made specially enjoyable because there were many old friends serving in the 325: Peanut Hinton, Bud Hillman, Lou Williams and many more. COL Wilson insisted I stand with him in the receiving line at the 325 club the night of the party. I must confess to a feeling of guilt, but it did my heart good when CPT William V Stieber came through the line and said, "Sir, how are you?"

During my visit to FT Bragg, I paid my respects to MG Joseph P. Cleland, the XVIII Airborne Corps Commander. When he heard that I was unhappy with my orders and wanted to come to Bragg, he offered to help. "I think I can get your orders changed. I'll call Jimmy Fry."

He did so while I was in his office, asking for me as his senior aide. As a Corps CDR he was entitled to a MAJ as aide and normally would get any OFF he asked for. But Fry was adamant about my assignment to KMI. He told Cleland that while he had the highest respect for him, he was not going to change assignments because of general officer interest; assignments would be made based on the needs of the Army and the needs of the officers concerned. After that episode I finally accepted the feet that I was going to the Kentucky Military Institute whether I liked it or not.

Almost a year after I had left the 9th IN so precipitously, Ewell and Steinbach collaborated in writing a recommendation for a Bronze Star Medal. The order and medal were forwarded to me at KMI.

CHAPTER 10

PROFESSOR

The pleasant stay with old friends at FT Bragg terminated; I drove to Louisville, still not sure where Lyndon or the Kentucky Military Institute were located. My orders directed me to report to the Commanding OFF of the Kentucky Military District (KMD), located in downtown Louisville. COL Wheaton, the CDR, gave me some general guidance and told me what little he knew about KMI. While completing the routine processing in the District Pers Office which handled records, pay and other administration for the ROTC instructors in Kentucky, the Pers OFF told me about the US Army personnel assigned to KMI. The Asst PMS&T was CPT William Sykes, an Armor Officer; there were two NCOs, MSGs Rustari and Faw. The Detachment (Det) was authorized four NCOs.

Someone in the HQ told me how to get to Lyndon and to KMI east of Louisville toward Lexington. About 1000 I left for my new assignment; a drive of about a half hour from downtown Louisville.

As I drove through the gate I was impressed by the campus. A long drive shaded by old trees, at this time of year in brilliant colors, led to the school complex. The administrative offices were in Ormsby Hall, an ante-bellum mansion. Student dormitories or barracks formed two sides of a quadrangle in the center of which was a tiny CQ shack. On the third side was a brick classroom building. The fourth side of the quadrangle was open and stretched toward the parade/football field and gymnasium. It was a pleasant physical plant.

Entering Ormsby Hall, I introduced myself to the first secretary I found and asked to see the head of the school, COL Richmond (an honorary Kentucky Colonel, with no actual military rank). The secretary called COL Richmond's office; she reported that he was tied up and would see me later. In response to my question, she directed me to the ROTC office, promising to call me when COL Richmond was free.

The ROTC office occupied a Quonset hut, with a desk for the PMS&T behind a partition; every one else was in the common front room. The ROTC staff which I would be working with appeared to be dedicated and effective. CPT Sykes was not as impressive in appearance as the ABN OFFs I had served with, but seemed to be competent. MSGs Rustari and Faw, older Regular NCOs, were enthusiastic and knowledgeable. Both were heavyset, no longer field soldiers. Rustari was the senior enlisted instructor, Faw the administrative NCO. The three of them gave me a quick introduction to the school, the ROTC program and my duties. CPT Sykes had set up the program for the fall term pending my arrival, but it needed my approval to continue. He went over it with me, explaining the rationale for his decisions; as it looked reasonable to me, inexperienced as I was, I accepted it. It proved to be a workable program.

No quarters were provided for the ROTC staff, but one of the secretaries found a motel in the vicinity where I could stay until I found something permanent. Eventually one of the staff members found a furnished room for me, just a bit better than a BOQ.

That first afternoon, I went to drill which followed the last academic class; what I saw was not pleasing. There was a great deal of standing around as the cadet officers talked with their units, but very little military drill was in evidence. There also seemed to be a large number of cadets excused from drill for various reasons. Drill appeared to be the logical target at which to launch my attack to improve the ROTC program. Certainly this was a purely military subject to be handled by the Army cadre.

During the next two or three days, I was completely read into the situation, met the faculty, became familiar with my duties and status, was instructed in the history and traditions of the school. KMI, a privately owned military school, was one of the oldest in the country. About 300 students were enrolled, 75 in the Junior School, hence not in the ROTC program.

My predecessor, LTC Kent, reassigned to Korea, was still in the area; his son was a student at KMI. He stopped by to talk with me, tendering some very bad advice. He counseled me not to make any changes immediately, certainly none in the first term. He said that the cadets resented changes. He further pontificated that I should make sure that I did nothing to antagonize the students because they could make my position untenable. Not only was this advice contrary to my basic philosophy of making changes when warranted, but it was inappropriate because I had been sent to KMI to make changes, to restore the ROTC program to conformity with Army policy and aims. Over the years, weak PMS&Ts such as Kent had yielded their authority to the school administration.

Meanwhile I was still waiting to meet the President of the school. His secretary, Mrs Tillie Rustari, my senior enlisted instructor's wife, kept me informed. She said the COL was avoiding me. This was a ploy to put me in my place. In other words, he was going to let me cool my heels. Wasting no time on that gambit I went about my duties. I called on the Commandant and Vice-president, LTC Hodgin, a tall, distinguished looking gentleman, and his brother the Headmaster, MAJ Hodgin. MAJ Hodgin held a legitimate commission as a RES OFF, the only faculty member to do so. Soon I knew all the faculty members except COL Richmond. CPT Sykes pointed him out to me as he went about the campus, but we still had not had an official opening interview during which we could exchange views on policies and procedures. As a matter of courtesy, I called at his office several times, but failed to see him. There was enough to keep me busy so I decided to let COL Richmond develop the situation.

The PMS&T traditionally taught Military History and Map Reading at KMI. Both were interesting to me so I prepared to carry on that tradition. Several days after my arrival, I met and had a conference with the cadet officers during which I told them what I intended to do and what I expected from them. Thus, I settled down to my tour of duty at the Kentucky Military Institute.

A week or ten days after I arrived, Tillie Rustari called to advise me that COL Richmond would see me. Walking into his office, I extended my hand, and introduced myself. He offered me a chair and we chatted for a few minutes. Then he got down to business. He told me what he expected me to do as the PMS&T, obviously what my predecessors had done. He emphasized that the former PMS&Ts had fitted into the school and adopted it ways. I listened to him carefully. When he finished, I said,

"COL Richmond, I appreciate the thoughts you have just expressed. Certainly I will take them under consideration. But you must realize that since I am the military officer here I'll have to determine what needs to be done to make this an effective ROTC unit. Assuredly we will work together to do whatever is best for the school and for the Army."

He blustered a bit, saying, "Don't let those generals fool you. I remember that before World War II they were ashamed to wear their uniforms in Washington and would scurry around in civilian clothes."

To avoid making a pointed and appropriate remark I clamped my jaws tightly. It incensed me that he would hold such feelings toward the military and yet run a military school. Refusing to rise to the bait, I waited for him to go on.

"Do you drink, MAJ?"

"Yes, I do, socially, sir."

"Well, I don't drink and I don't permit my faculty to drink. I expect the ROTC Det to adhere to the same rules as the faculty."

"COL Richmond, I respect your views in this matter. I assure you that no member of the ROTC Staff will ever appear on this campus under the influence of alcohol or after he has been drinking. But under no circumstances am I going to abstain from drinking myself or ask my staff to do so. If you feel that you cannot live with this, you are at liberty to call the Military District and request my transfer. But I am not going to pledge myself to abstinence."

Richmond, obviously unhappy, mumbled something I could not catch. Determined to get the matter settled, I continued, "If you aren't happy with my position on drinking, now is the time to take action. You have only to call Colonel Wheaton at the Military District and make known to him that you do not approve of my life style and I am sure the Army will transfer me."

He wasn't willing to go that far. He still blustered and tried to get me to commit myself to abstinence. I refused to do so. We parted shortly, not too amicably. This is the way our relation remained throughout my tenure. We were studiously courteous to each other, but there was no cordiality between us.

Returning to the ROTC office, I reviewed my conversation with COL Richmond with my staff, enjoining them that under no circumstances would any of them appear on campus if they had been drinking. But I repeated the same thing I told COL Richmond; I was not going to keep them from drinking. As a matter of fact, after drill ended at 1530 each day, it became customary for the entire Det to drop by a local bar, the "Eight Mile House", for a beer or two. It was removed from the campus so there was no intent to flaunt Richmond. But it provided a means to relax and discuss the events of the day.

Certain privileges were accorded to the military staff and faculty at KMI. All faculty members, including the military faculty, could eat with the cadets free of charge. Each faculty member was assigned a table, at which he maintained discipline and insured that every cadet got his share. Table 2 was assigned to me. I usually ate lunch in the school dining room. Occasionally I would eat the evening meal there, but never breakfast. A senior sitting at Table 2 kept order in my absence. The cadets got a bit more to eat when I was not there, as food was served family style.

A few weeks after I reported to KMI, I received official notice from the Finance Officer that I was held pecuniarily liable for the sum of $1, 100.00. This resulted from disapproval by the Surveying Officer of the Report of Survey submitted to cover the loss of properly in F Co, 508th RCT. While in the 9th IN, I had received papers from the 508 informing me that LTC Krebs, the Surveying OFF, contemplated holding me pecuniarily liable for approximately $1,400.00 for property lost while I commanded F Co. This was a surprise. I had expected Lattimore to keep his promise to make up the shortages since he had been Supply OFF at the time. Though authorized to submit any information to support the report of survey, as the S-3 I was busy at the time, and only took a few minutes to write a statement, explaining the turbulence during Longhorn, the difficulty on the DZ with the injured, and the rapidity of our move to the R&S line. It seemed a convincing statement. The papers had been mailed to the 508 and promptly forgotten.

Now, I owed the government $1, 100.00. Before paying this amount I had another opportunity to rebut the charge and provide additional information. If I accepted the judgement, I could pay in full or it could be deducted from my pay in monthly instalments of $100.00.

It was a shock! Not only did being held liable for the F Co loss rankle, but paying the government that much money would be burdensome, as I had just taken out a monthly allotment for $100.00 to buy mutual funds. In a carefully worded and relatively lengthy rebuttal, I reviewed the entire period of my command of F Co, setting out the procedures that had been established to control the property and naming the three Supply OFFs - Whitelaw, Reese and Lattimore. The many inventories I had taken were recorded. It was apparent that the loss covered by the survey was the result of the Longhorn maneuver. The problems incident to that maneuver were enumerated. The statement concluded that everything possible had been done to safeguard government property.

In about two months I was informed that my rebuttal had been denied and that effective with the next pay day $100.00 would be deducted from my pay each month until the judgement against me had been liquidated. Though unhappy, there was nothing more I could do. It would be necessary to watch my finances until the debt was paid.

Of course I was at fault, which made the loss more infuriating. I should have remained at Benning to make up the shortages. A commander should never trust anyone with the property he is signed for. It was foolish to take Lattimore's word that he would take care of the matter. It was a bitter lesson. I had failed on two accounts: managing property and judging character. After that I never thought of Lattimore as a trustworthy OFF. Fortunately, I never served with him again.

In a letter to Henry Tucker, my former Unit Administrator, I mentioned the fact that I had been held liable for the loss. He answered that as soon as I had left F Co Lattimore had executed the Report of Survey, without making any attempt to reduce the shortages, though both Tucker and the Supply SGT were sure they could be found within the 2/508 if not F Co.

Despite the financial problem, I settled into a routine. Working with boys was enjoyable, if not as challenging intellectually, as working with college students. They were an average lot, many fine boys, a few disciplinary problems, some from broken homes. Doubtless a few of the parents had put their sons into military school hoping that they would be straightened out. In my limited experience, that was a false hope; military schools, or any boarding school, can do just so much. Based on my observations while PMS&T at KMI, I am not impressed with military schools; at least at the high school level. Kentucky Military Institute was as good as any of them I suppose. But children, particularly younger ones, need parental guidance, love, affection and discipline. Teachers are of limited value as surrogate parents. There are limits to what they can do; cadet officers are not the answer to disciplinary problems. Certainly the Army cadre was ill-equipped to offer much help.

In November 1953, CPT Sykes received word that he was being relieved from active duty as part of another RIF. Sykes did not want to leave the Army and thought that LTC Kent's efficiency reports were largely responsible for his elimination. He took leave to review his files in Washington. When he returned, he told me that Kent had rated him based on his personality rather than performance. Sykes was not the most diplomatic officer I ever met, but I had been impressed with the way he had stepped in when Kent left, before I arrived, and had gotten things underway for the fall term. One of the remarks Kent had made was that he was disdainful of the students and talked down to them. I had audited several of Sykes1 classes and had not found that to be true. He did not tolerate any nonsense in the classroom, he made the students behave, but there was no improper attitude on his part. And I had not been impressed with Kent's approach to the military-student relationship.

Despite the fact that it was late to make an appeal, and not overly sanguine about the consideration that such actions were given, I offered to write a letter requesting reconsideration. Elimination should not be based on the opinion of one individual. In my letter recommending his retention I stated that in the short time I had been at KMI Sykes had impressed me. The letter was accompanied by a special efficiency report I rendered on him. In about three months Sykes received word that he had been retained on active duty. Both of us were pleased.

KM had a ten point outdoor rifle range (small bore) on the Lyndon campus. The KMI Rifle Team fired against other Junior ROTC units throughout the country. While observing the cadets fire, I became concerned about the safety limits of the range. Although only 22 caliber rifles were being fired, the range was near the boundary of the campus close to a well traveled road. The targets were against the base of the bill on which the "Alumni Hut" was located. CPT Sykes was directed to check the regulation on range safety. He found that the KMI range did not meet the safety limits even for 22 caliber firing. Obviously we either had to reconfigure the range to meet the safety limits or close it. When I spoke to COL Richmond, he dismissed the matter, saying that the Army was over-cautious.

KMI had been firing on that range for a hundred years without an accident. How-ever, in recent years the area had been developed; now more and more people came within the vicinity of the range.

Sykes developed a plan which provided ample safety, but its implementation required the expenditure of funds for construction. COL Richmond would not consider it. I closed the range. Fortunately, we were able to obtain permission to use an indoor range in a local NG Armory several afternoons each week at no cost to the school. Thus we were able to continue practice and match firing.

Most of our matches were fired on our own range. The certified targets were then sent to the school firing against KMI. The coaches decided the winners. The cadets found the few shoulder-to-shoulder matches more satisfying, but they were difficult to arrange. CPT Sykes coached the rifle team until his departure. KMI won about half its matches.

During my wanderings about Louisville I discovered an excellent restaurant called Leo's Hideaway. Located in the Fish Market Area, a deteriorated neighborhood, I was skeptical when it was recommended to me, but it proved to be outstanding. After a confrontation with the owner over a poorly prepared steak (the first two served were overdone), I had a truly fine meal. As a result of my refusal to accept a free meal, I became a special customer; there was always a table for me, and Charles, the first waiter I had, usually took care of me. This provided the means to encourage the rifle team. I made a standing offer to take to dinner at Leo's any cadet who won his match or fired a perfect score. The cadets found this a tempting incentive, because the food at KMI was not too good. A visit to Leo's also meant getting out of evening formations. Several times a year I made reservations for the six or eight boys who had done well; we all enjoyed the excellent fare at Leo's.

KMI had a two week Christmas recess from 19 December until 3 January. The military staff, having no duties, was authorized administrative leave which did not count against annual leave time. On 3 January, KMI resumed classes at its Venice, FL campus. Venice, a small town south of Sarasota, is the only city on the Gulf Coast of Florida which has no keys or islands shielding the mainland from the Gulf of Mexico. A train was chartered to take the students from Louisville to Venice. Each year several faculty members were assigned to supervise the train trip and maintain order. In the past, one of the Army personnel had shared that duty. On COL Richmond's request that this policy be continued, I agreed; either MSG Rustari or CPT Sykes made the trip in 1954.

After an enjoyable Christmas in College Point, I drove to Florida, stopping off in Baltimore to see the Rotherts and in Jacksonville to see the Reilly's (friends from Roswell).

At Venice, I found KMI housed in two old hotels, the San Marco and the Venice, originally built by a railroad union, which had selected Venice because it was supposed to have the best sunlight, the most actinic rays, in Florida. During the depression, COL Richmond, an astute businessman, had bought them for back taxes when the union had run short of money. The plant, now worth several million dollars, was badly in need of maintenance. Each faculty member, including ROTC instructors, was provided a room and bath without charge. Though MSG Faw and his wife had a small son, they still were authorized only one room, with a cot in it for the boy. The rooms were comparable to those in a BOQ and about as austerely furnished. To live off campus at the height of the tourist season in Florida was prohibitively expensive. Meals in the several good restaurants in the area were likewise costly, so most faculty members, myself included, ate the majority of their meals with the cadets in Venice. But I ate out as frequently as finances permitted.

The ROTC program, which had become a bit more military in the three months following my arrival, also resumed. In Florida, parades and pageants highlighted the military nature of the school. On alternate Sundays, the Cadet Corps conducted afternoon dress parades. The San Marco Hotel fronted on a park in the heart of Venice, which by arrangement with the City Administration, KMI used for daily drill and Sunday parades. These parades were tourist attractions, drawing several thousand spectators. Such an audience prompted the cadets to march their best.

Over the years many non-military gimmicks had been added to the parades to please the crowd, hence it was over the parades that I really clashed with COL Richmond for the first time. A unique system, colorful perhaps, but decidedly unmilitary, had been devised to get the cadets onto the parade field. Each Co appeared from a different door, clump of trees or corner of a building, making its way to its position on the Field by a route which intersected that of other companies, thus presenting problems in timing and control which were not readily handled. This was circus stuff, not military drill. The day after the first parade I announced at drill that the cadets would march on in proper military fashion. COL Richmond, who had heard the announcement, asked me to step into his office. He told me that the spectators liked and expected the other system; a change might cause a drop in attendance, so he wanted the current procedure continued. It appeared that it was time to establish my authority over military matters.

"COL Richmond, you are not running a carnival. You are running a military school. These cadets are supposed to be learning proper military drill. I cannot countenance military formations being made into circuses. There are many interesting and different parades that we will use, but they will be authorized formations. There is nothing more stirring than a well drilled military unit. We will put on a fine performance, but it will be a military one."

After some argument, he grudgingly yielded when he saw that I was unshakeable. I had made my first big point on policy.

The two weeks following my conversation with COL Richmond were devoted to preparing for the next scheduled parade, which was to be a Retreat Parade. We not only practiced Company drill, but formation of the Cadet Battalion prior to marching on the field. One of the shortcomings of the former procedures was the disregard of the colors. I made an important issue of designating the Color Company for that parade and the presentation of the colors to it and the Battalion before marching onto the field. I believe that the boys were impressed by the simple courtesy to the National Flag.

Despite the radical change in procedure the cadets put on a colorful military parade the next scheduled Sunday. Although it was cool, there was a good crowd which seemed to enjoy it.

Following that first successful parade, I determined that the Corps would conduct a different type of parade each Sunday. Successively we held the Retreat Parade, an Escort of the Colors, and an Awards Review. To demonstrate the flexibility of military formations, we developed a routine for the final parade at Venice, which would honor the sponsor of each Company (the girl friend of the Cadet Company Commander as it turned out in most cases). Once the Battalion was in formation, each Company Commander in turn went to the stands bowed to his young lady, escorted her to his Company, presented her to it, then stood in formation until all of the sponsors were on line. During this period, MSG Rustari, who had a remarkably sonorous and musical voice, announced the name and home town of the Company Commander and the name and home town of the sponsor. As the band played a waltz, the Company Commanders then escorted their sponsors to the reviewing stand, from which they accepted the honors as the Corps Passed in Review. This, too, made a hit. Both the cadets and the spectators seemed to enjoy the variety and color of the strictly military formations.

The ROTC Office, classrooms and arms room were in an old garage just across the street from the San Marco Hotel. There was also a 12 point indoor rifle range in the building. The major part of the former garage was occupied by a basketball court. Chapel and assembly functions were held in the bleachers in this part of the building. All of the military instruction continued at Venice. Rifle team practice and matches were also uninterrupted. Drill was over by 1530, the weather was warm, the beach close by. It was pleasant to work under these circumstances.

A new face appeared at the school when we convened in Florida. First Lieutenant Charlie Norman showed up in my office. A tall, slender, blond OFF, he wore a starched khaki uniform, highly polished jump boots, and parachutist wings and cap patch. Charlie had just gotten out of the Army. His last assignment had been with the 508, hence we had many mutual friends. A talented musician, Charlie was the new bandmaster. Because he felt more at home with the Army personnel than with the pseudo-military faculty, he gravitated to the ROTC Det. Although each member of the faculty was addressed as captain or major, only MAJ Hodgin and Charlie had the right to their grade. Since all teachers were CPTs until they had been with KMI for twenty years, at which time they became MAJs, COL Richmond wanted to make Charlie one, but he insisted on his actual grade of 1LT, wearing his uniform properly and proudly.

This was another matter on which COL Richmond and I disagreed. I did not think it proper to call the faculty by a military grade if they did not in fact hold one. COL Richmond and LTC Hodgin at least were commissioned in the Kentucky Militia, so-called Kentucky Colonels. But none of the other teachers had claim to the titles they used. I told COL Richmond that if the faculty was to be military, they should wear some sort of distinguishing uniform and insignia. Some effort was made toward getting them in uniform, but it was not overly successful, so I finally dropped the topic.

The matter of cadet insignia of rank also created friction when I insisted that the cadets officers and NCOs wear the approved ROTC insignia. They were wearing sleeve insignia similar to that used at the USMA. The senior cadet was the "First Captain" rather than a cadet LTC as authorized in the ROTC program. Not only was the sleeve insignia costly when grades were changed, but it was more cumbersome than the metal pins prescribed by ROTC regulations, disks for company grade and lozenges for field grade officers. Standard sleeve stripes were authorized for cadet noncommissioned officers. Working with COL Richmond and the cadets this change was finally achieved.

While the school was in session at Venice, the cadets participated in several pageants. The organizers of the pageants wanted KMI in their parades because the cadets wore colorful uniforms, marched well and the cadet officers with their sashes, sabers and plumed tarbooshes made a brave display. COL Richmond was eager to have the cadets on parade because it was good advertising for KMI. The band played marches well; Charlie Norman saw to that. In the 1954 term the cadets participated in the Sara-De-Soto pageant at Sarasota, the De Soto pageant at Bradenton, the Fort Myers "Pageant of Light", and the Gasparilla Parade in Tampa. The ROTC Det made the necessary liaison and, with Charlie Norman, went on each of these trips as supervisors and chaperons since they were made under its purview. Usually the sponsors, the Chamber of Commerce or Civic Group, provided bus transportation so KMI had no expenses incident to participating in the pageants. In addition, some provided lunch. The cadets liked the pageants as they provided an opportunity to get away from the routine of the school and a chance to show off. We practiced for the parades during normal drill sessions as a regular part of the ROTC program.

In an effort to establish better rapport with the boys, I also chaperoned some of the cadets on many of the basketball trips. KMI had a good basketball team which played in the Florida High School League. Most of the games were played away; on each occasion I took a carload of boys.

It gave me a chance to see a bit more of Florida and to eat in some of the excellent restaurants. The cadets were gentlemen and never a problem.

KMI had no drill team; early in the Florida session I suggested that one be organized. The cadets enthusiastically endorsed the initiative. We immediately set about forming and equipping the Kentucky Rifles. As every cadet wanted to be a member, it was difficult to pick the 40 who could drill best. Cadet LT Gandolfo, a trim, dark haired student with boundless energy and enthusiasm, an excellent posture, poise, and a resonant command voice, was the best drill master in the Corps. He was the obvious choice to be the drill team leader. The platoon was the envy of every cadet as it quickly mastered the basic drill team maneuvers. As soon as we formulated plans for the drill team, I had MSG Faw request through Army supply channels Ml 903 Springfield rifles. As they had better balance and were slightly lighter than the M-1 rifles used by the cadets in the daily drill, they enabled the team to execute the Manual of Arms more precisely. The '03s (as they were called) arrived with unusual dispatch. Richmond agreed to purchase white leather slings for them. A uniform was developed from items the cadets traditionally wore or were available through the Army: white shirt and trousers, gold scarf and enameled helmet liners. The commander wore his sash and feathered tarboosh.

The Kentucky Rifles made their official debut before a Sunday parade at Venice. They were an instant hit. Not only the cadets and their families, but also everyone who watched them execute their precision drill, acclaimed them. While the ROTC cadre provided the initial guidance and instruction, the success of the team resulted from the hard work, enthusiasm and determination of the cadets and the leadership of Cadet LT Joe Gandolfo. The cadets vied with each other to devise more intricate maneuvers which they practiced until execution was perfect.

Later, during a performance of the Kentucky Rifles for the President of Valley Forge Military Academy, LTG Milton Baker, the cadets were at their best. Baker was so impressed that he donated to the team a replica of the guidon used at Valley Forge by Washington's Guard. This enhanced the appearance and performance of the platoon.

The Venice Little Theater had an active season while KMI was in residence. Someone talked me into trying out for one of the parts with the result that I was selected for the male lead in *A Shop at Sly Corners*. The heroine was played by an attractive young lady from Sarasota. As a result of the hours we spent together rehearsing, we found we had much in common, and began to date. Some of the cadets were ushers during the performances and reported to the Corps on my performance and activities.

In conjunction with the pageant in Sarasota, a ball was held the night before the parade. The cadet officers were asked to provide a guard-of-honor for the Queen of the Pageant. As chaperon for the cadets, I was given tickets and a table. I took the young lady I had been dating, which occasioned much talk among the cadets who immediately had us romantically linked.

On my return from Korea, I had visited Christianson's, an old New York firm which tailored officers' uniforms, and ordered a full set: dress blues, dress whites, blue and white mess jackets and cape. At the Sara-De-Soto Ball, I wore the white mess jacket for the first time. The cadets were impressed, finding it difficult to believe that it was actually an Army uniform. In subtle ways such as this, I tried to indoctrinate the boys in the traditions of the Army. They had never seen the blue mess jacket, either, until I wore mine to chaperon a dance after our return to Lyndon. I acquired an unearned reputation about KMI as an Army gay blade.

The three months in Florida passed swiftly and pleasantly. I took the opportunity to see many of the attractions in the State as well as to visit old friends. Among the latter were George and Gladys Good, friends from Roswell, who had retired to Santa Maria Island, and Tom Samartino, my classmate at LICM, who was an Orthopedic Surgeon in Miami. The flatness of the landscape, the humidity and insects made Florida unattractive to me as a place of residence.

Before I had become fully familiar with the Florida campus and its environs, it was time to return to Lyndon. The end of March found us recrating the rifles and other impedimenta. Over the years, suitable sturdy containers had been constructed for the equipment, so the packing problems were minimized. The cadets again traveled by special train, while those of us not required for duty on that trip drove to Lyndon.

Orders were awaiting me on my return placing me on TDY to inspect the ROTC units in the high schools in Washington, DC. All ROTC units have annual inspections to make sure that they are complying with the Program of Instruction (POI) and other Army regulations. It was, in fact, an Annual General Inspection or AGI. KMI would have its inspection in May.

In early April I drove to Washington, where LTC Kerlin and I formed a team to inspect the eight high schools. The ROTC Coordinator had scheduled an inspection each morning and after-noon. I was interested in what other high schools were doing in the ROTC program. While they were not military schools, they generated many ideas for the program at KMI. It was an enjoyable TDY.

When I returned to KMI the final two months of the school year were in full swing. There was a parade with a different theme every Sunday afternoon, but always a proper military review. On

Mother's Day for instance, the Mother who traveled the farthest distance to be with her son, was honored. The cadets presented a fine appearance in their dress uniforms. Following the parade, they quickly returned their rifles to the arms room under the gym/chapel and reformed for the chapel service.

The ROTC cadre worked hard preparing for KMTs annual inspection, which the school passed with high grades. The cadets were at their best and turned out smartly for the occasion. MG Smith, Dep CDR of 2nd Army at FT Meade, MD took the review and made the inspection during his annual visit to the KMI ROTC Det. Since MG Smith endorsed my efficiency report, I was pleased that the cadets put on a smart parade for him.

COL Wheaton, Chief of the Kentucky Military District, and my immediate CDR, rarely saw me. He visited KMI in Florida in conjunction with a vacation, but never came to the Lyndon campus. This bothered me because as my rater he should have observed me more frequently to have a better idea of what I was doing. My rating would be based on the results of the AGI, and to some extent, on comments received from COL Richmond. This was a real worry!

Preparations for graduation and the closing of the school year began early in May. There were many competitions to select the best squad and platoon, the best drilled junior cadet, the best drilled cadet, and the outstanding cadet of the year. The ROTC Det was busy compiling evaluations and statistics to determine which cadet company would be designated Honor Company for the year.

Early in November I had announced that I would present a "PMS&T Cup" to the cadet who I thought the finest potential officer in the Corps. A small sterling silver julep cup, suitably engraved, was the prize displayed in my office. This created much interest; as graduation neared many seniors put out extra effort in an attempt to win it.

During the pre-graduation activities a circular announcing the Arctic Warfare Summer Indoctrination Course at FT Greely, AK, came in the routine correspondence from Kentucky Military District. Since J had never been to Alaska, this would be a good time to see part of it as well as a profitable way to spend the summer. The 30 day course ran from the middle of July to the middle of August, which fit my schedule. It was with both surprise and pleasure that I learned that my application to attend the course was approved.

Pre-graduation activities increased in intensity. The squad and platoon drill competitions were the last of many. The results remained secret, as the winners of all competitions, including Best Company, would be announced at a Military Awards Ceremony the afternoon before graduation.

Pre-graduation activities did not prevent me from attending the Kentucky Derby. Sipping an expensive, weak, almost tasteless mint julep, I watched the race from the infield. The Derby is a pageant worth experiencing, but for the next two years, I went to Derby parties where it was viewed on TV.

The day of the Military Awards Ceremony, the cadets, in undress uniform, formed a hollow square. The least significant awards were presented first. As the awards increased in stature and desirability, I deliberately built up the tension, referring occasionally to the "Best Company Award". Even at this age, personal ambitions and animosities were subordinated to unit pride; every cadet wanted his Company to be named "Best Company". The only award I did not present at the Military Awards Ceremony was the "PMS&T Cup" which would be given at the graduation ceremony the following day. The last thing on the agenda was the announcement of the "Best Company of the Year", selected on the overall performance of individual members of the company as well as the unit in drill, ROTC academics and total awards earned. As we reached the end of the awards the tension was palpable I made a short speech and procrastinated. The cadets were on edge. Finally I pronounced A Company the "Best Company". Pandemonium broke loose! A Company cadets jumped and screamed, losing control of themselves. The other companies, dejected, turned away in disappointment. It meant a great deal to these young men that they could wear a patch on their sleeves which said, "Best Company". The Military Awards Ceremony was over.

A formal graduation dance was held in the Brown Hotel in downtown Louisville each year. I attended in white mess jacket which again occasioned comment. During the dinner, the Senior Class President announced that *The Saber,* the cadet year book, had been dedicated to MSG Rustari. Each year the seniors honored their favorite instructor. I was delighted that MSG Rustari, a truly outstanding NCO, had been so recognized.

COL Richmond paid MSG Rustari to supervise "The Beat", the punishment program. The cadets walked "tours"; marched a given "Beat" with their rifles at right soldier arms, to remove demerits. At my urging, he changed the formation and procedure to make it more military. Despite his association with this punishment, he was well liked. He was a favorite counselor of the junior school students and contributed greatly to KMI; his recognition was well deserved.

Before the graduation ceremony, there was a last dress parade. The commencement speaker, The Mexican Ambassador to the United States, had been invited to take the honors at the parade. He was selected as speaker because several of the seniors were from Mexico. Charlie Norman worked with the band many hours to insure that it played the Mexican National Anthem correctly. The cadets marched their best for their parents and friends.

Graduation itself was held in front of Ormsby Hall, the antebellum mansion which served as Administrative Building for the school. Guests and cadets sat in folding chairs on the lawn under giant old trees facing the columned porch. The speaker, honored guests and faculty sat on the porch. COL Richmond, a true showman, was deeply committed to KMI. As the band softly played "My Old Kentucky Home" he presented academic awards while tears streamed down his face. The PMS&T Cup was awarded to Joe Gandolfo, the Leader of the Kentucky Rifles and later commander of A Company. Following graduation and the departure of the students, the ROTC Detachment settled down to administrative work.

The KMI cadet uniforms were patchwork quilts. Over the years a myriad of decorations and accouterments, some very unmilitary, had been authorized by the school administration. These were worn with little regard for uniformity or precision. To correct this, I determined that during the summer months an SOP would be developed to clarify the rules governing the uniform in an attempt to make it more military. The more I thought about the SOP the broader its scope became, one of the pitfalls of such a document. As a result the ROTC staff spent the summer codifying and clarifying all of the procedures used in the ROTC program at KMI. The school needed a better institutional memory to pass information from one PMS&T to the next, and the cadets needed a reference with specific and detailed information. CPT Sykes, MSG Rustari and I immediately set to work to develop the SOP.

MSG Faw, reassigned at the end of the school year, was replaced by MSG Richard Norcross. Norcross, an experienced administrative NCO, quickly adjusted to the KMI routine. SFC Schenck, an intelligent NCO but a problem drinker, was not a good choice for assignment as an enlisted instructor. SSG Andrew Condee, a quiet but effective supply sergeant also joined the cadre.

A major task that summer, and every summer, was the selection of cadet OFFs for the following school year. COL Richmond and I had a great deal of discussion and controversy over this. My list was based on my evaluation of the leadership potential of the individuals and on their appearance and general military demeanor. COL Richmond's list, while considering the same criteria, was weighted toward those students whose parents made contributions to the school or who might have potential in persuading others to enroll in it. Actually the two lists differed only on two company commanders and the Battalion Commander. We finally reached a compromise acceptable to both of us by the time I was ready to depart for Alaska.

The trip to Alaska caused me to miss my good friend Frank Mashburn's wedding. He had asked me to be his best man, but the dates conflicted. During a stop-over in Seattle, I did get to see my Deadeye buddy, Fred Steed. From Seattle I flew to Anchorage, where it was necessary to change again for Big Delta, close to FT Greely where the Arctic Warfare Center was located.

The Summer Arctic Indoctrination Course was concerned with three basic techniques: glacier crossing, mountain climbing and cross country movement through muskeg and by means of rivers. The latter would involve the use of the so-called Tananaw River Boats. The course reviewed cross country navigation as well as movement. The ground in Alaska never completely thaws, but softens two or three inches in the summer. The permafrost beneath this layer holds rainwater, creating a marsh or bog called muskeg, which covers most of the open area. The decaying vegetable matter nourishes a low, stringy grass, which flourishes in summer, making cross country movement on foot difficult. Because of this problem, movement during the summer is accomplished on rivers when possible. Land navigation poses problems because the compass needle points to the Magnetic North Pole, located some distance from true North.

It was a fascinating course. Articulate and experienced instructors taught the various techniques employing mostly practical work. There were many interesting students in the class. My partner on most problems was a civilian instructor at the Mountain Warfare Course at FT Carson whose knowledge of mountain climbing techniques helped me a great deal. He was in the course to observe the Arctic Warfare Center teaching methods as well as to learn the river, glacier and survival techniques covered.

Basic land navigation training, conducted at FT Greely, served as an introduction to the problems which would be encountered if the Army had to fight in Arctic regions during the summer. It was a short, unpleasant phase, during which we were plagued with swarms of mosquitoes and other insects.

The mountain climbing phase of training covered balance climbing, party climbing, belays and practice falls, piton work, rappelling and the use of ropes to cross ravines or lower casualties. My partner or buddy (all practical work was done with a buddy) from FT Carson helped me to master the techniques quickly. There is a thrill in descending a cliff by rappelling.

Included in the mountain training was a walk up Rainbow Mountain, a long gradual slope of several thousand feet. It was astounding to experience the effect of altitude on activity when an individual has little or no acclimatization. Because of the lighter air, the rate of breathing is increased to obtain the same amount of oxygen. By the time we reached the top of the Mountain we were all panting. The descent was much easier, accomplished by use of a long "scree slope". Scree is rotting rock that has deteriorated into fine pebbles and sand. In going down a scree slope, you dig your heels in at the end of each long stride; the scree begins to move, "floating" you a down. If you stumble, you could be covered the scree, but it is not a dangerous technique and was great fun.

Glacier crossing was probably the most interesting phase of the course since glaciers were an unknown environment for me. Instruction was conducted on the Black River Glacier by Albert Hople, a Swiss mountain climber. Although in his sixties, he was very spry and agile, and thoroughly knowledgeable in mountain climbing and travel over glaciers. We learned to cross the glaciers using cramp-ons (spikes strapped to ski boots); to cut ice steps; and to probe for hidden crevasses. Members of a party traversing a glacier are roped together as in mountain climbing. If one person breaks through a snow bridge and falls into a crevasse, instantly everyone else in the group goes on belay to secure him. The instructors demonstrated the technique of recovering from a fall into a crevasse; essentially climbing up the sheer ice wall using rope and cramp-ons. Each four man group practiced the technique. I volunteered to go into the crevasse to be extracted by our group. As the three members of my team went on beiay, I dropped over the side of the crevasse almost pulling the three of them with me! It was a foolish thing to do. I hadn't realized how my weight, suddenly snubbed by the rope, would strain the belay. Fortunately, their cramp-ons were firmly anchored in the ice. When I finally climbed out, the instructor roundly and properly chewed me out for taking an unnecessary risk. He informed us that the crevasse we were working on was almost a thousand feet deep!

The river phase began at FT Greely base camp. Alaskan rivers are traversed in long, flat boats, called Tananaw River Boats, with outboard motors mounted on a bracket. The bracket makes it possible to tilt the motor up in rapids or shallow water to keep the blades from striking rocks or bottom, shearing the cotter pin which holds the propeller to the shaft, or doing other damage. We learned to operate the boats in both deep and shallow water, pushing the lever to raise the motor at the last possible minute as we approached low water. We also learned to carry a number of extra cotter pins and how to replace them rapidly. There was also camping and survival work in the Alaskan wilderness. The crystal clear waters of the rivers and lakes comes from melting snow and ice, hence they are too cold to swim in; several of us tried. We dove in and immediately scrambled out - instantly blue with cold. During the river training we took a long trip up the Tananaw River and through its many sloughs. We camped on beautiful lakes, did a little fishing, and greatly enjoyed a paid vacation.

Alaska is beautiful There is a sense of silence, of space, of peace, of freshness. The terrain seems clean and unspoiled. Everywhere, snow-capped mountains are visible forming a breath-taking backdrop to each scene.

The night before graduation, our class took over the Greely Officers' Club. The course had been stimulating, challenging, and physically demanding. After four weeks of life in the open we were ready to relax. Liquor flowed freely; what reserves remained soon melted. The one USMC OFF in the class, an enthusiastic and professional CPT, had held his own when kidded about being the only "jar head" around. When the telephone rang late in the evening he answered with the words, "Kelley's Whore House. All the girls are busy."

On the other end of the line, the CO's wife sputtered, fumed and began berating the captain, who shrugged his shoulders and hung up. The Colonel's Lady was not content to drop the matter, but called the OD, who arrived and asked who had answered the telephone.

The advent of the OD sobered us somewhat. We rallied to the defense of our Marine class-mate. Obviously he had not meant to insult the CO's wife or any other lady. It was a flip remark said in jest and alcohol. Most military wives would have taken it in that light and dismissed the matter. Either our Colonel's wife had an inflated opinion of her importance or was overwhelmed by Alaska. In any event, she chose to make an issue of the matter. We evaded the OD's questions, but eventually he determined the culprit.

The next morning we learned that the COL had threatened to withhold the CPT's diploma and was considering keeping him at FT Greely for disciplinary action. The class supported the Marine; a delegation talked with the CO, but was unable to convince him to forget the incident. Graduation was held in glacial silence, the students indignant with the command.

Most of the class was flying in an Air Force C-124 from Big Delta to Elmendorf Air Force Base with a few hours in Anchorage before the connecting flight to Seattle. Several of us went to HQ, USA Alaska where we explained the situation to the CofS. He assured us that nothing would happen to the CPT, who appeared to be too fine an officer to have his career adversely affected because of a minor prank.

After an uneventful flight, I arrived back at the KMI campus, where COL Richmond offered me the use of a room in the attic of Ormsby Hall. It was well constructed with its own bath. But access was through the unfinished attic where the cadets kept their trunks. The disadvantage of living on campus was, of course, being too close to the cadets, especially if I had a few drinks in the evening. The major advantage was that it was free lodging. SFC Schenck was bemused; he couldn't imagine an RA Off living under such circumstances; to me it was no worse than living in a WWII BOQ.

Upon my return from Alaska, the ROTC Det completed the KMI SOP, which had grown into a formidable 55 page document. It detailed each of the parades the Corps would hold, including those for special occasions such as Mother's Day or Escort of Company Sponsors. My purpose in setting down the procedures was to make the parades and other events more meaningful to the cadets and their parents. The uniforms were cleaned up by establishing a ribbon system for awards and honors. Each commendation, academic or military, such as honor roll or neatest cadet, was represented by a specific multi-colored ribbon. The order and position of each was specified. Many cadets had quite a bit of "fruit salad" to decorate their uniforms. The item that proved the most controversial was the requirement for junior cadets to salute the cadet officers. In retrospect this was probably not a wise provision. The entire SOP was controversial and the cadets' reactions to it were varied. Shades of the FT McClellan SOP!

By the time the cadets reported back to school, the ROTC cadre was ready for them. The SOP was complete, the lesson plans had been redone. A copy of the SOP was issued to each cadet. Because it was so detailed and thick, it created some apprehension; the cadets thought they would be tested on it. We intended it as a reference only, and hoped in time that experience and familiarity would permit us to reduce the volume. In the long run, the effort was a good one because it clarified things that had formerly been left to chance. It was my theory that the cadets should know exactly where they stood, the limits in which they could operate, and what would happen to them if they failed to do so. It was my impression that I got along with the cadets because I would not deviate from the rules. The civilian instructors would yield to pressure or to emotional outbursts, but I insisted that the ROTC instructor staff hold fast to the limits. If a boy deserved to be punished, he was punished. The cadets liked this. Every teenager likes to know where he stands. When the limits aren't defined, when those in authority vacillate or yield, when one day rules are rigidly interpreted, the next day leniently, it confuses them. This makes them rebellious and unhappy. At least that was my view of the situation.

In addition to the SOP, another innovation greeted the cadets. Shortly after school began a commissioning ceremony was held in the chapel to impress on the cadets the privileges and responsibilities of command. The cadet officers enjoyed special status, including being excused from certain formations and details. To enhance their prestige and at the same time emphasize their responsibilities to the school and to the other cadets, the solemn ceremony was initiated.

Early in the 1954/55 school year, KMI played a football game against Culver Military Academy. Because Culver was a military school comparable to KMI, I went to the game on the bus with the team. While at Culver I had an opportunity to exchange ideas with the PMS&T there.

During the game, the Cadet Bn CDR, Harry Lee Bailey, broke his leg. When the team returned to KMI, I stayed with him at the hospital. Harry's father arrived the next day with an ambulance in which the three of us returned to Louisville. Due to an infection, Harry's absence from school promised to be a long one. Fortunately, he not only had good leadership potential, but was an outstanding student. He continued to study while in the hospital, hence he had no difficulty in completing his academic work for graduation.

The Corps of Cadets needed a temporary Bn CDR until Harry got back on his feet. With COL Richmond's concurrence, I appointed Charles Warren Upton, one of the Cadet Co COs, Acting Bn CDR. Harry returned to KMI while still on crutches, so he was unable to participate fully in the ROTC activities. The problem of parades, formations and other duties which required an ambulatory commander remained. Harry could not be deprived of his well earned position, nor could Upton be expected to handle two jobs. As a compromise, Bailey was confirmed as Bn CDR with Upton as his Deputy. Upton would take care of all parades, ceremonies and drill. There were some awkward moments, such as the graduation parade, which were solved by letting Harry take the honors at special parades.

The Lyndon session passed quickly. Once again I spent Christmas with the family in New York. To share the burden on the ROTC Detachment, I scheduled myself to ride the train to Venice in January. I drove my car to Florida, then returned to Louisville by plane. KMI paid the plane fare. The cadets straggled in to the Louisville Railroad Station, all of them on time. The trip to Florida took about 25 hours; though it entailed remaining on board overnight, it was an all-coach train. The Cadets were well behaved and posed no problems other than those resulting from excessive energy and the normal mischievousness of such a group. There were several members of the faculty aboard; between us we made sure that the boys were fed and got a little rest. It was a pleasant trip, not like the troop trains I knew in the Army.

On arrival in Florida, the cadets settled into the school routine. The ROTC program continued without interruption. Parades were held on alternate Sundays as in the past.

It occurred to me that a Garrison Flag would add much to the Sunday parades. The huge flag is flown on holidays and special occasions; surely the parades were special occasions. The flag pole in the park where the parades were held was not the height prescribed by Army Regulations, but would do. The Florida NG HQ located in St Augustine agreed to lend me a Garrison Flag on hand receipt. The following Sunday, the cadets enthusiastically raised the Garrison Flag, which was caught by the breeze and waved bravely. It was a glorious spectacle at which many people came to stare.

The parade began well. Upton gave the order PARADE REST, SOUND RETREAT. A reinforced Color Guard took position at the flag pole. The cadets were brought to ATTENTION and PRESENT ARMS. The band struck up the National Anthem. The Color Detail failed to lower the flag. After waiting a few seconds I terminated my salute and walked across the parade field to the flag pole. The Color Detail informed me unhappily that the ropes were stuck. Apparently the heavy flag blowing in the breeze had unseated the rope from the pulley.

In a hoarse whisper I told them to exert more pressure on the rope, hoping that it would free itself. Two sturdy football players gave a strong pull. The rope did not give, but the flag pole bent! Both the audience and the cadets laughed. Fortunately, the flag was now at a level at which the Detail could remove it. The cadets passed in review before that oddly bent flag pole, a mute reminder of my own improper staffing of the problem. It took us a week to get the flag pole repaired. The Garrison Flag was returned to St Augustine, never to be flown in Venice again.

As in past years, KMI participated in the local pageants. This year we took the Kentucky Rifles, commanded by Cadet CPT Herschel Murray, a husky, handsome football player. They created quite a sensation. The boys outdid themselves; justifiably proud, they marched tall. Some of the fancy drill, such as a silent manual of arms sequence was adapted to street marching, so the drill team would not hold up the parade. Every time the column ground to a halt, the team would go through one of its routines.

During the parade in Bradenton, it rained, soaking the cadets. Several people commented to Charlie Norman and me as we were marching beside the formation that we were foolish to walk in the rain getting our uniforms soaked. I wore a tropical worsted (TW) blouse and trousers, while Charlie was in TW shirt and trousers. The kibitzers were told that a leader belongs with his troops, a commander does not desert his men to protect himself. If a situation cannot be alleviated, the commander shares the unpleasantness. This was a strange concept to the civilians.

The cadet officers were again asked to act as honor guard for the Queen and her court at the Sarasota Pageant Ball. They made a colorful group in their dress uniforms. I took a date and stayed for the dance.

Several unpleasant incidents occurred during the season. At the Pageant of Light in Fort Meyers some of the cadets were caught drinking and one was involved unpleasantly with a girl. One cadet officer was reduced and all concerned reprimanded. Shortly after that incident, KMI played a basketball game against Venice High School on their court. After the game the cadets streamed across Highway 41, the Tamiami Trail, a well traveled road. Several cadets narrowly missed being struck by cars. The cadet officers who were supposed to march the cadets back to the KMI barracks were reprimanded and some of the privileges granted by the ROTC staff were rescinded. The cadets, unhappy with these actions, wrote letters to the editor of the cadet newspaper. One, very much to the point, decried the mass punishment meted out by the PMS&T. Seizing this opportunity to explain my position, I wrote a letter to the editor outlining my reasons for disciplining the Cadet Corps: the officers and NCOs failed in their responsibilities; the cadets failed to follow instructions or to act in a responsible manner. The onus was put on the Corps to prove that it deserved special privileges.

Since my arrival at KMI, I had written three letters to MG Fry, requesting reassignment from ROTC duty based on my perceived lack of suitability for it. Once again I wrote, once again MG Fry promptly replied, disapproving my request and reiterating that I was going to stay at KMI for three years.

The 1955 session at Florida passed quickly. The rifles and other equipment were repacked for the return to Lyndon. We arrived in time to enjoy a spectacular spring. Activities at Lyndon in 1955 paralleled those in 1954, though I did not make an inspection trip. KMI passed its annual government inspection with no serious deficiencies. The ROTC Det began preparing for a new, more intensive program to be introduced to all military schools in the fall, it required more hours of ROTC instruction to include field training and crew served weapons drills. After a careful study of the new program, I wrote an analysis of it to include its anticipated impact on KMI. Based on this, COL Richmond and I had many conferences.

In addition to preparations for the fall program, the activities which preceded the Military Awards Ceremony and graduation were underway. This year I invited several officers from nearby ROTC units to judge some of the more highly contested competitions.

An obsolete 105mm howitzer together with an adapter for firing blank rounds arrived early in the spring. These had been offered to any military school desiring them. Thinking it would make the campus look more military, I had requested one. The blank rounds were expensive so there was little chance of firing it very often, though COL Richmond did authorize me to purchase 24 rounds. Subsequently one of the arsenals made an adapter which would fire blank shotgun shells, which we bought. The first salute was fired on graduation day for MG Willems, the guest speaker.

The commencement of the class of 1955, KMI, passed into history. At the Military Awards Ceremony, pandemonium greeted the designation of the Band as Best Company. The cannon fired the 13 round salute to MG Willems with only two misfires; the addition to the review was duly appreciated. COL Richmond seemed to attain new emotional heights during his remarks and presentations. The barracks emptied rapidly as soon as the ceremony was over.

The selection of cadet officers for the next year was a difficult one this time because there were no strong leaders among the cadets. In the past two years there had been eight or ten who demonstrated good leadership potential, which meant that there were good Co COS backing the Cadet Bn CDR. COL Richmond and I huddled and argued. Because I had no better candidate to offer, I finally yielded to COL Richmond's choice, Perrin McGhee, a cadet whose character was unassailable, but no leader. The few cadets I thought might make good leaders had other short-comings, so McGhee got the nod. He was willing and motivated, but just not up to it. Events the following year confirmed my pessimism.

In 1955 all of the US Army personnel assigned to KMI had orders as cadre for the ROTC Summer Camp at FT Campbell, KY. We reported immediately after school closed. My assignment was as the D Co CO. CPT Sykes was on one of the training committees and the NCOs were assigned administrative or instructional duties. My request to have MSG Norcross as my 1SG and SSG Condee as my Supply Sergeant was denied. My XO, CPT Glenn Hill, an MP OFF with the ROTC Det at Michigan State University, did an outstanding job for me. 1SG Mitchell, also on ROTC duty, was a bust. An ABN Plt Ldr from the 11th ABN Div and an ROTC instructor NCO were assigned to each cadet Plt to rate and counsel the trainees. The 11th ABN Div also provided the cooks, supply personnel and other detail men for the summer camp.

One of the officers assigned to the summer camp from another ROTC Det, was an old friend, CPT Alvin Roegge, who had been assigned to CCRAK HQ in Korea. He had recently married another old friend, Daria Federonko! We had some interesting times together!

Shortly after I arrived at Campbell, I applied to make a jump with the 11th ABN Div. Based on a recommendation from his CofS, COL "Poopy" Connor, the CG turned it down. "Poopy" did not want to take the chance of having an ROTC instructor injured. I was disappointed; my last jump had been on Paengnyong Do in January 1953.

The ROTC Summer Camp lasted an intensive six weeks. The ROTC students were assigned to companies alphabetically. D Co had the H's through the K's. By chance a large number of these cadets were football players; there were 55 first string players from the various colleges out of the 200 cadets assigned to D Co. Many more were second string or in other sports; most of the Cadets were in excellent physical condition. Initially, however, they did poorly on hikes, phased in over the period starting with a very short one and working up to 20 miles. I could outwalk any of the cadets though I was almost twice their age. It was a question of knowing how to conserve and utilize energy. The cadets horsed around, expending much energy doing nothing.

Cadet John Juracek, Jr reported in with a sparse, unkempt beard. His Plt Ldr counseled him to shave it off; when he refused, he was sent to me. The untrimmed beard added to Juracek's unsoldierly appearance. After briefly explaining why Army Regulations banned beards, citing the problems they posed in the field, I ordered him to shave it off. He protested, declaring that his personal religion forbade him to shave it off. The chaplain told me that if the cadet was a member of a religion which had such a tenet he should be allowed to retain the beard, but the Army was under no obligation to permit every individual to develop his personal religion or to use such a religion as an excuse for disobeying uniform and personal appearance regulations. I pushed the issue vigorously. It finally went to the Deputy Camp Commander for a decision.

Unfortunately, the PMS&T of the school Juracek attended was at the summer camp. He asked the Dep CDR to permit Juracek to retain his beard, because he feared that if he was forced to shave or if he was eliminated, it would discourage other students at his school from joining the ROTC program, which was on probation because of low enrollment. My reaction was that if this was the sort of cadet produced, the program at that school should be closed out. But the Dep Camp CDR, the PMS&T at another college, decided that Juracek could keep his scraggly beard. I was ashamed to be associated with such officers in the ROTC program!

Despite this setback, we all kept working on Juracek. The problems he would face as a Plt Ldr when he inspected his unit were pointed out. How could he tell a soldier that he needed a haircut or a shave when he looked so slovenly himself? Juracek did not like this, but he had no answer for our argument. He asserted that he would exert enough leadership to overcome the situation. This was a laugh.

Activities settled into a routine not unlike the ones I had become accustomed to when commanding other companies. D Co was inspected by the ROTC Staff daily. The PMS&T from the University of Kentucky, a brilliant officer with a PHD in Chemistry, but not an effective leader, decided that the Cadet DOs should have additional duties. He directed that they report to him each morning the cadre personnel who were at Reveille. There was no requirement that any cadre personnel be present at the first formation, rather it was left to the Co COs. Normally I was present at Reveille, indeed, at all formations. When I could not be there Glenn Hill was. One morning on my way to Reveille I stopped to talk with one of the other ROTC officers. CPT Hill expected me to make the formation so when I did not appear there was no cadre officer present. Arriving in the D Co area about 15 minutes after Reveille, I found a worried young cadet waiting for me in the Orderly Room. A member of D Co, he was the DO. He told me he had been given orders to report any companies that did not have a cadre officer present. D Co was the only one that had no OFF present for Reveille that morning. The cadre had not been informed of such instructions. The cadet was concerned about reporting his own Company not wishing to get his Co CO in trouble. Though irritated about the requirement, I concealed it from the cadet, telling him that he had no alternative. He had been issued an order which should be executed; he should render his report truthfully. "Don't worry about getting me in trouble Do your duty." He reluctantly made his report.

Later that morning I went to see the Dep Camp CDR. The CG of FT Campbell was the Camp Commander in title, but a senior colonel, a PMS&T from a college with students at the camp, actually ran the Camp. I asked the Commander to relieve me as Co CO because I found it impossible to serve where subordinates were directed to report on their commanders. We had a heated talk. He told me in no uncertain terms that he would decide when and if I would be relieved. He agreed with me, however, that the original order was not proper and rescinded it.

D Co was a fine one though it did not win many administrative prizes. I simply did not emphasize spit and polish. The barracks were neat, about the standard of any RA unit, but never won the "Best Company Award". D Co did earn an enviable reputation in physical training. The cadets who won first and second places in PT for the Summer Camp were from Dog Co. The Outstanding Cadet in the Summer Camp was also from D Co. These awards satisfied me. I learned much from the cadets, hopefully they learned something from me. The major point I stressed to them was that they must assume that every order received was a lawful order. They had to presume that the officer who issued it had more information at hand and had thought it through. They could and should question it, strongly, if warranted, but once the decision was made, they had no alternative but to obey.

At the end of the summer, D Co had a party at one of the lakes. It was a tradition that the cadets threw the Summer Camp Cadre into the water. Most of us prepared for this by leaving our wallets and watches in our cars. We were all enjoying the beer and picnic supper when a couple of huge football players descended on me. They picked me up easily, trotted to the edge of the lake, and tossed me in. That started it. Glenn Hill and each of the Plt Ldrs in turn were immersed. Spirits ran high. Next the NCOs were good naturedly thrown in without protest. The only cadreman who fought them was 1SG Mitchell, who was not well liked by the cadets. He had not done a good job for me; like most soldiers, the cadets sensed this. At first they were inclined to ignore him, but he made such a fuss about not wanting to be thrown into the lake that they decided they would do it. He tried to fight them, but he was helpless in the hands of those big tackles; in he went. He emerged from the lake furious, spluttering, berating the cadets, making an ass of himself. The cadets were ready to lay hands on him again. To avoid an unpleasant situation, I ordered Mitchell back to his barracks. The party concluded happily.

On my return to KMI, I wrote letters of commendation for most of the ROTC and 11th ABN Div OFFs and NCOs who had worked so hard for me. Glenn Hill had especially earned such a letter as no efficiency reports were rendered on the cadre officers. All of the Plt Ldrs except one received letters. One 1LT, a USMA graduate, had been relieved from duty with D Co because of his poor performance. Clearly ineffective, he eventually was eliminated from the service. All of the NCOs received letters except 1SG Mitchell, who had been told my opinion of his performance before he left. He had the audacity to write a letter requesting that I send him a commendation! He found out that I had sent letters to other NCOs because one of the PSGs, assigned to the same college, proudly showed him his letter. Mitchell did not get a letter.

The few weeks before school opened were hectic ones. There was much work to be done to implement the new ROTC program this term. The comprehensive POI entailed the preparation of many new lesson plans. To accommodate the storage and issue of the equipment authorized, the

ROTC classroom at the other end of the Quonset Hut in which the ROTC office was located was converted into a Supply Room. SSG Condee was busy receiving, unpacking and shelving fatigues, web gear, field jackets, helmets and other individual and organizational equipment.

Crew-served weapons, light machine guns and 81mm mortars, had to be taken out of cosmoline and prepared for use. The panel truck authorized was put to immediate use picking up the new equipment. Later it was used to transport the Rifle Team to the NG Range, for supply trips to FT Knox and other purposes.

CPT Sykes left KMI upon our return from FT Campbell, replaced by 1LT Ray McClean, a stocky, gung-ho ABN OFF from Iowa. SFC Schenck was reassigned on my request, succeeded by athletic, square-jawed, ABN SFC Bill Pruitt. I was delighted to see these Airborne Troopers arrive; they would help set high standards of appearance and performance. MSGs Rustari and Norcross, now well oriented in the KMI ROTC program, provided stability and continuity to it.

School opened as did the eyes of the cadets when they saw the new equipment and heard me outline the new program. They were particularly interested in the bivouac, planned for early April on our return from Florida. Issue of equipment was as disorganized as I remembered it at FT Dix when I was first inducted into the Army in 1942.

The ROTC program was quickly underway. The Cadets were given classes in the nomenclature and functioning of the machine gun and mortar, and how to live in the field. The initial classes in pitching shelter halves, or pup tents, had many hilarious moments. Not a few cadets crawled into the one they had erected only to have it collapse on them. The first field packs reminded me of those the AA OFFs had devised during the Basic Course at TIS in 1944!

Mrs Norcross and Mrs Pruitt, the wives of two of the Army NCOs, helped the School QM at the beginning of the academic year, and throughout the year, by altering uniforms for the cadets. They worked at the large library table in Ormsby Hall. Just before the first parade, one of the Junior School Cadets rushed in and tearfully asked if they could shorten his trousers. His Cadet Co CO had given him ten minutes to get in proper uniform. There was not time for the normal procedures. The resourceful seamstresses stood the boy on the table, pinned his trousers at the proper length, then laid him on the table. Mrs Pruitt rotated the boy as Mrs Norcross stitched the terrified cadet's trousers on the sewing machine! The task was completed and the cadet back in formation in proper uniform in the prescribed time.

The Kentucky Rifles began to practice early in the school year. The leader this year, Cadet LT Stephenson, lacked the charisma of Gandolfo and Murray, though he tried his best. By now, cadets had been on the drill team for two years, which made it easier to bring it up to precision. Its first performance at Home Coming weekend was greeted with satisfying enthusiasm.

The three months at Lyndon passed rapidly; this was especially pleasing as it meant that I was closer to reassignment. The list of OFFs selected to attend the Command and General Staff College (C&GSC) at FT Leavenworth was released in the fall, happily, my name was on it. Since I would not be assigned to duty at the ROTC Summer Camp in 1956, I requested permission to attend the Ranger Course at FT Benning. My request was approved for the course beginning at the end of May. By leaving immediately following the graduation ceremony and driving through to FT Benning, I would miss only the first day of class. With these schools in my future, I almost enjoyed the last year at KMI.

An amusing incident occurred that fall. A newspaper clipping appeared on the bulletin board one morning. The cadets read it, laughed, then glanced slyly at me. After breakfast, I read the clipping. It reported that twins had been born to MAJ and Mrs Donald W. Seibert of Louisville and FT Knox. The middle initial had been changed to A! Donald W. Seibert, an Armor Officer, had plagued me for some time. He was the cause of the misunderstanding over my recall to AD in 1949 that had elicited my momentary panic. The puzzling orders which had assigned me to various Armor units over the years were always resolved when I looked at the middle initial. The boys made several comments in calculated undertones the remainder of the week as I maintained an impassive front.

Lyndon was only an hour's drive from FT Knox, which I visited frequently. Since the ROTC Det was authorized to borrow training aids from the Post, a program of Army Training Films was organized on Mondays, the cadets' day off. Attendance was voluntary, but surprisingly good. The cadets especially liked the leadership and combat training films. In addition to providing training aids and films for the ROTC instruction, Ft Knox also took care of our medical and dental needs. In my second year at KM I had a hernia repaired there.

One morning I was on my way to the Training Aids Center when an MP sedan with flashing lights appeared behind me. I pulled over puzzled, knowing that I had not been speeding or made any improper turns. The MP sedan pulled ahead of me, stopped and a PFC got out and slouched to my car. He leaned on my open window and growled,

"Why aincha car registered on post?"

Incensed at his lack of courtesy to an OFF (I was in uniform), I snapped, "Let's start all over again, soldier. You go back to your sedan, get in it, then come back, salute, and begin our conversation properly. As you can see I am an officer and expect you to accord me the proper military courtesy."

He was unhappy, but after one look at my face he reluctantly complied. On his return he rendered a perfunctory salute.

"Sir, we have noticed that you drive this car on FT Knox quite a bit, but you do not have it registered on Post. There is a drive to get all personnel assigned to the Post to register their POVs. I'll have to issue you a ticket."

"Now wait a minute. I am not assigned to FT Knox and do not have to have my car registered on Post."

"Do you have any orders to prove that, sir?"

I blew up! "Are you questioning my word, soldier? I am an officer in the United States Army and my word should be sufficient for you."

"Just the same I need some proof."

I cut him off. "Get in your sedan and follow me", I ordered. I started my own motor and drove directly to the Provost Marshal's office with the MP sedan in trail. Striding into the office, I asked the secretary if the Colonel was in. The MP was dejectedly in my wake. She also looked at my face then at the MP and motioned me into the PM's office. Knocking on the door, I entered, saluted and launched into my tale, explaining my status. I concluded by requesting that the MPs be instructed to observe proper military courtesy in handling all individuals they stopped. The COL thanked me; I saluted and left. The PM was laying down the law to the MP as I walked out of the office. Needless to say, I drove with extreme caution when I visited FT Knox from then on. My black and white convertible was too conspicuous.

Christmas leave and the move to Venice followed the pattern of other years. In 19561 did not ride the train. While the cadets were in Venice, they practiced crew drill with the machine gun and mortar. The seniors, the only ones who had this training, were required to wear fatigues on the days they had weapons instruction. This caused comment because they stood out in formations. The cadets became quite proficient in putting the machine gun and mortar into action. It seemed to me that this training was a bit too advanced for Junior ROTC, but it did inject additional interest into the program. As in the past, the cadets marched in various pageants, as well as in the Sunday Parades.

Back at Lyndon, the big topic of conversation, understandably, was the pending bivouac. FT Knox had assigned KMI an area in which to maneuver. Norman was pressed into service to act as instructor and umpire. After a recon of the area, McClean, Norman and I wrote a simple field exercise on the free maneuver concept. This meant that the two opposing forces would operate against each other and the outcome would be decided by the umpires based on the plans and actions of the opposing sides. The cadets had received no instruction in small unit operations or basic tactics, consequently the problem had to be simple. The primary purpose of the bivouac was to acquaint the students with Army life in the field.

The famous bivouac would be conducted Saturday and Sunday, with a critique and return on Monday. When the Corps fell out preparatory to boarding the buses for FT Knox, it was quite a spectacle. Some cadets looked as if they had been in the Army for some time. These were mainly Boy Scouts. Others looked as if they had been hurriedly bundled in cast-off clothing. But all were enthusiastic. The Junior School Cadets watched the buses depart wistfully.

The bivouac was an adventure for most of the cadets. Though they got little from the tactical aspects of the problem, the opportunity to live in the field like soldiers, for even a few days, was fascinating to them. Establishing a tactical assembly area and providing for basic creature needs, filled them with awe. COL Richmond had agreed to buy C Rations for all of the meals; the NCOs showed the cadets how to heat and enjoy them. The Post provided Protestant and Catholic Chaplains for services in the field. It was a memorable experience for the cadets, even more so for the cadre.

After the bivouac, the school buzzed for days; incidents were recalled and recounted with gusto. Every cadet had a different version to relate. In a week or two, the normal routine was reestablished. The Corps prepared for and passed the Annual Government Inspection. Preparations for graduation began.

During the year, I raised the question as to why the ROTC Staff was required to pay their way to Florida and back. It is true that KMI provided quarters for the military personnel there. Whenever an individual is ordered on TDY in the Army, travel expenses are paid. But the KMI ROTC Staff was required to move itself; the orders transferring it to Florida specified at no expense to the government. My request that the Det be paid mileage was denied. KMI was an unusual case, one of the few schools in the county that moved in this fashion. Officially the Army personnel assigned to KMI were based at Lyndon and drew rations and quarters allowances. There were no funds in the budget for TDY at Venice. Failing with the Army, I then initiated a request that the school pay the expenses. Of course, COL Richmond objected, claiming that he was providing rooms and meals in Florida and that the military personnel were getting a paid vacation. I didn't look at it that way. This was our duty assignment; the military personnel should not be out of pocket in order to accomplish their mission. The matter was still pending as the school year ended.

SFC Pruitt, a stern-looking Airborne NCO, and an excellent athlete, coached the KMI Baseball Team that spring. The cadets were most respectful of him. He invited me to his home for dinner; during the evening I complimented Mrs Pruitt on the many complicated crocheted dollies and antimacasars.

"Oh, I didn't make those", she said. "Bill did. He is always crocheting."

Seeing my amazement they explained that SFC Pruitt had been taught to crochet as therapy while recovering from a wound. He found it relaxing while listening to the radio or talking. I wondered what the cadets would have thought had they known!

As a result of my three years at KMI I had become concerned with the value of the Junior ROTC Program. Some figures the Admissions Officer and Alumni Secretary provided me demonstrated that few of the KMI graduates went on in military training. A few were admitted to one of the Service Academies each year, about five percent went into the Senior ROTC Program in college and about three percent actually served in one of the armed forces. This appeared to be a poor return for the expense the Army incurred. There was a six-man cadre at each military school and two or three at each high school. The official purpose of the Junior ROTC Program as stated in Army Regulations was to instill patriotism. Based on these facts, I wrote a paper questioning the purpose and value, anticipating, I suppose, McNamara's Cost Effectiveness Program. The paper was forwarded to the Military District before I left KMI. I never heard about it, though one of my recommendations, the use of retired military, has since been implemented. I wonder if my paper started someone thinking?

The excitement associated with graduation was heightened, at least for me, by my pending reassignment. There was much to be done in getting me paper work completed; an efficiency report on LT McClean, letters of commendation for the NCOs, thanks to various individuals who had supported the program throughout my three year tour. MAJ HODGIN, a Res OFF, had taught classes throughout my tenure to earn retirement points, I had to be sure that he was credited. My footlockers and books had to be packed an shipped. I started on a basic PT program to prepare for Ranger School; it was not overly successful. All this was accomplished while conducting the various competitions and determining the recipients of awards to be presented at the Military Awards Ceremony.

As in the past the Military Awards Ceremony was of great interest to all the cadets. As each cadet was called to receive his award, speculation increased as to which company would be named Best Company. The Cadet Bn CDR, Perrin McGhee, did not receive any military award and had not, in my opinion, earned any. His mother spoke sharply to me after the awards ceremony about this. I made no comment. There was the expected pandemonium when the Best Company was announced.

There was so much going on that I decided to miss the Senior Banquet. My uniforms had been packed and shipped, I had only a TW blouse and trousers which seemed inappropriate. But the NCOs urged me to go as this was my last commencement at KMI. When the President of the Senior Class announced that *The Saber,* the senior yearbook, had been dedicated to me, I was surprised, honored and flattered. The copy presented to me was cherished until the footlocker in which I kept it was stolen. It was a good feeling to know that the cadets recognized what I had tried to do.

My successor, MAJ Poff, had been asked to come for the graduation activities. This would give him an opportunity to see what we were doing, and also a chance to discuss with me my experience over the past three years. I could point out many pitfalls I had found. But he made no effort to do so.

There were other activities in addition to graduation that May. Several of the parents hosted farewell parties for me at which I was given gifts. One, most useful, was a traveling bar kit, complete with three quarts of liquor. The cadets presented me with two official Kentucky Derby sterling julep cups. The Rustaris and Norcross' joined forces to hold a cookout for me at the Rustari's house. I hosted a farewell party for the ROTC Staff at a local restaurant, at which we all had a good time. LT McClean was concerned about everyone being in condition to drive home. He was the only one who got a ticket that night!

Ray McClean wrote me later about the end of my effort to get the Staff paid TDY. "The arrival of MAJ Poff as PMS&T was a disaster. He was very sly, almost a recluse. I once had to get on the Cadet Adjutant for reading his name in a formation as MAJ Poof. I forget who the kid was.

"My experience with COL Richmond on the matter of TDY or travel pay was explosive, and I suppose I lost my cool somewhat, which was very likely his game. Poff had let me get in the middle as the spokesman for the NCOS. Richmond had at first requested an audience with MSG Norcross, but Norcross wouldn't go and at a meeting in the ROTC Hut had then suggested that I represent the NCOs. I agreed, feeling we had a good case, but after a violent session with the Colonel, we were all transferred.

"The CO of the Military District talked to me afterwards and was sympathetic, but also had a few words to say about the need for diplomacy which you gain with more experience."

The three years at KMI were frustrating in many respects, but in retrospect were not as bad as I had anticipated. The cadets were responsive and friendly, it seemed some good had come from my tenure there. Although I was disappointed in the small number of graduates who entered the military service, many of the cadets went into other professions and became distinguished and successful citizens. Though the ROTC cadre could claim little credit for the success of those graduates, it made a significant contribution toward the development of their character. The cadets, aware of my difficulties with COL Richmond, viewed them with humor, though they generally sided with me. Despite this newly awakened satisfaction, I was glad to leave KMI and head for the Ranger Course at Benning.

CHAPTER 11

STUDENT

Immediately after the graduation exercises at KMI, I changed into civilian clothes and headed for FT Benning. Due to my late departure and the long and tiring drive, I arrived at the Post late at night. Rather than taking time to sign in and get a room in the BOQ at that hour, I spent the night in the Visiting Officers Quarters (VOQ). Early the next morning I reported to the Ranger Training Center at Harmony Church. While I processed and arranged for a room in the BOQ, the class was taking the PT test and getting a general orientation. Both awaited me the next day.

The Army Ranger Course is perhaps the best training in leadership, other than actual command, that a young OFF can get. It is designed for LTs and junior NCOs. Hence the composition of Ranger Class 11 surprised me when I joined it the next day; the bulk of the students were CPTs who had just completed the Infantry Officers Advance Course. Many of them had seen combat in Korea. A few senior 1LTs from the Advance Class and several other LTs were also in the class, as well as a dozen or so NCOs, several of whom dropped out during the course.

In addition to myself, there were two other MAJs in Class 11, Phil Toon and Al Alphonso. Phil, an ARTY OFF, was a wiry, energetic USMA graduate. Alphonso, a stocky, dark, reserved individual was dependable in any situation. Phil and I were assigned rooms in the Harmony Church BOQ, a short distance from the Ranger area. Alphonso lived off Post with his wife. MAJs did not have to set up a bunk and display or stand inspection in the barracks as all the other OFFs did. The company grade officers had to maintain the same standards and displays as the enlisted students including cleaning the barracks, though most of them lived with their families off post.

Two of the students in the class were old friends, Tom Tackaberry and I had served together in the 504 in 1949 and 1950, and Ken Mertel had lived in the BOQ with me at FT Bragg during that same period. I was delighted to see them again, even happier to learn that they were going on with me to the C&GSC. Ken Mertel, the senior CPT in the class, was selected as the first Student Co CO, a position which was rotated among the company grade officers during the course. Tom Tackaberry was the Student Co CO during the Florida phase.

Throughout the course, each Ranger candidate had a "buddy" or partner at all times. These might change during some problems as habitual buddies were not always assigned to the same patrols. It was natural that the MAJs formed buddy teams. Phil Toon "adopted" 1LT Bobby Booth, who seemed overwhelmed by the Advance Course graduates in the class. Booth formed the fourth member of our group during most of the early work in the course.

The three majors, Toon, Alphonso and I, were looked at with some suspicion, if not disdain, by the rest of the students. They were convinced that we were receiving special treatment. The only consideration field grade officers were given was being able to live in the BOQ without having to stand inspection beside a barracks display. We did everything the other students did, perhaps a little more, as I will relate later on.

The Ranger Course was conducted in three phases; a very short introductory phase at FT Benning, a jungle and amphibious phase in Florida, and the key phase at Dahlonega, in north Georgia near the end of the Appalachian Trail. The Dahlonega phase included mountain climbing and patrolling. The initial phase at Benning consisted of orientation, PT, and map and compass work. The PT was needed because I had never weighed as much in my life as when I left KMI. The lack of exercise and almost daily sessions in the local beer joints had raised my weight to 195 pounds. The rudimentary PT program I attempted at KMI when I was approved for the Ranger Course had done little to improve my condition. Somehow I made it through the PT test that first day. The initial runs posed no problems, but the third day the pace was stepped up and the distance increased. It was my undoing. Although I finished the run, I did not finish it in formation. That was the only time I ever fell out.

The orientation phase passed rapidly. There were a few short, practice patrols designed to acquaint the students with the procedures that would be followed in Florida and Dahlonega. They also served to introduce us to the system of "lane graders", cadre officers assigned to every patrol who critiqued and evaluated the performance of the patrol leader and the patrol. Periodically they would interject new situations or require another student to take command of the patrol. Lane graders were key personnel in the course. After each patrol there was an on-the-spot critique of the group and the performance of each of the patrol leaders.

At the end of the orientation at FT Benning, the class went by bus to Eglin AF Base in the Florida panhandle where the Ranger Camp was located. Here MAJs shared the same barracks and circumstances as other Ranger students, and took their turn as barracks or latrine orderlies and at doing whatever was necessary to pass the daily inspections.

The Florida training emphasized movement through jungle and swamps as well as the amphibious infiltration of patrols. We were taught to use inflatable rafts to make amphibious landings as if from submarines. The techniques of survival, escape and evasion, living off the land, and avoiding capture were demonstrated and emphasized. Each student assembled a survival kit, which included first aid items, razor blades, fish lines and hooks, a small compass and whatever else was thought to be useful if cut off from friends and supplies. Some had large, elaborate kits, others very basic ones. Mine was contained in a metal band-aid box, each item wrapped so it would not rattle, which fit into my pocket.

Snakes were a favorite training aid during survival classes; we learned to recognize poisonous snakes, those that were good to eat and how to catch and handle them. The NCO who taught snake handling appeared the first period with a large rattlesnake around his mid-section under his fatigue jacket. Handling snakes posed no problem for me because I had handled zoological specimens all of my life.

The essence of the course was the patrol, the primary training medium. Every effort was made to create stressful situations to determine how the patrol leader would react. Much of the stress was the result of fatigue engendered by lack of sleep and the arduous physical exertion. Whether by chance or design, the patrols always encountered streams and swamps and were wet most of the time.

The patrols varied in length from several hours to several days. A company from the 82nd ABN Div was on TDY at Eglin Air Force Base to provide aggressor play for the problems. Patrols were ambushed, fired on, or subjected to other activities normal in a combat zone. Often, there were counter-patrols which had to be evaded. It was realistic training.

A patrol was initiated by posting a roster on the bulletin board. From eight to 20 men were assigned to each one, depending on its mission and type, reconnaissance, combat, or prisoner snatching patrol. The initial patrol leader, designated on the roster, received his order from the cadre then proceeded on his own. He was given a limited time in which to make his plan. He could organize his patrol as he saw fit, select the weapons to be carried, ask for special equipment such as ropes, rations or boats, designate formation and time of departure, and issue his order when and where he chose. He was critiqued on that order; its clarity and the amount of information passed on were major items stressed in the critique. He was downgraded if he required the patrol to carry equipment for which there was no eventual need. In the preparation phase, during which his men drew weapons and other equipment, packed gear and camouflaged themselves, he was graded on his inspections and rehearsals and getting the fully prepared patrol to the starting point on time.

The patrols were interesting but demanding. At any time the lane grader might declare the patrol leader a casualty requiring someone else to take over. A succession of command was specified as an essential element of every patrol order. This insured that each member of the patrol knew who would replace the leader if he became a casualty, and who would take over from the second leader and so on. Depending on the length of the problem, three or more members of the group might act as patrol leader. On very long patrols, all members would get a chance. The patrol leader who was declared a casualty became a replacement so that he remained with the group and did not lose any training time.

The patrol problems were well conceived and presented a variety of situations. Rubber rafts, canoes, trucks, helicopters and bicycles could be used, though occasionally they were declared not available. Ingenuity was required. Often "friendly partisans" assisted the patrol in finding equipment or food, or provided other assistance.

One patrol was required to reconnoiter a rocket site and get back with vital information by a specified time. Toward the end of the long patrol when time was running out and everyone was tired and discouraged, I became the patrol leader. The situation had fallen apart; several earlier patrol leaders had missed key contacts which had put us behind schedule. By some hard cross country movement immediately after I took command, the patrol made a time-sensitive rendezvous with partisans who provided us with a boat. To get the information to our HQ on time, it was necessary to paddle down the river about five miles in a very short time. By dint of tremendous effort on the part of every member of the group, we got to HQ in time to deliver accurate and complete information about the rocket site. At the end of the problem, the 1LT lane grader had some harsh things to say about several of the patrol leaders. He dismissed my performance with the statement, "Everything went well under Ranger Seibert except that he lacks force as a leader; he needs to develop more aggressive leadership."

Though incensed, I said nothing until he dismissed the group, at which time I told him that I would like to talk with him.

"I want to question your judgement on that critique. Nobody has ever accused me of lacking force as a commander, so I am interested in why you said that."

"Well, you didn't growl. You give your orders too quietly. There doesn't seem to be any enthusiasm in your orders. You don't use the Ranger growl to inspire the troops."

"Let me ask you a question. Did we accomplish our mission?"

"Yes."

"Did we get it accomplished with minimum casualties?"

"Yes."

"Did we get the information back on time?"

"Yes."

"Well, what is the problem?"

"You just didn't show any force."

"Was there any question about who was in charge when I had the patrol?"

"No."

"Did everyone respond to me?"

"Yes."

"Well, what is the problem?"

"I just think you lack force."

What he could not bring himself to say was that I did not make a big to-do when I told someone to do something. Without bluster, I treated the patrol members as intelligent, professional soldiers whom I expected to obey my orders without question. He could not understand how or why I got results. Like so many lane graders, his leadership experience was limited - he did not know how to get gung-ho Airborne/Ranger/Infantry soldiers to execute orders without hesitation unless he shouted at them. He had no idea of command presence, the importance of mutual respect and confidence between leader and follower, the essentials of leadership. I tried to explain them to him.

"I'm not faulting you," I ended up saying. "I'm trying to help you in your own business, helping you to develop your own leadership. There is a place for the rough-tough approach but it is not the only, or the best, approach to leadership."

I am not sure I got through to him. He reminded me of Lt Anderson from whom I took over command of B Co in Korea; he was young, aggressive, Airborne, and not only a Ranger, but a Ranger Instructor. I was merely a student trying to excuse my own lack of force. Who was I to tell him what leadership was all about? But we parted amicably. I hope that some of what we discussed sank in eventually. Unfortunately, though lane graders were the key personnel in the course, they were often less qualified than some of their students.

Although Alphonso, Toon, and I made every effort not to capitalize on our rank, there was widespread belief that we got special treatment. Invariably, when a patrol requiring heavy weapons (machine gun, recoilless rifle or mortar) was being organized, the MAJs initially carried them. Heavy weapons were rotated routinely among all members of a patrol, but one of the three of us started out with them, and we seemed to carry them most of the way. There was an unconscious conspiracy to make sure that the field grade carried their share of the load; the company grade OFFs were not going to let us get away with anything. It amused the three of us and we took it in good part. It wasn't that much of an imposition - we accepted our role as the "junior privates".

After three weeks of exhausting but invaluable training in the Florida jungles and swamps, we returned to Benning. The class was given two days to get clothing and equipment cleaned and in order. Then buses took us to Dahlonega. There were some small rugged mountains on which to practice climbing, rappelling and rope work. My month in Alaska paid dividends here; I was familiar with the Swiss Seat, rappelling, belaying and balance climbing.

In Dahlonega the patrols were longer and more physically demanding than any we had made so far. Though the terrain was well drained, there were many streams and it rained quite a bit. We were wet most of the time. But in North Georgia it also got cold at night. Because of the rugged terrain and the longer patrols the stress was greater than in Florida. Even the nights seemed darker. The training culminated in a three-day combat patrol with the mission of blowing up a power station at one of the dams. TIS had arranged for the patrol to get into the power house to lay its charges. Everyone was briefed on not interfering with the operation of the hydroelectric plant, and we were carefully watched to see that we avoided any contact with the machinery. It was a realistic problem. During its course many different situations were developed. One required contact with friendly partisans after 24 hours without food, they were to provide us with air-dropped supplies. The patrol missed the rendezvous the script required. We would have gone hungry except for the chickens in the area which we could catch, kill and bake. Though convinced that this was part of the scenario, I must admit my morale sagged when there was no chow waiting for us. I was pretty "beat" physically and mentally at the time. But Alphonso and Toon kidded me out of my funk, the rest of the problem went well.

During this problem, as on most, we had to wade in icy streams, usually hip deep. As we plunged through a swiftly running stream, the water reached to our crotches. Just at this time, the leader stopped the patrol and ordered, "Pass up the count."

This was a technique employed to insure that the patrol was complete and that it had not been infiltrated. Each member of the group had a number which was passed up from rear to front. Our leader had picked a most uncomfortable spot for the count. He was almost mobbed for it.

At the end of this long and demanding problem the class was subjected to a confidence test. A cable had been secured almost at the top of a towering tree and anchored at the base of another tree on the opposite side of a small, cold lake. Each Ranger had to climb a ladder to two logs spanning a narrow part of the lake, walk across that very unsteady bridge 25 feet above the water, then climb a rope ladder to the top of the tree where the cable was fastened. Arriving there cold, wet, tired, hungry (it was about 0500), and somewhat shaken, the student was required to grip a handle on a pulley and slide down the cable to the opposite bank. At a given time the grip on the handle had to be released, insuring immersion in the icy water. Releasing the handle too soon meant longer exposure in the water; releasing it too late could result in smashing into the tree to which the cable was fastened. If a Ranger failed to let go, and some froze, the cadre shouted to break his tension. It was actually fun, though certainly anti-climatic after the demanding patrol. As I climbed out of the icy water I was thankful that I had gone through the course in June rather than January. I could imagine those cold mountain streams rimed with ice or standing around in freezing wet clothes waiting to go back to base camp.

After the "Slide for Life" there was a short critique. Then the cooks served on the spot the most welcome breakfast I ever ate. There was everything, all the eggs you wanted cooked to order, bacon, sausage, juice, milk toast, jam, hash browned potatoes, coffee. We were hungry, wet, tired and cold, but the course was over and we ate like wolves.

Most students lost weight in Ranger School but I just reduced to my regular weight of 170. Getting rid of the fat accumulated at KMI was one of the benefits of the course.

On returning to base camp, we had to clean all the weapons before they could be turned in. This was SOP throughout the course. An eagle-eyed NCO inspected them and was only too happy to reject them for the slightest imperfection. We learned early in the course to clean fast and thoroughly to avoid loss of free time resulting from having to reclean a weapon. We wanted that time to snatch much needed sleep.

During the return to Benning and while preparing for graduation, there was time to assess the Ranger experience. Certainly it had been an outstanding course in small unit leadership. The pace had been fast, the patrols demanding and tiring, the entire period full of stress. Several students had dropped by the way, some gladly, others unwillingly. CPT Wyatt got a twig jammed in his eye and was in danger of losing his sight. He refused go to the hospital until ordered to do so. There was a real desire to earn and wear the Ranger Tab.

But the more experienced OFFs had derived less benefit from the course than the junior OFFs and NCOS. It did teach good basic field skills: techniques of patrolling, small unit maneuvers, escape and evasion, survival and living off the land. It inculcated greater confidence in less experienced OFFs. Those who had commanded Plts and Cos, either in combat or garrison, and had already formulated their concepts of leadership and learned to know their abilities in that area by actually handling men in various situations, still learned a great deal. It appeared to most that the course should be limited to LTs and NCOs.

Before graduation a picture of the class was taken as the photographer tried to get us to give the "Ranger Growl". We graduated in fatigues, on which we pinned the tabs after a short, provocative speech. Ken Mertel, a painfully conscientious OFF, was selected as the Outstanding Ranger in the class and awarded the class guidon. He had more than earned it.

Immediately after graduation I drove to College Point, taking Phil Toon as far as Manhattan, where he caught a train to West Point. Mother and Dad and I then drove to Prince Edward Island where we spent a week in a farmhouse. We enjoyed a quiet time, walking on the beaches, swimming, sight-seeing, relaxing, reading and eating all too much delicious farm fare. On the way back to College Point we stopped off to see Gladys and George Good, friends from RAAF, at their camp on Brantingham Lake. After a few days in College Point I drove to my new post.

Fort Leavenworth is the oldest post established by the US Army west of the Mississippi River still in use, an historic and beautiful place for a military school. Many of the buildings are steeped in history, formerly home to famous generals; some of the quarters surrounding the tree shaded parade field were built in the 1850s. Dating back to 1827, it has seen continuous use since, and is included in the National Register of Historic Places. The stone Protestant Chapel contains plaques memorializing individuals and units prominent in the taming of the west. Old trees lend beauty and its location on the Missouri River adds to its charm. It is the home of the US Army Command and General Staff College (C&GSC) and the US Army Disciplinary Barracks. In 1956 the Staff College was an intermediate-level school which stressed division and corps operations, dealt with the administration and logistical support of fighting forces, and taught staff procedures, emphasizing personnel, intelligence, operations and logistics.

The Disciplinary Barracks is a prison for military personnel convicted of serious crimes. The Federal Penitentiary is located at Leavenworth, adjacent to the Post, but is a separate installation. As part of their rehabilitation, the military prisoners learn many trades which they practice on Post. They operate a barber shop, an upholstery shop, a picture-framing concession and other enterprises. Military personnel are authorized to use these facilities; the incredibly low prices and careful workmanship make them popular. A haircut was 25 cents in 1956 and the barbers did a good job. Prisoners work under the careful guard of military and civilian police on duty at the Disciplinary Barracks.

In-processing at the C&GSC was well organized and efficient. All agencies concerned with student support had desks in a single large building, Gruber Hall. New students moved from desk to desk or station to station. Credit cards were issued on the spot for the PX service station and for several Kansas City department stores. Everything possible was done to get students settled quickly. A fine family post, every conceivable activity was available for wives and children to keep them occupied while husbands and fathers studied.

Bachelors were assigned a suite of two rooms in the BOQ, McClellan Hall, which was over a hundred years old. Each Off had a living room, bedroom and bath, both living rooms and bedrooms had fire places. Prisoners cut and delivered wood to the quarters, family and bachelor, for a nominal fee.

Married OFFs were housed in a variety of buildings, historic old quarters, converted WWII barracks, Wherry Housing and newer Capehart Housing. Those with large families were assigned quarters in the 'Beehive', a long brick Infantry Barracks complete with sallyport, which had been converted into spacious apartments with four or more bedrooms. A few OFFS lived off post either from necessity or choice.

After completing my processing, I began to move into the BOQ. I had just climbed the steps to my second floor apartment, dumped an armload of books onto the bed and sat looking at the footlockers and boxes that were waiting to be unpacked, when there was a knock on my door.

"Come in", I called.

A tall, heavy, smiling individual came in wearing civilian clothes. "Hi, I'm Wick. I have the rooms across the landing. Have a drink." He had a bottle with him. I invited him to sit down while I got glasses and ice. Wick was MAJ Howard T. Wickert, Jr, an ARTY OFF and USMA graduate. He had come to the C&GSC from West Point, where he had been teaching English. Wick is a master raconteur who makes the most mundane incident into a dramatic event. He has a biting wit which he does not hesitate to unleash on those deserving his scorn, we shared many interesting times and became inseparable during our stay at Leavenworth.

In the class were many people I had known over the years, Tom Tackaberry, John Kiser, Joe Fix, Hal Moore and Bill Sibert from the 504, Big Jim McClurkin and George McLendon from the 508, Bill Graves, Lou Williams and Bill Lindahl from the 9th IN, Brick Krause, Al Parker, Bob Selton, Gene Walters and Woody Shemwell from the Advance Class, Phil Toon and Ken Mertel from the Ranger Course, and, surprisingly, LTC Vince Abrignani, who had been the advisor to the 305th IN and helped me get back on AD in 1949. I made many new friends during the year, that is one of the bonuses of all Army schools, meeting people with whom you will associate for the rest of your career.

There were several Air Force and Marine OFFs in the class, and a goodly number of foreign OFFs: many from various South American countries, several from each of the NATO countries, about a half dozen from the British Commonwealth, two from Yugoslavia, one from Ethiopia, four from Thailand. Among the Thais was COL Chalard, who had been the S-3 of the Thai Bn attached to the 9th IN in Korea. There were seven OFFs from Vietnam who were delighted to find Wick fluent in French. From the Mid-east were OFFs from Iraq, Iran and Israel. The senior OFF in the class was LTG Shin from Korea.

The Foreign OFFs were billeted in one BOQ, probably with the thought of giving them a greater sense of comradeship; most of us thought they should be mixed in with the US bachelors. A few, mostly OFFs from South American countries, had wives with them and lived off post in the city of Leavenworth. Some of the houses, the leases for which had been passed on year after year to students from the same country, had become identified as the Chilean Quarters, the Guatemalan House or the Brazilian Manor.

The first morning of class we assembled in the Post Theater for our welcome and orientation. After the class had been called to attention, MG Lionel C. McGarr, the Commandant, destined to become a legend in that theater, marched smartly in followed by a gaggle of aides and faculty members. He stood stiffly at the podium, in ribbon bedecked uniform.

With clipped tones he welcomed us, outlined the course and gave his views on what we should carry away with us. It was the first time we heard him use the words "worldwide, atheistic communism" which he would manage to interject into every lecture or speech he made or attended. He introduced the principal staff and then turned to leave. The class came to attention as his aide held a door open for his exit. McGarr and his aide disappeared and the door closed. Just as the Director of Instruction (DOS) was about to give us more detail on the course, and after only a minute had passed, the door opened and a red-faced MG, followed by a cowed and embarrassed aide, exited the closet they had just entered. The class dissolved in laughter; was this an omen of things to come? Little more was accomplished that morning as one or another student thought back on the incident and began chuckling, precipitating gales of laughter from adjacent students.

During that initial orientation, the CMDT was given a nickname which stuck with him for the rest of the course. Because his hair was parted down the exact middle of his head and with great emphasis plastered to his scalp, he became "Spilthead McGarr" or just "Splithead".

Regular classes were held in Gruber Hall, a former riding hall, converted into 12 classrooms, each having tables for about 50 students, by folding walls. For large Command Post Exercises (CPXs), in-processing and other special events, these walls could be pushed out of the way to make one huge room. I was assigned to room 4; it and the class therein were referred to as "Gruber 4". Other class groups were similarly denoted. Three times during the year the groups were redistributed, though four or five us stayed in the same group. Each class had a leader; LTC Jim Gettings headed Gruber 4 with LTC Ed Markey, the 1948 Pine Camp S-4, as his assistant. By luck, Wick was also in Gruber 4. The groups were organized for social and administrative functions as well as for classroom instruction. Jim Gettings gave both Wick and I duties, as a result, we remained in Gruber 4 together with Jim and Ed throughout the course. The other 45 students shifted so that we got to know a good cross-section of the class, though less than a third of the 600 members were assigned to Gruber 4. We got to know many more at other functions.

"Issue the tissue", was the word of the day! The enlisted cadre seemed forever issuing requirements or advance information. The school day ran from 0800 to 1600. Occasionally we had "Commandant's Time" from 1500 on. PT periods were scheduled during which we could go to the gym or play golf or volleyball. But unless we finished an examination early, we rarely had a free hour. It was an intensive program until we learned to organize our time, then it became less demanding. Added to the plethora of subjects was the requirement that every American Officer be qualified with a "Prefix 5", that is, qualified in nuclear warfare. The last weeks of the course would be devoted exclusively to the study of classified nuclear warfare material. Other subject matter was compressed to accommodate the nuclear warfare instruction.

There was always homework: background material to read, advance requirements to digest, maps to color contour. Luckily, I am a rather rapid reader, hence I was able to finish the studying in a relatively short time. There were many officers in the class much smarter than I and with a greater desire to be first in academic work. I had no desire to be number one, if indeed, I had the ability to be. Early in the term I decided to take the course comfortably, learn as much as I could, but not neglect health, social life or the opportunity to make friends. In other words, I approached C&GSC pretty much as I had most of my college work; I set a reasonable standard and pace and operated at that rate.

The academic routine was basic. The class was issued an "advance sheet" which gave background material for the next lecture or practical exercise. When we met in Gruber 4, the instructor, a COL or LTC lectured for an hour or two. The school was cognizant of the fact that the attention-span is limited, that if students sat for more than one or two hours listening to the same voice their concentration dropped off. After the lecture there was usually a map exercise, a planning session or other practical work in staff procedures.

After each bloc of instruction such as Airborne Operations or Division Staff Functions there was an examination. In all there were perhaps 15 examinations on which we were graded superior, satisfactory or unsatisfactory, the latter a failure. Although I did not flunk any exams, I only "maxed" two. The rest were graded satisfactory. After each test there were the inevitable postmortems. Walking back to the BOQ we could not refrain from talking about various questions, distasteful as such discussions were.

Most of the instructors were good; their platform manner was not as polished as those at Benning, but they knew their subject and presented it in an understandable manner. In spite of careful screening, we did get one LTC who was a miserable instructor. Finally the section prevailed upon Jim Gettings to report him to Director of Instruction. Jim explained that the class was not getting anything from this instructor, who was scheduled to present several long and intricate problems. After lunch, someone from the DOI"s Office sat in on the class. The next day a new instructor took over. It was unfortunate for the OFF concerned; undoubtedly, he was conscientious, but he was not a teacher and was wasting our time.

All of the instruction was given in Gruber Hall or the Post Theater except one terrain appreciation problem during which we went out to look at the ground before doing some tactical planning. We traveled by bus in duty uniform and hardly got dust on our shoes. Leavenworth was a Staff College, not a field training school.

An important part of the curriculum was the guest lecture program. Senior military officers and selected civilians spoke to us about military and national policy matters. After the first lecture the CMDT got up and recapitulated what we had just heard, though the lecturer had expounded his topic thoroughly and then summarized his key points. In his recap, MG McGarr again used the words "world-wide, atheistic communism" several times. From then on he managed to work them into every closing statement regardless of their pertinence to the subject. The pattern was set, after each lecture, "Splithead" summarized and expostulated against world-wide, atheistic communism. They became watchwords; we waited at the end of each lecture to see how he would work them into his closing remarks.

MG McGarr had been the Asst Div CDR when I joined the 2nd Div in Korea, but had left to command at Koje-Do shortly after I arrived. He had a reputation as an exacting officer with high standards; a smart, strictly no-nonsense CDR, a bit of a martinet. About two months into the course, McGarr took the podium in the theater and informed the class that he was dividing the faculty into two groups; one group would teach the "Slant 7 Course" - our class which would graduate in 1957, the other would rewrite the course of instruction to bring it up to date so that it would be more meaningful for the "Slant 8 Class". This did not set well with the "Slant 7 Class". While attending one of the Army's most important courses, we had been told, in effect, that what we were learning was obsolete and in pressing need of revision. It hit the student body hard; MG McGarr probably never realized just how adversely it did strike us.

In November, Wick and I decided to pool our resources and give a cocktail party. We had enjoyed the hospitality of many friends and wanted to repay our social obligations. We intended to open both our apartments; to make sure that people wandered from one to the other, we planned that Wick would serve martinis and bourbon and I would serve Manhattans and Scotch. Wick made up a huge pitcher of martinis. "Ink" Gates came with his wife, Pat, and a great thirst. He opted for bourbon and water, walked over to Wick's bar, put ice and bourbon in a glass, grabbed a pitcher and poured what he thought was water. He took one gulp and spluttered! He had mistaken the martinis for water! After recovering from that double whammy, he got another drink and enjoyed the party with the rest of our guests. It was a pleasant affair, one of several we had that year.

Once the school routine had been established, I began to seek other diversions. While in Kansas City one day I wandered into a music store that was having a special sale on Hammond spinet organs. One of my life-long ambitions has been to play the piano or organ. The sale included a number of lessons, in addition to a rent-to-own plan in which the rental payments could be applied against the cost of the organ if later purchased. I signed a contract and the organ was delivered to my BOQ at Leavenworth. No doubt my insistent practicing annoyed my neighbors, particularly Jim Connell who lived just below me, but I had great fun and it was relaxing for me. However, I never really made much progress because I am not a musician.

The gym at Leavenworth was not particularly well-equipped. I was determined not to repeat the deterioration I had experienced at KMI and joined a health club in Kansas City. Despite the long drive, I managed to work out at least twice a week. The exercise helped with the weight problem and also proved relaxing.

The faculty and students of the Staff College supported an active Little Theater group. Scottie Allen, wife of one of our Gruber 4 classmates, was to direct the play, *LAURA*. Wick and I decided to support her. I read for one of the roles, Wick opted to help with the stage settings. Clarke Baldwin was selected for the male lead, I was cast as the villain, Waldo Lydecker. A very sexy, I use the term in less than a complimentary fashion, wife of one of the faculty members had the title role. She had a well developed figure which was accentuated by the clothes she wore and was the object of much comment around the post. When she entered any room she became the focus of all eyes.

Rehearsals began in November and by the time we went on Christmas leave, most of the cast had their lines memorized. Those who know the play recall that Laura's portrait is the pivotal prop and focus of the plot Wick, an accomplished artist who had done considerable portrait work, was asked to paint Laura. He produced a larger than life-size painting which depicted her as a true bitch. It had to be big because it was the centerpiece of the bedroom set. Wick's depiction left little to the imagination, all who viewed it thought it a perfect likeness. Scottie was a good director, who soon had us performing naturally. When performed, Laura was a huge success.

Meanwhile, back at Gruber Hall, the class was engaged in a series of map exercises involving a division attacking across Europe as a part of a larger force. The initial objective of the division was Lamballe, France. Caught up in the spirit of the problem a class motto was coined, "On to Lamballe!" Ollie Patton, Managing Editor of the Class Yearbook, wrote a letter, in the name of the class, to the Mayor of Lamballe asking for some words of wisdom for the Yearbook. In the problem, Lamballe had been liberated from an aggressor force and Ollie thought the local populace would be grateful to the class. The Mayor responded with a flowery letter, expressing disappointment in our delay in liberating his city, but welcoming the Americans to Lamballe. He declared the class honorary citizens of Lamballe. The exchange of amusing letters became a feature of our Yearbook.

All year we collected items for the yearbook. As the Gruber 4 representative I sent in many pictures and vignettes to be included. Wick contributed a number of cartoons as did Bill Sibert. One of my tasks was to get the names and nicknames of the OFFs, their wives maiden names, and the names of all their children. I asked MAJ Rafael Guimera Ferrer, one of the Spanish OFFs, the names of his children. He raised his hands and began ticking off his fingers, "Let me see. There is Neunuca, Rafael, Blanca, Elena, and... and... and... now wait a moment." But he could not remember the names of all of his children! He had to write home to his wife to get the names of their ten offspring. The class found this vastly amusing and Guimera was kidded unmercifully.

In 1956 there was a large American advisory effort in Greece assisting the Army in their efforts against the guerrillas. Toward the end of 1956, the US Army was preparing to change from the OD uniform to the new green uniform. As our olive-drab jackets and trousers were similar to those worn by the Greek Army, it was suggested that we give our OD uniforms to that Army. Just before Christmas, a box was placed at the entrance to Gruber Hall with a sign reading, "Donate your ODs to the Greek Army". Whoever was responsible had not coordinated the effort with the Greek OFFs in the class, who became highly incensed and insulted! They thought the Americans were patronizing them, implying that they could not afford their uniforms. As soon as it became apparent how they felt, the box and sign disappeared. The author of the effort had acted in good faith and apologized, but it was some time before the Greeks got over it.

The uniform change sparked a great deal of comment. The olive-drab uniform had been worn proudly in WWI and WWII and served well as both a combat uniform and, after brushing and pressing, one for ceremonial occasions. Brown shoes were also considered a symbol. And of course the "Ike Jacket" had become dear to the hearts of many, especially the Airborne. That it looked terrible on the short and stocky was beside the point. Soldiers should not be obese! But the greatest outrage among officers was the elimination of the semi-dress "Pinks and Greens" uniform, which was cherished by all, and considered one of the most distinguished looking uniforms in the world.

Everyone accepted the need to spruce up the enlisted men's undress uniform; the green uniform did that. There was strong criticism of the hat which many thought too German looking. The "scrambled eggs" on the visor of field grade officers caps was ridiculed as a "MacArthur Touch". There was no green shirt to wear without the jacket as with the OD uniform. Certainly it was not a uniform in which to fight. But that was taken care of by changes in the field uniform. So the controversy raged.

As the school year progressed, plans were made for the two week administrative leave (not chargeable) at Christmas time. I planned to go home for the holidays, but wanted to buy my Christmas presents before I left. Wick was painting my portrait which was to be a gift to Mother and Dad. He caught a good characterization of me dressed in blues with white gloves and cape, glancing at a map on the wall one more time before I went off to a social engagement. My only complaint was that he rendered me pasty-faced, the result of too much in-door work. Wick, who was preparing to spend Christmas with his family in Washington, also wanted to do some shopping. We decided to go into Kansas City one Saturday for that purpose and asked LTC Shifferaw Tessemma, the Ethiopian OFF, if he would like to go with us. A stranger in a strange country, he delightedly accepted our offer. Kansas City, MO still had some racial restrictions in 1956. We thought we had better check to see if Shifferaw would encounter any problems eating there, we certainly did not want to embarrass him. I called the Foreign Liaison Office, explained our plans to take LTC Shifferaw to Kansas City to shop and eat lunch and dinner there. Would there be any problem? The LNO asked, "What do you mean?"

"Will there be any problem because he looks black? Ethiopians are of Semitic ancestry but are black skinned, of course. Will he be subjected to any embarrassment if we take him to any of the better restaurants?"

The LNO dismissed the question. "Of course not. You know they are integrated in Missouri now and he can go any place he wants, particularly since he is an officer."

"Are you sure? We don't want to embarrass Colonel Shifferaw."

"Oh, I'm sure. There will be no problem."

Taking him at his word, we drove into the city, where we parted, I went to the gym and to take an organ lesson, Wick and Shiff to shop. Later in the afternoon, when I arrived at the hotel bar where we had planned to meet, I could tell from Wick's face that something was wrong. He explained it to me while Shiff was in the men's room. On an earlier foray into Kansas City, Wick had a delicious lunch in the restaurant in Macy's. The house specialty thoroughly Kansas City was a huge slab of roast beef au jus served on a round of brown bread. It seemed to Wick, and I concurred, that this was just the ticket for a cold, bitter day. With great anticipation, they went to the top floor of Macy's. They were somewhat early so there were many empty tables, but there was already a sizeable line formed at the cafeteria-style steam tables and much crowding, hanging up of coats and milling around.

They eagerly took their places in the line, Shifferaw's eyes dancing around the festive room in delight. Suddenly a man came directly toward them, calling out loudly, "Oh, no! Oh, no! Oh, no!" He strode up to Wick, now the target of hundreds of eyes and brayed, "He with you?" Wick, stupefied, said yes. "Well, he can't come in here" this grey-suited functionary loudly proclaimed.

Wick, horrified, seized the man's arm and yanked him out of earshot, saying, "What do you mean? This is an officer in the Imperial Ethiopian Army, an official guest of this country. How dare you carry on this way?" The little man unblinkingly answered, "I don't care. He's black! I just enforce the policy. Black is black! We would make one exception and nobody knows his story. He is black! That is what folks see. You got to get him out of here."

All but speechless with rage and humiliation, Wick turned back to Shiff on the line, still apparently unaware of anything but the busy scene of holiday Americans enjoying the food and the view out of the window. As best he could, Wick summoned a casually-annoyed tone and said to him, "Wouldn't you know! The very dish I wanted you to taste they aren't serving today. But there's another place I wanted to take you to, so let's go. This cafeteria is no good. We have enough of cafeterias at the Post." They departed to the amused and blatant Midwestern stares of at least a hundred people.

A thoroughly shaken, almost ill Wick took Shiff to the one haven he could be sure of- the Muhlbach Hotel, where there was no problem. However, the incident at Macy's troubled him. Later he took Shifferaw to Wolf Brothers, a fine men's store. While there, Shiff saw a pair of field glasses in a self-contained case which he liked. He told the salesgirl that he would take them if she could ship them.

"Oh, yes sir. Give me the address."

"Send them to Her Imperial Highness, the Empress of Ethiopia, Addis Ababa, Ethiopia."

The salesgirl gasped, gulped and finally wrote down the address, assuring LTC Shifferaw that the package would be mailed that day. She was certain the package would arrive in Ethiopia in time for Christmas.

In the meantime, Wick called the excellent gift shop run by the firm which makes Hallmark cards. He told the manager that he was bringing an Ethiopian Colonel to their store. Would they have someone show him their merchandise? The manager said that they would be delighted. When they entered the store a short time later, a charming lady walked up to them, saying to Shiff, "You must be Colonel Shifferaw".

She shook hands with him and welcomed him officially to the store. She was the chief buyer for Halls and took him through the store, showing him the merchandise, the stockroom and shipping room where not only gifts, but bulk quantities of Hallmark cards were sent out. Shiff was pleased that she had called him by name. The treatment at Hall's did much to lighten Wick's forebodings.

When I finally met them at the hotel bar, Wick was still very tense over the incident at lunch. After hurriedly telling me about it he asked where we should go for dinner. We had planned to go to the Golden Ox in the stockyards, but Wick was unsure of our reception.

"We had better check to be sure we'll be welcome", I said. When Shiff returned I excused myself, ostensibly to go to the men's room. Actually I called the Golden Ox and asked the woman who handled reservations if there would be any problems. After explaining to her that we were escorting a LTC from Ethiopia, she said, Oh, there will be no problem, we welcome the foreign OFFs from Leavenworth."

"I want to make sure. As you know Ethiopians are largely Semitic, they look like colored people."

She paused a moment, then said, "Well, we can put you in a private dining room."

"No. We do not want a private dining room. I just want to make sure that you will accept us with our guest as you would any other group of people."

She mumbled, hesitated, and finally said, "Well, unless you eat in a private dining room, perhaps it would be best not to come."

"We will not come. Rest assured that I will get this word out at FT Leavenworth and you can expect that no one from the Post will patronize your place from now on."

"Oh, we don't want that. You must realize that we have problems."

"Of course you have problems, but you are not going to inflict your problems on a guest of the United States Government."

I hung up. After calling another restaurant, I finally hit upon a well known Italian Ristorante in the heart of the city and not too far from the hotel where we were having a drink. The owner assured me that LTC Shifferaw would be most welcome. "I'll make sure that you have a good table," he said.

Much relieved, I thanked him after confirming our reservation for 1800. The cars were handy, but we decided to walk the short distance in spite of the freezing wind. We were glad that it was close by, it was bitter cold and Shiff was not used to winter weather. As soon as we walked into the restaurant a man strode up to meet us. "You must be Colonel Shifferaw from Ethiopia," he greeted Shiff, who beamed. The owner introduced himself and welcomed us to his restaurant. He escorted us to a choice table and insured that we had excellent service. Despite the unpleasantness at lunch, Shiff had a memorable day.

To this day neither Wick nor I can fathom how much of this harrowing byplay was perceived by Shifferaw. He was sensitive and amiable beyond belief. But he was urbane, on-the-ball, and no man's fool. The more we reflected on his demeanor throughout, the more there was to admire. Whether knowing or oblivious, his actions and reactions were beyond reproach. The terrible incidents he must have encountered when he ventured into the civilian community without even our bumbling intervention or precautions, are staggering to think of. These experiences, which must have been shared daily by our own black officers, were multiplied hundreds of times in those days, as black-skinned people eagerly arrived for their once-in-a-lifetime visit to the land of the free.

Instruction was suspended for the Christmas holidays. Wick took the train to Washington while I drove to New York. Christmas in College Point was festive as always. Mother and Dad had a huge Christmas tree and the traditional roast turkey dinner. All the noisy grandchildren were there with their parents. The family group was complete for the first time in many years making this a very special Christmas.

Wick had invited me to spend a night with him in Washington and to attend a cocktail party his Mother was giving. His Mother was called "Mappy" by the Wickert family and all their friends for reasons that are still a mystery to me. She insisted that I call her Mappy too. Wick had asked if I had any special friends in the Washington Area. Sam King, a fellow company commander in the 508, was assigned to the Military District of Washington. Mappy invited Sam and his wife, Betty, to the party. Betty and I were talking when the door opened and in walked a striking lady with a man I presumed to be her husband. Betty grabbed my arm saying excitedly,

"Do you know who that is?"

"No.

"That's the girl I invited to dinner at Benning the night you fell asleep."

She had married one of Wick's West Point classmates! I finally got her off to the side and we laughed over how I had fallen asleep and been awakened in time to take her home. One of the fascinating attributes of military service is the way people come into your life, leave, and then come back again.

In order to participate in the New Year's festivities, I drove back to Leavenworth early. There was the usual big party at the Club on New Year's Eve, the Post welcomed 1957 with gusto! Lou and Laura Williams had an open house on New Year's Day which prolonged that welcome.

Classes started again early in January. The routine was now familiar, guest lecturers, reading at home, formal class room instruction, practical work. Fortunately, some of us had other diversions. The organ continued to mystify me, rehearsals for Laura became more frequent as First Night in early February approached. We were finally ready for the presentation. The three performances went well. On the third night, Wick and I ate at the Club and I had a martini. During one of my key moments on stage, I forgot my lines. Fortunately Norm Allen realized I had forgotten his cue and burst on stage to arrest me as required. But that martini almost ruined the performance. I would have been humiliated had that happened after so many people had put that much work on the production. At the cast party later, there were many comments on my lapse. Years later, Wick told me that he had bumped into someone stationed at FT Knox who to his horror exclaimed, "Oh, you're the painter of that astonishing full-length portrait which hangs in splendor in their dining room."

One of the guest lecturers early in 1957 was the Deputy Chief of Staff for Personnel (DCSPER), LTG Walter Weible. He explained the new organization of the Army, the Pentomic Concept, and outlined the phase out of IN Regts and Bns. They were to be replaced with the "battle group". This seven-company maneuver organization was to be commanded by a COL. During the question and answer period, a senior IN COL on the faculty posed the problem of command and leadership training and experience, since there was a hiatus between the CPT Co CO and the COL battle group CDR. LTG Weible glibly dismissed the question and its implied criticism of the Pentomic Div with the remark, "If you can command a squad, you can command an army." Immediately he lost his audience, which knew quite well that many do not make the transition from command of a smaller to a larger unit easily.

Shortly after this blood-curdling insight into Pentagon thinking, one of the USMC LTCs in the class, Bob Elder, was visited by what he chose to consider an Army vendetta against him. Bob lived in the apartment just under Wick. One evening while Wick was studying he suddenly got warm. For some reason he put his hand down beside his chair and noticed that the floor was hot. He called me and we rushed down stairs. Looking in Bob Elder's window, we found that his apartment was on fire. We did not know whether Bob was in the apartment or not. Wick ran to call the fire department as I started to bang on Elder's door, trying to arouse him. The banging attracted the residents of the BOQ. Elder wandered up casually asking what was happening. He had been talking to Bill Cox at the other end of the BOQ! He arrived just in time to unlock his door so the firemen didn't have to break it down.

Bob moved across the street to another BOQ. In the middle of February he came to class one morning looking distraught.

"What's the matter, Bob?" I asked.

"You Army people have it in for us Marines."

"What's wrong?"

"Well, first you burned me out of my BOQ. Then, this morning as I was lying in bed gathering energy to get up, I happened to look up just as the ceiling fell in on me. Fortunately, it missed my face, but I am bruised all over. What do you guys have against Marine Officers?" Everyone in the group laughed.

At this time the US students began to receive instruction in nuclear warfare. There was to be a complete block of such instruction later on, but the faculty thought it best to ease us into the subject. The allied officers were excluded from these classes, as from all classified instruction. This was embarrassing to all of us. We thought that it would have been better if all of the classified material had been presented at one point in the course, either at the beginning, at the end, just before we went on Christmas leave, or after we came back. The allied officers could have been given those days off or had some special instruction so that they would not have felt excluded. No doubt this had been discussed with them during their orientation, but there was still something unpleasant about the system.

At the same time that the "Slant 7" Class was introduced to nuclear warfare, the school was conducting a series of VIP courses in the same subject. My former commander in the 9th IN, Richard Steinbach, recently promoted to BG, wrote to tell me that he would attend one of the VIP courses. The one-time Manchus in the class - COL Chalard, S-3 of the Thai Bn, LTC Bill Cox, the 2nd Div Surgeon, Bill Lindahl, Lou Williams, Carl Earles, Bill Graves and I - had a dinner party at the Club for BG Steinbach at which we swapped lies about the 9th Infantry.

My Course Advisor, LTC Mac Austin, had headed the Intelligence Section in CCRAK in Korea when I was in the Guerrilla Section of FEC/LD. Mac debriefed me after the frightening recon over North Korea. We had also had a number of other official contacts there and had attended the Episcopal services together whenever I was in Seoul. He and his delightful wife, Peg, had me to dinner several times. Mac did much to make the course smoother for me.

There was no thesis to write for the course, but several shorter papers were required - a complete staff study and an exposition. The purpose of these papers was to determine whether or not the students could write. That it was a good idea was proven when the papers revealed that some of the officers could not organize a paper or put their thoughts into clear prose. It was especially surprising since in those days, almost everyone who graduated from high school was capable of writing grammatical English. The faculty graded the papers carefully, criticizing organization, content, syntax, punctuation, and spelling.

In March 1957, a team from Career Management in the Pentagon came to Leavenworth to give the class its post-college assignments. Wick was assigned to the Southern Europe Task Force, a missile headquarters at Verona, Italy, which pleased him very much. But I drew duty with the Office of the Deputy Chief of Staff for Operations (ODCSOPS) in the Pentagon. My request to go back to FT Bragg preferably to the 82nd, had been disapproved. The Pentagon assignment meant that I would be away from troops seven straight years. With the new organization and changes in doctrine, this was not a good time for a staff job in my opinion. When I protested, the "Career Managers" told me that I needed high level staff duty to round out my career! I was not convinced.

The evening we received our assignments, we went to the Club for dinner, I to drown my sorrows, Wick to celebrate his opportunity. While we were drinking our second round, two LTCs, one AG, the other SC, passed our table. They both lived on the third floor in our stair well, considered sub-standard quarters and hence given to officers in bachelor status who were drawing quarters allowance for their wives or families who were not with them. They were accompanied by two ladies we presumed to be their wives. The AG officer said, "Good evening. It is a wonderful day, isn't it?"

That was probably the first time either of them had even acknowledged Wick or me. Over the year they had turned down several invitations to join us for a drink, or to attend our parties. Neither of them had been in Gruber 4 so far. We thought it odd that an officer would voluntarily spend a year separated from his wife. With the Pentagon in my future, I was not convinced it was a wonderful day.

"There is nothing good about the day as far as I am concerned. An assignment in the Pentagon is for the birds. I hate the Army!" I retorted.

They stiffened and passed on without further comment.

The next day, Wick and I were sitting in my room after lunch. There was a knock on the door. I called, "Come in." It was the AG LTC from above us.

"I would like to talk with you, major." he said without greeting.

"Come in and sit down. It is not anything you do not want Wick to hear is it?"

"I prefer to stand. No, perhaps it is just as well that MAJ Wickert is here. I want to ask you why you insulted me in front of my wife last evening. She is terribly upset about the incident at the Club. She can't understand why you dislike me so much. This is her first visit to Fort Leavenworth and it has been ruined for her. Now what prompted you to say what you did?"

"COL, if I offended your wife, I apologize. But I did not insult you or anyone else. All I did was gripe about my assignment. I can't see how my remarks could possibly be construed as being antagonistic toward you."

"Well, both COL Schreiber and I thought you were completely out of line, and I want to know what you are going to do about it."

"COL, you are making an issue out of a harmless, offhand and impersonal comment. If you have no sense of humor, I can't explain it to you. But I do not intend to do anything about it. Now if you will kindly leave us we have to get to class."

He had to be almost pushed out the door. He wanted to talk more about it. When he had gone, Wick let out a whoop! He could not believe what he had heard! Where had those two been all their Army careers? We had thought them odd the way they kept to themselves and did not mix with the other students in the class, and attending a full year course without their wives, but this was too much! We dissolved in laughter. We made it a point to limit our conversation with them in the future to the barest amenities.

Several days after the receipt of orders, Wick and I were discussing our plans. I mentioned that I wanted to get an apartment in the vicinity of the Pentagon. The BOQs provided for MAJs in Washington were described as grim, I wanted no part of them. Besides, I wanted to entertain, to start living like a civilized individual instead of like a nomad out of a footlocker. I asked Wick if he knew of any apartments close to the Pentagon. He knew of several in addition to the apartment complex his Mother lived in, but suggested that he ask his brother and sister-in-law, Tom and Ede, to see if they could find one for me.

In several weeks I received a packet with information on several apartments, complete with scale drawings of the layouts and comments about colors, light, and access to the Pentagon. Tom and Ede recommended an apartment in Arlington Towers near Key Bridge. Based on their recommendation, the drawing of the arrangement and the map showing its location, I wrote to the management and sight unseen, committed myself to a one year lease. The apartment removed one concern but it created another, I had no furniture except the organ, a college chair and my books and records. But with a place to live in I looked forward to setting up a bachelor "Pad". I even started to look forward to the Pentagon tour!

As the school year began to draw to a close, "Slant 7" prepared for its intensive block of nuclear instruction Just before the start of that instruction, a fire destroyed one of the oldest buildings on the Post, the original HQ, now dedicated to atomic warfare studies. Since most of the classified material was in that building, there was concern as to whether or not the faculty would be able to give us the nuclear weapons course. Fortunately, material for "Slant 7" was in the vaults in the main building, Grant Hall.

In each of the classrooms in Gruber Hall there was a large double-doored safe where classified material used by students was kept. Inside were individual locked boxes stacked up like safety deposit boxes in a bank vault. Each student was issued a combination for the lock on the box assigned to him. It took some time before each period began to get all the boxes out, and to put them away at the end of the period. Those boxes became very familiar to every American student in the class during the nuclear weapons instruction. This block was totally classified with the result that the allied officers were given other instruction during that time. The last week of nuclear instruction, the class returned to Gruber Hall each evening; all studying had to be done there because the classified material could not be removed from the building.

The nuclear weapons instruction included complicated calculations of fallout, yields, the number of megatons to use for the specific amount of destruction desired, the effect enemy nuclear weapons of a given yield would have on friendly troops, the extent of the area of contamination, and how long it would be before the contaminated area could be safely entered. Considerable math was involved. Those who had "slip sticks" or slide rules, got through it fairly easily, but I was never comfortable with math, nor was I able to use the slide rule, so I had to do all of my computations by longhand. The engineers in the class did well.

Graduation was imminent. Mother and Dad had accepted my invitation to attend the exercises and were looking forward to the train trip out as well as the visit. Wick had invited Mappy, and Bill Lindahl, his parents. The three of us decided to have a dinner party at Putsche's, an outstanding restaurant in Kansas City. After cocktails we planned to have Chateaubriand for the entire group. It would be expensive, but we were sure to have a superb meal. Because of the many social functions going on prior to graduation, dinner at Putsche's had to be on the day that Mother and Dad were to arrive. The guest house on Post was jammed, so I made reservations for them at the Cody Hotel in Leavenworth. Mappy and the Lindalhs were staying there, too. Mother and Dad's train was due to arrive at 1500 which would give them time to check into the Cody and freshen up before we drove to Kansas City.

On the day Mother and Dad were to arrive I got to the Leavenworth Station early. The agent told me their train was running late, but was not sure how late it would be. Suddenly a train came in which I thought was theirs, but it proved to be the morning train! Since the train stopped first in Kansas City, I decided to go there to get Mother and Dad off the train to save the time needed to drive from Leavenworth to Kansas City.

Just as I got to the station in Kansas City the errant train came in. I identified their car and retrieved two very wilted parents. They hurriedly told me that there had been a derailment which held them up. The air conditioning had broken down on one of the hottest June days, hence they were exhausted and hot. We found a convenient motel in Kansas City where they had a quick shower and got into dry, clean clothes. On our arrival at Putsche's about a half hour late, we found the others having cocktails. There was time for one drink before the delicious Chateaubriand was served. We enjoyed the evening; the Lindahl's, the Seiberts and Mappy were very compatible. Mother formed a close attachment with Mappy who was exactly her age.

Throughout the school year there had been a number of parties to which Wick, Bill Lindahl and I had been invited. We therefore gave a final cocktail party at the Club to introduce our parents to our friends as well as to repay our social obligations. In addition there were several other parties to which we were invited, so Mother and Dad were drawn into a whirlwind of social activity. This was the first time since I had been commissioned that they had visited me on any Army post. They were delighted with my friends who welcomed them warmly; I had indeed made many wonderful friends at Leavenworth.

Graduation was held under the old trees on the historic parade ground. GEN Maxwell D. Taylor, the CofS of the Army, spoke to us of the contribution he expected us to make to the future of the Army. It was a simple, dignified function. One representative student received the diplomas for all the students in his row, which reduced the time considerably.

Immediately after the goodbyes, Mother, Dad and I headed east in my black and white Pontiac convertible. Our first stop was St Louis, where we had an excellent roast beef dinner with Clarence and Elizabeth Kettler (Kett was with me at RAAF) at Stan Musial's Restaurant.

We then drove to Asheville, NC, where we picked up the Blue Ridge Parkway. Mother and Dad enjoyed the scenery; I fought the curves and hills. We had Communion in St Stephen's Cathedral at Harrisburg, PA, where my friend Howard Clark was Dean, then visited the Goods at Brantingham Lake. In all respects it was a relaxing leave.

On arriving in Washington, I finally found my way to Arlington Towers. The apartment Tom and Ede Wickert had found for me in the Tyler Building was well located and ideal for my purposes. Though it looked mighty bare at the time, I thought I would be comfortable there. My first full day in Washington, still on leave, was spent at a furniture store which agreed to deliver my purchases the next day. The organ, books and footlockers were also delivered the same day. Within three days, I was essentially settled, though there was still much to do and buy. The superintendent of the building found a maid for me who would clean the apartment once a week. With these chores behind me, I was ready to take on the Pentagon.

CHAPTER 12

PLANNER

To the newcomer the Pentagon is a huge, impersonal and confusing building. Locating the Administrative Office of the ODCSOPS introduced me to the system of floors, rings, bays and corridors. With several side excursions and considerable retracing of steps, I found the correct office and signed in. After the inevitable processing I was escorted to the Office of the Director of Plans.

A secretary took me to COL Samuel McC. Goodwin, who was sitting at a small side table, apparently a fifth wheel in the operations. Later I learned that he was being briefed as the new Asst Deputy Director of Plans. COL Goodwin, who greeted me warmly, asked various questions about my education and military background. He overwhelmed me with the following statement,

"You know, Don, my father was a planner and my grandfather was a planner. All my life all I wanted to be in the Army was a planner. Finally, here I am in Army Plans. This is the greatest job in the Army and you are privileged to be a member of the Army Planning Team. You have a great responsibility; a great opportunity to influence the future of the Army. Make the best of it."

This struck me as an effort to convince himself of the importance of his job. After my interview with Goodwin, I was introduced to COL Vernon P. Mock, the Deputy (Dep) Director, and then to BG James K. Woolnough, the Director of Plans. BG Woolnough was a tall, slender, imposing officer who greeted me with quiet courtesy. He was a gentleman, the more I got to know him, the more I liked him. COL Mock was an effusive, nervous individual who seemed to need to dominate any conversation. He said that I was assigned to the Campaign Plans/War Games Branch of Army War Plans Division of the Director of Plans, Office of the Deputy Chief of Staff for Military Operations! The organization as well as the building awed me. In turn, I was conducted to the offices of COL Moe Boylan, Chief of Army War Plans Division (AWPD), his Deputy, COL George Mayo, and COL Al Dequoy, the Chief of the Campaign Plans/War Games Branch. The other officer in the Campaign Branch was LTC Jean Hollstein, a tall, good-looking, slow talking, Airborne officer.

COL Al Dequoy, the Branch Chief, was a NG OFF on active duty for three years. NG OFFs from selected States were called to active duty for a three-year period to serve on the Army Staff and provide the viewpoint and experience of "citizen soldiers". The practice brings to the Army Staff many talented people. Because of his interest in computers and war gaming, COL Dequoy had been assigned to Plans. He was a short, energetic, brilliant officer from Massachusetts, who had practiced law in civilian life, but loved the Army and war gaming. The office was just becoming involved in war games as its recent name change to Campaign Plans/War Games Branch attested. COL Dequoy was authorized a civilian assistant, he finally chose a bright young man from the Army Map Service, John Onufrak, who was promoted to GS15 when he reported for duty in Plans. As a GS15 he had prerogatives similar to those of a BG, yet he would be working under a COL, an odd set-up, but typical of Army organization.

It became obvious that COL Mock did not like war gaming and I don't think BG Woolnough was particularly sympathetic to it at that time. The Air Force and the Navy were ahead of the Army in developing this technique. Once Kennedy and McNamara were in power, it became the "in" thing. At first the Air Force and Navy consistently bested the Army in Joint Staff Actions by alluding to the results of their war games. The Army belatedly recognized the value of and need to develop a war gaming capability.

COL Dequoy faced resistance from almost the entire Army Staff in his war gaming efforts. Though a fine mathematician and logical thinker, he was an extreemely poor briefer. Despite being a lawyer, he was not convincing, as a result, he had great difficulty in selling the conclusions of his war gaming.

The secretary in Campaign Plans Branch was a striking young black, Kitty Jones. Very capable, bright, efficient, brash, she loved to argue with everybody. But she never failed to get an action out on time and in excellent condition.

Because of the war gaming, the Branch was authorized another secretary. Edie was finally acquired to fill that vacancy. She was not nearly as efficient or effective as Kitty, in fact, on several occasions I recommended to COL Dequoy that she be fired. Dequoy was reluctant to take such action because of the difficulty in firing a civil service employee. However, he asked me to counsel her. One day I asked her to stay after quitting time. When everybody else had gone, I told her that her performance was not satisfactory. She began to cry but I was unmoved. I explained that I was trying to help her, to point out why we were dissatisfied with her work: she did not follow through, did not make notes when there were telephone calls, was often late, slow in her work, made errors which she failed to catch or correct, and did not keep us informed. Eventually she left to go to work for the Air Force, where she was given a promotion!

In the first week in ODCSOPS I learned to find my way around the Pentagon, attended several briefings for new officers, was staggered by the size, organization and complexity of ODCSOPS, and found that I had many friends in the Pentagon and in the Washington Area. Once the system of rings, bays and corridors was mastered and the numbering system understood it was easy to find anyone in the Pentagon if his or her room number was known. The briefings covered organization, policies, guidelines and administrative matters. The make-up of the Department of Defense (DOD), the Department of the Army (DA), its General Staff, and ODCSOPS became clear, alive and important rather than the incomprehensible wiring diagrams that I had scanned and forgotten. There were several hundred military and civilian personnel in ODCSOPS, which had four other Directorates in addition to Plans: Operations, Organization and Training, Aviation, and Guided Missiles. Plans consisted of the Directorate Office, The National Security Office (NSC) and four Divisions, Army War Plans (AWPD), Joint War Plans (JWPD), International Policy and Plans (IPPD) and Mobilization Plans (MPD).

A number of my Leavenworth classmates had been assigned to agencies in the Washington Area including Bill Cox and Jim Connell, both of whom lived in the Tyler Building, Ink Gates, Rod McFadden, Jim Munson, Jim Gettings, Woody Shemwell and Frank Camm. Tom Tackaberry went from Leavenworth to Tulane University. When he graduated with a Master's degree in psychology, he was assigned to the Pentagon resulting in frequent visits with him and Lilian. Bill Lindahl was at FT Meade near Baltimore. We saw each other often and I was an usher at his wedding in 1958. Though Norm and Scottie Allen went to Hawaii I became the Godfather of their first son, Norman III, by proxy. With such a large contingent of the Slant 7 class in the area, there were frequent reunions, especially of Gruber 4.

Sam and Betty King had quarters at FT Myer. Many evenings were spent with them either in their quarters or in the Officers' Club under Wainwright Hall. At least once a week I enjoyed Betty's gourmet cooking. Sam, in his job as the Ceremonies OFF for the Military District of Washington, handled the arrangements for honor guards and other affairs in the which the 3rd Infantry, The Old Guard, was involved. He asked me to take Betty to the interment of the Unknowns of WWII and Korea. We had VIP parking and seating. It was a most solemn occasion with President Eisenhower presiding.

Jack Wright, from the Advance Class and 508, was in the office across the corridor from Campaign Plans Branch. We reminisced frequently about the Red Devils. There were also frequent visits to Owings Mills to see Bill Long (IGMR) and his family and to Baltimore to see Ted Rothert (Walter Reed) and his family.

On the second or third day after completing the processing and briefings, before I got to know the people I was going to work with, or fully settled at my desk, a phone call shattered the quiet of the office about 1100. Campaign Plans Branch had a requirement to prepare a paper justifying a joint exercise in the Far East to demonstrate the mutual capability of the Southeast Asia Treaty Organization (SEATO) allies to reinforce or support each other in actual combat. By default, the action fell to me. Army General Staff procedures were still puzzling me, but Joint Staff actions were enigmas I had never tackled. This was a Joint Staff Action, First Kitty pointed me in the right direction, then an action officer in another branch told me that a similar exercise called "Firm Link" had been held the year before. The Joint Action Control Office (JACO) provided me a copy of the plan for "Firm Link" and the after action report. Based on that file I developed my initial paper, the Army position on the exercise. The matter was to go to the Joint Chiefs of Staff (JCS) for approval. The procedure, which I learned as I careened along, was to prepare a "purple", a tentative recommendation to the Joint Staff. When the DCSOPS of all the services approved the purple, it became a "green", which was considered by the JCS. If they approved the action it was red striped. Though not fully conversant with the procedure, I had received instructions in this process during the extensive briefings given me when I joined DCSOPS. Now I was getting on the job training!

The draft was completed by noon. COL Boylan looked at it, approved it and told me to take it "up the tape" to COL Mock, who put every new action officer in the Office of the Director of Plans through a drill over his first paper. If he measured up, he left him alone from then on to do his job. If anyone flunked the initial test, COL Mock badgered him for the rest of his tenure in Plans or DCSOPS. This had been impressed upon me by everyone in Army War Plans. The "purple" that I was writing had to reach the Director, himself, by 1330 since it was to be considered by all of the service Operations Chiefs at 1400 so expeditious action was essential. It appeared that extensive revision of the paper was impossible, a thought which calmed me as I went to face COL Mock. Fortunately I had a voluminous stack of files with me, partially digested. Backup material apparently impressed the Deputy Director, who started to tear my paper apart as soon as he had read it Despite his patronizing sarcasm I was confident of my work and defended my position vigorously. It seemed that Mock liked people who refused to back down when questioned. After approving the paper with minimal changes, he told me to get BG Woolnough's sanction before it was reproduced.

BG Woolnough, a gentleman, a fine officer and a great planner, had one habit which frustrated every action officer. He reached for his pencil before he read a paper, ready to mark it up or change it as he read. A newcomer to Plans, I was not aware of this idiosyncrasy; when he reached for his pencil I pointed out to him that there was a 1330 deadline on the paper and that COL Mock had already approved it. This took him aback; few action officers ever rushed General Woolnough, but I was new and brash. He hesitated, read the paper through, made a few minor word changes (I learned later that every word in a Joint Staff paper is important, a fact which Woolnough appreciated fully), then told me to have it put in final form. COL Mock's secretary, Margaret, typed a clean copy, with which Woolnough and I proceeded "up the tape" to brief LTG Clyde Eddleman, the DCSOPS. Woolnough recommended that the Army "buy" the draft. LTG Eddleman seemed satisfied that it would do for a trial run. We reproduced enough copies to meet all requirements, after which I turned it over to the JACO to be distributed to the other services. I had passed my first hurdle in the Pentagon.

COL Dequoy had not passed his initial examination with COL Mock, who took great delight in humiliating the Campaign Plans Branch Chief. Every time COL Dequoy took an action to the front office, COL Mock was particularly vicious. As a result, Dequoy hated dealing with him, preferring instead to bypass him and go directly to Woolnough.

A short time after my inauguration all action officers newly assigned to the Army Staff were assembled in the fifth floor auditorium where General Taylor, Army CofS, gave his monthly welcoming address. One of his comments struck me as being short sighted.

"You know, we are not going to waste our energy and time fighting the small battles. We are going to save our ammunition and our clout for the big ones."

This was a time when the three services were fighting each other for funds, roles and missions. Eisenhower had embraced the strategic deterrence concept which apparently blinded him to the importance of the role the Army played in national policy. As a result, the Army was losing ground in the assignment of rotes, missions and resources. These words came back to haunt us again and again because the Army never did fight the "big battles". It lost the entire war as a result of the little skirmishes that the Army Staff did not spend the time and energy to address.

So began three years marked by work days often 14 hours in length, by many frustrations, by the assignment of equal priority to highly significant actions and ridiculous exercises of no value. On balance, it turned out to be an enjoyable three years and one of the most valuable educational experiences of my career Some of the finest officers in the Army were assigned to ODCSOPS; it was a rare privilege to work with them. Most important of all, I learned, how the Army functions, how it is controlled, and how it makes plans for everything from opening a new base to deploying forces overseas. Plans was involved in almost every action initiated by the Army Staff, hence the action officers assigned there got into many diverse matters.

When I had been in AWPD about four months, I became involved in a nuclear war game being conducted by COL Dequoy. We analyzed the effects of nuclear weapons on the battlefield under many different situations. One interesting side study attempted to determine if nuclear weapons would have affected the outcome of the French defense of Dien-Bien-Phu. After plotting all of the possible nuclear weapons strikes, it became apparent that the use of nuclear weapons would not have altered appreciably the course of events leading to the French withdrawal from Vietnam.

Although I had completed the nuclear weapons instruction at C&GSC, I requested permission to attend the VIP Atomic Weapons Orientation Course at FT Bliss, TX. The course offered information on the characteristics, mobility and employment of nuclear delivery means. I was already familiar with calculations of fallout and destruction from the training at Leavenworth. The request was approved.

It was indeed a VIP course. As a MAJ, I was the junior officer in the class, admitted only because I was on the Army Staff. The school took care of the students in royal fashion. Classes were held from 0800 to 1600, after which the cadre made arrangements for entertainment and sight-seeing. The big attraction in the area was the Mexican border town, Juarez. Every night the school provided bus transportation to the International Bridge across the Rio Grande between El Paso and Juarez. There were some excellent eating places in Juarez as well as many night clubs which featured exotic dancers.

The week at Fort Bliss was a pleasant one, and in spite of all the fun and games across the river, I learned a great deal which proved valuable in my work. On returning to the Pentagon, I again plunged into the sea of paperwork; almost immediately I was over my head in actions.

My trip to FT Bliss made me the nuclear action officer in AWPD. Thus, I was the Plans action officer on the Davy Crockett Weapons System. Davy Crockett was essentially a spigot mortar designed to fire low yield nuclear rounds directly in front of Army troops. It was one of the Army's attempts to get into the nuclear club. After witnessing a test firing at Aberdeen Proving Ground, using conventional warheads, considering its limited range, and seeing how fragile the weapon itself was, I became convinced that it was not a useful weapons system. The R&D project officer, LTC Bill Fulton, who had instructed my Advance Class at Benning, was very proud of Davy Crockett. In the end, the Army adopted it, kept it for about 10 years, harassed the troops with the annual stereotyped ritual of Technical Proficiency Inspections (TPIs), only to discard it when its obvious shortcomings could no longer be ignored.

Members of the Army Staff were making plans for major wars, for troop movements affecting thousands of soldiers, for expenditures of hundreds of millions of dollars, yet they were unable to plan their own lives. Time after time I planned leaves which were canceled because of "emergency actions" or "hot actions", some of which proved to be unnecessary. One Saturday I was Plans DO, a task rotated among all action officers in the Directorate, which entailed receiving and screening all messages, notifying appropriate personnel of any requirements, monitoring the telephone, assisting BG Woolnough who usually came in every Saturday, and ensuring that all of the safes were locked when everyone left. BG Woolnough departed that day about 1230. By the time I had locked the safes, made the required security checks and threaded my way through the Saturday it was 1300. I had just gotten home when the phone rang. It was LTC Elvy Roberts, an OFF in the Office of the Secretary of the General Staff (SGS). He told me that there was a "hot action" from GEN Taylor which required that I return to the Pentagon immediately. Getting into uniform, back to the Pentagon I went.

LTC Roberts, one of MG Westmoreland's many assistants in his capacity as the SGS, told me that the CofS wanted, by 0800 Monday, a study of the capability of the Army to fight a limited war in the Middle East. This was early in 1958; after the announcement of the Eisenhower Doctrine in March of 1957, this subject had been studied and restudied; less than six months before Charlie Jackson had briefed the Chief on that very question. The requirement to do another analysis of the same area was such a surprise that I told Elvy that I couldn't believe the Chief wanted it on short notice since he had closed the issue months before. Elvy was adamant. He told me that he had gotten the action directly from GEN Taylor; it was once again a burning issue.

Unconvinced, I called BG Woolnough, voicing my suspicions about the study. He agreed with me; Elvy Roberts assured him that this was a hot action direct from the CofS. Woolnough, skeptical, called the SGS, MG Westmoreland; if the requirement was a valid one it meant that about 100 action officers would have to work all Saturday afternoon and night and all day Sunday. Then on Sunday evening every general officer who headed one of the agencies of the DA Staff would have to be briefed, their concurrences obtained, or their non-concurrences considered. This would be sheer harassment if Elvy had misinterpreted what GEN Taylor wanted.

Woolnough didn't get very far with Westmoreland. He even suggested that he, Woolnough, call GEN Taylor at his quarters to find out the exact nature of the requirement. Westmoreland vetoed that. Woolnough finally capitulated. He called me, saying, "Well, go ahead with it, Don. There's nothing I can do. This is apparently a legitimate requirement."

The matter still bothered me; before I called in the action OFFs, I went back to LTC Roberts. "Elvy, you'd better give me a memorandum outlining exactly what the Chief wants. It will save me a great deal of grief when I call all these people in and they start to beat on me over a requirement that they are sure to think unnecessary."

Elvy growled a bit but dictated a memorandum to his secretary which he signed and gave to me. When the action people came in muttering and grumbling, I handed each a copy of Elvy's directive and explained what was wanted them.

To initiate the action I quickly drafted a campaign plan which postulated a situation and developed a course of action for meeting it. This "strawman" was given to each element of the staff so that it could prepare its part to make the complete plan: an intelligence estimate; a plan of operations; a troop list; logistics requirements including movement of troops and supplies; personnel, morale and welfare considerations; cost and budgeting; training; medical; even mobilization and Reserve Component annexes.

The Staff worked most of Saturday night; I finally got away from the Pentagon about midnight. Everyone was back at 0800 on Sunday. By about 1000 a reasonable study had been put together. Then began the tedious work of getting concurrences, analyzing comments and objections, substituting words, deleting the objectionable parts of the plan so that the major agencies of the Army Staff would "buy" it. By 1600 the action officers had completed their work, agreed to the proposed draft and had begun briefing up the tape through the various elements of the Staff. My briefings began with COL Boylan, Chief of AWPD, who approved it without change; Woolnough approved it about 1800. LTG Eddleman, the DCSOPS, approved it about 2000. Concurrences from the other Staff agencies came in just as LTG Eddleman "put his chop" on it. Everybody else left as I set about putting a briefing together, completing the summary sheet which would accompany it and getting the visual aids made. Woolnough told me he would be in at 0630 on Monday morning to go over the final briefing and summary sheet with me. LTG Eddleman would then be briefed in time to sign off on the action before we took it to GEN Taylor at 0800.

About midnight Sunday, I went home to get a little sleep. At 0500 I was back at the Pentagon to make a final check of slides the visual aids people had worked all night to prepare, the briefing and the paper itself. Everything was in order; the final actions went as planned.

At 0800 I was standing tall behind the podium in GEN Taylor's office and began my briefing, "Sir, this is a decision briefing to evaluate our capabilities to fight a limited war in the Middle East." GEN Taylor looked up quickly, saying,

"Why are you giving me this, today? That action doesn't seem very pertinent now. Is there a particular reason that I'm getting this briefing?"

I looked pointedly at LTC Elvy Roberts, who looked away. I then looked at MG Westmoreland; he also looked away. I looked at my boss, Woolnough, for some support; he shrugged his shoulders. Nobody in the room said a word. Finally I muttered,

"The situation in the Middle East is so unstable that it is essential that we periodically re-evaluate our capability in that area."

I then hurried on with my briefing. GEN Taylor was not particularly satisfied, but he let me talk for a few minutes. Then he interrupted again, "I still don't understand why you are giving me this briefing. We went over this about six months ago and I thought we had established a firm set of guidelines on what we would do and what was needed. Why are we reviewing it again?"

It was quite evident that he was irritated. Once again I looked at Elvy Roberts, Westmoreland, the entire group for some help. None was forthcoming. Again I attempted to justify the paper, then hurried on with the briefing. I'd gotten out about three more sentences when GEN Taylor slammed his hand on his desk and said, "Stop. This is ridiculous. I have many things to do that are more important than this. I can't comprehend why you are wasting my time."

By this time I was irate because I was taking the brunt of General Taylor's displeasure. I looked around one more time for help. When none was forthcoming I took a copy of Elvy Robert's memorandum, walked deliberately over to GEN Taylor's desk and literally slammed it in front of him saying, "Sir, you asked for it"

GEN Taylor was a little surprised. He read the memorandum hastily, then looked at Westmoreland and Roberts, quite coldly I thought. He looked up at me, half smiled and said,

"Yes, I guess I did. Proceed, MAJ Seibert."

Returning to the podium I dutifully went through the briefing. I closed by saying, "Sir, this concludes the briefing."

General Taylor said, "Thank you very much. That will be all gentlemen." That was the end of the exercise. It was obvious that Taylor had not wanted that briefing nor had he wanted to put the Staff through the weekend drill. What most of us surmised later was that he had probably made an off-hand remark, or wondered aloud whether we were getting on with our capability to fight or redeploy to the Middle East. The hotshots in the office of the SGS, trying to anticipate his every thought, translated that immediately into a crash project which exercised some 100 members of the

Army Staff and brought at least 15 Generals in late on Sunday night for no real purpose. This was all too typical of the make-work actions in the Pentagon. I only wish that Generals would stop making casual remarks in front of eager young subordinates. All they do is create unnecessary work for many dedicated people.

The functioning of the Army Staff system was a never-ending marvel. Some wag said that a group of five or six bright MAJs strategically assigned to key slots in such elements as Plans, Personnel, Logistics and the Comptroller's Office could run the Army; if they were persuasive enough to convince their chiefs to support their positions they could get almost any action approved. Of course this is not true. The generals and senior colonels have experience and intelligence enough to analyze actions presented to them and will not approve a paper unless it is a well thought-out one. But it was a heady thought.

One of GEN Taylor's idiosyncrasies was his dislike of a large group of people in the room when he was being briefed. He preferred six or less. Once, Charlie Jackson was scheduled to brief him in the ODCSOPS conference room which was fairly large; I was the viewgraph operator. It was an important decision briefing so the principals of all of the Army Staff Agencies were present, at least six general officers, together with their action OFFs. In addition there was the SGS, an assistant SGS, BG Woolnough, Jackson and I. A total of 15 or 20 people. GEN Taylor walked in and looked around. Apparently he was in a bad mood. He turned to MG Bonesteel, the SGS, and said, "Tic, I told you that I didn't want so many people present when I am being briefed. Now why can't we limit this to six people?"

MG Bonesteel attempted to explain that since it was a decision briefing the staff agencies which had input to the action were present to answer questions or receive the CofS's decision and guidance. GEN Taylor, not convinced of the need for so many people, ordered, "Clear them out."

As a result, all of the action OFFs, the people who had the background and information to answer any questions, were sent out; the generals who had only a minimum knowledge of the action remained. They had been briefed on the action, of course, and had approved it, but they did not have the details at their fingertips. The burden to defend the action fell on Charlie Jackson. It was a strange idiosyncrasy, not in keeping with GEN Taylor's stature as CofS. He short-changed himself in this way several times, in my opinion.

When the Army Green uniform was adopted in 1956, its wearing was restricted by very stringent regulations. OFFs were forbidden, for example, to wear it in public after 1800, at which time they were either to wear civilian clothes or blues. This posed a hardship on those working in the Pentagon who rarely left the building before 1800. For bachelors like myself it was particularly difficult because we were precluded from stopping to shop, eat or have a drink before we got home. Legally, we had to go home and change clothes before going out for any purpose. By the time I got home and changed it was usually 2000; if I had to be in the Pentagon early the next morning I had no desire to go out at that time.

This was the subject of a heated conversation one evening at an ODCSOPS cocktail party at the FT Myer Officers' Club. A striking lady happened to overhear the conversation, joined us and asked me to repeat the problem. Since I did not know who she was, I was reluctant to do so but she persisted. Finally, I told her the gist of the conversation. She kept nodding and saying, "Of course, that's absolutely right." "It's ridiculous." "It puts an awful burden on people." "That should be changed. Let's talk to Max about It."

With that she grabbed my arm and started dragging me across the room toward GEN Taylor, the Max she wanted to talk to about it. Unknowingly, I had been talking to Mrs Taylor. The CofS was with LTG Eddleman and BG Woolnough as we came up.

"Max, you've got to listen to this young man. There's something that needs to be changed right away," she said.

Donald A. Seibert

GEN Taylor raised his eyebrows quizzically as he looked at me. My bosses glared. Though I tried to evade the issue and leave, Mrs Taylor insisted I tell the CofS about the problems the current uniform regulations created for Pentagon action officers. In concluding, I pointed out to GEN Taylor that it was particularly galling because officers on TDY were not subject to this same restriction and could wear their green uniforms after 1800. He was surprised about that aspect, apparently unaware of it. He thanked me and told me he would look into it. I beat a hasty retreat followed by the glower of Eddleman and Woolnough. Shortly thereafter the regulation was changed, whether as a result of this conversation I do not know.

Mother and Dad came down to visit me several times. Usually they would arrive late on Friday and return to New York on Sunday. With much coordination and back-up from friends, it was possible to break free for most of their visits. They attended several of my parties, thus getting to know my friends. During one trip we went to Williamsburg. On the way back to Arlington I drove them through many familiar streets in Richmond. They were shocked at the deterioration of the two neighborhoods we had lived in on West Carey Street during the twenties. Dad insisted on visiting Broad Street Station where the RF&P, for whom he had worked at the time, had such wonderful Christmas displays each year They included scale models of the RF&P trains, made by the mechanics in the round house, which ran around a huge Christmas tree. On another visit, we drove to Charlottesville to see Monticello and Ashlawn.

In addition to Mother and Dad, there were many other visitors to the apartment: my two sisters and their families, Elizabeth and Howard Clark, Milan and Ellen Hartz, Ted and Amy Rothert, the Longs from Owings Mills, Betty and Bill Ankley (Bill was attending the Marine Staff Course at Quantico). My phone would ring frequently, alerting me that an old friend passing through Washington would like to spend the night with me. These were always pleasant interludes, but some wanted to party all night, forgetting that I had to be at the Pentagon early each morning.

Occasionally, Ted Seely, from the 508 would pop in for a day or two. He introduced me to Erik and Rita Johnson, who became such close friends that they asked me to be their son Richard's Godfather. I was more than happy to do so. Richard and his twin sister, Melanie, were christened in the Children's Chapel at the National Cathedral.

When I first reported to the Pentagon, COL Wilson was assigned to Infantry Branch. We got together for dinner occasionally, usually at the Army Navy Club, of which he was a member. It was said to have the best food in Washington. A visit to the Army Navy Club was always interesting. Many retired OFFs lived there; some had participated in the wars against Spain and in the China campaigns. It was fascinating to overhear snatches of conversations detailing some vignette of combat with the Spanish, the Filipinos, or the Chinese. One evening two officers at the next table were discussing the building of the first airfield at FT Stotensberg north of Manila and its development into Clark Field.

COL Wilson suggested that he sponsor me for membership in the Army Navy Club. After looking into the matter carefully, I opted to join the Army Navy Country Club of which I am still an absentee member. It offered a greater variety of facilities, such as golf and swimming. Several friends, including the Homens and the Gates were members, adding to the attraction there.

Once I joined the Army Navy Country Club I tried to do something about my golf game by taking a few lessons. These were intermittent because I could never be sure when I could keep an appointment with the Pro. Bill Homen and I played a few times, but he was assigned to a secret AF intelligence gathering agency and was gone frequently. Golf suffered because duty in the Pentagon consumed most of my time and energy.

Ted Seely received orders to attend the Spanish Staff College. I told him to look up Rafael Guimera Ferrer and Luis Saez-Larumba, the two Spanish OFFS in my C&GSC class, who were assigned to the faculty of the Spanish Staff College. When they heard that Ted and I were friends, they welcomed him like a brother. Guimera had been promoted and was the Asst CMDT of the College. He made sure that Ted met people and got any help he needed. Saez-Larumba, a bachelor and a swinger, took him in tow, showing him how Spanish officers relaxed! Consequently, Ted met many Spanish OFFs in addition to getting to understand the Spanish Army well. In typical Pentagon fashion, the Army assigned him to South America instead of Spain, because it was not "Infantry Branch's turn to provide an OFF to Spain".

Herb Mansfield, my former 508 BN CO, periodically came to Washington on XVIII Airborne Corps business. Usually he would stay with me which provided an opportunity to eat Chinese food, or have dinner with Betty and Sam King. On one occasion, he flew up in uniform, bringing no civilian clothes. He had an early briefing the following day, after which he was to return to FT Bragg immediately. We went to a Chinese take-out restaurant, picked up an assortment of food, and drove to the King's quarters. As Herb was getting out of the car, he squeezed a container of plum sauce which spilled down the front of his blouse. Betty worked on it for some time, but it still looked terrible when he put it on the next morning. He took refuge behind a podium during the briefing.

During my residence in the Tyler Building, the Army conducted a Military Assistance Institute there. Many people I had served with attended the course enroute to their MAAG assignments. When Glen Hill attended the Institute, I invited him to stay with me rather than rent a place or stay in a motel. Although I had only one bedroom, it had twin beds. We were compatible so there was no discord. Most of the time I was home, Glen was studying. We took turns cooking. It was good to renew the friendship with a fine OFF like Glen.

Some of the students spent their time at the Institute on a perpetual party. One evening as I picked up my mail in the lobby, I bumped into LTC "Paddy" Nealson, already half inebriated. Nealson had been the one who had questioned my judgement on selecting the cadre for the 187 when I commanded K Co, 504. He recognized me, so there was no way to avoid asking him up to the apartment for a drink. He had a couple more there. As he got up to leave, he said, in all sincerity, "You know, Bill, I always liked and admired you. But I could never stand that other Seibert, what was his name? Don?" Was there ever a more classic case of *In Vino Veritas?*

Charlie Jackson, a stocky, intelligent, hard-driving IN OFF from South Carolina, whom I liked and admired, frequently had actions which required a scenario from Campaign Plans on short notice. Working together repeatedly, we developed a close friendship which continues to this day. On many occasions he would give me some general guidelines for a study in a given area from which I would type or dictate to Kitty a quick campaign plan. Charlie was always appreciative of the response he got from our Branch, but for me the drafting of a campaign plan became a routine matter after several attempts and a bit of research. Charlie and I would then go over this outline, flesh it out with the problems we wished addressed, and send it out to the Army Staff as a basis for a study. Such a paper was called a "strawman" because it was put together loosely so that it could be changed as the other staff agencies commented on it. If a paper was given to an action OFF to consider, it became quickly apparent, he responded more rapidly and effectively than if he was asked to submit a draft input to a study. The "strawman" effort always paid off.

The Middle East again became the subject of a disturbing action. This was another study to determine the tactical forces necessary to keep open the lines of communications there. Once again, I had the action, though this one did not entail a weekend drill. I wrote a scenario which called for three Army Divs, backed up by a fourth. After getting concurrences from all the staff agencies, I took the action up the tape. BG Woolnough accompanied me when I went to brief LTG Eddleman. The forces, their axis of advance and their objectives were displayed on a map. Eddleman got up from his desk to examine the map more closely, where Woolnough and I joined him. We all began moving units; every OFF is basically a tactician; LTG Eddleman was no exception. He became intrigued with the campaign plan, almost ignoring the rationale for the study. He approved the plan but directed that one USMC Div be included.

"Sir, I think that is wrong. The purpose is to see what the Army needs in the way of forces. To bring in the Marines will complicate the issue." I argued.

"Well, if we ever fight there, we are going to have a Marine Div whether we like it or not. We might just as well take a look at it to see what we need to support them. As you know it takes more to support a Marine Div than to support an Army Division. That is a fact of life."

"GEN Taylor will never buy it if we put a Marine Div in it. He is adamantly opposed to joint operations with the Marines when they can be avoided."

BG Woolnough's look indicated that I should stop arguing, but I continued until Eddleman said, "No, this is the way I want it. That's all."

Walking back I told BG Woolnough that I was sure we were going to get in trouble with the CofS if we left the USMC Div in the plan. He told me to prepare two briefings, one with and one without the Marine Div, and to prepare a Reclama to present to the DCSOPS the first thing in the morning. Working half the night I came up with the two briefings as well as my arguments against including the USMC Div. Early in the morning, Eddleman listened to my Reclama, disapproved it, retained the Marine Div in the plan, then announced that he was not going to go with us to the CofS! He had another appointment, MG Wheeler, the Asst DCSOPS (ADCSOPS), would accompany us to General Taylor's office.

MG Wheeler, who had just returned from TDY the night before, had no knowledge of this action. As we walked from the DCSOPS' office to the Chiefs I briefed him, emphasizing my concern about the USMC Div. MG Wheeler reassured me, saying, "Don't worry about it. If GEN Taylor questions it, I'll take care of it."

And he did indeed. As expected, GEN Taylor questioned the inclusion of the Marines, Wheeler gave some rational arguments for it which satisfied the CofS and he approved the action.

About eight months after I joined AWPD, Col Moe Boylan was replaced by COL "Poopy" Connor. COL Connor was a delightful person with a beautiful and charming wife. AWPD enjoyed many parties under his guidance, several at his home. But he was not a particularly astute staff officer and had the reputation of being an "intellectual prig". It was a standing joke in AWPD that if there was a split infinitive in the first paragraph of a paper, Poopy would pounce on it gleefully, make a bold correction, then give short shrift to the rest of the study. Many controversial actions got to the front office by this means. Their fate was usually foredoomed if the paper was not a good one, but at least it got a hearing before it was killed. That was one of the action OFFs1 laments, that novel or controversial ideas rarely got a hearing. They were usually killed by low-level chiefs who wanted to avoid anything new.

Jean Hollstein, by now a good friend, moved to Short Range Plans. His lovely wife, Jeanne, a gourmet cook, invited me to enjoy many delicious meals. Hollstein had two uniforms. One had the 101st ABN Div patch on the right sleeve which he wore when he briefed GEN Taylor, who had commanded the 101 in combat. The other had the 11th ABN Div patch on the right shoulder, which he wore when he briefed GEN Lemnitzer, who had commanded the 11th in Japan. Jean was replaced by LTC Frank Carpenter, another IN OFF, with whom I worked well and who also became a friend.

Shortly after Poopy became the Chief of AWPD, I was transferred to the front office as Asst XO of Plans. It was a move not to my liking, I would have preferred to remain in AWPD as an action OFF. The person I was replacing, Barney Broughton, one of the few CPTs in ODCSOPS, was moving to International Policy and Plans Division (IPPD).

The Asst XO was strictly a junior administrator or gopher (go-for) as they were called in the Pentagon. My immediate overseer was MAJ, later LTC, Grover Nash, but I worked closely with COL

Mock. One of my tasks was to secure and screen the cables of interest to Plans which had come into the Army Communications Room during the night. The ones I thought of significance were put in a looseleaf notebook, to be read by COL Mock, BG Woolnough and the Div Chiefs. COL Mock initially tried to arrive at the office before I had finished putting the cable book together. It was his way of testing me, I suppose. To thwart him, I came in earlier and earlier, finally arriving one morning at 0530 to beat him. COL Mock arrived at 0600 that morning to find the completed cable book waiting for him. Normal duty hours were 0800 to 1700. After that, the Dep Dir came in at a more reasonable hour unless there was a pressing action.

The Dep Dir gave me many tasks, constantly sending notes directing me to look into something, to do something, to inform someone of something. These notes (we called them Mock-o-grams) were addressed to others in Plans as well as Nash and me. If he worked late, I might find a hundred of them in his out-box when I came in. Each morning, before he took up routine matters, he would write out more requirements that he had thought of during the night.

COL Mock was a brilliant individual and probably the most unforgettable character in Plans. He was also one of the nastiest people I have ever had to work with. He had almost total recall which was of great assistance to BG Woolnough and the Directorate. He remembered every joint action he had ever read, even recalling the JCS number. He had the ability to handle several significant actions at one time; one day I watched as he dictated to three secretaries on three separate actions, shifting from subject to subject without losing thought or structure. But this was in part an ego trip; in spite of such talents I always felt that he hurt people deliberately. BG Woolnough had to constantly smooth the ruffled feathers his deputy had raised.

The Pentagon Officers Athletic Center (POAC) was an exceptionally well-equipped health club with swimming pool, weight room, steam room, squash, handball, and badminton courts. Whenever there was a lull, I would spend an hour or so there. Occasionally I would work out in the health club on weekends or in the evenings. It was the only way any of us could keep in reasonable condition while on duty in the Pentagon. Unfortunately, I did not get to use the facilities on a regular basis.

COL Robert Parker, the Dep Chief of JWPD, was a thick-set individual who played squash in the POAC almost every day. One day, while in the middle of a game, he received word that he was wanted in GEN Taylor's office immediately. After a quick shower he hurried to the Chiefs office. On arrival he was perspiring and still breathing heavily from the squash game as well as his race from the POAC. GEN Taylor looked at him critically.

"COL, you seem to be out of shape, if the short walk to my office affects you this way. I suggest you get into condition and lose some weight."

"Sir, I was called from a squash game, that's why I am sweating and puffing."

"They should not have called you off the squash court. I certainly did not want them to do that. I don't want to interfere with anyone's exercise unless it is unavoidable."

The CofS, an avid tennis player who rarely let anything interfere with his games, then issued instructions that anybody engaged in athletics at the POAC was not to be disturbed for a briefing in his office unless he personally decided that it was urgent enough to have the officer called off the court.

While wandering the corridors on the fifth floor on an errand for COL Mock, I noticed a sign identifying the office of BG John C. Horton, USAF. On impulse, I stepped in to see if "Jack" was in. His secretary, thinking I had an action to coordinate, showed me in without delay. When I recalled to BG Horton that I had been the Chemical Officer at RAAF in 1943, he remembered me immediately. We had a pleasant 15 minutes reminiscing about our duty together during WWII. Any rancor between us was lost in the euphoria of nostalgia.

One of my duties as the Asst XO of Plans was to screen the records of OFFs being considered for assignment there. At that time the Director had a veto over assignments. To assist in evaluating officers nominated, I screened all officers' 201 files for the Director and his Deputy. It soon became a routine operation, picking out salient comments from efficiency reports, outlining jobs held, listing military and civilian schooling, and finally noting the Officer's Efficiency Index (OEI). These notes were used by BG Woolnough and COL Mock to decide whether they wanted to look at the OFF further. It was a grave responsibility which I treated as such; the notes I made could well affect the career of an officer.

Joint War Plans developed a need for an OFF with a nuclear background. BG Woolnough wanted a MAJ or LTC who had troop experience as well as academic training. The requirement was passed to the Administrative Officer of ODCSOPS who sent down file after file. By this time I had reached the point where I could look at a file and determine whether the OFF would be acceptable to the Director. After the rejection of eight or ten files, the Admin OFF, a COL, came into my office, threw a file on my desk and said, "If you don't take this officer, you don't know what you want."

After a quick look at the file, I replied, "We won't take him."

"What is the matter with him? This guy has a max OEI. One fifty."

"Yes, but that was based on a single efficiency report rendered seven years ago for a one year period. Since then he has had nothing but schooling, the Atomic Energy Commission and another civilian type assignment for which he was not rated. He is not what the General is looking for. He wants someone grounded in troops as well as having a nuclear background."

The COL grunted, grabbed the file and left. Eventually he sent us the file on an officer I thought acceptable to the General; he was. It was frequently difficult to find the right officer for some of the jobs we had.

Another of my duties as the Plans Asst XO was the periodic review of the job sheets of the civilians who worked in the Directorate. That chore opened my eyes! As I read the job descriptions for the first time, it was apparent that the secretaries were not performing the duties called for in them. I pointed out to Grover Nash that the job sheet of BG Woolnough's secretary, Gladys, a delightful older lady, a GS9 and a good secretary, indicated that she performed many of the duties that he, our WAC SGT and I were in fact discharging. It was difficult to believe that a responsible officer had approved her job sheet. I rewrote it to reflect what she actually did do. COL Mock, who signed such papers for the Director, called me in immediately.

"What are you trying to do to Gladys?"

"What do you mean, sir?"

"You are going to get Gladys reduced to a GS5 with this job sheet."

"Well, sir, that is an exact description of her duties. I think the Director should have a GS9 secretary, but she doesn't do those things. We do them."

COL Mock explained the civil service system to me.

"This is the only way we can justify her grade. The same is true for my secretary, Margaret. You have to include such duties to beef up their responsibility so that the grade is authorized."

Though I remonstrated that this was dishonest, COL Mock would not listen. Under protest, I rewrote the job sheet according to his direction, glad that I did not have to sign it. Certainly, I did not want to see any of our civilian personnel reduced in grade, but neither did I want to render a false report.

One of the strange things in the Pentagon was how closely intelligence information was guarded. It was harder for an action officer to get access to good intelligence estimates than to our more sensitive plans. The rationale behind this was that if the enemy knew how much and what type of information the United States had, he could take countermeasures to deny us additional information. In addition, this knowledge could possibly reveal its source. This was not convincing to me; I thought that the intelligence community did a disservice to itself and to the military by over classifying information. The result was that all too many action officers were content to use less accurate, less complete, less current intelligence because it was too much trouble to get the latest and best. The best intelligence is of no value if it is not available to those who need it. I hope that this policy has been reviewed and that intelligence is now more readily available.

The Joint Strategic Objectives Plan (JSOP) was the big action of the year. While JWPD had primary action on the Plan, other divisions contributed to it; Mid-range Plans Branch of AWPD, for instance, did the force structure. It was a top secret plan which spelled out the forces for achieving US objectives in the immediate future, and it covered almost every contingency. It specifically set the military goals on which the budget was based, hence all the services considered it important. On many occasions, JWPD action officers walked down the Pentagon corridors pushing super-market carts filled with back-up papers to support the Army position on the JSOP!

One year the JSOP was leaked to the Alsop brothers who printed the essential elements of the plan in one of their syndicated columns. There was an intensive investigation to find the culprit who had given them the plan. Everyone who had handled any part of it was questioned. The felon was never found.

One Saturday, after I had locked up the Plans office and gone home, I received a call from the Security Police. When checking the safes in Plans, they had found one open. I rushed back, only to find that it was a safe that I had initialed as being closed. Monday morning, COL Mock was not happy when I reported the matter to him. Because of several leaks to the press of classified material, including the top secret JSOP to the Alsops, security was a sensitive subject at that time. He appointed an investigating officer. Although I distinctly remembered checking all of the safes before I initialed them, the fact was undeniable that one I had checked was found open. The investigating officer recommended that I be given an Article 15 for negligence, failure to follow proper procedures and several other derelictions. COL Mock came to my defense; with BG Woolnough's approval, he gave me a written reprimand, which was removed from my file when I left the Pentagon. It was a potent lesson. I was even more careful from then on. But I still cannot account for that open safe.

The Army component of the National Security Council (NSC) had an office to itself with access through the Plans Administrative Office. It was a separate Division, albeit a small one, of Plans, with only one COL and a clerk assigned to it. This office provided the Army input to all deliberations of the NSC. The clerk, a male civilian, maintained the sensitive files, logging each document in and out. Everything was considered "need to know". One morning there was a note on my desk asking me to call the DO of the Pentagon Security Office, who informed me that the civilian clerk in the NSC Office had been picked up by the police the night before on charges of soliciting a policeman. He had been booked as a homosexual. His security clearance was immediately withdrawn and a complete inventory of the NSC Office ordered. The rationale was that homosexuals, more easily pressured by threat of exposure, might be coerced into yielding secret documents. The clerk was reassigned to a less sensitive office.

While I was assigned to the Plans Office, five paratroopers were killed on a jump at FT Campbell. MG Bonesteel had replaced MG Westmoreland as SGS when the latter left the Pentagon to assume command of the 101st ABN Div at Campbell. Elements of the 101 had jumped in a marginal wind using T-10 parachutes, which were difficult to collapse since they had not yet been equipped with quick releases; the troopers were dragged across a rocky, hard drop zone, resulting in the five deaths. MG Westmoreland immediately jumped in the same winds without injury. The SGS called for a paratrooper to brief GEN Taylor on the problem with the T-10, the difficulties in collapsing it, and why the Army did not have quick releases on them. BG Woolnough picked me to do so. Just as I was leaving the office, COL "Hacksaw" Holcombe, Dep Dir of IPPD, came into the office. He had jumped in combat in WWII, and had much more airborne experience than I, so I suggested to BG Woolnough that COL Holcombe explain to GEN Taylor the problem with the T-10 and the probable causes of the fatalities at Campbell. COL Holcombe answered all of GEN Taylor's questions fully.

LTC Harrison J. Merritt joined the Short Range Plans Branch of AWPD while I was Asst XO of Plans. John was an old jumper with whom I formed a warm friendship. His wife, Rose, a fine cook, found out that I liked Lasagna, one of her specialties. There were many fine Italian meals at the Merritts.

Snow was the winter nightmare of everyone in the Washington area. Neither the city nor the surrounding counties knew how to cope with it, and local drivers became panic-stricken when the first flakes fell. On one occasion it began to snow about 1130 in the morning. At 1400 it was announced that the duty day was ended; all personnel were free to go home before the roads became impassable. This created a monumental traffic jam as thousands of people tried to get out of the parking lots at the same time. Normally, departures from the Pentagon were staggered due to differing schedules as well as the duties of the people concerned. The worst problem was the crush on the concourse, the area on which shops were located and from which access to the bus platforms was gained. To get to all buses, which ran in tunnels under the Pentagon, it was necessary to use stairs which led only to the concourse. The authorities who controlled such matters had failed to notify the bus companies of the early release, hence only the routine buses which ran every twenty minutes were available. It took many Pentagonians longer to get home than usual due to the back-up, since the transit companies did not get the rush hour buses operating until 1630.

In 1958, there was a heavy snowfall. I walked to the Pentagon through the drifts for several days. Only a skeleton force made it to work for the first three days. But COL Mock managed to get to FT Myer the first day from which he drove to the building on a snow plow! I was there with the cable book to greet him, however.

Merritt could not get into work for a week because the road from Waynewood was blocked with snow. Finally on Friday, he called to tell us that he was coming in; he was out of liquor and had to make the trip for supplies!

Bill Ankley, a friend from the 504 and 508, on graduating from the Staff Officers' Course at Quantico, was assigned as the Army LNO to the Marine Corps Amphibious Warfare Center at Little Creek, VA. He found it an interesting job and his status as one of the few Army OFFs on a Navy/Marine installation even more so. The first time he made reservations at the Officers' Club, he gave his name as CPT Ankley. When he and his party arrived, there was a quick switch in the arrangements when they found that he was not a Navy Captain.

Despite the heavy work schedule, I managed to visit Bill and Betty several times. On one visit they took me to FT Storey, close to Little Creek, for a picnic. FT Storey's fine beach and picnic area enabled all of us to enjoy a day in the water, especially young Jeff and Steve, who seemed to grow as I watched them. It was hard to believe that those strapping lads were babies when Bill and I were assigned to the 508 at Benning.

During the time I spent in Plans, there was a continuing rivalry between the Army, Navy and Air Force for a larger share of the DOD dollar, and for additional roles and missions. Though action officers from the various services were friendly and cooperative, the rivalry was serious and some times vicious. BG Woolnough was the Army member of the Defense Strategic Planning Board which met regularly in attempts to reconcile many of the differences in positions held by the services. Often the Army and Air Force would collaborate against the Navy and Marine Corps which were considered the arch foes of both. The Director's habit of reaching for a pencil when a paper was placed in front of him, became more understandable in the light of this rivalry. Pres Eisenhower was backing the Air Force and the "Big Bang" concept of nuclear deterrence, making it difficult for the Army to develop its case.

Though Nash and I were not involved directly in actions, all of them created work for the front office. In October, 1958, BG Woolnough was having a difficult time with the Planning Board, involved in a prolonged and complex session when word was received that the Army had successfully launched Explorer I, placing the satellite in orbit. Since Sputnik, DOD had been frantic to counter the Soviet lead; all of the services were vying to be first. Both the Navy and the Air Force had experienced failures. The word was sent down to Woolnough in the JCS conference room. He came back shortly with a broad smile on his face. He told us that he had received the note at a tense moment; when he told the other planners of the American success, the difficult problem was resolved in short order.

Periodically, DA sent a briefing team to each of the major commands to inform it on current actions in the Pentagon and in the Army worldwide. In 1958 I was selected as the ODCSOPS briefing officer for the team going to Alaska. There were three presentations to give, none of which I had written; one on the "Spectrum of War", one on the force structure, and one on future deployments.

The briefing team was headed by a BG from ODCSPER. The presentation on the force structure was well received, that on future deployments of interest, but the audiences quickly became visibly restless with the "Spectrum of War". This was a theoretical exposition of military actions available for use in foreign policy from a show of force to a nuclear exchange. Each time I gave it, I shortened it until finally I did little more than define the phases. Rightly or wrongly, I tailored the presentation to the audience.

Since Plans was currently looking at the defense of Alaska, I requested permission to drive from Big Delta to FT Richardson, at Anchorage. There were several critical areas in the mountains that posed special tactical problems. I thought it would be helpful to look at the terrain. This was arranged; another officer and I drove in a staff car from FT Greely, our last stop on the briefing circuit, to FT Richardson. It was only the second time I had been to Alaska and this trip gave me a better appreciation of the area. We had given our first briefing at Richardson where HQ US Army Alaska was located. From there we had flown to FT Wainwright, formerly Ladd Air Force Base, near Fairbanks, then to FT Greely, which I remembered well from the Arctic Indoctrination Course. On my return to the Pentagon, I felt confined and stifled by the routine after experiencing the purity and spaciousness of Alaska. Things settled back into the old routine.

The year in the front office of Plans passed quickly. When over, I was reassigned to AWPD, but this time to Mid-range Plans Branch, which was concerned with the period five to ten years in the future. The major action of Mid-range Plans was the Army Force Structure; the organization of the Army, the number and types of divisions (Infantry, Armor, or Airborne), separate brigades, battalions and companies as well as combat and combat support elements such as Artillery, Engineer, Signal and Aviation. For the combat units the necessary service support had to be provided in maintenance, logistical and medical units. It was a demanding and continuing action which required frequent briefings of the CofS.

MAJ Jim Owens was the principal authority on the force structure. Jim was a slender, bespectacled, energetic Armor Officer; an excellent briefer, he knew more about the structure of the Army than anyone in the Pentagon. Jim and I shared many interests and became close friends. LTC "Buzz" Glover, the chief of the branch, was the other force structure expert; I became their assistant and back- up in addition to my regular duties.

The first few months in Mid-range Plans most of my actions were involved with studies being done by Charlie Jackson. We worked well together, I developed a great appreciation for his ability to analyze complex problems and come up with the best solution. At that time, one of his major actions was a briefing for the JCS on the Army's readiness posture in Europe; specifically, how the Army would respond to an emergency situation there. Since it was an involved matter, I was assisting him. It immediately became evident that the detailed information needed was not available in the Pentagon. The only way to get it in time to complete the briefing by the deadline set by the Joint Chiefs was to bring someone to the Pentagon from US Army Europe (USAREUR) who was informed on the alert procedures. With Woolnough's approval, Charlie and I prepared a TWX (cablegram) requesting that USAREUR send some knowledgeable OFF to Washington to discuss its response to an emergency. The immediate reply informed us that two COLs, familiar with all USAREUR alert procedures, would arrive on the Blue Plate Special (a courier plane from Europe to Andrews AF Base) on a Saturday morning at 0630, the time the Blue Plate Special usually landed.

That Saturday morning Charlie and I met the two officers, COL Donald R. Ward from ODCSOPS, USAREUR, and COL Donald V. Bennett, the G-3 of 7th Army. After breakfast we took them to the Pentagon to "pick their brains," forgetting that they had been enroute for 18 hours. They explained the exact steps each unit took to implement alerts; how the alert was initiated, the information given in the alert notification message, the time involved in mustering the troops, the location of and move to alert positions, and the time/distance factors. Based on this information, a briefing was drafted which we asked them to look at. About midafternoon COL Ward gave out and excused himself.

COL Bennet stayed with us all afternoon. At 1800, when he began nodding, it suddenly occurred to us what a long day it had been for him. We quit for the night, but determined to complete the briefing with his help the following day, Sunday. Kitty cooked a big dinner for all of us Saturday night. COL Ward had other arrangements, so he did not join us. We managed to get a couple of drinks into COL Bennett and he did justice to Kitty's cooking, but by the time the meal was finished he was asleep on his feet. Although the BOQ at South FT Myer, an old WWII wooden barracks, was not adequate for a senior officer, COL Bennett was too tired to complain. He said he would move the next day; all he wanted at that time was a shower and sleep.

By 0900 on Sunday morning we were again at the Pentagon where we worked steadily all day. Finally the briefing was complete. During the next few days COL Bennett and COL Ward worked with us to polish it. He revealed that he was on PCS orders; he and his family had been scheduled to sail on the SS *United States* the day we finished the briefing. Because of our action he had been forced to cancel his scheduled voyage. His family was already enroute to the CONUS by air. COL Bennet would fly back to Europe to debrief and clear, and then return permanently. Charlie and I were apologetic about having deprived him and his family of luxurious and enjoyable trip aboard the SS *United States.*

COL Bennett decided to stay in Washington until after the briefing in the event there were questions by the JCS that Charlie was unable to answer. The briefing went well, after which we put Ward and Bennett on the plane to Europe. Charlie and I were dumbfounded a month or so later to be introduced to our new boss, COL Donald V. Bennett! He grinned when we were formally introduced, saying, "Now I've got you where I want you". He was a considerate boss and an outstanding officer. Our relationship during the time we served together was ideal.

Each year there was a joint exercise to rehearse the relocation of the DOD and the military services in the event of an impending major emergency. The idea was to move key people on short notice to continue the operation of the Services. The Army would relocate an Alternate CP to FT Bragg in the 1959 exercise, from which it would control the Army for the duration of the problem.

That year I was selected as one of the ODCSOPS personnel to go to Bragg. LTC George Rehkopf was the senior OPS representative. Designated personnel relocated on the given day, some like myself driving personally owned vehicles (POVs). The exercise went well, though a few people thought they were at Bragg for fun; they were more interested in drinking at the club then they were in taking care of their duties during the play of the problem. Rehkopf had to call several of them down, which he handled firmly but tactfully.

While at Bragg, COL Wilson arranged a jump out of a Piasecki helicopter. BG Woolnough gave me permission to make the jump, the first in six years. It was an interesting jump for me as it was the first time I jumped from the Piasecki helicopter, but jumping with old friends such as COL Wilson and Tom Tackaberry made it a special event.

Charlie Jackson left Mid-range Plans a few months after I joined it to move to Short Range Plans Branch. He was replaced by LTC Larry Blakely, a tall, slender, likeable individual. On many occasions, Jim Owens, Larry and I stopped off at my apartment after duty hours for a drink, before they made their way home. Often I would go to either home for dinner with them. Both their wives seemed to accept my presence on short notice without concern.

On the rare occasions when there was a lull in our work, Jim, Larry, and I, together with one or another action officer from Plans would go to the Market Inn near the Capitol for lunch. This was a favorite spot for many federal employees, probably because it featured the "Bird Bath Martini". The "Bird Bath" was served in a triple sized martini glass. Once we had one of those in us, we did not mind the noise, the smoke or the crowd at the Market Inn. When we got back to the Pentagon after such a lunch, we were not good for much. These infrequent forays convinced me that I could not drink in the middle of the day; the drinks made me logy. It was obvious that I would never become a three martini lunch man!

While in Mid-range Branch, my principal action was the Mid-range Estimate. However, I handled other interesting actions. Plans got into everything that went on in the Army. The opening and closing of installations, such as FT Polk, was a matter of concern to every section of the Army Staff. FT Polk had been opened and closed several times. There was a major political battle each time the Congressmen from Louisiana learned of plans to close the post, and each time it cost more money to do it. Finally a long range study made it clear that it should be kept open, but as the Army was reduced in strength, Polk was one of the first casualties.

Plans also had to concur in the requirements for construction throughout the Army. When a new classroom building was proposed for The Infantry School, the Plans action was mine; based on my recommendation, Plans concurred. But I blocked for three straight years the building of a new service station at West Point. Because the Military Academy is built on bed rock, construction costs are high. In addition, efforts to maintain architectural purity also increased the price. The cost of the proposed new station seemed exorbitant when construction dollars were scarce. It was my position that the Army Exchange System should finance such construction, not Army appropriated funds. It also seemed to me that construction of a new HQ building for CONARC at FT Monroe was questionable at a time when serious consideration was being given to moving the command from that post. I successfully urged nonconcurrence based on priorities. It was exciting to realize that a junior MAJ like me could influence the Army by coming up with logical reasons for or against a position.

Several actions involved officers in Training Directorate of ODCSOPS, in particular Arch Hamblen who had been in my Advance Class and the 508, and COL Steve Fuqua, who had commanded the 38th infantry in Korea when I was the S-3 of the 9th. Not only did I have occasion to coordinate with the 38th, but COL Steinbach and COL Fuqua were friends; on several occasions I was included in a conference or luncheon when they had gotten together.

COL G.G. O'Connor headed up JWPD. Several of my actions involved major Joint War papers, so I got to know him well. He eventually became the Asst Dep Dir of Plans, a much easier individual to work with than COL Mock. Hence, most of us tried to take our actions through him. The Chief of Mobilization Plans Div was COL Donn R. Pepke. A principal section of the Army Force Structure was devoted to the Reserve Components, the structure and readiness of which were of primary concern to Mobilization Plans: the priorities assigned to units and the order in which Reserve Units would be called into federal service. As a result, there were many actions involving both AWPD and Mobilization Plans Division.

Long hours became the norm again. To beat the traffic, I still got to the Pentagon by 0700. Whenever the weather was good, I walked, which took about half an hour. To get from Arlington Towers to the Pentagon, I had to cross Route 50 as there were no foot crossings or bridges. This posed no problem with the light morning traffic, but it was impossible to scoot across Route 50 in the face of evening traffic. I therefore took a bus home. It was a rare day when we left Mid-range Plans before 1800.

In the Pentagon, paper was the measure of the work performed. The more that was turned out the higher the individual rated in the scheme of things. This was especially true in AWPD. We turned out plans, studies, force structures and position papers by the gross. Each had to be prepared in 75 copies, it seemed to me. Much time was spent marching around the large conference table in the Midrange Plans Branch Office collating, assembling and stapling various products of our industry. Most action officers became quite adept at the collating task and could get 75 copies of a 20 page document together in short order. It was one of the many arts I learned in the Army! Walking the halls with a sheaf of paper in hand was a good way to avoid work; no one challenged an officer who was apparently coordinating an action.

An abbreviated Estimate of the Situation was used to reach quick decisions in many actions. It is a technique which presents a quick, hard look at given alternatives or options, listing the advantages and disadvantage of each. A fast decision could be made for use as the basis for developing major plans. Like all action officers I became adept in using this technique as well as writing answers to criticisms or nonconcurrences.

During my three years in the Pentagon I developed an admiration and respect for most of the civilian employees of the government. There were those few who did not meet the standards; who did not live up to their job descriptions; who tried to get away with the minimum amount of work and the maximum amount of benefits from the job. Eventually they were eliminated, though it was a lengthy and messy process. Frequently the only recourse was to eliminate or downgrade the job. Poor performers were fired only by "keeping book" on them for extended periods of time; this was almost impossible for the three-year tour officer to do. It was necessary to write periodic letters of reprimand, eventually building up a file to support firing. The normal procedure, unfortunately, was to reassign bunglers to another office, sometimes with a promotion, which simply placed the problem elsewhere.

The differences in the civilian personnel I came in contact with in the Pentagon were striking. Most Civil Service Personnel are dedicated and effective. Bill Garrahan, in Plans Division of ODCSPER, was always available whenever needed, willing to come in on weekends or work late into the night. Bill was one of the finest civilians I have served with. Others were less effective or dedicated. Most of the secretaries were good; they would work long hours or stay late if asked. Plans officers were always working late. When secretarial help was needed at night, it was customary to ask for volunteers; usually the same group came forward.

One of the frustrations an action officer faced in the Pentagon was that of rarely seeing the results of his work. Occasionally, as in the case of construction projects, more rarely as in the example of the ABN Bde action cited below, an OFF enjoyed the satisfaction of having one of his ideas approved and implemented during his tenure in the Pentagon. But this was the exception, particularly in Plans, which dealt with long-range actions such as the force structure and the stationing plan for the Army. These were implemented in the future, long after the officer who had worked on them had been reassigned.

With the recent inactivation of the 11th ABN Div in Europe, there was considerable conjecture as to whether any Airborne capability would remain there, or indeed, be based outside the CONUS. During a discussion of the future of parachute units with Jim Owens, I maintained that there should be an ABN capability of at least brigade strength in both Europe and the Far East. Refining the idea, I suggested that the Far East Bde be located in the Philippines or on Okinawa where it would be close to the probable areas of deployment. COL Bennett agreed with my concept and told me to develop a plan to brief up the tape. In a matter of days I completed a draft plan which confirmed an ABN Bde in Europe and deployed one to Okinawa. Okinawa was selected because it was closer to likely areas of employment and also because there was a great deal of prepositioned materiel there that could be used by the brigade, thus minimizing the amount of shipping needed to move it. My counterparts in the other Staff agencies, amenable to the idea, quickly supplied their input to the plan, which was then distributed for concurrence. It was amazing how swiftly concurrences from all elements of the Army Staff were received. Because every OFF considered himself an expert on tactics and strategy, plans developed in ODCSOPS were criticized or "nit-picked", not only on matters within the expertise of the other staff agencies, such as personnel, logistics, intelligence and comptroller, but on the tactics and strategy recommended. In this case everyone seemed in accord with the strategy. In short order the plan was ready for presentation to the CofS, GEN Lemnitzer.

As the principal action OFF, I had the privilege of briefing the plan to GEN Lemnitzer. It was a decision briefing which meant that if he approved the plan, it would be implemented. Accordingly, the heads of every Army Staff Agency, together with their action officers, were present in the room. All went well until I started to talk about the movement of the Bde to Okinawa. The point that there was pre-stocked equipment on the Island had been stressed previously.

"Therefore it will only require 180 short tons of equipment to be moved with the brigade," I said rather smugly.

At this point General Lemnitzer exploded.

"One hundred eighty short tons!" he exclaimed. "That's enough to supply an Armored division."

His vehemence startled me into making an off-hand remark that it included personal gear. All of the general officers and action officers nodded sagely.

GEN Lemnitzer was unconvinced. He settled down, however, so the briefing could continue. Several other times I mentioned the 180 short tons; each time GEN Lemnitzer flared up, then settled back down. Finally I reached the end of the briefing. Just as I was about to ask for approval of the plan, I glanced at my notes. There, staring me in the face was the figure 18 short tons of equipment! What to do? Should I admit my mistake? That would cause consternation among the Staff, who had supported my briefing. On the other hand, having made an error, I could not in conscience let GEN Lemnitzer make a decision based on incorrect information. Drawing a deep breath, I said,

"Just a minute, sir. Before you make your decision I want to correct something. I made an error. In my briefing notes the figure is in fact 18 short tons, not 180 short tons."

He looked at me closely as be said, "Now do you really mean that, Seibert? Or are you just changing it because I'm unhappy about the excessive tonnage?"

"No, sir, the figure is in fact 18 short tons. I misread the decimal point in my briefing. I'm sorry."

GEN Lemnitzer was relieved and smiled, but the other generals scowled because they had been put in the embarrassing position of supporting an erroneous figure. In fact, BG Woolnough me hell later on. But I think the error really sold the action to General Lemnitzer; the plan was approved.

It was turned over to the Director of Operations for implementation. Because I was the principal author, GEN Lemnitzer and LTG Oakes, the DCSOPS at that time, directed me to monitor and assist in implementing the plan. It was a real satisfaction to know that I had conceived an idea, written a plan, sold it to the DA Staff, briefed it to the CofS, received his approval, and now was helping to carry it out. The ABN Bde that went to Okinawa was the 173rd, one of the first elements deployed to Vietnam when it was decided to put American troops into that area.

BG Hamilton Howze, in 1959 the Chief of Army Aviation, was an aggressive and imaginative Officer who advocated the air cavalry concept. It was largely through his efforts that it was adopted by the Army and the 11th Air Assault Div activated to test the concept. BG Howze headed a study group which was exploring the initial concept, I was the Plans member of the group.

Many members of the Study Group, including BG Howze, were enthusiastically thinking in terms of large air cavalry units, up to a corps in size. Since I worked with the force structure, I kept telling the group that the Army could not support such an organization. The Army had a fixed end strength, 870,000 at the time, thus, for each AVN unit added to the current Army organization, some other unit had to be eliminated to keep the Army at the strength Congress had mandated. In addition, if an AVN Co was added, maintenance and logistical support elements for it had to be activated, further increasing the end strength. So it was not simply a matter of deciding that the Army would have 16 AVN Cos or three air cavalry divisions. It required hard decisions on what units to drop, an AR Div, an IN Div, or an ABN Div. Which was the most versatile, the most useful division for the Army? Which could best accomplish the Army's missions?

After more than three months of study, a position paper was developed. BG Woolnough was reluctant to concur in the study, though I made a strong argument for it. He recognized the merit of the concept, but had reservations about the impact on the force structure. Could the Army give up one of its combat divisions for this test division? What additional support would it require and how would that affect the "division slice", the percentage of the total Army strength required to support each division? BG Woolnough also had some tactical reservations. He told me to raise the question "Where are the horseholders?" Horseholders, he explained, were the troopers detailed to take care of the horses when cavalry units dismounted to fight; the men whose mission was to "hold the horses" to insure that they would be immediately available when it became necessary to remount. Woolnough thought that concept might well apply to air cavalry. What happens to the helicopters after they drop their Infantry? Do they return to their departure areas, again recrossing the enemy's front lines with all its sophisticated weaponry, or do they remain in the enemy rear prepared to extract the friendly forces if necessary. When I raised the question, BG Howze gave a vague answer, but never specifically addressed that problem. The Air Cavalry concept was approved and the 11th Air Assault Division activated to test it.

Late in 1959, when I had been in ODCSOPS 2 1/2 years, I was awarded the much prized "Liver Patch", a green, multi-leaf breast badge, the DA Staff insignia which was worn on the left pocket. Not everybody assigned to the Pentagon was authorized to wear it, only those who served with the definitive DA Staff.

COL Bennett did not remain in AWPD very long, but I got to know him well. He was replaced by COL Julian J. Ewell, who had commanded the 9th IN Regt in Korea; for a short time I was his S-3. All of the AWPD action officers wanted to know what kind of an OFF COL Ewell was. In telling them about him, I mentioned that I had been his S-3 in Korea. Everyone immediately assumed that the two of us were very close because of that special commander/S-3 relationship. When COL Ewell was introduced to the action officers in AWPD, he shook hands, saying, "How are you, Seibert?", just as if it was the first time he had seen me. This was typical of Ewell, who is a rather cool individual. It in no sense reflected on our relationship; as soon as he could, he had me in his office to talk about the Manchu times. But that initial reserved greeting gave my friends a chuckle.

COL Ewell was a dynamic officer, a go-getter, a comer When he became Chief of AWPD I was involved with the Mid-range Estimate, a plan directed to the period 5 to 8 years in the future. It was a long, complex plan with a wordy intelligence appreciation and many, many annexes. When it was finished very few people bothered to refer to it; in fact one had not been approved in some years. In discussing it with COL Ewell, I mentioned some wild ideas I wanted to put in it, but told him the stereotyped format made the document worthless. Ewell told me to forget the accepted format and develop my own. He also told me to put all my wild ideas into the draft to let the Staff chew on them.

A short, controversial Mid-range Estimate resulted. It contained such novel ideas as a trade off with the Air Force giving them the total air defense mission and in turn having them give the Army the Troop Carrier Command so that it could control its own aircraft for ABN and air movement operations. Needless to say, the AF never even considered such a trade off. But it forced a reassessment of the roles and missions by the Army which was healthy. Finally the controversial Mid-range Estimate was sent out for coordination. There wasn't a single concurrence!

Since every staff agency had nonconcurred, COL Ewell simply by-passed everyone, and went directly to GEN Decker who had replaced GEN Lemnitzer as CofS. Bob Selton later told me about the action, which he inherited when I left the Pentagon. COL Ewell apparently said something about as follows"

"Sir, everybody nonconcurs with this Mid-range Estimate but it has some good ideas for consideration. I recommend that you approve it for planning purposes only." GEN Decker glanced through it and approved it for planning purposes only! Thus the Army had a Mid-range Estimate approved but never implemented.

In 1958 I put in for advanced civil schooling, requesting to go to Duke University for a Masters in history. The USMA accepted me as an instructor in Military History contingent upon the award of the degree. As a history buff this seemed to be an ideal assignment. Just before I was to report to Duke in the fall of 1959, the Army ran short of funds; money for civil schooling was re-allocated to activities of higher priority. BG Reuben Tucker, Chief of Infantry, called the five IN OFFs approved for civil schooling that year to his office to assure us that when the Army restored the money to the school budget, we would be the first IN OFFs to go to school. Money was made available for civil schooling in Fiscal Year 1960. When informed that the Army had the funds and that I would be sent to Duke, I immediately called USMA to see if my assignment could be postponed a year; it could. My elation was dashed when the Schools Officer told me that when money for civil schooling had been deleted from the budget the previous year, the quota for the Masters Degree in history for IN OFFs had also been canceled. However, there were quotas in psychology, geography, operations research, and business administration. None of these fields interested me; international affairs or history were the only subjects I wanted to study. When I reminded the Schools Officer that I had put in for those two disciplines, he said, "They canceled the quotas for IN OFFs in those fields last year when they took away the funds. Infantry Branch has quotas in only these four areas, so you'll have to pick one of them. BG Tucker insists that no IN OFF go before you and the other OFFs who were canceled the year before."

"Just take me off the list. I do not want to get a Masters unless I can get it in a field that interests me."

The Schools Officer persisted in trying to convince me to study one of the other disciplines, but I was not interested in getting a Masters just for the sake of getting an advanced degree. Finally, the Schools Officer insisted that I discuss the matter with BG Tucker; reluctantly, I reported to him. We had a pleasant chat before getting to the issue I had come to see him about. As forcefully as possible, I explained that I wanted a Masters in international affairs or history, the only two disciplines that interested me. He regretted that the quotas in those fields had been canceled for IN OFFs, but wanted to make sure that I had the opportunity to attend graduate school this year. He suggested I think in terms of management which was going to become more and more important in the Army. A Masters in business administration would give me a jump on my contemporaries. Again, I demurred. "No, sir. Once I get an MBA, I will be tagged as a comptroller from then on and will get only staff assignments. I want to remain an Infantry commander or operations officer."

He assured me that though Infantry Branch would have to give me a utilization tour in management, business administration or as a comptroller, once that was completed I would not be assigned to such a position again. He did not convince me, and I remain convinced that once awarded such an Management MOS, I could not get out of that field. Again I asked to be taken off the civil schools list.

"Don't make a decision now, Seibert. Go and talk to BG Woolnough about it."

"Yes, sir."

Saluting, I walked out. BG Tucker apparently called BG Woolnough to ask him to convince me to go to a civilian school, because when I got back to my desk, there was a message to report to the Director of Plans. Woolnough went over the same arguments that Tucker had used; get an advanced degree in any field so long as you get one, but preferably get it in business administration or management since this was the coming thing in the Army. Again I stated my lack of interest in a degree for the sake of having it on my record. What did interest me was learning more history or international affairs and getting a teaching assignment at West Point in either of those fields. I reminded Woolnough that I had been accepted at the Military Academy if I got my degree in history.

"I am not interested in studying in any of those disciplines. I request that they cancel my quota," I said firmly.

BG Woolnough called BG Tucker, who reluctantly agreed to cancel the quota, and requested that I return to his office. Back I went to Infantry Branch.

"Since I am not going to send you to civil schooling, I'd like to send you to the Armed Forces Staff College. You'll be on orders in June."

Again I demurred. "General Tucker, I appreciate your efforts to help me with schooling, but I have been working on Joint Staff actions for the past three years in ODCSOPS. Although I am not in Joint War Plans, I still get into many of the joint actions. I think that I am thoroughly familiar with joint procedures and I would just as soon not go to the Armed Forces Staff College."

Tucker exploded! "What do you want to do, young man?"

"Sir, I want to go back to troops. I would like to go Europe assigned to one of the Airborne Battle Groups (ABGs)."

"Which one do you want to go to?"

"The 504th, since I served with the 504 before."

BG Tucker had commanded the 504th Parachute Infantry Regiment during WWII, so this struck a responsive cord.

"I can get you assigned to Europe, but I am not sure I can get you further assigned to the 504. That is up to USAREUR. However, I have a little pull and I'll see what I can do."

After thanking BG Tucker for his efforts on my behalf, I returned to work. By coincidence, the OFF who handled the assignment of MAJs in ODCSPER USAREUR was in the Pentagon on TDY. He had been in my Leavenworth class though never in Gruber 4. When I tracked him down he assured me that there would be no problem in assigning me to the 504. When the assignment to Europe was approved I asked the action officer handling it to send me to FT Benning on TDY for the IN OFFs' Refresher Course as well as an ABN Refresher Course before I went overseas. Within several weeks orders assigning me to US Army Europe in an ABN IN CDR's MOS with TDY enroute at US were published.

The receipt of orders initiated a flurry of action in preparing to leave the Pentagon. The Mid-range Estimate action was turned over to Bob Selton who had been in my Advance Class as well as at Leavenworth with me. Other actions seemed to keep me occupied, however. Between them I made arrangements for storing my furniture, shipping my stereo, books, uniforms and clothes to Europe and vacating my apartment.

Phil Toon, my Ranger buddy and Leavenworth classmate, saw my orders and called to tell me that he too was attending the IN Refresher Course. Although he was an ARTY OFF, he had convinced his branch that it would benefit the Army as well as himself to attend the course. He wanted to drive to Benning with me; we arranged to rendezvous at Union Station the day before the course started. He would take the train from West Point.

Up until the day of my departure I was involved in an action which required frequent telecons with Europe. A telecon was a teletypewriter conference which facilitated the discussion of classified material. Messages, questions and answers would appear on a large screen in sequence of transmittal. Permanent copies were made of them for the record. At 1800 on my last duty day in ODCSOPS, I completed the final telecon. AWPD had arranged a little party for me, but everybody had gone home by the time I left the telecon room. COL Ewell gave me a card signed by my co-workers, together with a small gift, and wished me well.

Many Officers have bitter feelings about their Pentagon tours, but despite many frustrations and long hours, I have fond memories of my duty there. It seemed to me that I served with the very finest officers in the Army, a select, carefully screened group. Those who labor in the Pentagon so long and hard, with little recognition, deserve great respect. My tour had been enlightening, I had learned a great deal about the functioning of the Army and the DOD, about staff procedures, how to get an action approved, how to deal with people who were opposed to an idea that I supported. Perhaps the greatest lesson was the proof of Murphy's Law; that which can go wrong will go wrong. It was amazing how a straightforward action could be fouled up or mired down in paper work. Equally amazing was how a little forethought, constant vigilance or a few intelligent comments could prevent or remedy the most impossible situation. The long hours, the horrendous parking problems, the traffic going to and from the building were things I never wanted to face again. When I signed out, I did so believing that I had accomplished something and learned much a good feeling but no regrets.

Most of my furniture with the exception of the stereo, records and books which accompanied me to Europe, were put in storage. Sam and Betty King offered to keep the organ and a few other items so they would not remain in a warehouse for three years.

Sam retired just as I left Washington. The Old Guard paraded especially for him in appreciation of his efforts in arranging ceremonies. Though an Active Duty MAJ, Sam was a Reserve LTC, hence he drew retired pay in that grade. Sam immediately joined the State Department where he handled the military ceremonies for foreign dignitaries. It was an inspired personnel action. I spent my last night in Washington with Sam and Betty.

Phil Toon was waiting at Union Station when I drove up. The trip to Benning was a pleasant one. The Infantry Refresher Course, consisted of demonstrations with little classroom instruction. It covered the organization of IN units from division down, reviewed IN weapons as well as both ABN and regular IN tactics, touched on combined-arms operations and emphasized logistics and other support at ABG level. There was also a short review of leadership techniques. It was a full, informative and rewarding three weeks.

At the end of the Infantry Refresher Course, I reported to the ABN Department, where I was turned over to a gung-ho SGT, who was very sharp, very courteous and very confident of his own ability. He put me through my paces! A "swing landing trainer" had been substituted for the suspended harness since I had completed jump school. Trainees were required to jump from a 14 foot platform with a parachute harness fastened to a rope passing through a pulley suspended from the ceiling. A fellow student or cadreman controlled the descent as the student practiced a proper PLF. PLFs were never my forte in the Airborne, and I had to go off that platform again and again. First I dove off, then I did not make a vigorous enough exit, then I was not landing on the three points of contact: the balls of the feet, the thigh, and the "push-up muscle". The SGT worked with me patiently, but he refused to let me jump until I satisfied him in every particular. I looked at him carefully to make sure he was not one of those cadremen who had harassed me in jump school in 1949. He was not. It seemed to me he was being overly critical, especially since I was an experienced jumper. But I had elected to go through the refresher course at Benning so I held my peace; I am sure that I received a more thorough refresher than most. Finally I was pronounced ready to jump.

The afternoon of my jump, the cadre was making a tailgate drop. It was my first tailgate jump as well as my first and only jump from a C-123. The C-123 was not a good aircraft for jumping, though designed for it The wheel wells took up too much of the fuselage of the aircraft, forcing the stick of jumpers to snake around them which made it awkward to exit from the side doors. The tailgate jump posed no such problems because the jumpers shuffled to the rear of the aircraft and stepped off. It was not necessary to hop, dive or jump out. The jumpmaster instructed me to keep on walking, step off, take up a proper position, count, then begin my five points of performance after the parachute deployed. It was an easier jump than from the door; the opening shock seemed considerably less than I normally experienced with the T-10. The jump went well, I even made a good PLF. As I left the DZI received a certificate attesting to my qualification to return to Airborne status. That eliminated any possibility of a delay when I got to Europe.

During the 15 day leave authorized by my orders, I took Mother and Dad to visit Bill and Muriel, my brother and sister-in-law, at Warwick, RI. Then we went to Niagara Falls which Mother and Dad had not seen in some years, and I had never seen. Dad was not feeling too well so he did not do much sight-seeing. But he perked up when we visited Gladys and George Good, my RAAF friends, at Brantingham Lake. This was always a treat for Mother and Dad. Dad and George talked baseball and Mother and Gladys talked whatever women talk about. I went swimming, walked in the woods or read. It was a pleasant trip which we all enjoyed.

On the way from Brantingham Lake to College Point, Dad complained that he did not feel well. When we got home he suddenly doubled over in pain. It was obvious that he had a heart attack. Mother and I made him comfortable and called his doctor, who told us what to do for him and prescribed medicine which I obtained from the local pharmacy. Winnie Buckley and I had a date that night. Since Dad seemed comfortable I went to pick her up. Just as we were leaving her house to go to dinner, the phone rang. It was my sister, Arlene; Dad had another heart attack and had been taken to the hospital in Jamaica. He was in an oxygen tent when I got there, but was obviously comfortable. Dr Lamberta assured me that everything was under control. The remaining days of my leave were spent driving Mother to and from the hospital.

Finally I had to report to FT Dix for transportation to Europe. Dad was still in the hospital, but was scheduled to be released within a few days. Bob, Arlene's husband, was going to take him home. I left with an uneasy feeling because of those heart attacks, both of which were severe. As it turned out, when I said goodbye at the hospital that was the last time I was to see Dad alive.

FT Dix is only a two-hour drive from College Point. After signing in and dropping off my luggage, I took the car to Newark for shipment, returning to Dix by bus. During the next two days, I shook down my luggage again, sending home a couple of packages of things I decided I didn't need. Finally, a group of us were taken by bus to McGuire Air Force Base, adjoining Dix, where we boarded a Constellation for the flight to Europe. We stopped overnight at the Azores where the plane was refueled. After an enjoyable meal at the Officers' Club and a good night's sleep, we continued on to Rhein Main Air Force Base in Frankfurt.

CHAPTER 13

TROOPER

Rhein-Main Air Base is a major aerial port-of-entry for military personnel arriving in Germany. It is a busy airport as the runways are shared by civilian air lines which have their terminal on the opposite side of the field from the USAF military facilities. On deplaning at the Military Air Transport Service (MATS) Terminal, I looked for someone from the 504 or from the 8th Div, but could locate no ABN personnel or any 8th Div members. The Army personnel on duty at the terminal assured me that I was expected. Experiencing the frustrations of the German telephone system for the first time, I finally got a call through to Mainz. A duty NCO answered, but immediately called to the phone Mr Roman Smith, the Personnel OFF, who was surprised that I had arrived; the 504 had been advised by Division that I would be on a later flight. Mr Smith told me that the Battle Group was at Baumholder, one of the maneuver areas, but that he would leave immediately for the 45 minute drive to Rhein Main to pick me up.

During my wait for Mr Smith, my baggage was unloaded, cleared, and I was ready to go. On the way to Mainz, Chief Warrant Officer Four (CW4) Smith gave me a quick summary of the 504 personnel and location. After I signed in he took me to the billeting office where I was assigned a two-room suite with a bath between. One of the rooms was furnished as a sitting room, the other as a bedroom, a comfortable set-up. Across the hall from me was the 505's Catholic chaplain, Father (MAJ) Ketchersid. In the same BOQ were a number of civilian school teachers, all-in-all an interesting group. The BOQ was located in the Mainz University Housing Area (MUHA) about a mile from Lee Kaserne in which the 504 and 505 were billeted. Married personnel lived in MUHA in three-story apartment buildings.

By the time I dropped my luggage and freshened up, it was close to 1700 so I walked to the Officers' Club next to the BOQ to have a drink and get something to eat. As I approached the Club, a 2LT ran out and stopped me, asking,

"Is your name Seibert?"

"Yes."

"Well, the General would like to see you."

His collar insignia indicated that he was aide to a brigadier general.

"What general?"

"BG Fuqua."

BG Stephen 0. Fuqua, Jr was the Asst Div CDR of the 8th Div. I had known him in Korea when he commanded the 38th IN and in ODCSOPS when he had been assigned to the Organization and Training Directorate. He welcomed me, genuinely glad to see me. Over a drink we had quite a chat. BG Fuqua commanded the ABN Bde, comprised of the two Airborne Battle Groups in Lee Kaserne and the supporting elements in the Kaserne at Biebrich.

While BG Fuqua and I were chatting a medical officer joined us. He had just completed his tour of duty with the 504 and would be rotating within the next few days. He took me to Wiesbaden that night to show me the city. We visited the Kurhaus, the spa hotel, which had a casino, stopping at the Spielbank, or gaming room to play roulette. The CPT promised to show me some of the finer eating places there if he did not leave immediately.

The day following my arrival I completed my processing. A full set of field gear was not obtainable because the Supply Sergeant was at Baumholder with the Battle Group. My footlockers, stereo, records and books sent two months before had not arrived. Fortunately, I had taken the precaution of bringing a pair of jump boots, a couple of pairs of fatigues and a field jacket in my hand luggage. That and a pistol belt and helmet Mr Smith found for me was about all the field gear available.

The 1st ABG 504th Infantry was at Baumholder for its ATT. It had just completed a week of field training during which it had gone through a practice ATT. The Adj, MAJ McPheron, had scheduled me to visit Baumholder to meet the 504 CDR, COL Joseph B. "Bo" Seay two days after my arrival. The doctor and I went back to Wiesbaden that evening and my luck at roulette improved.

The next morning I was driven to Baumholder in a jeep, a trip which took about an hour and a half. After a short chat with McPheron, I reported to COL Seay, a slightly built, wiry officer, who seemed to be a bit nervous and unsure of himself, I thought. During his brief discussion of the 504 with me, he informed me that I was to remain at Mainz to act as the rear area commander. Since the 5 04 was now keyed up for its ATT, he thought that a new comer, unfamiliar with the OFFs, men and SOPs of the Battle Group, would be more of a burden than an asset during the test. COL Seay told me that I was to be his S-3. Both by grade and secondary MOS, 72162, I was suited for that assignment; immediately following the ATT I would take over from CPT Jon Carney, the current S-3, who was being transferred to the Division G-3 section. The 504 had "failed" its practice test, which may have accounted for COL Seay's apparent lack of confidence; he was determined that nothing be done to jeopardize the outcome of the actual ATT. Although willing and anxious to make the plunge and take over my duties right away, I offered no objections to Seay's cautious arrangements. It appeared to me that had I gone through the ATT I would have gotten to know the 504 officers, troops and procedures, which would have made my assimilation into the unit much easier. But the COL opted to play it safe.

After my interview, I had a long talk with MAJ McPheron, the S-1. Mac had been the H Co CO of the 504 at Bragg in 1949 and 1950. We brought each other up to date on mutual friends. Then I went in to see LTC Ernie Hager, the XO, who had also been the XO of the 2nd Bn of the 504 (2/504) at Bragg. Although I knew him, we were not intimate simply because ABN Bns were rather close knit. We had a pleasant talk during which Ernie was able to give me some good information about the unit.

As we talked, Hager suddenly doubled over. He told me that he had a severe pain in his chest, which indicated that he had suffered a heart attack. When I wanted to call a doctor, Ernie told me not to. He realized that it was a heart attack, I suspect, but he didn't want to go to the hospital. When the pain became too severe, I insisted that a doctor be called. He immediately ordered Hager to the hospital. Even as they put him in the ambulance, Ernie protested that it was nothing and that he would be back shortly.

When the ambulance drove off, I headed back to Mainz. COL Seay was obviously upset about Ernie and the ATT. On my arrival back at Mainz, Mr Smith informed me that Hager had suffered another heart attack, much more serious than the initial one. He would be in the hospital at least a week, and would not be available during the ATT. COL Seay needed a field grade officer as XO, so I was ordered to get as much field gear together as possible and return to Baumholder immediately, prepared to stay. There were only four field grade officers in the 504 at that time: COL Seay, LTC Hager, MAJ Spurgeon Moore, the S-2 and MAJ McPheron. Mac was scheduled to rotate before the ATT began, and COL Seay did not want to use Moore as his XO because the S-2 play would be significant in the ATT. That made me the obvious choice to be Executive Officer.

The supply clerk was not able to give me much more field equipment. Everything was either locked up or at Baumholder. He managed to find an extra field jacket, a holster and a blanket, but a sleeping bag, field trousers, additional fatigues and other gear for field duty were unavailable.

Early the next morning my meager field equipment was loaded on a jeep trailer. The driver stopped at Bad Kreuznach, where the 8th Div HQ was located, to pick up CPT Lew Letgers, who had been the 504 Group Surgeon when it gyroscoped (moved as a unit) from Bragg, but had been reassigned to the Division Surgeon's Office. As the 504 surgeon had just rotated, Lew was going to fill that slot for the ATT since he was familiar with the 504 SOP. A fine field soldier as well as an excellent doctor, he impressed me favorably.

Once settled in the BOQ at Baumholder, there were only three days before the start of the ATT in which to become familiar with the organization of the Battle Group, the key personnel, especially COL Seay, and the policies, procedures and SOPs of the 504. Though everyone else in the unit was thoroughly familiar with the terrain of Baumholder, this did not bother me at first. The other problems were more pressing.

The battle group organization was not impressive. GEN Taylor had reorganized the IN Div to convince Congress and other critics that the Army was preparing to fight the next or nuclear war and not the last one. Little did he dream that the next war would be a counterinsurgency effort, not a major war, or that another reorganization of the Army would precede it. The battle group had five rifle companies, a mortar battery which later became the Combat Support Co, (CSC) plus a multipurpose HHC. The mortar battery contained 4.2 inch mortars and 90m self-propelled antitank guns (SPATS). Later the SPATs were replaced with wire guided missiles. HHC contained medical, engineer, personnel, logistical and administrative sections, a real hodgepodge! The theory on which such an organization was developed was that the nuclear battlefield would require small, independent organizations fighting alone or in cooperation with one another. The weaknesses were the lack of organic support in the rifle companies, and the inability of the commander to control or maneuver the five rifle companies effectively. Although there were five battle groups in the IN Div, it lacked the combat power of the earlier division. The problem was to use the organization to its maximum advantage in the upcoming problem.

The key personnel were not difficult to evaluate. COL Seay, who had been qualified as a parachutist a long time, struck me as a weak commander. He had spent more time on various staffs than in units, which was reflected in a lack of confidence in himself. He was most gracious to me; with the exception of one or two major flare-ups, we got along well. But it appeared, even this early, that he would have to be pushed into making decisions. The S-2, MAJ Spurgeon Moore, was a stocky, black officer with an outgoing personality and the ability to work well with anyone. There was instant rapport between us which ripened into a warm and lasting friendship. CPT Jonathan Carney, the S-3, was an intense, direct OFF who appeared to have a tight hold on every detail in his shop as well as a good sense of tactics. The S-4, CPT Tworek, was unflappable and solid. Since MAJ McPheron was rotating, the S-1 functions were to be handled by CPT Ross Goddard, a Judge Advocate General (JAG) OFF serving a two year tour with the Infantry (an Army policy designed to increase the rapport between branches). It appeared on quick appraisal that the key staff OFFs were more than up to their jobs and would carry the 504 through the ATT with few problems.

During those three days I met many of the other officers and NCOs, most of whom impressed me as sharp, hard-charging, confident, young officers and professional, seasoned NCOs. CPT Ralph Peterson, the commander of the CSC and CPT Sam Barth, the Asst S-3, immediately struck me as truly outstanding. Many of the LTs impacted on my consciousness most favorably, but it was some time before I could recall which companies or jobs they were in.

The biggest problem was to learn the policies, procedures and SOP of the 504. There was a written, cryptic SOP which I could follow, though it would take some time to become completely familiar with it. How COL Seay would use me as his XO was to develop. One of the difficulties I now faced was the fact that all of the OFFs and men were familiar with the Baumholder maneuver area. A former German training area, only recently given back to the German Army by the French who had used it almost exclusively, the terrain was mountainous and contained several abandoned villages which the German Army had forcibly evacuated prior to WWII. Each terrain feature had a special name given to it by American units, especially the 504. The OFFs and NCOs referred to such places as "Hitler's Crossroads", "the place where the jeep turned over last winter" or some similar nickname. Everyone knew exactly the place in question, everyone except me. So I had to learn the organization, the people, the SOP and the terrain in less than three days. But I was delighted to take the plunge. Moore and Carney and most of the other officers were of great assistance. The OPS SGT, MSG Byers, an outstanding NCO, also helped me a great deal.

The ATT, a short maneuver of three and half days, went very well. COL Seay, obviously concerned, acted almost like a caricature of a commander. He wanted to make sure that he and the 504 got credit from the umpires for every decision he made. He would emphatically say "Approved" each time a recommendation was made, then look pointedly at the umpire to make sure that he noted it. As XO, it was my job to coordinate the staff, to make sure that everybody was kept informed, and to take care of the administration of the 504 while Seay took care of the tactical details. I insinuated myself into all of the planning, trying not to interfere, but knocking heads together when there was a breakdown in coordination. However, the 504 was a professional unit which did well on its ATT.

Despite the preoccupation with staff work, I did manage to get among the troopers to inspect some positions. Once again I got into as many foxholes and gun emplacements as I could, to talk with the men about their fields of fire, to be sure that the machine gunners understood where the dead spaces were, to insure that all troopers knew where the preplanned concentrations were located in front of their defensive positions.

It was amazing how little had been passed on to the troopers in one company I checked. The PltLdrs knew the situation, but they hadn't oriented their men. This was due to inexperience; it was quickly corrected when called to their attention. But this is an all too common failing in the Army, the chain of command doesn't get the word down to the private on the front line. Despite my discomfort in the rain and the early fall chills each evening, it was good to be back in the field with enthusiastic, energetic, dedicated troopers. The ATT came to a satisfactory end, and the convoy back to Lee Kaserne at Mainz went well.

Shortly after our return to Mainz, COL Seay visited LTC Ernie Hager in the Landstuhl Hospital. His condition was serious; the second heart attack had been extremely severe, with grave complications. We were deeply concerned.

Before I could settle into my duties at Mainz, I was summoned by BG Fuqua, who told me that I was to assist him in putting on a demonstration at Finthen Army Air Field in Mainz, to "sell" the Pershing Missile to the NATO countries. The 8th Div had been given the mission of showing the missile; I was to be the project officer under his supervision. In turn, he and the 8th Div were being closely supervised by LTG Paul D. Adams, the V Corps Commander.

CPT John Hermann, CO of C Co, designated as the Demonstration/Support Co, became my assistant. John, a tall, quiet, effective, USMA graduate, and I worked out the schedule for the entire day. There was to be an initial briefing on the characteristics and capabilities of the Pershing Missile, a display of its mobility and ease of emplacement, and a lunch. The demonstration would not include firing, since no actual missiles had been deployed to Germany. The 8th Div's task, hence the 504's mission, was to take care of the housekeeping while a DA team briefed and answered questions. The guidance from LTG Adams was that it was to be a typical US Army display, spit and polish of course, but under austere field conditions. He wanted the 504 to have the noon meal in the field using a typical GI field mess to serve baked beans and apple pie. This appeared to me to be poor sales technique. The senior commanders invited to attend were primarily three and four star generals from all of the NATO countries, who were accustomed to having a gourmet type meal in the middle of the day with good wine, comfortable surroundings and excellent service. They could hardly be interested in going through a GI mess line to see how American soldiers ate in the field. With some difficulty I persuaded BG Fuqua that LTG Adam's approach was wrong; that we should have an elegant luncheon.

Where to serve the meal was a problem. By a process of elimination, we concluded that the Von Steuben Hotel in Wiesbaden was the ideal location. The Von Steuben was an AF Officers' Club which could handle a large group and serve a superb meal. I suggested that the very senior generals be flown by helicopter from Finthen Airfield, site of the demonstration, to the Von Steuben, and the MGs and below be driven in staff cars. It was only a half hour drive from Finthen to the Von Steuben and a police escort would be arranged under NATO auspices.

The plans progressed. John Hermann and I drew up two plans, one to conduct the demonstration in a hanger, the other out of doors. It was getting chilly and there was a possibility of rain. In our final plan we kept the spectators in the hangar. Initially, they would sit in bleachers and chairs facing the interior of the hangar for the briefing. After a break they would be seated in a second set of bleachers and chairs facing the open doorway of the hangar to witness the movement and emplacement of the missile launcher on the apron outside.

The 504 was given sufficient carte blanche to get enough Herman Nelson Heaters to blow hot air under the stands to keep the VIPs warm if necessary. There was also an allowance for coffee and cake at the break. Blankets and cushions were collected to pad the bleachers for those not senior enough for the front row arm chairs.

The completed plan was presented to BG Fuqua, who had certain reservations, but finally approved it after I explained the reasoning for each part. It was then briefed to MG Lloyd Moses, the 8th Div CG. He, too, had reservations in view of LTG Adams rather specific guidance on the meal in the field. Adams inspired a certain amount of terror in many of his subordinate commanders. His penchant for ways to demonstrate the American Soldier's capability to live in the field was respected; his sensitivity to criticism that America was a luxury loving country whose citizenry disliked austere conditions should be honored, but this was not the time to do so. After much persuasion, MG Moses approved the plan. It was now necessary to brief LTG Adams to obtain his approval. As the action officer, I would make the presentation to Adams for the 8th Div with BG Fuqua present.

Early one morning, BG Fuqua and I drove to the I.G. Farben Building in Frankfurt with our charts and diagrams. The Corps G-3, COL Ciccolella, had asked to hear the briefing before it was presented to LTG Adams. Having heard it, Ciccolella declared that the Corps CDR would throw us out of his office if we went in with the plan. He suggested several changes which BG Fuqua was almost ready to accept. Realistically, however, there was no time to make changes, since we were due to brief in 15 minutes. In addition, I thought that Ciccolella's proposed changes were completely wrong.

Finally I said, "This briefing has been approved by MG Moses, the 8th Div CG and we can not make any changes without his consent. We appreciate your help and guidance, COL Ciccolella but the plan is firm as far as the 8th Div is concerned. I think we should give it to General Adams just as it is."

Ciccolella said, "Well, it's your ass, Seibert, but I know that the General will throw you out."

In the few minutes before we were to brief the Corps Commander, BG Fuqua asked if we were right to insist on briefing the plan as it was. I reassured him that we were. Our task was to sell the missile, not the American Army. The way to sell it was to make sure the senior NATO generals were comfortable, their creature comforts cared for while they concentrated on the missile. They were not interested in spending a day in the field with the American Army in addition to hearing about the missile. Fuqua agreed reluctantly.

We trooped into Adam's office where the briefing went without interruption until I reached the matter of the luncheon at the Von Steuben. LTG Adams questioned the decision to serve the noon meal there instead of in the field. When the reasoning behind the decision was explained to him, he accepted it without further comment. His only concern was about moving so many people so far. But he approved the plan as it was briefed to him. BG Fuqua and I left his office with a great sigh of relief.

The demonstration went as planned. It was a major undertaking which took almost the entire 1st ABG 504th IN to support; C Co could not provide all of the guides, guards and details required. It was a sharp looking group of soldiers that prepared the demonstration and looked after the NATO generals; I was proud of the troopers of the 504. It was a rare privilege for me to see GEN Lauris Norstad, the Supreme Allied Commander, Europe (SACEUR) and the other senior allied generals, most in colorful semi-dress uniforms. Since the AF handled the luncheon, I did not see how that went, but am sure it was handled in an outstanding manner. The Pershing Missile was approved for NATO and acquired by some of the NATO countries. Certainly the 504 contributed to that sale.

Immediately after the demonstration, COL Seay took leave. Since I was the ranking field grade officer, I became the acting CDR. Moore was my junior by several years, and newly assigned MAJ Ed Cavanaugh had just been promoted. Ed was an outgoing Irishman, a USMA graduate, who handled all actions with great facility and humor. By that time LTC Hager had been dropped from our rolls and assigned to the Detachment of Patients at Landstuhl. The perquisites of power were exhilarating and enjoyable; a sedan and helicopter at my disposal on call. As Acting CO I inspected training, made the daily runs with the Group as usual, and attended several functions for COL Seay. One was a boxing match at a sports club in Nierstein. A young specialist fourth class (SP4 or speedy four) who spoke fluent German accompanied me as interpreter. It was expected that the visiting American Commander make a short speech after which he was designated the honorary judge of the match. The troopers routed the German fighters; it embarrassed me to present all of the trophies to Americans.

During this period I was notified that my car was at Bremerhaven ready to be picked up. This entailed a two-day trip, which I could not possibly make while acting CO. SGM Boone had an NCO pick it up after I signed the necessary authorization papers; he took the train to Bremerhaven and drove my car back. It was good to be independently mobile again.

Several days after COL Seay left, MAJ Cavanaugh, the S-1, told me that some personnel problems needed immediate attention. The HHC CO was due to rotate within a week which required a joint inventory of the property with his replacement before he left. CPT George Tworek was to become the HHC CO, replaced as S-4 by MAJ Moore. Although the table of Organization and Equipment (TO&E) provided for a major in each of the principal staff positions, 1LT Wayne Smith, the Asst S-2, was to take over Moore's duties. I would, upon Col Seay's return, take up my duties as the S-3. Ed had discussed these inter-related personnel actions with COL Seay before he left. He had approved them in principle, but had been reluctant to authorize implementation of the plan. Now time was running out. After reviewing the plan, I told him to make the changes immediately.

While the helicopter was available I decided to go to Landstuhl to visit Ernie Hager; I hadn't seen him since his heart attack at Baumholder. Enroute the pilot suggested that my visit with Ernie be limited if possible so that we could leave early in the afternoon to get back to Mainz before the predicted bad weather developed. On arriving at the hospital I found that Emie was nearing a crisis. Both of his legs had been amputated very close to his hips because blood clots had caused gangrene in them. In addition, he had been unable to take care of the poisons in his system which had affected his kidneys. He was in a sterile room on a kidney machine. Ernie, had a fierce will to live and was fighting valiantly, but was sinking fast. Betty, his wife, was very worried and the doctor did not give Emie long to live. In fact, he thought the crisis might come that very night. In view of this, I decided to spend the night at Landstuhl and sent the helicopter back.

Betty and I had a serious talk over dinner that evening. When we went back to see Ernie, it was evident that he was dying. Luckily, some force had prompted me to visit Ernie that day, so that someone was with Betty when he died. She had to make certain decisions immediately, including granting permission for an autopsy. The sedan came down from Mainz, enroute there we stopped at the mortuary center to make arrangements for the shipment of Ernie's body to the CONUS, where he would be buried in Arlington Cemetery.

CPT John Hermann, a friend of the Hagers, designated as Survivor's Assistance Officer, would escort Ernie's body and take care of many of the details for Betty. He did an outstanding job. Before Betty left, the Battle Group held a memorial service for LTC Ernest Hager, its former XO. The chaplain, MAJ Williams, wanted to have an empty casket at the service, but I vetoed that. If the body was not present, there would be no representation of it. Chaplain Williams assured me that it was normal at military services, but I was adamant in my refusal to permit it. The service was held at the flagpole in the courtyard of Lee Kaserne. LTG Adams, the V Corps CDR, and MG Moses, the 8th Div CG were both present. COL Seay returned the night before the service. It was a simple, but effective service; a tribute to Ernie's reputation as an old jumper and to his ability as a soldier.

The day after the memorial service, COL Seay had a Commander's Call, with all of the company commanders and staff. He was incensed that I had made personnel changes in the Battle Group while he was away. He never did tell me directly that he was unhappy with me, nor did he chew me out, but at the Commander's Call, he spoke at great length, in very strong terms, about loyalty to the commander; not undercutting him while he was away on leave; not reorganizing the unit while the commander was gone. Everyone was uncomfortable because they agreed that the changes should have been made long before. Although I was being indirectly chastised in front of the assembled officers, I shrugged it off.

Shortly after his return, COL Seay was forced to make another personnel change. The A Co CO, Miller, a handsome Irishman, was more interested in sky diving than in his company. Indeed, he put skydiving above his wife and children, all of whom he treated badly. As a result of his poor leadership, there was a fight in A Co one night; some called it a riot. COL Seay moved Sam Barth from the S-3 Section to face the challenge of A Co. When Hermann returned from LTC Hager's funeral he turned over C Co to newly assigned CPT Vince Guide, and became the Assistant S-3.

Things settled into a routine. The Army, experiencing a gas shortage due to lack of funds at this time, allocated gas on a very strict schedule. There was plenty of gasoline in the tanks at the Kaserne to permit the 504 and 505 to move in an emergency, but each unit was permitted to use only a specified amount at a given time. The 504, and all USAREUR units, given one allocation for administrative purposes and one for training, was required to account for each gallon used. The Div G-4, MAJ George Stoeckert, who had been in my Advance Class, monitored the gas situation. He was an arrogant character who constantly threw his weight around. As the Acting Battle Group XO (in addition to being the S-3) I supervised the consumption of gasoline in the 504.

Two or three days before the end of October, the '04 ran short of administrative gas. MG Moses, the 8th Div CG, had placed a strict requirement on the 504 and 505 to conduct courtesy patrols in Wiesbaden each night. Wiesbaden was an Air Force town; in addition to the Air Base just outside the city, there were the huge Exchange shopping center, Officers' and Enlisted Clubs and a housing area in the city. While AF personnel were in the majority, the troopers liked to go there because of the many fine places to eat, the gambling, the bars and the women. The troopers all too often let their animal spirits overcome their judgement. To avoid confrontations between paratroopers and AF personnel or German nationals, courtesy patrols were considered essential. As Wiesbaden was about 15 miles from Mainz, the patrols required vehicles, which used gasoline.

On that Saturday, the 504 did not have enough administrative gasoline to take its patrol to Wiesbaden. COL Seay was gone so I called the DO at Div to request a special gas allocation for the courtesy patrol. The DO, after checking, informed me that our request had been disapproved.

"Then please make it a matter of record that the 504 will not have its scheduled courtesy patrol in Wiesbaden tonight or tomorrow night due to the lack of administrative gasoline."

Within 20 minutes Stoeckert was on the phone.

"Who is the stupid ass that canceled the courtesy patrol in Wiesbaden because of gasoline? You know the CG insists on those courtesy patrols."

"I'm the stupid ass that canceled it because we have run out of administrative gasoline. Div refused to let us borrow against next month's allocation. So there is no way to move the trucks legally."

"Well, this is a question of not being able to handle your resources. If we have to do it from here, we can and will." He then gave me a lecture which I took only because I was not talking with him face to face and don't like to argue with people over the telephone. Finally he ended up by allocating us the necessary gasoline for the courtesy patrols.

The gasoline problem, like that in 1949, plagued us throughout 1960 and 1961. Every activity, training need, or administrative run had to be anticipated, the gasoline required estimated, and the fuel requested in advance. To this had to be added the known requirements such as laundry and supply runs to Bad Kreuznach, gas for the sedan and jeeps used for conferences, reconnaissances and the courtesy patrols. Unforeseen traffic jams or detours or an unexpected supply trip could play havoc with the allocation. There was no pad for contingencies. The gasoline problem is typical of those the Army creates when it refuses to trust commanders to handle the resources of his unit.

At this time, LTC Bob Tully was assigned as the XO of the Battle Group. With relief, I relinquished my exalted position to devote full time to my duties as the S-3. The S-3 Section was a good one. CPT Hermann was the Asst S-3 and Plans OFF, 1LT Fred Amie, the Tng OFF, and 1LT Charlie Sarkiss the OPS Off. With these officers, an outstanding OPS SGT, MSG Byers, and a good clerk, SP4 Blasingame, my job was easy. I got to see a lot of the Battle Group as well as the people in it.

One of my priorities on reporting for duty with the 504 was to get a jump since I could not draw jump pay until I did. For two months, I couldn't make one. First the weather was bad. In Germany fog frequently forced delay or cancellation of jumps. Next, aircraft were not available. Then, when the 504 did have jumps scheduled, some priority work prevented me from jumping. It was frustrating. Finally, I made a tailgate jump, my first from the B model C-130.

Because of the high pitched whine of the propellers, jumpers were required to use ear plugs to prevent hearing problems. The C-130, specifically designed for Airborne operations, proved to be excellent aircraft to jump from. Once the pitch of the propellers was toned down, I found little wrong with it.

That first jump in Germany was made on a DZ in Alzey South, where we leased a number of farms as drop zones. Most of the DZs were farmed during the summer, then leased to the US Army in the fall and winter.

Life in the 504 settled into a pattern. The Battle Group was constantly in the field, either as a unit or by company. There seemed to be something going on every minute, permitting little time for sightseeing or other relaxation. I did walk through Mainz on Sunday afternoons. In most areas of Germany the WWII damage had been repaired, but Mainz had been in the French Zone until recently, and the French had deliberately blocked all efforts to erase the scars. There were still many buildings which showed signs of bombing or artillery fire. The Cathedral and Rathaus (city hall), being meticulously restored, were completed before I left the 504. Just outside MUHA were several ruined houses, grim reminders of the war. But these impressions were obtained on many weekend walks, and it was months before I felt that I knew the area.

Physical training was scheduled every morning. Both COL Seay and I usually made the HHC PT formation. There was always a run at the end of the session, through the local woods and over small sand hills which made it even more demanding. COL Seay insisted on running with the company, indeed, leading the formation on most runs. He seemed on the verge of collapse many times, causing concern that he was overdoing it. But he always managed to finish every run.

Since Airborne units have limited transportation after a parachute assault, it is necessary to insure that troopers can march long distances. As part of the training program, a 50 mile road march, conducted over a three-day period, was scheduled. Setting up the route and locating overnight bivouac areas was an interesting exercise for me and I was looking forward to making the trek. But COL Seay decided that he would make it and I would stay back because of other pending plans. Despite my arguments, COL Seay was firm, so I resigned myself to remaining at Mainz. Everyday I drove to the bivouac site to keep Seay current on Battle Group affairs. He developed serious problems with his feet, which were bloody most of the time, but he made the entire march in spite of that. The Div Band met the troopers on the last day and escorted them to Lee Kaserne. Most of the men arrived in good shape, though several straggled in after the main body.

Every month there was an alert signaled by a message from Division. The DO would then activate the alert notification system by telephone and messenger to insure that everyone was informed. The siren on the Mainz Ordnance Plant wailed and woke the neighborhood. The civilians must have asked themselves each time if it was really an attack. The alerts were supposed to be on a random basis, without warning, but occasionally word did trickle down through the grapevine that one was scheduled for a certain night. Alerts were called at various times, but usually at night. Every unit had to secure equipment and ammo, clear its Kaserne, and occupy its assembly area within two hours of notification. Periodic progress reports were made to Div, which in turn notified V Corps, and the Corps, 7th Army HQ. A certain percentage of personnel had to be out of the Kaserne the first half hour, another percentage in an hour, and all in two hours. It was a rigid time-table, but a well thought out plan. Once in the initial assembly areas the units could then move to their General Alert Order (GAO) Positions on the east side of the Rhine River. In most cases the 8th Div units simply went to their initial assembly areas, had a meal there, then returned to their Kaserne. Every so often a unit would be ordered to move to its GAO position.

Sometimes the alerts were very disruptive, especially if called at chow time or just before. Then there was the problem of transporting the cooked or cooking food to the assembly area; if called at other times the entire meal was cooked in the field. Most alerts were called between 2200 and 0300. Ammunition was kept loaded on trailers in an ammunition holding area I 1/2 miles from Lee Barracks; the prime movers had only to back up to them, hook up, and pull them out of the revetments.

As I watched the men and vehicles scramble to clear the Kaserne during the first alert after my arrival in Germany, the session with COL Bennett during which he acquainted Charlie Jackson and me with the alert system in Europe flashed through my mind.

During an alert, POVs were not permitted to be driven from MUHA to Lee Barracks. This was to prevent traffic jams as well as to provide clear roads for the ammo vehicles which had to leave the Kaserne immediately. Most married personnel had their wives drive them close to the Kaserne, though trucks and buses were dispatched to pick them up at MUHA. As a bachelor, I had special permission to drive my vehicle to the Kaserne during alerts. Since there would be no one to care for the vehicles belonging to personnel without dependents if there were an actual emergency, they would be secured there.

All personnel owning POVs were required to have the gas tanks at least half filled at all times, and each was equipped with an alert kit containing food, water and other necessities. The families were prepared to evacuate the Mainz area and go to a safe area in France or Spain. These plans were carefully developed; all dependents had to attend Non-combatant Evacuation Order (NEO) briefings every six months.

Gasoline for US military personnel was cheap, though rationed. Coupon books were purchased at the PX for the monthly quota. The coupons could be used at specified service stations throughout Europe authorized to receive them. It was a simple and effective plan, one which could be used in the United States should gas rationing ever be required. Of course, military personnel were free to purchase gasoline on the local market, but then they had to pay the very high prices which all European civilians were charged. Additional coupon books could be purchased for leaves.

The 8th IN Div, which had the USAREUR ABN capability, maintained a special alert unit, the Alpha Prime Co. This duty rotated between the 504 and the 505. The Alpha Prime Co was restricted to the Kaserne 24 hours a day. It had the "prime" mission for a week at a time, although the Battle Group had it for a month. All company equipment, including jeep trailers loaded with ammunition, was rigged with parachutes attached; personnel parachutes were fitted so that the Alpha Prime Co could move out within 30 minutes. The routes to Rhein-Main or Wiesbaden Air Base were well known to all drivers as these would be the most probable aerial ports of embarkation to any of the areas for which the Army had ABN contingency missions. The ABN Bde had contingency plans for most of northern Africa, the Middle East and all of Europe; there were many plans to monitor.

At a dinner party at the Schutzenhaus, the first social affair I attended after joining the 504 I became aware of the existence of a clique composed of those who had gyroscoped with the 504 from Bragg to Mainz. One of the ladies, who made it known that she was one of the of the wives who had gyroscoped, asked me where I had come from.

"I came from the Pentagon. But when did your husband first join the 504?"

"He joined in January 1958."

"I first joined the 504 in February 1949."

At that she turned away; it ended that nonsensical little problem. From then on there was no more comment about who had gyroscoped or first joined the unit.

The 504 and 505 had an excellent football team called the Mainz Troopers. The team, drawn from the two ABGs, was coached by CPT Ralph Peterson, who commanded the 504 CSC. One of the things that made the Mainz Troopers almost unbeatable was their fine physical condition. As Airborne troopers they did more PT than the average soldier, in addition they had the true Airborne spirit. The important factor was that they did not tire toward the end of the game. Opposing teams put on a good effort the first half but soon lagged; they couldn't sustain that effort. The Mainz Troopers could; they were particularly strong in the last quarter of any game. To add to their effectiveness the members of the team were better than average players and Peterson was an excellent coach.

The 8th Division Band came to all games played by the Troopers. The drum major had a spectacular routine during which he would throw one leg straight out, then pivot on the other leg to make a turn. He didn't use the regular facing movements and his gymnastics fascinated everyone. The Band played "The All American Soldier", the 82nd ABN Div march (adopted by the Mainz Troopers as their song) after every touchdown. Supporters from the ABN Bde sang along lustily each time.

In 1960 the Mainz Troopers again swept the football opposition to win the USAREUR and EUCOM championships. The deciding game was played in the Mainz University Soccer Stadium. EUCOM was lucky to get it; Germans take soccer seriously, take special care of soccer fields, and are reluctant to let it be used for football because cleats tear up the sod.

LTC Sidney M. Marks (Mickey), a legend among the NCOs and OFFs of the 504, and many others who had been reassigned from the Battle Group, returned for the games. At the first game I met Sybil and Mickey Marks. Little did I suspect how well I would get to know them both in the future!

In spite of football, the relationship between the 504 and the 505 was not as cordial as would be expected between the only two ABN units in Europe. This was especially unfortunate since they shared Lee Kaserne. COL Ted Mataxis, commanding the 505, was not very cooperative with COL Seay. It appeared to me that he was overly competitive, probably because he was obsessed with a desire for promotion to BG, making that foremost in any consideration. He was inordinately conscious of the publicity he and the 505 obtained, which generated an unhealthy competition between the two units. COL Seay was not an avid competitor, hence the 504 was at a disadvantage. Because of the many plans and joint actions the two ABGs had in common, I worked closely with the S-3s of the 505, Bob Siegrist, and later Jerry Collins. Hence, I got to know many of the OFFs and NCOs in it.

Late in the fall of 1960, the 504 ABG was scheduled for the annual Expert Infantryman Badge (EIB) test. My S-3 section developed a plan to test the 504, but it was decided that a Div team should test both battle groups. Since the 504 plan was complete it was designated for Div use with me as the Team Chief. This made good sense as the test required many stations manned by a large group. In setting up the test we were careful to meet the criteria set forth in the regulations, stipulating very specific rules. This caused some grumbling because the '05 had not adhered to the same strict standards.

The first run of the EIB test produced a marked disparity in the number of troopers from the two units who qualified. Twenty-eight 504 troopers passed, while only eight passed from the 505. An irate COL Mataxis all but accused me of favoring the 504, which was not true. Div directed a retest under the watchful eye of an observer they named. On the retest a few more passed, six from the '04 and four from the '05. The Div observer was impressed with both the standards established for the test as well the fairness of administration. He vindicated my conviction that the Expert Infantryman Badge test should measure the ability of the soldier against an Army-wide standard and the badge itself represent something the soldier could be proud of as truly earned.

Later that fall it was announced that COL Seay was being reassigned to Div HQ as the XO of the ABN Bde and that LTC Marks was to be the new Battle Group CDR. LTC Mickey Marks had been Dep CO of the 504 when it gyroscoped from Bragg. He was now in a promotable status, assigned as commander pending promotion. The troops were delighted because they had a high regard for Marks as a commander, a field soldier and an individual. Everyone eagerly anticipated his return. I had never served with LTC Marks, and was looking forward to doing so. He bounced into the HQ unannounced one day, full of vim and vigor; a relatively short individual with a dynamic personality, he radiated confidence, enthusiasm, and professionalism. It was apparent why the troops rallied to him as a commander.

The assignment of the new commander posed an interesting situation since LTC Bob Tully outranked him. But Bob Tully had not been selected for promotion. As a result, Mickey was assigned by Direction of the President (DP), a device used in such cases. The DP would get around the differences in rank until Mickey was promoted.

At about the same time, LTC Townsend reported for duty. Battle groups were authorized two LTCs, a Dep CDR concerned with tactical and training matters and an XO who supervised administration. There was no real need for both officers, but since battle groups had replaced Regts and Bns, it was necessary to find assignments for LTCs. Mickey decided that Townsend should be the Deputy with no Executive; Bob Tully was made the coordinator of the Mainz Kaserne, an arrangement satisfactory to COL Mataxis. Tully was in effect the Kaserne or Post CDR who took care of such housekeeping details as the EM Club, the PX, the hiring and paying of local nationals, and the coordination of guard and police details.

Mickey hit the Battle Group with resounding force. The night he took command there was a fight in the EM Club which an excitable OD labeled a race riot. The following morning at the PT formation, before the run, LTC Marks got up on the platform on which the flagpole was erected and called out three outstanding NCOs he had known from his previous association with the 504. One was white, one Hispanic and one black. He had them stand with their arms around each other.

"Now these are three soldiers," he said. "They aren't black soldiers or white soldiers or Puerto Rican soldiers. They are just plain vanilla American soldiers, Airborne Troopers. I don't want to hear any talk about Mexican soldiers or black soldiers or whatever."

He then gave a short pointed speech about equality within the armed forces. And that ended it. This was typical of the way he handled things.

The senior PSG in D Co was MSG Richter one of my NCOs from F Co, 508. He was still a MSG with a fine reputation as a tactical NCO; but he also had a reputation for having a short temper which catapulted him into fights periodically. In fact, I had to get him out of at least one scrape while I was with the 504. Later MSG Jerome Sullivan reported for duty with the 505, still the sharp soldier who so often had taken the award for Outstanding Trooper of K Co, 504 in 1950.

COL Wilbur Wilson, now in Heidelberg, and I had corresponded over the years. The story of his assignments in Europe make interesting reading. Originally ordered to the Army Element of the Joint HQ in Naples, he was given the task of reorganizing it. One of the essential elements of his plan was the elimination of his own job, indeed, his entire section. When his recommendations were approved he was reassigned to the 8th Div as the ABN Bde CDR.

From the 8th Div COL Wilson had been reassigned to USAREUR HQ at Heidelberg. So far, I had not been able to get down to visit him, but shortly before Thanksgiving he called to ask if I would like to go to Switzerland with him during the Thanksgiving holidays. Assuming that I would be able to get leave over that four-day period, I leaped at the chance. One of my main reasons for asking for an assignment in Europe was to see that part of the world, but I had been so involved in my job that I had not been able to do much traveling. COL Marks approved a five day leave. COL Wilson drove up from Heidelberg to pick me up.

That trip to Switzerland began a love affair with the Continent that has never ended. The day we came in sight of the Alps was a clear, sunny one. The glistening snow-capped mountains were every bit as awe-inspiring as I had imagined them. Zurich was a bustling, interesting city, but Interlaken was a delightful and beautiful town. Most of the hotels were closed as it was between seasons, but we stayed at a gasthaus. As the only paying guests, we ate with the family, sampling good Swiss home cooking. The last stop was Bern, another fascinating city. Of course we visited the bears, reviewing the prophecy of evil overtaking the city if they deserted it. The plethora of fine cheeses caused me to eat too much, but I could not seem to get enough of them.

It was good to see COL Wilson again. The four-day trip was spent discussing the Army and various officers we knew. His views were always interesting, though I did not agree with all of them. It was a delightful break, after which I returned to Mainz and the waiting actions, prepared for long hours and constant pressure. During the next few months I visited Heidelberg on several weekends. One I spent with Kitty and Charlie Jackson, friends from the Pentagon, during which I also saw Barney Broughton and Art Hyman. Most of those weekends I visited COL Wilson.

In December, LTG Paul D. Adams was reassigned and LTG Brown replaced him as CDR of V Corps. The 504 was tasked to provide a reinforced rifle Co for the change of command ceremony. The uniform specified was Class A with service cap, the cap with the bill and grommet to keep it round. Paratroopers derisively called it the "flying saucer". Most of our troopers did not have one, although it was a required item of the uniform. Those having service caps had crammed them into duffel bags when they left FT Bragg for Germany, from which they had never dug them out. Because few troopers had service caps, which were anathema to the Airborne, the 504 ABG requested permission to wear the garrison cap, the "overseas cap" or "go to Hell cap" with the Airborne Patch on it. V Corps disapproved this request, but negotiations continued. Finally, in large part because of our protests, the field uniform with helmets and packs was specified. This was standard for the Airborne, which looked as sharp in starched field clothing as in Class A uniforms. The 504 troopers stood out in that formation.

Later that month there was an 8th Div maneuver in which the 504 participated. Communications throughout the Division did not work well in the cold wet weather. When the maneuver failed to accomplish some of the goals established for it, it was concluded early. LTC Marks got on the radio and ordered all units to move back to Lee Barracks. CPT Sam Barth, Commanding A Co, with tongue in cheek, asked for authentication of the order. Mickey never did understand codes, a fact Sam was well aware of, but his voice and language over the radio were so typical that it was difficult to mistake the fact that it was Mickey Marks talking. He told Sam in colorful terms that if he didn't believe that it was an authentic order he could stay out in the field as long as he wanted, but the rest of the units were proceeding home. Sam capitulated, "Rogered", and joined the convoy back to Lee Kaserae.

Immediately after the maneuver everyone was relieved to hear that MG Moses, considered a martinet, would be reassigned. MG Edgar Doleman, his successor, was reputed to be a highly able leader. MG Doleman was a superb tactician. After studying a map for five minutes, the terrain was indelibly printed on his mind. Thus, he could maneuver units over the ground easily. COL Jack Wright, who had been in my Advance Class, the 508 and in the Pentagon when I was there, was now CofS, having replaced COL Taber. Jack Wright was an excellent Chief of Staff, as I had occasion to learn later on.

Mickey Marks instituted a mandatory happy hour every Friday night at the Franklin House, the Officers' Club in MUHA. The officers relaxed, let off steam, aired gripes, and became a more cohesive group as a result of these gatherings, but the wives were not too happy about them until Mickey told them that they were welcome too.

Because I was a senior bachelor, I was appointed the 504 representative to the Officers' Club Council, and eventually elected its President. Exercising my prerogatives I insured that all of our meetings were relatively short. There wasn't a lot of argumentation or debate; we discussed any problems, made our decisions and ended the meetings. At the annual general meeting some of the more vocal officers accused me of being a dictator because I limited open discussion from the floor. There was always a group that wanted to sound off about the food, service, facilities or prices. They never made recommendations to the Council at its regular meetings or sent in suggestions, but wanted an audience to speak to. At the outset of the meeting I silenced them by telling them to give any complaints directly to me or one of the other members of the Council rather than taking the member's time.

During my tenure as President of the Board of Governors of the Franklin House, two young men in civilian clothes came into the club bar one Saturday afternoon. An OFF told me that they were both NCOs. I asked for their identification which they refused to show me. They said that they were agents Smith and Jones of the Criminal Investigation Division (CID). As such they did not have to provide any identification. Quickly disabusing them of that notion, I informed them that every law enforcement officer was required to identify himself, and that anyone entering the Officers' Club had to be a member, the guest of a member or a visiting officer. When they again refused to show any identification when I demanded it, I summarily ordered them out of the Club. Several days later the 8th Div PM called to tell me that I had exceeded my authority. He said that I had no right to throw an agent out of the club. After explaining their refusal to produce any identification I asked the PM how I was to know that they were indeed CID agents, and to cite the regulation that gave an enlisted agent the privileges of an Officers' Club. The Officers' Club bylaws as well as Army Regulations set aside the club exclusively for officers. Unless an enlisted man was invited for a special function as a guest of a command, he was not authorized to use an Officers' Club. Possibly a case could be made for permitting enlisted agents to use the club while investigating an incident, but then they should be required to produce some identification. Those agents were there to defy the system for their own pleasure.

The matter of enlisted CID agents is another example of the lack of trust the Army places in its officers. The Army is wrong in giving agents a spurious rank. When an agent, whether OFF or EM, wears the initials US instead of stripes or bars, it is a blatant attempt to create a special class. The theory that the agents will get better cooperation if their actual rank is not known is utter nonsense. Any OFF or NCO who fails to cooperate with an agent who is doing his job and his duty ought not to have a position of trust. In fact, the unidentified grade of the agent makes him more conspicuous in a military setting. The PM blustered in vain. No other agents ever came in the Franklin House during my tenure there.

As Christmas approached there was a spate of social affairs. It seemed that everybody was having a Christmas party. In addition there was the official 504 party. Being a bachelor, I was invited to many of them to fill out the table or to pair off with a wife whose husband was on TDY or a sister who was visiting. People were most generous in their invitations, making sure I thoroughly enjoyed the holidays.

COL Wilson called to invite me to go to Holland with him for Christmas. Mickey gave me a week's leave. Again, we had an interesting trip by car, up the Rhine to Cologne or Koln to see the great cathedral, then through the Ardennes Forest to St Vith, Bastogne, Vielsalm, Malmady and other areas associated with the Battle of the Bulge. Finally we arrived in Rotterdam. COL Wilson had made reservations for us in the Rijn Hotel. The eight course Christmas Eve dinner was superb! The fourth course was a sorbet to permit the diners to catch their breath before the entree. It was preceded by assorted hors d'oeuvres, soup and fish. Then the main course of roast goose, followed by salad, dessert and finally cheese and fruit. Everyone sang along with the band; it was a gala occasion which we enjoyed thoroughly. For the next few days we drove through Holland, arriving back at Mainz on 27 December.

John Hermann and five other 504 officers had made reservations for the New Year's Eve party at the Von Steuben in Wiesbaden. They asked me to join them, which I was delighted to do. It was a gala evening, as usual I wound up buying champagne for everyone in the party. The food, the atmosphere, the people, the music, all contributed to a most enjoyable evening.

Immediately after the first of the year (1961), preparations began for the annual maneuver, Winter Shield II. It was held in the winter so that the forces could transit farmlands leased by the Army without damaging crops, but there was always maneuver damage to settle up. Fences would be broken, minor damage done to ditches and buildings, or roads would be torn up by tanks. All units were enjoined by higher headquarters to minimize damage.

Selected OFFs had an opportunity to go to the Grafenwohr Tng Area (Graf), where the maneuver would start, to reconnoiter the area in which they were to operate. Each Co CO was authorized to take one jeep with four people in it. Three vehicles including LTC Marks' and mine were authorized for HQ. The recon party went in convoy. It was cold in the jeep going to and from Graf and during the reconnaissance. Fortunately it was warm in the BOQ at Grafenwohr. SF units from Bad Tolz would participate in Winter Shield II; some of the OFFs in those units had been with the 504 when it had first come to Europe, so we had immediate rapport with them.

Just before the Battle Group moved to Graf for the exercise, several new OFFs joined it, including 2LT James Sullivan and 1LT Gordon Corcoran. Most of the officers were assigned to companies, but I grabbed Sully, a personable and dynamic young Notre Dame graduate, as a badly needed LNO. He was gung-ho, just out of jump school, and extremely unhappy about his assignment. Despite his plea for a platoon, which I sympathized with fully, I retained him, promising him a Plt as soon as the maneuver ended. He did an outstanding job and got his fill of excitement driving around the German countryside or briefing at Div HQ.

The movement of the Battle Group to Grafenwohr by truck convoy was uneventful. It was frigid during the entire trip, but the troops had their field gear with them in the trucks which enabled them to keep warm. The S-4 arranged to have hot soup and coffee at each of the rest stops enroute. There was no snow on the Autobahn, though the countryside was covered. The quartering party, which had preceded the main body by one day, had already allocated company areas, so the 504 was able to move into its assembly area and begin setting up without delay. Snow and ice made digging in difficult.

The S-3 Section had a van which was used as a mobile CP. In it were the communications, maps and tactical operations center (TOC). The CO and S-3 were usually in the van if they weren't in the field. Mickey and I were inseparable during maneuvers; as his S-3, I was in his back pocket, actually in the back of his jeep, monitoring both the Division and Battle Group radio nets. It gets mighty cold in the back of a jeep without a top! The Asst S-3 and Plans OFF, CPT Hermann, spent most of his time in the van developing plans, writing orders or monitoring the situation.

A Red Cross worker from the 8th Div Red Cross team, attached to the Battle Group for Winter Shield, was constantly complaining about being cold or not having proper facilities. The S-1 had put him with Chaplain (MAJ) Denny Williams. It was not a happy combination, Denny was not much of a field soldier. But they managed to exist. Everyone was cold; the diesel space heaters were not very effective in keeping squad tents warm.

In the initial phase, the 504 and the 505, together with the rest of the 8th Div, would move south to defend against the 24th Div, the opposing force in the maneuver. The Div Order, unnecessarily complicated, had the 505 crossing the 504's position in order to precede it. The 505 had road priority for a specified time, after which the 504 took it over. At the briefing I tried to convince Stoeckert, now the G-3, to let the 504 go first since it was in position to lead off, vastly simplifying the entire move, but he would not alter his plan.

The night of the move there was a freeze. Because of the icy roads all units had great difficulty getting started, creating concern that the schedule would not be maintained. Mickey and I were at the initial point (IP), a crossroads, waiting for the 505 to pass. Instead, our CSC, under CPT Peterson, appeared. He was scheduled to wait until the 505 had cleared but had cut them off. His Co also had trouble getting out of its assembly area because of ice.

Mickey was aghast! He wailed, "This is definitely the end of my career. Mataxis is going to skin me in front of the Old Man and I have no excuse."

After considering all of the possible courses of action for the 504, I suggested that we move the entire Battle Group immediately and let the 505 follow it. This would have been the logical move in the first place. Mickey, not wanting to compromise the Div March Order, was reluctant to move, but the '04 was already holding up the '05 so the best course seemed to be to move the '04 on and clear the road. Finally, Mickey was persuaded to order the move. The Battle Group moved and moved fast. As it turned out, the 504 did not hold up the 505 since it had trouble with icy roads and was unable to clear its assembly area on time. Despite the initial foul-up, the two ABGs were able to get on line in good time; soon the entire 8th Div was in position with a minimum amount of confusion. Later Mickey went to the Div CP for a commanders' call with me in the back of his jeep as usual. There was coordination to be accomplished with the Div G-3 and the Signal Officer, so I did not attend the meeting. Driving back to our position Mickey said that Mataxis hadn't said a word about the 504 going before the 505. The 8th Div CG, MG Doleman, was happy with the move, so Mickey's concern was groundless.

Shortly after that commanders' call, the battle began. The 8th Division's quick move had taken the 24th Div by surprise, throwing it off balance. Doleman took advantage of the situation by ordering the 504 to make an end run. The first phase ended with the 8th Division credited with a decisive win.

All units went into temporary bivouacs preparatory to the next phase. One day, Mickey, John and I were in the van discussing the upcoming maneuver when there was a timid knock on the door.

John Hermann opened it; the Red Cross man was outside. He wanted to talk to me. He had asked for a jeep earlier; as coordinator of tactical vehicles, I had turned him down because there weren't enough of them. The S-1 arranged for the Chaplain and the Red Cross worker to share a jeep.

Certain that another plea for a jeep was to be made, I stepped outside to find MA Denny Williams, the Battle Group Chaplain, there also. Both of them looked at me solemnly as Denny told me that the Red Cross had received notification that Dad had died. He was to be buried three days hence. It was not unexpected; I was more or less prepared for this after Dad's two heart attacks before I left home. They told me that arrangements were being completed to get me out immediately on an emergency leave.

Thinking of the problems the Battle Group was facing in the next phase of the maneuver, I told them that I would not go home for the funeral. When I told Mickey that Dad had died but that I was not going home because of the maneuver, he exploded.

"No way, Don," he said. "You've got to go home. They'll get you out tonight and you'll be home in the morning. Your Mother will feel terrible if you don't go home. You owe it to your family and to your Father, too. And we will get along without you. Suppose you were a casualty? Go home!"

Convinced, within 15 minutes I was on my way from the maneuver to Mainz by light aircraft. John Hermann, who was completely familiar with the entire operation, assumed the duties of S-3. Mr Smith, back in Mainz, had been notified. He met me at Finthen Airfield with emergency leave orders already prepared. After a shower, I got into a clean uniform, packed a bag, and drove to Rhein-Main where I caught a plane that evening. Personnel on emergency leave take priority over everyone except those being medically evacuated, so I got the first plane out. It stopped at Goose Bay, Labrador to refuel. There I called Arlene and told her that I would get into McGuire that morning, and take the train to New York so no one had to meet me.

Once home, I was glad that Mickey insisted I go. Although wakes and viewings seem barbaric to me, I got to see many friends who paid their respects to Dad. Mother was happy that I had been able to make the funeral and we talked seriously about her future on several occasions. She thought she might go into one of the Episcopal Homes for the Aged; she was 71, the same age as Dad. The rest of the family and I persuaded her that this was wrong. She was still young; she had her health, energy, and faculties; she enjoyed her grandchildren and many friends, her church work and singing in the choir. We convinced her to get an apartment and lead a normal life for as long as possible. She finally decided she would do that. Once that matter was settled I knew that my two sisters, Margaret and Arlene, and their husbands, would help her move. Relieved, I headed back to Germany.

Personnel returning from emergency leave do not have any priority. Fortunately, with only a one day delay, I caught a flight from McGuire. As the aircraft approached Frankfurt, fog caused it to be diverted to Koln. Civilian buses took the military passengers to Frankfurt. It was a hair-raising trip. The bus drivers as well as civilian drivers were oblivious of the fog and the slippery Autobahn. At high speed, they whipped in and out of lanes, passing on the right, and tailgating. After several close calls, we arrived safely in Frankfurt. I reclaimed my car and drove directly to Mainz without delay. By that time, Winter Shield II was over and the 504 was back in Lee Kaserae. There were numerous "war stories" which gave me a second hand account on how well the maneuver had gone. John Hermann had done an excellent job as the S-3, working well with Mickey.

The Battle Group quickly settled back into its busy, crowded routine, immediately, after the refitting was complete, it resumed training. When everything was back to normal, Mickey suggested that the 504 have a traditional Dining-In. It sounded like a good idea, even if I was not quite sure what a Dining-In was; though I had heard references to them, I had never attended one. Mickey described it as a stag dinner party in formal uniform, during which rigid protocol was observed up to the conclusion of the meal, at which time all restraints were lifted. Essentially, it provided an opportunity to weld the officers of a unit more closely together with a dose of rigid discipline, followed by horseplay. With no further guidance, Marks told me to set it up. Almost as an afterthought, he said,

"We ought to invite a prominent guest speaker. Who do you think we should ask?"

"Why not go for the top and invite General Norstad," I suggested.

"He would never come," Mickey said a little unsurely. "He's too busy and too important."

"We'll never know unless we ask him. Let me draft a letter for your signature inviting him." Mickey shrugged. Within a week, he received a cordial letter from General Norstad apologizing for not being able to make our Dining-In because he had a NATO commitment. He hoped that we would invite him at some other time because he enjoyed visiting tactical units.

Mickey showed me the letter, saying, "Well, what next?"

"The next guy is the Commander-In-Chief, US Army Europe (CINCUSAREUR), GEN Bruce Clarke."

"Okay, let's go," Mickey said, grinning.

Almost the day after the letter was mailed, I received a phone call from GEN Clarke's aide, telling me that the General had accepted. He would arrive in one of the two trains provided the CINC by the German Government, and would sleep on the train. Thus we would not have any billeting problems. When Mickey heard the news he told me to inform Div that GEN Clarke would be in the 504 area. This I did immediately.

Within two days Div notified the 504 that GEN Clarke would make an official visit to the 8th Div coincidental with the Dining-In. MG Doleman directed that since the 504 had invited GEN Clarke for the Dining-In and he would be in our area, that we would also host his official visit. As the S-3 I was tasked to set up both the Dining-In and the official visit, which would be on the day after the Dining-In. The plan Marks and ultimately Doleman approved, included a briefing on our alert procedures, an inspection of the Alpha Prime Co, followed by a coffee break. After that Mickey would take GEN Clarke out to see 504 training.

The CINC in Mainz arrived on schedule. The Dining-In was most enjoyable, though the procedure we used was non-traditional, to put it charitably. There was no "Mr Vice", no bell or smoking lamp or other appurtenances and procedures usually associated with such affairs. Despite these short-comings it was a memorable occasion. GEN Clarke gave a fine talk on leadership, aimed at lieutenants.

The morning after the Dining-In, Mickey picked up The CINC at the railroad siding where his official train was located. Promptly at 0800 he arrived at the Battle Group HQ. At the same time, MG Doleman arrived. As Mickey escorted the now impressive entourage to the conference room where the CINC would be briefed on the Alpha Prime Mission, the Alpha Prime Co was preparing for inspection. The troopers had fallen out with all of their equipment including parachutes and the rigged heavy drop loads. There was the last-minute chaos which would suddenly resolve into the orderly precision of the inspection procedure.

GEN Clarke noted the activity and the shivering troopers. Nodding toward them he enquired, "What are those men doing, Colonel?"

"That is the Alpha Prime Company, Sir. They are preparing for your inspection after the briefing."

"I don't like to have troops standing out in the cold waiting for me. I'd like to inspect them now so they can be dismissed and get warm."

"Sir, the company is not quite ready for your inspection," I interposed. "I am sure that you will have a better understanding of their equipment and capabilities after the briefing. We are scheduled to inspect them at 0830."

Ignoring my comments, GEN Clarke said to Mickey, "I don't care about the schedule. We'll inspect them now and get them out of the cold."

"Yes, sir." Mickey turned to me saying, 'Tell Sam that we will be over to look at A Co in five minutes."

Saluting smartly, I hurried over to CPT Barth, who went into shock when I told him about the change of schedule. "We're not ready. The damn company will look like a leg outfit if they check it now. Can't you stall them?"

"No! The CINC wants to get the troops out of the cold. Better get moving."

Sam darted off shouting orders. Even as the CINC's party approached, there was a last frenzied effort before the company was perfectly alined, its equipment carefully displayed, the former chaos replaced with orderly military precision.

The Co CO reported smartly and each trooper in turn became ram-rod stiff as the General stepped in front of him. GEN Clarke asked pertinent questions, which the troopers answered respectfully and knowledgeably. After the inspection, the General took a few minutes to talk to the Company, complimenting the men on their appearance and obvious professionalism, telling them of the importance of their mission, and concluding with his confidence in their ability. That was one of GEN Clarke's strong points, his ability to communicate with junior OFFs and EM. It was good leadership to which the troopers responded.

Immediately after the inspection the visitors headed for the briefing room, the Alpha Prime Company already picking up its gear to clear the parade field. Everyone was thoroughly chilled by now, so Mickey suggested that we have coffee. This was the second change in the itinerary. The coffee was not scheduled to be served for another hour, however, Mickey nodded to me whereupon I sent a runner to the mess hall to inform the mess personnel to bring over the coffee. It took several trips; the first trip produced the coffee urn and cups, but no spoons, sugar or cream; the second produced the spoons, sugar, and cream but no cake; the third produced the cake and a knife, but no plates or napkins. With each trip some of Mickey's patience evaporated and his ire grew. He glared at me, at the CINC, at the cooks. When he looked at the cake he almost had apoplexy. The cooks had misspelled the General's name. The beautifully decorated cake read, "Welcome General Clark". The CINC was very sensitive to this, as Mickey well knew. Muttering to me, "I'm ruined," he approached GEN Clarke.

"Sir, will you cut the cake?"

GEN Clarke strode to the table, glared at the cake, then cut a corner slab. It was then that the absence of the plates and napkins was discovered. For a brief moment there was a deathly silence, not even the sound of breathing in the room as if everyone held his breath hoping the situation would resolve itself. Then Clarke turned to Doleman.

"Have a piece of cake, Ed." With these words he seized MG Doleman's hand and slapped the slab of cake, gooey icing side down, into the reluctant palm.

Mickey visibly wilted. I could hear his groan, "There goes my career."

The coffee break then came to a quick end as the briefing began. It, at least, went well. The CINC was alert and interested. He asked searching questions; the prompt, frank answers appeared to please him. Mickey then escorted him to the waiting jeeps for an inspection of the training scheduled for that day. GEN Clarke was impressed with the enthusiasm with which the training was being conducted in the four companies visited. As he left, he complimented the 504 highly, and Mickey particularly. As this was done in front of MG Doleman, it completely erased any adverse impression the coffee break gaffe might have created. Later, LTC Marks received a letter through channels expressing the CINC's appreciation, and a personal letter thanking Mickey for the fine time at the Dining-In.

The '04 settled back into its training and refitting cycle. It was soon back to what passed for normal in the busy schedule.

Taking advantage of a rare lull in the pace, I visited COL Wilson in Heidelberg for a weekend, arriving the day that MG Edwin C. Walker was relieved of command of the 24th IN Div. Walker, a controversial figure by this time, had taken a strong and vocal anticommunist stand which included a proscription of communist literature in his Div area. He had tried to bar the *Overseas Weekly* and other liberal papers, but had been thwarted on this. His relief was the result of many such incidents. He was in the same BOQ in Heidelberg as COL Wilson while awaiting orders. When MG Walker was a colonel commanding the Ranger Department at FT Benning and I was in the 508, COL Wilson had introduced me to him. He was an impressive officer.

Wilson suggested that the three of us have dinner together. We went to the Europaische, the best hotel with the finest restaurant in Heidelberg. The delicious meal was marred to some extent by Walker's conversation. He had earned my admiration as a soldier. He had a fine combat record in WWII as Dep CDR of the 1st Special Service Forces, and what I had seen at the Ranger Command and at Bragg when he commanded the V Corps Artillery, reinforced his reputation. Now he was obsessed with the idea that the communists were going to take over America. He dominated the dinner conversation, castigating everybody, even accusing President Eisenhower of being a fellow traveler. It was obvious why he had been relieved; a sad ending to a distinguished career.

One of my Leavenworth classmates, Bruce Babbitt, was the Staff Judge Advocate (SJA) of the 8th Div. Although I saw him rarely, we talked frequently on the telephone. He helped me over some difficult problems when I was the President of the 504 Special Court.

On several occasions I got into controversies with one of the civilian lawyers who had established himself in the Frankfurt area. He promised the troopers he would get them acquitted if he represented them; for a substantial fee. He was probably a competent lawyer, but his ethics were suspect and he used questionable tactics in the courtroom, where he was frequently out of order. In several cases he accosted me in court, challenging some of my rulings in an offensive and demeaning manner. Finally, during one trial, I told him that if he did not stop harassing the court, I would find him in contempt. Bruce Babbitt supported me, assuring me that I could indeed hold a lawyer as well as anyone else in contempt of court. He further informed me that I had the authority to levy a fine against the lawyer if he persisted in disrupting the court. Although this curtailed his flamboyance for a time, resulting in the loss of several cases, he still forced himself on the troops. He tried to get some of his clients to buy cigarettes and other items for him in the PX, an illegal act punishable in the German courts. But he escaped prosecution for such activities.

As one of the few field grade officers in the 504, I made several Article 32 investigations which were analogous to grand jury proceedings, as well as answering several congressional inquiries. One involved a SGT in Sam Barth's Co. Sam had reduced the SGT to CPL for several violations of orders. The SGT's wife wrote to her Congressman accusing Sam of conducting a vendetta against her husband. She rambled on about the Sergeant's outstanding career up to that point, "and then CPT Barth appeared on the scene". My investigation indicated that Sam was not only justified in his action, but that he should have reduced the sergeant to private! I wrote a strongly worded draft reply (by this time DA no longer trusted its junior subordinate commanders to answer congressional inquiries; the unit concerned furnished a draft reply to Div which edited it, retyped it and forwarded it under the signature of either the AG or CofS). In addition I investigated an allegation against a WO1 who took pictures during his off-duty time. An EM complained that he had paid for photographs which he had not received. The WO1 was cleared when my investigation revealed that he had withheld the pictures because the check drawn on the Boy Scout Fund, had bounced because of an improper signature. The matter was quickly resolved when a new check was tendered.

Although Alzey South was the DZ used most frequently by the Americans, the US Army jumped throughout Germany. One of the favorite DZs was Leipheim. This was a peat meadow near Augsburg. The peat was so soft and springy it was almost like jumping on a mattress. In the spring of 1961, the 504 was scheduled to jump at Leipheim. Charlie Sarkiss, my OPS OFF, went down to coordinate with the German Air Force the use of their facilities which were close by. He made arrangements for billeting our DZ control team, refueling our vehicles, and handling serious medical cases. He urged me to come down to meet the German Air Force personnel. Since I wanted to check on the DZ and arrangements, I caught a flight to the German air field, where Charlie picked me up. The CO of the German Air Base, a LTC (Oberstleutnant), insisted I call on him. He was most cooperative. As three of the German officers had been especially helpful, I took them out to dinner. Charlie was of course with us. It was the first time I tasted weisbier, a very light beer with a squeeze of lemon in it. It was very good! After dinner we went to a night club in Augsburg. An enjoyable evening.

The jump at Leipheim went well, although the troopers found it a bit disconcerting to come in for a landing near mowing machinery. The German farmers were cutting hay and would not stop, though they kept a sharp lookout for jumpers.

MG Steinbach, who had been my Regt CDR in Korea, was Chief of the Army Military Assistance Advisory Group (MAAG) in Germany, and would soon become head of the MAAG. He invited me to spend a weekend with him and his wife at Bad Godesberg. Although the US Embassy was in Bonn, most of the Diplomatic Corps lived in Bad Godesburg. He had a large set of quarters directly on the Rhine, with a beautiful view, though the river traffic was noisy. It was a delightful visit. He and his wife, Roz, entertained me royally.

Steinbach offered me a job with his organization, which carried with it a jump slot. The offer was tempting; the job involved travel throughout the country and provided an opportunity to get to know the Germans and to see Germany. In addition, I would work with the German Parachute School. Steinbach and I had worked well together when I was his S-3 in Korea; he was a good boss, and I liked him which made it difficult to turn down his offer. But I had been away from troops for seven years. Despite my staff position, I enjoyed duty with the 504, liked Mickey, liked the esprit of the '04, liked our field duty. Reluctantly, I turned down his offer.

Probably the most outstanding attribute of the 1st Airborne Battle Group, 504th Infantry was the wealth of superb officers it possessed. Most of the Co COs were true professionals who demanded the highest standards from their LTs. The LTs were young, eager, enthusiastic and inexhaustible! They made mistakes, but achieved outstanding results. Perhaps this was the result of the continuing training they received from their Co COs. Whether in garrison or the field, this training never ceased. Many of the companies had formal classes for the NCOS, but the LTs were never slighted. Initially, the Battle Group staff conducted classes dealing with the responsibilities of officers. But the most important training the young LTs received was from the senior NCOs. Though it took them a long time to recognize just how much these noncommissioned professionals could teach them, the more alert LTs soon learned to listen carefully to their senior sergeants.

The Co COs were harder on their OFFs than on their EM. They were experienced and professional, and demanded complete obedience, maximum effort, loyalty and dedication. Among those that impressed me were: CPT Sam Barth, who commanded at one time or another, HHC, A and B Cos; CPT Ralph Peterson, who in addition to his demanding duties as CO of CSC, still found time to coach the Mainz Troopers to three European championships; CPT John Hermann who turned over command of C Co to become my Asst S-3 and Plans OFF; CPT John Mess, who made an outstanding unit of E Co; CPT Al Barnes, a black OFF who succeeded John Mess as CO of E Co and did an equally fine job; and CPT Dan Palmer, who commanded D Co most ably and was promoted to MAJ before I left the 504.

There were, of course, some OFFs who were not up to these standards. Several who had left the Battle Group before I arrived were mentioned with disdain. Phil Miller, the sky diver, was a sorry Co CO. Long was a weak commander who eventually had to be replaced. During my tenure, the worst of the captains was Vince Guide. After several counseling sessions which did nothing to stem the continuing deterioration in the morale and performance of C Co, he was reassigned to the S-3 Section so that I could keep a close eye on him. My efficiency report was very critical, which surprised him in spite of the many counseling sessions I had with him. Although I could not show him the report, I wrote him a letter outlining the salient points I made.

The enthusiastic LTs in the 504 were too numerous to list. Those I saw after reassignment, and who impressed me with their dedication and potential, were Dick Hooker, a talented musician from Louisiana, Wayne Smith, who did an outstanding job as S-2 as well as A Co CO, but who let liquor sully the end of his career, Doug Craver, who proved to be one of the best Co COs in the Battle Group although still a 1LT, Bill Posey the tall, outgoing Medical Platoon Leader, and Keith Barlow, a handsome USMA graduate. All except Wayne Smith were eventually promoted to colonel. Most of them were married to lovely young ladies who seemed hardly old enough to be out of school. An outstanding group of officers with whom to serve.

One of the greatest joys of duty in Germany, one that the demanding schedule and constant duty in the field rendered all the more desirable because of its rarity, was dining in German restaurants, "on the economy" as the troops called it. There were many outstanding eating places in the area, but even the meanest village boasted a gasthaus which served delicious, hearty food and local wines. Everyone learned quickly to order the Hauswein, as no self-respecting Gastwirt would risk his reputation by serving poor wine. The tart Rhine wines appealed to me, and I developed a strong liking for them. With the Deutsche Mark at about four to the dollar, these gastronomic treats were cheap as well as enjoyable.

The best restaurant in Germany was the Krone Hotel in Assmannshausen, a short drive from Mainz. The Rhine Salmon, the Rehsteaks and the local sparkling burgundy, a rarity in the Rhine Valley, were truly gourmet treats. Wiesbaden boasted many fine restaurants, my favorite being Mutter Engles. The Kurhaus in Bad Kreuznach and the Fausthaus in the same city were excellent. Many of the 504 OFFs liked the Lennenberg Vald "Castle" a short drive from Mainz. Its specialty was chicken which was always good. And the spiesbraten in a small village near Baumholder was a rare treat. There was much truth in my often repeated and facetious comment that I "ate my way across Europe".

Early in April 1961, the 504 went to Baumholder for extensive field training. Just before we left Mainz, decided that the unit would have a Prop Blast there. The Officers' Club at Baumholder had a vaulted, unfinished basement, with a dirt floor, which looked like a vine cellar. It lent itself well to such an affair because it would permit good control over the officers. Preparations were completed before we left Mainz Most of the LTs in the 504 had recently completed jump school, hence they had never been Blasted.

The Prop Blast, the traditional airborne initiation ceremony is usually a stag affair. COL Cleland had invited the wives to the 508 Prop Blast at Benning in 1951, but many of us thought that the resulting affair lacked the spirit usually associated with Prop Blasts. Transportation to the club and back to the billets would be provided, and if a few of the officers had a little too much to drink, it would be handled by our unit. Mickey thought that MG Doleman should be Prop Blasted and invited him to the event. He also suggested to Ted Mataxis that the 504 Blast him. Ted was planning a similar ceremony for the 505 shortly after ours; as yet he had not been Blasted himself. Mickey told him that it would not be good to have his own unit Blast him. They would either be too easy on him or be too vindictive, which could lead to a very nasty situation. In any event, he should already be Blasted when his unit held their Prop Blast. Ted agreed.

The blastees were put through their paces, including MG Doleman and Ted Mataxis. There was some harmless harassment such as making the blastees duckwalk, do push-ups and swallow vegetable dye which would color their urine. LTs Jimmy MacGill and Bill Posey were in their element here. A few OFFs were turned back when they appeared before the "Board", and had to go through "training" at the hands of MacGill and Posey. Doleman was given a short count and Mataxis got a long count. During the course of the evening, Ted backed me up against the wall.

"You don't like me do you, Seibert?"

Tact conflicted with honesty but finally I said, "No, I really don't".

"Why not?"

"Well, I just don't like the way you operate."

"You think I am just a publicity hound don't you?"

"That's one thing."

"Well, I'll tell you. I'm not a Military Academy graduate and I want to be a general. I think I would make a good general. The only way I can get promoted is to make sure that my name is always in front of the generals who are going to sit on the promotion board. So I take every opportunity to get publicity for the 505 and myself. And that is the reason for it."

"Well, I can't argue with that, Colonel."

During the Prop Blast several OFFs got a bit obstreperous. 2LT Jebavy failed to do things in the ritual way the "board", of which I was a member, thought he should and sent him back for "more training." When he again foiled to measure up, the "board" wouldn't Blast him. At this he started to fight. He challenged LTC Marks and the members of the "board" and had to be physically restrained. He obviously had too much to drink. Finally some of the brawny NCOs who were standing by took him back to the BOQ and put him to bed.

After the Prop Blast was over, I wandered over to the dispensary. There were about eight 504 OFFs there getting all kinds of medication for hangovers, split knuckles, scrapped shins and other minor injuries. It was almost a disaster area! But it had been a good Prop Blast with no serious problems, which everyone had enjoyed.

Shortly after the Prop Blast the 8th Div was levied for one combat arms MAJ, who had a knowledge of tactics and knew the contingency plans of the Div. The OFF was to go on TDY to HQ, 7th Army, in Stuttgart for three months, to participate in a war game. The 8th Div nominee was MAJ Donald A. Seibert. Because of my tour in ODCSOPS, I was apparently the only MAJ who met all of the requirements. Mickey agreed with my argument that the S-3 of the Battle Group should not go. He protested, but Div wanted to send "good people". Mickey capitulated, all too easily I thought, saying, "Well, I think Don's good people. So he will go." Sam Barth, who had relinquished command of A Co to become the Asst S-3, would assume my duties.

Stuttgart is an old city, one I wanted to visit, but not this way. On arrival I was assigned a BOQ room. The group was to work under the G-2. It was rumored that LTG Davidson, the Army CDR, had directed his G-3 to conduct the war game, but COL Mel Zais had pleaded lack of personnel to handle it. Davidson had then turned it over to his G-2 and levied the divisions for people. The task was to examine the 7th Army's requirements for high performance aircraft in the event of a Russian invasion of Western Europe, looking especially at the need for reconnaissance and tactical air support of 7th Army. The need for troop lift aircraft was also included, but LTG Davidson thought that problem in hand.

There were four MAJs, one from each division in the 7th Army. Gus Braun from the 3rd Armored, Dale Taylor, who had been in my class at Leavenworth, from the 4th Armored and a fourth from the 24th IN Div. Three of us were very compatible, but the MAJ from the 24th Div did not fit in with the rest. He tried to impress everyone with his capability, background and contacts. He only succeeded in convincing us that he was a poor OFF. The proof came later when the promotion list to LTC was published. Both of us were in the zone of consideration, I made it but he did not. Gus and Dale were not in the zone.

The first six weeks we read ourselves into the situation, getting all of the intelligence information we could and developing procedures. Because of my experience with COL Dequoy in AWPD of ODCSOPS, I assumed the lead, but all four of us collaborated to develop the parameters, methodology and scenario. Decisions were made by random throws of the dice. It was an interesting exercise once we finally got to the guts of the game during the last six weeks of our TDY.

Dale Taylor was an easy person to work with, and Gus Braun proved to be a gem. Gus, the Asst G-3 of the 3rd AR Div, lived in a housing area north of Frankfurt. He was a stocky, round-faced officer, with a hearty laugh and a keen sense of humor. He was also a very effective staff officer. Almost every weekend he and I drove home together. Dale had only a short distance to go to the 4th AR Div, and the 24th Div was at Augsburg, Since I had my car, Gus left his with Maggie, his wife. Frankfurt was only a short drive from Mainz so I would drop him off at his quarters and then go on to Mainz. About half the time I stayed for dinner. Maggie was a good cook. The Brauns had two lively daughters, and I got to know the entire family well. Several weekends Gus and I stayed in Stuttgart to do some sightseeing. One week end we drove to Munich to see the Nymphenberg Palace, the Hofbrau Haus, the Frauenkirchen and other famous sights.

It was an interesting period of TDY. Finally, we briefed the study, first to the Army G-2, then the G-3. Both were unimpressed. When it was briefed to LTG Davidson, he said that it was what he wanted. The war game developed a formidable list of aircraft requirements. Davidson said that he needed something substantive to back up his request for aircraft if 7th Army was going to hold its position; the major mission of the AF in the opening days of war is to insure air superiority and then to interdict the battlefield. Close air support is a poor third priority. This war game was designed by LTG Davidson to be used in his argument for priority air support for 7th Army.

After briefing LTG Davidson our TDY terminated. The 504 was back in its normal training posture at Mainz, and I quickly settled down to my duties as S-3. Mickey was promoted late in June; shortly afterwards he had an elegant promotion party at the Franklin House. Activity again became routine.

COL Wilson called late in June to ask if I was interested in flying to Finland for the long 4th of July weekend. The '04 was not committed at the time and Mickey approved a four-day leave. COL Wilson and I flew from Frankfurt to Helsinki. We spent most of the time in Helsinki itself, although we made one trip by boat to Porvoo, which was only about 50 miles from the Soviet Union, the closest I had ever been to Russia during my Army career. Due to my assignment in ODCSOPS, and the high security clearances I had held, I was not permitted behind the Iron Curtain except to Berlin on the duty train. It was a pleasant leave. Helsinki is a delightful city and the Finns seemed friendly, independent, and prosperous.

Since Dad's death, I had worked to pick up Mother as a dependent. Finally, the paperwork came through. Because I would be paid quarters allowances for Mother, I was no longer authorized two rooms in the BOQ. All of my belongings were moved into one of the rooms I had occupied and I shared the bath with another officer, whom I rarely saw.

Early in August while we were in the field on a training exercise, Mickey formally promoted me, pinning silver leaves on my uniform. Actually my date of rank was 20 July, but the orders had been delayed.

Everyone I knew in Germany was invited to a promotion party at the Franklin House. The club put on a spectacular affair for me. The centerpiece of the buffet table was a huge cheeseboard featuring about ten European cheeses bought in local market in Mainz. The party cost a paltry $239.00, dirt cheap considering the amount of food and liquor consumed. It was a happy party at which I had more to eat and drink and more fun than any of the guests.

As a LTC I became the Battle Group Executive Officer and Sam Barth became the S-3. It was strange to have no real responsibilities. AH I did was wander around, see where I could help and try to keep out of everybody's way. A battle group really did not need two LTCs. There was always a question in my mind, and in Townsend's, as to which of us had purview over a given action. Mickey continued to lean on me, as we had established a fine rapport. It delighted me that he included me in most of his thinking and discussion. As the XO, the staff OFFs were rated by me so I got to know a great deal about their work. Most of my time was spent with Spurge Moore, the S-4, and with Sam Barth, the S-3. Ed Cavanaugh had been reassigned first as a student at the Armed Forces Staff College and then to the faculty of the Air Force Academy. Dick Cann, who had worked with Mickey before, joined the 504 and became the S-1.

The Battle Group was scheduled to go to Baumholder again in September for its annual ATT. Since Sam would rotate before me ATT, Dick Cann was made the S-3 and the S-1 functions were again assumed by Ross Goddard. Perhaps because of his legal training, Ross seemed a little lenient in dealing with some of our court-martial cases.

BG William B. Rosson, who had replaced BG Fuqua as the Asst Div CDR as well as the ABN Bde CDR was going to supervise the ATT. Rosson was an impressive OFF, he looked and acted like a general in the best sense of the term! Previously assigned to the staff of US Army Europe, he was a friend of COL Wilson's. He had hosted a cocktail party for Wilbur Wilson when he left Heidelberg for Vietnam, to which I had been invited. Earlier in the summer BG Rosson and I had become acquainted during a jump in France. The ABN Bde flew to the air base at Chaumont, France where we marshaled. It was the first time we had operated as a brigade since he had assumed command. He impressed me. He insured that everyone knew what was going on. His aide had put their sleeping bags on benches in one of the hanger offices without checking them. The bench on which Rosson was to sleep had a nail in it which punctured his air mattress. The aide did not offer his mattress to his boss, nor did Rosson ask him for another, he simply made the best of it. This was typical of BG Rosson.

The lady mayor of Chaumont invited BG Rosson to call on her to tour her home, the Chateau Val Des Escoliers, which had been built from the ruins of an ancient abbey several hundred years before. The beautiful chateau had been in her husband's family for generations. During WWI General Pershing had used it as his HQ. Rosson asked Mickey to accompany him; since Mickey had something else to do and was not particularly interested in old buildings, I was asked if I wanted to go. I jumped at the chance since I was both a history buff and interested in old houses. The mayor remembered General Pershing and had many things that had belonged to him or that he had used while he was in residence at the chateau, as well as many pictures of Pershing with both the mayor and her husband. It was a fascinating afternoon.

Since BG Rosson was supervising the ATT, we suspected that we were in for a really unique one. That turned out to be the case. Rosson decided that the normal routine of an intensive three-day exercise did not measure the ability of a unit or its commander and staff. In a three-day ATT every one functioned without sleep for the 72-hour period, which was totally artificial. He insisted instead on at least five days so that the staff would have to work in shifts and the commander and staff had to sleep. He also interjected many unusual features. The scenario covered the usual tactical maneuvers: movement to contact, defense, attack, withdrawal. But BG Rosson included a relief, a nuclear attack, a natural disaster and other situations. It was an unusual and demanding test.

During this ATT I had all of my field gear and experienced no discomfort, due in large part to my driver, PFC Oswald, an outstanding soldier. I only had to tell him something once; from then on he followed those instructions without prompting. On the first field exercise he drove for me, I told him to dig in every time we stopped. He did so and was kidded by COL Marks' driver and other staff drivers for being eager. But he dutifully carried out my instructions. He took care of my creature comforts so that I could devote my energies to my duties. Oswald also had a fine sense of direction; I rarely had to navigate for him except on reconnaissance of a new area.

As XO my duties were light. Mickey and Dick Cann, his S-3, were seldom in the CP. Townsend, the Deputy, was given various tactical missions. My chief function was to make sure that the staff was fully coordinated, to insure that everyone, staff as well as troopers, knew what was going on at all times, and to make sure that all elements of the plans were carried out. I made a point of getting around to the companies periodically, which was principally Mickey's and Townsend's job; but I checked support; supply, ammo, food; and to see if the word had gotten down. Although most of my time was spent in the CP, I did get out on reconnaissance now and then and even got to lead a convoy or two.

The exercise, unusual and interesting, taught me much. It was my first real assignment as XO of a unit larger than a company. The 504 did well. BG Rosson was complimentary in his critique of the Battle Group, of Mickey in particular, and of the S-3. He also commented that the XO had done an outstanding job keeping the staff coordinated and informed!

Shortly after the 504 returned to Mainz, planning for an ABN Bde operation in the British Zone at Sennelager was initiated. The Bde (the 504 and the 505) would marshall in Lee Barracks, truck to Frankfurt, emplane at Rhein-Main, then jump at Sennelager. By this time COL Arch Hamblen, who had been in my Advance Class, in the 508, and in the Pentagon with me, had replaced COL Mataxis as CDR of the 505. Bob Siegrist had become the XO of the 505 and Jerry Collins was now the S-3.

The DZ at Sennelager was a tank gunnery range; aerial photographs revealed many steel tank hulls with jagged metal edges scattered over it. The British or a detail under the DZSO covered the sharper edges with mattresses so that if our troopers struck them, they wouldn't be cut to pieces. We all looked forward to jumping on an unfamiliar DZ. The weather was cool with considerable rain forecast, we wanted to make the jump before the weather turned really bad.

The marshaling at Lee Kaseme as well as the movement to Rhein-Main went as planned. At Rhein-Main we encountered problems with the Air Force; the load masters of the C-l 30s, who have a great deal of authority, did not want to accept the heavy drop loads as they were rigged. I argued in vain. The loads had been rigged under the supervision of CW4 Olin Baggett, my Unit Administrator in K Co 504, who was now a heavy drop expert and in charge of the riggers at Biebrich. He assured me that they had been rigged in accordance with agreed Army/Air Force doctrine. Though load masters were the experts on heavy drop in charge of loading, securing and dropping equipment from aircraft cargo bays, they were not infallible. MAJ Will Chambers, the Army LNO to the AF, supported the load masters. He said the SOP called for a different rigging. Not only was there not time to rerig the loads, but I trusted Baggett. If he was satsified that the loads had been rigged in accordance with approved procedures, I was too. When Chambers told me we were wrong, I exploded. "Bull! These are the loads that we routinely rig for the Alpha Prime and for other alerts; these are the loads we are going into combat with. If the AF can't take them, we are in bad shape as far as our mission accomplishment is concerned."

Though I pressed the issue, Chambers insisted that the loads be modified. It was impossible to do so and make the station times, which are as important to the Army as to the Air Force.

"Well, if that is the case, we'll scrub the drop. If we can't drop our loads the way they are rigged, there is no point in wasting time or fuel," I said turning away.

Just then the CDR of the Air Wing, a BG, came up and wanted to know what the hold-up was. After explaining the situation to him I concluded, "I'm just about to scrub the mission. If the AF can't drop these loads, you can't support us in a real emergency. There is no point in going forward with this practice. We'll have to go back and work out procedures that we both agree on. These are rigged under currently agreed methods."

The wing CDR looked at them, then called the load masters together. They explained their objections; a few projections which the load masters claimed could hang up the loads as they exited the air craft, and the matter of the height of the rigged 3/4-ton trucks. The wing Commander decided that the AF would go with the loads if we could remove some of the minor projections. Baggett said his people could make the changes in a few minutes. The solution satisfied everyone and we were soon airborne.

The formation of the aircraft was Vees in trail. Mickey and I were in the lead ship of the first Vee, with MG Doleman in the left wing ship and BG Rosson in the right. All were to drop on silk. That meant that when the two wing ships saw silk from the lead ship, they would execute the drop; if there was no silk, there would be no jump. There were still controversies with the AF as to who controlled the jump; whether paratroopers must go on the green light or whether the jump master had discretion depending on his appraisal of the DZ and the conditions on it. At this time the jump-master still made the decision to go or not go when the green light came on. It was unusual for the CO and his XO to be in the same aircraft, however, Townsend was in a different ship.

As our aircraft made its approach to the DZ, it was waved around because the winds on the ground were marginal. The C-130 banked sharply to come around for a second approach. Second Lieutenant Ted Bara told Mickey that he felt sick and asked if he could stand in the door for a minute. The red light had remained on since the turn around would take less than 10 minutes, so the troopers were standing and hooked up, Mickey stepped aside to let Bara get to the door. As he stood there, Bara popped his reserve chute. This is serious inside the aircraft, especially at the door. The air current caught the reserve chute and sucked it out the door, pulling the suspension lines between Mickey's legs. Bara's reserve chute deployed when it reached the slip stream, jerking him from the plane about a mile or so from the DZ. Mickey was almost pulled from the ship with Bara, but managed to scramble aside as Bara exited. Mickey looked out the door and gasped.

"Oh, my God. They're jumping on Bara's silk," he shouted. Out of each of the wing ships came a body from which a parachute blossomed. Obviously the pilots of the wing ships had seen Bara's silk and turned on the green light. Realizing that there was some problem, they immediately switched back to red so only the two generals jumped. As BG Rosson recalled later, "Before exiting on the green light, I looked from the door to the DZ ahead. It was about two miles away with woods below. I did not see Bara's chute, and was startled when the green light went on. I jumped on a reflex action and landed in the woods near Bara, who was hung up in a tree. The landing having cost me a sprained ankle, I experienced some difficulty in walking the mile or so to the DZ, where I met General Doleman at the observers' stand."

Just then there was a call from COL Jack Singlaub, the DZSO, who reported that the winds were marginal and recommended that the jump be scrubbed. Mickey vehemently disagreed.

"Hell, no. With two generals in the air, we are going, regardless of the winds," he decided.

There was no question about jumping he told the pilot through the load master. Shortly the aircraft were in jumping attitude, the green light came on, and the entire 504 jumped. Mickey fumed all the way down to the DZ. The DZSO scrubbed the jump for the 505 and they air landed about 25 miles away.

When Mickey got on the ground all he could say was, "Where is that lieutenant? Where is that lieutenant? He's ruined my career."

Finally he calmed down. The first thing, of course, was to find the two generals and the lieutenant. Fortunately, as soon as the three had exited their aircraft, Singlaub saw Bara's reserve and understood what had happened. He dispatched several jeeps to pick up the jumpers. One of them found MG Doleman, but BG Rosson limped all the way back to the DZ. We made sure that Mickey Marks did not see 2LT Bara until the 504 got back to Mainz.

The 504 ABG had gone in light; each of us in the command section was carrying a part of the CP: an arctic tent, radios, drafting supplies, etc. The Co's jeep, two scout vehicles and some weapons carriers were in the heavy drop load, but the battle group would be operating on foot.

Once the generals were accounted for, excitement over their early exit evaporated and the maneuver proceeded. Doleman was called back to Div HQ and rumors began to fly about the 504 might move to Berlin.

There had been a lengthy debate before we left Mainz as to whether the basic load of ammunition should be taken. Under most circumstances, whenever a unit left its Kaseme for the field, it took its basic load with it. The Div G-4 questioned whether we should drop our basic load on a practice jump.

Most of us thought we should; if there were any problems with rigging those loads, we would discover them. On the other hand, if the ammunition spilled all over the DZ, it would be difficult to police it up or reconstitute the load. The decision was made at Div, or higher, to leave the basic loads in the ammo dump at Mainz. This was an unfortunate decision for the 504 as later events proved.

The Berlin Wall was erected the night before the 504 jumped. The next day, the 8th Div was ordered to reinforce the American Garrison in Berlin with one battle group. Initially the 504 was considered because it was close to the Berlin Autobahn at Sennelager and could move rapidly. Since the 504 did not have its basic load, that course of action was dropped. Instead, the 1st Battle Group of the 18th IN, commanded by COL Glover S. Johns, Jr, moved from Mannheim. We were unhappy, it would have been a great opportunity for the unit, for the CDR and for all of the OFFs and men. The experience would have been outstanding; but more important, it would have gotten the 504 into the middle of things, which we all wanted, since that is the essence of being a Regular.

Due to the situation in Berlin, the maneuver was shortened. The 504 and 505 were airlifted back to Wiesbaden. The ABN Bde was placed on alert when it returned to home stations, but nothing further came of it.

One day, shortly after the Sennelager jump, I stopped by Mickey's office to pick him up for lunch. The phone rang; the call was evidently from someone senior to Mickey because he kept saying, "Sir, Yes, Sir, No, Sir" and was trying to argue as politely as possible. Thinking he would prefer to talk privately, I started to leave the office but Mickey vehemently motioned for me to stay. "He is not going to want the job... But he is doing a great job for the Battle Group and the Division right here... Is that final, Sir? Well, all right, Sir."

Mickey hung up and looked at me somberly, saying, "That was Jack Wright. He just informed me that you're being reassigned to Div as the G-4." Mickey dropped dispiritedly into his chair as I vented my displeasure. Aside from not wanting to be a logistician, I didn't want to leave the '04; I enjoyed working for Mickey Marks and liked the people I was working with.

"Now calm down, Donald. You heard me argue with Jack. There is nothing that he can do about it. The decision has been made by General Doleman."

"I want to talk to Jack Wright. Let me argue with him. I am sure I can persuade him to forget it."

Mickey gave his permission. After lunch I drove to Bad Kreuznach (BK). First, I went to see the G-l. He told me that the matter had not been settled; two other officers under consideration, but I was the prime prospect. It looked as if I was going to get the nod to be the G-4. When the G-l told me there was nothing he could due to influence the decision, I went to see COL Wright. We chatted a bit about the Advance Class and the 508.

"Now about this G-4 thing, Sir," I said. "It's not my bag and I don't want any part of it."

Wright smiled and began to discuss the matter with me seriously. He said I needed staff experience, that the Div needed good officers on the general staff, that this seemed an ideal assignment for both. It was important that the G-4 be somebody who appreciated what the troops needed in the way of support. When he failed to sway me after 20 minutes, COL Wright said, "I see I can't persuade you. You might as well go talk to the General."

He announced me to MG Doleman. I walked in and reported to him. Doleman left his desk and we sat in adjacent armchairs. He lit his pipe; I talked for 15 minutes straight. MG Doleman didn't say a word, he nodded his head occasionally as he puffed on his pipe, but he just let me talk on. When there is no rebuttal or argument even the most agitated speaker soon winds down. Obviously, this was the technique Doleman used on me because I finally stopped talking and looked at him pleadingly.

"Don, I appreciate everything you have said and I agree with you. I understand your feelings. I think you're doing an outstanding j ob for the 504 and the Division, but I think that you will do more for the Division as my G-4. The decision is made. You are going to be the G-4."

There was nothing further to be said, the CG had made his decision. All I could do was say, "Yes, Sir", salute, about face and walk out.

COL Wright wanted to know the gist of the conversation after which he informed me that I was to report for duty within four days. That meant completing whatever projects I had at Mainz, executing efficiency reports on the 504 Battle Group staff OFFs, clearing the 504 and the BOQ and moving to BK. The move posed no problem as I could get a 3/4 ton truck from the Battle Group to move all of my belongings in one trip. Before I returned to Mainz, I stopped by the Billeting office and was assigned a room in the BOQ. In some respects life at BK would be more convenient than at Mainz, because I could walk from my BOQ to the HQ, the PX and the club. I liked the BK area, but I liked Mainz better.

After a hectic clearance and a pleasant hail and farewell party at Mainz, I settled in at Bad Kreuznach. My duties as G-4, different from anything I had done previously, immediately immersed me. There was much to learn; so much I did not know.

As the G-4 of the 8th IN Div I had staff supervision over all logistical functions: supply, medical service, maintenance, buildings, graves registration, food service and transportation. The 8th Div Support CMD (DISCOM) personnel were the logistics operators; the G-4 personnel were the logistics planners and policy-makers. The DISCOM CDR, a COL, was a professional with whom I had no difficulty working.

There were many contingency plans for crises in various parts of Europe and North Africa to become familiar with. As the S-3 of the 504, I had knowledge of many of the plans, but now I had to become acquainted with a different aspect of them. There were also plans for movement of the 8th Div in the event of a Soviet attack; these included stockpiles of supplies which had to be rotated and maintained. Some of the most intricate plans dealt with the refueling requirements for the Div in the event of a move.

There was a major ammo area east of the Rhine, manned by displaced persons (DPs), mostly Latvians and Lithuanians. They were organized as a semi-military unit with a DP in charge who had been given the rank of major. He ruled with an iron hand. I envied that discipline.

A week or so after I assumed my duties as the G-4, COL Wright announced at the morning conference that the 8th Div was to be mechanized. All IN units were to be provided with armored personnel carriers (APCs). Several questions, including the fate of the ABN Bde, were still being resolved by DA. This change meant that the Div faced a major task in receiving and distributing the mechanized equipment, and from then on, servicing it. In addition, there would be monumental training tasks to acquaint the troops with their new equipment and tactics. There were many problems to be solved: working with the G-3 to decide the priorities of issue and mechanization of the units; insuring that the maintenance capability was phased in simultaneously with the mechanization; disposing of old equipment replaced by the APCs; obtaining adequate tools and spare parts; and, finally, insuring the availability of petroleum, oil and lubricants (POL).

Since the 24th Div at Augsburg had just completed its mechanization, I suggested that I visit it to discuss with the G-4 the problems that Div had encountered phasing into mechanization. COL Wright approved and I made a three-day visit to Augsburg. In addition to many profitable discussions with the G-4 and DISCOM Commander, I also saw several old friends, including Charlie Jackson who commanded a mechanized battalion at Ulm. Many pitfalls were pointed out to me that the 8th Div could avoid; I returned to BK with copious notes. The mechanization of the 8th Division began smoothly enough.

COL Wright had an effective technique as Chief of Staff. Each morning he met with the principal staff (the G-l, G-2, G-3, G-4 and G-5) during which each of us summarized what was going on in our area. Once a week he met with the combined staff, both principal and special, including Aviation (AVN), Chemical (CW), Engineer (Engr), Medical (MC), Ordnance (ORD), Quartermaster (QM) and Signal (SIG) OFFs, the AG, the PM and the SJA. Once a month the Div CG held a Commanders' Conference with the staff in attendance. This insured that both CDRs and Staff were fully informed on what was going on in the Division.

BG Rosson was also instrumental in insuring that everyone was kept informed. He was constantly on the go, as was MG Doleman. As ABN Bde CDR, Rosson paid particular attention to the units at Mainz. The G-4 section was very much involved in airborne mission support and my Asst was the Bde S-4, hence I saw a great deal of Rosson as well as visiting Mainz occasionally.

Based on the many ABN contingency plans, I applied for jump status, maintaining that my job necessitated jumping periodically. It was approved without much delay. Toward the end of November I managed to get a jump at Finthen from an Army aircraft (Beaver).

The motto of the 8th IN Div intrigued me. It was adopted during WWII. BG Charles D.W. Canham, the Asst Div CDR, was preparing to receive the surrender of a large force of Germans. The German CDR asked him, "What are your credentials?"

Canham gestured toward the 8th Div soldiers covering the proceedings with their weapons and said, "These are my credentials."

That phrase caught the imagination of the troops who adopted it as the motto of the Division.

The third week after I moved to Div HQ, it was announced that MG Doleman was being reassigned to HQ, USAREUR, and that MG Andrew J. Goodpaster was replacing him. Immediately, the staff was plunged into a frenzy of activity to bid farewell to Doleman and to welcome Goodpaster. COL Wright maintained that the staff could not serve two masters at one time: he directed that up until the day of the change of command, all activities be directed toward MG Doleman; once the change of command took place, the staff would focus on MG Goodpaster.

The night before the change of command there was a dinner dance for MG and Mrs Doleman. During the evening I had an opportunity to talk with MG Doleman privately. *In vino veritas;* shedding my awe of stars under the influence of alcohol, I attacked Doleman humorously.

"Sir, I have never called a General Officer a son of a bitch, but I am certainly tempted to do so in your case. You must have known before I was reassigned to Div HQ that you were leaving. Why did you insist I move?"

MG Doleman grinned.

"You know it was an interesting coincidence, Don. Just before you came in to see me, I had a call from General Bruce Clarke. We talked for about a half hour on the phone. I used the identical arguments you did as to why I should remain with the 8th Division as its Commanding General and should not be reassigned to a staff position in Heidelberg. General Clarke considered my reasons carefully before making the decision that I was going to be his DCSOPS in spite of them. It is ironic that ten minutes later you and I went through the same sequence. In answer to your question specifically, I wanted to make sure that my successor had the best possible staff available to him when he took over the Division. I wanted you for my G-4 had I continued in command. So I went ahead with your reassignment." We parted good friends.

The change of command ceremony at Bad Kreuznach included representative elements from each of the battle groups and major units. BG Rosson was the CDR of Troops, supported by the primary staff of the Div, including me as G-4. It was a simple but impressive ceremony which went well. GEN Clarke passed the 8th Div colors from MG Doleman to MG Goodpaster.

Goodpaster's personality was different from Doleman's. He was a more academic individual, which is not to say that he wasn't equally as capable as a CDR and as a tactician. Doleman was a field soldier, an Infantryman. Goodpaster, an Engineer, had a more scholarly approach to the solution of tactical problems.

To familiarize MG Goodpaster with all of the activities of the 8th Div, each staff agency in turn briefed him. This was good for me because it served to crystalize in my own mind many of the things that I had been struggling with in trying to orient myself.

In late November I went to Berlin to represent MG Goodpaster at Thanksgiving dinner with the 18th IN Battle Group as well as to check up on supply and maintenance problems resulting from the precipitous move. It was an interesting trip on the duty train, which was sealed at Frankfurt. The seals were not broken until the train arrived in Berlin. This procedure was agreed upon by the US and USSR to avoid problems.

The 18th IN was well housed in a fairly modern Kaserne. A provision of the WWII Peace Treaty required the Federal Republic of Germany to pay all expenses of the four occupying powers in Berlin. Hence US units there received excellent support.

COL Johns was bitter about the after-action report the 8th Div Staff had prepared on his Battle Group's move. He said that he was given commendations by everyone from CINCUSAREUR to President Kennedy, "but there is no honor within my own family". He claimed that the Division Staff tore him apart. Although I had not participated in the preparation of the report, I had read it. I tried to explain to COL Johns that it was a means of analyzing areas that could be improved if such a move was ordered again. It was not a reflection on him or the 18th IN, rather, it was a criticism of the Div and the support it had given him in his move. He was not particularly mollified, although he accepted my explanation. Certainly the 18th IN had made mistakes which were pointed out in the report. Any unit sent forward under those circumstances would have made mistakes. These were pointed out together with suggested corrections. A CDR who cannot accept constructive criticism does not deserve his command. COL Johns had taken umbrage with the after-action report which had been forwarded to him for comment; rather than trying to learn from the mistakes of all parties concerned. He gave me back the report with his personal remarks.

During my three-day visit, I had an opportunity to see a bit of Berlin, to walk down the Kurfurstendamm, the main avenue of the shopping district and visit the Kaiser Wilhelm Memorial Church, destroyed in an air raid. The ruins of the bell tower have been preserved as a symbol. Next to it an octagonal glass tower houses the new church. The contrast between the two structures is a vivid reminder of the war.

Of course the most interesting sights in Berlin were the wall itself as well as Check Point Charlie. A guide led me through attics and across rooftops to get to one of the OPs from which to see across the wall. Immediately after the wall had gone up, these OPs had been established in an attempt to aid anyone trying to get into West Berlin without provoking any incidents.

Spandau Prison was also of interest. As the Russians were guarding it during my visit my escort suggested that we not get too close because they were touchy about visitors. To cap my tour I visited the stadium where Hitler had made a mockery of the 1936 Olympic Games. The trip was profitable to me as G-4 and interesting and enjoyable personally.

On returning to BK, the mechanization of the Div faced me. I also became involved in planning a Rhine River crossing exercise that was to be held early in December. In the event that the 8th Div had to occupy its GAO positions, the bridges across the Rhine might be blown, requiring the use of pontoon and foot bridges as well as rafts. The FTX was an opportunity to rehearse such a crossing. This would be my first field exercise as G-4. It was a strange feeling to be in the rear instead of at the cutting edge. But such matters as the huge amount of equipment needed by the engineers in constructing the bridges, the gasoline supply, main supply routes (MSRs), march tables and medical evacuation occupied me. My section did an outstanding job in planning the logistical aspects of the exercise. I consulted frequently with the DISCOM CDR, the logistical operator. As a result we worked out many of the problems which might otherwise have crept into the plans.

The river crossing operation required careful coordination because the Rhine River, a major artery of commerce, had to be closed to all traffic for the period of the actual crossing. The captains of the barges which ply up and down the river day and night, as well as the shippers, are not well disposed to the river being closed to their traffic. However, they recognize the need for these practices during which every effort is made to minimize the length of time that the river is closed.

The morning of the actual crossing was cold and foggy. An early breakfast was served in the CG's Mess on the west side of the Rhine, after which we followed MG Goodpaster to watch the engineers launch the assault boats. When the Infantry had secured a bridge head on the east bank, a rafting operation was initiated, followed by the construction of the pontoon "swing bridge" for vehicular traffic, as well as a foot bridge for troops. The bridges remained across the river for three days; periodically, sections were opened to permit commercial traffic to pass. The operation went well.

Once across the Rhine, the Div moved to a temporary exercise area. Whenever elements of the US Army operated outside the major training areas such as Baumholder, Grafenwohr or Hohenfels, it leased farms over which to maneuver. This was the reason that most FTXs were conducted in the wintertime after the harvests were in. The farmers reaped substantial profits from leasing their frozen land for such purposes.

As G-4, I operated from the Div Main Area, shuttling back and forth between the Forward Tactical CP, the Main CP, and the Rear. Much of my business was with the DISCOM CDR who was at the Div Rear. There were few major incidents. Several vehicles turned over on the trip back and a few tanker trucks had to be towed in.

It was an instructive maneuver for me. As a new G-4 I made many mistakes, but MG Goodpaster did not become concerned. As he pointed out, that is why we practiced. During the problem I occasionally saw Mickey Marks and elements of the 504, but most of the units I saw were support rather than combat outfits.

Once the maneuver was over, we again took up the task of mechanization. Together with my staff, I set up a schedule to visit each of the battle groups as well as every Kaserne occupied by 8th Div troops to see for myself the physical condition of the buildings and hard stands. It was instructive to look at the units and Kasernes from a logistical point of view rather than from the perspective of operations or command.

In late November I was invited to attend another 504 Prop Blast at Baumholder. The Battle Group had adopted the custom of holding its Prop Blasts there because the officers were away from wives and civilians, were on post, did not have to drive and could be more easily controlled. As it was on a Saturday night I was able to make it. I had a room in the BOQ so did not have to drive back to BK that night. The day after the Prop Blast the Mainz Troopers, now the 8th Div Team, were playing for the European Command Championship. The team had a few players from other elements of the Div, but was essentially the old Mainz Troopers. Both Mickey and I wanted to see the game. We decided that since we both had our cars at Baumholder, we would drive back to Bad Kreuznach, leave my car, and then I would ride with Mickey and Sybil to Karlsruhe, where the game was being played.

On Sunday, I was delayed in clearing the BOQ and did not leave with Mickey and Sybil. In the short interval between our departures, a freezing rain made the road from Baumholder to the autobahn a sheet of ice. There was a steep hill leading from the cantonment area which I gingerly began to descend. When only a short distance down the hill, my car began to slide. The only way I could stop or control the car was to steer on the shoulder of the road, which was less slick because of the leaves and other vegetation. Looking down the hill, I saw that a 5,000 gallon tanker truck had jack-knifed at the bottom. There was a very narrow path around it that I thought I might negotiate even without chains. Cautiously, I eased the car down the shoulder of the road, occasionally sliding. It was a hair-raising experience, which took about an hour. Finally I got around the truck and proceeded to the autobahn. By the time I got to BK it was 1500.

Mickey had given me up and gone on. I was glad that he got to see the game, I had to be content with hearing it described on the Armed Forces Network. But I cheered as loudly as the rest when the Troopers won.

One of my problems was COL John Acuff, CO of the 16th Infantry. COL Acuff was a firm believer in the adage that the squeaky wheel gets the grease. Consequently, almost every morning I got a phone call from him or his Deputy about some problem in the 16th IN. Most were bona fide but not urgent problems, which were being taken care of in the normal course of business. One of them was the mess hall stoves at Baumholder. They needed a complete overhaul, hence there was a project underway to replace them. There was also a long term plan for the rehabilitation of the barracks there. But COL Acuff was not satisfied. After several weeks I told him that we were doing the best we could, but that we could not give the 16th special attention every time he demanded it. This was reported to COL Wright who recognized the situation. He instructed me to keep him informed of any problems with the battle groups, especially the 16th. He also received many calls from COL Acuff. There is a virtue, of course, in making known any legitimate needs, but it can be overdone with the result that any clout a good complaint carries is lost.

As mechanization and other projects proceeded, I began to think about Christmas. My brother, Bill, had written to tell me that his ship, the *Essex,* an aircraft carrier, would be in Rotterdam over Christmas. Bill and I were never close, but we got along as well as most brothers. Since I had no plans for Christmas, I suggested that we spend it together in Rotterdam. We arranged to rendezvous on the 23rd of December.

Leaving Bad Kreuznach about 0600, I arrived at Rotterdam in the early afternoon. After registering at the Rijn Hotel, the same one I had stayed at with COL Wilson the year before, I dropped my luggage and drove to the docks. The *Essex* was having open house, so there were three liberty boats operating, one for visitors, one for sailors and one for officers. The crowd was large at the visitors' landing; the officers' liberty boat had just left and the next one would not leave for another hour, so I walked over to the sailors1 area. A boat was just getting ready to depart, I jumped aboard. As I was in civilian clothes the coxswain asked for my ID. He merely glanced at my current Armed Forces ID card, nodded his head and we were under way. At the hanger deck, where we debarked, a Marine guard requested my ID as civilian visitors were supposed to go to another area. When he saw that I was a LTC, he wanted to have me escorted to "officers' country".

"Hell, I'm only here to see my brother, Chief Petty Officer Bill Seibert. Just tell me how to find him."

When he was convinced that I was not going to adhere to normal protocol, the guard had someone escort me to the Chiefs' Quarters. Bill had just gotten off duty. We went ashore by the enlisted liberty boat.

We spent a pleasant leave together. I had made reservations for the Christmas Eve Dinner in the Main Dining Room of the Rijn Hotel, the same affair COL Wilson and I had enjoyed so much the previous year. In Holland there are two Christmas dinner celebrations, the big one on Christmas Eve, a dinner dance, with much singing and too much food, and a more restrained one on Christmas Day. Again the atmosphere was joyous, with everyone joining in the singing, swaying from side to side. Many of the of the songs I knew. The sumptuous eight-course dinner, served over a four-hour period, followed the same format with the sorbet offered just before the roast goose to permit the hors d'oeuvres, fish and soup to digest. The meal was delicious and the Gemutlichkeit catching. We enjoyed the evening.

The next day we drove around the area, but since it was Christmas, everything was closed. That night we ate in a restaurant at the top of the observation tower overlooking the harbor, where we had another fine meal. The view of the harbor was spectacular. All of the ships, including the *Essex,* were decorated with strings of lights. The scene looked unreal.

The day after Christmas we planned to drive into Germany, I wanted to show Bill a bit of the area as well as get him some good sauerbraten. Just as we were leaving the hotel, my assistant called to inform me that I was to return within the next 48 hours as the G-l had received orders reassigning me. He couldn't tell me where I was going having only an alert from the G-l. With that much leeway, I decided we would go ahead with our planned trip on the 26th and I would return to BK on the 27th. It was an interesting drive through the north German countryside. The sauerbraten was good, but compared critically with Mother's, we agreed that hers was better. That was one of her specialities.

On the morning of 27 December I took Bill to the *Essex* after breakfast, and then headed back to BK. The following morning the G-l gave me orders reassigning me to the 1st Armored Division at FT Hood, TX. The tours of all personnel in Germany had been extended because of the Berlin Wall. Hence, I was puzzled about my reassignment. The G-l speculated that I was getting command of a Bn. He suggested I call COL John Spears, now Chief of The Infantry Branch, in the Pentagon. After much delay, I got through to COL Spears. I explained to him that this was my first tour in Europe that I had come prepared to spend at least three years there to see something of the Continent, and hoped to get command of one of the USAREUR Armored Infantry Battalions, the only IN Bns in the Army.

John enlightened me, "They are reactivating the 1st Armored Division under the Golf Series TO&E. Under it there will be battalions grouped under a brigade rather than a regiment. You have been selected to command one of the battalions."

When I discussed the merits of waiting for a Bn in Europe, Spears pointed out that the possibility of getting one of those in USAREUR was slim. He assured me that I was going to get command of a battalion in the 1st AR Div, the first to be organized under the so-called "ROAD Concept". It took only a little thought to convince me that the important thing was to get command of a BN and I told John I would accept gladly.

After only three months in Bad Kreuznach I was going back to the CONUS. The Transportation Officer, under my staff supervision, made arrangements to have my car shipped two weeks before I left, insuring that it would be available as soon as I got home. The BOQ was within walking distance of the office and club; a staff car was available for official business outside the area. The sudden orders made it necessary to complete my paperwork and projects in a very short time, so one of my NCOs drove my car to Bremerhaven for processing and shipment. This required only a special form, actually a limited power of attorney. The Transportation Officer also arranged to ship my footlockers by military air so that my fatigues and field gear would be available at FT Hood when I arrived.

John C. Bennett, a MAJ in the G-3 section, who was on the outstanding promotion list to LTC, had been selected to replace me. He moved into my office immediately. Since he knew all of the staff OFFs in the Division, and was aware of the mechanization effort, he needed only a short briefing before he was ready to assume his new responsibilities. Because I do not believe in overlaps, I turned over the reins to him as soon as he felt ready to take them.

Four days before I left the Div, I made my last jump with BG Rosson from a Beaver at Finthen. Rosson was making three or four jumps he needed to earn his senior jump wings. Since I had many things to do, I made only one jump, though I would have preferred to make the seven I needed for qualification as a Master Jumper. In spite of a lowering overcast, the winds were not high and we made a good jump.

The G-4 Section Officers arranged a dinner party for me several nights before I was scheduled to depart. They invited many of my friends throughout the Division including MG and Mrs Goodpaster and BG Rosson.

The day before I was to fly out of Rhein-Main, I told COL Wright that I was going to Mainz to say goodbye to friends, have dinner with Mickey and Sybil and other friends, and perhaps to spend the night. The CofS seemed strangely uneasy about the trip and suggested that I stick around the HQ.

Donald A. Seibert

With no duties, I saw no point in hanging around BK rather than spending the time with friends. Finally COL Wright told me that there was to be an awards ceremony at 1600 at which I would be given the Army Commendation Medal (ARCOM). Ceremonies of this sort never appealed to me, this was no exception, especially since it meant I had to curtail my farewells at Mainz. But it had been arranged, so I promised to be back by 1530. The farewell visit at Mainz was short but pleasant.

On my return to Bad Kreuznach I was told to see the CofS immediately. Everyone seemed ill at ease. COL Wright looked at me glumly, saying, "We don't know our General too well. We just assumed he would follow current Div policy. When I took your citation for the ARCOM to him to sign, he announced a new policy. He doesn't believe field grade officers should be given the ARCOM, but that it be reserved for Co grade OFFs and EM. He is giving you a Certificate of Achievement. He said we should give you credit for your fine job as G-4 in your efficiency report. He wanted me to warn you in advance so that you would not be taken aback.

It really made no difference to me. There is some virtue in getting a medal rather than a piece of paper; the ribbon can be worn on your breast as a visible token of a job well done. But fundamentally I agreed with the CG, too many medals are given to officers with little justification. This cheapens awards. The important thing is what is said in the efficiency report.

A short time later we trooped into the CG's office. BG Rosson, the principal staff, as well as most of the people I had worked with were there. After the presentation, there was coffee and cake, during which the Generals and others present said goodbye.

The next morning I was driven to Rhein-Main in a staff car, shortly I was manifested and airborne. Upon landing at McGuire Air Force Base, I changed into civilian clothes, before traveling to College Point. It was good to see Mother and the rest of the family. The next morning I picked up my car at the Brooklyn Army Terminal, delighted to have wheels again.

Most of my ten-day leave was spent in New York with the family and friends. As I headed south I stopped in Washington to see Wick and Betty and Sam King.

My orders required me to report to FT Hood on the 31st of January. Arriving on the 30th, I signed in at Combat Command A (CCA) of the 1st Armored Division, a separate unit commanded by BG Roy Lassetter. The 1st AR Div had not yet been reactivated.

334

CHAPTER 14

REGULAR

FT Hood, and more specifically CCA of the 1st AR Div, was the scene of great activity my first week there. Many others, like myself, were reporting in for the reactivation of the Division. Among them were several old friends: COL Donn Pepke and MAJ Barney Broughton from Pentagon days, LTC Dick Wise from my Leavenworth class, and LTC Dick Cann recently of Mainz. Dick Wise, Dick Cann and I were slated for battalion command positions. Barney, though on the promotion list to LTC, would have to be satisfied with an assignment as a Bn XO until he was promoted, COL Donn Pepke was to be the 1st AR Div CofS.

The Army's discriminatory policy on quarters for bachelor officers once again confronted me. Each Bn CO was authorized a set of family quarters on post into which he could move on arrival. These were "designated or position quarters", a privilege of command, which provided a suitable setting for the commander to entertain his officers and other guests. My application for an exception to policy for the assignment of the family quarters authorized the commander of my battalion to a bachelor was disapproved. Seeking an alternative, I requested assignment of one of the 12 small cottages built during WWII to house regimental commanders and other colonels. These had two bedrooms, a living room, a dining room, kitchen, and bath, even an orderly's room. One of them would have served me admirably, but again my request was turned down because these houses were reserved for transient married officers, those who were awaiting assignment of quarters or clearing post. There were no quarters available on post for a senior bachelor officer; the billeting personnel (and apparently the senior commanders on post) were completely indifferent to the needs of their bachelor officers. I had to settle for a room in a WWII wooden BOQ. The billeting officer proudly pointed out to me that the room he was assigning to me had a sink in it, the only room in the BOQ so equipped!

Since I had picked up Mother as a dependent, I was only authorized one room in the BOQ. I had offered to drop her as a dependent if given suitable quarters. This would have meant the loss of my quarters allowance which was sent to her each month. However, I could have increased my monthly allotment to her to make up the difference. Though willing to do so to get adequate quarters, I was not going to give up that money just to get an additional BOQ room! Consequently, I moved my luggage into the BOQ (my household goods were still in storage), putting my name on the list for the first available room in the modern brick BOQ.

Meanwhile, I looked for my footlockers. The BK Transportation OFF had shipped them via military air freight so that my field equipment would be waiting when I arrived at Fort Hood. But none of my baggage could be located on Post. The FT Hood Transportation OFF finally wired to BK to trace the shipment. He sheepishly informed me that while the footlockers had, in fact, been air lifted from Germany to Dover Air Force Base in Delaware, they would be transported from Dover by truck when there was enough baggage to make up a full truckload! My uniforms finally arrived at Hood 2 1/2 months after I did!

Having found a place to sleep, I set about becoming acquainted with the personnel with whom I would be serving as well as the units, currently active, which would be absorbed into the 1st AR Div. CCA had one IN Bn, one AR (tank) Bn and a HHC. The 1st Battalion, 6th Infantry was tasked to cadre the 5th Battalion, 6th Infantry which I would activate, organize, train and command. Rather than develop a cadre list, it had been decided that Co D would form the nucleus of the 5th of the 6th (5/6). CPT Ernest K. Gruene, Jr (Kyle) the D Co CO reported to me. He was tentatively slated to be my S-3 when D Co was redesignated Co A, 5th Bn, 6th IN. Co D had been tasked by CCA with writing lessons plans for the Advanced Individual Training (AIT), and Basic Unit Training (BUT) to be given to all Infantry filler personnel.

The 1st Armored Division was officially reactivated on 3 February. Cadre personnel began pouring into the Bn HQ located in a WWII wooden HQ building. The first to report in was MSG Oliver E. Allen, a slender, intense, extremely talented Noncommissioned Officer. He was one of the finest NCOs, soldiers, men, I have ever been privileged to serve with. MSG Allen became the Bn Sergeant Major (SGM). Next came MAJ William E. Smith, a stocky IN OFF who would be my XO. Then CPT Harry B. Porterfield, a quiet, reserved, but experienced Infantryman reported for duty. He was made the Bn S-4, and immediately became immersed in receiving and distributing the tons of supplies and equipment assigned an Armored Infantry Bn (AIB). He was invaluable in getting things organized initially. Five other CPTs followed; four were to command companies, the fifth was assigned as the Adj or 8-1. In bunches, 22 newly commissioned 2LTs arrived. Interspersed with the OFFs, NCOs with various military occupational specialty (MOS) codes joined the unit. Soon, each of the Cos had a 1SG, Supply SGT, Mess SGT and at least two PSGs. In addition, the 5/6 received a Maintenance SGT, Personnel (Pers) SGT, Commo SGT and several clerks. Within two weeks a skeleton organization was in place.

CPT Gruene, who was fully acquainted with Fort Hood and would have been of great help to all of us in learning our way around the Post, had been detailed by BG Lassetter to put on a series of demonstrations of Armored Infantry tactics for the newly-assigned OFFs and NCOs. These demonstrations were part of an indoctrination course designed to ensure that all of the personnel serving with an armored division for the first time were familiar with the tactics and techniques employed. Every OFF and NCO got to act as an APC and tank crew member and to fire the tank gun during the course. Company D and one of the tank Cos put on several excellent demonstrations which assisted me in getting into the "Armor frame of mind".

Gruene insisted that the demonstrations start on time; one night his OFFs and maintenance personnel went to the tank firing range to scavenge parts from abandoned APCs used as targets, in order to insure that the demonstration went off as scheduled the following day. An entire ramp assembly was among the parts cannibalized that evening. Gruene impressed me; a Texas A&M graduate, was sharp, precise in his military courtesy, very professional in his duties, demanding of his subordinates, but also much concerned with their development. He gave his LTs and NCOs careful instructions on each mission and afforded them an opportunity to ask questions. He did not tell them how to do a job, but offered many suggestions that enabled them to avoid manifest mistakes. If I had one criticism of CPT Gruene it was that he was overly competitive resulting in a little less than full cooperation with the other Co COs. In the few opportunities we had to talk, it became obvious to me that the Gruene had something on his mind. It came out while we rode in a jeep to one of his demonstrations.

When I asked if he was ready to take over his duties as S-3, he turned to me with a resolute expression on his face, almost as if to say "It's now or never". "Sir, I've been meaning to talk to you about that. I know that it would be great experience for me to be the S-3 of a battalion. And I've already commanded two companies, so I suppose I should be looking for some other experience, but damn it, Sir, I think there is nothing like being a company commander. Can't you let me stay in A Co? I'll be the best company commander you have."

His outburst did not surprise me. He reminded me of my own desire to remain with a company, probably the most satisfying job in the Army. Though his experience in Co D would have made him invaluable as the S-3, I appreciated his desire to remain with A Co. Just that morning, the 1st Bde

S-1 had asked me if I would accept an AR CPT as the Bn S-3. The Div, which had been assigned too many AR OFFs, was trying to find appropriate jobs for them. Though I had hesitated about accepting an AR OFF as the S-3 of an IN Bn, Kyle's plea triggered my decision.

The expression on Gruene's face had become more and more grim as I hesitated in answering him. He appeared convinced that he had overstepped himself, perhaps getting off to a bad start with me. Suppressing a smile, I answered, "If you feel that strongly about it, Kyle, you can keep the company. But don't expect it to remain intact. I am going to need some of those officers and NCOs you have trained."

A look of disbelief, then relief, followed by sheer joy swept over Gruene's face. "Do you really mean it, Sir? I can keep the company?"

"Yes, I mean it. Division offered me an Armor captain as S-3 today. I was reluctant to accept him but you obviously want to keep your company so much that I can't deny it to you. You keep A Co and I'll take Kiggen as my S-3."

The normally taciturn Gruene was almost voluble for the rest of the trip to the demonstration area. On arrival there he called his OFFs together and apparently told them the news. There was a whoop, and much excitement, which quickly dampened as Kyle returned them to the realities of the pending demonstration. There was unusual enthusiasm in the performance that day.

With Gruene in command of A Co, the 5/6 began to take shape. CPT Francis P. "Pat" McDermott, an outgoing, conscientious Irishman and an Army Aviator, assumed command of B Co. Co C was given to CPT Ernie Brant, a sharp paratrooper who had spent most of his career as an NCO in Airborne units. He reflected the spit and polish of the professional ABN NCO; having been a 1SG before he went to OCS, I anticipated little difficulty with his unit administration. Some long-time NCOs approach their duties as OFFs much as they did when they were EM, finding it impossible to delegate authority. This proved to be the case with Brant. The HHC CO was CPT Willie Ballard, initially the only black OFF assigned to the Bn. He had one of the most demanding jobs of all; HHC had all of the supply, maintenance, communications, reconnaissance, medical, administrative and fire power elements in the Battalion. It was a large, complex and unwieldy command, but Willie handled it well.

In all, I was pleased with the personnel assigned to the 5/6. In particular, the NCOs were of high caliber. Rumor had it that they were a select group, their performance did much to substantiate that claim. They were truly professional. This was especially important in light of the very green LTs in all of the battalions. As Dick Wise remarked, "Given the experience level of our OFFs and the pace at which we attempted to create ready units from a standing start, I daresay our cadre NCOs contributed more, man for man, than the Army at large is accustomed, or entitled to expect of its Noncommissioned Officers."

Our LTs must be given due credit. A few had been commissioned from OCS hence had some prior service, but most were recent ROTC graduates with little knowledge of the Army or of company duties. Of necessity, a tremendous burden was placed upon them; on the whole they responded well. Like many Bn COs and all Co COs, I sometimes became impatient with them; they were woefully ill-prepared for the duties they had to undertake in a newly-organized, untrained Bn. That they performed as well as they did is a reflection of their great dedication, determination and enthusiasm. No one could have asked for greater effort from them.

Slowly, the pieces started to fall into place as the organization took shape. Fillers were expected momentarily, but as we waited for them we developed the policies and procedures which would carry the 5th Battalion, 6th Infantry through the next year. One of the interesting sidelights on life in the 5th of the 6th, was the fact that there was no "colonel's lady" of the Battalion. By default, MAJ Smith's wife, Yvonne, assumed the role. She was a delightful lady who seemed to have time for everything. Living with the Smith's and their three teenagers was Yvonne's invalid mother. Since I had been denied the command set of quarters assigned for the CO of the 5/6, I persuaded the Post Commander to turn them over to MAJ Smith. As it turned out, I spent a great deal of time in those quarters being entertained by the Smiths.

The delay in receiving fillers also provided the opportunity to complete the organization of the Bn as well as affording me the chance to outline my views on command and training. The problems in organization were reflected in A Co. Despite Gruene's valiant fight, most of his trained LTs were transferred; each of the other Cos received one of A Co's 1LTs as XO, a job they handled well. In addition, HHC was given a Texas A&M graduate, 1LT Dan Gates, as Scout Plt Ldr.

Gruene was able to retain 1LT Emil "Bud" Schaerer, a husky personable and effective OFF from Chattanooga, TN, whose thick southern drawl belied his unlimited energy. Commissioned in the Military Police Corps, Bud was serving an orientation tour with the combat arms. He was better trained than most Infantry LTs, largely as the result of the time and effort CPT Gruene had spent on him and his other OFFs. Schaerer was the A Co XO, its Weapons Plt Ldr, and "guiding light" for newly commissioned 2LTs Cotton, Durbin and Wilson. The three of them frequently became lost when in the field - Bud had to go out and find them. Cotton and Durbin learned to find their way, but Wilson continued to lose his.

Probably the nadir of Schaerer's career with A Co was when his Weapons Plt failed its mortar test. Bud had worked with it, but busy with other duties, had delegated much of the instructing to his NCOs. As Plt Ldr he could not delegate his responsibility. To the great mortification of that young 1LT, CPT Gruene did not soon let Bud forget his dereliction.

Because Gruene was permitted to retain A Co, CPT Jim Moore, who was to have commanded it, was made the Asst S-3. He provided a calming balance to Kiggen's Prussian brusqueness. Almost before I got to know him, the S-1, CPT Johnson, was reassigned. Though several LTs were rotated through the S-1 position from time to time, most duties were handled by MAJ Smith or SGM Allen. It is my firm belief that all newly commissioned LTs belong in line companies as Plt Ldrs. The HQ was shorted to keep as many LTs in such positions as long as possible. On occasion a LT was brought up as a liaison officer or Adj when the work load became impossible, but most of them stayed in companies. It was necessary to give CPT Porterfield an assistant to handle the mass of supplies and equipment the Battalion was receiving. Reluctantly, I had to assign 2LT Don Strittmatter as the Supply Officer. Porterfield, Strittmatter, and later C WO Carter, the Property Book Officer, made an effective team

A slender, comical but highly knowledgeable intelligence specialist, MSG Henderson, immediately dubbed "Spook", acted as the S-2 most of the time I commanded the 5/6. Spook was inclined to drink too much; it was some time before I realized what he meant when he said he was going over to the NCO Club for some "soup". He was never drunk on duty and handled himself well. A natural wit, he was a good person to have in the HQ as he would invariably break any tension with a comic comment.

In a series of early meetings with the Co COs, I acquainted them with my policies and philosophy of command. The activation and training of a battalion offered a unique challenge and a rare privilege. Calling on my experience with F Co, 508 AIR, I was able to guide and assist the Co COs over many pitfalls. To accomplish our mission of making a combat-ready battalion of the 5th of the 6th as soon as possible, all other considerations had to be subordinated. The same three goals which I aimed for when I commanded K Co, 504 and F Co 508 were now set for the 5/6 in order of priority: discipline, physical fitness and tactical and technical proficiency. Regardless of how well trained a unit is, if it is not disciplined it will not function well in combat, where soldiers must respond rapidly and fully to instructions. Lives and the success of the mission depend on instant obedience to the orders of the commander, hence discipline was my first priority. If troops are in good physical condition and are well disciplined, they can accomplish anything. After leaving the APCs, the ability to fight, to travel many miles on foot, to run when required, to continue with little rest, to carry combat loads, requires great fitness and stamina. A sense of timing and coordination results from physical conditioning and is complementary to discipline. The third priority was tactical/technical proficiency. Certainly the tools of the trade were not to be neglected, but effective utilization of weapons, equipment and military skills could only be achieved by disciplined, physically fit soldiers. These three priorities, discipline, physical conditioning and tactical/technical proficiency, would order the training program. Another basic tenet which I have stated before and repeat for emphasis, and which I hold contrary to the views of many, is that it is more difficult to train a rifleman than it is to train a weapons crewman. The weapons crewman learns rote movements which quickly become instinctive. It is far more difficult to train the rifleman in the largely judgmental techniques he needs to survive in combat: terrain appreciation, movement over varied terrain, utilization of cover and concealment, silent movement, accurate range estimation, fire discipline, fire distribution. The training of a rifleman is a lengthy process which cannot be shortened.

Having learned a good lesson from LTC Mansfield, I announced that every man assigned to the 5/6 would be qualified to drive every vehicle in the Bn. That move to San Angelo, TX from FT Benning impressed me with the advantages of having an abundance of drivers. In a unit that would enter combat in armored personnel carriers (APCs), this seemed even more important. By the time the fillers arrived, I had licenses authorizing me to drive the M59 APC, the M8 tank, and of course, all of the wheeled vehicles. Later I qualified to drive the M88 recovery vehicle. All of the OFFs and NCOs were similarly qualified.

It quickly became apparent that I knew little or nothing about Armored units. My ignorance of time distance factors, maintenance, and logistics (especially POL requirements), was appalling. As this was a matter of first importance to me personally, I determined to learn as much as I could about these matters. The Maintenance Officer, Mr Trimer, or the Maintenance Sergeant, MSG McCulley, both highly knowledgeable about the "tracks", were hunted down whenever I failed to understand a problem. They ceased to be surprised when I crawled under a vehicle to see for myself the malfunction to be corrected or to identify the part under discussion. In retrospect, that short tour as the G-4 of the 8th IN Div had given me a head start on the logistics problems, but there was still much to learn. TIS had barely mentioned mechanized Infantry. Confident of my basic Infantry tactics which would be employed once the 5/6 dismounted, I could concentrate on those problems peculiar to mechanized units.

When I arrived, BG Ralph E. Haines, Jr was serving as the Asst Div CDR of the 2nd AR Div. Since he was to command the 1st AR Div, his promotion was a matter of time When we gathered for the first Commanders' Conference, we were presented with an impressive individual who looked every inch a general, tall, rather spare, thin-faced with piercing eyes. It took only a short while to realize that here was one of the rare Army officers who towered above his contemporaries. He so dominated the 1st AR Div that the Asst Div CDRs are almost faceless now. Only COLs Donn Pepke and Charlie Hollis seemed to move in his orbit. Though he never engendered affection, he commanded admiration and respect for his professionalism. On all but two of the few occasions when I disagreed with his decisions or programs, I had to respect them. It soon became apparent that competition was to be a key element in his command philosophy. In everything the 1st AR Div did, he pitted Bn against Bn: ATTs, AWOLs, Command Material Maintenance Inspections (CMMIs), deadline rates, tank gunnery, bond sales. At times, competition became so intense that it was counter-productive; perhaps never really out of control, but very close to it.

However, it was in training that Haines made his mark with the Bn COs. He established a climate which enabled all of us to exercise our ingenuity and daring. This was particularly true in his emphasis on live fire exercises.

Suddenly the Battalion was inundated with young privates fresh from their basic training. Since few had received their Advanced Individual Training (AIT), it became our task to impart to these largely untrained men the basic skills of a soldier, then to mold them into teams at squad, platoon, company and battalion level. It was a great privilege and a challenge, a most satisfying prospect. Here were troops to guide, train, assist and lead, the ultimate duty any officer could wish for.

The arrival of the fillers brought problems to the Battalion. Their morale was low, caused in part by the prohibition on having dependents accompany them. Despite official warning not to bring their families, the men either did not hear or did not want to hear. Consequently women and children were sleeping in cars, in single rooms with no toilet facilities, in lean-tos, in any place they could be sheltered. Those that became ill were unable, at first, to receive medical attention at the clinics because they were not recognized dependents. The Battalion Surgeon, CPT Milton Goldman, lanced a festering boil under one wife's arm in a parking lot one night. Things finally settled down as the men found housing for their families. The Army discouraged the marriage of trainees and recruits because of its inability to care for them, but Army Regulations could not dampen romance!

The 5th Battalion, 6th Infantry developed a routine to get the AIT completed as soon as possible. The S-3, CPT Kiggen, wanted to set up Bn Committees to accomplish the AIT, but I insisted that the training be handled by each Commander. While there was a possibility that the training might not be as uniform as under committee control, the development of unit pride and esprit would be facilitated. Though the program of instruction (POI) was dictated by DA and Div, Kiggen set up workable training schedules which enabled the companies to conduct the instruction. As mentioned before, Kiggen was ably assisted by CPT Jim Moore, a fme soldier, an Army aviator and Infantry officer from Buena Vista, GA.

Shortly after we began training, each Battalion was notified that it would provide a jeep which was repainted, always polished and clean, with a driver required to have a starched Class A uniform ready, both available on call at all times, This vehicle was for the mounted band. Along with other commanders, I protested that I needed all of my vehicles and the men needed their training; but MG Haines himself had issued the order making it a hard-and-fast requirement. The CG had been familiar with the mounted band of the 1st AR Div during WWII and was determined that the reactivated Div would have one. Each jeep carried two musicians, who played lustily as the band lead the mounted Div in reviews.

Activation Day was March 3rd, by this time every unit had enough qualified drivers to make a mounted review possible. Two brackets had been welded onto each commanders' APC, one to carry the American Flag, the other to hold the Battalion Colors. The bracket for the Battalion Colors was hinged so that the colors could be dipped as the track passed the Reviewing Officer. It was an impressive ceremony during which each of the Bn COs received his colors, affixed them to his command track which he then proudly rode in the mounted review.

After the formal activation ceremony the Battalion settled into a schedule as the training commenced in earnest. Every day I visited each company at least once, more frequently twice, to see what was going on, to make suggestions or corrections if required, or to critique the training. While I wanted to give the Co COs as much latitude to train their units as possible, it was my responsibility to see that the 5/6 was ultimately prepared to fight. At every break I tried to talk to the men instead of the OFFs or NCOs whom I could talk with during the instruction or at other times. Soon I knew many of them by name. Whenever possible, I took PT with one of the Cos. As each scheduled PT at a different time, fitting it into their overall program and the training areas they were allocated, it was hard to work it into my own schedule. Those ABN days when the entire Bn ran as a unit were a wistful memory.

My visits to the units served a second, perhaps even more important purpose. My own experience indicated that the commander who is seen by the troops, who evidences genuine interest in his men, exerts greater influence on them. My soldiers could never say that they seldom saw their commander; in addition to my daily visits to the training areas, I was at the Bn reveille formation which was held each morning in garrison. Usually I was an observer more often than a participant, though I presided at the monthly muster formation or at those during which I wanted to put out special orders or instructions. Most Co COs were present at reveille, or were in the area checking their mess halls or otherwise preparing for the training day. Before reveille I visited each of the mess halls. The cooks soon learned to expect me with the result that I found fewer and fewer items to criticize. Whenever there was creamed beef on toast (SOS) the cook on duty would insist I try it, knowing it was one of my favorites. They would wait anxiously as I tasted it, visibly relieved if I assured them it was good. At times I would be forced to tell them it was too watery, too lumpy, not properly seasoned or for some reason not up to standard. Company messes are a great asset in building morale and esprit. Consolidated dining facilities, while perhaps more efficient, detract from unit pride. The mess personnel in the 5th of the 6th were proud of their contribution to their unit; the men appreciated their efforts.

The Co COs and I talked frequently. Battalion policy gave them direct access to me at any time. They did not have to go through the Adj or XO. Most simply asked the Sergeant Major if I was free, knocked at my door, and reported. Or they accosted me in the area if they had something to discuss. This ready access paid off in mutual trust and respect.

Starting as soon as the company commanders were assigned, scheduled meetings were held with them at which I verbally gave guidance and policy. After each meeting the Bn Clerk typed up my "Commander's Notes" which MAJ Smith or SGM Allen had taken down. This provided both the Commanders and staff with a reference which enabled them to check their implementation of the policies announced.

After about six months there was a considerable file of policy-notes; most were of only transitory interest, some were duplicatory, but many of permanent concern. MAJ Smith codified mem into a Commander's Policy File. It was helpful to me to review the guidance I had given, as well as helpful to the commanders and staff. Once established,, that policy file was comprehensive, detailed, and always kept current.

The practice of hoarding proved difficult to eradicate, even through the Commander's Notes. Co A brought to the 5th Bn, 6th IN some of the practices followed in CCA, specifically the hoarding of spare parts and other materiel. For instance, they had four barrels for each machine gun - one to fire, one for inspections and two for trouble. In addition, coffee was accumulated, about half of the regular ration being put aside into a trading fund. At one time D Co of CCA had between 500 and 1,000 pounds of coffee which was traded to the Post Engineer personnel for lumber for paneling, and to the 123rd Maintenance Bn for lost or damaged ordnance equipment. When a 50 Cal machine gun was lost, coffee purchased a replacement. While this was strictly against regulations, most supply and maintenance sergeants followed the practice which was tacitly supported by the Co COs who would benefit when transferred from the unit. It was difficult to stamp out this system, though Harry Porterfield tried to convince the Co COs that the supplies were available when needed. Even stern warnings and periodic inspections failed to root out the practice.

SGM Allen picked an outstanding young soldier, Rick Perrin, as my driver. Rick, from California, was a husky, intelligent young man whose primary recreation before he had been drafted, was driving hot rods on certified tracks. He was an excellent driver, could take the jeep any place, was conscientious, and was always available when I needed him. Just at this time the Army was replacing the M38 jeep with the M51. Most units were having problems with the new vehicle because the adjustment of the torque on the wheels was not fully understood. The engineering of the suspension system as well as tightening the bolts on the wheels too much, caused the M51 to corner in a markedly different manner from the M38. There were a number of accidents until drivers got used to the vehicle.

But Rick had no problems with the M51 jeep. He was delighted when challenged to take it up a steep incline to see what it would do.

When the M51 jeeps were first issued they were a disaster. The Army had accepted them but had neglected to consider that the prime use for a jeep in an IN unit was to carry the commander's radios. This had not been provided for; there was no bracket or other means of mounting a radio. Moreover, the jeep body was too thin to permit the attachment of a radio directly to it. My motor pool personnel jury-rigged a bracket for the command jeeps which worked until instructions for a standard bracket were received.

In addition to the friends I had in the 1st AR Div, there were others at FT Hood. The Madisons and Ted Voorhees, whom I had known at Mainz were in the 2nd AR Div. Tom Modisett, who had been one of my Plt Ldrs in K Co, 504, was assigned to Post HQ. Maxine and Bill Chippeaux from RAAF were in Fort Worth. In 1962 the 96th IN Div Reunion was held in Dallas. I was able to attend the session on Saturday, but I only knew three or four people, including Walt Cohen, my SGM in the 2nd Bn, 382nd IN, who now lived in Laredo.

It was interesting to watch the 5/6 develop. CPT Gruene ran A Co well, very much as I had run mine. He made an effort to keep aloof, obviously concerned about being accused of "apple polishing". Whenever there were meetings, he remained grim-faced, accepting each piece of guidance with a doubtful look. During one of my counseling sessions with him, I mentioned this. "Kyle, during my meetings you look at me with a jaundiced eye when I issue instructions. I want you to look at things in a more positive light." He grimaced at this, but did ask me what I meant by a jaundiced eye, then made haste to assure me that he was not questioning my instructions. Later he told me that my remark had upset him very much; first because he did not know what the hell a "jaundiced eye" was and secondly because he thought he was going to be relieved.

All of my Co COs were counseled periodically, Brant possibly more than the others. In my opinion he was too GI, more of a 1SG than a Co CO. He must have given his First Sergeant fits because he knew as much about company administration and handling the duty roster as that NCO. On the whole I was pleased with the way the companies were developing. Pat McDermott was a steady, solid commander; there were few problems in B Co. Willie Ballard had the biggest challenge with HHC because of the many elements in it, but he handled his myriad problems well.

Soon after the 5/6 was organized I directed that all OFFs would attend happy hour once a week. These informal get-togethers enabled them to know each other better, to talk out any imagined or real jealousies or animosities which might have developed between or within units because of a lack of communication, and to exchange ideas. Every Friday night after training, the OFFs would assemble at the Officers' Club Annex in the hospital area to have one or two drinks before going home. The guidance was explicit: they must appear, but what they drank or how long they stayed was their own business. The important thing was to get to know their brother OFFs. It helped to weld the OFFs and the Bn into a very close unit.

Sometimes my efforts to challenge the thoughts of the junior officers appeared doomed. On one occasion, while sitting with a group of 2LTs I tried to explain to them that the military is simply an instrument of national policy. It was a concept completely foreign to them; that a show of the flag, a demonstration of force, ultimately war itself, were all extensions of United States National Policy, or even remotely related to diplomacy was quite an abstract idea. I am not sure that I got my point across.

The Club Annex at the hospital was also the scene of many after hours bull sessions during which the Bn COs compared notes, exchanged views on their problems and their solutions or offered each other valuable suggestions. We discussed the Div, its strengths and weaknesses, ultimately reaching an informal consensus on the standards we wanted set. Not only old friends such as Dick Wise, Barney

Broughton and Dick Cann were there, but at these sessions I got to know many other COs such as Ken Althaus, Ben Carroll and Dick Hoffinan.

Shortly after activation, I assigned to each of the lieutenants a research project on the history of the Regiment. The 6th Infantry was an old, highly decorated unit, with 44 campaign streamers on its colors. Each LT in the 5/6 had the task of researching one of those campaigns and writing a summary of it. While this was a bit academic, I wanted those young officers to not only know the history of their Regiment, but to be able to discuss it with their fellow officers as well as their men. Whether this effort achieved its purpose is questionable, but at least every LT was informed on one campaign in which the 6th Infantry had participated. In addition, I put my rather extensive military library in my office and urged any of the Bn OFFs to borrow and read the books. At least a few were used, because I lost one book on small unit actions in the Korean War.

COL Hollis, the 1st Bde CDR, was socially minded, so there were gatherings of all sorts. The COL invited his Bn COs to his quarters several times. In garrison, we wore a neck scarf of our branch color. The 5th of the 6th wore IN blue, the tank Bns and Bde HQ wore gold or yellow. COL Hollis, an AR OFF, always wore a gold scarf, though I chided him that he had as much IN in his Bde as AR (two IN Bns, two tank Bns). At one party he did appear with a blue scarf. But before he left he took off the blue scarf to reveal a yellow one beneath it.

Late in the spring, quotas for promotions were received in the 1st AR Div. The first of the NCOs to be promoted was SGM Allen. MG Haines had a Div formation at his HQ to which the wives of the Sergeants Major being promoted as well as their Bn COs were invited. Haines made a special ceremony of the Sergeants Major promotions, calling them the "generals of the noncommissioned officer ranks". Whenever he could, the CG continued the policy of promoting personally all first three graders.

A number of other NCOs were promoted at the same time Allen became a SGM. After the official promotion ceremony, CPT Pat McDermott came to see me, visibly disturbed. When asked the trouble, he said, "Sir, the best NCO in the Bn was passed over for promotion. SFC Johnson is head and shoulders above any NCO in B Co and I will stack him up against any NCO in the Bn or Div. Can you do anything about it?"

If Pat thought that much of SFC Johnson, who more than lived up to the reputation given him as time passed and I got to know him myself, then it seemed to me I had to try to do something about the situation. Not only did I want to support my Co COs, but I wanted to enhance and develop the prestige and leadership of the NCOs. Working with my Personnel NCO, the Div G-l and the Div AG, an unused slot was found and given to me. A bit late, but well ahead of many others in the 5/6, Johnson was promoted to MSG. Years later, Pat McDermott told me that my esteem among the black personnel in the Bn was greatly raised because I had gone to bat for a black NCO. As he put it, "It was the fact that you did something right away, and did not wait for the next quota or list. That impressed everyone."

Among the OFFs, Tom Kiggen was the first to be promoted. When he was given his gold maple leaves, there was a palpable sigh of resignation from the Co COs. They were sure that their lot would deteriorate even further under Kiggen as a field grade officer. In contrast, Harry Porterfield's promotion to MAJ was greatly applauded, because he was most helpful to everyone in the BN. Toward the end of the year, Smith became a LTC and was transferred to Div HQ.

Training continued to go well resulting in a marked improvement in the morale, discipline, physical fitness and military proficiency of the men. With this well in hand, I decided that the OFFs could take time off periodically for a formal Dining-In. The XO set up the procedure, using much of the same ritual developed for the Dining-In of the 504 at Mainz. The blind leading the blind! It still did not conform to the traditions that most Army units used, but it served us well.

In developing the procedures for the Dining-In, I resolved to develop a punch that symbolized the unique, colorful history of the 6th Infantry. On several evenings SGM Allen, Kiggen, Porterfield and I gathered in Yvonne Smith's kitchen where we concocted various noxious brews which we attempted to relate to the 6th Infantry heritage. Yvonne never commented, though she occasionally looked in on us with an amused expression. Finally a recipe was developed which satisfied the historical requirement, but which left much to be desired in a gustatory sense. Roughly it was composed of a fifth each of: Canadian whiskey for the War of 1812, Tequila for both the 1847 and 1916 Mexican campaigns, Corn whiskey for the Civil War, and another fifth of Corn for the Indian wars, rum for the Spanish-American War in Cuba, sugar and lime juice for the Philippine Insurrection, brandy for WWI in France, Chianti for WWII in Italy and bourbon for the training periods between wars. It was potent! Though we tried various means to improve the taste such as adding tea or fruit juice, that com whiskey dominated the palate.

For the first Dining-In MG Haines was the honored guest. During the cocktail hour which preceded dinner, every OFF in the Bn, under strict orders from me, went up to him, introduced himself and chatted a moment with his Div CDR. Keeping in the background as much as possible during this period, I noted that Haines carried most of the conversation. The young officers were almost tongue tied in the presence of their Commanding General. This was one of the things I hoped the Dining-In would remedy.

At 1930 everyone repaired to the table. The Colors were posted after which one of the LTs read his resume of the Battle of Chippewa as another officer identified the battle streamer hanging from the staff. Chaplain Saunders said grace, a 2LT previously designated, proposed a toast to the President. During the meal, the junior 2LT in the 5/6 sat on MG Haines' right, while I sat on his left. Haines again carried the conversation with the 2LT. Occasionally, he and I talked briefly together. Following dinner, MG Haines spoke to the OFFs, stressing the importance of the traditions of the service.

The punch climaxed the evening. At that first Dining-In a ritual was established which was followed from then on. The XO announced a war or campaign; an OFF stepped forward and poured the appropriate liquor over a cake of ice in the punch bowl. Later dry ice was used which fumed and heightened the effect. When the last ingredient had been added, everyone was given a cup of the punch. Those who did not drink were not required to take one. Toasts were drunk to the 6th Infantry, to the members killed in action while serving with the Regiment, and to the ladies. With the potent punch to lower inhibitions, the party got underway with much singing and horse-play. MG Haines left shortly to avoid inhibiting the fun, and I followed him a half hour later. By the time I left the punch had done its work - the group remaining was fully relaxed.

Because of its potency, and the amount made by using a fifth of each type of liquor, there was a great deal left. Kiggen and several others bottled the dregs to use for the rest of the quarter until the next Dining-In. It was a shock to visit the Kiggens and be served that concoction!

The successful Dining-In highlighted the need for official silver for the 5th Battalion, 6th Infantry for such affairs. The 1st Bn, 6th IN had all of the official memorabilia of the Regiment, leaving the 5th few tangible assets on which to build traditions. The 5/6 needed a silver punch bowl, tray and cups which could be used not only for OFFs' formations, but at NCO or Co functions.

Just at this time, an official title or nickname was adopted for the Battalion. All personnel assigned to the 5th of the 6th had been asked to think of a short, distinctive and descriptive name for it. The 6th IN Regt crest carried a ladder and crocodile with the motto "Unity is Strength", but I wanted something that would characterize the 5th Bn. Someone, perhaps MAJ Smith, thought of a name based on the resume of the Battle of Chippewa read at the Dining-In. During the Battle, the 6th IN Regt arrived on the scene at a critical point. The British/Canadian Commander cried, "Those are Regulars by God." The name THE REGULARS was proposed, and struck an instant chord. It was exactly right for the 5/6 and was adopted forthwith.

The following order was put out the next morning at reveille, "From now on everyone will refer to the 5th Battalion, 6th Infantry as THE REGULARS." The troops took this literally; from then on it was never the 5th of the 6th, it was THE REGULARS. The approved routine when answering the telephone was "Headquarters, THE REGULARS, Sir." Many callers insisted at first, "But I wanted the 5th of the 6th Infantry".

"This *is* THE REGULARS, Sir."

Despite some initial razzing from other units, the name stuck, becoming a rallying cry. The troops took it seriously, always referring to their Battalion as THE REGULARS. With not a little pride, I noted some years later, that the Office of the Chief of Military History, or the heraldry branch or whatever element in the Army makes such decisions, officially dubbed the entire 6th Infantry Regiment THE REGULARS.

Having a name, I pursued the need to get silver to go with it. While discussing with SGM Allen the problem of financing the purchase of such items, I mentioned my hope that the troops would pledge their loyalty to THE REGULARS, and stopped in mid-sentence. "That's it, Sergeant Major. That's the solution. We'll call the bowl THE REGULARS PLEDGE. It will be a pledge of loyalty, and that pledge of loyalty will be engraved on it. Let's see, how about this?"

"We pledge ourselves to uphold the high standards of courage, discipline and professional skill first established by THE REGULARS during the Battle of Chippewa and to add to the outstand-ing reputation, fame and glory of the 6th Infantry."

"That's good, Sir. I think the men will like that."

There was a talented draftsman in THE REGULARS S-3 Section, who inscribed on a large parchment scroll THE REGULARS PLEDGE. He did a superb job, also embellishing the document with the Regimental crest. A letter was sent to each member of THE REGULARS explaining the desirability of purchasing a sterling silver punch bowl, tray and cups for THE REGULARS to be used by all for social occasions, the bowl to be called THE REGULARS PLEDGE. The pledge was then spelled out. Each EM was asked to take THE REGULARS PLEDGE and to donate ten cents for each pay grade held, each officer taking the pledge would be asked to donate one dollar for each pay grade. At the next monthly reveille muster, a table with the scroll on it was set up on a PT platform in front of the Bn. After the muster, I read the pledge aloud, then signed the scroll, followed by SGM Allen. The Sergeant Major had selected two sharp privates who then signed it. After the four Co COs, the formal signing ended.

The scroll was sent to each company in turn, to permit everyone to pledge and sign. Of course, it was supposed to be strictly voluntary, but knowing how units operate in the Army, I was sure that the first sergeants put pressure on any men who hesitated. Finally, the scroll was returned to Bn HQ. The list of names was impressive, though I am not sure that everyone signed it, nor was this ever checked. Over a thousand dollars was donated by the members of the Bn but it was not enough even at the low cost of silver at that time. To make up the difference, I put in several hundred dollars. I suspect that SGM Allen did also, though I was never sure since he handled the actual purchase and accounting for the funds.

The SGM contacted a jeweler in San Antonio, who engraved the largest available sterling Revere bowl with the 6th IN crest on one side and THE REGULARS PLEDGE on the other. The space between was reserved for the names of the Bn COs and SGMs. In addition, several hundred julep type cups were ordered. The NCOs bought a tray for the bowl and cups.

The Sergeant Major was made custodian of THE REGULARS PLEDGE in official orders. He had the responsibility of securing it as well as making it available to any of the units when they wanted it for parties or ceremonies. I wanted the silver used, without concern for the possibility of dents or scratches, not treated as a museum piece. Harking back to those days in the 504 when I fought to use the Tucker Tumbler, now in the 82nd Airborne Division Museum and rarely if ever used, I determined that this was to be readily available to everyone assigned to THE REGULARS.

The bowl and cups were the tangibles but they depicted the spirit. THE REGULARS developed a very strong esprit, unusual in my limited experience. There was a sense of belonging epitomized in the motto "Unity is Strength". But it went beyond that. There was a sense of identity that made for high morale; all of us were proud to be one of THE REGULARS.

Shortly after the acquisition of THE REGULARS PLEDGE, the men completed then-Advanced Individual Training. This was the occasion for the first Bn parade during which the men donned the blue Infantry cord, worn on their left shoulders to announce that they were Infantry Soldiers. It was an impressive parade, a sort of graduation review.

Next we undertook Basic Unit Training (BUT) - squad, platoon, company and finally battalion training. This entailed much field work. While the Co COs retained control of the training, a great deal more direction was exercised by my staff and me. It was important to make maximum use of training facilities and training tune. In addition, live fire exercises were conducted which required positive safety controls. MG Haines stressed live fire exercises, urging every unit to schedule as many as possible. But there never seemed to be enough of them. Limitations on ammunition, the availability of ranges, and the number of units requiring overhead artillery fire dictated the frequency of live fire exercises.

Live fire problems also included combined arms training. One of the most effective drills that we conducted was one in which the APCs loaded with troops advanced under overhead artillery fire. Held in the Jack Mountain area, it gave the troops confidence in the ability of the APCs to protect them from small arms and artillery fragments. Of course, the APCs could not sustain a direct hit by an artillery shell, nor would it stop a 5O caliber machine gun bullet, but the troops gained confidence in the limited protection afforded and got a thrill out of riding in the tracks listening to the rattle of artillery shell fragments on the roof and sides.

During the Squad, Plt and Co tng the COs were authorized and encouraged to take their men into the field for a week at a time. A rifle Co CO would call an alert early Monday morning, sometimes at 0300, move his unit to the field, train all week, then return to the Bn area on Friday. Sometimes a Co made a night march back on Thursday night. Friday was devoted to cleaning equipment and preparing for the next week's training. An inspection was held every Saturday. This was a fast pace; only rarely was anything scheduled on a weekend. I wanted the weekends free so that the men and officers could relax. It was good training, which the men reflected. To get the OFFs away from their Cos after inspection, I urged them, especially the Co COs, to stop by the club to have lunch or a drink before they went home.

The Scout Platoon, the recon element of the Bn, contained two M8 tanks as well as many jeeps. The men in the Scout Plt developed a special esprit and were a gung-ho bunch. They thought of themselves more as Cavalry (CAV) than IN. They would need such spirit if they were to perform their mission in combat. The Plt acted as aggressors against the Bn or the Rifle Cos on many occasions. Needless to say, the companies usually "won" the engagements primarily because of their greater firepower and larger numbers.

Battalion communications were good. The Commo Plt LDR, a young 1LT, was convinced he had the most important job in the Bn. He would work himself and his Plt unsparingly to insure that there was good communications whenever the Battalion was in the field.

The lieutenant who commanded the 4.2 Platoon, a scholar, easily mastered the artillery procedures which were used by the Plt. Later, he was moved to the newly activated Davy Crockett Section which demanded even more of an academic mind. Davey Crockett was the tactical atomic weapon for the Infantry. As mentioned before, I considered it a poor weapon. Its range was limited, it was complex and cumbersome and had marginal utility at the Bn level. The thought of many IN Bns popping atomic rounds over the battlefield was a frightening prospect. Since it had an atomic warhead, the unit that handled it was required to undergo periodic "Technical Proficiency Inspections" or TPIs. Regulations required that two people be present during every step in getting the round ready to fire: removing it from security, inspecting it, handling it, transporting it under guard, developing the fire plan, mounting the round on its launcher and simulating firing it. It was detailed, but this young 1LT organized, trained and developed the Section into a highly proficient unit. The several preliminary TPIs administered by Div were passed easily. Before the official DA TPI, however, I left the 5/6.

All of these elements were in HHC. Willie Ballard did a professional job in training that unit, in keeping the Bn Staff happy, and in making me comfortable in the field. MSG McCulley's maintenance people built a small hut on a three-quarter ton trailer that could be towed behind an APC or 2 1/4 ton truck. It provided me a place to sleep, to do some paperwork and to keep some personal items and clothing. The major problem was that it was not airtight, when pulled behind one of the tracks a fine powdery dust seeped through the cracks. The trailer would arrive in the field loaded with dust, giving Rick a difficult task to thoroughly clean it before it could be used.

The men were urged to attend chapel every Sunday. An Episcopal chaplain, CPT A. Donald Davies, in another Bde, held a Communion Service at 0800 each Sunday. Whenever possible I attended that service and then went to the General Protestant Service in the Brigade Chapel. It was not that I was overly pious, but I believed that my presence at the General Protestant Service would foster a greater attendance of THE REGULARS. Many of the OFFs in the 5/6 also attended these services. By requiring a different Co to sponsor the service each Sunday, the Protestant troops were encouraged to go to chapel. At all appropriate formations the men of all faiths were urged to attend their particular services. But other than by example, suggestion and the sponsoring of the services, I refused to pressure the men on the matter of church attendance.

Attendance at two Sunday services earned me a reputation I did not deserve. One Sunday, Chaplain Saunders preached on Demas. During the course of his sermon, he mentioned that there were only two references to this martyr in the Bible, and cited them. By chance, the gospel at the Episcopal Service contained a reference to Demas, taken from a text not mentioned by Chaplain Saunders. After the service, I jokingly corrected the good chaplain, citing the text I had heard in the Episcopal service. Immediately, he looked on me as one well read in the Bible - far from fact. Despite my attempts to correct this impression, it persisted. Long after I had forgotten the incident, it was recalled dramatically by Chaplain Saunders under strange circumstances.

THE REGULARS did not have a Bn Chaplain or chapel, but Bde HQ was authorized three chaplains by TO&E. Chaplain Saunders, a 1LT and a Baptist minister, became in fact if not in assignment, THE REGULARS Chaplain. He was an enthusiastic officer on whom I called for any affairs in which the services of a chaplain were needed: invocations at all ceremonies, funerals, character guidance, and counseling. He and his wife were included in all of our social activities.

Chaplain Saunders became involved with me in the one semi-religious controversy I had. THE REGULARS were scheduled to be in the field the week following Easter. An intensive training program was planned. To make maximum utilization of the training time, I decided to move to the field on Sunday, an exception to my firmly stated policy of leaving the week ends free. The fact that it was Easter had not registered when I set the departure time for 1000. Almost immediately there were questions and complaints, initially through Roman Catholic chaplain channels. The Bde Roman Catholic chaplain called to ask me to defer moving the Bn until Monday. Delay of the movement would entail cancelling some important tng which could never be made up, so I determined to go ahead with the Sunday move. By this time some emotional appeals to permit families to attend church together on Easter had been received. Finally, I relented to the extent that departure would be delayed until 1400, enabling the men to go to Easter services with their families, as well as to have Easter dinner with them. This was not fully satisfactory to the chaplains, as evidenced by continued rumblings. MG Haines called to question me about the matter. After hearing my reasons he told me that it was my decision though he would prefer that I delay movement until Monday. Chaplain Saunders supported me and saw no problem with the afternoon departure, so I decided to go ahead as scheduled. In my view on and off schedules are a greater harassment to the troops than duty on Sunday afternoons.

Easter was a glorious, sunny day. After attending chapel services I had dinner with B Co. Immediately thereafter the area was alive with preparations for departure. This was THE REGULARS first Bn move by APC. The leading unit crossed the initial point (IP) exactly on time - the move was underway. Suddenly, my radio crackled with the transmission, "Jumpmaster Six, this is Hobo Six on your push, over," The expression "on your push" was new to me, and Hobo was not a station in the Bn net. Later I learned that the phrase "on your push" was used by armored units meaning "on your net". It was COL Hollis, the 1st Bde CDR, in a helicopter over the convoy. He had called to comment on the way the vehicles were spaced in the convoy. The matter was corrected without disrupting the forward movement of the Bn. The practice of senior commanders entering a subordinate command net to talk to the commander when all of the stations of the unit are privileged to the conversation, always struck me as wrong. This was one of the rare instances when it was justified, since the Bde net was not open, but the use of the procedure should be severely limited by senior commanders.

The bivouac area was reached with several hours of daylight left. By dark all of the units were settled into their campsites. Training began early on Monday. A great deal was accomplished during the week. SGM Allen, who had been checking with the men, reported no complaints from them concerning the Easter departure.

Insects posed an interesting problem for us in our early days in the field, particularly caterpillars and tarantulas. In the spring, the caterpillars came out in untold numbers. On human skin they caused an irritation and raised welts hence everyone had to sleep under mosquito bars or to protect themselves in some other way when the millions of caterpillars were hungrily crawling over everything. Tarantulas have hairy bodies, often up to two inches in diameter, with their eight legs spreading more than five inches. They have a unique ability to jump straight up about the height of a jeep floor; quite often one of these creatures would hop into my vehicle. While they are essentially harmless to man, though they can inflict painful bites if provoked, most of the troops were convinced that they were deadly and were afraid of them. The Easter bivouac was crawling with caterpillars and tarantulas.

As spring gave way to summer, the heat became intense. Problems with heat exhaustion surfaced early. THE REGULARS sent two men to the hospital with what was thought to be heat exhaustion. The doctors informed us that the men were simply hyperventilated, another result of the heat, but less severe than either heat exhaustion or heat stroke. Everyone learned to recognize those three ailments. Specific instructions were issued by Div concerning the availability and use of salt tablets and other preventive measures. Immediately, the incidence of heat casualties was equated with poor leadership; it became another item of comparison between Bns. Later, when the weather turned cold, the same criterion would be used if any of the troops suffered from frostbite. With a severe wind-chill factor this was indeed a problem in Texas. Both of these considerations were stressed to all officers, who watched their men carefully.

Early in the summer, THE REGULARS celebrated the anniversary of the activation of the 6th Infantry. A training holiday, parade and field day marked the event. There were military as well as athletic contests. The NCOs even got me to play softball, a game which I never played well. The company messes served a picnic lunch at the athletic field, for wives and children as well as soldiers. In the evening there was a party at the NCO Club which I attended briefly. The officers held a dinner dance at the Officers' Club. It was a relaxing and enjoyable day, one steeped in tradition.

In July, CPT Gruene received orders for Vietnam. He was replaced by CPT Angel Mejia-Flores. Angel was from Puerto Rico and spoke with a pronounced accent. When he became excited, it was difficult to understand him, particularly if he was transmitting over the radio. Most of us who communicated with him routinely by radio, soon got used to his accent. Mejia easily phased into A Co, doing an excellent job as Co CO. Fortunately, Bud Schaerer, the XO under Gruene, remained under Mejia. He provided continuity during the transition between commanders so there was no loss of momentum.

Schaerer a RA Military Police (MP) OFF, manifested an interest in transferring to the Infantry. I encouraged him, and wrote a strong endorsement of his application for transfer. It was disapproved. My friends in the Pentagon, to whom I appealed for help, were unable to break the bureaucratic bottleneck, so Military Police remained Bud's basic branch. There is a possibility that he would have made the Army his career had he become an Infantryman, but he did not want 30 years as a policeman. The Army lost an outstanding officer.

As soon as APCs began to be used, first for driver training, then for Co exercises, finally for Bn marches, maintenance problems developed. At all times there were APCs on deadline (inoperable). Maintenance frustrated all commanders. Though I had an outstanding Maintenance WO, Mr Trimer, and an effective group of mechanics under MSG McCulley's capable direction, we never seemed to get all of our vehicles operative at one time. One of the difficulties was the M59 APC itself which had two engines requiring synchronization. This was a technique which all mechanics did not master. When the engines were "out of sync" other problems developed. Another difficulty was the age of the vehicles, which had been driven many miles over rough terrain by inexperienced or careless drivers. Much time and energy was devoted to maintenance in order to reduce the deadline. When the new M113 APCs arrived, the deadline rate dropped to zero for a time.

Predictably, the deadline rate became an indicator of the leadership of a unit; this quickly became a major issue in the Div as MG Haines pitted the deadline rate of one unit against that of others.. While every Bn and Co commander recognized the limitations a high deadline rate imposed upon his mobility, the matter seemed to be an obsession with the chain of command; the distractions and diversions of energy engendered by this concern on the part of the senior officers materially hampered training and the effort to make the Infantry battalions combat ready. There is probably no solution to the problem, except constant vigilance, training, the availability of spare parts, and immediate repair, but the Army must end its infatuation with complex and maintenance-wasteful machines and look for simpler, maintenance-free equipment. When testing new equipment for the Army, the need for maintenance should receive major consideration. This problem was finally formally addressed by including RAM (Reliability, Availability, and Maintainability) as an integral part of the procurement process.

As one means of solving the deadline problem, the Div requested quotas for the Senior Officers Preventive Maintenance Course at FT Knox, KY. It was a one-week course designed to train commanders to inspect vehicles to identify problems which could cause breakdowns, and to determine if the proper preventive maintenance was being performed. It was a short, intensive, but informative course.

One of the first quotas was given to me early in the fall of 1962. Not only did I get a great deal of useful instruction, but I also had the chance to see many of my friends from the 504 in Mainz. About ten IN OFFs from the 504 and 505 were attending the Armor Officers Advance Course. There was a mini-reunion with Dick Hooker, Charlie Sarkiss, Warne Meade and others.

Upon completion of squad and Plt unit training, every Bn was required to submit a monthly report on its readiness for overseas movement or for combat. This was a report I took very seriously and made out myself. The first report was returned by Div with a note that it lowered the Division's overall score. This was based on the question, "Do you have adequate trained NCOs?" While impressed with the performance of the initial cadre NCOs as well as with the potential of the junior NCOs, recently promoted, I put the Bn in C category in answer to this question. Most of the Squad Leaders and all of the fire-team Leaders were acting NCOs, privates who had recently completed their Advanced Individual Training and were now going through Basic Unit Training (BUT) with the other men. They had been selected because they showed leadership potential, but they were in no sense trained to lead in combat; hence I graded in accordance with the regulation. COL Pepke, the CofS, called me to suggest that I change the rating. "You can change it at Div but this is the way I see the Bn," I said. "I think THE REGULARS is as good or better than any Bn in the Div, but there is a definite shortcoming in trained leadership in the NCO ranks which should be noted." Nothing further was said and I do not know if Div changed my rating or not. In spite of my recalcitrance, the 1st AR Div received its STRAC (Strategic Army Corps) rating indicating it was ready for combat. This incident was indicative of a growing problem in the Army; the rendering of paper reports which did not, in fact, reflect the true status of units.

THE REGULARS held several parades with varying formations during the course of the year that I commanded it. One was an "Escort of the Colors", a formation that few of the troops or Officers had seen. In fact, the Division Band Master told me that he had never participated in an Escort of the Colors. After the Bn was assembled on the parade field, the band and Color Company paraded to Bn HQ, received the National Colors, and escorted them to the waiting Bn. Unfortunately, the distance from the parade field to the Bn HQ was almost a quarter of a mile. It took the band and Color Co about 15 minutes to march to HQ and back, a dead time for the troops in formation as well as the spectators. But it was an impressive ceremony. It probably should be conducted only by units whose parade fields are immediately adjacent to their HQ. There were also retreat parades, reviews and awards formations.

Social functions were very much a part of life in THE REGULARS. In addition to the Dinings-In and happy hours, a social function of some sort was scheduled each month for OFFs, so that their wives were involved with the Battalion. Both the Corps and Div CDRs were invited to most of these affairs. LTG Thomas W. Dunn, the III Corps CDR, attended many affairs at the Club, those hosted by THE REGULARS among others. His wife, "Curlie", a delightful lady with whom I enjoyed dancing, took an interest in me because I was a bachelor. Her favorite dance was the Varsoviana, or "Put Your Little Foot." Curlie would dance it only with "Tommy", her husband. Several times when we were dancing together and the band struck up the Varsoviana, she excused herself and ran over to LTG Dunn. The two of them then began to dance gracefully. "Put Your Little Foot" was a favorite at Hood, indeed in the southwest, I first learned it at Roswell. We all got to know the catchy, yet stately dance.

In the fall, Mother wrote that she was going to visit her friend, Jean Messineo in California and would swing by to see me on her way home. Her plane arrived at Love Field late in the afternoon, so after meeting her, we had dinner and remained in Dallas overnight. Although the Billeting Officer would not assign one of the WWII cottages to me, he did make one available for Mother. It was comfortable for her since it had everything she needed including a kitchen in which she could make coffee for breakfast. The 5/6 OFFs wives took care of her. They had her for coffees, luncheons, and short trips. The first evening she was at FT Hood I gave a cocktail party to introduce her to my OFFS, their wives and my friends. She and I were invited to dinner by the Kiggens, the McDermotts and SGM and Mrs Allen. All of the officers' wives took great pains to make sure that she enjoyed her visit. Before she left she asked what she could do to thank them all. Just at that time the new Cowhouse Motel opened in Killeen; its restaurant was reputed to be excellent. I suggested she give a luncheon there for all the wives. Mother liked the idea, so I set it up without giving consideration to racial matters. Late in 1962 there was still resistance to full integration in Texas. There were now two married black officers in the Bn, CPT Willie Ballard and a second lieutenant.

On the day of the luncheon as one of the wives picked up Mother, I thought of the fact that there would be two black ladies in the group. Hurriedly I mentioned this to Mother, telling her to call me if there was any problem. We did not want to have our black ladies embarrassed. The ladies all met in the lobby. When it was time to go in to lunch, Mother took the two black ladies, one on each arm, and swept into the dining room. There was no reaction from the manager. Later I kidded her about integrating the Cowhouse Motel.

As was the custom in most units, I held a special conference session for EM once a week. It was widely advertised throughout the 5/6 that I would be in my office after duty hours every Thursday, at which time anybody could come to talk with me about any problem without going through channels (seeing the 1SG or Co CO). In announcing these sessions it was made clear that the chain of command was to be the first and most important channel for solving problems. But when the chain of command did not operate successfully or promptly, the open door policy was available for use. There was always a suspicion in my mind that the SGM controlled these sessions since he remained in the outer office to keep order and to make sure that only one person came into the office at a time. It is possible that he discouraged some from using the privilege.

One evening a black soldier came in to ask for a transfer to a post in the northeast. When asked his reason for the request, he told me that he was from Philadelphia, where he had married a white girl while in college. Texas laws prohibited miscegenation. Hence, he could not bring his wife to Hood because a private could not get quarters on Post, nor could he legally rent an apartment in town.

After giving the matter serious consideration I told the soldier that I would not approve the request for a transfer. Though the law was wrong and should be changed, I did not believe that it was up to the Army to bear the burden of reform. He had married a white girl in the face of widespread, and almost universal condemnation of mixed marriages. While I personally found nothing to censor in this, he and his wife had to be prepared to accept the consequences of their actions. To expect the Army to transfer every individual who had a personal problem would create an impossible personnel situation. However, I told him that he should submit the request, giving his reasons for the transfer. Though I would recommend disapproval based on the rationale I had just explained, I was not the approving authority. The request would go to The Department of the Army in Washington, which might well reassign him over my negative recommendation.

The soldier's request for transfer was approved over my recommended disapproval. His transfer was a loss; I had previously discussed with him the possibility of attending OCS.

Several Thursdays later another black soldier knocked on my door, entered, saluted and said, "Sir, I have this problem in my company. The people are prejudiced against me. They are not giving me a fair deal in the company."

This startled me as I thought all of my Co COs were beyond that. "What Co are you in, soldier?" I asked quickly.

"B Company, Sir. Captain McDermott's Company."

"I can't believe CPT McDermott would treat you differently from any other soldier in his company."

"Well, it's not CPT McDermott, it's the LT. He does just like the civilians do."

"Who's your Platoon Leader, Soldier?"

"Second Lieutenant Kenyon, Sir." Again I was astounded, Kenyon was a fine officer with a high moral code. It was difficult to believe that he was prejudiced against any man in his platoon.

"Soldier, I find it hard to believe that LT Kenyon is prejudiced against you."

"Well, sir, it's not really the lieutenant, it's the Platoon Sergeant."

"Who is your Platoon Sergeant."

"Sergeant Johnson, Sir."

Sergeant Johnson was one of the finest NCOs in the Battalion - a husky, intelligent, disciplined, sensible, professional, black NCO.

"Young man, Sergeant Johnson is a black soldier, also."

351

"Well, Colonel, he just don't like me and he's prejudiced against me because I'm black."

"If Sergeant Johnson is prejudiced against you, it is not because you are black. It's because you are not a good soldier. Now you go back and show Sergeant Johnson that you know how to soldier."

"Well, Sir, I would rather have a different sergeant. One that is not so hard on us privates."

"Soldier, that will be all. You report back to your company and shape up. Dismissed."

He saluted, did an about face and walked sheepishly out of my office. SGM Allen chuckled in the outer office.

Black officers and NCOs faced a difficult situation in the sixties. Those who held commissioned or noncommissioned grades had earned them by hard work, loyalty and proven competence. As more and more black activists were drafted or enlisted into the Army the black OFFs and NCOs became the target of abuse. They were accused of being "Uncle Toms" and called "Oreos", black on the outside, but white inside. As they attempted to maintain the same standards of discipline for all soldiers they were pressured to give preferential and less demanding treatment to blacks. They were caught in a no-win situation with blacks against them if they did not openly support civil rights movements regardless of military policies, and criticism from whites if they showed favoritism toward blacks. A most unfortunate position to be in and one which many excellent officers and NCOs had difficulty in handling.

There were relatively few disciplinary problems in THE REGULARS. There was, of course, a Special Court-martial on orders in the 5/6 which had very little to do. As a result of one of the rare trials that came before it, the Court sent one soldier to the stockade. He was convicted of going AWOL. He had been AWOL two or three times, the last period being just short of a month. Based on this record I approved the sentence of the Court and put him in the Post Stockade. One day I got a call from MG Haines, who told me that he had visited the Post Stockade and talked with my AWOL Soldier among others.

"He looked me in the eye and told me that he wanted to soldier," Haines said seriously. "Don, that young man was sincere. He wants a chance to soldier. Why don't you release him from the stockade and let him prove to you what a good soldier he can be."

"Sir, this man has been AWOL three times. That is why he was put in the stockade. I don't want to take him out. He will just go AWOL again. I don't think it is right."

After some discussion, MG Haines said, "Don, I am convinced that he really wants to soldier. Take him out of the stockade."

"Yes, Sir."

The paperwork was quickly processed and the man released from confinement. Three days later he was AWOL again. The next time I saw MG Haines I mentioned to him that the soldier was AWOL. He grinned at me rather sheepishly, saying, "Perhaps I should have listened to you, Don. But he appeared so earnest and I was sure you could straighten him out. I thought he had changed."

In my opinion no convict is ever really rehabilitated. When a hood is identified he ought to be punished and then dishonorably discharged. It is a waste of resources to try to reform hoods.

As squad training gave way to Plt tng, which was in turn followed by Co tng, THE REGULARS developed into an effective tactical organization. Though weak initially in AR/IN techniques, I soon learned that my knowledge of basic Infantry Tactics was the most important thing. Few AR OFFs really understood how the IN should fight on a battlefield dominated by tanks, or what contribution the IN could make to combined Armor/Infantry operations. They had no better ideas about where to position the APCs after the IN dismounted than we Infantrymen did.

On a number of occasions I had differences on tactics with staff officers and commanders at Bde and Div. While not pretending to be a great tactician, I considered myself firmly grounded in Infantry Tactics. Like many others, I believed that the APC was simply another means of transportation, such as the parachute, truck or airplane, to carry troops to the combat area. Once in combat, the troops would dismount to fight as Infantry. There were some people in the 1st AR Div who thought that the APC was a tactical vehicle from which the IN should fight, but it was not designed for that purpose. A few APCs had machine guns mounted on them. But the troops within the personnel carrier could not fire as there were no firing ports.

Most of my disagreements on tactics were with the Div G-3, MAJ Lawrence L. Golston. As an AR OFF, he looked at tactics from the point of view of a tank commander. He visited the 5/6 during many of its training exercises, particularly during combined arms training. He often gave suggestions or made criticisms I thought wrong. I would listen to his comments, then make up my mind based on my analysis of the situation. During one exercise he directed me to change the disposition of my Infantrymen, after a sharp interchange, I ordered him out of the area. He returned shortly with MG Haines. After hearing my plans and reasoning, Haines reluctantly agreed that my dispositions were correct. It appeared to be a hard admission for him. It struck me as odd that he seemed more anxious to support one of his staff officers than he did to support one of his commanders.

Late in the summer THE REGULARS received an unexpected weekend mission. I was unhappy about this second violation of my stated "no week-end duty" policy, but the men seemed delighted with the mission: aggressor against an Airborne Brigade. Strike Command at MacDill AF Base, Tampa, FL, had directed the move of an 82nd ABN Div Bde from FT Bragg on a readiness exercise. The weather in the drop area precluded a parachute assault, so an air landed operation at Killeen Base, adjacent to FT Hood, had been substituted. Killeen Base, a closely guarded atomic storage site, had an airfield which could handle any type of aircraft. The C-130s loaded with paratroopers landed there for a two-day maneuver during which THE REGULARS would act as the aggressor force.

At that time the Bn radio call sign was "Jumpmaster", which drove the ABN troops berserk. While monitoring THE REGULARS radio transmissions they repeatedly heard Jumpmaster and were convinced we were toying with them.

It was a good exercise for THE REGULARS. The APCs could move the troops rapidly from point to point, while it took the ABN Infantrymen hours to get to their objectives on foot. We knew the terrain thoroughly, having maneuvered over it many times. Although it was a "free maneuver", with both sides at liberty to operate as they saw fit, we did know the mission of the ABN Bde and their initial assembly area, so had an advantage. We learned a great deal from that exercise.

Later, during a Strike Command exercise under GEN Paul D. Adams, COL Mel Zais, in charge of field maneuvers at that HQ, came to FT Hood. COL Wilson had introduced me to Zais when they were both assigned to the Pentagon, and we had visited Zais and his wife at their home. During the three-month war games TDY at Stuttgart I had also seen quite a bit of him as he was then the G-3 of 7th Army. One Saturday afternoon I wandered into the Officers' Club bar, where Mel was in a corner, drinking by himself. No man should drink alone, so I went over to say hello. During our conversation it developed that he was depressed because a BGs' promotion list had just been published and his name had not been on it.

"Don, I'm not going to make it. They passed me by and I'm getting too old."

"Wait until next year," I consoled. "You are certain to make the next list, It's too early to give up. You have several years of eligibility left, you will surely be picked." He was promoted in 1963 and went from brigadier general to four star general in a matter of six or seven years.

During one of our training exercises in August, The Regulars crossed the Cowhouse Creek in APCs. All of the units had practiced floating the tracks, making sure that the troops understood how to control them in the water and that everyone was proficient in this technique. The area selected for the crossing had a steep bank on the far side. As B Co was crossing, one of its APCs failed to make the grade. The driver started to back down for another approach, but as he did so the track flooded, shorting out the bilge pump, which caused the track to sink. Most of the men got out but two were unaccounted for. Attempts to recover the men continued into the night. Everybody in the immediate

353

area who had any lifesaving experience, including MG Haines' aide, dove in to try to find them. Just before dawn scuba divers found them snared in the weeds and bushes at the bottom of the creek. The loss of two young soldiers due to an accident that nobody had anticipated was tragic. All of the troops were saddened, and Pat McDermott, the B Co CO was visibly shaken. The exercise was completed under a cloud of depression. Chaplain Saunders conducted an impressive memorial service for the men once THE REGULARS returned to base camp.

To preserve the regular roads, track marches were conducted on special "tank trails" at FT Hood. For some reason these were never called tank trails over the radio but were always referred to as "Tango Tangos". It was never clear why the military phonetic words were used; tank trail is as easy to understand as Tango Tango. These tank trails were churned into a powdery dust by the tracks. The lead track had good visibility, but unless the wind was blowing at right angles to the direction of march, the rear tracks in a serial caught hell as they moved in a dense dust cloud. This was a real test for our drivers, posing serious safety problems. There were several accidents in other units due to the dust. Fortunately, THE REGULARS did not have any incidents. The dust cloud was a give-away, of course, of the movement of an armored unit. In actual combat tracks would not be confined to trails, but would deploy across country or use paved roads.

As THE REGULARS moved out on a night march to begin the Bn ATT, both blackout and dust caused problems. The column was starting and stopping frequently; the uneven movement indicated to me that the Co COs were confused. MAJ Kiggen was ahead of me at one check point when the column halted for the fifth time. In response to my radio query, the lead Co CO admitted that he did not know which way to go. He had made a turn and was disoriented. After consulting the march table it appeared to me that the lead track had turned incorrectly. I called Kiggen on the command net, reporting that the column appeared to be lost. Kiggen assured me that the turn was correct, referring me to the footnotes on the march table, which spelled out alternatives for several contingencies. This startled me, foot notes to march tables with alternate routes for a night tactical march complicated matters. It meant that each march unit commander had to check all the foot notes under blackout conditions to determine which way to go. There had been no contingency to trigger use of alternate routes, nor had I heard any communication over the command net informing them to do so. Kiggen, a good but abrasive OFF, exerted undue pressure on the Co COs. Though it was clearly understood that Co COs had direct access to me, and that he was a staff officer, his desire to get things done his way frequently had to be curbed. The Co COs took delight in hearing my irritation with Kiggen vented over the air. Normally, I did not reprimand anyone on the radio, but I was so provoked about the unnecessarily complicated march table which required a survey of six or seven footnotes each time a check point was reached, and this on an ATT, that I let him know my displeasure. Despite the road march, THE REGULARS passed the ATT handily.

Late in October, 1962, the Cuban Missile Crisis struck the nation and the 1st Armored Division. The Div had just been declared combat ready, morale was high, especially with the possibility of combat in Cuba. There had been several alerts; it was well known that MG Haines had been getting orders on a continuing basis. One evening the Bn COs were called to the Div CP where we were informed that the 1st Bde was going to Camp Stewart for a possible invasion of Cuba. However, the Bde was to be reconfigured, THE REGULARS were to be left behind. This was like being hit in the stomach. I was stunned! In my opinion we had the best battalion in the Div. Apparently MG Haines and COL Hollis did not think so. But this was the first indication that they had reservations about THE REGULARS.

That THE REGULARS was not going with the 1st Bde was bad enough; not knowing why it wasn't going was worse. After the meeting I protested but could not get a satisfactory answer from either Haines or Hollis. Suspecting that it might have been my outspoken views on tactics, I told COL Hollis that if that was the reason he should take THE REGULARS without me. But there was no change and no reason given. Admittedly I was a maverick. But I thought I was a team player. The only time I had not gone along with the crowd was on the STRAC rating. But that had changed nothing. I got along well with COL Hollis and the Bde Staff, and I knew the policies and procedures of the 1st Bde. Barring some major foiling in me or the battalion, there seemed no logical reason for leaving THE REGULARS behind. COL Hollis, thinking to ease the blow, told me that he was taking one company from THE REGULARS. Glumly I agreed that it should be A Co.

Both COL Hollis and MG Haines had clearly been derelict in their leadership responsibilities in failing to counsel me concerning reservations they had about my performance or that of THE REGULARS. There had been nothing but glowing praise of the morale and progress of the unit during training. To permit any unit to be declared combat ready, without pointing out shortcomings that might be corrected, to me was unthinkable.

But the situation was made worse. The 1st Bde was given priority on personnel and equipment. Rather than insisting that the Post Support Agencies get the Bde to first class fighting condition, the rest of the Div was levied for top flight personnel and good equipment. As a result, there was one first class Bde, the 1st, and two second class brigades in the 1st AR Div. The cannibalization of those units not going to Camp Stewart left the remainder of the Div in terrible shape and it was never again a balanced unit. As it turned out this was an extremely bad decision.

The 1st Bde was loaded on trains for the move to Camp Stewart, GA, just outside Savannah. All of the resources of THE REGULARS were at the disposal of CPT Mejia; his loading and movement became a Battalion project.

The 1st Bde had no sooner cleared Ft Hood when orders were received directing the entire Div to proceed to Camp Stewart. Now there was a mess, because all the remaining battalions, particularly THE REGULARS, had nothing but junk to take with them. The resentment over the loss of carefully maintained radio and motor equipment to the 1st Bde reached a new level. In a frenzy of activity, tracks were repaired and new equipment drawn. It took great effort to make the unit even marginally effective. Deadline rates were high. Eventually, the 5/6 minus was combat-ready. Loading was accomplished by driving the tracks from the rear of the train forward. Spanners were laid between the cars so that the vehicles could be driven ahead. Once on the proper car, the APCs or tanks were chocked, blocked and cabled to the cars. Fortunately, the experience of outloading A Co made things easier for the rest of THE REGULARS.

Just before departing from Ft Hood, I was checking the Bn reveille formation. Before turning the companies back to their commanders the Duty Officer announced some last minute changes I had instructed him to pass on to the units. As CPT Brant dismissed C Co, he said aloud, so that everybody in his company, indeed in the immediate area, including SGM Allen and myself could hear him, "What stupid son of a bitch made that decision?"

Outraged that a Co CO would criticize an order from Bn HQ in front of his men, I determined to take Brant to task. There was no objection to any of the commanders coming in to talk about an order or policy -1 welcomed their comments and criticisms. After careful consideration of their points I would then decide the issue. But I did not approve of any commander taking issue with an order in front of his men. Returning to the Bn CPI called CPT Brant and ordered him to report to me immediately. After discussing the matter with him I told him that I was disturbed that he would criticize my decisions in front of his soldiers. He acted amazed. "But sir, I don't understand what you are talking about. I didn't say such a thing."

This was not true, I had heard him; there was no question in my mind that it was Brant who had spoken. He had uttered his remarks loud enough so that I heard them across the street so I was sure that his entire company had heard them. His bold lie shocked me into an instant decision. "CPT Brant, you are relieved," I told him. "Go back to your Co and clean out your desk immediately. I'll take the necessary steps to have a new Co CO replace you."

Brant protested, saying, "I really didn't mean that."

"Ernie, I can stand anything but lying. I will not tolerate an officer who lacks integrity. I want to be able to depend your word, to know that any report or statement you make to me is true. I no longer have any confidence in your word. You are relieved."

Brant saluted with exaggerated precision, snapped, "Yes, Sir", did an about face and stalked out of my office. He reminded me of a sulky kid. Ernie came back later and apologized. He said he had spoken without thinking; he tried to explain his action and asked me to give him a second chance. I told him that having once been lied to, I could never again trust him to tell the truth. Under those circumstances I thought it best for him, C Co and the Bn that he be transferred.

Immediately, I called COL Jenson, CDR of the 2nd Bde to which THE REGULARS was now attached, telling him of my decision and requesting that orders be cut transferring Brant from the 5/6. Command of C Co was given to 1LT Gates, who was gung-ho, and who had done an excellent job as the Scout Plt Ldr. I thought that he might inspire C Co to move out with him.

There was little time for Gates to do anything but inventory the property, sign for it and assume command. Fortunately, all preparations for the move were complete - he had only to follow the plan Ernie had made. He could make other changes, if warranted, when C Co closed into Camp Stewart.

The tracks, accompanied by a guard detail, went by train, the rest of the personnel by motor convoy. The motor march took about three days. The convoy moved well, though not as efficiently as the 508 had moved from Benning to San Angelo, TX, in 1952. CPT Jim Moore, an Army Aviator, was asked to ferry one of the helicopters, thus he arrived at Stewart a day before the convoy did. He was able to recon the area assigned to the 5/6, and tentatively assign Co areas before THE REGULARS reached the Post. I approved his dispositions on sight.

Camp Stewart was an inactive Army post used by NG units for their summer encampments. It did have some barracks, but mostly frames on which to erect tents. There were WWII type mess halls, combined orderly and supply rooms, latrines and Bn HQ buildings. Each Bn, including THE REGULARS, was assigned the required number of buildings and tent frames. Since A Co had been detached, THE REGULARS had an extra mess hall. This was made into a club and recreation center for both EM and OFFs. THE REGULARS was the only battalion so fortunate; it proved a boon to morale. A bar was set up which dispensed both beer and hard liquor. Almost every night, I stopped by to have a drink with the OFFs before going to my quarters. The companies set up their messes in the WWII mess halls; I ate with each of them in turn.

There were many other units marshalling at Camp Stewart. While at the Officers' Club one evening, I met MAJ Zolton Kollat who had been my PSG in I Co, 504, and one of my PSGs in F Co, 508. He had left F Co to accept his commission in 1951. We enjoyed a long talk over a couple of drinks.

Bn COs were billeted in the nurses' quarters of the inactive hospital. Two officers shared each suite, consisting of a living room, bedroom with two beds, and a bathroom. My roommate was Barney Broughton, an old friend from the Pentagon. Barney was amazed at my ability to fall asleep quickly once in bed. He reported that on many occasions while we were talking he would hear regular breathing indicating that I was asleep. This ability to sleep anyplace, under any circumstances served me well in my career.

The fact that THE REGULARS had not remained with the 1st Bde continued to plague me. After much thought I wrote a letter to MG Haines requesting to be relieved. SGM Allen typed it for me because I did not want the matter to get around the Bn. In the letter I stated that it was obvious that the Div CDR did not have confidence in me as a Bn CO. Since I did not want THE REGULARS penalized because of his reservations about me, I asked to be relieved. I showed the letter to Barney before I forwarded it. He took me to task for even thinking of such an action. He was certain that personalities were involved and persuaded me not to submit the letter. But the matter continued to bother me.

THE REGULARS had been attached to the 2nd Bde commanded by COL Lloyd K. Jenson. He was not the dynamic, strong commander that COL Hollis was. We tangled shortly after closing into Camp Stewart. When I wrote the efficiency report on CPT Brant, the Co CO I had relieved, I directed that an extra copy of the comments be made. I then instructed SGM Allen to get the copy to Brant unofficially. In those days DA decreed that officers would not be shown their efficiency reports. The theory was that the rating officer would be more objective if he did not have to show and explain his ratings to his subordinates. This was ridiculous, but I could not officially discuss the report with Ernie. In my comments I pointed out that Brant was a strong disciplinarian and a good tactician, but indicated my loss of confidence in his integrity, the reason for his relief. It appeared to me that he had reached the level of his capability as a CPT Co CO and should not be promoted.

COL Jenson told me several times that he wanted me to change the report. He had been impressed with Brant who was a sharp Airborne type. In refusing to change the report, I told COL Jenson that I considered the rating of officers a very grave responsibility and that I gave each report careful consideration. In the case of Brant, I had given his report more than usual thought; as a result I could not in conscience change it. If he disagreed with my rating, he could make this known in his indorsement even though he had not observed Brant during the rating period (it seemed to me that COL Hollis should have indorsed it). COL Jenson finally ordered me to change the report. This precipitated a heated exchange during which I pointed out to him that he had issued an illegal order. Finally he recognized that I was hardheaded and was not going to make any change. What he said in his indorsement was never made known to me.

After that experience it seemed to me that the only bright spot in the 2nd Bde was Chaplain Davies, who replaced Chaplain Saunders as the de facto chaplain of THE REGULARS. Davies was an excellent preacher, an effective chaplain and an Episcopal priest. He left the Army and was later consecrated Bishop of Dallas

Because it had been anticipated that the 1st AR Div would be committed to combat in Cuba, the troops had been instructed to bring minimal clothing, though most had brought a sport shirt and slacks. Those who did have civilian clothing were permitted to go into Savannah on pass on week ends. On two occasions I got into Savannah with Barney Broughton for dinner at one of the fine restaurants. But we did not have much time to see the city as we had to be back to Camp Stewart by midnight. Since the Division was on alert, a curfew had been imposed.

Thanksgiving at Camp Stewart was very festive. As usual, the Army had provided many extras for the troops. The Co COs exerted themselves to decorate the mess halls and make it a pleasant meal. The Asst Div CDR, BG Norvell, inspected the mess halls and was highly compli-mentary, especially of C Co; 1LT Gates, who had artistic abilities, had decorated his mess hall colorfully. Though invited to eat with all of the Cos, I elected to have Thanksgiving dinner with B Co.

On several occasions I visited A Co. CPT Mejia asked me to have dinner with the company one evening, during which I talked with the men to make sure that they were getting everything they needed. All indicated that they were eager to rejoin THE REGULARS. Before A Co had left Ft Hood CPT Mejia had come to me almost in tears. He wanted to stay with the Bn - wanted to remain a REGULAR. Touched by his loyalty to the unit, I assured him that until notified otherwise, A Co was still part of THE REGULARS. He did not want to take the 5th of the 6th Infantry insignia or designations off the A Co vehicles. He had been almost as dejected as I was at A Co's detachment.

The missile crisis passed. The Soviets yielded to President Kennedy's conditions and the 1st AR Div was left at Camp Stewart without a mission. All units embarked on an intensive training program which included foot road marches (there was no place to maneuver the tracks), and the firing of most weapons. With MG Haines' backing, many live fire exercises were conducted.

President Kennedy visited Camp Stewart to review the 1st Bde which was to have made the initial landing. The President complimented the Div on its rapid move and thanked the men for their service and performance. He was briefed on the 1st AR Div's readiness. For two weeks before the Presidential visit, work-men were busy remodeling the briefing room. It cost about $10,000 to refurbish it; Camp Stewart had a beautiful briefing room after that one hour session. Following the briefing there was a ten-minute period unallocated. It was suggested that the President meet with the battalion commanders or sergeants major. MG Haines, ever concerned with the prestige of the noncommissioned officers, decided that the President should meet the sergeants major. Though denied the opportunity to meet him formally, the other Bn COs and I were in the reviewing stand where he talked to us all briefly.

In mid-December it was announced that the Div would return to Ft Hood by various means, train, motor convoy and ship. LSTs had been chartered for the movement of the 1st AR Div to Cuba. They did not belong to the US Navy, but were privately owned, under Liberian or Panamanian flags. Most of the captains were experienced Scandinavian seamen, but the crews were a polyglot rabble picked up from various Caribbean ports. As the vessels were still under charter and available, part of the Div would return to Texas by that means. THE REGULARS was selected to go by LST. There was an uneasy feeling that Goldston, now a LTC, had a hand in this decision. It would be a slow, not too pleasant way of movement, but it would be different! Co A, still attached to the 1st Bde, would return with it, but the rest of the 5/6 would travel by LST.

The move was made in three stages, a motor march from Camp Stewart to Port Everglades; the sea voyage by LST to Galveston; then another motor march from Galveston to FT Hood. The tracks returned by rail. The trip to Fort Lauderdale (Port Everglades) took 1 1/2 days. THE REGULARS bivouacked overnight in Deland, FL, where Herb Mansfield had retired. After the troops were settled for the night, SGM Allen and I had dinner with Herb and Irene at their home. During the pleasant visit SGM Allen was forced to listen to many lively jump stories. Herb was then a student at Stetson University and had lettered in soccer at age 46!

On arrival at Port Everglades, the LSTs were loaded quickly. B Co embarked on one LST, C Co on another, and HHC on the third. Bn HQ was split with a field grade officer on each LST. It took much effort to clean up the filthy vessels to make them liveable. The troop compartments had been neglected over time. On the LST with B Co, I was given a stateroom crowded with gear but reasonably clean. Most of the OFFs and all of the EM were crowded into staterooms and troop compartments.

By prior arrangement THE REGULARS took over the mess on each of the three ships on which it would travel. Army mess personnel served food for both the crew and the Bn. The galleys were particularly dirty; a great deal of energy was expended before our mess sergeants considered them fit to use.

The small convoy sailed around Key West and into the Gulf of Mexico. Once in the Gulf the rudder on the LST carrying B Co was damaged during a storm - there was no means of steering the ship. The Captain stopped the engines and we bobbed about until the storm was over, while the other LSTs stood by. It took two days to fix the steering gear. Fortunately there was enough food and water on board so that the delay created no problems. It was a monotonous trip for the troops; once the initial excitement wore off there was little for them to do. Finally, the LSTs reached Galveston. A Div representative welcomed us as we debarked. Without delay a convoy was formed and the Bn started for FT Hood. This trip, too, took about a day and a half.

It was good to be back in our own area. On inspecting the facilities to make sure that all was in order, C Co found that a pipe had burst and water had spewed all over the mess hall. It was a shambles; cobwebs, mildew and dirty water covered everything. Just before Brant had been relieved, the C Co mess hall had been painted to make it a very attractive place. Now it could not be used. While repairs were being made, one of the C Co Plts ate with each of the other companies. As soon as it had closed into FT Hood, A Co returned to Bn control, me officers and men were delighted to be REGULARS again.

Throughout the holiday period, Christmas festivities held sway. The traditional Army Christmas dinner was even better than Thanksgiving. Co A asked me to have dinner with them -I was delighted to do so. There were many parties on Post, including a Bn Christmas party. Determined that THE REGULARS would have a New Years' reception, I had to work around COL Jenson's and MG Haines1 affairs. As a result, THE REGULARS New Year's reception began about 1600 in a private room at the Officers' Club Annex in the hospital area. The officers were in dress blues and their wives in beautiful gowns. Of course, REGULARS Punch was served. It was a gala start for 1963.

Early in February, there was the usual monthly formation, a cocktail party during which people joining or leaving THE REGULARS were recognized. At that party, THE REGULARS bade farewell to the Smiths and the Kiggens. Smith, now a LTC, was transferred to Divas the G-l. MAJ Kiggen was reassigned to a tank Bn. They were presented with small replicas of THE REGULARS PLEDGE in appreciation of their contribution to the 5/6. Harry Porterfield become the XO, replaced as S-4 by a newly arrived CPT. Jim Moore became the Bn S-3. This delighted the Co COs. Moore, though equally competent, was easier to get along with.

At that party Bud and Caroline Schaerer received a baby cup for their first born, Burt. I believe that he was the first child born into THE REGULARS. The Schaerers had just returned from leave in Tennessee. Bud had brought back some strong "white lightning". Because the ladies did not like corn liquor, a modified REGULARS Punch had been mixed. Bud surreptitiously spiked it with white lightning not only giving it a strong taste but adding to its potency!

In the middle of January, THE REGULARS was selected to conduct ranger type training for the Div. The mission had been assigned because I was one of the few Bn COs who was ranger qualified. Before writing the training program, arrangements were completed for Jim Moore and me to go on TDY to Benning to review some of the ranger training techniques. At the same time, I was selected to go to FT Huachuca, AZ to take the Aerial Surveillance Sensor Course. Moore and I went to Benning together. He had a chance to visit his parents in Buena Vista, just outside the Post. We were able to get to Dahlonega to review such training procedures as rappelling, mountain climbing and long-range patrolling. Upon completion of that phase of the trip, Jim left me at the airport in Dallas where I caught a flight for El Paso, Tucson and Ft Huachuca.

Just after my plane became airborne, a handsome young man came from the first class section and dropped into the seat next to me. Traveling under orders, I was in uniform in the tourist section. My new seat mate introduced himself as SSG Haywood from F Co of the 508. He had gotten out of the Army and was now with an engineering firm (perhaps it was his own). Our long talk was spiced with recollections of our days in F Co of the 508.

The one-week Aerial Surveillance Sensor Course covered the use of drone aircraft equipped with various types of intelligence gathering devices, radar, infrared, and photographic. It was an interesting course which I enjoyed thoroughly. My oldest friend, George Gabelia, was also on TDY at FT Huachuca We had dinner together; one of the few times our paths crossed on active duty.

On returning to FT Hood, Jim Moore and I began to write the POI for the ranger training. Meanwhile, normal activities continued. The Battalion was in refresher training. One day in February, while visiting one of the companies firing on the rifle range, Rick, my jeep driver, received a message from the CP directing me to report to the Chief of Staff s office immediately. Enroute to Div HQ my thoughts ran over the last few days wondering what had gone wrong that the Chief should want to see me. Nothing untoward had happened that would have upset the Div CDR, an unusual situation in itself, because I was frequently in hot water. My readiness report had been approved so I could think of nothing the Chief would call me to his office for.

Arriving at the Div CP, I found Barney Broughton there. Barney, now promoted and a Bn CO, was equally puzzled. We reported to COL Pepke, the CofS, who was no more communicative than anybody else had been. He merely told us that the CG was waiting to see us in his office. Barney and I walked in, followed by COL Pepke, saluted and reported to MG Haines. He looked up from his desk with an odd expression on his face, I am not exactly sure what it did portray. He told us that he had just received a call from the Pentagon informing him that the two of us were being reassigned from the Div. I was to go to MacDill AF Base for duty with STRICOM, while Barney was to go to FT Ritchie for duty with the Joint Alternate Command Element (JACE) of the Joint Chiefs of Staff.

Both of us immediately protested, I had commanded THE REGULARS for just over a year, and Barney had yet not completed a year as a Bn CO. MG Haines appeared sympathetic, telling us that he, too, had protested, but had been told that our assignments were final. Immediately my mind reviewed all the people I knew in the Pentagon. I asked MG Haines if he had any objections to my calling the SGS, MG Mock. Although Mock and I had never been close, I had worked for him a year and apparently had satisfied him in all the requirements he had placed on me. Barney had also worked for him, and asked me to plead his case at the same time. MG Haines' aide placed the call, when MG Mock answered, I explained the situation, told him that the Bn was at the peak of its training and that I wanted to stay another six months at least in order to develop it. Warming to the argument I explained Barney's plight, having had less than eight months as a Bn CO. Mock was extremely cool, informing me in no uncertain terms that this was a matter for the staff in which he would not interfere. There was no doubt that we were going to be transferred.

However, MG Haines felt that because Barney was married and had children, duty at JACE, which necessitated alternate weeks away from home, would not be good for him or his family. He asked me if I had any objections to changing jobs with Barney. Though not particularly interested in the JACE job, and really preferring the duty at MacDill which might be an Airborne slot, I could not deprive Barney of the opportunity of remaining with his family, so I concurred in the change. Haines arranged for the change in orders.

We were told to talk with the lieutenant colonel's assignment officer in Infantry Branch, for instructions and timing. On contacting the action officer at the Pentagon, he wanted to know how soon I could report for duty. Looking at the calendar, I told him that it would be two weeks before I could turn over the Bn, I wanted a minimum of two weeks leave plus the four days I was entitled to for travel time, hence it would be sometime in mid-April before I would be available for duty. He told me that was unacceptable, that I had to be available not later than the 25th of February. Duty on the Joint Staff is normally a three-year tour and replacements are programmed far in advance. This precipitous assignment did not make sense and I wanted to know the reason for the urgency. He would not tell me the problem, so we argued back and forth. Reluctant to give up my leave, I eventually compromised on the third of March.

Leaving THE REGULARS would be difficult. There was a closeness with all of the officers which is rarely experienced. Apparently the other officers in the Battalion felt the same way -I was overwhelmed with the farewell activities arranged for me and the gifts showered upon me. THE REGULARS was a tight-knit organization, and I was one of the first few to leave. Following an emotional change of command ceremony, at which MG Haines pinned an ARCOM on me, I departed with regret.

After a short visit with Mother in New York, I drove to Washington to look for an apartment. The one I located was just off Columbia Pike, in Dominion Towers, a ground floor apartment with a private entrance onto the parking lot. It had one bedroom, with a large living room, dining area and kitchen. My furniture was delivered from storage along with the items I had left with Sam and Betty King. Shortly, I was comfortably settled and ready for my new assignment.

CHAPTER 15

CHAIRBORNE

The Pentagon was as hectic as ever when I reported for duty on 3 March 1963. It was easier for me to find the Administrative Office of the Joint Alternate Command Element (JACE), my new HQ, than it had been to find ODSCOPS when first I reported for duty in 1957. After signing in, the processing officer informed me that I would need summer uniforms immediately as the Battle Staff Team I was assigned to was getting ready to go to the Caribbean. My baggage, which contained all of my summer uniforms, had not arrived from FT Hood, hence, I was completely unprepared for such a trip as I had expected duty in the Washington area. Eventually, the officer I replaced, who luckily was my size, lent me enough khaki and TW uniforms to get me through the trip.

During routine processing, an explanation of the precipitate orders emerged; an officer originally assigned to a Joint HQ at FT Meade, MD, didn't like that assignment and prevailed upon a friend, a general officer, to get his orders changed. When this was accomplished, it became necessary to find someone to replace him. Army Personnel selected the LTC I was now replacing, thus triggering the chain reaction. What it amounted to was that some selfish officer, because of his personal desires, abetted by a meddlesome general, fouled up the personnel system. In so doing he made it difficult for two brother officers. I now understood MG Fry's strong position on assignments. This is an object lesson or at least a thought that some of those bright young lads who are trying to run their own careers should consider. Every time they succeed in getting their orders changed, it is going to affect one or more OFFs. My own action in calling Mock now appeared to be the same selfish action; I was relieved, on reflection, that he had taken no action. This is not to say that an OFF should not ask for or fight for any assignment he wants, but he should do it through the proper personnel channels, not through the intervention of senior officers.

The JACE Battle Staff Team I was going to work with was at FT Ritchie; I joined it there. The Team, headed by an AF COL, was composed of about 40 OFFs and EM from all services.

While the team slept at FT Ritchie, it worked in "The Rock", a cave hollowed out of a solid limestone mountain, with great steel doors which could seal it from a nuclear blast, fallout or chemical attack. An underground city had been built in the cave.

COL G. C. Willms, the Team Chief, assigned me as an "Emergency Action Officer" (EAO) charged with handling a communications console to set up conferences, pass orders, record conversations and keep in contact with US military elements throughout the world. The EAO had access to very highly classified, top priority orders in the event of any major mobilization or attack. A second EAO was always on duty; on this Team he was MAJ Richard Gaudsmith, USAF, who undertook to break me in on the necessary procedures. The Emergency Action Team (EAT) was completed by a strapping Marine Gunnery Sergeant, Chris Melonson. The rest of the Battle Staff Team consisted of operations, intelligence and logistical personnel who would man the Command Post (CP) in an emergency.

There were five Battle Staff Teams manning JACE in turn: two Teams were in the FT Ritchie area pulling twelve-hour shifts at the Rock; another two were on alert in the Washington area; and the remaining team was off duty. Teams were on duty for five days, then off four to eight days; the schedule constantly rotated so that teams had night duty one tour, day duty the next.

The Emergency Action Teams conducted a check of the world-wide communications at least once during each twelve-hour shift. During this check, called WHITE EXPRESS, the procedures that would be used in the event of an emergency to convene a world-wide conference or pass special orders or messages were followed. Every JCS Unified and Specified Command, each of the military service operations centers and many other important HQ were included in this check. The console had 30 or 40 buttons, each connected directly to similar consoles in all HQ throughout the world. By pressing a button, the connection to the NATO CP, for instance, could be completed instantly. A WHITE EXPRESS check was initiated without notice whenever we decided it should be accomplished. Dick and I checked each other as we raced through the procedure, depressing each button in turn and saying, "WHITE EXPRESS, standby". When all HQ had responded, the check was terminated. This procedure took little more than a minute to complete. It was always timed and recorded. Communications to the SAC Airborne Command Post, called LOOKING GLASS, were also checked during WHITE EXPRESS. Another important check on the ability to send messages to nuclear submarines, involved a separate communications system.

In the Emergency Action Office, a locked room with bullet-proof glass windows looking out on the general conference room, was a "Red Box", a small safe actually, with two locks. Each of the EAOs had a key to one of the locks, thus it took both to open the safe. Kept in the "Red Box" were prepared, pre-recorded messages which could unleash nuclear retaliation in the event of war. It was an awesome responsibility with which each Emergency Action Officer was deeply imbued. The EAOs were the only members of the Team who carried loaded side arms while on duty.

The EAO who routinely relieved me on one of the other teams, LTC Sid Hack, an AR OFF, became a good friend after many reliefs. We had much in common and enjoyed a few minutes of interesting talk at each change over.

Because each team had the 12 hour night shift every other duty period, many of the team members had difficulty sleeping during the day. It was hard to go to bed at 0900 and get a good sleep. The medical personnel gave each of us a packet of sleeping pills, but I took one only one time. Fortunately, I experienced little difficulty in sleeping, because the taking of any drugs while faced with the responsibilities of the EAO concerned me.

The team I joined had one week of duty at FT Ritchie before going to the Caribbean; in that time I became proficient in all emergency action procedures. Immediately following a three day break, I drove to Norfolk and reported aboard the USS *Northampton*. Another team also reported for duty at the same time. The Command Center Afloat was to provide communications back-up and an emergency refuge for President Kennedy when he visited Costa Rica on his first visit out of the country. The *Northampton* would cruise in international waters off the coast; helicopters would be available to evacuate him to the *Northampton* in the event of any difficulties there; the EAT would provide immediate communication facilities

The *Northampton* was a WWII cruiser which had been converted into a command ship. There was a suite of rooms for the President, a large briefing room, an area for the Battle Staff Team, including an Emergency Action Room, and cabins for the two teams plus members of the President's entourage. Dick Gaudsmith and I found the communications console and immediately checked to make sure that the *Northampton* was in contact with all of the major US HQ in the world.

It was a pleasant trip; the 12 hour tours were not overly demanding. By careful scheduling each team got as many day as night tours. We officers ate our meals in the Ward Room with specified seats at the tables for each sitting. The Navy lives more lavishly than the Army, though also more stuffily, and the food was good. Even the sea remained calm. The only thing missing was a before dinner drink. There was time to read, to sun on deck and enjoy the sea voyage.

The *Northampton* went first to the international waters off Costa Rica, cruised for the two days of the President's visit, then proceeded to Cristobal on the Atlantic side of the Canal Zone. There was an opportunity to see Colon, some of the ruins in the area, and the Atlantic Terminus of the Canal.

The seafood was excellent; the chance to stretch sea-legs welcome. It was the first time I had been in that part of the world.

On the way back to Norfolk, the *Northampton* stopped off at San Juan, Puerto Rico, for three days. It was another opportunity to see old fortifications, enjoy superb seafood, gamble a bit in one of the many casinos, and see another part of the world. By the end of the voyage the new job seemed more acceptable, although I still resented the precipitous departure from THE REGULARS.

On returning to Washington, the Team reverted to the regular schedule, one week at FT Ritchie, then off four to eight days, back to Ritchie a week, then off four to eight days. Each time we went to Ritchie we would go on a different schedule, first the 2100 - 0900, next the 0900 - 2100. Ritchie is about 75 miles from Washington, a drive of about an hour and a half. Every third week was free, a golden opportunity to visit friends, travel or just relax.

At the start of each shift tour, there was a general meeting of the entire Team in the conference room. Dick Gaudsmith usually stayed at the console but could see and hear the proceedings since the Emergency Action Team was in a glass enclosed room which looked out on the conference room, thick with microphones so all proceedings could be taped. During one such meeting COL Willms called me to the front of the group and presented me with an Appreciation Certificate from the Armed Forces Chaplains Board. Chaplains Davies and Saunders at FT Hood had recommended me for the award. I was surprised and a bit non-plussed.

As part of the Team's readiness training, a daily briefing was presented to each shift. This insured that everyone was constantly recording and evaluating all information coming through the system. Most of the briefings were stereotyped, but they provided practice as well as keeping us current on world events.

There were many old friends in the Washington Area which made duty there pleasant. Jim Owens was back in the Pentagon and I saw him and Joan often. Of course many evenings were spent with Sam and Betty King; Betty's gourmet cooking was better than ever. Sam's tales of the visits of foreign dignitaries were fascinating; his duties in the State Department Protocol Office brought him in contact with many of them. Peanut Hinton had the Special Forces Desk in OPO; I visited Marjie and Peanut at their home in Annandale frequently. Bill and Lucy Homen were again in Washington, now living in the River House. They had just had another son, Gregory. Bill and I got out on the golf course once or twice, but my game was as bad as ever.

An enjoyable surprise was to find Wick assigned to DCSPER in the Pentagon. We began doing things together much as we had at Leavenworth. Wick had bought a log cabin at Scientists Cliffs, MD, on the Chesapeake Bay, which he called *Far Niente,* literally translated from the Italian as the Doing of Nothing. I spent many hours there helping him make improvements or just relaxing on the Bay.

A number of old friends visited me in the apartment at Dominion Towers: Frank and Lucy Mashburn, Harry Porterfield and his wife Millie Jo, Willie Ballard, Charlie and Kitty Jackson and Gus and Maggie Braun. The latter two couples spent a week each with me while they looked for houses in the area. Charlie Jackson attended the National War College, while Gus Braun was assigned as Comptroller of the National Guard Bureau upon his graduation from Syracuse University with an MBA. The opportunity to renew so many friendships was the real attraction of that tour. Of course members of the family visited also. During the breaks I explored Washington, visiting all the museums and places of interest I had missed during previous tours in that area.

Toward the end of July, BG Tibbets, the Commander of JACE (and the pilot of the Enola Gay from which the atomic bomb had been dropped on Hiroshima) assembled the team to announce that because of a reorganization of the National Military Command Center (NMCC), some Team members were being reassigned to duty with it in the Pentagon, while others would remain with JACE. Shortly, orders were published assigning me to the NMCC effective 2 August.

When I signed in at the JCS Administrative Office, LTC George Wear, a Leavenworth classmate and now the JCS Administrative Officer, oriented me. Then he escorted me to the NMCC, where the Battle Staff Team Leader, Navy Captain Sid Baney, assigned me to the Europe Desk as an Operations Staff Officer (OSO). My area of responsibility was Europe and the Middle East which I had to keep under surveillance, maintaining familiarity with current intelligence as well as with all plans pertaining to those areas. At all times each OSO had to be prepared to brief on the plans, status of the forces, and the current intelligence pertaining to his area. As in JACE, the teams had staggered shifts; after a break a team might work 3 days from 2000 to 0500, 3 days from 0500 to 1200, and 3 days from 1200 to 2000, then be off for 3 days. After each break, the team would report for a different shift, so that the schedule kept rotating. It became a monotonous routine; the 3 days off were useful, but the constant changing of schedules was not good.

The NMCC was a suite of rooms in the bowels of the JCS area on the second floor of the Pentagon. There was an Emergency Action Office with a console and the ever-present EAOs; a large room in which the on-duty Battle Staff Team worked, and a large JCS conference room with multiple rear projection screens, electronic displays of time of burst of nuclear weapons and other data concerned with nuclear warfare. In addition there was the room in which the US terminus of the "Hot Line" teletype was housed and a utility room for draftsmen. There was also a small office for the General or Flag Officer on duty, but the Battle Staff Team Chief, an Army, Air Force or Marine Colonel or Navy Captain, had his desk in the large room with his team. The General/Flag Officer was a later addition found necessary as a result of several incidents involving Bobby Kennedy and other Administration Big-wigs who wanted to play general. The movement of troops to the University of Mississippi for the purpose of integrating it was one example. Attorney General Kennedy wanted to know the name and race of every individual in the Army contingent sent to Jackson and literally wanted to give each soldier specific instructions. He was not a pleasant person to deal with. It was then decided that the NMCC needed a little more muscle at the military end, so the General/Flag Officer was assigned. Working with the Navy Rear Admiral on our shift was frustrating. He was an intellectual prude, more interested in the structure than the substance of the paper, who had a fetish about commas. He took the commas out of all messages, making them more difficult to read.

During my ten months in the NMCC many interesting events transpired. In Europe and the Middle East there were crises in Skopje, Yugoslavia, when an earthquake killed over 1,000 people in Cyprus when the Turks moved in; in Dar es Salaam when American lives were threatened during a mutiny; and in Berlin, when the Russians blockaded the autobahn and refused to permit Allied convoys to traverse East Germany. Although free access to Berlin was guaranteed by treaty, the Russians would periodically hold up trains or convoys entering or leaving the city. Such blockades always created a furor, requiring the Battle Staff Team on duty to brief the JCS on minute-to-minute actions during any stoppage.

Other OSOs handled the integration of the University of Mississippi, the Alaskan earthquake and the Tonkin Gulf incident. The night of August 4, 1964 every member of the team followed the *Maddox* and the *C. Turner Joy* as they faced the North Vietnamese gun boats in the Tonkin Gulf. The NMCC received the reports at the same time the Navy did. Although none of these were related to my specific areas, I became involved by helping out the over-worked officer who had the action. They in turn helped me when a stalled convoy on the Berlin Autobahn swamped me.

After the Dar es Salaam incident during which the USS *Manley* had done an efficient job in evacuating 61 Americans endangered by a mutiny in Tanganyika, I prepared a message to the ship which I concluded with the words "Well Done". The Admiral on duty immediately struck this out, saying, "You don't do that in the Navy. When you send a well done to a captain it amounts to a citation. This action does not warrant a citation." It seemed a juvenile policy, not being able to compliment individuals or units for doing a good job; perhaps the Navy had a reason which escaped me.

The amount of detail the White House, the State Department, the Justice Department and other Executive Agencies demanded of the NMCC was unbelievable. Almost before the first spot report had been received, the concerned OSO was besieged by questions and demands for details he was, in most cases, not able to supply. It was over-kill of the worst sort; direct supervision from the highest to the lowest echelon. This resulted in large part from the fact that communications were too good; the Emergency Action Team was able to patch a call from the Oval Office directly to a Plt Ldr on the ground. Scores of intermediate commanders were by-passed; the result was chaos. Such circumvention breeds not only a lack of confidence or trust in subordinates, but also aggravates frustration. Reluctance to delegate authority reflects the lack of confidence the senior official has in himself. When he believes that he alone can handle the details of a situation, he is overwhelmed with minutiae and drowned in trivia. This tendency in the Army leads to the development of OFFs and NCOs who depend on someone else to do their thinking or make their decisions. Our junior OFFs and NCOs are denied experience in the exercise of command.

While I was assigned to the NMCC, Mother visited me occasionally. She would hop the shuttle at LaGuardia Field and I would pick her up an hour later at National Airport. Wick invited her to Far Niente several times when his Mother, Mappy, was there. The two ladies spent hours talking and watching ships go by. Wick and I never found out the subject of those long and absorbing conversations.

While talking to Hal Long on one of my frequent visits to Owings Mills to see his parents, he expressed some interest in attending the USMA. After consulting with Keith Barlow, with whom I had maintained correspondence after our service together in the 504 at Mainz, a weekend orientation visit was planned. Keith, assigned as an English instructor at West Point, agreed to give the boys a tour of USMA including the new academic building, take them to a home football game, after which we would have dinner with Keith and Kay and several cadets. Since Charlie and Kitty Jackson's oldest son, Charley, was also in the throes of deciding what he wanted to do after graduation from high school, he was included in the trip. It was fun! The boys were impressed with the Military Academy in spite of a humiliating defeat suffered on home territory. They were especially taken with Keith, who got so carried away with rhetoric, some of the 18th Century poets, and drink, that he let the steaks burn. But this recruiting effort was in vain; both boys went on to other pursuits.

During my first months in the Pentagon the famous "Hot Line" was completed. As mentioned previously, this was a teletype machine located in a separate room. There were linguists on duty in addition to the communications personnel, who were constantly conducting checks to make sure both the Russian Terminus as well as the American Terminus were operational. It took several frustrating weeks to get the teletypewriters on line and operating satisfactorily. Subsequently there were frequent outages.

On 22 November 1963, I left the NMCC at noon looking forward to a three-day break, which included dinner with Lucy and Bill Homen the following night. As I drove toward FT Myer to get a haircut, the radio program was interrupted with an announcement that President Kennedy had been shot. There were no details. The radio in the barbershop was not on when I arrived. When I told the barber that the President had been shot, he immediately turned it on; it now carried nothing except bulletins concerning the shooting.

Immediately after getting to my apartment, I called the NMCC. There was a long wait to get through as the lines were all busy. Finally the on-shift team chief answered. When I enquired on the need for additional people to man telephones or to assist in any other way, he assured me that though the JCS had ordered a greater readiness posture, everything was under control and no augmentation was needed.

Throughout that afternoon while doing my chores, I listened to the bulletins. All TV stations had stopped broadcasting their regular programs, between bulletins classical music, such as excerpts from some of the great Bach Masses, was played. Finally it was announced officially that the President was dead.

On Saturday evening I had dinner with Lucy and Bill Homen as planned. About 2100 we watched on TV as the Capitol Rotunda was opened to let the general public file past the casket of President Kennedy lying in state. Bill suddenly proposed, "Don, let's go over there. He was our Commander-in-Chief and we should pay our respects. We'll put on our uniforms and salute him for the last time."

Although I had voted for Kennedy, I was not an ardent admirer of his and was not enchanted with the idea of viewing a casket, but as Bill seemed bent on going, I agreed to accompany him. Bill changed into his Air Force uniform with bow tie to make it formal, then drove me to my apartment where I put on dress blues. After circling the Capitol, we finally found a parking place four blocks from the grounds and joined the end of the line which wound from the East Front around the Capitol toward the Mall. When we joined the line it was almost to the Garfield Statue on the West Side. The line inched along slowly. It was cold and neither of us had on overcoats. Seven to ten across, the line was fairly compact. Bill and I tried to stay in the center of the mass to take advantage of the body heat radiating from the crowd. Everyone talked to everyone else. The main topics were the assassination, what Johnson would be like as President, where we came from and what we did. The people around us were interested in Bill and me since we were in uniform, and asked about our careers. One youth, about 18 years old, was captivated by the ribbons and insignia which decorated our uniforms. He attempted to keep us talking about military life, our experiences, and what each device on the uniform meant. The line inched forward as it grew colder and colder. At midnight we reached the drive on the East Front.

When we reached the bottom of the East Front steps about 0300, a Capitol Policeman informed us that service men in uniform did not have to stand in line, they went right on in! If we had only known this five hours earlier! By this time we had established a close rapport with the people around us and thought it would be unfair to leave them and move to the head of the line. So we waited our turn, another hour.

Finally we entered the Rotunda. As the line narrowed to a single file, Bill fell in behind me with our young admirer on his heels still talking. Marching to the foot of the catafalque I came to attention, saluted and moved quickly off. Bill was immediately behind me. Just as he raised his arm to render his smartest salute, the lad behind him bumped into him, almost causing him to fall to the Rotunda floor. Hastily recovering and scarlet with mortification, Bill managed an atrocious salute and slinked away after me. Lucy's sister in San Francisco saw the incident on television and recognized Bill. Shivering and half frozen, Bill and I got back to River House about 0500 where Lucy quickly cooked a hot breakfast for us.

The weekend seemed interminable. Most entertainment, both live and TV, had been canceled, and many businesses had closed in respect for the slain President. On the day of the funeral, Joan and Jim Owens stopped by. They arrived Just as the funeral proceedings began. Joan wanted to watch the ceremonies, so we sat, drinks in hand, and witnessed the theatrical spectacular which was the burial of an assassinated President: the removal of the casket from the Capitol to St Matthew's Cathedral; the forced march of dignitaries from the White House to the Cathedral; the ballet of Cardinal Cushing on the high altar; the funeral procession to Arlington; the interment; the igniting of the eternal flame. Certainly no President's place in history had been arranged with more elaborate panoply.

During most of the time I was assigned to the NMCC, one of my fellow desk mates was LTC Marshall, who all too frequently came to work with alcohol on his breath; several times he was almost unfit for duty. The first several occasions I covered for him, but after four or five such incidents I told him that I would no longer do so. He had to straighten himself out or take the con sequences. Captain Baney had at first ignored the situation, but then he gave Marshall a stem warning. There was only marginal improvement. The matter never became serious enough to warrant relief, but his efficiency, and consequently, his efficiency report, suffered, Marshall was a competent OFF when sober.

Immediately after Christmas, 1963, I was astounded to find my name on the War College List. Based on my age, plus the break in service from 1946 to 1949, my chances for selection to attend any of the War Colleges seemed slim. The orders required me to report to the Army War College (AWC) at Carlisle Barracks, PA, in mid-August. A thick packet of material came in the mail containing a list of books to read, forms to fill out, as well as information about the course and the post.

Included was information concerning the opportunity to get a Masters Degree in International Affairs during off-duty time. George Washington University (GWU) maintained a branch at Carlisle for resident instruction and granted credit for one half of the required hours for studies at the Army War College. During the school year courses were offered in the evening and at the conclusion of the course, a two week "cram session" provided two additional courses. The War College thesis could be submitted to fulfill that requirement for the Masters. The opportunity was too good to pass up so I immediately enrolled in the program.

In July 1964, movers packed my household goods, most of which would go into storage because I would live in the BOQ at Carlisle. Only my stereo, records and some books would accompany me to the AWC. Peanut and Marjie Hinton agreed to keep the organ for me to avoid having it in a dusty warehouse. Marjie played and would enjoy it.

After a short leave I drove to Carlisle. Harrisburg was familiar territory because of duty at Indiantown Gap and visits to June and Howard Clark at the Cathedral, but for some reason I had never been to Carlisle Barracks. It was a thrill to report to that historic post. During the processing a BOQ was assigned, but it was a wooden WWII barracks, with few improvements over those I had lived in as a lieutenant. I decided to look for an apartment in Carlisle. When the Billeting Officer heard of my intention to live off post he told me that a vacancy was opening in "The Castle". This was a fieldstone mansion built by a contractor for his wife in the mid-30s. It was a copy of the English manor house in which they had spent their honeymoon. When the Army bought additional land on which to build family housing, this huge mansion became government property. Four bachelors were permitted to live in elegance in The Castle; one had just been reassigned; I was given his room.

It was gracious living! Each officer had a bedroom with a private bath. There was a mammoth living room, with a fireplace big enough to stand in; a kitchen; butler's pantry; dining room; and library, also with a fireplace. The entrance hall was about thirty feet high with more area than many homes. It was unbelievable that four Army bachelors could live in such baronial splendor. There were many elegant parties in The Castle during the course of the year.

My housemates were a compatible group: the State Department Representative to the AWC, Ray Leddy, Mac Smith and Ed Ramsey, both Infantry Colonels. As the junior officer, I had the back bedroom, formerly the housekeeper's room, which was most comfortable. All of the rooms on the lower floor were used in common.

The year at the AWC was enjoyable and rewarding. There were many old friends in the course: six from my Infantry Advance Class, 14 from my Leavenworth Class, and many I had served with in various assignments. Brick Krause, Gene Walters and I had attended all three courses together. Ken Althaus, Dick Cann, Frank Walton and I had commanded battalions in the 1st Armored Division. Ed Cavanaugh and Bob Siegrist had been with me at Mainz and Sid Hack at JACE. In addition I met many interesting people, some of whom became life-long friends, others who would serve with me in future assignments.

The course was primarily concerned with the development of US National Policy: military, foreign, political, economic and domestic. The guest speaker program was extensive and varied;

almost every day an authority in some field spoke on a problem facing the US: labor, the population explosion, economics, commerce, productivity, pollution, management, manufacturing, military strategy or political and foreign affairs. Following each talk an extended question and answer period permitted detailed probes of issues.

In retrospect the curriculum may have been a bit esoteric, too lofty to accomplish the purposes of the War College. Few of the students would ever deal on such a high level in world politics, economic affairs or even military strategy. The country was faced with the expanding Vietnam involvement, but this problem was never addressed in either seminars or instruction. Several guest speakers, including General (Big) Minn and Bernard Fall, gave their views on the situation, but the concept of counterinsurgency, the wars of liberation, or the role of the US in such situations received scant attention. There was a reluctance to tell the President how things really were or to instruct McNamara in military matters. All shared the guilt, the senior generals, the guest speakers, the faculty and the students. But these thoughts came later; during the year we were interested and intrigued by the course.

In addition to the AWC curriculum, mind-broadening courses were offered by GWU in its Masters program. Because I had no language credits, my degree would be a Master of Science in International Affairs. The courses in International Law, Political Science, Sociology (Culture, Contact and Change) and Diplomacy Since WWII, complemented those presented by the AWC and provided new ideas and concepts.

One of the important decisions each student faced was the subject and classification of his thesis. Since the peace-keeping efforts of the UN had always interested me, I chose that as my topic. Though I tried to keep it unclassified, some of the references quoted were confidential. One from the State Department was critical, and despite my efforts, reclassification was refused. Fortunately, the resident GWU faculty was cleared for confidential material which permitted the use of the same thesis for both AWC and GWU.

During the year the Army made yet another extensive study of its educational system which this time included the graduate program at Carlisle. LTG Ralph Haines, Chairman of the study group, came to Carlisle to look at both the AWC and GWU programs. The Officers from the 1st AR Div who were in the class hosted a cocktail party for him at The Castle. Unfortunately, his group recommended that the masters degree program be eliminated because it conflicted with the regular AWC curriculum. In my opinion, this was a bad decision made on bad information. I know of no GWU students who were interviewed or whose opinions had been sought. It was alleged that those enrolled in the graduate program neglected their AWC duties, studies, and committee assignments to work on their GWU courses. From personal knowledge I can say that this was not so. The GWU experience enhanced that of the AWC. As a result of my studies at GWU, I was a more informed contributor to my seminars in the War College. Regardless, the Army discontinued the graduate program only to reinstate it in a modified form as an integral part of the curriculum, but using a local college.

The Army War College did not make any major trips during the school year; we envied the students at the National War College and the Industrial College the trips they took outside the CONUS. We did go to New York for a week to attend sessions of the United Nations and to hear discussions of UN affairs. This trip provided an opportunity to see Mother and the rest of the family as well as a chance to work on my thesis. We stayed at a nearby hotel so we could walk to the UN. It was a good week during which we saw several plays and ate at some of the better restaurants. Most wives accompanied their student husbands.

During the year, several students developed a need to visit Redstone Arsenal to talk with Werner von Braun and other missile experts in conjunction with their theses or studies. The College was able to get a C-47 to take about 30 students to Redstone. Through subtle machination, I managed to be on the roster. It was a good trip which gave us a close look at the facilities at Redstone Arsenal plus the opportunity to meet the people who had made possible the first US space shot.

Each year the faculty put on a skit recording the momentous three days of the Battle of Gettysburg. This was done on a Friday evening. On the following Saturday those interested toured the Gettysburg Battlefield. Tom Wickert came up for the weekend, we both thoroughly enjoyed the presentation and the tour.

Wick also spent a weekend at Carlisle during which we had a great time exploring the area. Wick's father had commanded Carlisle Barracks in the 1930s when it was the Army Field Medical School. Hence Wick had numerous recollections of life on the post and in the surrounding area during the days of the "old Army". He showed me many interesting things in the vicinity: the various gaps in the mountains, several old covered bridges, historic buildings.

In November we all went to the Army Navy game. There was more than usual interest since there were several Navy and Marine officers in the class, some of whom had graduated from the USNA. Buses were hired to take us to Philadelphia and back. With ice and chasers available on each bus, it was a hilarious group that proceeded to Philadelphia. Father (LTC) Len Stegman, my seat-mate, made Bloody Marys using a special brand of tomato juice that he ordered. Lunch was served at the Defense Supply Depot; after the game a reception was held there. Army won the game that year (1964) so most of the group was happy.

As Christmas approached, the four of us residing in The Castle planned to have a party, a real bash. After many consultations and much thought, we adopted a theme and a format. It would be a formal affair; though most hosts shied away from asking their guests to dress formally, the men to wear dress blues, mess jackets or tuxedos, the ladies long gowns, we concluded that The Castle cried out for formality.

The theme adopted was "The Four Knights of The Castle". Invitations were issued in their name. A costume house in Philadelphia provided pageboy and squire costumes. The sons of our classmates, Dale and Mamie Greenleaf, agreed to dress in them. The squire was to stand outside the door with a saddled horse to lend atmosphere as the guests arrived. He would open the door and the page would announce each couple. Unfortunately, people swarmed in overwhelming the page; he didn't have a chance to announce anyone. Finally he just closed the door after each entrance.

Each of the "Knights" invited 50 friends; another 50 faculty members and wives were invited jointly. The 250 guests filled the huge mansion. Mother came from New York and June and Howard Clark from Harrisburg. Despite complaints about the dress, the party was a huge success. A tall Christmas tree dominated the entrance hall, fires burned in the living room and library, and flowers from the Farmers Market were scattered about in great profusion. We had hired the Commandant's enlisted aide to prepare the food: turkey, ham, cheese, dips of many kinds and a relish tray. The large dining room was always crowded, as were the four bars strategically placed. The NCOs hired as bartenders were kept busy by the thirsty crowd. When the allocated amount of liquor was exhausted -and relatively early at that - each of us raided our own liquor cabinets to keep the party going. It was a festive affair appropriate to the season. The last guest left about 0400.

The next day The Castle was a shambles. Although Lucky, our housekeeper came in at 0800, there was too much for her to do; all of us pitched in to help. Even Mother was pressed into service. About noon, when things appeared to be in hand, Mother and I left for New York for the holidays.

Again, it was a good Christmas. During the first week I spent much time at the NYU and UN libraries doing research for my thesis as well as several papers for my Masters program.

A few days after Christmas I went to Washington to visit friends, seeing Wick and Sam and Betty King among others. COL Wilbur Wilson was back from Vietnam, so I spent several days with him. I was the only person present when he retired from the Army on 31 December. There was no ceremony; he merely turned in his active duty ID card and received a retiree ID card. This was an ungracious end to a long career during which Colonel Wilson had contributed so much to the Army. No official thanks or recognition were tendered to this outstanding officer from whom I had learned so much. He was controversial, but a true professional; the fact that he had not been promoted to BG was a disappointment to everyone who knew and admired him.

The note on the Christmas card from Sara and Dave McNaught informed me that Dave was in Walter Reed Hospital. The day I stopped to visit him, I was shocked to learn that Dave had died that morning. Wilbur and I went to see Sara, Dave's wife, that evening; both of us attended his funeral.

While in Washington I took the opportunity to visit the Office of Personnel Management to talk about my next assignment. Every student had filled out a preference sheet on reporting to the War College; I had indicated my desire to go to Vietnam in any capacity. The LTC who handled my records was very evasive, refusing to give direct answers to my questions. Assuring him that I understood that no assignment was final and would not be final until the orders were published, I tried to get him to tell me my chances of getting to Vietnam, and if I was not going there to give me some indication of where they were thinking of assigning me. He evaded my queries and refused to discuss my assignment. Finally, I demanded to see the Chief of Infantry, COL Bill McKean. Bill, too, was evasive. By this time I was outraged.

"Dammit, it's my career and you ought to be able to talk to me on the level about it. What are you considering?"

Reluctantly, Bill reached in his desk, took out a sheaf of papers and handed it to me. It was a Summary Sheet to the Army CofS which forwarded my Form 66 and complete 201 file. The Summary Sheet informed the Chief that in response to the requirement levied on Infantry Branch, LTC Donald A. Seibert was nominated as the Army Aide to the President of the United States! I was staggered; the recommendation was flattering, but I told Bill that I did not want the job. I had never been an aide, had always fought being an aide, did not know how to be an aide and did not want to be an aide. The political beliefs and machinations of President Johnson disturbed me; it would be hard to support concepts I did not believe in.

"Forget it, Don", Bill said. "We've gone through the whole business. Your nomination has been approved by the Chief of Staff, the Secretary of the Army and the Secretary of Defense and your file is at the White House. I am sure you have the job. To my knowledge, no President has ever turned down a service recommendation. So forget it. Don't say anything to anybody about it."

"Okay, but can I discuss it with one guy?"

"Yeah, that will be all right, but don't let it get around until its final."

That evening at dinner, I talked to Wilbur about my projected assignment. He convinced me not to fight the assignment but to accept it with a positive approach that it would be both rewarding and interesting. There was still the possibility that the President for some reason might decide against me. From what Bill had said, however, this was most unlikely; once the file went to the White House from the Pentagon, it was unprecedented for the President to turn down the Army's recommendation.

On returning to Carlisle after Christmas leave, I was still unhappy because I did not look forward to my next assignment. Gradually, I reconciled myself to it by considering its advantages, the people I would meet, the historic meetings I would be part of.

In the middle of March a personnel team came to Carlisle to give the Array students then-orders. Copies of the orders were put in each student's mail box. After a general briefing on the principles governing the assignments, students were permitted to open their boxes to learn their next assignment. Waiting until the crowd in the mail room thinned, I reached in my box expecting mat I had been assigned as the Army Aide to the President; however, the orders directed me to report to The Infantry School for duty with the Staff and Faculty. Though relieved at not being an Aide to the President, I was unhappy about going to FT Benning rather than to Vietnam. With fire in my eyes I again went to see Bill McKean who was with the team from the Pentagon. When asked about an assignment to Vietnam, Bill said, "Don, there just aren't any requirements for Infantry Lieutenant Colonels in Vietnam."

"Bill, I can't believe that there is any place in the world where Army troops are assigned for which you have no requirement for Infantry Lieutenant Colonels. Please change my orders."

Bill was adamant, so after a bit more blustering I started to leave. "Bill, I don't want to part with any acrimony, and I will go where I am ordered. But I have a question to ask you. Why didn't I get the job as Aide to the President? Now don't misunderstand me; I didn't want it; I am not disappointed because I did not get it; but to satisfy my curiosity, tell my why I did not get it."

A grin came over his face as he looked at me, saying, "The President sent your file back with a hand written note on it, 'This officer is eminently qualified but I want a black aide at this time.' So the Army nominated a black officer." MAJ Hugh G. Robinson, CE, was the first Negro to serve as a Military Aide to a President of the United States.

We both laughed about the reverse discrimination, but I was relieved, though unhappy about not going to Vietnam.

Just after Christmas, Mac Smith, one of my housemates, started to have problems including difficulty walking and occasional mild seizures. Ed Ramsey was convinced that he was drinking too much; over my protests, he went to the CMDT, MG Eugene Salet, a good friend and former commander of Mac's, to request help for Mac. Salet talked with Mac, who curtailed his drinking, but the problems persisted. As Mac was not drinking more than the rest of us, it seemed to me that he had some serious health condition. He was persuaded to have a physical examination at the hospital where his ailment was diagnosed as a mild form of diabetes. The doctors believed his seizures were the result of low blood sugar. Mac appeared to have none of the symptoms associated with diabetes, but the doctors were more competent at diagnosis than I, so I said nothing.

One Saturday evening while we were preparing to leave for a party, Mac and I sat in the kitchen having a drink, deciding what we would do after the cocktail party. Suddenly, Mac was contorted by a muscular spasm and fell off his chair onto the floor. Shouting for Ed Ramsey, I put a wooden spoon between his teeth to prevent him from biting or swallowing his tongue and made sure he did not hurt himself while the seizure lasted. Ed Ramsey called an ambulance and Mac was taken to the hospital. Once again his condition was diagnosed as a mild case of diabetes. This simply did not square with the facts so I went to MG Salet and asked him to get Mac to Walter Reed. Salet called the Post Surgeon who reluctantly agreed to send Mac to Valley Forge General Hospital, only a short distance from Carlisle. In a short time the diagnosis was made; Mac had a tumor on his brain. He was transferred to Walter Reed Hospital in Washington where he was to undergo surgery to remove the tumor.

When I visited Mac at Valley Forge, just before his transfer to Walter Reed, he confided to me that he was apprehensive about the operation, but was sure it would correct his problem and so faced h with courage.

Later I visited him at Walter Reed before the operation. To prepare those who faced brain surgery, the hospital recruited people who had undergone such operations to talk to those awaiting the ordeal. Mac was scheduled for one of those talks during my visit. With surprise and pleasure I welcomed the NCO who was to talk with Mac, SGM Henry Hand, my old 1SG from F Co, 508. As a result of an accident, Hand had required brain surgery after which he volunteered for the counseling program. Between us, we made Mac forget momentarily his concern.

The operation was apparently successful. Mac was quite weak when he came back, but he insisted that he be re-admitted to the class. He was determined to finish both the War College Course and also his GWU studies for his Masters. His friends were concerned that the load would be too much for him, but Mac was determined. It took him a bit longer to complete his thesis; he had missed almost a month of school and he was slow in getting back all of his faculties, but he completed both courses. At graduation, when Mac's name was called and he climbed to the stage to receive his War College Diploma from GEN Eisenhower, the student body gave him a spontaneous standing ovation for his courage, will and spirit. It was a great moment for him, a great moment for his family and for all of us who knew Mac and admired him. Later he was awarded his Masters Degree by GWU. Unfortunately the tumor recurred in October and he died.

While Mac Smith was in the hospital for his operation, another big party was held at The Castle. By this time Ray Leddy had moved into an apartment off post and Ed Ramsey had been married. Now Herm Phynes, a civilian from the Army Security Agency, LTC Dick Kerr and LTC Will Waschoe lived in The Castle with Mac and me. This bash had been planned before Mac went to Walter Reed, so he insisted on being listed as one of the hosts and contributed his share of the liquor and food. This was typical of him. We missed Mac at that party.

Suddenly, June arrived and we were busy with the National Strategy Seminar, finishing our theses, taking exams, and preparing for the two weeks of concentrated study with G WU which would complete the formal academic work for the Masters Degree.

Graduation, preceded by many parties, was a great event. Mother came down for the activities. The night before, several of us had dinner at the Club. Mac and his wife Millie (who had remained in Laurel, MD because their children were in high school there), Mother, MG and Mrs Salet, and several other close friends were sitting in the lounge after dinner. I ordered Rusty Nails for Mother and myself; she had never had one before. During the course of the evening others in the group ordered her refills. She must have had three or four. When it came time to take her to the guest house, she had difficulty getting up from her chair! She was slightly tipsy. We laughed as I supported her over to Washington Hall.

Just before graduation, I learned that COL Bill McKean had been reassigned to Vietnam and COL Don Hickman was now Chief of Infantry. I immediately called him, explaining my interest in going to Vietnam, and asked if there was any chance of having my orders changed. After checking, he called back and said, "I see no reason at all why you can't go to Vietnam, Don. We have a host of outstanding requirements for lieutenant colonels in Vietnam. Although they are getting more than their share of War College graduates, we can manage that. I'm changing your orders. You'll get them shortly."

Following the GWU term I went to College Point on leave. My orders were sent to FT Totten, an hour's drive from home. Once they were in hand, I prepared for Vietnam.

After an enjoyable leave, I said another tearful goodbye to Mother. She was reluctant to see me off to my third war. Fortunately, Arlene and Bob were on hand to console her.

On arrival at the Port of Embarkation (POE) at San Francisco, I asked for the next flight out. The AF SGT was happy to oblige; he manifested me on a four-day flight on a C-130 from California to Saigon. The AF occasionally flew C-130s to prove that MAC could transfer people and cargo from the CONUS to Vietnam with current assets. Planes departing as much as three days later beat me to Saigon. The other unlucky OFF on the plane with me was MAJ Charlie Norton, a Special Forces (SF) Officer. We stopped at Hawaii, Guam and the Philippines enroute. Finally we reached Saigon.

CHAPTER 16

ADVISOR

The Military Assistance Command, Vietnam (MACV), was dispersed in several buildings widely scattered throughout Saigon. Though a HQ building which consolidated all of the staff under one roof was eventually built at Ton Son Nhut Air Base, in 1965 it was necessary to go from building to building to complete the processing, including briefings, interviews and the issuance of field equipment. The chaplain's briefing provided a welcome reunion; Chaplain Saunders, who had been de facto chaplain of THE REGULARS at FT Hood, mounted the dais and was as surprised and delighted to see me in the audience as I was to see him on the podium. He called the attention of the group to me and recounted the incident when I corrected him following one of his sermons. He had said in that sermon that there were only two references to Demas in the Bible. After the service I had pointed out to him a third which had been mentioned during the 0800 Episcopal Communion I attended prior to the General Protestant Service. After his orientation we had a long talk over dinner. It was good to see him, as I had a high regard for him as a soldier and a chaplain. We recalled with relish those exciting days with THE REGULARS.

The Billeting Officer assigned me a room in the Majestic Hotel on the Saigon River. The dining room and bar were on the top floor which made it possible, while enjoying an after dinner drink on the balcony, to look west and see tracers, artillery and flareships firing. Someone told me that the action was in Hau Nghia Province (Prov) where the 25th Army of Vietnam (ARVN) Div was located.

Though I slept in the Majestic Hotel, I spent much of my free time at the Rex Hotel in the heart of Saigon. The open air bar and restaurant on the top floor was a popular meeting place for most of the American officers in the Saigon area. One evening I ran into Wayne Smith there. He told me that several of the old 504 Mainz crowd were in Saigon. He contacted some of them and several days later he informed me that we were invited to GEN Westmoreland's villa for dinner the next evening. The General was out, but Dick Hooker, his junior aide, arranged the dinner. Wayne and I arrived at the villa in a pedicab, a three-wheeled bicycle with a double seat in front. A tiny Vietnamese man astride the bicycle frame behind provided the locomotion. MAJ Tallman, an AF OFF and the General's senior aide, was present; we found him an interesting character. Jimmy MacGill also attended; it was an hilarious evening. Jimmy drove us back in his jeep, clipping the General's fence as we roared out of the compound.

The orientation lasted about four days for field grade officers. Company grade officers, most of whom were far better prepared for duty in Vietnam by virtue of having attended the Military Assistance Training Advisor (MATA) Course at FT Bragg, were required to undergo a ten-day course. By the end of the third day, all of the other field grade officers had received assignments and were preparing to depart. However, there were no orders for me. When I spoke to the personnel people, they told me that I wasn't supposed to be in Vietnam because the security clearances I had held while with the NMCC precluded anyone being assigned to a combat area for several years, I was being considered for duty in MACV HQ in Saigon; some thought was being given to sending me back to the CONUS. At this nonsense I exploded and again violated my own principles by calling MG Rosson, CofS of MACV. After explaining the problem to him and assuring him of my desire to get into combat in any capacity, advisor, recon team member or preferably with one of the American units which were just beginning to deploy to Vietnam, I asked him to get me reassigned out of Saigon.

No doubt my readers are smirking over the two actions to affect my assignment after my vehement comments about the change of orders which sent me to JACE. My pontifications about fouling up brother officers were applicable then, but now I had negotiated two changes. In defense I can only point out that my actions did not interfere with the normal process; my first request was to Infantry Branch which had the requirements, knew who was available and where they could best be utilized. The second was to break a policy SNAFU. Perhaps I am guilty of rationalization; in dealing with the proper authorities rather than circumventing the system, I saw no adverse impact on any other officer. MG Rosson was sympathetic; in a short time I was assigned as the Deputy Senior Advisor to the 25th ARVN Div stationed at Due Hoa, Hau Nghia Province, just west of Saigon. That night following dinner at the Majestic Hotel, I went out on the balcony after dark. Across the Saigon River in the west, flare ships were illuminating an area in which a fire fight was going on. Although close to Saigon, there was considerable enemy activity in Hau Nghia. As I sipped a Rusty Nail while watching the tracers and flares, I mused that I had gotten everything I wanted; duty in Vietnam, an assignment to an advisory unit with a Vietnamese division engaged in actual fighting, my third combat tour.

The next day a jeep, driven by a SGT, took me to Bien Hoa where the ARVN III Corps HQ was located. Here, the III Corps Advisory Team, which would be my next higher headquarters, was also located. The road from Saigon to Bien Hoa was subject to sniper fire and there was an occasional shot at the jeep. The vehicle was not hit, but the driver did some fast driving, permitting only a glimpse at the rubber plantation, now the bivouac area for the advance element of the 1st IN Div which had recently arrived in country, and soon to become the Long Binh complex.

The Senior Advisor (SA) to the III Corps was COL Frink who had commanded the 504 before I joined it at Mainz, Germany. The fact that we had served in the same unit, even though at different times, established a rapport which enabled me to get off to an initial good start with him.

That afternoon was given to briefings on the general situation and the advisory effort as well as specific discussion of the problems in the 25th ARVN Div area. During the afternoon and later in the evening I met all of the Corps' Advisory Staff. In the morning a UH1 -B helicopter took me to Due Hoa. It was an interesting flight; over rice paddies, lush green with growing rice in the Bien Hoa/Saigon area, across the Saigon River; then over sere and dry rice fields after crossing the river; over roads pitted by mine explosions, and over hamlets either deserted or in which people kept out of sight.

The pilot indicated a large hamlet ahead which we circled before landing at a chopper pad in a barbed wire enclosed compound. MAJ John Tracy, the S-1 Advisor and Adj of Advisory Team 99, met the chopper. After introducing himself he took me to the Advisors' Compound which incorporated a Buddhist temple and monastery. The actual temple had been boarded up, but the advisors were living behind it in the monastery enclosure. Several prefab buildings had been added but the offices, supply room and sleeping quarters for most of the OFFs were in the monastery buildings. The EM lived in prefab barracks. A mess hall, water tanks, showers and latrines had also been added.

MAJ Tracy introduced me to the Senior Advisor, COL Jesse Ugalde, and to the other advisory personnel. They were a disparate group, coming from many branches of the Army and different backgrounds. A cubicle had been set aside for me which contained a bed with mosquito bar, a chest of drawers, a chair and a table. Most of the other OFFs either shared a cubicle or lived in a dormitory type arrangement. COL Ugalde occupied a large Jamesway, comfortably furnished, situated alongside the main monastery building in which I was billeted. Plans were underway for the construction of a more efficient compound for the advisors. The temple would then be turned back to the Vietnamese, Several times during my stay at Due Hoa, the Buddhists held services in the temple. This was done with our permission, since everyone had to come through the guarded compound gate. It was interesting to hear the chanting and throbbing drums.

Once settled, the Advisory Staff gave me detailed briefings about the area with which we were concerned. The 25th Division Tactical Area (DTA) encompassed the provinces of Tay Ninh, Hau Nghia and Long An. Tay Ninh was largely forested with several rubber plantations in the southern part. It was in the forests that the Viet Cong (VC) concealed their War Zone C, the major HQ and supply area in the immediate vicinity of Saigon. Hau Nghia had many rubber plantations along the major roads, Highways I and 22. The western part of the province was almost treeless, with sugar cane fields, rice paddies and swamp. Long An was delta type country, given over almost entirely to rice cultivation; it was one of the most important food producing provinces in the country.

Tay Ninh Province, with its capitol at Tay Ninh City, had four districts in which there were US Advisors: Khiem Hanh, Hieu Thien, Phuoc Ninh and Phu Khuong. Bao Trai was the capitol of Hau Nghia which also had four districts, but there were US Advisors at only three: Due Hoa, Trang Bang and Cu Chi. Due Hue, close to the Cambodian border, was considered too vulnerable, though an advisory team was established there before I left the area. Tan An was the capitol of Long An, which had six districts in which US Advisory teams were assigned: Can Giuoc, Can Duoc, Thu Thua, Ben Luc, Tan Tru and Binh Phuoc. Later a team was located in Rach Kien.

The 25th ARVN Div had three Regts: the 46th and 50th in Long An and the 49th at Cu Chi. Long An Province was considered the most critical in the DTA. The two Regts not only guarded the rice fields, but also the bridges on Highway 4, the major rice supply route from IV Corps (the Mekong Delta area) to Saigon. There were US Advisors with each of the regimental and battalion commanders. The 25th Div also had four Ranger Bns attached to it. COL Chinh, the Div CDR, controlled a substantial force.

During my initial discussions with COL Ugalde, he told me that he was concerned about the low morale of the advisors. The 25th ARVN Div had recently moved from I Corps to Due Hoa in III Corps. COL Chinh had been a cell mate and was a trusted friend of the flamboyant Premier Nguyen Cao Ky. The Div had been relocated to the Saigon area by Premier Ky as an anti-coup force to prevent his overthrow and that of the current government. As a result, Chinh had severe restrictions placed on his tactical operations; he could not commit to combat more than one Bn from each Regt at any one time. The remainder had to be available for the defense of critical installations, bridges and roads, and to prevent Vietnamese troops from moving into Saigon for a coup. One of the major reasons for the low morale among the advisors was the fact that the combat power of the Division was held in check. There were other reasons. Living conditions were primitive. Due to the recent move of the Division, there had not been time to develop decent living areas for Advisors. There were also problems with personnel assignments. COL Ugalde pointed out that despite the low morale of the Advisors he was convinced that they were doing an effective job. He also briefed me generally on the 25th ARVN Div, and outlined my duties: to advise the Asst Div CDR, LTC Luyen and the CofS, LTC Giai; to function as XO of Advisory Team 99; and to supervise the administration of the Team for him.

Col Ugalde explained that the advisors were in one of two categories. One group with the Regts and Bns was concerned only with military matters. There was talk of putting advisors down to Co level, but this never came about. The advisors were OFFs; each had one or two EM working with him, primarily as radio/telephone operators (RTOs), but also as assistant Advisors. Most of the EM were senior NCOs, E-6s or E-7s who had considerable tactical and field experience.

The other set of Advisors encompassed those in the government area, the province and district advisors, who were involved not only in security and pacification operations, but in other matters of government. Few of the Advisors were proficient in these areas, but their counterparts continually asked their advice on administrative matters. They had to rely on common sense and whatever training and background they had in responding.

Because Vietnam had an essentially military government, the Division Commander in each DTA was the chief official there. COL Chinh, as the 25th ARVN Div CDR, had under his direct control the Province Chiefs of Tay Ninh, Hau Nghia and Long An. They didn't like it. They preferred to deal directly with the bureaucratic government in Saigon rather than go through military channels. As a result of this situation the Senior Advisor to the Division Commander also supervised the province and district advisors as well as the regimental and battalion advisors. Province and district advisors were assigned to advise on security matters, especially on the training and employment of "regional (district) forces" and "popular (hamlet) forces" commonly known as RFPF forces. RFPF were militia-type units, organized primarily for local employment, especially defense. Most were poorly trained and equipped. These RFPF or "Ruff Puffs" were not held in high esteem except in rare instances.

In addition to the Army Advisors, there was a USAF Tactical Air Control Party (TACP) attached to the 25th ARVN Division living in our compound. Then- small, fixed wing, single engine spotter aircraft was kept on the Division strip. There were also Army L-19s, Bird Dogs, with American pilots, in support of each province. The pilots and maintenance personnel lived with the advisory teams.

Advisory Team 99 had a sizable communications group with radio/telephone as well as both voice and code radio. The Team was rarely out of communications with the Prov and Regt advisors or with our higher HQ, III Corps Advisory Team at Bien Hoa. Team 99 had more than 300 officers and men assigned to it, including advisors at Div, Regt, and Prov, communications personnel, security guards, mess and administrative personnel.

Due Hoa, as noted earlier, was in Hau Nghia Province. The advisory team to the Dist HQ there, headed by MAJ Jim Rapkock, lived in a separate compound adjacent to their counterparts. The Dist Chief was nominally in charge of security at Due Hoa, but since the 25th Div HQ was there, he had problems executing his functions. Understandably, COL Chinh wanted to control the security of his own HQ. However, he was finally persuaded to divide responsibility; the Div CP, the Advisory Compound and the air strip remained under ARVN security, but the remainder of Due Hoa was guarded by RFPF forces. Because of occasional harassing fire, the helicopter supporting Advisory Team 99 did not remain at Due Hoa overnight. This often posed problems when it was necessary to react rapidly.

After several days of processing, orientation and getting acquainted with the Team, I finally met my two counterparts, LTC Hoanc Van Luyen, the Asst Div CDR, and LTC Do Ke Giai, the CofS. Both spoke excellent English and welcomed me warmly; an immediate rapport was established between us. LTC Luyen was married to the daughter of the sister of the former Emperor Bao Dai and so had connections with the aristocracy of Vietnam. LTC Giai, a paratrooper who had commanded a parachute battalion in the ABN Bde before it became a Div, had an enviable combat record. He was a very energetic individual, constantly involved in tons of paperwork. It seems the Vietnamese Army was as bad or worse than the US Army in the amount of paperwork generated in day-to-day operations.

The Advisors' offices were in the 25th ARVN Div Compound, just across the road from our own. Advisory Team 99 shared to a limited extent their facility. COL Chinh not only had his office but his quarters in a school building in the ARVN compound. Both the Division and the Advisory Team had separate briefing rooms and tactical operations centers (TOCs).

Shortly after my arrival a plan was completed and implemented to collocate the Advisors with their counterparts. This was a radical departure. The Vietnamese were rather secretive about what they were doing, while the Americans, suspicious that the Viet Cong had infiltrated the Vietnamese Army, were equally secretive. As a result the two elements did not always act in concert. COL Ugalde approved a plan which would have Americans and Vietnamese looking at each other constantly, talking to each other, developing plans together, working in concert and trusting each other. It was a novel idea and tough to sell, but finally COL Ugalde convinced COL Chinh of its merits. Both LTC Luyen and LTC Giai agreed to the plan. Soon the Advisors were sharing the offices of their counterparts. COL Ugalde kept his own office next to COL Chain's. I collocated with LTC Luyen, rather than with LTC Giai. By sharing an office with Luyen, I gave Giai the privacy and opportunity to fulfill his administrative duties. There was a constant parade of people into his office to talk to him about various matters. Perhaps this was a mistake; if I had been with Giai I would have learned more about the administration of the Division. But I didn't think that I could have helped him much; he could not take the time to discuss everything with me, and I did not read, speak or understand Vietnamese.

Most Vietnamese officers were equally fluent in French and Vietnamese. Vietnam had been under French control for almost a hundred years. As a result most ARVN OFFs had served under French OFFs either as senior NCOs or junior OFFs and had been required to learn and speak French. Those Americans who did not speak Vietnamese but did speak French could communicate effectively with their counterparts. Unfortunately, I have no linguistic ability, so spoke neither language. Luyen and Giai spoke adequate English enabling us to communicate effectively.

Shortly after my arrival, Luyen and Giai gave a dinner parry to welcome me. It was held in the evening in the ARVN Compound. The two counterparts had sent to Vung Tau, a major fishing center, for crabs, oysters, clams, huge prawns, nine or ten inches in length, and frog legs. These were broiled on a grill and served with a tasty, but piquant sauce called Nuoc Mam, made by placing fish in crocks and permitting the weight of the fish to squeeze out the oil, which, if pure, is colorless and almost odorless. Impure Nuoc Mam has a terrible odor. Tiny red peppers are usually cut up in the Nuoc Mam to make it very hot. It is delicious with fish and meat. There was a local Scotch, not very good, which when mixed with coconut milk made a smooth, potent, but sickeningly sweet drink. COL Chinh and COL Ugalde attended, but no other Advisors were invited. It provided an opportunity for the two Vietnamese officers and I to get to know each other.

At a conference COL Chinh held shortly after my arrival, I met the regimental commanders and Province Chiefs as well as their Advisors. Following this, I began to visit each of the subordinate Advisory Teams by helicopter. It took several weeks to get to all of them.

About a week after joining Advisory Team 99, my counterpart, LTC Luyen, told me he was going to attend a "Hop Toe Meeting" in Bien Hoa. Hop Toe (cooperation in Vietnamese), also called the "oil drop concept", was a plan for pacifying Vietnam by concentrating all resources, military, economic, social, medical, agricultural, political, in a given area until it was pacified. As it became secure and the VC were driven out, the government would expand its security and resources into the adjacent area, building on the central safe zone. In theory, security would expand similar to the way oil spreads out in an ever-widening circular layer when dropped on water. The "drop" in III Corps was Saigon, it was hoped that the area of security would spread from that focal point into the surrounding provinces, including Hau Nghia, Tay Ninh, and Long An, the area of OPS of the 25th ARVN Div. On a smaller scale, the Div HQ, and in turn each Regt HQ, were also "oil drops" which would expand and coalesce until the country was entirely secure.

The Hop Toe Council in III Corps held periodic meetings with representatives of all of the governmental services, particularly the military, which headed it. LTC Luyen invited me to attend the meeting with him which I agreed to do. He refused my suggestion that we go by helicopter, electing to go by jeep so that he would have transportation in Saigon. Although concerned about the security of the roads, I agreed. The 25th ARVN Division provided a jeep for me with an ARVN soldier as driver. The trip to Saigon and then to Bien Hoa where I spent the night at the Advisory Compound was uneventful. LTC Luyen stayed with his wife in Cholon, the Chinese Section of Saigon. His wife ran an ice company which had a virtual monopoly on ice sold in downtown Saigon; she was wealthy.

The next morning LTC Luyen met me at III Corps HQ, but the meeting had been moved to Saigon. Disregarding speed laws and traffic control, Luyen sped along the highway with my driver in hot pursuit. Once in the Saigon maze, the drivers got lost. We arrived just as the meeting started.

It was an interesting meeting; each element of the government, fiscal, police, medical, sanitation, and military had its say and made recommendations on how to handle various problems. Those were particularly Vietnamese problems. Although the French colonial system, unlike the British, had placed little emphasis on providing indigenous civil servants, the Vietnamese appeared to handle routine administration fairly well. Certainly they understood municipal management and government. Some advisors made occasional recommendations but basically it was a Vietnamese meeting.

During the return trip to Due Hoa, LTC Luyen showed great concern about mines in the road. A well sandbagged security vehicle proceeded our jeeps. Fortunately no mines were encountered; we arrived at Due Hoa without difficulty. The drive from Saigon to the Advisory Compound in Due Hoa took about an hour.

After making a complete tour of the 25th DTA and visiting all of the advisor detachments, which took almost a month, I began to work on the problem of advisor morale. Housing and creature comforts were finding their way to the subordinate teams; that aspect of the problem appeared to be clearing up. But we still had to "sell1 the job to our advisors. This became even more important as the buildup of American units got underway. Everyone, including me, wanted duty with a US tactical unit. Suppressing my own feelings, I suggested that newly assigned advisors get to know COL Ugalde and myself, as well as the other Div Advisors they would be working with, before they went into the field. At least they could then put a face at the end of the radio net or telephone line. More thorough briefings, providing as much background information on their counterparts and organizations at the Prov, Dist, Regt or Bn level as was available, were scheduled before new advisors went to their units.

Following my suggestion, each newly assigned advisor had dinner with COL Ugalde and myself to get to know us on a more personal basis. It also gave them an opportunity to discuss their responsibilities, efficiency reports and duties, and to ask questions they might have been reluctant to ask in a briefing or more formal atmosphere. In addition, it gave COL Ugalde and me a chance to clarify the constraints placed on Col Chinh so that his apparent lack of aggressiveness was put in proper perspective. Ugalde and I usually sat at a separate table with a number of the senior staff advisors and could always find room for any officer newly assigned.

There was a bar in the dining room where both OFFs and EM could buy drinks. It became the custom for me to buy after dinner drinks for the table when newly assigned officers ate with us. To simplify the matter, the bar tender, on my instructions, automatically served everyone a Rusty Nail, made of equal parts of Scotch and Drambuie. It is a tasty after dinner drink which most people like, though apparently not too well known, thus something different. These dinners did tend to draw the team closer together.

Among the OFFs in the 25th DTA was George Laland, who had been on Paengnyong Do with me in Korea. He was the advisor to the 49th Regt at Cu Chi. His promotion to LTC in November resulted in his transfer; Regt advisors were all majors. George had settled down a bit, though still gung-ho and "Airborne All The way"!

Several advisors impressed me immediately. Coming from different branches, I looked at them closely to see how they handled the Infantry problems. Most did very well. CPT Jim Parlier, an Ord OFF, was a district advisor, who did a noteworthy job, earning his CIB on a series of operations with the RFPF. Jim was the vindication of the system of assigning technical service branch officers to one of the combat arms for an orientation tour. CPT Rudy Holbrook, an AR OFF, readily adapted to his advisory duties with the 2nd Bn, 49th IN Regt. CPT Doug Morgan, an ARTY OFF, was initially assigned as an advisor to the 2nd Bn, 46th IN Regt, later as the G-3 Air Advisor at Div. He told me about his introduction to the advisory effort, which seemed typical for most company grade officers. This is his story,

"My arrival at the 2nd Battalion, 46th Regiment was something neither my training in the MATA Course at FT Bragg nor my twelve-week course in the Vietnamese language at Monterey had prepared me for. I was picked up in Saigon after a ten-day in-country orientation and driven in a jeep out of Cholon. As we exited the White Mouse (ARVN MP) manned check point, the sergeant instructed me to load my carbine and keep a sharp eye on the right side of the road. The driver, a Vietnamese soldier, instinctively speeded up to about 50 MPH, a speed well above that which the road condition demanded. I realized that I was now in 'hostile territory'. It took only about 25 minutes to reach the Regimental CP where MAJ Ed Benedict welcomed me to the outfit and the town of Can Giuoc. Moments later CPT Dan Brown arrived; the Battalion Advisor with whom I was to work. I immediately felt comfortable with both advisors for they appeared confident, easy going and unconcerned with the heavily bunkered buildings, the machine gun emplacements guarding the CP entrances and the proliferation of weaponry, ammunition and concertina wire in all directions.

"After a brief orientation at the Regimental Advisor's CP which was in actuality only two 10 by 10 rooms, Brown and I drove to a modest house on the road leading out of town to the south. This was to be 'home' for the next two days. We arrived just prior to supper, so I had a chance to meet the Vietnamese officers with whom I would be working in the coming months. Most spoke a little English and with my Vietnamese language training we could at least introduce ourselves, discuss our families and talk about basic military topics.

"That first meal with the Vietnamese was a difficult one for me to handle. Not only was I the center of curious attention, but also rather nervous with this first real encounter with chop sticks. My fingers and hand cramped for the first several weeks when using these new eating implements, but I finally learned to relax. The meal of rice and soup made of greens and generally tasteless and indigestible small chunks of nondescript meat was filling, though the hot wine did not satisfy my need for fluid replenishment from this first day's encounter with the battlefield and the friendlies. I slept little that first night, partly from the stress of the day, but mostly from the inability of my bones and muscles to conform to the hard flat surface of the wooden platform that was called 'bed'. The weeks ahead had to get better and they did."

Morgan's first combat operation, representative of those faced by most advisors, is retold as he narrated it to me,

"On my second day in the Battalion, we were alerted to conduct a sweep and clear operation, a regimental operation involving also the 'ruff puffs'. Our team had CPT Brown, myself, a sergeant first class and a spec four RTO. Brown designated the sergeant and myself to go along with the lead company. Such an arrangement facilitated the coordinating of helicopter gunship support or TACAIR, both US-supplied commodities for the most part. Departing town prior to dawn we moved along the edges of the rice paddies. It was spring and most of the paddies were dry so the pace was fast. The Battalion used an intelligence squad to act as we would employ a scout platoon to assure that we did not walk into an ambush. The intelligence squad normally departed several hours in advance and radioed clearance to proceed.

"At about 1000 we approached a series of paddy fields 500 to 800 meters across. On the far side we could see the green foliage of the river bank. It was in this heavily overgrown area that the VC elements we were searching for were supposed to be situated. It was my understanding that an adjacent unit was approaching from the north while we were approaching from the east. We commenced walking across the open paddy fields with no scouts visible to our front. This tactic did not appear sound to me at the time, but as a two-day warrior, I did not consider it wise to question the judgement of a Vietnamese Regular Army Captain who must have employed this same tactic on numerous occasions and had obviously lived to try it again. Enroute we paused several times to check our flank units and to conduct communications checks. The Vietnamese soldiers considered American cigarettes a luxury, and on rest breaks I found myself sharing puffs with the nearest soldier. I enjoyed this association as it helped me feel less an outsider who had just arrived from the CONUS two weeks ago.

"Subsequently we continued approaching the river line when suddenly, only 150 meters from our objective, we were in a hail of bullets coming from the front and right front. The bastards had caught us in the open with no where to go but forward. I stood up on several occasions to assess the situation but was met by a hail of fire and the firm hand of the sergeant who advised that 'they shoot the advisors, for the advisors control the gunships and TACAIR'. Hadn't really thought about that until it was mentioned. I was scared and pissed at the stupidity of the tactic we had just executed. We eventually got artillery fire into the tree line and assaulted it but were driven back. I made it to the edge on the second assault. With us closing in and the sound of helicopters which Brown had called for in the background, the VC vanished into the trees, but only far enough to take cover in a series of foxholes. We lost 16 or 17 men that day including the Vietnamese medic to whom I had given a cigarette just prior to the assault that cost him his life. I felt that day a sense of frustration at the senseless loss of life due to poor tactics, slow fire support, and lack of aggressiveness, a frustration I retained when I departed on the Freedom Bird almost a year later."

Morgan's account of the living conditions he first encountered was characteristic; the Advisory Teams lived much like their counterparts. During my initial flights and visits throughout the DTA, the paucity of adequate advisory housing became apparent. The US teams operated from different types of structures. Some used existing buildings, abandoned or confiscated, which the Vietnamese government made available to the advisors. Where possible the advisors were located close to their counterparts to minimize reaction time and communications. As the American stay in Vietnam lengthened, advisory compounds were built at most tactical and Prov HQ. The Team at Tan Tru was in buildings on an island in the river which could be reached only by sampan or a rickety bridge. The Khiem Hahn Dist HQ was located in a compound on a flat plain, visible from a great distance. Although surrounded by at least five barbed wire fences, with mines between each fence, a determined enemy could penetrate to the Team House at any time.

The Hau Nghia Province Team Compound in Bao Trai, built especially for the advisors several years before, was very suitable. It included billets for both officers and enlisted men, a mess hall, recreation room, latrine with showers, arms room, advisory offices and helicopter pad. The team at Tay Ninh City used pre-existing buildings augmented with some built by the Special Forces. The Long An Province Team occupied a villa confiscated by the Vietnamese for it; several buildings had been erected in the courtyard to provide additional facilities. Most district, regimental and battalion advisory teams lived more primitively.

The Division Advisory Team Compound at Due Hoa was a patchwork of Vietnamese buildings, prefabricated American buildings, and buildings constructed locally by Vietnamese and GI labor. Shortly after arriving at Due Hoa I became involved in the construction of a new compound. RMK, a combination of two contract construction firms, was building it. The local supervisor of the project and I were in constant consultation. Prior to my arrival the new advisory area had been fenced. The first decision that had to be made was on the disposition of some Buddhist graves in the area. The initial inclination was to move them because they concealed an approach into the compound and would mask defensive fires if the compound was attacked. However, the Vietnamese are ancestor worshipers who consider the moving of the bones or dust of an ancestor a sacrilege. To do so would create animosity among the local residents. Hence, I decided that the security in that particular sector would have to suffer to leave the graves intact. This required modification of the plans for the defenses, the leach field, and the relocation of several buildings. The biggest modification was the change in the location of the septic tank and leach field because the graves were in the area in which it was originally planned to put them.

One of the first projects was to insure a water supply. RMK brought in a well-drilling rig, but there was difficulty in finding adequate water. Finally, a source that was pure and plentiful was struck. As work proceeded steadily I was consulted more and more on the arrangement or dividing of buildings and on the defenses of the area. Team 99 moved into the new compound in January 1966, before I left the 25th ARVN Division.

Hau Nghia was the major infiltration route to Saigon. It bordered on Tay Ninh Province just below the VC War Zone C, as well as on the Plain of Reeds, a swampy area to the west under control of the Viet Cong. Hence there were many routes for the Viet Cong (VC) and North Vietnam Army (NVA) to use to get into Saigon, in the past, this area had been used by the Viet Minh in their struggle for freedom from the French. There were many caves and tunnels which the VC enlarged and exploited. One of the missions of the 25th ARVN Div was to sever these routes into Saigon. This was difficult because Hau Nghia had many pockets of VC and many VC sympathizers. It was not possible to travel from one hamlet to another on the majority of the roads in the province because they were mined. The ARVN would sweep them periodically to open them for convoys to get supplies from Saigon to the district or province headquarters, but normal traffic could not flow on most of the roads without serious risk.

The Hau Nghia Province Chief was a political individual frequently at odds with COL Chinh, the 25th DTA CDR. The advisors were sometimes impressed to mediate their differences. One advisor had to be transferred because he began taking the side of the Province Chief against the Division Commander. It was MACV policy to keep out of the internal politics of Vietnam if possible, and not to push one individual over another. There was, however, a requirement to recommend to MACV the relief of any Vietnamese officer thought to be ineffective. Both the Province Chief and the Division Commander were dynamic and apparently effective within their limits. To take sides with one against the other seemed to Ugalde counter-productive. It was particularly bad when the reports from the Province Advisor began to get to MACV HQ that were in conflict with the Div Advisor's reports being rendered by COL Ugalde. When the Province Advisor was questioned on this, he pointed out that he was doing his job advising and reporting as required. He was informed that the policy was not to support one or the other; that the US advisory effort must speak consistently; it was harmful to have Americans, advising at two different echelons of command, take conflicting positions. Unconvinced, he continued to fight the problem, so on my recommendation to COL Ugalde he was reassigned to MACV HQ.

The road between Due Hoa and Saigon was usually open, although as time went on, the VC mined it more and more. LTC Luyen and I drove it occasionally to visit the 49th Regt or the Dist HQ in Cu Chi. The Cu Chi District Chief had a pet boa constrictor; when he had guests, he would proudly bring out his pet. On many occasions I had to hold it to have my picture taken.

Toward the end of 1965, LTC Luyen informed me that he was driving to the 49th Regt CP in his jeep. By this time there was considerable enemy activity on the road to Saigon, so I decided to take with me an American bodyguard. The 1SG of Advisory Team 99 selected a soldier from the Security Section who was a good shot and a well-trained Infantryman. Specialist Fourth Class Charles A. Totten was a husky, sharp, good-looking young man who had been a guard on the Tombs of the Unknowns before his assignment to Vietnam. He was delighted to get away from the routine and proved to be a capable and alert guard. During the trip I mentioned to him that I needed to learn more about the M-16 rifle, which I hadn't had an opportunity to work with it. said that he was familiar with the rifle and had fired expert with it; he suggested that I let him give me some instructions. When we returned I arranged to have <u>him</u> instruct me in the assembly, disassembly and dry firing of the M-16; we also did a bit of familiarization firing with it at the edge of town.

The return from Cu Chi was made in a convoy of four jeeps; in the lead vehicle was an ARVN LT, two soldiers and a driver, then LTC Luyen's jeep, followed by mine, with a guard jeep in the rear.

The convoy was about two thirds of the way to Due Hoa when there was a loud explosion; the lead jeep was blown into the air. Obviously it had run over a mine. The LT lost an eye and eventually died; one of the other ARVN soldiers was killed instantly. The other two were badly wounded. We gave them what first aid we could while scattering the soldiers, including SP4 Totten, for security. Fortunately the jeeps had radios with which we called for assistance. Shortly a force came out from Due Hoa to escort us into town.

This was the sort of thing we now expected each time we drove on the roads in the area. Mining the roads was a tactic which the VC used effectively to isolate hamlets. Unfortunately, the tactic killed more civilians than military personnel or advisors. It was a shotgun approach which did as much damage to the people the VC were trying to woo as it did to the forces in control of Vietnam they were trying to displace. This must always be kept in mind when evaluating the fight in Vietnam. Civilians were the pawns of the VC, and to a lesser extent, of the Vietnamese authorities. The media and other uninformed individuals accused the South Vietnamese and the Americans of callously killing civilians with artillery and napalm, but there was little mention of the toll the VC took. There were deaths, of course, from friendly fire; a battle cannot be fought without killing innocent civilians if they will not evacuate the area. But a large percentage of the civilians killed or wounded were the result of VC activities: terrorist bombings, indiscriminate mining of roads, shelling of villages and hamlets and deliberate assassination of government officials.

MAJ Chuck Yarborough was the Advisor in Long An Province, a principal agricultural area crowded with rice paddies, sugar cane fields and hamlets. So aggressive and eager that he could not abide delays, he was never satisfied with the system as it operated, constantly trying to bypass channels to get things done by any means. While normally welcoming initiative, I found some of his methods beyond reason and had to curb him occasionally. A capable advisor and a good soldier, he unfortunately antagonized people with his abrasiveness. He was replaced by George Dennett, a War College classmate, who understood the system. We worked well together.

The Long An Province Chief lived in a magnificent French Villa on the Vam Co Dong River. It was always enjoyable to lunch with him because he had a fine chef. Cultured Vietnamese enjoyed food that was an admirable mixture of Chinese and French cuisines. Crisp French bread was served at every meal as well as other delicacies I enjoyed. Some did not find the food as palatable as I. Fortunately, I never got sick from eating the local food. The peasants did not fare so well; they ate everything including dog and monkey meat.

At the 50th Regiment change of command ceremony which I attended with LTC Luyen, a formal dinner was served consisting of "seven kinds of beef": chopped beef, beef stew, beef dipped in a sauce, beef soup, roast beef, beef wrapped in green leaves and steamed, and a seventh way I disremember. The Vietnamese also ate a great deal of seafood because most of the country bordered the coast. Rice was of course, a staple at all meals, but there were many vegetables also.

Doug Morgan described one peasant meal, "On one festive occasion, a national holiday, we were 'treated' to a bowl of duck blood, plenty of rice, and semi-cooked duck sliced for chopstick handling. The trick was to put the rice in the blood, cover it with sliced duck and greenery from the table, and ENJOY. While I did not lose my stomach, I credit the feat with my lack of sobriety that evening. I rapidly learned that a great quantity of beer can make even duck blood palatable. While I learned to enjoy the bulk of Vietnamese cooking, I could not stomach quantities required to maintain my body weight. As a consequence, I lost 32 pounds in the first two months with the Battalion, and retained that loss until I reported to the TOC at Due Hoa to work as G-3 Air."

The most prominent terrain feature in the 25th DTA was a lone hill in Tay Ninh province which rose about 250 feet from the flat plain. Called Nui Ba Dinh or the "Black Virgin Mountain", it was used by both Americans and ARVN as a communications center. The top was reached by helicopter, as the VC were entrenched about a third of the way up on the hill. Periodic operations were mounted to clear them out, but none fully succeeded. On the other hand, the VC never overran the communications facilities on the top of Nui Ba Dinh.

Tay Ninh was an interesting province, dominated by a single religious sect, the Cao Dai. Among its saints were Buddha, Confucius, Jesus Christ, Joan of Arc, Victor Hugo and Sun Yat-Sen. There was a huge Cao Dai temple in Tay Ninh City, a unique structure; the characteristic "All Seeing Eye of God" painted on the roof was clearly visible when approaching the city by helicopter. On one visit with my counterpart, I was given a detailed tour of the temple, but only after I had removed my boots.

The Tay Ninh Province Chief was a competent, effective administrator whose advisor was MAJ Bill Radtke, a SF OFF. SF Teams had been established in Tay Ninh Province very early in the American presence. Because of the three or four SF Teams in Tay Ninh, it was decided that the Prov Advisory Team should be made up in large part of Green Beret personnel. MAJ Radtke was both the Prov Senior Advisor and the B Team Chief.

The Province Chiefs home was a show place; his garden contained many bushes trimmed to represent animals: elephants, peacocks, water buffalo, monkeys, tigers and dogs. It was quite a display of which the Chief was justly proud, He, too, set a fine table.

On one occasion at a luncheon in Tay Ninh, both dog and monkey were served. Monkey, a pinkish meat which looked and tasted like veal, is stringy and tough. Dog is a darker meat which tasted like rabbit. As long as you do not think about what you are eating, it is not too bad. As a matter of necessity, the Vietnamese use almost every animal for food. Dogs were not only pets, but also live stock. Once the concept of dog as food is accepted, it was possible to eat and even enjoy it. Always interested in food, I was willing to try anything.

As a result of many visits to Tay Ninh with my counterpart or to visit US Advisory Teams, I got to know the Province well. This stood me in good stead on a later assignment. Although there were no ARVN troops in Tay Ninh, the VC did not seem to control the Province or interfere too much with the normal life there. The explanation given was that the Cao Dais were so nationalistic and aggressive that the RFPF, made up in large measure from followers of the sect, were able to hold their own against the VC. In addition, there were the troops recruited and trained by the SF. Despite the fact that the VC War Zone C was in Tay Ninh there was less enemy activity there than in Hau Nghia.

The concept of using Special Forces as advisors was under attack because they reported to two headquarters. The Advisors in Tay Ninh, of course, reported to COL Ugalde, Senior Advisor of the 25th DTA. They also reported to the 5th SF Group, which provided most of their support. Their loyalties were therefore divided. MAJ Radtke, a dedicated officer who did an outstanding job as Province Advisor, posed no problem. Some of the other areas in which the dual system operated did not fare so well. There was, understandably, a resentment of the SF by the MACV advisors, largely because the SF Teams got far better supply service than did the MACV Teams. SF Teams had access to funds and supplies through 5th Group that were not available to other advisory teams. This caused animosity, particularly in areas where there was a mixture of the two teams. Radtke as Prov Advisor had under his control both SF and MACV advisory teams.

In Vietnam it was unfortunately true that there were several different wars: The ARVN war, the RFPF war, the CIA war, the secret SOG war, the SF war, and eventually the American forces war. All of these were not completely coordinated; a single command structure such as we had in Korea was never achieved.

Because of Radtke's split responsibilities, he was not always able to get to see his subordinate teams as often as he wanted to. Even in Tay Ninh the roads were sometimes mined, so he traveled throughout the large Province by helicopter for the most part. These were not readily available. Often he could not get to some of his advisory teams for several weeks. It was not surprising, therefore, that I received word through one of the NCOs on the Team at Go Dau Ha that there was a problem with the Senior Advisor there. Since the NCO seemed highly concerned, I visited the Team without delay. During a long talk with the District Advisor, he appeared ill at ease, unable to relax completely while I was there. When asked how much he had gotten around with his District Chief, he gave an evasive answer. He was unkempt and looked as if he needed a shower; though there was a primitive shower available at Go Dau Ha. I sensed that this officer had not made a good adjustment to his assignment, a conclusion borne out when I talked with the junior OFFs and senior NCOs on the team. Reluctantly, they told me that the CPT was so frightened that he never left the compound; he never took off his boots, even when sleeping, because he wanted to be prepared to "bug out" in the event the Team House was overrun. This accounted for the Senior Advisor's apparent lack of personal hygiene. He obviously was of no help to the District Chief, so I ordered him back to Due Hoa and replaced him. As he was a MACV Advisor, I could do this without infringing on Radtke's authority, though I notified him at once of my action. It was a case of poor assignment, although as an IN OFF he should have been able to handle the situation.

The 25th ARVN Div rarely mounted operations controlled by Div HQ. Most of the military action was under regimental or task force commander control. Occasionally, however, Div would order an operation with a mixed force: a Bn from one of the Regts, a Ranger Bn and RFPF forces. The Div Tactical CP would be deployed on these occasions. Since COL Chinh had been restricted in the combat forces he could field, and there was always a limited involvement, he elected to remain at his Div CP to control the bulk of his forces in the event of a crisis. As a result, LTC Luyen commanded such operations; I accompanied him to the field. These were usually fruitless efforts; I am convinced that they were compromised. Too many people got to know about them in advance. It was a common belief among the advisors that all echelons of command and control, Div, Regts, Bns, Provs and Dists, had been infiltrated by the VC. This was one of the objections to having integrated offices for the advisors and their counterparts. But it was a fact of life in Vietnam so we made the best of it.

One such operation under LTC Luyen's control was in the area of the Hep Hoa sugar mill. Long An, Hau Nghia and Tay Ninh grew a great deal of sugar cane; the government had built a mill on the river to produce sugar, molasses and rum. The sugar was not well refined; though crystalline, it was dirty brown because all of the impurities had not been removed. The molasses, thick and syrupy, smelled and tasted strong. The rum was miserable. It sold quite well in Saigon only because it was cheap. The sugar mill was an important money-maker for the government.

Due Hue Dist HQ, near the sugar mill, had a strong force of RFPF to secure both the HQ and the mill. Routinely, the only access to the mill was by helicopter or boat; in Due Hue all roads were mined, hence sugar cane reached the mill by boat. LTC Luyen's mission was to open the road to the mill so that supplies and personnel could be moved. Like most Div operations, this one had little enemy contact. The mission was accomplished as the supplies and personnel reached the Dist HQ and the mill without incident. Much sugar, rum and molasses was trucked back to Saigon. The lack of contact appeared to be no reflection on Luyen's ability or integrity.

Advisory Team 99 was assigned a helicopter, which reported daily, and was used for command and control, supply, medical evacuation and other tactical or administrative purposes. Some-times additional helicopters were made available which were given to Prov or Regt advisors. When a large operation was planned, sufficient helicopters to move one or more companies could be obtain-ed. Each month, on pay day, COL Ugalde, an Army Aviator, would satisfy his flight time requirement by flying the helicopter around the DTA on the "pay day circuit". If he couldn't go, I made the circuit. It was an opportunity to see each of the advisory teams, to find out how they were living, what their problems were, and how we could help them. Whenever possible I used the helicopter to visit some of the advisory teams. Frequently, LTC Luyen and I would visit Prov chiefs or Regt commanders.

Interpreting COL Ugalde's instructions to look into the morale of the advisors to require frequent visits, I saw every team at least twice a month. Transportation was the big problem since the chopper was in constant demand for tactical use, resupply, or administrative purposes. COL Ugalde often took COL Chinh to visit one of the Regt or Prov HQ, so scheduling was involved. The L19s, fixed wing aircraft, were good for reconnaissance, but could only land at those advisory team locations with airstrips.

Because of the shortage of helicopters, I had occasion to fly with many people. John Paul Vann, the USAID Advisor to Hau Nghia, and I frequently toured the Prov together. Vann, a dynamic individual, was a former Army LTC, who had been Advisor to the CG of the 7th ARVN Div in IV Corps. He had left the Army in protest because he disagreed with MACV policies, indeed, the policy of the Administration in prosecuting the war. He advocated a central command through which the US would assume overall control of all forces fighting in South Vietnam. He had other strong beliefs, which he still attempted to get implemented. He had returned to Vietnam as a civilian under the auspices of USAID. Due to the split responsibility in the US advisory effort, he was free to make any recommendations he thought appropriate. As a USAID advisor he was not responsible to MACV. This posed problems because the Province Chief looked to his military advisor for all advice, particularly on military matters. Vann would volunteer both military and political advice without regard to the MACV military advisor. This conflicting advice was used by the wily Province Chief, who played the MACV and USAID advisors against each other. Since MACV provided most of his support, including helicopters, weapons, ammunition and rice, he was careful not to alienate the MACV advisor, but pushed his luck to the limit. It was a bad situation. Vann, though dedicated and sincere, also thought he was better qualified than most MACV Advisors; but he did not have all the answers and confused rather than clarified a ticklish situation.

On one occasion I flew with Bernard Fall, who had written extensively on Vietnam and was considered an expert on the country. During our flight from Due Hoa to Tay Ninh City we had an interesting discussion on the indicators of VC influence. He considered the number of hamlet chiefs killed per month one of the most reliable indicators; others were the number of attacks on hamlets, as well as the percentage of a given crop harvested and recovered. He maintained that such statistics were a key to the actual influence of the VC in the country. We agreed on many items, but had different approaches to the problems, particularly on tactics for defeating the VC.

One day COL Ugalde was alerted to show the entire 25th DTA to a VIP who would arrive shortly. The VIP, LTG John Heintges, was both commanding and impressive, tall, built proportionally, with grey hair. COL Ugalde was tied up with COL Chinh, so it was my privilege to escort LTG Heintges throughout the area of operations (AO). We visited all of the advisory teams in one day, quite a feat. Obviously we stayed at each one a very short time. As it happened, several times when the helicopter took off from an area it was fired on by VC. After the third time Heintges looked questioningly at me and asked if such fire was typical.

"Yes, sir", I replied. "We control the district and province headquarters and the area immediately around them, but that is about all."

Heintges commented that it was necessary to get out and patrol more. He had a particular interest in RFPF as that was to be his major concern as Deputy Commander, MACV (DEPCOMUSMACV). He questioned everyone about what could be done to upgrade RFPF and push them out into saturation patrolling.

During the stop at Due Hue, we visited the sugar mill. Enroute, LTG Heintges was briefed that the manager of the mill was a physically disabled ARVN MAJ. Wounded in combat, he had been put in charge of the mill because he was no longer combat worthy. As he showed us through the mill, LTG Heintges complimented him on his job and evidenced interest in the production. The major poured us a drink of rum; the general made the mistake of praising it highly. About a week later a message came from Hep Hoa that there was a case of rum for LTG Heintges at the sugar mill. On my next swing through the DTAI picked it up. It was presented to LTG Heintges on his next visit to our area.

As a result of my visits throughout the DTA, I became acquainted with most of the Vietnamese officers in the area. The older officers had fought with the French against the Viet Minh, and were experienced combat leaders. Though they did not always show the aggressiveness and dedication that we desired, most were effective. The younger officers, many of them graduates of the Vietnamese Military Academy at Dalat, appeared unsure of themselves and displayed little leadership. Obviously, these generalizations did not fit every officer, but the differences were notable. Typical of the older group was CPT (Dai-Uy in Vietnamese) Di. As commander of the 2nd Bn, 46th IN Regt, he had made his unit into a capable fighting force through dynamic leadership. Again I quote Doug Morgan, an advisor with the 2/46,

"Di was educated by the French, schooled at Benning, and was a forceful and feared commander; feared not only by the VC, but also by his own soldiers because of the tirades he would occasionally lapse into when the situation was deteriorating, or when the soldiers were displaying a weak or indifferent attitude. I have watched him take a new group of recruits, stand them at attention in front of the Battalion Headquarters and lecture them while slapping each to the ground several times over the course of two or more hours. He was a stern disciplinarian, but his troops never fled in the six months we were together. He was honest and straightforward with the advisors. While he rarely accepted our advice at face value, he valued it and used part to conduct that or the next operation. He appeared to recognize that reports were not as exact or precise as he expected, for on more than one occasion he asked for an American verification of a command report that a unit was where it reported it was, or that the unit had in fact searched the area in question with negative results. Unfortunately, his company commanders were not as thorough or precise in their reports as he expected them to be. On one occasion, when I had been with the Battalion for about four months, I was asked to verify that the company I was with had searched a heavily entangled area suspected of harboring VC which had been seen to enter that area. The company commander reported that the area had been searched with negative results, when, in fact, the company had never entered the area. My report to Brown revealed the discrepancy and also created a void with the company commander that I am sure was never closed.

"Di was married to a beautiful French-Vietnamese lady. She and their three year old son lived in Saigon. Di's bodyguard would occasionally arrive unexpectedly with the family in Di's early fifties model Oldsmobile. No other wives, girl friends or families were ever allowed to visit the CP, but on at least six separate instances when we were standing down from an operation, Di and his family would join us for dinner. No officer ever questioned or doubted his authority or wisdom. His word was absolute.

"The advisors were equally diverse in background and ability. Some were dedicated, knowledgeable and effective; others were content to let their counterparts set the pace; if the ARVN officer was non-aggressive they became the same way. On the whole, however, the advisors were competent officers who tried their best. Even the MATA Course at FT Bragg was not equal to preparing advisors for their duties; many, like myself, arrived in country with only their American training and experience to guide them. That they accomplished as much as they did is a tribute to their ingenuity and determination."

As mentioned earlier, CPT Jim Parlier, an ORD OFF assigned as a Dist Advisor, was awarded the CIB by virtue of participating in many operations with the RFPF. He deserved it; without denigrating him, I became involved in an emotional controversy in Vietnam. Any advisor at District or Province, could earn the CIB if the requirements, other than being assigned to the Infantry, were met. Up till this point, the CIB had been reserved solely for Infantry troops. Not even Artillerymen in WWII or Korea could earn it. As American units came into Vietnam, OFFs or EM of other branches were denied the badge even though they fought with Infantry battalions or brigades, in Vietnam this exclusivity of this award was violated; soon Ordnance, Chemical, Medical Service Corps, Adjutant General, and even Judge Advocate General Officers s sported the Combat Infantryman Badge. A case can be made for the award to other than Infantrymen if they truly operated for thirty days in a ground combat role and were exposed to enemy fire. But such awards clearly frustrated the original purpose of the badge, the enhancement of the Infantry soldier. As a result of my concern for the integrity of the CIB as well as my appreciation for the service rendered by many non-Infantry troops such as Jim Parlier, I wrote a strong letter recommending establishment of a Combat Badge, which could be awarded to any OFF or EM, regardless of service, provided he met certain criteria such as operating against an ground enemy for 30 days during which they were under hostile fire or being wounded while engaged in such operations. This recommendation was never approved, though MACV continued to award the CIB to members of other services, in clear violation of the Army Regulation establishing it. Perhaps MACV had been granted an exception to policy; if so this was never communicated to the troops. American units continued to deny the badge to Artillery Forward Observers who were on the front line at all times with the Infantrymen.

During one of my flights over the DTA, I noticed that there were many water buffalo which seemed always to be drifting across the area. When the movements of the buffalo were called to the attention of the G-2 Advisors, they came up with the theory that the water buffalo might indicate the movement of the VC. They passed instructions to all pilots flying over the DTA to note the movement and render periodic reports or "buffalo counts". This became a standing joke as the continuing reports of buffalo herds sounded almost like a comic western drama.

One of my duties was to sit on the MACV Promotion Board. The six officers interviewed all recommended NCOs, many truly outstanding. Advisory Team 99 recommended for promotion SFC Peddie, a dedicated, capable Engr NCO, with no formal education, either military or civilian. He could do almost any engineering task and was a natural leader, but made a poor impression on the Board every time he appeared. Despite my arguments to the Board members, faced with too much talent and too few vacancies, they denied Peddie the additional stripes he deserved.

During my tenure with Advisory Team 99, official duties took me to Saigon at least once a month. There was always some free time which I used to see the city. On each visit I tried to eat in one of the excellent restaurants there. LTC Luyen, who lived in Cholon, took me to several superb Chinese restaurants in that part of the city. Caruso's, a French restaurant, served delicious food. There were many outstanding Vietnamese eating places, the Floating Restaurant being the most famous. It was bombed shortly after my arrival, so was closed. Cheap Charlie's, close to the Brink Hotel, served delicious crab and asparagus soup among other things. Most restaurants had wire screening or grills over the windows so that passers-by could not throw grenades into them.

Tu Do Street, the "red light" district, lined with bars, massage parlors and souvenir shops, was the favorite hangout of most GIs. SF troopers gathered at the Sporting Bar, more of a club than a bar. Passing it one day, SGM Heinzelman, from Mainz, Germany, grabbed me and hauled me in for a couple of drinks and talk about the old times in the 504.

Saigon had an impressive cathedral and an excellent zoo, both still open to the public. The two civilian hotels flanking the Legislative Building were the Caravelle, where most of the reporters and diplomats stayed, and the Continental. Saigon was a cosmopolitan city which offered a great deal of diversion. Of course prostitutes were available anywhere and at any time, walking the streets, in the bars, and in the massage parlors frequented by soldiers.

While driving from Saigon to Bien Hoa on one of my trips, I noted much activity in the huge rubber plantations just south of Bien Hoa. Trees were being cut down and buildings erected. The driver told me that the area was being prepared for the 1st Infantry Division, the first US Army division-sized force deployed to Vietnam. It eventually became the Long Binh logistical complex and US Army, Vietnam (USARV) HQ. The first large Army tactical unit in country was the 173rd ABN Bde from Okinawa. My role in stationing that unit in the far east gave me great satisfaction.

Late in 1965, Advisory Team 99 received word that the US 25th IN Div was coming to Vietnam and would be located in the 25th DTA. There was a great deal of coordination to be done with the Vietnamese requiring the best efforts of the advisors. Initially it was proposed that several self-propelled 8-inch guns be positioned at Bao Trai, but after it was pointed out that the roads not only needed major upgrading for the heavy traffic, but also daily mine, sweeping before vehicles could traverse them, it was decided to put them elsewhere. Though the guns would have been able to fire into the VC stronghold in the Plain of Reeds, it was considered too risky. The US 25th Div base camp was to be at Cu Chi, where Div HQ and one Bde would be located.

COL Chinh had been kept apprised on the plans, as they developed. Finally it became necessary to brief the 49th Regt CO at Cu Chi. It was to be a briefing strictly for Vietnamese personnel, an OFF from the US 25th IN Div was to make the presentation to the Vietnamese OFFs concerned. In discussing the briefing with the G-3 Advisor at III Corps, he informed me that COL Frink wanted a representative from the III Corps Advisory Team present. COL Ugalde had no objections, but I pointed out that since it was to be a briefing for ARVN, Americans must be unobtrusive, hence no interruptions or questions by the Americans. The G-3 Advisor assured me that this was understood.

On the day of the briefing a self-important LTC from the III Corps Advisory Team came to Cu Chi. When the briefing got underway, he began interrupting to ask questions, distracting the briefer and confusing the Vietnamese. Leaning over so that only he could hear me, I asked him to please be quiet as this was a briefing for the Vietnamese, not for him; his Team would get the same information directly from the 25th Div. But he persisted in interrupting. Finally, after the Vietnamese had become visibly upset, I told him in no uncertain terms to shut up. He became highly miffed; on his return to Bien Hoa he told COL Frink that I had embarrassed him in front of the ARVN, compromising his prestige and that of the US Advisors. COL. Frink called COL. Ugalde to get our version of the matter. Although Ugalde had been given a detailed account of the incident, he put me on the phone to tell Frink exactly what had happened and what I had said to his representative. COL Frink demanded that I apologize. I refused. Ugalde discussed the matter with me, but I was adamant; the LTC, a guest, had tried to usurp the briefing; he had distracted the briefer and confused the ARVN. It was he, in fact, who had embarrassed the US Advisors and the Vietnamese; it was he who should apologize. COL Frink ordered me to Bien Hoa to discuss the matter. He chewed my butt royally, but was unable to get me to apologize. Finally he dropped the matter, but on my efficiency report he rated me low in tact. This was not unusual, my lack of tack was well documented.

The III Corps Advisory Team or MACV HQ periodically directed the advisory teams to push the Vietnamese into greater combat activity. Due to COL Chinh's restriction on the amount of troops he could employ at any one time, the 25th ARVN Div's combat record was not very impressive. On the other hand, the routes to IV Corps and Tay Ninh remained open with bridges intact. Unfairly, the advisors were faulted for this lack of aggressiveness. Attempts to explain the restrictions on the 25th ARVN to higher HQ were not heeded.

Many senior officers failed to understand the advisory effort, holding advisors responsible for the performance of their counterparts. An advisor could persuade, could withhold support if he thought a particular mission unsound, could provide or deny helicopter and other support, but his influence was limited. It was unfair for higher HQ to condemn advisors for actions which were not under their control. Strong advisors could sometimes dominate weaker counterparts, in effect, usurping command. But this was rare. Since there was no unified chain of command in Vietnam, advisors could neither direct nor order. This inability to get obvious things done was a continuing cause for the advisors low morale.

Although he took every opportunity to explain to higher HQ the situation in the 25th DTA, COL Ugalde frequently received directives to increase the combat activity in the area. One day BG DePuy, MACV J-3, visited Due Hoa. As was the custom, he was given a joint briefing on operations. All Americans as well as Vietnamese were given joint briefings so that they understood the Vietnamese thinking and actions, a very effective technique. After the briefing DePuy, Ugalde and I were talking in the back of the TOC with no Vietnamese present. DePuy berated Ugalde, saying that he had to get the 25th Div moving; it had the worst combat record of all the ARVN divisions. He kept insisting that Ugalde and Advisory Team 99 had to get more ARVN troops out in the field, to get more operations underway. After making another attempt to explain the restraints on Chinh, Ugalde merely listened; there was nothing he could do about the matter. Stung to indiscretion, I interrupted,

"General, go to your counterpart, the J-3 of the Vietnamese JGS and get him to order COL Chinh to operate. If you do that, this Division will move out immediately. COL Chinh is an experienced soldier, he'll move anytime he gets orders, or the restrictions placed on him are lifted. But at this time he can only commit a limited amount of combat power. So if you want the Division to fight, go to your counterpart and influence him."

DePuy looked at me as if I was insane, saying, "I have no control over my counterpart."

"Do you think that we have more control at this level?"

"Well, you are the advisors down here."

"Aren't you the advisor to the J-3 of the Joint General Staff?"

"Well, that's different."

It is doubtful if DePuy ever did fully understand the relationship of the advisors to their Vietnamese Counterparts.

Occasionally, highly classified messages were received requesting that the Team helicopter orbit in a given area for half an hour or more. This was to provide a beacon on which B-52 aircraft could home-in for "Arc Light" strikes. Arc Lights were massive, saturation bombings of known or suspected VC concentrations. Several times COL Ugalde and I watched these strikes from the helicopter which flew just off the target zone. The Arc Lights were tremendous! The Shockwaves from the bombs were actually visible. The area in the 25th DTA most frequently struck was the Hobo Woods just north of Cu Chi, a well-known and heavily infested VC assembly area.

The Vietnamese Ranger Training Center at Trung Lap, on the fringe of the Hobo Woods, was in the 25th ARVN Div AO, consequently the Div had a commitment for its security. During LTC Luyen's periodic checks of the Center, I got to know most of the Ranger Advisors there and to witness some of the training. The Ranger Bns were generally well lead, aggressive units. COL Chinh used the four Ranger Bns assigned to his Division on most operations.

During one visit to Trung Lap, a Ranger Advisor asked me if Team 99 could spare a radio operator for a month. Due to rotation and lag in the replacement system, his Ranger Team would be minus an RTO for the time the battalion he was advising was in training. Battalions undergoing training went on maneuvers in the jungle outside their camp. These exercises were actually in the Hobo Woods and often became live fire exercises against a real enemy, as the VC frequently tried to ambush them. Hence, the advisor needed some one to handle his communications. The first name that popped into my head was Totten, an eager Infantry soldier who had acted as my bodyguard on occasion. The 1SG was able to arrange the guard schedule so that Totten could go to Trung Lap. While there, the Battalion he was with had several fire fights. When Totten came back, he was proudly wearing a CIB.

CPT Brown, who had been MG Salet's aide at the War College, was the advisor to a Ranger Battalion which had a hot battle between Bao Trai and Cu Chi. One of his NCOs recommended him for a Silver Star because he had called in and adjusted close air support. After considering the matter carefully, I recommended disapproval. Brown had done only what an Infantry soldier was supposed to do. Before recommending disapproval, I talked with both the SGT and CPT Brown to determine if he had exposed himself to an unusual degree. He had not. Because the Tactical Air Support Brown had directed on the VC was credited with the victory, the Team thought he deserved an award. There was no unusual valor associated with his act, however. The matter of awards was a problem, as there appeared to be different standards throughout Vietnam. In many cases, particularly in US units, awards were given rather freely, but in MACV awards for valor were made strictly according to the regulations. The SF awards system fell somewhere in between. This was unfortunate; perhaps I was overly protective of the system, but it seemed to me that when an award was given it should be earned. In my judgement the standards seemed lower in Vietnam than they had been in Korea, and Korean standards had been lower than those I experienced in WWII.

Immediately after the battle, I went to look at the area. VC bodies still littered the landscape. The intelligence people were interested in how well nourished the VC were, what kind of uniforms they wore, what kind of equipment they had and how many and what kind of weapons were recovered. It was only when there were large numbers of killed in action (KIA) that the bodies could be seen because as soon as a fire fight was over, the Viet Cong would attempt to drag their casualties off the battlefield. If that was impossible, they would strip them of all usable equipment. Their first priority appeared to be the recovery of weapons; it was rare that any were left behind. This was a statistic that MACV stressed, weapons vs body count. The body count was just coming into prominence as an index of combat effectiveness. Because weapons were so valuable to the VC, they were the first things policed up, consequently it was unusual to get a weapon for each body. Later, as the VC escalated the intensity of the combat, there was a corresponding increase of the ratio of weapons to body count.

At Christmas, Team 99 had a party for the children of the Vietnamese who worked in the compound: cooks, guards, drivers, laborers and cleaning personnel. All of the EM and OFFs donated gifts sent from home. There was ice cream, cake, coke, favors, hats and candy. The EM decorated the mess hall for the afternoon party. Almost a hundred children arrived dressed in their best. They were initially shy, especially when Santa came with deep "Ho-Ho-Hos" and gave each a gift, an apple and an orange. Eventually the little tykes thawed out and became as happy and active as children their age all over the world. The Americans enjoyed the party more than the Vietnamese.

When the 25th ARVN Division moved to Due Hoa from I Corps, its HQ and Advisory Team were initially located in Saigon and operated out of that city. The advisors went to the field during the day and returned to Saigon at night. Just before my arrival, the Div HQ and the Advisory Team had relocated to Due Hoa. As a result of contracts and connections the advisors had in Saigon, a villa had been rented for the use of officers when in Saigon on business. Each officer paid a minimal sum every month for rent, utilities, and a woman to keep the house in good order. It was kept locked, but any officer who had business in Saigon could get the key and use the quarters to sleep in. There were cots and other minimal furnishings, electricity as well as undrinkable running water. The villa lacked screens and mosquito bars but when "punk coils" were burned, the smoke kept away the pests at night. This was a satisfactory arrangement in the latter part of 1965 because there was little terrorist activity in Saigon men. The villa we rented was just around the corner from a Vietnamese police station in Gia Dinh, a suburb of Saigon, so officers felt secure. In retrospect everyone who stayed in the villa was vulnerable, particularly when only one was in the villa. It did provide handy lodgings, otherwise the officers would have had to drive to Bien Hoa to stay at the III Corps Advisory Team Compound as billets in Saigon were usually full.

Just before Christmas, I put in for Rest and Recuperation leave (R&R) in Hong Kong. Approved for early January, it was a relaxing and enjoyable trip. Hong Kong is a fascinating city. From my 18th story room in the Hilton Hotel on Hong Kong Island I watched the teeming traffic in the harbor;

the funicular to the highest hill on Hong Kong Island afforded a spectacular view of the harbor, especially at night; the ride on the Star Ferry from Hong Kong Island to the Kowloon Peninsula was a delight: fast, cheap, frequent. I gorged on delicious food, including Peking Duck (I inadvertently ordered a whole duck when I went into a restaurant frequented only by Chinese; the waiter was most grateful when I presented the remains, almost the entire bird, to him as a tip). The millions living in the high rise apartments or on thousands of sampans or junks in the harbor gave new meaning to the concept of population explosion, the tours were interesting.

After a delightful five days I returned to Saigon. The plane arrived at Ton Son Nhut in the late afternoon, so I went to the villa to spend the night. Almost as soon as I got into bed I fell asleep. Suddenly, heavy automatic and small arms fire sounded all about me. I bounced out of bed and cautiously looked out the window. Tracer bullets, antiaircraft fire and all sorts of explosions lit the sky. It appeared that Saigon was under attack by the VC. Strangely, no vehicles were moving, nor was there much activity on the streets. People were not evacuating the area, so I decided to lie low. I didn't have a weapon; my pistol had been left at Due Hoa. Finally the firing ceased; I went back to sleep, puzzled and concerned.

The next morning I made my way to MACV HQ, called Due Hoa for helicopter transport, and visited with officers in the J-1 Section. LTC Dave Presson mentioned the tremendous waste of ammunition during the firing the night before to celebrate Tet, the Vietnamese New Year. Since there was no ready supply of firecrackers, the Vietnamese soldiers fired their weapons. The incident made me realize how vulnerable Advisors were in the villa. On my return to Due Hoa, I initiated action to close it, directing all of our people to stay in MACV billets.

During my conversation with Dave Presson, who handled the assignment of field grade officers for the J-1 section, he told me that the Senior Advisor of the 24th Special Tactical Zone (24th STZ) was being reassigned and that the job would be open shortly. The position called for a colonel, but he thought that since I was fairly senior and might be on the next promotion list, he could persuade the DCSPER to assign me there. To get the job I would have to extend my tour in Vietnam for a minimum of six months in order to have a full year in the new job. The opportunity to be the Senior Advisor was irresistible, so I signed and Dave processed the papers.

With high hopes that I would soon head an advisory team in the highlands, I returned to Due Hoa just in time to organize the move into our new compound. Late in January 1966, orders were published transferring me to the 24th Special Tactical Zone as Senior Advisor with a reporting date of I February. John McGiffert, a Gruber 4 Leavenworth classmate was named as my replacement. His arrival several days before I left provided an opportunity to tell him about our two counterparts, and to catch up on news of our Leavenworth classmates.

The night before my departure, Advisory Team 99 gave a party for me in the mess hall of the new compound. Almost all of the advisors who had joined the Team after me were present, as well as many who had been there before me. It was a gala affair to which COL Ugalde had invited both of my counterparts. There were speeches and a few presents. Each of my counterparts had received from me a pen and pencil set engraved with their names. They reciprocated; LTC Luyen presented me with a rifle captured on one of the operations he had commanded, and LTC Giai gave me an invitation to a dinner party.

After dinner one of the captains asked permission to make a presentation on behalf of the American Dai-Uys. In their name he presented me with a loving cup made from an artillery shell, following which he inducted me into The Order of The Rusty Nail. A large rusty spike fastened to a blue ribbon was hung around my neck. As the citation was read, each of the officers who had dined with COL Ugalde and me and had partaken of a Rusty Nail came up and poured one into the loving cup. At the conclusion of the reading, urged on by cheers, the captain informed me that as a member of The Order of The Rusty Nail, I was expected to chug-a-lug the contents of the loving cup. Forsaking common sense, I took the cup and downed most of it. There must have been at least a dozen Rusty Nails in the mug, more liquid, more alcohol than I could possibly handle. Almost as soon as I resumed my seat I slumped over in a drunken sleep. The Dai-Uys laughed as they triumphantly carried me to my hootch and put me to bed. The Team doctor took my blood pressure periodically during the night. Finally I staggered to the latrine, vomited all of the alcohol, and went to bed to sleep it off.

The next morning I had the katzenjammer of all hangovers! Every movement was painful, but I was told that there would be a formation in the ARVN compound at which COL. Chinh was to award several officers, including myself, Vietnamese medals. Though in no condition to stand at attention for an award, past training enabled me to do so. Chinh pinned on me the Republic of Vietnam Cross of Gallantry with Gold Star, roughly equivalent to the American Silver Star. Finally the ceremony was over! Then came the revelation! It is the Vietnamese custom to "wet down" an award. My two counterparts literally led me by the hand to the conference room where Chinh's aide opened a bottle of champagne. Chinh poured a little wine on my award and those of the other advisors who had been "gonged". Then we had to drink a toast, the last thing I wanted at 1000 hours that day.

The Team helicopter took me to the III Corps Advisory Team at Bien Hoa, where the staff debriefed me. Elmer May, who had been a star and later coach of the Mainz Troopers, was the Artillery Advisor at III Corps. He was still in superb physical condition. We had a long talk about our Mainz friends. After signing out I reported to MACV HQ for transportation to Pleiku, where the II Corps Advisory Team was located. While waiting for my flight, I stayed at the Rex Hotel.

During that period, LTC Giai hosted the dinner party he had invited me to the night of the farewell party. He had arranged the dinner at a restaurant in Saigon and invited LTC Luyen, many of the advisors and most of the 25th Div Staff. Because he knew I enjoyed it, "seven kinds of beef" was the entree. It was an enjoyable evening, one I appreciated. It appeared that this would be the last time I would see Luyen and Giai, but later both entered my life again.

Finally, I was notified to report to the Fixed Wing Section of the MACV Aviation Det at Ton Son Nhut for my flight to Pleiku. A pleasant surprise awaited me; Pat McDermott, who had commanded B Co of THE REGULARS, was my pilot. During the flight north we reminisced about THE REGULARS.

On arrival at Pleiku Airfield, LTC Barney Broughton, who had been with me in the Pentagon and had also commanded a BN in the 1st AR Div, met me. Now the II Corps G-3 Advisor, he was my sponsor. He left to command a BN in the 1st Air CAV Div several days after my arrival. Before his departure, he made sure I was comfortably settled and briefed. He introduced me to the II Corps Senior Advisor, COL Pat Timothy, a dynamic, but volatile officer, who gave me a hasty overview of the highlands after welcoming me. Later, Barney and his S-3, John Hermann, who had been my assistant in the 1st Battle Group, 504th ABN IN in Mainz, visited me in Kontum; his battalion operated in the 24th STZ area for some tune.

During the next few days the II Corps Advisory Staff briefed me on the area, emphasizing Kontum and Pleiku, the provinces making up the 24th Special Tactical Zone. They outlined the history of the Zone, gave me a summary of the enemy activity in the area, and introduced me to the IIARVN Corps Staff. While there I was constantly reminded that COL Wilbur Wilson had been instrumental in building the advisory compound at Pleiku. It was two hollow squares; OFFs lived in rooms on two sides of one; the mess and recreation rooms were on a third, and the Advisory Offices formed the fourth. EM lived in an adjacent square which shared the side housing the offices. Defensive positions surrounded the two squares. Timothy introduced me to MG Vinh Loc, a tall Vietnamese prince, who commanded II Corps.

DAI-UY ORDER
NUMBER   1

11 February 1966

    1. TC 001. The following AWARD is announced.

SEIBERT, DONALD A 060224 LT COL INF USA
  Awarded: Order of the Rusty Nail
  Date action: 2 February and 5 February 1966
  Theater: Republic of Vietnam
  Reason: For heroism in connection with social operations against a
        hostile force. Lieutenant Colonel Seibert distinguished him-
        self by heroic action on 2 February and 5 February 1966 and
        many previous dates too numerous to mention, in that he ex-
        hibited exceptional fortitude, courage, and zeal and a mag-
        namious capacity. Lieutenant Colonel Seibert consistantly
        undertook overwhelming odds and forces superior in number (and
        infrequently in rank) and drove them to their knees in liquid
        defeat. Never did he question the field of battle but immedi-
        ately displaced his forces to that location, displaying except-
        ional foresight by maintaining an adequate reserve. Disregard-
        ing his personal safety, Lieutenant Colonel Seibert repeatedly
        exposed himself to caustic verbal attacks, often times simul-
        taneously from the front and both flanks. Never did he balk,
        but pursued onward to colorful victory. Only due to his out-
        standing logistical operations and never ending source of
        supply, combined with unswerving endurance, was he able to
        maintain this rapid pace. Lieutenant Colonel Seibert's actions
        reflect great credit upon himself and the ancient order of Field
        Grade Officers and commands the highest respect from that dis-
        tinguished group known as Company Grade Officers.

FOR THE SENIOR DAI-UY:

R. B. FREEMAN
Dai-Uy, AGC

The II Corps Advisory Team reported to First Field Force, Vietnam (IFFV) at Nha Trang on the coast, commanded by LTG "Swede" Larsen. On the few visits I made to Nha Trang, the white beaches fronted by luxurious but decaying villas impressed me. There were several old friends there, BG Don Bolton the CofS and COL Alec Kovalevsky the G-4. Alec was a pre-WWII friend I had met through my pal George Gabelia; he later visited me at Kontum.

After two days with the II Corps Advisory Team I went to Kontum by chopper. The Huey landed inside a barbed wire enclosure which surrounded the 24th STZ MACV Advisory Compound, where COL Archie Hyle, the Senior Advisor, greeted me. Tenza Compound was typical of those constructed for American advisors: wooden and stucco buildings with tile roofs, the upper half of the walls open and screened; they could be closed with wooden shutters in the monsoon season. Until COL Hyle left I occupied the "VIP Suite", which was in fact just another room with a little better furniture. There was a separate "hootch" for the Senior Advisor, a prefab building with a latrine, a large comfortable set of quarters as I found out when I talked with COL Hyle there.

During the afternoon I settled into the VIP room, after which I changed into civilian clothes. When I walked into the officer' Club about 1700, I was shocked to find that I was the only person not in uniform. It was common practice throughout Vietnam at that time to change into civilian clothing when off-duty. Even at Pleiku this had been sanctioned. Seeing my discomfiture, the officers grinned; later they told me that COL Hyle had put out an order that no one in the 24th STZ Advisory Team would wear civilian clothes at any time. The matter had not been mentioned to me. Once the American troop concentration built up, this became MACV policy.

The Officers' Club was a comfortable facility with a bar, a large room used as a movie theater, and a circular patio. The enlisted men had a larger, but separate club and recreation facility. At the club that evening, the Adj, CPT Freeman, introduced me to LTC Herschel Lane, the Deputy Senior Advisor, MAJ K.C. Brown, the G-3 Advisor, MAJ John Stewart, the G-2 Advisor and MAJ Bill Tyler, the Kontum Province Advisor. After talking a few minutes over a drink, we went to the mess for dinner. A cubicle had been partitioned in the mess hall for field grade OFFs; other OFFs ate in the main dining room with the EM, though at separate tables. The field grade dining room contained a rectangular table with COL Hyle sitting at the head. After hearing me comment that I preferred round tables because they facilitated conversation, K.C. Brown found a circular table which could accommodate 12 people.

The first morning in Kontum, the 24th STZ Advisory Staff briefed me, after which COL Hyle introduced me to Colonel (Dai-Ta) Nguyen Van Phuoc, Commanding Officer of the 24th Special Tactical Zone. The Zone Headquarters was about a half mile from the MACV Advisory Compound; although it was within walking distance, personnel usually drove back and forth by jeep. The Advisors1 offices were located in buildings separate from those occupied by the Zone Staff. In time, limited collocation of some advisors with their counterparts was achieved as in the 25th ARVN Div.

Two days after my arrival, CPT Freeman informed me that COL Phuoc was hosting a party to honor COL Hyle's departure and my arrival. COL Phuoc's house in downtown Kontum, a large French-type villa with a huge Bougainvillaea vine growing over the front porch, was the scene of the party. The Bougainvillaea was in bloom and added color to the scene. In the courtyard was a pen in which a small, tame Vietnamese deer was kept; when anyone wearing short sleeves walked into the pen, the friendly deer would run to lick the salt from his arms. There were also several peacocks, ducks and other animals; many referred to the house and grounds as Dai-Ta Phuoc's zoo.

The dinner party, laid under the trees, was complete with excellent food, music, entertainment, and speeches by COL Phuoc and MAJ Doan, the Kontum Province Chief. COL Hyle was presented with mementos of his tenure as Senior Advisor. Most of the ARVN Staff, as well as many prominent Vietnamese townspeople, including Roman Catholic, Buddhist and Protestant clergy were in attendance. COL Phuoc had also invited a number of the advisors, including MAJ Bill Tyler, the

Kontum Province Advisor and LTC Ed Smith, the Pleiku Province Advisor. Ed was a big, gruff, open, likeable individual. It was an entertaining and interesting evening which gave me an opportunity to get to know COL Phuoc and his officers. The following morning, after COL Hyle left for his new assignment, I assumed the duties of Senior Advisor, 24th Special Tactical Zone.

The 24th STZ encompassed two of the largest provinces in Vietnam, Pleiku and Kontum; its area was greater than that of the 25th DTA. American Advisors were assigned to two districts or subsectors in Pleiku, Thanh An and Le Trung, and one in Kontum, Dak To. The Thanh An Dist HQ was in a very indefensible position; a move of a few hundred yards would have placed it on highly defensible terrain. MAJ Churchman, the Thanh An Dist Advisor, told me that the site had been selected by a former Province Chief in consultation with his astrologer, despite the advice of his American Advisor. Although it was never overrun during my tenure in the 24th STZ, there was considerable concern about it.

Pleiku Province was more densely populated that Kontum. The Prov Chief, LTC Ho Vinh, had as his advisor initially, LTC Ed Smith, who left shortly after my arrival, followed by LTC Jack Miller. Ed, a dynamic and hard-charging OFF, browbeat Ho Vinh on occasions. Jack, a USMA graduate with previous advisory experience in Vietnam, was a more diplomatic officer. He had helped set up the Vietnamese Military Academy at Dalat. I was pleased to have him as Ed's replacement.

Advising MAJ Nguyen Hop Doan, the Kontum Province Chief, was MAJ Bill Tyler, a tall, handsome, gung-ho IN OFF. Because of the location of the 24th STZ HQ in Kontum, and because Bill Tyler lived in the same compound, I saw more of him than I did of Jack Miller. Having his boss sitting on top of him no doubt posed some problems for Bill, but it did not faze him. After becoming acquainted with all of the advisors, I was convinced that they were dedicated and qualified people.

The only tactical unit assigned to the 24th STZ was the 42nd ARVN IN Regt with HQ at Tan Canh, about 25 miles north of Kontum City in Kontum Province. The ARVN II Corps HQ in Pleiku City had a task force under its control. Used mainly as a Palace Guard, it had three Ranger Bns and two AR CAV Regts in it. There were also many RFPF companies throughout the Zone. In addition, there were eight SF Camps in the two provinces. These were under a B Det, located at Kontum, adjacent to the MACV Compound. It was in turn under a C Det at Pleiku which reported to the 5th Special Forces Group at Nha Trang.

Before my arrival in Kontum, LTG Larsen, the IFFV Commander, upset with the lack of responsiveness and coordination by the Special Forces in relation to the general military efforts throughout the II Corps area (coterminous with the IFFV area), demanded that the SF camps be placed under his operational control (OPCON). GEN Westmoreland had placed all SF Camps in II Corps OPCON to CG, IFFV who, in turn, had delegated OPCON to the Senior Advisors in each of the DTAs as well as the 24th STZ. Hence, Team B24, commanded by LTC Frank Dallas, and the eight SF Teams in the 24th STZ were under my OPCON.

Although there was only one ARVN Regt, there was considerable combat power in the 24th STZ which could be mobilized if necessary. As a result of the OPCON of the SF Teams given me, it was possible to insure that the camps did cooperate in any military operation COL Phuoc mounted. In theory he had a similar ARVN chain of command, which included a not very cooperative Vietnamese SF commander. The SF or Civilian Irregular Defense Group (CIDG) camps were nominally under Vietnamese SF command. In fact, the US Green Berets recruited, trained and paid the Montagnards (local tribesman in the Highlands) and, in fact, controlled the camps.

Montagnards, the original inhabitants of the Highlands, were so-called "primitive people". There were about 21 different tribes of Montagnard, the Rah De being the most numerous in the 24th STZ. The Montagnard wore loin cloths and were armed with blowguns, crossbows and spears. But they made good soldiers under the tutelage of the US Special Forces. The Vietnamese looked down on them and refused them equal status or rights because they had no concept of cleanliness or sanitation, they farmed in a primitive fashion using a "slash and burn" technique to clear the ground, they had distinctive, primitive dances and music, much of which was played on various sized gongs, and they engaged in animal sacrifices. This second class status had precipitated a revolt in 1964, sparking a serious confrontation between the Vietnamese and the US SF advisors who had great loyalty to their Montagnard troops. As a result, they had begun to interpose themselves between the Montagnard and the Vietnamese. It was unfortunate, though understandable, that the Green Beret advisors took sides, creating problems which should not have arisen.

COL Phuoc, a stocky, round-faced man about 5 feet 8 inches tall, with a mane of raven black hair, lived in his villa with two aides and several EM who did the cooking and took care of him. His wife, who lived in My Tho with their children, came to visit Phuoc on several occasions. COL Phuoc, a Roman Catholic, had been an Intelligence Officer in the Diem regime before the first coup. He had a keen sense of humor, was knowledgeable, spoke excellent English, and was easy to work with. K.C. Brown, the G-3 Advisor, fluent in French, was able to determine any subtle issues that Phuoc found difficult to put into English.

COL Phuoc was amenable to suggestions. Frequently special intelligence (SI) information which could not be divulged to the Vietnamese would be forwarded from Pleiku. Based on this information, I would recommend an operation which he usually agreed to mount. It was obvious that he knew about such classified sources of information. As a long-time intelligence officer, Phuoc had his own sources, frequently he already knew about the enemy concentrations reported in the SI. He maintained a complex intelligence network in the 24th Special Tactical Zone.

The briefings by the II Corps and 24th STZ advisors indicated that COL Phuoc was not held in high esteem by MG Vinh Loc. Whether this was because he was a Roman Catholic or because he had been associated with Diem, was not clear. It soon became obvious that he did not have the resources and support the area and the enemy threat warranted. There were many problems that COL Phuoc and I had to work out together, I looked forward to an interesting and rewarding year in the 24th Special Tactical Zone.

As a first priority, I visited all of the advisory elements within the Zone. COL Phuoc accompanied me on most of the visits, but when visiting only MACV advisory dets or some of the SF (CIDG) camps, I went without him. The eight CIDG camps were of special interest. The most northern one was Dak Pek where CPT Sam Sanford, a husky, confident, effective officer was the A Det CO. The most southern was Plei Me, scene of a major battle the year before about which MG Vinh Loc had written a book called "Why Plei Me?" Due Co, very close to the Cambodian border in Pleiku Prov, had also been the scene of several major battles in the last year. Most of the camps were near the Cambodian or Laotian borders. Three of them were not, Mang Buk and Plateau Gi were in the mountains to the northeast of Kontum City and could be reached only by aircraft. The A Teams at those camps were really out of the main stream of military life. They had to make do with what could be airlifted to them and were in constant danger of being overrun. The Plateau Gi camp was on a large plateau, the Mang Buk camp in a beautiful valley. The other camp that was not near the border was Plei Do Lim, southeast of Pleiku City. It was located on a major VC infiltration route, but its usefulness was now under question.

Major Haywood B. Allen, a stocky, outgoing IN OFF, was the Senior Advisor of the 42nd ARVN Regt. As Tan Canh and Dak To were about a mile apart, the Dist Advisory Team at Dak To and the larger Regt Advisory Team at Tan Canh were in close contact.

The 24th STZ Advisory Staff consisted of the SA, the Deputy, LTC Lane, CPT Larry Freeman, G-l Advisor and also the Team Adj andS-1, MAJ Stewart, G-2 Advisor, actually assigned to the 519th Military Intelligence Command in Saigon, Brown, G-3 Advisor, CPT Jim Fowler, G-4 Advisor, and CPT Dick Hervert,G-5 Advisor. Dick, a USMA graduate and Ordnance Officer, was interested in the Vietnamese people as well as in G-5 work. Jim Fowler was replaced by CPT Charles Chesak shortly after I arrived. CPT Chuck Vemity, originally advisor to the 1st Bn, 42nd IN at Kontum City, later became the Asst Subsector Advisor at Kontum Subsector when it was activated. CPT John Bates commanded HQ Co as well as the MACV Compound. Pleased with the personnel and the area of the 24th STZ, I welcomed the challenges, both military and administrative. There were a few leadership problems, American as well as Vietnamese.

Two weeks after my arrival, COL Phuoc announced that he was mounting an operation to open the road from Kontum City to Dak To. The Vietnamese did not fully control the roads at that time. Occasionally a single jeep or truck could drive without incident from Kontum to Tan Canh, as MAJ Allen periodically attested when he drove down to consult with me or talk to his advisor to the 1st Bn. But whenever a convoy moved it was necessary to mount an operation to secure the highway. This involved having elements of the 42nd Regt, RFPF or CIDG patrol on either side of the road, check it for mines, and then outpost it as long as the road was "open". In critical areas troops would "sweep" the roads with mine detectors. COL. Phuoc established a CP in the RFPF post at Kon Trang Mone, about halfway between Kontum and Tan Canh, he and I drove back and forth checking the troops on outpost. The military discipline of the Vietnamese was generally abominable; once the troops got into their positions, ponchos were stretched between trees under which the troops dozed. Promptly at 1130 the soldiers cooked their meals; no activity went on from 1130 to 1330, siesta time. It was normal procedure with all of the Vietnamese to take a siesta at noon; even the Viet Cong did so, hence most military activities ceased unless there was actual contact. It was difficult for me to accept this way of military life, but no amount of talk altered it. Even COL Phuoc shrugged off my expostulations. Fortunately the road was kept open only one day. An uninspiring beginning to operations (OPS) with COL Phuoc.

All 24th STZ operations were given a Dan Thang number, a phrase which was supposed to bring luck to the operation. The road opening was Dan Thang 49; it was followed by many Dan Thangs with allied units, with ARVN forces alone, and with mixed ARVN, CIDG and RFPF.

Whenever COL Phuoc and I were in the field together, I made it a point to eat with him. He had food prepared for the two of us. Usually there was crisp, fresh French bread, rice, and soup, a satisfying meal. To minimize the cost, and bear my share, I would provide C Rations, five-in-one, canned fruit or vegetables. COL Phuoc's mess never served a bad meal nor did I ever get sick from eating Vietnamese food.

That first one-day road clearing action initiated a series of almost 100 OPS conducted in various parts of the Zone during the ensuing year. At times Phuoc would get OPCON of one of the Ranger Bns in Pleiku to augment the 42nd Regt. Most of the OPS were conducted in Kontum Prov. COL Phuoc had to get special permission to operate in Pietku Prov; only rarely did the 24th STZ forces operate there.

Just as I settled in as SA of the 24th STZ, the 1st Brigade of the 25th US Infantry Division (1/25th Bde) arrived in Pleiku. Its initial camp was located just west of the II Corps Advisory Compound. Shortly after it's base camp was established, the colonel commanding the Bde was replaced by BG Glenn Walker. The 24th STZ conducted many joint OPS with the 1/25 Bde, during which I not only got to know Walker well, but developed a great admiration for him as an officer and as an individual. One of the major joint operations conducted by the 24th STZ and the 1/25 Bde, was the opening of the road between Kontum and Dak Pek. The ARVN wanted to recover engineer equipment used in the construction of the camp and left at Dak Pek. The only way to do so was to open the road and drive it out. The plan was to open the road from Pleiku City to Dak Pek using the 1st Bde, 25th Div, the 42nd ARVN Regt, CIDG and RFPF forces. It was an interesting operation during which both the ARVN and US units probed into the mountains on either side of the road through the Dak Bla Valley without significant contact. MAJ Allen, the 24th Regt Advisor, and I drove by jeep from Tan Canh to Dak Pek. On arrival, covered with fine dust which adhered because of our perspiration, we found LTC John Bennett there. John, the Dep CDR of the 5th SF Group, had flown into the camp for an inspection. We hadn't seen each other since he had replaced me as the G-4 of the 8th IN Div, so we had a lengthy talk. The operation concluded as the engineer equipment was convoyed back down the valley, with frequent pauses for minor road repairs. Security was withdrawn as the convoy moved toward Kontum.

It was decided to build a SF camp near Polei Kleng almost due west of Kontum City. This would be the ninth CIDG camp in the 24tii STZ. To get equipment and materials to the site by convoy, a number of road operations were conducted using ARVN, CIDG and RFPF, during which ARVN engineers installed a pontoon bridge across the Dak Bla River. CPT Mark Monroe, an impressive, energetic, enthusiastic SF OFF was in charge of building the camp.

Next there were several operations in the Chu Prong Mountains, northwest of Pleiku City, on the Kontum/Pleiku Province boundary. One was in conjunction with the 1st Bde, 25th Div. Again, no significant contact was made.

About a month after I became the 24th STZ Senior Advisor, MAJ Charlie Norton, who had flown in the C-13G with me from San Francisco to Saigon, appeared in the area. He was with the Studies and Observation Group (SOG), which planned to put a Forward Operation Base (FOB) just south of Dak TO. There was a concrete runway there which could accommodate C-130 aircraft, and an abandoned SF camp was nearby. As a first step, Charlie wanted to establish a small camp at the Dak To runway from which operations could be launched. My advisors and I assisted in effecting coordination with ARVN, Province, and Special Forces. COL Phuoc agreed to almost every request made by SOG. The facilities of the MACV Compound were made available to Charlie and his US personnel during the construction of the FOB. The camp, between the river and the airstrip, was completed rapidly; soon operations were being launched from it. SOG operations were classified because of their cross-border nature, however, Charlie kept me informed of everything he was doing. Later he established a training and supply base south of Kontum City. After he left, security became tighter and during the briefing of the new US CDR in the area, his replacement barred me because he did not believe that I had a "need to know"! It struck me as odd that there would be operations in the area, which required coordination, to which I was not privy. This sort of thing gave rise to animosity between elements fighting in Vietnam and was in part the reason that military operations were not more successful.

While the Dak To camp was under construction, I walked into our Officers' Club one night and found sitting on a bar stool my K Co machine gunner CPL ZAKY. Thinking he was a sergeant major, I greeted him and then in a friendly fashion, started to chew him out for drinking in an Officers' Club. With a smirk, he showed me an ID card indicating he was an IN 1LT. His duties with SOG required him to fly in L-1 9 spotter aircraft frequently. Poor ZAKY suffered with the GIs (diarrhea) causing him great discomfort on the two and three hour flights.

The Vietnamese did not man their offices on Sundays, so most advisors had the day off. Sundays, therefore, provided an opportunity to visit the advisory teams without embarrassing COL Phuoc by going without him, and also to fly, at least twice a month, a fixed wing recon over the boundaries of the 24th STZ. A fixed wing det was assigned to the Advisory Teams in both Kontum and Pleiku Provinces. The Prov Senior Advisors controlled them for recon and other missions, but I had access to the planes for operations or reconnaissance.

The fixed wing det in Kontum was manned by some interesting characters. Joe Hibbs, a young 1LT, looked like a teenager. He had been GEN Westmoreland's driver in the 101 st ABN Div before he had gone to OCS, and was a superb pilot with whom I enjoyed flying. CPT Arlie Deaton, CDR of the Kontum det did an outstanding job both on aircraft maintenance and reconnaissance. He insisted that I learn to land the L-l9 in the event something happened to the pilot, so each time I flew with him we shot a few landings. The L-19 pilots were alert to new trail patterns and other changes in the area.

There was also an AF det called Barrel Roll housed in our compound. They provided reconnaissance and tactical air support for a highly classified operation to cut the Ho Chi Minh trail in Laos. Barrel Roll was a demanding routine requiring lengthy flights. The detachment also supported some SOG operations. LTC Gibson, the Barrel Roll Det CDR, briefed me on their orations.

The concrete runway at Kontum could accommodate all American transport aircraft used in Vietnam. As the buildup of American units and other forces in the 24th STZ continued, a great deal of air traffic was generated; eventually a C-130 courier plane stopped everyday. The airmen assigned to the aerial port det handling cargo and passenger traffic at Kontum, who lived in the MACV Compound, caused a minor problem. All EM in the compound pulled guard duty. Everybody who lived in the compound was on the alert roster regardless of job. Even the pilots had alert stations. When the aerial port det reported in, the First Sergeant put the men on the guard duty roster. The senior NCO protested, eventually escalating the matter to my attention, claiming that his men were not supposed to be given any extra duties. Except for guard, none of the EM pulled any but their primary duty; civilian men and women were hired as KPs, cooks and orderlies to police the area. They even made the beds for the men and cleaned their rooms. However, guard duty was essential for the security of all; therefore no one was exempt from it. After listening to the aerial port detachment's complaint, the policy was carefully explained to the NCO-in-charge. Still adamant, he said, "We were told that we did not have to pull guard duty, and my men are not going to do it."

"It's a simple matter, sergeant," I responded. "You and your team can move down to the airfield and stay there. You don't have to remain in the MAC V Compound. Down at the airfield you can do as you like. But here you will follow the rules. If you are not willing to do your share towards securing the compound, the other men have no need to secure you."

"But, colonel, there is no security at the airfield."

"That's right. But you aren't willing to do your share to provide it here, so you can leave."

That did not set well with the NCO, who called his CDR at Ton Son Nhut Subsequently, I received calls first from a MAJ, then a LTC and eventually a COL. Each of them was given the same explanation, all refused to see my position. Finally I told the COL, "I'm giving the sergeant 24 hours. Unless he agrees to pull his share of guard duty, I'm going to move him out of the compound."

Though not sure I had the authority to do that, I made the statement and would have done it. Shortly, a pleasant brigadier general called saying that he understood that there was a problem with some of his men. The situation was quickly explained to him. In concluding, I told him that I did not believe that anybody should be exempted from security duty. Even I had my duties during alerts and periodically checked the guard at night.

The general agreed with me, saying that he did not understand what the fuss was about, but he would straighten it out. The sergeant sheepishly reported to me that evening that he had been ordered to pull his share of security duty. To put him at ease, I told him that he had been right to get the matter clarified, to stand up for his men No one held any animosity toward him.

When I had been at Kontum about four months, the 1SG brought my driver, a clean-cut young man from a farm family in the Midwest, to my hootch with the report that he had been caught smoking marijuana; the 1SG gave me a package of marijuana cigarettes which he had taken from the driver. This was my introduction to the drug problem in Vietnam. Since it was the first incident, and it did not appear it would become a major problem in our Team, I decided to take no official action against the driver. He could not have been disciplined because the evidence against him had been illegally obtained. He was reprimanded and relieved as my driver. In combat there was no place for anybody who might be under the influence of marijuana or other drugs.

Donald A. Seibert

In Tenza Compound, named in honor of LTC Tony Tenza who had been killed in Kontum several years before, there was a flag pole on which the American and Vietnamese flags were flown. To remind the advisors that they were still in the US Army, I decreed that there would be a retreat ceremony every evening and that a formation would be held every Friday, at which awards and decorations would be presented, policies announced or explained, or other matters attended to. To enhance the ceremony, MG Donald V. Bennett, then Superintendant at West Point, was requested to send tapes of the retreat music used at the Military Academy. Almost by return mail, two tapes arrived with a note from Bennett explaining that the extra tape was to take care of any loss or damage to the other one. Each evening the flag was lowered as "To The Colors" played, while on Fridays, with the troops in formation, the National Anthem was played. Many of the troops received awards thereafter in an appropriate manner.

The 1st Air CAV Div, whose base camp was located east of Pleiku in Binh Dinh Prov, operated in the Due Co/Plei Me area in the summer of 1966. During this operation I had a chance to talk with BG Jack Wright the Asst Div CDR, and COL Jack Hennessey, who commanded a Bde of the Div, both of whom had been in my Advance Class, as well as other old friends. It was a thrill to walk out of II Corps HQ in Pleiku and see the myriad helicopters parked in the 1st CAV laager across from the building. Strangely, the VC did not mortar the aircraft there.

The 42nd Regt mounted an operation north of Dak To to remove the Montagnards from one of the isolated villages where they were subject to VC harassment. The 42nd had organized a convoy of refugees which was proceeding to Dak To. About five miles north of Tan Canh the column was ambushed; a number of refugees were killed, vehicles were set afire, and the entire relocation operation was thrown into disarray. COL Phuoc and I were at the 42nd CP when the word came. Alerting the chopper pilot, I asked COL Phuoc if he wanted to go to the scene to see what help we could give the 42nd Regt. COL Phuoc hesitated, then told me we should not go. This was very unlike my counterpart. He told me that he did not think that he or I should go at this time because the Regt CO and his Advisor were there and we could not do any more than they were doing. He thought that we should let the 42nd Regt, whose operation it was, get the matter reorganized first. This made me unhappy; I told him that we should demonstrate our interest, find out what was needed in the way of additional combat force, medical assistance or other support, and attempt to obtain it for the 42nd Regt. I also thought that there might be casualties that our chopper could get to the hospital for immediate care. He still refused. I suspected that it was a question of saving face; he did not want to embarrass his Regt CDR by appearing at a disaster. But if this was the case, it was giving priority to the wrong facet of the problem. I told him that since there were American advisors there, I was going whether he came or not. He still refused. After dropping me off, the chopper returned to the 42nd Compound on call for MEDEVAC if required and available to Phuoc if he decided to go to the ambush site.

MAJ Allen briefed me quickly on the situation. The convoy was still under fire at *the* time, he had requested gunships to strafe the positions from which the enemy was firing. He had also requested MEDEVAC and medical aid for the refugees which were enroute, so that my ship was not needed. He had done everything he could to assist his counterpart as far as I could see. The ARVN were still exchanging fire with the VC, thus it was difficult to determine if additional troops would be needed. Just then Allen made contact with the gunships. He directed them to fire east of his green smoke not to fire west of it. The gunships zoomed in on their strafing run, but reversed the instructions, firing west of the green smoke, not to the east of it, hence they strafed the friendly column. It is a terrifying sensation to be strafed by your own gunships, which were firing both 40mm and 30 caliber machine guns. Luckily, they were slightly off target and did no further damage to the convoy. Along with the others, I pressed into the ground hard enough to imprint the outline of my body, I thought. Allen quickly contacted the gunships, which made another pass, this time firing on target, either killing the VC or causing them to withdraw. As the enemy firing stopped, COL Phuoc landed near our position; he had been airborne when the gunships strafed the convoy. He took hold immediately; the convoy was quickly reorganized; within a matter of hours it was safely into Tan Canh. COL Phuoc never discussed the matter with me or explained his reluctance to go out to assess the situation at first hand.

In June, John Stewart, the G-2 Advisor, left. He was replaced by MAJ Dick Gallant. Shortly thereafter Larry Freeman rotated. CPT Ferguson, a QM OFF, became the G-1 Advisor and Adjutant. "Fergy" was a parachute rigger officer who wanted to get with the heavy drop unit at Cam Ranh Bay. There were so many applications for the few Airborne positions available that his chances of getting the assignment were slim. He resigned himself to being an advisor. Although his heart was not really in the assignment, he did a superb job.

COL Timothy also left in June, replaced by BG Dick Lee, who was less volatile than Timothy, a typical hard-charging ABN IN CDR. MAJ Tyler, the Kontum Province Senior Advisor, also rotated in June and was replaced by LTC Don Creuziger, a quiet, highly effective AR OFF who immediately established good rapport with MAJ Doan, the Province Chief. Then MAJ Allen, the Advisor to the 42nd Regt left. The loss of so many experienced advisors in such a short time, an event repeated several times each year, even though replaced by equally capable individuals, made progress erratic and adversely affected the advisory effort.

When Allen left the 42nd ARVN Regt, MAJ James (Buck) Bukowski replaced him. Buck was an aggressive young Infantryman, who had not earned a CIB, one of the things he wanted most. During the six months he spent as Advisor to the 42nd IN, he pushed the Regt into the field as much as he could. Fate was against him; the few times the Regt made contact or came under fire, he was not in the area. He was always elsewhere with the Regt CO. He was frustrated each time he heard that I was under fire, or some of his subordinate advisors were. On his departure he had still not qualified for the CIB. Considering the six months he had spent in combat, though never under fire, the rules might have been stretched in his case, but I was a stickler for the regulations governing that award.

Shortly after BG Lee arrived, he made a tour of Pleiku and Kontum Provinces, which included a visit to the leper colony close to the Kontum/Pleiku boundary. Sister Maria Theresa, a French peasant, who ran the leprosarium, had come to Vietnam thirty or forty years before as a nurse.

Gradually she had become involved exclusively with lepers. Truly concerned about their condition, she ran the leprosarium with stern discipline. Sister was a typical French peasant, tall, big boned, very positive in her opinions, frugal, an able administrator and accomplished beggar, who would do anything to aid her cause. The Americans helped whenever possible, transferring critical patients by helicopter, turning over excess food and supplies, abandoned or captured rice, or providing limited engineering help.

Accompanying BG Lee on the visit was the new II Corps Advisory Team Chaplain, a Roman Catholic priest, who had just been elevated to Monsignor. K.C. Brown interpreted for the group since Sister Maria Theresa only spoke French and Vietnamese. When making the introductions, K.C. first introduced BG Lee, then the Chaplain. He told the Sister that the Chaplain had just become a Monsignor. At that Sister Maria Theresa began talking excitedly, stabbing the Chaplain in the chest with a bony forefinger. K.C. grinned broadly; when she finally stopped he turned to the priest, saying, "The Sister is telling you to go to the Holy Father and tell him he must do something about birth control. If something isn't done about it, there will continue to be lepers in the world. In order to stop this we must organize a system of birth control." There was more about her rationale for birth control. The Chaplain, taken aback, did not know how to handle the matter.

During the summer of 1966, intelligence indicated a VC buildup to the west of Pleiku City for a possible attack on II Corps HQ. As a result, an element of the ARVN ABN Div was ordered to the area for a large-scale operation to flush out the enemy. At the several planning conferences at II Corps

HQ, which I attended with COL Phuoc, I saw another old friend, COL Jim Bartholomees, the Senior Advisor to the ABN Div. Jim was arguing for committing the entire Div rather than just one Bde as had been planned. He told me that he was trying to get MG Dong, the Commander, out of Saigon. MG Dong (he was later promoted to LTG) was a good soldier but also a playboy who did not like to take to the field. Jim was trying every means possible to get him out on an operation. This led to a controversy between Jim and me over who should command the operation; I insisted that COL Phuoc should as he was the commander of the 24th STZ in which the operation was to be conducted. Jim, of course, argued to get MG Dong to Pleiku as commander. The advisors did more talking than the Vietnamese! Just as MG Vinh Loc was about to decide in favor of MG Dong, I said, "Now General, you must remember that COL Phuoc has the mission of operating in Pleiku and Kontum Provinces. Yet you always take the command away from him when there is a major operation. Either you should give him the command or you should relieve him."

There was a silence. MG Vinh Loc looked startled, while BG Lee glared at me, unhappy that I had put Vinh Loc on the spot. Jim didn't know what to say; he wanted Dong to get out of Saigon but he saw my point. Vinh Loc looked at me strangely as he said, "You're right, COL Seibert. We will make COL Phuoc the overall tactical commander."

Eventually, the entire ABN Div did come up to Pleiku, at which time MG Dong assumed overall command. But it was a split responsibility. COL Phuoc was his Deputy Commander, with responsibility for certain elements of the operation while Dong exercised overall command. Jim succeeded in getting Dong out of Saigon for the operation, though Dong commuted between the two areas. COL Phuoc was in command during MG Dong's absences so his authority in Pleiku was established. As it developed, the VC were not located, nor was there any major contact with the enemy. The threat to II Corps evaporated.

In July MAJ Doan, the Kontum Province Chief, was promoted to LTC. MG Vinh Loc pinned on his new insignia, two silver hibiscus flowers. A colonel rated three. Some of the advisors wore the Vietnamese insignia on their fatigue uniforms, in addition to their own, so that those not familiar with the US insignia would know their comparative rank.

Late in the summer at a conference in II Corps HQ, GEN Westmoreland briefed MG Vinh Loc and his staff on the arrival of the US 4th Infantry Division and established its area of operations. For some reason the AO did not coincide with the province boundaries, but was cut off just north of the southern boundary of Pleiku Prov. This split advisory and Vietnamese command lines and appeared to multiply problems of coordination. GEN Westmoreland and I had quite a discussion about it. He listened to my arguments, but adhered to his original plan.

MG "Ace" Collins brought the 4th US Div over but was shortly replaced by MG Ray Peers. When the first contingent arrived, Prime Minister KY welcomed it to Vietnam. He really won the hearts of the GIs, when he hopped on the top of a CONEX container and talked to them with his hands on his hips. A flamboyant individual who spoke excellent English, KY really made the American soldiers feel that they had an important contribution to make in defeating the enemy and pacifying the country. It was an interesting formation, with the troops gathered around the CONEX containers and the diminutive but very dominant Vietnamese Major General talking to them. As this was the monsoon season the area was muddy, though it stopped raining long enough for the ceremony.

With the arrival of the 4th Div came the opportunity to see Charlie Jackson who commanded one of the brigades. Initially his unit was on the coast where I visited him; eventually it moved to the west of the Chu Prong in Pleiku Province where it was possible to visit his CP often.

While in the field with COL Phuoc one day, my HQ notified me that an important message had been received which required my immediate attention. My Deputy called to urge me to return to Kontum immediately. Since we were engaged in an operation, I told him that I did not want to leave my counterpart. In a short time LTC Lane drove out to the field with the message, an invitation or request or order to attend a dinner party, in Saigon, hosted by COL Sam Wilson, for former Vice President Richard Nixon. Apparently Mr Nixon came to Vietnam periodically to be briefed on the situation so that he would remain current concerning that part of the world. Lane was instructed to send my regrets; political and social affairs in Saigon did not interest me; even the visit of the former Vice President should not take precedence over combat operations, in my view. When BG Lee heard that I had refused the invitation, he ordered me to go. Representatives of all facets of military operations had been carefully picked: an advisor to a Bn CDR, an advisor to a Prov Chief, an advisor to a DTA or tactical zone (me), and commanders of a US Bn, Bde and Div. Before leaving the field I explained to COL Phuoc why I was going to Saigon.

The trip to Saigon, made in a single motor Beaver, a reliable but slow De Haviland aircraft, took over an hour. Since there was some time available, I stopped to see Charlie Reidenbaugh, who had served with me in DCSOPS, and was now the Senior Advisor of the 10th ARVN Division at Xuan Loc. Charlie was unhappy with his counterpart, MG Lu Lan. He thought he was a poor commander, a comment I was to remember at a later date. He also commented on the designation of the Div. The common expression in Vietnam for anything that was very bad was "Number 10". People referred to the Div as "Number 10" which further depressed Charlie. Eventually the Div was redesignated the 18th Div.

On arriving in Saigon, I secured billets at the Rex, put on a clean uniform, then proceeded to the villa where the dinner for Mr Nixon was to be held. MG DePuy, now CG of the 1st IN Div, was present as the senior American commander. Drinks were served while we waited for Mr Nixon and Ambassador Lodge. Mr Nixon arrived before the Ambassador, who was attending a diplomatic party at another embassy. When he came, it was obvious that he had been drinking quite a bit. As Ambassador he held the highest precedence in the group, so soup was served to him first, Without waiting for Mr Nixon to be served, he started to spoon it into his mouth.

Mr Nixon was an interesting person, likeable and intelligent. He asked incisive questions showing concern about the situation in Vietnam. During the course of the evening, the conversation focused on military matters, advisory efforts and US tactical operations. MG DePuy made several blunt statements, some critical of the current American policy in Vietnam. At one point Ambassador Lodge interrupted him and said, "Who do you work for, General DePuy?" DePuy, taken aback, was not sure how to take that question. "Why General Westmoreland, of course," he said.

"Well, I work for the President of the United States," Mr Lodge said, cuttingly. "I thought you did too. I also thought that we were implementing the same national policy in Vietnam."

There was a dead silence in the room until Mr Nixon made some comment which broke the tension. Conversation resumed slowly. Later MG DePuy made another comment which displeased the Ambassador. Turning to the General he said bluntly, "General, why don't you go back and supervise your Division? We don't need you here any more."

Thus dismissed, DePuy got up and made his exit. Mr Nixon again smoothed over the situation. Shortly after that the rest of us made our farewells and returned to our billets.

On my return to the 24th STZ, I resumed my routine which included learning more about the Vietnamese people and their culture. The Vietnamese are sociable people. As Senior Advisor, I attended many affairs with COL Phuoc. All of the religious organizations in the area, Buddhist, Cao Dai, Protestant and Roman Catholic, periodically held memorial services or other rites to which the Zone and Province Advisors were invited. LTC Doan, Kontum Province Chief, and LTC Ho Vinh, Pleiku Province Chief, frequently gave official dinners, luncheons or other functions; there was an active "cocktail circuit" in the area. The advisors reciprocated at times, with a dinner at the MACV Compound. MACV funds were available for such affairs.

American soldiers had difficulty adjusting to Vietnamese culture. They were amused and somewhat abashed to see two ARVN soldiers, in full combat array, weapons slung over their shoulders, walking hand in hand. It took them some time to realize that this was not a sign of effeminacy but a way of life. Vietnamese people took strong exception to anyone waving them forward or toward them with the palm up. This was reserved for animals or inferior menials. The proper way to call a taxi or individual to you was to wave the fingers, palm down. This, too, took some time to sink in. The Vietnamese, who have little body hair, were fascinated by the body hair on Americans. In particular, a hairy armed person seemed to intrigue them. School children liked to run their hands over the forearms of Americans, getting great delight from the silky hair which covered them.

LTG Heintges, DEPCOMUSMACV, primarily interested in RFPF, but also in the Special Forces, visited II Corps often. Whenever he could, he enjoyed eating at our mess. My only criticism of him was that he loved to talk to the Vietnamese, in fact he loved to talk to everybody, and would get so involved in a conversation as to forget time. Hence he never kept on schedule. Exasperated and out of patience, I talked to his aide many times about this, pointing out that his boss kept busy people waiting, particularly the Province Chiefs. As a remedy, I suggested that his aide cut down on the number of appointments made for Heintges to give him more time at each stop. The aide told me that he had tried to do this but the General insisted he had to make a certain number of visits each day. He always met every commitment, but was often as much as three hours late to an appointment. It was the lament of many advisors that they spent almost as much time waiting on the helipad, not only for LTG Heintges but for other visitors as well, as they did on their job.

One reason LTG Heintges enjoyed eating at the Kontum mess was the fine fresh vegetables served. Kontum was a successful experiment in American advisory effort. US agricultural experts, sent to certain areas to study the feasibility of truck farming, had determined that Kontum Province was ideal for such an activity. As a result, there were many truck gardens in the area which grew scallions, cucumbers, carrots, lettuce, egg plant and other vegetables. The MACV cooks bought the vegetables from the local markets, but disinfected them even though the farmers did not use night soil to fertilize. The medics wanted to ban the use of local vegetables, but as long as I was in Kontum they were served without causing problems. It was good to have fresh vegetables; they were delicious; even my discriminating taste found little fault with the food at the MACV Compound or in the field with COL Phuoc.

The Swiss maintained a hospital unit in Kontum, which was allegedly neutral. However, many of the personnel were anti-American and pro-Viet Cong, though most were pleasant and easy to get along with. The MACV clubs and PX were available to them; on several occasions the team of doctors and nurses was invited to dinner or other affairs at the Compound. But this soon stopped, when we learned that some of the doctors were dealing directly with the Viet Cong, giving food and medical supplies provided by the American government to them. When this was called to the attention of the head of the team, he said, "Well, we are neutral so we should be aiding both sides." But they did not in fact maintain the spirit of neutrality. Finally I cut them off and had nothing further to do with them.

Dr Smith, an American civilian doctor, a woman with a worldwide reputation, ran a hospital exclusively for the Montagnard in Kontum. A legend in the area, she was quite a recluse who rarely came to the MACV Compound. During several talks with her, she pointed out to me cases she claimed were the result of "American" bombings or artillery. When challenged, she never could state positively whether the wounds resulted from American or Vietnamese artillery or VC mortars or rockets. She was opposed to the American involvement in the war; the alternative, Communist takeover of the country, did not seem to concern her. I was not impressed with her objectivity or logic.

COL Phuoc, with me in tow, made many trips to various Montagnard villages, often taking a medical team to treat cases not serious enough for hospitalization. He also distributed rice and other supplies. On most of these visits, we had to go through the "rice wine ceremony". The Montagnard make a rice wine fermented in tall ceramic or clay crocks. Visitors were invited to drink from a communal rice wine jug through bamboo or reed straws. It was abominable wine. Though I had qualms about the sanitation of the jugs, I never did get sick. During ceremonial drinking, everyone could see the level of the wine in the jug recede so there was no way to avoid swallowing the foul tasting wine, or eating the half-cooked chicken which was served. After many of these rice wine ceremonies, the Montagnard gave visitors a bracelet made of brass or gold as a token of friendship and everlasting peace. Many advisors had ten or twelve on their arms. Those from the Rah De were prized because the Rah De, a bit more advanced, made very handsome bracelets. COL. Phuoc gave me one as a token of friendship when I left Kontum in 1967.

The 1st Bde oft he 101st ABN Div, a separate brigade commanded by BG Willard Pearson, came to Kontum periodically to conduct operations, usually in conjunction with the ARVN. On their first visit after my arrival, I was pleased to see SFC Chasson, whom I had known in the 504 in Mainz. He was one of the long-range reconnaissance patrol (LRRP) leaders. We had a quick talk recalling old friends in Mainz. Chester McCoid, who had been in my Advance Class and in the 2nd Div in Korea, was Deputy of the 1/101 for a time. During one operation the Bde, camped at the Kontum airstrip, planned to make a pay jump to qualify their personnel for the extra pay ABN troopers are authorized. Jerry Collins, the S-3 of the Bde, set up a jump for me with one of the Bns. There were several old friends among the OFFs in the 1/101, Bill Hankins from the 504 at Bragg commanded the Support Bn, and Ted Mataxis from Mainz, who replaced McCoid as Deputy Commander. In January of 1967, Jerry Collins, whom I had last seen in Mainz, and I received the ARVN Gallantry Cross with Palm.

An operation conducted by the 1/101 and the 42nd ARVN Regt was targeted on the Tou M'Rong area northeast of Tan Canh. During the operation LTC Doan and MAJ Dave Hackworth, who commanded a Bn of the 1/101, met unexpectedly. The two had known each other when Doan had been in the ARVN ABN Bde and Hackworth had been his advisor. They had a joyous reunion on Tou M'Rong Mountain, in a tenuously secured area that eventually had to be evacuated. Tou M'Rong was constantly raided by the VC; the Vietnamese had no means of reinforcing the area because the roads were mined and the enemy was between Tan Canh and the mountain.

During one of the joint operations conducted by the 24th STZ and the 1/101 there was minor contact in the vicinity of Tou M'Rong, but it faded and could not be regained. Finally the ARVN ended their participation. The 1/101 elected to remain in the area, patrolling and probing, trying to regain contact. Suddenly, they uncovered a large concentration of VC, precipitating a major battle. It was during this fight that CPT Bill Carpenter, West Point's famous "lonesome end", called in napalm to prevent the VC from overrunning his position. He directed it be dropped so close to his own unit that several of the men, including himself, were burned. For this he was later awarded the Distinguished Service Cross (DSC). Hank Emerson, a War College Classmate, was the Bn CO during this action. BG S.L.A. Marshall reported this battle in his book, "War in the Monsoons".

Occasionally celebrities in the entertainment world visited throughout Vietnam, but few of them came to Kontum or Pleiku. Some athletes, star football players and golfers, came up to talk with the troops. George Jessel brought a show to Kontum which played in the small theater in the MACV Compound. The real prize was Martha Raye who came to Kontum three times during my assignment there. She was a real trooper, genuinely interested in the GI. She had a particular spot in her heart for the Green Berets, but was interested in all GIs and would go any place to talk to them or entertain them. Whenever she came, she stayed in our Compound. Arrangements were made so that the latrine was available to her at certain times; the officers could always use the enlisted latrines. Martha always put on a fine show, after which she would have a couple of drinks and then go over to the B Team Compound adjacent to ours and play poker all night. She loved poker and drank martinis like water. Though she would play until 0300 or 0400, it never affected her; she always got up, ready to go when scheduled.

During one of her visits, I took her on a helicopter flight over the 24th STZ. As we were flying over an area in which an operation was going on, I told her that the Advisory Team with the ARVN had not been able to see her show. Immediately she wanted to go down to talk to the men. Told that the operation was in progress, she said, "That doesn't make any difference. I've been under fire before."

She insisted on landing. When contacted by radio, the Team reported that it was at a secure landing zone (LZ). We landed, Martha spent 15 or 20 minutes joking and talking with the men. It not only boosted the morale of the men there, but of all advisors to know that she cared enough about them to take time to talk to only one or two of them. She was a tremendous gal.

The NCO running our PX was extremely aggressive. Given a relatively free hand, he made many deals with larger PXs and with the PX warehouse. As a result, the Kontum PX was better stocked than most. People flying across the area would stop to buy items they could not get elsewhere. When possible, transients were permitted to buy even controlled items. There was always a good stock of cameras. The instamatic I had brought to Vietnam with me no longer worked, so I bought an idiot-proof Kodak Instamatic at the PX. This started a picture taking binge which spanned two tours, during which I took 5,000 or 6,000 slides. Many were unique, most turned out well. All are now irreplaceable and have been deposited with the Military History Institute at Carlisle Barracks. They covered many subjects: local color, school children, the Montagnard, their villages and "happy houses", Buddhist monks, Cao Dai temples, operations, ARVN and American, troops, fortifications, gun positions, even VC KIA.

Montagnard happy houses were large, central meeting structures found in every Montagnard settlement. They were called happy houses by the Americans because until they were married the bachelors slept there at night. It was the center of activity of every Montagnard tribe. During the day it was used as a meeting place or for entertaining important visitors. They were unusual structures, woven of reeds and raffia, with steeply pitched roofs which towered over the rest of the shacks in Montagnard villages. All were elaborately decorated.

Early in the fall I took an R&R to Bangkok. The flight to Thailand stopped at Pleiku so it was convenient to board the plane there. Bangkok was enchanting, the R&R delightful. An inveterate tourist, I visited all of the major temples, palaces and museums. I also took several boat rides through the floating markets. The rivers were filthy, but teeming with sampans loaded with colorful vegetables of all descriptions, as well as hand made objects, house wares and other merchandise. Of course I tried Thai food, which is hot, as I remembered from eating with the Thai Bn in Korea, but I enjoyed it.

A special treat was a visit with Bob and Ruth Ann Clark, who had been at Carlisle with me. Bob, the USIS Director in Bangkok, invited me to a fantastic dinner party in their home. From the first wash cloth wrung out in icy water, which greatly refreshed everyone in that hot climate, to the final cloth wrung out in hot water, which served in lieu of a finger bowl, the party was singular. There was an interesting mixture of Thai, American and other nationals. The tangy food was served by a lovely girl in a colorful native dress. One of the guests, Jim Thompson, a controversial figure in the silk business in Bangkok, disappeared several weeks after that dinner party. No one knows what happened to him.

After that relaxing and enjoyable trip, the routine resumed. The ARVN continued to mount operations, most of them without significant contact or results. In many cases roads were opened to villages that were isolated so that supplies could be delivered. In that respect the operations accomplished something, though I was always suspicious that each operation was compromised.

During Dan Thang 119, an extended operation in the Dak Akoi Valley northeast of Kontum City, several helicopter assault landings were made, some in conjunction with the 1/101, some ARVN only. During one insertion there were insufficient UH-1B helicopters, or "slicks" as they were universally called in Vietnam. Eight had been requested but only three reported for the operation. COL Phuoc and I discussed the risks involved in shuttling the troops to the landing zone. If it was "cold", that is, no contact was made, there was no great danger. But if it was a "hot" LZ, where the VC contested the landing, the few troops that could be landed in three slicks would be cut to pieces before additional soldiers could reinforce them. COL Phuoc, who considered the operation important, wanted to proceed. Normally a slick could take eight fully-equipped American soldiers. The pilots assured me that there would be no trouble transporting ten ARVN soldiers to the LZ. This was still too few in my estimation.

COL Phuoc had already directed the artillery to prep the LZ, as I still debated the risks. Finally a thought occurred to me;, turning to the pilot of the Zone Command and Control (C&C) helicopter, I asked him if he would be able to carry eight ARVN soldiers in addition to COL Phuoc and me. He looked at me oddly for a moment, then grinned. "Sure we can, Colonel. We haven't made an assault landing in some time. What say we lead the flight?"

COL Phuoc appeared happy with the solution, so I nodded. The other pilots were briefed as Dai-Ta Phuoc barked an order. Eight soldiers obediently peeled from the formation and headed for the C&C ship. After Col Phuoc and I had taken our places and donned head sets, the formation became airborne. The pilot of the C&C ship knew the LZ since we had reconnoitered it several days before. As it came into sight, a smoke round landed nearby, indicating the end of the artillery preparation. Both door gunners commenced firing at the tree line as the C&C swooped down, hovered a few inches from the ground while the tiny Vietnamese leaped out and raced toward the concealment of the tree line, then lifted swiftly for the return to Kontum City. No shots greeted me assault. It took three lifts to land the entire force. The ARVN soldiers were delighted to be riding with COL Phuoc and me, mistakenly believing that they were safe with the Dai-Tas. By the time the third lift was on the ground, it was growing dark. COL Phuoc and I were thoroughly chilled, and highly keyed up due to the excitement of the insertion. When the final report was received from the force on the ground that it was proceeding with its mission, we turned back to the MACV Compound with relief.

BG Lee came to Kontum to present me with my Third Award of the CIB, designated by a second star on the badge. Before he left, MAJ Allen had initiated the recommendation, attesting to the fact that I met the criteria for the third award of the badge; under fire more than once while accompanying the 42nd ARVN Regt on operations and more than 30 days in combat in Vietnam. This was not the way I wanted to earn that award; I wanted to earn it in combat with an American unit. In my view this was getting the CIB the easy way, though technically I fulfilled the requirements.

MAJ Ted Frost assumed command of the B Team, when LTC Dallas and MAJ Price left. Though Frost was an IN OFF with long service in SF, he did not seem to share the prevailing view of most Green Beret officers that SF operations should be conducted without consultation with the ARVN. Frost was very cooperative; as a result many remunerative operations utilizing ARVN and the CIDG were mounted. At about the same time LTC Bill Patch took over the C Team in Pleiku. All problems in coordination and cooperation in the 24th STZ seemed to vanish at once. Bill, a War College Classmate, understood the need for mutual coordination and cooperation between all military elements in the area. A good man for the job, he was cognizant of what was going on in the Highlands. We worked well together.

When the colonels' promotion list was published in August, 1966, I was delighted to find my name on it. Only 45% of those considered had been selected by the Promotion Board that year so it was a great boost to my morale. Actual promotion, however, was several months in the future as the list moved slowly. Fortunately, time passed quickly in the 24th STZ.

Finally, one day in November, BG Lee flew up from Pleiku to pin eagles on me. The officers were ready for the occasion, I was presented with a number of gifts including a set of underwear with a huge eagle on the T-shirt and another on the front of the drawers!

Plans for a promotion party were quickly completed. Everybody I knew in Vietnam was invited, but official duties kept most from attending. Mac Austin, from Korea and Leavenworth, was able to get up from Nha Trang.

It was a spectacular promotion party. There was plenty of liquor, a panoply of seafood, which had been brought up from Vung Tau especially for the occasion, and much entertainment. In addition to the OFFs' promotion party, I also had a party for the EM, during which I spent a half hour or so at the NCO club.

Shortly after my promotion a tragic incident happened at Dak To. About three weeks after MAJ Dick Lowery and CPT Ed Starr, two talented officers, were assigned as advisors at Dak To Subsector, the Dist HQ was attacked. Both Starr and Lowery left the compound to rally the RFPF and pursue the Viet Cong. Both were killed. It was a blow to all of us. A memorial mass was held in the Catholic Church in Kontum which COL Phuoc, LTC Doan, Don Creuziger, and all of the advisors attended. There were other memorials and tributes to these two fine soldiers, the first advisors killed while I was the Senior Advisor of the 24th STZ.

Because the Plei Do Lim SF Camp southeast of Pleiku City had out-lived its usefulness as a CIDG camp, plans were made to remove the SF team and convert the CIDG to RFPF. The first such conversion in Vietnam, it was considered a great step forward in the administration and security of the area. At a formal ceremony, Plei Do Lim became a Dist HQ, and the Montagnard were discharged from the CIDG and sworn in as RFPF by MG Vinh Loc. In time the Team House was memorialized for Sergeant Lawrence Harris, an advisor who had been killed in an operation in Pleiku Province.

As Christmas approached there was a flurry of activity. The distribution of gifts to the children of the ARVN and RFPF by MACV had become traditional over the years. Both toys and clothing were collected for the youngsters. The French had converted many of the Montagnard to Catholicism; there was a French Bishop in the Highlands and many Vietnamese priests. Early in the summer, I sent letters to several newspapers in New York asking to have Christmas gifts and clothing sent to the advisory teams. The response was good, many packages arrived in the mail. Of course, my family helped, but packages from people I did not know arrived in response to my letters. By Christmas we had a respectable collection of supplies to give out.

Just before Christmas, COL Phuoc received word that MG Vinh Loc planned to spend Christmas Eve with the 42nd ARVN Regt at Tan Canh. Apparently, it was a tradition with him to spend Christmas Eve with a troop unit. He provided beer, liquor, and food. There was to be a bonfire, singing and dancing. COL Phuoc, of course, had to go; he asked me to accompany him. It was an interesting evening; Vinh Loc affected the pose of a field commander so taken with his troops that he had to spend this great holiday with them. The bonfire was lit in the middle of the ARVN Compound at Tan Canh. At separate fires calves and pigs were roasted on spits. Rice and other food was available and beer flowed freely. At 0200, though MG Vinh Loc was still with the troops and the partying continued, I stumbled to bed in the Advisory area. Despite the bonfires providing aiming points for VC mortars and rockets, there was no enemy fire.

The next morning COL Phuoc and I returned to Kontum City to visit each of the ARVN and RFPF units to distribute gifts, some from my store, some from his. Most of the gifts were for the children who were dressed in their finest for the official visit.

COL Phuoc joined me for Christmas dinner with the Advisory Team. The cooks had outdone themselves and the mess hall was lavishly decorated. That afternoon I visited each of the Advisory Teams to wish the men a Merry Christmas. At each stop pictures were taken of the teams and a brief time was spent with them. I apologized to the helicopter crew for imposing on them that day, but they brushed it aside, they were interested in seeing the teams also, as they knew them all.

Early in 1967, the 1st Bde, 101st ABN Div came back for an operation in Kontum. They set up a base camp at the air strip at Tan Canh. During that period the 1/101 was visited by GEN

Harold K. Johnson, the CofS of the Army. BG Pearson hosted a luncheon for GEN Johnson, GEN Westmoreland and LTG Lemley, the DCSOPS, and invited both BG Lee and me to attend. In the course of the luncheon, Johnson turned to me, asking about my duties as an advisor, what we were doing, what my thoughts on the effort were. He asked specifically my opinion about expanding the advisory effort. Westmoreland had just announced that the effort would be expanded, so this posed a problem. However, my opinion had been solicited so I gave GEN Johnson an honest answer; that in my view it was time to re-evaluate the entire advisory effort, which was an interim measure, adopted until the Vietnamese could build a training base. A similar program had been adopted in Korea, where advisors had been used early, but only until the Koreans were able to train themselves. Once they had established their training base the advisors were withdrawn. Relating this same logic to Vietnam, it appeared that the time had come to remove advisors. They were a crutch at this point; Vietnamese officers depended on them for artillery and tactical air support, airlift, MEDEVAC, coordination and logistical support. In answer to the question I suggested that we start cutting the advisory effort, substituting for it liaison teams to handle the coordination of firepower, gunships and helicopters, and let the ARVN commanders fight their own battles. The Vietnamese should do their own planning, they had enough training, experience and background to do so. Although ARVN junior leadership was not strong, most of the senior commanders had been fighting with or against the French for many years, hence were seasoned campaigners; if the advisory effort was phased out, the Vietnamese officers would gain more confidence in their ability to fight. The liaison teams could still exert some influence through the support rendered or withheld. GEN Johnson, intrigued, asked LTG Lemley to make a note of my idea. Of course, GEN Westmoreland immediately disagreed. No doubt as soon as he got back to Saigon, he briefed the CofS thoroughly on his views. Perhaps his logic was more valid than mine. Certainly he had access to more information, but I was convinced that we had overstayed our role as advisors in Vietnam.

In my role as advisor, I made several trips to Dalat, a beautiful city. Once I had the good fortune to go there with Jack Miller who had been an advisor to the Vietnamese Military Academy located outside the city and who knew the area well. Jack borrowed a jeep and showed me the sights; Dalat reminded me of some of the cities in the French/Swiss Alps. There were French type houses in the hills, many beautiful trees, especially huge flame trees, almost solid red. The bougainvillaea, which covered most villas, was in bloom. We usually stayed at the Dalat Palace Hotel, a luxurious old French hotel with very high ceilings for coolness. The first time there was in the monsoon season and the rooms were dank even with fires in them, though the public rooms were pleasant. There were conical mosquito nets over each of the beds, providing an almost regal canopy. Dalat was the center for growing flowers and vegetables, and was renowned for its fine strawberries. Strangely, most were white rather than red. The Vietnamese made delicious strawberry jam and a strawberry wine, which I found too sweet.

In February 1967, I again went on R&R, this time to Taiwan. It was an enjoyable week during which I gorged myself on Chinese food. I acquired some interesting souvenirs, including porcelain stools, marble vases, and two Batik paintings.

On returning to Kontum, I bade farewell to MAJ Bukowski and welcomed his replacement, MAJ "Dutch" Passailaigue, as the Senior Advisor to the 42nd ARVN Regt. Dutch was a bachelor, a gourmet cook, a gung-ho Airborne type, and a great outdoors man. During the many operations we were on together, I found him to be a highly competent officer.

One of the most interesting ceremonies that occurred while I was Senior Advisor of the 24th STZ was the welcoming back of the Montagnard to full participation in the life of Vietnam. Since their revolt in 1964, they had been looked upon by the Vietnamese with great suspicion; this suspicion was reciprocated by the Montagnard. Negotiations had been going on for some time to convince the Montagnard to give their full loyalty to the South Vietnamese Government. The Vietnamese could not afford to have these fierce fighters at their back while they were fighting the Viet Cong. Most of the tribes finally agreed to pledge their loyalty to the Government. An elaborate ceremony was planned in Pleiku on the plain across from II Corps HQ. A reviewing stand covered with parachutes, was erected for VIPs, with a spacious arena marked out in front of it. The Montagnard, in their tribal dress, camped in this area. Montagnard cloth, woven by the women, is very colorful, each tribe incorporating different designs and color combinations.

The day of the ceremony was bright and sunny, VIPs from all over Vietnam had come to Pleiku. As the advisor to COL Phuoc, who was in nominal command of the security for the area, I was invited to the festivities. Prime Minister Ky, Ambassador Lodge and GEN Westmoreland were among the important people there. Ambassador Lodge was the ranking American at the ceremony, I was seated directly behind him. As part of the ritual, a water buffalo was killed in a gruesome way. The animal was tethered to a pole around which Montagnard men danced, darting in to cut the beast with their long, sharp knives. First it was ham-strung; finally it bled to death. Immediately, the carcass was cut open, the liver and heart taken out and the blood drained. Ambassador Lodge, along with other VIPs, was invited to drink the blood and eat of the raw liver and heart. This was supposed to transfer the strength and courage of the beast to those who partook of this "feast". Only VIPs and higher ranking tribesmen were permitted to share this prize. When Ambassador Lodge came back to his seat, he muttered, "I regret that I have but one stomach to give for my country." The Americans dissolved in laughter.

Finally, the Montagnard assembled before the stand and on bended knee pledged loyalty to the Vietnamese Government. Following this impressive pledge, Prime Minister Ky readmitted them to full participation in the life of the Republic of Vietnam. Afterwards there was much dancing and feasting. The Montagnard danced to the accompaniment of a band consisting of a series of gongs ranging from two to three feet in diameter to one only several inches in diameter, each held by a separate individual who struck his gong at appropriate times to play music akin to an out-of-tune carillon. There was also the inevitable rice wine ceremony. It was a full and interesting day.

Early in 1967 orders assigning me to command a Training Bde at FT Benning arrived. This was not what I wanted, so I again extended my tour in Vietnam in an attempt to obtain command of a Tactical Bde. All of my career had been pointing toward this goal, command of troops in combat. The experience and training obtained over the years, as well as my feel for the situation in Vietnam convinced me that I could do an excellent job in this respect; such a command would be the ultimate assignment in my Army career. Certainly the responsibility and privilege of commanding American soldiers in combat is the highest honor any officer can hope to attain. For over six months I had pursued this goal, personally requesting a command from all but two of the Div CDRs in Vietnam. I wrote to the CGs of the 9th and 25th Divisions. While all were sympathetic, all told me that they had waiting lists for brigade command, people they had known and promised a brigade should one open in their division.

Unable to get down to see him, I wrote to MG Weyand, commanding the 25th Division. After some delay a letter arrived from him in which he told me that when a brigade commander had been wounded he had asked for me. USARV sent the request for my reassignment to MACV, but someone in the MACV J-l disapproved it. The 25th Division was told that MACV was "tired of providing top-flight colonels to USARV", and that unless an officer of comparable stature was available to replace me, I would not be released. MG Weyand went on to say that obviously he had no replacement for me so had been forced to look elsewhere for a Bde CDR.

This so infuriated me when it came to my attention, that I took the next plane to Saigon and stormed into MACV HQ. The MACV J-l was in the CONUS, so I spoke to his Deputy, COL Kenneth R. Lamison, who told me that he had made the decision during the J-1 's absence. As he put it, he was "sick and tired of having USARV milk off the best colonels in the theater". He declared that MACV also had requirements for outstanding colonels and that he was going to stop the one-way movement of senior officers. Lamison had been in my Leavenworth class, but this did not deter me from berating him, not only because of what he had done to me but what he was doing policy wise; it was inconceivable that any headquarters would deliberately establish a policy keeping an officer who sincerely wanted a command from getting one if it was available.

After venting my wrath on Lamison, I went to see the Chief of Staff of MACV, MG William B. Rosson. In an angry torrent, the story was related to him, and my opinion of that particular personnel policy expressed at length. Rosson, in his usual calm style, let me rattle on, but it was obvious that he was concerned. Finally, when I ran out of words, he told me that nobody made decisions about the assignment of colonels, particularly assignments for command, except the COMUSMACV himself, GEN Westmoreland. This was the first time that the matter had come to the attention of the Command Group. Although it was too late to do anything for me in this instance, he assured me that no one would be turned down for a command in the future without the personal approval of GEN Westmoreland. He went on to say that Lamison had made his decision contrary to approved policy and without the knowledge of General Westmoreland or his Chief of Staff.

While in the III Corps area, I called Mickey Marks, who commanded a brigade in the Big Red One, the 1st IN Div. He suggested that I talk to MG DePuy about a command, so I went to Lai Khe. Mickey showed me around his AO while we waited for BG Hollingsworth, the Asst Div CDR. Later Mickey introduced me to Hollingsworth and forcefully urged him to give me a brigade. Hollingsworth told me to report to Div HQ later that afternoon to talk with MG DePuy. When I talked with DePuy, I was informed that though well qualified, the Big Red One also had a waiting list. After spending the night with Mickey, I returned to Kontum discouraged but not defeated; though there seemed little hope for command after contacting every Division Commander in Vietnam.

Finally, in desperation, I wrote a personal letter to GEN Westmoreland. Excusing the informality of my request, I asked for command of a brigade. Reviewing my background and experience, I stated that I was the best qualified colonel in the theater to command a brigade, based on my advisory experience. Westmoreland responded within a few days, saying that I was being considered for command later in the summer. Nine days later, the Personnel Officer at Pleiku called to tell me that orders had been received assigning me as Commanding Officer of the 1st Bde, 9th IN Div. With a whoop, I hung up, not believing my good fortune.

My affairs were quickly put in order in the 24th Special Tactical Zone. COL Phuoc was informed that I was leaving to command a brigade in III Corps, and that COL Eldeen H. Kauffman would replace me. There would be no turnover because I was to assume command of the brigade before COL Kauffinan arrived. CCL Phuoc, as pleased as I was at my command assignment, gave me an impressive dinner party to which he invited all of the senior ARVN OFFs in the Zone as well as most of the advisors. He presented me with an award, The Staff Service Medal, as well as several mementoes including a heavy Rha De friendship bracelet. The advisors also gave me a farewell party. I was leaving the 24th STZ with the feeling that I had contributed something to the Army of Vietnam and to the effort in the Zone.

During the time I was with the 24th STZ, about 100 operations had been conducted, ranging in length from one to twenty-three days. The results had not been impressive in terms of enemy killed or weapons gathered. However, they were important because they kept the Viet Cong off balance and provided security to the area. An operation is hard to evaluate, but one measure of success, perhaps, is the fact that there was only one major assault on any of the villages in the 24th STZ, except Tou M'Rong. Dak Pek occasionally got mortared or had a probe, and some of the SF camps came under fire because of their exposed positions. But there was no serious attack on districts or provinces except the raid on Dak To in which the two advisors had been killed. There was the big battle north of Tan Canh in which the 1/101 was involved, but that was the result of aggressive patrolling which uncovered VC hiding places and served to throw the VC or NVA off balance.

9 Dec

Dear Colonel Seibert:

I appreciated your letter of 17 November. You have an outstanding record and I am certain that you would be a great asset to any unit.

Last week, I had to deck a commander for my 2nd Brigade. I requested you, however,

USARV informed me that you could not be released unless I furnished a replacement. I, therefore, had to look elsewhere.

I have talked to Don Bolton and Gen O'Connor and they both say that you will undoubtedly be offered a brigade in the 4th Division.

Best of luck,
Sincerely,
Red Culbyred

30 December 1966

General William C Westmoreland
COMUSMACV
APO 96222

Dear General Westmoreland,

Please pardon the informality of this letter, however, it appears to be the best way to handle this matter. I would prefer to make my request to you in person, but your time is so fully occupied that I did not want to intrude upon it.

This letter is a request for consideration as a brigade commander in one of the US divisions in Vietnam. I have completed seventeen months as an advisor (six and one months as DSA of the 25th ARVN Division and ten and one half months as Senior Advisor of the 24th Special Tactical Zone). I have seven months remaining on my extension (DEROS 31 July 1967). I am certain that my experience and training makes me as well qualified to command a brigade as any officer in the Army. The insight and knowledge gained as an advisor will be an added advantage in dealing with ARVN units and GVN officials. I am convinced that I can do the best possible job for you as a brigade commander.

My special reason for writing is to solicit your approval of my assignment as a brigade commander. I recognize that you give your commanders the greatest possible latitude in such matters and rarely are involved directly in the selection of brigade commanders. I intend to make every effort to obtain command of a brigade in one of the US units in Vietnam. Your approval of such a reassignment is of course essential.

Be assured that if afforded the opportunity, I will more than justify the confidence reposed in me by such a command.

Sincerely Yours,

DONALD A SEIBERT
Colonel, Infantry
Senior Advisor

For my year plus service as Senior Advisor to the 24th Special Tactical Zone, BG Lee awarded me the first Oak Leaf Cluster to the Legion of Merit, as well as an ARCOM with Oak Leaf Cluster and "V" device.

Early one sunny morning, a large group gathered at the Kontum Airstrip. There was a full company of the 42nd Regt in dress uniform; the Regt Band played bravely if raggedly. All of the advisors were there, as well as most of the senior Zone ARVN OFFS. We all watched the skies for the Beaver which was to take me to Long Binh. Finally it lumbered into sight. Immediately, a bugler sounded a clarion call, and the ARVN Co hastily adjusted its lines- COL Phuoc, LTC Doan and the 42nd Regt CO escorted me in a review of the honor guard. The advisors and Vietnamese officers formed a long file, down which I passed, shaking hands in farewell. By this time my footlocker had been loaded onto the aircraft. With a final wave of hands, I climbed aboard. Immediately, we taxied to the end of the runway and took off. As we gained altitude, I took what I thought would be my last look at Kontum.

CHAPTER 17

COMMANDER

The DeHaviland Beaver rumbled into the air from the Kontum Air Field and settled into a slow, steady flight to the south as I sat back in the small uncomfortable seat pondering the fate which awaited me as Commander of the 1st Bde 9th IN Div. After what seemed an interminable journey, the aircraft rolled to a halt at the transient terminal at Long Binh Airstrip. A 1LT trotted out to the aircraft, saluting as I deplaned. "Sir, I am LT Greenwood, Liaison Officer, 9th Infantry Division. I will escort you to Bearcat," he said. An NCO with him unloaded my luggage, which was transferred to a waiting Huey. As the chopper became airborne, my eyes widened as I looked down on the sprawling complex that had replaced the orderly rubber plantations in only two short years. Greenwood attempted to point out the installations as we flew over them: the two hospitals; USARV HQ; the various supply and maintenance facilities. Suddenly, the organized clutter gave way to jungle.

In only a matter of minutes, we were again over a military camp, this one still in the throes of construction. "This is Bearcat, Sir. The northern sector of the perimeter is the 1st Brigade area," my escort said. But already we had overflown it and were descending to land at a helipad in front of Div HQ.

My luggage was transferred to a jeep as Greenwood led me to the HQ. COL Miller, the CofS, met and welcomed me to the 9th IN Div. After some small talk, he took me in to see BG G.G. O'Connor, the Asst Div CDR. O'Connor, who had been in Plans, DCSOPS, in the Pentagon when I was there, welcomed me cordially. We had an interesting few minutes recalling those days under BG Woolnough and COL Mock. O'Connor gave me a brief summary of the disposition of the 9th Div and its activities, informing me that the Staff had prepared detailed briefings to acquaint me fully with the Division, its policies and procedures.

After our conversation, 1LT Greenwood led me to a van fitted out as a set of quarters which I would occupy while being briefed. That evening at dinner, I met MG George S. Eckhardt, the Division Commander, a tall man, who looked old and tired. He too, welcomed me to the Division. BG Morgan Roseborough, the other Asst Div CDR under whose supervision I would operate, also welcomed me. Roseborough was a big, energetic and open individual whom I liked immediately. During the meal LTC Charley Meek, The Division Chaplain, an old friend from the 508, and LTC Ross Goddard, the Division Staff Judge Advocate, whom I had known in the 504 at Mainz as a captain, both greeted me. We talked briefly of those great days in the 508 at Benning and the 504 at Mainz.

During the next two days, the Staff gave me a complete account of the Div since it had arrived in Vietnam a few months before, and explained the major policies governing its activities. The orientation also included a visit to the other two brigades. The 2nd Bde, called the Riverine Force, operated in the Delta Area just at the HI Corps/IV Corps boundary. At its HQ, at Dong Tarn, I met Bill Fulton, the Commander, an acquaintance of long standing. The 3rd Bde was in Long An Province. Enroute to its Headquarters, the pilot of my helicopter obligingly stopped off at Due Hoa where I marveled at the completed advisory compound, and had a brief chat with BG Chinh, only recently promoted. He told me that COL Giai was now commanding the 18th ARVN Div at Xuan Loc, and that COL Luyen was en route to Pleiku.

The 3rd Bde was commanded by an old friend and War College classmate, George Everett, who was able to give me some good information about the 9th Div, although he had only recently assumed command. These visits completed my orientation; by now I was eager to get to the 1st Bde and assume command.

The third day after joining the 9th Division, I flew to the 1st Bde CP at Loc Ninh. The Brigade was attached to the 1st IN Divs for Operation Junction City, one of the many efforts to search out and destroy major enemy strongholds. When ever an effort was targeted against a specific enemy force or stronghold, it was called an operation (OPN) and given a name. Junction City was targeted against the Viet Cong HQ in the area. The 1st Bde was deployed along Highway 13 guarding the Big Red One's supply line. Two days before, the 3rd Squadron, 5th Cavalry (3/5 CAV), attached to the 1st Bde, had fought a fierce battle at Ap Bau Bang during which the Squadron Commander, LTC "Hap" Haszard had earned a recommendation for the DSC. The 4th of the 39th Infantry (4/39 Inf) had been alerted to reinforce the 3/5 CAV but had not been needed. The destruction the NVA or VC had inflicted when they penetrated the CAV's perimeter was still evident when I visited the 3/5 later

The 1st Bde (1/9) was composed of HHC, commanded by CPT Martin Jagles, two Infantry battalions, the 2nd Bn, 39th IN (2/39), commanded by LTC Ken Trinkler and the 4/39 commanded by LTC Clyde Bell, and a mechanized Infantry battalion, the 2nd Bn, 47th IN, Mechanized (2/47 MECH) commanded by LTC Bill Cronin. The 3/5 CAV routinely operated with the 1st Bde but was occasionally placed OPCON to another brigade.

The 1st Bde Commander, COL Maurice W. Kendall, welcomed me, gave me a short orientation on the current situation and took me on a tour of the four Bns. Even this fleeting visit revealed a manifest tension in everyone in the Brigade; it was wound up tight. Obviously Kendall kept his commanders and staff on a very short leash and gave them little leeway. It was apparent that the staff officers were afraid to act on their own recognizance for fear of being overruled or reprimanded for any initiative they might take. Each individual commands differently, adapting his leadership to his own experience, personality and views. Kendall seemed to oversupervise and to be reluctant to delegate authority. Something needed to be done immediately so the commanders and staff officers could begin to operate in the way I thought they should. I could hardly wait to take command.

COL Kendall and I returned to Bearcat where an abbreviated change of command ceremony was held. Immediately afterwards, I returned to the 1st Bde which was still OPCON to the 1st Div. After reporting to MG Hay, the CG, and to COL Bill Kitchen, the CofS, I went to see Mickey Marks, who still commanded the 2nd (Iron) Bde of the 1st Div. He briefed me on the area and on MG Hay's policies. Then I settled down to learn my new command and its personnel. There was little activity during the remainder of Junction City; the battalions outposted the roads, patrolled extensively and occupied likely ambush sites. Whenever convoys moved, my S-3, MAJ Fitzmorris, and I would fly the route in the C&C ship. We had no major contact during the period; within a week the 1st Bde returned to Bearcat.

Two concepts which persist in the Army have never seemed persuasive to me. One is that upon assumption of command a new commander should make no changes in the first few days or weeks; he should wait before making those changes which appear obvious or necessary to him. Such a delay is unwarranted. If a commander sees something that is wrong or if things are not functioning the way he wants them to, he should take action immediately. There is no virtue in making changes just to impress one's presence on a command, nor is there merit in the wholesale repudiation of existing policies without determining why they were established, but if change is warranted, it should be effected without delay. The second concept is that a commander has to make his presence felt by doing something dramatic or drastic to call attention to his assumption of command. The troops know when there has been a change of command; they do not need to have it headlined. If a new commander visits his troops, talks to them, is seen, makes necessary changes in policy, guides the unit his way, in a word, commands, then he has done all that is necessary to impress his personality and leadership on the unit.

Following this precept, I spent a great deal of time with the units of the 1st Brigade during the first two weeks I was with it. It was a fine outfit, with a capable staff; the battalion commanders were competent; the troops were good. It appeared to me, though I cannot document it, that the problem with the 1st Bde, as with the entire 9th Div, was that it had never really made the transition from the training areas at FT Riley, KS, to the jungles of Vietnam. The units were still going on training problems or maneuver exercises rather than on combat operations. It was most likely this perception had filtered up through channels and prompted the shuffling of senior commanders.

One of my own long cherished hopes, that of activating and training a unit and then leading it in combat, one I thought might be realized by my assignment to F Co, 508 RCT, began to look less desirable. The alleged advantage of commanders training the units they will lead in combat now seemed questionable. On the one hand, the commander who trains his unit develops confidence, respect and loyalty, establishes SOPs and routine procedures, and gains an insight into how his commanders and staff officers operate and think. On the other hand, such a commander may become too emotionally involved with the men and the unit, resulting in a reluctance to commit the element to combat, to fight it aggressively, or, as I suspected was the case with the 1st Bde, to make the transition from training to combat. There appeared to be some definite shortcomings in the 9th Div as a result of having the commanders who trained the units lead them in combat.

On returning to Bearcat, I learned that my Executive Officer was being reassigned to II Field Force HQ. The XO of the 2nd Bn, 39th IN, LTC Hassett, recently promoted, was now too senior for his job. As he was highly recommended as a doer and impressed me when I met him, he was reassigned as the 1st Bde XO. What I wanted in my XO was somebody who could command and build the base camp. Construction of semi-permanent buildings had already been started, but there was still much to be done. The Brigade would be out of Bearcat on operations most of the time, hence I would be able to devote little time to supervising construction. There was also need for someone to handle routine administrative and logistical matters in the base camp. LTC Hassett joined Bde HQ and did exactly what I wanted him to do: pushed forward needed supplies to us when we were operating out of Bearcat, handled routine administration for the Brigade, built a comfortable and efficient area virtually without guidance from me, and commanded the base camp effectively. He also supervised the construction of the three battalion areas while the commanders were on combat operations.

MAJ Fitzmorris, the S-3 was transferred to the Div G-3 Section within two weeks after I took command; again I raided the 2/39. MAJ Art Davies, the Bn S-3, had been recommended to me by Fitzmorris as his replacement. The 2/39 had two strong captains in its S-3 Section, Shaw and Pack, either of whom could replace Davies. Without qualms, I moved Art to Brigade. He made an outstanding S-3.

Again, the inconsistency of the awards system came home to me. I recommended MAJ Fitzmorris for a CIB, based on his duty as the 1st Bde S-3 in combat for a period in excess of 30 days during which he was under fire many times. Division disapproved the award because his basic branch was Armor. My argument that he had been acting as an IN OFF during this assignment was not considered. Had he been an advisor, he would now be wearing the CIB.

While the Brigade was in Bearcat, I went to Xuan Loc, HQ of 18th ARVN Div, to pay a courtesy call on COL Giai, Commander of the Division. The 18th ARVN Div's AO was to the east and north of Bearcat, within the 1st Bde's area of interest. It was apparent that we would operate frequently with elements of the 18th Div. COL Giai was delighted to see me and assured me of his full support on any combined operations. He offered to place ARVN troops under my OPCON whenever it was justifiable. The rapport established at Due Hoa was more firmly welded.

During this time I visited all of the 9th Div units (ARTY, AVN, EN, MC and SC as well as Technical Service elements) that had supported the 1st Bde, on Junction City as well as on previous operations. On these visits I talked to the troops and commanders whenever possible, thanking them for the support they had given the Brigade, and emphasizing how much it depended on their support. This began a policy pursued throughout my tenure; the visits were followed by letters of appreciation or commendation to the supporting units through channels. This was the least that any commander could do for the people who gave him such excellent support.

The 1st Bde did not stay at Bearcat long. Toward the end of March 1967, I received orders to operate with the Australian Task Force in Phuoc Tuy Prov, southeast of Bearcat. The mission of OPN Port Sea was to find and kill Viet Cong in the area and to destroy their living quarters, supplies, and fortifications. In addition, families were to be relocated from the operational zone to more secure areas so that they would not be subject to the harassing fire, raids or patrol actions necessary to secure allied bases, the Prov Capitals, and Dist HQ.

It was an interesting operation because the Australians function differently than do Americans. They were a bit more relaxed in the field, although they had even more rigid rules of engagement than did the US. The 9th Div was in overall command since MG Eckhardt was senior to the Brigadier commanding the Australian Task Force. This command arrangement also precluded my being OPCON to the Australian Task Force. During Port Sea there was little contact. Twice it appeared that a sizeable force had been encircled, but few VC were found when the troops moved in on the location.

The 1/9 was minus the 4/39 during Operation Port Sea because that unit was committed to the security of Long Binh in a continuing operation called Uniontown, which I commanded whenever the Brigade was not involved in another operation. The 2/39 IN, the 2/47 MECH, the 3/5 CAV, the 11th Direct Support (DS) ARTY Bn and other support units were the 9th Div troops committed to Port Sea. The 2/39 moved by USAF C-123s from Long Thanh air strip to the Australian Task Force Airfield, but assaulted into the combat area by helicopter. The rest of the Brigade went by road with the 2/47 leading initially. On reaching the area suspected of being the VC base camp, I pushed the 3/5 ahead of the 2/47; the CAV seized crossing sites on the river, emplaced an Armored Vehicle Launched Bridge (A VLB) which was attached to it for this operation, and moved their tanks across the river.

Numerous airmobile assaults were conducted; in the 12-day action some 300 UH-1D sorties and 17 CH-47 sorties were made, not unusual in this type of warfare. OPN Port Sea concluded with five friendly KIA, 48 wounded in action (WIA), 44 confirmed enemy KIA and six prisoners of war (POWs). One tank and three of the CAVs APCs were destroyed and two tanks, one APC and the AVLB damaged. We captured 77 weapons as well as thousands of rounds of ammunition of all kinds. The Brigade was under fire several times. The 3/5 had the most protracted engagement in which two of its troops were involved. This fight resulted in the destruction of the two tanks and three APCs.

During one contact, DUSTOFF, a medical evacuation (MEDEVAC) helicopter, was needed for a seriously wounded soldier. As it was taking off from a hastily constructed LZ, its rotor blades hit some trees causing it to crash, further injuring the wounded soldier as well as the crew members. After considerable work on the LZ, all casualties were evacuated, but the helicopter had to be destroyed as it was impossible to extract it.

Many bunker complexes were located in which a large amount of ammunition, almost 18 tons of rice and other food were stored. Most of this was evacuated for distribution to Vietnamese civilians. The VC ammunition was destroyed in place after samples were taken for intelligence. Although no major contact had been made, and the mission had been only partially completed, it was a significant operation; the VC were located though not destroyed; needed supplies were denied them; and friendly Vietnamese civilians were relocated to more secure areas. It provided me an opportunity to shake down the Brigade under relatively simple requirements, and to establish the command relations between BG Roseborough and myself.

The 2/39, after making contact, was engaged in a fire fight. LTC Trinkler, the Battalion Commander, conducted the action from one of the Brigade OH-23 helicopters, closely observed by my staff and me in the C&C ship above him. Trinkler appeared to have everything under control, so I made no attempt to interfere with his handling of the fight. Suddenly the radio came to life, "Shining 6, this is Python 66. Over." Python 66 was the Asst Div CDR, BG Roseborough, who normally contacted the Brigade on the Division Command Net. However, he had entered the Brigade Command Net, obviously intending to give Trinkler instructions directly. Recognizing that Roseborough was in effect usurping my command, I cut in saying, "Unknown station this is a restricted net. Cease traffic immediately. Out".

In a matter of seconds an irate brigadier general's voice crackled over the Division Command Net, "Stalwart 6, this is Python 66. Over." MAJ Davies grinned at me as I answered, "Python 66, this is Stalwart 6. Over."

An angry voice lashed out, "Stalwart 6, I have been trying to contact Shining 6 (CO 2/39) on your net and have been cut out. What is the matter? Over."

"Python 66, Shining 6 is engaged in a fire fight which I am monitoring. My Command Net is therefore restricted to authorized stations until contact is lost. Please transmit your traffic on this net. Over."

"Stalwart 6, I have instructions for Shining 6, which I want him to have immediately, Over."

"Python 66, send me your instructions. The situation is under control but Shining 6 needs to give it his full attention. I will relay if necessary. Over."

"Stalwart 6, never mind," this last in an injured tone. "Call me when contact is broken. Out"

It was almost possible to feel across the air waves the heat of BG Roseborough's rage. The three helicopters continued to circle at three different altitudes. The firing below sounded like tiny firecrackers, which blazed and then stuttered to a halt. The Brigade Command Net came to life, "Stalwart 6, this is Shining 6. Contact broken. I have three lightly wounded. There are no confirmed VC K1A. I am landing to check the situation, and will give a complete report as soon as possible. Over."

"Shining 6, this is Stalwart 6. Roger your transmission. Good job. Out." Switching to the Division Command Net I intoned, "Python 66, this is Stalwart 6. Over."

"Stalwart 6, this is Python 66. I monitored. Where can we meet to talk? Over."

"Python 66. LZ Able is just to the northeast and is secure. I will meet you there in zero five. Over." "Python 66. Roger. Out."

The two helicopters swerved and headed to the nearby cleared area. Both touched down simultaneously, Roseborough leaped out of one as I jumped out of the other. We strode toward each other purposefully.

"Seibert, what the hell was that all about?"

"Sir, Trinkler had everything under control and did not need any advice from you or me. But if you had instructions, you should have given them to me. You saw me over the area in obvious control. I don't appreciate any one giving my battalion commanders orders except through me."

"Well, as Assistant Division Commander, and supervisor of the 1st and 3rd Bdes, I intend to give any orders I deem necessary to any one regardless of the chain of command." By this time his color had risen and his voice became irate.

Equally heated, I replied, "General, I command the 1st Brigade. If you don't trust me to command it, then relieve me. But as long as I command, I insist that all orders to my subordinates be given through me. There was no emergency which warranted bypassing channels. Orders from two people only confuse the situation. Trinkler had enough on his hands without sorting out conflicting orders. I want to command this Brigade, not be a figurehead."

My words had a chilling effect on the General as well as on me. We both lost our heads simultaneously. Roseborough flushed a bit, but relaxed visibly.

"I guess you are right. I got caught up in the situation and when I saw a couple of VC firing from the flank, I wanted to make sure Trinkler knew about them."

"I appreciate that, General Roseborough. But Trinkler had already seen them and told his people about them. I guess I got a little hot for a minute, and I apologize. But I do want to command this Brigade completely."

"I understand, Don. And I respect your right to do so. I'll confine my transmissions to the Division Command Net unless I see a real emergency."

"Thanks, sir. That's all I ask."

We shook hands and headed for our choppers. My pilot waited until the General's aircraft was airborne before taking off. Roseborough kept his word and never again attempted to tell any of my battalion commanders what to do when I was present. Our relations were cordial and amicable from then on. The Asst Div CDR gave me every opportunity to exercise my leadership and ideas.

It was a common practice in Vietnam, for general officers to rush to the sound of the gun, take command from their subordinates and run battles themselves. Certainly someone in the air, seeing things the commander on the ground cannot see, should advise him of them. On the other hand, the situation on the ground may be entirely different than its appearance from the air. A commander must permit his subordinates to exercise their leadership and authority unless the situation is in doubt or troops in unnecessary jeopardy. To rush in and take control each time a shot is fired is hardly the way to inspire confidence or to give junior officers needed experience. Every combat operation may be considered a training vehicle though not a deliberately contrived one. There is no question in my mind that in Vietnam too many senior officers attempted to usurp the authority of their subordinate commanders. Their exact motives are unclear, probably they were not ulterior nor were they doing it for their own self-aggrandizement, although this was a suspicion that many junior officers entertained. Most likely they were caught up in the in drama of the action. Unfortunately, some senior officers showed little or no confidence in their subordinates.

Back in Bearcat, I again made the rounds of the supporting units; where feasible, I thanked the troops personally for their aid, and put through channels letters of appreciation. In the case of the non-divisional aviation units, it was almost impossible to find an opportunity to talk directly with the pilots and crew chiefs. They were always committed. One aviation battalion commander called to express his appreciation for my letter; he said that it was the first time his unit had ever been thanked by a commander they supported. It was incredible that its outstanding airlift and gunship support had been accepted without acknowledgment!

Shortly after we got back to Bearcat, word came through ARVN channels that BG Giai, just promoted, wanted to present some awards to members of the 1st Bde for their participation in OPN Port Sea. Delighted, I went to see him to arrange a time and formation. On the appointed day, I brought him to Bearcat in my C&C ship where he pinned ARVN decorations on a representative group of officers and soldiers from the Brigade. The men appreciated this gesture.

After only three days in Bearcat, the 1st Bde was once again on its way, this time to Tay Ninh where it became OPCON to the 25th US Div for OPN Junction City III. As is apparent, the 1/9 was a swing brigade living up to the motto of its component 39th IN Bns "Anything, Anywhere, Anytime, Bar Nothing". It was sent anywhere additional forces were necessary for operations. The Bde moved to Tay Ninh by road, although the 4/39 Inf was airlifted to Tay Ninh West Airfield to relieve the 2/12 Inf. It was a long, hard movement, through Bien Hoa, Saigon, and Cu Chi. The Command Group; the S-3, ARTY LNO, AF LNO, RTO/runner/driver and I spent long hours in the air policing the convoy. Fortunately there were no incidents on the way. The 2/39 remained in Bien Hoa Province on the Uniontown security mission. On reporting to MG Tillson, now the 25th Div CG, I was given my mission: secure Tay Ninh Prov. Certain 25th US Div and Vietnamese units were placed under my OPCON from time to time: the 36th ARVN Ranger Bn, a Co of the US 3/4 Armor, and the US 2/12 IN Bn. Thelst Bde area of operations extended from Tay Ninh City north. Located in the AO were several SF Camps: Trai Bi, Prek Loc and Ben Soi. To accomplish the assigned mission, limited search and destroy operations were conducted to prevent VC movement, or to deny their resupply. An attempt was made to find and destroy enemy safe areas so that the VC were kept off balance at all times. This would provide security for all of Tay Ninh Prov as well as the 196th Bde's base camp west of Tay Ninh City (the 196th was involved in Junction City III), the rock quarry at the foot of Nui Ba Dinh, the laterite pit, and the major routes to Sui Da and Dau Tieng. Enough combat power was available to reinforce Ben Soi, Prek Loc., Trai Bi and the Sui Da base camp if necessary. The month-long operation was successful from that aspect; only one of the installations for which the 1/9 provided security was subjected to a minor probe, easily repulsed.

Prek Loc, a SF/CIDG camp, had received a heavy mortar and ground attack a few weeks before and was in the process of being rebuilt. MG Tillson directed me to monitor that effort and if necessary to take charge of it. Specifically, I had responsibility for the external security of the camp until it was able to defend itself.

The Bde CP, located in an area known as the French Fort, occupied the site of the CP of the 3rd Bde, 4th US IN Div (attached to the 25th Div) which was involved in Junction City III. COL Marshall Garth, the Bde CDR, generously left some of his facilities there, including his own living quarters, a trailer, which had been dug in and sandbagged. To reduce the number of troops needed for the security of the C P, the perimeter was reconfigured. Although this thinned the defenses of the CP, it was never probed.

The 2/47, commanded by LTC Bill Cronin, while operating north of the Bde CP area, found an extensive complex of caves and tunnels. It was apparently part of the safe area the VC were using as a base from which to harass the installations farther south. Bill reported that he could not destroy it with the troops and equipment he had and asked my guidance on it. Before any decision was made, it was necessary for me to look at the complex.

The C&C ship, with the usual command group, landed in a natural clearing in the jungle which 2/47 troops secured. After the command group disembarked, I sent the chopper back to the CP to await a call when it was needed again. My RTO, SP4 Rick Hanes, with his back-pack radio, was in contact with the TOC at the CP.

Bill led us through the jungle about a half a mile, to the complex. It was far too extensive to destroy with demolitions, so I decided to put air strikes on it at a later date. It appeared to be abandoned, perhaps it was an alternate site, hence it did not seem important to destroy it immediately.

Having given Bill my estimate and decision, the Command Group prepared to leave the 2/47 area. Hanes called for the chopper, instructing it to be prepared to pick us up on call. The 2/47 had troops throughout the area, therefore Bill called for a minimal security force to secure the Bde Command Group as we started back to the LZ. Neither Bill nor I realized that the sergeant, who was acting as point, had elected to take the exact route back to the LZ that had been used coming from it. This was a mistake. It was common practice, indeed SOP, not to backtrack on the same route if it could be avoided. To return on the same route gave the enemy an opportunity to position forces to ambush a unit or to zero its mortars on it. Despite the presence of friendly troops in the area, it was not a wise decision. There was a fire team forward and one behind, but I didn't realize just how thin our combat escort was. This is hindsight, other than directing a different return route, I'm not sure I would have done anything more about security.

As we moved out, I positioned myself behind the point man to see what was going on. Suddenly, a burst of AK47 fire shattered the stillness, the point man went down, killed instantly. Everyone hit the ground. Since I had no other weapon than my pistol, I started to squirm forward to secure the point man's M-16. As I inched forward, the enemy fired again, preventing me from reaching the point man. When the escort and command group drew back into a small perimeter, we discovered that there were only six or seven effective weapons in the little force, most, like myself, had pistols and Hanes had a carbine. Bill immediately contacted the company closest to him and Hanes notified the Bde CP. The area was heavily vegetated, though not triple canopy jungle. Visibility was limited and movement difficult and noisy. Bill Cronin and my S-3, Art Davies, tried to reposition themselves to see where the fire was coming from and to insure that the limited fire power available was used to the best effect. As they moved, another burst of AK47 fire ripped out, killing both Bill Cronin and Art Davies.

The few effective weapons fired at likely targets, but the VC were well concealed. It appeared from the enemy fire that it was only a small group, probably five or six individuals. Then we began to receive fire from several different directions, indicating that additional enemy had reinforced the original group. Taking the handset of Hanes' radio, I called for artillery, warning the TOC to clear with the 2/47 CP because I was not sure of the location of the troops in the area. Meanwhile, the commander of the 2/47 unit closest to us, reported that he was moving troops immediately into the area. Having fixed the exact position of the Command Group and the friendly forces, the ARTY LNO, CPT Wes Comfort was able to adjust the fire, placing it on the side of our small perimeter away from the advancing friendly troops. On my instructions he called it in as close as possible. Occasionally, pieces of shrapnel landed in our position but the fire kept the VC off balance until the 2/47 Co reached us. Although there was a lack of weapons, only one radio and few Infantrymen, we were able to hold our position. But with our limited firepower, there was no way to maneuver without exposing unnecessarily everybody in the group. Shortly, elements of the 2/47 Co joined us. I saw some excellent team work by those American troops, particularly one machine gunner who constantly repositioned himself to bring fire on the enemy. He effectively neutralized most of the VC almost single handed.

The VC withdrew; if our fire killed any of them there was no evidence of it. Not wanting to further jeopardize either the Command Group or the 2/47 troops, I decided that we would not go back to the initial LZ, we would go to one of the company positions, cut an LZ, and MEDEVAC the wounded. Then the Command Group would be extracted. Meanwhile, some of the 2/47 APCs moved into the area to assist in breaking down the vegetation, After much hard work, an LZ which could handle a DUSTOFF and a Bde OH-23 was cleared.

All of the Command Group was shaken. It hit me particularly hard, losing three good men, including a Battalion Commander and my Brigade S-3, and having several wounded. With great remorse I reviewed the situation and questioned my judgement. As the senior officer present, I was responsible for what had happened, I had not questioned Bill Cronin's assessment of the situation, and had not insured adequate security. This is not said in criticism of Bill or the NCO leading our security force, everyone acted in accordance with his estimate of the situation, and to that extent, acted soundly. Obviously, we should not have taken the same route back to the LZ, indeed we probably should not have used that LZ again. I fault myself for not realizing that there were enemy in the area. A second time, I would do things differently. Hopefully, there would be no second time. But from then on, every member of the Command Group carried an M-16 with adequate ammunition.

Once back at the CP, the immediate task facing me was to make sure that Bill's death did not adversely affect the morale and combat effectiveness of his Battalion. He was much admired and beloved by his men, an outstanding OFF with a brilliant future. After giving the facts to Ken Renaud, who was in charge of the TOC, so that a complete report could be made both to the 9th and 25th

Divisions, I went to the 2/47 CP, talked with MAJ Jim Steel the Executive Officer, and formally put him in temporary command. Steel was an Academy Graduate, apparently a stable officer, though events proved that he was not the strong commander I hoped he'd be. But he kept the Battalion under control and effective until a new battalion commander arrived.

BG Don Bolton, who had served with me in Korea in the 9th IN and now one of the Asst Div CDRs of the 25th, visited me shortly after the reports reached his HQ. He was assured that there was no untoward effect on the 2/47 or the 1/9, and that the Command Group, other than the S-3, was in good shape. Later in the afternoon the TOC received word from the 9th Div HQ that BG Roseborough was enroute to talk to me. He arrived just after dark, a rather ticklish experience because the LZ was neither lighted nor apparent. The Bde aircraft normally returned to Tay Ninh for the night rather than remain at French Fort exposed to mortar rounds or sniper fire. It was obvious that Roseborough wanted to find out how the experience had affected me, whether I had lost my nerve. He asked if the Brigade could continue its mission and was still combat effective. There was no question about that in my mind. Despite my sorrow and remorse over the deaths of Bill Cronin, Art Davies and the sergeant, I did not believe that my ability to command had been impaired. BG Roseborough was assured of that. He informed me that a new battalion commander, LTC Art Moreland, had been designated but would not arrive for several days. Steel would fight the Bn until he took command.

The Asst S-3, CPT Ken Renaud, a CWS Officer, was a competent individual who had been assistant to MAJ Fitzmorris as well as MAJ Davies and was thoroughly familiar with Infantry tactics, the Div SOPs and my method of operation. There seemed to be no need to make a hasty decision on Major Davies' replacement, Ken handled the S-3 duties in an outstanding manner for about ten days. By that time I had selected MAJ Al Rozon, S-3 of the 4/39, to be the new Brigade S-3. Al reported for duty during the closing days of OPN Junction City III.

It was my difficult task to write the letters of condolence to the wives of the men who had been killed, Bill Cronin, Art Davies, and the sergeant. Once this had been completed, recommendations for awards were submitted. The 2/47 machine gunner was recommended for a Silver Star as were Bill Cronin and Art Davies, and my RTO for an Army Commendation Medal (ARCOM) with V. A few days after the incident, MG Tillson came to French Fort to present "Impact Awards" (on the spot decorations without waiting for the paperwork or formal recommendations.) He had already visited the 2/47 CP on a similar mission. Most of the Command Group was included in the formation, which he insisted I join. He pinned a Silver Star on me, which made me indignant because in my view I had done nothing to earn it. When MG Tillson heard my protest, he told me that he believed that whenever a senior commander assumed control of an operation on the ground and handled it satisfactorily he deserved a Silver Star. It was his view that most commanders perform acts which deserve such recognition but are rarely recommended for it because they stop the action on it themselves, or the people who observed the incident were too busy with other things and never got around to making the recommendation. Though not fully convinced, I accepted MG Tillson's logic and the award, albeit reluctantly.

During Junction City III, I visited all of the SF camps in Tay Ninh. Special attention was given to Prek Loc, but I made it my business to check all of them periodically to offer assistance and to make sure of their external security.

One evening there was a probe of Prek Loc. In a matter of minutes a helicopter was on its way from Tay Ninh City and I was soon airborne. LTC Happersadt, who commanded Prek Loc, became excited and tied up the radio nets. The probe, consisting of a few mortar rounds and some small arms fire, could easily be repelled by the garrison at Prek Loc. When I attempted to direct a flare ship on target and to put artillery on possible locations from which the VC might be attacking the camp, Happersadt kept filling the air with useless communications which were completely incoherent at times. Finally, I directed him to get off the net and assumed command of the operation until it was over. It was a minor probe that should have caused no problems.

The next morning I went to Prek Loc to talk to Happersadt. He apparently had lost control of himself because of the condition of the camp's defenses. We reached an understanding on our responsibilities. The 2/47 saturated the area around Prek Loc with patrols but found little evidence of a ground attack. Perhaps a small VC element with mortars had infiltrated within range of the camp, fired a few rounds, and covered their withdrawal with small arms fire. But no large unit had been in the area.

The 4/39 had responsibility for the security of the quarry, laterite pit and the roads to the east of Tay Ninh City. As was my custom, I visited each company at least once a day checking their defenses, their needs and their wants. On many of these occasions I bumped into COL Dave Ott, a Leavenworth classmate, the 25th DIVARTY CDR. Dave insured that the 1/9 never lacked artillery support. On his visits to our DS ARTY Bn, the 1/11, he had only the highest praise for it and its commander, LTC Jack Sadler.

One day as we left French Fort in the C&C ship, the pilot told me over the intercom that he had lost his hydraulics, with the result that he had only limited control over the aircraft and could make only shallow turns and restricted maneuvers. He was going to put down at the Tay Ninh City Airfield, but since he could control the aircraft only if he maintained some air speed, he would have to make a running landing. He advised us to prepare for a crash landing and called ahead to alert the airfield. Long before the helicopter reached the airfield, he lined it up with the runway and slowly eased it down until the skids made contact. There was a slight jolt before friction stopped the aircraft. It was a professional performance. The helicopter had to be towed from the runway, but another C&C ship picked us up shortly.

In my experience, there were relatively few malfunctions with the helicopters in Vietnam. The Bde helicopters, the OH-23s, were in top-flight condition. MAJ George Cockle, the Bde AVN OFF, ran a very tight shop and kept our choppers in good condition, the Aviation Section was justly proud of its maintenance. Its call sign was ANTEATER, hence the maintenance and parking area had been dubbed the "Anthill". There were four OH-23s in the Section and four pilots, MAJ Cockle, CPT Earl Malchow, CPT Bill Shawn, and CWO Hans Hoffman. Hoffman was an especially adept pilot. It was my policy to put the helicopters out to the Bns to the maximum extent possible, but on the advice of George, always concerned about maintenance, we tried to rotate them and keep one in maintenance at all times.

The 1/9 Chaplain, a Roman Catholic Priest, Father (Major) McGonigal, was an outstanding troop chaplain but he rarely kept Brigade informed of his location, hence we could never account for his movements. Periodically he would turn up missing, necessitating a search of all of the units in order to find the good father. Several times I told him that he must keep us informed, he promised to do so, but he was really indifferent to administration, believing that his main job was with the troops whose spiritual needs he looked after so well.

Ten days before the end of Junction City III, MAJ Al Rozon reported to Bde as the S-3. He had been doing an outstanding job as the 4/39 OPS OFF, and Clyde Bell protested his reassignment vehemently. Since both Art Davies and Hassett had been transferred from the 2/39, however, he had little complaint. Al proved to be a superb S-3 and we worked well together. No doubt he found me difficult to work with, my temper was ever on short leash. When anything went wrong, I let everyone nearby know that I was unhappy. Like Wilbur Wilson, I often let go in front of others, chewing out people publicly. Afterwards I was always remorseful, but my best intentions seemed to effect no cure. Unfortunately, Al, who as S-3 was almost always with me, came in for the brunt of my temper, somehow he managed to live with it and we soon established a close rapport.

There were a few minor engagements during Junction City III, but the Bde had no significant contact during that month. Shortly after Rozon assumed his duties as S-3, orders were received to abandon French Fort and move southeast to link-up with the 1st Bde, 25th Div near Dau Tieng.

The work of closing out French Fort commenced. It was necessary to return all of the equipment left there by the 25th Div, including COL Garth's trailer. In devising the plan for the link-up, Rozon and I determined that it was necessary to move a battery of the 1/11 so that it would be in range to support the 2/47 when it crossed the river. It was easy enough to select the position, but not easy to find troops to secure the fire base, the Bde had run out of Infantry. Al suggested that we use the attached Engineer Company to seize and hold Fire Support Base Fang. When the Co CO, CPT Frank Miller, was told that his company was going to make a combat assault the following day, his jaw dropped. Miller was a brilliant officer who had done an outstanding job on all of his engineering tasks. Now he was faced with a mission he hadn't anticipated. He stammered something about the Engineers' mission, but I quickly pointed out to him that the Engineers' secondary mission was to fight as Infantry. Intelligence indicated that the area selected for the fire support base was mined, use of the EN Co in a combat assault would serve the dual purpose of putting Engineers on the ground to clear it of mines as well as enemy. Frank called the Div Engineer at Bearcat to get guidance, LTC Read told him to "do as the man says , that's what you're there for". Miller then entered into the mission with a great deal of enthusiasm, in fact he asked whether his men would get the CIB if they made contact. Luckily, the LZ was cold, although the AVLB was blown up in a shallow stream where detectors did not locate the mine. An APC was also partially disabled as a result of undetected mines. The Engineers did succeed in removing most of the mines enabling the artillery to go into position without trouble.

The link-up at Dau Tieng was effected with no further problems as the operation ended. Though there was little significant contact during Junction City III, it did throw the VC off balance. The amount of equipment and food-stuffs captured or destroyed, and the routing of the VC out of their safe hiding places, set back their plans considerably.

The 1/9 consolidated at Tay Ninh City to make the long motor march back to Bearcat. The day of the move, Al Rozon and I spent almost ten hours in the C&C ship monitoring the movement and getting the convoy through critical areas. The move went well.

Back at Bearcat, there were many personnel changes to reckon with. O'Connor was promoted to Major General and replaced Eckhardt as CG of the 9th Div. This was a welcome change which infused new energy and direction into the Div. Eckhardt, apparently worn out and ailing, had given lackluster leadership to his command. LTC Art Moreland joined the 1st Bde as the 2/47 MECH Bn Commander. He was a competent, effective, but colorless leader.

Clyde Bell, reassigned as the Division G-1, relinquished command of the 4/39 to LTC Dan Baldwin. Dan was a sturdy, dynamic, gung-ho, Airborne type who was bursting with energy and enthusiasm. He had a minor stuttering problem, which in most cases was under control, but occasionally flared up in arguments with me. He had wide experience in Vietnam, both as an advisor in the ARVN ABN Bde and as a Province or District Advisor. He knew many of the Vietnamese officers in the Bien Hoa area, most importantly, the Province Chief, LTC Hai and BG Giai. This cemented the rapport the 1/9 had established with those two officers. Dan was a controversial officer who rubbed many people the wrong way. Despite his propensity to take action before his plans were complete and to talk before he thought, he did an outstanding job for me as a battalion commander in combat. On occasions, there was liquor on his breath. Though I had no objections to a social drink while at Bearcat, I did not countenance drinking on operations, and spoke to Dan about this. He was never under the influence of alcohol to my knowledge, certainly it did not affect his performance of duty. Nevertheless, it did give me some concern. Al Rozon had been replaced as the S-3 of the

4/39 by CPT George Skinner, an unflappable individual who was a good counter to Dan Baldwin's mercurial personality. He did an excellent job as Bn S-3.

Ken Trinkler also received orders transferring him to the III Corps Advisory Team at Bien Hoa. These were not effective for a month. During that time he tried to have the orders revoked so he could remain with the 2/39, he was not happy with the assignment as an advisor. Ken was an effective battalion commander, so I also tried to have him remain with the 2/39, but both our efforts were unsuccessful.

The Bde Sergeant Major also left. The OPS SGM, who impressed me as a doer, was my choice as the new SGM. But just at that time the Command Sergeant Major (CSM) Program was implemented Army-wide, and my choice was not on the CSM List. The Div SGM informed me that SGM Graham of the 4/39 would be the next Bde SGM. This did not sit well with me, not only because I had a very poor opinion of SGM Graham, but also because I did not think that the Div SGM should dictate personnel changes in my Bde. We had words on this, the matter was finally referred to MG O'Connor. For the first and only time, O'Connor did not back me, but approved the Div SGM's choice. He explained that because the program was just being implemented he wanted to show his support of it and his senior non-commissioned officer. Had my choice been on the CSM List, he would have approved my choice. At any rate, SGM Graham was foisted on the 1st Bde.

CSM Graham was a former captain, past experience made me wary of ex-officers in senior NCO ranks. A few, such as MSG Rustari at KMI, were outstanding, but most were obviously poor officers, hence poor NCOs. CSM Graham was of the latter group. In all fairness, it is possible that I did not give him the confidence I might have given one of my own choice. But Graham seemed more interested in following me around, than in doing the job I wanted him to do. Because of the heavy radio console and full load of fuel the C&C always carried, the Command Group was limited to five; myself, Al Rozon, the S-3, Wes Comfort, the ARTY LNO, MAJ Larry Johnson, the AF LNO and my RTO/driver, Rick Hanes. Even Rick was periodically left behind. There was no room in the chopper for the SGM. During my initial talks with Graham, I emphasized that he would not ordinarily fly with me. Indeed, I wanted him to move about the Brigade independently, to visit all of the companies, talk to the men and keep me informed of their morale and problems. Graham was assured that each day he would be taken to any unit he desired to visit, and picked up again that evening. But every day, without fail, Graham would accost me as I prepared to leave the CP and ask wistfully if he could accompany me in the C&C ship. The answer was always the same. Graham did not move about the Brigade as I wanted him to, but seemed always on his way to Div HQ to a meeting with the Div SGM. He did the Brigade little good.

As may be apparent, the Command Sergeant Major program was not well received by me. It seemed to me that the Army had created a job for senior NCOs which had little substance. Again, I must assume responsibility for not using CSM Graham more effectively, but he would not do what I wanted him to do. One day on my return to the CP, one of my battalion commanders called. He asked if I had any problems with the quality or punctuality of the officer efficiency reports submitted by him. Puzzled, I told him that there was no problem with his reports. "Where did you get the idea that anything is amiss?"

"CSM Graham informed the Battalion Sergeant Major that Division was unhappy with the way efficiency reports were being rendered, and the fact that so many were submitted late. I wondered if we were guilty on that score?"

"No, there are no problems with efficiency reports in the Brigade. Believe me, if there were, you would be the first to hear it from me. Forget whatever you heard from the Sergeant Major."

Hanging up, I summoned Graham. "What is this you are putting out to the units about efficiency reports, Sergeant Major?"

"I was going to tell you about that, Colonel. At a Division Sergeants Major meeting today, the G-l Sergeant Major told us that there is a serious problem with efficiency reports in the 9th Division, and that General O'Connor was getting upset about it. I thought I would jack up everyone in the 1st Bde before he lowered the boom on us."

"Did you talk to MAJ Townsley, the S-1, about it first?"

"No, sir, I didn't get a chance."

"Well, how do you know there is a problem in the 1st Bde?"

"Oh, the G-l Sergeant Major told us that all of the units were in trouble."

"Well, get this straight, Sergeant Major. Efficiency reports are of great concern to me as well as to my officers, and I keep close check on them. There is no problem with them in this Brigade. You have neither the authority nor the responsibility to put out matters of policy to the subordinate units unless you have been given specific instructions, as you have been given in the cases of police, courtesy and uniforms. In particular, I never want you to go to a meeting at Division and pass on information to the units, except in the areas mentioned, without first checking with the Adjutant, Colonel Hassett or me. You are not in the policymaking chain. I will not tolerate a shadow chain of command. Is that clear?"

"Yes, sir. I was only trying to help."

The Command Sergeant Major program continued to trouble me over the years. There were many outstanding people in the program, such as CSM Dunn of the 101st Airborne Division. But there were also many outstanding Sergeants Major who were not in the program, such as SGM Allen of THE REGULARS, and SGM Batton of the Ace Board. One of the most effective Sergeants Major I ever served with was a staff NCO, a medic, SGM Pace. I continued to be uneasy with the shadow chain of command which developed as a result of this program. There was a lot of wheeling and dealing going on, particularly in the assignment of NCOS that I did not think was good for the Army. Ultimately, clearly defined responsibilities were assigned to Command Sergeants Major and these experienced and dedicated professionals now seem to be making a meaningful contribution to the Army.

The 1st Bde spent about three weeks in Bearcat this time which gave the new S-3 and Bn COs a chance to take hold of their duties. LTC Hassett had done an outstanding job in building the Brigade area; I was well pleased with the comfortable lay-out within the Bearcat perimeter.

An officers' dining room had been set up in the HHC Mess Hall. It was an addition to the enlisted mess, using the same kitchen but with a separate entrance. There was a bar so that officers could have a drink before dinner. The enlisted men had beer, and used the mess as a club. The mess was a good one, considering the situation, due in large measure to the excellent supervision of a dedicated warrant officer, Tom Lash, the Brigade Food Service Supervisor.

A house trailer had been provided for each brigade commander. It was part of a shipment of several hundred house trailers purchased as temporary housing following a hurricane and then sent to Vietnam for use as offices or quarters. The 9th Div received enough trailers so that one was assigned to each Brigade for the Commander's quarters. It had a bathroom, two bedrooms and a living-room, dining-room-kitchen combination. LTC Hassett had it wired for electricity; I could shave and use the refrigerator, but since there was no sewage, I used the officers' latrine and shower.

While in Bearcat this time, I became concerned about the continuing security mission for the Long Binh area called OPN Uniontown. The CG of IIFFV had assigned the responsibility for the security of Long Binh to the 9th Div, the CG had passed the mission to the 1st Bde. When I was out of the area on other missions, the DIVARTY CDR or the 9th DISCOM assumed command of Uniontown. One Bn from each Div in II Field Force, the 1st, 9th or 25th, was rotated into the Uniontown area for a one-month tour of duty. A base camp had been constructed for the Uniontown force in the eastern part of the Long Binh complex. All units hated the duty. Eventually MG DePuy and MG Tillson talked LTG Weyand, now the IIFFV Commander, out of the mission and it devolved

428

on the 9th Div to handle it entirely. During my tenure as Commander of Uniontown, I did have one battalion from the 1st and 25th Divisions, but most of the time one of my units, the 2/39, the 4/39, or the 2/47 had the mission. As CDR of Uniontown I tied in closely with the IIFFV G-3, initially Tom Tarpley from the Infantry Advance Class.

After a thorough study of the mission and fire plans, I became alarmed about split responsibility and the complex nature of the coordination of fires. The Uniontown Bn CO had responsibility for security outside the perimeter of Long Binh. The CDR of Long Binh Post had responsibility for security inside the perimeter. ARVN units in the area were involved as was the Bien Hoa Province Chief. There was also a special Bien Hoa Military District, which was not responsible to either the Province Chief or the local ARVN commander. There appeared to be no effective coordination between these HQ. After much effort and talk, I was able to persuade everyone involved that some sort of joint tactical operations center was needed, if only with an LNO from each element concerned. The clearance of fires would be expedited, if nothing else. This was eventually established.

USARV HQ, commanded by LTG Bruce Palmer, was located at Long Binh. The Chief of Staff, USARV, was BG Robert Taber, who had been CofS of the 8th Div in Germany. The USARV DCSOPS was BG George Young, with whom I had served in the past.

While studying the Uniontown mission, I stopped by to see George Young. He asked me to give him an informal briefing on the external security measures for Long Binh. As a personal favor, I was happy to do so. Security was provided by patrolling. Each night the Uniontown Bn sent out listening posts, moving patrols and ambush patrols; of course, the pattern varied each night. George thanked me for the briefing. I mentioned the matter to MG O'Connor the next time I saw him.

A few days later George called and apologetically asked if I would brief BG Taber, who had evinced great interest in the security of Long Binh. This briefing concerned me, not only did I have reservations about briefing BG Taber based on our past relationship, but the matter was getting out of channels. USARV was dealing directly with a subordinate commander three echelons below. This is never in the best interests of the Army. Reluctantly agreeing because George had asked, I told him of my concern about getting out of proper channels. He agreed, but said that BG Taber had specifically asked for the briefing. In my opinion the request should have gone to IIFFV, then to the 9th Div, finally to me. I did not have a chance to talk with either the 9th Div CofS or the CG before the briefing.

When George and I entered BG Taber's office, he greeted me cordially. The briefing was completed without interruption. After the formal presentation, Taber asked several questions. Then he began to take the plan apart; he "felt" that more patrols should be in "this area" than "that"; ultimately he told me to reconfigure the entire plan. Politely but firmly, I resisted his instructions, but he kept insisting that the changes be made. For instance, he was concerned that LTG Palmer's office window was within rifle range of the perimeter of Long Binh Post and wanted a permanent patrol in that area. When it was pointed out that there were always patrols in that general vicinity but that it would not be tactically sound to maintain a constant patrol there, he became incensed. Again, I resisted; to pattern the patrol plan would be counter-productive as well as dangerous, exposing the men to possible ambush. Taber insisted the plan be altered. Finally, losing patience, I told him that the plan had been approved by the 9th Division Commander, MG O'Connor, and by the IIFFV Commander, LTG Weyand, and that his comments or recommended changes should be directed through those channels. In conclusion, I told him that it was not proper for me to make changes based on his recommendations or orders. Obviously unhappy, he let me go.

George was apologetic when we left, but offered no solution. On returning to Bearcat, I immediately went to see MG O'Connor. When he heard my story he was amused, saying "Well, we will never hear any more about it, Don, but I'm glad you told me." That ended the matter.

After three weeks in Bearcat, the 1st Bde was ordered to conduct an operation in the northeast of Bien Hoa Province, across the Song Be River, in conjunction with the 18th ARVN Div. Intelligence indicated that the rocket attacks on Bien Hoa Airbase were coming from that area. Our mission was to search for rocket sites or VC assembly areas.

While Al Rozon was drafting the plan, I went to talk with BG Giai. Happy to cooperate, he placed all his troops north of the river OPCON to me: one 18th ARVN Div Bn and one Vietnamese Marine Bn. The only command problem I had during the operation was with the USMC LTC advising the Vietnamese Marine Bn who wanted to use gung-ho USMC tactics. It was not that kind of an operation, but he was assured that if contact was made, the Vietnamese Marine Bn would be involved.

OPN Rocket was conducted by the 2/39 and 2/47, the 4/39 had the Uniontown mission and the 3/5 CAV was operating elsewhere. No contact was made during the relatively short operation, though several possible rocket sites were located which we planned to keep under surveillance. Its importance to me was that it gave Al Rozon and me a chance to shake down together as CO/S-3. I was very happy with Al as the S-3.

During Rocket, Ken Trinkler reluctantly departed for his assignment with the III Corps Advisory Team. MAJ Vidal Rodriguez, the XO of the 2/39, assumed command. He was an intense Puerto Rican who took his command responsibilities very seriously. He did not have the 2/39 long, because of his grade, but while in command he did a competent job. The Bn S-3, CPT Gene Shaw, and his Asst, CPT Dick Pack, a handsome, aggressive ABN OFF, almost overwhelmed Rodriguez on several occasions, but he managed to curb their enthusiasm.

During OPN Rocket, Al completed the plans for the next operation, Akron I. The Brigade returned to Bearcat only long enough to resupply; in two days it was operating a few miles to the southeast of it. Akron I involved an air assault by the 2/39 and one company of the 4/39, and a ground movement by the 2/47 MECH, the 3/5 CAV and the remainder of the 4/39. The mission was to locate the Hot Dich and Phuoc Chi VC base areas, flush out the enemy and destroy his installations. A secondary task was to locate the 274th VC Regiment which intelligence said controlled VC operations in the area southeast of Bien Hoa.

There was no major fighting during Akron I. Several small contacts were made in which 17 VC were killed, 1 captured and 26 suspects were detained. In addition, 50 weapons were captured and 7,461 rounds of ammunition destroyed. The Bde suffered 7 killed and 72 wounded, mostly from mines. A number of large tunnel and bunker complexes were located and destroyed. GEN Abrams, DEPCOMUSMACV, visited the area to observe the technique used in flushing the tunnels; an air blower forced smoke and tear gas into the underground complex. When the smoke surfaced, alternate entrances were revealed, identifying the entire complex, which was destroyed

It was during Akron I that the 1/9 Bde was introduced to the Rome Plow. Rome Plows are heavy-duty bulldozers with large cutting blades honed to keen sharpness. Under the protection of the 2/47 and 3/5 they cut into the jungle, opening trails and roads to permit safer passage, as well as exposing and destroying bunker complexes. The blades, which could cut down sizeable trees, easily knifed their way through the jungle.

Toward the end of Akron I, LTC Mike Lee joined the Bde and assumed command of the 2nd Bn, 39th IN. Lee was a handsome, articulate and ambitious officer who quickly asserted his control over the 2/39. Rodriguez once again reverted to XO.

Ten or 15 miles to the east of Bearcat was the 11th Armored Cavalry base camp, Black Horse; at that time the 11th CAV was commanded by COL Bill Farley, a War College classmate. Since the 11th CAV was OPCON to the 9th Div, I saw Bill at many meetings.

The road between Bearcat and Black Horse was heavily overgrown. During Akron I, the Rome Plows cut the jungle back a hundred yards on either side to give better observation, thus permitting safer movement. The 2/47 and 3/5 did not like the task of securing the Rome Plows, but it was an important one. The duty gave each of the units an opportunity to saturate the area with patrols and to check out possible VC base camps.

About this time civic action, a centerpiece of President Kennedy's counterinsurgency program of 1961-63, was revived and once again became an important element in Vietnam. All military units were ordered to get involved in civic actions, including "MEDCAPS". During MEDCAPS, a team of medical specialists, including a doctor if he could be spared, was sent to hamlets or villages to give emergency medical care. Though not a satisfactory solution, it did provide some medical coverage to areas in which the Vietnamese had none. On occasion a "county fair" was held, with entertainment, instruction, and distribution of food and supplies. These county fairs were normally held in conjunction with MEDCAPS. Units built playgrounds for children, repaired schools, temples and churches, and did other civic action work; such activities became routine during many operations when there was limited contact. During Akron I, one MEDCAP was conducted and one playground built. With the conclusion of Akron I at the end of June, the 1/9 returned to Bearcat.

The lack of any major contact or sizeable body count on Akron I and preceding operations concerned me. An increasing importance was being put on body count in Vietnam at this time. The success of an operation was equated with the size of the body count; those operations in which no large numbers of enemy were killed or large numbers of weapons collected, were looked upon as unsuccessful. MG O'Connor, unconvinced that this was the ultimate criterion, did not put undue emphasis on it. However, MACV was beginning to take body count very seriously; most divisions used it as a measure of effectiveness. The result was predictable; soldiers began counting two bodies where there was only one. An additional category, "probable body count", made its appearance; imaginations were unleashed estimating these "probables". In time, the body count system got out of control.

Since the 1st Bde had no major contacts or great body counts, I looked over our operations carefully. Were we too cautious? Were our tactics sound? Was our intelligence reliable? Were operations compromised during coordination with the Vietnamese? What was the problem? The result of my analysis was reassuring. The Bns were aggressive and effective, the tactics sound, and intelligence reliable. The 1st Bde was doing a good job, carrying out its real mission, which was to provide security to the area. The enemy was avoiding contact, perhaps driven into base areas outside the Bde AO. The matter of body count ceased to distress me.

And so the pattern evolved. The 1st Bde would return to Bearcat for a week or so, get itself cleaned up and resupplied, then leave on another operation. Most of the operations were in Bien Hoa Prov. As a result there was considerable coordination and cooperation with the Province Chief, LTC Tran Van Hai, and his Senior Advisor, LTC Erik Johnson. Erik's son Richard, was my godson. Erik and I conferred frequently. The Bde received good cooperation from LTC Hai, not only because of Erik's influence, but also due to the fact that Dan Baldwin had been Hai's advisor in the past. Bien Hoa, considered a critical province, always had a senior ARVN officer as its Province Chief.

The 39th Infantry Regiment was called the Fighting Falcons. LT Jimmy Vanderpool of the 4/39 wrote a Fighting Falcons rallying song to the tune of a popular song. Dan Baldwin seized upon it, insisting that all of his officers and men learn it. They would sing it at the slightest pretext. For some reason, this irked Mike Lee and the 2/39. Dan, knowing this, made sure the song was sung whenever there was a mixture of the two battalions. This served to underline the rivalry between the two, which was on the whole, healthy. Sadly, it became a personal matter between Danny and Mike. Luckily, no major difficulty developed; the Bde was not in garrison long enough and the two commanders did cooperate effectively in combat.

On 3 July 1967, the 1st Bde initiated a continuing operation called "Riley" a cover operation for the external security of the Long Binh/Bien Hoa/Bearcat complex. A major mission was the support of the "revolutionary development" program in Bien Hoa Province, providing security for MEDCAPS, civic action programs, and the clearing of the verges of roads so that vehicular traffic would be less vulnerable to ambush.

In the first 60 days of OPN Riley, the 1/9 conducted seven battalion, 14 Co and 247 Plt airmobile assaults. A number of "buddy operations" were conducted in conjunction with ARVN and RFPF units. The results were not spectacular: 108 VC KIA, 18 POWs, five Chieu Hoi (ralliers), and 133 detainees processed; but the penetration provided security for the major complexes and for revolutionary development programs. There were no attacks on any of the villages or hamlets in the Riley AO during its lifetime; this I took as a measure of its effectiveness. In one week of the operation, 22 - 29 Aug, 23 weapons, 17 directional mines and over 12,000 rounds of ammunition were captured.

The Chieu Hoi program, also called Open Arms, was an attempt to get the VC to defect. In it the Government of Vietnam (GVN) offered communists who "rallied" a political pardon, the opportunity to take vocational training, and help in finding jobs. I was unable to assess its effectiveness, since only limited numbers crossed over to our units.

Whenever the Bde operated in the Riley mode, the 4/39 moved into the Nhon Trach Dist of Bien Hoa Prov, southwest of Bearcat. The terrain in the northern part of the District, along the Song Tri Vai River, was high, relatively dry ground. Since it then sloped toward the sea, southern Nhon Trach was mostly swamp and marsh, cut by estuaries from the Song Tri Vai and Saigon Rivers and the ocean itself. Dan Baldwin established his CP in the Phu Thanh Rubber Plantation in central Nhon Trach, from which he conducted many operations.

The 2/47 was assigned Cong Thanh Dist, north of Long Binh and east of Bien Hoa City. The terrain there was relatively high and open, permitting the use of the APCs. Each time the Bde assumed the Riley posture, LTC Moreland moved his tracks up Highway 15 to get to his District.

The 2/39 covered Long Thanh Dist, just south of the Bearcat perimeter. Much of it was covered by the Binh Son Rubber Plantation. The plantation was infested with VC who threatened the workers in an attempt to keep them under communist control. A lovely villa, the home of the plantation manager, located in a park-like clearing in the center of the plantation, became a permanent CP for one 2/39 Co, which used it as a base for operations. One of its patrols was lost; when found after a major search, three of the men had been shot through the back of the head. Initially it was reported that they had been executed by the VC. This was never proven to my satisfaction, but the suspicion remained in the minds of the troops.

In mid-July, the 3rd Bde temporarily relieved the 1/9 of the Riley Mission, putting one company in each district; a 25th Div Bn assumed responsibility for the Uniontown OPN. The 1st Bde then moved to Phuoc Tuy Prov (southeast of Bien Hoa) for OPN Paddington. Just before we left Bearcat, while on my way to see BG Giai to coordinate the use of ARVN forces for Paddington, the C&C ship was forced to land in the area between Bien Hoa and Xuan Loc. The pilot called a "May Day", and indicated that a "Code 6" (colonel) was involved. While it wasn't known VC country, it was definitely not under friendly control. In a very short time there were gunships and other helicopters in the area. I'm sure that all pilots took comfort from the fact that a "May Day" call resulted in such prompt protection and assistance. The first aircraft to arrive, a CH-47 cargo helicopter, took me to Bearcat. It was indicative of the effective communications enjoyed in Vietnam as well as how the entire aviation community was geared to assist any aircraft in trouble.

Paddington, targeted against the 274th VC Regiment, was conducted jointly with the 1st Australian Task Force. The 2/47 was placed OPCON to the Australian Task Force, while the 1st Bde operated with the 2/39, 4/39, and the 3/5 CAV; BG Giai placed the 2/43rd ARVN Bn under my OPCON. It was a moderately successful operation in which there were 28 VC and 5 US killed, but only three weapons captured. We succeeded in sealing the area in which intelligence indicated the

VC Regt operated, but during the night a procession of women, children and Buddhist monks left the area. The 4/39th wanted to fire on them, but I refused to give them permission, directing them to round up the refugees instead. This was difficult to do; many escaped, including members of the 274th VC Regt, no doubt.

During Paddington, I had an altercation with the Div Provost Marshall (PM). Whenever the 1st Bde went on an operation, the "Brigade Slice" of Div support was attached to it. This included the DS ARTY Bn, the 1/11, Co A of the EN Bn, a medical det, an ordnance det, an MP Plt and an intelligence section. According to the PM the MP Plt was provided for internal traffic control in the Bde CP and for securing and handling POWs. In order to put the maximum number of men out scouring the area for VC, I pared the CP security to the bone. To insure that only people authorized access to the TOC were admitted, I directed the MP Plt Ldr to place a man at the entrance with a roster of those cleared for entry. The PM visited the Bde CP shortly after Paddington started; he informed me that using MPs on the TOC was an improper use of military police and that I should cease such a practice immediately. His timing was poor; I lit into him, making it clear to him that I commanded the 1st Bde and would use the assets provided me in any way I saw fit. He then stated that if I did not take the MP off the TOC, he would order the MP Plt back to Bearcat. I locked his heels and pointed out that he no longer had control of the MP Plt once it was attached to the Bde by the Div CG. Those MPs were mine to use as I saw fit. He became excited, declaring that he was going to pursue the matter with the Chief of Staff and the Division Commander. Nothing happened. On returning to Bearcat, I mentioned the matter to Maury Kendall, the CofS. He grinned as he said, "Yes, he came in and talked to me about it. I told him that they were your troops and you could do with them what you liked." It was essential to use assets to get maximum return. A tactical CP in the field required no traffic control, most people came by helicopter. POWs, when captured, would be handled as the situation required. Hence the MPs had no real function. It was ridiculous to take soldiers from a rifle platoon to control access to the TOC when MPs were available. The matter was resolved and no more was said about it.

As a result of contacts made during Paddington, Danny Baldwin arranged an officer exchange program with the 1st Australian Task Force. He would send one of his lieutenants to the Task Force, which in turn would send him an Australian of similar grade. The Australian officers sent to the 4/39th were truly outstanding and aggressive. They remained in one of the 4/39 rifle companies for two to four weeks.

On returning to Bearcat, the 1/9 once again assumed the Riley mission; the battalions deployed to the districts they were securing, the 3/5 CAV reverted to Division control. During a minor engagement, one company entered a village in which it received small arms fire. The Co CO, enraged that his men were being fired upon from the Vietnamese houses, ordered four of them burned. On receiving word of the burning, I went to look at the situation. Once the facts were clear, I relieved the Co CO on the spot. As soon as possible, I informed his Bn CO that the captain had been relieved for violating the Rules of Engagement. It was contrary to those rules to destroy any Vietnamese dwelling unless there was a military necessity to do so. Every attempt was made to minimize the damage and destruction resulting from American operations. In justifying his action, the Co CO claimed that the houses were VC strongholds and that he could not operate in the area without jeopardizing his men unless the houses were destroyed. This did not appear to be the case, the captain had knowingly violated the Rules of Engagement; this could not be condoned.

General Harold K. Johnson, the Chief of Staff of the Army, visited the 9th Div and the 1st Bde during Riley. First briefed on the operation, he was then taken to visit the positions of the 2/39 and 4/39. He indicated concern over some of the bunkers under construction. MG DePuy, CG of the 1st Div, had devised what was called the "DePuy Bunker", a good defensive position, but one that had to be modified to fit the high water table in the Nhon Trach. GEN Johnson questioned these modifications, concerned that they might not provide maximum protection to the troops, an objective everyone was trying hard to achieve.

During the visit the SGM of the Army attended all of the briefings given to GEN Johnson, rather than going out on his own, as I thought he should have, to talk with the NCOs and soldiers. Hence he gained no additional insight into matters in Vietnam. He did little to help the CofS assess the situation. The CSM Program continued to disappoint me.

"OPN Corral", a unique action conducted during Riley, was evolved by Mike Lee and his S-3, Gene Shaw, based on constant intelligence reports of VC infrastructure in Bien Go Village, due west of Long Binh. The village had originally supported the workers of the rubber plantation which was destroyed in order to build the Long Binh complex. The plan was to seal the village, and in conjunction with RFPF and National Police, search it thoroughly, house by house, interrogating every inhabitant. The major problem was to coordinate with the RAG (River Army Group) boats, RFPF, and National Police without compromising the target area. Erik Johnson was invaluable in accomplishing this; he and LTC Hai arranged matters without disclosing the objective.

Bien Go was to be cordoned using US troops, after which the RFPF and National Police would be brought in. Experience had demonstrated that the best time to conduct a successful cordon and search of a village was between 1200 and 1400. The VC, like other Vietnamese, rested at this time, hence were less alert. Lee chose 1200 as the time to spring his trap. One Co, using RAG boats, sealed the river side, elements of the other two Cos made simultaneous airmobile assaults on three sides, completely sealing the area without warning. When notified that the cordon was complete, LTC Hai brought in RFPF and National Police to conduct the search and interrogation.

Although no fire fights developed, several US soldiers were wounded by exploding land mines, booby traps and snipers. After several days, tempers began to fray, the troops became convinced that the village was inhabited solely by VC. They treated the villagers more and more harshly, even taking personal objects as souvenirs. One soldier took a small statue of Buddha from one of the temples, causing great indignation among the local population. The situation was explosive. Erik Johnson, who had learned of it through Vietnamese channels, notified me. Together with LTC Hai and Erik, I went to Bien Go immediately. Between us, we managed to defuse the situation before it erupted into violence. On my orders, Mike Lee called together his OFFs and NCOs, to whom I re-emphasized the Rules of Engagement and reviewed American policy in Vietnam. I ordered that the statue be found, even if it required a shakedown inspection of all US troops, and the culprit punished. Finally, I directed the OFFs and NCOs to talk with their men to insure that no additional difficulty developed. With LTC Hai and Erik Johnson working in the same manner with the Vietnamese, an ugly confrontation was avoided.

During the four days Bien Go was cordoned, the 2/39 conducted MEDCAPS and other civic actions. American and Vietnamese intelligence people interviewed every adult in the village as well as many children. In all, 64 villagers were actually detained for further interrogation. Some were draft dodgers, one was an ARVN LT AWOL from his unit. Only a handful were identified as part of the VC infrastructure. These were taken to the National Police HQ in Bien Hoa; their disposition was never reported to the Brigade.

Also during Riley, the 4/39 Recon Plt conducted OPN Martz. For three days the Plt patrolled the Song Tri Vai River in engineer boats, searching the lower reaches of the Nonh Trach where the rivers and estuaries cut up the land. During that one-platoon operation 12 VC were killed and 11 weapons captured. A search of the area a few days later by an ARVN unit produced nine additional weapons which the intelligence people assumed had been hidden by wounded. One US soldier was killed and 16 wounded in the operation, however.

While operating in the Nhon Trach, the 4/39 experimented with Plt assaults at the conclusion of which the platoon minus one squad was extracted. The squad was left on the ground to ambush any VC who came to search the area formerly occupied by US units. This technique resulted in good contact on several occasions.

With the three battalions deployed in their Riley configuration, I operated from the Bde CP at Bearcat. Everyday, I spent most of the daylight hours visiting Bns and Cos, returning late in the afternoon to attend to administration.

Being in Bearcat I got to know the Div Staff well. In addition, there were opportunities to discuss Bde operations and other matters with BG Roseborough and MG O'Connor. I saw eye to eye on most matters with Bill Richardson, an imaginative G-3, and Fitzmorris, who had been the 1st Bde S-3 when I assumed command, was in his section. Every Sunday evening, MG O'Connor had a meeting which all brigade commanders attended. The purpose was to allocate resources for the ensuing week. Each brigade commander presented his proposed plan of operations, including those they wanted to undertake if not directed by Div. O'Connor, on the recommendation of his Staff, would then allocate the resources, particularly helicopters and artillery. There was keen competition as the Bde CDRs vied with each other to get the resources they needed for the week. I doubt whether the 1st Bde got more than its fair share of assets, but I was usually satisfied. It appeared that I enjoyed MG O'Connor's confidence; certainly he was tolerant of my idiosyncrasies. Another advantage of working out of Bearcat was the opportunity to attend the evening briefings at the Div CP to find out what was going on, what the other brigades were doing, and what resources I might obtain that were found to be excess to the needs of the other brigades.

Being in Bearcat also made it easy to keep abreast of supply and personnel matters, stay on top of paperwork and visit the wounded in the hospitals. Every Sunday it became routine to visit the hospitals to talk with members of the 1st Bde confined to them. A Liaison NCO was stationed at one of the hospitals to keep track of 1st Bde officers and men. He had a list with the hospital and ward number of each of those hospitalized. It was a sad chore for me to visit them, though the morale of most seemed high. Some were badly shot up and could look forward only to permanent disability, but they remained cheerful. Happily, most had less serious wounds. CSM Graham always accompanied me on these visits.

One of the advantages of the Vietnamese War (if such it can be called) was almost immediate availability of helicopter (DUSTOFF) ambulances which evacuated casualties from the battlefield to a hospital in record time. There was minimum delay between the time men were wounded and the time they received definitive medical care. This played a major role in reducing deaths or permanent disability. Like most commanders in Vietnam, I believed that it was my obligation to make sure that my wounded soldiers understood that they weren't just a cipher in the medical system. Though they had been dropped from our rolls, everyone in the 1st Bde was still interested in their welfare and would continue to look out for them. On these visits periodic complaints surfaced: they weren't getting their mail, or they weren't getting personal items they needed such as shaving gear. CSM Graham would take the list, follow up on the complaints, and report on the action taken. This was one of the missions I had assigned him and he did a good job in this matter. He was also urged to make other visits to the hospitals on his own.

Bill Fulton was promoted to BG and COL Bert David assumed command of the 2nd Bde (Riverine Force). Fulton was given supervision of that particular part of the 9th Div AO because of his experience with the Riverine Force and his knowledge of the area. It seemed to me that this was unfortunate because he continued to look over Bert David's shoulder. Since Bill had organized, trained and commanded the Riverine Force, he was naturally tied to it. His presence didn't give Bert full opportunity to exercise his own ingenuity and leadership. However, Bert took this in stride, doing an outstanding job.

George Everett was reassigned from the Div; before he left, I determined to see him, MAJ Townsley, my Adj, called the 3rd Bde and was informed that it was on an operation with its CP in the village of Roch Kien in Long An Prov. My pilot, who knew the area, put me down in the small village. Immediately, I sensed that something was wrong. Normally when a chopper lands, children, and many adults, crowd around it. When Americans walk into a village, the children smile and wave. There were no children in evidence in this village and the few adults visible were furtive and obviously frightened. This was clear evidence the VC controlled the village. Without more ado, I hurried back to the helicopter. Fortunately, the pilot had not shut down the engine, and I shouted to him to take off immediately. We left without incident. Later I learned that I had been given the wrong village. The 3rd Bde did in fact occupy Roch Kien later on.

Bearcat was a huge, sprawling complex with an extended perimeter, protected with barbed wire, bunkers, and an earth wall. The 1st Bde had no responsibility for the security of the perimeter, OPS Riley and Uniontown occupied it fully. The 9th DIVARTY and DISCOM shared the onus for the Bearcat security. During one stand-down, the Base Security CDR wanted the Bde to man part of the perimeter, insisting that it do this whenever in garrison. This was not reasonable, in my view; these occasional, short stand-downs gave the riflemen a chance to relax and rehabilitate themselves and their equipment. Under pressure, I agreed to provide a few troops for a sector of the perimeter on a permanent basis. The 1st Bde sector would be manned by the rear detachment, mostly maintenance, supply and administrative personnel. This was not particularly onerous; the sector manned was small, the duty rotated throughout the Bde so no man had it more than once every five or six days. The 1st Bde did have a counterattack role if it was in camp. To insure that all troops were ready for an attack, Div held periodic Red Alerts, during which all troops prepared to defend the perimeter or assembled as a counterattack force.

One evening a cold made me so miserable that I went to bed about 2230. Routinely, I did my administrative work in the evening. During the daytime I was out visiting units, reconnoitering, effecting coordination, or checking defenses. This evening the paperwork was put aside; after taking a couple of aspirin I finally got to sleep. Immediately, the phone rang, Al Rozon informed me that a Red Alert had been declared. Normally, I would be heading for the TOC before Al could hang up, but this evening he was instructed to carry on; if anything serious developed, he was to give me a call. In about 15 minutes, Al called again to tell me that MG O'Connor was in the TOC asking for me. He periodically visited each of the units during a Red Alert, so it was no surprise, though I was a bit chagrined because I had not been there when he arrived. When I explained why I hadn't been at the TOC when he arrived, O'Connor dismissed the matter. He wanted to discuss the build-up in intelligence in the Hot Dich area that Al had called to his attention. We were watching it as a possible area for an operation, though I had not yet approached Div about it. O'Connor, interested in it based on Al's enthusiastic talk, wanted to know what I had in mind.

My plan for Akron II or Bolt was to put a B-52 strike in the area, followed immediately by an airmobile operation. Intelligence indicated that it was the HQ of the 274th VC Regiment which controlled the area southeast of Bien Hoa. The target was about 15 miles east of Bearcat. MG O'Connor was particularly interested in the operation because of the special intelligence (SI) reports on the area. He wanted to study it a bit more but told me to develop the plan on a priority basis. Within the next three days the intelligence became conclusive; by means of radio intercept the VC HQ was pinpointed. MG O'Connor requested that an Arc Light be diverted to that area and allocated enough helicopters to lift a full battalion. The day selected, the slicks were on the Long Thanh Airstrip, just outside Bearcat, ready for the 2/39 to load for the initial assault. The 4/39 would follow on the second lift; the 2/47 was on Uniontown, but would join the Bde later.

The Arc Light went as scheduled; the Command Group, airborne in the C&C, saw it hit the target. Immediately, the 2/39, already loaded in the slicks, was ordered to commence its air assault. The LZs were cold, though it was evident that the B-52 strike had hit the enemy CP. There were only a few bodies, but a great deal of ammunition, weapons, radios, signal equipment and other materiel was policed up. The equipment, especially some RPGs, switchboards and radios, was new and of the latest issue. Understandably, it was of great interest to the intelligence community. For one week the Bde conducted an intensive search of the area, which was checker-boarded, each square being carefully searched in turn. GEN Westmoreland visited the 1/9 CP during OPN Bolt, especially interested in the new RPGs. Finally, the 2/47 joined us by land and although we spent another week looking for the 274th VC Regiment, we never did make contact with it.

During Bolt, Danny Baldwin received a quick lesson. Before assuming command of the 4/39, he had been briefed on the shortage of helicopters for command and control (C&C) at Bn level. The Staff had impressed on him, however, that an OH-23 could always be diverted for his use in the event of a contact. Dan the consummate Infantryman, dismissed this airily, asserting that he would control his Battalion from the ground. After one day of operating in the Hot Dich area, he suddenly realized that though he could talk with his companies, he had no idea where they were, what their situation was, what sort of terrain they were in, or where they were heading. He was only aware of the situation in the company he was with. Sheepishly, he asked for an OH-23 for the next day, and spent over eight hours in the air.

While the 1st Bde was on Akron II (Bolt), the Div celebrated MG O'Connor's birthday. The CofS had notified all brigade commanders that there was to be a celebration in the CG's mess to which they were invited. Maury Kendall, the Chief, suggested that each unit think up some gimmick as a birthday gift for the Div CG. It needed little thought for me to determine that the 1st Bde was going to give him a python. MG O'Connor's call sign was Python 6; a six-foot python was needed. Word went out to find a python. Periodically, some unit would come across one in the jungle. All Bns were told that if any of their troops came across a python, they were to capture it. Luckily, just before the birthday, an SF Team came upon a six-foot python. Al Rozon, who had served with the Green Berets, had put out a desperate call to them.

On the evening of the celebration one of the Bde units was in a fire fight, so I refused to leave the area. The Bde S-5, MAJ Adams, stood in for me. He did not partake of the dinner but sat unobtrusively in the rear of the room. When the presentations were to be made (he had already coordinated with COL Kendall) the 1st Bde was called on first. MAJ Adams walked forward and said, "Sir, on behalf of COL Seibert and the "First and Foremost" Brigade, I wish to extend heartiest wishes to the Commanding General on his birthday". With this, Adams extended his hand. The python was wrapped about his arm with the head in the palm of his hand. As O'Connor reached out to shake hands, he glanced down to see the snake's head weaving back and forth. He quickly retracted his hand. Adams unwrapped the six-foot python and gravely presented it to the CG, who gingerly passed it to his aide. The aide hated snakes! The python became quite an attraction; a cage was constructed for it located outside Div HQ. Every ten days the Div HQ CMDT would buy a live chick or duck from the local market. Quite a group gathered each time a fowl was put in the cage to watch the python coil around it, break all of its bones, then swallow it whole. Python Six would then lay quietly for a week digesting its meal.

During Akron II, the weather turned bad as the monsoon season approached. On one occasion the Command Group was going into a battalion CP located adjacent to a natural clearing in the jungle.

Fog suddenly completed engulfed the C&C, causing the pilot to experience vertigo, he didn't know whether he was going up or down; he was, in fact going down when he should have been going up. Everyone became excited. Finally the co-pilot wrenched control to take the chopper above the fog. The AF LNO refused to fly in the helicopter after that experience. It was a scary moment. Weather was a constant problem in Vietnam; because of fog or other adverse climatic conditions, it was not always possible to depend on the use of the helicopter for evacuating casualties, resupplying units or maintaining personal command and control.

Bolt or Akron II ended in late August with a body count of 41 VC KIA, 4 VC POW/WIA, and 4 US KIA, 4 WIA; 29 weapons were captured (including the new type RPGs), much communications equipment found, and about 11,500 rounds of ammunition were destroyed.

After Bolt, the Brigade resumed the Riley posture. In conducting the numerous platoon helicopter assaults, someone questioned why we never put the units in at dusk or even darkness. It was normal procedure to make airmobile assaults as early in the day as possible to give the unit maximum time to get away from the landing zone, find a defensive position, and get settled for the first night. In addition, visibility was important to the pilots for safe insertions. However, we began to question this logic, particularly with smaller units. Inserting units at dusk or immediately after dark might confuse the VC.

The first night insertion the 1st Bde tried was conducted by the 4/39 in the Nhon Trach area. Danny Baldwin ran the insertion, but I observed it from one of the ANTEATER OH-23s. It was highly successful. Though there was concern on the part of the Huey pilots about safety - their visibility would be reduced, hence their depth perception and judgement affected - neither the pilots nor the unit experienced difficulty. None of the night insertions resulted in immediate contact. We began to push this as an alternate to our set tactics.

LTG Weyand, Commander of IIFFV, which had its HQ at the "Plantation" in the Long Binh complex, had a weekly meeting with his division commanders, to which MG O'Connor occasionally invited me. The prominence John Vann, now USAID Advisor to the II Field Force Commander, assumed at these meetings was striking; he always sat in front with LTG Weyand, and had no hesitation in voicing his opinion on matters that were primarily military. He did not restrict himself to USAID considerations: political, economic or social. As a retired LTC, who had left the Army in part because he disagreed with the military policy of the administration, it seemed presumptuous of him to intrude his military views when LTG Weyand, MG O'Connor, MG DePuy and MG Tillson were discussing tactics. I disagreed with many of his views.

At one such meeting, I was sitting directly behind O'Connor. Danny Baldwin was with me, because the CG's call to join him at the meeting reached me while I was inspecting the 4/39 with Danny in the C&C; I brought him to the meeting. LTG Weyand told the division commanders that COMUSMACV wanted to upgrade the ARVN by having the US Army retrain them on a battalion by battalion basis. He asked the three Div CDRs how soon they could implement such a program, emphasizing the need for quick action. While the others were collecting their thoughts, MG O'Connor turned, saying, "The 1st Bde will have the mission. How soon can you be ready?"

After mulling the matter a minute, I decided to give the mission to the 4/39, Not only were they in a relatively static location in the Nhon Trach making it easier for them to handle such a mission than it would be for either of the other two battalions, but Danny's experience as an advisor would greatly enhance their understanding and execution of such a task. In turn, Danny was told that the 4/39 would conduct the training and asked how soon he could start it. Danny, ever the optimist and gung-ho type, said, "Sir, I can start in two days."

This was obviously not reasonable, so I told MG O'Connor that we would be ready for the first battalion in a week. With such an early start there was a possibility of problems with the initial ARVN Bn which entered training because we would be shaking down the course as we put them through the instruction. O'Connor nodded. MG DePuy and MG Tillson, sputtered and stammered, finally stating that it would be at least a month, perhaps two months, before they could possibly start such a program due to their commitments, the need to write lesson plans, assemble training aids and prepare an area. MG O'Connor announced, "Don Seibert will have the mission for the 9th Div. He tells me that he can take the initial battalion one week from today." Weyand was pleased; since GEN Westmoreland had made this a priority matter, he was not particularly happy with the delays the other divisions had forecast. "Good. We are going to monitor this program closely."

The 1st Bde was under the gun. Danny returned with me to Bearcat, where I outlined to him a Program of Instruction (POI), and how I thought the training should be conducted. It would include communications, mortar, machine gun and individual weapons training, scouting, patrolling, and squad, platoon and company tactics. Taking my general guidance, Dan and his staff developed an excellent program. His XO, MAJ Kamakahi, a heavy-set Hawaiian, directed the training supported by one Co, while Dan conducted operations with the remainder of the 4/39.

It was an effective training program, The ARVN responded well, largely due to BG Giai's direct interest and the fine instructors MAJ Kamakahi selected. On one visit to the training, I was astonished to find the Bn Chaplain, CPT Kirk, instructing in the Browning Automatic Rifle (BAR). Since the US Army had phased out the BAR, most junior officers were unfamiliar with it. Chaplain Kirk, who had been an enlisted BAR gunner before he went into the ministry, was a competent instructor. During the tactics training, the ARVN units conducted several air assaults and search and clear operations in the Nhon Trach with the 4/39. Dan and Kamakahi did a skillful job integrating training and actual operations.

As anticipated that first training cycle was closely supervised. Commanders and staff officers from the 9th Div, II Field Force, and MACV as well as from the 1st and 25th Divisions, visited the training site. When I checked the instruction the first time, the ARVN Bn CO called his unit to attention, completely disrupting the class. After that first incident, I gave specific orders that the class would not be interrupted for anyone including general officers. It was necessary to have a senior NCO, or officer, available at the rear of the unit to report to visitors and explain what was going on. Everyone seemed pleased with the training the 4/39 was conducting, I thought Dan and his Bn did an outstanding job.

As that program progressed, it spawned a similar one for the RFPF. But in the Ruff Puff program, American teams, usually an OFF and two or three NCOs, were placed with the RFPF companies. The teams were to train, to show by example, to upgrade the RFPF. This procedure made me uneasy because I didn't like having my soldiers with RFPF units whose dependability in combat I was not sure of. Some RFPF were good fighting units; others were poorly trained, poorly led and would run at the first shot. The possibility of having my troops abandoned in a fire fight by squeamish RFPF concerned me. Fortunately, no disasters occurred though one team had a close call-At the height of the program the 1st Bde had as many as nine teams deployed. The Bn COs were unhappy because it took OFFs and NCOs from their units. Though my policy was to take no more than one team from each company, the loss of any officers or NCOs posed problems in Vietnam.

During one phase of Riley, the 4/39, with troops in engineer boats, was sweeping the river, stopping sampans, challenging river traffic and monitoring both banks. One of the engineer boats struck a submerged mine; several men were lost when the boat was blown up. Immediately, concealed VC opened fire on the survivors and on the troops on the banks. A nasty situation developed when the company commander panicked. This sharp looking officer, who had been in the Bde S-3 Section, had pleaded for a company. After observing him for a month or so, I made him a Co CO in the 4/39. This was his first real experience commanding his company in a fire fight. Losing control, he began screaming for help over the radio, tying up the net so that his platoons could not report to him and Danny could not give him instructions or find out what he needed. Baldwin was in an OH-23; I told him over the Bde Command Net to get on the ground and straighten things out. He landed immediately, quickly got things organized, the casualties evacuated, and security restored. Later, Danny discussed the matter with me, uncertain how to proceed since I had made the decision to give the captain the company. He was a liability who should be relieved, certainly I would find it hard to trust him to lead men again. Danny, with my approval, relieved the CPT of his command. This incident concerned me because I had made an obvious error in judgement; my assessment of that CPT could not have been worse. It is hard to anticipate how anyone will react under fire; it was the only case in my experience in which an officer I trusted panicked in combat. It left me with an uncomfortable feeling.

In September, on completion of six months of command, a major decision faced me. According to the policy then in existence in Vietnam, another officer would replace me in command of the 1st Bde. This was a controversial policy, I shared the view of most officers that commanders were rotated too often and too soon. However, after 25 months in Vietnam I was reluctant to extend again. Colonels' Branch of Officer's Personnel Office (OPO), had sent several letters outlining various jobs for which I was being considered. In anticipation of my rotation I had written to COL Red Ayres, who headed Colonels' Branch, asking for an inter-theater transfer to Germany. My first tour there had lasted only a year and a half. I wanted to get back to that part of the world. Ayres' first response informed me that there was no requirement for an Infantry COL in Germany; in fact, there was an excess of Army COLs in Europe. Later, he told me that there would be an opening for a COL in HQ, USAREUR, after the first of the year, against which he had programmed me.

MG O'Connor assured me that if I stayed I could keep the 1st Bde for a full year. However, he advised me to leave Vietnam; 25 months was long enough to be exposed to the stress, climate and conditions there. During that time I had been in and out of combat situations much of the time, although as a COL I was never as fully exposed as the men in rifle companies. Based on his advice, I finally decided that when my current extension expired, at which time I would have commanded the 1st Bde seven and a half months, I would leave Vietnam. The assignment to Heidelberg was confirmed.

My request for orders authorizing me to take the Embassy Courier Flight around the world was approved. With almost 90 days of accumulated leave time, there would be leisure to visit Thailand, India, Pakistan, Arabia and Spain. From Torrejon, there was flight to Charleston, SC. In anticipation of getting off the flight at each of those countries, spending a week, then picking up the next courier as it came through, I secured the necessary visas. The trip would start by taking an R&R flight to Australia, spending a week there, then taking a courier flight to Christ Church, New Zealand, to visit my friend from Korea, Jim Denby. The courier would return me to Sydney, where I could hop an Australian Air Force plane to Singapore, only a short hop from Bangkok, where the courier flight to New Delhi would be boarded. If the itinerary was followed as planned, I would still have 15 days at home with the family at the end of December.

While working out my travel plans, a Thai Div arrived in Vietnam. The 9th Div sponsored the Thais, and a base camp was built for them on the north of the Bearcat complex. The 1st Bde, whose area was adjacent to the Thai area, was the sponsoring unit within the 9th Div. MG Chalard, now the G-3 of the Thai Army, came to effect liaison, but was not going to command the division. It was the 1st Bde's task to introduce the Thais to combat in Vietnam. Their initial baptism of fire was in the Nhon Trach with the 4/39. Later they operated with the 2/39 in their Riley AO. The Thais did not impress me in Vietnam as much as they had in Korea. For some reason it took them a long time to adjust to jungle operations, which seemed odd because the area was typical of that in which they normally operated in Thailand. They seemed hesitant to close with the enemy, lacking the aggressiveness which had characterized the "Little Tigers" in Korea. In time, part of the Riley AO was to be turned over to them.

While these plans were being developed, the 1st Bde again left the Riley configuration to operate in Phuoc Tuy Province. In addition to a determined search for VC base camps, the Brigade would again provide security for Rome Plows cutting a 200-yard swath through the jungle along trails and roads. For the first week, the operation proceeded without major incident. Then, as the Rome Plows approached the twin mountains west of Ba Ria, the "Great Find" was uncovered. LT Ron Jordan of B Co, 4/39, noted a slight depression in the ground as he was taking a break. Intrigued, he investigated, becoming convinced that it was the entrance to a tunnel. He put a claymore mine face down and detonated it. A hole opened revealing the entrance to what appeared a large complex of tunnels, storage bunkers and living quarters.

After a preliminary exploration, it was necessary to divert more and more troops to the area to explore the extensive works and to remove the supplies and equipment found. Tons of rice, mountains of ammunition, quantities of medical supplies and 1300 weapons were evacuated. Many of the weapons were new, still in cosmoline; others were older but serviceable weapons; some were junk. There were two 75mm pack howitzers, several kinds of mortars, and machine guns of every description. The Brigade had quite an arsenal when all of the materiel was collected in the CP area of the 3/5 CAV, the only unit that could provide the necessary security.

As reports of the "Great Find" were forwarded through channels, swarms of visitors descended on the area. GEN Westmoreland, LTG Weyand and MG O'Connor came almost every day to see what else had been uncovered; and each day more weapons, more ammunition, more medical supplies and food stuffs were extracted. It was the largest weapons find in Vietnam to that date. Prime Minister Ky came with GEN Cao Van Vien, Chief of the Vietnamese Joint General Staff. Vien, who had been in my class at Leavenworth, greeted me effusively. BG Giai and other ARVN OFFs also came for a look and to congratulate the 1st Bde. Reporters and photographers came in such numbers that they became a problem.

The troops liked to take pictures of the visitors. One soldier, sitting on top of an APC, attempted to take a picture of GEN Westmoreland. He seemed hesitant about it, so I asked the General if he would mind standing beside one of the weapons for a moment while the young warrior took his picture. Westmoreland, of course, agreed. Just as the soldier was about to snap his picture, the General grinned and walked over to him, saying, "Son, if you really want that picture, you had better take the dust cover off your lens." The embarrassed cameraman hastily removed the cap as GEN Westmoreland laughed and walked back to the weapon. The young man got his picture.

This haul made headlines in the papers in the United States. I was ordered to attend the MACV evening briefing for the press to talk about it. That MACV briefing was a side show! Most of the well-known reporters were there. The technique used was "show and tell". Various commanders from units which had engaged in significant actions were there along with soldiers who were being recommended for awards of valor. The MACV Press Officer had requested that I bring Ron Jordan and several weapons, which were photographed for the television programs. Some of my friends later wrote that they had seen me on TV or heard about the find on the radio. It was a shot in the arm for the 1st Bde and the troops.

The big problem was what to do with the weapons. Many of them were junk, some had intelligence value, some would make excellent hunting rifles. All of the troops wanted souvenir weapons. There were about 200 new carbines with sniper scopes that were highly desirable. MACV gave me permission to allocate most of these weapons as bona fide souvenirs. Each Bn was given an equal share, the Bn COs deciding on the ultimate distribution. Everyone insisted that I take one of the weapons. Knowing the keen interest in the sniper rifles, I elected to take a pistol, a Chinese copy of a Belgian version of the American 45 pistol. As fair as the distribution could be made, there were some hard feelings about who should or should not get souvenirs. My decision to distribute them equally among the four battalions on the operation was criticized. Even though the 4/39 had made the initial find eventually all of the units were involved in the extraction, hence the 3/5 CAV, the 2/47, the 2/39 as well as the 4/39 got their fair share of the weapons. Not all of the weapons could be kept; only rifles, pistols and carbines were legitimate souvenirs. Division, II Field Force and MACV wanted souvenirs, so the Brigade had to make do with what was left.

Shortly after the "Great Find" it was time for me to leave the 1st Bde. As the time for the change of command approached, I was certain that I had made a mistake, I really did not want to go. It was a great honor to command a brigade of American soldiers in combat, the 1st Bde had acquitted itself well and I was proud of it.

Before my departure, BG Giai invited me to Xuan Loc for a farewell dinner. He also had an 18th ARVN Div presentation ceremony during which he pinned on me the Cross of Gallantry with Palm, the Army Distinguished Service Order, and the Vietnamese National Order Fifth Class. All were high awards, which were no doubt granted as the result of my 27 months of service in Vietnam, but which really reflected BG Giai's friendship and regard.

Erik Johnson and his counterpart LTC Hai also had a party in my honor. One of the ANTEATERS flew me to Bien Hoa Prov HQ on the night of that occasion. It was a most enjoyable affair. LTC Hai gave me a bronze statue of a Vietnamese peasant plowing his field behind a water buffalo. It is a beautiful thing which I treasure to this day. There were many other gifts from the advisors and the Vietnamese. It was fortuitous that the Bde was in Bearcat for a brief stand-down. The social whirl in combat was almost too much for me! Each of the Bns had a party, dinner or luncheon at which I received mementoes of my service with them. MG O'Connor had me to dinner at his mess.

COL Williams, my replacement, arrived several days before I left. We had a chance to discuss personalities and he got a brief orientation on the terrain.

The day before the change of command there was a flare-up in the Tan Canh/Dac To area of Kontum; the1st Bde was alerted to move there. When I tried to convince MG O'Connor to let me take the Bde to Kontum since I was thoroughly familiar with the area, he refused.

Several old friends came to the change of command ceremony: COL Jack P. Pollock, the USARV Dental OFF, who had been at Carlisle with me, and COL Howard Leifheit, who had served with me at Pine Camp. Howard had visited me during a Bde stand-down; he was the Chief of Lab Service in one of the hospitals at Long Binh.

Since it was raining, the change of command ceremony, with the colors of each of the battalions together with a token force present, was held in the large maintenance tent in the "Ant Hill". As MG O'Connor pinned a Bronze Star on me he told me that it was an interim award until the Legion of Merit could be processed and approved. His intention was never fulfilled; no Legion of Merit was awarded. Since the Legion of Merit, and one Oak Leaf Cluster, had been previously awarded for service in Vietnam, I made no issue of it. But after commanding the Brigade for seven months and receiving an outstanding efficiency report, the lack of the Legion of Merit was unusual. In fact, I took perverse pride in the fact that I was probably the only colonel who commanded a brigade in Vietnam who did not receive that award. Obviously it was an administrative error. Certainly BG Roseborough and MG O'Connor had been most flattering and generous in their comments on my efficiency report. The 24th Oak Leaf Cluster to the Air Medal was also awarded as a result of over 2900 hours spent in L-19s or helicopters during the 27 months in Vietnam.

All of the awards and functions tendered me gave me a feeling that I had made some small contribution the US effort in Vietnam. But my greatest satisfaction on leaving the 1st Bde was that my tour as commander had validated the third award of the Combat Infantryman Badge. I no longer felt that I had gotten it the easy way on technicalities. It is worthy of note that only about 300 Infantrymen ever earned the third award of the CIB.

Immediately following the change of command ceremony, I went to Tan Son Nhut Airfield to catch the R&R flight to Sidney. When the Officer-in-Charge of the R&R in Sidney learned that I was not going to make the return flight he became alarmed; a colonel AWOL? He was reassured to know that my orders covered this.

The next three weeks were both enlightening and enjoyable. I found Australia a delightful country to visit. Unfortunately, my letter to Jim Denby and his letter to me crossed; when I got to Christ Church, New Zealand, and called his home, a strange voice informed me that he was in Scotland as an exchange teacher. The person on the phone was his counterpart from Scotland. Despite this disappointment, I enjoyed seeing part of New Zealand. Singapore and the Raffles Hotel were as I pictured them, though the city had grown to a modern sprawl. Bangkok was as fascinating as on my first R&R there. I toured New Delhi, drove to Agra to see the Taj Mahal and to Jaipur to see the elaborate maharajas' palaces, then flew to Khajaraho to see the famous, old temples adorned with erotic carvings. An overnight trip to Benares completed the Indian interlude. Seeing sick and diseased people, many with open sores, bathing in the filthy waters of the "Holy Ganges River" to be "cleansed" was depressing. Many were brought there to die and be cremated on the banks of the Ganges, a somber sight.

When I returned to New Delhi to catch the next courier flight, I was worn out. The letdown from Vietnam was setting in, home beckoned irresistibly. The planned visits to Pakistan and Saudi Arabia were canceled; I stayed on the plane to Torrejon, catching glimpses of Karachi and Riyadh during the brief stopovers. Finally the plane arrived at Torrejon. Because of higher priority passengers, there was an overnight wait for the next flight to Charleston. Fortunately, my orders permitted me to travel in civilian clothes.

The advantage of being a colonel became obvious as the plane neared Charleston. The crew chief asked if I wanted transportation on arrival; the pilot called ahead and ascertained that a flight to New York was leaving within a half hour after we were due to arrive. Though it seemed impossible, I determined to make that plane. Things moved swiftly after the plane landed: as the senior officer aboard, I was the first person to debark; an escort officer and staff car were waiting for me; the driver quickly retrieved my luggage and sped me directly to the terminal; the escort officer expedited my way through customs. Hurriedly thanking the escort officer, I raced to the civilian terminal. Fortunately the line was not long and in minutes I was heading for the New York plane, pausing only long enough to call Mother and tell her my flight number and ETA at Kennedy Airport. Bob, Arlene and Mother met me at Kennedy. It was a happy reunion. I could look forward to 20 days of relaxation, including Christmas with the family.

The local papers had carried the story of the 1st Bde's "Great Find" and the commander of the local American Legion post asked me to talk at their next meeting. The WWII veterans were fascinated by my account of operations in Vietnam.

Just before Christinas a teletype message (TWX) from my new boss in Heidelberg, MG Rowny, arrived. It directed me to attend during the first week in January, a VIP orientation course on the characteristics and capabilities of computers at the IBM Center in Washington.

After the first of the year, 1968, loaded for departure to Germany, I drove to Washington in the car I had bought my first day home. Wick put me up at his apartment for the duration of the course. It was an instructive and valuable orientation on computers. During that week I attended a Carlisle Class Reunion at which I saw many friends. MG Julian Ewell, who was going to Vietnam to command the 9th IN Div, had a luncheon with the members of the "team" he was taking with him. He invited me to talk with the OFFs about the Div and its operations.

At last, the computer course behind me, I drove to McGuire Air Force Base. After turning my car in at Newark for shipment to Germany there was an overnight wait for the plane to Frankfurt. Once airborne, the flight was smooth and swift, a decided contrast to the former 24 hour flight. At Rhein Main, COL Bob Borman, my sponsor and the officer I was going to replace in DCSLOG, Headquarters, US Army Europe (USAREUR) met me. Driving to Heidelberg, he gave me a brief overview of duty there.

CHAPTER 18

LOGISTICIAN

On arrival at Heidelberg, the inevitable processing was accomplished swiftly. Two rooms similar to those I had originally occupied at Mainz in 1960 were reserved for me in the BOQ across from HQ, US AREUR. While convenient to the office, they were small and offered no facilities to entertain. My query about the possibility of getting a set of family quarters was met with consternation; in agitated tones the billeting clerk told me that housing was at a premium in Europe, and that no family housing could be diverted to bachelors. Jet lag prevented me from exploding; I got to bed early that evening.

The day after my arrival in Heidelberg, I met my new boss, COL Carl Leidy, who told me to take time to get settled. The problem of quarters occupied me fully. Some helpful person in the office of the Secretary of the General Staff (SGS), suggested that one of the VIP suites at Patrick Henry Village (a housing area for US military personnel in Heidelberg about a five-minute drive from HQ) might serve my needs; each had a bedroom, bath, living room and a small kitchen. As a last resort one of those suites would have sufficed, but I wanted a place in which to entertain or to have friends stay overnight. The search continued. Eventually, someone told me of an apartment in Sandhausen, a small town about 10 minutes drive from Heidelberg. The American civilian working for US AREUR who was currently renting the apartment was about to return to the CONUS. He wanted to find an American to take it over because he had carpets, drapes and some furniture he wanted to sell. The apartment was spacious: a huge living room, a fair-sized dining area, a compact kitchen, toilet, separate bath, two bedrooms, one large, the other adequate. It was on the ground floor with a patio out back. The house, not yet completed on the outside (it was to be stuccoed), was owned by two brothers who had an apartment in the basement; two other apartments, on the second and third floors, were occupied by Americans. After one look, I signed a lease for one year, and bought whatever the departing occupant had for sale, curtains, rugs and chairs. The Billeting Officer agreed to provide any furniture needed; within two days a refrigerator, electric stove, kitchen table, a complete living room set, a dining room table with six chairs, a sideboard and furniture for two bedrooms including schranks or armoires (German houses rarely have closets) were delivered. My stereo, records, books, pictures, and other things shipped from Carlisle arrived at the same time. In short order I was comfortably situated.

It was necessary to transfer responsibility for the utilities. This became a chore; I was introduced to the famous **_Beamte_** (German Civil Servant) intractability. It was too simple to merely sign over the records; instead, each utility had to be reprocessed. Fortunately, MAJ Jaan Kurgvel volunteered to help me. Jaan was a former Displaced Person (DP) from one of the Baltic Countries, who had joined the US Army and earned his citizenship. He spoke German and several other languages fluently, and knew the German mind With his help, the telephone service was restored, the electricity was turned on again, the water flowed and finally the garbage was collected. This latter was a true triumph. Because I planned to do considerable entertaining, it appeared that a single garbage/trash can might not be enough. On applying for the sticker which had to be affixed to each can if it was to be emptied, the **_Beamte_** refused to give me approval for two cans. He told me, through Jaan, that one person could not possibly fill up more than one can per week, let alone two. One was all I would get. Jaan expostulated in vain. But the **_Beamte_** reckoned with an equally stubborn American, descendant of

Germans on both parental lines; he had met his match! Between Jaan and me, we overwhelmed even that bastion of officialdom, and left the office triumphantly with stickers for two cans. Subsequent events proved the wisdom of that battle.

Since my car would not arrive for some time, I rented one from a German car rental agency. It turned out to be expensive, but in a few weeks notice was received that my car had arrived at Bremerhaven. Apparently the timing had been good; when the car was turned in at Newark it was put on a ship which left shortly. One of the NCOs from the office went to Bremerhaven by train, picked up the car and drove it back to Heidelberg for me. That was one of the advantages of being in the Transportation and Services Directorate of DCSLOG. All transportation matters funneled into one of the sections of the Directorate, so things like the car could be handled with dispatch.

Once settled, I found that there were a number of old friends in the area. The Carlisle Class was well represented: Sid Hack was XO of DCSLOG, Bob Young was assigned to ODCSOPS, Verne Bowers (just promoted to BG) was about to leave, and Jim Ursano was replacing him as XO of DCSPER, Jack Rhett was with an Engineer command, Tom McGuire was the XO to the CofS, USAREUR, and Dick Chapin and Rod McFadden were in Mannheim, a short drive from Heidelberg. There were other old friends there also: Gus Braun was the Comptroller at Saarbrucken, Jim Russell, who had been in my Advance Class, was CofS of Headquarters Command, Al BettelH, from the 504 and 508, now a civilian, was in DCSOPS, Al Roegge (and Daria) was in the Communications Directorate. Dutch Passailaigue, Jim Ryan, Rudy Holbrook, Ron Weisenborn, John Stewart, Charles Chesak and Larry Freeman, all people who had been with me in Vietnam, were in and around Heidelberg. As time passed others surfaced: Jim Gettings from Leavenworth, Dick Gaudsmith from JACE, Al Rozon, Hans Hoffman, Tom Lasch, George Skinner and Bud Harris from the 1st Bde, 9th IN Div, Roy Atteberry from Plans, DCSOPS. Don Creuziger, the Senior Advisor of Kontum Province, had an Armored Cav Squadron on the border.

Ron Weisenbom found me as the result of a letter he had written which finally caught up with me in Heidelberg. Ron had been passed over for promotion to major as the result of an efficiency report he had received for his tour in Kontum, flying reconnaissance and target identification missions on the highly sensitive Barrel Roll operation. He was requesting my help in appealing the report. Of course he had not worked for me and I had no definitive knowledge of his flying performance, however, I had been with him for many months in Kontum, knew him well, and could attest to his personal habits and character, which were impugned in the report.

The derogatory comments had been made by the indorsing officer based in Saigon. Ron was an air lift pilot who normally flew C-130s, while most of the Barrel Roll pilots were fighter pilots who looked with disdain on those who did not fly the faster, more maneuverable aircraft. Ron asked me to write a letter for him, which I was happy to do, commenting on those matters within my competence. The appeal was successful, Ron was promoted to major. He was stationed in Wiesbaden, but attended many parties I gave in Sandhausen. Whenever he and his wife came to a party at DAS SCHLOSS, as I called my apartment, they stayed overnight at the Gasthaus Gruner Baum in Sandhausen. They soon enjoyed a special relationship with the owner.

The first time I saw MAJ Jim Ryan in Heidelberg I was shocked. He was unkempt, seedy-looking and little resembled the sharp young officer who had worked for me in Kontum. He had deteriorated mentally and physically; I was sorry to hear that he had been placed before a Board of Officers which was considering his fitness for retention in the service. Called to testify in Ryan's behalf, I was startled at the thrust of the questions asked by his Defense Counsel.

When asked to describe my association with MAJ Ryan, I reported that he had worked for me as a District Advisor in Kontum Province. The Board asked questions concerning his courage, competence and general performance of duty. Then I was asked if I was aware of any homosexual activities in the Dist HQ during MAJ Ryan's assignment there. My stunned reply was an emphatic denial of such

Donald A. Seibert

knowledge. The advisory teams lived in isolation as closely-knit groups by virtue of their relationship with the Vietnamese which might foster any tendencies to abnormal relationships. No reports of such conduct on the part of Ryan had been brought to my attention, and I found it hard to credit them.

Even during the hearings, Ryan was not up to the same standards of appearance he had maintained under the harsh conditions in Vietnam. I was saddened by the change. He was transferred from the area and I never received word of the final outcome of the Board.

After getting settled, I was interviewed by the DCSLOG, MG Edward L. Rowny, later promoted to LTG and given the rank of Ambassador as an arms limitation expert in talks with the Soviets. He gave me a special job; I was to look into the possibility of recovering equipment, surplus to the needs of the troops in Vietnam, which had accumulated because the supply system was automatically shipping materiel there in excess of the rate of consumption. I was to see about getting some of those surpluses for Europe.

Given a small office and the services of a secretary, I went to work. Many phone calls, much reading and a great deal of computer research verified the existence of surplus items in Vietnam which were available to US AREUR. However, US AREUR would have to pay transportation charges and the initial cost of the items might be deducted from its budget. In a detailed report my findings were fully documented. MG Rowny thanked me, then dropped the project, USAREUR did not have the funds to buy the surplus commodities. It was a good exercise which introduced me to the logistics problems of a major command.

COL Carl Leidy, Transportation Corps (TC), Chief of the Directorate of Transportation and Services, was a highly effective officer who ran a good shop. I was happy working for him. Just as my surplus study was completed, Bob Borman was reassigned as Leidy's Deputy, and I was made the Chief of Services Division. This was a shock to a number of people; traditionally the Chief of Services was a QM OFF. But Rowny wanted someone in that position who was a decisive policy-maker, not a technician. Fed up with the ineffectiveness of many technical service officers, MG Rowny eagerly embraced Sid Hack's recommendation to give the job to a combat arms officer who would look at the services functions from the point of view of the troops. An Infantry officer, myself, was assigned the task. The choice was not viewed with universal approval in DCSLOG!

As Chief of Services Division, my duties, as spelled out in my job description, consisted of developing policy and exercising staff and technical supervision of Food (Class I Supply), the food program and commissary operations; Petroleum, Oil and Lubricants (POL) and chemical supplies (Class III Supply); laundry and dry cleaning facilities; mortuary and graves registration programs; property disposal activities; clothing sales store and shoe repair facilities; and administrative and Interservice support to the US Navy, Air Force, civilian agencies, non-governmental agencies and individuals including foreign liaison personnel.

In addition, as Chief of Services I was charged with advising the DCSLOG on construction requirements, and recommending policy on all engineer activities in which the DCSLOG had general staff supervision responsibilities. As Chief of Services I also held two positions which crossed service boundaries: Joint Area Petroleum Officer (JAPO), charged with directing and supervising the Joint Area Petroleum Office, Heidelberg, which handled the fuel requirements for all Army, Navy and Air Force units in Europe; and Theater Joint Graves Registration Officer (TJGRO), charged with the disposition of the dead of the three services.

Services Division did not get into actual operations; these were handled by the Communications Zone (COMZ) headed by a MG. There was some friction between the DCSLOG staff and the operators who constantly accused the staff of getting into their business. With the responsibility for technical supervision such friction was unavoidable. Usually the difficulties arose as the result of personality clashes, rather than any attempt to usurp authority.

446

In this connection, I was fortunate. On an early trip to Worms to visit the COMZ HQ, I found Roy Atteberry was the CofS with Dick Chapin his deputy. Whenever there was a problem in my area, it was only necessary to pick up the phone and call one of them; the matter would be resolved quickly. Roy left shortly, replaced by Dick as Chief of Staff. When Rod McFadden, Comptroller of COMZ, took command of the 4th AR Div DISCOM in Nurnberg, Gus Braun moved from Saarbrucken to replace him. While none of this removed all of the problems, it helped smooth the way for amicable, speedy and satisfactory solutions that might otherwise have taken weeks of acrimonious wrangling.

As far as I was concerned the two most important facets of my job were Class I and Class III Supply. Class I, food, was a major factor in troop morale; any effort in this area contributed to the welfare of the troops. Class III, POL, was also important; the US Army, indeed the US forces, could not move or fight without it. There was some consternation in POL circles when an IN OFF was assigned as the Joint Area Petroleum Officer, traditionally a QM position. The Class III Office also negotiated contracts for the purchase of the gasoline by PX service stations.

Although not happy with being a logistician, it became obvious as time went on that I could do more for the individual soldier in Europe as Chief of Services Division of DCSLOG than in any other assignment in USAREUR other than command of a unit.

Once settled in the apartment and my job, a housewarming party to corral all of my friends in the immediate area appeared to be a priority effort. Invitations were printed and mailed, but a week before the party, I came down with a strange malady which necessitated postponement of the festivities. Leaving the office for Sandhausen one evening, I developed all the symptoms of flu: a tired, aching feeling, loss of appetite, and a stuffed head. Thinking I was coming down with a cold, I took a couple of aspirin before going to bed early that night. The next morning the symptoms not only persisted, but I had a touch of diarrhea. Despite this, I went to work as usual. By the time I climbed the stairs to the third floor of the German Barracks in which my office was located, I was exhausted and out of breath. This was unusual; normally I ran up those three flights with no difficulty. It was necessary to relax before I started to work.

Just as I recovered, a phone call summoned me to the office of the Deputy DCSLOG, BG Richards. While talking with him, I almost passed out; my eyes blurred and my knees turned to water. Excusing myself, I went to the latrine close by to get a grip on myself. It was obvious that I had better get to the dispensary.

Although as a colonel I got a little more expeditious treatment man the average officer or soldier on sick call, the medics were remarkably unimpressed with my symptoms. They assured me that it was simply a 24-hour virus and prescribed the routine symptomatic treatment. Turning to leave, I mentioned the diarrhea and that the stool was black. Immediately everything changed! The doctor became concerned and demanded a stool specimen, forthwith. After seeing it, he hospitalized me on the spot, not letting me get toilet articles or other items. When questioned about the sudden turn he told me that a black stool indicated internal bleeding.

Once in bed, a captain (doctor) examined me, confiding that he suspected that I had a perforated ulcer. Since Dad had suffered with ulcers for years, the symptoms were familiar to me, I had none of them. My immediate response was, "Doctor, I give ulcers but I do not have them."

The doctor saw no humor in this statement; he had already made up his mind that the only possible cause for my internal bleeding was a perforated ulcer, hence he proceeded on that premise. He completed a thorough examination, after which he ordered every conceivable test, including the entire GI series. After a week in the hospital the bleeding finally stopped spontaneously. A diagnosis was never made, though finally, and reluctantly, the doctors ruled out an ulcer.

Following my release from the hospital, the long-delayed housewarming was held. It was very special because so many old friends, as well as new friends I quickly made in Heidelberg, attended it.

As part of my orientation in the services activities, I set up a program of official trips throughout Germany to see as many of the operations under my staff supervision as possible in order to understand fully my responsibilities. I wanted to see the warehousing of food, the salvage yards, the laundries and dry cleaning plants, the graves registration (mortuary) process, and the clothing sales stores. The routine was to send a message a week in advance to advise people of the visit, and request a briefing followed by a walk-through to show me everything about each operation. On every visit I took with me the staff officer actually concerned with that activity. Suddenly those logistics functions became interesting. Due to a fortunate knack for organizing my work, there was ample time for both visits as well as the routine staff work in Heidelberg. All of the authority that could be delegated to my subordinates was given them; things worked smoothly. The officers and civilians working for me were conscientious, dependable and knowledgeable; given my guidance they worked better without me there.

A commander or staff officer is only as good as the people who work for him. The secret of success is to surround yourself with effective, loyal people. While this is not always possible, weak personnel can be used to maximum capability if they cannot be reassigned. In Services Division there were many outstanding OFFs and civilians. Madeline Peel, my secretary, the wife of a Signal Corps LTC in the Communications/Electronics Staff Agency, was unusually competent. She knew much more about administration than I did. LTC Clise, the Class I Officer, left shortly after my arrival and was replaced by LTC Swank. Clise had been an asset who knew his business and ran a good section. Swank, not as professional as Clise, needed more supervision. MAJ Jaan Kurgvel, the Food Service Advisor, was knowledgeable not only in his primary field, but in other QM duties as well. CWO Roberts and SGM White were the Food Service experts. Both had started as assistant or apprentice cooks, become skilled cooks, then mess sergeants and finally food service supervisors. They were truly experts.

Originally the Engineer Officer was LTC Baswell; his assistant LTC Bruce Carswell. Bruce was a USMA graduate. Both he and Baswell were effective officers. Baswell was replaced by LTC Jack Frankeberger, an ARTY OFF, who looked like a linebacker for the Dallas Cowboys. He had, in fact, played football for VMI, was an excellent organizer and did an outstanding job for me. MAJ, later LTC, John E Murphy, who had a degree in petroleum engineering, headed the POL section. A USMA Graduate, formally an IN (Special Forces) Officer, Jack was facing a disability discharge. His transfer to the QM Corps was an attempt to remain in service (he was retired for disability just after I left Services Division). He was knowledgeable and dedicated and managed the Class III section effectively. CPT Rocco Bruno, a QM OFF, was a lawyer from New York who handled clothing sales stores. For a short time a WAC MAJ was assigned to the Division, but she did such an outstanding job that Carl Leidy moved her to his office. The military complement of Services was completed by several EM, headed by MSG Charlie Monroe, who handled the paperwork for the Division. He kept the suspense file and knew where every paper in the Division was located.

Services had many highly competent civilians, most of them GS 12s who had been in Europe for many years, some since the early days of the occupation. Sid Steele, a GS13, watched over laundry, dry-cleaning and mortuary and graves registration activities. Sid was a true professional who managed his affairs well. Ralph Zimmer, a retired EN LTC, was the General Engineer, the staff officer for installations for DCSLOG. He lacked formal engineer schooling, but his practical knowledge of the construction business was invaluable to the DCSLOG. Although he had an enormous ego, I respected him and learned to depend on him. Mr Jeffers, the junkman (a term used in an affectionate sense), in charge of salvage and property disposal, was later promoted to GS13. Mr Porter, the commissary expert, had been on the job for many years. Though highly knowledgeable, he let his personal views on civil rights interfere with his job. He was abrasive, hence not as effective as he could have been. Russell Burk, the petroleum expert, was a GS12. The personnel classification people wanted to downgrade his position to GS 11; this controversy raged all during my tenure in DCSLOG. I supported the GS12 grade, considering the duties he performed. When I left, he had not been reduced.

Jim Travis, whose primary concern was Interservice support agreements and clothing sales stores, had a heart attack shortly after I arrived. He was hospitalized during most of the time I was in DCSLOG. The attack left him partially paralyzed, but he insisted he could do his job, though he had no stamina. I thought he should take a physical disability retirement. However, he needed to complete several more years for maximum civil service retirement, and also needed several more years in the Reserves to qualify for a Title III Reserve Retirement, so he refused to retire. He put in an appearance, but was not effective. This was still a problem when I left.

Services Division was a good team. With the exceptions mentioned, the people could be depended on without much supervision. My relationship with them was not only rewarding, but professionally and socially enjoyable. The wives of the Services Officers, Enlisted Men and Civilians, all delightful ladies, adopted me. Ann Frankeberger, a nurse (MAJ) at the Heidelberg

Military Hospital, was charming, as was Chris Bruno, the youngest of the wives in the Division. Linda Zimmer must have believed that I was undernourished; on the frequent occasions she asked me to dinner, she prepared enough of her outstanding German food for twice the number invited. In addition, Ceil Kurgvel, Pat Murphy, Helga Monroe, and Andree Steele made special efforts to make my tour in Heidelberg enjoyable.

Problems, of all kinds and in every area, were identified during official trips which took me all over Germany - to Munich, Stuttgart, Kaiserslautern, Karlsruhe, Geissen - wherever there were major service-oriented logistical installations. Every mode of transportation was used; aircraft, private car, sedans and train. On each trip I managed to find some time to look around the cities I had not been to before. Constantly, I met old friends. In Numberg Rod and Toni McFadden always welcomed me. On one visit I got to see the famous Kriskindelmart, which featured over a thousand booths selling Christmas toys, ornaments, candy and cakes. On a trip to Stuttgart to attend a JAPO meeting at European Command (EUCOM) HQ, I saw Jim Gettmgs who had been the leader of Gruber 4. I made trips to Holland and Italy in connection with my duties, to attend meetings or represent the DCSLOG. Unfortunately, I got to visit few tactical units, though I wanted to see if there were logistical support problems in them.

Early in the spring of 1968, I was designated the DCSLOG representative for the annual Army Youth Association (AYA) Fair, which raised money for the activities and recreation of the young dependents of military personnel assigned to the Heidelberg area. The fair was a major undertaking; a German carnival set up a full range of carnival rides in traditional county fair style in the Patrick Henry village Housing Area. There were German concessions which sold such eatables as bratwurst, pretzels and cakes, as well as two beer tents, both with bands playing rollicking German drinking songs.

Each HQ staff agency had a booth on the midway; the Communications Section ran a hamburger stand manned by their personnel. Many friends including the Roegges and the Peels were behind the grills preparing hamburgers. The DCSLOG booth sold ice cream. Germans love American ice cream; the COMZ plant at Kaiserslautern made many gallons which were sold to Germans as well as Americans. The fair was open to anyone with dollars. Many times when I was on duty at the booth, I sold several gallons to a German family, and watched with disbelief as they packed them into suitcases. Later, I saw some of my customers on the midway, ice cream dripping from the luggage!

The fair entailed a lot of work; it seemed to me that the US Army, rather the US taxpayer, underwrote it for thousands of dollars. Considering the man-hours diverted from assigned duties, the use of government transportation and facilities, not to mention the manufacture of the ice cream, the accounting for which always remained a mystery to me, a sizeable investment in manpower and resources was diverted to the affair. Certainly no actual money was involved, though it might have been cheaper to finance the youth activities from appropriated funds.

One of my principal interests was Food Service. MAJ Kurgvel and CWO Roberts were vitally concerned with it, but SGM Don White was the enlisted expert on messes. He visited most of them during the course of the year. On occasion, when a particular mess was in bad condition and making no improvement, he would ask me to provide clout to stir those responsible to action. One day he told me that the worst mess in Germany at that time was the one in Lee Barracks in Mainz. This shocked me because the messes there had been excellent when I served with the 504. But SGM White did not enlist my clout without good reason, so I told him to set up a visit. On the occasions that White and I visited a mess, the headquarters concerned was notified a week in advance that a senior staff officer from USAREUR HQ would make an official visit to the mess. SGM White set up such a visit to the Mainz mess; I was interested in seeing how the ABN Bde looked. I had last been to Mainz in 1962.

We arrived at Mainz in a staff car to find the Bde CDR "unavailable". This was odd, normally when a senior staff officer from a higher HQ scheduled a formal visit to a unit, the commander made it a point to meet him. The ABN Bde was not in the field, but no reason was given for his absence. The XO greeted me; after talking briefly with him, White and I went to the mess hall.

The ABN Bde had one consolidated mess in the mess hall formerly used by the 505. A 1LT reported to me, informing me that he was the Mess OFF; his Co CO was responsible for the mess, but he was the OIC. We chatted a bit before I went about my inspection.

SGM White made the detailed inspection; as the expert he looked at the technical aspects, while I made a general inspection, covering the personnel, overall appearance of the mess, the menu for the day, and a spot-check of the records. As a former Co CO I had enough experience to recognize a good mess.

About 1100 several troopers were served "early chow". USAREUR had put out guidance (or recommendations) that "early chow" be discontinued because the cooks prepared the meals for ten or twelve early eaters (guards and CQs). By the time the majority of the troops came in the food was overcooked, dried out, or otherwise below standard. It was suggested that messes have "late chow" so that only ten or twelve men (usually rotated daily) would be subjected to the less palatable chow rather than inconveniencing the majority of those eating in the mess.

During "early chow", first the Co CO (captain) then the Bn CO (LTC) came in. Both made a point of checking the mess, both were in the chain of command having responsibility for the mess, both were going to have lunch with me. No member of the Bde staff appeared. We discussed the mess in general terms for a few minutes. The mess sergeant told us that they were ready to serve us, if I would go to the large table near the window a DRO would bring chow to us. My response startled them. "No, I haven't finished yet. We'll eat a little later. I want to see the serving line in operation." This disconcerted everyone, Bn CO, Co CO, mess officer, and mess sergeant. SGM White smiled.

First I watched the sign-in to see that someone was checking mess cards and collecting from separate ration men. Then I took a position behind the serving counter to watch the mess personnel serve the food. After concentrating on the service for several minutes, I talked with the cooks who were manning the steam table. They appeared to be capable men who knew their job, and were interested in a food service career. One "speedy four" commented on "all of the brass" in the mess hall, volunteering that it was unusual to have either the Bn CO or the Co CO there, indeed to have any officers at all. "This is the first time they have been in the mess in the six months I have been here."

This, of course, explained why it was such a bad mess. The chain of command was not checking it. My next question was blunt. "Don't any of the officers eat in the mess?"

"Oh yes, the duty officer comes in and has one meal a day to comply with regulations, but none of them ever say anything; it's a drag for them. They couldn't care less."

Again the mess sergeant came up to me, saying, "Are you ready to eat, sir?"

"No, I'll spend about 45 minutes behind the line until it is obvious that the majority of the troops have eaten."

Finally the line thinned; only sporadic troopers were coming through. At that time, I told the mess sergeant that I was ready to eat. SGM White, having completed his inspection, had told me the essentials of his findings, which I was prepared to discuss with the Bn CO and the Co CO. An official written report would be sent through channels, of course.

The mess sergeant said, "Sir, how would you like your steak?"

"Sergeant, the menu does not call for steak. The men are eating pork chops."

"Yes, sir. But we have steaks for you and the Battalion Commander and the official party. We're just ready to put them on. How would you like yours?"

"Sergeant, you are not going to serve me steak. I'm inspecting your mess and I want to eat the food the troops are eating to see how it is."

This took him back because there was little food left, though troopers were still drifting through the mess line.

"Well, sir, if you will just sit over there, we will bring you a tray."

"No, sergeant. We'll go through the mess line."

The Battalion Commander apparently had never been through the line in his own mess, he didn't know how to go about it! SGM White was grinning broadly, though he had expected this. With me in the lead, the party trooped to the head-count NCO and signed in. As an inspector, I did not have to pay the surcharge, though I did pay for my meal. Again leading the group, I took a tray and went through the mess line. There was not very much left, and that little was not very palatable. But the official party, including the Bn CO, the Co CO and his mess officer, solemnly ate as if it was a gourmet meal.

As we ate, I explained to the group what was wrong with the mess. My first and most important observation was the lack of command interest and supervision, neither the Bde CDR, nor anyone in the chain of command seemed interested in how the troops ate. After several other general comments, SGM White discussed the details. When he was finished, the Battalion Commander was informed that an official report would be submitted through channels.

After lunch SGM White and I stopped at Bde HQ, but again the Commander was not available. His XO was briefed on our findings, told that a full report would be forwarded through channels, and warned that we would be back to reinspect in six months. Someone else reinspected because by that time I was back to Vietnam. I wondered if any improvements were made.

One of my Food Service duties was participation in the selection of the Best Mess in US Army, Europe, which would then compete for the Connelly Award, given each year to the best troop mess in the Army. Actually there were two awards, one for the best consolidated mess and one for the best unit mess. Each area or major command in USAREUR nominated its best mess, from which a USAREUR team made the final selection. In 1968 that team consisted of Burt David, SGM White and myself. Burt David, selected for promotion to BG but not yet promoted, had replaced BG Richards as Deputy DCSLOG. We visited each of the nominated messes, always for the lunch meal, inspected the mess hall, examined the records, watched the preparation, the service, and ate lunch.

One of the unit messes checked was that of the Berlin Bde ARTY Battery. On a fast, one-day trip, we flew into Templehof, the West Berlin Airport, spent a few hours at the mess, and returned to Rhein Main. The Berlin mess was selected as the best unit mess in USAREUR: it placed second in the Army competition. The USAREUR consolidated mess selected that year won the first place Connelly Award.

Shortly after the completion of the best mess competition, I made an official visit to Berlin, going by duty train which was sealed from Frankfurt to Berlin. A room at Harnick House, the VIP quarters in Berlin had been reserved for me, and the Berlin Command placed a sedan at my disposal. BG Sam MacC Goodwin was in the Berlin Command HQ, the first time I had seen him since those days in DCSOPS. CPT Burl McDaniels, who had been in the 504 in Mainz, was the SF S-4 in Berlin. He took me to East Berlin to buy Czechoslovakian crystal.

It was official policy that US officers make periodic trips to East Berlin to demonstrate freedom of access, hence we went in uniform in an official sedan. The difference between East and West Berlin was striking. Whereas West Berlin was busy, thriving, gay, with lots of shoppers, sightseers and cars, East Berlin was depressing, had few cars, few people on the streets and the shops had very little merchandise. I did purchase the crystal I wanted. I also explored West Berlin using the staff car (part of the West German WWII reparations since Berlin was still officially occupied).

The West German Government also paid for the occupation force, providing housing, fuel and other items not peculiar to the US Army. There were few logistical problems there.

Back in Heidelberg, work, trips and sightseeing continued. A number of visitors made their way to Germany to see me. Bill Long spent a week with me. After two days at DAS SCHLOSS, as I called my digs, we drove around Austria stopping to see one of his old friends in Steyr. My sister Arlene's son and his wife visited me for several days during which I showed them the area. Dan Baldwin, one of my Bn COs in the 1st Bde, 9th Inf Div, spent several nights in DAS SCHLOSS. There were others, I was only sorry I could not convince Mother to visit me, but she felt that at age 80 the trip would be too much for her.

Wick visited Europe for three weeks in mid-1968. We drove about the Continent: Aachen, site of my favorite cathedral, Wurzberg, to see the Tiepolo ceilings in the Residenz of the Prince-Bishops, Bavaria, where I bought a beautiful hand carved creche and where we visited famous castles, Western Austria, to see Charlottenburg in Innsbruck, finally across the Brenner Pass into Italy to spend four glorious days in Venice. A quick trip to Verona where we saw a spectacular operatic performance in the ancient Roman Coliseum there, ended our joint venture. While I took the car-train through St Goddard Pass and returned to Heidelberg, Wick did more traveling in Italy.

Such trips as the ones with Wick and Bill Long were possible because I still had much leave accumulated during my tour in Vietnam, was able to organize my work to minimize the impact of my absence, and had an understanding boss.

In June 1968 I planned a party for all of the people I knew in Germany who had served with me in Vietnam. The first of several "Vietnam Rallies", I was delighted that so many made it. Those who did, included, Dutch Passailaigue, George Skinner, Hans Hoffman, Ron Weisenborn, Jim Parlier, John Stewart, AI Rozon, Jim Lasch and Jim Harris. All but Dutch and Jim Harris were accompanied by their wives, the first time I had met most of them. It was a gala affair, at which many lively stories were rehashed.

In all I hosted four Vietnam Rallies during the 18 months I spent in Heidelberg. LTG and Mrs Heintges attended several of them. At the first one they attended, LTG Heintges, Deputy Commander-in-Chief, US Army, Europe (DCINCUSAREUR) and CG 7th US Army, very formally presented me with a bottle of Hep Hoa Rum. He said that he had been carrying the case with him since the manager of the Sugar Mill had given it to him in 1966! Though it was terrible rum, he saved it for very special occasions, such as the Vietnam Rally! He was delighted to get rid of one more bottle of that foul stuff.

Late in the summer a team came from the CONUS to present a three-week, concentrated course in computer technology. It covered the theory of programming, as well as the mathematical computations on which programs are based. Because I had attended the IBM orientation in Washington, MG Rowny insisted I attend this longer course. My protests concerning the press of business or my lack of mathematical background fell on deaf ears. So each day from 0800 to 1630 I sat in class and tried to grasp the material the instructors were presenting, but it was over my head. Several young LTs in the course who had recently graduated with degrees in computer science or in mathematics, took turns trying to make sense out of the theory for me; though they managed to pull me through the course, they were not able to make me understand it all.

Shortly after the computer course, MG Rowny was replaced by BG "Nick" Maples. Maples had the reputation of being a "hard nose" who was being brought in to shape up the logistical program in USAREUR. There were many problem areas, some in the services. MG Rowny was an intelligent and dedicated officer, but he seemed unable to establish priorities. Every action had precedence; he attacked USAREUR logistics with a shot gun, thus diluting the effectiveness of the staffs efforts. BG Maples set out very positive priorities; in the Services area he gave me a detailed list.

Sid Hack left about the same time MG Rowny did and was replaced by Bob Selton, whom I had known for many years. Burt David was promoted to BG, I saw much of him. There were still close friends in the front office.

Between trips, work in Services Division continued unabated. As in all commands, The G-1 or Deputy Chief of Staff, Personnel (DCSPER), was responsible for matters affecting troop morale in USAREUR. Services Division was the point of contact in DCSLOG for morale actions.

MG Julian Wilson, whose service had been in the Adjutant General's Corps, was the USAREUR DCSPER. It seems to me that it is a mistake to make an AG OFF a DCSPER or G-l. Indeed, I believe it is a mistake to make a technical service officer a general staff officer. Most look at matters in terms of numbers or statistics rather than people. This was the case with Wilson.

Since Services Division provided the ODCSLOG input to actions affecting troop morale that originated in ODCSPER, it was inevitable that MG Wilson and I had many disagreements on policy. Unfortunately, Jim Ursano, as XO of ODCSPER, frequently got in the middle of these disagreements. Though unhappy about arguing with Jim, a good friend, I had to call the shots as I saw them.

The first action we clashed about was a policy on command housing. DCSPER set the policy for the assignment of quarters; DCSLOG had staff purview over the buildings; Services Division, as the DCSLOG agency for housing, had to comment on every action which affected quarters. The ODCSPER sent over for coordination an action which called for the designation of certain housing as "command quarters". It was a good policy which set aside specific quarters for commanders of battalions and brigades, and for key staff officers such as Div CofSs. All general officers already had command housing. An officer assigned to command a unit would automatically move into the house designated for that particular command. Such quarters, commensurate with the prestige of the position, would be suitable for entertaining. Thus, no senior commander would have to live on the economy or commute from one place to another.

CPT Bruno, who had action on the paper, came in to see me, saying, "Sir, this is a routine action in which I recommend you concur." He then briefly outlined the policy.

When he had finished, I said, "Yes, we will concur provided the quarters are made available to bachelor officers if they command such units."

CPT Bruno protested, "Sir, I don't think the DCSPER will buy that."

"If he won't buy it, his policy will not work. We will not concur unless that stipulation is in the policy."

He looked perplexed. I explained my reasoning, "Suppose there is a house set aside for a Bde CDR at Baumholder. If I were assigned to command that Bde, would I get that set of quarters?"

"No. What would you do with such a house?"

"I would live in it like any other commander and entertain in it. Now, if It don't get the house and the command tour is 18 months, would the house remain vacant?"

"No, Sir, obviously not."

"It would be assigned to somebody else then?"

"Yes, Sir, housing is very critical in Europe."

"When I am reassigned, will the house be available for the next commander?"

"I don't know. If your tours exactly overlapped it would. But that is not likely is it?"

"No, it isn't. That is why we must insist on that provision. How many bachelor officers are there in USAREUR that will be given command of brigades or Battalions? Not more than one or two. Perhaps once in five years a bachelor might occupy command housing, but you have to make provision for him in the policy. Do you understand why?"

"Yes, Sir."

The provisional concurrence went over to ODCSPER as the official ODCSLOG position. CPT Bruno reported that the ODCSPER action officer had protested our provision: even after he had cited my example, the ODCSPER action officer was convinced that MG Wilson would not buy it. My counterpart in DCSPER called me, accusing me of being obstructive. Patiently, I explained to him that I was only attempting to insure that the policy would work, I heartily indorsed it, but it could only work if provisions were made for bachelors. He agreed, partially, "Yeah, that's a problem all right, but we can't back off from our position on diverting family housing to bachelors."

"Well, the policy will not work unless you do, and DCSLOG will not concur without that provision."

Eventually, BG Maples called me to his office. He said that MG Wilson accused me of being an obstructionist concerning a very good command housing policy, which he, Maples, thoroughly approved. Why did I non-concur? Again I explained my rationale.

"Of course you are right! It is very simple. It just will not work unless bachelor officers are included."

He called MG Wilson, informing him that my provisional concurrence was the official DCSLOG position, and explained why. Rather than giving a bachelor a house, perhaps once every five years, MG Wilson dropped a good policy. I lost much respect for him because of his lack of flexibility.

There were other actions with ODCSPER and MG Wilson. As the DCSLOG representative, I made a trip with him on the CINC's train from Heidelberg to Bremerhaven. CINCUSAREUR had available two trains: a four-car train and a two-car train. Since early occupation days, they had been provided by the Bundesbahn at no cost to the US Government. CINCUSAREUR was also the commander of the Central Army Group, a combined German-American command, hence the trains, which could go any place in Europe, were at his disposal. The trains were available to general officers for staff visits. MG Wilson and his party used one for the trip to Bremerhaven to inspect housing and other facilities.

It was an interesting trip. Excellent meals were served on the train and the accommodations were comfortable. At Bremerhaven we visited the out-processing facilities for the shipment of troops, household goods and cars. In one warehouse we discovered a stock of old Rosenthal china which had been bought for general officers' quarters. MG Wilson asked me to get it into the supply system, which was done on my return to Heidelberg.

Wandering through the commissary in Heidelberg one day, it struck me that no cigarettes were on sale there. In the CONUS, cigarettes were a popular item in commissaries. The experts in the Class I Branch assured me that commissaries could sell cigarettes for a dollar a carton cheaper than they were being sold in PXs. This would be a real savings to our junior enlisted men. I directed the Class I Branch to draft a proposal to sell cigarettes in commissaries. The paper was returned from ODCSPER, which had purview over troop morale matters as well as PXs with a nonconcurrence based on the adverse impact such sales would have on PX profits.

At that time the PXs in Europe were returning to the Army Air Force Exchange Service (AAFES) profits totaling about 36 million dollars a year; only six million of which was returned to European welfare funds. The ODCSLOG position was that there was little advantage in making all that profit for the PX system, if Europe was getting only a token return. The DCSPER informed the DCSLOG that most of the money was going to Vietnam to take care of shortages and pilferage there. We persisted in the position that cigarettes should be sold in commissaries to save the soldiers money. The matter escalated to general officer level, and "back channels" (fast, direct personal cablegrams between general officers) began flying back and forth from HQ DA to HQ USAREUR. Apparently the head of AAFES, worried about the possibility of a decrease in profits, asked the Army CofS to intervene in the matter. I wondered which position really benefitted the soldiers most.

While representing the DCSLOG on the PX Council, the matter of the pricing of items was raised. In exasperation, I asked MG Wilson, "Aren't you interested in the Speedy Four and the junior officer?"

Wilson looked at me calmly and said, "No. I am only interested in the career soldier, the NCO. He can afford to pay those prices."

Stunned, I should have let the matter drop but could not. "How do you expect to convince the Speedy Four to stay in and become a Regular soldier if you don't take care of him at that level?"

Wilson made no answer.

Another battle Services lost was on the price of PX gasoline. LTC Murphy's Class III Branch negotiated the contracts for the purchase of gasoline sold by the PX. When new contracts were being considered, Murphy told me we could reduce the cost of gasoline by four or five cents a gallon, in 1968, the cost of gasoline at the PX pump was about 19 cents for regular and 24 for high-test, exceedingly cheap compared with the prices on the German economy. Murphy said that he could negotiate the contract so that the PX could sell regular gasoline for 14 cents and high-test for 20, and still make the five cents profit per gallon it was now making. Again the ODCSPER said no; this time the rationale was safety. With cheaper gas the safety experts foresaw more mileage exposure to accidents. The argument was specious; the price of gasoline was not a factor in the number of miles Americans were driving. Liquor, tobacco, coffee, tea and gasoline were rationed items for US military personnel in Europe, consequently the cheaper price would not have resulted in increased driving. It took all the allowable gas to fuel the American "gas-guzzlers" for routine driving. Extra gasoline coupons were available for those on leave orders to other countries, again not a function of price. Lower gas prices would save the soldier and his family money. The DCSPER apparently was not interested in saving the soldier money.

In the fall of 1968 MG Wilson took SGM White and me to Chiemsee to check on the recreation center there. The DCSPER was responsible for all recreation facilities while the DCSLOG was charged with the food service. We had dinner, evaluated the service, the food, the entertainment and the facilities. All were excellent. On this matter the DCSPER and the DCSLOG were in full agreement. The US military recreational facilities such as those at Chiemsee and Garmisch were truly outstanding.

Late in the summer of 1968, Dave Presson, an old friend, was assigned to ODCSOPS. Dave and his wife Mike (Muriel) frequently had me to parties or dinner in their quadriplex. At one of their informal dinners, I got into a discussion of deadlines with MG "Hook" Almquist, the Deputy Chief of Staff, Operations (DCSOPS). He had needled me in a friendly fashion about an action that his office had sent over to ODCSLOG for coordination. We had missed the deadline; indeed, I had requested an extension of that deadline. He commented on our lack of professional staff work; I countered with a remark on the unnecessarily short deadline. Almquist immediately became defensive. "You know very well, Don, that no action officer touches a paper more than three days before the deadline. If I gave you a month, nobody in your shop would look at it until just before the deadline."

He had forgotten his days as an action officer; the lead time necessary to develop data or effect coordination, the mental gymnastics of writing the paper in the back of the mind while working on other actions, the slow development of arguments, consideration of the best approach to "selling" your position. He was probably correct in his statement that an action officer did not write a paper more than a few days before the deadline, though three was stretching the truth. But the need for adequate time to think it through had been forgotten.

When I posited these arguments, he would not accept them. As there was no point in disrupting the dinner the Pressons were having, I uncharacteristically dropped the matter. But it struck me that all too many senior officers who set deadlines forget their days as action officers and the mechanics of developing a completed staff action. This accounts for much of the poor staff work and faulty reasoning that goes on in many headquarters. If those who establish deadlines would give a quick thought to the information which must be obtained and the details the action involves, perhaps they would not set such arbitrary limits on time, perhaps they would begin to anticipate the need for information or recommendations. Some actions, in response to crises, must be handled expeditiously, but they are few in number.

As I had learned while with the 504 in Mainz, monthly alerts to check the reaction time of units in Europe were a fact of life. For HQ, USAREUR, these were more harassment than training for people like myself who had little more to do than throw alert gear (kept packed in a duffel bag) into my car and report to a given point near the HQ. Once my name was checked off I went back to Sandhausen, unloaded my alert gear, changed uniform (we reported in field uniform) and returned to work. For personnel assigned to tactical elements, these were important training exercises as they often went to their General Alert Order (GAO) positions, but the HQ staff did not do so. Because of the unreliable German telephone system, I missed several alerts when the DO could not get through. Regardless of how pointless I thought my participation in alerts was, I was not happy about missing them. It was a duty; I did not like to neglect any duty.

There had been little opportunity to travel during my first tour in Europe with the 1st ABG, 504 IN at Mainz, so I took leave whenever my duties permitted. In addition to the trips with Wick and Bill Long, I spent a few days in Copenhagen, where I saw all the sights, including a side trip to Elsinore, the setting for Shakespeare's Hamlet. Over Thanksgiving I flew to Vienna, where I visited the Vienna Woods, Schloss Mayerling, the birthplace of Beethoven, the cathedral and the mile-long apartment building. On Sunday morning I saw a performance of the famous Lippizaner horses at the Spanish Riding School. The Concierge at my hotel obtained a ticket for a performance of Don Giovanni at the beautifully restored opera house; the Viennese love Mozart next to Straus, and with Don Giovanni their favorite, they were extravagant with their applause. There was also wonderful food. Again, I had occasion to boast that I ate my way across Europe!

In the Spring of 1969 I visited Athens and Rome. My arrival in Athens on the Greek Orthodox Good Friday enabled me to witness the Good Friday Parade. Troops, civilians and clergy marched in funereal cadence to a dirge played by a military band; a coffin representing the body of Christ was borne on the shoulders of an honor guard; the crosses, icons, candles and clergy, resplendent even in funeral vestments, were too numerous to count.

Greece is delightful. My regret was that I saw so little of it. More time was spent at the Acropolis, only a short walk from my hotel, than in any other part of Athens. On an excursion to Delphi to see where myth claims the oracle hid, there was a chance to visit the famous circus and amphitheater as well as a Byzantine Church with magnificent mosaics. Thermopylae impressed me, especially the mound supposed to contain the remains of the Spartans killed there. And there were special Easter dishes to enjoy.

After a wonder-filled week in Greece, I flew to Rome. The director of the USO, which offered the best tours at reasonable rates, arranged for a VIP seat at a general audience with the Pope, though I protested that a Roman Catholic might value this more than I did. It was most interesting. The Pope, seated on a throne borne on the shoulders of the Swiss Guards, was carried the length of St Peters to the High Altar. Great pageantry!

In one short week I saw monumental Rome: St Peters, the Vatican Museum, the Sistine Chapel, the Coliseum, the Catacombs, most of the great cathedrals and basilicas, many Roman ruins. Of course, I enjoyed trying the local Italian food; every area has its specialities and Rome had some delicious ones. Rome was all I expected, I could have spent a month there instead of a week.

Meanwhile, back at Services Division a dedicated staff continued to look after the interests of the troops. When present for duty, I contributed what I could to the effort. Since the Division exercised staff supervision over commissaries, I received many phone calls from irate customers regarding service, stockage, hours and prices. The most frequent question asked was "Why don't they have (item) in the commissary?" My stock answer was, "If enough people want it we will get it." The USAREUR commissary system was limited in the number of line items it could stock; only 22,000 separate items were authorized. This was simply a matter of expediency; there was not enough warehousing, transportation, or shelf space to stock every item everyone wanted. Items were carefully selected based on packaging, perishability (shelf-life), demonstrated desire, and current fads. Due regard was given to ethnic tastes. Twice a year the European Commissary Resale Item Board, ECRIB, met to consider new products or to change items already stocked. If a new item was accepted, an old item had to be dropped. The Board included representatives from each of the major units as well as Army wives, so it had an appreciation of what the customers wanted. Though not a regular member of the Board, I attended two of its meetings at Geissen. Sales representatives demonstrated new products, offering samples to taste if edible, and provided information on package size and other matters. The Board then voted to accept, reject or drop items. It was a slow, cumbersome system, but one that gave the commissary patrons the best possible selection under the circumstances.

One of the customers of the commissary system was GEN Polk's mess. USAREUR HQ was in a German Army Kaserne. The Command Section was in one building and the staff occupied five or six barracks, each major staff section in a separate building. The Command Building contained the offices of the CINC, GEN Polk, his Deputy, LTG Heintges, the CofS, SGS, conference rooms and a dining room. The dining room was famous because of its round table which could seat fourteen people. Every day at lunch every seat at the table was filled. GEN Polk ate there only about two days each week; he was rarely in the HQ during the day more than that. If the other general and special staff OFFs were on trips, then the SGS would have COLs from the various staff sections fill in the spaces. Each section had a roster of COLs available to attend the lunch. Often notification was received only an hour or so before noon. Most officers disliked eating in the CINC's mess and tried to avoid doing so (no COL ate there more than once a month). Though I would never volunteer, I enjoyed eating there occasionally. The food was excellent, although usually too much, and there was always good conversation. Only rarely was there a discussion of policy. Normally everyone talked about matters of interest outside the office. Each officer paid for his meal; the reason to fill the table each day. Otherwise the mess would not remain solvent. Drinks were available before or during lunch. These I avoided; I have never been able to drink in the middle of the day; drinking before 1700 (tradition dictates that the military drinks after retreat) makes me sleepy or listless in the afternoon. On rare occasions I will have a Bloody Mary at a brunch, or a drink at a family gathering.

The CINC periodically hosted official, formal parties for visiting dignitaries, to which colonels in USAREUR HQ were invited. At least twice each year, the CINC hosted a dinner dance for the senior members of his Staff. It was a shock when I found that I was the thirtieth colonel assigned to ODCSLOG USAREUR, though not the 30th in rank; this was indicative of the number of senior officers in the HQ. The CINC's parties, held in the Casino, the Officers' Club at Patrick Henry Village, were elegant. There was always excellent food and entertainment.

Dinner partners were assigned; husband and wife rarely sat together. Each officer attending the party found an envelope marked with his name on a table at the entrance to the ballroom. In the envelope was a slip on which was the name of his dinner partner as well as his table and seat number.

Only once did I draw a partner I knew, Mrs Welch, the wife of a buddy, the other times I drew complete strangers. It was an interesting method of mixing people.

Observing my friends buying distinctive Hems for their "final" home stirred an interest in getting some items for my future "digs". US personnel assigned to duty in Europe brought only linens, silver and china, pictures and other personal items, and kitchen utensils with them; furniture was provided, in quarters as well as in economy housing. Most quarters had upholstered, comfortable, good-looking chairs called "barrel chairs" which I liked very much. Since the factory that made them was close to Heidelberg, I was able to purchase four of them at a good price. From an Army wife who had collected antiques during a three year tour, but who found herself grossly over the household goods weight allowance, I bought a handsome bureau with marble top at the ridiculously low price of $35.00. A beautifully hand-crafted inlaid coffee table, containing 122 different woods was displayed in the Officers' Club one day, I bought it. Like most Americans stationed in Germany, I purchased four wall clocks, all of them antiques.

During one of the periods I spent at my desk in Heidelberg, my long-time friendship with Bob Selton was almost destroyed. Bob had replaced Sid Hack as XO of ODCSLOG. Periodically, if everything was in order at the office, I would leave early. With a real sense of dedication to my duty, the concept of an eight to five duty day, mentally punching a time clock, or a 48 hour work week, simply never occurred to me. It was a rare day that I did not spend ten hours in the office or on duty; always an early riser, I was usually the first officer in the HQ each morning except for the duty offer. If my duties were accomplished, I saw no virtue in sitting in the office until an arbitrary departure time. One such day as I was leaving to go home, one of my NCOs suggested that it might not be a good time to depart because the ODCSLOG XO was sitting in his car noting the people who left before 1700. The SSG, very apologetic, said that he did not want to see me get into trouble, but I obviously was not aware that COL Selton had been doing this for several days. I thanked him for the tip, inwardly seething, I couldn't imagine anything more juvenile than a COL checking OFFs, or NCOs for that matter, in such a HQ as USAREUR. If there was a problem with work not being accomplished or people not available when needed, the division chiefs should be told to take care of the matter.

Despite the NCO's warning I continued downstairs. As I left the building, I saw Bob sitting in a car, he did not look at me when I stared at him before getting into my own car and driving off. The next morning I went to see COL Leidy, but he was out; his Deputy COL Foelsch (Bob Borman had left), with whom I had several clashes before, asked what I wanted. Foelsch wanted everyone to take all matters through him before going to see Leidy, a waste of time and effort. The idea of a colonel supervising a colonel supervising a colonel is the ultimate farce in military organization. When the situation was explained to him, he thought it was a great idea! Before our discussion became too heated, COL Leidy returned. After explaining the matter to him, I told him that I thought I should talk to Bob Selton and BG Maples about it. Carl very wisely calmed me down, saying that he would take care of the matter. Had i confronted Bob or Maples in my current frame of mind, I would have said things I would later regret. Carl never told me if he had talked with Bob or to Maples, but there was no more checking, I never found out if it was Bob's idea or BG Maples' to check on ODCSLOG personnel. Perhaps it was best that I did not know.

The DCSLOG was a member of the Class VI Board. The Class VI operation, liquor sales, a multi-million dollar business, generated a great deal of money for troop Welfare Funds. Unlike PX profits, these did not go back to the CONUS, but remained in Europe where they were used for the benefit of the troops stationed there. The Class VI Board made decisions on operations, prices, what to buy, stockage levels, operating hours for Class VI stores, whether to rehabilitate a particular store or close it. Whenever BG Maples could not make the meetings, I sat in as his alternate. One of the items always on the agenda was the handling of ready cash. There was always a great deal of money on hand, the result of a good cash flow system, often in excess of a half million dollars. The Class VI system discounted all its bills, stocked when prices were right, and maintained a cash reserve for rehabilitation, losses, or special buys. Frequently there was a motion to put this ready cash out on short term loans; it amazed me how much interest could be made in three or six months with such loans.

It was also interesting to learn that Army regulations precluded the sale of foreign liquor cheaper than a comparable American whiskey such as Bourbon. The USAREUR Class VI System could have sold Scotch, for instance, at least $2.00 a quart cheaper than its current price, but had to sell it for $1.00 above that charged for Bourbon. A fifth of Chivas Regal was $6.00 and the more common brands $4.00 because Bourbon was $3.00. There was no tax on this liquor, a large part of the price elsewhere. The military is a creature of politicians who are sensitive to lobbies and pressure groups. Hence, many regulations made little sense in terms of troop welfare.

As Chief of Services, it was my fate to attend or host many conferences. Sid Steelesetupa Joint Graves Registration Conference in Heidelberg. Graves Registration OFFs from all of the US Army, Navy and Air Force commands in Europe and the Middle East attended. Though not apleasant subject to talk about, it was necessary to insure that the recovery and disposition of the dead could be handled in the best possible fashion. As TJGRO I was the official host. It was an interest-ing conference at which I learned much.

Murphy and Burk set up a JAPO conference at Chiemsee. Murphy asked a SF Team from Bad Tolztomake a demonstration water jump for us. When he found that I wanted to make a jump, he arranged for a wet suit and parachute for both of us; it was my first water jump. The JAPO conference was most productive.

Services Division also sponsored a Food Service Conference at Munich. BG Maples at first opposed it because he thought it was an attempt to attend the Oktoberfest on government time and expense. Actually these conferences served many useful purposes; due to their Europe-wide representation, they provided a forum for the discussion of troubling Food Service problems. Maples did address the conference on the need for reducing the amount of paperwork in Food Service and getting on with the important matter of providing better food for the troops. The Brigadier in charge of Food Service for the British Army also attended.

The conference was held the first few days in October, so everyone had a chance to go to the Oktoberfest in the evenings. It is a fun time, with much singing, dancing, eating, and, of course, drinking. The crowd was rousing, drunken, roistering, loud, but generally good-natured, everyone was out to enjoy the fun. We did.

LTC Charles Drake, an action officer in ODCSPER, called to tell me that I had been selected to address the British Staff College at Camberly on "US Operations in Vietnam". Fortunately, I had brought the many slides I had taken in Vietnam to Germany. About fifty of them provided the basis on which I wrote the presentation in accordance with the guidelines received from the British Staff College. It was to address the tactics and techniques utilized, not the rationale for the US involve-ment there.

The British Staff College paid my way by commercial air. This was my first visit to the British Isles, so I asked for a few days leave in London. At Heathrow I was met by a British MAJ with a staff car in which we rode to Camberly. A suite of rooms in the main building of the Staff College was provided for me. To an old building buff like myself it was an exciting structure, probably 300 or 400 years old with extremely antique plumbing. But the visitors accommodations were comfortable. The bat-man assigned to look after me brought me a mug of hot, muddy, sweet tea in the morning. Some of the staff had me to dinner in the dining room of the College; the old silver and trophies on display represented centuries of tradition.

The American LNO, a LTC, escorted me to the auditorium. My presentation was preceded by a discussion of the political and diplomatic considerations of the US involvement in Vietnam, and why our presence there was a mistake. The journalist/historian making the presentation roundly berated the US for its policy toward its southeast Asian ally.

It was not opportune to rebut the biased presentation of the first speaker. I merely introduced my subject with the words, "The US involvement in Vietnam is a matter of national policy, we in the military simply implement such policies." The students appeared far more interested in my presentation than in the former one, asking many incisive questions. The talk was received well.

My escort officer drove me to London, where I had reservations at Columbia House, an USAF transit billet, which was comfortable and cheap, in three short, crammed days, I saw all of the great sights I had read about; the changing of the guard at Buckingham Palace, St Paul's Cathedral, Westminister Abbey, the British Museum, the Tower of London, Runnymeade and Windsor Castle. In the evenings I was able to see several plays. It was a fine introduction to England which whetted my appetite for further visits.

Later in the year I was again tasked to speak on Vietnam, this time to a German Veteran Officers Association at the Officer Candidate School in Hamburg. The retired group paid the expenses. This presentation provided another opportunity to see a part of Germany I had not been to. Two sights in Hamburg intrigued me; the enclosed street just off the Reeperbahn devoted entirely to prostitution, and the great working display of miniature trains in the Town Hall. My hosts treated me to a gourmet German meal the night of the presentation.

My talk had been translated into German for distribution to the audience; as I spoke in English they followed me in the translation. There was an interpreter, of course, whose major function was during the question and answer period. I was not proficient or confident enough in German to answer without one.

The day after the presentation, a staff car took me to Bremerhaven where I inspected the cold storage facilities. Almost all of the meat and other food destined for the troop messes and commissaries came through that port. Here the meat was sorted, thawed, or shipped immediately to various depots. It was an essential element in the food system for Europe.

Late in 1968 I was designated as the 7th Army Chief of Services. Certain officers in HQ, USAREUR were "double-slotted" as both USAREUR staff officers and 7th Army staff officers. In the event of an emergency, 7th Army HQ would take to the field to direct operations. As 7th Army Chief of Services I would play an important role in wartime as food and fuel were essential for combat operations. Command Post Exercises (CPXs) were conducted by 7th Army HQ periodically to train its personnel in communications and staff procedures. For the duration of the CPX, the staff moved to a Kaserne in a city other than Heidelberg. While there was usually only routine logistical play, the CPXs did serve to familiarize the personnel with each other and with the procedures established for 7th Army.

About this time, work was completed on the Tactical Operations System, TOS, a project to computerize the reporting and display of tactical information. All intelligence and operational reports were tunneled directly from their sources, platoon leaders, company commanders, the TOCs of maneuver units, reconnaissance elements, or intelligence gathering agencies, to a computer which almost instantaneously displayed them on an automated map. In theory the information was collated and processed so the Corps Commander had detailed, up-to-the-minute information on which to base his decisions.

During the Test CPX, MAJ Kurgvel was designated to play the 7th Army G-4. Kurgvel was assisted by a Reserve officer, a schoolteacher in the USAREUR school system on active duty for two weeks, and five junior NCOs. Though I protested that such a small group could not do justice to the job, working 24 hours each of the seven days of the exercise, BG Maples refused to augment the ODCSLOG element, believing that there would be only minor logistics play. He instructed Kurgvel to report that "all operational requirements could be supported".

But LTG Heintges, the exercise commander, who wanted to test TOS thoroughly, insisted on the movement of all barrier materials and ammunition called for in the Emergency Plan. This developed many realistic logistics requirements. After a major protest, another ODCSLOG CPT was assigned to handle the day shift. During the night shift, Kurgvel handled all of the activity. He wrote the briefings, including considerable back-up data and rationale to enable the briefer to answer LTG Heintges detailed questions. When the 7th Army Engineer element failed to answer the questions on atomic demolitions, Kurgvel was tasked to find the answers on transportation and time requirements. It was a difficult period for Kurgvel, one he handled well.

Upon conclusion of the CPX, a demonstration of TOS was given to the USAREUR Staff. During the question period, I asked, "How do you build delay into the system?" The briefer and technicians were aghast at my question, carefully explaining that the purpose of TOS was to get information immediately to the Corps Commander. The flood of unevaluated information directly to Corps or Army was the point that concerned me.

"Having been a green lieutenant in combat, I remember my first fire fight. I was sure that my platoon was being held up by a battalion of the enemy. It turned out we were facing one or two squads. Now who is going to assess such reports from inexperienced people? Is a report, unevaluated at company, battalion, regiment or brigade, going to flash directly from a platoon or squad to Corps Headquarters and be displayed? I believe that a false picture will develop causing the commander to make faulty decisions."

No one had an answer, indeed, no one would listen to me. TOS was a wonderful instrument which its civilian designers proudly claimed could receive and display every scrap of data, regardless of its reliability, obtained from the lowest element to the most sophisticated intelligence gathering devices. The sheer magnitude of the reports would saturate even a large computer. Unreliable communications or electrical current would distort the picture. Such a system, in my view, would lead to further usurpation of the authority of subordinate commanders, in addition to resulting in many poor decisions.

Christmas of 1968 was spent in Heidelberg. Ann and Jack Frankeberger had asked me to have dinner with them late in the afternoon. At noon, I had a delicious traditional German Christmas dinner at the Hotel Ritter on the Haupstrasse; goose, dumplings, red cabbage, apple sauce. That evening, at the Frankebergers, I enjoyed the traditional American turkey dinner.

Maples was promoted to MG at the end of the year. He and his wife had not only a New Year's Day reception, but also a promotion party.

In the spring of 1969 Services was again the ODCSLOG representative for the AYA Fair. There was initial panic when the COMZ Class I Officer proposed using ice cream being made for the fair, the large supply of rancid butter in the commissary warehouse, which because of its strong taste could not be issued to the troops or sold in commissaries. He assured me that not only would the taste of the ice cream be unaffected, but it was the logical way to get rid of the sizeable inventory of unusable butter. As it turned out, we sold more ice cream than ever without complaint as to taste!

Though by this time comfortable with Services operations, I was still not happy as a logistics staff officer. After much thought, I applied for a second tour in Vietnam. It was approved only after LTG Goodpaster, Deputy COMUSMACV, found a job for me as G-3, I Field Force, Vietnam (IFFV).

Just at this time, I was made the 7th Army G-4. My last official action was an interesting trip to Morocco with LTG Heintges. Since 7th Army had a contingency plan for Morocco, Heintges wanted his Staff to get first hand information on the country and terrain. LTG and Mrs Heintges and five staff officers made the trip as tourists; actually, we went to reconnoiter. Dave Presson, representing G-3, and I teamed up and shared a room wherever we went. On arrival at Rabat via Air France, my luggage was missing. The State Department took care of all formalities so there were no problems with customs, but customs without baggage posed no problems in any event! The embassy commissary was opened so that I could buy enough toilet articles and underwear to make do until my luggage caught up with me. Fortunately, we were not traveling in uniform. The baggage reached me three days later, just before we left Rabat. The trip across Morocco, made in three cars driven by Moroccans, included visits to Fez, Jebel, Marrakech, and Casablanca. At each city, acting as tourists, we went to the great markets or bazaars, haggled with rug merchants and other vendors, and were fascinated by the teeming hordes of people. Several actually bought rugs which were taken to Germany on an embassy courier plane.

We visited a Moroccan Army Training Camp. The skills which were in critical shortage in the Moroccan economy had been identified, and a program had been set up in the Army in which every draftee was trained in a career field: aviation, ground transportation, utilities, medical or food service (actually tourism and hotel management as well). Our group was briefed on and toured the training camp after which the soldiers learning to be chefs, waiters or hotel managers put on a formal luncheon for us that was superb. It included such Arabian delicacies as roast lamb picked off the carcass with the fingers, couscous, rice and other delicious foods I was unable to identify. The Director of the Training Camp presented each of us with an unstuffed white Moroccan leather hassock.

It was an enjoyable trip which enabled us to see a great deal of Morocco. One of the memorable features of the country was the Muezzins calling the faithful to prayer from the minarets. Their cries were particularly eerie in the early morning or late at night.

When the group returned to Heidelberg, I prepared for my return trip to Vietnam. Because of his anti-American stand, I would not go to France as long as DeGaulle was President of the country. Fortunately for me, he died at that time, so I determined to go through France on my way home. The trip back to America was to be made on the SS *United States,* the last of the American luxury liners. To fill the steamship, the government bought up all vacant space and made it available to military personnel. As a member of Transportation and Services Directorate, there was no problem getting assigned to the first June sailing. In order to spend a week in Paris, I would board the ship at LeHavre.

Packing and processing began; an officer assigned to ODCSOPS took over my apartment, bought the drapes and carpets I had purchased from my predecessor, and signed for all the furniture on loan from the Billeting Office. Finally, two days before my departure, movers packed the furniture, books, records and clothing that would go into storage. Packed in one of the footlockers going into storage were all of the insignia and memorabilia of my career, regimental crests, my first pair of 2LT bars, souvenir cigarette lighters and many other items impossible to replace. That footlocker was obviously marked, because when my household goods were assembled several years later, it was missing.

Since I had not picked up my car on its arrival in Germany, I drove it to Bremerhaven to see how car shipments were handled. Unfortunately, very few cars could go on the SS *United States* and my application was too late. Those lucky few who could get their cars on the ship could pick them up within hours after the ship docked.

The processing of the car for shipment to the United States was fast and efficient. COL Kittrell of Transportation Division had advised me when to turn it in to get it on a ship that was leaving at once, so that it would be available to me on my arrival in New York. For the remainder of my time in Heidelberg, Carl Leidy loaned me his Volkswagen to get back and forth from Sandhausen to the office, so I was not inconvenienced.

There was the usual round of farewell affairs: an office party at which the award of the second Oak Leaf Cluster to the LOM and the traditional stein were presented; an NCO luncheon Charley Monroe arranged at which he presented me a Buck knife engraved with the best wishes of the NCOs. But I drew the line at a Directorate dinner party which Carl Leidy wanted to have for me.

Finally, the processing completed, I boarded the train for the short trip to Paris. On detraining at Le Gare Du Nord, a hostile cab driver took me to the Hotel Lotti just off the Place de la Concorde. It was an intimate pension-type hotel, which Wick had recommended.

The four days in Paris were most enjoyable. I was a typical tourist, awed by Versailles, Notre Dame, the Left Bank, Sacre Coeur, the Louvre, the Rue de la Paix, the Eiffel Tower, the Champs Elysees, the Arc de Triomphe and the Invalids. The Invalids especially impressed me; the original purpose of the building was a retirement home for veterans of the French Army. Napoleon's tomb was an afterthought. The Invalids is now a museum in which history of the French Army is eloquently displayed. Paris is a beautiful city; it is understandable why people fall in love with it. If only the Parisians were less rude and inconsiderate, it would be a glorious city.

At last it was time to take the boat train to LeHavre from Gare St Lazare, a short pleasant trip. The boat train is a tradition in which I was delighted to participate. The tracks terminated at the dock where porters picked up my luggage, and took it directly to my stateroom.

The SS *United States* was a luxury ship. As an officer, I was entitled to first class passage; though staterooms were assigned by the Army according to the number of members in a family, rather than by grade, many junior to me had larger cabins. This was of no concern; my stateroom was adequate since I had no intention of doing anything but sleeping there.

The trip was a unique experience; the food was superb, the service outstanding, the facilities complete and luxurious. The best part of the trip was that it took only five days. Had it been longer it would have been too much; too much to eat, too much to drink, too little exercise, too close quarters. It was a smooth crossing; the weather was perfect, the ocean calm.

As the ship neared America, we were told that landfall would be early in the morning, I was up and packed by 0530. As the SS *United States* steamed past Sandy Hook and into New York Harbor the view was spectacular. From 0600 on the decks were crowded as people watched Long Island pass on our starboard. A cheer went up as the Statue of Liberty came into view.

We docked without incident about 1100. Arlene and Bob had driven Mother down to meet me, though I could not pick them out in the crowd. Customs took only a few minutes; all of my bags cleared without inspection. There was a fond reunion when the family found me.

The ten-day was full and enjoyable. My car was available in Brooklyn the day after I arrived in New York. After spending a few days with Mother, I drove to Washington to see friends there, then spent a night with G.G. and Hope O'Connor, who lived in the original Quarters No I on FT Monroe, a most historic house.

When the leave ended, I sold my car to Arlene and Bob, who drove me to Kennedy Airport where I caught a flight to Seattle. Once again I spent a night with the Steeds. Fred drove me to McChord Air Force Base. After checking in, I was informed that my flight would depart at 1600. With six hours to kill, I called Sid Hack who commanded an Armored Cavalry Regiment at FT Lewis. We had lunch together and a good talk.

The trip to Vietnam was shorter and more pleasant this time. The flight went non-stop to Tokyo; after only a short stopover, we proceeded to Cam Ranh Bay. Upon my arrival there, an IFFV LNO met me. He had arranged for billets as I was scheduled to spend a night in the Replacement Depot for processing, even though orders assigning me to IFFV had already been published. The following morning we went by helicopter to Nha Trang. It was interesting to note the changes since my last tour as we flew up the coast. As always the water was clear and blue; the beaches wide and white.

CHAPTER 19

STAFF OFFICER

The drive from Nha Trang Airfield, where the helicopter landed, was along a broad tree-lined boulevard with the white beach and blue ocean on one side, and large, stately houses set in lush gardens on the other. Though the former French villas were a bit seedy, their grandeur was still apparent. As on the few occasions when I had visited the city while assigned as Senior Advisor of the 24th STZ, the beauty of the city impressed me. It was a grand setting.

HQ, First Field Force, Vietnam (IFFV) was in the Grand Hotel, a former grand-lux hostelry on the Boulevard facing the beach. My escort took me to the office of the G-1, COL Ted Hervey, who welcomed me, had me sign in, and suggested that I get settled in billets before beginning me inevitable processing. A room had been reserved for me in the King Duy Tan Hotel, a structure completed under the auspices of the US Government as billets for senior American officers. The comfortable room with a bath, was cooled by a window air conditioner. The hotel was also on the Boulevard, only a short walk from the HQ. The dining room in the King Duy Tan Hotel was, for some strange reason, used by junior officers who lived in different billets. King Duy Tan residents ate at The Salamander Club, a senior officers' mess and club in a former French villa. The Salamander (actually Gecko, a small lizard) had a good bar and (air mess. One of its enjoyable features was a Saturday night cook-out during which members selected and grilled their own steaks. On occasion we became sick of the typical Army fare, which was, however, for a "combat situation" as this was designated, unusually good. The US had gone to great lengths to make tours in Vietnam attractive, but it was hard for me to consider Nha Trang a "combat situation", with an air conditioned room and a pleasant club, despite the threat of an occasional ground or rocket attack.

After the administrative processing was over, my indoctrination began. COL McClellan, the G-3 I was replacing, laid on an extensive orientation for me because I had arrived earlier than anticipated. Stan was not scheduled to leave until 18 July; I had arrived on 29 June. The orientation included a trip to Saigon and Long Binh for briefings at MAC V and USARV. At US ARV HQ I met Ed Cavanaugh, from the War College and Mainz, Ralph Peterson, the former coach of the Mainz Troopers, as well as Jean Hollstein from me Pentagon. They gave me some pointed, honest views of things in Vietnam. The Long Binh complex had grown and expanded in the year and a half since I had last seen it; II Field Force Headquarters was similarly changed since my last inspection of the Uniontown operation. While in the area, I spent me night with the Senior Advisor to the 18th ARVN Div. MG Giai greeted me warmly, hosting a fine dinner in my honor. Since coordination with HQS in III and I Corps would, at times, be required, visits to IIFFV, the 3rd Marine Amphibious Force (MAF) and XXIV Corps HQ had been included in my schedule. After leaving Long Binh and the IIFFV area, I went to Da Nang. COL Ollie Patton, a Leavenworth and War College classmate, the XXIV Corps G-2, brought me up to date on mutual friends as well as on the situation in I Corps. While in the area, I visited MG Jack Wright (Advance Class, 508 and 8th Div), CG of the 101st ABN Div, whose CofS, COL O.G. Garrett, was a War College classmate.

Back at Nha Trang there were detailed briefings by all of the IFFV Staff. Here I renewed several old friendships: MG Joseph R. Russ the Deputy IFFV Commander, COL Jim McClurkin from the 508, Col Kenny Bull from the Advance Class and Leavenworth, and COL Al Lockhart, also a Leavenworth classmate. With these old friends and many new ones, I immediately felt comfortable.

Continuing the orientation, I visited the Korean (ROK) Task Force HQ and 5th Special Forces Group HQ at Nha Trang, as well as all of the tactical units in II Corps; the US 4th IN Div and 173rd ABN Bde, the two ROK Div, the ARVN 22nd and 23rd Divs and the 24th STZ. It was interesting to see the changes the TET offensive had wrought in Kontum and Pleiku. George Miller, a Carlisle classmate, was Senior Advisor of the 24th STZ. LTC Doan, still the Kontum Province Chief, appeared delighted to see me again. BG Pat Timothy was once again the Senior Advisor of II Corps; his Deputy Sam Barth, was an old friend from the 504 in Mainz. Later Sam became the Senior Advisor to the 22nd ARVN Div. On a few occasions, Sam called me in desperation when he needed helicopters or other resources; I was happy to help him out when I could. MG Lu Lan, who had commanded the 10th ARVN Div when I visited Charlie Reidenbaugh in 1966, now commanded II Corps. There were a few friends on the II Corps Staff; COL Luyen my counterpart in the 25th ARVN Div, was Deputy for RFPF and LTC Ngo Than Nghia was still the G-2. Both of them seemed genuinely glad to see me.

The leisurely orientation gave me a sound footing to take over as G-3 and avoided a long overlap with Stan, but I fretted at the delay. I almost pushed him onto the aircraft the day he left; finally I assumed the duties of G-3.

LTG Charles A. Corcoran, CG, IFFV, a thin almost ascetic officer, filled with nervous energy, at times displayed a temper like my own. He was a superb writer, though he had not completed college, if, indeed, he had attended one at all. His Deputy, MG Joseph R. (Bud) Russ, was a quiet, easy-going, but very effective OFF who always had a word of encouragement for everyone. BG Richard H. Johnson, the CofS, a tall, thin, intellectual OFF, seemed to find it hard to relax with his subordinates. He set high standards, which no one could quarrel with, but was too demanding, failing to make allowances for the problems faced by the staff: the unclear guidance often given, the lack of information available, the need for sleep, as well as the frequently arbitrary deadlines. The action officers, who considered him a "hard nose" called him "Zoot" or more frequently "Snake" because he struck without warning, most of them dreaded taking actions to him.

The situation reminded me of the one which had existed in Plans ODCSOPS when COL Mock terrified many of the action officers. But Johnson was not as difficult as Mock. The last of the complement of general officers at IFFV HQ was BG Winant Sidle, Commander of Corps Artillery, a friendly, helpful individual.

To coordinate the civilian functions of government, a separate HQ section had been created at the Field Force or Corps level. Because Vietnamese Military Commanders also exercised civil powers, the Office for Civil Operations and Rural Development Support (CORDS) was a staff section of IFFV HO; the senior civilian, usually from USAID, was a Deputy of the CG, called DEPCORDS. Jim Magellas, the DEPCORDS, IFFV, was a likeable, cooperative individual. As a paratrooper with the 82nd ABN Div in WWII, he had earned the DSC. We hit it off well, holding similar views on most matters; whenever I dealt with Jim we accomplished a great deal in a short time. This was not true of his assistant, Will Chambers, with whom I had tangled at Rhein Main before the Sennelager jump in 1961, which was incidentally, the last time I had seen him. He had retired from the Army as a LTC and joined USAID. He liked to assert his power, often intruding his views into purely military decisions. While he was free to point out the effect contemplated military actions might have on civil actions, I thought he overstepped himself when he began arguing tactics.

The G-3 office was well manned with outstanding OFFs and NCOs. The Deputy G-3, LTC Stan Ward, an ARTY OFF, a competent, well-organized OFF who moved papers expeditiously, quickly familiarized me with the G-3 routine. The Chief of the Operations Division (OPS DIV), LTC Don English, a sharp, efficient IN OFF, was a bit of a martinet, who literally bit off his words as he spoke. But he was on top of everything going on in II Corps; as a result, he kept me well informed. LTC "Skip" MacDonald, an AR OFF, headed the Plans Division. A quietly competent individual, who had been denied an opportunity for command when he was retained at IFFV, was of great help to me. The G-3 Air, LTC John Trankovich, and the Chief of the Security Section, LTC Bruce Bidwell, filled the complement of LTCs. There was a sizeable group of effective MAJs and CPTs. MAJ Dick Hooker, whose ability I knew from the 504 in Mainz, had written to me when he heard that I was assigned as G-3 IFFV to ask for a job. Ted Hervey, the G-I, was able to get him assigned to the HQ shortly after I assumed the duties of G-3. The most impressive CPT in the G-3 office was Ron Ray, a tall, well-built, handsome, ABN IN OFF. He struck me immediately as one who could be depended upon to get things done.

SGM Jim Graham headed a well-trained and dedicated group of NCOs. Graham, a muscular, athletic, highly effective soldier, ran on the beach every day and kept himself in excellent physical condition. He would have made an outstanding SGM for the 1st Bde 9th Div in contrast to his namesake, F.C. Graham, with whom I had been saddled. Graham handled administrative and enlisted personnel matters quickly and well. Periodically he arranged Sunday afternoon beach parties for the G-3 Section; everyone who could be spared was coerced to attend them. One of the finest beach areas, set aside for the American troops, had barbeque pits, shaded picnic tables, volleyball courts and other amenities. The swimming, frolicking and eating, accompanied by cold beer, were a welcome relief from the demanding schedule the G-3 personnel followed.

One of the first tasks given me by LTG Corcoran was an evaluation of Task Force South (TFS). This was a separate brigade-size command with HQ at Dalat. Commanded by a COL with only a skeleton staff, it controlled three Bns: the 3rd Bn, 506th ABN IN (which had come to Vietnam as the 4th Bn, 1st Bde, 101st ABN Div); the 1st Bn, 50th Mech IN, and the 2nd Bn, 1st CAV Regt. Corcoran was not happy with the performance of this provisional organization, which had only limited artillery and other support. My mission was to determine if the commander should be relieved or other changes made. After three days in and around Dalat looking closely at TFS, I concluded that there were no grounds for relieving its commander, though he was not particularly impressive. It did appear to me that the location and mission of the Task Force were questionable, and that its Bns could be better employed elsewhere. There was a definite morale problem in the 3/506. which wanted to return to the 101st ABN Div, now that the entire Div had been deployed to Vietnam. The 101 was also eager to have the 3/506 back; in time it was reassigned to the Screaming Eagles. Meanwhile I reported my findings to LTG Corcoran. Eventually, TFS, relocated to the coast with HQ at Phan Thiet, operated in the two southern provinces of II Corps on the South China Sea.

Shortly after I assumed the duties of G-3, BG Johnson directed my Section to evaluate the security of districts and hamlets. Ron Ray, given the task, was well-suited for it, since he was solidly grounded in Infantry tactics, had served a combat tour with the 173rd ABN Bde, and was an intelligent, energetic, and careful staff OFF. In addition, Ron defended his views staunchly if he thought he was right. Johnson, who had some preconceived ideas on the study, tended to over-ride any conclusions not in consonance with his own. Ron refused to accept the CofS's predetermined views, and defended his position well. He had considerable data to back up his arguments; though the discussions often became heated, Ron refused to back down. Since I was not always able to be present during these briefings, Ron took the heat directly. After Johnson learned to respect Ron's judgement, things settled down. Later I learned that Ray had been recommended for the Medal of Honor for an action during his tour with the 173rd. Subsequently, the President presented him with the Nations' highest award for valor. Although he walked with a limp at the time, the result of a wound suffered during the action for which he was cited, through determined exercise Ron finally regained full use of his limb.

In the first few weeks of my duty with IFFV, I was struck with the constant criticism LTG Corcoran and BG Johnson made of the 4th Div; they repeatedly decried its "lack of aggressiveness". It seemed to me that Johnson was making unfair comparisons, recalling the battles about Dak To in 1967 and 1968 when he commanded one of the 4th Div's Bdes, but I did not understand Corcoran's criticism. On several occasions he intimated that he might relieve commanders or make other changes. After several days of this sort of talk, I could contain myself no longer and asked, "Has anyone discussed this with General Pepke?" MG Pepke, the 4th Div CG, was an old friend from the Pentagon and 1st AR Div days, an OFF for whom I had great respect. At my question, LTG Corcoran and BG Johnson looked at me in surprise as they slowly answered, "No".

"If the 4th Div is not as aggressive in its operations as you think it should be, and you are dissatisfied with it in any way, shouldn't MG Pepke be told?" Silence greeted this question. It was evident that no one at IFFV had ever discussed the matter with MG Pepke.

"Sir, I think that before we criticize a commander or unit we ought to tell them where they are lacking. What do you want from the 4th Division? What do you expect of them?"

There was obvious discomfort but no response which I interpreted to mean that LTG Corcoran did not want to tell MG Pepke of his dissatisfaction. However, he still held to his view that the 4th Div was not aggressive. At length, I recommended that, as a friend rather than as a staff officer representing the Commanding General, I talk with MG Pepke informally, informing him of the concern at IFFV about the aggressiveness of the 4th Div. This would alert him so that he could take a hard look at his operations. Both generals agreed that this might be the best solution to the immediate problem.

The next day I flew to Camp Enari in Pleiku Prov to have lunch with MG Pepke. Before earing I told him that I would like to talk with him privately about 4th Div operations; however, he elected to have COL Gordon Duqueman, his CofS, sit in on the conversation. With complete candor, I told him of the feeling at IFFV HQ. Being new in country, I had no detailed knowledge of the 4th Div's operations, so was in no position to advise Pepke what he should do to change Corcoran's views. Pepke and Duqueman were surprised and shocked; they had no idea that there was any concern about the 4th Div at IFFV. It was awkward for me, but with the situation now in the open, Pepke was able to deal with it. The few reports I had read did not support the view that the 4th Div lacked aggressiveness. True, it had not had any major contact in the past month, but that frequently happened. The VC at times faded away, knocked off balance by US, ROK or Vietnamese attacks, or in need of rest and resupply, they withdrew into one of their base areas, or turned their attention and resources to other areas. There was an evident increase in operational activity in the 4th Div AO following my visit, but little contact immediately.

Shortly after my visit to the 4th Div I learned that MG Giai had been reassigned from the 18th ARVN Div to the ARVN Training Center north of Nha Trang. As soon as activity subsided enough to permit a free afternoon, I went to visit him. Added to the pleasure of seeing Giai again, was finding COL Angel Torres, one of my K Co Plt Ldrs as his Senior Advisor. Both Giai and Torres insisted on showing me the entire camp, a carbon copy of a US Army Advanced Infantry Training Center. The facilities and the training were impressive. Even more interesting was their briefing on the Center's contingency missions, one of which was to reinforce Nha Trang if it was attacked. During the year I was able to visit Giai and Torres several times.

In a short time, my activities became second nature. Because the situation in II Corps constantly changed, things never became routine in the G-3 Section, but a pattern began to form. Always an early riser, I got to the office shortly after 0600. The shift on duty in the TOC briefed me on significant developments during the night, after which I read the message traffic. At my direction, the OPS Div compiled a loose leaf note book which I called my "brain". It listed all current operations in the II Corps area, US, Vietnamese and Korean, the Army aircraft allocation for the day, and other data concerning combat support and organization of the forces in II Corps. This was necessitated by the sheer volume of detail and my inability to recall every one of the myriad operations ongoing in the area. After giving some attention to paperwork, I walked to the Salamander Club for breakfast, Returning to the office I discussed with the G-3 personnel their current projects. At 0800 we all trooped into the briefing room on the second floor of the Grand Hotel, the floor on which the

Command Section offices were located, where the generals and the Staff were briefed on II Corps events during the previous 24 hours and on activities planned for the day. Following this, those who had Special Intelligence (SI) clearance went to the SI briefing room for an update on information received through radio intercept and other sophisticated means. Immediately after these briefings, I hastily gave my division chiefs guidance based on instructions received from the generals, before heading out to the airfield. Almost every day I visited one of the units in II Corps, conferred with the Vietnamese or Korean G-3s, or attended meetings or ceremonies.

Often I did not return until after the evening update held at 1700. When I did get back, there were conferences with my division chiefs or action officers, as well as a mountain of paperwork which kept me busy until it was necessary to break away for dinner or give up that pleasure entirely. By the time I got to the Duy Tan about 2130, I was ready for bed, though I usually had a short conversation and a drink with friends before I turned in. It was a demanding schedule, but a fascinating assignment, I was in the middle of everything, and I reveled in it

When I finally left my desk in the evening, I would normally find my division chiefs waiting for me at the bar of the Salamander Club, already deep in a game of Ship-Captain-Crew. This was the accepted method for determining who paid for the drinks or the wine for dinner. For some strange reason, I enjoyed a phenomenal run of luck; the dice responded nightly to my pleas. The entire G-3 Section would gang up on me, trying to get me to pay for a round, but only once did they have that satisfaction. It was a hilarious and friendly game which relaxed all of us after a full day. Invariably the G-3 Section was the last group to eat; the mess was about to close when we finally sat down to dinner.

There were several places to eat in Nha Trang, at least during the early part of my tour there. In addition to the Salamander Club, there were the Air Force, Corps Artillery and Special Forces Clubs at the airfield. The 20th Evacuation Hospital had a fine bar and dining room which many of the junior officers frequented for the female companionship as much as the food. But the real treats were the Vietnamese restaurants. My favorite was La Fregates owned and run by the wife of the Darlac Prov Chief. It served excellent Vietnamese and French food with a touch of Chinese. The speciality was langouste or spiny lobster which were caught just offshore and brought in immediately for the evening meal. These lobsters do not have large claws, but the abdomen (erroneously called the tail by most people) is a solid piece of delicious meat. These were served in three sizes, small, medium and large, the latter from six to nine pounds. Anyone who ordered half a large lobster usually got more than he could eat About every two weeks the G-3 crew ate at La Fregates. Another favorite was Francois's run by a retired French Foreign Legion SGT and his Vietnamese wife. It too served excellent food. In all restaurants in Vietnam, wonderful, crisp-crusted French bread was served. There were several good Chinese restaurants in Nha Trang, so there was no lack of variety as long as the local eating establishments were on limits. Unhappily, because of security considerations and sanitary conditions, all were placed off limits to US personnel some six months after I joined IFFV.

Toward the end of the summer, rotation caused several personnel changes in the G-3 Section. LTC Ward was replaced as Deputy by LTC Forest Rittgers, a sharp IN OFF who had been wounded while commanding an IN Bn in the 25th Div. He was assigned to the staff until he regained full use of his legs, after which he returned to command. He made a superb deputy, not only because of his command experience in Vietnam, but also because he was a well-organized and careful staff officer. We worked well together. Bruce Bidwell was replaced by LTC Bob Bond, an AR OFF, and two additional LTCs were assigned, Les McGee, (who became the Asst OPS OFF until Don English left in November, at which time he took over as Chief of Operations), and Ray LaFrance. With these officers, the resources were available to reorganize the G-3 Section along more functional lines. Working with Rittgers and the division chiefs, a new organization was devised and implemented. A coordinating group comprised of LTC Rittgers, an Admin Off, SGM Graham, and several clerks supported me.

The many G-3 functions were handled in six divisions, OPS under Don English, Plans under Skip MacDonald, Security under Bob Bond, Organization and Training (O&T) under Ray LaFrance, Air under "Trank" Trankovich, and Chemical under Len Martin. In addition, the 13th Military History Det functioned as a part of the G-3 Section with MAJ Ron Duchin in charge. It was quite an empire, but it worked efficiently, possibly because I was away from the office so much.

There was a constant turnover of junior OFFs and EM; scarcely a week went by without a ceremony at which I awarded an ARCOM or some other recognition and presented a plaque to someone leaving the Section. Periodically the officers had a hail and farewell party atone of the clubs at the Nha Trang Airfield. At one such party, I welcomed a hard-charging ABN IN OFF, MAJ Paul "Mickey" Leary, who took over Special Operations in OPS Div, handling all matters dealing with SF, Long-range Reconnaissance Patrols (LRRPs), and Ranger Co missions. Later he requested reassignment from IFFV; reluctantly I released him. He was killed in Cambodia shortly thereafter, a fine officer cut down before his time.

Les McGee recommended highly a CPT he knew who had been assigned to Vietnam. He urged me to try to get him for OPS Div. Ted Hervey was able to get CPT Joe Sarakaitis assigned to IFFV. Joe lived up to McGee's recommendation. A round-faced, stocky officer, he elected to remain on the night shift in the TOC all the time he was with the G-3 Section. He came to IFFV as a "promotable" CPT; his MAJ's leaves were pinned on him shortly after his arrival. Joe told me about his first taste of the "field grade syndrome"; as a CPT he was not deemed knowledgeable or experienced enough to head a shift in the TOC, but the day he was promoted he became officer-in-charge (OIC) of the night shift! Joe, a hard worker and a highly-competent officer, relaxed during the night by slipping up to the roof of the Grand Hotel about 0230 each morning when everything was quiet, to daydream while listening to the surf break on the beach. He said that 30 minutes of such solitude refreshed him more than anything he could think of. As OIC of the night shift, Joe was responsible for preparing the morning briefings, a recapitulation of the activities in II Corps during the preceding 24 hours. In time, I gained so much confidence in his ability and reliability that I no longer required a rehearsal of the briefings, satisfied with a quick review of the highlights and the information in my "brain" book.

During these personnel changes, one problem bothered me. Bob Bond, the senior LTC in the G-3 Section, would normally have been assigned as Deputy G-3. However, he was unable to get an SI clearance because he was married to a foreign national who had relatives behind the iron curtain. For about a month I tried to operate with Bob as my Deputy, in spite of his lack of clearances, but so much of the information used in the papers prepared by G-3 personnel involved SI, that he was bypassed on most actions, hence was of little assistance to me. It was at this time that I moved him to Security and brought Rittgers in as Deputy.

While these personnel changes were taking place, the billeting of junior OFFs was reorganized. Most MAJs lived in beautiful, old villas with faded glory, scattered throughout the city, usually four or five to a villa. Though the MAJs enjoyed both privacy as well as the freedom to cook their own meals when they wanted to, the dispersed locations posed problems of security and control. CPTs lived in several hotels scattered about Nha Trang. Hastily built, two-story, tin roofed, wooden barracks, screened and open to the weather, were being constructed at Camp McDermott, which surrounded the airfield on the south side of the city. The overhanging eaves shielded the occupants from the rain and sun, shutters were provided for the monsoon season. By the end of the summer all OFFs in the grade of MAJ or below were concentrated in these quarters at Camp McDermott (LTCs and COLs lived in the Duy Tan, while the generals occupied a spacious villa). Each OFF had a room about 8X15 with a cot, ceiling fan, plywood wardrobe and steel folding chair. Ingenuity provided tables and bookcases. The OFFs used communal latrines. Most of the G-3 OFFs protested vigorously the concentration at Camp McDermott, finding the accommodations less comfortable than those vacated. But the decision had been made for security reasons; the scattered billets were potential targets for VC terrorists.

Security at first proved illusory, even lessened. The crowded BOQ area became a target for VC mortar men; shortly after the junior OFFs moved to Camp McDennott, 15 or 20 rounds were "walked" through the area. A 81/82 mm round hit the tin roof of one barracks, putting holes everywhere in the building. Although there were several such attacks, fortunately no one was seriously injured. Indeed, most of the injuries resulted from the chaos as OFFs grabbed weapons and steel pots and ran for the bunkers adjacent to the barracks.

An immediate problem surfaced in that first attack. Officers from various units were billeted at McDermott; each unit represented had its own defense plan, which involved M60 machine guns sited down the streets between the barracks, effectively covering the routes to the bunkers used by officers from other units. Indeed, the fields of fire seemed more calculated to destroy the BOQs and friendly bunkers than any potential VC. Luckily, there was no ground attack before protests of the occupants resulted in a general defense plan, fully coordinated and focused on the outer perimeter.

The EM lived in similar barracks on the grounds of the Grand Hotel. There was also a mess hall, club, movie and a small PX. But the major facilities were located at Camp McDermott The large PX there even stocked small refrigerators and electric appliances. The Korean officers and soldiers made more extensive use of that PX than the Americans.

The mortar attacks on Camp McDermott were a source of concern. MAJ Sarakaitis' room was hit while he was on duty; sadly he reported the loss of a wall full of pictures his children had sent him, and six bottles of Chivas Regal Scotch! Joe "pulled rank" and moved to the first floor "to put a layer of captains between me and the VC mortars", as he put it.

Dick Hooker described one attack to me, "One night, a small group, including the American Red Cross representative, was winding up an evening by visiting the quarters of MAJ Gordy Sullivan of the G-l Section. About midnight we were listening to his newly-arrived tape of Hair. A particularly wistful piece was playing when we heard a distant explosion. The music played on. Another mortar explosion, closer. Nobody moves, glances are exchanged, the music plays on. A third explosion, definitely closer, was followed immediately by one very close. The lights go out, everybody dives for cover (there was none), as a round hits the end of the building. When a flashlight finally revealed the scene, the ARC representative was discovered, unhurt, stuck halfway under an overturned three hundred pound wardrobe."

MAJ Leary suggested I visit the MACV School operated by the 5th SF Group. A particular pet of GEN Westmoreland, the school trained personnel for the LRRPs. During the visit, I was delighted to see CPT Arif Zaky, one of my NCOs from K Co, 504, the Asst Cmdt of the School, who insisted that I address the next graduating class. Mickey Leary prepared some appropriate remarks, which I tailored to my own style and views. The students were delighted with my speech, remarkably short!

While personnel and billeting changes were being effected, the Plans Division became involved in a Base Area Targeting Plan, a follow-on to Ron Ray's Hamlet Security Study. Dick Hooker., the project officer, LTC MacDonald and I spent long hours going over the details. This plan established the priority in which IFFV would attack VC and NVA base camps. It included a proposed scenario, the forces deemed necessary, and locations of possible artillery fire support bases. The plan proved remarkably accurate and helpful in two major battles, the first of which occurred early in October.

Close to the Cambodian border in Quang Duoc Province were two villages, Due Lap and Bu Prang, ;and a SF Camp, which could be reached only by an almost impassable road. One of Hooker's scenarios involved an attack on the SF Camp or the two villages with the subsequent reinforcement of them, by the 23rd ARVN Div from Ban Me Thuot. Almost as if rehearsed, the VC attacked first Bu Prang, then Due Lap, and finally the SF Camp; the 23rd ARVN Div sent forces to assist in the defense: of the two villages. The logistical, air and artillery support called for in the plan was positioned very much as Hooker had proposed. The fighting was intense at times, and the 23rd Div was hard-pressed. More and more US artillery was repositioned to support the battle. To achieve full coverage of the area, standard US artillery doctrine was violated. Over the protests of BG Sidle, LTG Corcoran, also a former Artilleryman, began decentralizing the artillery until some sections were firing from forward bases which were only supported by another section of artillery at maximum range. It was a touchy situation, hut finally the VC were forced to withdraw into Cambodia.

On several occasions, LTG Corcoran, BGs Johnson and Sidle, and I huddled to review the Rules of Engagement which governed US fire across the Cambodian border. Specifically authorized was the; return of fire received from Cambodia, hot pursuit of forces crossing the border to avoid US or ARVN fire and the destruction of recognized base areas from which attacks on friendly installations were launched. Based on the situation, we frequently directed artillery and gunship fire across the border, even programming one or two B-52 strikes on identified base areas.

Just as the Battle of Bu Prang and Due Lap was drawing to a close, BG Sidle was reassigned to the CONUS, replaced by COL (P) Charley Hall. Hall a likeable, energetic, ABN Artilleryman, was faced with the wide dispersion of the artillery and some very poorly defended fire support bases. It took C barley a month or more to reposition the artillery into a more conventional and more defensible configuration.

Even during the height of the fighting around Bu Prang and Due lap, LTG Corcoran rarely took me with him when visiting units. In fact, I recall going to Due Lap only once during that time. Unlike most commanders, LTG Corcoran and his G-3 were not inseparable. While he did not forbid me to travel with him, he discouraged it, usually giving me other missions. On many occasions, he would drop me off in his U-21 while enroute to another area. In some respects this gave us wider coverage since we saw different units or actions on the same day.

It was necessary to spend more and more time in the Ban Me Thuot area during those days, coordinating support for the 23rd ARVN Div. It was a city which held many memories of my tour with the 24th STZ. The Advisory Team lived in the Imperial Bungalow, a rambling wooden structure somewhat patterned after a Montagnard Happy House, built by former Emperor Bao Dai as a hunting lodge. In 1970 it was burned down by a careless advisor cooking over a hot plate in his room. Tim Gannon, the Darlac Province Advisor, was replaced toward the end of 1969 by Wayne Smith from the 504 at Mainz.

As the situation in the Bu Prang/Due Lap area became critical, LTG Corcoran kept GEN Westmoreland apprized of what was going on by a nightly "back channel", a personal message sent over the secure and very fast SI net. Every night I would draft a report, take it to BG Johnson, who would revise it before getting LTG Corcoran's approval. In a short time I became adept at drafting those back channels; slowly Johnson made fewer corrections in them. The point was finally reached at which I could sit down at my typewriter, review the events of the day, and dash off the draft in a matter of minutes. This was a time-saver because by the time I usually returned from Ban Me Thuot or wherever I happened to be that day, the clerical personnel would be gone. This rough back channel I hand carried to the Generals' quarters, a fine French villa, several blocks from the Duy Tan. After the CofS and CG edited the draft, which fortunately took less and less time as my experience grew, the message was delivered to the SI Section for dispatch. Then I rushed to the Salamander Club, which was usually ready to close, kept open only because Forest Rittgers forcefully impressed on the Vietnamese mess personnel that they could not close until they had fed me!

As operations around Due Lap drew to a close, things settled down once again into a "normal routine". Since I had been in Vietnam six months, it seemed time to take an R&R. I had not been to Manila since the end of WWII in 1945, so I decided to go there to see what changes had been made.

Just before my departure for Manila, George Miller, the Senior Advisor of the 24th STZ and his counterpart were shot down in a helicopter north of Tan Canh. A memorial service was held for George in the chapel in Tenza Compound in Kontum. Of course, I attended. Father Van, the Roman Catholic Chaplain of the 24th STZ and MG Russ both took part in the simple ceremony. I had become well-acquainted with George at the War College; a dedicated officer, a good friend, he was making a real contribution to Kontum.

The R&R in Manila was an enjoyable one. Since the plane left from Cam Ranh Bay, it was an easy trip. There was still evidence of the destruction done to Manila during WWII, though a great deal had been accomplished in rebuilding the city. I stayed at The Hilton Hotel, which was new and guaranteed "earthquake proof. But one night I awoke to find myself on the floor. The building was shaking so violently, I found it difficult to get to my feet. My first thought was that if the elevator shaft was bent I would have to walk down 18 floors. Though the quake was a severe one, that did not prove to be the case.

During those few days in Manila, I saw many of the sights I had seen in 1945: the cathedrals and churches, the City Hall, the opera, and others. Most had been repaired, others were no longer standing. I visited the US National Cemetery just outside the city. On the marble walls of the memorial were maps of the WWII campaigns, as well as the names of those who had been killed in the fighting in that part of the world. I found listed the names of some of the members of F Co, 382nd IN who had been killed on Okinawa.

In 1945 the most popular Philippine resort was Baguio, in northern Luzon. Since I had not gotten there in 1945, I spent two days in that beautiful area. The Army maintained a leave center there, but I stayed in the Pines Hotel.

On my return to Manila, the gentleman who ran the tours to Corregidor flew me to the island. On a private, leisurely tour, I saw much more than those on regular tours, even getting into Malinta Tunnel. I finally understood the terms "topside", "bottomside" and the "long barracks" that Wick had used in describing his life on Corregidor when his father was assigned there.

After much persuasion, a taxi driver took me to a seedy part of the city to see my first and only cock fight. The furious betting, conducted by arm and hand signals used to make and acknowledge bets, was more interesting than the fighting.

Manila was beautifully decorated for the Christmas holidays, the lights and gaiety enhanced the visit. Adding to the color were the brightly decorated and largely modified jeeps used as cabs and buses. These "Jeepneys" careened recklessly about the streets overloaded with laughing, shouting passengers. At last an aircraft returned me to Can Ranh Bay in time to spend Christmas at IFFV.

Personnel turnover continued unabated. In November, I attended the ceremony at Camp Enari at which MG Pepke relinquished command of the 4th Div to MG Glenn Walker. Walker had commanded the 1st Bde, 25th Div in Pleiku during much of the time I was with the 24th STZ. Al Burdette, Advance Class and 508, invited me to his change of command ceremony when he left the 1st AVN Bde. LTG Corcoran also attended the ceremony so I flew to Long Binh with him for that occasion. In the G-3 Section Don English left and Les McGee took over OPS from him. When Rittgers went back to a battalion, LTC Steve Dotur became my Deputy. Bond took command of the 2/1st Cav in TFS, and LTC George Rozsypal took over Security Division. There were other changes. Skip MacDonald was turned down when he requested reassignment, though if an AR CMD assignment had been available he would have gotten it.

Dick Hooker, promoted to LTC, immediately wanted to command a BN. As a result of a letter I wrote to O.G. Garrett, CofS of the 101st ABN Div, he went for an interview and was accepted by Jack Wright. But on his return, IFFV turned down his request for reassignment. Al Lockhart refused to let him talk to BG Johnson about the transfer, and I was unable to break the deadlock for him. As it was obvious that he would not get out of the II Corps area, he asked BG Cunningham about an assignment to the 173rd ABN Bde and was put on the waiting list. He finally settled for the opportunity to command the 1/50 Mech Bn in TFS when the commander rotated.

In February, LTG Corcoran turned over command of IFFV to LTG Arthur S. Collins, Jr. At dinner party prior to his departure, Corcoran was both spoofed and lauded. At the change of command ceremony in front of the Grand Hotel, BG Johnson was Commander of Troops with the IFFV Staff standing tall behind him. He put us through our paces! LTG "Ace" Collins - dynamic, energetic, short - was a different type of commander than his predecessor, more of a field soldier, much interested in training.

In April MG Russ departed after a fitting farewell party, replaced by MG Charles P. Brown. Brown, a distinguished looking officer, was a dedicated Artilleryman who touted his branch at every opportunity. As proud of the Infantry as Brown was of the Artillery, I naturally got into some good-natured disputes with him about the relative virtues of Infantrymen and Artillerymen. But we shared common views on tactics, leadership and personnel, and worked well together. Though his primary concern was RFPF, we consulted together often. It was through him that I met LTC George Nelson. MG Brown and I frequently traveled in the same aircraft, sharing some interesting adventures.

Shortly after MG Brown arrived, BG Johnson was replaced by BG Richard Powers. Though more friendly than Johnson, I did not hold Powers in the same high esteem, professionally, in which I held Johnson. It was my responsibility to adjust to him, but I found him difficult to work with. I was especially concerned when he tried to interpose himself between LTG Collins and the Staff; he attempted to keep from the CG information and recommendations from his staff I thought he should have.

Powers and I became involved in a heated manner over efficiency reports. A WO in the AG Section sent an efficiency report I had submitted on a G-3 officer back to me with a note that the comments were not adequate. I returned the report with an explanation of my position. COL Ledda, the AG, called me to discuss the matter, insisting I add additional comments concerning supply economy, which I did not think appropriate. He quoted the regulations; I pointed out that they suggested those remarks be included but did not require them; in the case of the officer involved, they were not appropriate. COL Ledda took the matter to BG Powers, who directed me to rewrite the report. Whenever challenged on efficiency reports I became very stubborn. My efficiency reports were carefully thought out and rendered in accordance with the regulations. During several heated discussions, I maintained that Powers should make any comments he thought appropriate, including the ones he insisted I make, in his review of the report. He finally yielded when he found out that I would not give in on this matter.

In 1969 and 1970, there was a quantum increase in the use of electronic sensors of all types in Vietnam. A considerable portion of the morning briefing was now devoted to sensors: the information gained from them, the plans for emplacing them and the allocation of resources to handle them. The sensors were highly sophisticated; some could detect and relay any voices in the area, others were sensitive to ground tremors from vehicles, still others were activated by footsteps. Each sensor had a microphone or other receptor, and either stored information received to be transmitted on demand, or continually broadcast the data as it was received. The location of sensors was a matter of serious concern, decided only after careful analysis of the patterns of infiltration of the VC and NVA. Some were individually planted; others were planted in a specific pattern, either in rows or in a checkerboard, others were randomly inserted. Insertion was made by high performance aircraft, helicopter or ground patrols. Specialists monitored the sensors at a reception station in Pleiku, analyzing the information received. By the sequence of activation of sensors in a line or in a geometric pattern, the speed and direction of movement could be determined; through differing intensities and sensitivities, vehicles and personnel could be identified. It was a fascinating subject, yet sensors yielded minimal useful information.

When the G-1 told me that I was entitled to another R&R in April, I went to Hong Kong again, staying on Kowloon at the Peninsula Hotel. This old, luxurious British hotel had recently been refurbished. Though expensive, I enjoyed the service and amenities. Again, I gorged myself on delicious Chinese food.

While in Hongkong, one of my former cadets from KMI, Harry Bailey, who had a one-year residency in the Children's Hospital, drove me out to the New Territories, the border lands with Red China. Harry and his colleagues, hearing of my liking for Peking Duck, arranged a dinner party at which we could enjoy that delicacy. On entering the restaurant, some sixth sense made me ill at ease. When I saw the huge picture of Mao Tse-Tung on the wall the reason was obvious. An American officer fighting the North Vietnamese Communists was sitting down to dinner in a Red Chinese Restaurant! My inclination was to withdraw politely, but the lure of the Peking Duck was too much. It was worth the discomfiture!

Returning to Nha Trang, I found a major battle developing in Kontum. This was the second Base Area Targeting Plan developed by Hooker which unfolded according to the script. Almost all of the SF camps came under attack, Dak Seang, Dak To, Dak Pek, Ben Het and Tan Canh itself. The most fierce fighting centered around Dak Seang and Ben Het. LTG Collins, MG Brown and I spent most days in the area; a liaison party from IFFV was positioned with COL Ollie Dillard, the new 24th STZ Advisor. This team coordinated the support IFFV provided to the ARVN and CIDG forces, Much of the artillery support was provided by the 52nd ARTY Group, commanded initially by Alan Toffler, a War College Classmate. During this period he was replaced by Bob Dingeman, a Leavenworth classmate. The 4th Div provided artillery and helicopter support and deployed troops into the threatened areas. The fighting raged fiercely throughout Kontum, now one camp taking the brunt of the attack, now another. Finally the NVA withdrew to Cambodia or Laos; a troubled calm settled over the Highlands.

MG Brown and I shared many unforgettable airplane trips to the Kontum-Pleiku area. Several times we made Ground Control Approaches (GCA) only to pull up sharply at the last moment when the pilot was unable to see the runway because thick fog hugged the ground. In each case, we let the pilot decide if the mission should be scrubbed because the risks were too great.

Personnel rotation continued apace. COL Wagonhurst, a War College classmate, assumed command of Task Force South. COL Ben Ambrose (promoted after he joined IFFV) replaced Kenny Bull as the G-4. COL Curtis Livingston, who had relieved me of command of THE REGULARS in 1963, replaced Lou Caraplis as G-2. COL Bud Bressler, who had commanded one of the tank battalions in the 1st Bde of the 1st AR Div when I was with THE REGULARS, joined CORDS. When Jim Magellas departed, leaving Will Chambers as the acting DEPCORDS, it was a trying time for all of us. Chambers, who stated at one meeting with LTG Collins and his staff, that he "yielded to no man in his knowledge of tactics", frequently tried to interject himself into discussions of purely military matters. His strategic views were given short shrift. In the G-3 Section, Dotur was replaced by Rozsypal as Deputy, and LTC Grubbs replaced Les McGee as Chief of Operations.

Early in 19701 attended the ceremony in which MG Jack Wright turned over command of the 101st Airborne Division to MG Jack Hennessey. Both had been in my Advance Class and were good friends. While there, I discussed with Jack Hennessey the possibility of becoming his Chief of Staff. He expressed genuine interest in having me as the CofS of the 101st ABN Div. On my return to Nha Trang, Ted Hervey processed the required paperwork. Since I would have been in Vietnam more than a year by the time such a transfer could be effected, it involved an extension of my tour. It was finally decided that I would leave IFFV in November, 1970, after 14 months as G-3, to assume the duties of Chief of Staff of the 101st ABN Div.

Late in May, I accompanied LTG Collins to Pleiku to brief LTG Lu Lan and the 4th Division on the proposed invasion of Cambodia to destroy North Vietnamese supply and training areas. President

Nixon had authorized an incursion across the border in the Pleiku area. The operation stirred up a storm, not only in Cambodia and Vietnam, but apparently in the United States as well. The area was critical to the enemy who reacted strongly to the ARVN operation. Considerable rice and weapons were found, but the results were somewhat disappointing. It did serve notice on the NVA that they no longer had a safe haven to which they could withdraw whenever the fighting became too much for them.

During the fighting in Kontum, Collins, in an attempt to enhance their combat capability, tasked the G-3 Section to develop a plan for field training ARVN squads. With the Vietnamese Training Command close by, it seemed to me to be an unnecessary duplication, but Collins was determined to go ahead with it. After many drafts, Ray LaFrance and his O&T Division devised a plan which LTG Collins approved. We monitored the pilot program which was set up east of Nha Trang. The actual training was less than satisfactory, and did not have the full support of the units giving it or receiving it; indeed its implementation left much to be desired. The project was not coordinated with the ARVN Training Command which was never enthusiastic about it. Perhaps MG Giai and I could have worked out something between us, but we did not collaborate on it.

In July, I flew up to Camp Radcliffe with MG Brown, to attend the change of command of the 4th Div, which had moved from Camp Enari to the former 1st CAV Div Base Camp on Highway 13 near An Khe. It was a better location from which to command the highway or to respond to a crisis in either the Highlands or on the coast. The trip to the Golf Course, as the landing field at Radcliffe was called, was uneventful. However, during the ceremony, at which GEN Rosson, now the Deputy COMUSMACV officiated, the weather deteriorated. To try to get ahead of the predicted severe thunderstorm, MG Brown alerted the pilot that we would leave immediately after the ceremony. As soon as we had paid our respects to GEN Rosson and MGs Walker and Burke, the outgoing and incoming 4th Division Commanders, we commandeered one of the jeeps waiting to shuttle people to the reception and rushed to the landing field.

The pilot had the U-21 prepared for takeoff. As anxious as we to miss the storm, he had obtained clearance and pre-flighted the plane. As soon as Brown and I were aboard, he taxied to the head of the runway and requested permission to take off. Permission was granted immediately; without delay, the plane started down the strip. Just then, a thunder squall struck, rocking the plane. Brown and I expected the take off to be aborted, but the pilot grimly continued down the runway, hoping no doubt, to get above the storm before its full fury struck. Rain lashed the plane, wind buffeted it, but we gathered speed. Even above the roar of the engines, the peals of thunder reverberated. Heavy clouds had darkened the day, but frequent flashes of lightning revealed that the plane had veered off the runway onto the turf, though the rocking of the plane was as much due to the wind as the rough ground. Shuddering violently the U-21 left the ground, dropped to earth again, then with shrieking engines, rose into the air, hesitated, dipped slightly, then surged aloft with a roar. Just as we left the tip of the airstrip, a helicopter ducked under one wing, frantically trying to avoid colliding with us, as it came in for a landing. MG Brown told me the next day that at dinner that night, LTG Collins had heatedly told of an incident at the Golf Course in which some idiots taking off in a U-21 in a squall had almost collided with his helicopter as it tried to get out of the storm and onto the ground. Brown, who like me had been petrified during that takeoff, silently nodded his head at Collins' exasperation.

A MACV policy designed to encourage OFFs and NCOs to extend their tours of duty in Vietnam, granted a month's leave in the CONUS to those extending for one year. In lieu of this leave, I requested two extra R&Rs when I extended for the assignment as CofS Staff of the 101st. Taking the first one in August, I went to Tokyo. Always an avid tourist, I saw the sights of Tokyo, the World's Fair at Osaka and the lower slopes of Mount Fujiyama. Though I found that Japanese food lacked the variety and delicacy of Chinese cuisine, I enjoyed tempura, shrimp, fish, beef or vegetables dipped in batter and fried lightly in fat. Prices in Tokyo were astronomical, quite different from 1952 when I had been interviewed there for assignment to the guerrilla force.

On my return to Nha Trang, I resumed my daily visits and nightly paperwork. During a visit to Phan Thiet, I talked with Dick Hooker, who had been tasked to upgrade the defenses of LZ Betty, HQ of Task Force South. His Bn, the 1/50, was manning the defenses of Betty, located on a high bluff overlooking the China Sea. A VC attack on Betty several months before had resulted in heavy US casualties. Dick had just reached an understanding with the TFS Staff, which had been tasking his companies for various missions without informing him. He was in the process of parking all except two platoons of his APCs and putting his troops into a typical Infantry role. Track operations were ineffective in the sandy, heavily-overgrown coastal plain, where small groups of VC were operating. Once his men adopted ground tactics, the Infantry patrols enjoyed fair success in interdicting VC movement to and from the populated areas.

Late in August, Charlie Hall celebrated his promotion to BG with a fine party in the generals' villa. When BG Powers left, he was to have been replaced by BG George Wear, an Advance Class and War College classmate. My joy at the prospect of working with an old friend as CofS was short lived, however. BG MacFarlane, who had been assigned to replace Gordon Duqueman as Senior Advisor to LTG Lu Lan, was 6'4"; LTG Lu Lan was 5'4"! Someone at MACV decided that the disparity in height might be embarassing to LTG Lu Lan, so Wear, who is relatively short, was assigned as Senior Advisor, II Corps, and MacFarlane became CofS of IFFV. Just after this change, Lockhart was replaced by Phelps Jones, who had been in Plans, ODCSOPS at the same time I was there. Phelps, a deep thinker and a staff officer in the best sense of the word, and I did not always agree on how the Asst CofS should operate. In his determination to be fully informed at all times, he demanded separate briefings which took a great deal of the staffs time. It was an extra echelon we learned to live with. Since I had a high regard for Phelps, we got along well.

After my promotion to colonel in 1966, I began to take a keen interest in the brigadier general promotion list each year. Most of the officers whose names appeared on the list were contemporaries, many were old friends, and many more had served with me. Hence, the names of a majority of those on each list were familiar to me. In all but a very few cases, I could find no fault with those selected, the greatest number were solid officers who would do a creditable job as general officers. Rarely I would disagree violently with a selection, but my quarrel was usually not with those selected, but with the many outstanding OFFs I knew who were not on the list.

My own name would never appear on the list. Since the Kennedy/McNamara era, the Army had a fixation on youth. Few colonels over 45 years of age could expect to be promoted and none over 50. Due to my break in service, I was 46 when promoted to colonel, five years older than most of the officers in year group 1948 in which I had been integrated into the Regular Army. Year group '48 would not be considered for promotion until I was 50 years old or very close to it. Based on age alone, I accepted the fact that I was out of the running. Nor had I worked long enough or close enough to any general who might "sponsor" me or advocate my cause. My record, though impressive, was not spectacular, certainly I was no "water walker". While convinced that I could do a better job than many nominated for promotion to BG, and as good a job as most, I had resigned myself to the fact that I would receive no more promotions. This in no way affected my attitude or performance, but was a recognition of the realities of the situation. Despite this, I must admit to a momentary twinge of disappointment, perhaps even envy or hurt pride, each time a new list appeared.

The most pitiful officer in the Army is the one who fails to recognize that he is not going to be promoted. For reasons which are obvious to all except the officer himself, he will never be recommended by a board. Especially true of colonels, such officers spend much time writhing in agony over their non-selection, seeking cause and placing blame on everyone but themselves. All else failing, the last resort is to blame "politics". In my view, politics has little to do with promotions. Of course there is the possibility of an exception, an aide to the President, a Service Secretary or the Chief of Staff of the Army could be selected considerably ahead of his contemporaries. Even in such cases, it seems to me that the officer must have had much to recommend him to hold such an assignment in the first place.

I believe that selection boards are conscientious and fair in considering officers for promotion. Certainly such boards have a difficult task; in the case of the BG Board, some 5,000 COLs, most promoted because of demonstrated ability, must be considered. Using arbitrary criteria such as age, schooling, and experience, perhaps 4,000 can be eliminated quickly. A careful perusal of efficiency reports further reduces the number to be seriously considered. Because the board members know the rating officers, those who tend to give inflated ratings, as well as those who pride themselves on being "tough raters", they can evaluate the reports realistically. But eventually, the board must select from between 100 to 300 truly outstanding colonels, the 50 usually promoted each year. This may become a matter of personal knowledge; a member of the board who was impressed with a particular officer while serving with him, will urge his selection. This is not politics in my view, but the luck of the draw. My luck has never been good, so I expected no miracles.

Early in September, I visited one of the ROK Divisions. The U-21 which was to return me to Nha Trang, was first taking BG Hugh Cunningham to LZ English, HQ of the 173rd ABN Bde. While enjoying a pleasant conversation with Hugh Cunningham as the plane neared LZ English, I noted abstractedly that we were landing from the seaside, which was unusual. Normally aircraft landed from the west, but there appeared to be no cause for alarm, perhaps the winds had changed, though the prevailing winds were from the sea. It did seem as if the plane was too high for the landing, was diving at much too steep an angle, and was going in with unusual speed. Could there be snipers this close to English? As I looked ahead through the cockpit, it appeared that the aircraft was going to touch down short of the undulating, PSP paved strip and land on the over-run. With speed undiminished, the U-21 slammed onto the over-run about sixty feet from the PSP strip. The impact caused the plane to bounce about four times, each time striking the ground with terrific force. At the second impact, the seat in which the CSM of the 173rd was sitting was wrenched loose and he was thrown to the floor. Everyone in the plane was badly shaken up.

The senior pilot, a sharp 1LT, immediately took control of the ship and gunned it aloft. He made a swing around the airfield to approach from the west, then made an easy landing on two wheels. As the plane settled on the runway, however, it tilted over on the left side. Unknown to the pilot, it had lost a wheel on the first landing. The propellers dug into the ground, slewing the ship around before they broke off. The left wing sheared off just as the plane caught fire. I was out of my seat and at the rear exit immediately. The crew chief ran forward to assist the pilots as the CSM and I got the door open in record time. Everyone cleared the plane without injury. Although the aircraft was blazing, it did not explode.

We were rushed to the 173rd HQ where a doctor gave us a quick check. None of us had any injuries, though the CSM had some bruises sustained when his seat tore loose.

A report had been flashed to Nha Trang immediately after the plane crashed. Shortly, the 173rd was informed that a helicopter was enroute to pick me up. An OH-23A arrived about 1600. Its pilot had apparently been told to keep my mind off the crash, so he had me fly the helicopter to Nha Trang, instructing me how to do it. It was the first time I had flown a helicopter, so the crash was soon forgotten as I became absorbed in the intricacies of maintaining a stable flight. After landing at Nha Trang, I had to relate the incident a hundred times. It was quite an experience; it took some time to get over a certain tension each time a U-211 was flying in came in for a landing.

Late in September, 1970, though the peace talks were deadlocked over the size and shape of the conference table, the phase-down of American forces was already underway. On several occasions I went to Saigon for conferences on the reduction, which involved detailed, highly classified planning;

the G-3 Plans Division worked around the clock to keep up with the many changes in "guidance" received from Saigon.

Just at this critical time, Skip MacDonald, the Chief of Plans, rotated. He had been unable to get a command assignment in Vietnam due to the few openings for Armor LTCs. Prior to his departure, I recommended him for a Legion of Merit (LOM). To my chagrin, it was disapproved, caught up in a change in awards policy to make them more selective. The LOM was to be reserved for those in more "responsible" positions. Believing that the Chief of Plans in IFFV was a very "responsible" position, and that Skip had done outstanding work, I went to LTG Collins about the matter. He personally approved it. MAJ Bob Riscassi replaced Skip. A sharp, effective officer who took over at a critical time without difficulty, he was shortly promoted to LTC.

Planning for the withdrawal of US troops continued. The 4th Div would be reduced Bde by Bde, the Div itself phased out gradually. The 173rd ABN Bde, the first US Army Combat Bde to arrive in Vietnam, would be one of the last to leave. Such units as Task Force South were the first to go, US Artillery units were reduced proportionally as Infantry battalions left.

TFS HQ was dissolved. COL Wagonhurst, designated as my replacement, was assigned to CORDS until my departure. Dick Hooker enjoyed independent command for a few weeks. The 1/50 shipped personnel with more than six months left in country to other units, and turned in all of the equipment assigned to it. The US presence at LZ Betty was closed out. When all personnel except a 15-man color guard had been reassigned, Dick left Bien Hoa with the remnants of his command. He turned over the colors to the 1st AR Div at FT Hood three days later.

In early September, orders were published assigning me to the 101st ABN Div effective in October. Jack Hennessey called to ask me not to report until I November, because he was moving the incumbent CofS, Hugh MacDonald, to a Bde at that time, and he did not want two Chiefs of Staff. This suited me. Entitled to another R&R because of my extension, I would go to Australia. On my return, I would visit several other divisions to see how their chiefs of staff functioned, get to MAC V and US ARV HQs for briefings, then proceed to the 101st for a minimal orientation before taking over from Hugh MacDonald. BG MacFarlane approved the plan. Wagonhurst, already familiar with IFFV HQ, needed only a day or so of overlap before replacing me as G-3.

The trip to Australia was again enjoyable. This time I managed to get "out back" for a day, to see kangaroos, koala bears and other animals in their natural habitat. That was worth the trip. On returning to Nha Trang, I said goodbye to MG Giai and COL Torres. While making my official goodbyes to the Vietnamese officers at II Corps, I was presented with the Vietnamese Award for Civil Action, apparently the only award for which Americans were eligible that I did not have. The ROKs also gave me the Order of Military Merit, and LTG Collins awarded me the third Oak Leaf Cluster to the Legion of Merit.

The comprehensive orientation program I had arranged proved valuable. At USARV HQ the staff briefed me on personnel and logistical policies and the few problems they had identified in the 101st. The Provost Marshal covered the drug problem as well as the situation in clubs and messes. During my visit to the 1st Air Cav Div, I met Art Hyman, recently promoted to BG. He was just assuming his duties as Asst Div CDR for Support (ADC-S). At the Americal, or 23rd Div, Tom Tackaberry, the CofS, a long-time friend, gave me many helpful tips. Finally it was time to report to the 101st Airborne Division.

AU-21 took me to PhuBai, northeast of Da Nang, where one of the Bdes of the 101st was located. The short flight from Phu Bai to Camp Eagle, was in a Huey. Camp Eagle was an impressive base camp. The pilot obligingly flew me around the perimeter before landing at the command helipad. As we settled on the pad, a sign saluting arriving or departing VIPs, read, "Welcome Colonel Seibert".

COL Hugh MacDonald, the incumbent CofS, welcomed me and escorted me to the transient VIP quarters, next to the CG's "Hootch". Hugh had arranged a six day orientation which included briefings, visits to XXIV Corps HQ (which had replaced III MAF), all of the installations in the 101st AO, and an opportunity to meet all of the commanders and key staff officers in the Division. This orientation occupied the time until MacDonald was due to assume command of his Bde, so the actual overlap was minimal. This pleased me as I do not believe in overlaps.

Camp Eagle had many excellent facilities, none better than the Commanding General's Mess, built by the Seabees in earlier days when the Marines had been stationed there. It had a huge stone fire place in the lounge, a large dining room and a complete kitchen. It was a comfortable place. The principal staff officers and certain key assistants ate at the mess by invitation of the CG, about 25 people in all. Of course, MG Hennessey, the Div CG, BG Sid Berry (a War College Classmate) and BG O. E. Smith, the Asst Div CDRs (ADCs) ate there. It was here that I was formally welcomed to the 101st Airborne Division. I was glad to see Jack Hennessey again, an old friend and a truly outstanding officer.

The G-l, LTC Keith Barlow, whom I had known in the 504 in Mainz, oriented me first. After the formal briefing we had a long talk, not only about G-l matters, but also about old friends. He brought me up to date on many of the officers who had been in the 504 at Mainz. He, the PM and the IG gave me a comprehensive insight into drug and race problems in the Div and what was being done about them.

The remainder of the staff briefed me in turn. Between briefings each of the brigades and separate battalions were visited. The XO of the 2nd Bde, which Hugh MacDonald was to take over, was LTC George Neroutsis, also from the 504 at Mainz.

The briefings and my visits throughout the Div area indicated that morale was generally good. But in all units, as in every outfit in Vietnam, the demonstrations and protests in the United States against the US role in Vietnam were a continuing source of irritation. Though the soldiers had been exposed to the ferment in the schools and streets before being drafted they had accepted their lot. Now, while they were risking their lives serving their country, helping South Vietnam, an ally, fight to prevent its subjugation by the communist North, naive idealists and calculating activists, safe at home, were aiding the enemy and further endangering their lives. The names Fonda, Weiss, Spock, Ramsey Clarke and their ilk were anathema to most. In addition, the distortions of the media angered and hurt everyone. Most did not recognize actions in which they had participated when they read the accounts in the papers and magazines.

Grand strategy and international politics mean little to the soldier facing the constant risk of death. Most never became involved either philosophically or politically in the Vietnam situation; they were there because they had been drafted, and made the best of it. Their concerns were survival, security and creature comfort. Men may volunteer to join the Army to serve their country, and rarely, for a cause, but they fight to save their own lives and the lives of the men in their squads, platoons and companies. Occasionally a charismatic leader at battalion or brigade level may motivate them, but their horizon seldom rises above the small unit level.

In addition, men fight for honor, though they would be the first to scoff at the idea. But they fight to maintain their image in the eyes of their friends, they fight so they will not let their buddies down, and they fight for their squad, platoon and company. Though they may not be conscious of it, they fight for their honor.

Now American soldiers were pawns in the struggle between the "establishment" and those who would destroy it. They were dismayed and hurt by the reports from home which portrayed them as vicious killers and mindless robots without regard for the lives and property of the Vietnamese civilians. Though the Vietnamese soldier was usually held in contempt, and the general populace looked on as potential or actual Viet Cong, civilians were usually left alone. My Lai was an aberration. Contrary to the impression created by the media, there was no callous destruction of villages, no thoughtless bombing or napalming of homes; when done, such acts were done with reason.

A few officers and enlisted men in Vietnam protested and openly admired those who sought to treat with the enemy to undermine their country. About the same number had strong convictions about the virtue of the US role in Indochina, these two factions, together a tiny minority, argued and fought, causing dissension in units. In addition, racial tension, drugs, poor leadership and the continuing turnover in leaders and personnel, which made identification with a unit difficult, combined to create serious morale problems in some units. This was evidenced most glaringly by "fragging"; the attempt to kill an officer or NCO with a fragmentation hand grenade. Most of these problems could be minimized, and were in the 101st, by strong, positive leadership. But the public protests by a vocal minority back home continually undercut the efforts of the best commanders.

Hopefully, The United States will never fight another war, but if it becomes necessary to do so, our National Leaders must insure that our own people unite behind the soldier on the battlefield. Never again should he be sent against an enemy while those he is risking his life for openly treat with the enemy, traitors to their country and saboteurs of their countrymen. Honest protest and dissent are cherished American traditions, treason is a despicable and cowardly act, the more despised when practiced by civilians not facing the enemy.

As part of my orientation, a day and a half visit to Da Nang was scheduled. XXIV Corps had taken over the functions of III MAF. Hence only a courtesy call was made on the Marines, but a detailed briefing was given to me at XXIV Corps. While at Da Nang I visited the I Corps Advisory Team, headed by BG Charlie Jackson. Charlie and I had a long chat during which he gave me a run-down on the situation in I Corps.

The detailed orientation gave me a good concept of what the 101st was doing and how it operated. Its standards were high; Hugh MacDonald was a perfectionist in the ABN sense of the word; he had set up the evening briefings to reflect a great deal of showmanship and snap. In my view there was too much "eyewash" for a division in combat. It did not seem appropriate that the briefings equal those at the Airborne School at FT Benning. Though I determined to take no specific action to reverse what had been set up, I wasn't going to push to keep the same spit-and-polish standard. The content of the briefing was of more concern to me that the way it was presented.

On I November 1970 I became the CofS of the 101st ABN Div. In a short time I got to know how MG Hennessey operated. He had written a letter of instructions outlining the duties and responsibilities of his Chief of Staff; in effect it directed the Chief to run the 101 administratively, while he and his ADCs fought it. This appeared to be a reasonable delineation of responsibility, it is the way I tried to operate until he left. MG Tom Tarpley, his successor, would never specify the duties of the Chief or the ADCs.

There were two ADCs, BG Sid Berry, Asst Division Commander for Operations (ADC-O), and BG O.E. Smith for Support (ADC-S). This organization posed a problem for me as CofS (and probably for other chiefs as well). There were, in effect, two Deputy Chiefs of Staff senior to the CofS, each of whom had oversight of certain Div Staff OFFs. Sid Berry, the ADC-O, was concerned with the G-3 and G-2, while O.E. Smith, the ADC-S, worked closely with the G-4, G-l and G-5. This created difficulties because the staff officers had two bosses. Nominally, the CofS was their supervisor and rating officer. But the ADCs, who gave them instructions directly, also indorsed their efficiency reports. Frequently the Staff received conflicting instructions from an ADC and the CofS. Though a workable policy was eventually developed, an additional workload was placed on the staff officers. I directed them to comply with any orders from the ADCs if not in conflict with orders from me, provide the generals with any information requested, and keep me informed of all orders and requests received. If any conflicts arose, they were to inform me immediately so that I could resolve them, relieving the staff of that problem. This is a continuing problem the Army has created by insisting on retaining two BGs in every division. While nice to have because they provide for greater promotion potential, the positions cannot be justified by an honest and logical evaluation of need.

As may be expected, I often got involved in controversies with the two ADCs. We had some serious discussions, some arguments. Certainly O.E. Smith and I did not see eye to eye on all matters. He insisted on escalating even minor problems to the general officer level. If there was a shortage of any equipment or a delayed delivery, whether or not it affected the Division's immediate combat capability, O.E. would jump into the matter. He would not wait for the G-4 or DISCOM to go through their approved channels to solve problems. As soon as any difficulty arose, BG Smith immediately took up the cause, delighted to have a reason to send a back channel message. The back channel was a new toy he had as a general officer, and he never permitted an opportunity to play with it to pass. In the end he did the 101 a disservice by giving it a reputation for whining and jumping channels. By over use of back channels, he lost his clout as people began to treat as routine all messages he sent. In several private talks I tried to explain this to him, tried to get him to settle down, but he would have no part of it. He appeared more interested in impressing MG Hennessey or MG Tarpley with his grasp of the situation than in actually solving the problem. After one of my candid talks with him, he told me that I was an ineffective CofS, because I did not intrude myself into every action; at least Jack Hennessey did not agree with him.

CSM Richard Dunn, the 101st ABN Div CSM, was a professional soldier for whom I had great respect. As we saw eye to eye on most matters, I leaned on him to get things done around the Division area. A high priority was given to improving the living conditions for the men. He followed this project for me. He also took care of minor disciplinary problems. Whenever anyone from the HQ came across a soldier who did not meet 101st standards, he was brought to the CSM who handled the matter with the man's ISG, thus saving much paperwork.

The 101st ABN Div had a Drug Abuse and Race Relations Council chaired by BG 0. E. Smith. When he was in the field, I assumed the chair. The Council had many lengthy discussions about race relations, one in particular regarding the accouterments black soldiers could wear. Many activists wore black woven wrist bands, carried sticks with one end carved into a fist, or wore earrings or other exposed jewelry. The use of these symbols was discussed in the context of Army regulations as well as racial pride. Black OFFs on the Council provided good insight into the problem. The "DAP, slapping hands in lieu of shaking them, a complex routine which often lasted several minutes, was explained and given tacit approval. The wearing of jewelry and other accouterments was permitted only as authorized in regulations. The Council attempted to insure adherence to existing regulations in all matters, the maintenance of good discipline and morale, while adopting policies which offended neither white nor black. It was a period of strong ethnic identification, which I found difficult to accept. It was my contention that people should identify as simply Americans rather than part-Americans: Afro-Americans, German-Americans, or Hispanic-Americans. Though less sympathetic to ethnic identity than I might have been, I gave each situation careful consideration. Certainly I agreed that within reason we did not want to deprive any soldier of anything that would enhance his morale in combat.

The drug situation was a matter of deep concern to all. We received frequent reports from the Surgeon, the Chaplain, the PM, the IG and commanders concerning the extent of the problem. The figures cited by the media appeared inflated and sensational in view of the operations of the Div. The problem should not be minimized: it was very real and very dangerous. But if the quoted figures were correct, there would have been no effective ground units. This was not the case. Although not in a troop unit, reports from Bde and Bn CDRs convinced me that their units were combat effective. If reports of drug use were accurate, more than a quarter of the troops would have been incapacitated by them.

A few units had leadership problems; there were several "fraggings", the attempt to kill OFFs or NCOs with fragmentation grenades or other means. As a result, several men were put in a temporary confinement facility made from a CONEX (Container Export, a large metal packing case with doors and means for locking or securing the contents) container with air holes. Fragging, a vicious practice, was a real source of concern to all OFFs and NCOs. It indicated a lack of leadership, a lack of discipline, a lack of morale which needed to be addressed immediately and forcefully. It was less a result disenchantment with the war in Vietnam as some have claimed, than an indication of the breakdown of order in our society; the permissiveness which has characterized the education and development of post-WWII children.

All three of the generals assigned to the 101st, qualified aviators, flew their own helicopters. As a result, they were gone most of the day visiting units or installations. MG Hennessey, in particular, visited almost all 101st units every day. BG Berry, as ADC-0, got to see the majority of the combat elements, especially if there was any contact. BG Smith, visited the support units as well as many combat elements to check on logistical matters.

The CofS was assigned a helicopter, but I used it rarely. My duties required me to stay in the CP to keep things moving, to meet visitors or to handle emergencies as they came up. When the three generals were out, the staff was often out too. Hence I was chained to my desk handling paperwork or routine matters, a situation not entirely satisfactory to me, but one which I accepted as my lot as CofS. My helicopter was used for utility missions, for staff visits, even combat assaults, after the Div AVN OFF checked with me to see if I had a requirement for it.

Initially the Bde CDRs were COLs Paul Gorman, Walt Root, and Ben Harrison. Hugh MacDonald replaced Walt Root, and Dave Grange, who commanded the 101st ABN Division Support CMD on my arrival, replaced Harrison when Ben became the Senior Advisor to the 1st ARVN Div in Hue Dave was replaced as DISCOM by COL Don Rosenblum, who had been advisor to one of the ROK divisions when I was G-3 of IFFV. The DIVARTY was commanded by COL Lee Surut and the AVN Group by COL Ed Davis. All of these COLs were impressive; in time, all but Hugh MacDonald and Ed Davis were promoted to BG.

A few days after Hugh MacDonald assumed command of the 2nd Bde at Phu Bai, MG Hennessey was called by LTG McCaffrey, Deputy Commanding General (DCG) USARV, who insisted that Hugh be relieved because of some remarks he had made a month or so before. Hugh had spent a few days at the R&R Center at China Beach j ust outside Da Nang, a fine beach resort built for the troops in the I Corps area. While there, he drank too much, interrupted a Philippine combo providing entertainment in the Club, took over the microphone and harangued the troops about combat versus noncombat personnel. He had belittled support troops as "rear echelon commandos", as well as disparaging soldiers who were not Infantrymen or from other combat arms. Several soldiers took exception to what he had said as well as the way he said it (he was crude and undiplomatic in his language) and wrote home or to their Congressmen; eventually the matter was investigated by the DA Inspector General.

Because of this incident, LTG McCaffrey demanded Hugh's transfer pending disciplinary action. Jack Hennessey did not want to relieve Hugh. He had done an outstanding job as CofS and was doing a commendable job as Bde CDR. He had made a serious error in judgement under the influence of alcohol while on R&R. Though a senior officer should not permit himself to become intoxicated, especially in the presence of enlisted men, Jack went to bat for Hugh. At first he was able to stave off the relief, but eventually pressure from the CONUS, where the war was vigorously protested by a very vocal minority and any incident such as this used to denigrate OFFs and the military, became so great that he was ordered to relieve Hugh. Reluctantly he did so. Joe Greene took over the 2nd Bde when Hugh returned to the CONUS to face further investigation.

Just after I took over as CofS, I got involved with the media. There was a plethora of reporters and photographers wandering about Vietnam, oriented toward disasters and the spectacular rather than success or objective reporting of routine events. Because of some bad experiences other divisions had with statements quoted out of context, or confidential remarks released, I told the Public Affairs

Officer, MAJ Ed Smith, to inform me whether or not any reporter who came into Division area to speak to one of the generals or me was friendly to the Army and the 101st ABN Div. This was to avoid talking off the record to a reporter only to find those remarks quoted out of context. These instructions somehow reached the media resulting in several articles which accused me of maintaining a press rating which influenced the 101st's handling of reporters and the information provided. This was not true; the Div provided the same facilities and information to all media personnel. It was a personal example of the self-serving way facts were twisted by reporters to fit their pre-conceived ideas, a microcosm of the misrepresentation and slanted reporting which poured out of Vietnam. It also caused me to question the loyalty of MAJ Smith the Public Affairs Officer.

Just before Christmas, Father Len Stegman, a War College classmate, notified me that he was escorting Cardinal Cook through Vietnam and would be in our area. Cardinal Cook, head of the Roman Catholic Military Ordinate, made an annual visit to Vietnam. When he arrived at Camp Eagle for his visit to the 101st ABN Div, all of the Generals were out, so I welcomed him to the Division. It was good to see Len Stegman, though we had little time to talk. Len came later on another visit to spend a night with me. That time we had a good session, recalling old friends.

As part of his annual Vietnam Christmas tour, Bob Hope was scheduled at Camp Eagle on 22 December 1970. The list of requirements he levied on us and the conditions he imposed to put on the show were unbelievable He played only to large audiences of 5,000 or more. The size of the stage, the number of electrical outlets, the dressing rooms, the seating were specified. Though I enjoyed Hope's shows, I was always aware that he sold for a princely sum the television rights to the shows he put on there. He used the military audience to further his ends and would stop the show if it was not taping as he thought it should, going back over the routine. The military expended tremendous resources of time, labor and material for each of his performances. Certainly the troops enjoyed the shows, but was the effort worth it? Planning and preparations began a month before the show. These included the physical movement of thousands of troops to Camp Eagle and back to their base camps to see the performance, for which large numbers of trucks and helicopters were required. Arrangements for site preparation and for receiving, feeding and caring for not only the Bob Hope troupe, but also the VIPs and media personnel who inevitably came for such a show had to be made. An elaborate buffet luncheon was to be laid out in the lounge of the CG's Mess for the VIPs and Bob Hope's troupe . The media was excluded from this function. About 15 or 20 OFFs and twice that many EM were placed on temporary duty with Div whose sole duty for several weeks was preparing for the event. The EN Bn devoted most of its efforts to site preparation for a month before the performance. For days before the show, extra patrols went out. All possible mortar and rocket sites were checked and many physically occupied. As a result of these security measures, one-third of the Div could not attend because they were out on patrol.

The day of the show was overcast, but the ceiling was high enough to permit fixed wing aircraft and helicopters to fly. Prime Minister Ky and LTG Lam (CG, IARVN Corps) who came with LTG Sutherland, CG of XXTV Corps, were among the large group of VIPs who arrived. It was a good show. MG Hennessey was the butt of many jokes, since Hope likes to needle the "brass". The huge three by four foot placards used to cue Hope and others in the cast were raised just behind me. Having talked to several OFFs and EM beforehand, he was able to bring local color to the performance by mentioning many areas from which the troops came. Afterwards Hope and some of his troupe visited the hospital to bring part of the show to the troops there. This was a much appreciated, thoughtful effort.

During my tenure as CofS S, several officers I knew joined the Division. CPT Dick Pack, who had been the S-3 Air of the 2/39 in the 1st Bde of the 9th Div when I commanded it, was the first. Dick, a tall, handsome, well-built paratrooper was not only an aggressive Infantryman, but also an aviator. He joined one of the Aviation units in the 101st. LT Hal Long, Bill and Madeline's son, arrived next. An ORD OFF serving an orientation tour with the IN, Hal was introduced to the generals and the staff while having dinner with me at the CG's Mess. I told him many stories of my service with his Dad during WWII. To insure that he received the most from his combat arms tour, I had him assigned to the 2nd Bn, 502nd IN, commanded by LTC Chuck Shay, one of the most aggressive Bn COs in the Division. I was sure that Hal would get good combat experience under him. Later I visited Hal in the hospital at Phu Bai, where he shamefacedly admitted that he was there as the result of a burst appendix, rather than a wound from enemy fire. He had stuck it out in the jungle too long, not willing to give in to an ailment not combat connected. Tall, handsome, 1LT Jeff Ankley, a fine Infantry OFF, son of Bill and Betty Ankley with whom I had served in the 504 (he was born just before Bill reported to Bragg) and the 508, was in the 2/502. He and his buddy came to see me; we had a long talk about his family.

The battalions of the Division, rotated on operations, spent more time in the jungle than in base camps. Contact with the enemy was all too frequent. As in every combat situation, there were several unfortunate incidents with our own support. DIVARTY fired into a 1st Bde unit just after Christmas, killing nine soldiers. A thorough investigation was made of this tragic accident. Occasionally gunships strafed friendly units or villages. Every precaution was taken to minimize these occurrences, but each incident, especially if it involved civilians, was played up by the media as a callous or deliberate act.

Just after the first of 1970, Jack Hennessey received orders transferring him from the 101st to become Commandant of the Command and General Staff College at FT Leavenworth. There was a lively farewell dinner for him in the mess at which fitting tribute was paid to this fine commander. Each battalion put on a skit or made a presentation to him. Three young soldiers who had composed songs about Vietnam sang them. One, "Tooey Louie", which I thought extremely good, was about a combat lieutenant's experiences in the "boonies"

The new commander, MG Tom Tarpley, would not join the Division until March, so there was no change of command. He was the third consecutive Div CDR who had been in my Advance Class: first Jack Wright, men Jack Hennessey, and now Tom Tarpley. The last time I had seen Tom was in 1967 when he was G-3 of IIFFV. Meanwhile, Sid Berry, the senior of the two BGs, would command the Div.

Shortly after Jack Hennessey left the 101, orders for an operation across the border into Laos, Lam Son 719, were received. Immediately planning got underway. Since this planning was to be very closely held, we decided to set up a separate planning and briefing room. My "hootch", fully sandbagged, was next to Div HQ; it had two rooms, a living room or lounge, a bedroom and a latrine. The living room, fairly large, was rarely used as I spent most of my time either in the HQ or the CG's Mess. It was well suited for a planning room. The door between my bedroom and the living room was blocked, since there was a side door into the bedroom.

The plans became extremely detailed, though still on a close-hold basis. Sid Berry decided that even the CofS was not authorized to have access to the material! I protested in vain, finding myself in the same anomalous position that Bond, my Asst G-3 in Nha Trang, had been in when he was denied access to information his subordinates had. The G-3 and the rest of the staff working on the plans, my subordinates, could not discuss them with me, nor could I assist them with advice or guidance. It was a stupid and thoughtless decision. That the CofS of the Div did not need to know what was going on or have a part in the planning for an operation involving the Div was absurd. Sid was carried away by the fact that the operation was across the border into Laos, and that only those who were actually involved needed to know about it. As CofS I certainly had need to know if I was to fulfill my responsibilities.

The Div began to prepare for OPN Lam Son 719 by moving support elements into position. The US was to support the operation with helicopters, artillery from in Vietnam, and logistically. No American units, other than aviation elements, were going into Laos. The plan was to cut the North

Vietnamese supply line, intelligence having indicated a massive movement of supplies south through Laos. There was information that the North Vietnamese were laying a POL pipeline through Laos to Cambodia, along the "Ho Chi Minh Trail", the main supply route to their units throughout Vietnam. Tactical elements of the 101 were repositioned closer to the border and Khe Sanh was reoccupied. BG Smith, actively engaged in this logistical build-up, asked for more and more assistance. Finally, LTC Simpson, the G-5, was assigned to help him set up a logistical HQ in Dong Ha, the 5th RCT area north of Camp Eagle. Simpson was a good G-5, but was a specialist. Smith, who was beginning to feel the pressure, decided that LTC Simpson was not responsive enough, and directed me to relieve him. Since he had been acting outside his normal assignment, I refused to do so. We argued about this. Smith was prone to rash decisions when excited; he was not a calm individual when things were not going right and he infected everyone with his panic.

The real work of setting up the supply base fell on the CDR of the DISCOM, COL Don Rosenblum, who apparently was able to handle O.E. Smith well. O.E. was always threatening that his career rested in his hands (slowly uncupping them as if what was in them fell out), but Don was not bothered. He did an outstanding job, particularly during Lam Son 719. Eventually he was promoted to LTG, a well-deserved reward.

OPN Lam Son 719 got underway just as MG Tom Tarpley took command of the Division. He decided to move a light command element to Dong Ha, where the 5th RCT could give it security. This put the tactical CP north of the hill mass which held fog clouds and frequently posed flying problems. As soon as Tarpley told me of his plan, I immediately sent the HQ CMDT to set up a forward CP and went there myself. It was my view that the CofS should be with the Div CDR, available to coordinate the staff, handle incoming traffic and keep routine matters moving so he could give his full attention to the tactical situation. A complete TOC was established in a bunker provided by the 5th RCT, with a briefing room for the CG. The G-3, G-2 and a few officers were there, a very light staff. BG Berry was forward as ADC-0. BG Smith remained back at Camp Eagle in charge of the elements remaining there. In support of Lam Son 719 two of the 101st Bdes were operating in the Khe Sanh area, so the bulk of the Division was focused there.

Smith began complaining that there were too many details to handle at Eagle and asked that I return to help him. Finally MG Tarpley told me to go back to the Div Rear to handle things there. I thought this was a mistake, but of course, I complied. By this time my relations with Smith were courteous but cool.

While the Division was fully involved in supporting Lam Son 719, Smith insisted that all of the Div HQ buildings be repainted white and green! I protested that in a combat situation eye-wash such as this was unnecessary, but was ordered to have it done; significant resources of manpower and material were expended on this needless project.

Lam Son 719 and the operations around Khe Sanh continued. As often as weather and my duties permitted, I went forward to keep abreast of the situation, to talk with the staff to insure that everything went well in the forward CP and to discuss various matters with MG Tarpley. On several occasions I got to Khe Sanh, but there was little I could contribute; BG Berry had his CP there.

After the operation many reports and evaluations were written. BG Berry wrote a report for the Infantry School concluding that Operation Lam Son 719 proved that helicopters could survive on the battlefield. The same data led me to the exactly the reverse conclusion. Many helicopters were lost because there were too few safe LZs. The ARVN did not push out far enough to secure the landing zones from fire; consequently helicopters were hit going into and out of them. Other aircraft were hit in flight. Lam Son 719 appeared to show that even unsophisticated anti-aircraft fire could deny available landing zones to helicopters.

During Lam Son 719, the Signal Officer, who was also the Signal Battalion Commander, was relieved. BG Berry was never satisfied with the communications in the Division. Apparently in several critical instances, communications went out or failed to get installed on time. This was no great surprise to me because I had seen several signal officers relieved in Europe. Technically proficient, they were not commanders. Several Infantry battalion commanders were also relieved before their normal tour of duty was over because of lack of leadership.

BG Smith also insisted that I get rid of the G-1, LTC Ferguson, who had replaced Keith Barlow when he assumed command of a battalion. Ferguson was doing things to my satisfaction, but he didn't seem able to please Smith. When first told to get rid of him, I refused, precipitating another argument with the ADC-S. Finally Smith went to Tarpley, who directed me to have Ferguson transferred. When asked if this was to be a relief, Tarpley said no.

Since he was not being relieved for cause, and had been on the job less than three months I suggested that no efficiency report be rendered on him. This would keep any derogatory remarks from his file. MG Tarpley agreed. Eventually, Smith insisted that an efficiency report be rendered on Ferguson and that it mention why he was transferred. After more argument, I finally yielded, giving Ferguson as honest an evaluation as I could, and not dwelling on the cause for his transfer. Perhaps I should have fought harder for the G-1, but there were so many things going on then that I did not find the time to defend him. With both Tarpley and Smith convinced of his shortcomings, it appeared that if he stayed his career might have been hurt even more. That incident bothered me; it was not one which I had handled to my own satisfaction.

Close to the Div HQ was a fenced compound containing several house trailers, in which the Red Cross ladies, the "Doughnut Dollies" lived. There was also one trailer used for putting up VIPs. Equipped with a shower and latrine, it was comfortable but not luxurious. BG Smith thought that the 101st ABN Div should have better VIP quarters; he directed that the trailer be spruced up. There was a plan underway to set up a really elegant VIP suite at Phu Bai, in one of the excellent facilities the XXIV Corps had vacated when it moved to Da Nang and occupied the III MAF area. Never a spit and polish worshiper, I was satisfied that under the combat conditions the 101 faced, there were adequate, comfortable quarters for VIPs. It became a question of where to put the priorities. Material resources and manpower were required to make any improvement in the VIP quarters at Camp Eagle - I did not think the results would justify the effort. To refurbish the quarters required some "scrounging"; I was not a scrounger, and did not approve of scrounging, which always resulted in a legitimate claimant being shorted. Undoubtedly I have benefitted from the scrounging of my subordinates over the years, but have never encouraged it. We made some improvements in the VIP quarters at Camp Eagle, but O.E. was never satisfied.

Late in April, MG Tarpley told me that the Deputy USARV CDR, LTG McCaffrey, was concerned that I had spent over four years in Vietnam and thought that I should be rotated earlier than my July ETS. COL George Viney, a friend from the C&GSC at Leavenworth and the Pentagon, who was due in country in early May, was slated to replace me. I protested, but Tom would not fight it. The Division Staff seemed genuinely sorry to see me leave. My relations with them had always been good. The principal staff OFFs were outstanding and functioned well. As a result of their expressions of respect I left the 101st ABN Div with a good feeling .

I was never sure whether or not I was eased out of my job, perhaps because of Smith's obvious lack of confidence in my performance which might have resulted in subtle suggestions to the CG to replace me. Tarpley had been less than enthusiastic in supporting me on several occasions including the matter of my reassignment. But when I left the 101 I was given the usual rewards: a party at the CG's Mess during which I received some fine gifts from the staff; a short ceremony on the chopper pad at which I was awarded the Fourth Oak Leaf Cluster to the Legion of Merit, a complimentary but not glowing efficiency report from Tarpley. The indorsement from LTG Sutherland, the XXIV Corps CDR, who rarely saw me, was less than enthusiastic. This was interesting because his endorsement on the report Jack Hennessey had rendered on me was most complimentary. Suddenly, four months later, his opinion of me had dropped. But I did not see this endorsement until a year later when I reviewed my file in the Pentagon. This caused me to wonder if I had failed as CofS; if I had been fired.

As soon as it was decided that I leave, I began negotiating with Colonel's Branch about a job. There was no chance to go to troops, so I asked for an assignment at the Army War College at Carlisle Barracks. It was a pleasant post, close to home. Instead, I was assigned to HQ Test and Evaluation Command (TECOM) at Aberdeen Proving Ground, MD. The reason I was not assigned to the War College, I learned later, was because my seniority would have required adjustment of the staff there. Some minor minion made the decision and passed it to the Pentagon.

With orders to Aberdeen Proving Ground, assigned to an organization I had never heard of, I began the trip back to the United States. A U-21 took me from Phu Bai to Long Binh where I spent the night with friends at USARV HQ, including MG Charlie Gettys and BG Jim Ursano. It was an enjoyable evening. The next day I flew back to the CONUS . The leave home was delightful, as always.

CHAPTER 20

TESTER

Aberdeen Proving Ground (APG), MD, as I vaguely recalled from the two brief visits made there while in OCS, was ten miles north of Edgewood Arsenal, located on the Chesapeake Bay. Other than the fact that it was the Ordnance School, I remembered nothing about the post. Intrigued by the assignment and anxious to get some idea of the quarters situation there, I called to make an appointment, then drove down to see my sponsor, COL Bill Mullen. Though he had written and given me some information, there were many questions still unanswered.

Bill was a pleasant, friendly, Irish, Quartermaster Colonel, whom I liked on sight. He was the Comptroller of the Command (TECOM), but was currently acting Deputy Chief of Staff for Support (DCS-S), the job I would hold. Mullen gave me a quick briefing on TECOM and my duties.

TECOM, subordinate to the Army Materiel Command, was charged with service and engineering testing of all equipment being developed or procured for the US Army. To accomplish this mission, TECOM had 16 boards, proving grounds and test centers: The Airborne, Communications and Electronics (ACE) Board at FT Bragg, NC; The Air Defense Board at FT Bliss, TX; The Armor Board at FT Knox, KY; The Field Artillery Board at FT Sill, OK; The Aviation Board at FT Rucker, AL The Infantry Board at FT Benning, GA; Aberdeen Proving Ground, MD; Dugway Proving Ground, UT; The Electronics Proving Ground at FT Huachuca, AZ; The Engineer Proving Ground at FT Belvoir, VA, Jefferson Proving Ground at Madison, IN, the Quartermaster Proving Ground at FT Lee, VA; Yuma Proving Ground, AZ; The White Sands Missile Range, TX; The Arctic Test Center at FT Greely, AK; and the Tropic Test Center at FT Amador in the Canal Zone. The Quartermaster and Engineer Proving Grounds were being phased out at this time. Most of the test facilities were tenant agencies on various Army posts, but APG, Dugway Proving Ground, Jefferson Proving Ground, White Sands Missile Range and Yuma Proving Ground were separate posts whose commanders were subordinate to the Commanding General, TECOM.

To control this large, diverse command, there was a sizeable staff at APG. MG Frank M. Izenour was the CDR and BG Edwin Powell was Dep/CofS/Chief of Testing. Powell had two Deputy CofSs: one for Administration and Support (DCS-S), the other for Testing (DCS-T). COL Harry F. "Pete" Grimm was the DCS-T. The former DCS-S, COL Warren Hodges, had been assigned as the Post Commander of APG several months before, at which time Bill Mullen had temporarily taken over his duties in addition to handling his own as Comptroller. Bill was happy to see me arrive.

The large number of senior military and civilian personnel in the HQ amazed me. In addition to the two generals there were 12 COLs, a PL313 (GS18), two GS16s and 10 GS15s. That was a great deal of rank, seniority and experience for one HQ. The fact that three of the COLs who were subordinate to the DCS-S were senior to me, caused me some concern; however, this was never a problem in our dealings, all three worked well with me. Bill Mullen, the Comptroller, Charlie Levy, the SJA, and Jim Chenault, the IG, all reported to the DCS-S for guidance and supervision, yet I would not be able to rate them because of their seniority. It was an odd situation which reinforced my belief that one colonel should not work for another.

Bill told me a bit about some of the personnel I would be serving with. MAJ Joe Foster, Chemical Corps, quietly competent, was the SGS. His delightful wife, Jane, was the mainstay of the Army Community Services organization at APG. Two GS15s, Pat Jordan, Chief of Personnel, Training and

Force Development Directorate, jokingly called "Peterfud", and the Chief of his Personnel Division, Duane Repke, would be key people in much of my work. LTC Bert Leach and Mr Ray Brownley (GS13) in the Plans and Study Program Division were working on a reorganization of TECOM, a task in which the Force Development Division under Joe Gisriel (GS15) was much involved. Their efforts would take much of my time. All of these people I got to know and respect; I found them hardworking and conscientious. More important, we became friends.

Bill also introduced me to Janet Atkinson, who was to be my secretary, and to Helen Simar, Pete Grimm's secretary. It was a quick, intensive overview, but it gave me a good idea of what I was going to be doing for the next few years.

One of my primary concerns was quarters, I wanted to know whether or not I could get a set of quarters on post. Bill was not optimistic, but suggested I talk to the CG. He took me to see MG Izenour. After a cordial welcome and a bit of discussion about my experience, I requested a set of quarters on post. MG Izenour told me that he would think about it, but that he was not favorably disposed toward my request. Eventually he decided that I could not occupy a set of family quarters on post. This was a disappointment, because as one of the ranking officers in TECOM holding a position which involved social and protocol responsibilities, I could not entertain properly in a BOQ.

Before returning to New York, I signed for a set of rooms in the BOQ, and spent some time looking for a house or apartment in the town of Aberdeen. While in the area I visited Bill and Madeline Long; their home in Owings Mills was only an hour's drive from the Proving Ground. They promised to look for an apartment for me. During the drive back to New York, I reflected on the good fortune which stationed me near so many old friends: Ruth (Bender) Daubert, whom I had known since high school, a widow, now, lived in Aberdeen; the Longs were at Owings Mills; Ted and Amy Rothert were at Fallston, just 20 miles from APG; and Sybil and Mickey Marks were at FT Meade, just a short distance away.

After my leave, I reported for duty and took up residence in the BOQ. As BOQs go, this one was not bad; I had a suite of rooms including a fair sized living room, a bedroom and bath; a kitchen was shared with the occupant of the adjoining suite. But this was not adequate as far as I was concerned, so I continued to look for something more suitable. In a few weeks I found a large, comfortable apartment only a from my front door to TECOM Headquarters. It had two bedrooms, a den, a large living room with a good-sized dining ell, an efficient kitchen and, of course, a bath. There was a small deck outside the living room on which I installed a hibachi which cooked many good steaks for me.. The current occupant would not vacate the premises for another three weeks, by which time I had arranged to assemble my belongings from the various places where they were in storage: Carlisle, Washington, New York and New Jersey. To fully furnish the apartment, I bought some good, traditional furniture. Bill Long spent several days helping me arrange the apartment; we enjoyed doing it and the results were most satisfactory.

That apartment was the scene of many enjoyable parties. Each time I hosted one, either my sister Margaret and her husband, George, or my sister Arlene and her husband, Bob, drove down with Mother to enjoy the festivities. In this way they got to know most of my friends. Other old friends managed to find their way to Aberdeen. In addition to the Longs, Rotherts, Marks and Ruth Daubert who were close by, Bonnie and Dick Hooker (504 Mainz and IFFV), Kay and Keith Barlow (504 Mainz and 101st), Joe and Marsha Sarakaitis (IFFV), and Hershell and Sharon Murray (KMI cadet) accepted invitations at various times. The guest room was constantly in use. My brother Bill and his wife Muriel drove down from Warwick, RI, several times to visit. Many friends passing through the area stopped off for a night or two.

When I became acquainted with TECOM and APG, I found much that I liked. The post, though small, was beautiful, situated, on the Chesapeake Bay. The buildings were handsome, particularly the senior OFFs quarters and OFFs club which were built of native stone. The Officers' Club had a fine view of the Bay. The Ordnance Center and School, the Proving Ground, the Limited Warfare Laboratory and the Army Materiel Systems Analysis Agency were tenant agencies on the post.

Several old friends were assigned to TECOM or were in the area. COL Bill DeBrocke, whom I had first met at Leavenworth, was Director of the Materiel Testing Directorate which operated the Proving Ground. He told me later of his "frustration in being the Director, but having very limited capability for influencing the system. I recall the battles with the senior civilians in trying to change the set ways. Usually the uniformed personnel lost out, because we were transferred every few years while their tenure could last a whole career. If they did not care for your directions, they merely had to wait until you were reassigned and then put things back the way they were."

COL Alec Kovalevsky, whom I had known since grade school days, was Chief of the Infantry Materiel Test Directorate. Alec's wife, Frances, and Jim Chenault's wife, Ruth, were sisters. Alec retired shortly after my arrival and was replaced by COL Lewington "Lew" Ponder. Later, Bill Young, a Carlisle classmate and Ben Ambrose, whom I had known in IFFV, reported in. It was a treat to be able to pick up those old associations.

Immediately after I reported for duty, MG Izenour directed me to go to the Electronics Proving Ground (EPG) at FT Huachuca to make an evaluation of the situation there. Displeased with the reports he was receiving, he was contemplating the relief of the Commander. Though not familiar with the situation, I urged restraint, suggesting that somebody talk to COL Enderle and apprize him of the fact that his performance was suspect. Certainly he had not been promoted to COL and given the responsibility for EPG without having some worth. When I asked if anybody had discussed his performance of duty with him, I was told that no one had. Thus I was given the mission of making an independent evaluation, to include a recommendation for relief or retention.

It took three full days to familiarize myself with the operation of EPG. It was apparent that COL Enderle, the Commanding Officer, while a highly qualified electronics expert, was a weak manager and commander. He left most of the routine administration and management to his Deputy, COL Beaumont. Beaumont, very much the wheeler-dealer, though competent in his field, was not the kind of OFF to handle details or a complex operation such as EPG. The Executive Officer, LTC Ralph Hill, was a competent, no-nonsense OFF who appeared to be holding things together. Before I left I spoke frankly with COL Enderle, explaining the purpose of my visit, and giving him a summary of my observations. There appeared to be no grounds to recommend relief, but I pointed out several areas he needed to give close attention to. I advised him to get more deeply involved in the administration and management of EPG. While at Huachuca I had dinner with George and Louise Everett. George was CofS of the Strategic Communications Command. We had served together in the Pentagon, had been classmates at Carlisle, and had Bdes in the 9th Div in Vietnam at the same time.

On my return to Aberdeen, MG Izenour approved my findings. He wrote a detailed letter to COL Enderle outlining his dissatisfaction with his performance, which he promised to watch closely. Though there was only marginal improvement, Enderle remained at EPG until his tour of duty was completed.

When I reported for duty at TECOM, it was standard procedure that one of the Dep Chiefs of Staff be in the HQ every Saturday morning. A skeleton staff also came in, though they accomplished little. TECOM did not function on Saturdays and there were no weekend crises which needed attention. There appeared to be no need for these people to be spending their Saturday mornings in the office. While looking into the matter, I noted that MG Izenour came to his office every Saturday morning to read or to catch up on his paperwork without interruption by telephone, visits or conferences.

The third Saturday I was on duty, I asked Izenour if there was any reason for me to be there. "I realize that you come in to work every Saturday, Sir, but you have never called for any of the staff, nor for any assistance, yet policy requires one of the Deputy Chiefs of Staff and a skeleton force to be here. Is there any real need for such a requirement?"

After discussing the matter, Izenour declared that he had no need for anyone on Saturday, indeed, he preferred to be alone to think and work. He agreed that the requirement could be terminated. When this was announced at the general staff meeting on Monday morning, there were audible sighs of relief. It was typical of a large HQ; perhaps the requirement had been valid when instituted, but it had long since outlived its need. However, since no one had seen fit to challenge it, a meaningless and wasteful personnel policy perpetuated itself.

After settling into my duties, I visited Sybil and Mickey Marks at FT Meade. They invited me to attend a cocktail party they were giving three weeks hence. One of the guests at the party was COL Ed Smith who had been the Pleiku Prov Advisor when I was Senior Advisor of the 24th STZ. He was currently in the G-3 Section of 1st Army. We laughed over the many "crises" we had shared in Pleiku.

At that party, I also met for the first time MG Sam Koster and his delightful wife, Cherie. Koster was temporarily assigned to 1st Army while awaiting the results of an investigation into his alleged culpability in the "My Lai Massacre". He had commanded the 23rd Div at the time of the incident, and had just resigned as Superintendent of the US Military Academy at West Point to avoid embarrassment to that fine institution. An exhaustive inquiry failed to find any dereliction or wrong doing on his part. Nevertheless, to satisfy the press and other vocal critics, he was administratively reduced to brigadier general.

This bothered me. The probe found no grounds for legal action against Koster, yet political expediency dictated that he be punished for guilt by association. With the furor over the US involvement in Vietnam, someone had to be sacrificed to still the public outcry. That someone was Sam Koster. An abbreviated version of LTG Peer's investigation of the MY Lai case had been made available to certain officers, including me. The only thing that struck me was that apparently no one in the chain of command had checked on the matter. Reports of a hundred or more casualties, whether friendly, enemy, or civilian, automatically triggered a check by Bde and Div CDRs in other units. If such a report had been made, no senior officer had looked into the matter. But other activities in the Div AO at the time might have made it impossible. It did seem to me that the Div CofS and the Bde CDR let down their CG.

At the time I met Sam and Cherie, I did not know that they were to be assigned to TECOM. When Sam became my immediate supervisor we got to be close friends. Before BG Koster reported for duty at TECOM, there were many parties and ceremonies marking BG Powell's retirement. These activities continued as we welcomed Sam and Cherie to the post.

The Kosters' arrival provided an excellent opportunity to have my first party. In addition to the principal staff officers and civilians of TECOM, I invited Mickey and Sybil Marks and Pat and Ink Gates (Ink was a classmate of Sam's at USMA). My sister Arlene and her husband, Bob, drove Mother down for the weekend. At that party I earned an undeserved reputation as a gourmet host. Patterned after my parties in Heidelberg, I had a mountain of shrimp, chicken livers and water chestnuts wrapped in bacon, four whole beef filets roasted to a delicate pink, an assortment of cheeses, a relish tray with an excellent curry dip (made from a recipe Janey Cox had given me), several other dips and caviar. Though I spent most of Friday night and Saturday preparing for it, I enjoyed it as much as the guests. A soldier from APG was hired as bar tender and clean-up man. It was one of many good parties at Aberdeen.

My job as TECOM's Deputy Chief of Staff for Support included all support and administra-tion activities indeed, everything that went on in or involved the HQ. This included supervision of 16 directorates and offices: Comptroller, IG, Legal, Safety, Plans and Programs, Logistics, Procurement, Personnel, Training and Force Development, Management Information Systems, Information or

Public Affairs, Equal Employment Opportunity, Chaplain, Surgeon, Security, Administration, Management and the SGS. The Deputy for Testing had an equally unwieldy group of directorates to supervise. Manning these 16 activities were both OFFs and civil service personnel. Though not working for me, one of the GS 16s, the Chemical Warfare Specialist, Ed Miller, became a close friend. He had attended OCS at Edgewood several classes ahead of me and we had a great time recalling those hectic days. My friendship with Ed and his wife, Gertrude, which continued until their deaths, was one of the best things that resulted from my tour at TECOM.

Since my duties required familiarity with the operation of all of the subordinate agencies of TECOM, I thought it necessary for me to get a first-hand look at them. MG Izenour approved my proposal, admittedly optimistic, to visit one agency each month. Though not able to adhere to that plan fully, I eventually visited every one. Because FT Bragg was one of my favorite posts and I had many friends there including COL Pete Kelley, a War College classmate who was President of the ACE Board, that was first on my schedule.

Next was FT Benning, also a favorite post; the Infantry Board was one in which I was particularly interested. Since I had already been to FT Huachuca, I deferred another trip to EPG in favor of one to Jefferson Proving Ground (JPG), Madison, IN. This was another case in which the Commander, COL Mayhall, was not highly esteemed at TECOM HQ. Since BG Koster also wanted to visit the subordinate agencies, he and I flew to JPG in TECOM's airplane. We were less than impressed with COL Mayhall who met us in disreputable shape. He wore a rumpled, unkempt uniform, a wrinkled shirt, tarnished brass, unpolished shoes and a wreck of a military hat. Despite his unprofessional appearance it became apparent that he had the strong and loyal support of the civilian personnel.

Jefferson Proving Ground tested much of the production ammunition being manufactured for the Army. A sample of each lot of ammunition was sent to one of the proving grounds to be fired to determine if it reacted the way it should. JPG was a predominantly civilian operation with limited military input. COL Mayhall appeared to know what was going on, but there seemed something missing, a lack of clear lines of responsibility. There was an impression that JPG operated in spite of, not because of, any direction from either Mayhall or TECOM. Koster and I had a frank talk with COL Mayhall, who was warned that we were concerned about the operation of JPG and given guidance concerning the items we thought wrong. As Mayhall was to retire shortly, no further action was taken.

On my visit to the Aviation Board, I saw COL Dan Gust, an old friend from the Advance Class and the War College, who was President of the Board, and his Deputy, Lou Williams. Lou had been with me in the 9th IN in Korea, had made the return on the POW ship with me, and had been in my Leavenworth class. It was an enjoyable visit, because in addition, I got to see MG Al Burdette, the CG of FT Rucker, and COL Jim Mapp, his Director of Training. The trips were not only informative and valuable from a professional point of view, but were providing a chance to see old friends.

The visit to White Sands Missile Range (WSMR) was combined with one to the Air Defense Board at FT Bliss, as the two installations are contiguous. White Sands was especially interesting as it was a joint test facility run by the Army. MG DeSaussure wore several "hats" which he balanced well. He was a subordinate commander of TECOM in charge of the test range there. He also commanded the Joint Test Range for which the Army was executive agent and so reported directly to the Pentagon. It was a fascinating organization which included highly sophisticated tracking and monitoring devices as well as a nuclear reactor. MG DeSaussure made sure I saw it all.

A staff car took me from WSMR to FT Bliss, a matter of an hour's drive. The President of the Air Defense Board, COL Bill Holcombe, was another War College classmate. After seeing the operation of the Board, I enjoyed the two days' leave I had requested to see Daria Roegge and Charlie Monroe.

Another interesting trip was to Deseret Test Center (DTC), with HQ at FT Douglas, Salt Lake City. Testing was actually done at Dugway Proving Ground (DPG) about 50 miles to the west. After talking to BG Max Etkin, the Commander of DTC, and being briefed by his staff, a helicopter took me to Dugway. At the Proving Ground my Chemical Warfare training stood me in good stead; surprised at how much I recalled, my prior training enabled me to ask intelligent questions. On this trip, too, I took a day's leave to see Salt Lake City, Temple Square, and a rehearsal of the famous Tabernacle Choir.

The trips to the Arctic and Tropic Test Centers were especially exciting. I had never been to Alaska in the winter, so I looked forward to seeing the perpetual dark. First stopping off at FT Richardson at HQ, US Army, Alaska, to talk with MG Charlie Gettys, an old friend from the 504 ABN IN days at Bragg, I flew in his U-21 to FT Greely. It was cold; there was a great deal of snow, but the Test Center Commander was concerned that some equipment had not been sufficiently "cold soaked" to conduct testing during my visit. Several miles from the cantonment area in the vicinity of Bold Lake, was a hollow where the coldest air settled; it was here the equipment to be tested was left for several days until every molecule of the material reached air temperature. The process was called "cold soaking".

Though warned about static electricity due to the cold, dry air, I continued to get shocked each time I reached for a door knob or a light switch. Cold air seemed to have substance and could be seen as it flowed into a building when a door or window was opened.

While at FT Greely I had the unexpected pleasure of seeing COL Angel Torres who had the unlikely assignment as Commander of the Arctic Warfare School. Some faceless personnel OFF deep in the bowels of the Pentagon must have chuckled as he assigned a Puerto Rican to the Arctic, but Torres seemed to enjoy the duty. Over elk stew we talked of MG Giai, our experiences in Vietnam, and those halcyon days when Torres was one of my Plt Ldrs in Co K, 504th Airborne Infantry.

The trip to the Tropic Test Center provided a nice balance to that to the Arctic. MG Maury Kendall, whom I had replaced as Commander of the 1st Bde 9th Div, was on the same airplane to Panama; we talked briefly about mutual friends in the 9th Div. I also bumped into Ray Leddy, the State Department advisor at the War College, who had lived in the Castle with me, but we had no time to talk.

Because of a shortage of accommodations at FT Amador, I stayed in a hotel in Panama City. As a result, I saw a bit of the city driving back and forth to the Canal Zone (CZ) and on walks I took between briefings. Several evenings I walked to the CZ to visit friends, GEN Rosson, now Commander-in-Chief South (CINCSOUTH), as delightful a dinner companion as I remembered from our association in the 8th Div, hosted a dinner party for me to which he invited some old friends: LTC John Mess, and his witty wife, Helen, and MAJ Hal Dyson and his wife, friends from the 504 in Mainz, and LTC Bill Tyler, who had been the Kontum Prov Advisor when I was with the 24th STZ. Bill introduced me to his lovely wife Carina.

Between these reunions, COL Hyrum "Hy" Dallinga showed me the activities of the Tropic Test Center (TTC). The effect of heat, humidity, salt air, fungus and insects on the equipment, and the ability of soldiers to carry, operate and maintain that equipment in the tropics were evaluated. There were problems, primarily of management, at the Center, which my visit helped me understand.

Dallinga took me to dinner at the Club Panamar, an elegant restaurant on the Pacific Ocean where we enjoyed delicious seafood on a patio under a canopy of stars. He also hosted a cocktail party in my honor at which I met all of the personnel assigned to the TTC. At that party I was introduced to seviche, a spicy delicacy concocted from raw fish cured in fresh lime juice,

In planning my itinerary, I had included several days of leave. The highlight of that leave was a trip through the Canal on a British freighter. The American pilot and I met at the dock at 0600 to go to the freighter in the pilot boat. The British captain gave me the freedom of his ship, but I spent most of the time on the bridge watching our passage through the locks and cuts. It was a fascinating experience. Because of a storm on the Atlantic side, I was asked to debark at Gatun Locks, no one wanted an inexperienced landlubber negotiating the Jacobs Ladder from the freighter to the heaving pilot boat in a high sea. It was only a short walk from the locks to the railroad station; the ride back to FT Amador provided an opportunity to see more of the Canal Zone. Later I had a chance to visit the Miraflores Locks which were being cleaned and repaired. Descending to the bottom of the compartments and standing beside the huge gates was a unique experience. The simplicity of the system, the ease of control of the locks, and the minimum maintenance required are a tribute to the engineers who designed and built the Canal.

Though not a subordinate agency of TECOM, I also visited Project MASTER at FT Hood. To accomplish its mission of testing tactical concepts, MASTER had a sophisticated, instrumented range which was able to measure movement and bullet strikes from various weapons fired on the range. Though not directly involved in the testing of equipment, its operational worth was frequently evaluated, hence TECOM coordinated with it fully.

The trip to Hood was particularly enjoyable because I saw many old friends. BG Charles Jackson was CofS of III Corps. I had dinner with him and his wife, Kitty. Woody Shemwell (Advance Class, Leavenworth, and the Pentagon), Ken Althaus (1st AR Div and War College), Ben Harrison (101st) and Joe Starker (IFFV) were all assigned to the post. During a nostalgic visit to the area formerly occupied by THE REGULARS, now being cleared to make way for modem barracks, I was happy to see that the WWII structures were finally being replaced.

MG Izenour announced early in November that he was retiring the first of December 1971. The staff had a lavish party for him which included a 'This is My Life" slide and talk show in which Izenour's life was portrayed in short vignettes and scenes. Bill McGolgin, Public Information OFF of TECOM, was primarily responsible for this well-done effort. The General's wife, Billie, contributed many old pictures and information on incidents in his background which nobody on the staff even suspected. It was an enjoyable evening at the APG Officers' Club during which MG Izenour received many gifts and good wishes. Most of the staff viewed his leaving with mixed feelings. He was a controversial commander; dynamic, aggressive, and dedicated, but overly demanding, sometimes inconsiderate, often thoughtless of his subordinates' dignity. The end of the party was in part a reflection of this latter side. As the evening advanced, more and more of the guests left. It was a mid-week evening; the following day would be a busy one for everyone. Some, who had attended the party only out of a sense of duty, used this as an excuse to leave early. Others became restless through the over-long slide show. For whatever reasons, by the time the last waltz was played at midnight, only the SGS, MAJ Foster and his wife, Jane, and Izenour's aide and his wife remained to dance that final set with the retiring couple. When Joe Foster told me this, I was ashamed of my own lack of consideration for a dedicated Regular Officer at the conclusion of his long career.

The day after MG Izenour retired, the new Commander, MG Charles P. Brown, with whom I had shared many interesting adventures in Vietnam, was welcomed. I was delighted to serve again with this outstanding OFF, whose broad knowledge, dynamic leadership and sound judgement I respected. He came to TECOM from Paris, France, where he had been the Military Advisor to the US Peace Negotiator with the North Vietnamese. He told me it had been a frustrating assignment. After the welcoming ceremony outside TECOM HQ, there was an informal reception for him and his wife, Evelyn, in the conference room. The Browns' arrival provided an excuse for another party; again my apartment rang with merriment. MG Brown kept me busy from the moment he assumed command. I believe we made a good team; we thought alike, had basically the same approach to problems, and Brown knew that I would give him an honest opinion.

Pete Grimm retired in mid-1972. After much consultation between MG Brown, BG Koster and myself, COL Lew Ponder from the Infantry Materiel Test Directorate was designated to replace him as DCS-T. It was a good choice. Lew, a solid officer, did an outstanding job for TECOM in that assignment. He was easier to work with than Pete, hence things moved more smoothly at the headquarters as a result.

Ed and Gert Miller held a spectacular party one Saturday night in June 1972. All week the weather service had been issuing bulletins on the progress of Hurricane Agnes. As luck would have it, on the day of the party the storm hit the Chesapeake Bay and Aberdeen area with all its fury. That afternoon, we all attended the wedding of Lew and Esther Ponder's daughter, Judie, at the Post Chapel. Lew and Esther became so involved in getting the wedding guests out ahead of the storm, they were unable to attend the party, but the other guests gathered at the Millers' in Bel Air, where we all enjoyed an evening of fun in spite of the wind and rain, Both MG Brown and COL Hodges, Commanding Officer of APG, were distracted by periodic reports from the post; damage done to facilities, requests for equipment from nearby communities, the rising Susquehanna River. Just north of Bel Air, the Conowingo Dam impounded the waters of the Susquehanna. Although all the gates had been opened, the pressure continued to mount, giving rise to the possibility that the dam might break and spread havoc throughout the area. Fortunately it did not.

Sam Koster, all business at work, was the center of fun and games that night. Able to put aside his responsibilities and relax at a party, he knew many unusual games which added to the gaiety. His tall, handsome appearance and great charm made him the center of an admiring group of ladies. That night Sam suggested we play TRAIN. No one knew exactly what TRAIN was, but everyone at the party was willing to play. He formed a human train with Joe Foster's wife, Jane, immediately behind himself, and snake-danced all over the room to whatever was playing on the stereo at the time. When Sam reached the laundiy room door, he stopped and asked Jane to enter the darkened room with him. Once inside, he asked her if she wanted a big surprise. "Yes, indeed." "Okay, close your eyes and pucker up your lips." Jane did so and got a big surprise, a smart slap on the cheek! The two of them came out of the darkened room to the questioning looks of the remaining people in the group. Sam went to the end of the train, as Jane led the snake dance again until it was her turn to give the man behind her "a big surprise". It was a kid's game, but a perfect to counter the howling wind outside. Finally we thought it best to beat our way back home, everyone left by midnight, unusually early to leave a Miller bash.

In November 1971, just before MG Izenour retired, The ACE Board, which was preparing to test sensors, presented their proposal for the construction of the sensor testing site. Since considerable equipment and a lot of money were required, MG Izenour directed a reduction in cost and greater justification for the expenditures. Early in 1972, COL Pete Kelley returned to brief MG Brown and the TECOM staff. The ACE Board finally got most of what it needed.

During the second visit, I mentioned to Pete that I had always regretted not qualifying as a Master Jumper. Though all of the specific requirements had been met, I needed to "fall out" of an aircraft six more times. Pete said, "Come down to the Board. We'll jump you and qualify you. No sweat." Since I planned to make a routine visit to the ACE Board, I asked MG Brown if he had any objections if I made a couple of jumps while I was there. I told him frankly that I wanted to get my Master Jump Wings. Brown, who was not Airborne, viewed jumping with amused tolerance. After kidding me about the stupidity of falling out on my head, he agreed to the venture. Pete was notified that during my upcoming visit I wanted to make six jumps. He assured me that he would have everything set up.

Early one morning the TECOM aircraft deposited me at Pope Field, where Pete picked me up for the short drive to FT Bragg. Donning fatigues and jump boots, I reported to Pete, who turned me over to COL Bob Apt, Chief of Testing at the Board. Bob in turn, passed me to MAJ Don Wolstenholme, a project officer in the Airborne Test Division. Pete had thought it best that I take a little refresher training. After five or six practice parachute landing falls (PLFs), I pointed out to Wolstenholme that I had never yet made a good PLF and did not expect to. However, we kept at it as Bob Apt watched.

Wolstenholme didn't know whether or not to OK me to jump. Finally, I said, "Let's knock it off. I'm not going to do any better in the time we have. I'm satisfied. I'll take the responsibility."

AT Holland Drop Zone Board personnel were already conducting jumps from an HU-1B helicopter. Strangely, I had never jumped a "Huey". As the DZSO gave me a few brief instructions, I chuted up. Together with seven other jumpers I climbed on the helicopter. Immediately we were airborne; the jumpmaster pointed to me and I pushed myself out (we were sitting on the floor) and went through the five points of performance.

It was my goal to make all six jumps that day because it was doubtful that I would get another opportunity to jump again. Certainly, I would never get another Airborne assignment. The first two jumps went quickly and easily, but then the wind began to rise, making jump conditions marginal. On the third jump I was dragged because sand had gotten into the Capehart Release, and I was not able to squeeze it to release the canopy. It is almost impossible to collapse a T-1O canopy by pulling on the lower risers, but I finally managed to get to my feet and run around the chute to collapse it. After that happened, the DZSO posted people around the DZ, one in a jeep, to collapse chutes should anyone have a similar problem.

The Safety Officer, concerned about the rising wind, wanted to call off the jumping. A number of people were still waiting to jump, so I persuaded him to continue. Each succeeding jump the conditions became a little worse, though the Capehart Releases worked well on those jumps. The T-1O is difficult to steer, you can climb the risers to the skirt of the canopy and still not exercise a great deal of control over your direction. Finally I exited the helicopter for my sixth jump; with a sigh of thanksgiving, the DZSO ended the jumping for the day. It had taken a little more than an hour to make those six jumps.

On the drive back to the post, I began to feel stiff, so I went to the Normandy House to take a hot shower and a nap before lunch. The ACE Board was to brief me at 1330. The next thing I knew, the phone awakened me; Pete, in that sarcastic voice of his, asked me whether I was going to make the briefing. When I tried to get up, I found that I was stiff, every movement was painful, and I ached all over. Chagrined, I told him I was not even going out for lunch. Pete and Coletta had invited me for dinner that evening and I was determined to make that date. About 1730, I took another hot shower which eased the creaking a bit. Although it was a delightful meal and evening, I did not stay long. It is apparent why physical training is so important to the parachutist. Although I had been going to the gym at Aberdeen fairly regularly, I was still not in good shape. I had forgotten just how demanding a parachute jump is.

When I completed my sixth jump, Pete called MG Brown to inform him that my escapade with the parachute was over, he could relax; I hadn't landed on my head. On my return, Brown greeted me with a sarcastic comment. Pete cut orders attesting to my qualification as a Master Parachutist and sent me my Master Jump Whigs which I wore proudly.

Shortly after the jumping visit, I decided to get to know the junior officers in TECOM better, to find out about their attitudes toward the Army and their jobs. To accomplish this, I planned a cocktail party to which I invited all of the company grade officers, then- wives or girl friends. The night before the party, I received a phone call from Pam Clark; Elizabeth, my godchild, had died and was being buried the next day. Elizabeth's death was not unexpected; she had been suffering from epilepsy and lupus and the severe side effects of the medications she was taking for both. It was too late to call the guests to cancel the party. I drove to Philadelphia early Saturday morning; immediately after the interment, I returned to Aberdeen, arriving about 15 minutes before the guests. Everything was ready for the party, but needed to be set out. As the guests arrived, they were given drinks, then put to work. In short order the party was going in fine fashion. It served its purpose, I got to talk informally with all of the company grade officers, to establish a rapport with them which was helpful to me as well as the command.

In addition to the active social life on and around APG, the lure of the many fine places to eat in the Baltimore area proved irresistible. All too often military people fail to explore the advantages of a particular location. Determined that such would not be the case at Aberdeen, an eating club was organized with the assistance of Ed Miller and Joe Foster. The purpose of the Dining-out Club was to meet with other TECOM people who enjoyed good food in order to sample the fare at restaurants in the greater Baltimore area. It was an informal organization without dues or specific membership. Dinners were scheduled every six weeks, with an average attendance of 25. We enjoyed many delightful evenings and superb food, but we could never convince MG Brown or BG Koster to join us. The hard-core members, other than the Millers, the Fosters, and myself, were Dan Watkins, the Canadian LNO, Ray Turner, a retired warrant officer, the Military Personnel Officer, and Dave Padgett, the Chief of Procurement, and their wives.

However, it was not all social activity at APG, TECOM was a busy agency in which there were many things going on. One of the most interesting and frustrating activities that TECOM was engaged in was the linking of all of the subordinate agencies with the large computers at Aberdeen Proving Ground and White Sands Missile Range. Each of the boards, proving grounds and test centers had a limited computer capability; the concept was to link them together so that the greater capability of the large computers could be made available to all agencies, using their smaller computers as terminals. Ed Goldstein, Chief of the Management Information System Office (MISO), a GS-15, had been with IBM for some time and was an expert in his field. Certainly he knew more about computer hardware and software than anyone I ever met. But he had difficulty communicating his expertise to others. There were monumental problems in setting up the complex system; everyone was impatient to have all of the agencies on line. Few understood the problems: software, dedicated lines, leakage on the lines, and scheduling. My two courses in computers while with ODCSLOG USAREUR gave me some insight into the task. I enjoyed working with Ed Goldstein and learned a great deal from him.

In the spring of 1972, just after MG Brown had things operating to his satisfaction, the Army began to re-study its system of testing. There had been some adverse publicity and considerable criticism of the Army for accepting equipment which turned out to be faulty or did not satisfy all requirements. Consequently, the testing procedure came under attack. The big question the Army General Staff wrestled with was whether to reorganize or, in typical Army fashion, form a new command. All too often, the Army's solution to a problem is to organize a special command to handle it. This proliferation of commands erodes the authority of major commanders without perceptible improvement in operations. Another question was whether testing should be divorced from AMC, the procurer of the equipment and placed directly under DA. The need for all boards, proving grounds and test centers was challenged. TECOM spent much effort justifying and rejustifying its existence, its methodology, its objectivity. Every facet was studied ad nauseum, as is done all too often in the Government.

During this period, MG Brown directed a searching review of TECOM's organization with a view toward streamlining it. After studying the manning tables, I had observed first to MG Izenour and then to MG Brown, that there appeared to be too many senior grade civilians in the organization. It was necessary to maintain a balance between military and civilian personnel to provide for continuity and to minimize parochialism in testing. TECOM HQ was staffed with 24 civilians in grade GS15 or above, but there were only 18 officers in the grade of colonel or above. Most of the civilians were outstanding people, but perhaps some jobs had been inflated. For instance, there were two GS16s, neither contributing a great deal at the time. After discussing the matter with Lew Ponder, I recommended that we eliminate those two spaces. MG Brown concurred. A lengthy personnel action ensued. Surprisingly, it is as difficult to get rid of a civilian space as to get one approved; this is particularly true of GS15s and above. It is hard to justify such spaces when requested, hence when action is taken to eliminate them, the Civil Service Commission is suspicious that the action is an attempt to get rid of the individual rather than the space.

At the same time there was an increasing requirement for greater reliability, availability and maintainability (RAM) analysis in testing. Accordingly, it was decided to create a new RAM Evaluation Directorate, headed by a PL313. Recruiting to fill that technical position was a long and involved process.

There were other organizational changes. The Administrative Office was eliminated, its functions given to the SGS. Lew Ponder was involved in changes in the test directorates. It was necessary to strip much of the evaluation capability from the Materiel Test Directorates (MTDs) to create the new RAM Directorate, a difficult matter because the MTDs had to retain some capability in order to interface with the new directorate. They also had to design new tests to provide the RAM data. It was essentially a shift of spaces from one directorate to another, involving no loss of personnel.

Finally, after consultation with Lew, it was decided that one secretary could handle both his work and mine, thus saving an additional space. Just at this time, MG Brown's secretary retired. BG Koster's secretary replaced her and Helen Simar, Lew's secretary became Koster's secretary. Janet took on Lew's work as well as handling mine. It worked out smoothly without need to let anyone go.

Simultaneously, the DA decided to merge Aberdeen Proving Ground and Edgewood Arsenal.

The gates of the two installations were about ten miles apart, but the property of both abutted, so it was decided that one HQ could administer both installations, eliminating one complete staff, thus saving considerable administrative funds. As the combined HQ was to be at APG, its commander, COL Hodges, was made responsible for the merger. The personnel at Edgewood Arsenal were understandably reluctant to relinquish the status of an independent post, nor did they relish control by an "unsympathetic" HQ. During the merger, considerable acrimony developed between the two staffs; many decisions escalated to TECOM HQ. Hodges briefed BG Koster once a week on the progress; I either sat in on those briefings or Warren stopped by later to keep me informed. Some of the matters were petty such as the disposition of the Army Community Services building at Edgewood, or the retention of two flying clubs, one at each post. This latter matter was complicated by the fact that the Edgewood Flying Club had elected one of its civilian members as an officer of the club in contravention of Army Regulations. Hodges insisted that a new election be held; though he was correct, it further exacerbated the strained relations.

There was also a problem with the purchasing and contracting authority, a sensitive legal area. Those of us on the TECOM staff sympathized with both Warren and the people at Edgewood. But the merger had been ordered, therefore it should be completed as quickly and fully as possible. This was the way MG Brown and the TECOM staff addressed each problem.

Though I rarely got involved in post affairs, parking was always a sore point with me. There never seems to be adequate parking any place with the result that untold man-hours (not to mention gasoline) are expended by visitors and workers seeking parking. All too often, people are forced to park on shoulders or grass resulting in unsightly areas.

The Pentagon was infamous for its parking. The 27,000 people who worked there fought for parking permits, subjected to great inconvenience. But visitors to the Pentagon found almost no parking whatsoever. The few lanes of visitors' parking were filled early in the morning. Although restricted to three hours, latecomers rarely could get a space. How any one conducted business at such a place was always a mystery.

Reserved parking is never satisfactory. It is usually allocated to convenience workers, rarely the people who have business in a HQ or on an installation. It is taken to extremes in some units where huge blocks of parking spaces are reserved for: company commander, executive officer, first sergeant, supply sergeant, mess sergeant, OIC, NCOIC, and charge of quarters. At all posts there are reserved spaces for sergeants major, but none for the battalion commanders for whom they worked!

But my greatest gripe was with the abuse of the system by dependents. Reserved parking is ostensibly provided to save the time of a commander or key staff officer so that he can concern himself with his primary duties. All too often, those spaces served the wives and children, even the enlisted aides of general officers, rather than the officers they were intended for. This was particularly true at APG. A number of spaces were reserved at the Officers' Club for general officers, colonels or GS15s and above, and one for "any 2Lt". Invariably when I drove to the club for a quick lunch, there was no parking; the reserved spaces were occupied by cars belonging to wives who were at the club for bridge or a social. I usually took a longer lunch break and ate off post.

This was true at the commissary, PX, hospital, indeed wherever there was reserved parking. The dependents assumed the prerogatives of rank. It was bad enough when wives did it. I found it impossible to believe that teenagers got away with it. I mentioned the problem to Warren Hodges and Bill Harris when they were Post Commanders. Both gave me a grim smile as they told me flatly they would not touch that issue under any circumstances.

The problem of healthy people usurping parking spaces reserved for the handicapped is even more infuriating. When I stopped one woman who had parked in a handicapped parking space at the commissary, she assured me that her husband was handicapped, didn't I see the decal? When I pointed out that her husband was not in the car, that she and her two children were perfectly healthy, and that a handicapped person might arrive who needed the space, she flounced away in a pique. So much for my efforts to reform the parking system.

In the fall of 1972, COL Pete Kelley told me that he was planning to retire from the ACE Board the first of February, 1973. Just after he had taken over TECOM, I had asked MG Brown to send me to one of the boards. The President of the Infantry Board retired in early 1972. When I asked to replace him Brown decided that I could be of more assistance to him in the early months of his command if I remained at APG. When Pete told me he was retiring, I determined to try again, the ACE Board was not only a challenging job, it was a jump slot. In addition, FT Bragg was one of my favorite posts where many friends were assigned.

MG Brown gave a great deal of consideration to the personal desires of his subordinates, and knew of my desire for the command. He also wanted someone at the Board he could depend upon and trust, now that it was becoming so deeply involved in sensor testing. To my delight he consented to my transfer.

The DA Office of Personnel Operations (OPO) was requested to effect the reassignment; soon, orders were cut transferring me to the ACE Board with a reporting date of 8 January 1973. This provided time to find quarters, get settled and be oriented before Pete left. Though I did not believe in overlaps, it would give me a chance to be introduced to the people I was going to work with by the officer I was going to replace. COL Bob Dingeman, who had been in my Leavenworth class and commanded the ARTY Group at Pleiku in 1970, was to replace me. Once the reporting date was fixed, I decided to take leave over Christmas, and go directly to FT Bragg after the holidays without reporting back to TECOM. Immediately after that decision was made, talk of farewell functions began to surface. It was because of my dislike of farewell parties and ceremonies that I had decided to go directly from leave to Bragg; such affairs always seemed to be an unnecessary harassment of the people involved.

Consequently, I tried to stop talk of farewell activities, letting it be known that I would appreciate it if my friends would have me over for a drink or dinner before I left. The matter received an unusual amount of attention. Many people on the staff who had become close friends were sincerely interested in sending me off in high style, but I continued to discourage any official function. The matter escalated to MG Brown; we knocked heads about it several times. Finally, he told me that while he understood my feelings in the matter, it would be a disappointment to many people if I went off without some function; he suggested I consent to one party. Flattered that people thought enough of me to take such a strong stand, I assented to one dinner party. MG Brown usually had a small intimate supper for departing colonels, particularly those in the command section, at which he said the official goodbyes. It was in terms of such a party that I acquiesced. Brown agreed to hold the guest list to a minimum, including only those who were close to me- The parry was to be held just after my Christmas leave; I would return for a day or so and then go on to FT Bragg.

Before clearing my apartment to depart on leave, I gave two back-to-back parties, a cocktail buffet on Saturday and an open house on Sunday. In this way I repaid all of my social obligations, said goodbye to my good friends, and recognized my co-workers. The packers then emptied the apartment, after which I drove to College Point. Christmas leave was good.

While I was on leave, and without my knowledge or consent, the intimate dinner escalated into a huge party for which TECOM took over the entire upper floor of the Officers' Club. It was a shock to walk in and find the room decorated with 25 cartoons, all of me. The TECOM illustrator, Gene Pondo, a talented cartoonist, had done a series of sketches spoofing me. Each office under my supervision had given him ideas; they remembered the stupid things I had done, and there were many of them, which he put into appropriate cartoons. Pondo had an uncanny knack of catching features and expressions. He really caught many of my idiosyncrasies and characteristics; I laughed harder than anyone at the wry humor displayed. Almost all of the TECOM Officers and civilians were present; each staff section presented me with a weird gift to help make the transition from TECOM to the ACE Board a bit easier. Though chagrined at the disregard of my wishes, I must admit that I was flattered by the thought and effort behind it all; certainly I appreciated it.

The day following the parry, I started for FT Bragg, stopping to see friends at Baltimore, Washington and Petersburg, where I spent the night with Anne and Dan Cleary, friends from the 504 at Bragg. Dan, who taught in the Logistics School at FT Lee, went to work at 0600 each morning. Before we went to bed, I thanked Anne and said goodbye, as I planned to leave with Dan at 0600. It had started to snow during the night and was still snowing when I left Petersburg; already the roads were powdered but still the storm did not did seem threatening. Certainly the farther south I got, the lighter the snow would be. But the storm was coming up from the south. That phase of the trip should have taken only three hours. As it turned out, it was six and a half hours before I finally got to Bragg. Each successive mile I drove the snow came down harder and stuck more; traffic slowed; the last 25 miles were driven at about ten miles an hour. There were times when it was doubtful that I would be able to get through, but finally I arrived at my destination. Pete had made reservations for me at the Normandy House, the Visiting Officers Quarters (VOQ), so I drove directly there. The post was officially closed because of the snow, but I was able to get settled in my temporary lodgings. About 1430 LTC William Cecil called; he was to be my escort and sponsor. Somehow he had made his way out to the post to offer his services. There was nothing to be done; I thanked him and told him to forget about me until the snow cleared up.

Prior to leaving TECOM, I had a lengthy correspondence with LTG Hay, CG, XVIII Airborne Corps, and BG "Brick" Krause, his CofS. Brick was an old buddy; we had been in the same classes at Benning, Leavenworth and Carlisle. When I wrote him that I would like to get quarters on post appropriate to my grade, he was initially receptive. Before writing him, I had contacted the DA office that handled family housing, and was assured of approval of any request for assignment of family quarters to me based on the job I was going to hold. Though that aspect of it was no problem, LTG Hay disapproved my request.

Brick had written to tell me that the staff had recommended that I be quartered in Hardy Hall, a high-rise BOQ. There were two room suites with a tiny pantry which were comfortably furnished. The staff had suggested that I could entertain in the large lobby! When I saw him, I really chewed him out about the stupid solution the Post staff had come up with. Trying to entertain formally in the lobby of a BOQ, with young officers wandering in and out in any dress made no sense.

On my arrival, LTG Hay relented a little. Though he would not give me senior officers quarters, he agreed to divert a duplex in Hammond Hills where CPTs and junior MAJs lived. On looking into this solution, it appeared to me that a senior COL living among junior OFFs would unduly inhibit them, as well as being uncomfortable for me. Reluctantly, I turned down Hay's offer and looked for housing off post.

Bill Cecil, my sponsor, drove me all over Fayetteville for a week; we looked first for a house to rent, then for an apartment. There were few apartments or houses available that were suitable for entertaining. While processing at the Personnel Center, I asked the billeting representative if she knew of any apartments or houses for rent in the area. She suggested I look at the Cedar Woods Apartments. When Cecil and I drove there, we found a large three-bedroom apartment that would suit my needs. Unfortunately, it was not yet finished, I could not move in for three weeks, but I signed a one year lease and arranged for the delivery of my furniture.

There were many friends at Bragg or in retirement in the area. In addition to Pete and Brick, O.G. Garrett and Hank Emerson were there from the War College class. Bob and Betty Whitelaw (504 and 508) were assigned to the SF R&D Command. There was a sizeable gaggle from the 504 in Mainz: Doug and Maryann Craver, Jean and Wayne Smith, Jim and Joanna Sullivan, and Gordon and Pat Corcoran. Chaplain Saunders from the 1st AR Div was the 82nd ABN Div Chaplain. Danny Baldwin, who had commanded the 4/39 in my Bde in Vietnam and Al Flynn, who had also been in the 9th Div, were on post. Dave and Mike Presson (Vietnam and Heidelberg), Bob and Kay Selton (Advance Class and ODCSLOG, Heidelberg), Charles and Alice Meek (508) were in post units, Jim and Sue Bartholomees (2nd Div, Korea, and Vietnam) and Frank and Dee Dee Bamhart (Advance Class) had retired in Fayetteville.

Because the Normandy House is a transient officers quarters, I was forced to move to Hardy Hall and occupy the suite Brick had told me about. The activity in the lobby confirmed my reservations about entertaining there. Immediately after that move, it snowed again, this time an 18-inch fall which paralyzed the surrounding communities and delayed completion of my apartment several more weeks. The post sent engineer equipment to help dig out Florence, SC.

On 1 February, the retirement and change of command ceremonies took place. We actually exchanged a flag that Pete had found somewhere, though the ACE Board was not a flag-bearing unit. In addition to many of Pete's friends, all of the senior officers on post were present, MG Brown represented TECOM.

Sometime after the ceremony, I moved to the Cedar Woods apartment. My driver, SP4 Gregory Dupuis, helped me get settled; in a few weeks I had a house-warming party to which I invited not only the officers and ladies of the ACE Board, but also friends on post. The apartment frequently harbored many refugees from the grueling trip down 1-95 the main north-south route on the east coast. I was always pleased when friends stopped to visit me.

The drive from the apartment to my office took about 15 minutes. Always an early riser, I was on the way by 0545, missing the morning traffic; there was rarely a crisis at the Board, so I left every day when duty hours ended, usually before the evening traffic built up. Our duty hours were 0730 to 1600, in contrast to the post hours, 0800 to 1630. This enabled Ace Board personnel, in particular civilians, to get on and off post with minimum traffic. Eventually the post adopted the early schedule, so everyone faced the same situation. There was no purpose in staying at the Board after duty hours, though many project OFFs remained to finish reports. I refused to add to their workload by staying myself.

My early arrival at the office each morning posed a problem for SP4 Dupuis. One of his duties was to dust my office and make sure it was ready for me. Since I usually got in about 0600, it made for an early morning for him. When I discovered that he was coming in at 0530, I told him to dust the office any time during the day.

Being President of the ACE Board was one of the most enjoyable non-troop tours that I had in the Army. There was a dedicated group of people at the Board doing interesting things. It seemed to me that the Board played a role in improving the equipment used by all Army troops. For the past year at TECOM I had listened to the plans and recommendations that were now coming to fruition; the sensor testing site was under construction; other activities were going on. The job was stimulating!

The Airborne, Communications and Electronics Board (originally the Artillery Board) is the oldest test board in the Army. It became Army Field Forces Board One after WWII; over the years its mission changed. Because of its location at FT Bragg it logically became the Airborne Board. It acquired a Special Forces title for a short time; though SF equipment continued to be tested, that part of the name was dropped (it was renamed the Airborne and Special Operations Test Board in 1987). The Board conducted Expanded Service Tests (EST) to determine if equipment could be effectively used by average troops with minimum training, and if it had any major deficiencies. It also conducted Check Tests (CT) to determine if modifications corrected the deficiencies they were designed for, as well as participating in Engineering Tests (ET). The Airborne Division tested equipment and systems including personnel and cargo parachutes, and aircraft used for airdrop or air transport of troops, supplies or equipment. The Communications and Electronics Division tested equipment used in Army Divs or lower units including radios, teletypewriters, power sources, and security equipment.

The soldiers borrowed from tactical units, preferably in squads and platoons, used the equipment as they would in the field. Under carefully observed conditions, any problems in training, functioning or maintenance were identified and the equipment evaluated against the specifications under which it was being procured or developed. The Board worked with all units on post as well as with agencies who provided specialized people when they were not assigned to FT Bragg.

The many facilities controlled by the Board contributed to the desirability of the assignment. It had its own workshops, aircraft and vehicles, riggers, test and maintenance personnel, indeed, the Board was a self-contained unit.

The Board had three aircraft: two T-20s, Navy trainers, and one HU-1B "Huey", flown by one civilian, two military pilots, as well as those test OFFs who were rated aviators. The T-20s were essentially "chase Planes", which followed the lift aircraft to photograph all personnel and materiel drops from exit to the ground. They were invaluable in documenting the attitude of personnel or equipment when opening took place, as well as the deployment of chutes. Three civilian photographers, on flight status, manned the cameras in the T-20s.

As a tenant unit, the ACE Board was not directly subordinate to the Post Commander. A written agreement between FT Bragg and TECOM set forth the responsibilities of the Board and Post to each other. Obviously, I was responsive to the CG, XVIIIABN Corps, my military senior, for any assistance I could provide in special areas. But the Board could not be tasked by the Post staff and my OFFs and EM were not required to perform post duties such as OD, CQ or post guard. Board duty was pleasant for all.

There were several reasons for the pleasant atmosphere which prevailed at the Board. Principal among them was the relationship which existed between the Board and its higher HQ. TECOM was some 500 miles away, and we had little direct responsibility to the Corps or Post. Deadlines, except for infrequent non-project associated events, were programmed in the test plans. Hence, artificial time constraints were rarely imposed. Since all its resources, with the exception of the test troops borrowed from post units, were under Board control, they were available when needed. Troops liked to work with the Board; it provided a stimulating change from routine training and a chance to see early versions of new equipment. Most units were cooperative in meeting our needs. The tenant arrangement with Corps worked well.

The Board offered the post many services. A USAF C-l 30 was available to the Board every duty day and we made the decision as to whether it should be rigged for heavy drop or troop jumps. In addition, the Huey was always available, hence jumps could be scheduled at will. A limited number of jumps could be made available to post personnel. As President, I was besieged by staff officers who wanted quick, easy jumps without the long marshalling required by tactical units. We also had facilities to put on unique displays and could provide expertise in many areas.

Immediately after assuming responsibility as President, I set about getting acquainted with every feature of the Board. It was obvious there was a professional group working for me, I wanted to get to know the projects they were working on as well as learn the methods of testing. While not wishing to get involved in the detailed testing, I was desirous of knowing all facets of it. COL Bob Apt, the Director of Testing, had under him two test divisions, Airborne under LTC Bob Reid and Communications and Electronics under LTC George Riviere. Both were competent officers who had knowledgeable test officers in their divisions. Apt, Reid, Riviere and their subordinates briefed me fully.

The Board was organized as a company to which all personnel were assigned. The Co CO, CPT Ron Amon, a Ranger, Airborne, Signal Corps OFF, ran an outstanding unit. The company was a Table of Distribution (TD) organization with mess, supply room and barracks. Less than 50 EM lived in the WWII barracks on Smoke Bomb Hill. Most of the EM had technical skills such as, parachute riggers, communications specialists, electronic maintenance technicians, combat engineers, Army AVN mechanics, motor mechanics, security, supply or administrative specialties. All were highly qualified. The majority of the EM and OFFs were married. It appeared that the current organization was a needless expense for the Army and unnecessary work for Ron Amon; certainly the men in the barracks should be closer to their work. It was my initial desire to put our enlisted men on the 3rd floor of the Board HQ building, but there were difficulties in getting approval. After much study, Ron recommended that our men living in the barracks be billeted with the Corps HHC. Negotiations with Al Flynn, the HQ CMDT, resulted in the assignment of one floor in the HHC barracks to the Board; our men were now only a few hundred yards from our HQ. When the men moved, the Co organization was phased out.

Several members of the Board had served with me before. CW4 Olin Baggett, who had been my Unit Administrator in K Co, 504, here at Bragg in 1949-1950, and in the ABN Bde in Mainz and Biebrich, was in charge of the ACE Board Hangar, where parachutes were packed and equipment rigged for test drops. He was a true professional, heading a group of competent, loyal NCOs who accomplished their duties without detailed supervision. Unfortunately, shortly after I joined the Board, Baggett retired. One of his NCOs, SGT Harvey Mundy had been in the Ranger Co assigned to IFFV and had participated in many long range reconnaissance patrols. On several occasions when I had visited the Rangers to commend them for a particularly hazardous action, I had met this sharp young man. The Chief of Plans, LTC George Nelson, had been assigned as Chief of RFPF for the DEPCORDS IFFV. These people made me feel at home.

The Board SGM, Roy Barton, a former SF soldier, was one of the most helpful NCOs I have ever served with. If all CSMs and SGMs operated as he did, I would quickly lose my prejudice against them. There were many other outstanding EM on the Board, my driver, SP4 Dupuis, being among them. Dupuis could do anything with his hands; he was a carpenter, electrician, motor mechanic, builder and artisan, an asset to the Board and to me.

As soon as I was thoroughly familiar with my duties as President, I determined to visit all of the agencies the Board worked with throughout the Army to become familiar with the people we dealt with and the work they did in connection with us. A spaced schedule was developed. The first visit was to the Aviation Systems Command in St Louis, to which I flew in an Army aircraft. Clarence Kettler met me at the General Aviation Terminal and I spent a pleasant evening with him and Elizabeth. During the briefing the following day at the Aviation Systems Command, I met the action people who worked with the Board. My luncheon companions were BG Leo D. Turner and BG Charles E.

Reed, Jr. Leo and I had served together in the 504 at Bragg and were War College classmates. Bill had been the 9th Div Engineer when I had the 1st Bde. He told me about Frank Miller's call to him when I had given his Engineer Co the mission of seizing an LZ. It was an enjoyable luncheon and a profitable visit.

From St Louis I flew to Natick, MA, where LTC Dick Hardman of the Airborne Test Division joined me for an orientation at the Natick Laboratories. This organization developed most of the Army Airborne equipment, as well as clothing, helmets, food and most QM items. It too was an informative visit.

Later Bob Apt and I went to Edwards AFB, CA, to check on a Sidelooking Airborne Radar (SLAR) test underway there. It appeared to be going well. From Edwards we flew to China Lake where the Board was conducting tests on the Special Atomic Demolition Munition {S ADM), a highly classified device. Again, the test was on schedule. Next on the itinerary was El Centro, CA, where the Army, the Air Force and the Navy/Marines were jointly developing uniform platforms and parachutes for heavy drop, and where Board personnel were involved with the AF on the C-5 aircraft. We flew in the C-5 during a test of the terrain guidance system. It was eerie to head directly for a mountain and have the plane climb to avoid it without the pilot touching the controls. CWO Dexter Hall, a member of the Board C-5 Test Group, met us and explained some of the difficulties the Army was experiencing with the big aircraft in heavy drop and troop jumps. Bob and I then flew to FT Huachuca to talk about some equipment EPG had engineer tested, and which we were now service testing. All these visits were helpful in giving me a better appreciation of where the Board fit into the testing system and its inter-relations with other agencies. Much of this I had gotten during my tour at TECOM, but not in the same detail or with the immediacy that I now faced.

Finally I visited the Rigger School at FT Lee, VA. While there I attended one of the Joint Air Movement Board (JAMBOARD) sessions as an observer, Bob Reid was the official ACE Board member.

The Board was involved in many interesting programs at this time. The Airborne Test Division was attempting to determine if every item of heavy equipment in the ABN Div could be parachuted into a combat situation. The Sheridan tank, a heavy dump truck, a tractor and scraper, indeed the entire Family of Engineer Construction Equipment (FAMECE) underwent testing during my tenure. An evaluation was underway to determine if the sight for the Dragon Missile, the Medium Antitank Assault Weapon System, was best dropped on the platform with the missile or delivered by individual parachutist. Working with SF personnel, an examination of the M-1 Grapnel, an Individual Aid and Survival Kit and a set of climbers for rope ascent were being tested. The High Altitude Delivery System, designed to drop A-22 equipment containers from altitudes up to 12,500 feet was an interesting project.

The test that intrigued me most was the Low Altitude Parachute Extraction System (LAPES). This involved the extraction of very heavy equipment such as the Sheridan Tank or bulldozers from a C-l 30 aircraft flying only inches from the ground. A parachute released as the plane skimmed the drop zone, dragged the piece of equipment from the aircraft; after dropping to the earth it skidded to a halt on a specially constructed platform. One C-130 crew became highly expert in the technique, but their very expertise may have given us unrealistic results. We needed average air-crews. Our riggers prepared the loads for extraction, attached the parachutes and monitored the tests. So far as I remember, there was only one malfunction with LAPES during the time I was with the Board. It is a good system which can put heavy equipment on the ground in a hurry. The low flying aircraft are highly vulnerable to ground fire, however.

Just as I assumed the Presidency of the Board, the testing of the C-5 aircraft began phasing out. Because of its complexity, a special evaluation group headed by COL A.K. Charles had been set up in 1971 to examine the plane's capability for jumping, heavy drop and airlift. The Army testing had disclosed certain shortcomings, primarily in accommodations for jumping paratroopers. Most of these deficiencies were rectified and the aircraft rechecked before the C-5 project was disbanded. The C-5 Army team had a separate office at Pope Air Force Base, close to the Board hangar. When A.K. phased out the C-5 program, he became my Deputy until he retired. LTC Steverson then became my XO in lieu of a Deputy.

The Communications Test Division was working with a new night sight, camera, antenna, generator and, of course, sensors. One of the initial sensor tests was a security system for arms rooms and other key installations. Sensors were installed in several locations: a SF consolidated arms room, the Corps MP Co arms room, and an arms room in the 82nd ABN Div, The principal problem with the system was false alarms.

The construction of the sensor test site became such a complex undertaking that I put LTC Steverson in charge of it. MAJ Bruce Gronich, the Project OFF, was doing an outstanding job but was getting bogged down in administrative and logistical matters. Steverson was made the overall supervisor so that Gronich could devote himself entirely to the testing. Many of the ideas Bruce, a highly intelligent Signal Corps OFF, thought up for testing sensors were difficult to comprehend. However, I had confidence in him and let him develop the program as he saw fit within specified budgetary and manpower limitations.

While driving around the Cottonade area one Sunday afternoon in March, I noticed a new house being erected. The walls had just been put up, enabling me to see the general floor plan, which I liked. The house seemed to lend itself to entertaining. It occurred to me that the purchase of a house would not only give me tax advantages, but also enable me to build up some equity, something I had neglected over the years. The Cottonade Realty Office told me the house would be ready for occupancy the first of May and quoted a price that seemed reasonable. With a VA loan, it was apparent that if I put down only $5,000, my quarters allowance would take care of the monthly payments. The deal was closed. I was able to select the colors and have some minor modifications made in the construction before it was turned over to me. My lease at Cedar Woods had a military escape clause, so that posed no problem.

When ready to move from Cedar Woods, there were many items I did not want the movers to pack, principally my books and some of the more fragile things I had collected over the years. This gave rise to a moving party. A bar was set up in the apartment and one in the house. Officers of the Board and their wives were invited to assist me, those who elected to do so were asked to bring boxes and baskets. Each person was to move a box of books or something fragile. After a drink at the apartment, boxes were packed and moved to the house, where additional drinks and hors d'oeuvres were available. It worked well. All of the small or breakable things were moved that night so that the movers only had to take the large furniture.

My driver, Dupuis, had helped me move into the apartment. CPT Amon had given him a three-day pass and I paid him well for his assistance. Between us we had set up the apartment in a day. Dupuis agreed to help under the same conditions when I moved into the house. He and another enlisted man from the Board, under a similar arrangement, put the house in order while I attended to my duties at the Board. From my rough sketches they hung pictures and memorabilia and arranged furniture so that the house was quickly in order

The house proved to be enjoyable and useful. It was a good place in which to entertain, as proven by the house warming party I had shortly after moving in. A parade of visitors came to see me, members of my family as well as friends driving through the area.

With housing and social activities in hand, I decided to reorganize the Board. It seemed to me that as Board President I was too isolated from the testing as a result of the interposition of the Director of Testing between me and the Chiefs of the Test Divisions. My concern was no criticism of Bob Apt, the Director. But in order to utilize him properly and to respect the chain of command, every time

I wanted to know anything about a test I had to go through him. This was not the way I wanted the Board to operate. I made Bob my Deputy and phased out the position of Director of Testing. The Chiefs of the Airborne and Communications and Electronics Test Divisions then reported directly to me. The new organization worked well.

At the same time other organizational changes were made. Just before I joined the Board, a Data Systems and Command Management Office had been established with an eager young civilian, Neal Cameron, in charge. I now eliminated the Administrative Office, under Jesse Fowler, a GS 11 and a retired CWO. Jesse went to another organization on post. Certain functions handled by the Administrative Office went to Neal Cameron's section. The purely administrative functions were consolidated under Nellie Salebee. Before reorganization, Nellie had managed the typing pool for the Test Directorate. She became the head of the Administrative Branch, with all filing and typing under her supervision. The spaces recovered from these changes were used to enhance the testing capability of the Board.

A noticeable coolness existed between the personnel assigned to the Airborne Test Division and those assigned to the Communications and Electronics Test Division. To eliminate this, I determined to get a recreational program going at the Board. With the assistance of CPT Amon and SGM Batton, a bowling league was organized. Officers, enlisted men and civilians bowled. The program brought all of the Board members closer together. Though not a bowler, I was spectator and cheer leader. In 1974, we were informed that we could not have the league again because of the civilians bowling with us. Bowling lane owners in Fayetteville had complained; the lanes at FT Bragg were for military only. Such pettiness did much to alienate the military from the civilians in Fayetteville.

A volleyball league was also established. I played on the HQ Team, handicapping it greatly. SGM Batton was the team captain; after his retirement, SGM Pace took over. It provided good sport, exercise, and many laughs.

Before Christmas, someone suggested that the Board have a pot-luck supper in the Hangar. Plans for a simple get-together rapidly became more elaborate. With money from the unit fund, we hired a band. As is usually the case with such affairs, the food was delicious and plentiful. I authorized brown-bagging in addition to the soft drinks and beer bought by the unit fund. When I left the party at midnight, it was still going strong.

Twice a year the Board played a golf tournament on the Special Service Course. The Officers competed against the Enlisted Men. That year (1953) the Officers managed to win both tournaments in spite my miserable playing. With many avid golfers among the Board Officers there was a golf ladder, with my name always on the bottom. Every Wednesday one of the Board Officers went to the pro-shop at the Officers' Course to get tee times. With adroit use of RHIP (rank has its privileges) I was always in the first foursome to tee off. Most of the officers were amused at my efforts, but I enjoyed walking the course with friendly people. Ron Amon tried to help me improve my game, but eventually he gave up that impossible task.

These activities did much to reduce the coolness between the two test divisions and weld the Board members into a more cohesive group.

As at Leavenworth, I joined a local health club. Since I could arrange my schedule so that I was able to leave the office early, I managed to work out three times a week which kept me in fair shape.

A tragic incident marred our serene life at the Board. A phone call one Saturday morning informed me that MAJ Don Wolstenholme, the OFF who had shepherded me through those final jumps for my Master Jump Wings, had drowned at Wrightsville Beach. He had taken his two children for a pleasant outing there. His son was caught in the undertow. Don tried to save him, but both he and the boy drowned. It was a sad task to comfort his wife and daughter and to bury Don and his son. The Board C-130 was diverted to fly a large group of his fellow OFFs and EM to Washington.

From Andrews AFB an Army bus took us to the FT Myer Chapel for the funeral services. To pay our last respects to Don Wolstenholme, I asked the Board members to march behind the caisson to the grave site.

Early in April, the staff suggested that we prepare for the annual "Airborne Reunion". Before Pete Kelley retired, he briefed me on this event; the two previous years he had invited a group of his old Airborne buddies to assemble at FT Bragg. The affair had been so well received that he wanted to perpetuate the tradition. It was a get-together of Airborne officers who had served together in various units and assignments over the years. No one Airborne unit was represented, the common bonds being Airborne qualification before 1950, service together in a TO&E ABN unit, and good party types. Pete had used the Board assets to support it and asked me to continue the custom. The mailing list he turned over to me contained many familiar names.

As I was hosting the 1973 Airborne Reunion, I included my Airborne friends. Most of the OFFs invited were retired, though a few like myself were still on active duty. We also invited the key OFFs on post. It was an enjoyable, though "wet" weekend. Liquor and lies flowed freely! Since 1971, there has been a reunion every year but one. The tradition continues today, but now fully divorced from the Board.

Since it was possible to jump at the Board anytime, I set a goal to jump at least once a week. In most cases I jumped from a helicopter because it was easier for the ABN Test Division to set up such a jump for me. This precluded having to re-rig the C-130 for troop jumps if it was going to be used for a heavy drop. On those occasions when there was a troop jump scheduled, I eagerly took advantage of it. Jumping once a week, I had greater confidence in myself and improved my technique in the air and in landing, though my PLFs were almost as bad as ever. The Board Huey would land at the ACE Board Hangar at Pope Field to pick us up. After a quick briefing, we chuted up, climbed aboard the chopper and sat on the floor with our feet dangling out. As the senior officer, I was always the number one man, the first one to jump. Pleasant enough in the summer, in the winter, exposed to the wind, we were thoroughly chilled by the time we jumped. The Huey would fly along Manchester Road from the Hangar to Holland DZ, usually assigned to the Board for its tests. After a quick pass over the DZ, during which the jumpmaster would throw out a crepe paper streamer to determine the speed and direction of the winds aloft, the pilot adjusted his approach for our jump. It was an easy way to jump.

In 73 the Army was phasing in the MC1-1, the so-called "steerable parachute". The Board was also testing the XT-1 harness which had two leg snaps and a cross-chest snap instead of the quick release box, a more comfortable and utilitarian harness. Once I jumped the combination of the two, I would jump no other way. The new harness and parachute eliminated much of the discomfort i always experienced in jumping. The riggers set aside an MC1-1 parachute rigged with an XT-1 harness carefully adjusted to my body, so chuting up was easy.

Also in 1973 the Board was tasked to test parachutes for SF HALO (High Altitude Low Opening or sky diving) operations. MAJ Scotty McGurk, the test OFF, together with five rigger NCOs, qualified in free fall at the SF HALO School. One of the parachutes tested was the MC1-1 configured for HALO with a special harness and termed the MC1-1-2. I made one flight to 12,000 feet with them and watched the exit technique; of course I observed many of the jumps from the ground. At first they landed all over the reservation, but as they acquired more skill, they began to land on the Tee. The HALO Test team had to take compression chamber training because at high altitudes, the use of oxygen was routine in jumps.

Troopers in the 82nd jumped a "naked" rifle slung over the shoulder; in several tragic incidents a static line wrapped around a barrel, preventing separation of the individual from the static line, resulting in his being towed behind the aircraft. Several men were killed because the C-130 crews were unable to pull them in, an extraordinarily difficult job for the static jumpmaster and the crew chief, even though the C-130 had a motor-driven winch to retrieve static lines and back packs. Division and Corps asked the Board to study the problem, providing a full TO&E Plt commanded by 1LT Bob Powers, for any tests we elected to make.

Powers was a muscular, dedicated USMA wrestler and graduate with an unusually high set of moral standards. In talking with him I found that one of his instructors at the Academy had been my friend Wick, for whom he had a high regard as teacher and friend. Bob not only took his own platoon through a number of jumps, but several others from the Division. The Board photographed actions both inside and outside the aircraft. In most cases, troopers exited with poor body position, although this was not the determining factor. Our moving pictures of the actions inside the aircraft clearly showed that the troopers let go the bight in the loop of the static line too early, thus creating considerable slack, which permitted the air stream to loop it over the rifle. In addition, the troopers crowded together at the door. The malfunctions were the result of poor jumping and poor jumpmaster procedures. The Board suggested that the 82nd jump with the muzzles down, though this posed a problem in keeping the bores clean. With greater emphasis on training not only of the individual trooper, but also of the jumpmaster, the problem was virtually eliminated.

One of the special privileges accorded the ACE Board President was the authority to qualify personnel as jumpers. Pete Kelley had conducted several jump qualification courses for selected personnel, primarily to qualify ACE Board members, but also open to certain post personnel. In 1973, I decided that the Board would again run a jump school. A sharp, able CPT, Jared (Jerry) Bates, who had instructed in the Ranger Department at FT Benning before joining the Board, was selected to head the course. He conducted a thorough and effective course. A senior COL on post was given permission to attend. During the training Jerry told me that he was concerned about the COL's progress, he seemed to lack confidence in himself when jumping from the 34-foot tower. Observing him, I noted that he did not make vigorous or proper exits from the tower. Jerry recommended that the COL be dropped from the course. Several EM who were experiencing similar difficulties, were to be dropped, but the COL presented a problem. I talked with him, explaining why I was contemplating dropping him from the course. Although unhappy about not completing the course, he was philosophical about it. He recognized my obligation to be sure that the people the Board qualified as jumpers were properly trained. He asked for another chance, which I gave him. Neither Jerry nor I noted any improvement in his next few exits. Reluctantly, I directed that he be dropped from the course on the Friday of the last week of pre-jump training. The next week the class would jump from aircraft in flight.

When LTG Hay heard that the COL was being eliminated, he called and asked me to reverse my decision. He declared that elimination from the course might adversely effect the COL's career. Though there would be no record in the COL's file of his attendance at the Airborne Board School unless he qualified, I was disturbed by the need to drop the COL as well as by LTG Hay's request. I explained that I had an obligation to insure that everyone certified by the Ace Board was a well-trained jumper. Hay insisted I make an exception in the case of the COL. The idea that any officer who volunteered to take a course must be passed was hard to justify in my mind. After careful consideration and a lengthy discussion with Jerry, I called together all of the people in the class about whom we were in doubt, and told them that if they were willing to make the effort, we would give them extra training over the weekend to try to qualify them. After this extra training, we did let the COL and two of the EM jump, two others were dropped. The colonel made better exits from the aircraft than he did from the 34-foot tower, which poses a problem to many people. Some find it easier to jump out of an aircraft than out of the tower. But I remained uneasy about the COL, never sure that he had become a fully proficient jumper.

As a result of my policy to jump weekly, I accumulated a considerable number of jumps. At the time, I was the Executive Vice President of the Airborne Association, which maintained an informal listing of those jumpers who had made 100 jumps or more. Such jumpers were inducted into the "Century Club" with the award of a certificate and a set of miniature gold Master Jump Wings for wear with civilian clothing. Unknown to me, SGM Barton had kept count of my jumps and submitted an application for my induction into the Century Club to an officer of the Airborne Association. One afternoon I was called to the Board Hangar where I found a formation headed by LTG Richard J. Seitz, who had replaced LTG Hay as CG of XVIII Airborne Corps, and LTG (RET) William P. Yarborough, the President of the Airborne Association. They presented the certificate and gold Century Club Wings to me. At the same time, SGM Batton gave me a gold jump helmet. ACE Board personnel routinely jumped with motorcycle helmets; jumpers with more than 100 jumps wore gold helmets.

Inevitably, changes occurred in the personnel assigned to the Board. Dexter Hall, who took charge of the Hangar when Olin Baggett retired, was assigned to Korea. CW03 Bob Page, an experienced and capable rigger, replaced him. LTC Pete Hayes, who had been on the C-5 test team, replaced LTC George Nelson as Plans Officer, when the latter retired. After Don Dyer, the Logistics Chief, left, I depended on CWO3 Morgan, Chief of the Logistics Management Office. MAJ Gronic left about the time the sensor testing peaked. On his retirement, SGM Batton was replaced by SGM Roy Pace, another fine ex-Special Forces NCO.

Wayne Smith, who had been in the 504 at Mainz and was the Darlac Prov Advisor when I was at IFFV, asked me for a job when he relinquished command of a SF Bn. Because there were reports that Wayne had a drinking problem, I was reluctant to take him. During a frank talk about this, Wayne assured me that he recognized his problem, but that he had it under control. With reservations, I accepted Smith as one of the branch chiefs in the Airborne Test Division.

For a while all went well; Wayne did a good job. In our initial discussion I had told Smith that if he needed help with his drinking problem, he should come see me. One morning, he came to my office to ask for help; he was not able to handle his drinking problem alone. Wasting no time, I called the CO of the hospital, COL Gore, a friend, and told him that one of my OFFs needed hospitalization to "dry out" and work on his problem. Al Gore's only question was whether the OFF was worth salvaging; when assured he was, he admitted Wayne to the hospital immediately. The doctor in charge of the alcoholic ward, pleased with Smith's progress, recommended he be sent back to full duty. Wayne came back somewhat chastened by his experience in the hospital, where OFFs and EM with similar problems were assigned to the same ward. He did well for a while, then slipped; again he took the necessary steps to bring his problem under control. When Bob Reid retired, Wayne became the Chief of the Airborne Test Division.

Just after Smith joined the Board, I was invited to address the Ranger graduation at FT Benning. Wayne, a Ranger, was tasked to draft a speech for me. He submitted a very gung-ho-you-are-the-best congratulatory speech, which did not satisfy me. Using as much of Smith's draft as I could, I dictated a speech to my secretary, taking as my theme "What are you going to do with your training". I challenged the graduates to use their expertise to make the Army more professional and to invigorate Infantry training.

A sharp Ranger 1LT escorted me from the Columbus Airport to Green Hall, where I spent the night. When my escort officer picked me up the next morning, I had on the starched fatigues specified as the graduation uniform. The Director of the Ranger Department, shook his head when we met, handing me an OD T-shirt which he asked me to substitute for my white one. He said that it was tradition in the Ranger Department to use the OD T-shirt so that no white was showing that could be used as a target by an enemy! With a grin, I donned the green shirt.

The ceremony was simple and brief, my remarks appeared to be well received. As I assisted in pinning the tabs on the men, I noted what a superb looking group they were. Finally, with the famous

Ranger growl, the formation was dismissed. COL Bowers asked for a copy of my speech, saying it was the most meaningful one that had been given to the graduates in some time.

Shortly after returning from FT Benning, I received an invitation to Sam Koster's retirement and the accompanying activities. The TECOM airplane picked me up the day before the ceremony. That afternoon, I conducted some business with the TECOM staff and had a talk with MG Brown, during which he told me the story of Sam's "non-award".

It is customary upon the retirement or reassignment of most general officers to award them the Distinguished Service Medal (DSM). MG Brown wanted to present the DSM to Sam in recognition of his outstanding performance as the Deputy CG of TECOM. However, as part of the "administrative action" taken against Koster as a result of the My Lai tragedy, the Army had revoked the DSM Sam had been awarded while commanding the 23rd Div, Therefore Brown took the precaution of asking the AMC CDR, GEN Miley, if he would support such a recommendation; Miley said he would. MG Brown then asked GEN Abrams, Army CofS, the same question. Abrams said that a recommendation for Sam Koster would be treated as one for any other general officer and considered on its merits. Heartened, but still concerned, Brown had submitted the recommendation several months before Sam was due to retire. As the time drew closer and he had not received word that the award had been approved, he called the AMC CofS to ask him to check into it. Weeks passed with no word. Finally MG Brown went to see LTG Kerwin, the DA DCSPER, who gave him no satisfaction. The week before Sam's retirement, no word had been received as to whether or not he was to get the DSM.

Two days before Sam's retirement, TECOM was informed that the DSM recommendation had been disapproved at "a very high level because it was feared the media might interpret it as restoring the award that had been taken away". This was in the early days of Watergate, which had made the Administration sensitive to any criticism, especially related to Vietnam. Brown accepted the disapproval with reluctance, informing AMC that he was recommending Sam for the Legion of Merit. With great mortification the AMC CofS told him that he could not do so; that the "authorities" did not want Sam to get any medal. "They" did not want any adverse publicity from

Sam's retirement; any award might be misconstrued. MG Brown was properly incensed; Sam wanted to dispense with the ceremony, but Brown insisted that it go on; his long and honorable career should be recognized.

The retirement party for Sam and Cherie the night before was a lavish one. TECOM had gone all out to wish them well because they were well-liked by everyone at Aberdeen. But the retirement itself was a grim affair. MG Stu Meyer happened to be on a staff visit to TECOM from AMC, and was the only officer not assigned to TECOM or APG at the ceremony. The whole matter was distasteful to me; it was a reflection on the leadership in the Army. It seemed a gutless group. Even GEN Abrams, whom I thought a fine troop commander, had let politics get to him, and had tarnished his image in my eyes.

The name of the new Deputy Commander/Chief of Staff of TECOM surprised me; BG O.E. Smith, whom I had known in the 101st ABN Div, was replacing Sam Koster. I did not have a high opinion of Smith and looked forward to working with him again with some dismay. However, O. E. was apparently overawed by Brown, and he did not interfere with my work at the Board.

Back at Bragg, testing continued apace. Though the sensor program was well underway, there appeared to be more Airborne testing than Communications or Electronics testing. The Board continued to perform its mission in a highly competent fashion with little direction from me.

Because units such as the ACE Board lack military tradition, I thought that a dining-in would keep alive the customs of the service among the officers. Ron Amon, given the mission of setting one up, used the procedures developed by the 504 at Mainz and THE REGULARS at FT Hood, neither conducted according to the traditions of the dining-in throughout the Army. Despite this, it was an exuberant affair combining good food, camaraderie, ritual and horse-play in a memorable fashion.

My relations with the XVIII Airborne Corps Staff were cordial and I had a good association with LTG Dick Seitz. He was a fine officer, a dynamic commander and a genuine individual; we developed a warm friendship. His wife, Betty, was a wonderful person who invited me to many dinner parties at their quarters. Just before Christmas, 1973, Dick and Betty had a small dinner party to which they invited me. Liqueurs were served in the living room, where Betty sat at the piano and led in singing Christmas Carols. During a lull we heard the poignant sound of caroling outside. Dick and Betty opened the door revealing a group of young officers and their wives from one of the units on post. The Seitzs cordially invited them all in for drinks. Most were lieutenants who were abashed at being invited into the Commanding General's quarters. After a drink and a short pleasant visit, they left.

Immediately after the departure of the carolers, someone suggested that we go out and carol. Without more ado, Seitz herded us all outside. We went from quarters to quarters in the Normandy area, sang one or two carols (not too well, I'm afraid), then rang the bell to wish the occupants a Merry Christmas. Some residents were reluctant to open the door; when they did, not knowing who to expect, and saw the CG and his wife in the group, we were made more than welcome.

As was customary when on a state-side assignment, I made plans to spend the Christmas holiday with Mother in New York. Three days before I was ready to leave, Pat Jordan, the Director of Personnel at TECOM, called to tell me that DA had reduced the Board's parachute duty positions (jump slots). GEN Abrams wanted to recover hazardous duty spaces for two Ranger Bns the Army planned to activate, but did not want to increase the overall number of jump slots in the Army. Pat asked what would happen if the ACE Board was cut to 25 Airborne spaces. Without hesitation I said, 'The first thing that would happen is that you would lose the President of the ACE Board. The second thing is that the Board could not perform its mission."

Pat immediately said, "Don't worry, Don. We are going to take care of your jump slot". This really irked me; Pat thought he was doing me a favor by taking care of my Airborne status.. Though his motives were good, he was doing the wrong thing. It wasn't my jump slot that bothered me, it was the jump slots of the specialists, the NCOs, and the junior OFFs who worked for me that were at stake. After my initial outburst, I explained to Pat that if the Board lost that many jump slots, it couldn't do its job. There were 49 parachute riggers assigned to the Board. Their Military Occupational Specialty Code required them to jump; if they didn't jump, they couldn't maintain their MOS. Thus we would lose many of the experienced riggers assigned. As it was we had too few for the tests we were doing. In addition, 25 airborne spaces would not take care of the test project OFFs. After explaining that to Pat, I repeated, "Pat, you are going to lose the President of the Board. I have just decided to retire." Pat argued with me, but finally hung up. Suddenly it seemed time to get out of the Army. The lack of leadership, lack of discipline, lack of integrity, which now pervaded the Army overshadowed everything I loved about it. The disgraceful treatment that had been accorded Sam Koster was typical of the current disregard for time-honored traditions. Political considerations were now driving the personnel actions of the Army. TECOM and the ACE Board were constantly having to justify their mission, indeed their very existence; now I had to justify the jump slots essential for the performance of my testing. The Army was no longer enjoyable; it was time to retire. Automatically I reached for the telephone to call MG Brown. When he was on the line, I said without preamble, "Sir, I have decided to retire."

"Now what's the problem, Don?" Brown asked.

"It's a lot of things, too many to discuss now. But the matter that triggered my decision was this idiotic cut in jump slots at the Board. If I am cut to 25 jump slots, I won't have enough riggers or project officers to do the testing. I am sick of trying to make do on a shoe string. I'm ready to get out."

"Now wait a minute. I don't know anything about the cut in jump slots. I am sure that something can be done about that. Don't go off half cocked without trying to remedy the situation. I am sure I can take care of that problem."

"Sir, it isn't just the jump slots, it is the whole attitude in the Army these days. The cut was just the straw that broke the camel's back. Things are not the same, I don't enjoy being in the Army anymore. I am getting sour, and before I sour any of the junior OFFs or NCOs I had better get out. I'll let you know after Christmas the exact date, but it will probably be the first of June."

"Don't make any rash decisions now, Don. Go on leave and think about it. I am sure that when you give it more thought, you'll stay. I want you to stay; you are doing a good job at the Board, and the Army needs people like you. Stick it out a little longer. Don't decide anything until you get back from leave."

"Okay, sir. I'll give it some thought. But I am pretty sure that I am going to get out. A Merry Christmas to you and Evelyn."

"Merry Christmas, Don. Give my best to your Mother. And give that matter some careful thought."

"Yes, sir. Goodbye."

For the rest of the day and all that night, I wrestled with the problem. My mind whirled with thoughts as, unbidden, people and events jostled for attention, were noted, then immediately thrust aside by other images. My life in the Army passed quickly in review. Posts, duties, places, events and people jumbled together, and then a clear picture would emerge. Those first days at FT Dix, OCS, Okinawa, that first soldier in my platoon who had been killed, bumping into Dana Federonko in the ward tent on Mindoro, medical school, my return to active duty, being sworn in as a Regular Army Officer, that muddy, sickeningly sweet tea on the British warship after the guerrilla band had been driven from the mainland, KMI, duty at the Pentagon, the jump at Sennelager, THE REGULARS PLEDGE, the expression on Frank Miller's face when I told him that his Engineer Co would make a combat assault, the many close calls in aircraft, those six jumps at the ACE Board to qualify as a Master Jumper, schools at Benning, Leavenworth, Greely and Carlisle. The phenomenal luck I had enjoyed during more than five years in combat zones, much of it in contact with the enemy. Yet I had never been wounded. Mrs Gabelia would probably tell me it was the icon she had given me. It suddenly struck me that I had never been afraid of dying, but had been terrified of being maimed or becoming incapacitated. There had been moments of paralyzing dread, but death was not an element of them. There was a glow when I thought of Bill Long, Clarence Kettler, Ted Rothert, Frank Mashburn, and all the other friends I had made in the Army. It was that, more than anything that I hated to give up. But of course I would not give up my friends when I retired, and I would make more friends out of the Army just as I had made friends in it. But a special chemistry operates in the services, which ripens friendships more quickly and cements them more firmly. There was the ability to separate the professional and the personal aspects of people. Many of my close friends were not outstanding OFFs or soldiers, but this did not affect that friendship. On the other hand, I respected the professional ability of many people I did not like. There had been many gratifying assignments, positions of prestige and authority. Though I had not been promoted to general officer rank, I had commanded many troops. Those days with F Co, 382nd IN on Okinawa, K Co 504, F Co 508, B Co 9th IN, with THE REGULARS, with the 1st Bde, 9th IN Div, gave me tremendous satisfaction. It struck me that the caliber of soldiers I had been privileged to serve with had not varied much from WWII, through Korea and Vietnam. Basically All were solid American men and good soldiers.

The reduction in jump slots could not be forgotten (they were restored). The constant rectification of mission, personnel, even organization would not fade. The treatment of Sam Koster would not go away. Management had replaced leadership in the Army and the managers seemed to have no personal interest in their subordinates. Their only concern was to get more effective use out of them. The personal had given place to personnel considerations. The military services had become instruments for social change. The need for aggressive, well- trained, combat-ready soldiers had been subordinated to the use of the military to further racial integration, provide an opportunity for high school drop-outs to complete their education, encourage ethnic identity and other social experiments. None of these ends could be challenged, but the military services were not the organizations to remedy society's ills. There was little integrity left even among officers. Reports were doctored to reflect expected results, and few officers had the courage to tell the emperor that he had on no clothes. Promotion was no longer based on selecting the best qualified individual, but a new concept, "fully qualified", now permitted arbitrary criteria such as age, sex and ethnic background to become determining factors. Indeed, quota systems were invoked to further vitiate selections.

Rewarding, satisfying, enjoyable as my career had been, it was obviously time to leave the service. By the next morning, my decision was irrevocable. Before I left for New York, I wrote to MG Brown and told him that I would retire 31 May 1974. That date was chosen so that I could host one more Airborne Reunion. In the letter I tried vainly to express to Charlie Brown my reasons for leaving the service at this time. On paper they looked selfish, self-centered, even bigoted. In the end, the fact that it was no longer exhilarating to be in the Army was the only one that made any sense.

During an enjoyable leave in New York, I determined that I would not "stack arms". In military parlance that term of opprobrium was applied to those who no longer performed their duties with enthusiasm or dedication, but were content to do only enough to get along until it was time to go. I returned to the ACE Board with as much vigor and energy as I had displayed before my decision to retire.

The question of my replacement arose immediately after Christmas. Because of my sudden decision, the personnel system was hard put to nominate a successor for me. When this posed a problem for TECOM, I recommended that COL Bob Apt be given the job. He had been with the Board almost five years, knew testing, the personnel assigned and the post. The Board President was traditionally a War College graduate; since Bob was not, MG Brown hesitated. Finally, on my recommendation, Bob was named the next President.

Just at this time, my driver, Gregory Dupuis, completed his enlistment. SGM Pace found an sharp, shy, earnest young Infantryman, PFC Darryl Rhodes, to replace him. Rhodes came to the Board from the 82nd ABN Div. When I commented that Rhodes was not wearing jump wings, Pace explained that he had requested to be removed from jump status in order to get the transfer. He had been appalled by the rampant use of drugs in the barracks and refused to yield to peer pressure and become an addict. His request for transfer to another unit had been disapproved; the only way he could get out of the situation was to sign a "quit slip" and leave jump status. Though he came to the Board under this cloud, Pace had recognized what a fine young man he was. He was not the technician that Dupuis was, but Rhodes did an excellent job as my driver, fully justifying Pace's judgement. Eventually, Pace was able to get his jump wings back for him, and he was promoted to specialist fourth class.

The use of drugs at the Board was never a serious threat to its mission, yet Board personnel, like most in the Army, dabbled in its use. In the great majority of cases, the use of marijuana was the most serious violation. The exception was one motor mechanic who used and sold to his friends mescaline and LSD as well as marijuana. He lived in the barracks and was caught during a routine shakedown. The MP "marijuana dog" alerted on this man's desk, where a stash of drugs was located. Several months later, the man was finally tried, but was not convicted because CPT Amon was unable to remember the exact sequence of events during the shakedown. The man was released from active duty a short time later and we heard mat he was burned to death in a house trailer following some sort of dispute. Alcohol abuse was also present though limited; in addition to Wayne Smith's problem, the 1SG had to be counseled by the hospital drug abuse personnel but was not admitted as an in-patient. On the whole, I was satisfied that the incidence of drug and alcohol abuse was limited at the Board.

In early spring the Board was temporarily allocated Normandy DZ while the engineers made an emergency landing strip on Holland DZ. I jumped from a C-l 30 onto Normandy, a good jump for every one but me. For the first and only time I landed in a tree. When it was obvious that I could not avoid the tree even with the MC1-1 steerable parachute, I did everything I had been taught to do, though I had not used the procedures before. My parachute caught on a limb about thirty feet from the ground. Using the prescribed procedures, I popped my reserve and slid down it. The riggers eventually recovered the chute with no damage to it, but the Airborne Test Division, especially Bob Reid, was chagrined at putting the "boss" in the trees, and I came in for some good-natured raillery. It was an interesting experience.

Airborne Reunion Number Four, the first weekend in May, was a spectacular success. Those attending thought it the best yet. Though it kept the Board Personnel busy, particularly those in Plans Division, it was worth the effort.

Finally the day neared for my retirement. Again the question of a farewell party surfaced. Although they knew my aversion to such affairs, Bob Apt, Bob Reid and George Riviere persuaded me that there should be a formal dinner dance at which the Board would say goodbye to me. The active social life at the Board included at least two formal parties each year, one at about this time, so it would not be an extra activity. In addition there were pool parties, "hail and farewells" and picnics. Hence this fit into the pattern.

However, I decided there would be no change of command ceremony which I believe should be limited to tactical units. In addition, I was going to retire with an assembly of my friends at the flag pole on the Main Post. With them at my side, I would salute the flag for the last time as it came down at retreat on the day I left active duty. There would be no awards, no speeches, no parade, no retirement ceremony. Those attending would be invited to be my guests at the club for a drink with me.

All my friends were invited to my retirement; I was pleased and flattered by the number who came. Bill and Madeline Long, (IGMR) two of my oldest Army friends, came down from Owings Mills, Frank and Lucy Mashburn (504 Bragg) came from Tennessee, the Clarence Kettlers (Roswell) from St Louis, the Brunos (Heidelberg) from Niagara Falls, Herb Mansfield (508) from Florida, and of course, many friends from the Post. Bill Ankley (504 and 508), on temporary duty in the United States from Japan, came with Steve, his son, a fine looking 1LT. Arlene and Margaret came with their husbands, Bob and George (George came despite the fact that he was terminally ill with cancer of the lungs), and Ed and Gert Miller came from TECOM.

The day before I was to retire, I made my final jump with the Board. The guests who were available, went out to Sicily Drop Zone to watch. It was a perfect day for a jump, a tailgate drop from a c-130, but I took no extra chances despite the ideal conditions!

At the formal dinner dance at Pope Air Force Base Officers' Club, many gifts, most of them made by members of the Board, were presented to me. Ron Amon's wife made a beautiful, unusual, Elizabethan ceramic chess set for me; to accompany it, Ron made a chess board, so huge that it could be used as a table. There were lamps made from artillery shells, a shadow box containing my medals and decorations, plaques and citations. One of the most unusual gifts was a huge, framed montage picture of my military life. Pete Hayes borrowed some of my scrap books, the Board photographers reproduced many of the pictures covering my entire career and Plans Division mounted them in a large frame made by the Maintenance Shop. The thoughtfulness and kindness of those wonderful people who expended so much time and effort to honor me was deeply appreciated.

The next day, Friday, 31 May 1974, MG Brown arrived in the TECOM C-47 with many friends from Aberdeen including Sam Koster. Brown wanted to award me another Legion of Merit at the ceremony, but I refused. Awards and speeches were not going to be a part of my official retirement. With SGM Pace and one or two others present in my office, MG Brown pinned on my chest a Legion of Merit with five Oak Leaf Clusters. After he had "gonged" me, he shook hands and thanked me for my service to the Army and TECOM. I removed the medal, and MG Brown and I drove to the main post flag pole. Assembled there were most of the Board personnel, the TECOM delegation, many senior Post OFFs, and a large number of friends. The 82nd ABN Div Band played some of my favorite military music, including "The All American Soldier". At 1700 everyone stood as the band played "To The Colors" followed by the National Anthem. As the flag slowly descended, I saluted, surrounded by friends. The folding of the flag following the ceremony marked the end of 32 years of military service. I thanked the band and the others who had participated in the ceremony, after which the entire group of friends, officers and enlisted men, followed me to the Fort Bragg Officers' Club to enjoy a gala party. My life with THE REGULARS was over.

Donald A. Seibert

APPENDIX A

MINDORO REVISITED

In July 1945 the US 96th Division, The Deadeyes, embarked on LSTs at Okinawa for Mindoro, The Philippines, to train for the invasion of Japan. The Mindoro beaches were similar to those the Deadeyes were expected to encounter in that amphibious assault. Enroute, news of the atomic bombing of Hiroshima and Nagasaki surprised and amazed everyone; word that the Japanese had agreed to unconditional surrender caused great joy and relief. The 96th Div arrived at Mindoro before the peace treaty was signed and its members impatiently awaited shipping for their return home. Finally, after five months on the Island, the last of the Deadeyes, myself among them, left Mindoro with scant possibility of ever returning there.

In February 1981 a propeller-driven aircraft left Manila at 0600 and droned over the mountains of Mindoro as I eagerly peered into the dawn for some familiar landmark. There was none. As the aircraft taxied to the terminal at San Jose, I searched the area for something that would identify the place for me. Nothing looked familiar.

After deplaning, I made my way to the terminal exit to get a taxi. There were several Jeepneys, the highly decorated miniature buses mounted on jeep frames, and a large number of tricycles, but no taxis. These tricycles, motorcycles with covered sidecars, brightly painted and decorated in the same fashion as Jeepneys, were the preferred mode of travel in much of The Philippines for short trips. A tricycle driver asked if I wanted transportation into San Jose; I indicated that I did and asked how much it would cost to get to the best hotel. The driver said that the trip would cost 2 pisos - about 15 cents in US currency. As I clambered into the rickshaw-like sidecar, the motorcycle sputtered to life; the driver accelerated and we bumped along the uneven road toward San Jose.

The road from the airport into town appeared to be the only one paved in the area; later exploration revealed several additional paved streets in San Jose. As we dodged our way past trucks, Jeepneys, bicycles, pedestrians with huge bundles balanced precariously on their heads, squawking chickens and emaciated dogs, I eagerly looked to the right and left but saw nothing that I remembered. After several near-misses, the tricycle driver pulled up triumphantly in front of Roda's Hotel, the largest and best that San Jose boasted.

At first glance, Roda's looked acceptable. Its five stories towered above the other buildings in San Jose and a concrete drive arched majestically from the street to the covered portico. Though it was fully light by this time, the lobby appeared dim. The ancient switchboard behind the counter, remarkably like one found at a WWII Division Headquarters, proved to be an omen of the adventures awaiting me at Roda's.

A pleasant clerk assured me that a room was available and enquired, "Air Con?" I indeed wanted an air conditioned room. After registering, the clerk handed me the key to Room 303 and pointed to the stairs; the elevator was not working. Two flights of stairs were not troublesome with only my handbag to contend with; I quickly found Room 303, unlocked the door and surveyed my lodgings. There was a thin, lumpy, cotton-filled mattress on a wooden platform, obviously the bed. A bamboo table stood against one wall with a stool and a mirror framed in the same material; a worn, tired looking straw mat covered the floor. A closet, without hangers or hooks, completed the appointments. I noted with satisfaction the air conditioner in the window over the bed; the window itself was covered by a bamboo blind.

516

A door led to the bathroom. When I switched on the light the bulb glowed dimly -1 estimated that it was a 45 watt bulb. There was a standard toilet and sink - and that was all. Closer examination revealed a showerhead projecting from the wall with two faucets under it, and a drain under the sink. It was indeed a bathroom.

Roda's was not a five star hotel by any means, but it was adequate; I had slept in worse places. Before leaving I checked to make sure the "air con" was working and was pleased when a stream of cold air issued from it in only a few minutes. Satisfied, I ate a quick breakfast and set out to explore San Jose.

The business man who had occupied the seat next to me on the flight to Mindoro had told me that it was one of the least developed of the larger Philippine Islands, primarily because of the severe malaria problem which had plagued it until heroic measures finally curbed the disease. The lack of progress was apparent as I wandered about San Jose. The main street, called GEN Dunckel Street, paralleled the shore from the airport to Caminawit Point, perhaps six kilometers, and was paved throughout, though indifferently maintained. A second paved street intersected Dunckel, traversing the city from the ferry docks to the outskirts and led past the Municipal Building in one direction and the Market in the other.

Sections of paved roads were scattered about the city, but most streets were hard packed earth. The buildings, largely wooden one and two-story frame structures with corrugated tin roofs, were huddled together. Several cement and stucco buildings, some like Roda's of five stories, were scattered throughout. Dogs and chickens slept, pecked and ran throughout the city. Smoking fires, apparently debris and palm fronds, marked most streets. A steady stream of tricycles, Jeepneys, and trucks surged along the main streets; the number of people moving about at this early hour surprised me.

San Jose seemed to be a typical Pacific island village with closely built open store fronts, abandoned vehicles and other debris profusely scattered about; business was conducted largely on the packed earth in front of the shops. Still, nothing looked familiar. The church was obviously of recent vintage. Some buildings looked old enough to have been there in 1945, but since they resembled so many of the buildings seen in this part of the world, I could not be sure if they were ones I recalled. The sizeable market, teeming with people and crowded with wares, could have been in Seoul, Saigon or on any of the Islands I had visited before. There were many fishing boats on the beaches and flies covered everything.

A little after 0900 I passed the Philippine Airlines (PAL) Office and stopped in to confirm my return flight. A smiling, polite and very helpful young man assured me that my reservation on the seven o'clock flight the next day was valid and also informed me that I was due a refund because a propeller driven aircraft had been substituted for the jet which normally made the trip. He suggested I wait until the next day before applying for the refund as it was probable that another substitution would be made on the return flight.

After concluding my business, I asked Mr Briones, the individual who had been so helpful, if there was anyone who could tell me about the American facilities which had been on the island in 1945.

"Oh, you were with the liberation forces, sir?"

"No, but my Division came to the Island later and spent about five months here. I am trying to find out where our bivouac was. First we camped along a small river and then we moved to the Navy Base on the beach. I wonder if anything is left of those camps?"

"I don't think so, sir. I have lived here all my life and don't remember them. I do recall a huge pile of equipment which was left -just bulldozed into a heap to get it out of the way: jeeps, cranes, steel matting, parts of buildings, trucks - all kinds of junk. But even that is gone now. But perhaps some others remember."

Briones turned to his co-workers and spoke in rapid Tagalog. Everyone looked puzzled at first and then one after another mentioned a name. Finally Briones, or Bert as I later came to call him, turned and said, "Florenzo Rodriguez was here when the Americans landed on December 15, 1944. He was the police chief in San Jose since the war ended and has just retired. He knows everyone in the area and all about the war. We will go ask him. And maybe the Mayor can help. We will call on him, too."

Closing and locking his drawer, Bert walked around the counter to the door.

"I don't want to impose on you or take you from your work," I said.

"Oh I am off now until two o'clock. I will take you to Mr Rodriguez." By this time we were outside the PAL office. "Do you mind riding on the back of my motorcycle, or should we take a tricycle?"

Up to that moment I had never ridden on the back of a motorcycle, indeed I had not ridden on a motorcycle at all in over 30 years. But Bert looked at me expectantly, and it was obvious that he wanted to take his motorcycle. "Okay, let's go on your motorcycle," I said.

Briones smiled and showed me where to put my feet. As he started the motor, I somehow scrambled on the seat behind him. My feet had barely found the rods provided when we were off into the traffic. Zigzagging past trucks, tricycles and pedestrians we soon arrived at the Plaza in front of an imposing building only a few blocks from the PAL office. As he brought the motorcycle to a halt, Bert called over his shoulder, "This is the Municipal Building. We will see if the Mayor can help us." We both dismounted; after conferring with a policeman at the door, Briones led me up a wide staircase. On a landing was a framed military aerial mosaic of the San Jose area. The legend indicated that it had been made in 1964 by a USMC Reconnaissance Group. Bert pointed out various buildings.

"Where is the sugar mill?" I asked.

"Oh, that is in Barrio Central," he replied pointing to a small village about 15 kilometers to the northeast of San Jose.

"I remember there was a sugar mill in the village close to our camp. We were on a small river. I thought that the village was called San Jose." The aerial photograph clearly showed a river running through the village, and Central looked to be in the location I thought San Jose should be.

"Oh, Central is a barrio of San Jose. In fact, during the war it was the principal barrio of the area. That is why it is called Central."

"Do you know where the Navy or the CB or the PT Bases were located?"

Bert looked puzzled and admitted that he had no idea where any of those installations had been. He started toward the Mayor's Office saying, "The Mayor is too young to know about the liberation forces, but he may have some records."

"If he does not remember the war, there is no need to bother him. He is no doubt busy."

"He will not mind. But maybe we should go first to Florenzo Rodriguez."

Returning to the motorcycle, we were soon weaving through the traffic again. After a dozen turns which completely confused me, Briones pulled up in front of a small house. He called out as we dismounted and a young boy ran out pointing to the left. Bert, with me in tow, walked to the door indicated, calling out as he went. An elderly Filipino appeared; Briones greeted him courteously in Tagalog. He then turned and introduced us in English. Rodriguez shook hands, looked at me closely, and invited us to sit on a bench on the porch.

"So, you were with the liberation forces, eh?"

"No, my Division came to Mindoro in August 1945, after it was secured."

"You were with the 96th Division? There was the 381st, 382nd and 383rdRegiments. Which were you with?"

"I was with the 382nd."

"Oh yes, and how long did you stay on Mindoro?"

"Until January, 1946."

Then ensued a fascinating discussion during which Rodriguez gave an account of the occupation of the Island by the Japanese and the landing of US forces on 15 December 1944. He had been a guerrilla and had joined the Americans as they came over the beach. He spoke familiarly of the Commander, BG William C. Dunckel, was disappointed when I told him that I did not know him, and explained that the main street of San Jose had been named for him. We then talked about the American installations established on the Island. Rodriguez confirmed that the 96th Division had originally been in camps around the base of the mountains and that the Navy had built its bases on Cominawit Point.

"Do you remember where the Red Cross Center was located?"

"Yes, that was in the administration building of the sugar mill at Central. There was a hospital, maybe two, on the hills we call Little Baguio. One was the 13th, I think."

"Wasn't the 96th Division Headquarters on a hill, too?"

"Yes, near the hospitals. There was a big amphitheater there, too."

"Was there an air field near the sugar mill?"

"Yes, at the foot of the hills. It was built immediately after the Americans came ashore, and planes from that airstrip and others built by the Japanese supported the landings on Luzon."

"Well, I guess Central was where our camp was."

After a few more remarks it became obvious that Rodriguez had things to do. I suggested to Bert that we leave. Briones wanted to go back to the Mayor's Office, but I told him there was no point in our interrupting his schedule.

"Then I will take you to my Lolo. He knows all about the war."

As we sped through the town on the motorcycle, Bert talked about his Lolo; I gathered he was a Godfather, was Bert's great uncle and had raised him after his father's death.

We stopped before an imposing residence, surrounded by a high wall over which branches of flowering trees arched. It was a mansion compared with the other houses I had seen in San Jose. A young girl opened the gate when Briones called out, and Bert walked to the front door as if he belonged there. Without knocking, he opened the door and walked in, calling out a greeting in Tagalog. A matronly woman kissed him fondly. Bert then introduced me to Mr and Mrs Sarmiento. I am sure they had no idea who I was, nor had my name registered.

Mr Sarmiento remained seated in an ancient Morris Chair. He appeared to be in his eighties and in poor health; certainly he was hard of hearing. After a brief exchange with Bert in Tagalog, Mr Sarmiento turned to me.

"So, you were with the liberation forces?"

"No, I came with the 96th Division in 1945."

Mr Sarmiento began to reminisce about the war, the arrival of the Japanese, and their brutal methods. A young lieutenant was in charge of the occupation force and treated everyone with cruelty and disdain. "He ordered that all of the important people in San Jose be rounded up - and told us that we must obey all of his orders - furnish everything his men required - and vacate our houses so he and his men could live in them. When we protested, he shouted at us, 'Who are you to question my orders?'

"'I am Ramon Sarmiento, an official of this city and own much land here.'

"'Then I will make an example of you and your friends.'

"He told his men to herd us out of town. The Japanese then gave us shovels and made us dig our own graves; they beat us if we did not dig fast enough. The Jap lieutenant was very stern. He ordered the first man shot. The Mayor of San Jose stood at the head of his grave and a firing squad shot him. Then the Mayor of Central was shot. I held up my hand and said,'You can't do this. We have law in The Philippines. You cannot execute a man without a trial.' The lieutenant turned on me and I thought he was going to order the firing squad to shoot me next, so I kept on talking. While I was talking an airplane flew over and the lieutenant ordered his men to form an honor guard for the general who got out of the plane. The general ordered the executions stopped. I was very lucky."

Mr Sarmiento paused as his wife brought in coffee. He continued, "Lieutenant Golden of the US Navy came to me after the Americans drove the Japanese out and said, 'Ramon, we will make a contract for your land. We want to build a Navy Base on the point.' I owned all the land from San Jose to Caminawit Point; I told Golden that I would give the land to the Americans free of charge for their use during the war. But Golden insisted on a contract and Captain Brown, US Navy, agreed. So we signed a contract. Did you know LT Golden or CPT Brown?"

"No, I did not."

"They were good friends. Perhaps you knew my friend Colonel Dill?"

"Yes, Colonel Dill was my regimental commander," I replied excitedly.

"Well, I remember him well. Where is Colonel Dill now?"

"He retired in San Antonio, Texas. But he is an old man and I am not sure if he is still living."

"He was a good friend. A short man, and a good officer. I can never forget him or his Supply Officer Lieutenant Seibert."

Stunned, I could only stare at Mr Sarmiento. The last month the 96th Division had been on Mindoro I had been acting Regimental Supply Officer of the 382nd Infantry. Apparently Mr Sarmiento had not heard my name when we were introduced.

"But I am Seibert and I was COL Dill's Supply Officer the last few weeks we were here. I helped close out the area before we left," I managed to say.

"Yes, COL Dill and LT Seibert called me in and asked me what buildings I wanted on the Navy Base. I selected the ones I wanted and the rest were bulldozed into a huge pile. They gave me Jeeps, uniforms and food, and told me that the facilities on the Navy Base were worth about one million five hundred thousand dollars. So I was a millionaire. And now you have come to see me."

Vaguely I recalled closing out the Navy Base before we left the Island. There were dim recollections of transactions with local Filipinos, but names, faces and events would not come into focus. "This is unbelievable," I said. "I can't imagine meeting you after all these years."

"Yes, I am pleased that you have come to see me. You must take supper with us tonight. And you and your wife come too, Bertie."

"Okay, sir. I'll skip school tonight." Briones was taking business management courses at the local college at night. He had taught school before going to work for the Philippine Airlines.

The conversation became animated; none of us could quite believe the thousand to one chance which had brought us together. When I gave Mr Sarmiento my card, he looked at it carefully and exclaimed, "Yes, Donald Seibert, Supply Officer for Colonel Dill. Take off your glasses and let me look at you."

He stared at me intently after I had removed my glasses. "Yes, I remember your face. You had more hair then and were thinner. But I remember you." At my insistence, Bert took a picture of Mr Sarmiento and me with my camera. I promised to send a copy back to Mindoro. We discussed the 96th Division, Colonel Dill and my trip. Briones recalled that as a young boy he had seen a "mountain of junk - equipment abandoned by the US Army, of no use to local Filipinos and too costly to remove. It had been bulldozed into a pile and jungle, nature and gradual development of the area had caused it to disappear. When asked about the various facilities, Mr Sarmiento told me that the Catholic Church now stood on "officers' country" where the Navy (and later the 382nd) Officers' Club and billets had been. He also confirmed that the original camp of the 382nd had been just outside Central. Finally, it was time to go. Bidding farewell to my rediscovered friend and promising to return about six thirty for supper, Bert and I again mounted his motorcycle.

A brief visit was made at the office of a local lawyer, Ramon Curva (SP?), who had lived in Grand Rapids, MI before WWII, had graduated from Calvin College and had received his law degree from a college in Holland, Michigan. We had a brief, enjoyable chat, during which Curva recalled his own days in the US Army.

Bert next drove the two or three kilometers from the center of San Jose to Cominawit Point, where it seemed to me the PT Base had been. The local wharf and shipping center now utilized the area; the dock could have been the one constructed by the CBs in 1945. We walked on the beach where the men of the 382nd had cavorted a long time ago. Bert declined my invitation to have lunch with me, explaining that his family was expecting him He insisted on taking me to a local restaurant and ordering my lunch, telling the proprietor that I would be back at noon to eat it. He claimed the meals at Roda's were too expensive and not very good. Finally he dropped me off at the hotel, promising to pick me up between 6:30 and 7:00.

On entering the lobby of Roda's it seemed even more dimly lit than it had been earlier that morning. Climbing to the third floor, I flipped the switch in the bathroom, but the light failed to come on. I checked the light in the bed room; it too failed to light when the switched was flipped. Obviously there was no electricity. In need of some freshening after the dusty motorcycle ride, I turned the tap in the wash basin. There was no water! Provisions had been made for the toilet, however. A large bucket of water and an oversized dipper had been placed in the bathroom to flush the toilet. Disappointed at not being able to freshen up before lunch, I retraced my steps to the lobby. On turning in my key, I was assured that the electricity would be on again by 4:45 - and that water would then be available. Water flow was dependent on a pressure tank which required electricity. Lunch was good: a platter of prawns cooked in spices, fried rice, salad and iced tea. There was too much of everything, but I did not leave any of those tasty prawns. All were peeled and eaten.

After lunch I walked about the city for a few minutes. It was almost deserted as most of the population took a siesta. In answer to my question about the propriety of bringing a bottle of whiskey to Mr Sarmiento that evening, Bert had assured me that it would be appreciated. When I hopefully suggested Scotch, he had urged that I bring brandy. During my walk I bought a bottle of Fundadore.

Returning to the hotel and leaving the brandy, I enquired about getting to Central. The clerk informed me that I could go either by Jeepney or tricycle. A young boy employed by the hotel to sweep out the lobby, handle luggage and do other odd jobs, offered to accompany me and make sure that I caught the correct Jeepney. We took a tricycle to the market, and on my guide's instruction, I paid the driver I piso. We transferred to a rather seedy looking Jeepney. The driver, a stout woman, insisted that my guide and I sit on the front seat rather than in the back where two bench seats stretched the length of the Jeepney bed. These soon became crowded with people and bundles; indeed a fourth individual was crowded into the cab with us and several men clung precariously outside the Jeepney when we finally left the market. My guide told me that the fare was 5 pisos per person.

The Jeepney careened through San Jose, the female driver playing the traditional Filipino game of "Chicken" with rare skill. After several near misses we left the crowded streets and close-packed buildings behind and headed northeast. Just outside San Jose we crossed a single Bailey Bridge, probably installed in 1945, and immediately the road and area seemed familiar. There were no landmarks I could identify, nothing that I could specifically recall, yet there was a very strong impression that I had been on that road before. The Jeepney stopped frequently to drop off passengers or pick up others, so the 15 kilometer trip took about 45 minutes. Finally Central came into view, dominated by the ruins of the sugar mill. Though now only a skeleton, the mill evoked clear recollections. I knew where I was.

Clambering out of the Jeepney and paying the two fares, my young guide and I headed toward the sugar mill. My guide spoke poor English, so communication was difficult, but we got to the mill. The administration building in which the Red Cross had operated a recreation center was largely intact, but the rest of the mill was a shambles. After I took several pictures, my guide started back toward the center of the barrio. I looked in vain for the house of the local school teacher who had opened a restaurant in 1945. A graduate of North Dakota Agricultural College, he managed to keep a supply of cold beer; most of us were convinced he had arrangements with willing supply SGTS. He served tough but tasty chicken and hamburgers of dubious ancestry, but a visit to his establishment broke the monotony of GI fare. The house was near the sugar mill, but though many in the area looked old enough to be the one, positive identification was impossible. The road leading east out of Central looked familiar; it was surely the same one that my Platoon and I had taken when they took me into San Jose (Central?) when I was transferred to HHC. 1LT Bill Stocks, SGT Monday and I had also used that road on our way back from a foray for cold beer and stringy chicken. We had marveled at the adroitness with which a Filipino lady, with a huge bundle balanced on her head, had avoided the Jeep as we drove past. I pointed along the road saying, "This looks familiar. Let's go up this road a little way."

After only a short walk we came to a bridge; the river flowing under it was the same width and depth as the one I remembered next to the 382nd camp. An overgrown trail, at right angles to the one we were on, led off to the south paralleling the river; I was sure it led to the site of our old camp. Unfortunately, time did not permit me to explore it. While standing on the bridge, my guide pointed to the area called Little Baguio several miles away. As I looked at the hills I could visualize the two hospitals and our Division Headquarters which stood on them. When we continued across the bridge, a wooden school building came into view. I knew that school house; it had been used as an Officers' Club by the 382nd Infantry.

"Do you know how long that school has been there?" I asked the youth.

"It was built about 1933," a strange voice said in excellent English. Turning, I saw a Filipino man about my own age. "Why do you ask?"

"I am sure that our regiment used that building when we were here in 1945."

"Yes, it was used by the 96th Division then. I am the chief teacher of the school, and I was here at the time. Come, I will show you."

We introduced ourselves and shook hands, but I did not get his name. He talked about the 96th Division and various members of it he had known. As we approached the building, a group of children was sitting on the steps singing. When I raised my camera to take a picture, they shouted in glee and quickly composed themselves primly. My instamatic could not take in the entire group, even though I backed off, but they posed for me as if for a portrait.

We climbed the steps and memories flooded back. I might have been racing up them with Daria Federonko, a nurse I had first met in 1942 as an enlisted man assigned to the Station Hospital at Indiantown Gap Military Reservation, PA. Our paths had crossed again when I visited my Platoon Runner, Bob Laird, in the 13th Station Hospital on Mindoro and discovered that Daria was his Ward Nurse We had danced many sets in that school house. I thought of the indefatigable COL Macy Dill, Commander of the 382nd Infantry Regiment, who was twice our age and could dance two or three polkas, one after the other, with no apparent effort. The faces of the many fine officers and enlisted men who had made the harrowing LST trip through a typhoon from Okinawa to Mindoro with me flashed through my mind. The sight of handsome, young 1LT Petsch, pinned under his overturned jeep and drowned in a few inches of water rose unbidden to my mind. He had been enroute to the Regimental Area from this same club that night he died. Recollections of the unbelievable trip to Manila to purchase $35,000.00 worth of locally produced whiskey for this and the enlisted clubs pushed to the fore. I recalled how frustrated and bored and impatient we were as we waited to get back home, and how the club had provided welcome relief and enjoyment to us. The steps, the porch, the construction of the building were completely familiar. The Chief Teacher led me to one of the doorways and pointed. Clearly visible under the weathering paint was a large 96 with the word DEADEYES superimposed on it. Under it was the subscription: Mindoro, 1945. After showing me through the school, the principal led me to his office, where he introduced me to his Assistant and handed me a sheet of paper saying, "Please sign your name and address. You are the first American to visit our school. Several Japanese have come - though they came to honor their ancestors who were buried here. But you are the only American who has come back."

After signing my name and bidding the principal and his assistant farewell, we left the school and walked to the market place in Central, to catch the Jeepney back to San Jose. When it approached, the gentleman sitting beside the driver called to us to join him on the front seat. I perched myself on the outside so I could take pictures enroute. The man sitting with us on the front seat, the Assistant Principal we had met at the school, maintained an interesting commentary on the area and the Japanese occupation of Mindoro as we drove to San Jose.

At Roda's Hotel electricity had been restored and water was again flowing. Feeling the need for a shower after the hot, dusty ride, I looked forward to a leisurely one before Bert was scheduled to pick me up. Already the "air con" was laboring valiantly to cope with the missing window pane concealed behind the bamboo blind. Entering the bathroom, I was delighted with the stream of water from the shower head; though water flowed only from the cold faucet, it was tepid due to the sun beating upon the tank on the roof, and was not unpleasant. Just as I completed soaping myself, the water pressure failed; it was a tedious task to rid myself of lather using a wet washcloth and the minuscule stream now flowing. So much for the joys of Roda's.

Bert appeared on his motorcycle just after 1830. With Fundadore clutched in my right hand, I mounted behind him and we were off into the maze that was Barrio Bocangay Payase. Enroute, I asked Bert if his wife was already at Mr Sarmiento's house. He told me that he would go for her after he dropped me off. We arrived with a flourish, and the same young girl opened the gate for us. Mr Sarmiento and his wife greeted us warmly. Already the table was laden with many dishes of food. My host graciously accepted the brandy and passed it to his wife. He introduced a pretty young lady, the youngest of his seven children.

Mrs Sarmiento led me to an armchair and pressed a frosted stein into my hand. A quart of San Miguel beer was on the coffee table in front of me. Bert left to get his wife as Mr Sarmiento and I picked up the threads of our morning conversation. Mrs Sarmiento brought in a cup of chicken soup with a chicken heart and liver in it; the broth was thick with Malanga leaves.

"This will make you strong and virile and enable you to live to an old age," she said. The soup was rich and tasty, the Malanga leaves pleasantly pungent. I alternated between sips of cold beer and hot broth until both were consumed. Another quart of San Miguel was placed on the coffee table, and my hostess made sure there was ice in my stein at all times. A beaming Mrs Sarmiento also placed another cup of broth before me.

Finally, Mr Sarmiento, who had not joined me in drinking because his doctor had forbade further indulgence in alcohol or tobacco, suggested that we take our places at the table. Surprised, since Bert and his wife had not yet appeared, I blurted out something about waiting for them. "Oh, they are family and will not mind if we start. I am hungry because I eat only one meal a day."

Although there were six places set, only Mr Sarmiento and I sat down. His daughter sat aside from the table busy with reading or other activities, while Mrs Sarmiento bustled from kitchen to table. Now I had good look at what was offered - it was a feast! There were two platters or bowls of everything: prawns boiled in spices and still in their shells, steamed crabs, fried chicken legs and thighs, duck roasted and basted with savory herbs and spices and cut up into small pieces, roast pork served with sliced, fried potatoes, spaghetti with a red sauce and liberally topped with sliced red peppers, a cole slaw-like salad with tomatoes cut up in it and a mayonnaise dressing and a mountain of sliced bread which looked homemade.

As I contemplated where to begin, Bert and his wife arrived. After the introductions, Bert and his wife joined us at the table. Mrs Sarmiento continued to bustle from kitchen to table and the daughter remained seated apart. Soup was served to Bert and me, but to no one else. Mr Sarmiento concentrated on the prawns, though he ate a bit from some of the other dishes. I tried everything on the table except the bread, deciding that I needed room for the more toothsome items. Each dish was delicious, and I ate more than I should.

Conversation was animated and stimulating, ranging from Mr Sarmiento's recollections of the war and the early days of the Philippine Republic to a discussion of the therapeutic value of various plants and leaves grown in the area. Bert's wife taught history and biology, so the conversation leaped easily from topic to topic as someone struck a new note. The beer flowed, at least in my glass. Bert drank both beer and brandy; when offered brandy, I deferred until later.

Finally I was stuffed. When she was convinced that I could not or would not eat any more, Mrs Sarmiento reluctantly removed my plate piled high with prawn and crab shells, chicken, duck and pork bones and other debris. She returned with a ripe papaya which she sliced and cleaned and offered to Mr Sarmiento and me. I managed to eat a small slice; it was delicious, fresh from the tree in the yard. The conversation during dinner had been so interesting that I had lost track of time. Now Mr Sarmiento looked sleepy. I glanced at my watch and noted that it was 2130.

"I'll have a sip of that brandy now, please," I said, "and then I will have to leave. I have an early flight in the morning." The Sarmientos protested, but after sipping brandy for a few minutes as the conversation continued unabated, I arose and suggested to Bert that he take me home. Farewells were genuinely warm and regretful. Each of us promised to write and keep in touch. Mrs Sarmiento was proudly embarrassed at my sincere compliments about her cooking.

The staccato roar of the motorcycle broke the stillness of the warm night and Bert and I were off into the dark. At the hotel, I thanked Bert for a most enjoyable and eventful day and made my way to my room. The "air con" which I had left running, had lowered the temperature in the room enough to enable me to get a good night's sleep.

The next morning I awoke at 0430 as usual. Not trusting the water pressure, I decided to forego my customary morning shower. Without a mirror in the bathroom, shaving was something of a guessing game, which I won, by feel and habit, without cutting myself. Someone knocked on my door and informed me that the hotel van would leave for the airport at 0545.

It was barely light when we arrived at the terminal. I was surprised and pleased to see Bert already behind the PAL counter. First, I paid the airport tax, then Bert issued my boarding pass and refunded 46 pisos, the difference in fare between a Jet and a propeller driven aircraft.

The flight was called promptly at 0650 and the aircraft was quickly loaded. As the plane rose and circled north, I had a quick look at San Jose and a better view of Cental. This time I left Mindoro convinced that there was scant possibility of ever returning there.

APPENDIX B

SUMMARY OF MILITARY CAREER

COLONEL DONALD A. SEIBERT, USA RET

BORN: 27 APRIL 1920 IN HEMPSTEAD, NY
GRADUATED FROM FLUSHING HIGH SCHOOL IN 1938; BA (BIOLOGY) FROM
WASHINGTON SQUARE COLLEGE, NYU; MS (INTERNATIONAL AFFAIRS) FROM
GEORGE WASHINGTON U. ENLISTED: 26 JANUARY 1942; COMMISSIONED 23
JANUARY 1943; RETIRED 31 MAY 1974

MILITARY EDUCATION:

1942 BASIC TRAINING (MEDICAL) FT LEE, VA
1942 SURGICAL TECHNICIAN COURSE, WALTER REED ARMY HOSPITAL, DC
1942-1943 OFFICER CANDIDATE SCHOOL, CWS, EDGEWOOD ARSENAL, MD
1942 FIRST AIR CHEMICAL OFFICERS' COURSE, EDGEWOOD ARSENAL, MD
1944 INFANTRY OFFICERS' SPECIAL BASIC COURSE, FT BENNING, GA
1949 PARACHUTE SCHOOL, FT BENNING, GA
1950-1951 INFANTRY OFFICERS' ADVANCE COURSE, FT BENNING, GA
1954 SUMMER ARCTIC INDOCTRINATION COURSE, FT GREELEY, AK
1956 RANGER COURSE, FT BENNING, GA
1956-1957 COMMAND AND GENERAL STAFF COLLEGE, FT LEAVENWORTH, KS
1964-1965 ARMY WAR COLLEGE, CARLISLE BARRACKS, PA

CAREER HIGHLIGHTS:

APR 43 - SEP 44 CHEMICAL OFFICER/GROUND TRAINING OFFICER ARMY AIR
FORCE, SANTA
ANA ARMY AIR BASE, ROSWELL ARMY AIR FIELD
DEC 44 - MAR 44 PLATOON LEADER/INSTRUCTOR, IRTC, FT MCCLELLAN, AL
APR 45 - FEB 46 PLATOON LEADER, F Co, COMPANY EXECUTIVE OFFICER, E Co,
BATTALION
ADJUTANT/COMMANDING OFFICER, HQ & HQ Co, 2nd BATTALION, 382nd
INFANTRY; REGIMENTAL S-4 AND SERVICE Co COMMANDER, 382nd
INFANTRY, 96th INFANTRY DIVISION, UNITED STATES ARMY PACIFIC MAR46-DEC48
COMMANDING OFFICER, HQ & HQ Co 305th INFANTRY, 77th RESERVE
DIVISION, NEW YORK, NY FEB49-FEB50 EXECUTIVE OFFICER, HQ & HQ Co, HEAVY
MACHINE OUN PLATOON LEADER,
M Co, RIFLE PLATOON LEADER, I Co, 504th AIRBORNE INFANTRY FEB 50- AUG 50
COMMANDING OFFICER, K Co, 504th AIRBORNE INFANTRY, 82ND AIRBORNE
DIVISION, FORT BRAGG, NC0 APR 51- JUN 52 COMMANDING OFFICER, F Co, 508th
AIRBORNE REGIMENTAL COMBAT

TEAM, FT BENNING, GA

JUN 52- JAN -53 GUERILLA ADVISOR, FECOM, KOREA

FEB 53- APR 53 COMMANDING OFFICER B Co, 9th INFANTRY, 2nd INFANTRY DIV, KOREA

APR 53- AUG 53 S-3 9th INFANTRY, 2ND INFANTRY DIVISION, KOREA

OCT 53- MAY 56 PMS&T, KENTUCKY MILITARY INSTITUTE, LYNDON, KY

JUL 57- JUN 60 PLANS OFFICER, ARMY WAR PLANS DIVISION, DA, THE PENTAGON

AUG60- OCT 61 S-3 AND EXECUTIVE OFFICER, 1ST AIRBORNE BATTLE GROUP, 504th, 8TH

INFANTRY DIVISION, GERMANY

OCT 61-JAN 62 G-4 8th INFANTRY DIVISION, GERMANY FEB 62- FEB -63 COMMANDING OFFICER 5th BATTALION, 6TH INFANTRY (MECH), 1st

ARMORED DIVISION, FT HOOD, TX MAR 63- JUL 63 EMERGENCY ACTION OFFICER, JOINT ALTERNATE COMMAND ELEMENT,

FT RITCHIE, MD JUL 63- JUL 64 OPERATIONS OFFICER, BATTLE STAFF TEAM, NATIONAL MILITARY

COMMAND CENTER, OFFICE OF THE JOINT CHIEFS OF STAFF, PENTAGON AUG 65- JAN 66 DEPUTY SENIOR ADVISOR, 25th VIETNAMESE DIVISION, VIETNAM FEB 66- MAR 67 SENIOR ADVISOR, 24th SPECIAL TACTICAL ZONE, VIETNAM MAR 67- NOV 67 COMMANDING OFFICER, 1st BRIGADE, 9th INFANTRY DIVISION, VN FEB 68- JUN 69 CHIEF SERVICES DIVISION, OFFICE OF THE DEPUTY CHIEF OF STAFF

LOGISTICS, US ARMY EUROPE, G-4 7th US ARMY, GERMANY JUL 69-NOV 70 G-3 FIRST FIELD FORCE, VIETNAM NOV 70- MAY 71 CHIEF OF STAFF 101st AIRBORNE DIVISION, VIETNAM JUN 71 - DEC 72 DEPUTY CHIEF OF STAFF FOR SUPPORT, TEST AND EVALUATION

COMMAND, ABERDEEN PROVING GROUND, MD JAN 73- MAY 74 PRESIDENT, AIRBORNE, COMMUNICATIONS, AND ELECTRONICS BOARD,

FT BRAGG, NC

QUALIFICATIONS AND BADGES

1 ST, 2ND AND 3RD AWARDS OF THE COMBAT INFANTRYMAN BADGE (CU3 WITH 3 STARS)
MASTER PARACHUTIST
RANGER TAB
GLIDERIST BADGE
ARMY GENERAL STAFF INSIGNIA
JOINT CHIEFS OF STAFF IDENTIFICATION BADGE

AWARDS AND DECORATIONS

SILVER STAR (OAK LEAF CLUSTER)
LEGION OF MERIT (5 OAK LEAF CLUSTERS)
BRONZE STAR MEDAL (OAK LEAF CLUSTER)
MERITORIOUS SERVICE MEDAL
AIR MEDAL (24 OAK LEAF CLUSTERS)
ARMY COMMENDATION MEDAL (2 OAK LEAF CLUSTERS AND "V" DEVICE)
AMERICAN CAMPAIGN MEDAL

ASIATIC PACIFIC CAMPAIGN MEDAL (1 STAR)
WORLD WAR II VICTORY MEDAL
NATIONAL DEFENSE SERVICE MEDAL (1 OAK LEAF CLUSTER)
KOREAN SERVICE MEDAL (3 STARS)
VIETNAM SERVICE MEDAL (7 STARS)
PHILIPPINE LIBERATION MEDAL
KOREAN (ROK) WHARANG DISTINGUISHED SERVICE MEDAL WITH GOLD STAR
VIETNAM (RVN) NATIONAL ORDER, FIFTH CLASS
VIETNAM DISTINGUISHED SERVICE ORDER, SECOND CLASS
VIETNAM GALLANTRY CROSS (2 PALMS, 2 GOLD STARS)
VIETNAM ARMED FORCES HONOR MEDAL, FIRST CLASS
VIETNAM STAFF SERVICE HONOR MEDAL, FIRST CLASS
VIETNAM CIVIL ACTION MEDAL, FIRST CLASS
KOREAN ORDER OF MILITARY MERTT, CHIN MUI
UNITED NATIONS SERVICE MEDAL
VIETNAMESE CAMPAIGN MEDAL WITH "60" DEVICE

APPENDIX C

ABBREVIATIONS USED IN THE REGULARS

AA Antiaircraft Artillery
AB Air base
ABG Airborne
ASCI Assistant CofS Intelligence
AD Active Duty
Adj Adjutant
Admin Administration, Administrative
Adv Advisor
AF Air Force (US)
AG Adjutant General ('s Corps)
AIB Armored Infantry Battalion
AIR Airborne Infantry Regiment
Ammo Ammunition
AO Area of Operation
APC Armored Personal Carrier
APG Aberdeen Proving Ground
AR Armor (branch) Armored
ARCOM Army Commendation Ribbon
ARTY Artillery (branch)
ARVN Army, Republic of Vietnam
ASR Available Supply Rate
Asst Assistant
ATT Annual Training Test
AVN Aviation (Branch) (aircraft)
AWC Army War College
AWPD Army War Plans Division
Bde Brigade
BG Brigadier General
Bn Battalion
BOQ Bachelor Officers' Quarters
Btry Battery
CAV Cavalry (branch)
CCF Chinese Communist Forces
CDR Commander
CE Corps of Engineers (branch)
CG Commanding General
C&GSC Command and General Staff Col
CIB Combat Infantryman Badge
CMD Command
CMDT Commandant

CO Commander
Co Company
CofS Chief of Staff
COL Colonel
Commo Communications Officer, SGT
CONARC Continental Army Command
CONUS Continental United States
CP Command Post
CPL Corporal
CPT Captain
CQ Charge of Quarters
CSC Combat Support Company
CSM Command Sergeant Major
CW Chemical Warfare
CWO Chief Warrant Officer
CW2 Chief Warrant Officer 2nd Grade
CW3 Chemical Warfare Service
DA Department of the Army
DCSLOG Deputy Chief of Staff, Logistics
DCSOPS Deputy Chief of Staff, OPNS
DCSPER Deputy Chief of Staff, Personnel
Dep Deputy
Det Detachment
Dir Director
DISCOM Div Support Command (CDR)
Dist District
Div Division
DO Duty Officer
DOD Department of Defense
DS Direct Support
DSA Deputy Senior Advisor
DSC Distinguished Service Cross
DTA Division Tactical Area
DZ Drop Zone
EAO Emergency Action Officer
EIB Expert Infantryman Badge
EM Enlisted Men
EN Enemy
Engr Engineer(s)
1LT First Lieutenant
1SG First Sergeant
FM Field Manual
FO Forward Observer
FSCC Fire Support Coordination Ctr
FT Fort
FWD Forward
GI Government Issue - US Soldier
G-1 Asst CofS, Personnel

G-2 Asst CofS, Intelligence
G-3 Asst CofS, Operations
G-4 Asst CofS, Logistics
G-5 Asst CofS, Civil Affairs
GEN General
Hel Helicopter
HHC HQ and HQ Co
H&I Harassing and Interdiction (Fire)
HMG Heavy Machine Gun
HQ Headquarters
I&E Information and Education
IFFV First Field Force, Vietnam
IIFFV Second Field Force, Vietnam
IG Inspector General
IN Infantry (branch)
IRTC IN Replacement Training Ctr
JACE Joint Alternate CMD Element
JAG Judge Advocate General (branch)
JCS Join Chiefs of Staff
JWPD Joint War Plans Division
KATUSA Korean Augmentation to USA
KP Kitchen Police
LD Line of Departure
Ldr Leader
LNO Liaison Officer
LST Land Ship Tank
LT Lieutenant
LTC Lieutenant Colonel
LTG Lieutenant General
LTJG Lieutenant Junior Grade
LZ Landing Zone
MAAG Military Assistance Advisory Grp
MACM Medical Administrative Corps
MACO Marshalling Area Control Officer
MC Medical Corps (branch)
Mech Mechanized
MG Major General
Mil Military
MLR Main Line of Resistance
MOH Medal of Honor
MOS Military Occupational Specialty
MP Military Police (branch) (-man)
MSG Master Sergeant
NCOIC NCO-in-charge
NG National Guard
NKA North Korean Army
NMCC National Military Command Ctr
NVA North Vietnamese Army

NYU New York University
OCS Officer Candidate School
OD Officer of the Day
OFF Officer
OG Officer of the Guard
OIC Officer-in-charge
OP Observation Post
OPN Operation
OPS Operations
ORD Ordnance (branch), Weapons
Pers Personnel
PFC Private First Class
PLF Parachute Landing Fall
Plt Platoon
PM Provost Marshall
POAC Pentagon OFFs Athletic Center
POI Program of Instruction
POL Petroleum, Oil and Lubricants
POV Privately Owned Vehicles
POW Prisoner of War
Prov Province
PSG Platoon Sergeant
PT Physical Training
PVT Private
PX Post Exchange
QM Quartermaster (branch)
RA Regular Army
RAAF Roswell Army Air Field
RCT Regimental Combat Team
Recon Reconnaissance
Regt Regiment(al)
RES Reserve(s)
R&R Rest and Recuperation (recreation)
RIF Reduction in Force
ROK Republic of Korea
ROTC Reserve Officers' Training Corps
RTO Radio/Telephone Operator
SA Senior Advisor
SC Signal Corps (branch)
SD Special Duty
S-1 Personnel Staff Officer
S-2 Intelligence Staff Officer
S-3 Operations Staff Officer
S-4 Logistics Staff Officer
2LT Second Lieutenant
SF Special Forces
SFC Sergeant First Class
SGM Sergeant Major

SGS Secretary of the General Staff
SGT Sergeant
SI Special Intelligence
SIG Signal, Signalman
SJA Staff Judge Advocate
SL Squad Leader
SSG Staff Sergeant
STZ Special Tactical Zone
TDY Temporary Duty
TIS The Infantry School
Tng Training
TOC Tactical Operations Center
TO&E Table of Org and Equipment
TWX Teletype Message, Wire
UGO Unit Gas Officer
USMA US Military Academy, West Point
USAREUR US Army, Europe
VC Viet Cong
WFTC Western Flying Training Command
WO1 Warrant Officer, 1st Grade
XO Executive Officer